CW01656573

T&T Clark Companion to Nonconformity

Forthcoming titles in this series include:

T&T Clark Companion to the Atonement, edited by Adam J. Johnson
T&T Clark Companion to the Doctrine of Sin, edited by Keith L. Johnson and David Lauber
T&T Clark Companion to Christian Prayer, edited by Ashley Cocksworth and John C. McDowell
T&T Clark Companion to de Lubac, edited by Jordan Hillebert
T&T Clark Companion to Pneumatology, edited by Daniel M. Castelo and Kenneth M. Loyer
T&T Clark Companion to Schillebeeckx, edited by Stephan van Erp
T&T Clark Companion to the Theology of Kierkegaard, edited by David J. Gouwens and Aaron Edwards

Titles already published include:

T&T Clark Companion to Liturgy, edited by Alcuin Reid
T&T Clark Companion to Methodism, edited by Charles Yrigoyen Jr
T&T Clark Companion to Reformation Theology, edited by David M. Whitford
T&T Clark Companion to Augustine and Modern Theology, edited by C.C. Pecknold and Tarmo Toom

T&T Clark Companion to Nonconformity

Edited by

Robert Pope

Bloomsbury T&T Clark
An imprint of Bloomsbury Publishing Plc

B L O O M S B U R Y
LONDON • OXFORD • NEW YORK • NEW DELHI • SYDNEY

Bloomsbury T&T Clark
An imprint of Bloomsbury Publishing Plc

Imprint previously known as T&T Clark

50 Bedford Square
London
WC1B 3DP
UK

1385 Broadway
New York
NY 10018
USA

www.bloomsbury.com

First published 2013. This edition published 2016

British Library Cataloguing-in-Publication Data
A catalogue record for this book is available from the British Library.

ISBN: HB: 978-0-56750-526-2
PB: 978-0-56766-993-3
ePDF: 978-0-56765-538-7
ePub: 978-1-47255-830-5

Library of Congress Cataloging-in-Publication Data
A catalog record for this book is available from the Library of Congress.

Typeset by Newgen Knowledge Works (P) Ltd., Chennai, India
Printed and bound in Great Britain

Contents

Preface

This book is about Protestant Nonconformity in England and Wales. While Nonconformists have consistently claimed the Puritans and Separatists of the middle to late sixteenth and the first half of the seventeenth centuries as their historical antecedents (and they duly make their appearance in the following chapters), it was the Act of Uniformity of 1662, requiring 'unfeigned assent and consent' to the Book of Common Prayer, Episcopal ordination and the swearing of allegiance to the restored monarch which defined them in law and, in fact, identified them as law-breakers. The Act also made outlaws of Roman Catholics, but whereas this virtually drove Catholics underground, those Protestants who refused to conform to the requirements of the Act forged their own religious traditions which survived a quarter century of official persecution before finally forcing a compromise when, in 1689, their existence was legally acknowledged albeit under tightly defined terms of toleration which still saw them officially excluded from public life and from certain other social privileges.

In subsequent years Nonconformists reinvented themselves as they responded to the Evangelical Revival of the eighteenth, the industrialization of the nineteenth and the ecumenism of the twentieth centuries. Their theology was transformed as it acknowledged the revivalism of the eighteenth century as well as the developments in thought stemming from the Enlightenment. Social and political witness became increasingly explicit especially following industrialization, the gradual widening of the franchise and the repeal of the Test and Corporation Acts in 1828. At the same time that the legal discrimination suffered from the seventeenth century was gradually being removed, so too Nonconformists found their ranks swollen by their new-found, if at times unwilling, allies – the Methodists. Indeed, such was their collective strength that they began to challenge the Established Church with the claim that, by the mid-nineteenth century, they represented a substantial proportion of religious observers in both England and Wales. Such a turn of events, apparently supported by the 1851 Religious Census, required the more positive appellation of the 'Free Churches', with the adjective supplying a theological and social confidence which enabled experimentation in belief and practice as well as in social and political witness.

During the twentieth century, traditional Nonconformist denominations suffered cruel and relentless numerical decline, though what could be considered 'a new Nonconformity', in David Bebbington's phrase, emerged through Pentecostalism, the Charismatic movement, the Black-Majority churches and the so-called 'New Churches'. There was not necessarily a direct association between these new groups and those of traditional Dissent. But their attempts to establish alternative forms of faith and order, and the (often implicit) conviction that they were free to do so, suggested that they had, in some senses, inherited the Nonconformist mantle.

All of this is touched upon in what follows, and much of it is elucidated in detail, but the primary focus is on the major traditional Nonconformist groups – the Independents (Congregationalists), Baptists, Presbyterians and Unitarians, with the Society of Friends (Quakers) entering the account as the most prominent Nonconformists who, if talk of 'mainstream' Nonconformity is truly justifiable, could also be considered to fall outside it. Methodists have their own *Companion*, and were not, at least initially, Nonconformists. Yet their growing affinity with Old Dissent as the nineteenth century proceeded has meant that they, too, have been included, where appropriate, in this volume.

Nonconformist history cannot be told without some reference to events in Ireland and Scotland, though religious dissent and Nonconformity in those nations is of a different nature and could not be covered judiciously here. As a result, England and Wales constitute the primary focus for this volume's chapters. The content is organized thematically and chronologically, rather than denominationally, as this enables the distinctive witness and contribution of Nonconformists to be most clearly outlined. This approach best suits the complex but richly fascinating history of religious Nonconformity constituted as it is by disagreement, persecution, the claims of conscience, the inadequacy of toleration, the battle to achieve social and political equality under the law, and – more than anything – the desire to worship God according to biblical norms and conscientious conviction rather than statutory requirements, the interference of the state and the mediation of a priest.

As the following chapters eruditely reveal, it is all too easy to read nineteenth-century denominationalism back into the seventeenth century. At that point, Presbyterians and Independents, at best, constituted a 'temper', a mood or a party within the national church rather than anything more substantial. Consequently capitalization denotes the emergence of a defined group, the use of a noun – rather than an adjective – as far as the early period is concerned. This policy has been adopted in order to ensure that the denominations of the nineteenth century, with their definite structures, are not seen as exactly compatible with the rather looser interpretations and practices of earlier times.

The contributors to this volume were given the freedom to treat their topic in as comprehensive a manner as possible within the limitations of space, to limit the discussion to a specific tradition or to present a representative case study. They were also encouraged to make use of the four volumes, produced under the overall supervision of Alan P. F. Sell, and titled *Protestant Nonconformist Texts*, published by Ashgate in 2006 and 2007. These volumes constitute a rich resource of source material for anyone considering further research into the history of Protestant Dissent and Nonconformity. Nevertheless, it was inevitable that some aspects of Nonconformist history and thought would appear more than once in the following pages, with each repetition enabling the reader to see the breadth of interpretation possible. Readers who wish to pursue particular themes are advised to consult the endnotes of the book, while Clive D. Field's 'structured bibliography' offers a comprehensive guide to the sources available to those interested in further study.

There are a number of acknowledgements which need to be made. First, I am grateful to T&T Clark and its then commissioning editor, Thomas Kraft, for commissioning the book. I note also my gratitude to his successor, Anna Turton, and to the editorial assistants Katie Broomfield and Caitlin Flynn for the patience which they demonstrated while this volume was being prepared. It has taken far longer to finalize the volume than originally envisaged, but the result was, hopefully, worth the wait. The project has been guided by a number of colleagues who have acted unofficially as editorial consultants. I am indebted to Professors Clyde Binfield, John H. Y. Briggs, D. Densil Morgan and Alan P. F. Sell whose knowledge of the Nonconformist traditions was invaluable in setting this project in motion and has been called upon on more than one occasion as work on this volume has proceeded. The vast majority of the essays contained here were easily commissioned, and I am pleased to record my thanks to all the contributors for their willingness to participate in this project as well as for the work they have produced. There were some mishaps along the way, and I am particularly grateful to Professor Keith Robbins for stepping in at the eleventh hour. This volume is all the richer for having his contribution.

Not all of the main contributors were free to contribute entries for the 'ABC of Nonconformity', rendering necessary an approach to other colleagues. Once again, I am grateful to each one for their willingness to contribute, particularly to Dr David Cornick and Dr Stephen Orchard, both of whom undertook a wide range of topics from all periods in

Nonconformist history, while Dr David Ceri Jones agreed to undertake a large number of articles on eighteenth century and evangelical topics. Dr Ralph Waller was kind enough to write an entry in the midst of what must be an exceptionally busy schedule, while Alan Ruston was most helpful in supplying entries from the Unitarian tradition. I am also grateful to Dr Richard C. Allen, Dr Alan Argent, Professor David Killingray, the Revd Geoffrey Roper and Dr Timothy B. Walsh for their willingness to contribute. But in all this, I must record a particular debt to Professor John H. Y. Briggs for his support, encouragement and unfailing help. His willingness to supply all that was asked of him is greatly appreciated and his assistance has contributed significantly to the successful completion of this project.

I would also like to record my thanks to the production company Newgen Knowledge Works, especially through the person of Srikanth Srinivasan with whom it has been a pleasure to work.

Part of chapter 7 has appeared previously as 'The Contribution of Protestant Nonconformists to Biblical Scholarship in the Twentieth Century', in Alan P. F. Sell and Anthony R. Cross (eds), *Protestant Nonconformity in the Twentieth Century* (Carlisle: Paternoster, 2003), pp. 1–32. I am grateful to the editors and to the publisher, through the office of Dr Mike Parsons, for granting permission to reproduce it here.

All the contributors to this volume have established themselves as experts in their various fields and their contributions here draw on an enormous store of critical knowledge. As a result, each chapter constitutes a unique contribution to our knowledge of Nonconformity. Their inclusion in this single volume enables a comprehensive picture to be painted of what was once a socially powerful movement and one which retains historical and theological significance. It should be clear, too, from what follows that, though much denuded, it continues, in various ways, to exercise a religious, social and political influence. For all these reasons, Nonconformity deserves scholarly attention. It is both my hope and my conviction that the collection which follows does justice to its subject and will serve as an authoritative resource for many years to come.

Robert Pope
University of Wales, Trinity St David
Epiphany 2013

Part I

Historical and Theological Topics

1 The Changing Shape of Nonconformity, 1662–2000

John H. Y. Briggs

Nonconformity finds its historical roots in those groups – Congregationalists, Presbyterians, Baptists together with the Quakers – which, for the most part, insisted on a radical Puritan theology, experience and liturgy and found themselves outside the national church after the restoration of the monarchy in 1660. In subsequent years its numbers grew as other groups emerged and developed outside the Church of England, and indeed outside the older forms of Dissent. In the eighteenth century Methodism, in all its forms, constituted a substantial body, which, not without struggle, came to identify itself with evangelical Dissent. In the nineteenth century bodies such as the Plymouth Brethren again sought to implement what they thought was a more apostolic pattern of ecclesiology, while in the twentieth century Pentecostal experience and the migration of peoples from the Caribbean and the continent of Africa have created further new churches which have increasingly sought to identify themselves as part of the 'Free Church' family.

I. Sect, Church and Denomination

Historians have borrowed from sociologists of religion, whose interests lie in the broad sweep of religious movements and organizations, language used to describe different ecclesiastical groupings. These were classically described by Max Weber and Ernst Troeltsch,[1] who wrote of 'church' or 'parish-type' and 'sect-type' groups, with the notion that the first were essentially *comprehensive*, embracing all citizens in a given area, while the second were *exclusive*, confined to those who had made a deliberate choice to join the committed and themselves to take on the responsibilities of membership; thus the frequent over-neat contrast that, whereas one was born into the church, one had to be reborn into the life of a sect. Some theologians have been less than happy with such distinctions because of the not unnatural deduction that sects are necessarily sectarian, without due appreciation of the catholic dimensions of ecclesiology.[2]

While some Dissenters were undoubtedly sectarian, others cherished contrary convictions. Indeed, a large part of the rationale for their separation from the national church was occasioned by their desire to reclaim the true catholicity and apostolicity of the church, in which 'the Crown Rights of the Redeemer' were truly respected without fear of state interference. This church was to have a defined covenanted membership of regenerate believers gathered out of the world, with powers through church meeting or through representative Connexional synod, to discern the mind of Christ for itself and for its mission in the world, and therefore to appoint its own officers. Within such a church the theology of the priesthood of all believers, without degrading the importance of ordination, underlined the participatory nature of the church with high responsibilities assigned to the laity

Thus, the influential Congregational theologian John Owen, sometime vice-chancellor of the University of Oxford, speaks of Christian congregations being 'obliged into mutual Communion among themselves, which is their consent, endeavour and conjunction in and for the promotion of the Edification of the Catholic Church, and therein their own, as they are Parts and Members of it'. As a consequence, to separate from other members of the Church Catholic was a denial of Christian truth:

> No Church therefore is so Independent, as that it can always, and in all Cases, observe the Duties it owes to the Lord Christ and the Church Catholick, by all those Powers by which it is able to act in itself distinctly, without conjunction with others. And the Church that confines its Duty unto the Acts of its own Assemblies, cuts itself off from the external Communion of the Church Catholick; nor will it be safe for any Man to commit the Conduct of his Soul to such a Church.

In categorical language Owen asserts:

> That particular Church which extends not its Duty beyond its own Assemblies and Members, is fallen off from the principal end of its Institution. And every Principle, Opinion, or Persuasion, that inclines any Church to confine its Care and Duty unto its own Edification only; yea, or of those only which agree with it in some peculiar practice, making it neglective of all due means of the Edification of the Church Catholick, is Schismatical.[3]

Accordingly, even in the earliest years there were difficulties with the church–sect classification, but over time H. Richard Niebuhr asserts that church and sect were necessarily compelled to acknowledge the other's continued existence, and even their capacity to be of service to the *Missio*

Dei. Accordingly, he argues, it is better to replace the older terms with the language of 'denomination'. A denomination is thus a church, or indeed for that matter a sect, 'which has accommodated itself to the reality of the permanent competition with other "churches" in its territory'. He also suggests a generational succession in the history of sects, by which they began to respond to a perceived need for institutional support (seen, e.g., in the emergence of theological colleges to train a clerical leadership, a denominational press, central administration, etc.). At the same time he argues that 'as generation succeeds generation, the isolation of the community from the world becomes more difficult',[4] with all the necessary adjustment of actions and attitudes therein involved.

At the same time churches, too, as Alan Gilbert has shown, even established churches, were compelled to move in a denominational direction. To demonstrate this he cites John Keble's frank admission in his famous 1833 Assize Sermon that henceforth the Church of England was 'only to stand, in the eye of the State, as one sect among many, depending for any pre-eminence she might appear to retain, merely upon her having a strong party in the country'. To support his argument Gilbert invokes Peter Berger who suggests that in the second quarter of the nineteenth century the Church of England moved towards 'a typically denominational solution as an ex-monopolistic institution in a pluralistic society', for whereas a church can behave 'as befits an institution exercising exclusive control over a population of retainers', a denomination must organize itself so as 'to woo a population of consumers, in competition with other groups having the same purpose'.[5] In this way the scene was set for the twentieth century and the birth of increasingly cordial ecumenical relations.

II. Dissent, Nonconformity and the Free Churches

The language describing Protestant Christians who do not belong to the Church of England has changed over the last five centuries or so, the language of opposition reflected in the terms 'Dissent' and 'Nonconformity' giving way to the more positive affirmations of the 'Free Churches'. Dissent described those Christians who in conscience *dissented* from the teaching of the Established Church, while Nonconformity described those unwilling to *conform* to its discipline and practice, and, in particular, the totality of its liturgical demands. Both these descriptions were dependent for the actuality of their definition on the faith and practice of the Church by law established, from which they wished to distance themselves. Thus they would describe different groups in Scotland from those they identified in England, and had no strict meaning in Ireland and Wales after the Anglican churches in those nations were disestablished (in 1871 and 1920 respectively).

The language of *Nonconformity* goes back to the sixteenth century: Elizabeth I, in her attempt to secure a broad-based religious settlement after the persecution of the reign of her sister Mary I, secured in 1559 an Act of Uniformity prescribing the use, with some conservative revisions, of the Prayer Book of 1552 introduced in Edward VI's brief reign, and the vestments and religious practice then authorized, which clearly set out the distinctiveness of the outlook of the new English Church from its Catholic roots, but falling short of that sought by more radical minds. But it was the 1662 Act of the same name which confirmed the nature of Nonconformity as we know it, for it required 'unfeigned assent and consent' to all that was in the Book of Common Prayer and for clergy, if not Episcopally ordained, to seek (re-)ordination at the hands of a bishop. This act forced moderate Presbyterians to choose whether to conform, or to decline assent and suffer the consequences of their nonconformity. Similar conformity was also sought of university fellows, schoolmasters and private tutors.[6]

The 'Toleration Act' (1689), which followed the failure of attempts to widen the terms of communion within the reconstituted Church of England to secure greater 'comprehension', provided a limited toleration for Protestant Dissenters professing an orthodox, Trinitarian confession. However, even its limited terms had to be defended, and the so-called Committee of the Three Denominations – Baptist, Congregational and Presbyterian – was set up in 1702 for this purpose. This was followed by the corresponding lay body, the (Protestant) Dissenting Deputies, established in 1732, to seek amendment of the penal legislation, which continued to circumscribe the freedom enjoyed by Nonconformists, often identified as 'Dissenting disabilities', that remained on the statute book.[7] While the Test and Corporation Acts were repealed in 1828, thereby removing the penalty from Nonconformists taking office under the crown and sitting on representative governing bodies, other disabilities, especially those associated with religious tests in the ancient universities, remained in force till the last quarter of the nineteenth century. Though such inequalities may not have inhibited Nonconformists from exercising their full citizenship in the way that they had once done, they did serve to foster Nonconformist militancy against such perceived injustices for which purpose the Liberation Society (founded in 1844 as the Anti-State Church Association, before being renamed nine years later), driven by its fiery secretary the Revd Edward Miall, engaged in passionate polemic.

Other pieces of language are also bound up in this identity; thus the early Nonconformists were uniformly considered to be 'Puritan', concerned both for purity of life and purity in the church, defined in relationship to biblical principles rather than church traditions or state legislation. However, not all Puritans were Nonconformists, indeed some would limit the term to those within the Established Church seeking more forthright reform.

Early Nonconformists were also necessarily 'Separatists', that is to say, in the seventeenth century they separated from the Established Church some going through a stage of semi-detachment sometimes known as semi-Separatism. In the process they came to reject both the principle of establishment and the rule of bishops. A third word is 'evangelical', descriptive of the new life brought to British Protestantism through the ministry of the Wesleys and George Whitefield, which led to both the spiritual and numerical growth of Nonconformity in the second half of the eighteenth century. Most Nonconformists were powerfully influenced by evangelicalism except those Presbyterians who adopted Arian, and eventually Unitarian, views, who, by contrast, finally took the title of 'Rational Dissent', although this must not be taken to mean that other Dissenters were not also influenced by the Enlightenment to develop great respect for a God-given intelligence, as part of the promise of being made in the image of God.

III. The Seventeenth Century

a. 'Old Dissent'

A convenient way of analysing Nonconformity is to consider the different groups by the date of their origin. Thus from the seventeenth century there emerge the Independents or Congregationalists, the Presbyterians, the Baptists and the Quakers, those groups often termed 'Old Dissent'. The doctrine of these groups was prescribed in various confessional statements of which the most important was the *Westminster Confession*, drafted in 1646 and approved by parliament in June 1648, articulating standard Reformed (Calvinist) doctrine and Presbyterian ecclesiology. The Congregational variation is found in the *Savoy Declaration* (1658) which reflects the same doctrine as the *Westminster Confession* but now allied to Congregational church polity. These two statements of faith were also reflected in the Baptist *Second London Confession* of 1677 which revised the earlier 1644 Confession in light of those of *Westminster* and *Savoy*, indicating a wide consensus on the understanding of the Reformed faith.

However, Nonconformist unity was not quite so complete as this might suggest. First, there were at least two kinds of Baptist[8] – General and Particular – reflecting different opinions as to the scope of the atonement, the General Baptists believing in the general salvation of all who believed, a belief derived as much from their Mennonite contacts as from Dutch Arminians, while the Particulars believed in the particular redemption of the elect only. The General Baptists were in this way separate from the main body of Calvinist Dissent from the very beginning, though their so-called Orthodox Creed of 1679, signed by some fifty-four 'messengers, elders and brethren' representing the more orthodox churches in the midland counties, in the interests of unity, did its best to minimize these differences. At the same time it refuted the aberrant Christological views of the Dutch Mennonite Melchior Hoffman, with his minimalist views of the incarnation which were gaining some currency in Kent and Sussex.[9]

In due course many Presbyterians revised their inherited Calvinism to give greater weight to Free Will in the manner of the Arminians. Both General Baptist and Presbyterian divines were in due course to go further in their search for what they took to be an intellectually defensible theology, adopting first Arian views in Christology, and later full-blown Socinian or Unitarian positions,[10] and therefore falling outside the scope of the 'Toleration Act' (1689) with its requirement of a Trinitarian subscription. Similar developments occurred, it should be said, within the Church of England notwithstanding its orthodoxy of liturgy, catechism and articles.

A variety of issues were at stake here, particularly the authority of humanly constructed creeds or confessions of faith, as well as the actual content of such statements. Thus the Nonconformist divines who met together at the Salters' Hall in London in February 1719, to advise the churches on the authority of credal statements spelling out the nature of the Godhead, decided by a vote of fifty-seven to fifty-three against 'human compositions' being authoritative. The alternative was to say that the only test of orthodoxy was scripture without any particular human interpretation being imposed upon it. At a further conference in March, the meeting divided into 'Subscribers' and 'Non-subscribers', those who stood for the Bible as 'the only and perfect rule of faith'. At the time the non-subscribers were eloquent in support of 'the doctrine of the blessed Trinity and proper divinity of Our Lord Jesus Christ', but insisted that such matters were to be tested only by the explicit teaching found in scripture. The make-up of the seventy-eight subscribing ministers who met at Salters' Hall were thirty Presbyterians, twenty-eight Congregationalists, fourteen Particular Baptists, one General Baptist and five whose denomination is not known. Among the seventy-three non-subscribers were forty-seven Presbyterians, nine Congregationalists, fourteen General Baptists, two Particular Baptists and one whose denomination is not known.

From these figures, Michael Watts deduces, 'the majority of Presbyterian and General Baptist ministers took their stand on the sufficiency of scripture, the majority of Congregationalists and Particular Baptists insisted on subscription to a Trinitarian creed'. Admirable though the defence of allowing only the Bible to determine the doctrine of the church may have been, with the benefit of hindsight, it has to be noted that the pulpits of most of the churches which adopted such a slogan were, by the end of the century, occupied by Unitarians, whereas most of the Particular Baptist and Congregational churches weathered the slight of being termed 'antinomian', and remained Trinitarian in their faith.[11]

While we happily use the language of Presbyterian, Independent and Baptist to describe the three historic strands within Nonconformity in the early period, especially under the pressures of persecution which all but destroyed the Presbyterian system of church courts, there was fluidity between the different groups, with local congregations moving from one group to another, and indeed beyond their confessional boundaries. In the seventeenth century there were some regional associations and indeed attempts at national assemblies but none of these were all-embracing. For robust, well-disciplined denominational organization and life was a creation of the nineteenth, and even the twentieth century. However, financial needs did lead to the establishment of a Common Fund in 1690 to aid destitute ministers and to train their successors, a prelude to the establishment of the so-called short-lived Happy Union between Congregationalists and Presbyterians, a year later, designed to bring the two traditions together. While the desire to come together represented a perceived need for organizational strength, the failure of the enterprise within a decade indicates the strength of fiercely held ecclesiologial and theological differences separating the two groups. In like manner General and Particular Baptists failed to find sufficient common ground for united action, with the Particular Baptist Fund resolutely refusing either to help or receive help from General Baptists. Thus organization of the separate Nonconformist congregations in the eighteenth century remained primitive and informal – in the hands of fund holders, meetings in coffee-houses or taverns and voluntary societies formed for specific objects such as itinerancy, ministerial training and the support of Sunday Schools.[12]

b. The Religious Society of Friends (Quakers)

Of the more radical sects born in the seventeenth century, the only one to survive into modern times was the Society of Friends, or the Quakers as they have often been known, who have their origins in the forty-year ministry of George Fox which began in the late 1640s. Quakers give special place to the 'Inner Light', or 'that of God within every man', speaking directly to the soul as their ultimate standard of truth, though the exercise of this was to be informed by the scriptures, and, at the time of their foundation, to operate within a distinctly Christian framework, though uncontrolled by any written creed.

A peace church which did not celebrate the sacraments, believing the whole of human life to have sacramental significance, the Society of Friends in its early history endured much suffering, of which it kept diligent records. Excluded from public life, they made a distinguished contribution to the changing industrial and commercial life of the nation, as seen in the Quaker biscuit and chocolate-making dynasties, as also in their banking partnerships and other industrial initiatives. They were typical of those Dissenters who were motivated by a high work ethic whose religious sensitivity eschewed a lifestyle lavish in display, which necessarily saw them accumulating considerable capital much of which they re-invested in their businesses with a handsome portion devoted to philanthropy.

Though never able to recover the numerical strength they had secured by the end of the seventeenth century, Friends played a distinguished role in exerting a moral influence in national life beyond that which their numbers could justify. In particular, alongside evangelical Anglicans, they led the churches in their campaign to secure first the abolition of the slave trade (1807) and then the emancipation of all slaves within the British Empire (from 1833), realizing that much continuing effort was needed to secure the welfare of the emancipated slaves.

IV. The Eighteenth Century

a. 'New Dissent' – Calvinistic Methodists and Wesleyan Methodism

The eighteenth century witnessed the inception of what has come to be known as 'New Dissent',[13] namely those denominations born out of the Evangelical Revival which gave rise to the birth of Wesleyan Methodism, which espoused a warm evangelical Arminianism, and to their Calvinist counterparts, manifest in the emergence of the Calvinistic Methodists in Wales and the Countess of Huntingdon's Connexion in England. Methodism began as a pietistic reform movement within the Church of England, similar to those which sought to reinvigorate the state churches of Europe, but which, like them, eventually found the parochial system of a state church too confining.

Thus it was that the success of Methodism's itinerant preaching, together with the antagonism of the leaders of the Church of England, meant that the movement found its future outside the Established Church. Separation from the Church was a cause of much heartache and was a cumulative rather than a sudden process. The question had been posed as early as the first conference in 1744, and the very appointment of preachers to itinerate throughout the land, from 1740 onwards, showed scant respect for the parish system. This was compounded when the Methodists began to build their own chapels, the first of which was built in Bristol in 1739, which from the late 1750s were commonly registered, much to John Wesley's regret, under the terms provided for Dissenters by the 'Toleration Act'. In 1760 three Methodist preachers in Norwich provoked a crisis in the Connexion by administering the Lord's Supper, which just over thirty years later was to become common practice within the Connexion. Many see the crucial turning point in 1784 when Wesley ordained two men as presbyters to work in the newly independent United States of America, and 'set apart' Thomas Coke to supervise the work, that is to exercise '*episcope*' over the American churches. Four years later, in 1788, Wesley ordained the first candidate for full ministerial service in England. Internal differences, mainly focused on regional differences and the respective roles of clerical and lay leaders, soon led to a shattering of the unity of the movement into a number of separate communities – Primitive, New Connexion and Bible Christian to name but three – the English sections of which were only finally reunited in 1932. 'Born in song', Methodism offered attractive popular services fruitful in conversions especially among the emerging working class.

New Dissent soon became more numerous than Old Dissent and was well represented right across the nation, both in the countryside and the newly emerging industrial communities of the midlands and the north of England. This is why historians such as Halèvy have argued that the Evangelical Revival saved England from suffering the same kind of social cataclysm that occurred in the French Revolution. Indeed this was an effect which was to continue through the generations, hence the judgement that the Labour Party owed more to Methodism than to Marx. These judgements have, however, been challenged by historians of the Left.

Not only did Methodism make a direct impact in Britain and worldwide, it also helped the older denominations to refocus and to gain a new confidence. Hence Geoffrey Nuttall's view: 'It was during the eighteenth-century that historic Dissent took the form in which it has been a recognizable part of the English scene, and the poles between which, by attraction or repulsion, it did so were Calvinism and the Evangelical Revival.' Here the thinking of Jonathan Edwards, the American Calvinist philosopher theologian, was most marked, as was that of George Whitefield, but the man who provided the Independents (Congregationalists) with a revised Calvinist theology was Edward Williams of Birmingham and Rotherham. Similar changes took place among the Baptists where the Particulars turned against the excesses of hyper-Calvinism to discover, or rediscover, a missionary-orientated interpretation of Calvin's teaching under the influence of Andrew Fuller, which soon led to the founding of the Baptist Missionary Society in 1792, in the midst of the French Wars, the first of Britain's modern missionary societies. Dan Taylor, also under the influence of the Methodist Revival, founded the New Connexion of General Baptists in 1770, which restored orthodoxy and missionary passion to that strand of Baptist life.

b. Rational Nonconformity

Little influenced by the Evangelical Revival were the old Presbyterians and General Baptists who were in the process of moving through Arianism and Socinianism to a full-blown Unitarianism. The movement's origins were to be found among those Dissenters who found it difficult to find a fully fleshed-out doctrine of the Trinity in the Bible, which, rather than creed or confession, they then believed to be the proper test of faith and practice. However, during the eighteenth century many of them, under the influence of ideas emerging out of the Enlightenment, came to give more authority to the divine gift of reason than to the biblical revelation.

Typical of the new emphasis was Theophilus Lindsey who did not have a background in Dissent: in 1773 after the failure of a petition to parliament to relax the terms of subscription, he resigned his living in the Church of England and opened a Unitarian Chapel in Essex Street in London. In this manner he 'first organized Unitarian Dissent as a working force in the religious life of England'. In 1790, with the former Presbyterians Thomas Belsham and Joseph Priestley, the chemist-cum-Unitarian minister who was the dominant figure in the movement for the earlier period, he founded the Unitarian Society, 'the basis of which was an assertion of the unity of God and the simple humanity of Jesus Christ in opposition both to the orthodox Trinitarian formulae and to ancient Arian teaching'.[14]

While numerically a decreasing interest (in the 1851 Census they could only muster just over 3,400 attenders in just 200-odd chapels), they did attract, in addition to their historic roots among the Presbyterians and General Baptists, a considerable number of clergy from Particular Baptist and Independent congregations, and even some from the various Methodist denominations. At an opposite extreme, however, the denomination suffered significant losses to total unbelief or to ethical humanitarianism.[15] Not surprisingly they became ardent champions of reform, making especially valuable contributions in the areas of public health, factory reform, women's rights and prisoners' welfare.[16]

In the ministry of James Martineau, who went on record as lamenting the 'sceptical origin' of the denomination, further theological changes took place for, in the context of an age of romanticism rather than rationalism, Martineau argued that Unitarians should base their faith on 'the intrinsically divine character of Christianity, a more penetrating appreciation of the mind of Christ and a more trustful faith in him for his own sake', a position attacked by his critics as nebulous and irrational.[17] Their non-subscription to any formal theological confession coupled with their rejection of major aspects of orthodox belief meant that formally they were unable to relate to proto-ecumenical or indeed ecumenical initiatives, though personal relationships in some cases transcended these barriers.

V. The World of Chapel

a. Sunday Schools, Temperance, Philanthropy and Missionary Endeavour

In a new, dynamic world, chapels became a major feature of the landscape in both cities and villages, though in the countryside a determinedly Anglican landlord could still deny them a convenient site for the erection of a chapel. On the other hand, Nonconformists were able to respond to the movement of population from the countryside to new industrial locations much more readily than the Established Church, when the parish church could be situated far distant from the new centres of industrial housing; for whereas the establishment of a new parish required legislation in parliament, all the Nonconformists needed was an ever-present abundant enthusiasm, for the skills both to erect and build a chapel and to furnish and equip it could often be found within the chapel community.

So successful were Nonconformists in this new world of capital and commerce that by the time of the one and only religious census in 1851 they could claim rough parity with the Anglican Church in terms of attendances at worship, while possessing in excess of five thousand more places of worship. This numerical strength raised questions as to the continued appropriateness of the disabilities under which they still laboured.

Chapel was, however, more than a place of worship, fundamentally important though this undoubtedly was. Most chapels had either an adjoining Sunday School or this could form a separate building. Either way it provided the chapel community with valuable social space for a wide range of educational and leisure activities. These came to play a large part in chapel life, increasingly occupying a major part of the Nonconformist believer's week. Sunday Schools, together with the other youth activities that they spawned, represented a foremost part of Dissenting outreach into the community, consuming large amounts of capital and vast human resources. Here the laity, and especially the female laity, came into their own. Sunday Schools, then 'one of the most significant social institutions of modern Britain', were 'the only religious institution which the nineteenth-century public in the mass had any intention of using'. They 'taught faith, duty and for much of their existence, literacy', training 'successive generations of children with dedication, often with flexibility, and usually with an intelligent concern for the welfare of their charges'.[18]

Children were also a special focus of the temperance movement which like Sunday Schools absorbed an enormous amount of Nonconformist energy in the nineteenth century, for the moral case for temperance often focused on the dire condition of the drunkard's family in years before the advent of the Welfare State. It was their pitiable condition that drove the most conscientious to adopt teetotalism and to campaign for restrictions on the sale of alcohol. Temperance was intrinsically a matter of social conscience rather than a moralistic peccadillo, a genuine attempt in a drink-sodden society to aid the poor, not a conspiratorial attempt to impose middle-class manners on a reluctant working class.

The movement also gave birth to its own juvenile branches such as the Sons of Temperance, a benefit society with strict temperance requirements, and the Band of Hope, which, with its own distinctive methodology mixing together educational and recreational activities, became a ubiquitous instrument for inculcating Nonconformist culture among the young. Thomas Cook, the General Baptist laymen, sometime missionary in the East Midlands for the New Connexion, began his famous career as a pioneer in the travel business by organizing a temperance excursion from Leicester to Loughborough in July 1841, and later ran several Temperance Hotels in a further attempt to furnish the temperance cause with every convenience. In its support of the temperance movement, Nonconformity increasingly promoted a sober culture of mutual improvement and self-help in contrast to the rowdy sensuous entertainment associated with drink and the public house.

The massive investment in philanthropy, both nationally and in the local community, was another mark of mature Nonconformity, conscientiously committed to aid the destitute and disadvantaged. This puts the lie to the jibe that nineteenth-century Nonconformists were more concerned with the welfare of the destitute overseas than those at home, particularly that they were more concerned for black slaves in the Caribbean and America than the white slaves of the newly emerging factory system at home.

Nevertheless, the interest in overseas missions was a major concern of all the Nonconformist denominations. Both the renewed interest in itinerancy at home and the propagation of Christian missions overseas have a common origin as fruits of the Evangelical Revival. Both emerged in the tumultuous 1790s when the nation politically was engaged with the turmoil in Europe and the ensuing wars with France, a less than auspicious context for such new endeavours. While Wesley expressed global concern in his famous aphorism that he claimed 'the world as his parish', the older Calvinist denominations throwing off the deadweight of antinomianism and aided by the fruits of exploration as secured by persons such as Captain Cook, threw themselves with gusto into the task of worldwide mission. The visionary here was the self-educated Northamptonshire cobbler William Carey, who in 1792 penned *An Enquiry into the Obligation of Christians to Use Means for the Conversion of the Heathen* which stirred the Particular Baptists to found their missionary society later that same year. Nervous of criticism from within their own ranks, they worked within narrow denominational boundaries, not even admitting General Baptist support for the new enterprise.

Rather different was the establishment of the London Missionary Society three years later in 1795. This aimed at a pan-evangelical enterprise, involving not only members of the three denominations but evangelical Anglicans as well – so universal were its ambitions that it was often referred to as *The* Missionary Society. 'As men cheerfully shouldered the great missionary burden, denominational divisions seemed to crumble', argued W. R. Ward. 'There was general euphoria at the end of bigotry and the triumph of Catholic Christianity.' These latter words were, of course, construed from a Protestant Nonconformist point of view, but it was not long before distinctly denominational instruments were being developed to aid mission and ministry at home and abroad. In 1799 a Church Missionary Society was founded on a specifically Episcopal basis, and other joint enterprises at home and abroad faced church–chapel conflicts in their governance. Between 1813 and 1818 Methodist missionary concerns came together in the Methodist Missionary Society.

Later a number of non-denominational societies, operating on the so-called faith principle, the most famous of which was the China Inland Mission, came into being with most of them deriving a large part of their support from the British Free Churches. Be it on a denominational or on a wider basis, missionary concerns formed a large part of the Nonconformist agenda, eliciting massive financial support, the consecration of many lives, some of whom only survived a few months in the country of their missionary service, many well-attended meetings up and down the nation, the exploitation of visual images by means of the new technology of the magic lantern and a prolific array of journals informing the constituency of the geography, customs and societies of the missionary world, making their readers much more aware of global realities in the process.

Such activities necessarily saw reluctant missionary societies becoming engaged with political issues, whether the institution of slavery in the Caribbean, or *sati* in India, or the abuses of labour for the benefit of the rubber trade on the Congo River. Moreover, the opening up of continents through exploration and the nurture of legitimate trade, in the Livingstone mode of championing the Bible and the Flag, involved the missionary enterprise in more than simply evangelistic activity as indeed had been seen from the very beginning with Carey's involvement in the study and promulgation of Indian language and culture.

b. The (Plymouth) Brethren

The nineteenth century saw further new divisions in the church. In the 1830s under the leadership of a former Anglican priest, J. N. Darby, there emerged the (Plymouth) Brethren who in 1849 split between 'Open' and 'Exclusive' strands. Upholding the authority of the Bible, they rejected an ordained ministry. Conservative-evangelical in theology, their worship focuses on the weekly unstructured celebration of 'The Breaking of Bread', partly as symbolizing Christian Union, and partly as indicating the centrality of Christ's death to Christian faith and experience. Internally they are split between the Exclusive (Darbyite) Brethren and more open groups. Though dissenting from the Established Church, in the United Kingdom they have been slow formally to unite in activities with other Free Churches, though they have been influential within interdenominational mission agencies both at home and overseas. In the twentieth century there was a tendency for people in this tradition to transfer to other churches, often taking Brethren ideas with them, such as a dispensationalist pre-millennial view of Christian history, widely disseminated through the use of the so-called Scofield Bible published in 1909.

c. The Salvation Army

Of a very different order is the Salvation Army, whose origins lie in Methodism, and more specifically that off-shoot of Methodism found in the North American Holiness Movement. It was founded in 1878 out of what had previously been the East London Christian Mission, established by William Booth in 1865. The Salvation Army committed itself to aggressive evangelism among the un-churched working classes, taking the Christian gospel to those who never darkened the doors of any church. For this Booth adopted the military metaphor to shape the structure of mission, with uniformed officers rather than clergy, a military command structure, citadels rather than chapels and its weekly journal *The War Cry*. Brass bands popularized its evangelistic liturgies with often the use of secular melodies – 'Why', asked General Booth, 'should the Devil have all the best tunes?' In putting its female officers in particular into a distinctive uniform, the 'Sally Army' played an important role in the emancipation of women, for the Salvation Army 'Lassies' became much respected for their ministry in public houses and more generally in the worst slums of Britain's inner cities.

The Army also became famous for blending social care with evangelism in the interest of those called 'the submerged tenth', vividly expounded in Booth's *In Darkest England and the Way Out* (1890), which metaphorically exploited comparison with H. M. Stanley's *In Darkest Africa and the Way Out* published in the same year. In the nineteenth century the Army saw itself as essentially a mission agency, and was so regarded by other churches who saw it as undertaking a specialist missionary task beyond their own competence. As the Army has participated in the ecumenical movement, it has become more denominationally self-conscious and so has been challenged to rethink its own ecclesiological status.

d. The Nonconformist Conscience

The nineteenth century also saw the emergence of the Nonconformist Conscience,[19] a set of common moral values espoused by the Free Churches. Its origins lie in the campaign first to outlaw the slave trade and secondly to abolish slavery within the British Empire. In their quest for legislation to secure religious equality, Nonconformists were also active in trying to ameliorate their remaining civil disabilities. Giving almost religious value to the principles of self-help they were, however, reluctant to become involved in 'political issues', but slowly they came to see that the great problems of society could not be solved by much philanthropy and a maximum of voluntary effort. Only the state was powerful enough to bring reform. Thus in their concern for temperance as also to control gambling, they necessarily moved from education to legal intervention, which was also the case with Sunday observance.

Other issues, such as factory reform, had already enlisted the state as ally, and housing reform was about to do so as well.

Sexual morality became a focus of concern with two significant literary presentations that emanated from Nonconformist pens: Andrew Mearns' *Bitter Cry of Outcast London* (1883) and W. T. Stead's *Maiden Tribute of Modern Babylon* (1885). The first was concerned with the relationship between sexual laxity and poor housing, and the second with the ease with which the trafficking of young girls from the continent occurred in Victorian London. Allied to this was the passing of a sequence of Contagious Diseases Acts (1864–69) which so offended Josephine Butler, an Anglican vicar's wife who instituted the campaign for their repeal. This series of Acts were aimed at providing English soldiers in garrison towns with 'clean' prostitutes by imposing an arbitrary system of female inspection, thus raising not only issues of morality but issues of gender inequality. If the government could legislate in favour of depraved behaviour, why should legislation not also be the instrument of moral reform?

The actual language of the Nonconformist Conscience emerged in a similar context, when in 1890 the leader of the Irish Party, C. S. Parnell, was cited in a divorce case. While expressing continued concern for justice for Ireland, the Methodist leader, Hugh Price Hughes, thundered, 'we stand immovably on this rock; what is morally wrong can never be politically right', echoing in fact the motto of the Dissenting Benjamin Flower's *Political Review and Monthly Register* (1807–11) from the beginning of the century.

Education was the issue which brought Nonconformity into politics at the end of the nineteenth century. The issue was Nonconformist hostility to any idea that public money should fund confessional education The context was the aftermath of the repeal in 1868 of the church's right to levy a church rate. But could its powers of securing public funds be making a return through the funding of schools rather than churches? Three years after the passing of Foster's Education Act of 1870 the *Baptist Magazine* made the charge: 'The school rate becomes the successor of the church rate.' The contentious finance involved in implementing the act was not large: exchequer grants by way of capitation fees were continued and in fact increased, though building grants came to an end, but clause 25 provided that children in Poor Law institutions should be sent to school at the expense of the local rate-payers. The monies involved were trivial but it was the principle to which Nonconformists objected: Nonconformists should not be forced to pay for the teaching of doctrines which they believed to be false. Worse was to follow with the passing of Balfour's Education Act of 1902 which allowed for denominational schools to be funded from the rates which led to the maximum of Nonconformist hostility and the founding of the 'passive resistance' movement with the withholding of the payment of the education rate, leading to the imprisonment of some 230 resisters over the next three years and thousands fined. Relations between church and chapel could hardly have been more tense.

Although Nonconformists allied with the Liberal Party in an attempt to secure their programme of reform, now including the establishment of a nation-wide system of non-denominational state education which would include simple Bible instruction but not confessional teaching, the Liberals never delivered what the Nonconformist Conscience demanded.

e. Free Church Unity

By the closing years of the nineteenth century, Free Churchmen were less enamoured with the virulent attacks of the Liberation Society on the Established Church, and its fight for disestablishment. In the post-industrial period, both sects and churches had to accommodate themselves to new social realities and to the permanent existence of each other. Thus while the Established Church was compelled to recognize the durability of Dissent, and even by the end of the century the need to work with it, that same Dissent came to shed much of the exclusive sectarianism of its past and to see its own life as but one legitimate way, among many, of being Christian. Thus church and sect alike have, in Niebuhr's sense of the word, become 'denominations' As a result, Noncomformists stressed the fostering of constructive relationships emphasizing the positive aspect of being 'Free Churches', and championing the idea of Free Churches existing in, and protected by a free, that is an increasingly democratic, state.

While many Dissenters shared in the work of the Evangelical Alliance from its beginnings in 1846, that alliance was essentially an alliance of individuals not churches. In 1892 the first national Free Church Congress was held, comprised chiefly of representatives of local Free Church Councils, leading to the establishment of the National Council of the Evangelical Free Churches four years later. The new body, while recognizing the autonomy of the participating denominations, developed the ability to speak on behalf of a wide spectrum of Free Church life, pursuing Free Church educational concerns, developing increasing confidence in recognizing one another's ministries, engaging in nationwide united mission. In many ways such sharing between the Free Churches, as also their involvement in the emergence of daughter churches in the Third World, prepared them for wider ecumenical participation in the second half of the twentieth century.

After the First World War, largely as a result of the persistent efforts of the Revd J. H. Shakespeare, the general secretary of the Baptist Union, a second body, the Federal Council of the Evangelical Free Churches was established, still respecting the autonomy of the participating denominations, but with an agreed Statement of Faith, and with its governing body made up of denominationally authorized delegates. In Shakespeare's mind this was to be the first stage in setting up a United Free Church, which he hoped might in due course enter into discussion about the reunion of all non-Roman Catholic Churches in Britain. His vision was ahead of his time: neither of these outcomes was to occur. In 1940 the two councils, the one founded on local energies, the other brought into being by the express wish of the participating denominations, united to form the Free Church Federal Council, which by the end of the twentieth century was working ever more closely with the national ecumenical instrument Churches Together in England, which then operated from the Council's premises in London.

VI. The Twentieth Century

a. Pentecostalism and the Charismatic Movement

Many historians see the twentieth century giving birth to a new strand of Christian experience – the Pentecostal. Included within that category there would also have to be included what have been called Independently-founded (in contrast with Mission-founded) African Churches. The earliest manifestations of the new movement were in the Welsh Revival of 1904, which had a major impact on the historic Free Churches, and in the Azusa Street Revival in Los Angeles two years later. Their growth worldwide has been amazing – Pentecostal churches alone accounting for more than fifty million members by the 1980s. In general terms their doctrine – in terms of the authority of scripture, Trinitarian views of the Godhead, justification by grace through faith, the call to a holy life, etc. – is similar to that of conservative evangelicals, but their distinctive doctrine is their belief in the baptism of the Holy Spirit, and the expectation of such phenomena as speaking in tongues and faith healing to occur in a post-apostolic age. In Britain three principal Pentecostal denominations emerged: Elim, the Assemblies of God and the Apostolic Church.

The movement cannot, however, be confined to those who have joined one of the Pentecostal denominations. For example, with the impact of the Charismatic movement, it has been claimed that close to 10 per cent of the world's Roman Catholics could be described as Catholic Pentecostals.

Thus alongside institutional Pentecostalism has to be placed the impact of the Charismatic movement within mainstream denominations, that is to say, the number of Christians who place the same kind of emphasis on the special work of the Holy Spirit, with baptism in the Spirit as a separate post-conversion experience, without feeling the need to separate from their parent denominations, was very considerable.[20] Thus from the 1950s onwards there have emerged Anglican Charismatics, Methodist Charismatics, Reformed Charismatics and Baptist Charismatics. More recent manifestations among these groups have been in the 'Signs and Wonders' movement and those who claim the Toronto Blessing.

b. Restorationism and the House Church Movement

A further development from the 1960s onwards has been the development of house churches within what has been called the Restorationist tradition, yet another group in history claiming to recover the primitive apostolic tradition. Their periodical, *Restoration,* was begun in 1975 by Bryn Jones in Bradford and Arthur Wallis, both of whom had a background in the Brethren movement, who believed that Christianity was moving into a post-denominational existence. Many people were attracted to these new lively fellowships from existing Nonconformist congregations. Indeed some whole churches moved over to the new networks which rejected the older form of congregational government in favour of the top-down authority of apostles, who exercised authority over a number of other ministers, who locally appointed elders, as against deacons elected by the church meeting. While many were attracted others were repelled by the triumphalistic, and often sectarian, tone of the new movement, for by the 1980s there were some ten distinct networks operating in the United Kingdom.

c. Black-Majority and Diaspora Churches

Social change has made a constant impact on the life of the churches – none more so than the migration of large numbers of people from the Caribbean to Britain from the 1950s onwards. Finding the worship of many Free Churches too constrained, and, truth to tell, the membership not always welcoming, or understanding of the religious needs of their new neighbours, many turned to Black-majority Pentecostal churches, such as the Church of God of Prophecy, the New Testament Church of God, the New Testament Assembly and many others. People coming from Africa have also often brought with them their distinctive denominations such as the various Aladura (Praying), and the Cherubim and Seraphim Church. A further feature would be the growth in congregations worshipping in languages other than English – for example, French, Spanish, Portuguese, Polish, Korean – catering for diaspora groups, often using the premises of existing Nonconformist churches. At the same time some of the largest congregations in the mainstream denominations came to have a largely non-white membership. All of this means that within the whole rainbow people of God the ethnic profile of the Free Churches has become much more varied with a corresponding diversification of patterns of worship and church life.

d. The Ecumenical Dimension

At the end of the nineteenth century the different Nonconformist denominations were in the process of establishing fraternal organizations crossing national boundaries in a search for worldwide fellowship.[21] The Presbyterians were first in 1877 followed by the Methodists in 1881, the Congregationalists in 1891 and the Baptists in 1905. The forming of these global networks changed the context in which the Free Churches had to identify themselves, no longer simply in terms of relations with the Church of England but now in harmony with the outlook of a worldwide fellowship of shared faith and practice.

In 1892 the Wesleyan layman, Dr (later Sir) Henry Lunn, invited all the territorial bishops, other Anglican dignitaries and representative leaders of the Free Churches to enjoy the majestic scenery of Grindelwald in the Bernese Oberland, there to consider in light of the Lambeth Quadrilateral (Holy Scripture as the rule and standard of faith; the Apostles' and Nicene creed; the sacraments of baptism and Holy Communion and the Historic Episcopate) agreed by the Lambeth Conference of Anglican Bishops in 1888, what might be possible in the realm of Christian reunion. The clause relating to the Historic Episcopate was particularly problematic for Free Church people but many good personal relations were established and Bishop Perowne of Worcester celebrated a joint communion, to the consternation of his High Church colleagues.

A further impetus to close relations with other churches both in this country and across the world was the World Missionary Conference held in Edinburgh in 1910. Thereafter a number of global networks, in all of which the Free Churches played their part, began to bring Christian people together: the International Missionary Council (1921), and the Life and Work (1925) and Faith and Order (1927) movements. A fourth strand was to be found in the World Council of Christian Education which had its roots in the Sunday School movement which had been holding world conventions from 1862, with the International Lessons Committee dating to 1874 and the International Bible Reading Association to 1882. These activities, in which the British Free Churches were prominent, came together in the World Sunday School Association in 1907, renamed the World Council of Christian Education in 1947, a year before the founding of the World Council of Churches at its Amsterdam Assembly in 1948. The British Council of Churches antedated the world body by some six years. In 1990, when the Roman Catholic Church decided to share in council with other Christians, the old British Council of Churches disbanded giving way to a new structure of national councils for England, Scotland, Wales and Ireland with an overarching council dealing with issues common to all four nations. The language also changed from 'Council' to 'Churches Together', symbolic of the vision that the work was to be owned by the churches themselves, rather than effected by a newly created ecumenical bureaucracy.

One of the fruits of the ecumenical movement has been the development of local experiments in churches of different denominations working together. From 1973 these were called Local Ecumenical Projects, but by the 1990s had come to be known as Local Ecumenical Partnerships (LEPs). While some may take the form of a general covenant between churches in a given location to do as much together as possible, others involved shared buildings, ministry, worship and witness in a united congregation. In 2001 some 750 such partnerships existed: many bring together several of the Free Churches, but quite a number cross the boundary between Established Church and one or more of the Free Churches. In particular, the Methodist Church entered into a covenant in 2003, committing itself to working towards closer co-operation and greater mutual recognition with the Church of England.

VII. Confronting Change

Sunday Schools, temperance, philanthropy and missionary endeavour, all so critical in profiling Victorian and early-twentieth-century Dissent were all challenged as essential parts of Nonconformist life as the second millennium came to an end. At the beginning of the twentieth century it has been estimated that four out of five children spent some time in Sunday School; by the year 2000 only 4 per cent of the appropriate age cohorts had that experience.[22] The Free Churches who had been strong sabbatarians were now confronted by a culture which increasingly embraced Sunday as a day for leisure activity and retail therapy rather than Sunday School and worship with effective evangelism suffering from the image of chapel community as a holy huddle of unrealistic spoil-sports. In the context of the welfare state, a generally more affluent society and holidays taken in the wine cultures of southern Europe, the drunkard's family no longer suffered as its predecessors had done, and social drinking became commonplace among Nonconformists, overturning earlier teetotal scruples, though excessive drinking remained a major and apparently intractable problem in certain segments of society.

While throughout the nineteenth century Nonconformist mission embraced not only an evangelistic concern for souls, its philanthropy strove valiantly to improve the context inhabited by the new urban populations.

Increasingly however it became apparent that the structural problems of poverty, industrial production and urban housing were of an order beyond the competence of individual or even communal philanthropy: only the state in either its national or local incarnation had the resources to intervene effectively, and so responsibility for these aspects of human welfare were transferred to them, making larger areas of Dissenting activity apparently redundant. Thus Jeffrey Cox argues, 'the chapels were hit all at once by the emergence of new philanthropic, administrative and educational bureaucracies which destroyed their claims to social utility'.[23]

Concern for global mission was also radically reformed in the latter part of the twentieth century as the old notion of sending churches and receiving mission fields was thrown into disarray, as people from the mission field migrated to the developed world, as the centre of gravity for Christian mission moved south, and the activity of missionary societies gave way to a world of partner churches.

A final question, then, would be whether there is continued justification for Nonconformity, even in the guise of the Free Churches, to remain separate from the Church of England, for the barriers between the different churches have become much more permeable than they were even in the mid-twentieth century, though this is not to say that all the difficult issues of ministry and sacramental practice have been resolved, though they have been, and continue to be, honestly addressed. Moreover with regard to actions of the state which offend the Christian conscience, in terms of war and peace, international economic justice, action to avert ecological disaster, it might be right to assert: 'We are all Dissenters now.'

All this, however, has to be set in the context of the ongoing march of secularization so that one distinguished author entitles his analysis *The Death of Christian Britain*. After plotting the gradual decline of religious commitment in the United Kingdom in the first half of the twentieth century, Callum Brown argues for a process whereby from the 1960s onwards 'a formerly religious people have entirely forsaken organized Christianity in a sudden plunge into a truly secular condition'. Indeed, 'quite suddenly in 1963, something very profound ruptured the character of the nation and its people, sending organized Christianity on a downward spiral to the margins of social significance'.[24]

Arguably this process has been more damaging to Nonconformity than to the Established Church. 'Nonconformity, by definition', argues Alan Gilbert, 'represents a positive commitment to one religious system rather than another; and for this reason it is much less likely than Anglicanism to survive as a residual loyalty in a secular society.'[25] But this is not the whole truth, for if one includes as Free Churches, the Pentecostal, Black-majority and New Church groupings, they remain numerically significant, though now sharing much less coherence of history and tradition. Indeed, in this context, David Bebbington argues that in Callum Brown's decade of crisis, there emerged 'a new Nonconformity'.[26]

In 1962, Christopher Driver published his *A Future for the Free Churches?* with a rather emphatic question mark, a year before Callum Brown's year of cataclysmic change. Even so the signs were there.

> [O]ver large tracks of the country . . . behind the peeling facades and the plaintive wayside pulpits there is nothing left but a faithful, ingrown remnant, whiling away its Pleasant Sunday Afternoons and its Women's Bright Hours in dingy rooms from which whole generations and classes and intelligence levels have long since fled.[27]

The sad truth was that it was not only society that had become secularized but a large part of chapel life as well. David Bebbington has argued that the chapels in their attempts to face the social challenges of the times had 'blunted the distinctly religious appeal of their message', drawing attention in particular to the impact of milder and less dogmatic understandings of the nature of hell and the afterlife.[28]

Questions therefore arise. Have the Free Churches in recent history properly deployed their freedom in the interests of the witness of the Church of Jesus Christ? How far were the marks of historic Nonconformity still vitally present in their witness? How far has the Established Church so radically changed as to lessen the need for Dissent – with better involvement of the laity, more congregational decision-making, and freer forms of worship blended with the structure of the liturgy? Were, then, the twin forces of establishment and episcopacy still obstacles to reunion in a secular world in which the actual form of establishment was changing so that Dissenting disabilities could hardly be seen as a cause of continued division? To what extent had the Charismatic movement created new relationships in and between the churches, and together with the emergence of new denominations, small as discrete entities but considerable in their combined force, and the growth of Black-majority churches created a new strength within the Free Churches?

However, even a Free-churchman, of such profound ecumenical commitment as Ernest Payne could argue that developments in church and state in Britain have not 'invalidated the basic Free Church contention that Faith comes before Order, the Gospel before the Church', continuing with the contention that 'Tradition, whether in doctrine or in practice, is a valuable guide but a poor master'. Given that the central principle of the Free Churches 'has been vindicated again and again in history', 'the way to unity cannot be by the sacrifice of truth or principle, or by the repudiation of the spiritual heritage of any branch of the Church'. Moreover, it remains true that there is a bond of kinship (e.g. in the mutual recognition of membership and ministry) which stretches across all the Free Churches, not only in these islands but around the world, which operates on a deeper level than many other ecumenical relationships. However, the very title of Free Church imposes an obligation that those of this tradition live up to their name.

Notes

1 Max Weber, '"Churches" and "Sects" in North America: An Ecclesiastical Socio-Political Sketch', *Sociological Theory*, 3/1 (1985), pp. 7–13, translated from the original publication in the *Frankfurter Zeitung* and the *Christliche Welt* both in 1906; Ernst Troeltsch, *The Social Teaching of the Christian Church*, 2 vols, trans. Olive Wyon (London: Allen and Unwin, 1931).

2 For example, Paul Fiddes, 'Church and Sect: Cross-Currents in Early Baptist Life', in A. R. Cross and N. J. Wood (eds), *Exploring Baptist Origins* (Oxford: Regents Park College, 2010), pp. 33–57.

3 John Owen, *The True Nature of a Gospel Church* (1689 edn), pp. 234, 244, 251.

4 H. Richard Niebuhr, *The Social Sources of Denominationalism* (New York: Meridian Books, 1957 [1920]), pp. 6, 20.

5 A. D. Gilbert, *Religion and Society in Industrial England: Church, Chapel and Social Change, 1740–1914* (London: Longman, 1976), pp. 142–43, citing Keble's *Assize Sermon on National Apostacy* as quoted in D. Bowen, *The Idea of the Victorian Church* (Montreal: McGill University Press, 1968), p. 43, and P. Berger, *The Social Reality of Religion* (London: Faber and Faber, 1969), pp. 137–38. See also J. H. Y. Briggs, 'Confessional Identity, Denominational Institutions and Relations with Others: A Study in Changing Contexts', in P. E. Thompson and A. R. Cross (eds), *Recycling the Past or Researching History? Studies in Baptist Historiography and Myths* (Milton Keynes: Paternoster, 2005), pp. 14–16.

6 Michael R. Watts, *The Dissenters, Volume I: From the Reformation to the French Revolution* (Oxford: Clarendon, 1978), pp. 17–18, 218–19. See also. Alan P. F. Sell (ed.), *The Great Ejectment of 1662: Its Antecedents. Aftermath and Significance* (Eugene, OR: Pickwick Publications, 2012).

7 Ibid., pp. 167–68; B. L. Manning, *The Protestant Dissenting Deputies* (Cambridge: Cambridge University Press, 1952).

8 There was a third group, the Seventh-Day Baptists, who believed that Saturday not Sunday was the appropriate day for Christian worship.

9 See W. L. Lumpkin and Bill Leonard (eds), *Baptist Confessions of Faith* (2nd edn, Valley Forge, PA: Judson Press, 2011), pp. 298–348.

10 Both Arians and Socinians made the second person of the Trinity subordinate to the Father, but whereas the Arians allowed pre-existence and divinity to the Son, conferred on him by the Father, the Socinians denied both the Son's pre-existence and his divinity and any doctrine of vicarious atonement.

11 Watts, *The Dissenters*, pp. 375–77. 'Antinomian', an epithet often used unjustly to vilify conservatives by those of a more liberal outlook, describes those High or hyper-Calvinists, who so emphasized the privileges of the elect as to put them beyond the requirements of obeying the moral law.

12 R. Tudur Jones, *Congregationalism in England, 1662–1962* (London: Independent Press, 1962), pp. 110–14. Roger Hayden, 'Coffee House Baptists in Eighteenth-Century London', unpublished paper.

13 Most commentators so label Old and New Dissent, distinguishing between those denominations with a seventeenth-century origin and those that were born out of the revivals of the eighteenth century. For his part Alan Gilbert uses 'New Dissent' not only to describe the various Methodist groups, but also the rejuvenated groups among Baptists and Congregationalists. Gilbert, *Religion and Society in Industrial England*, pp. 47–48.
14 E. A. Payne, *The Free Church Tradition in the Life of England* (London: Hodder and Stoughton, 1965 [1944]), p. 81.
15 Michael R. Watts, *The Dissenters, Volume II: The Expansion of Evangelical Nonconformity, 1791–1859* (Oxford: Clarendon Press, 1995), pp. 81–97.
16 See R. V. Holt, *The Unitarian Contribution to Social Progress* (New York: Lindsey Press, 1952 [1938]).
17 C. Gordon Bolam, Jeremy Goring, H. L. Short and Roger Thomas, *The English Presbyterians: From Elizabethan Puritanism to Modern Unitarianism* (London: G. Allen and Unwin, 1967), pp. 254–57.
18 See Stephen Orchard and John H. Y. Briggs (eds), *The Sunday School Movement: Studies in the Growth and Decline of Sunday Schools* (Milton Keynes: Paternoster, 2007), commendations by David Bebbington, David Thompson and W. R. Ward, cited pp. 42–43.
19 D. W. Bebbington, *The Nonconformist Conscience: Chapel and Politics, 1870–1914* (London: G. Allen and Unwin, 1982).
20 Ian Randall, *Evangelical Experiences: A Study in the Spirituality of English Evangelicalism, 1918–39* (Carlisle: Paternoster, 1999), chapter 8.
21 For this section consult A. P. F. Sell and A. R. Cross (eds), *Protestant Nonconformity in the Twentieth Century* (Carlisle: Paternoster, 2003); Randall, *Evangelical Experiences*.
22 D. Rosman, 'Sunday Schools and Social Change in the Twentieth Century', in Orchard and Briggs (eds), *The Sunday School Movement*, p. 150; D. Bebbington, 'Evangelism and Spirituality in Twentieth-Century English Protestant Nonconformity', in Sell and Cross (eds), *Protestant Nonconformity in the Twentieth Century*, p. 203.
23 Jeffrey Cox, *The English Churches in a Secular Society: Lambeth 1870–1930* (Oxford: Oxford University Press, 1982), pp. 198–201, 253 and chapter 8.
24 Callum Brown, *The Death of Christian Britain: Understanding and Secularization, 1800–2000* (London: Routledge, 2000), p. 1.
25 Gilbert, *Religion and Society in Industrial England*, p. 206.
26 Bebbington, 'Evangelism and Spirituality in Twentieth-Century English Protestant Nonconformity', pp. 214–15.
27 Christopher Driver, *A Future for the Free Churches?* (London: SCM, 1962), pp. 16–17.
28 Bebbington, 'Evangelism and Spirituality in Twentieth-Century English Protestant Nonconformity', pp. 191–92.

2 Nonconformity in Wales

D. Densil Morgan

Late-Tudor Wales was rural, poor and staunchly royalist. Its towns were few and small and it hardly possessed the middling, mercantile class among which English Puritanism flourished. There is little wonder, therefore, that Wales, John Penry apart, does not garner a mention in Patrick Collinson's authoritative study *The Elizabethan Puritan Movement*.[1] Puritan influence, when it arrived, was purely a Stuart, and post-Stuart, phenomenon.

I. Pre-Restoration Wales, 1639–60

Even in the Stuart period Puritanism was localized, in the border town of Wrexham in north-east Wales, where links with the principal towns of the English midlands were strong, and in east Monmouthshire similarly linked with Gloucestershire and Bristol. 'Puritanism', according to Geraint H. Jenkins, 'spread along the trade routes in South Wales and tended to prosper best among the well-to-do and middling sorts'.[2] Precise dates are hard to ascertain, but it seems that William Wroth (1576–1641), a graduate of Jesus College, Oxford, and incumbent of the parish of Llanfaches, Monmouthshire, underwent a conversion in ca 1630–31 and began preaching in an awakening way, while William Erbury (1604–54), first as curate in St Wooloo's church, Newport, and in 1633 as vicar of St John's parish, Cardiff, made his Puritan credentials clear to all. A native of Cardiff, he had studied both at Brasenose College, Oxford, and Queens' College, Cambridge. Walter Cradock (1610–59), from Llangwm, Monmouthshire, a graduate of Jesus College, Oxford, and like the other two from a fairly substantial yeoman background, became Erbury's curate, and after clashing with his bishop (who referred to him memorably as 'a bold ignorant young fellow') in 1634, transferred to Wrexham for a year, where a Puritan lectureship had already been established. There, during 1635–36, he made quite a stir not least among the town's publicans who accused him, through the effects of his preaching, of curtailing their trade. Among his listeners was a schoolboy from Merionethshire, in the heart of north Wales' Snowdonia, called Morgan Llwyd (1619–59), who was drawn to his radical message. Along with Vavasor Powell (1617–70), a schoolmaster from Radnorshire, Cradock and Llwyd would form the triumvirate who would take the lead in the Puritan advance of the Cromwellian period a decade later.

The first Nonconformist congregation or church (notwithstanding the claim by the eighteenth-century Baptist historian Joshua Thomas that there was a Baptist fellowship in Olchon, on the border of Breconshire, Monmouthshire and Herefordshire as early as 1633[3]) was that established by William Wroth, a semi-Separatist congregation within his own parish, set up in 1639 according to 'the New England way'. This meant that it did not wholly reject the Anglican compact as being apostate, but invited members to covenant together in a sacramental fellowship voluntarily undergoing church discipline with an open policy regarding baptism, whether believer's baptism or paedo-baptism: 'They represented a godly community of saints whose worship supplemented rather than undermined the parochial system.'[4]

What gave Welsh Puritanism its edge during the 1630s and, paradoxically, its advantage however localized, was Archbishop Laud's policy of enforcing uniformity from 1634 onwards when he was appointed to the see of Canterbury. His overzealous use of the Star Chamber and the Court of High Commission, before which Wroth, Erbury and Cradock were all summoned, afforded their views publicity which otherwise they would not have attained. However, with the collapse of the Laudian regime in 1641, and the ensuing tension between parliament and king, Welsh Puritans – Cradock especially – came to wield considerable influence within parliamentary circles. If Puritanism gained strength among the better off in the towns, Swansea, Cardiff, Haverfordwest, Wrexham and the like, the inveterate conservatism of the bulk of the Welsh everywhere else made them staunch supporters of the king. The onset of the Civil War, in 1642, made it difficult for the incipient nonconformist or 'gathered', non-parochial churches to survive. Many from the Llanfaches congregation relocated to Bristol, and when the king took that city in 1643, to London. Due to the weakness of parliamentary influence outside the principal conurbations, the attempted introduction of Presbyterian polity within the national church from 1643 never extended to Wales. This meant that where Puritanism persisted, it would develop as Congregationalism or Independency: 'Rigid, middle-class Presbyterianism did not commend itself to the disciples of William Wroth, who increasingly endorsed the independence of individual congregations and pressed for religious toleration and godly reformation.'[5] By the mid-1640s a spirit of revival had registered in the mountain areas north of Llanfaches, and in a sermon before parliament in 1648, Cradock could report that he had observed 'the most glorious work that ever I saw in Britain, unless it were in London; the Gospel is run over the mountains between Brecknockshire and Monmouthshire, as the fire in the thatch'.[6] This was the year of Colonel Thomas Pride's 'purge' of the Long Parliament and the institution of radical political reform culminating in the execution of Charles I a year later. A campaign of vigorous, government-sponsored evangelism ensued, its main impact being channelled through the Act for the Better Propagation and Preaching of the Gospel in Wales (1650) by which the state seized church assets and used them to finance the employment of evangelical preachers to replace parish clergy unacceptable to the new regime, and the establishment of a system of primary education. In operation between 1650 and 1653, 278 clergymen were ejected from their livings while a committee of twenty-five 'approvers' selected their replacements.[7] The most high-profile campaigner for the Act was Vavasor Powell, a firebrand by any measure, who drew huge opprobrium due to both the radical nature of the measure and the inept way in which it was put into practice. The most effective centres of activity were, once more, the border area of south-east Wales and Wrexham in the north-east, where Morgan Llwyd and his successor Ambrose Mostyn (1610–63?) were based. Following the cessation of the Act in March 1653, the task of appointing permanent incumbents to Welsh parishes was transferred to London, to the Committee for Approbation of Public Preachers, the so called Triers.

The former unanimity among the Welsh Puritan leaders was destroyed in 1655 when Erbury and Powell, both of whom held to millennialist or Fifth Monarchy doctrines, challenged Oliver Cromwell's claim to be Lord Protector, believing this to be an affront to the unique authority of the returning Christ. Cradock, for his part, actively supported the Protector's regime, while Llwyd, the most introspective and theologically creative of the group,[8] became disillusioned by the strife and took to contemplation and mysticism. By this time the early promise of Puritan renewal had diminished, while its leaders, still relatively young men, passed from the scene. Erbury died, aged 50, in 1654; Cradock, aged 49, in 1659; Llwyd, aged 40, in the same year. Only Powell survived beyond the Restoration, dying in 1670 still aged only 53: 'By the time of Cromwell's death in 1658 the Puritan movement in Wales was hopelessly fragmented . . . Robbed of a common cause, the Welsh saints drifted apart and were never again able to stimulate a genuine spiritual revolution.'[9]

The radicalism of Welsh Puritanism, such as it was, was never that of the Ranters, the Levellers or the Diggers, only being displayed in the influence of the millenarian Fifth Monarchists as illustrated by the witness of Powell and the early Morgan Llwyd, the Baptists and, more pointedly, the Quakers. The first Baptist community was established in 1656 in mid-Wales, not far from the English border, by Hugh Evans, a local man who had been won to the General or Arminian Baptist cause during his time as an apprentice mercer in Worcester before returning intent on evangelizing his home area, the parishes of Llan-hir, Cefnllys and Nantmel in Radnorshire.[10] Yet the undoubted leader of the Baptist cause in Wales was John Myles, a native of

Welsh-speaking Herefordshire and graduate of Brasenose College, Oxford, who was dispatched by the London Particular (or Calvinistic) Baptists in 1649 to evangelize south Wales. Unlike the Llanfaches semi-separatists or the Radnorshire open-communion Arminians, Myles' vision was ecclesiastical as much as it was individualist. The creation of specific church communities was as important as the salvation of individual souls. Between 1649 and 1653 a network of five closed-communion Calvinistic Baptist churches bound together tightly in an association had been established between Carmarthen in west Wales and Abergavenny in south-east Wales with Ilston, on the Gower peninsula, as its headquarters. Like Cradock, Powell and Llwyd, Myles (1621–83) was a leading Welsh Puritan, an approver under the Propagation Act and a born administrator, and between 1649 and 1660, 261 people were baptized, 153 of them women (in Ilston itself the percentage was higher), putting themselves under a bracing doctrinal and moral discipline.[11]

If the Baptist faith was thought to undermine both social convention and the contract between church and state, Quakerism with its radically subjectivist piety and violently anti-establishment temper, was even more disturbing. The link between the English Quakers and Wales was Morgan Llwyd who, in 1653, sent emissaries to Swarthmoor Hall in Lancashire to explore common ground between his own increasingly interiorized spirituality and the 'inner light' of the followers of George Fox. Quakerism filled the void left by the collapse of Fifth Monarchist speculation following Cromwell's appointment as Protector. The one man who took on the mantle of leadership was John ap John (1625–97) from Rhiwabon near Wrexham, formerly a member of Morgan Llwyd's congregation, who became Fox's lieutenant in Wales. Quakerism rooted itself in Merionethshire, especially the area around Dolgellau in the shadow of the Cader Idris range, and parts of Montgomeryshire flourishing there from 1656 onwards. John accompanied Fox on his famous tour through Wales in 1657, translating the leader's message into the vernacular and preaching himself in Welsh. Like Puritanism generally, the movement drew support from the lesser squires, farmers and yeomen in the rural areas and craftsmen and artisans in the towns as well as some very spirited women. Even more than with the Baptists, Quakerism afforded women the opportunity to practice their talents within the context of worship, but here they were given full parity with the men. They were, in fact, a 'radical, turbulent and bellicose people who proclaimed their message with fearless candour'.[12]

II. Restoration and 'Toleration', 1660–89

By the mid-1650s there was a yearning for peace, tranquillity and the earlier *status quo*. With the restoration of the monarchy in May 1660 came the settling of old scores and the first to suffer were those Puritans whose convictions had been the most radical. The town gaols in Carmarthen, Haverfordwest and Cardiff were filled with Quakers who refused to take the oath of loyalty while Vavasor Powell, the most pugnacious of the Welsh Puritans, would spend all but ten months of the next decade in the Fleet and other prisons before his premature death in 1670.

The Cavalier Parliament lasted for eighteen years between 1661 and 1679, during which time the fortunes of those Protestants who were least enamoured of the renewed Anglican compact were most strained. Many of the 120 or so Puritan ministers who had been installed in Welsh parishes during the Commonwealth quit well before the enactment of the Act of Uniformity on 24 August 1662, St Bartholomew's Day. In fact, seventy-eight did so in 1660, thirteen in 1661 and only thirty or so in 1662. Only conscientious Presbyterians (of whom there were few) like the diarist Philip Henry (1631–96) in Hanmer, Flintshire, and John Jones in Llanarmon, Denbighshire, held out to the end, hoping for comprehension within an inclusive if re-formed establishment. When it was made known that Episcopal ordination was a requirement of the new regime, unfeigned acceptance of the whole of the Book of Common Prayer and unreserved allegiance to the system, they felt they had no choice but to refuse to conform. Thereafter the stipulations of the Clarendon Code – the first Conventicle Act of May 1664, the Five Mile Act of October 1665, the second Conventicle Act of May 1670 to say nothing of the previously ratified Corporation Act of December 1661 and Quaker Act of May 1662 – placed conscientious Puritans wholly outside the establishment's pale. 'Welsh Dissenters', states Geraint H. Jenkins, 'were confronted by a dispirited array of penal laws whose avowed aim was adamantly clear: to inflict upon them untold pain, suffering and humiliation'.[13] The effectiveness of these measures, nevertheless, depended on local circumstances. Not all magistrates were happy to fulfil the minutiae of the rulings, and with the Declaration of Indulgence in 1672 the regimen was suspended. Now allowed restricted rights under the law, some 185 Welsh Dissenters including Baptists, Independents and a few Presbyterians were granted licences to register their meeting places. The one sect which was wholly impervious to the Penal Code was the Quakers. From 1681 onwards they emigrated, recreating in the townships of Haverford, Merion, Tredyffrin, Bala-Cynwyd and Bryn Mawr on the banks of the Schuylkill River near William Penn's Philadelphia, those communities which had flourished previously at the foot of Cader Idris. It would spell the virtual demise of Quaker influence within Wales itself.

According to the Compton Census of 1676 there were some four thousand Dissenters in the four Welsh dioceses: 247 in Bangor, 463 in St Asaph,

905 in Llandaff and 2,401 in St Davids. This was still a small minority, some 1 per cent of the Welsh population as a whole. Dissent, like Puritanism, prospered best in populous, busy and thriving urban centres, along the borders and in south Wales. In Glamorganshire and parts of Monmouthshire it was proving to be sturdy: 'Ministers had evidently preserved the fellowship of their churches and old Puritanism was still very much alive'.[14] Some rural networks also flourished: Independents in the Cilgwyn church situated in mid- and north Cardiganshire, the Baptists of north and north-west Carmarthenshire, the Teifi Valley and a wide area beyond, who established a new church, at Rhydwilym, in 1667, when the Penal Code reigned supreme, which soon measured its membership in hundreds. By this time Myles' church in Ilston had declined seriously. The leaders of post-1660 Welsh Dissent were not destined to achieve the fame of their predecessors, but the sometimes clandestine preaching of the Independents Stephen Hughes (1622–88) 'the apostle of Carmarthenshire', Henry Maurice (1634–82) in Breconshire and Radnor, Hugh Owen (1639–1700) in Merionethshire and the tenacious Baptist William Jones (d. 1701) at Rhydwilym ensured not only the survival of Dissenting witness but its confirmation and ensuing strength. 'In short', to quote Geraint H. Jenkins again: 'Dissent was here to stay.'[15]

With the 'Toleration Act' of 1689, Dissent was legalized though its adherents still suffered considerable disadvantages. Provided they took out a licence and worshipped behind unlocked doors, they were now allowed to congregate and to build their own meeting houses. William III's policies were substantially more enlightened than those of his predecessors, yet his Dissenting subjects remained excluded from civil and political activities, their sons were barred from attending the English universities – Wales would not have its own university until the nineteenth century – and they were expected to contribute both church rate and tithe. Nevertheless, the historiography of Welsh Dissent registered 1689 as a time of respite if not wholesale rejoicing. 'With this', wrote Joshua Thomas, 'peace at last prevailed throughout the kingdom.'[16]

III. 'Toleration' and Revival, 1689–1735

With the cessation of persecution came a period of calm. Welsh Dissent had weathered the storm and emerged the stronger. If the revolutionary drama of Puritanism had abated in 1660 and the more pointed post-Restoration hardships had ended in 1689, the years leading up to the spectacular energies of the Evangelical Revival witnessed the consolidation and even modest expansion of the cause. It has been claimed that 'the period from 1660 to 1689 was, truly, the heroic age of Welsh Dissent'.[17] If that is the case, heroism gave way to a sense of sobriety, doctrinal exactitude and deep seriousness of purpose. Evangelism and church expansion remained a priority but the piety of what can now be termed the Older Dissent was characterized by a restrained and measured classicism. 'As the cultured congregation sank deep into its pews in the meeting houses at Llwynrhydowen, or Pen-dref (Llanfyllin), or Rhydwilym, in order quietly to savour its worship, its members could be forgiven for thinking that their sobriety and cultivated demeanour were an aspect of the predestination in which they revelled daily.'[18] In other words, the gilded age of Dissent had arrived.

The Anglican ideal in 1662 had been to impose a virtually absolute uniformity between the Established Church and the state.[19] Such, however, was the resolute quality of Protestant Dissent (and the durability of the Roman Catholic community which was, in Wales, much less extensive[20]) that the ideal had proved unworkable. The 'Toleration Act' had, in fact, institutionalized Dissent and the Established Church was obliged to act accordingly. By the beginning of the eighteenth century not even the exquisite prose of such High Church apologists as Ellis Wynne in *Gweledigaethau'r Bardd Cwsg* ('The Visions of the Sleeping Bard', 1702) or Theophilus Evans in the polemical sections of *Drych y Prif Oesoedd* ('A Mirror of the Early Ages', 1716), his imaginative history of the early Welsh nation and church,[21] could disabuse Protestant Dissenters of the validity of their claim to exist and indeed to prosper. Accusations of schism, undermining the social order and a disdain for legally instituted authority increasingly rung hollow, while Dissent took full advantage of the Church of England's weaknesses, its unwieldy structures, its large parishes especially in the sparsely populated uplands and its often indifferent spiritual discipline. Even the most loyal Anglicans were conscious of their church's faults, as the famous lament *A View of the State of Religion in the Diocese of St David* (1721) by Erasmus Saunders, prebendary of Brecon, makes abundantly clear.[22] Seizing their opportunity, Dissenting fellowships became even sturdier and expanded their bounds. By 1715 the Baptists had some twenty-one congregations or fellowships within a dozen churches, while the Independents and Presbyterians – which, in Wales, had become virtually indistinguishable from one another[23] – possessed some eighty congregations grouped together within some sixty separate churches. Baptist strength was in north Pembrokeshire and on the Carmarthen–Cardiganshire border, mid-Glamorgan, west Monmouthshire as well as parts of Radnorshire, while the Independents were also strongest in west Wales namely Pembrokeshire, Carmarthenshire and Cardiganshire; in Breconshire in mid-Wales; Glamorganshire and Monmouthshire in the south, as well as having a limited presence in such north Wales towns as Pwllheli, Rhuthin, Denbigh and Wrexham. In all by 1715 the Dissenting denominations had an estimated membership of some 17,700 which, although still a small proportion of the Welsh people, had expanded from the 1 per cent recorded in 1676 to nearly 4 per cent of the population as a whole.[24] The figures, collated by Dr John Evans of London's Hand Alley Church in response to the request made by the Committee of the Three Denominations, illustrate the relative strength and extensiveness of the movement. They 'reveal that Welsh Dissent was a small but influential minority'.[25]

The churches of Welsh Older Dissent were populated, for the most part, by 'the middling sorts': artisans, craftsmen, tradesmen and their families as well as among many yeoman farmers. As such they were sufficiently independent to be distanced from the social hierarchy which was represented by the Church of England and were equally far from the rural and urban poor. As for their ministers, 'these were sober, knowledgeable, well-to-do men, and most . . . were landowners'.[26] Church membership incurred a religious and moral responsibility which was not undertaken lightly. It entailed discipline and the detailed mutual supervision of members' lives. The single Sunday service, usually in the morning, included the reading of scripture, communal prayer, hymn or psalm singing and the exposition of the Word. This was complemented by catechizing within families in the home on Sunday afternoons. Apart from the Quakers and, in mid-Cardiganshire, a small move towards Arianism and Rational Dissent,[27] the doctrinal underpinning of Welsh Dissent was Calvinism. The movement possessed a coherent dogmatic theology and a clear, high churchmanship. The sacraments, both baptism and the Lord's Supper, were objective witnesses to God's sovereign grace, while both Baptists and Independents had a high concept of the ordained ministry. The minister's principal task was the preaching of the Word, while it could be said that, in Wales, the history of post-Restoration Dissent is that of its preachers.[28] Philip Pugh, Edmund Jones and Lewis Rees had prominence among the Independents while Enoch Francis, Miles Harry, Morgan Griffiths and Timothy Thomas were most renowned among the Baptists.

Philip Pugh (1679–1760), who did so much to preserve the doctrinal rectitude of Cardiganshire Independency in the face of the encroachment of Arianism, would become the virtual mentor of Daniel Rowland, the Anglican clergyman who became one of the mainsprings of the Evangelical Revival. Edmund Jones of Pontypool (1702–93), the so-called *Hen Broffwyd* ('Old Prophet'), functioned virtually as an archbishop among the Independents with influence far beyond his Monmouthshire base, while Lewis Rees (1710–1800), a native of the Neath Valley in Glamorgan, pastored the notable congregation at Llanbryn-mair, Montgomeryshire, before returning to oversee the significant growth of the Independent cause in the environs of Swansea. The Baptist Enoch Francis (1688–1740) fulfilled a distinguished ministry in the Teifi Valley on the Cardiganshire–Carmarthen border. Miles Harry (1700–60), leader of the Monmouthshire Baptists and associate of the Methodist revivalist Howell

Harris, would ensure that the energies of the Evangelical Revival would be channelled (at least for a while) into the Older Dissent, while Morgan Griffiths (1699–1748), a zealous evangelist, led the movement in the eastern part of Glamorganshire. Timothy Thomas (1720–68), minister at Aberduar, Carmarthenshire, combined literary gifts with a consummate doctrinal precision. For the Older Dissent ecclesiastical purity, doctrinal exactitude and evangelical zeal went hand in hand. An openness to the missionary task and a yearning for a fresh outpouring of the Spirit meant that the Evangelical Revival, when it arrived, would be afforded a cautious welcome. It would be only by the 1780s and 1790s however, that the revival would turn Welsh Dissent from a select and somewhat marginal body into a vibrant popular movement which would transform the nation's life.

IV. The Methodists and Their Influence, 1735–1811

Despite the movement being, on the whole, evangelistically orientated and spiritually lively, it was from among those wholeheartedly committed to the Established Church that widespread renewal would occur. The Evangelical Revival in Wales is dated from the conversion experience of the Anglican schoolmaster Howell Harris (1714–73) of Trevecka, Breconshire, at Eastertide 1735, and the awakening of Daniel Rowland (1713–90), curate of Llangeitho, Cardiganshire, at roughly the same time. Neither man knew the other, and at the beginning at least, the spiritual revival which spread from these two centres in mid- and west Wales remained independent of one another.[29] Within a few years William Williams of Pantycelyn (1717–90), soon to become immortalized as the hymnist *par excellence* of the revival in Wales, and by the early 1740s Peter Williams (1723–96), latterly best known as a commentator of scripture and supplier of bibles, would join them in leadership roles. Rowland and both Williamses were ordained clergymen while Harris, a layman, was doggedly committed to perpetuating the Methodist message from within the bounds of the Established Church.

Between 1735 and 1740 all the signs were that the renewal of spirituality and heightened evangelistic verve which emanated from the new Methodist movement would energize Calvinistic Dissent as well. Daniel Rowland found in Philip Pugh, his neighbour and pastor of the Cilgwyn church in Cardiganshire, a wise mentor and sound advisor in the evangelical way. It was Pugh who counselled him to emphasize the gospel rather than the law and to apply the balm of free grace to afflicted souls sooner rather than later while entreating them to come to Christ.[30] Hearing of his startling effectiveness as a peripatetic evangelist, Edmund Jones, supported by the Baptist Miles Harry, invited Howell Harris to the uplands and valleys of Monmouthshire in 1737–38 to hold public preaching meetings for the edification of all. These were but two of a number of Dissenting ministers from south-east Wales – David Jones of Caerphilly, James Davies of Merthyr Tydfil, Henry Davies of the Vale of Neath and the Baptist James Roberts of Ross were others – who worked in tandem with the young Methodist leaders, contributing to the administrative structures that Harris was beginning to put in place to provide pastoral oversight for new converts. The first Methodist 'associations' were open to the evangelical clergy and Dissenting ministers alike.

It was not, however, to last. By 1740 the Dissenters had become wary of Harris' autocratic ways. Also, rather than assisting in the work of establishing fellowship meetings or 'societies' of the newly converted who still owed an allegiance to the Established Church, a far more instinctive response among the ministers was to form them into gathered Dissenting congregations. This was anathema to Harris and Rowland, both of whom would remain staunch Church of England men. Theological dissension occurred, especially in Harris' case concerning the doctrine of assurance, while for the Baptists the question of believer's baptism emerged. The Trevecka Methodist would soon accuse Miles Harry of bigotry and a proselytizing zeal,[31] and by October 1740 all meaningful collaboration had ceased. For the next four decades Welsh Methodism (which unlike John Wesley's English movement was Calvinistic in tone) and evangelical Dissent would develop independently of each other. Until the 1780s it would be Methodist exhorters, often untutored and invariably not ordained, who would provide the energy for the spread of the Evangelical Revival: 'Every Methodist preacher required stout legs, a good pair of lungs, a willingness to travel in fair and foul weather in order to bring the gospel to wretched sinners.'[32] Although still attached to the Established Church, they were free from Episcopal control and often as critical of conventional religion as the regular Church of England clergy were of them. It was an anomalous position which would lead, after the demise of its original leaders, to the secession of the Welsh Calvinistic body from the mother church.

During these decades Welsh Dissent grew slowly rather than spectacularly. Indeed, by the 1760s there were regular complaints, among the Baptists at least, of lifelessness and spiritual torpor. 'The lives of many professors are too similar to those of the world',[33] complained the annual letter of the South Wales Association of 1760; 'a lack of success in the means of grace'[34] was noted in 1767 while four years later 'the churches were complaining bitterly of deadness and fruitlessness'.[35] Then, quite unexpectedly, baptisms rocketed from 93 to 337.[36] Thereafter the membership graph climbed steadily, and sometimes startlingly, upward with renewed eagerness from within the Dissenting churches to propagate the gospel and uncommon willingness from without to accept it. 'This year', wrote a south Wales pastor in 1785,

'God saw fit to pour out the spirit of revival on many of our members' and so intense had the outpouring been that 'many are smitten and convicted to such a degree that they cleave to the godly imploring of them what they must do to be saved'.[37] 'Our commission', enthused the 1783 letter, 'is to preach to all men going forth into the highways and hedges to proclaim the glad tidings of great joy and that to all sinners'.[38] Whereas such exuberance, especially following the revival of 1762,[39] had been characteristic of Methodism alone, by now the Evangelical Revival was permeating the ranks of the Older Dissent. 'We received much more news', it was recorded in 1786, 'which would cause the hearts of those who love Zion to rejoice. She is giving birth to many sons and daughters, and the hand of the Lord is with his servants prospering the Word uncommonly in many places both north and south.'[40]

What was true of the Baptists was equally true of the Independents. For them the pivotal year was 1785.[41] Just as Baptist ministers like Christmas Evans (1766–1838) shed their Older Dissenting reserve for the spirit of enthusiasm, Independents of the calibre of Benjamin Jones, Pwllheli (1756–1823), George Lewis, Llanuwchllyn (1763–1822), Morgan Jones, Tre-lech (1768–1835), David Peter, Carmarthen (1765–1837) conjoined the older emphases on learning and sound doctrine with a renewed, more extrovert zeal. There were others like David Davies of Swansea (1763–1816) and Azariah Shadrach (1774–1844) who had more in common with the Methodist exhorters than with those who had previously adorned the Dissenting pulpit. 'Towards the end of the century', wrote Tudur Jones, 'there arose a generation of proletarian ministers, not educated and not well provided for, whose dowry was their enthusiasm'.[42] It was this enthusiasm which brought the Older Dissent into the mainstream of the Evangelical Revival, and brought the common people into the meeting houses of a rapidly increasing evangelical Dissent. 'Perhaps there never has been such a nation as the Welsh who have been won over so widely to the preaching of the gospel', wrote Christmas Evans in 1813. 'Meeting houses have been erected in each corner of the land and the majority of the common people, nearly all of them, crowd in to listen. There is virtually no other nation whose members have, in such numbers, professed the gospel so widely, in both south Wales and the north.'[43] By the dawn of the nineteenth century Welsh Dissent and with it the life of the people of Wales was about to be wholly transformed.

V. The Years of Growth, 1811–51

The year 1811 is an important milestone in the history of Welsh Dissent in that it witnessed the secession of the Calvinistic Methodists from the Established Church to become a separate Nonconformist denomination. Howell Harris had died in 1773 and Daniel Rowland in 1790, and however reluctant the next generation of Methodist leaders, Thomas Charles of Bala especially, were to sever the link with the Anglican Church, the break with the parent body had become inevitable. 'What strikes my mind with great force', wrote Thomas Jones of Denbigh, the Methodists' premier theologian, in 1810, 'is [that] . . . I do not recollect seeing a visible church described by any writer but as a congregation of people having the Word of God truly preached and the sacraments duly administered among them'.[44] For two generations the sacraments had been administered not by Methodists for Methodists in their fellowship meetings but in the parish churches, frequently by parish clergy who had scant sympathy for Methodist teachings. With the passing of the episcopally ordained Methodist clergy and the burgeoning popularity of the younger Methodist preachers, there was a clamour for the Welsh Methodists to ordain ministers for themselves. 'That compelling of any of our members', continued Jones, 'to seek for either of the sacraments from without the pale of our own connexion is a thing we ought not to be guilty of, as being contrary to the Word of God and to the universal custom of the churches of God in every age and every country'.[45] The time was ripe for the Methodists to pronounce themselves not an unofficial sect nominally attached to the Anglican Church but a functioning church in their own right. Consequently on 19 June 1811, in the north Wales town of Bala, Thomas Charles, a clergyman of the Church of England and (along with Thomas Jones) the movement's undisputed leader, ordained eight Calvinistic Methodist preachers to administer the sacraments of baptism and the Lord's Supper. Two months later, in Llandeilo, south Wales, he repeated the process ordaining a further thirteen preachers.[46] The Welsh Calvinistic Methodist Connexion, or what would become the Presbyterian Church of Wales, had been born.

By then the Connexion was the largest popular religious grouping in Wales. Although detailed statistics for membership are not available, 407 new meeting houses or chapel buildings were erected between 1763 and 1814, ensuring the Calvinistic Methodist presence throughout Wales and among the expatriate Welsh in London and the great conurbations of the English midlands.[47] By the same year (1814) the Welsh Independent churches had risen to 257,[48] while Baptist membership rose from 14,600 in 1810 to 21,499 a decade later.[49] By this time the Wesleyan Methodists were also making significant inroads, especially into north-east Wales, the Vale of Clwyd and north Cardiganshire.[50] This was the golden age of preaching with such exquisite exemplars of the craft as the Baptist Christmas Evans, the Calvinistic Methodist John Elias (1774–1841) and the Independent William Williams of Wern, near Wrexham (1781–1840) forging Wales' reputation as being the home of 'preaching second to no other under the sun'.[51] Dissent was rapidly becoming the chosen religious option of a large percentage of the Welsh people and it was still growing. What Tudur Jones says of the Independents was true of Dissent as a whole: 'Between 1800 and 1850 there was a tremendous increase in the number of Congregational churches in Wales. Nothing like it had been seen before, and nothing like it has been seen since. For a period of half a century a new cause was established, on average, every five weeks.'[52] Fed by a spate of local revivals, culminating in the Great Revival of 1859 which effected deeply churches of all denominations,[53] more and more ordinary people were being swept into the Dissenting congregations leaving the Established Church virtually bereft. 'The Church spell has lost its charm for the people', remarked a character in the autobiography of Robert Roberts, 'the Wandering Scholar', during the 1840s, 'there is no question about it: they have found out a tune more pleasing to their ears'.[54] These people were, on the whole, less educated than previous generations of Dissenting members and less well-off, though even then the very poor, like the very rich, would never become the denizens of Welsh Dissent. In a word, the age of popular or mass Nonconformity had arrived.

This brought losses as well as gains. The high ecclesiasticism of the Older Dissent gave way to an individualized evangelicalism which had less time for the communal aspect of the church covenant and its specific discipline, while theology itself became more pragmatic in tone. The bulk of the preachers (the Wesleyans apart) remained Calvinist, though their creed became attenuated, reflecting the 'New System' of Edward Williams and the Independents, the 'Fullerism' of the Tredegar minister J. P. Davies and the Baptists – replicating in a Welsh language idiom the doctrinal scheme of the Kettering theologian Andrew Fuller – and the moderate Calvinism which was championed among the Calvinistic Methodists by John Jones, Tal-sarn and others. This in turn, especially among the Independents, led to a more aggressive emphasis on human choice, first in procuring salvation and then in the social and political realm. Preachers began to challenge the older scheme which stressed the exclusiveness of the elect and the individual's helplessness in the face of the divine decree, reminding hearers of their absolute moral responsibility to yield to the gospel call. Even the revivals employed 'the new measures' including direct preaching, specific exhortation and the need for an immediate public response to the preached message.[55] This had implications in the social and political realm. The 'New System' inaugurated by Edward Williams of Rotherham and popularized by his pupil John Roberts of Llanbryn-mair, became 'the doctrinal springboard of the Welsh radicalism of the nineteenth century'.[56] The activist tenor of the age, including the successes of the Baptist Missionary Society, the London Missionary Society, the British and Foreign Bible Society (which had been instigated by Thomas Charles of Bala) and the proliferation of catechizing meetings and all age Sunday Schools, taught Welsh Nonconformists to think for themselves, to take matters into their own hands and soon to challenge the socio-political *status quo*. Led by the Independents David Rees (1801–69) and William Rees ('Gwilym Hiraethog') (1803–83), Baptists such as Thomas Price (1820–88) and taken up increasingly by the previously quiescent Calvinistic Methodists,[57] by mid-century popular Nonconformity was becoming a potent political force of the Whig persuasion, set to challenge the Church of England-Tory hegemony in Wales: 'In creating an articulate, literate and self-confident people, Nonconformity was preparing the way for a great political revolution.'[58] When the 1851 Religious Census provided the statistical proof that four-fifths of all worshippers in Wales were outside the pale of the Established Church,[59] the scene was set for the creation of what seemed to be a whole nation imbued with the values of Protestant Dissent.[60]

VI. A Nation of Nonconformists, 1851–1914

'It may be stated in general terms', wrote Henry Richard, soon to be elected as Liberal MP for Merthyr Tydfil, 'that the Welsh are now a nation of Nonconformists'.[61] With the triumph of Nonconformity came the flexing of political muscle and a move to meet the challenge of late-Victorian modernity. The granting of the vote to working class males in 1868 changed the political complexion of the nation. The division became stark: a small anglicized gentry whose allegiance was to the Anglican Church and a large working and agricultural class – the middle class remained negligible – now possessing growing parliamentary representation, which was Welsh in speech and Nonconformist in religion. The Chapel–Church divide would characterize Wales well into the twentieth century. Soon most long-standing Dissenting grievances would be allayed: the tithe would be commuted, church rates would be abolished, burial and marriage laws were amended to allow Nonconformists full and binding rights, while the two ancient English universities were opened up to (male) Dissenting undergraduates. The one burning cause to remain was that of disestablishment. As it happened the Church of England would be disestablished and disendowed within the four Welsh dioceses in 1914 (enacted in 1920), but the protracted and bitter campaign both for and against disestablishment did more harm than good to the reputation of institutional Christianity.[62] By the end of the Victorian era more and more people were being disengaged from specifically religious questions and drawn to matters of temporal improvement and change. Though hardly in decline, Nonconformity – as Dissent was now called – was being wracked by serious internal tensions.

The reasons for Welsh Nonconformist anxiety can be listed succinctly: Anglicization, increasing social mobility, the influence of sports, entertainments and pastimes hitherto deemed inimical to the puritan ethos, the rise of the socialist cause and the labour movement, and the intellectual challenge to Christianity per se. The leading Nonconformist intellectual of the latter part of the nineteenth century was Thomas Charles Edwards (1837–1900), great-grandson of Thomas Charles of Bala and son of Lewis Edwards (1809–87), Wales' leading theologian of mid-century. One of the first Dissenters to graduate from Oxford following the abolition of religious tests, he was ordained into the Calvinistic Methodist Church and became the first principal of the new 'national college', at Aberystwyth, in 1872. 'In our fathers' days', he told his church's general assembly in 1888, 'it could be taken for granted that theology was the abiding concern of a huge swath of the Welsh lay folk, but can that be said of today? Now it is politics or scientific theory, and is it not a fact that our young men not only have no theology but have no appetite for it at all?' In the same year, he informed the Pan-Presbyterian Council in London: 'In the present condition of things in Wales you have a people actually weary of contending systems, keenly alive at the same time to the fascination of new ideas, political and scientific, and, for this reason, in danger of drifting away from theological truth altogether.' It was not that the gospel was not being preached. The basic soundness of the evangelical pulpit could not be faulted. What was new was that the listeners, still active in their chapels, were becoming more and more sceptical as to the reality of divine truth. 'In our age agnosticism has come to the front as a conscious phase of the human intellect and teaches our young men not that this or that solution to the problem is fallacious . . . but that the problem itself need not be solved either way.'[63] Theology itself was changing, and even the benign or liberalized Calvinism which had become the mid-Victorian norm was being challenged by an increasingly potent philosophical Idealism. A theology of atonement was being eclipsed by an immanentist doctrine which harmonized, in an optimistic fashion, human potential with the divine.[64] By the first decade of the new century and despite its still flourishing outward appearance, Welsh Nonconformity was being tested as never before.

This being the case, the astounding religious revival of 1904–5 remains something of an enigma. Beginning in south Cardiganshire in the spring of 1904, rapidly spreading throughout the whole of Wales and beyond, and only abating around Christmastide 1905, it brought myriads of people either back into the churches having received a fresh vision of the glory of the gospel or else brought them to a saving knowledge of Christ for the first time. Prepared for assiduously by a band of committed younger ministers, its most high-profile leader would be Evan Roberts (1878–1951), a former coal miner and ministerial candidate with the Welsh Calvinistic Methodists. Unlike the revivals of the past, its doctrinal content was muted. Its emphasis – under Evan Roberts, at least – was upon the divine love sometimes at the expense of the divine wrath, while its most obvious characteristic was not powerful preaching but high emotional intensity. Roberts, though patently sincere, was theologically untrained and given to intense subjectivism, a cause of much controversy at the time. As a result of the revival church membership in the Nonconformist denominations increased by some 80,000, a rise of 18.6 per cent, though much backsliding and disenchantment was recorded during the subsequent years. An objective assessment, even at this juncture, is difficult to make. For some it was 'the swansong of the old religious tradition of Wales . . . the consumptive's flush of death'.[65] For others it was, and remained, a turning point in their lives and the basis of a lifetime's commitment and faithfulness. Although stubbornly difficult to evaluate,[66] it remains 'one of the most remarkable events in twentieth-century Welsh history'.[67]

VII. 1914 to the Present

Lack of space prevents a full description of the development of Protestant Nonconformity during the twentieth century and beyond, but statistically speaking the high point came in 1926 when as many as 530,000 people, over a quarter of the population, were in communicant membership with either the Calvinistic Methodists, the Congregationalists, the Baptists or the Wesleyans.[68] Numbers would fall steadily until the 1970s and calamitously thereafter. The First World War had little immediate effect on church membership but severe consequences for Christian faith more generally: it would signify a divide between a religious and increasingly post-religious worldview. Although Anglicanism and Roman Catholicism gained ground – the disestablished Church in Wales, independent of Canterbury and forming a separate archiepiscopal province within the Anglican Communion, came into existence in 1920 – the main characteristic of Wales during the inter-war years was social dislocation and economic hardship. Formerly allied with the Liberal Party, Welsh Nonconformity struggled to find a role within an increasingly class-bound and socialist inclined country.[69] Political nationalism, via Plaid Cymru, the Welsh Nationalist Party which was established in 1925,[70] would be attractive for some, but mostly the denominations would fight shy of an overt political stance. The chapels, however, could no longer afford to be socially disengaged. The quest for a theologically responsible social gospel along with a renewal of biblical orthodoxy inspired, as in Scotland, by the thought of the Swiss theologian Karl Barth, would characterize sections of the Welsh pulpit up to and beyond the Second World War.[71]

That war was not nearly as traumatic as the conflagration of 1914–18, though by the 1950s Welsh Nonconformity, unlike Welsh Anglicanism or Roman Catholicism, was undergoing significant attrition. Nominally the link between chapel and nation was still intact. 'By the first quarter of the nineteenth century', wrote the cultural commentator W. J. Gruffydd in 1951, 'Wales had become what it substantially is today, a nation of Evangelical Christians'.[72] This 'Nonconformist nation', nevertheless, was in an increasingly parlous state. In a volume celebrating the tercentenary of the Act of Uniformity of 1662 which created Protestant Dissent, its author described the *mores* of an increasingly affluent generation in which the chapels had been called to witness: 'This is the atmosphere in which Nonconformity is forced to exist and today it is fighting for its life.'[73]

Despite attempts at renewing chapel life by conservative evangelical means on the one hand and ecumenical methods on the other, by the 1960s and 1970s the movement was being buffeted by both secular theology and the forces of secularity itself. There occurred one belated attempt, on the verge of the millennium, to establish a single Welsh Free Church body, which came to nothing. By then institutional Christianity had become infinitely diverse while the older denominations, now complemented by different strands of Pentecostalism, fellowship networks and a plethora of new 'emerging' churches, underscored the exceedingly diffuse nature of contemporary faith. That having been said, the traditions which trace their roots back to the Puritan movement, early Dissent and the Calvinistic Methodism of the post-1811 era still exist, and there are those who continue to draw sustenance from what remains an exceedingly rich and engaging heritage.

Notes

1 John Penry (1563–93), a native of Breconshire, assumed Puritan views at Cambridge in the early 1580s. Although active in London, the English midlands and Scotland, his concern for his native land became manifest in his three treatises: *The Aequity of an Humble Supplication* (1587), *An Exhortation unto the governors and people of . . . Wales* (1588) and *A Supplication unto the High Court of Parliament* (1588); see David Williams, *John Penry: Three Treatises Concerning Wales* (Cardiff: University of Wales Press, 1960). It was for his involvement in the Marprelate controversy, however, his trial for sedition and susequent execution that he is principally noted. Patrick Collinson, *The Elizabethan Puritan Movement* (Oxford: Clarendon Press, 1967), pp. 391–95, 428.

2 Geraint H. Jenkins, *Protestant Dissenters in Wales, 1639–89* (Cardiff: University of Wales Press, 1992), p. 10.

3 Joshua Thomas, *Hanes y Bedyddwyr Ymhlith y Cymry* (Carmarthen: John Ross, 1778), pp. 66–86.

4 Jenkins, *Protestant Dissenters in Wales*, p. 13.

5 Ibid., p. 15.

6 'Glad Tydings from Heaven', in T. Charles and T. Oliver (eds), *The Works of the Late Revd Walter Cradock* (Chester: W.C. Jones, 1800), pp. 380–81.

7 See S. K. Roberts, 'Propagating the Gospel in Wales: The Making of the 1650 Act', in *Transactions of the Honourable Society of Cymmrodorion*, NS, 10 (2004), pp. 57–75.

8 M. Wynn Thomas, *Morgan Llwyd: Writers of Wales* (Cardiff: University of Wales Press, 1984).

9 Jenkins, *Protestant Dissenters in Wales*, p. 27.
10 T. M. Bassett, *The Welsh Baptists* (Swansea: Ilston Press, 1977), pp. 14–15.
11 B. G. Owens, *The Ilston Book* (Aberystwyth: National Library of Wales, 1996); D. Densil Morgan, *Wales and the Word: Historical Perspectives on Welsh Identity and Religion* (Cardiff: University of Wales Press, 2008), pp. 5–16.
12 Jenkins, *Protestant Dissenters in Wales*, p. 37.
13 Ibid., p. 46; idem, *The Foundation of Modern Wales, 1642–1780* (Oxford and Cardiff: Clarendon Press and University of Wales Press, 1987), pp. 183–88.
14 Jenkins, *The Foundation of Modern Wales*, p. 192.
15 Ibid., p. 194.
16 Thomas, *Hanes y Bedyddwyr Ymhlith y Cymry*, p. 39.
17 Jenkins, *The Foundation of Modern Wales*, pp. 193–94.
18 R. Tudur Jones, 'Yr Hen Ymneilltuwyr', in Gomer M. Roberts (ed.), *Hanes Methodistiaeth Galfinaidd Cymru, Cyfrol I: Y Deffroad Mawr* (Caernarfon: Llyfrfa'r Methodistiaid, 1974), pp. 13–42 [p. 14].
19 The most recent account of Welsh Anglicanism during the post-Restoration period is contained in William Jacob's section in Glanmor Williams et al., *The Welsh Church from Reformation to Disestablishment, 1603–1920* (Cardiff: University of Wales Press, 2007), pp. 65–206.
20 Ibid., pp. 79–81; cf. Jenkins, *The Foundation of Modern Wales*, pp. 188–90.
21 Gwyn Thomas, 'Two prose writers: Ellis Wynne and Theophilus Evans', in Branwen Jarvis (ed.), *A Guide to Welsh Literature, 1700–1800* (Cardiff: University of Wales Press, 2000), pp. 45–63.
22 Erasmus Saunders, *A View of the State of Religion in the Diocese of St David* (Cardiff: University of Wales Press reprint, 1949), cf. Geraint H. Jenkins, *Literature, Religion and Society in Wales, 1660–1730* (Cardiff: University of Wales Press, 1978), pp. 1–15.
23 Consequently the analysis for Wales used by Michael R. Watts, *The Dissenters, Volume 1: From the Reformation to the French Revolution* (Oxford: Clarendon Press, 1978), pp. 267–88, is only partially correct.
24 Jones, 'Yr Hen Ymneilltuwyr', pp. 15–16; cf. Bassett, *The Welsh Baptists*, pp. 54–58; R. Tudur Jones, *Congregationalism in Wales*, ed. Robert Pope (Cardiff: University of Wales Press, 2004), pp. 79–94.
25 Jenkins, *The Foundation of Modern Wales*, p. 195.
26 Jones, *Congregationalism in Wales*, p. 80.
27 Jenkins, *Literature, Religion and Society in Wales, 1660–1730*, pp. 187–89.
28 See D. Densil Morgan, 'Preaching in the Vernacular: The Welsh Sermon, 1689–1901', in Keith A. Francis and William Gibson (eds), *The Oxford Handbook of the Sermon* (Oxford: Oxford University Press, 2012), pp. 199–214.
29 William Jacob, 'Welsh Methodism', in Williams et al., *The Welsh Church from Reformation to Disestablishment*, pp. 165–83; David Ceri Jones, Boyd Stanley Schlenther and Eryn Mant White, *The Elect Methodists: Calvinistic Methodism in England and Wales, 1735–1811* (Cardiff: University of Wales Press, 2012), pp. 11–14.
30 Eifion Evans, *Daniel Rowland and the Great Evangelical Awakening in Wales* (Edinburgh: Banner of Truth Trust, 1985), pp. 38–45.
31 Geraint Tudur, *Howell Harris: From Conversion to Separation, 1735–50* (Cardiff: University of Wales Press, 1998), pp. 76–77.
32 Jenkins, *The Foundations of Modern Wales*, p. 350.
33 *Llythyr, oddiwrth y Gymmanfa* (Carmarthen: John Ross, 1760), p. 5, cf. (1763), p. 4.
34 *Llythyr, oddiwrth y Gymmanfa* (Carmarthen: John Ross, 1767), p. 3
35 *Llythyr, oddiwrth y Gymmanfa* (Carmarthen: John Ross, 1771), p. 4, cf. (1772), p. 4.

36 See D. Densil Morgan, '"Smoke, Fire and Light": Baptists and the Revitalization of Welsh Dissent', *The Baptist Quarterly*, 32 (1988), pp. 224–32.
37 Quoted in John T. Griffiths, *Hanes Eglwys Pen-y-fai* (Carmarthen: Gwenlyn Evans, 1916), p. 26.
38 *Llythyr, oddiwrth y Gymmanfa* (Carmarthen: John Ross, 1783), p. 3
39 Jones, Schlenther and White, *The Elect Methodists*, pp. 123–28.
40 *Llythyr, oddiwrth y Gymmanfa* (Carmarthen: John Ross, 1786), p. 7.
41 Jones, *Congregationalism in Wales*, p. 114.
42 Ibid., p. 118.
43 'Cyflwr crefydd yng Nghymru' (1813), in Owen Davies (ed.), *Gweithiau Christmas Evans* (Carmarthen: Gwenlyn Evans, 1899), II, p. 13; cf. Morgan, *Wales and the Word*, pp. 17–30.
44 Gomer M. Roberts (ed.), *Hanes Methodistiaeth Galfinaidd Cymru, Cyfrol II: Cynnydd y Corff* (Caernarfon: Llyfrfa'r Methodistiaid Calfinaidd, 1978), p. 293.
45 Ibid., p. 294.
46 Jones, Schlenther and White, *The Elect Methodists*, pp. 223–32; D. Densil Morgan, 'Thomas Jones of Denbigh (1756–1820) and the Ordination of 1811', *The Welsh Journal of Religious History*, 6 (2011), pp. 19–30.
47 Roberts (ed.), *Hanes Methodistiaeth Galfinaidd Cymru*, II, pp. 529–42.
48 Jones, *Congregationalism in Wales*, p. 149.
49 Bassett, *The Welsh Baptists*, p. 211.
50 Lionel Madden (ed.), *Methodism in Wales: A Short History of the Wesley Tradition* (Llandudno: Welsh Methodist Conference, 2003), pp. 23–38.
51 Morgan, 'Preaching in the Vernacular', pp. 205–9; idem, *Edward Matthews, Ewenni* (Caernarfon: Gwasg Pantycelyn, 2012), pp. 55–60.
52 Jones, *Congregationalism in Wales*, p. 149.
53 J. Gwynfor Jones (ed.), *Hanes Methodistiaeth Galfinaidd Cymru, Cyfrol III, Y Twf a'r Cadarnhau c.1814–1914* (Caernarfon: Gwasg Pantycelyn, 2012), pp. 42–48.
54 J. Burnett and H. G. Williams (eds), *A Wandering Scholar: The Life and Opinions of Robert Roberts* (rev. edn, Cardiff: University of Wales Press, 1991 [1923]), p. 63.
55 Richard Carwardine, 'The Welsh Evangelical Community and "Finney's Revival"', *The Journal of Ecclesiastical History*, 29 (1978), pp. 463–80; Jones, *Congregationalism in Wales*, pp. 133–37.
56 Pennar Davies, *Episodes in the History of Brecknockshire Dissent* (Brecon: The Brecknockshire Society, 1959), p. 45.
57 Robert Pope, 'Methodistiaeth a Chymdeithas', in Jones (ed.), *Hanes Methodistiaeth Galfinaidd Cymru*, III, pp. 355–66; D. Densil Morgan, *Lewis Edwards* (Cardiff: University of Wales Press, 2009), pp. 118–28.
58 Jones, *Congregationalism in Wales*, p. 159.
59 Ieuan Gwynedd Jones, *The Religious Census of 1851: A Calendar of the Returns Relating to Wales*, 2 vols (Cardiff: University of Wales Press, 1976, 1981).
60 It should be remembered however that for the 975,000 Nonconformists (out of a total Welsh population of 1,163,000) recorded as attending worship on census Sunday, it seems that as many again were beyond the reach of organized religion: 'The irreligious are a lost element in Welsh historiography', John Davies, *A History of Wales* (Harmondsworth: Penguin Books, 1993), p. 427.
61 Henry Richard, *Letters and Essays on Wales* (2nd edn, London: James Clarke, 1884 [1866]), p. 2.
62 K. O. Morgan, *Freedom or Sacrilege? A History of the Campaign for Welsh Disestablishment* (Penarth: Church in Wales Publications, 1966); D. Densil Morgan, *The Span of the Cross: Christian Religion and Society in Wales, 1914–2000* (2nd edn, Cardiff: University of Wales Press, 2011), pp. 30–37.

63 Quoted in Morgan, 'Preaching in the Vernacular', pp. 210–11.
64 See D. Densil Morgan, 'Credo ac Athrawiaeth', in Jones (ed.), *Hanes Methodistiaeth Galfinaidd Cymru*, III, pp. 149–64; idem, 'Et incarnatus est: The Christology of Thomas Charles Edwards (1837–1900)', *Transactions of the Honourable Society of Cymmrodorion*, NS, 18 (2012), pp. 56–66.
65 D. R. Davies, *In Search of Myself: An Autobiography* (London: Geoffrey Bles, 1961), p. 37.
66 Cf. D. Densil Morgan, 'Diwygiad Crefyddol 1904–5', *Cof Cenedl*, XX (2005), pp. 167–200; Robert Pope, 'Evan Roberts in Theological Context', *Transactions of the Honourable Society of Cymmrodorion*, NS, 11 (2005), pp. 144–69; idem, 'Demythologising the Evan Roberts Revival, 1904–1905', *The Journal of Ecclesiastical History*, 57 (2006), pp. 515–34.
67 R. Tudur Jones, *Faith and the Crisis of a Nation: Wales 1890–1914*, ed. Robert Pope (Cardiff: University of Wales Press, 2004), p. 283; chapters 12–14 in Tudur Jones' study remain the most detailed and perceptive account of the event.
68 For this section see Morgan, *The Span of the Cross*, passim.
69 See Robert Pope, *Building Jerusalem: Nonconformity, Labour and the Social Question in Wales, 1906–39* (Cardiff: University of Wales Press, 1998).
70 Morgan, *Wales and the Word*, pp. 224–26; Keith Robbins, *England, Ireland, Scotland, Wales: The Christian Church, 1900–2000* (Oxford: Oxford University Press, 2006), pp. 189–98.
71 Robert Pope, *Seeking God's Kingdom: The Nonconformist Social Gospel in Wales, 1906–39* (Cardiff: University of Wales Press, 1999); D. Densil Morgan, *Barth Reception in Britain* (London: T&T Clark, 2010), pp. 48–62, 156–60, 194–200.
72 Quoted in Morgan, *The Span of the Cross*, pp. 205–6.
73 R. Ifor Parry, *Ymneilltuaeth* (Llandysul: Gwasg Gomer, 1962), p. 175.

3 Church and State, 1550–1750: The Emergence of Dissent

John Coffey

The history of Dissent has usually been written with the end in view. Church and Dissent were to become separate entities, and historians of Anglicanism and Nonconformity were inclined to write a teleological history of the sixteenth and seventeenth centuries, explaining why this came to pass. This was not an illegitimate approach, for one of the duties of the historian is to explain why things have come to be the way they are. But too often, weak teleology became strong teleology, and a sense of inevitability crept into the narratives.[1]

Anglicans tended to assume that the current shape and temper of the Church of England was the natural state of things, an expression of 'the genius of Anglicanism'. When P. E. More and F. L. Cross assembled their major anthology of *Anglicanism* (1935), their selection of texts was heavily skewed towards the high church and latitudinarian traditions. Although a few Calvinist and Puritan icons made the cut (notably James Ussher and Richard Baxter), the anthology thoroughly obscured the Reformed identity of the Church of England under Elizabeth I and James I. Richard Hooker loomed large, but there was no space given to William Perkins, who in his own day was much more famous across Europe as a spokesman for the English Church.[2] Puritanism was seen as an alien force, quite out of keeping with Anglicanism. The same editorial principle was at work in a much more recent anthology, *The Anglican Tradition* (1991), which contained many medieval sources (such as the Fourth Lateran Council's statement on transubstantiation), but not a single extract from the continental Reformed divines who, according to Eamon Duffy, 'played so decisive a role in shaping the emerging Church of England: no Calvin, no Bucer, no Bullinger'.[3] As a result, the low church, Reformed character of early Anglicanism was thoroughly obscured, so that the split between Anglicanism and Puritanism, Church and Dissent appeared to be entirely predictable. The latter was a malignant growth that was always going to be rejected by the Anglican body.

Ironically, this polarized account suited historians of Dissent, who were only too happy to underplay the early Nonconformists' attachment to the Established Church, while exaggerating their affinities with modern Free Churches. The eighteenth-century historian Daniel Neal set the pattern by emphasizing the tyranny of the bishops, the persecution of the Puritans and the affinity between Puritanism and liberty. As a consequence, Puritanism was understood not as the cutting edge of the English Church but as the natural precursor of Dissent.[4] The story of Presbyterianism and Congregationalism was written as teleological denominational history, even though both groupings operated within the national church until 1662.[5] Radical (and unrepresentative) Puritans like Thomas Helwys and Roger Williams were singled out as heralds of a liberal future, pioneers, prophets and apostles of religious freedom.[6] John Owen was credited with instilling tolerationist principles in his pupil John Locke, even though Owen's toleration was strictly bounded and Locke had favoured religious uniformity at the Restoration.[7] Milton and Cromwell were reclaimed as champions of 'civil and religious liberty' (language they themselves had popularized).[8] The result was a Whig interpretation of history, which emphasized those aspects of the past that had triumphed in the present.[9]

In recent times, historians have become wary of teleological narratives, and more acutely aware of our tendency to read the present into the past. We are more likely to emphasize the foreignness and difference of the past. In this chapter, I want to offer an account of church and state between 1550 and 1750 that does not point inexorably towards the separation of Church and Dissent. Instead, I want to stress that the story of Dissent can only be told in conjunction with the story of the Church of England. Until late in the seventeenth century, most Dissenters remained thoroughly invested in the State Church, and deeply committed to the ideals of the magisterial Reformation. While the sects did sever links with the Established Church, the parting of the ways between the Church and a broader Dissent was a slow and painful business, one that was contingent rather than inevitable. What we call Puritanism was imbricated with Anglicanism. To set these abstractions at war with each other is to distort the story of post-Reformation England. Much of early Protestant Dissent was not dissent *from* the Church of England, but dissent *within* it and on its behalf. The religious settlement continued to be hotly debated long after 1559, and there were numerous attempts to remake the English Church – by Puritans and Laudians, Presbyterians and Independents, Latitudinarians and High Churchmen. Only after much struggle and various contingencies did Church and Dissent become rival ecclesiastical blocs.[10]

I. The Birth Pangs of Protestant England

The eventual schism between Church and Dissent set England apart from other Protestant nations. By the eighteenth century, the Established Church had decisively distanced itself from the Reformed tradition, and Dissent had split into four denominations (Presbyterians, Congregationalists, Baptists and Quakers), a situation without parallel elsewhere in Protestant Europe. But in the sixteenth century, the English were less exceptional. Henry VIII, of course, was unique, a monarch who broke with Rome while repudiating Luther. But England's *Protestant* Reformation was emphatically part of the broader European Reformation. During the reign of Edward VI (1547–53), the English Reformers were in close contact with their continental brethren. Indeed, the English state recruited three major European Reformed theologians – Jan Laski, Martin Bucer and Peter Martyr Vermigli – appointing the latter two to chairs at Cambridge and Oxford respectively. Thomas Cranmer himself moved beyond his early Lutheran positions to a distinctly Reformed theology, eloquently expressed in his second Book of Common Prayer (1552) and the Forty-Two Articles (1553). And the Edwardian Reformation was unequivocally magisterial, complete with a programme of state-sponsored iconoclasm that whitewashed the internal walls of churches and removed 'idolatrous' images. While the Radical Reformation made a fleeting appearance in the shape of Free Willers and anti-Trinitarians, neither fared well. In 1550–51, the Edwardian regime burned Joan Bocher and George van Parris at the stake for heresy. The executions prompted no public debate on the rights and wrongs of religious coercion. The Reformed were firmly committed to religious uniformity. And as in the reign of Henry VIII, church and state were unified under the supreme authority of the monarch.[11]

Under Mary I (1553–58), Protestants suffered ferocious persecution, with almost three hundred being burned to death for heresy. Yet if this was a traumatic decade, it also witnessed a dramatic surge of Reformed (particularly Calvinist) expansion. This new wave of Protestantism swept across France, claiming up to 10 per cent of the population, and made great inroads into the Netherlands. In Geneva itself, Calvin consolidated his authority, both through the sheer force of his personality, piety and learning, and with the support of the state. In 1553, Geneva imitated the Edwardian regime by executing an anti-Trinitarian, the notorious Servetus. Calvinists persecuted others even as they underwent persecution themselves. Although a few – like Sebastian Castellio – denounced the killing of heretics, most Protestants shared the Augustinian assumption that rulers had been established as 'nursing fathers' to the church and 'agents of wrath' against its enemies. Of the numerous Reformed confessions drawn up in the mid-sixteenth century nearly all included an article on the civil magistrate. Here the Reformed repudiated the Anabaptist notion that Christians should not hold civil office; instead, they taught that Christian magistrates were like the kings of Old Testament Israel who overthrew idolatry and punished teachers of false religion.[12]

This union of church and state was reaffirmed by the Elizabethan Settlement. England followed Zurich rather than Geneva, preferring an 'Erastian' policy of royal supremacy to the Calvinian view that the church should be independent of the state.[13] Elizabeth I was determined to keep the church under a tight rein. A traditionalist kind of Protestant, her faith had taken shape in the early phase of evangelical reform in the 1530s and 1540s and she was unenthusiastic about the more militant Reformed Protestantism that had swept the board in the 1550s. She insisted on clerical vestments and was a stickler for conformity to the Prayer Book. She disliked long sermons and would have preferred a celibate clergy. However, much to her chagrin, almost the entire episcopal bench resigned soon after her succession, and she was forced to replace them with convinced Reformers, a number of whom had spent the last few years in exile on the continent, participating in the advanced religious reforms of continental cities such as Strasbourg and Basel. These Reformed bishops set the tone for the early Church of England. They were Calvinist in theology, believing that the doctrine of predestination was necessary to protect the Reformation principle of *sola gratia*. They read and recommended the writings of European Reformed divines, and identified strongly with their sister churches in the Reformed world – in Switzerland, France, the Netherlands, Hungary and elsewhere.[14]

Of course, in certain respects, the Church of England looked different to other Reformed churches. It retained the medieval ecclesiastical hierarchy and a traditional threefold model of ministry (bishops, priests and deacons). Although the Scots and the Hungarian Reformed Church also had bishops (or superintendents), the Reformed had adopted a fourfold model of ministry (pastors, doctors, elders and deacons). The English Church retained a prescriptive liturgy, whereas most Reformed churches had directories of worship that allowed the clergy to extemporize. The English clergy wore (or were meant to wear) traditional vestments, including the surplice and cope, whereas most other Reformed clergy wore plain academic robe. Finally, the Church of England retained cathedrals and choirs, which contrasted sharply with the plain congregational psalm-singing heard in most parishes.

It was the 'half reformed' character of the Elizabethan church that provoked the rise of 'Puritanism' and Dissent. In the mid-1560s, a Vestiarian Controversy broke out over clerical dress. The Puritan protestors were not marginal extremists – two of their leaders were heads of Oxford colleges. But the queen was appalled at the 'diversity, variety, contention and vain love of singularity' in the church, and demanded 'uniformity of order'. The advocates of conformity argued that 'things indifferent' – *adiaphora*, or things not determined by scripture – could be decided by the magistrate. Puritans either replied that the cope and the surplice were not indirectly condemned by scripture, or that things indifferent should be left to individual conscience. In 1566, thirty-seven Puritan ministers were suspended from office and threatened with deprivation if they failed to conform within three months. In the event, however, most clergy compromised and very few were deprived of their livings. The Puritans were dissenters within the Established Church, and few of them could contemplate separation.[15]

When the next wave of Puritan agitation arrived in the 1570s, it was bolder and more far-reaching. Once again, though, it came from within the establishment, as a Cambridge divinity professor, Thomas Cartwright, gave a series of lectures calling for the government of the church to be remodelled along the lines of the New Testament church. Cartwright was removed from his chair and left England for Geneva. Two other Presbyterians, John Field and Thomas Wilcox, published *An Admonition to the Parliament* (1572), sparking the extended Admonition Controversy. Yet the title of their book indicates that theirs was to be a magisterial reformation, carried out by parliament. And while both men were imprisoned for a spell, their pastoral ministry was soon resurrected thanks to powerful patrons like the Earl of Leicester and Lord Burghley. The struggle between the bishops and the presbyterians did become increasingly fierce, and by the late 1580s, the polemicist who wrote under the pseudonym 'Martin Marprelate' was denouncing Archbishop Whitgift as 'a monstrous Antichristian Pope: a most bloudie oppressor of Gods saintes'. The new bishop of London, Richard Bancroft, succeeded in breaking the back of the Presbyterian movement in the 1590s. Although Presbyterian ideas continued to circulate among some Puritan clergy, most learned to live with bishops and work effectively within the Established Church.[16]

A small number of radical Puritans, however, became so disaffected with the national church that they separated to form pure congregations. Separatism was brutally suppressed by the authorities. A royal proclamation against Robert Browne and Robert Harrison in 1583 described them as 'lewd and evil disposed persons . . . ready to violate and break the peace of the church, the realm, and the quietness of the people'. Separatism was not mere religious opinion, it was a seditious breach of civil order. Many separatists were imprisoned and a number were executed, including John Greenwood, Henry Barrow and John Penry in 1593.[17] Because separatists lived in fear of their lives, many migrated to the Netherlands, especially during the reign of James I. It was among these exiles that English Puritanism took its most radical turn, as John Smyth and Thomas Helwys adopted believer's baptism. Smyth eventually joined a Mennonite sect, the Waterlanders (identifying explicitly with the continental Radical Reformation), while Helwys returned to England, founding the first English Baptist church in Spitalfields in 1612.[18]

With the separatists and the Baptists we see a gulf opening up between Church and Dissent. But these were tiny groups, entirely unrepresentative of the mainstream of English Puritanism. The vast majority of the godly remained within the church. Even the arch-Separatist Robert Browne returned to parish ministry, only finally losing his living during the Laudian crackdown on nonconformity in the 1630s. Moreover, the main separatist leaders before the Baptists continued to accept some of the key assumptions of the magisterial Reformation, including the duty of Christian magistrates to suppress idolatry and punish heresy. Dissatisfied with their current magistrates, they refused to 'tarry for the magistrate', and proceeded to reform the church from the grass roots. But they retained the ideal of the godly state.[19] Smyth and Helwys, by contrast, issued sweeping condemnations of religious coercion. Probably influenced by Dutch multi-confessionalism and by the Mennonites, they demanded the toleration of all religions. 'Let them be heretikes, Turcks, Jewes, or whatsoever it appertynes not to the earthly power to punish them in the least measure', wrote Helwys.[20] This resounding call for religious liberty would eventually become synonymous with Dissent.[21] In 1612 it was highly eccentric.

II. A Church Divided

By calling for radical reform of the Church of England and even breaking away from it, Puritans provoked a fierce backlash. And from the 1590s onwards, anti-Puritanism would serve to legitimize a new style of conformist churchmanship that sought to distance the Church from the Reformed tradition. Historians have struggled to find a name for the advocates of this hierarchical and sacramentalist tendency within the Established Church. At the time, they came to be called Arminians and eventually Laudians, and more recently they have been labelled avant-garde conformists or high churchmen. Among them we can count famous figures in the Anglican tradition like Lancelot Andrewes and Richard Hooker, along with less celebrated divines like John Overall, Samuel Harsnet, Hadrian Saravia and Peter Baro. They first rose to prominence during the anti-Puritan drive of the 1590s, in what has been called 'the Anglican moment'.[22] The label 'Anglican' can be misleading, for in many respects these figures were themselves dissenters, as hostile to the *status quo* as the Presbyterians. They simply wanted to pull the Church in the opposite direction to the Puritans – away from the Reformed churches. For them, the English Church was (or was meant to be) unique, and they lamented its drab services, its low view of the sacraments, its predestinarian doctrine, its warm relations with continental Calvinists, its nonconformist clergy and their populist appeals to the laity. The Church of England, they believed, should aspire to something better, something more elevated. It should be the perfect embodiment of patristic Christianity, it should reinforce the dignity and authority of its bishops, it should rediscover 'the beauty of holiness' and it should emphasize the real presence of Christ in the Eucharist. In mapping out a unique identity for the Church of England, these divines were busy inventing 'Anglicanism' as something set apart from the vulgar Reformed churches of the continent.[23]

Initially, these would-be reformers of the Church were no more successful than their Puritan enemies. The majority of the bishops were staunchly Reformed in their theology and ecclesiastical identity, and feared that this avant-garde tendency was intent on reversing the Reformation. Barrett and Baro's careers were ruined by their reckless attacks on Calvinist predestinarianism, and Howson's progress was also damaged. Much of Hooker's great work *The Laws of Ecclesiastical Polity* remained unpublished, and only in later years would he acquire the reputation as the supreme exponent of Anglicanism. The Church's centre-of-gravity remained with the conformist Calvinists, men like George Abbot, archbishop of Canterbury from 1611 to 1633, and his brother Robert, bishop of Salisbury and author of a major work in defence of William Perkins' Calvinist and anti-Catholic apologia for the English Church. Although James I was attracted to high church clergy like Lancelot Andrewes, the king remained firmly committed to Calvinist orthodoxy, sending a delegation to the Synod of Dort in 1618 which joined in the condemnation of the Dutch Arminians.[24]

Because the Church of England remained within the Calvinist international, the vast majority of Puritans remained within the Church.[25] Some Puritan clergy were disciplined or suspended for nonconformity – for refusing to wear clerical vestments, or use the sign of the cross in baptism, or require kneeling at Communion. Others were discreet in their nonconformity, or were indulged by sympathetic Calvinist bishops. And many 'moderate Puritans' poured their energies into pastoral work.[26] Frustrated in their drive to reform the church's government and liturgy, they learned to make the best of their ample opportunities within a half-reformed church. If Puritanism as a movement of ecclesiastical reform was derailed in the 1590s, Puritanism as 'the first Protestant Pietism' was thriving.[27] The godly clergy pioneered 'a hotter sort' of Protestantism, marked out by a strenuous programme of voluntary religion beyond the parish services. It involved 'gadding' to hear the sermons of Puritan incumbents and lecturers, reading godly books, intensive personal prayer and fasting, family worship and psalm-singing, and gathering in small groups and conventicles. This kind of fervent Protestant religion took hold in numerous parishes across England. Towns like Dorchester and Banbury became renowned for their godliness. Cambridge colleges like Emmanuel and Christ's produced several generations of eager and talented Puritan clergy. And moderate Puritans learned to work with bishops, defending Reformed orthodoxy and participating in the translation of the Authorized Version of the Bible in 1611. Under James I, Puritanism appeared to be not an oppositional movement but the cutting edge of English Protestantism. Only a tiny minority seceded, and according to Patrick Collinson, there seemed little prospect of a major schism between Puritanism and Anglicanism, Church and Dissent.[28]

Events, however, would intervene. First, there was the outbreak of the Thirty Years War in 1618. It began when the Calvinist nobles of Bohemia revolted against the Catholic Holy Roman Emperor and offered the crown to James I's son-in-law, Frederick of the Palatinate. Puritans and many conformist Calvinists believed that England should support the Calvinist rebels and the Calvinist Palatinate, and were deeply disturbed when the king stood on the sidelines and watched as the revolt was crushed and the Palatinate was sacked. Increasingly, the king turned to the high church 'Arminians', who had little sympathy for continental Calvinists and the highest reverence for the authority of kings. The elevation of this high church faction was accelerated when Charles I succeeded his father in 1625. By 1628, their rising star William Laud had been made bishop of London, and in 1633 he succeeded George Abbot as archbishop of Canterbury.

The rise of the Laudians was accompanied by a fresh assault on Puritanism. As the godly clergy came under increasing pressure for nonconformity, some decided to emigrate. As in the early seventeenth century, a number chose to go to the Dutch republic, where they could establish godly congregations undisturbed by the authorities.[29] But there was now a new option – America. In 1619–20, a group of Separatists, later lionized as the Pilgrim Fathers, established a colony at Plymouth in New England. By the mid-1620s, leading Puritan aristocrats like Lord Saye and Sele and the Earl of Warwick, were exploring the possibility of colonization in the West Indies. This eventually came to fruition in the short-lived Providence Island colony.[30] But the most successful venture was launched by the Massachusetts Bay Company. Between 1628 and 1640, during the Great Migration, around 15,000 English settlers moved to Massachusetts, with seventy-six Puritan clergy among them. Unlike the Pilgrim Fathers, the Massachusetts colonists were not Separatists. They continued to profess loyalty to the Church of England, and when the opportunity came to reform it in 1640, many returned to their homeland. In Massachusetts, they were theoretically under the jurisdiction of the bishop of London, but since he was 3,000 miles away, their congregations were essentially autonomous. They introduced a system of church membership, which was only open to those who professed faith and showed evidence of conversion in their godly lives. This was a radical departure from English arrangements, where all parishioners were members of the church by virtue of their baptism. But the Massachusetts Congregationalists continued to practice infant baptism and their meeting houses functioned as parish churches, with the whole population expected to attend. In line with the magisterial Reformation, the civil authorities had the power to punish heresy and blasphemy. The churches of Massachusetts were still established, state churches.[31]

Some Puritans, however, were moving in more radical directions. The godly clergy had forged a hot Protestant subculture in which the laity were galvanized and mobilized. It proved difficult to control, producing a troubling succession of exorcists, prophets, heresiarchs, lay preachers, sectaries and controversialists.[32] On both sides of the Atlantic, Puritanism was troubled by antinomian controversies over law and grace.[33] There were signs that its energies were all too fissiparous. The Laudian decade was radicalizing the godly, turning them towards outright dissent. Separatism was growing, and a few Separatists were baptized as adult believers, forming the first Calvinistic Baptist congregations. Like the General Baptists, they were few in number, but they reflected a growing militancy.[34] There was widespread outrage in 1637 when three leading Puritans – a minister, Henry Burton; a lawyer, William Prynne; and a doctor, John Bastwick – had their ears cropped and were branded with the letters 'S. L.' for seditious libel against the bishops. Moderate Puritans had once come to terms with bishops, but with hard-line conformists in power, they were rapidly becoming more sceptical. This was especially so after the Glasgow General Assembly abolished Episcopacy in Scotland at the end of 1638, held in the wake of the Covenanter revolt against the imposition of a Scottish Prayer Book. The situation now looked ominous, and the setbacks of Protestant forces in the Thirty Years War contributed to a sense of apocalyptic foreboding. A group of leading noblemen – led by the Puritan Earl of Warwick and the Calvinist Earl of Bedford – began plotting against the Laudian regime. When Charles I failed to suppress the Covenanter revolt in the First Bishops War of 1639, he found himself caught between Scottish rebels and an English fifth column.[35] In 1640, he had no choice but to recall parliament for the first time in eleven years. His Personal Rule was over, and the struggle for a new religious settlement was underway.

III. The Puritan Revolution, 1640–60

The Elizabethan Settlement of 1559 had lasted for eight decades, but it had always had its discontents. For Puritans, it was only 'halfly reformed'; for Laudians, it was too Reformed by half. The Puritans were now in the ascendancy. The Short Parliament of April–May 1640 witnessed fierce attacks on the high church bishops, and when the king lost the Second Bishops' War to the

Covenanters in the summer of 1640, the Laudian experiment was halted in its tracks. The Long Parliament that assembled in November of that year was to sit until 1653, presiding over a religious revolution, one that historians have dubbed 'The Puritan Revolution'. Puritans, Dissenters and Nonconformists now became the establishment, and they were determined to remake the Church of England.[36]

This is a vital point, easily missed. We are so accustomed to pitting an oppositional Puritanism against an establishment Anglicanism that we forget that Puritans *were* the establishment in the mid-seventeenth century. We know that the Puritan reformation of the national church ended in failure, and so we think of the mid-seventeenth century as the period when the great dissenting denominations were formed – the Presbyterians, Congregationalists, Baptists and Quakers. But that was not the goal, at least for the vast majority of English Puritans. The Presbyterians and Congregationalists were not merely interested in founding denominations; they aimed higher – at the reform of the national Church.

Historians have sometimes talked as if the Church of England was driven underground in the 1640s and 1650s.[37] While happy to refer to 'the Interregnum Church' or the 'Cromwellian Church' they have been clear that this was not 'the Church of England', an entity only 'restored' or 're-established' with the monarchy after 1660.[38] Some contemporaries took the same view, insisting that the removal of bishops, canons and prayer book entailed the death of the Church. In December 1660, the earl of Clarendon praised the English Church as 'the best and the best-reformed church in the Christian World'. It had been 'buried so many years, by the boisterous hands of profane and sacrilegious persons'; now, God had 'miraculously . . . raised it from the grave'.[39]

Reformed Protestants indignantly rejected this claim. A year before the Restoration, Richard Baxter chided those advocates of prelacy who 'confidently . . . appropriate the title of the Church of *England*'. Militant anti-Calvinists like Thomas Pierce pretended to follow the Church of England, when in reality they had deserted it.[40] To the question 'where is your Church of England now?', Baxter retorted: 'it is living still'.[41] Far from dying or disappearing, the Church was being reformed and renovated. The Puritan ambition was that England's State Church (the *ecclesia Anglicana*) would finally assume its providential role as the first among equals, the purest of Europe's Reformed churches, the spearhead of the Protestant cause. The Puritan Revolution was a second Reformation of the Church of England.[42]

As such, it was a *magisterial* Reformation. Its headquarters were in Westminster, seat of the houses of parliament. Here, the politicians observed forty-two monthly fast days between 1642 and 1649, days when they listened to long sermons from the country's leading Puritan divines who urged them to build the temple of the Lord like Solomon or restore Jerusalem like Ezra and Nehemiah. From here there issued a constant stream of ordinances and statutes for the reform of the English Church and people.[43] In 1641, parliament ordered churchwardens to reverse Laudian 'innovations' by removing communion rails, altars, crucifixes and images from parish churches. State-sanctioned iconoclasm, such a marked feature of Calvinist reformation, and so prominent under Edward VI, was happening once again. In 1643, parliament signed the Solemn League and Covenant with the Scottish Covenanters, agreeing to reform the English Church 'in doctrine, worship, discipline and government, according to the word of God and the example of the best reformed churches'.[44] In 1644, it proscribed the Book of Common Prayer, replacing it in 1645 with a new Directory for Public Worship. In the same year, Archbishop Laud was beheaded on Tower Hill, and in 1646, the Westminster Parliament abolished Episcopacy.

Westminster was also the venue for 'the Assembly of Divines', the body tasked with advising parliament on the reform of the national Church. The Assembly met from 1643, and although the majority of its members were divines, it also had thirty lay representatives from among peers and MPs. It was parliament's largest standing committee, a reminder that this was an Erastian reformation, on which the politicians had the final say. The Assembly drew up a new directory of worship to replace the Prayer Book, a new confession of faith, catechisms, and a form of church government which advocated a Presbyterian system. Parliament ensured that the final settlement secured lay control of the church, and the clericalist ambitions of many of the Assembly's divines were curtailed.[45]

Had English Puritans united behind this Erastian-Presbyterian programme it would have had broad appeal. Few tears had been shed for the Laudians, and there was widespread agreement that the Church needed to reassert a robust Reformed Protestant identity. Of course, the abolition of bishops and liturgy had been deeply controversial. While many agreed that the power of bishops should be reduced and the liturgy reformed, it came as a shock to see them removed altogether. There was powerful grass roots nostalgia for the Prayer Book.[46] And the ejection of over two thousand beneficed clergy from their livings testified to the radicalism of Puritan reform.[47] Nevertheless, once parliament had won the Civil War, the prospect of a stable settlement was alluring. If the godly had coalesced around the Assembly's recommendations, it could have become a reality.

Instead, Puritan reformers became bitterly divided. In the Westminster Assembly itself, a small minority (the Dissenting Brethren) had objected to elements of Presbyterianism, and argued in favour of Congregationalism – self-governing churches made up of the godly rather than the whole parish. Outside Westminster, in the City of London and elsewhere, radical

Puritanism flourished. Separatists and Baptists established numerous congregations, and (perhaps more importantly) they acquired notoriety through pamphleteering and preaching.[48] Heterodox ideas were openly aired, and England appeared to be having its own Radical Reformation.[49] Presbyterian divines demanded the suppression of heresy and schism, calling on godly magistrates to imitate Old Testament kings like their sixteenth-century forbears. But they were countered by a vigorous campaign for religious toleration, involving radical Puritans such as John Milton, Roger Williams, John Goodwin and William Walwyn. Tolerationists threw into question some of the fundamental assumptions of the magisterial Reformation tradition. In particular, they started to deny that the magistrate had coercive powers in matters of religion. Taking up the slogan 'liberty of conscience', they argued that even ill-informed consciences ought to be respected.[50]

This would not have mattered had radical Puritans been isolated and denied political support. But by the mid-1640s, an Independent coalition had formed that included some powerful Westminster politicians (such as Sir Henry Vane the younger, former governor of Massachusetts) and military commanders (such as Oliver Cromwell). The Independents supported toleration (though they differed on how far it should extend), and were wary of, if not hostile to, the Scottish Covenanters. And they quickly became dominant in parliament's armies, reorganized in 1645 as the New Model Army. Although the political Presbyterians were the majority at Westminster, they had lost control of the army by 1647, when it was in open revolt. After it won the Second Civil War against the king in 1648, the army purged parliament. In January 1649, Charles I was put on trial and executed for treason.[51]

The Presbyterian reformation was now stymied, though not as emphatically as its Laudian predecessor. But where did this leave the national church? Here the triumphant Independents were deeply divided between radical and magisterial impulses. For radicals like Milton, Williams and their friend Vane, the best thing the state could do was to leave the church alone. Interfering magistrates had been the bane of Christian history, and religious coercion was the tool of Antichrist.[52] This radical Puritan defence of religious liberty was much celebrated by later Dissenters, but it was heavily contested even among Independents. At times, John Owen could sound like Roger Williams, but he remained more attached to traditional Protestant ideals. Godly magistrates should uphold true religion by ensuring that orthodox teachers were placed in parishes, and by using their power to punish heresiarchs (like the anti-Trinitarian John Biddle).[53] Influenced by Henry Ireton and then by Owen, Cromwell was firmly committed to magisterial reformation. The Cromwellian religious settlement maintained the parish churches and tithes, and set up a system of Triers and Ejectors, the former to examine new clergy, the latter to remove the politically, morally or theologically unsound.[54]

The great majority of the godly – and the overwhelming mass of their clergy – remained within the Church of England. Presbyterians, though deeply frustrated by the failure of their own system, soon participated as Triers and Ejectors. They deplored the regicide and the proliferation of sects and heresies, but recognized that the Cromwellian settlement offered real opportunities. Richard Baxter lamented the rise of the New Model Army and the triumph of the Independents, but he also looked back on the 1650s as a golden moment. Through his writings and his regional associations, he tried to transform the parish ministry into a dynamic force for the evangelization of England. The Congregationalists, of course, had a formative influence on Cromwell's religious policy, although they constituted only a small proportion of the parish clergy. John Owen rejected the concept of a 'national church' on the grounds that the only true churches were local congregations, but he worked hard (though unsuccessfully) to draw up a confession of faith that would be binding on all parish ministers; he and Philip Nye were satirically compared to the archbishops of Canterbury and York. The Congregationalists did assemble gathered churches beyond the parish, voluntary fellowships of the godly. Yet many of them also held parish livings, and they remained committed to parochial and national reformation.[55] Recent research has suggested that their *Savoy Declaration* of 1658 was no narrow denominational project, but a response to the Humble Petition and Advice, which had mandated a national confession of faith.[56] Although the Baptists were mostly separatists, even they had pastors who doubled as parish clergy. Indeed, several Baptists – including John Tombes and Henry Jessey – sat on the national committee of Triers, examining men for the public ministry.

With hindsight, of course, the Puritan Revolution can be seen as the crucible in which denominational identities began to form. The Westminster Assembly produced the seminal texts of later Presbyterianism; Congregationalists and Particular Baptists drew up confessions of faith that revised Westminster's; and Quakers emerged as a brand new movement, growing rapidly from a standing start to as many as 60,000 by 1660. Most Baptists and all Quakers stood outside the Established Church. Quakers, in particular, experienced persecution, from both mobs and officials. In 1656, after a ten-day debate in the Presbyterian-dominated parliament, their most extravagant minister, James Nayler, was sentenced to be branded, flogged, bored through the tongue with a hot iron and imprisoned.[57] Altogether around two thousand Quakers were imprisoned by local magistrates.

Yet Cromwell himself was averse to persecuting the Quakers, and he regarded Presbyterians, Independents and Baptists as godly brethren. In the 1650s, these groups were the insiders; the true Protestant Dissenters were the dissident Episcopalians, who resorted to clandestine ordinations and illegal conventicles using the Prayer Book, some of which were disrupted by the authorities. The Church of England was under Puritan hegemony, and at the height of Cromwell's Protectorate, the people we call 'Anglican' Royalists despaired of the future.[58] In 1657, when he was offered the Crown and re-inaugurated as Lord Protector, Oliver was not yet sixty years old, and it was hard to imagine an imminent restoration of the Stuarts and the bishops.

IV. Church and Dissent in the Restoration, 1660–88

This, however, was exactly what transpired in 1660–62, soon after Cromwell's unexpected demise in 1658. Suddenly, finally and irreversibly, Puritans became Dissenters. Presbyterians had eagerly backed the Restoration, anxious to end the anarchic constitutional and religious experiments of 1659. But they had hoped – even expected – to continue where they belonged, within the parishes, within the national Church. In their own eyes, they were establishment men, utterly distinct from the wild sectaries who had supported the regicide and disrupted the unity of the parish. To many of their countrymen, however, they were the ministers whose incendiary sermons had sparked the Civil Wars and unleashed all that followed. The regicide, the sects, the wars and the chaos of the preceding decades were blamed on the Puritan ministry, hundreds of whom were unceremoniously ejected from their parishes in 1660. The Presbyterians, however, still held out hope of a favourable settlement. Several had been offered bishoprics and while Baxter and Edmund Calamy declined, Edward Reynolds accepted the see of Norwich. In October 1660, the Worcester House Declaration suggested generous terms of accommodation for the Puritans, though its status was unclear. In April 1661, twelve leading Puritans met with twelve Episcopal clergy at the Savoy Conference to discuss liturgical revision. Baxter took the provocative step of presenting a new Reformed liturgy, which was firmly rebuffed by the conference convenor, Gilbert Sheldon, who was determined to restore the Prayer Book.[59]

Sheldon and his allies prevailed, and he became archbishop of Canterbury in 1663. His anti-Puritanism resonated powerfully with the Cavalier Parliament which was to sit from 1661 to 1679. It was dominated by Anglican Royalists who were in no mood to compromise with the zealots who had preached up the Great Rebellion. In December 1661, they passed a Corporation Act, which required all civic office holders to submit to a sacramental test. Then MPs trained their sights on Nonconforming ministers. The Act of Uniformity (1662) required all clergy to renounce their non-Episcopal ordinations and the Solemn League and Covenant, and to give full assent to the Book of Common Prayer. Altogether, almost two thousand Puritan clergy were removed between 1660 and 1662.[60]

With hindsight, we can see that it was a decisive parting of the ways between Church and Dissent. Before the Civil Wars, 'nonconformists' had been parish clergy who scrupled at certain ceremonies; now they were ejected ministers. This wholesale purge of the Puritan ministry was a dramatic break with the Church's past, something that is obscured when we talk of the Church being 'restored' or 're-established'. This was no longer the Church of late sixteenth and early seventeenth century – by expelling its Puritan tendency more thoroughly than Laud had ever dared, the Church was realigning itself and striking out in a new direction. Increasingly, its Reformed identity would be downplayed, its uniquely Anglican identity celebrated. The restoration of the bishops and the liturgy can obscure the fact that this too was a second Reformation.

Other legislation was designed to shut down the religious marketplace that had opened up under Cromwell, reasserting the monopoly of the Established Church. During the 1650s, even Quaker meetings were legally permissible; under the Quaker Act (1662) they were outlawed. The Conventicle Act (1664) prohibited any adult from attending a Nonconformist meeting of five or more people outside the household. The File Mile Act (1665) banned ejected ministers from coming within five miles of their former parish or any corporate town. The second Conventicle Act (1670) was more draconian than the first, with heavier penalties for Nonconformist clergy and incentives for informants.

The enforcement of these laws varied considerably across the Restoration era.[61] Chronologically, persecution was intense during the first decade when there was considerable fear of a Dissenter revolt led by disbanded New Model Army soldiers. It levelled off during the Cabal ministry (1667–73) which supported Charles II's Declaration of Indulgence in 1672, before intensifying under the earl of Danby in the mid-1670s, who persuaded the king to align himself more firmly with the Church party. In the Exclusion Crisis (1678–81), Dissenters experienced a new period of relief, as public anxiety focused on a Catholic plot and the Whigs took advantage. But the association of Dissenters with Exclusion and Whig radicalism provoked a Tory-Anglican reaction after 1681, the nadir of Nonconformist fortunes. As in the early 1660s, the worst persecution coincided with fears that civil war might break out again. Relief only came with the Declarations of Indulgence issued by James II in 1687 and 1688.

Persecution fluctuated according to geography and denomination. In many communities, local magistrates were sympathetic to Dissent, and some bishops favoured a policy of lenience too. Elsewhere, the law was rigorously implemented. As for the denominations, militant Anglicans tended to see all Dissenters as sectaries and schismatics, but others recognized that there was a broad spectrum extending from moderate Presbyterians to radical Quakers, with Congregationalists and Baptists somewhere in between. Presbyterians like Baxter acknowledged that Quakers bore the brunt of the repression, though no group was immune.

While the Restoration state stopped short of using the death penalty against Dissenters, persecution was fierce. Thousands were heavily fined or had property sequestered, with a good many suffering financial ruin. Thousands were also imprisoned. Among the Quakers alone, it has been estimated that as many as 11,000 went to gaol between 1660 and 1686, and around 450 died as a result of their sufferings. Among the Quaker leaders who met their death in prison were Richard Hubberthorne, Edward Burrough and Francis Howgill, young men who had played a key role in creating the national movement. Nor was imprisonment reserved for the sects alone. In 1682, at the start of the Tory Reaction, fifty-two Presbyterians were consigned to Bristol gaol together with eighty-six Quakers, 'almost stifled' with up to thirty in a single room. Over 200 of the ejected clergy served time in Restoration prisons, including Richard Baxter. In this respect, at least, the persecution of the Puritan clergy in the Restoration was harsher than that inflicted on their Anglican counterparts during the Civil War era. In its scale and intensity, this was a persecution of Protestant by Protestant unparalleled in seventeenth-century Europe.

Despite this, there is a danger in viewing Restoration Puritanism 'through the lens of a denominational future' rather than 'through the lens of a dynamic and unsettled national church past'.[62] As Mark Goldie observes, 'many, perhaps most, of the ejected ministers were careful to maintain their loyalty to the national Church', while 'the great majority of the Dissenting laity were likewise partial conformists'. As a consequence, 'the boundary between the Church and moderate Dissent' was 'highly porous'.[63] Quakers and most Baptists were adamantly separatist, but even among the Baptists there were exceptions – John Tombes, the former Trier, 'came constantly' to Edward Fowler's parish church in Salisbury, 'heard common prayer and received the sacrament kneeling'.[64] Congregationalists were divided over whether it was legitimate to attend the Established Church to hear sermons – John Owen and William Bridge argued strenuously against such a compromise, but Philip Nye thought it a duty to do so, though he agreed that it was wrong to join in Common Prayer and take the Sacrament. Some Presbyterian clergy took Nye's position, but in general they were more willing to participate in parish worship and communion.[65] Unlike the Episcopalians of the 1650s, they were extremely reluctant to ordain new ministers; whereas the bishops had conducted around 2,500 ordinations between 1646 and 1660, the Presbyterians may have ordained as few as twenty new pastors between 1662 and 1694.[66] They regularly attended parish services and scheduled their own meetings so as not to clash with the official Prayer Book services, clinging to the hope that they would soon be accommodated within the national church.[67] They had not come to terms with being Dissenters.

The Puritan gentry and aristocracy remained even more firmly ensconced within the parish churches, even as they attended the sermons of Nonconformist clergy and employed them as domestic chaplains.[68] A significant number of Puritan MPs were re-elected, and they were to emerge as a significant force during the Exclusion Crisis, led by a veteran of 1640s parliamentarianism Sir Denzil Holles. These 'Puritan Whigs', like the older Presbyterian clergy, worked hard to promote schemes of comprehension, designed to reincorporate the Presbyterian ministers within the Church of England.[69] And comprehension enjoyed considerable support from moderate episcopalians, both clergy and laity.[70] As Michael Winship notes, we should not equate 'the Church of England' with its militant conformists or even with the majority of its legally active clergy. Their hostility to Nonconformists was not universally shared by other 'Anglicans', and the identity of the Established Church was still being hotly contested. The debate about Puritanism 'was ultimately a debate about who could claim possession of the Church of England'.[71] Had comprehension worked, it would have entailed a new religious settlement, one with a more Reformed flavour.

Comprehension, however, proved more difficult to implement than a policy of toleration. In 1672, the Declaration of Indulgence allowed the Nonconformists to seek licences for their meeting places and their ministers. This was an important turning point, because among the sixteen hundred who took up the offer were almost a thousand Presbyterians. By formalizing their conventicles, the Presbyterians consolidated their separate identity, even though they continued to attend parish worship. The Indulgence was soon recalled after pressure from parliament, but a younger generation of Presbyterian clergy (the 'Ducklings') became more reconciled to their dissenting status than the older 'Dons' like Baxter. Whereas the Dons still sought comprehension, the Ducklings were more likely to join with the Independents in lobbying for toleration.[72] These years witnessed a vigorous debate over 'liberty of conscience', with powerful contributions being made by a range of writers sympathetic to Dissent, including John Locke (in his unpublished *Essay concerning Toleration*); John Milton in *Of True Religion*; the poet and MP Andrew Marvell in his satire *The Rehearsal Transposed*; the republican Slingsby Bethel; the Presbyterian John Humfrey; the Congregationalist John Owen; and the Quaker William Penn.[73] When Penn was granted a royal charter to found the colony of Pennsylvania in 1681, he called its capital Philadelphia (brotherly love); its laws stipulated that no theistic believer was to 'be molested or prejudiced for their religious persuasion, or practice, in matters of faith and worship, nor shall they be compelled, at any time, to frequent or maintain any religious worship, place of ministry whatever'.[74]

Presbyterians had once lambasted toleration as a doctrine of Anabaptists and Socinians, Arminians and Sectaries. But as the ejected ministers became victims of religious intolerance, they were slowly (and painfully) weaned off their attachment to the principle of enforced uniformity.[75] They found their own words quoted against them, as Anglicans defended the suppression of Dissent by republishing the anti-toleration tirades of earlier Presbyterians. Thomas Long, for example, reprinted Baxter's spicy denunciations of toleration from 1659 alongside similar quotations from Calvin, Thomas Edwards and other 'Presbyterians'.[76] But by 1679, Baxter himself was sounding very different notes, as he complained about the 'many and many books . . . that cry down liberty and toleration'. He observed that those who supported toleration were usually 'they that are lowest', while those who condemned it were the ones 'in power'. They typically talked of the 'mischiefs' it occasioned – the Japanese and Chinese had done so to justify the suppression of Christians, the Papists to justify their Inquisitions, while 'Lutherans cry down the toleration of Calvinists'. Yet as Baxter pointed out (like Henry Robinson before him and John Locke after him): 'If all the princes on earth should force their subjects to be of one religion, it would be their own.' Toleration, he concluded, was preferable to uniformity.[77]

The experience of persecution was also hardening ecclesiastical identities. While leading Congregationalists were willing to countenance attendance at parish services, they held out little hope for comprehension. John Owen, once the vice-chancellor of Oxford University, used his high-level contacts to promote a policy of indulgence. Freed from the distractions of parish ministry, Congregationalists gave undivided attention to building their gathered churches. Many Baptists had refused to participate in the Cromwellian state Church, and they were adamantly hostile to the Church of the Restoration. Quakers were now less inclined to heckle the parochial clergy than in the early days of their movement, and in some cases they even held minor parish offices, but they were the uncompromising epitome of Dissent. Their most famous work during this era was begun in prison by William Penn and entitled *No Cross, No Crown* (1669/1682).

The stubborn persistence of Dissent became one of the central issues of Restoration politics. By the Exclusion Crisis, it was an issue that divided those nascent political parties, the Whigs and the Tories. These were initially terms of abuse that bore witness to the fact that Restoration politics was the politics of religion.[78] Whigs were named after militant Scottish Covenanters, Tories after Irish Catholic Confederates. Although the majority of Whigs were conformists, they had strong Nonconformist support, and were committed to the toleration of Dissent. Tories were the Church and King party, the party of religious uniformity, and during their brief period of triumph after 1681 they 'aimed at nothing less than the annihilation of Dissent'.[79]

Ironically, this last and greatest persecution was ended during the reign of the Catholic James II. Quakers and Baptists were brought in from the cold, as the king sought to construct an alliance of Dissenters and Catholics against the hitherto privileged Church party. Most Dissenters were very wary of his motives, and inclined to believe Halifax's warning that the king was embracing the Nonconformists so that he might squeeze them later. Had James survived, the prospects for comprehension may have increased, as Dissenters and Anglicans drew together to defend the Protestantism of the English nation. Yet his strategy was a disaster, particularly since it coincided with the brutal suppression of the Huguenots by Louis XIV. By 1688, some of England's most powerful statesmen and bishops were preparing to invite a Dutch invasion.

V. 1689 and After

The Glorious Revolution that followed the Williamite coup brought toleration and denied comprehension. Bills for both had been introduced into parliament, but comprehension was once again blocked by Anglicans, who now had to worry about a Dutch Reformed king.[80] Presbyterian clergy – who had long hoped to resume service as pastors of the *ecclesia Anglicana* – now had to accept their status as Dissenters. The year 1689 saw 'the victory of the Independent concept of toleration over Presbyterian hopes of Comprehension'.[81]

The 'Toleration Act' (1689) was limited – it neither mentioned 'toleration' nor offered a principled defence of liberty of conscience; it simply suspended the penal laws against Trinitarian Protestant Nonconformists; it excluded Unitarians, Catholics, deists and atheists; and it left Dissenters as second-class citizens, who could only hold civil office if they took communion within the Established Church. Nevertheless, it was a landmark piece of legislation that liberated Dissent. Dissenters were legally free to erect chapels, administer communion and baptize infants. In the two decades after 1689, they registered thousands of meeting houses. By 1715, there were at least 400,000 Dissenters in England and Wales, comprising around 7 per cent of the population.[82]

Even the Presbyterians now accepted their status as a denomination. They held their services on Sunday mornings, in competition with parish worship, and the practice of partial or semi-conformity went into steep decline. Instead, lay Dissenters practised 'occasional conformity', taking Anglican Communion once a year simply to qualify for civil office. In 1697, the Lord Mayor of London caused offence when he brazenly received Anglican Communion in the morning before parading in full regalia to a Dissenting meeting house in the afternoon. The same loophole allowed Presbyterians to occupy the mayoralty of Nottingham for two-thirds of the eighteenth century.[83] While finding ways to retain civil office, Presbyterians increasingly identified more closely with other Dissenters than with Anglicans. In 1691, they banded together with Congregationalists to form the 'Happy Union' and set up a Common Fund. Both were short-lived, but they were merely the first in a long series of cooperative schemes. Another symbolic turning point was the first public ordinations of Presbyterian ministers in 1694. 'Denominationalism', as Mark Goldie explains, had been 'a slow and reluctant process, and its decisive moment was neither 1662 nor 1672, but 1689'.[84]

Many high churchmen were infuriated that the state had abandoned the hallowed principle of religious uniformity and caved in to religious pluralism. Some churchmen called for the 'Toleration Act' to be repealed or restricted in its effects. Daniel Defoe parodied their zeal in his satire *The Shortest Way with Dissenters* (1702), only to be gaoled for his efforts. In 1709, the 'High Church' divine Henry Sacheverall preached an incendiary sermon against Dissent and toleration. When he was put on trial the following year for libelling the Revolution, mobs shouting 'High Church and Sacheverall' attacked and partially destroyed some of the largest Dissenting chapels in London. In 1711, high church MPs pushed through an Occasional Conformity Act, aimed at preventing Dissenters from qualifying for public office by taking Anglican Communion once a year. In 1714, the Schism Act was passed, with the intent of shutting down the flourishing Dissenting Academies, which provided higher education to those excluded from Oxford and Cambridge. Both Acts were repealed by the Whig administration in 1719, but for a time, toleration had looked fragile. In Birmingham, for example, there were major anti-Dissenting riots in 1714 and 1715. Only after 1719 could Dissenters breathe more easily.

The days in which Presbyterians denounced toleration seemed distant. In Part II of his *Defence of Moderate Nonconformity* (1704), Edmund Calamy redefined Dissenting identity on Lockean lines. Although he accepted the venerable Reformed conception of kings and queens as 'nursing Fathers and . . . nursing Mothers to the Church under the New Testament', Calamy denied that they had coercive powers or could pass penal laws. Every congregation should 'manage itself in an entire independency', and there should be no imposition by magistrates or synods. Moreover, 'every Man' should be left free in matters of religion to act according to his conscience and 'has none to controul him, as long as the Civil Interests of Mankind . . . remain untouch'd'.[85]

Later Rational Dissenters highlighted Calamy's book as a key turning point in the intellectual history of English Presbyterianism. Andrew Kippis admitted in 1773 that seventeenth-century Presbyterians had 'never entertained any just sentiments on the subject of toleration', but thanks to Locke and Calamy there had been an 'alteration in . . . the Dissenters' sentiments'. This was a posthumous vindication for the Puritan tolerationists whose ideas had been so emphatically condemned by Presbyterians in the 1640s. As Goldie comments, the new Presbyterians, with their emphasis on godly magistrates who suppress immorality and irreligion while allowing Protestant diversity to flourish, remind us 'how close Lockean toleration was to Cromwellian independency and how far from Enlightenment secularism'. Locke himself wrote to Calamy expressing approval of his work, and John Toland agreed that the Presbyterians had now 'expressly declared their minds' on liberty of conscience, especially in Calamy's writings, 'which they generally approve'.[86] Anglican critics pointed out the contradiction between 'how very violent the Presbyterians in 1645, &c were against any Toleration in Religion, when they had the Power in their Hands; and how very clamorous they are now for it'. A pamphlet subtitled *1645 against 1710* contrasted the opinions of 'the Old and the New Presbyterians', devoting five pages to anti-tolerationist quotations from Calamy's grandfather.[87]

Such Anglican critics implied that 'the new Presbyterians' were hiding their true intentions, but there is every reason to think that their change of tune was more than a pragmatic move. In 1703, London Presbyterians joined Baptists and Congregationalists in writing to the New England authorities, asking them to overturn anti-Quaker legislation. Calamy reproduced the letter in one of his works to show that Dissenters were not 'Enemies to the Liberty of others', as their Anglican critics claimed. The letter stated that it was against 'the Principles of the Gospel' and 'the undoubted Rights of Mankind' for anyone to be punished for 'conscientious and peaceable Dissent from the Establish'd Way of Religion, whilst they are not justly Chargeable with any Immorality, or what is plainly Destructive of Civil Society'.[88] This was an essentially Lockean view of toleration and its limits.

By the 1720s and 1730s, a younger generation of more liberal Presbyterians went further than Calamy, engaging in an explicit attack on the intolerance of the Reformed tradition. In 1722, the Presbyterian Samuel Chandler translated the Dutch Arminian Philip van Limborch's famous treatise on the history of the Inquisition. In a later tract, he honestly admitted that the Presbyterians of the 1640s had no intention of tolerating other religions (and he quoted the *Westminster Larger Catechism* to prove it).[89] Chandler and other Rational Dissenters such as Caleb Fleming, John Taylor, Micaiah Towgood, drew on Locke, Bayle and Benjamin Hoadly to craft a 'consistent Protestantism' that eschewed the enforcement of religious doctrine as 'the very ESSENCE of Popery'.[90] In their periodical of the 1730s, the *Old Whig*, this new generation of Presbyterians, steeped in Enlightenment texts, launched attacks on bigotry and intolerance, including a lengthy account of the execution of Servetus that was fiercely critical of Calvin.[91] Such English Presbyterian divines now sounded like the most radical tolerationists of the 1640s, as they rejected religious establishments altogether, and insisted, as Towgood did, that 'Human Lawgivers have Power only over Bodies and Estates . . . but to Matters of Conscience and Religion their Authority cannot extend'.[92] For English Presbyterians this was a remarkable *volte-face*. In 1659 Baxter had condemned 'Universal Liberty' in religion and the denial of the magistrate's power in religion as 'a wicked doctrine' – by the 1730s, that very doctrine was being trumpeted by leading Presbyterian divines as the heart and soul of Protestantism. The principles of magisterial Reformation were giving way to religious voluntarism.

Ironically, Dissenters struggled to take advantage of this new world. Having survived the storm of persecution, they now found themselves becalmed in the smooth sea of toleration. By the 1730s, there was growing anxiety and debate about 'the decay of the dissenting interest'. While some lamented Dissent's lack of sophistication, others feared that it was losing its spiritual edge and vitality. Around fifty Dissenting ministers had conformed to the Established Church since 1714, among them Joseph Butler and Thomas Secker, and many others were swept along by the fashion for 'rational religion'. Among Presbyterians especially, Calvinism and Trinitarianism were in steep decline, and the number of converts and worshippers seemed to be falling too. Between 80 and 90 per cent of Quakers were the children of Quakers. Dissent seemed to be losing its expansionist, evangelical energy. England was now a religious marketplace, but Dissenters seemed ill-placed to exploit it.[93]

Among those who did rise to the challenge were the Congregationalists Philip Doddridge and Isaac Watts. Both were emphatically Lockean in their commitment to religious liberty and religious voluntarism, but also wary of Locke's minimalist theology. In their hymns and writings they promoted traditional Reformed doctrine and Puritan piety, believing that these were the best means of 'reviving the Dissenting interest'.[94] They found a kindred spirit in the New England Congregationalist Jonathan Edwards, who was an acute participant-observer of local and regional 'revival'. In England and Wales, ironically, revivalism would be spearheaded by Anglicans like George Whitefield, John Wesley and Howell Harris, who took to the fields and the streets to preach. To Dissenters, who had worked so hard to establish their 'polite' credentials in the face of Anglican disdain, this was a surprising development. But as the eighteenth century progressed, growing numbers of Congregationalists and Baptists were swept along by the Evangelical Revival. In the religious marketplace that had opened up since the 'Act of Toleration', the congregations that flourished would be those that embraced the new evangelical style – populist, participatory, expressive and missionary. England's Reformation had been driven forward by the state; the revival would come from the grass roots. Instead of 'tarrying for the magistrate', evangelicals would put their faith in voluntary religion.[95]

VI. Conclusion

The religious settlement ushered in by the Glorious Revolution proved to be remarkably durable, lasting until 1828 when the repeal of the Test and Corporation Acts brought Dissenters civic equality. But we have seen that there was nothing inevitable about this outcome. The triumph of toleration and the emergence of Dissent was the result of a long, convoluted and contingent history. For two-thirds of our period (i.e. 1550–1689), the majority of Nonconformists wished to belong to the national Church and remained drawn to magisterial reformation. They had good reason to hope that they could avoid becoming Dissenters outside the Church of England. At numerous junctures in the story, alternative futures had opened up and then closed. Various ecclesiastical factions had attempted to remake the Church of England in their own image, only to meet with failure. New religious settlements had been forged in the 1640s and 1650s, in 1662 and 1689.

Eventually, even the Presbyterians had to concede that the game was up. Comprehension was not going to work. Church and Dissent were to go their separate ways. For Baptists and Quakers (and even for Congregationalists) this was easier to accept, since they did not share the Presbyterian devotion to parochial ministry and the ideal of a 'national church'. But these bodies accounted for less than half of the Dissenters – in 1660, they probably only numbered between 100,000 and 150,000 adherents (2 to 3 per cent of the population). It was the Presbyterians, with their élite support and their mass following, who constituted the greatest loss for the national Church. The state churches in other Protestant lands had produced minor splinter groups; the English Church had ejected one-fifth of its own clergy. Dissent was set to become a major force in national life.

Notes

I am most grateful to Professor Anthony Milton for his comments on this chapter.

1 For the distinction between 'strong' and 'weak' teleology, see Glenn Burgess, 'On Revisionism: An Analysis of Early Stuart Historiography in the 1970s and 1980s', *Historical Journal*, 33 (1990), pp. 609–27.

2 P. E. More and F. L. Cross (eds), *Anglicanism: The Thought and Practice of the Church of England, Illustrated from the Religious Literature of the Seventeenth Century* (London: SPCK, 1935). On the agenda of the original editors see W. B. Patterson's 'Foreword' to the new edition, More and Cross (eds), *Anglicanism* (Cambridge: James Clarke and Co, 2009), pp. xvii–xxiv. See also W. B. Patterson, 'William Perkins as Apologist for the Church of England', *Journal of Ecclesiastical History*, 57 (2006), pp. 252–69.

3 Eamon Duffy, 'The Shock of Change: Continuity and Discontinuity in the Elizabethan Church of England', in S. Platten (ed.), *Anglicanism and the Western Christian Tradition* (Norwich: Canterbury Press, 2003), p. 42. The anthology to which he refers is Gillian R. Evans and J. Robert White (eds), *The Anglican Tradition: A Handbook of Sources* (London: SPCK, 1991).

4 John Seed, *Dissenting Histories: Religious Division and the Politics of Memory in Eighteenth-Century England* (Edinburgh: Edinburgh University Press, 2008), chapter 2.
5 For one distinguished example, see R. W. Dale, *History of English Congregationalism* (London: Hasell, Watson and Viney, 1907). The language of liberty runs through Dale's book, and he celebrated Puritanism as the movement that led to 'the inalienable rights of man' and the principle of 'religious liberty' (p. 173).
6 See, e.g., E. B. Underhill, *Struggles and Triumphs of Religious Liberty: An Historical Survey* (1851). For the Hanserd Knollys Society, Underhill edited *Tracts on Liberty of Conscience and Persecution, 1614–61* (1846) and Roger Williams, *The Bloudy Tenent of Persecution* (1848).
7 William Orme, *Memoirs of the Life, Writings and Religious Connexions of John Owen* (1820), p. 106.
8 For one example, see the Baptist Joseph Ivimey's study, *John Milton: His Life and Times* (London: E. Wilson, 1833). On the origins of the language of 'civil and religious liberty' see Blair Worden, *God's Instruments: Political Conduct in the England of Oliver Cromwell* (Oxford: Oxford University Press, 2012), chapter 8.
9 The Nonconformists' Whiggish appropriation of seventeenth-century Puritanism is explored in Blair Worden, *Roundhead Reputations: The English Civil Wars and the Passions of Posterity* (London: Allen Lane, 2001), chapters 8–10.
10 The finest overview of Dissent during this period remains Michael R. Watts, *The Dissenters, Volume 1: From the Reformation to the French Revolution* (Oxford: Oxford University Press, 1978). The best anthology is R. Tudur Jones et al. (eds), *Protestant Nonconformist Texts, Volume 1: 1550–1700* (Aldershot: Ashgate, 2007).
11 See Diarmaid MacCulloch, *Tudor Church Militant: Edward VI and the Protestant Reformation* (London: Allen Lane, 2000).
12 For the continental context see Philip Benedict, *Christ's Churches Purely Reformed: A Social History of Calvinism* (New Haven: Yale University Press, 2004).
13 On the contributions of Zurich and Geneva see Diarmaid MacCulloch, 'The Church of England, 1533–1603', in Platten (ed.), *Anglicanism and the Western Christian Tradition*, pp. 34–40.
14 On this generation of English bishops see Patrick Collinson, *Archbishop Grindal, 1519–1583: The Struggle for a Reformed Church* (London: Jonathan Cape, 1979).
15 See Patrick Collinson, *The Elizabethan Puritan Movement* (London: Jonathan Cape, 1967), pp. 21–97.
16 Ibid.; Peter Lake, *Anglicans and Puritans? Presbyterians and English Conformist Thought – Whitgift to Hooker* (London: Unwin Hyman, 1988). On the persistence of Presbyterianism after the 1590s see Polly Ha, *English Presbyterianism, 1590–1640* (Stanford: Stanford University Press, 2011).
17 B. R. White, *The English Separatist Tradition from the Marian Martyrs to the Pilgrim Fathers* (Oxford: Oxford University Press, 1971); Stephen Brachlow, *The Communion of Saints: Radical Puritan and Separatist Ecclesiology, 1570–1625* (Oxford: Oxford University Press, 1988).
18 James Coggins, *John Smyth's Congregation: English Separatism, Mennonite Influence and the Elect Nation* (Harrisonburg, VA: Herald Press, 1991).
19 Brachlow, *The Communion of Saints*, chapter 7.
20 Thomas Helwys, *The Mistery of Iniquity* (1612), p. 69.
21 Timothy Larsen, *Friends of Religious Equality: Nonconformist Politics in Mid-Victorian England* (Woodbridge: Boydell and Brewer, 1999).
22 Peter Lake, 'The "Anglican Moment"? Richard Hooker and the Ideological Watershed of the 1590s', in Platten (ed.), *Anglicanism and the Western Christian Tradition*, chapter 5. See also Anthony Milton, 'Anglicanism by Stealth: The Career

and Influence of John Overall', in Peter Lake and Kenneth Fincham (eds), *Religious Politics in Post-Reformation England* (Woodbridge: Boydell and Brewer, 2006).

23 See Nicholas Tyacke, *Anti-Calvinists: The Rise of English Arminianism, c.1590–1640* (Oxford: Oxford University Press, 1987); Anthony Milton, *Catholic and Reformed: The Roman and Protestant Churches in English Protestant Thought, 1600–1640* (Cambridge: Cambridge University Press, 1995); Jean-Louis Quantin, *The Church of England and Christian Antiquity: The Construction of Confessional Identity in the Seventeenth Century* (Oxford: Oxford University Press, 2009).

24 Anthony Milton (ed.), *The British Delegation and the Synod of Dort (1618–19)* (Woodbridge: Boydell Press, 2005).

25 See Patrick Collinson, 'England and International Calvinism, 1558–1640', in Menna Prestwich (ed.), *International Calvinism, 1541–1715* (Oxford: The Clarendon Press, 1985), chapter 7; idem, *Godly People: Essays in English Protestantism and Puritanism* (London: The Hambledon Press, 1983), chapter 20.

26 On the origins of this tradition see Peter Lake, *Moderate Puritans and the Elizabethan Church* (Cambridge: Cambridge University Press, 1982).

27 Dwight Bozeman, *The Precisianist Strain: Disciplinary Religion and the Antinominan Backlash in Puritanism to 1638* (Chapel Hill, NC: University of North Carolina Press, 2004), chapter 4.

28 See Patrick Collinson, *The Religion of Protestants: The Church in English Society, 1559–1625* (Oxford: Oxford University Press, 1982). But see Peter Lake's review in the *Journal of Ecclesiastical History*, 34 (1983), pp. 627–29.

29 Keith Sprunger, *Dutch Puritanism: A History of English and Scottish Churches of the Netherlands in the Sixteenth and Seventeenth Centuries* (Leiden: Brill, 1982).

30 Karen Kuperman, *Providence Island, 1630–1641: The Other Puritan Colony* (Cambridge: Cambridge University Press, 1993).

31 Virginia DeJohn Anderson, *New England's Generation: The Great Migration and the Formation of Society and Culture in the Seventeenth Century* (Cambridge: Cambridge University Press, 1991); Stephen Foster, *The Long Argument: English Puritanism and the Shaping of New England Culture, 1570–1700* (Raleigh, NC: University of North Carolina Press, 1991).

32 David Como, 'Radical Puritanism,' in John Coffey and Paul C. H. Lim (eds), *The Cambridge Companion to Puritanism* (Cambridge: Cambridge University Press, 2008), chapter 14.

33 David Como, *Blown by the Spirit: Puritanism and the Emergence of an Antinomian Underground in Pre-Civil-War England* (Stanford, CA: Stanford University Press, 2004); Michael Winship, *Making Heretics: Militant Protestantism and Free Grace in Massachusetts* (Princeton, NJ: Princeton University Press, 2002).

34 Stephen Wright, *The Early English Baptists, 1603–1649* (Woodbridge: Boydell and Brewer, 2006), pp. 68–74.

35 John Adamson, *The Noble Revolt: The Overthrow of Charles I* (London: Weidenfeld and Nicholson, 2007).

36 See William Shaw, *A History of the English Church during the Civil Wars and under the Commonwealth, 1640–1660*, 2 vols (London: Longmans, 1900). For a recent assessment of success and failure, see Bernard Capp, *England's Culture Wars: Puritan Reformation and its Enemies in the Interregnum, 1649–1660* (Oxford: Oxford University Press, 2012).

37 Indeed, John Pocock and Gordon Schochet write of 'the Church of England's temporary disestablishment and underground survival'. See their essay, 'Interregnum and Restoration', in J. G. A. Pocock (ed.), *The Varieties of British Political Thought, 1500–1800* (Cambridge: Cambridge University Press, 1993), p. 156. As Robert Bosher noted, 'the now-well established tradition of depicting Anglicanism as

a persecuted underground movement began soon after the Restoration, when Laudian writers preferred to ignore the inconvenient truth that Anglican conformity to the Cromwellian Church was widespread'. Bosher, *The Making of the Restoration Settlement* (Westminster: Dacre Press, 1951), p. 24 n.1.

38 See, e.g., Anne Whiteman, 'The Restoration of the Church of England', in Geoffrey Nuttall and Owen Chadwick (eds), *From Uniformity to Unity, 1662–1962* (London: SPCK, 1962), chapter 1; I. M. Green, *The Re-Establishment of the Church of England, 1660–63* (Oxford: Oxford University Press, 1978).

39 'Speech to Both Houses on the Dissolution of the Convention Parliament, 29 December 1660', in John Kenyon (ed.), *The Stuart Constitution: Documents and Commentary* (Cambridge: Cambridge University Press, 1986), p. 347.

40 Richard Baxter, *A Key for Catholics* (1659), pp. 335, 30. See also p. 453.

41 Richard Baxter, *Catholic Unity* (1659), in *The Practical Works of Richard Baxter*, 4 vols (1846), IV, p. 689.

42 For a full development of this thesis we await Anthony Milton's major monograph, *England's Second Reformation: The Battle for the Church of England, 1636–66*, forthcoming.

43 See C. H. Firth and R. S. Rait (eds), *Acts and Ordinances of the Interregnum, 1642–1660* (London: H.M. Stationary Office, 1911).

44 Gerald Bray (ed.), *Documents of the English Reformation* (Cambridge: James Clarke, 1994), p. 484.

45 Our understanding of the Assembly will be transformed by Chad Van Dixhoorn (ed.), *Minutes and Papers of the Westminster Assembly, 1643–1652*, 5 vols (Oxford: Oxford University Press, 2012).

46 See Judith Maltby, *Prayer Book and People in Elizabethan and Early Stuart England* (Cambridge: Cambridge University Press, 1998), chapter 5; John Morrill, 'The Church of England, 1642–49', in idem, *The Nature of the English Revolution* (Harlow: Longman, 1993), pp. 148–75.

47 I. M. Green, 'The Persecution of "Scandalous" and "Malignant" Parish Clergy during the English Civil War', *English Historical Review*, 194 (1979), pp. 507–31.

48 Murray Tolmie, *The Triumph of the Saints: The Separate Churches of London, 1626–1649* (Cambridge: Cambridge University Press, 1977).

49 The classic work on heterodoxy in the period is Christopher Hill, *The World Turned Upside Down: Radical Ideas during the English Revolution* (Harmondsworth: Penguin, 1975 [1972]).

50 See John Coffey, 'The Toleration Controversy during the English Revolution', in Christopher Durston and Judith Maltby (eds), *Religion in Revolutionary England* (Manchester: Manchester University Press, 2006), chapter 2.

51 The best short account of factional politics is David Scott, *Politics and War in the Three Stuart Kingdoms, 1637–1649* (Houndmills: Palgrave Macmillan, 2004).

52 Carolyn Polizzotto, 'The Campaign against the Humble Proposals of 1652', *Journal of Ecclesiastical History*, 38 (1987), pp. 569–81.

53 John Coffey, 'John Owen and the Puritan Toleration Controversy, 1646–59', in Kelly Kapic and Mark Jones (eds), *The Ashgate Research Companion to John Owen's Theology* (Farnham: Ashgate, 2012), chapter 14.

54 Ann Hughes, '"The Public Profession of these Nations": The National Church in Interregnum England', in Durston and Maltby (eds), *Religion in Revolutionary England*, chapter 4; Worden, *God's Instruments*, chapter 3: 'Toleration and the Protectorate'.

55 See Joel Halcomb, 'A Social History of Congregational Religious Practice during the Puritan Revolution' (unpublished PhD thesis, University of Cambridge, 2009), chapters 3 and 8.

56 Hunter Powell, 'The Last Confession: A Background Study of the Savoy Declaration of Faith and Order (1658)' (unpublished MPhil dissertation, University of Cambridge, 2008).
57 Leo Damrosch, *The Sorrows of the Quaker Jesus: James Nayler and the Puritan Crackdown on the Free Spirit* (Cambridge, MA: Harvard University Press, 1996).
58 Jason McElligott and David L. Smith (eds), *Royalists and Royalism during the Interregnum* (Manchester: Manchester University Press, 2010), pp. 13–15, 18–43.
59 E. C. Ratcliff, 'The Savoy Conference and the Revision of the Book of Common Prayer', in Nuttall and Chadwick (eds), *From Uniformity to Unity*, chapter 2.
60 See A. G. Matthews (ed.), *Calamy Revised: Being an Revision of Edmund Calamy's Account of the Ministers and Others Ejected and Silenced, 1660–62* (Oxford: The Clarendon Press, 1934).
61 For the account of persecution that follows, see the surveys by Gerald Cragg, *Puritanism in the Period of the Great Persecution* (Cambridge: Cambridge University Press, 1957); John Coffey, *Persecution and Toleration in Protestant England, 1558–1689* (London: Longman, 2000), pp. 169–79; John Marshall, *John Locke, Toleration and Early Enlightenment Culture* (Cambridge: Cambridge University Press, 2006), pp. 94–115.
62 Michael Winship, 'Defining Puritanism in Restoration England: Richard Baxter and Others Respond to a Friendly Debate', *Historical Journal*, 54 (2011), p. 692.
63 Mark Goldie, 'Roger Morrice and the Puritan Whigs', in *The Entring Book of Roger Morrice, 1677–1691* (Woodbridge: The Boydell Press, 2007), I, pp. 229–30.
64 Mark Goldie and John Spurr, 'Politics and the Restoration Parish: Edward Fowler and the Struggle for St Giles Cripplegate', *English Historical Review*, 109 (1994), pp. 574.
65 Douglas Lacey, *Dissent and Parliamentary Politics in England, 1661–1689* (New Brunswick: Rutgers University Press, 1969), pp. 16–21.
66 Compare Kenneth Fincham and Stephen Taylor, 'Episcopal Ordinations and Ordinands in England, 1646–1660', *English Historical Review*, 125 (2011), pp. 319–44, with David Wykes, 'The Minister's Calling: The Preparation and Qualification of Candidates for the Presbyterian Ministry in England, 1660–1689', *Nederlands Archief voor Kerkgeschiedenis*, 82 (2004), pp. 271–80.
67 See Goldie, 'Roger Morrice and the Puritan Whigs', pp. 225–51.
68 J. T. Cliffe, *The Puritan Gentry Besieged, 1650–1700* (London: Routledge, 1993).
69 Goldie, 'Roger Morrice and the Puritan Whigs', I, chapter 4.
70 See Roger Thomas, 'Comprehension and Indulgence', in Nuttall and Chadwick (eds), *From Uniformity to Unity*, chapter 4.
71 Winship, 'Defining Puritanism in Restoration England', pp. 709–10.
72 Bolan et al., *The English Presbyterians*, pp. 98–101.
73 Gary De Krey, 'Dissenting Cases for Conscience, 1667–1672', *Historical Journal*, 38 (1995), pp. 53–83.
74 'Laws Agreed Upon in England, &c, 1682', in D. Dreisbach and M. D. Hall (eds), *The Sacred Rights of Conscience: Selected Readings on Religious Liberty and Church-State Relations in the American Founding* (Indianapolis, IN: Liberty Fund, 2009), p. 118.
75 See M. Goldie, 'Toleration and the Godly Prince in Restoration England', in J. Morrow and J. Scott (eds), *Liberty, Authority, Formality: Political Ideas and Culture, 1600–1900* (Exeter: Imprint Academic, 2008), chapter 3.
76 Thomas Long, *The Letter for Toleration Decipher'd and the Absurdity and Impiety of an Absolute Toleration Demonstrated by the Judgment of the Presbyterians, Independents, and by Mr Calvin, Mr Baxter, and the Parliament of 1662* (1689).
77 Richard Baxter, *Reasons for Christian Unity and Concord* (1679), in *The Practical Works of Richard Baxter*, IV, pp. 727–28.

78 Tim Harris, Paul Seaward and Mark Goldie (eds), *The Politics of Religion in Restoration England* (Oxford: Wiley-Blackwell, 1990).
79 Goldie, 'Roger Morrice and the Puritan Whigs', p. 21.
80 John Spurr, 'The Church of England, Comprehension and the 1689 Toleration Act', *English Historical Review*, 104 (1989), pp. 927–46.
81 Watts, *The Dissenters, Volume 1*, p. 260.
82 Geoffrey Holmes, *The Making of a Great Power: Late Stuart and Early Georgian England, 1660–1832* (London: Longman, 1993), pp. 353, 459–61.
83 Watts, *The Dissenters, Volume 1*, pp. 265–66, 482–83.
84 Goldie, 'Roger Morrice and the Puritan Whigs', p. 238.
85 Edmund Calamy, *A Defence of Moderate Nonconformity*, 3 parts (1703–5), II, pp. 24–30, 90.
86 M. Goldie, 'The Dissenters and Toleration: The Impact of Locke', unpublished paper delivered at the Yale Conference on Civil and Religious Liberty, 2008.
87 [Anon], *1645 against 1710* (1710).
88 Edmund Calamy, *An Abridgement of Mr Baxter's History*, 2 vols (1713), I, pp. 670–72.
89 See Samuel Chandler, *The History of Persecution in Four Parts* (1736), p. 381. The Fourth Part is devoted to persecution conducted by Protestants.
90 Micaiah Towgood, *The Dissenters Apology* (1739), p. 30. See also [John Taylor], *A Narrative of Mr Joseph Rawson's Case* (1737).
91 See A. C. Thompson, 'Popery, Politics and Private Judgement in Early Hanoverian Britain', *Historical Journal*, 45 (2002), pp. 333–56. George Benson's account of the Servetus case, first published in the *Old Whig* in 1738, was later republished in Benson, *A Collection of Tracts* (3rd edn, 1748), pp. 163–210.
92 Towgood, *The Dissenters Apology*, pp. 14–15.
93 Watts, *The Dissenters, Volume 1*, pp. 382–93.
94 Isabel Rivers, *Reason, Grace and Sentiment: A Study of the Language of Religion and Ethics in England, 1660–1780* (Cambridge: Cambridge University Press, 1991), chapter 4.
95 These themes are explored in Mark Noll, *The Rise of Evangelicalism* (Leicester: Inter-Varsity Press, 2003).

4 Nonconformity and the State, ca 1750–2012

Keith Robbins

It would be foolish to suppose that a summary treatment of Nonconformity and the state, over some two and a half centuries, can do justice to the complexity of all the strands and elements involved.[1] Neither the Nonconformity nor the state of 1750 was that of 1850, 1950 or the present. 'Dissenter' is used in what follows interchangeably with Nonconformist and indeed was initially the more frequent usage. Both words carry the same implication of opposition to a prevailing *status quo* and a desire, more or less strongly held, to bring about 'change'. The issues under consideration may seem similar, from century to century, but the context shifts substantially.

Nonconformity indicates a refusal to accept a prevailing set of 'norms' as defined by government and expressed in law, that is to say the constitution (written or unwritten) of the state. The form of that Nonconformity may be 'weak' or 'strong'. In turn, what 'Conformity' requires may vary widely in scope and consequence. Refusal may bring social exclusion, legal penalty, or both. The gap between Conformity and Nonconformity, however, may sometimes be clear-cut, but at others hard to identify. The two constantly co-exist, shaping and refining each other. The 'boundaries' as experienced in one century may disappear in the next, only to reappear subsequently. Dissenters may be perceived, and perceive themselves, as 'a people apart'. As quintessential 'outsiders', they may be 'everywhere spoken against' and, in certain circumstances be perceived as a threat to the well-being of the state by those who control it.[2]

These, of course, are broad initial generalizations. What might be called the intrinsic dissidence of Dissent itself makes precision difficult in writing about its relationship with the state. Nonconformity, in a sense, was only ever 'one' in the fact of its Nonconformity. Theological and ecclesial differences between and among Baptists, Congregationalists, residual Presbyterians, Calvinistic Methodists, Quakers and others could be acute and preclude a common stance. While Dissenters might possess a certain family likeness, they knew they were different from each other. Quakers patrolled their ranks by excluding any who 'married out'. On the other hand, those Nonconformists who 'married across' within Nonconformity, often incorporated themselves into their new denominations without difficulty. The Nonconformity of Unitarians raised difficult boundary questions. An emerging but internally fractious 'Methodism' also began its awkward relationship with 'historic Dissent'. Wesleyans, in particular, supposed they might still have a 'special relationship' with the Church of England.[3] There were, of course, other differences on the ground. Dissenters were more numerous in some cities, towns and countries than in others. Wales was not England. Pastors and people did not invariably speak with one voice.

These and other differences need no further elaboration and are discussed elsewhere in this volume. They caution against any notion that Nonconformity and the state invariably grappled with each other in solid formations. They point too to an inherent and inescapable tension in the nature of much Nonconformity, looked at in structural and organizational terms. There was often a divide between 'the local' and 'the national', between the 'sovereignty' of a local congregation and the collaboration of an 'association' or 'union'. Both Baptists and Congregationalists in the early nineteenth century edged hesitantly towards national 'Unions'. Dissent grew 'spontaneously'. Its congregations were not 'planted' by a controlling 'authority', though a nervous state insisted on ministerial licences. Its ministers owed no obedience to a superior. It flourished or faded in its own internal freedom and perhaps contradictions. It might be, however, that if Dissent was to deal with the state in order to defend 'freedom of conscience', it needed 'representative bodies' or 'spokesmen' to act on its behalf. It was no easy task, however, to constitute such bodies or identify such individuals without giving them unwelcome authority, indeed power. The corollary was that the state could not know with certainty which Dissenters were 'representative voices'. Without them, however, Dissent might seem a messy inchoate fractious mass, huddled together in voluntary obscurity, unable to deal with the agencies of the state.[4]

'The religious opinions of dissenters are so various, that there is perhaps no point in which they are agreed, except in asserting the rights of conscience against all human control and authority.' So declared Robert Hall, Aberdeen graduate and Cambridge Baptist minister, a vigorous writer of political tracts at the time of the French Revolution.[5] Dissent was not then, and did not subsequently become, a body of opinion with settled and detailed views on the state. There is no single document, declaration, statement or confession which sets out, beyond doubt, 'what Dissenters believed' about the state. To look for such a document would be to miss the point. If Dissenters really did only agree among themselves in 'asserting the rights of conscience' against all human control and authority, conscience could and did yield different conclusions. It produced plurality not uniformity. The central requirement of Dissent, in dealing with the state, was that it should recognize 'the rights of conscience' as paramount. What they might precisely be was not easy to define.

That brings us to a consideration of the state. In the eighteenth-century United Kingdom, in theory and in practice the state 'contained' the church just as the church 'contained' the state. In dissenting from the state's 'national church', and rejecting its religious authority, Dissent could not avoid some kind of dissent from the state. It might even be directly seeking to replace one form of state with another. What religious Dissent wanted could potentially be limitless. James VI and I had famously declared 'No bishop, no king'. Two centuries later, Dissenters had no bishops, and displayed no sign of yearning for them. The skeleton in the Dissenting cupboard was the head of Charles I. It was an awkward inheritance requiring careful political handling. Son of a Baptist pastor, Robert Hall had been born in 1760. In his view, long before 'the final catastrophe which issued in the king's death' parliament had been oppressed by Cromwell's arms. The execution of Charles had been 'the deed of a faction', condemned 'by the great body of puritans as a criminal severity'.[6] Oliver Cromwell was perhaps still to be treasured in collective Dissenting memory as 'our chief of men', but he neither could nor should be 'our once and future Protector'. He had too many warts. Now, Hanoverian kings were on the throne. By their actions in 1715 and 1745 Dissenters had established their loyalty, Hall claimed, 'beyond suspicion'. Hostile opinion was not so sure.

Dissenters might be loyal to the Hanoverian State, but they were not content with it. Looking back on the Restoration, and on 1662, and even on the 'Glorious Revolution', it had not given them full civil rights in England. Hall himself, to give a small example, could only obtain his university degree in Scotland. Other restrictions and subordinations applied. Yet it would be wrong to speak of persecution. *De iure*, and even more *de facto*, under the 1689 'Toleration Act', Dissent had had a 'tolerated' existence for over a century. It was allowed its own places of worship, teachers and preachers. Toleration, however, might be withdrawn. Clouds could soon gather and the halcyon days be over, as the prominent Dissenter Philip Doddridge put it (his mother was from Bohemia and knew about such things). The 1673 Test Act excluded Dissenters from civil and military office. Office holders had to swear allegiance to the monarch, affirm his supremacy as head of the Church of England, and receive communion in it. However, Anglo-Welsh religious Dissent probably had more religious freedom than obtained in most contemporary European countries with state churches, Protestant or Catholic. Legislation was one thing, its regular enforcement perhaps another. It is by now well-known that such Dissenters as were so inclined could play a part in civic or even, to small degree, national political life by means of 'occasional conformity'.[7] This, however, for them, was still the sophistry, subterfuge or ecclesiastical hypocrisy required of 'second class' subjects of the Crown. It was not parity. That a state should grant such toleration was welcome, but toleration nevertheless still presupposed that the state itself, in its organs and institutions, constituted the orthodoxy of national life. It still aspired to some kind of uniformity even if, in practice, it could not be achieved. Annual Indemnity Acts which granted exemptions from the penalties of the Test and Corporation Acts were, however, only an 'indulgence' by the state, no more. Such indulgence, to some irate bishops, looked like flabbiness. Whigs and Tories clashed on the subject of 'rights'. Whig luminaries did not sit in obscure Dissenting chapels, but they did like talking about rights.

The nineteenth century saw Dissent pressing to move from this 'toleration', and its accompanying accumulated but imprecise 'accommodations', to one in which the state ceased privileging, in legal and financial terms, one church over another. Dissent, in a sense, wished to abolish itself. It might still *differ* from the church in theological principle or ecclesiastical organization but its inferiority should disappear. Indeed, the *ancien régime* state should itself disappear. Might its replacement be in some sense 'democratic', and by what means and over what span of time? Looking at the position in the 1790s, this would be no mere tinkering at the edges. Religious liberty and civil liberty would have to hang together. A wholesale reconstruction of the state would be needed. Here was a quandary for Dissenters. If they were to achieve such fundamental change, what they wanted for themselves had to be part of a wider political agenda. Political Tracts were published by Hall in the early 1790s addressing such topics as the Freedom of the Press, the Right of Public Discussion, the Reform of Parliament, and Theories of the Rights of Man. There were ambitious schemes which had come from the fertile brain of Richard Price, citizen of the new world. These, however, were the years of the French Revolution. Dissent might again be portrayed as 'dangerous' and 'disloyal'. Opponents suspected that these new Sunday Schools bred Jacobinism. There was a war on against France. Were Dissenters 'Friends of Peace?' In short, their path at this time was contentious and internally divided.

What was the state confronted by 'Anglo-Welsh' Dissent (if we can use such a term, at least for this immediate purpose)? Since 1707, what was now the United Kingdom of Great Britain had ceased to be uni-confessional. In England/Wales it was an 'Anglican' confessional state and in Scotland it was a 'Presbyterian' state (though in a different manner). The monarch was the Supreme Governor of the Church of England, but had no such position in Scotland. The split personality of the monarch and the state had important consequences for Anglo-Welsh Dissent. It meant that Conformity could mean different things. The English state, in the terms of the Act of Union, had abandoned the notion, more than once entertained in the past, that Scotland should be 'Anglican/Episcopalian'. Now a diversity of church establishment existed within the one state. Scottish Presbyterianism was certainly different from religious Dissent in England and Wales but its universities, as Hall and other prominent Dissenters had found, were hospitable to it. Calvinistic Methodism in Wales might eventually blossom as 'properly' Presbyterian. Even so, the Church of Scotland was 'established' and firmly attached to its particular form of partnership with the state. It was, however, always prey to modest internal Dissent, though there had been nothing on the scale of the 'Great Disruption' that occurred in 1843. The emergence at that point in Scotland of a separated Free Church, not considered in detail here, changed the ecclesiastical landscape, and not only in Scotland. It meant that in Great Britain the numerical balance in mid-century between Dissent and Established Church shifted.

The British–Irish Union of 1800 brought another dimension to the question of Dissent. The United Kingdom now contained a constituent part which had a Roman Catholic majority. The English–Welsh–Irish part of the state was formally Anglican (the Church of England and the Church of Ireland, in theory at least, were one). In a more general sense, the entire state was 'Protestant'. Yet the numerical strength of Irish Roman Catholicism could not be disguised. It looked likely to be able to withstand periodic bouts of 'Protestant' proselytism. It therefore seemed likely that the security and viability of the new United Kingdom made some accommodation with Irish Roman Catholicism imperative, though there was their awkward monarch for British politicians to deal with, not to mention 'Protestant' opinion in Britain. Here there was a complication. In England, Scotland and Wales, Protestant Dissenters and Roman Catholic Dissenters stood together as minorities 'outside' the state. There were senses in which their cause was common, yet the scope for joint action scarcely existed. Protestant Dissent suspected, looking to Europe, that it was only in their minority position that Roman Catholics favoured 'freedom'. Nevertheless, both sets of Dissenters received their 'emancipation' at more or less the same juncture. It had been a long road. Attempts to repeal the Test and Corporation Acts had failed in the Lords in the 1780s (and not again considered between 1794 and 1804). The urge to contain Dissent had not disappeared, not least among the episcopate. Papal footwork in reining in 'political priests', and the British need for Irish troops (and 'peace' in Ireland), combined with other factors to cause Prime Minister Peel in 1829 to bring in 'Catholic Emancipation' and thus 'complete' the Repeal of the Test and Corporation Acts of the previous year. He upset his Oxford tutor, now the bishop of Oxford, in the process. Electoral punishment followed. A pragmatic prime minister became a traitor.

Taken together, these measures are sometimes taken to be the end of 'the Protestant Constitution', or perhaps one should say 'the Anglican Constitution'. Their implications were profound, though neither immediate nor totally transforming. Not least in the existence and function of monarchy, some elements of an 'Anglican Constitution' still exist in the twenty-first century. Thus we cannot speak of 1828–29 as the complete liberation of Dissent from the restrictions of the state. Rather, through the remaining 'long nineteenth century' we see a religious pluralism evolving in erratic stages but not according to a timetable. 'Repeal', for some historians, constitutes a more profound change in the country's self-understanding than the succeeding 'great' Reform Act of 1832. Even if that is the case, it was the successive phases of parliamentary reform that thereafter determined what happened. Dissent, church and state have all been involved.

Nonconformity has been the first actor. The repeal of the Test and Corporation Acts did not in itself bring 'equality'. There were still areas where structures and practices discriminated against it (or so it believed). For example, the state, when it began to give some financial support to education, did so initially through schools maintained by societies under the aegis, respectively, of 'church' and 'chapel'. Since the former had more than the latter, it got more money. Dissenters resented that its advantage was thereby reinforced. Education remained a battle ground for many decades to come.[8] Dissent feared that increasing state intervention would buttress the Anglican position. The 1870 Education Act, however, made provision for a religious instruction which was to be 'non-denominational'. It seemed to be a solution. But the church said that education in its schools was not simply a matter of 'religious instruction'. Nonconformists still came up with examples, particularly rural examples, where their children had no option but to attend church schools and thus be corrupted. The issue rumbled on, erupting again when the state's involvement in education increased further. The 1902 Education Act was held by Dissent to privilege the church and was met by far-reaching civil disobedience. The 'Passive Resistance' campaign mounted by such figures as the Baptist John Clifford was determined to reverse the legislation. Some Nonconformists paid fines and even accepted imprisonment, so strong was their opposition. The legislation remained and, in fundamentals, was not altered when a Liberal government came into office after 1905.

There was, however, a lingering uncertainty, even in their own ranks, about what Dissenters really wanted. Perhaps, some thought, the school education system (and the new university colleges of England and Wales as they emerged in the late century) should be secular. That did not mean that the system should be 'secularist' but that the church should not prescribe or proscribe. Dissenters would nurture their own young in Sunday Schools in their own particular tenets. The danger was, however, that generations fed on a diet of 'non-denominational' religious teaching in schools might not see much need for any church. They had as much religion as they needed. In practice, Nonconformists did not have the resources to develop a comprehensive school system of their own, even if they had wanted to. A paradoxical situation was perhaps developing. Dissent battled against the state's support for, or acceptance of, church hegemony in education, but if Dissenters succeeded in reducing or even eliminating the church's position, they might be paving the way for a secular education which might be even more unpalatable. The issue manifested itself later in the 1944 Education Act, and at subsequent intervals ever since, regarding both Roman Catholic and Anglican schools. Even into the 1960s, however, the Dissenting voice tended to be critical if not hostile to such schools and echoes of 'Passive Resistance' could still be heard, but by the end of the century this agitation had faded – and Dissent itself had substantially faded.

The 'education debate' was perhaps the most conspicuous issue which required thought about the role of the state. Speaking generally, one might regard the period from 1828 to 1914 as one in which Dissent functioned on two fronts, the one uneasily related to the other. The first involved steady and constant effort to remove continuing irksome restrictions, burdens or exclusions as Dissenters experienced them. There was the question of where they could be buried. Another argument centred on payment of the Church Rate. Why should Dissenters pay in support of a church to which they did not belong? This last question brought a young Quaker into action in his native Rochdale. Many Quakers looked askance at such agitation.

Decades later, this same John Bright became the first Dissenter to become a cabinet minister – in Gladstone's 1868 Liberal government. Other Dissenters moved into political prominence locally and nationally. As the electorate expanded in 1867, and again two decades later, it seemed to be ever more important to court the Nonconformist vote. Leading Dissenting ministers appreciated the status they appeared to have achieved. 'Influence' was supposed to work both ways. Yet John Bright was neither comfortable nor successful as a cabinet minister. He resigned his then office when the government of which he was a part authorized the bombardment of Alexandria in 1882.[9] In foreign affairs, perhaps to their credit, it could be said that Dissenters often found more to criticize than to applaud.[10] The state's *Realpolitik* and the 'Nonconformist Conscience' did not easily co-exist. Over subsequent decades, only one committed Free Churchman was entrusted by a prime minister with the office of Secretary of State for Foreign Affairs – the Methodist Arthur Henderson, a zealot for the League of Nations – in 1929.

The Liberal Party, as it developed after 1868, was the Dissenting vehicle. Yet other sections of that party were wary of Nonconformist influence. Dissenters were 'faddists', they thought, with narrow obsessions. Dissenters did indeed face an ideological difficulty. How were they to move from being 'against' to being 'for'? They had struggled against the state, increasingly successfully, it seemed, and were now indeed becoming part of its public face. As a body, they certainly did not control the state, but they had a share in determining its stance. A place, modest to be sure, could increasingly be found for their representatives on solemn symbolic state occasions. Their emphasis had been on 'freedom', but did they not now want to restrict the freedom of others (even if, of course, for their own good)?[11] 'Temperance' and the 'drink question' was a case in point, but there were other comparable issues and broader economic questions. Dissenters, not least John Bright, passionately supported Free Trade. Perhaps they also wanted a 'nightwatchman' state, without burgeoning bureaucracy, 'centralization' and an ever-widening concept of the state's sphere. For others, however, and perhaps it was a matter of generations, Dissent should extricate itself from an archaic individualism. Since the 'Nonconformist Conscience' is considered elsewhere in this volume nothing further is said about it here. The important point, however, is that Nonconformity reached its political zenith before 1914 in a House of Commons in which Liberal MPs wrestled with 'New Liberalism'. Liberal legislation, with general Dissenting support, certainly extended the role of the state, even if it did not 'lay the foundations of the Welfare State'.

When that Welfare State did arrive, after the Second World War, Nonconformists generally supported it, but some were in two minds. Those who had abandoned a distressed inter-war Liberalism, and had come to support Labour's 'New Jerusalem', thoroughly welcomed the National Health Service, even if they were somewhat reserved about 'the Socialist state'. Others, however, were worried about the likely demise of 'Voluntarism'. Dissenters were by nature believers in the voluntary principle. They had been involved in myriad societies for the relief of poverty and social deprivation. Sometimes elaborated into a 'Social Gospel', Dissenting charity had displayed itself conspicuously in 'good causes'. Maybe more could have been done on a 'voluntary' basis, but was there not at least the possibility of atrophied consciences and a corrosion of individual responsibility if the state extended its long arm everywhere? 'Freedom' might be as much in danger in the United Kingdom as it was elsewhere in post-war Europe. Critics, however, thought this line far-fetched and suspected that what churches were most worried about was their own future. It is sometimes argued that poor people came to church for 'charity'. When the state stepped in to provide for their 'welfare', the churches would lose their 'clients'. Argument about what a Welfare State should be has never completely disappeared but Dissenters, as such, have only had a small voice in its evolution.[12]

This is not the place to embark on a discussion of 'the decline of Nonconformity'. However, in relation to matters discussed thus far, as a coherent religio-political force in its dealings with the state, 'Nonconformity' had run its course, shall we say by 1950. Decade on decade, its earlier exclusions had been nibbled away at; it was no longer everywhere spoken against. The universities of Oxford and Cambridge gave Dissenters degrees. Dissenters scurried to insert their own colleges into such venerable locations. One could surely not ask for more. They were no longer waiting at the door for admittance but sat at the cabinet table or at the High Table of an Oxbridge College. Dissent had largely become part of the 'fabric of national life'. A sort-of Welsh Baptist had been prime minister. He had won the greatest war the United Kingdom had ever fought. He had made sure that the army had its Nonconformist chaplains. It was true, on the other hand, that Nonconformists had been disproportionately numerous among those who had 'conscientiously' objected to fighting in that war. They had obeyed the dictates of conscience not the will of the state. Yet they were few in number.[13] The great majority of Nonconformist men, whether prompted by their conscience or, later, compelled by the state, believed that it was their duty to fight for King and Country. Passive Resistance was not what John Clifford wanted to offer to a German army. During the second such war, a noted Baptist historian, writing in one of those new colleges in Oxford, wrote a well-received book significantly entitled *The Free Church Tradition in the Life of England*: Dissent had become a Tradition.[14] 'Incorporation', as we have seen, had indeed been happening for decades. Free Church leaders, although not sociologists, had experienced in their own lives the erosion of boundaries. 'Success' made it increasingly difficult to stake out the old ground, wallow in the heroism of the past and sustain community cohesion into the future.

Indeed, in the later nineteenth century, 'Nonconformity' as a term, had been slowly phased out, without fanfare. In its place came a new brand – 'The Free Churches' – trying, without entire success, to display some kind of 'federal' unity. The intention was to be positive. Their constituent bodies were now not routinely *against* anything. They neither Dissented nor Conformed: they were now simply 'free' with a proper place in the public space. Had the 'Free Church in a Free State' therefore come to pass? The aspirations advanced in the heady atmosphere of the early 1790s, in the agitation and writing of Edward Miall and the Liberation Society in mid-century, or in the cogent case advanced by Henry Richard, with Wales particularly in mind, might be thought to have been achieved.[15] 'The Union of the Churches with the State is doomed', declared Baptist Wriothesley Noel confidently in 1848 on page 627 of an essay on the subject issued as he left his ministry in the Church of England for that among Baptists.[16] He pointed to the 'grand results' of spiritual liberty in the United States. All the principles on which the existing union rested were unsound. The word of God was against it. Its blighting influence was everywhere. It could not be allowed to injure the nation any longer. The 'Free Church in a Free State' was surely imminent. A century later, however, Nonconformists of this era might consider that the United Kingdom state, taken in the round, had arguably not quite achieved this obvious Elysium. The remainder of this chapter makes some suggestions as to why, if so, this has been the case.

The second actor throughout has been the Church of England itself. 'Establishment', throughout its post-Reformation history (if one can put it like that) had always been a double-edged condition. Intimacy with the political manoeuvres of the state had always brought both advantage and disadvantage. It left obscure, for long periods, what a church might be. Was it sufficient for the parliament of the state to be its parliament? Was it distinctive 'in its own right' or was it the form the religious expression of the English people? Writers from S. T. Coleridge through to Thomas Arnold and far beyond into the twentieth century had pondered what it meant to be a Christian society and how the church 'fitted' such a society. Perhaps the church should adjust itself, become more 'inclusive', and express the Christian sentiment of the people, however vague. Points of theological detail or ecclesiastical practice which got in the way of such a task were annoying. The state needed the broadest kind of church possible. Such a church, for its part, could guide the state. Here, with variation, was the continuing expression of the Burkean view that the church and state were one. If, in reality that was not the case, every effort should be made to 'accommodate' Dissent. It should not be scorned and excluded.

On the other hand, quite a different view could be taken. The extent to which the government of the day had 'rationalized' the top-heavy structure of the Church of Ireland had been one of the triggers of Tractarianism. The Church of England, it was being said, was not 'the ecclesiastical department of State' or at least not just that. But what was it? It is not our purpose here to answer that question. Trying to do so led B. W. Noel to the Baptists, and J. H. Newman to the Roman Catholic Church, to name but two examples. Indeed, it has led to nearly two centuries of debate in the Church of England, with no single conclusion acceptable to all its members. If the Church of England constituted a *via media* between 'Protestantism' and 'Catholicism', as some minds have supposed, so its destiny, or perhaps its fate, was to find, in parallel, some kind of middle ground in its relationship with the state. It could have 'a mind of its own' yet should not detach itself from the wider community of the nation. It did not want to turn history on its head and become itself 'just another set of Dissenters'. What all these matters entail had many ramifications and, still, leave many unresolved aspects. They touched, to no small degree, on money. They involved government. The life and liberty of the church, some said, required that it should have its own 'Assembly', though still 'National' and still ultimately responsible to parliament. The church found, when it did have such a body, that parliament in 1927–28 could throw out its Revised Prayer Book. This particular reversal, as it were, at the hands of the state, led some prominent churchmen, even a senior bishop, to change their minds and themselves advocate disestablishment. However, they were a clear minority and did not succeed. Nevertheless, over subsequent decades, the Church of England sponsored further reports on 'church and state' and edged itself towards further changes in its own government (a Synod) while still, for the most part, continuing to assert the benefits of a 'working partnership' with the state. It scarcely needs to be said that all this is ongoing business, without internal consensus.[17]

The result, however, is that the Church of England in 2012 is not what it was in 1812. Free Churches, certainly since 1945, and arguably earlier, have lost the Disestablishment fervour of earlier generations. Free Churches do not want the state to 'establish' them but what establishment has come to mean in the twenty-first century does not constitute a fundamental obstacle to fraternal (and, latterly, sisterly) relations with the Church of England. Obstacles to 'reunion' between the Church of England and English Free Churches do not lie, to any substantial degree, in the fact of the church's continuing state connection, as that now exists. Even in 1935, the Congregational historian B. L. Manning, in his evidence to the Commission of that year, said he did not know whether he wished to see disestablishment.[18] The differences that are now poured over in ecumenical 'conversation' (and very often remain there) are 'theological' and 'ecclesial'. Recent decades have illustrated that successive archbishops of Canterbury have not refrained from criticizing the state, both in respect of domestic and foreign policies. Indeed, the Free Churches have come to believe that in a certain sense they speak for them too.

The third actor, however, has been the state itself. The above discussion has centred on Free Churches and the Church of England within the United Kingdom state, but that is only part of the picture. The relationship must be seen in the context of the evolution of the United Kingdom as a whole. The state disestablished the Church of Ireland in 1872 and established no other church in its place. It had, thereafter, to negotiate its way through complex relationships with the three major churches. A minority Anglican church in Ireland could not be sustained. Thus the United Kingdom, as a whole ceased to be simply a 'Protestant State' (Anglican and Presbyterian). It had been numbers and political prudence that had prevailed and impelled Gladstone, the prime minister concerned, to jettison views which he had put in print as a younger man.

And it was numbers, too, which disrupted 'Anglo-Welsh Dissent' as the single bloc – though a complicated one – which it has been taken as being in the century after 1750. The prospects for disestablishment were brighter in Wales than in England. Once it could be plausibly maintained, after the 1851 Religious Census, though with much argument, that the Welsh church-going majority was Dissenting, the campaign had a momentum which it lacked in England. However the Church of England in Wales might defend itself, it could not ultimately hold out against that reality, particularly when, at last, pre-1914 Liberal administrations could be persuaded to pass the necessary legislation (and implement it after the First World War). Linguistic and cultural concerns sharpened the campaign. The message that the Welsh were 'a Nonconformist people' was forged. The successful outcome in Wales ended whatever slim chance there might have been that 'Anglo-Welsh-Scottish Dissent' would be strong enough in Britain to make a United Kingdom government feel compelled to 'Disestablish' throughout the country. In Scotland, after some further adjustments, the Church of Scotland and the United Free Church came together again in 1932. That left English Nonconformists on their own (albeit with a good many Welsh and Scots living among them). They had always been a minority, a significant and sometimes vociferous minority, but a minority none the less. The majority of the English people might not be ardently Anglican but neither was it, in bulk, hostile. The Church of England might even be the only thoroughly English institution they had. Manning had also said that as an Englishman he venerated parts of the Church of England and had not wished to trust them to 'self-governing episcopalians'. Therefore nothing very dramatic changed. It was also the case, in Wales itself, after all the heat that had been generated, post-disestablishment 'Nonconformity' did not have a 'golden age'. Quite the contrary. In the decades after 1945 in particular, it was impossible to believe, as had once been claimed, that the very act of Disestablishment would inject fresh vigour. The individual Free Churches hovered over the creation of a single Free Church but failed to land. The 'Old Church' was still arguably the largest individual church, with an all-Wales parochial coverage. It now had its own archbishop and constituted a separate Anglican province. Whether, in the process, it had sufficiently 'Welshified' itself (or needed to) was a matter of opinion.[19]

Therefore, only if the state itself took the initiative in England and disestablished the Church of England would the still theoretical aspiration of the Free Churches there be realized. Even before 1939, however, the example both of the Soviet Union and Nazi Germany, showed them, perhaps, that there was no such thing as a 'Free' state disinterestedly and in 'neutral' fashion dealing with 'Free' Churches. It had been accepted by the churches in the United Kingdom, almost without question, that the state, expressing the country as a whole, would still be in a general sense 'Christian' if Disestablishment did take place. But that might not in fact always be so. Nor, in the nineteenth and for the first half of the twentieth century, could it have been foreseen that the United Kingdom would become 'multi-faith', 'multi-ethnic' and, some said, 'secular'. Such a state would perhaps have no option but to disentangle itself from any kind of Christianity. The issue moved to the fore in the twenty-first century. Issues in sexuality, ranging from 'women bishops' to homosexuality and marriage, indicated a similar division of opinion between the 'liberal state' and all churches. A 'great divorce' was predicted (as it had been in the past). Nonconformity and the state, however, seemed now to have long lost resonance as a self-contained question. The stakes were now much higher. The surviving Free Church voice would only be modest in determining the outcome. It is not for a historian, however, to say what that outcome will be.

Notes

1 K. Robbins, *England, Ireland, Scotland, Wales: The Christian Church 1900–2000* (Oxford: Oxford University Press, 2008). This book considers the Nonconformity discussed in this chapter in a broad ecclesiastical and political context.

2 D. Davie, *Dissentient Voice: Enlightenment and Christian Dissent* (Notre Dame, IN and London: University of Notre Dame Press, 1982); V. Cunningham, *Everywhere Spoken Against: Dissent and the Victorian Novel* (Oxford: Oxford University Press, 1975).

3 J. Gregory, '"In the Church I Will Live and Die": John Wesley, the Church of England and Methodism', in W. Gibson and R. G. Ingram (eds), *Religious Identities in Britain 1660–1832* (Aldershot: Ashgate, 2005), pp. 147–78.

4 The 'Protestant Dissenting Deputies' who had been engaged in day-to-day activities to protect the civil rights of Dissenters were essentially London based. B. L. Manning, *The Protestant Dissenting Deputies*, ed. O. Greenwood (Cambridge: Cambridge University Press, 1952).

5 O. Gregory, *The Works of Robert Hall, A.M.*, 3 vols (London: Henry Bohn, 1835), III, p. 142.

6 Ibid., p. 140.

7 J. E. Bradley, *Religion, Revolution and English Radicalism: Non-Conformity in Eighteenth-Century Politics and Society* (Cambridge: Cambridge University Press, 1990); R. Hole, *Pulpits, Politics and Public Order in England 1760–1832* (Cambridge: Cambridge University Press, 1989).

8 P. T. Marsh, 'For Christ and Secularism: R. W. Dale and the Fight for Civic Education in Birmingham', in C. Binfield (ed.), *The Cross and the City: Supplement to the Journal of the United Reformed Church History Society*, 6 (1999), pp. 77–90.

9 K. Robbins, *John Bright* (London: Routledge and Kegan Paul, 1979).

10 M. Hughes, 'Nonconformity and Foreign Policy', in K. Robbins and J. Fisher (eds), *Religion and Diplomacy: Religion and British Foreign Policy, 1815 to 1941* (Dordrecht: Republic of Letters Press, 2010), pp. 33–60.

11 P. Mandler (ed.), *Liberty and Authority in Victorian Britain* (Oxford: Oxford University Press, 2006).

12 G. Finlayson, *Citizen, State and Social Welfare in Britain 1830–1990* (Oxford: Oxford University Press, 1994).

13 K. Robbins, 'The British Experience of Conscientious Objection', in H. Cecil and P. H. Liddle (eds), *The British Experience of Armageddon* (London: Leo Cooper, 1996), pp. 691–708; idem, 'Protestant Nonconformists and the Peace Question', in

A. P. F. Sell and A. R. Cross (eds), *Protestant Nonconformity in the Twentieth Century* (Carlisle: Paternoster, 2003), pp. 216–39.

14 In 1941, Payne was the senior tutor at the (Baptist) Regent's Park College, Oxford.

15 K. Robbins, 'Church Establishment, Disestablishment and Democracy in the United Kingdom of Great Britain and Ireland, 1870–1920', in idem (ed.), *The Dynamics of Religious Reform in Northern Europe 1780–1920: Political and Legal Perspectives* (Leuven: Leuven University Press, 2010), pp. 69–92; A. Miall, *Life of Edward Miall* (London: Macmillan, 1884); W. H. Mackintosh, *Disestablishment and Liberation* (London: Epworth Press, 1972); H. Richard and J. C. Williams, *Disestablishment* (London: Swan Sonnenschein, 1885).

16 B. W. Noel, *Essay on the Union of Church and State* (London: James Nisbet, 1848).

17 K. Robbins, 'Political Anglicanism: Church and State in the Twentieth Century', in N. Yates, (ed.), *Anglicanism: Essays in Theory, Belief and Practice* (Lampeter: University of Wales, Lampeter, 2008), pp. 89–104.

18 *Commission on Church & State* (1935), London: Church Assembly, II, p. 89.

19 K. Robbins, 'Establishing Disestablishment: Some Reflections on Wales and Scotland', in S. J. Brown and G. Newlands (eds), *Scottish Christianity in the Modern World* (Edinburgh: T&T Clark, 2008), pp. 231–58.

5 Nonconformists and Polity

David M. Thompson

What do readers think of when they hear the word 'polity'? Many might immediately say 'episcopalian', 'presbyterian', 'congregational', or similar adjectives. So one might expect a consideration of the polities of the different Nonconformist churches to examine each in turn, with reflections on the justification for each 'ideal type'. This is certainly tidy, but it is also essentially backward-looking, because the final form of each polity is taken as a guide to its origins. Such a strategy is misleading, both in content and priorities. This chapter is therefore a historical analysis, intended to show how and why different groups came to different eventual resting points in their views.

I. Elizabethan and Jacobean Nonconformity

The first point is simple but obvious; the individuals and groups that wished to pursue reformation further than the Elizabethan Church of England had a common starting point in their rejection of diocesan Episcopacy in its then existing form. The twists and turns of the Protestant Reformation were still within the living memory of the chief protagonists in this debate; furthermore a number of bishops were still involved in the Court with political responsibilities; and the one thing not reformed in the English Reformation was the diocesan structure of the church. Hence many radical reformers regarded the Elizabethan Church as crypto-papist. One of the commonest terms of abuse used to describe both bishops and clergy in the Church of England was 'dumb dogs', a reference to Isa. 56.10, which was translated in the Geneva Bible (1560) as: 'Their watchmen are all blinde: they have no knowledge: thei are all dome dogs: thei cannot barke: thei lie & slepe and delite in sleping.' There was also a note: 'He [the prophet] sheweth that his affliction shall come through the fault of the governours, Prophetes & pastors, whose ignorance, negligence, avarice & obstinacie provoked God's wrath against them.'[1]

The concern about Episcopal government was not only anti-papist, though the underlying significance of that aspect should never be underestimated. It reflected a concern about Christian living and the lack of what was regarded as essential church discipline within the congregation. The Church of England, like the Catholic Church before it, was organized on a territorial basis. Everyone who lived in the parish was a member of the church. But many did not live up to the standards expected of Christians by the more radical reformers. The problem was that the only system of church discipline was that enforced by the church courts. This was a time-consuming process, with no guaranteed result. More than anything else, what the radical Reformers wanted in asserting the role of the local congregation was an effective system of church discipline.

A third issue concerned the relationship of local congregations to one another. This lay behind the arguments over synods – or initially the 'classis' of ministers, later better known by the term 'presbytery' – and in particular whether such synods had ecclesiastical or 'spiritual' power over congregations. 'Classis' remained the standard term from Thomas Cartwright's initial attempt to introduce them in the Elizabethan Church until the latter years of the Commonwealth in the 1650s. Both these attempts ultimately failed. The underlying mistake in many previous analyses of this subject has been the effort to classify the various views advanced by individuals, in terms of what the different systems came to be, rather than in understanding the words used by different individuals against the setting of the contexts in which they found themselves.

Thomas Cartwright is therefore usually called a Presbyterian. Certainly he believed that elders should be appointed for each local congregation, selected from the leading men in the community, who would assist the minister in the enforcement of discipline.[2] This was modelled on the pattern introduced by John Calvin in Geneva from the 1530s, which had the advantage of working in a small city state where the local laity were also civil magistrates. Such a system respected the existing social hierarchy. He also worked to introduce 'classes' in the 1580s. Cartwright had the advantage of royal patronage to publish a confutation of the 'Rhemists Translation' of the Bible, organized by the Jesuits. Because of this Cartwright was unwilling to do anything which might be interpreted as disloyal to the queen, even though when the book was ready Archbishop Whitgift forbade its publication in 1586. (It was eventually published in 1618.) Cartwright also kept quiet after Whitgift's ban, to the disappointment of his followers. However, the idea of elders as such is not unique to Cartwright, since many later Separatists also appointed elders. Where Cartwright did differ from other more radical voices was that he did not believe that the Church of England as such was a 'false church'.

Cartwright's disagreement with Robert Harrison and Henry Greenwood, who were more radical in their criticism, was not made public by him in his life time. (He died in 1603.) But Robert Browne, also a Cambridge man, who became a minister in Norwich, published a book allegedly by Cartwright criticizing Browne as well as answering it. Whereas Cartwright defended the credentials of the Church of England as a true Church of Christ, Browne did not. His solution involved separating from the Church of England altogether (hence they were called Separatists) and putting the responsibility for discipline into the hands of the church meeting, that is all the members of the local church under the guidance of their pastor. Perhaps the most famous phrase associated with Browne is in his book of 1582 (published in Holland), *A Treatise of reformation without tarying for anie*. He denied the authority of civil government (in which he included the bishops) over the church, and claimed that preachers would not guide and reform the church aright because the magistrates forbade them to do so. The excuse they offered was that 'they doo but tarie for the Magistrates authorities, and then they will guide and reforme as they ought'; but this was to put the magistrate in the place of Christ.[3]

Eventually Cartwright was forced by Whitgift to stop teaching (though he continued to write); Browne submitted and was received back into the Church of England. However, Browne's friends Robert Harrison and Henry Barrow developed many of his ideas. Barrow's book *A Brief Discoverie of the False Church* (1590) led to his being charged with treason before the Court of High Commission. There is some suggestion that he hoped that the intervention of Lord Burghley might mitigate the wrath of Archbishop Whitgift, but he was mistaken. Barrow and his colleague John Greenwood were executed in 1593. Browne died in 1633, having lived long enough to be presented for Nonconformity again during his tenure of various Church of England livings in Charles I's reign.

A further stage in this development is represented by Henry Jacob (1563–1624), who fled to Holland after the failure of the Hampton Court Conference in 1604.[4] Before that Conference he had published a book, which criticized the views of Francis Johnson's church in London, the other minister of which was Greenwood. However, his views seemed to have changed later, possibly because he met Johnson in prison. His movements in the years after the Conference are unclear, but by 1610 he was in the Netherlands. Here he published a book on *The True Beginning and Institution of Christ's True Visible or Ministeriall Church* (1610). His definition of such a church begins to look like a characteristic Independent (or Congregational) one:

> [A] nomber of faithfull people joyned by their willing consent in a spirituall outward society or body politike, ordinarily comming together into one place, instituted by Christ in his New Testament & having the power to exercise Ecclesiasticall government and all Gods other spirituall ordinances (the meanes of salvation) in & for it selfe immediately from Christ.

The phrase 'willing consent' may be taken as a precursor of the later practice of the church covenant. The meaning of the phrase 'spirituall ordinances' was spelt out later, not only as the power to dispense the Word and Sacraments, but also to appoint and depose ministers, and 'to receave and cast forth the soules of men out of the Kingdom of heaven'. Yet Jacob envisaged the Pastor being assisted in the latter task by 'the grave assistant Elders', such that this government was not 'simply & plainly Democraticall, but firstly Aristocraticall, and partly Monarchicall'.[5] Jacob also envisaged some kind of place for synods. They had not power to impose their decisions on local congregations, 'yet it is true (beside the Magistrates honourable assistance) verie oft there is great, and singular, yea sometimes in a sorte necessarie helpe to bee had by Synodes. Which are meetings of choyse men out of many Churches . . . Whose counsailles, advises, and determinations are most expedient and wholesome always.'[6] At best therefore Jacob has to be regarded as a 'semi-Separatist'. The division of scholars over where to place him is a perfect illustration of the problems involved in reading history backwards.[7]

By 1610–11 yet another tradition had appeared on the scene – the General Baptists, founded by John Smyth and Thomas Helwys. The extent to which this group had been influenced by earlier Anabaptists in sixteenth-century England has been discussed by various scholars, but seems impossible to resolve with any certainty. In origin the group probably derived more from the Separatist tradition, but their time in Amsterdam brought them into contact with the Mennonites there. When Smyth baptized himself in 1608 or 1609, he deliberately chose not to ask a Mennonite to perform the baptism for him. Of greater significance is Smyth's adoption of an Arminian theology, rather than a Calvinist, which justified an individual's right to choose to be baptized. This made the confession of faith at baptism the equivalent of participation in the church covenant in the Separatist tradition. It could be argued that the rejection of infant baptism was a logical consequence of the Separatist tradition, and certainly the General Baptists saw it in this way; but Separatists, on the other hand, were keen to emphasize the importance of infant baptism, because this preserved the covenant of grace. John Smyth's *Short Confession of Faith* (ca 1608) affirmed that 'the church of Christ is a company of the faithful; baptized after confession of sin and of faith, endowed with the power of Christ'; and also that 'the church of Christ has power delegated to themselves of announcing the word, administering the sacraments, appointing ministers, disclaiming them, and also excommunicating; but the last appeal is to the brethren or body of the church'.[8] Thomas Helwys in his Confession of Faith of 1611 amplified the second point when he stated that a congregation is complete even without officers, so that its members 'may and ought, when they are come together, to pray, prophesy, break bread and administer in all the holy ordinances although as yet they have no officers'.[9] Barrie White appropriately observes that this provision may have been influenced by the experience of persecution and the imprisonment of their ministers, but it nevertheless represents a step further than Separatists were prepared to take. However, in normal circumstances churches did elect officers, including elders and deacons, as well as ministers. Between the 1610s and the 1640s there are only small clues to precisely what was happening, but it is clear that the English Baptists differed from the Dutch Mennonites in two significant ways by being prepared to take oaths, and by permitting members of the church to be magistrates. At this stage therefore it is more helpful to think in terms of a spectrum of belief and practice from Presbyterians *via* Separatists of various hues to the General Baptists rather than clearly distinct positions.

II. The Crucible of the Civil War and Commonwealth

Thus far the discussion has centred on different religious parties, with only occasional political implications. The 1640s inexorably tied politics and religion together. At the Hampton Court Conference James I had memorably remarked, probably in exasperation at the more radical Puritan ideas, 'No bishop, no king'. But the idea of the 'divine right of kings', to which James himself made a contribution, had not been fully developed before; no more had *jure divino* Episcopacy. By the late 1630s both ideas had advanced considerably and both were threatened by the Long Parliament, which assembled in 1640. The king's power to rule by prerogative was under attack from the beginning, and it was recognized from early on that some kind of reform of the Church of England was desirable: the Grand Remonstrance of 1641 called for 'a general synod of the most grave, pious, learned, and judicious divines of this island'.[10] It was against this background that the Westminster Assembly of Divines was convened by a Parliamentary Ordinance[11] of 12 June 1643, with power to confer on matters 'concerning the liturgy, discipline and government of the Church of England . . . and to deliver their opinions . . . as shall be most agreeable to the Word of God as by both or either of the said Houses of Parliament shall be required'.[12] The Ordinance constantly repeated the subordination of the Assembly to parliament, and the way in which parliament eventually treated the Assembly's work demonstrated that.

Space forbids a detailed account of the Assembly's work, and it will therefore be necessary to note a few of the main conclusions and consequences.[13] The majority of the members of the Westminster Assembly were conservative English Puritans, and there were also two distinct but influential groups – the so-called Dissenting Brethren, who were Independents and were members of the Assembly, and the commissioners from the Church of Scotland who were not members but representatives of a sister church. These two groups were influential as much because of the support they drew from outside the Assembly as within it: in the first case, from the Army, and in the second case, from Scotland, since the Scots had been drawn into what was originally an English conflict. When they agreed, as in the early discussion of the necessity of the Ruling Elder in November-December 1643, along with the London Presbyterian ministers, they were able to demonstrate that the real dividing line in the Assembly lay not so much along lines of polity as between conservatives and those who believed that scripture justified a change from the *status quo*.[14] The Directory for Public Worship was approved by the Assembly in the later part of 1644, and became law by an Ordinance of 3 January 1644/45. The speed of that reflected the need to replace the Book of Common Prayer and the fact that the Directory had only minor ecclesiological implications.[15] What Robert Paul described as the 'Grand Debate' in the Assembly, between Presbyterian and Independent ecclesiologies, was eventually won by the Presbyterians by default, not so much because of a conviction about the Presbyterian form of church government as because of a depressed recognition that this was the only way to secure uniformity between England and Scotland. The Independents did not put forward an alternative proposal, but were increasingly driven to argue for toleration, which was the one thing the majority were determined not to concede.[16] So the Confession was drafted on the basis of a Presbyterian ecclesiology.

However, the battle then shifted to parliament in the spring and summer of 1646. Here the issue was whether the church in general and Presbyteries in particular enjoyed a separate power by divine right, or whether all such power was dependent upon parliament. The likely answer from the parliamentary side was never really in doubt. First, the House of Commons asked the Assembly to specify the sins which would justify exclusion from the Lord's Supper. The Assembly responded by asserting the *jus divinum* of the church's censures. Thereupon the Commons addressed nine specific questions to the Assembly, which they failed to answer beyond approving the proposition 'that Jesus Christ as King and Head of His Church hath Himself appointed a Church government'.[17] When the Commons received the complete text of the *Confession* in December, they called for the proof texts, which were provided in April 1647. Although parliament approved the setting up of a system of Presbyterian church government in 1648, it declined to approve those chapters of the Confession which impugned parliamentary sovereignty.[18] The effect of the Westminster Assembly, set as it was in the context of a civil war, had been to sharpen divisions between Presbyterians, Independents and the majority of moderate Puritans, and goes a long way towards explaining what happened at the Restoration.

The religious melting pot of the Civil War in the 1640s, as the fundamental organs of the Church of England in the episcopate and church courts were dismantled or deprived of their authority, provided conditions for the rapid growth of those religious groups more radical than Independents. Sometimes university-educated ministers found their position and authority challenged by people of humbler social origins who were members of the Army. White describes the career of William Lambe, a soap-boiler who became a travelling General Baptist evangelist, and was arrested by the lord mayor of London in 1645 for preaching in contravention of a City of London ordinance forbidding anyone other than ordained ministers to preach. But after a short prison sentence, Lambe continued as before, eventually becoming a chaplain in Cromwell's army. Another was Henry Denne, formerly a minister of the Church of England in Huntingdonshire, who became a Baptist travelling preacher, despite being arrested by the Parliamentary Committee for Cambridgeshire. After being the only one of four 'Levellers' pardoned in 1649, he became pastor of the Fenstanton Baptist Church (near St Ives, Huntingdonshire), whose records are some of the oldest in the country. The records also indicate the existence of area meetings in Cambridgeshire, perhaps in some sense a precursor of the later Baptist Associations.[19]

These developments also indicate the division emerging between the Puritan authorities in parliament and the army, and those often called 'sectaries', who were regarded as disturbing the social, as well as the religious, order. A prime example of this was the emergence of George Fox's Quaker movement, more properly known as the Society of Friends, at the end of the 1640s. Fox (1624–91) was the son of a weaver from the village now known as Fenny Drayton on the Leicestershire–Warwickshire border, an area that saw some of the major battles of the Civil War. Apprenticed as a shoemaker, he became convinced that what mattered above all was to follow 'the Light within'. Consequently, unlike other radical Christian groups, he did not give the same priority to scripture, even though he saw himself very much as part of the Christian tradition. After Fox moved to accept the hospitality of Thomas and Margaret Fell at Swarthmoor Hall in North Lancashire in 1652, he lost his originally dominant position in the movement.[20] Nevertheless his expeditions both to Europe and the West Indian and American colonies spread the Society outside England quite early on. Like the Baptists and Separatists, the Quakers organized themselves into local meetings, but unlike them the Quakers developed a more organized national manifestation earlier, through the Meeting for Sufferings (the original name for London Yearly Meeting), which was concerned to intervene on behalf of Quakers who were suffering under persecution. Because Quakers refused to pay tithes, or take oaths, or (eventually) take up arms, the occasions for such intervention became more frequent. The Quaker Peace Testimony was originally given to Charles II in January 1661 in order to reassure him that Quakers would not take up arms against the king.[21]

Fox's itinerant evangelism, while owing something to the example of the General Baptists and certainly different from the pattern of the early Separatists, influenced John Wesley in the next century. Although Quakers did not ordain ministers (as Separatists and General Baptists did), their local meetings did choose elders to lead them. Another activity in which they led the way was in counting their members, which they did partly as a consequence of agreeing to look after their own poor. John Wesley also counted his class members.

Quakers began in the turbulent times of the Civil War and Commonwealth, but nearly half of Fox's life was spent in the reigns of Charles II and his brother James II. In 1676, Robert Barclay, a Scottish Friend (and a member of the Scots Privy Council from 1679) published *An Apology for the True Christian Divinity*, arguing against Calvinist understandings of predestination and scriptural authority, and instead for universal salvation and direct revelation. Atonement and communion therefore became inward experiences. The 'day of visitation' received less emphasis by comparison with the need to live a sober life, free from frills and human pomp.[22] It was in the Restoration period that systematic organization of the Quaker movement began, and the same was true in varying degrees of the other groups so far considered. Presbyterians had instituted a 'classis' system in the 1650s, the records of a few of which survive; but it was not as effective as the presbyteries in the Church of Scotland (which themselves still encountered difficulties in gaining the effective support of ministers). After the Act of Uniformity of 1662 the majority of those ministers with strong Presbyterian convictions left the Church of England; but their numbers were never sufficient to establish a Presbyterian structure beyond the local church. Effectively therefore they became ministers of local congregations and their defining characteristic was the greater authority given to elders in the congregation, which meant that they could take decisions without reference to the church membership.

Traditional Separatists, now more often described as Independents (and occasionally Congregationalists), had defined their difference from Presbyterians in the *Savoy Declaration* of 1658, which, while for the most part repeating word for word the text of the *Westminster Confession* of Faith of 1646, omitted Westminster's affirmation of the role of magistrate, and instead had a separate statement on 'the Institution of Churches and the Order appointed in them by Jesus Christ'. This declared the independence of each local congregation from 'any Church more extensive or Catholique' (article VI) and an emphasis on the calling of any minister, teacher or elder in the church 'by the common suffrage of the Church itself, and solemnly set apart by Fasting and Prayer, with Imposition of Hands of the Eldership' (article XI) as the means of appointment of ministers. Thus the essence of the call consisted in the election by the church and the minister's acceptance of it, not the imposition of hands. As with the General Baptist understanding of baptism, therefore, there is a *prima facie* similarity with more Catholic tradition, but such a Catholic interpretation is expressly denied. Although the *Savoy Declaration* allowed a place for synods in which the Messengers of the churches might meet to advise on differences in the peace, union and edification of the churches, such synods were expressly denied any 'Church-Power, properly so called, or Jurisdiction over the Churches' (article XXVI). In this respect therefore *Savoy* was consistent with Henry Jacob's understanding some fifty years earlier.[23]

However, the *Savoy Declaration* was undoubtedly designed for a church which saw itself as a potentially dominant one in the country (even though formally separate from the political power), rather as emerged in Massachusetts or Connecticut. Instead within five years, Independents were reduced to an illegal minority. This undoubtedly weakened their capacity to develop and grow; for the moment their main task was survival. Only after the 'Toleration Act' of 1689 was it possible for a new era to begin.

For the General Baptists the Commonwealth was not primarily a time of sunshine, as it was for the Independents. Hence the effect of the Restoration, though severe, did not mean such a reversal of fortune. But by now they were no longer the only Baptists on the scene. The 1640s had seen the emergence of Calvinistic Baptists, significantly many of them from the family of congregations associated with Henry Jacob's congregation in Southwark. In 1644 seven congregations published a *Confession of Faith* (revised in 1646), which was substantially based on the *Separatist Confession* of 1596. There were, however, three significant differences, which made it a more radical statement. The first concerned the affirmation that baptism should be by immersion upon Confession of Faith. Initially the General Baptists had retained baptism from a basin, rather than insisting on immersion. The second was that the ministry was accorded a lesser place by comparison with the will of the congregation as a whole. This was similar to the General Baptist position outlined above. The third difference was a statement that the duty of obedience to God overrode that of obedience to the magistrate.[24] So whereas the difference between the relative authority of ministers and church officers in relation to the congregation distinguished Presbyterians from Independents in one direction, the same difference distinguished Independents from Baptists in the opposite direction. The later Particular Baptist Confession of 1677, reaffirmed by the representatives of 107 congregations at a general assembly of September 1689, was similarly based largely upon the *Savoy Declaration*, while specifically stating that 'the work of Preaching the Word, is not so peculiarly confined to [the bishops or pastors of the churches]; but that others also gifted, and fitted by the Holy *Spirit* for it, and approved, and called by the *Church*, may and ought to perform it' (article 11).[25] Notwithstanding these emerging differences between Baptists and Independents, a number of congregations, particularly in the provinces, remained essentially 'mixed' congregations containing members with paedobaptist and Baptist views. Philip Doddridge in his *Lectures on Theology* outlined the arguments for and against infant baptism and baptism by immersion, and in each case concluded that to separate from those believing the opposite would be to act without sufficient warrant. Indeed he suggested that 'Christians whose persuasions relating to infant baptism are different, should . . . avoid all severe and unkind censures on account of such difference'.[26]

Confessions of Faith in the seventeenth century were usually justified by proof texts from scripture – at least the references were given. Baptists were scrupulous in justifying the positions they took from scripture, and the same was true of Independents also. This signified an increasing tendency to look directly to scripture for the justification of church order, rather than to classical Reformers like John Calvin. Precisely such a tendency justified the adoption of baptism upon confession of faith by the Particular Baptists instead of the infant baptism practised in the Separatist congregations where they began. In the eighteenth century some ministers originally brought up in Presbyterian backgrounds moved to Independent congregations, or turned their congregations into Independent congregations (often by the adoption of a church covenant), in order to preserve a Calvinist orthodoxy against the encroachments of Arian or Socinian ideas. In the same way, some Independents turned their congregations into Particular Baptist congregations at the end of the eighteenth century in order to preserve their Calvinism against the weakening of the idea that Christ died only for the elect. But the scripture underlying Calvin, rather than the authority of Calvin himself, was the driving force.

III. The Evangelical Revival

The eighteenth century witnessed the appearance of a new kind of religious movement, which bore little resemblance to any of the dissenting churches so far described. It was largely the creation of one man, John Wesley (1703–91), a minister of the Church of England, and Wesleyan Methodism very much reflected the idiosyncrasies of its founder. There were other kinds of 'methodists' in the eighteenth century – those associated with Howell Harris in Wales emerged at very much the same time, save that they were Calvinist in their theology rather than Arminian; but Wesley's Methodism was the most tightly organized, and indeed that organization led to subsequent divisions after Wesley's death. Unlike the older Dissenters Wesley never claimed any New Testament precedent or authority for his organization. His view was that church order should be 'simply what is expedient and necessary for sustaining the preaching of the gospel and fostering its fruits'.[27] This approach has tended to condition many evangelical approaches to church polity ever since.

The fundamental unit was the society ('seiadau' in Welsh), following the pattern of the Holy Club at Oxford, to which the Wesley brothers had belonged while undergraduates at Oxford, the various Anglican religious societies of the early eighteenth century and particularly the Moravian societies. All sincere seekers of salvation were welcome to join such societies – as yet they had no specific denominational implications; proof of conversion was not required, so they were not comparable to the Dissenters' 'gathered churches'. Those who had experienced spiritual assurance (the term generally used in preference to conversion in the eighteenth century) were also gathered into select bands, a grouping copied from the Moravians. A few years later the societies were further divided into classes of about a dozen members who met weekly under the guidance of a leader for spiritual conversation. Membership was indicated by the possession of a class ticket, which was renewed quarterly on the basis of regular attendance and payment of a shilling.[28] Ironically the success of the Methodist societies in gathering new members may have made it more difficult for those with prior denominational loyalties to remain; and certainly from the point when meeting rooms were built and Sunday worship held it became difficult to distinguish Methodists from other churches.

The class leaders met regularly (initially every week) with the stewards, who were responsible for finance and the care of meeting rooms, and the travelling preacher. Ordinary members of the societies had no role in governance at this stage. Local preachers, that is, those who remained in their trade and did not travel, were not clearly defined until the 1751 Conference, and did not meet regularly until the end of the century. Quarterly meetings of preachers, stewards and leaders from the societies became established in the 1750s, probably based on the Quaker pattern of quarterly meetings.

From 1744 Wesley met annually with his travelling preachers in what eventually became the Conference; its Minutes were published from 1765. From these we may gain some idea of what Wesley meant by using the term 'Connexion'. Rack notes that in secular usage it referred to the clients of a tradesman, the followers of a politician, or the religious followers of an individual, such as George Whitefield or the Countess of Huntingdon. Wesley defined it in a paper read to the 1769 Conference. Addressing the travelling preachers he said: 'You are at present one body. You act in concert with each other, and by united counsels . . . As long as I live, there will be no great difficulty: I am under God, a centre of union to all our Travelling as well as Local Preachers . . . But by what means may this connexion be preserved when God removes me from you?'[29] His solution was to establish a committee of three, five or seven preachers, who would act according to articles of agreement. This was eventually embodied in the Deed of Declaration of 1784, which was enrolled in Chancery, and provided for the 'Legal Hundred' Preachers to have ultimate responsibility for governance.[30] In other words the unity of the Wesleyan Connexion was first personal, and then vested in a leading group of Travelling Preachers. Wesley certainly ensured that in his lifetime, as he wrote in 1790, '[w]e are no republicans, and never intend to be'.[31] In that he was strikingly different from Henry Jacob's careful balancing of different kinds of polity nearly two centuries before.

Wesley's organization was tighter at a national level than any other in the Britain of his day. Both civil and Anglican government were much more localized in practice than Wesley's Methodism set out to be, quite apart from that of other Nonconformist churches. This may have been the underlying cause of the problems that beset it after his death. The issue of the representation of the Methodist people as a whole lay at the heart of the implications for polity of most of the ensuing splits. The Methodist New Connexion, which separated in 1797, had a Conference in which laymen were represented in equal numbers to ministers, and the Primitive Methodists, which were formally constituted in 1811, had two laymen to every travelling preacher in their Conference. The Bible Christians, which did not hold a Conference until 1816, welcomed women into ministry, while the Independent Methodists, who separated in 1806, established a system in which local churches were not subordinate to any higher authority at all. The Wesleyan Methodist Association of 1836 declined to specify any ministerial-lay proportion, but left it to the circuits to decide; the Wesleyan Reformers, who either left or were expelled from the original Connexion after 1849 never did specify a constitution before uniting with the Wesleyan Methodist Association to form the United Methodist Free Churches in 1857.[32] Eventually in 1861 the Wesleyans set up mixed preparatory committees of preachers and laymen to meet before Conference, and in 1877 the Conference decided to admit laymen to its membership from 1878. It may be that Wesley's basis in expediency would have led him to adopt and rationalize these developments in due course, as he was prepared to ordain ministers for the United States of America and Scotland in the 1780s.

It was not until well into the nineteenth century that Methodism began to come to terms with the fact that it was effectively a church, symbolized by the adoption of the ordination of itinerant preachers from 1836. But that only serves to emphasize the extreme reluctance with which Wesleyans were persuaded to adopt a sacramental basis for membership and to regard the celebration of the Lord's Supper as normal. The development of Methodism marked the last distinctive type of local organization to emerge in the ranks of Nonconformity. There were, of course, other new religious groups which appeared in the nineteenth and twentieth centuries, but essentially their local organizational structure was a variant on one or other of the models that had already appeared. What did begin to change, particularly in the twentieth century, was the way in which the various features of the different polities were understood theologically.

In so far as Wesleyan Methodism embodied a national organization for the purposes of evangelism, it was a precursor of significant changes in the older Dissenting churches. As noted earlier, what was lacking in those (with the exception of the Quakers) was any effective national manifestation of the church concerned. What might have been a first step happened in the late 1720s and 1730s in London with the formation of two groups, the General Body of the Dissenting Ministers (1727) and a corresponding group of laymen, the Dissenting Deputies (1732). Since the purpose of both bodies was to represent Dissent to the court and government of the day, membership was confined to those congregations within ten miles of the City of London. While from a practical point of view this made sense, not surprisingly it provoked the criticism of Dissenters in the provinces. The three denominations represented were the Presbyterians, the Independents and the Baptists. One of the first tasks of the Dissenting Ministers was to administer a fund of £500 (soon increased to £1,000) per year set up by the government to assist poor ministers' widows. It is easy to see why such a fund could easily provoke jealousy and accusations of favouritism, since it was relatively small to handle the situations involved. The solution was to invite laymen to administer the fund, so as to avoid such accusations, and advantage was taken of a separate decision by the ministers in 1732 to establish a committee of 'gentlemen of weight in the three denominations' to consider what steps might be taken to repeal the Test and Corporation Acts. Behind this lay a feeling, which had existed since 1714, that the Hanoverian dynasty so loyally welcomed by Dissent had done very little to improve their status from that of simply being tolerated rather than recognized as part of civil society.[33] It took nearly another century before the campaign would be successful, but the Dissenting Deputies, formally constituted by annual elections in 1736, continued to exercise a watching brief, in consultation where necessary with country congregations, on issues affecting Dissenters from that time onwards.[34]

IV. The Beginnings of Modern Denominational Organization

More significant for the future development of denominational organization was a quite different development at the end of the century. In 1792 the

Baptist Missionary Society was formed, followed by the London Missionary Society in 1795 and the Church Missionary Society in 1799. Their purpose was to gather finance to support the sending of missionaries to proclaim the gospel overseas. The societies sought personal contributions, like any other eighteenth-century society of subscribers. Thus the various missionary societies were not directly representative bodies of the churches, from which their support was drawn. The London Missionary Society, indeed, was founded on an undenominational principle in 1795 and was supported by a variety of churches, although eventually it became predominantly Congregationalist. The Missionary Society model was followed by a number of other religious societies at the same time, for example, the Religious Tract Society, the British and Foreign Bible Society and the British and Foreign Schools Society. The Societies usually had one or more Secretaries and they employed missionaries, or other workers. For the Church of England, they posed a problem because they cut across diocesan structures of authority.

But they posed even greater challenges for the Nonconformist bodies. They were national in scope, rather than local. Yet they were essentially parachurch organizations rather than parts of any national structure, since the requisite national structures did not exist. Initially the significance of such issues could be contained because the missionary societies worked outside Great Britain; and this remained true to some extent in relation to the distribution of tracts or Bibles, or the establishment of schools. However, very soon consequences were drawn from the field of overseas missionary work for the methods of evangelization at home. A number of the Congregational County Associations formed from the 1790s had as one of their main objects evangelization within their area; and Baptists had their Village Itinerant Societies. The Congregational Home Missionary Society formed in 1819 was in fact primarily confined to London, though that was a rapidly growing city. These societies brought at least a county, if not a national, perspective to their work; their committees decided where work should be undertaken and who should do it. In practice, they were much more like the Wesleyan top-down organization than anything within the tradition of the old Dissent. Neither, like Wesley, did they attempt to justify the form of their organizations on anything other than the principles of expediency; their justification lay in their results. But they were handling funds on a quite new scale, and attracted the kind of interest that money always does.

Those results, initially, were somewhat mixed, both in their endurance and their geographical spread. There is little doubt that the various village itinerancy groups were responsible for the significant expansion in the number of Congregational and Baptist churches in rural southern England during the Napoleonic Wars and immediately afterwards. They were also innovatory, in that, although the ideal was always that a new church should be able to call and support its own pastor, in practice this was rarely immediately possible, and sometimes it never happened. This presented new problems for the ecclesiology of these denominations in that in earlier times the minister had always been seen as the hub of the congregation. Moreover, there was a thin line between the provision of support for the work of evangelization and what was effectively a stipend for the evangelist; and for the first time this system subjected congregations to the oversight, and ultimately control, of a committee outside the local congregation. For the time being the full significance of these innovations lay in the future; but they illustrate the influence that the evangelistic success of Methodism had on the older Dissent.

A rather different consequence of the Missionary Society and other religious societies was the attempt to introduce General Meetings of ministers and congregations, corresponding to the annual 'May meetings' of the evangelical societies. The *Evangelical Magazine* in 1806 advertised a meeting 'at St Paul's Coffee House, on Saturday morning in the Missionary Week, 17th May, 1806, at Ten o'clock' to consider the formation of a General Union among the Congregational or Independent churches in Great Britain. Among the possible advantages of such a Union were financial assistance for new congregations until they could call a settled minister, advice to such congregations on appropriate trust deeds, introducing young men to the academies and a method for 'free communication between the County Associations and that formed with the regular churches in the metropolis'.[35] Although the meeting was duly held, and a series of attempts were made to draft an appropriate constitution, in the end the proposed General Union failed to materialize, essentially because those in London failed to appreciate the importance of appropriate consultation with the County Associations, possibly because there was not one in London itself.

The idea did not die, however, and the periodicals continued to publish letters and proposals from various parts of the country in the 1810s and 1820s lamenting the lack of a national body. When the London Congregational Union was formed in 1826, notwithstanding its explicit disavowal of any intention to form a 'General Union', private conversations began between ministers and leading laymen and by May 1830 a Provisional Committee for a Congregational Union had been formed. As Albert Peel notes, 'once more the promoters were men actively associated with Congregational missionary enterprise at home and abroad'.[36] Further work led to the preparation of a plan for 'a voluntary Union of Independent Churches and Ministers' with every County Association considered as a part of it. There would be an annual subscription, together with a committee of twelve ministers and the same number of laymen, a treasurer and a secretary; and it would be clear that such a Union might advise churches if invited to do so, but would not consider any business that would interfere with church discipline or with the independency of the churches. On this basis the Union was formed in May 1831, and the meeting spent most of its time in preparing and approving a Declaration of Faith and Order.[37]

A similar pattern was followed, with rather more initial success, by the Baptists. On 25 June 1812 a meeting was held under the chairmanship of the Revd John Rippon, minister of the Carter Lane Particular Baptist church in Southwark, which resolved to form a nation-wide union of Particular Baptist churches. On the previous day, the sixty ministers who supported this resolution had attended special meetings in support of William Carey's mission to India under the BMS. Both churches and Associations were invited to send messengers to a meeting in June 1813 – the Baptists did not repeat the Congregationalists' mistake of ignoring the Associations. A constitution was approved in the following year, which included among its objects the opportunity for ministers to get to know one another better and support the missions. There was to be a committee, composed of the London ministers, with a treasurer and three named secretaries; nevertheless committee meetings were open to ministers and messengers from the country who wished to attend. Instead of establishing any new institutions itself the Union commended the support of various existing societies to aid the mission, their academical institutions, societies for itinerant and village preaching, and the Particular Baptist and Widows Funds. In other words, while making a similar disclaimer to the Congregationalists about any wish to exercise authority or power over local congregations, the Union sought to gather together support for existing institutions.[38]

Although the General Union's aims were more modest than those of its Congregational equivalent and to that extent more realistic, it found itself the victim of declining interest on the part of its major constituents in the tumultuous events of the next twenty years. It might be argued that, despite the acknowledged tendency of Baptists to co-operate with one another more during the nineteenth century, in practice it seemed to be little more than another meeting. While it was not split by the Baptist controversies of these years, especially over hyper-Calvinism, open communion and the Serampore mission, there was no real way in which it could be anything more than another forum in which such issues were argued. In 1832 a revised constitution was adopted with four objects: to extend brotherly love and union among Baptist ministers and churches 'who agree in the sentiments usually denominated evangelical'; to promote unity in the cause of Christ and the interests of the Baptist denomination; to collect accurate statistical information about Baptist churches, societies, institutions and colleges; and to circulate an annual report of the proceedings of the Union.[39] This was still a relatively minimalist constitution, not least doctrinally where any reference to particular redemption (as in the 1812 resolutions) was omitted; but it did make possible some drawing together of both Particular Baptists who had adopted a 'Fullerite interpretation of Calvinism'[40] and General Baptists, particularly those of the New Connexion of 1770, who were more evangelical in their approach to church-planting than the older General Baptists had become. However, it is important to note that both the Baptist and the Congregational Unions were unions of individual ministers and churches, and a number of congregations in both denominations remained outside, for a variety of local reasons. Furthermore the careful eschewing of any 'church power' over individual congregations limited their representative function, but also freed them to take initiatives, which a more formal structure might have inhibited. Eventually it was their fund-raising capacity that made them significant; with their establishment we have the beginning of modern denominational structures. In the short term in the 1830s both Unions became involved in co-ordinating co-operative action for the redress of the outstanding Nonconformist grievances albeit with limited success at that time.

Meanwhile the situation among Presbyterians had begun to change. The theology of many Presbyterian ministers (or congregations) in the eighteenth century became Arian, Socinian or Unitarian. In 1813 an Act of Parliament was passed to legalize Unitarianism, and in 1825 the British and Foreign Unitarian Association was formed. In its general structure it was comparable to the Congregational and Baptist Unions of these years, and therefore demonstrated that the Unitarians had abandoned most of the principles that would have made them recognizable to a Presbyterian like Thomas Cartwright or John Knox. Unitarian congregations were effectively autonomous in the way that the Independent tradition had advocated. Those Presbyterian congregations that remained orthodox and retained elements of a Presbyterian form of church government were concentrated in particular parts of the country, mainly Manchester, Liverpool and the Lancashire towns, Northumberland and Tyneside, and London. Here there were classes or presbyteries, which either survived from the late seventeenth century or were re-established in the eighteenth century as toleration for Dissent allowed. Northumberland in particular suffered no shortage of ministers, being able to call upon a variety of Scots particularly after the secessions from the Church of Scotland after 1733 produced a number of ministers looking for a charge.[41] Nevertheless it is misleading to describe eighteenth-century English Presbyterianism as essentially a branch of the Church of Scotland, because the majority of the congregations were English in origin.

The Act of Union in 1707 and the political disturbances in Scotland until 1745 encouraged a number of Scots, particularly middle-class entrepreneurs, to move south into either the ship-building or textile industries of northern England. Many became pillars of Independent congregations, but a similar number reinforced the indigenous Presbyterian congregations in England. This largely explains the geographical concentrations. Although the Church of Scotland had elders in its church courts from the seventeenth century, at first the English classes seem to have been confined to ministers, as the sixteenth- and seventeenth-century predecessors had been. But the Presbytery of Newcastle-upon-Tyne introduced elders as members in 1783, London in 1787 and Northumberland in 1820 (though in the north-west of Northumberland Presbytery they were invited in 1818).[42]

In 1835 the General Assembly of the Church of Scotland received a report from its Committee on Presbyterian Churches in England and also heard Dr Hugh Ralph and Mr Alex Munro, ministers in Liverpool and Manchester respectively, who were a deputation from the presbytery of Lancashire in favour of a closer connection between the two churches. It resolved to recommend that the English presbyteries form a Synod constituted on principles in accord with the constitution and laws of the Church of Scotland, and to consider how the difficulties in the way of closer connection between the two churches might be removed. Presumably the initiative for this came from Lancashire, but in the following year the presbyteries of Lancashire and the north-west of England came together to form the synod of the Presbyterian Church in England. The two members of the deputation in Edinburgh the previous year were appointed Moderator and Clerk respectively. The first action of the synod was 'to adopt the Westminster Standards, as received by the Church of Scotland, in doctrine, discipline, government, and worship'.[43]

Wherever the precise impulse for this action came from, it explains why from 1836 the doctrinal standards of the English Presbyterians were so closely identified with those of the Church of Scotland. It does not mean that before 1836 such churches should necessarily be regarded as 'Scotch Churches', as some historians have suggested, even though a few were the result of outreach by congregations that had been associated with the Church of Scotland since the sixteenth century. Nor does it nullify the point that some English Presbyterian churches were 'saved' for Presbyterianism by the action of Church of Scotland ministers, such as Alexander Macdonald in Stafford in the 1830s.[44] But John Black, the first general secretary of the Presbyterian Church of England, denied in 1887 that 'the essence of the Presbyterian idea was the *organisation of Presbyteries and Synods*'. Rather, 'the *Presbyterial organisation of the individual congregations* stands much closer to the essential principle of Presbyterianism than their *organisation in Presbyteries*'. Then in a move which would have shaken the Westminster Divines, with their determination to prove everything from scripture, he asserted that 'no intelligent Presbyterian pretends to find in the New Testament a regular system of Presbyterial and Synodical organisation'; but they did hold that the New Testament contained the fully developed *'rule of the eldership or presbyterate over the Congregation'*.[45] This principle contrasted with the Congregational emphasis on the supremacy of the church meeting.

The 'difficulties' referred to in the 1835 General Assembly resolution concerned the question of the legal jurisdiction of the Church of Scotland in England. These difficulties were not resolved and were caught up in the wider questions of the legal competence of the General Assembly raised in the 'Ten Years Conflict'.[46] By 1843 the presbyteries of London and Newcastle-upon-Tyne had been admitted (1839), as were Berwick-upon-Tweed (1840) and Northumberland and north-west Northumberland (1842). But at the Disruption of the Church of Scotland the overwhelming majority of the English churches took the Free Church side and the words 'in connection with the Church of Scotland' were henceforth deleted from the title of the synod.[47]

Although the presbyteries of the Presbyterian Church in England had agreed to include elders by 1836, they were considerably outnumbered by ministers, and this position only gradually changed. In other churches, however, the question of lay representation was pressed more strongly. Both the Congregational and Baptist Unions were initiated by committees of ministers, acting in consultation with various gentlemen; and since the national assemblies had no authority, the issue was less important. But it was recognized from an early point that in so far as initiatives required the raising of funds, the co-operation of the laity was essential. The same was broadly true of Quakers and Unitarians.

Methodism had more difficulties. There was no division in British Methodism between 1797 and 1849 that did not involve in some way the rights of the laity. As has been seen above, Wesley envisaged his preachers being under him or in connexion with him, rather as Catholic bishops are in communion with the bishop of Rome. Class leaders and local preachers had no voice directly in the governance of Methodism. After Wesley's death the immediate conflicts that arose essentially concerned the relative rights of the trustees, who were usually, if not invariably, laymen. The breakaway Methodist bodies all made provision for the representation of the laity, whether trustees or local preachers in various proportions, as has been seen. The Wesleyan Conference eventually resolved the issue by creating two sessions of its Conference – one exclusively ministerial, with certain questions reserved to it, and the other a representative session containing an equal number of laymen and ministers. By the time of the final stage of Methodist union from 1910, the issue had shifted to that of the survival of the ministerial session. It did, and still does, though the range of its business was limited in the later twentieth century.

V. The New Involvement of the State

Until the twentieth century it was possible to consider Free Church polity without any reference to the civil law, apart from the crucial acts of parliament from the 'Toleration Act' of 1689 onwards, which removed public restrictions on what Nonconformists could do. (The term 'Free Church', derived from the example of the Free Church of Scotland, increased in popularity in the later nineteenth century as a more positive description than the rather negative – though accurate – terms Nonconformity and Dissent.) When the union between the Free Church of Scotland and the United Free Church of 1900 was challenged in the courts, however, matters changed. In 1904 the House of Lords ruled on appeal that the Free Church of Scotland did not have the power to enter into a union with the United Free Church without changing the trusts on which its property was held, and therefore awarded its property to the continuing minority. This was resolved by an Act of Parliament in 1905. Consequently when the Methodist New Connexion, the Bible Christians and the United Methodist Free Churches came together to form the United Methodist Church in 1907, they secured an act of parliament to ensure their legal right to do so. That precedent was followed in the wider Methodist Union of 1932. However, this had the odd consequence that churches which held that the state had no jurisdiction in matters spiritual were actually depending upon acts of parliament to determine their future polity – even though the presenting issue concerned property law, which clearly was within statutory jurisdiction.

Trust law has, in fact, been the driver for greater statutory involvement in Free Church life through the twentieth century, even though by the twenty-first it did not stop there. Interestingly the legal provision for incorporation of trust bodies was used by both the Baptist and Congregational Unions to incorporate their county unions or associations, so they could hold the property of local churches as a corporate trustee, avoiding the inconvenience caused when churches forgot to replace their local trustees on death. Another development was the use of Company Law through the device of the Company Limited by Guarantee to make those trust bodies companies with limited liability. In these sensible ways churches were able to secure their property and also to limit their liability in relation to it. The Baptist and Congregational Trusts Act of 1951 also widened the scope of investments that churches and related bodies might hold, enabling them to invest in the equity market. However, in other ways these developments blurred the question of the autonomy of local congregations, which had been such a hallmark of the Separatist tradition.

All churches have been subject to the jurisdiction of the Charity Commission since the mid-nineteenth century. From 1993 successive Charities Acts have tightened up the process of central oversight. Accounts have to be submitted according to Statements of Recommended Practice. Finally in the twenty-first century legislation concerned to eliminate discrimination, to ensure child protection and to establish equality across a range of fields has increasingly occupied the time and money of local congregations, regardless of polity, raising new questions of the ability of small congregations to cope with these official requirements.

The ecumenical movement, despite its relative lack of success in forwarding organic union, had significant consequences in the area of polity. Apart from the internal Presbyterian and Methodist unions in Scotland and Britain, the major achievement in organic union has been the formation of the United Reformed Church between the Presbyterian Church of England and the majority of member churches of the Congregational Church in England and Wales (1972), subsequently enlarged by the adherence of the majority of Churches of Christ in Great Britain and Ireland in 1981 and the majority of member churches of the Congregational Union of Scotland in 2000. The United Reformed Church adopted a conciliar structure more akin to that of the Presbyterian Church of England than that of Congregationalism. Not surprisingly the minorities that stayed out on the Congregational side at each stage did so because they were unwilling to sacrifice local autonomy.

However, the proposals for Anglican–Methodist Union in 1972 and those for a Covenant between five of the English churches in 1982 failed to secure sufficient majorities in the Church of England. Each would have involved the acceptance of Episcopacy by the Free Churches involved. In principle the Anglican–Methodist Covenant of 2003 entailed the acceptance by the Methodist Church of Episcopacy, but it has so far failed to come up with a version of it which satisfies the Methodist Conference. In principle this may be possible among the Covenanted Churches of Wales as a result of a meeting in 2012, but it is too early to comment on the possible success of that. In general around the world it seems to be assumed that any reunited church will involve the acceptance of some kind of conciliar episcopate, thereby addressing the problem with which this chapter began.

Nevertheless the growing Christian communities of the later twentieth century have been of the community church and Pentecostal type. Community churches follow an essentially autonomous pattern, with a limited development of ministerial structure. Pentecostal churches, on the other hand, while in many respects fostering local independence, exercise a central control over matters of faith, with the power to expel errant churches from their fellowship. The same is true of Christian Scientists where all local churches are technically branches of the 'mother church' in Boston, Massachusetts. Seventh day Adventists have a similar international structure, which ensures that all local churches follow similar patterns of worship and teaching. Jehovah's Witnesses also have a tightly controlled international organization. It is interesting that the last three have their headquarters in the United States, representing an international element, which was largely lacking in the English Reformation. Certain evangelical churches, such as the Apostolic Networks as well as some African Pentecostal churches established in Britain as a result of migration, use the title bishop for their leaders, but without the overtones of apostolic succession associated with Catholic theology. The various churches described in this chapter have all set up organizations, collectively known as Christian World Communions, in the course of the twentieth century; the one thing which is common to all, even the Anglican Communion, is that at the international level organization is essentially advisory, and does not impinge on the freedom of the national unit.

Notes

1 The term 'dumb dogs' was also used to describe ministers who could only read prayers and read from the *Homilies* rather than praying *ex tempore* and preaching their own sermons.
2 See, e.g., Cartwright's *Short Catechism* (first printed in *The Treatise of Christian Religion*, 1616), in A. Peel and Leland H. Carlson, *Cartwrightiana* (London: George Allen & Unwin, 1951), pp. 159–73, esp. p. 171.
3 Robert Browne, *A Treatise of reformation without tarying for anie*, in A. Peel and Leland H. Carson (eds), *The Writings of Robert Harrison and Robert Browne* (London: George Allen & Unwin, 1953), pp. 154–55.
4 The Hampton Court Conference was an attempt by James I to settle religious disputes in 1604 at which he presided. It was not successful in achieving this aim, and its only result was the Authorized Version of the Bible in 1611.
5 Extracts from Jacob's *True Beginning* in R. Tudur Jones et al. (eds), *Protestant Nonconformist Texts, Volume 1: 1550 to 1700* (Aldershot: Ashgate, 2007), pp. 115–16.
6 H. Jacob, *Reasons Taken out of God's Word and the Best Humane Testimonies Proving A Necessitie of Reforming our Churches in England* (1604), 30, 31: *Transactions of the Congregational Historical Society*, 19/3 (1962), p. 122.
7 See Stephen Brachlow, 'The Elizabethan Roots of Henry Jacob's Churchmanship: Refocusing the Historiographical Lens', *Journal of Ecclesiastical History*, 36/2 (1985), pp. 228–54; amplified in the same author's *The Communion of Saints: Radical Puritan and Separatist Ecclesiology 1570–1625* (Oxford: Oxford University Press, 1988).
8 John Smyth, 'Short Confession of Faith in XX Articles', articles 12 and 13, in Jones et al. (eds), *Protestant Nonconformist Texts, Volume 1*, p. 117.
9 Quoted in B. R. White, *The English Baptists of the 17th Century* (London: Baptist Historical Society, 1983), p. 26.
10 'The Grand Remonstrance', §185 in J. P. Kenyon (ed.), *The Stuart Constitution: Documents and Commentary* (Cambridge: Cambridge University Press, 1966), p. 238.
11 That is, without the approval of the king.
12 Kenyon, *The Stuart Constitution*, p. 262.

13 There is a detailed analysis in Robert S. Paul, *The Assembly of the Lord* (Edinburgh: T&T Clark, 1985). See also Chad van Dixhoorn (ed.), *The Minutes and Papers of the Westminster Assembly, 1643–1652* (Oxford: Oxford University Press, 2012).
14 Paul, *Assembly of the Lord*, pp. 163–74.
15 Ibid., pp. 358–75, 518.
16 Ibid., pp. 437–91.
17 Ibid., pp. 492–514. In its original form, the words 'in the hands of Church Officers distinct from the civil government' appeared at the end.
18 Ibid., p. 518. The offending chapters were XXX and XXXI on 'Church Censures' and 'Synods and Councils'; and passages from XX 'Of Christan Liberty and Liberty of Conscience', XXII 'Of the Civil Magistrate' and XXIV 'Of Marriage and Divorce'.
19 White, *English Baptists of the 17th Century*, pp. 32–54; cf. Edward Bean Underhill (ed.), *Records of the Churches of Christ, gathered at Fenstanton, Warboys, and Hexham* (London: Hanserd Knollys Society, 1854). The Levellers were essentially a political rather than a religious group, although the Fifth Monarchy Men (taking their name from the fifth world empire following the four prophesied in Daniel 2 under the rule of Christ) were an Adventist group, expecting the Second Coming in 1666.
20 Pink Dandelion, *An Introduction to Quakerism* (Cambridge: Cambridge University Press, 2007), pp. 13–37.
21 See Jones et al. (eds), *Protestant Nonconformist Texts, Volume 1*, pp. 232–35.
22 Dandelion, *Introduction to Quakerism*, pp. 54–58.
23 A. G. Matthews (ed.), *The Savoy Declaration of Faith and Order 1658* (London: Independent Press, 1959).
24 White, *The English Baptists of the 17th Century*, pp. 58–64; William L. Lumpkin, *Baptist Confessions of Faith* (rev. edn, Chicago, IL: Judson Press, Chicago, 1969), pp. 144–71.
25 Jones et al. (eds), *Protestant Nonconformist Texts, Volume 1*, pp. 330–31.
26 Philip Doddridge, 'Lectures on Divinity', in *The Works of the Rev. P. Doddridge, D.D.* (Leeds: Edward Baines, 1804), V, pp. 324, 334.
27 Henry D. Rack, *Reasonable Enthusiast: John Wesley and the Rise of Methodism* (London: Epworth Press, 1989), p. 237.
28 Ibid., pp. 238–40; cf. Frank Baker, 'Polity', in Rupert Davies and Gordon Rupp (eds), *A History of the Methodist Church in Great Britain* (London: Epworth Press, 1965), I, pp. 213–28.
29 Extract from the *Minutes of the Methodist Conferences*, I, pp. 87–89 in Rupert Davies, A. Raymond George and Gordon Rupp (eds), *A History of the Methodist Church in Great Britain* (London: Epworth Press, 1988), IV, pp. 162–63.
30 See W. J. Townsend, H. B. Workman and George Eayrs, *A New History of Methodism* (London: Hodder & Stoughton, 1909), II, pp. 551–56.
31 Letters, viii, 196; cited *A History of the Methodist Church in Great Britain*, I, p. 226.
32 Rupert Davies, A. Raymond George and Gordon Rupp (eds), *A History of the Methodist Church in Great Britain* (London: Epworth Press, 1978), II, pp. 288–91, 297–98, 306–10, 317, 319–22, 323–26.
33 Bernard Lord Manning, *The Protestant Dissenting Deputies*, ed. Ormerod Greenwood (Cambridge: Cambridge University Press, 1952), pp. 21–22.
34 Ibid., pp. 23–33.
35 *Evangelical Magazine*, XIV (May 1806), p. 234, quoted in Albert Peel, *These Hundred Years* (London: Congregational Union of England and Wales, 1931), p. 31.
36 Peel, *These Hundred Years*, p. 46.
37 Ibid., pp. 42–74.
38 Ernest A. Payne, *The Baptist Union: A Short History* (London: Carey Kingsgate Press, 1959), pp. 15–27.
39 Ibid., pp. 60–61.

40 The significance of this is explained in more detail by Payne, but in essence it justified the preaching of the gospel to all without sacrificing the principle of predestination.
41 W. Thorp, *Brief Sketch of the Rise of the Northumberland Presbytery* (Privately printed: Chatton, Northumberland, 1925), pp. 13–15.
42 Ibid., pp. 16–17.
43 Leone Levi, *Digest of the Actings and Proceedings of the Synod of the Presbyterian Church in England, 1836–76* (London: Publications Committee of the Synod, 1877), pp. 1–2.
44 Kenneth Macleod Black, *The Scots Churches in England* (Edinburgh: William Blackwood, 1906), pp. 294–95.
45 John Black, *Presbyterianism in England in the Eighteenth and Nineteenth Centuries* (London: Presbyterian Church of England, 1887), pp. 13–14 (italics original). The importance of this passage justifies extended quotation.
46 The 'Ten Years Conflict' is the phrase often used to describe the struggle between Moderates and Evangelicals in the Church of Scotland over its attempt to modify its laws concerning the call of ministers and creation of new parishes. See Andrew L. Drummond and James Bulloch, *The Scottish Church, 1688–1843* (Edinburgh: The Saint Andrew Press, 1973), chapter 11.
47 K. M. Black, *The Scots Churches in England*, pp. 20–22. Black's Appendix contains copies of the different minutes recorded by the two sides in the presbytery of London.

6 Nonconformists and the Bible, ca 1559–1804

John Gwynfor Jones

It was Thomas Cartwright, a pioneer of Puritanism in the latter half of the sixteenth century in England, who referred to the significance of the scriptures in acts of worship:

> When as the like of the sacrament dependeth on the preaching of the Word of God, there must of necessity the Word of God be, not read, but preached unto the people amongst whom the sacraments are ministered.[1]

He, like his fellow Presbyterians, considered that the Bible was central to the proclamation of the gospel to the masses. The Presbyterian wing of Puritanism believed that the scriptures were more authoritative than the sacraments as a means of grace. To Puritans it was the new revelation of God and had to be interpreted literally. Continental Protestant influences ensured that the Bible became central to the creed in England and reformists regarded each human being as individually responsible before God.[2] Their beliefs differed from those of Richard Hooker in his *The Laws of Ecclesiastical Polity* (1594–97), the most erudite *apologia* for the Church of England, when he argued that the scriptures were not the only authority in religion for, in his mind, historical expediency and the law of nature also had a role in the creation of social relations, and divine law and the law of nature are similar entities signifying that the universe, governed by God's will and society, is a product of nature. Consequently, he rejected the Calvinist creed.[3]

Cartwright's argument was endorsed by John Penry, the Welsh Presbyterian-turned-Separatist during his short life, in his treatise lamenting the dire spiritual condition of the Welsh people in the early Reformation period. 'We desire to have the knowledge of our God, and the lawes of his kingdome . . . made known and taught to us', he stated, a direct reference again to the centrality of the Bible and its role in the life of the Christian.[4] Puritans regarded the scriptures as the pattern established by God for the ideal church. The revelation of the Bible and its divine authority were accepted by them alongside the Calvinist belief that the church, as a congregation of visible saints called through grace, constituted the true church, and in this respect they differed from the official church which stressed formal ritualism. The true church established in 1559, however, was regarded as being invisible, accepting natural philosophy and Calvinism as its spiritual criterion.

I. Puritans and the Bible

Puritanism had its early growth in the decade before the accession to the throne of Elizabeth I when Protestant exiles were resident in the Calvinistic centres of Frankfort, Basel and Geneva during Mary Tudor's reign. It was at Geneva in 1557 that William Whittingham, together with Anthony Gilbey, Thomas Sampson, William Cole and Christopher Goodman, published a new edition of the New Testament, and in 1560 he published a version of the English Bible, known as the 'Breeches Bible', which was dedicated to Elizabeth soon after her accession. It was based in part on the Great Bible of 1539 and in part on William Tyndale's New Testament, its sources being the original Hebrew and Greek versions. It was also a Bible which had detailed annotations which were attached, but not always approved, in the margins and the text was divided into verses and not in continuous prose as in the past. The Geneva Bible proved itself to be more popular than the Great Bible and the Bishops' Bible of 1568, and it went through well over a hundred editions, many of them during Elizabeth's reign. The Bible's vocabulary and phraseology deliberately added Puritan interpretations which gave offence to Church of England leaders as well as to Roman Catholics. The influence of Calvin and French translators such as Lefèvre d'Étaples was clearly felt on the work and those who produced the 'Authorized Version' in 1611 also incorporated parts of it.[5]

The return of Protestant exiles from the continent on Elizabeth's accession led to increasing opposition to the Book of Common Prayer (1552) and there was a demand for a revised Presbyterian form of church government and liturgy. Thus began the Puritan movement to reform the church from within after the passing of the Acts of Supremacy and Uniformity (1559). The Episcopalian system and the rites and ceremonies of the church were attacked, and to further the Reformation there was an increased demand for a revised edition of the Bible. Consequently, in 1568 the Bishops' Bible appeared based on the Great Bible. It was authorized by Matthew Parker, archbishop of Canterbury, and was approved to be read publicly in all churches.[6] Unfortunately it lacked the quality and appeal of the Geneva Bible, which continued to be popular until 1611 when the 'Authorized Version' of the Bible appeared. There was little collaboration among those scholars appointed to revise the 1568 Bible, which accounted for its deficiencies, and it is not surprising that the Geneva version still remained widely used in parish churches. The Bishops' Bible, however, continued the division of the text into chapter and verse but marginal notes were abandoned to avoid theological controversies which might be harmful to the development of the new faith.

At the Hampton Court Conference in January 1604, where a deputation of Church of England clergy and moderate Puritans convened to discuss matters of reform regarding rites and practices, the lasting legacy was the new revised edition of the Bible.[7] It was not an 'authorized' version but was approved by the conference and the king despite the less than enthusiastic support it obtained from the bishops present. Although James opposed what he regarded as 'suche brainsicke and headie preachers, their disciples and followers' he was, however, prepared to listen to Puritan views at the conference: 'I am so farre from beeing contentious in these things', he stated, '(whiche for my own parte I euer esteemed as indifferent) as I doe aequallie loue and honour the learned and graue men of either of these opinions.'[8]

Although James expressed his anger when Dr John Rainolds, the chief Puritan spokesman of the delegation, used the term 'presbytery' when proposing organizational changes in the church and in ritual and ceremony, vowing to 'harry' them and their followers from the land if they did not conform, he eventually did agree that a revision of the Bible was necessary and should be undertaken.[9] It was clearly a way of placating the Puritan group who did not obtain support for their proposals with the exception of some minor concessions. In the introduction to the reader it is stated as follows:

> [V]pon the importunate petitions of the Puritanes, at his Maiesties coming to this Crowne, the Conference at Hampton Court, having bene appointed for hearing their complaints [following the Millenary Petition of 1603]; when by force of reason they were put from all other grounds, they had recourse at the last, to this shifte, that they could not with good conscience subscribe to the Communion Booke, since it maintained the Bible as it was there translated, which was as they said, a most corrupted translation.[10]

It appears that the decision to revise was mainly to please the Puritan deputation. Bancroft, the most outspoken of the bishops at Hampton Court, expressed his disapproval of the publication of yet another version of the Bible but Rainolds, in referring to the existing versions, argued that they did not meet required standards and cited examples of mistranslations, for example, Ps. 105.28, 106.30 and Gal. 4.25 where the translation of both Hebrew and Greek versions respectively was unclear. He also drew attention to the marginal notes, many of which were misleading, others being seditious or heretical. William Barlow's account of the discussions on this matter of providing a revision of the scriptures was biased against the Puritans, and he believed that the conference had been unnecessary. As Miles Smith, later to be elevated bishop of Gloucester, stated James favoured a revision:

> And although this was iudged to be but a very poore and emptie shift; yet euen hereupon did his Maiestie beginne to bethink himself of the good that might ensue by a new translation, and presently after gaue order for this Translation which is now presented vnto thee. Thus much to satisfie our scrupulous Brethren.[11]

The process of revision over the following six years revealed the influence which Tyndale's translation and the Geneva Bible had on the fifty-four scholars, most of whom are known by name, who devoted themselves to the task. Instructions stipulated that there were to be six companies, two centred at Cambridge, two at Oxford and two at Westminster, the prime aim being to revise, not translate anew, the Bishops' Bible which seriously needed amendment, and that was declared by Smith in the introduction to the reader:

> Truly (good Christian Reader) wee neuer thought from the beginning, that we should neede to make a new Translation nor yet to make of a bad one a good one . . . but to make a good one better, or out of many good ones, one principall good one . . . that hath bene our indeauour, that our marke.[12]

Of the four members of the Puritan deputation at Hampton Court two were chosen to join the large group of translators, namely Dr John Rainolds, president of Corpus Christi College, Oxford, and Laurence Chaderton, master of Emmanuel College, Cambridge. Rainolds joined the first Oxford Company who revised Isaiah to Malachi, and Chaderton was a member of the first Cambridge Company responsible for I Chronicles to the Song of Solomon. Both were reputable scholars, Chaderton, a moderate Puritan, being a distinguished linguist and powerful preacher who rose to prominence in the church, and Rainolds, also a moderate, accepting the apostolic succession and retaining the sacraments, and an eminent Greek scholar who died prematurely three years after joining his Company.

On its publication the 'Authorized Version' of the Bible was widely acclaimed and had a powerful influence on Church of England litterateurs such as George Herbert, John Donne, Henry Vaughan and Lewis Bayly. Bayly, appointed bishop of Bangor in 1616, betrayed traces of moderate Puritanism in his famous *The Practice of Piety* (ca 1611) which gained popularity among Puritans and Anglicans. It is the work of an erudite scholar on the ladder of promotion at the time of its publication. It contained quotations from the Bible and early church fathers and offered guidance on pietism and moral discipline similar, in parts, to Arthur Dent's *The Plaine Man's Pathway to Heaven* (1590). Bayly stressed 'true piety' and was less argumentative than Dent. Since he did not reject ceremonial or any part of the Prayer Book his work can be regarded as being more pietistic than puritanical.[13]

In Wales of the mid-seventeenth century Oliver Thomas – an Anglican priest who became a Puritan preacher – emphasized the Bible's teaching on piety in his *Car-wr y Cymry* (1631), one of the few original religious works in Welsh of the seventeenth century. He was one of the Approvers appointed under the Act for the Better Propagation of the Gospel in Wales (1650) and his puritanical tendencies are clearly revealed before and after. He became a Presbyterian during the Civil War. This major work of his urged the Welsh people to read the Bible now that the 'small' five-shilling Welsh Bible had been published a year earlier in 1630, sponsored by Sir Thomas Myddleton and Rowland Heylin, two prosperous Puritan London-Welsh merchants. Thomas emphasized that Bible-reading was essential and he specifically noted the sections which should be read at appropriate times. Constant reading, Thomas explained, would offer the reader benefits destined to enrich his spiritual experiences and to attain salvation:

> It is in the deep that the wonders of the Lord are to be seen . . . Gold and silver ore and the priceless treasures are not found on the face of the earth but in the depths of the earth, and because of this one must dig deep and descend into the abyss before they are brought out: in the same way the Scriptures must be searched, and searched closely and assiduously, in order that people may obtain the treasures of wisdom and knowledge to the comfort of their souls.[14]

Thomas' contemporary Rhys Prichard, vicar of Llandovery, Carmarthenshire, again a priest with strong Puritan tendencies, exhorted his parishioners to purchase the 1630 Bible and acquaint themselves with its contents. His advice that parishioners should read it is clearly revealed in his simple, homely carols in the vernacular published fully in 1681 as

Canwyll y Cymry by the Puritan preacher, writer and publisher Stephen Hughes of Meidrim:

> The Word's a candle, to give light,
> The Word will shew thee where to tread,
> The Word will guide thy airy flight,
> The Word to heaven will thee lead.
>
> The Bible in thy native tongue,
> May now e'en for a crown be got,
> Sell then thy all, and be not long,
> E'er thou this precious book hast bought.[15]

In a letter to Sir Marmaduke Lloyd of Maesyfelin in Cardiganshire in 1626 Prichard praised his Christian demeanour in public service as follows:

> I blesse God for his goodness & hartily wishe that o'r churche now (*in senio mundi*) when the light of the gospel is growne dimme, may shine gloriously with suche lights, as yourselfe, who are to the people of those parts, A lanterne to their feete & a light to their paths.[16]

The year 1630 was a significant turning-point in the history of Welsh religious literature described as 'the beginnings of a proto-modern sense of national identity'.[17] It signified a remarkable landmark in the publication of religious prose in the early seventeenth century following the appearance of the first Welsh Bible in 1588 and its revision in 1620 by Richard Parry, bishop of St Asaph, and the renowned scholar Dr John Davies of Mallwyd. William Morgan, the sole translator of the complete Bible into Welsh, was graciously praised by contemporary litterateurs and poets for his fine achievement but its major disadvantage, as in 1620, was that its use was confined to public reading in churches, the majority of the population being illiterate. The 1563 Act which led to its translation was not intended as a means of saving the native language but rather to ensure that the new faith might be understood and accepted by a monoglot population in Wales.[18] The Welsh people had to wait until the 1670s and from then on to benefit from the educational provisions which were, in due course, to have significant repercussions on the nation's religious life and experience.

A system had been devised in 1625, known as the 'lecture system', to provide a preaching ministry and education in the more backward areas of the kingdom, namely Wales and the north of England. It was an effort by Feoffees (trustees) for Impropriations, chiefly in urban centres like London and Bristol, to use impropriations purchased by them to provide suitable preachers. The Puritan John Preston of Lincoln's Inn, in a sermon before the Commons in July 1625, drew attention to the need for such a ministry to preach to the needy and illiterate. 'Is it not a lamentable case', he declared, 'to see how many perish for want of knowledge in Wales, in the Northern counties and in many places besides? . . . Where doth popery abound so much as in the dark places of the kingdom?'[19] These preachers were required to select texts from parts of the Catechism, the Creed, the Ten Commandments or the Lord's Prayer which seriously restricted their choice and were subject to many regulations. In addition, for fear of the spread of Puritanism, the government gave little support and Archbishop William Laud, who opposed the project, suppressed it in 1633.

The 1630 Bible in Wales, however, was a means by which those who were literate might read it for themselves, and in Puritan, as well as Anglican, households the head (or *paterfamilias*) was responsible for holding daily prayers and devotions. This practice had increased during the early Reformation era, and heads of households thereby familiarized their dependents with the scriptures and Christian virtues. In his preface to his translation of Arthur Dent's *The Plaine Man's Pathway to Heaven* (1590) the priest Robert Llwyd, vicar of Chirk, drew a comparison between physical and spiritual sustenance, urging the father to care for his family's moral wellbeing:

> Because, although you feed your children and your family's bodies, and leave it at that without caring for their souls, what are you doing more to them than you do to your horse, your ox, yes your dog? Read this [the 1630 Bible], therefore, to your wife and children.[20]

Family prayers, sermons and catechizing were readily available in print and Bayly stressed the need for private devotional practices to improve Christian values:

> [A]s therefore if thou desirest to have the blessing of God vpon thyselfe, and vpon thy Family . . . calle every morning all thy Familie to some convenient roome, and first, either reade thyselfe vnto them a chapter of the Word of God, or cause it to be reade distinctly by some other.[21]

Dent also realized the value of private exhortation and reminded his readers of the links between the Word, faith, Christ and eternal life, and the need to preach the Word of God:

> [T]he preaching of the Word is not a thing of human invention, but it is God's own devise, and came first out of his wisdom as the best nearest way to save men's souls . . . where the Word of God is not preached there the

> people perish . . . take away the word; take away faith, take away Christ; take away Christ; and take away eternal life. So then it followeth . . . if we will have heaven . . . we must have the word preached.[22]

Throughout the seventeenth century the Bible continued to be the chief literary work in the lives of people for it was regarded as the guide to an understanding of spiritual experience and endurance. In that context a section of a letter sent by Lady Brilliana Harley, wife of the Puritan Sir Robert Harley of Brampton Bryan in Herefordshire, to her eldest son Edward at Oxford reveals her Puritan tendencies. It encourages the young student to read the scriptures and pray constantly:

> [W]e must feede vpon the worde of God, which when we haue doun we must not let idell, but we must be diligent in exersiseing of what we knowe, and the more we practes the more we shall knowe . . . let nothinge hinder you from performeing constant priuet duties of prayeing and redeing . . . priuet prayer is one of the beest meanes to keepe the hart cloos with God.[23]

Like many other families the Harleys were typical rural Puritan gentry whose religious principles governed their domestic and public life. Harley was described locally as a 'pillar of religion', primarily because of his staunch Puritan behaviour and outlook. The spiritualization of the household was a central feature of their existence, based on devotion to Bible-reading, prayer and meditation. The household, as Christopher Hill states, was the 'lowest on the hierarchy of discipline and obedience', a moral mainstay which maintained the family's unity from the head of the household down to the most menial of servants.[24] The nuclear family was an essential entity in the task of fulfilling God's will. Study and exposition of the scriptures, Hill continues, 'both contributed to the stability of Protestantism' whereby the educated minority were able to disseminate and interpret the Word to their subordinates. The Puritan Thomas Taylor likewise referred to the role of prayer and devotion in family life in his tract in 1653: 'Let every master of a family see to what he is called, namely, to make his house a little church, to instruct every one of his family in the fear of God to contain every one of them under holy discipline, to pray with them and for them.'[25]

In his preface to the 1630 Bible, Michael Roberts, fellow of Jesus College, Oxford, made this point clearly when he recalled the close bond which the good Christian established between himself and God through reading and studying the scriptures: 'it must dwell in thy chamber, under thine own roof', he stated, 'as thy friend, eating thy bread like a dearest companion and chief adviser'. It was insufficient to leave it in church 'as a strange man', or to read it every week, or every three months, for it had to be the reader's constant companion.[26] The turbulence of the 1640s and 1650s made it a means of interpretating the radical revolution as, for example, the Fifth Monarchy beliefs. Of those two decades Christopher Hill states that 'society was in turmoil and the Bible was expected to find solutions to pressing problems, biblical texts being constantly used to defend radical ideas'.[27] In 1645 the Presbyterians in the Long Parliament banned the use of the Book of Common Prayer and replaced it with the Directory for Public Worship, and an ordinance was provided for the election or appointment of elders in a new Presbyterian system.[28] The purpose was to establish a Reformed national church but that was not acceptable to all since sectarians rejected it. In this Directory it was stated that the 'singing of psalms' was to occur 'to praise God . . . in the congregation, and also privately in the family'.[29] Those who could read were to use the Psalm-Book but 'where many in the congregation cannot read, it is convenient that the minister or some other fit person . . . do read the psalm line by line, before the singing thereof'.[30] The Presbyterians, often wrongly identified as radicals, were intent on establishing order and uniformity in view of the increasing pressures by radical sects described as 'sectarian excesses' and generally as dissenters 'who refused to accept the principle that Christ's Church could be conterminous with the Tudor or Stuart state'.[31] Psalms became popular among Puritans from the late sixteenth century onwards, and they regarded their obedience to authority comparable to that found in the Old Testament.[32] In 1648 they provided a new Psalter, the versification producing simple metrical versions for congregational singing.[33] John Milton published his metrical Psalms in 1623, 1648 and 1653, his latter versions being closer in style and vocabulary to the 'Authorized Version' of the Bible.[34] His version of Psalm 1 bears a close resemblance to the 1611 translation:

> Bless'd is the man who hath not walked astray
> In counsel of the wicked, and i' th' way
> Of sinners hath not stood, and in the seat
> Of scorners hath not sat.[35]

In fact, the versifying and singing of Psalms became increasingly popular and appealed to Puritans because they expressed the central truths of the Bible and were published in a much more convenient manner than the scriptures. The role of the Bible, however, was pre-eminently central in their lives, as the Puritan Thomas Taylor declared when he explained that concord and order in society could only be established by dutifully embracing the Word of God:

> If Christian religion confirm civil authority then the way to bring men to become subject to superiors is to plant the gospel . . . It is not power, it is not policy, that will still, subdue and keep under a rebellious people without the power of the Word and their consciences.[36]

John Milton lived in an age of marked radical religious tensions in the 1640s and 1650s, the era when Particular and General Baptists, Quakers, Ranters, Seekers, Fifth Monarchists and other religious groups publicized their beliefs in the press. They all believed in liberty of conscience and religious toleration but differed regarding the extent to which they should be separate from the church, an issue which became clearer during the Civil War and Interregnum. Puritanism still remained at the base of radical beliefs, such as predestination, associated with Particular Baptists as opposed to the salvation through God's free grace preached by the General Baptists. Also, Fifth Monarchists believed in the second coming of Christ proclaiming that they were the true saints on earth destined to welcome Him. Elements of millenarianism characterized a number of these radical movements, and Puritan thought had adhered to it as taught in the Book of Revelation. Quakers, on the other hand, believed that the spirit of God, as an 'inner light' resided within the individual and that the Bible, the orthodox teaching of the church and the Protestant tradition were not absolutely necessary to guide them in their devotions.[37] There were atheists as well, and Levellers such as Gerrard Winstanley and William Walwyn denied that the Bible was the Word of God.[38] Such indications of extreme radicalism, however, increased the campaign against the 'antichrist' from the end of the Civil War onwards.

Puritans linked the spirit of God with the Word of God, and they upheld scriptural authority, but that did not appeal to some groups such as the Ranters who believed the authority of the Spirit was superior to that of the scriptures.[39] Changes did occur and were allowed, even in moderate 'gathered churches' on points of doctrine, but their ministers accepted the Word of God as being central to their beliefs. Puritan thought stressed that godly virtue, a belief in the individual relationship with God and responsibility in the sight of God were fundamental to scriptural teaching.[40]

John Milton, one of the prime Puritan poets of the mid-seventeenth century, was remarkable for his prodigious learning and literary output as well as his radicalism.[41] He was well-informed about the politics of his day serving as Latin secretary for the new Council of State after the execution of Charles I in 1649. He was also a lapsed Presbyterian apologist, a regicide, a profound thinker and epic poet. Doubtless, his most magnificent poetic creation was *Paradise Lost* with its biblical context revealing knowledge of Jewish commentators and the Christian Fathers essential to master the theology needed to portray the 'Fall of Man'. He adopted Tyndale's style, the central matter of the poem being a manifestation of God's sovereignty according to Calvinistic doctrine, the depravity of man and God's mercy and grace. Underlining all this is his critical comment on the deception and betrayal of secular rulers. It is considered that Milton was the best of all English biblical poets, adapting the scriptures as a means of displaying poetic skills. His works, both poetic and prose, demonstrated the influence of the 1611 Bible as well as the Latin version by Junius-Tremellius, revealing his remarkable skill in being able to read these sources even in his early days. He was well-acquainted with other kindred sources as well and believed that the songs of the Old Testament were superior in quality to those of the classics. In *Paradise Regained* he describes Christ making this point in his debate with Satan:

> if I would delight my private hours
> With music or with poem, where so soon
> As in our native language can I find
> That solace? All our law and story strewed
> With hymns, our Psalms with artful terms inscribed,
> Our Hebrew songs and harps in Babylon,
> That pleased so well our victor's ear, declare
> That rather Greece from us these arts derived,
> Ill imitated, while they loudest sing
> The vices of their deities, and their own,
> In fable, hymn or song, so personating
> Their gods ridiculous, and themselves past shame.
> Remove their swelling epithets thick laid
> As varnish on a harlot's cheek, the rest,
> Thin sown with aught of profit or delight,
> Will far be found unworthy to compare
> With Sion's songs, to all true tastes excelling,
> Where God is praised aright, and Godlike men,
> The Holiest of Holies, and his saints;
> Such are from God inspired, not such from thee[42]

Although Milton often used classical illusions doubtless his main source was the Bible, the Word of God as the spiritual guide to eternal life. *Paradise Lost* portrays a God who allows man to fall from grace, *Paradise Regained* describes the temptation of Christ and *Samson Agonistes* depicts his betrayal of God by misusing the gifts given him to remain faithful. This latter work was a bitter comment on the republican movement which had forsaken God's will in mid-century. In his tract *Areopagitica* he stated, when defending the freedom of the press, that 'Truth is compared in scripture to a streaming fountain; If the waters flow not in perpetual progression, they sicken into a muddy pool of conformity and tradition' (cf. 'The words of a man's mouth are as deep waters, and the wellspring of wisdom as a flowing brook': Prov. 18.4).[43]

Another Puritan author of immense literary importance was the Baptist John Bunyan, a tinker by trade who became a preacher and author. He was of a lower social class than Milton and his work lacks Milton's splendour and magnanimity but his magnum opus *The Pilgrim's Progress* (1678), written when he was in Bedford prison, and his autobiography *Grace Abounding to the Chief of Sinners* (1666) are admirable examples of the impact which the 'Authorized Version' of the Bible had on style and content. *The Pilgrim's Progress* was a remarkable allegory which gained popularity beyond all recognition, and the style and imagery is aptly described in J. R. Green's words: 'the English . . . is the English of the Bible . . . so completely has the Bible become Bunyan's life that one feels its phrases as the natural expression of his thoughts. He has lived in the Bible till its words have become his own'.[44] So deep was the influence of the Bible on *The Pilgrim's Progress* that Bunyan was convinced that it was a gift from God. Generations of Christians have read it as a second to the Bible. In this allegory he used the scriptures as his chief source to portray the sinner's search for spiritual peace and salvation. *The Pilgrim's Progress* is not only a study of and meditation on Christian values but the allegorical character Christian's efforts to divest himself of his burdens during his journey through life is a study of Bunyan himself. It is a work which, as N. H. Keeble states, 'is at once realistic, allegorical in the old medieval sense, picturing forth theological abstractions . . . investing particular experiences with figurative significance'.[45] *The Pilgrim's Progress* has been recognized as the 'classic allegory of Puritan endeavour', Bunyan's concern being to portray the attainment of spiritual victory in a sinful world. It ends on a triumphant note of victory over sin in the 'other world' through God's grace and Christian's personal effort to gain God's favour in salvation.[46] Calvinists believed in the reality of Satan and the literal interpretation of the scriptures through which they obtained experience of the Holy Spirit. Christian read only the Bible and Evangelist is his guide. Although he was well-versed in the works of Dent, Bayly and others his prime authority was the Bible. 'I depend on the sayings of no man', he stated, 'I found it in the Scriptures of Truth among the sayings of God'.[47]

In addition to John Bunyan dissenting authors such as Richard Baxter, Edmund Calamy and Daniel Defoe were actively engaged in publishing works which had the Bible as their central theme. Baxter, for example, set about paraphrasing the New Testament in 1684. The years between 1662 and 1688, R. Tudur Jones states, 'was the Golden Age of independency' when the sect, together with other Nonconformists concentrated principally on 'the fundamentals of faith'.[48] Edmund Calamy was a moderate dissenter and a prolific writer who, with Baxter, sought to save the reputation of their fellow Dissenters down to the 'Toleration Act' of 1689. Interestingly, in his *Reliquiae Baxterianae* Baxter recounted his early upbringing in Shropshire, referring to his father, who had mended his ways, and become a moderate Puritan, teaching himself to read the Bible and helping to guide his son in the Christian faith: 'by the bare reading of the scriptures in private, without either preaching or godly company or any other Books but the Bible. And God made him the instrument of my first Convictions and Appropriation of a Holy life, as well as of my Restraint from the grossest sort of Lives.'[49] Baxter continued by stating that reading the Word in his home was no easy task because of the frequent dancing that took place outside under a maypole. Owing to his change of heart his father was scornfully called a 'Puritan, Precision and Hypocrite'. 'By this Experience', he continued, 'I was fully convinc'd that Godly people were the best, and those that despised them and lived in Sin and Pleasure, were a malignant unhappy sort of people'.[50]

II. The Age of Benevolence

The closing decades of the seventeenth century represented an awakening of an age labelled 'the age of benevolence'. In addition to political change with the Whig ascendancy and the gradual emergence of a new industrial society there had also appeared a philanthropic movement associated with the founding of charity schools in Britain. The movement has been called 'puritanism in action' which was associated with the drive towards literacy, the emphasis on moral rectitude and the elimination of ignorance. Central in this movement was Puritan piety, an outgrowth of post-Restoration Nonconformity which, despite the severe persecution suffered by Dissenters down to 1689 and to a lesser degree for many years after, made valiant efforts to use the Bible to improve the quality of religious life by means of this experiment known as the Society for the Propagation of Christian Knowledge (SPCK), established in London in 1699 in a more tolerant age. The Puritan spirit played a major role in the spread of philanthropy, and charity was associated with humanitarian endeavour.[51] Puritanism meant more than mere adherence to dogma and was more closely related to discipline and good conduct. Pietism was associated with 'the reformation of manners', implying practical Christianity in public and private demeanour.[52]

Although Puritanism had suffered following the Restoration of the Stuart monarchy in 1660 it left a strong legacy for future generations, a moral code indicating an attitude of mind which was to have significant repercussions on eighteenth-century society. In fact, Puritan dissenting cultural and religious heritage served to enrich the evangelical movements in England and Wales in days when rationalist thought, liberalism and bitter theological controversies became trends which caused much division between sects, a common feature which continued over many years as they developed, in due course, into denominations. In the established Charity Schools Christian standards were raised and social bearing became a major factor in the religious instruction based on the Bible and other devotional works. Central to this education was the teaching of godly discipline, and sermons, hymns and prayers were provided for children. The catechism was used as well as the Book of Common Prayer, the Psalms and the New Testament together with some sections from the Old Testament, especially from the prophets and Ecclesiastes. Richard Allestree's *The Whole Duty of Man,* first published in 1658 and possibly the most widely read manual in the eighteenth century, regarded as a defence against the threat of popery, was a work which had a deep influence on Howell Harris, one of the leaders of Welsh Methodism, who, through his reading of it, learnt of salvation through his understanding of faith, repentance and the individual's duty towards God and his fellow men.[53] It was a 'manual of godly living' of which Harris thought highly: 'As soon as I began reading it', he declared, 'I was convinced that in every branch of my Duty to God, to myself and to my neighbours, I was guilty and had fallen short'.[54]

It was Thomas Gouge, a London ejected minister, who formed the Welsh Trust in 1674 following on from the schools established by the Act for the Better Propagation of the Gospel in Wales (1650). During the period after the Restoration, even at times of persecution, Dissenters were determined to use education as a means of improving spiritual life as revealed in the Welsh Trust. The eighteenth century was an era in which revival and the evangelical movement in the Church of England formed a bridge between biblical publication activity and the founding of the British and Foreign Bible Society in 1804, a significant landmark in the history of the Bible in modern England and Wales. Evangelization was to become a movement of considerable influence with its background extending to the time of Lewis Bayly, Rhys Prichard, Richard Allestree and other like-minded litterateurs who produced translations of catechisms, the Psalms and the New Testament. The trust divided its work into two parts, the publication of devotional literature and the founding of schools, and in 1678 Stephen Hughes, the Carmarthenshire Puritan minister ejected in 1660, published

8,000 Bibles in Welsh. The aim of all this activity was to implant Christian principles to foster good citizenship and literacy. Although the Trust lapsed in 1681 on Gouge's death, its achievement was remarkable for its attempt to bring about co-operation between moderate Anglicans and Dissenters, the emphasis being placed on the Bible and other religious works. Owing to the pioneering spirit of its leaders it was called 'the parent of eighteenth-century educational movements' which functioned during a short period before toleration was granted to Dissenters.[55]

In London groups of philanthropists appeared eager to relieve the suffering of the poor and ill-endowed as part of their Christian endeavour, and in 1697 a small but popular publication by Dr Josiah Woodward, a Church of England clergyman, correspondent of the SPCK and a moral reformer and philanthropist, appeared describing their activities entitled *An Account of the Religious Societies in the City of London, and of Their Endeavours for the Reformation of Manners*.[56] Although the intention was to identify manners with good conduct the use of the Bible was central in their activities, and the result was the establishment in the Church of England of 'Societies for the Reformation of Manners' in 1691. Dissenters were allowed to assist in propagating their message within this movement until the 1730s when it came to an end having served Anglicans and Nonconformists well.

Education was designed to improve the quality of religious life and advance a 'campaign against illiteracy', and in Wales Dr Thomas Bray, an Oswestry clergyman and eager supporter of libraries, with four laymen formed a society for that purpose 'to promote Christian knowledge', the forerunner of the SPCK.[57] One of the instructions which gave guidance to the society ran as follows: 'To read pious Books often for their [i.e. those taught in the schools] Edification, especially the Holy Bible, [and] to be continually mindful of the great obligation of this special Profession of Religion'. The puritan ethic was acceptable in these schools, and some Nonconformist ministers were allowed to teach in them. They were at first supported by Dissenters who withdrew after the Schism Act of 1714 which prohibited dissenting preachers from teaching in their conventicles, a serious blow to Presbyterians who wished to continue their aim to establish an educated ministry. They had, however, set up their own charity schools and Dissenting Academies, many reputed to be of good quality. Schools were set up in small market towns such as Caernarfon, Wrexham and Denbigh, and Bibles and Catechisms were provided. The degree of intolerance, however, should not be exaggerated for churchmen and Nonconformists co-operated in certain areas.

The SPCK had been established in Wales as well as England, the prime leader being Sir John Philipps of Picton Castle, Pembrokeshire, a prosperous landowner and Anglican who was eager to promote Christian education.[58] Prior to this development in Wales the Welsh Trust had been founded, a dissenting movement which formed a close association with the latitudinarian movement in the Church of England. It was an effort to improve moral standards through education on a co-operative basis which involved church leaders such as John Tillotson, a distinguished preacher who became archbishop of Canterbury in 1691, Edward Stillingfleet, bishop of Worcester, and Benjamin Whichcote, philosopher and theologian, regarded as the spiritual founder of the Cambridge Platonists, together with leading Dissenters such as Baxter, Thomas Fermin and William Bates.

Geraint H. Jenkins states that between 1660 and 1730, 14.7 per cent of Welsh books were Bibles, the Book of Common Prayer, Psalms and catechisms.[59] Although social and economic factors stemmed the constant call for more devotional literature it is remarkable that between 1640 and 1740 six new editions of the Bible appeared, the chief publisher being Stephen Hughes who believed that God's people should be literate and knowledgeable in the scriptures.[60] He and others like him in Wales and England were fully aware that Roman Catholic threats could undermine the Protestant faith and they were convinced that a Bible-reading nation would overcome the problem.[61] Hughes, like Griffith Jones of Llanddowror or his mentor Madam Bevan of Laugharne, might also be considered a 'morning star' of the Methodist Revival. Jones established his circulating schools in the 1730s in Carmarthenshire and they quickly spread throughout Wales, teaching children and adults to read the Bible and catechism in the vernacular. The Bible was the chief cornerstone of the education obtained in Griffith Jones' schools; its authority was a revelation of God's will to humanity which contained every essential truth for salvation: 'The will of God, and all Things necessary to the salvation of Men', he stated, 'are revealed in the Holy Scriptures, which He appointed for the only infallible light'. He continued:

> They contain the saving Truths which none but the wisdom of God could reveal . . . Without the diligent and conscientious Use of them, the Christian Religion cannot thrive, nor be kept alive in the World. Is not the Gospel the sacred Field, where the hidden Treasure, and the Pearl of great Price are to be found . . . The sacred Volumes cannot be too much studied, or too seriously perused by those who would cherish, purify, and improve themselves in a devout Frame of mind.[62]

His contribution was immense for he fostered the movement which created a literate and morally edified society.[63] That is witnessed in a letter by the curate of Gelli-gaer, Glamorgan, in July 1741 in which he stated when referring to the change of heart which the schools had engendered among those who previously had disregarded the Sabbath:

> Many of them . . . are as fervent for the sanctification of it as before they were in prophaning it . . . neighbours associate now on the Lord's Day evening to read their Bibles . . . and to repeat what they remember of the instruction given them . . . They gratefully own the light and reformation they are now blessed with to be owing (next under God) to the charitable supporters of these schools.[64]

There are many, Vavasor Powell states, when listing instructions for those who neglect God and practice all kinds of sin and depravity and are ignorant of the Word,

> although they are invited by the preaching of the Word and by the holy scriptures to turn to God away from their sins with repentant hearts, through faith in Jesus Christ, so that they are forgiven for them and are freed from the damnation it is owed them, and be partakers at the end of eternal life in heaven.[65]

In his conversation between Christ and the doubting individual he also declared that he should 'search the scriptures for they can make you perfect and wise to salvation and apply you to all good deeds'.[66]

The prolific publication of Bibles in the eighteenth century was sufficient proof that Dissent was not in any state of decay. In fact, the tradition assumed a significant role in the progress of the Methodist Revival in England and Wales from the 1730s onwards. There was some opposition, as in the case of William Lucy, bishop of St Davids, in a letter to Gilbert Sheldon, archbishop of Canterbury, in 1673 referring to schools in his diocese which caused disruption between conformists and others – 'wch highly advances the growth of Schisme . . . wch in despight of law & coercion are . . . erected by seminarys of the dissenting party.' Nevertheless, Independents played an active part in the progress of evangelization for they themselves had come under the evangelical influence of the charity and Methodist movements which gave their dry intellectual sermons an emotional appeal.[67]

It was from the late seventeenth century onwards to the nineteenth that hardened Nonconformists participated in several theological disputes regarding such profound matters as redemption and the person of Christ, a distinct indication of the education provided in the Dissenting Academies, described as the 'bedrock of rationalism and radicalism' and as the main agency of education for Nonconformists who were denied entrance to the English universities.[68] Of the numerous contributions which were disseminated by the presses on theological beliefs the Antinomians, Arians, Unitarians and Arminians assumed prominence. The Synod of Dort (1618–19) had decided only to accept High Calvinist doctrine based on unconditional election, particular atonement to the elect only, man's total incapacity before God, effective calling (i.e. that grace cannot be rejected) and continuation in a state of grace. More extreme sects, however, continued to adhere to their own beliefs on the nature of God and Christ, especially the belief that Christ was a man only, that by faithfully following his virtues that salvation was possible, that there was no original sin and that it was human reason which best explains the scriptures. Thus emerged ongoing debates between Calvinists and Arminians, between Unitarians and Trinitarians, and High and Low Calvinism, conducted by theologians well-versed in the intellectual life of their age. Suffice it to say that all these bitter disputes were based on individual interpretations of the Bible, and in this context, as so often in the past, the Word of God had become open to reinterpretation by intellectuals who considered that their own vision of God was indisputable.[69] It was such a controversy which led to the famous Welsh Methodist preacher Peter Williams being excommunicated in 1791 from the Connexion for his Sabellian interpretation of the first verse in St John's gospel in his edition of the Bible in 1770, and the Independent minister John Canne's pocket edition twenty years later, in which he rejected the belief in the separate entities of the Holy Trinity.[70] It is interesting to note that Williams' Bible was the first in Welsh to attach commentaries at the end of each chapter, and the first to be printed in Wales.[71]

III. The Evangelical Revival, the Missionary Movement and the Bible

Methodists were not Dissenters but rather continued the evangelical mission to reform the Church of England from within. John Wesley's Arminian sect finally seceded in 1784 and the Calvinistic Methodists in Wales ordained their first ministers in 1811 when a new denomination was formed. It was an age when many editions of the Bible were published and the demand was increasing at a time when the power of the Methodists fostered spiritual regeneration through open air preaching and their societies. Methodism rapidly grew in popularity since it appealed to the emotion, arousing the spirit of an active faith and individual conscience. In the account of his conversion in May 1738 at Aldersgate in London, John Wesley referred to his heart being 'strangely warmed', a feeling that he trusted in Christ which gave him an assurance that He had taken away his sins and had saved him 'from the law of sin and death'.[72] Biblical study and meditation played a central role in Wesley's conversion. He emphasized faith and salvation which he regarded as a blessing that the individual sinner acquired through God's free mercy and faith, meaning that a spiritual light had revealed to the soul God's eternal being in his life. In a preface to a selection of his sermons Wesley stated firmly:

> I have accordingly set down in the following sermons what I find in the Bible concerning the way to heaven, with a view to distinguish the way of God from all those which are inventions of men. I have endeavoured to describe the true, the scriptural, experimental religion, so as to omit nothing which is a real part thereof and to add nothing thereto which is not.[73]

The Bible was the source of wisdom to Wesley and in his sermons he constantly referred to its content as the way to salvation. In his preface he again clarified the essential role of the Bible in preparing the way to eternal life:

> I want to know one thing – the way to heaven . . . God himself has condescended to teach the way . . . He hath written it down in a book, O give me that book! At any price give me the Book of God! I have it: here is knowledge enough for me. Let me be *homo unius libri*. Here then I am, far from the busy ways of men. I sit down alone: only God is here. In His presence I open, I read His book: for this end, to find the way to heaven.[74]

He was aware that many misrepresented or misunderstood the scriptures, but he saw it as the Word of God which could not be excelled. So also were Howell Harris' experiences in his role as the pioneer of the evangelical movement in Wales. After his conversion in the summer of 1735 he proclaimed that the Bible was the genuine mouthpiece of God, and in his Diary in March 1741 he wrote: 'God speaks to none but thro' His Word now.' In his mind God's revealed will was undisputable and the Methodists were 'in His Will and love'.[75] Consequently, in the early years of his ministry, Harris began to place great emphasis on quoting texts when conducting his meetings and preaching.[76]

In the years between 1710 and 1759 about 221 editions of the Bible appeared in English, the majority being reprints of the 1611 'Authorized Version'.[77] In Welsh nineteen versions were printed before 1797, six of them by the SPCK. In 1792 the first denominational missionary society was established, when the Baptist Missionary Society sent William Carey to India where he translated the Bible into Bengali Hindi, Sanskrit and part translations to other languages. He was of humble origins in Northamptonshire, reared an Anglican but in his young days joined the Baptists and contributed immensely as a Christian missionary in Bengal. Many Nonconformist missionaries were sent from England and Wales to various mission fields. The first Calvinistic Methodist from Wales to visit the Khasi Hills in India was Thomas Jones of Montgomeryshire in 1841, who translated St Matthew's version of the gospel into the native language. William Lewis, born of Welsh parents in Manchester, also went to the same area in 1843 and translated most of the New Testament and, with his wife, published *The Pilgrim's Progress* in Khasi. In 1800 John Davies set sail for Tahiti and the surrounding Tahitan islands and contributed to the mission there, translating parts of the New Testament and Psalms, the catechism and John Bunyan's classic. The evangelical spirit in England and Wales was largely responsible for the progress in various mission fields by the Anglican Church and Nonconformist denominations.

It was on 7 March 1804 that the British and Foreign Bible Society was founded, based on the London Missionary Society and Religious Tract Society, the aim being to make available an abundance of Bibles in the home and foreign missionary market. The publication of the Bible at home and abroad was essentially a missionary venture, designed to extend knowledge of God's word in communities deprived of spiritual regeneration. It was an interdenominational society and contributed significantly to publishing translations of the scriptures into several languages. The British and Foreign Bible Society was an urgent necessity for the supply of sufficient copies to satisfy the spiritual needs of an increasing population.

With new printing techniques the New Testament and the whole Bible appeared in English in 1805 and 1806 respectively and the increase over the period to 1850 was tremendous reflecting the enterprise shown by Anglicans and Nonconformists alike to spread the faith. Thomas Charles of Bala in north Wales made representations to the Religious Tract Society for Bibles to be published in Welsh, an incentive given him to improve literacy among a largely monoglot nation in his newly founded Sunday Schools. Joseph Tarn, treasurer of the Religious Tract Society, in his letter to him in 1804, on the day when the British and Foreign Bible Society was founded, informed him of the good news, and in his reply Charles stated how successful his Sunday Schools were and emphasized the necessity for a supply of Bibles in them:

> The Sunday-Schools have occassioned *[sic]* more calls for Bibles within these five years, than perhaps ever was known before among our poor people. The possession of a Bible produces a feeling among them, which

> the possession of no one thing in the world besides could produce . . . I have seen some of them overcome with joy, and burst into tears of thankfulness on their obtaining possession of a Bible as their own property and for their free use.[78]

In this context the romantic story of Mary Jones of Llanfihangel-y-pennant, in south Merioneth, whose home was almost thirty miles away from Bala, where Thomas Charles resided, is relevant. According to tradition she travelled barefoot in 1800 to seek a copy from him, and despite the scarcity, according to tradition, he gave one of his own copies to her.[79] It is said that it was her enthusiasm which inspired Charles when he took part in the discussions which, again according to tradition, led four years later to the establishment of the Bible Society.[80] The dedication which inspired it followed innumerable difficulties in the missionary campaigns conducted abroad by Nonconformist denominations to propagate the Christian faith. To support the central society in London local societies were formed, and the first in Wales appeared on 27 April 1810 at Swansea, and the second at Neath on 24 September of the same year.[81]

The labours of Robert Raikes of Gloucester, Morgan John Rhys of Hengoed, Dr Edward Williams of Oswestry, George Lewis of Carmarthenshire and Thomas Charles, among several others, were founded on the teaching of the scriptures as the previous Circulating Schools had been in the days of Griffith Jones in Wales and, in 1785, the Sunday School Philanthropic Societies in England. The broad aim of these devoted individuals and the establishments which they founded was to improve literacy and the moral standards of a socially deprived peasantry and proletariat, and 'the basic requirement was an exact knowledge of the Bible in adequate numbers quickly and cheaply'.[82] In *The Christian Observer* in July 1810 one excited witness described the first arrival of a cartload of Bibles in Wales as follows:

> The Welsh peasants went out in crowds to meet it [i.e. the load of Bibles] and welcomed it as the Israelites did the ark of old; drew it into the town and eagerly bore off every copy as rapidly as they could be dispersed. The young people consumed the whole night reading it, and labourers carried it with them to the fields that they might enjoy it during the intervals of their labours.[83]

No further details are given but the wider truth is evident, that a reading public had by then increased and that the work of Griffith Jones and Thomas Charles and others had been amply rewarded.

The Revd John Owen, secretary of the Bible Society, during one of his journeys on the continent to survey those societies affiliated to it, described his meeting with a Pastor Oberlin at Woldback near Basel in September 1818 praising his support for the Society's work: 'when I announced to him . . .', he stated, 'that I appeared before him, as the Secretary of the British and Foreign Bible Society . . . our conversation became familiar . . . upon the things pertaining to the kingdom of God [and] . . . never ceased to be deeply interesting, and pregnant with edification'.[84]

In this spirit the Bible Society proceeded with its work, thus opening up a century of Bible publication, private reading and study in Victorian times. Thomas Charles' massive *Y Geiriadur Beiblaidd* (Bible Dictionary), published in 1808 was a compulsory guide for the Welsh people, not only, as Ieuan Gwynedd Jones states, to 'open up a world of new intellectual experiences' but also to serve more like an encyclopaedia than a conventional Bible dictionary. In a broader perspective its contents taught readers to go further and to question social, political and ethical values.[85] Christopher Hill, in his erudite study of the impact of the English Bible in the seventeenth century, notes that it not only enlightened readers in the scriptures but also enabled them to appraise the essence of human existence. 'They,' he declares, 'found lessons and consolation for living on earth as well as the path to heaven . . . the Bible has established cultural norms which survived religious beliefs'. Horizons were broadened and intellectual powers enhanced.[86] By the early Victorian era the 1611 English 'Authorized Version' and the 1588 Bible in Welsh had 'come of age'.

Notes

I wish to thank Brian Ll. James for reading this contribution and for his useful comments and suggestions.

1 P. McGrath, *Papists and Puritans under Elizabeth I* (London: Blandford Press, 1967), p. 39.
2 P. Collinson, *The Elizabethan Puritan Movement* (London: Cape, 1967), pp. 27–28; idem, *English Puritanism* (London: Historical Association, 1983), pp. 12–24.
3 R. Hooker, *Of the Laws of Ecclesiastical Polity*, ed. A. S. McGrade (Cambridge: Cambridge University Press, 1983), pp. 1, 26, 32.
4 J. Penry, *Three Treatises Concerning Wales*, ed. D. Williams (Cardiff: University of Wales Press, 1960), p. 13.
5 D. Daniell, *The Bible in English: Its History and Influence* (New Haven, CT: Yale University Press, 2003), pp. 290–319.
6 Ibid., pp. 338–47.
7 M. H. Curtis, 'Hampton Court Conference and Its aftermath', *History*, 46 (1961), pp. 1–16; F. Shriver, 'Hampton Court Re-Visited: James I and the Puritans', *Journal of Ecclesiastical History*, 33 (1982), pp. 48–71; P. Collinson, 'The Jacobean Religious Settlement: The Hampton Court Conference', in H. Tomlinson (ed.), *Before the English Civil War: Essays on English Stuart Politics and Government* (London: Macmillan, 1983), pp. 27–51.

8 J. Craigie (ed.), *The Basilikon Doron of King James VI* (London/Edinburgh: William Blackwood Press/Scottish Text Society, 1944), pp. 16–17.
9 Daniell, *Bible in English*, pp. 427–60; D. H. Willson, *King James VI and I* (London: Cape, 1956), p. 207; C. Bingham, *James I of England* (London: Weidenfeld and Nicolson, 1981), pp. 38–39.
10 A. W. Pollard (ed.), *The Holy Bible* (Oxford: Oxford University Press, 1911), p. vii.
11 Ibid.
12 Ibid., p. ix.
13 A. H. Dodd, 'Bishop Lewes Bayly of Bangor *c.*1575–1631', *Transactions of the Caernarvonshire Historical Society*, 28 (1967), pp. 14–18.
14 R. G. Gruffydd, 'Anglican Prose', in idem (ed.), *A Guide to Welsh Literature c. 1530–1700* (Cardiff: University of Wales Press, 1997), p. 182.
15 R. B. Jones, *'A Lanterne to Their Feete': Remembering Rhys Prichard 1579–1644, Vicar of Llandovery* (Porth-y-rhyd: Drover Press, 1994), p. 60.
16 Ibid., p. 22.
17 M. Wynn Thomas, 'Seventeenth-Century Puritan writers: Morgan Llwyd and Charles Edwards', in Gruffydd (ed.), *A Guide to Welsh Literature c. 1530–1700*, p. 190.
18 Many publications have appeared on the 1588 translation of the Bible, such as Glanmor Williams, *Wales and the Reformation* (Cardiff: University of Wales Press, 1997), pp. 338–60; Eryn M. White, *The Welsh Bible* (Stroud: Tempus, 2007), pp. 17–37, 39–52; R. G. Gruffydd, *The Translating of the Bible into the Welsh Tongue by William Morgan in 1588* (London: BBC, 1998).
19 J. Preston, *A Sermon Preached. . . . Before the Commons House* (2 July 1625). See Christopher Hill, *Change and Continuity in Seventeenth-Century England* (London: Weidenfeld and Nicolson, 1974), pp. 16–21.
20 G. H. Hughes (ed.), *Rhagymadroddion 1547–1659* (Cardiff: University of Wales Press, 1951), p. 127.
21 Lewis Bayly, *The Practice of Pietie* (London: Printed for Andrew Crooke, 1639), p. 343.
22 A. Dent, *The Plaine Man's Pathway to Heaven* (Pittsburgh, PA: Soli Deo Gloria Publications, 1994), pp. 266–67.
23 T. T. Lewis (ed.), *Letters of the Lady Brilliana Harley . . . of Brampton Bryan* (London: Camden Society, 1854), XV, p. 15.
24 Christopher Hill, *Society and Puritanism in Pre-Revolutionary England* (London: Secker & Wartburg, 1964), pp. 49, 443, 455.
25 *The Works of . . . Dr Thom[as] Taylor* (London, 1653), p. 190.
26 Hughes, *Rhagymadroddion*, p. 124 (author's translation).
27 Christopher Hill, *The English Bible and the Seventeenth-Century Revolution* (London: Penguin, 1994), pp. 4–5.
28 B. Coward and P. Gaunt (eds), *English Historical Documents 1603–1660* (London and New York: Routledge, 2010), pp. 1003–4.
29 Ibid., p. 1002.
30 D. Cressy and L. A. Ferrell, *Religion and Society in Early Modern England* (London and New York: Routledge, 1996), p. 192.
31 Basil Hall, 'Puritanism: The Problem of Definition', in G. J. Cuming (ed.), *Studies in Church History*, 2 (London: Thomas Nelson, 1965), p. 294.
32 A. C. Partridge, *English Biblical Translation* (London: Deutsch, 1973), p. 142.
33 D. Norton, *A History of the English Bible as Literature* (Cambridge: Cambridge University Press, 2000), pp. 179–80; D. Bush (ed.), *Milton, Poetical Works* (London: Oxford University Press, 1973), p. 5.
34 Norton, *English Bible as Literature*, pp. 179–80.
35 Ibid., p. 180.

36 Thomas Taylor, *A Commentary upon the Epistle of St Paul Written to Titus* (London: 1658), pp. 398–99.
37 H. Barbour, *The Quakers in Puritan England* (New Haven, CT and London: Yale University Press, 1964), pp. 139–40.
38 Hill, *English Bible*, p. 232.
39 F. D. Dow, *Radicalism in the English Revolution, 1640–1660* (Oxford: Basil Blackwell, 1985), pp. 61–62.
40 Ibid., p. 36.
41 Norton, *English Bible as Literature*, pp. 174–83. For a study of Milton's interest in and involvement with revolutionary ideas see Christopher Hill, *Milton and the English Revolution* (London: Faber, 1977).
42 Norton, *English Bible as Literature*, p. 177; Bush (ed.), *Milton, Poetical Works*, pp. 504–5.
43 B. Bobrick, *The Making of the English Bible* (London: Phoenix, 2002), p. 292; M. W. Wallace, *Milton's Prose* (London: Oxford University Press, 1949), pp. 307–8.
44 J. R. Green, *A Short History of the English People* (London: Macmillan, 1888), p. 627; Norton, *English Bible as Literature*, p. 183.
45 N. H. Keeble, *The Literary Culture of Nonconformity in later Seventeenth-Century England* (Leicester: Leicester University Press, 1987), p. 264.
46 J. Marlowe, *The Puritan Tradition in English Life* (London: The Cresset Press, 1956), p. 132.
47 Keeble, *Literary Culture*, p. 157.
48 R. Tudur Jones, *Congregationalism in England 1662–1962* (London: Independent Press, 1962), pp. 63–64.
49 Richard Baxter, *Reliquiae Baxterianae* (London: Printed for T. Parker, 1696), pp. 1–2; N. H. Keeble, *The Autobiography of Baxter* (London: Dent, 1974), p. 4.
50 Keeble, *Autobiography of Baxter*, p. 3.
51 For the background to the Societies for the Reformation of Manners see M. G. Jones (ed.), *The Charity School Movement: A Study of Eighteenth-Century Puritanism in Action* (Cambridge: Cambridge University Press, 1964), pp. 2–4, and D. W. R. Bahlman, *The Moral Revolution of 1688* (New Haven, CT and London: Yale University Press and Oxford University Press, 1957).
52 Jones, *Charity School Movement*, pp. 6–7.
53 Geraint Tudur, *Howell Harris: From Conversion to Separation, 1735–1750* (Cardiff: University of Wales Press, 2000), p. 38. Allestree's work was translated into Welsh by John Langford (1672) and Edward Samuel (1718).
54 Howell Harris, *A Brief Account of the Life of Howell Harris* (Trevecka: Trevecka Press, 1791), p. 12; Tudur, *Howell Harris*, p. 12.
55 Jones, *Charity School Movement*, pp. 281–9.
56 Josiah Woodward, *An Account of the Religious Societies . . . in the City of London*, with introduction by D. E. Jenkins (Liverpool: Brython Press, 1935), pp. 5–19.
57 M. Clement, *The SPCK and Wales, 1699–1740* (London: SPCK, 1954), pp. 14, 18–19; E. D. Evans, *A History of Wales, 1660–1815* (Cardiff: University of Wales Press, 1976), pp. 42–56; White, *Welsh Bible*, pp. 52–71, 73–100.
58 Clement, *SPCK and Wales*, pp. xiv–xv onwards.
59 Geraint H. Jenkins, *Literature, Religion and Society in Wales, 1660–1730* (Cardiff: University of Wales Press, 1978), pp. 38–39.
60 Ibid., pp. 55–60.
61 White, *Welsh Bible*, p. 69.
62 Griffith Jones, *Welch Piety* (London: Printed by J. Oliver, 1759), p. 11.
63 F. A. Cavenagh, *The Life and Work of Griffith Jones of Llanddowror* (Cardiff: University of Wales Press, 1983); Geraint H. Jenkins, 'An Old and Much Honoured Soldier:

Griffith Jones of Llanddowror', *Welsh History Review*, 11 (1983), pp. 449–68; Jones, *Charity School Movement*, pp. 297–314.

64 Ibid., p. 301.

65 Vavasor Powell, *Cyfarwydd-deb i'r Anghyfarwydd* (London: Thomas Dawks, 1677), p. 146.

66 Ibid., p. 56.

67 Geraint H. Jenkins, *Protestant Dissenters in Wales 1639–1689* (Cardiff: University of Wales Press, 1992), p. 93.

68 Michael R. Watts, *The Dissenters, Volume 1: From the Reformation to the French Revolution* (Oxford: Oxford University Press, 1978), pp. 366–71; R. Tudur Jones, 'The Puritan contribution', in J. L. Williams and G. Rhys Hughes (eds), *The History of Education in Wales* (Swansea: Christopher Davies Press, 1978), pp. 40–44; idem, 'Relations between Anglicans and Dissenters: The Promotion of Piety, 1670–1730', in D. Walker (ed.), *A History of the Church in Wales* (Penarth: Church in Wales Publications, 1976), pp. 79–102.

69 Watts, *The Dissenters, Volume 1*, pp. 394–478. For the broader background of dissenting theology see J. Gwili Jenkins, *Hanfod Duw a Pherson Crist* (Liverpool: Brython Press, 1931).

70 For the life and work of Peter Williams see G. M. Roberts, *Bywyd a Gwaith Peter Williams* (Cardiff: University of Wales Press, 1943); Derec Ll. Morgan, *Pobl Pantycelyn* (Llandysul: Gomer Press, 1986), pp. 37–52. For Canne see *Oxford Dictionary of National Biography* (Oxford: Oxford University Press, 2004) [hereafter *ODNB*], pp. 903–4.

71 *ODNB*, pp. 269–70.

72 N. Curnock, *John Wesley's Journal* (London: Epworth Press, 1949), p. 51; F. Whaling and A. C. Outler (eds), *John and Charles Wesley: Selected Prayers, Hymns* (New York: Paulist Press, 1981), p. 107; J. H. Plumb, *England in the Eighteenth Century 1714–1815* (London: Penguin, 1951), p. 92.

73 A. C. Outler, *Sermons on Several Occasions* (Oxford: Oxford University Press, 1970), p. vi.

74 Ibid.

75 Tudur, *Howell Harris*, p. 25.

76 Ibid., p. 42.

77 Jones, *Charity School Movement*, pp. 409–50.

78 D. E. Jenkins, *The Life of the Rev. Thomas Charles of Bala* (Denbigh: Llewelyn Jenkins, 1908), II, pp. 492–94, 517–18.

79 Ibid., pp. 492–94, 518–19. For Mary Jones, see E. W. James, 'Ann Griffiths, Mary Jones a Mecca'r Methodistiaid', *Llên Cymru*, 21 (1998), pp. 74–87; idem, 'Bala and the Bible: Thomas Charles, Ann Griffiths and Mary Jones', *Journal of the Merioneth Historical and Record Society*, 15 (2007), pp. 185–200 (esp. pp. 194–96); M. E. R., *Mary Jones and Her Bible* (Harpenden: Gospel Standard Trust Publications, 1994); Elisabeth Williams, *To Bala for a Bible: The Story of Mary Jones and the Beginnings of the Bible Society* (Bridgend: Evangelical Press of Wales, 1988).

80 This tradition is rejected by the celebrated Welsh bibliophile Bob Owen of Croesor. University of Bangor MS. 2384. See also D. Evans, *Bywyd Bob Owen* (Caernarfon: Gwasg Gwynedd, 1977), pp. 224–25.

81 W. Canton, *A History of the British and Foreign Bible Society* (London: J. Murray, 1904–10), I, p. 472.

82 I. Gwynedd Jones, 'Thomas Charles (1755–1814)', in Charles Gittins (ed.), *Pioneers of Welsh Education: Four Lectures* (Swansea: Swansea University Faculty of Education, n.d.), p. 49.

83 Jones, *Charity School Movement*, p. 321.
84 J. Owen, *Extracts of Letters on the Object and Connexions of the British and Foreign Bible Society* (London: British and Foreign Bible Society, 1819), p. 11.
85 Jones, 'Thomas Charles (1755–1814)', p. 50.
86 Hill, *English Bible*, pp. 438–39.

7 Nonconformists and Biblical Scholarship: The Nineteenth and Twentieth Centuries

John Tudno Williams

> It is the continent of Europe, and in particular its German-speaking parts, that was responsible for the changes and challenges to how the Bible was interpreted in the nineteenth century. Britain and America (New England) first resisted and later embraced these challenges, albeit with modifications that were dictated by local factors.[1]

Thus begins John Rogerson's chapter on 'The Bible and Theology' in *The Blackwell Companion to Nineteenth-Century Theology*. In the first half of this chapter I propose to outline the reactions of leading scholars in the main Nonconformist denominations in England and Wales, that is, the Baptists, Congregationalists, Presbyterians and Unitarians, to the developments in the employment of historical criticism of the Bible by continental scholars from the beginning of the nineteenth century. As the issues raised in the treatment of either Testament differ considerably, at least initially, those raised by the critical approach to the Old Testament will be considered first, and then there follows consideration of issues affecting the New Testament.

It can be demonstrated that 'acquaintance with German Old Testament critical scholarship in England can be traced back to the 1790s, if not earlier. On the whole, this knowledge was at its deepest and keenest in the Unitarian circles which took over from Deism the spirit of radical dissent.'[2] Then Rogerson adds: 'We should probably conclude that the knowledge of German criticism possessed by Unitarian circles in England did not significantly influence non-Unitarians.'[3]

I. The Nineteenth Century

a. The Emergence of Old Testament Criticism

The first significant event of the nineteenth century with regard to the study of the Old Testament was the publication of the 1804 doctoral dissertation of Wilhelm Martin Leberecht de Wette (1780–1849) which linked the composition of the book of Deuteronomy with King Josiah's reform of Judah's religious practices in the year 621 BC. This set a marker by which other parts of the Pentateuch could be judged. What, therefore, could be their relationship as regards sources, origin and dates to this book? Later, in a work published in 1869, *Der sogenannte Grundschrift des Pentateuch* ('The so-called Basic Source of the Pentateuch'), on the basis of ideas first propounded by his teacher at Strasbourg Eduard Reuss (1804–91), Karl Heinrich Graf (1815–69) showed that, since neither the book of Deuteronomy nor Judges-Kings presuppose the laws and narratives of a so-called Priestly Source, that source must be regarded as the latest source of the Pentateuch. This view was later developed by Julius Wellhausen (1844–1918) into a fully-fledged Four Document Hypothesis to account for the composition of the whole of the Pentateuch. De Wette in his *Beiträge zur Einleitung in das Alte Testament* (1806–7) had also proposed a reconstruction of the history of Israelite religion, whereby the priestly institutions were to be regarded as later developments within it. Indeed, it was Josiah's reform, with its insistence on centralizing the sacrificial worship in the Jerusalem temple, which placed power in the hands of the priesthood. Wellhausen built upon such ideas and developed a detailed picture of the historical development of Israelite religion up to the Babylonian exile and beyond.

Such ideas were anathema to Nonconformists nurtured on Puritan and pietist teaching and the later influences emanating from the Methodist revivals (both Arminian and Calvinist) of the eighteenth century. They had learned about them through the English translations, available from the 1830s, of works by conservative scholars in Germany, such as Ernst Wilhelm Hengstenberg (1802–69) and Friedrich August G. Tholuck (1799–1877), who rejected them totally. Indeed, they expressed the hope that these radical views were ephemeral and would be, indeed had already been, fully refuted.[4] In fact, it is claimed that as late as 1880: 'It was still possible for orthodox Bible scholars in England to consider higher criticism as the temporary form taken by infidelity in Germany and confidently to predict the scholarly victory of tradition.'[5]

However, the study of the Old Testament in England in this period was not always plain-sailing as far as the traditionalist, orthodox position was concerned. What can probably be termed the *cause célèbre*, at least within Nonconformist circles, was that which led to the dismissal of Samuel Davidson

(1806–98) from his position as Old Testament Professor at the Lancashire Independent College near Manchester in 1857. The previous year he had, at the request of the publishers of T. H. Horne's *Introduction to the Critical Study and Knowledge of the Holy Scriptures*, rewritten the second volume, under the title *The Text of the Old Testament*. 'In fact', says Rogerson,

> Davidson's contribution to Horne's work was very orthodox when compared with de Wette and [Wilhelm] Vatke [1806–82]. He did, however, allow that the biblical writers were not infallible on every matter of historical detail, and that while Moses had certainly written *parts* of the Pentateuch he had not written all of it. He accepted that the Pentateuch contained an Elohim document, written in the time of Joshua, and a Jehovah document, written during the period of the Judges. On other matters he upheld the unity of authorship of the whole of Isaiah and the book of Daniel, and defended the independence and reliability of the books of Chronicles.

Thus, concludes Rogerson, '[i]t seems incredible that Davidson should have been dismissed from his post for holding such mild critical views, but the incident is an indicator of opinion at the time in part of British non-conformist circles'.[6] In response to his dismissal Davidson wrote *Facts, Statements, and Explanations* (1857), in which he argued for the essential orthodoxy of his position, but his reply was not acceptable to a narrow majority of the College Committee.[7] The result was that biblical criticism was banished from the curriculum of the College.[8] As John Kelly, a Congregational minister from Liverpool and member of the College Committee, said: 'We are hardly prepared for this style of teaching yet.' Furthermore, it is recounted that his successor Alexander Thomson (1815–95), when Wellhausen's *Prolegomena to the History of Israel* arrived in the college library in the 1880s, took it out and refused to return it so that students' minds should not be poisoned.[9]

Perhaps two of the most famous examples of the clash between traditionalist and radical views about the Old Testament in the nineteenth century involved Anglicans. They were the publication of the volume *Essays and Reviews* in 1860, and the case of Bishop J. W. Colenso (1814–83) in Natal. However, they were not without their effect upon Nonconformists. *Essays and Reviews* raised doubts about the historicity of miracles and whether the Bible was historically reliable and divinely inspired.[10] More than four hundred books and articles were written in response to it and in 1864 it was formally condemned by the Church of England.

Colenso, when questioned by local Zulus about facts in the Pentateuchal narratives, was obliged to admit to the indefensibility of many of them, and he published the first part of his *The Pentateuch and Book of Joshua Critically*

Examined in 1862, the final part appearing in 1879. A synod of the South African Church deposed him, but the Judicial Committee of the Privy Council in England supported his retention of his bishopric.[11] The Nonconformist reactions to the positions propounded in both instances were overwhelmingly negative.[12]

A third example of high controversy led to the dismissal of William Robertson Smith (1846–94) from his post at Aberdeen, and it certainly had its effect on Nonconformists south of the border. Described as 'arguably the greatest, certainly the most brilliant and original of modern Old Testament and Semitic scholars',[13] Robertson Smith, the Old Testament Professor at the Free Church College in Aberdeen, believed that biblical criticism embodied 'the principles and aims of a truly Protestant study of Scripture',[14] and so insisted on emphasizing the Reformation principle that the core of religion was a personal relationship with the living God.[15] He also deemed it to be a means of rescuing the Old Testament 'from obfuscation and of affirming its message in an age increasingly dominated by scientific discoveries'.[16] Of his teachers, A. B. Davidson (1840–1902) of Edinburgh, in particular, had exerted most influence upon him, as he was also to exert on two later doyens of Old Testament studies among the Nonconformists, William Gray Elmslie (1848–89) and John Skinner (1851–1925).[17] The initial furore had been caused by the publication of his article on 'Bible' in the ninth edition of the *Encyclopaedia Britannica* in 1875. Although his later introduction to biblical criticism *The Old Testament in the Jewish Church* (1881) 'was written with evangelistic fervour',[18] Robertson Smith was still considered to be too much in advance of his own church, and was dismissed from his post in 1881. He moved to Cambridge where he pursued Arabic studies, and thus by leaving Scotland became a Nonconformist as regards his religious allegiance. Owen Charles Whitehouse (1849–1916) stated that Davidson 'and his illustrious pupil, Professor Robertson Smith, may be regarded as sharing with [the Anglican, T. K.] Cheyne [1841–1905] the honour of being the real "Bahnbrecher" [trailblazers] of our modern British Old Testament research by the work contributed by each during the eventful decade 1870–1880'.[19]

However, the unease of Nonconformists regarding the whole affair was palpable. Seeing that Robertson Smith had reiterated the Reformation call for the believer's individual responsibility, guided by the Holy Spirit, to interpret the Bible, Glover comments: 'The removal of all doctrinal questions from the controversy left the central issue whether Smith had the right to interpret the Bible for himself. Reduced to this issue, the matter was likely to be decided in Smith's favour by the English nonconformists. They were not yet ready to accept his critical opinions, but on the whole the nonconformists were pleased that so able a scholar was a firm evangelical.'[20]

Other nineteenth-century controversies involving Nonconformist attitudes to critical scholarship need to be mentioned. One was the case of Archibald Duff (1845–1934), a staunch evangelical and an able Bible scholar, and one of the earliest Nonconformists to accept the Wellhausen theory, who agreed in 1881 that religious history should be seen as centred in Christ.[21] Duff became professor of Hebrew and Old Testament Theology at Airedale College, Bradford, in 1878. It was A. M. Fairbairn who had appointed him, and although his Old Testament criticism was said to be 'pre-Wellhausen', nevertheless, 'he threw his growing influence behind a critical approach to the Bible'.[22] Duff assumed a number of advanced critical positions, such as that the sufferings of the Servant of Isaiah were not those of Christ but Jeremiah's. However, the main thesis of his work was that the Old Testament testimony to the evangelical doctrine of the atonement was affirmed.[23] As a result, Glover could comment: 'Orthodox theology could cover a multitude of critical sins.'[24]

Then, there was the so-called Down Grade controversy in the course of which Charles Haddon Spurgeon (1834–92) accused fellow Baptists of rejecting biblical inerrancy, but, more essentially, doctrinal matters such as the atonement and the fate of the wicked.[25] The term 'Down Grade' derived from the title of unsigned articles published by Spurgeon in his journal *The Sword and the Trowel* in 1887. In fact, they dealt with the defection of eighteenth-century Nonconformists from Calvinism. The implication of the articles was that any defection from evangelical truth (which was equated with Calvinism) put individuals or bodies on 'the Down Grade'. Spurgeon himself published later in the year 'Another Word Concerning the Down-Grade', in which he opposed higher criticism because he thought it led to heresy. In fact, as Glover says: 'Higher criticism was involved in the whole affair but only in a minor and subsidiary way.'[26] The whole incident led to Spurgeon's resignation from the Baptist Union in 1888, but he received only minority support for his position from his fellow Baptists.[27]

Controversy also surrounded *Inspiration and the Bible* (1888) by Robert Forman Horton (1855–1934) in which he adopted a critical attitude to problems posed by the Bible.[28] Incidentally, Horton, a Congregational minister in London, had been included as one of the 'Down Grade' preachers by Spurgeon. 'Horton's book had caused alarm because it lacked the emphasis on evangelical theology that made higher criticism acceptable to the Nonconformists', said Glover. However, this may be termed a 'low-grade' controversy, and it just serves to show how 'higher criticism moved downward from scholars through pastors to the general religious public'.[29]

In 1880, according to Alfred Cave, 99 per cent of biblical scholars in England, Scotland and America accepted the Mosaic authorship of the

Pentateuch. 'Higher criticism did not get a foothold in England until after 1880', claims Glover. 'Before that time the reaction of the English to foreign criticism was almost wholly negative.'[30] However, he adds:

> The period between 1880 and 1887 did not see a mass capitulation to criticism, but it is important as a period when a large proportion of the foremost scholars, teachers, and denominational leaders either adopted a critical approach to the Bible themselves or learned to tolerate such an approach on the part of their colleagues.[31]

Glover explained its success in winning approval partly because of the weakness of conservative scholarship in England,[32] and also because fundamental doctrinal questions were not involved.[33]

A significant event in the history of Nonconformity was the opening of Mansfield College in Oxford in 1886, an event which coincided with the general recognition among both Nonconformist and Anglican scholars of the importance of biblical criticism. We are told that from the outset, its students were introduced to the critical 'scientific' study of the Bible. The principal, A. M. Fairbairn, arranged for his students to be taught by the recently appointed Old Testament Anglican scholars T. K. Cheyne and S. R. Driver (1846–1914), both exponents of the new German-influenced critical scholarship.[34] Among its early students and members of staff were two who were to become pre-eminent in Old Testament study – George Buchanan Gray and H. Wheeler Robinson; it is also to be noted that A. S. Peake began his teaching career at Mansfield (1891–93). In addition, George Adam Smith, the eminent Scottish Old Testament scholar, was a frequent visiting preacher and lecturer at Mansfield between 1894 and 1900.[35] Thus an atmosphere was formed which was receptive to the new criticism. A further indication that the critical method had been accepted in Britain was demonstrated by the *Cambridge Biblical Commentary*, which from the 1880s saw contributions from English and Scottish scholars of high quality.[36] They included *Isaiah 1–39* (1896) by the Presbyterian John Skinner.

It has been said that '[t]he Nonconformists produced no first-rate critics until near the end of the century',[37] but such scholars certainly emerged by then, one of whom was George Buchanan Gray (1865–1922). His most original publication *Studies in Hebrew Proper Names* (1896) 'is still cited as one of the most thorough treatments of the subject'.[38] He also produced *A Critical Introduction to the Old Testament* (1913) and *The Forms of Hebrew Poetry* (1915), and his treatment of *Sacrifice in the Old Testament* (1925), published after his death, is truly comprehensive in its scope. He also contributed two commentaries to the important *International Critical Commentary* series, *Numbers* (1903) and *Isaiah I–XXVII* (1912), as well as being responsible for the completion of S. R. Driver's Commentary on *The Book of Job* (1921). It has been well said that Buchanan Gray 'came to be recognized as the greatest Old Testament scholar of his generation in the English-speaking world'.[39]

Thus, attitudes among Nonconformists towards biblical criticism changed markedly in the last decade or so of the nineteenth century. Although penned a little later, the following words of W. H. Bennett (1855–1920) from the introduction to a volume entitled *The Bible and Criticism*, written jointly by him and W. F. Adeney (1848–1920), faithfully reflect the standpoint assumed by leading Nonconformist teachers in theological colleges by this time: 'Biblical Criticism is not to be equated with "finding" fault with the Bible.'[40] However, in the part he wrote about the Old Testament he conceded that 'in very wide circles [traditional or orthodox] views are still taken for granted; the presuppositions of popular religion can only be changed very slowly'.[41] Again, in the Preface to the volume of Essays by Congregationalists, *Faith and Criticism*,[42] the authors, among whom were both Bennett and Adeney, began by stating: 'The writers of these Essays have been drawn together and led to issue this volume by a strong desire to help those very numerous seekers after truth whose minds have been disturbed by the work of criticism in Biblical and Theological questions',[43] and end it by venturing 'to hope that their efforts may encourage the younger generation of inquirers to face bravely the necessary changes of theological development in the certainty that the essential truths of Christ and Christianity can never be shaken by criticism or discredited by growing knowledge'.[44] In his essay on the Old Testament Bennett reviewed what he perceived to be the beneficial outcomes of critical study of the Old Testament,[45] while Adeney, in his essay on the New Testament,[46] expressed his confidence that, after dialogue with conservative scholars, he and his ilk had gained 'a sure footing on the free soil of open discussion'.[47]

b. The New Testament

With respect to New Testament studies the most significant topic of debate, certainly in the first half of the nineteenth century, was the so-called Quest of the Historical Jesus. The origins of this quest lay at the end of the previous century. It was Hermann Samuel Reimarus (1694–1768), a Deist, who in his *Fragments*, published anonymously between 1774 and 1777 and after his death,[48] who set out the need to clarify the historical task of distinguishing between the proclamation by the historical Jesus and the preaching of the early church,[49] and had concluded that the Jesus of history differed substantially from the Christ of faith. It has been well said that after centuries of Christianity and a Christology which tended to put all the emphasis on the divine rather than the human nature of Christ, 'Reimarus' question about

Jesus' purpose for himself put Jesus back into the sphere of human history and asked how his life and teachings were related to the particular condition of Judaism at the time'.[50]

However, the life of Jesus which attracted most attention, and that usually of a hostile kind, was *Leben Jesu* published in two volumes in 1835–36 and written by David Friedrich Strauss (1808–74).[51] His greatest error in the eyes of his critics was to suggest rejection of the supernatural elements in Jesus' life and teaching, for which he employed the rather ambiguous term 'mythical'. The early Christians, he claimed, had devised myths about Jesus. His insistence on all sources being 'myth' 'made everything, without exception, historically uncertain'.[52] It was a young Unitarian Mary Anne Evans (later known as the novelist George Eliot) who was given the task of translating Strauss' work into English. Her stated unease with regard to the task is recorded, but it was completed by 1846.[53] Glover commented: 'Of all German criticism it was the writings of the more radical New Testament critics that first became widely known – or rather widely known about – in England. The translation of Strauss's *Leben Jesu* was the first real impact of higher criticism on England.'[54] A basic weakness in his methodology was his failure to address questions about the sources for the gospels and also to draw out a history of the development of primitive Christianity. These weaknesses, especially the latter, were comprehensively dealt with by Ferdinand Christian Baur (1792–1860) and the Tübingen school, who put forward the novel idea that a development of thought can be traced throughout the New Testament.[55]

Not unexpectedly, negative responses were voiced in Nonconformist circles with regard to the theories of Strauss and Baur, which were deemed to be wholly extreme, and Glover commented: 'After that England retired behind the protection of the conservative critics, the Cambridge trio, Godet, Charteris, Reynolds, Sanday, and others.'[56] However, by the final decade of the century, in a reference to Baur, Adeney could state:

> The inherent historicity of the New Testament in its description of the age of the Apostles is also becoming more apparent. This is seen in what is known as the Tübingen hypothesis. We owe much to Baur, the celebrated author of that hypothesis; the conservative school would have been wiser if it had calmly examined what he had to say and opened its eyes to the real discoveries he was making, instead of shouting itself hoarse in defence of every jot and tittle of its old uncritical opinions. To Baur we owe an incalculable debt of gratitude for teaching us to read the New Testament from the inside. He has shown us how to look for the minds of the writers, and how to detect the processes of thought out of which their writings grew.[57]

II. The Twentieth Century

By the beginning of the twentieth century the results of the surge in historical-critical scholarship of the Bible needed to be conveyed to a wider public, and Nonconformist scholars were in the vanguard in this task, and none more so than the Primitive Methodist Arthur Samuel Peake (1865–1929), who had begun his academic career in the service of two Congregational Colleges. In fact, his first book *A Guide to Biblical Study* (1897) sought to do this.[58] In this context, it is interesting to note that in a review of it in *The Times* there occurred the comment: 'The line of study suggested by it cannot well be neglected if the Church of England is to maintain herself at least upon a level with Nonconformist bodies in theological learning.'[59] Peake, says Ian Sellers in a reassessment of his work, 'saw the dichotomy in church life as that between fundamentalist ignorance and modern learning'.[60] An anonymous writer in the Peake Commemoration volume wrote in 1929:

> Perhaps it was Peake's greatest service, not merely to his own communion but to the whole religious life of England, that he helped to save us from a fundamental controversy such as that which had devastated large sections of the church in America. He knew the facts which modern study of the Bible had brought to light. He knew them and was frank and fearless in telling them, but he was also a simple and consistent believer in Jesus, and he let that be seen too.[61]

A lasting legacy of Peake's efforts at the dissemination of the fruits of biblical scholarship is the famous *Commentary* on the Bible bearing his name which, beginning in 1919, went through a number of editions and was resurrected later under the editorship of H. H. Rowley. He was succeeded in the John Rylands Chair of Biblical Criticism and Exegesis in the University of Manchester (incidentally, the only theological chair in England open at the time to Nonconformists[62]) by Charles Harold Dodd (1884–1973), a Congregationalist, born and brought up in Wrexham, north Wales, who like his predecessor concerned himself in his first major publication *The Authority of the Bible* (1928) with 'progressive revelation', that is, that the Bible records the character and purpose of God in the history and experience of man.[63]

G. B. Caird identified the principle of unity running through Dodd's work as 'the conviction that God is Lord of history, and that the Word of God spoken in scripture is so inextricably interwoven into the fabric of historical events that it can be let loose into the modern world in the fullness of its relevance and power only through historical criticism exercised with the utmost integrity and thoroughness'.[64] Throughout *The Authority of the Bible* Dodd laid heavy stress on the importance of the historical element in the Bible, and in particular on the way it relates to the life and ministry of Jesus Christ. In *History and the Gospel* (1938) he stressed the need to ask the historical question about the life, death and resurrection of Jesus. He recoiled from the nineteenth-century quest of the historical Jesus with its seeking after the bare facts of history. The gospels were written 'from faith to faith' he asserted.[65] However, he refused to follow Bultmann and his disciples in denying the importance of the historical Jesus for faith: 'We need not be so sceptical as some recent critics have shown themselves of the possibility of getting behind the early church to the real Jesus of history.'[66] His belief in the fundamental trustworthiness of the Synoptic traditions (and in part those of the Fourth Gospel as well) is nowhere better exemplified than in his last published work *The Founder of Christianity* (1970).[67] This little volume embodied his assured results in setting forth the 'Historical Jesus'.

In his work he embraced many of the insights of form-criticism, albeit in a much less negative way than that of such German pioneers of this method of studying the gospels as Bultmann.[68] Dodd turned their methods, as Caird put it, 'to more constructive use'.[69] In his essay on 'The Framework of the Gospel Narrative' he countered the arguments of the form-critics who had propounded the view that no credence could be placed on the Markan order of events regarding the ministry of Jesus with the view that 'in broad lines the Marcan order does represent a genuine succession of events within which movement and development can be traced'.[70]

Similarly the English Presbyterian Thomas W. Manson (1893–1958), Dodd's successor in the Rylands Chair at Manchester, believed that the gospel tradition could be used as respectable historical material and that eye-witness tradition could still be relied upon in assessing the value of the gospel narratives as history.[71] He also, in a justly famous lecture titled 'The Quest of the Historical Jesus – Continuing' reaffirmed the need for such a quest in the second half of the century,[72] and the Congregationalist G. B. Caird (1917–84), has been called the pioneer of the so-called Third Quest of the historical Jesus.[73] This is a description coined by N. T. Wright in 1992 of a quest that regards Jesus as an eschatological prophet and emphasizes his location in first-century Judaism.[74]

There flourished in the 1940s and 1950s the so-called Biblical Theology Movement. It has been noted that 'there were certainly significant groups within Britain – particularly from the Free Churches – which shared many of the goals and attitudes of the American Biblical Theology Movement'.[75] Undoubtedly Dodd may be counted among the precursors of this trend, for the idea of revelation through history was basic to it and it was also deemed to form the underlying basis of its inner unity.[76] Similarly a constant feature of Dodd's interpretation of the New Testament writings was his search for their unity, and indeed it was his emphasis on the kerygmatic unity of the New Testament which provided a major impetus to the growth of biblical theology itself.[77] This has to be seen as his personal reaction to the older liberal criticism with its emphasis on the search for sources and analysis of the material. 'In the end', he said of it, 'we were presented with a New Testament of bits and pieces. Each separate constituent was characterised and appreciated in depth, often to its great illumination, but they scarcely seemed to form a whole. The relation they bore to one another was obscure.'[78]

In *According to the Scriptures* (1952) he sought to demonstrate how the writers of the New Testament made use of the Old Testament scriptures, and how they favoured certain sections from the prophets and the psalms, with the whole context of such passages having to be taken into consideration. Such treatment of them formed what Dodd called 'the substructure of all Christian theology' and 'its chief regulative ideas'.[79]

Dodd also approached the question of the existence of a common tradition within the early church underlying the whole of the New Testament from another angle. It was here that he pointed to the common proclamation of the gospel message by the apostles and also to the ethical teaching common to various epistles of the New Testament. 'Broadly speaking', he said, 'we may recognise two aspects of this central tradition. On the one hand it is a preaching or proclamation (*kerygma*) about God's action for the salvation of men . . . On the other hand, it embodies an ethical ideal for a corporate and individual life. The most general term for this is "teaching" (*didache*).'[80] Dodd himself called the *kerygma* the 'ground-plan of New Testament theology'. In his pioneering work *The Apostolic Preaching and Its Developments* (1936), he set out the main elements in the preaching or proclamation (*kerygma*) of the early church, which he reconstructed on the basis of the relevant contents of Paul's epistles, the pattern being repeated, it was claimed, in the early speeches of the book of Acts.[81] He also believed that a common practice of ethical teaching from a very early period in the history of the church could be traced in the epistles.

a. The Old Testament

Throughout the twentieth century Old Testament studies in England and Wales has been to a large extent dominated by Baptist scholars, whose contributions now come under review. I shall concentrate on four of them: Harold Henry Rowley (1890–1969), Henry Wheeler Robinson (1872–1945), Theodore H. Robinson (1881–1964) and Aubrey R. Johnson (1901–85).

Since he was a proponent of the Biblical Theology movement, the unity of the Bible was a recurring theme in Rowley's publications,[82] as was the need to recover a theological dimension to the Bible and to restate its contemporary relevance for people in the modern world:[83] 'No single word seems more cogently to express Rowley's belief in the evangelical message of the Old Testament, or the purpose of the scholar's task, than does this one word *relevance.*'[84] It has been said that 'Rowley was at his best in the disentangling of complex critical problems where the proliferation of rival views had tended to obscure the essentials',[85] and that his many critical surveys of outstanding Old Testament problems 'were notable for their lucid analysis of the issues involved, their comprehensive documentation, their unbiased presentation of the views of other scholars, and the combination of caution and sound judgement with which the conclusions were presented'.[86]

Rowley understood his work to be in direct continuity with that of his mentor Wheeler Robinson,[87] principal of the Baptist Regent's Park College, Oxford, whose concept of 'corporate personality' influenced not only studies of the Old Testament but also topics in New Testament studies such as the concept of the church in Paul. He first used the phrase 'corporate personality' in his book *The Christian Doctrine of Man* (1911), and his essay titled 'Hebrew Psychology in Relation to Pauline Anthropology'[88] contained *in nuce* some of the ideas later developed in his influential paper 'Corporate Personality',[89] which has been called 'a classic of British Old Testament scholarship'.[90]

He defined what he meant by it thus: 'Corporate personality means for us in this place the treatment of the family, clan, or the nation, as the unit in place of the individual.'[91] Thus the concept 'recognized the social solidarity of the ancient Hebrew people in their relation to God, emphasizing the singular identity of individual, family, clan and nation. Corporate personality means that in community the individual has meaning only in relation to the group.'[92] The conception 'largely removes the sharp antithesis between the collective and the individualistic views'.[93] Thus, it has been claimed that, along with the Danish scholar Johannes Pedersen and A. R. Johnson, 'he opened up a new vista on the Old Testament world that proved immensely exciting to his contemporaries'.[94] Despite trenchant criticism of his standpoint, it is unlikely the term 'corporate personality' will disappear without trace from scholarly writing.[95]

The concept of corporate personality attracted the attention of New Testament scholars also, and in particular T. W. Manson, who applied it to the term Son of man in the gospels. So the corporate interpretation of this expression is usually associated with Manson, although he was by no means the first scholar in history to have adopted it.[96] It is based on the portrayal of the 'one like a son of man' in Dan. 7.13, who is generally understood to be a symbolic figure representing the 'saints of the Most High', that is, the kingdom or people of God.[97] For Manson the Son of man is 'an ideal figure and stands for the manifestation of the Kingdom of God on earth in a people wholly devoted to their heavenly king'.[98] The term becomes a designation of Jesus alone when his mission to create the Son of man, the kingdom of God's people, succeeds neither among the people nor among his disciples. Then he stands alone, embodying in his own person the perfect human response to the regal claims of God.[99] However, his view has not been in the main acceptable.[100]

Wheeler Robinson also contributed substantially to our understanding of the primitive Semitic idea of man. In it 'there is', he wrote, 'no distinction of the psychical and ethical from the physical, so that the actual breath of man can be thought of as his "soul", and the reek of hot blood identified with this "breath-soul"'.[101] 'This breath-soul is conceived as the animating principle of man's life, its essential constituent.'[102] Thus 'there is no trichotomy in Hebrew psychology, no triple division of human personality into body, soul and spirit'.[103] Man is no 'immortal soul, imprisoned in a body', but an interreaction of 'breath-soul, spirit and the body with its various organs', that is in short, 'an animated body'.[104]

According to R. A. Mason, another in the distinguished line of Baptist Old Testament scholars, the most important contribution of Wheeler Robinson was his suggestion of how divine inspiration works: he called it the 'invasion' of the human personality by the Spirit of God.[105] He developed his ideas about revelation through the Spirit in his *The Christian Experience of the Holy Spirit* (1928),[106] and concluded that the only real spiritual authority was intrinsic, an intuitive response to the inward working of the Spirit.[107]

Theodore Henry Robinson is particularly known for a number of textbooks. In co-operation with the Anglican W. O. E. Oesterley, he produced *Hebrew Religion: Its Origin and Development* (1930); *A History of Israel* in two volumes, he himself being responsible for the first volume: *The Exodus to the Fall of Jerusalem* (1932), and *An Introduction to the Books of the Old Testament* (1934). Not unexpectedly, Old Testament studies had by later in the twentieth century superseded a number of standpoints set forth in these volumes and certainly by the end of the century Old Testament scholars had cast doubt on the very notion of a 'history of Israel'.

Undoubtedly T. H. Robinson's most important contribution was to the study of the prophets. Rowley in a survey of the study of Old Testament prophecy stated that no contemporary British scholar had contributed more towards an understanding of the prophets.[108] Indeed he pioneered two aspects of these studies in particular by emphasizing the ecstatic element in prophecy and by suggesting how the prophetic oracles were transmitted and committed in writing in the literature of the Old Testament.[109] In the preface to his volume *Prophecy and the Prophets in Ancient Israel* (1923) he claimed that it was he, along with John Skinner of Westminster College, Cambridge, in his book on Jeremiah, *Prophecy and Religion* (1922), who had presented the new ideas from Germany to the English-speaking world about the psychology of the prophets, although, he claimed, 'some of the greatest of British Old Testament scholars still deny that there was any ecstatic element in the life of the canonical prophets'. The volume itself lay great store by this element in prophecy, although there is little doubt that Robinson exaggerated the ecstatic element in prophecy.[110]

T. H. Robinson was succeeded in the Semitics chair in Cardiff by one of his former pupils, Aubrey R. Johnson, whose main contribution to Old Testament scholarship lies in the study of the psalms. Following the innovative work of Hermann Gunkel and Sigmund Mowinckel in interpreting the psalms in the context of worship, liturgy and the cult of the Jerusalem temple, Johnson concentrated on the place of the king in worship, naming the main festival 'the Festival of Kingship'. After delineating the close connection between the king in Israel and the cult, as it is portrayed in the historical books of the Old Testament,[111] he followed Gunkel in demonstrating that some psalms, namely the 'Royal Cult-Songs', portray particular events in the Enthronement Festival of the King.[112] However, Mowinckel and Johnson went further in their researches and sought to uncover a form of divine or 'sacral' kingship in Israel, with Johnson himself preferring the neutral term 'sacral kingship' to the more common term 'divine kingship'.[113] He described the ritual drama in which the kings or nations of the earth who represent the forces of darkness and death oppose the representatives of light and life, the king of Israel and his people. The king is sometimes referred to as the Son, the Servant, and the Messiah of the Lord, and it is upon him that the whole nation depends for its welfare as a whole.[114]

Ronald E. Clements, also a Baptist, has suggested that a result of studies such as those of Johnson 'has been a better understanding of the nature and significance of a number of passages in the prophetic books which refer to a future king, and which have loosely been regarded as messianic'.[115] Johnson's standpoint, however, was not without its critics among whom was the Methodist Christopher R. North, who concluded: 'There is little evidence for the conception of "the divinity of the king" in ancient Israel; indeed, such evidence as we have seems definitely to point against it.'[116]

Following Mowinckel again, Johnson sought to show the role of cultic prophets in Israel. He claimed they were present at all the sanctuaries of Yahweh, but especially in the Jerusalem Temple. They stood side by side with the priests and played as important a part as they in it.[117] In his final published work *The Cultic Prophet and Israel's Psalmody* (1979),[118] Johnson tried to reconstruct the activities and aims, with their setting in a festival, of the cultic prophets, deriving the picture from a detailed study of many psalms. This work, which was a long time in gestation, has not on the whole been favourably received.[119]

Stimulated by the work of Johannes Pedersen,[120] Johnson contributed extensively to our understanding of the psychology of the Israelites. In his monograph *The One and the Many in the Israelite Conception of God* (1942, second edition 1961), a work greatly influenced by Wheeler Robinson's notion of 'corporate personality', he described the natural movement from the individual to the group or the many in common parlance about man and about God. An extension in God's personality is found in the Spirit, the Word, the Name, and the Ark,[121] and at the end of this study Johnson recommended its value as a new way towards the doctrine of the Trinity.[122]

In his monograph *The Vitality of the Individual in the Thought of Ancient Israel* (1949, second edition 1964), he discussed every example in the Old Testament of terms relating to man.[123] Such a study could have been tedious to read, but in reality the author succeeded in making it remarkably lively and interesting, especially as he associated the Hebrew words and expressions with English colloquialisms. Throughout these discussions Johnson sought, in the tradition of Wheeler Robinson, to picture the Hebrew notion of man as a psychosomatic unity rather than in dualistic terms as a body and soul.

In 1970 the German Old Testament scholar Klaus Koch published *Ratlos vor der Apokalyptik* (which might be rendered 'Clueless or Perplexed with regard to Apocalyptic'). It pointed to the comparative neglect of apocalyptic literature in German circles over much of the century. The English translation of this work was called *The Rediscovery of Apocalyptic*.[124] H. H. Rowley has been credited with reviving interest in this form of literature. Indeed, his book on the subject was titled *The Relevance of Apocalyptic* (1944),[125] and later another Baptist David S. Russell produced a comprehensive study of Jewish Apocalyptic literature.[126] It is remarkable that this literary form was so long neglected by biblical scholars during the twentieth century, especially when one recalls how the century had begun in a blaze of interest in the subject. In particular Johannes Weiss and Albert Schweitzer had set an agenda for New Testament study in the very first decade of the century in which the eschatological Kingdom of God was believed to be central to the teaching of Jesus.

b. The New Testament

It must be remembered, however, that Weiss and Albert Schweitzer (in his famous *The Quest of the Historical Jesus*) had emphasized one side of the Jewish hope about the Kingdom, namely the supernatural element.[127] It was as a reaction to Schweitzer's views that C. H. Dodd developed his ideas about eschatology, and he did so in the context of his study of Jesus' parables of the kingdom, setting out his evidence for the concept which is usually linked with him, namely 'realized eschatology'. Indeed, the term was first used by him in his book *The Parables of the Kingdom* (1935).[128] There are passages in the synoptic gospels, he claimed, which demonstrated that

> in the earliest tradition Jesus was understood to have proclaimed that the Kingdom of God . . . had come. It is not merely imminent, it

> is here . . . Whatever we make of them the sayings which declare the Kingdom of God to have come are explicit and unequivocal. They are moreover the most characteristic and distinctive of the Gospel sayings on the subject. They have no parallel in Jewish teaching or prayers of the period. If therefore we are seeking the *differentia* of the teaching of Jesus upon the Kingdom of God, it is here that it must be found.[129]

However, in countering the over-emphasis of Weiss[130] and Schweitzer[131] upon the futurist element in the eschatological teaching of Jesus, Dodd probably went too far in the opposite direction when emphasizing that the Kingdom had come with power, and appeared to lose sight of the real futurist element in Jesus' teaching. In fact, in stressing the 'realized eschatology' in Jesus' teaching, he claimed that those sayings which imply a future Kingdom of God did not refer to a future coming in this world, but rather to something beyond time and space.[132] Later, in *The Coming of Christ* (1951) he talked of expectation passing into realization and of realization in turn kindling fresh expectancy: 'There is always more to hope for', he claimed.[133] Furthermore, the Second Coming refers to 'a coming beyond history: definitely, I should say, *beyond* history, and not a further event *in* history, not even the last event'.[134] However, his views on the matter appear to have mellowed over the years, so that G. B. Caird could claim, 'he soon made the necessary adjustments and declared his belief that the New Testament eschatology was summed up in the Johannine phrase "the time is coming and now is"'.[135] So despite the many criticisms of his concept of a 'realized eschatology', nothing can detract from the fact that, in the words of one of the most radical of twentieth-century Nonconformist scholars, the Baptist Norman Perrin, this has been deemed 'the most important single contribution made to the Anglo-American discussion of Kingdom of God in the teaching of Jesus'.[136]

However, history's verdict on Dodd who, it has been claimed, 'is by any account the most influential of twentieth century British scholars' in the field of New Testament studies,[137] may well direct us to his contribution as a Johannine scholar.[138] His second magnum opus on John's Gospel *Historical Tradition in the Fourth Gospel* (1963)[139] greatly influenced a trend towards what has been termed the 'New Look on the Fourth Gospel' with its emphasis on the historical value of the Johannine narrative.[140] His main conclusion arising from a detailed study of *Historical Tradition in the Fourth Gospel* was that behind this gospel there 'lies an ancient oral tradition independent of the other gospels, and meriting serious consideration as a contribution to our knowledge of the historical facts concerning Jesus Christ'.[141]

In his earlier volume *The Interpretation of the Fourth Gospel* (1953)[142] Dodd provided a wide-ranging examination of possible backgrounds to the thought of the gospel. In an article published some years before this volume appeared he had written: 'The Evangelist shows himself to be deeply versed in Judaism . . . His mind moves with equal freedom in the Jewish and in the Hellenistic ways of thought . . . as though both were native to him, so that they are deeply fused into a theology that is neither Jewish nor Greek, but intelligible from both sides.'[143] It has been aptly said that Dodd's 'writings are a mirror of the transition which has marked our time from a predominantly Hellenistic to a more Semitic approach to the New Testament'.[144] That was a tribute to him by the Welsh Congregationalist William D. Davies (1911–2001), a student of his at Cambridge, who in his first major study *Paul and Rabbinic Judaism* (1948),[145] published while he was lecturing in the Yorkshire United Independent College, Bradford, before he emigrated to the United States, located Paul firmly within the context of first-century Judaism. It was in its own right a highly influential work and delineated clearly Paul's religious background in the first century of the Christian era.

In the letter dedicatory in the *Festschrift* presented to him in 1954[146] Dodd was called 'a prince of exegetes'. Nowhere are these exegetical gifts better exemplified than in his attempts to expound the teaching of the Apostle Paul. The title of his earliest published volume *The Meaning of Paul for Today* (1920) showed his constant concern to make the New Testament relevant to modern contemporary life. Likewise his lucid commentary on *The Epistle of Paul to the Romans* (1932) in *The Moffatt New Testament Commentary* series exhibited a similar concern to make scripture relevant: 'The task of the commentator', he maintained, is 'to try to discover as exactly as possible what Paul meant, in his own terms'.[147]

It has not been in the nature of British scholars, unlike their counterparts in Germany, to form themselves into schools as followers of a particular scholar or viewpoint.[148] However, if, as has frequently been said, Bultmann's influence was the dominating one in New Testament scholarship in Germany and the United States over the greater part of the twentieth century, it can legitimately be claimed that it was Dodd's influence which was the guiding one in the United Kingdom.

Outside the world of scholarship he will probably be most remembered for his work in connection with *The New English Bible*. He was appointed general director of the project in 1947 and held this position for over twenty years, seeing the task through from inception to completion. The New Testament was published in 1961 and the Old Testament with the Apocrypha in 1970. In a tribute to him published in *The Times* after his death, Donald Coggan, who became chairman of the Joint Committee, recalled what he had written in his preface to the complete Bible: 'As director, Dr. Dodd gave outstanding leadership and guidance to the project, bringing to the work scholarship, sensitivity, and an ever watchful eye.'[149] It is also necessary to record the considerable contribution of other Nonconformists from England and Wales to *The New English Bible*. Of the eleven members of the Old Testament panel, six were Nonconformists, two out of seven of the Apocrypha panel, and three out of nine members of the New Testament panel.[150]

Nonconformity throughout the twentieth century produced Pauline scholars of the very highest order. Besides Dodd and Davies, we could name G. B. Caird, C. E. B. Cranfield, C. K. Barrett and F. F. Bruce. The latter two in particular produced major commentaries on the Pauline corpus of letters and in addition volumes on the apostle's thought and circumstances.[151] At the end of the century James Dunn published a massive study of his thought *The Theology of Paul the Apostle* (1998).[152]

The middle part of the twentieth century has been termed by J. Munsey Turner 'the golden age of Free Church scholarship'. He continued: 'The glory of our theology is the ability of scholars to be "middle men" between research work and the preacher, teacher and worshipper. Peake and Dodd were supreme here.'[153] Both had held the Rylands Chair in Manchester. Its occupant between 1959 and 1978 was the Scotsman Frederick Fyvie Bruce (1910–90), a member of the Open Brethren, who spent the whole of his academic life in England. He too, like his predecessors in that chair, made an immense contribution in writing on the whole span of the Bible for a popular audience as well as for scholars. Coming as he did from a religiously conservative background it was his particular contribution to demonstrate 'to his fellow-evangelicals that biblical criticism can help them understand the Bible better and lead to positive conclusions as well as negative ones'.[154] Howard Marshall claimed: 'It is not too much to say that [Bruce's Commentary on the Greek text of *The Acts of the Apostles* (1951)[155]] marked the real beginning of conservative evangelical scholarship',[156] and '[i]n all this Bruce was something of a bridge-builder between different schools of scholarship'.[157] His biographer states that 'he paved the way for widespread evangelical acceptance of critical methodologies as having a part to play in reverent and submissive biblical study, and for wider academic acceptance of evangelicals as genuine scholars'.[158]

Thus we appear to return at the end of the twentieth century to a situation very similar to that prevailing at the end of the nineteenth century when critical scholarship was really taking hold on Nonconformity in England and Wales. Similar sentiments were being voiced in both epochs and the leading Nonconformist biblical scholars of both periods were acutely aware of the danger of perpetuating the chasm in understanding with regard to biblical interpretation between their publications, on the one hand, and believers in general, on the other. They too strove might and main to be bridge-builders in overcoming these difficulties.

Notes

1 John W. Rogerson, 'The Bible and Theology', in David Fergusson (ed.), *The Blackwell Companion to Nineteenth-Century Theology* (Chichester: Wiley-Blackwell, 2010), p. 455.
2 J. W. Rogerson, *Old Testament Criticism in the Nineteenth Century: England and Germany* (London: SPCK, 1984), p. 158.
3 Ibid., p. 162.
4 For the conservative reactions in Wales see R. Tudur Jones, 'Astudio'r Hen Destament yng Nghymru, 1860–1890', in Gwilym H. Jones (ed.), *Efrydiau Beiblaidd Bangor 2* (Swansea: Gwasg John Penry,1977), pp. 153–65, 169–71. For England see Willis B. Glover Jr, *Evangelical Nonconformists and Higher Criticism in the Nineteenth Century* (London: Independent Press, 1954), pp. 41–43.
5 Glover, *Evangelical Nonconformists*, p. 36.
6 Rogerson, 'The Bible and Theology', p. 461; cf. also idem, *Old Testament Criticism*, pp. 197–202. For further accounts of the whole affair see Glover, *Evangelical Nonconformists*, pp. 44–47, who attributes Davidson's dismissal to his holding too loose a view of biblical inspiration. Cf. also F. Roger Tomes, '"We Are Hardly Prepared for This Style of Teaching Yet": Samuel Davidson and Lancashire Independent College', *Journal of the United Reformed Church History Society*, 5/7 (1995), pp. 400–2, and idem, 'Samuel Davidson and William Robertson Smith: Parallel Cases?', in William Johnstone (ed.), *William Robertson Smith: Essays in Reassessment* (Sheffield: Sheffield Academic Press, 1995), pp. 67–77; Elaine Kaye, *For the Work of Ministry: A History of Northern College and Its Predecessors* (Edinburgh: T&T Clark, 1999), pp. 80–85.
7 Rogerson, *Old Testament Criticism*, p. 202.
8 Tomes, '"We Are Hardly Prepared"', p. 411.
9 Leslie Peake, *Arthur Samuel Peake: A Memoir* (London: Hodder and Stoughton, 1930), p. 132, quoting Robert Mackintosh.
10 See Rogerson, *Old Testament Criticism*, pp. 209–19; Ieuan Ellis, '*Essays and Reviews*', in R. J. Coggins and J. L. Houlden (ed.), *A Dictionary of Biblical Interpretation* (London: SCM, 1990), pp. 203–4.
11 For Colenso, see Rogerson, *Old Testament Criticism*, pp. 220–37.
12 See Glover, *Evangelical Nonconformists*, pp. 48–52; 54–55. For Welsh Nonconformist reactions, see R. Tudur Jones, 'Astudio'r Hen Destament yng Nghymru, 1860–1890', pp. 150–53.
13 Edward Ball, 'W. Robertson Smith', in *A Dictionary of Biblical Interpretation*, p. 633. See also Rogerson, *Old Testament Criticism*, pp. 275–81.
14 W. Robertson Smith, *The Old Testament in the Jewish Church* (2nd edn, London: Adam and Charles Black, 1892), p. 16.
15 Ibid., pp. 1–20.
16 Rogerson, 'The Bible and Theology', p. 465.
17 Glover, *Evangelical Nonconformists*, pp. 59–61.
18 Rogerson, 'The Bible and Theology', p. 465.
19 Whitehouse, quoted by Glover, *Evangelical Nonconformists*, p. 61.
20 Ibid., pp. 125–26.
21 Cf. ibid., p. 34. See A. Duff, *On the History of the Idea of the Atonement* (Bradford, 1881), pp. 2–3.
22 Glover, *Evangelical Nonconformists*, p. 111.
23 Ibid., pp. 111–12.
24 Ibid., p. 112; cf. also Kaye, *For the Work of Ministry*, pp. 130–31.
25 Glover, *Evangelical Nonconformists*, pp. 164–76.
26 Ibid., p. 174.

27 For an account of the whole matter see ibid., pp. 163–76.
28 See ibid., pp. 176–84.
29 Ibid., p.184.
30 Ibid., p. 36. Cf. Rogerson, *Old Testament Criticism*, p. 219.
31 Glover, *Evangelical Nonconformists*, p. 110; cf. pp. 37, 157, 161.
32 Ibid., pp. 71, 184–85.
33 Ibid., pp. 110, 162.
34 Elaine Kaye, *Mansfield College,Oxford: Its Origin, History and Significance* (Oxford: Oxford University Press, 1996), p. 117.
35 Ibid., p. 118.
36 Rogerson, 'The Bible and Theology', p. 466; cf. idem, *Old Testament Criticism*, pp. 286–87. For the increasingly favourable reception of biblical criticism in Wales see Gwilym H. Jones, 'Beirniadaeth yr Hen Destament yng Nghymru oddeutu tro'r ganrif (1890–1914)', in E. Stanley John (ed.), *Y Gair a'r Genedl: Cyfrol Deyrnged i R. Tudur Jones* (Swansea: Gwasg John Penry, 1986), pp. 63–78.
37 Glover, *Evangelical Nonconformists*, p. 134.
38 F. Roger Tomes, 'George Buchanan Gray', in John Taylor and Clyde Binfield (eds), *Who They Were in the Reformed Churches of England and Wales 1901–2000* (Donnington: Shaun Tyas/United Reformed Church History Society, 2007), p. 82.
39 Kaye, *Mansfield College*, p. 122; cf. also pp. 156–57; Glover, *Evangelical Nonconformists*, p. 212.
40 W. H. Bennett and W. F. Adeney, *The Bible and Criticism* (London: T. C. and E. C. Jack, n.d.), p. vii.
41 Ibid., p. 9.
42 Bennett et al., *Faith and Criticism: Congregationalist Symposium* (London: Sampson, Low Marston and Co., 1893).
43 Ibid., p. v.
44 Ibid., p. vi.
45 Ibid., pp. 1–17.
46 Ibid., pp. 51–93.
47 Ibid., pp. 66–67. Adeney was the editor of The Century Bible series of critical commentaries to which a number of Nonconformist scholars contributed.
48 For an English edition of the work see C. H. Talbert (ed.), *Reimarus: Fragments*, trans. R. S. Fraser (London: SCM, 1971).
49 W. G. Kümmel, *The New Testament: The History of the Investigation of Its Problems*, trans. S. McLean Gilmour and Howard C. Kee (London: SCM, 1973), p. 90.
50 J. K. Riches, 'Lessing as Editor of Reimarus' Apologie', in E. A. Livingstone (ed.), *Studia Biblica 1978, II, Papers on the Gospels* (Sheffield: JSOT Press, 1980), p. 251.
51 See further Kümmel, *The New Testament*, pp. 120–27; Stephen Neill, *The Interpretation of the New Testament,1861–1961* (London: Oxford University Press, 1966), pp. 12–19.
52 Karl Barth, *Protestant Theology in the Nineteenth Century: Its Background and History*, trans. Brian Cozens and John Bowden (London: SCM, 1972), p. 560.
53 See Glover, *Evangelical Nonconformists*, p. 38; Neill, *The Interpretation of the New Testament*, p. 17 n.1; Rogerson, *Old Testament Criticism*, p. 250; idem, 'The Bible and Theology', p. 458.
54 Glover, *Evangelical Nonconformists*, p. 38.
55 Kümmel, *The New Testament*, p. 141.
56 Glover, *Evangelical Nonconformists*, pp. 29–30; cf. also pp. 63–64.
57 Adeney in *The Bible and Criticism*, p. 65.
58 Cf. John T. Wilkinson, *Arthur Samuel Peake: A Biography* (London: Epworth, 1971), pp. 86–88. For a fuller account of Nonconformist biblical scholarship in the twentieth century, see J. Tudno Williams, 'The Contribution of Protestant Nonconformists to Biblical Scholarship in the Twentieth Century', in Alan P. F. Sell and Anthony

R. Cross (eds), *Protestant Nonconformity in the Twentieth Century* (Carlisle: Paternoster, 2003), pp. 1–32.

59 *The Times* (21 October 1897), quoted by Wilkinson, *Arthur Samuel Peake*, p. 88.

60 Ian Sellers, 'A. S. Peake Reconsidered', *Epworth Review*, 24/4 (1997), p. 83.

61 John T. Wilkinson (ed.), *A .S. Peake, 1865–1929: Essays in Commemoration* (London: Epworth, 1958), p. 12.

62 Kaye, *Mansfield College,Oxford*, p. 177.

63 Wilkinson, *Arthur Samuel Peake*, p. 93. For Dodd's discussion of the term see his *The Authority of the Bible* (rev. edn, London: Fontana, 1960), pp. 248–63. Cf. idem, *The Bible Today* (Cambridge: Cambridge University Press, 1956), p. 98.

64 G. B. Caird, 'C. H. Dodd', in M. E. Marty and D. G. Perman (eds), *A Handbook of Christian Theologians* (Cambridge: Lutterworth, 1984), p. 321.

65 Dodd, *History and the Gospel* (London: Nisbet, 1938), p. 14.

66 Dodd, *Authority*, p. 215; cf. also his *The Apostolic Preaching and Its Developments* (new edn, London: Hodder and Stoughton, 1956), p. 56.

67 Dodd, *The Founder of Christianity* (London: Fontana Books, 1973).

68 For Dodd's remarks on form-criticism see his inaugural lecture as Norris-Hulse Professor at Cambridge, *The Present Task in New Testament Studies* (Cambridge: Cambridge University Press, 1936), pp. 19–22, and idem, *History and the Gospel*, pp. 91–103.

69 Caird, 'Dodd', p. 324.

70 Dodd, 'The Framework of the Gospel Narrative', *The Expository Times*, XLIII (1932), p. 400.

71 T. W. Manson, *Studies in the Gospels and Epistles*, ed. Matthew Black (Manchester: Manchester University Press, 1962), pp. 6, 40–42.

72 The lecture is reproduced in *Studies in the Gospels*, pp. 3–12.

73 Cf. Mark A. Powell, *The Jesus Debate: Modern Historians Investigate the Life of Christ* (Oxford: Lion, 1999), p. 200 n.35. Cf. James Barr, 'Obituary of G. B. Caird', *Proceedings of the British Academy*, 71 (1985), pp. 504–5.

74 N. T. Wright, 'Quest for the Historical Jesus', in D. N. Freedman (ed.), *Anchor Bible Dictionary* (New York: Doubleday, 1992), III, pp. 796–802.

75 Brevard S. Childs, *Biblical Theology in Crisis* (Philadelphia: Westminster Press, 1970), p. 26.

76 Barr, *Explorations in Theology 7: The Scope and Authority of the Bible* (London: SCM, 1980), pp. 4–5.

77 See W. D. Davies' tribute to Dodd, 'In Memoriam Charles Harold Dodd, 1884–1973', *New Testament Studies*, 20 (1973–74), p. iii.

78 Dodd in his Introduction to P. Gardner-Smith (ed.), *The Roads Converge: A Contribution to the Question of Christian Reunion* (London: Edward Arnold, 1963), p. 4.

79 Dodd, *According to the Scriptures: The Sub-structure of New Testament Theology* (London: Fontana, 1952), p. 127; cf. p. 27.

80 Dodd, *History and the Gospel*, p. 50. He propounded his theory about the *Kerygma* in *The Apostolic Preaching*, and that on the *Didache* in *Gospel and Law: The Relation of Faith and Ethics in Early Christianity* (Cambridge: Cambridge University Press, 1951).

81 This theory has been heavily criticized: see, e.g., H. J. Cadbury, 'Acts and Eschatology', in W. D. Davies and D. Daube (eds), *The Background of the New Testament and Its Eschatology: Studies in Honour of C. H. Dodd* (Cambridge: Cambridge University Press, 1954), pp. 313–20; C. F. Evans, 'The Kerygma', *Journal of Theological Studies*, VII (1956), pp. 26–41; J. P. M. Sweet, 'Second Thoughts: viii. The Kerygma', *The Expository Times*, LXXVI (1964/5), pp. 143–47. More recently, James D. G. Dunn, *Unity and Diversity in the New Testament: An Inquiry into the Character of Earliest Christianity* (London: SCM, 1977), pp. 11–32, has suggested we should think rather of *kerygmata* in the plural.

82 Cf. Harold H. Rowley, *The Unity of the Bible* (London: Carey Kingsgate Press, 1953). Cf. Henning Graf Reventlow, *Problems of Biblical Theology in the Twentieth Century*, trans. John Bowden (London: SCM, 1986), pp. 4–5.
83 Cf. Rowley, *The Relevance of the Bible* (London: James Clarke, 1942); idem, *The Rediscovery of the Old Testament* (London: James Clarke, 1945).
84 Ronald E. Clements, 'The Biblical Scholarship of H. H. Rowley (1890–1969)', *Baptist Quarterly*, 38/2 (1999), p. 77.
85 George W. Anderson, 'Obituary of Harold Henry Rowley, 1890–1969', *Proceedings of the British Academy*, 56 (1970), p. 316.
86 Ibid., p. 314. Three volumes of Rowley's essays were published: *The Servant of the Lord and Other Essays on the Old Testament* (London: Lutterworth, 1952); *From Moses to Qumran: The Authority of the Bible and Other Major Issues in Old Testament Studies* (London: Lutterworth, 1963); *Men of God: Studies in Old Testament History and Prophecy* (London: Nelson, 1963).
87 Childs, *Biblical Theology in Crisis*, p. 24.
88 H. Wheeler Robinson, 'Hebrew Psychology in Relation to Pauline Anthropology', in W. B. Selbie (ed.), *Mansfield College Essays: Presented to the Reverend Andrew Martin Fairbairn, D.D., on the Occasion of His Seventieth Birthday* (London: Hodder and Stoughton, 1909), pp. 265–86.
89 Cf. John Reumann in 'Introduction' to the second edition of *Corporate Personality* (Edinburgh: T&T Clark, 1981), p. 20.
90 By Cyril S. Rodd in 'Introduction', ibid., p. 7.
91 Wheeler Robinson, 'Hebrew Psychology', in A. S. Peake (ed.), *The People and the Book: Essays on the Old Testament* (Oxford: Clarendon, 1925), p. 376.
92 R. A. Coughenour, 'Henry Wheeler Robinson', in Donald K. McKim (ed.), *Historical Handbook of Major Biblical Interpreters* (Leicester: IVP, 1998), p. 516.
93 Wheeler Robinson, *Corporate Personality*, p. 38.
94 Rodd in *Corporate Personality*, p. 14.
95 Cf. ibid., pp. 8, 14. For the criticisms, see J. R. Porter, 'The Legal Aspects of the Concept of "Corporate Personality" in the Old Testament', *Vetus Testamentum*, XV (1965), pp. 361–80; J. W. Rogerson, 'The Hebrew Conception of Corporate Personality: A Re-Examination', *Journal of Theological Studies*, (ns) 21 (1970), pp. 1–16.
96 Cf. Delbert Burkett, *The Son of Man Debate: A History and Evaluation* (Cambridge: Cambridge University Press, 1999), pp. 35–37.
97 Manson, *Studies in the Gospels and Epistles*, pp. 126–27. Cf. Wheeler Robinson, *Corporate Personality*, pp. 29–30.
98 Manson, *The Teaching of Jesus* (2nd edn, Cambridge: Cambridge University Press, 1935), p. 227.
99 Ibid., p. 228.
100 Cf., e.g., Barnabas Lindars, *Jesus Son of Man* (London: SPCK, 1983), p. 215; Burkett, *The Son of Man Debate*, p. 37.
101 Wheeler Robinson, 'Hebrew Psychology', p. 353.
102 Ibid., p. 357.
103 Ibid., p. 362.
104 Wheeler Robinson, 'Hebrew Psychology in Relation to Pauline Anthropology', p. 277. Cf. also 'Hebrew Psychology', p. 362.
105 Rex A. Mason, 'H. Wheeler Robinson Revisited', *Baptist Quarterly*, 37/5 (1998), p. 220.
106 London: Nisbet, 1928.
107 Wheeler Robinson, *Redemption and Revelation in the Actuality of History* (London: Nisbet, 1942), p. 165. Cf. Mason, 'H. Wheeler Robinson Revisited', p. 222.

108 Rowley, *The Servant of the Lord*, p. 92 n.6.
109 Cf. C. R. North, 'Living Issues in Biblical Scholarship: The Place of Oral Tradition in the Growth of the Old Testament', *The Expository Times*, LXI (1949/50), p. 293; Otto Eissfeldt, 'The Prophetic Literature', in Rowley (ed.), *The Old Testament and Modern Study* (Oxford: Clarendon, 1951), p. 126.
110 Rowley, *The Servant of the Lord*, pp. 96–102.
111 Cf. A. R. Johnson, 'Living Issues in Biblical Scholarship: Divine Kingship and the Old Testament', *The Expository Times*, LXII (1950/51), p. 37; idem, 'Hebrew Conceptions of Kingship', in S. H. Hooke (ed.), *Myth, Ritual and Kingship: Essays on the Theory and Practice of Kingship in Ancient Israel* (Oxford: Clarendon, 1958), pp. 204–35.
112 Cf. Johnson, 'Divine Kingship', 36–37; idem, 'The Psalms' in *The Old Testament and Modern Study*, pp. 167–68; idem, *Sacral Kingship in Ancient Israel* (Cardiff: University of Wales Press, 1955), passim; idem, 'Hebrew Conceptions', pp. 204–35.
113 Johnson, 'Divine Kingship', p. 41.
114 Johnson, 'The Psalms', pp. 196–97; cf. also 'Divine Kingship and the Old Testament', pp. 37–40.
115 R. E. Clements, *A Century of Old Testament Study* (rev. edn, Cambridge: Lutterworth, 1983), p. 108.
116 North, *The Old Testament Interpretation of History* (London: Epworth, 1946), p. 123.
117 Johnson, *The Cultic Prophet in Ancient Israel* (Cardiff: University of Wales Press, 1944). Rowley disagreed with this position: cf. his *Worship in Ancient Israel: Its Forms and Meaning* (London: SPCK, 1967), pp. 171–72.
118 Cardiff: University of Wales Press, 1979.
119 Cf. Clements, *A Century of Old Testament Study*, p. 117.
120 At the same time Johnson conceded that it had to be used critically and with caution: cf. his *The Vitality of the Individual in the Thought of Ancient Israel* (Cardiff: University of Wales Press, 1949), p. 1 n.3.
121 Johnson, *The One and the Many*, pp. 17–37.
122 Ibid., p. 41.
123 Wheeler Robinson had carried out a similar exercise in 'Hebrew Psychology', pp. 354–66.
124 Studies in Biblical Theology, second series, 22 (London: SCM, 1972).
125 Rowley, *The Relevance of Apocalyptic: A Study of Jewish and Christian Apocalypses from Daniel to the Revelation* (London: Lutterworth, 1944).
126 David S. Russell, *The Method and Message of Jewish Apocalyptic, 200 BC–AD 100* (London: SCM, 1964).
127 Albert Schweitzer, *The Quest of the Historical Jesus*, trans. W. Montgomery (London: A & C Black, 1910). Cf. Owen E. Evans, 'Kingdom of God', in G. A. Buttrick (ed.), *The Interpreter's Dictionary of the Bible* (Nashville, TN: Abingdon, 1962), III, p. 20.
128 Dodd, *The Parables of the Kingdom* (London: Nisbet, 1935), p. 51.
129 Ibid., p. 49.
130 Weiss' views are summarized by Norman Perrin, *The Kingdom of God in the Teaching of Jesus* (London: SCM, 1963), pp. 16–23.
131 Likewise a summary of Schweitzer's views appears in Perrin, *Kingdom of God*, pp. 28–35.
132 Dodd, *The Parables of the Kingdom*, p. 56.
133 Dodd, *The Coming of Christ* (Cambridge: Cambridge University Press, 1951), p. 10.
134 Ibid., p .17.
135 Caird, 'The Study of the Gospels, p. iii. Redaction Criticism', *The Expository Times*, XXXVII (1975/76), p. 170. Cf. Dodd, *According to the Scriptures*, p. 74.
136 Perrin, *Kingdom of God*, p. 58.

137 I. Howard Marshall, 'They Set Us in New Paths. I. The New Testament: Paths without Destinations', *The Expository Times*, 100 (1988/89), p. 11.
138 See his obituary in *The Times*, (24 September 1973). Cf. also the view of Marshall, 'They Set Us in New Paths', pp. 11–12.
139 Cambridge: Cambridge University Press, 1963.
140 See John A. T. Robinson, *Twelve New Testament Studies* (London: SCM, 1962), pp. 94–102.
141 Dodd, *Historical Tradition*, p. 423.
142 Cambridge: Cambridge University Press, 1953.
143 Dodd, 'The History and Doctrine of the Apostolic Age', in T. W. Manson (ed.), *A Companion to the Bible* (Edinburgh: T&T Clark, 1939), pp. 411–12.
144 W. D. Davies' tribute in *New Testament Studies*, XX (1973/74), p. iv.
145 London: SPCK, 1948.
146 W. D. Davies and David Daube (eds), *The Background of the New Testament and Its Eschatology: Studies in Honour of C. H. Dodd* (Cambridge: Cambridge University Press, 1954).
147 Dodd, *The Epistle to the Romans* (London: Hodder and Stoughton, 1932), p. xxxiv.
148 Cf. John Painter, 'C. K. Barrett', in McKim (ed.), *Historical Handbook*, p. 428.
149 Donald Coggan, *The Times* (26 September, 1973).
150 The full list is: B. J. Roberts, A. R. Johnson, L. H. Brockington, N. H. Snaith, H. H. Rowley and T. H. Robinson (OT); W. H. Cadman and G. B. Caird (Apocrypha);and C. H. Dodd, W. F. Howard and T. W. Manson (NT).
151 C. Kingsley Barrett, *Paul: An Introduction to His Thought* (London: Chapman, 1994), and F. F. Bruce, *Paul: Apostle of the Free Spirit* (Exeter: Paternoster, 1977).
152 James D. G. Dunn, *The Theology of Paul the Apostle* (Edinburgh: T&T Clark, 1998).
153 J. Munsey Turner, 'The Free Church Traditions – Treasures Old and New', *Free Church Chronicle*, 41/2 (1986), p. 24.
154 Marshall, 'Obituary of F. F. Bruce', *Proceedings of the British Academy*, 80 (1991), p. 251.
155 F. F. Bruce, *The Acts of the Apostles* (London: Tyndale Press, 1951).
156 Marshall, 'Obituary of F. F. Bruce', p. 254.
157 Ibid., p. 251.
158 Tim Grass, *F. F. Bruce: A Life: The Definitive Biography of a New Testament Scholar* (Milton Keynes: Paternoster, 2011), p. 217.

8 Nonconformists and the Person of Christ

Alan P. F. Sell

Every Christian doctrine may, and perhaps should, be viewed through a Christological lens. There are, however, specific matters concerning the person of Christ as such – among them his two natures, his eternal Sonship, his relation as Son to the Father, kenotic theories, and modern reappraisals of the Chalcedonian Formula – and these are our concern here. The objective is to sketch the main lines of Nonconformist reflection on these topics, understanding by 'Nonconformist' the major traditions of historic Dissent: the Congregationalists, Presbyterians and Baptists; together with the Calvinistic and Arminian Methodist products of the Evangelical Revival, the Unitarians, and those streams which came together in 1876 to form the Presbyterian Church of England.

In an important sense reflection upon the person of Christ may be said to be an afterthought. While temporally and logically the incarnation precedes the atoning act at the Cross, for Bethlehem comes before Calvary, and Jesus can do what he does only because he is who he is, the question Jesus addressed to the Pharisees, 'What is your opinion about the Messiah? Whose son is he?' (Mt. 22.42) can be given its most satisfactory answer only by those who have experienced God's saving grace. As P. T. Forsyth put it: 'Our approach to Christology is through the office of Christ as Saviour. We only grasp the real divinity of His person by the value for us of His Cross.'[1] Not, indeed, that our grasp is always firm; and no matter how much our knowledge and experience grow we shall never fully plumb the mystery of the incarnation. We may, however, have confidence that the puzzling reflections in the mirror that we see are reflections of the truth.

I. Early Dissent

The early Dissenters – not least those who, because they believed that the Holy Spirit had further guidance to impart, would never have formally subscribed to 'the words of men', were for the most part by no means reluctant to set down the things commonly believed among them. Thus, for example, in 1596 the members of a Baptist church, some of whose members were in London, others in exile in the Netherlands, published *A True Confession*. They declare that the Lord Jesus 'is the everlasting Son of God, and the engraven form of his Person; co-essential, co-equal, and co-eternal . . . [he] was made man of a woman . . . and was also in all things like unto us, sin only excepted'.[2] This confession was used by the seven Particular Baptist Churches of London when devising their *London Confession* of 1644.[3] Meanwhile in 1609 the General Baptist John Smyth (1570?–1612) had published his *Short Confession of Faith in XX Articles*. Here we learn that 'Jesus Christ is true God and true man, viz. the Son of God taking to himself, in addition, the true and pure nature of a man . . . as pertaining to the flesh, [he] was conceived by the Holy Spirit in the womb of the Virgin Mary'.[4] Smyth is not as specific as others regarding the eternal generation of the Son and the divinity of Christ.

Of all the seventeenth-century declarations of faith the *Westminster Confession* of 1647, one of a number of products of the Westminster Assembly, is the most important. In saying this I do not have in mind so much the global reach it subsequently attained through Presbyterianism, but the fact that both the Congregational *Savoy Declaration* of 1658 and the Baptist *Second London Confession* of 1677 adhere closely to Westminster's doctrinal sections. We might note that while the confession was composed largely by Presbyterians, five Congregationalists, Thomas Goodwin (1600–80), Philip Nye (1596?–1672), William Bridge (1600?–70), Sidrach Simpson (1600?–65) and Jeremiah Burroughes (1599–1646), were prominent members of the Westminster Assembly. Where the person of Christ is concerned the Congregationalists and Baptists slightly elaborated upon Westminster, but did not repudiate any of its claims, which are as follows:

> In the unity of the Godhead there be three Persons, of one substance, power, and eternity; God the Father, God the Son, and God the Holy Ghost. The Father is of none, neither begotten nor proceeding, the Son is eternally begotten of the Father . . . The Son of God, the second person in the Trinity, being very and eternal God, of one substance, and equal with the Father, did, when the fullness of time was come, take upon him man's nature, with all the essential properties and common infirmities thereof, yet without sin: being conceived by the power of the Holy Ghost in the womb of the Virgin Mary, of her substance.[5]

Many Dissenting theologians echoed these words. Thus, for example, John Owen (1616–83), the greatest of them (if also one of the most prolix), affirms that Jesus Christ 'was truly, really, completely a divine person from eternity, which is included in the notion of his being the Son, and so distinct from the

Father'. At the incarnation Jesus, who could not cease to be the perfect Son of God, assumed the 'substantial adjunct' of a human nature free from sin.[6]

We may say with some confidence that to the end of the seventeenth century the major traditions of Nonconformity were in accord with classical orthodox teaching on the person of Christ and, indeed, this line of thought survives to this day. Already, however, alternative views were being published (often clandestinely, it being illegal to deny the Trinity). In 1605 the views of Fausto Paolo Sozzini (1539–1604), known as Socinus, were advanced in the *Racovian Catechism*, a work which first reached England in 1609. Jesus, we are informed, was truly a mortal man by nature, but is now immortal. He was the only begotten Son of God, but was not of the very essence of God, and hence was not divine in that sense. But if 'divine' refers to the fact that the Holy Spirit was indissolubly united to Christ's human nature, 'I certainly do so far acknowledge such a nature in Christ as to believe that next after God it belonged to no one in a higher degree'.[7]

In 1652 John Biddle (1616–62), a Gloucester schoolmaster, published an English translation of the *Racovian Catechism*. In his own writings he affirms that Jesus' nature is human only (and hence not eternally generate); yet as the second person of the Trinity, and hence as sovereign over us, he is worthy of worship as our Lord and God in human form, but 'he is not the most high God, the same with the Father, but subordinate to Him'.[8] For his pains Biddle was imprisoned, but on his release in 1652 he published further Socinian tracts and catechisms for adults and children, and these earned him a further term in prison, where he died in 1662. Meanwhile in 1654, and in a context in which many were convinced that heterodoxy threatened the stability of the nation, John Owen was required by the state to write a refutation of Socinianism, and this he did in *Vindiciae Evangelicae; or, The Mystery of the Gospel Vindicated and Socinianism Examined* (1655). Owen argues that since Christ the Son is the agent of creation the doctrine of the Son's eternal generation, which Biddle denies, must be upheld.

If the Particular Baptist *London Confession* was largely on all fours with *Westminster* and *Savoy*, the *Standard Confession* (1660) of the General Baptists was less Christologically definite. It thus reflects the differences of view expressed by the more latitudinarian General Baptists of Kent and Sussex, and those of Buckinghamshire and neighbouring counties, an area which had been influenced by Lollardy. This may in part explain why Matthew Caffyn (bapt. 1628–1714), 'the Battle-axe of Sussex' who was challenged at the General Baptist Assembly on a number of occasions between 1672 and 1700, was able to avoid censure. His opponents accused Caffyn of being in sympathy with the views of the German Anabaptist Melchior Hoffman, who argued that since humanity is under the curse of sin Jesus could not be our redeemer if his flesh were of Mary's flesh and blood, and hence the eternal

Word became incarnate. The problem is that Caffyn himself had denounced Melchorism. It may therefore be that his opinion was more in accord with that of Caspar Schwenckfeld, namely that Christ's truly human flesh was given to him by the Father, Mary being the vehicle for his birth. Be that as it may, Caffyn's opponents, among whom Thomas Monk was prominent, published an *Orthodox Creed* (1679) in which they affirmed the co-equality of the persons of the Trinity, upheld the eternal generation of the Son, and ruled out adoptionism, Arianism, Socinianism and Melchiorism. In 1696 a more decidedly orthodox General Association was constituted over against the General Assembly, and it was not until 1704 that the breach was temporarily healed, and both parties united around a document, comprising six articles, entitled *The Unity of the Churches*. The Christological clause does not state in so many words that the Son was eternally generate, but it does indicate the felt need of the drafter to rule out Melchiorism: Jesus took 'to himself our nature, in the womb of the blessed Virgin Mary, of whom, in respect of the flesh, he was made'.[9]

During the 1690s discussion of Socinianism was rife. Thomas Firmin, the Church of England businessman, sponsored a series of *Unitarian Tracts*, one of them written by the clergyman Stephen Nye, whose father John had written an anti-Socinian tract, and whose great-uncle was Philip Nye of the Westminster Assembly and the *Savoy Declaration*. Meanwhile the 'Happy Union' of Congregational and Presbyterian ministers, achieved in 1690 with a view to advancing the cause of Dissent, foundered in 1693 because the Congregationalists suspected the Presbyterians of Socinianism, while the Presbyterians challenged the Congregationalists to repudiate antinomianism, which they refused to do. Not, indeed, that all Presbyterians were flirting with Socinianism. On the contrary, to Oliver Heywood (1629–1702) it was 'a thousand Pities that in England, a Goshen, a Land of Light, where the Gospel-Sun hath shined in its Meridian Splendour, such black Fogs should rise out of the bottomless Pit as to darken our Horizon'.[10]

II. The Eighteenth Century

If Socinians were especially concerned with the full humanity of Jesus as such, those of an Arian disposition focused on the relations between the Father and the Son, holding that Jesus was not the Son of God from eternity, for although he was an original creation of God, he was a creature (and hence subordinate) only, and that which is generated requires a prior generator. Eighteenth-century Arians did not see eye to eye on all points, and two Presbyterians will exemplify the fact. Micaiah Towgood (1700–92) thought it appropriate to worship Christ at the Lord's Supper, whereas Richard Price (1723–91) thought that God alone should be worshipped. We should also note that some who were labelled 'Arian' disowned the name. The Presbyterian James Peirce (1674–1726) of Exeter asked, 'Why should we, I pray, be denominated from Arius? Did we ever propose any particular veneration for him? Do we pretend, nay, do we not most positively deny, that we have received our opinions from him?'[11] Yet another Presbyterian, Samuel Bourn the Younger (1689–1754), went further. 'Can any conscientious Men call them [Arians], while they profess not to have received one Notion from him, to have no acquaintance with him, and to have seen none of his Writings, and while they disclaim such as are reported to be his peculiar tenets?'[12] Whence, then, came their teaching? Peirce, Bourn and many others branded heterodox consistently appealed to the sufficiency of scripture, but so, too, did the orthodox. There was, however, a difference of tone as between the two appeals to scripture. In the wake of Locke, the heterodox were more likely than the orthodox to emphasize the right of private judgement and to exalt reason. 'By our *reason*', declared the Presbyterian Arian George Benson (1699–1762), 'we are to make trial of what is offered to us, as a *revelation* from God. Otherwise; how could we distinguish between the *Koran of Mahomet*, and the *Bible*?'[13]

It was during the course of reading William Sherlock's defence of the Trinity that the Presbyterian minister Thomas Emlyn (1663–1741) became attracted to Arianism. In 1702 he published *An Humble Enquiry into the Scripture Account of Jesus Christ*, in which he argued that Christ 'is indeed the *Lord of Lords*, but that Notes an Inferior Character, compared with that of *God of Gods* . . . if he have a God above him, then he is not the Absolutely Supream God, tho' in relation to Created Beings, he may be a God (or Ruler) over all'.[14] Emlyn's reward for advancing his case was a spell of more than two years in prison.

Meanwhile Arthur Bury, a clergyman expelled from the Rectorship of Exeter College, Oxford, in 1689, published an anti-trinitarian work, *The Naked Gospel*, in the following year. This fuelled the debate, and further coals were added when Samuel Clarke, Rector of St James', Piccadilly, published *The Scripture Doctrine of the Trinity* in 1712. That there were three divine persons he did not doubt, but 'The Father (or first Person) Alone is Self-existent, Underived, Unoriginated, Independent; made of None, begotten of None, Proceeding from None'.[15] Clarke's book was influential, not least among West-country Dissenters, among them James Peirce, around whose head the storm broke. Because he could not find it affirmed in the Bible, he denied that Father, Son and Holy Spirit together comprised the one God.[16]

Doctrinal strife became so widespread that a conference was convened at the Salters' Hall in 1719. The subject of discussion was, ostensibly, the Trinity, but it became clear that the really divisive question was whether formal subscription to that doctrine should be required of Dissenting ministers. Of those who voted fifty-three ministers favoured subscription, fifty-seven did not. The Master of the Rolls, Joseph Jekyl, afterwards observed: 'The Bible carried it by four.'[17] The matter is further complicated by the fact that the victorious non-subscribing party included only two avowed Arians, the Presbyterian Benjamin Avery (d. 1764) and the Congregationalist Nathaniel Lardner (1684–1768),[18] while Luke Langdon and Martin Tomkins were veering in that direction. The remaining non-subscribers published a pamphlet in which they appealed to the principle of the sufficiency of scripture, affirmed the Trinity and repudiated Arianism.[19] It is proper to add that some prominent Presbyterian ministers took no part in the proceedings, Edmund Calamy and Henry Grove (1674–1738) among them.

During the two decades from 1720 onwards the focus of debate was upon the eternal generation of the Son. The High Calvinist Congregationalist Abraham Taylor (fl. 1721–40) took no less a person than his fellow Congregationalist Isaac Watts (1674–1748) to task over the issue. Watts had written *The Christian Doctrine of the Trinity* (1722) in the wake of the Salters' Hall conference in an attempt to reconcile the opposing parties. In Taylor's view the attempt had failed miserably. He called upon Watts to seek pardon for 'obtruding upon us the Socinian scheme . . . yet not knowing that he does so', and 'for representing the doctrine of the eternal generation of the Son . . . to be a popish and scholastic hypothesis'.[20] In the following year Taylor followed up with a two-volume work on *The Scripture-Doctrine of the Holy and Ever-Blessed Trinity, Stated and Defended, in Opposition to the Arian Scheme*, in which he insisted against Clarke that the three persons of the Trinity are one in nature and substance, that the Son is consubstantial with the Father and eternally generate.

In 1729 another staunchly Calvinistic Congregationalist John Guyse (d. 1761) preached two sermons on *Christ the Son of God the great Subject of a Gospel Ministry*, in which he affirmed the eternal generation of the Son; whereupon the Presbyterian Samuel Chandler (1693–1766) entered the lists. Chandler, who was liable to tease, probably deliberately launched a hostage to fortune by declaring that the distinctions between the persons of the Trinity are beyond our comprehension and 'of very little importance for us to know'.[21] Chandler says that he affirms 'the proper Deity of our Lord Jesus Christ',[22] but cannot affirm the Son's eternal generation. He urges Guyse to supply the scriptural evidence for the doctrine. In a reply, Guyse failed at this point, Chandler replied again, whereupon Guyse fell silent.

Thirty years after his death, the orthodox Congregationalist Thomas Ridgley (1667–1734), who had been a subscriber at Salters' Hall, was taken to task by the High Calvinist Baptist John Gill (1697–1771) over the question of eternal generation. Gill was determined to rule out the pre-existarian claim that the human soul of Jesus existed eternally (which Ridgley did not maintain), and to defend the doctrine of the eternal generation of the Son on the ground that if it were repudiated, the relation between the first and second persons would be obscured. Ridgley's point was that the orthodox were imprudent if they asserted the Son's eternal generation, for this entailed the Father's communication of his essence or personality to the Son; and this could be held to be an endorsement of Socinian and Arian logic which turned upon the insistence that the one who communicates is prior to the recipient, and hence that the Son is subordinate to the Father. Ridgley's motive was thus orthodox, but he did tempt those of Gill's persuasion when he wrote: 'When we read of the Son of God as dependent on the Father, inferior and obedient to him, and yet as being equal to him, and having the same divine nature, we cannot conceive of any character which answer to all these ideas of sonship, except that of Mediator.'[23] This, to Gill, amounted to the Socinian doctrine of Christ's Sonship by office, and he would have none of it;[24] moreover, he blithely overlooked Ridgley's careful qualifying statements, among them this: 'When . . . we speak of the person of Christ as [Mediator], we always suppose him to be both God and man',[25] whereas to the Socinians' Christ remains ever a creature.

With more justification, Gill's friend John Brine (1703–65) turned his polemical weapons upon James Foster (1697–1753), a General Baptist who by now was minister of the Congregational church meeting at Pinners' Hall. According to Walter Wilson, Foster was 'far gone in the Socinian scheme', and 'it is no injury to him to observe, that the grand doctrines of human redemption, and divine influence, formed no part of his creed'.[26] Wilson quoted Foster's assistant and successor Caleb Fleming (1698–1779) as saying of Foster, that 'he was convinced that the great design of Christ's ministrations was *moral,* viz. to promote virtue, and advance the interests of morality in the world'.[27] To Brine, Christ's purpose was far otherwise, hence, *A Vindication of some Truths of Natural and Revealed Religion: In Answer to the False Reasoning of Mr. James Foster* (1746). Among other things, Brine rebuts Foster's position on regeneration, justification and the mediation of Christ; and there follows a long appended *Dialogue between a Calvinist, a Socinian, an Arminian, a Baxterian, and a Deist.* We can guess who wins without delving into the tome.

With the appearance of *Discourses on Various Subjects of Natural Religion and the Christian Revelation* (1760) by the third Presbyterian Samuel Bourn (1714–96) we reach something of a watershed in eighteenth-century discussions of the person of Christ. Hitherto the Arian challenge regarding the relation of the Son to the Father, and the question therefore of the Son's eternal generation, had been to the fore; but with Bourn's work a turn is taken in a more decidedly humanitarian direction. That is to say, the discussion centres more strongly in the nature of Jesus as such; so that Bourn becomes a harbinger of Unitarianism. The nub of his case is that Jesus is 'sometimes . . . stiled *a God*: not on account of his metaphysical nature or essence (which Scripture saith not a word of), but on account of the dominion or government, which God hath committed to him for the eternal salvation of men', and '[t]o this dominion or empire our Saviour rose by his virtue, or his most perfect and exemplary obedience to God'.[28] We note the continuing appeal to the sufficiency of scripture, and the humanitarian claim that Jesus *earned* his status.

Some divines, like Towgood and Price, remained Arians – Price to the distress of his ministerial uncle Samuel, who opined that 'he had rather see [his nephew] transformed into a pig, than that he should have been brought up to be a dissenting minister without believing in the Trinity'.[29] Others increasingly felt that Arianism was an unstable half-way-house, and they proceeded to Unitarianism. Some, however, reached the latter destination without passing through Arianism at all. Among these was Theophilus Lindsey (1723–1808), who left the Church of England in 1773 and spent the rest of his life disseminating Unitarianism. He, like Thomas Belsham (1750–1829), and others, was reluctant to admit Arians to the Unitarian Society; this body, they thought, should be the preserve of humanitarians only. However, Price, for example, became a member in 1791, the year of his death. Without question the most significant Unitarian author was Joseph Priestley (1733–1804), who was raised in Congregational Calvinism, turned rational (as distinct from evangelical) Arminian, and thence Unitarian. Relying on the sufficiency of scripture, Priestley insisted that the doctrine of the Trinity yielded more objects of worship than one, whereas to Paul, Jesus was '*a man approved of God*', and that the one mediator between God and man was 'the *man* Jesus Christ'.[30]

By now the Arminian Methodists were in the ascendant, and John Wesley (1703–91) was in no doubt as to the identity of his doctrinal foes: 'We believe Christ to be the eternal supreme God; and herein we are distinguished from the Socinians and Arians.'[31] In Wesley's opinion, Priestley was 'one of the most dangerous enemies of Christianity that is now in the world', for which reason he urged John William Fletcher (1729–85) to reply to Priestley's book *The History of the Corruptions of Christianity* (1782) – a task that Fletcher began and, following Fletcher's death, Joseph Benson (1748–1821) completed.

In the closing decade of the eighteenth century the evangelical Calvinist Baptist Andrew Fuller (1754–1815) rose up against Socinianism. Positively, Fuller upheld the eternal generation of the Son, opposed pre-existarianism and adoptionism, and maintained that 'in the order of nature the Father must have existed before the Son; but, in that of duration, he never existed without the

Son. The Father and the Son, therefore, are properly eternal'.[32] On this foundation Fuller sallied forth with *The Calvinistic and Socinian Systems Examined and Compared, as to Their Moral Tendency* (1793). The last clause in his title is important, for the Socinians and Unitarians were great upholders of morality. Fuller was convinced that if the deity and atonement of Christ were neglected – as he thought they were by his opponents – 'practical religion is divested of its most powerful motives'.[33] He expressed the alternatives thus: 'If the Socinians be right, we are not only superstitious devotees . . . but habitual idolaters. On the other hand, if we be right, they are guilty of refusing to subject their faith to the decisions of heaven, of rejecting the only way of salvation, and of sacrilegiously depriving the Son of God of his essential glory.'[34] The Unitarians were slow to respond, perhaps because they were waiting for Priestley to do so, but he did not; so Joshua Toulmin (1740–1815) and John Kentish (1768–1853) entered the lists against Fuller, the arguments went round and round, and neither party was able to persuade the other.

III. The Nineteenth Century

When we come to the nineteenth century we find that denominations as we have come to know them are beginning to be formed, and some of these published statements of their faith. Among these were the Calvinistic Methodists or Presbyterians of Wales who, in their *Confession* of 1823, declared:

> In the fullness of time, God's own Son, eternally begotten, an infinite Person in the Godhead, equal with the Father, the express image of his Person, true God, took upon himself human nature, in the Virgin's womb, – true, entire humanity, but holy and free from its defilement . . . [A] divine Person and human nature have been indivisibly united in the one Mediator, without conversion or confusion of the Divine and human natures. The infinite Person, Jesus Christ, is true God and true man; yet, one Mediator, between God and man.[35]

Ten years later the infant Congregational Union of England and Wales unanimously adopted a fresh *Declaration of the Faith, Church Order, and Discipline of the Congregational, or Independent Dissenters.* Interestingly, in their covering letter which accompanied the *Declaration* when it was circulated among the churches, the secretaries explained that the document was not so much for the information of Congregationalists themselves; rather, the objective was to correct the views of 'a very large proportion of our countrymen [who] take us to be either SOCINIANS or METHODISTS'.[36] Overall, the *Declaration* proclaims moderate Calvinism, but what is of interest here is the fact that its statements regarding Christ's person are not as robust as those of the *Savoy Declaration*. It is affirmed that Jesus was born of the Virgin Mary, and that he was 'both Son of Man and Son of God; partaking fully and truly of human nature, though without sin – equal with the Father and the "express image of His person"';[37] but there is no specific reference to eternal generation, and the statement that Christ was fully man is not balanced by one which declares that he is fully divine. For its part, *Savoy* affirms 'two whole perfect and distinct natures, the Godhead and the manhood, were inseparably joined in one person, without conversion, composition, or confusion; which person is very God and very man, yet one Christ'.[38] When, in 1899 the National Council of the Evangelical Free Churches published its *Catechism for Use in Home and School*, its clauses on the person of Christ were weaker still, perhaps owing to the popular use for which it was intended.[39]

In Adam Clarke (1762–1832) the Wesleyans found their first significant theological scholar. A polymath, his multi-volume *Commentary on the Whole of Scripture* was published between 1810 and 1824. At the end of his commentary on Proverbs 8, Clarke declares his hand on the person of Christ:

> I believe Jehovah, Jesus, the Holy Ghost to be one infinite, eternal Godhead subsisting ineffably in three persons. I believe Jesus Christ to be, as to his Divine nature, as unoriginated and eternal as Jehovah himself; and with the Holy Ghost to be one infinite Godhead, neither person being created, begotten, not proceeding, more than another: as to its essence, but one Trinity, in an infinite, eternal and inseparable unity . . . But I believe not in an eternal sonship of generation of the Divine nature of Jesus Christ.[40]

Clarke is aware that supporters of eternal generation might charge him with tritheism or Sabellianism; they in turn, he thinks (after the manner of Thomas Ridgley before him), might be challenged to show how they avoid Arianism. But it is not his way to stir up controversy: 'I will have nothing to do with ill-tempered, abusive men; I wish them more light and better manners.'[41]

It was not an 'ill-tempered, abusive' man who queried Clarke's position, but his friend and younger contemporary Richard Watson (1781–1833), Wesleyanism's first systematic theologian. The appearance of Watson's *Remarks on the Eternal Sonship of Christ and Use of Reason in Matters of Religion* (1818) coincided with Wesleyan concern that Unitarianism was spreading among them. Indeed, in 1818 the first annual meeting of the Methodist Unitarian Association was held in Rochdale. Watson is especially concerned to rebut Clarke's claim that in the New Testament the term 'Son of God' refers only to Christ's humanity. Among other examples, Watson argues that Peter's confession that Jesus is the Christ=Messiah, the Son of the living God, shows that the term 'Son of God' refers to Christ's divinity, for Jews did not normally think of the Messiah as a divine person. In his larger *Theological Institutes* (1836) Watson came forth in stout defence of the classical Chalcedonian Formula.

The Congregational theologian George Payne (1781–1848) regularly pursued Socinians, Arians and Unitarians well into the nineteenth century, but he also concedes that high orthodox scholastic divines tend 'either to degrade the Lord Jesus Christ, or to throw impenetrable obscurity over all our statements concerning the Trinity'.[42] He further grants the undeniable fact that in ordinary usage the term 'son' implies 'posteriority, derivation, inferiority', and hence that 'as a divine subsistent [the second person of the Trinity] does not bear the name of Son . . . that title is given to him on account of the office he assumed as Emmanuel, of God with us'.[43] For this reason he, like Ridgley and Clarke, cannot endorse the doctrine of the eternal generation of the Son. He discusses five objections to his view, of which the most important is that Christ is referred to as Son before the incarnation. Payne retorts, 'he was so in intention and appointment, though not in act and accomplishment . . . He became actually the Son of God by his miraculous incarnation'.[44] Payne does not deny the eternal existence of the second person of the Trinity; his point is that Christ did not exist eternally as Son. In this way he hoped to hold Arianism at bay by closing the door to suggestions of posteriority.

The doctrine of eternal generation caused a fluttering in Strict and Particular Baptist dovecotes during the middle decades of the nineteenth century, and lines of demarcation were drawn then which are still operative today. John Stevens (1776–1847) did much to initiate the debate with his repudiation of the doctrine of the eternal generation of the Son, and his claims that Jesus was both eternally God and the Son of God. He supported the latter claim by adopting pre-existarianism, namely the view that Christ's human soul predated his incarnation. He published his view in his *Verses on the Sonship of Christ and the Pre-Existence of His Human Soul* (1812), and *A Scriptural Display of the Triune God and the Early Existence of Jesus's Human Soul* (1813). It would seem that when Samuel Collins (1799–1881), the proprietor and editor of *The Gospel Herald, or Poor Christian's Magazine*, opened his pages to Stevens, John Gadsby (1808–93) was prompted to launch *The Gospel Standard* in 1845. The most prominent advocate of eternal generation was J. C. Philpot (1802–69), who resigned his Church of England curacy in 1835, became a Strict Baptist and was editor of *The Gospel Standard* from 1849 until his death. Like orthodox and heterodox divines before him, Philpot takes his stand on the sufficiency of scripture. He stoutly denies that Jesus became Son at the incarnation, as if he were not Son previously; and against the view that generation presupposes a prior generator and implies the subordination of the one generated, he insists that to call Jesus the eternal Son is to declare his co-eternity with the Father. The controversy rumbled on. James Wells (1803–72) opposed eternal generation in *The Earthen Vessel*, while Thomas Row (1786–1868) reiterated the pre-existarian case in the same magazine, and also criticized sermons of Philpot in *The Gospel Herald*.

Meanwhile an intellectually aggressive Unitarianism was making headway in many parts of the country under the leadership of J. J. Tayler (1797–1869) and James Martineau (1805–90), while in the north-west a more evangelistic and socially orientated Unitarianism associated with the names of William Gaskell (1805–84) and Charles Beard (1827–88) was making inroads, to the dismay of many orthodox Dissenters. There were tensions of various kinds within Unitarianism, especially as the transition occurred from the more biblical-rational Unitarianism of Priestley, Belsham and others, to the Romantic-immanentist Unitarianism of Martineau and others, associated as it was with a turn from scripture sufficiency and the denial of the miraculous. A number of Unitarians, not to mention orthodox writers, took exception to Martineau's declaration of 1861: 'The Incarnation is true, not of Christ exclusively, but of Man universally, and of God everlastingly.'[45]

Orthodox Dissent in Wales was likewise disturbed by the advance of pockets of Unitarianism, especially in south Cardiganshire, which became known to the orthodox as 'the black spot'. The publication in Welsh of *The Atonement* (1860, E.T. 1887) by the Welsh Presbyterian Lewis Edwards (1809–87) was a significant event. His title notwithstanding, he makes a number of points concerning the person of Christ. Given the union of divinity and humanity in Christ, Edwards acknowledges the difficulty of believing that Jesus had a human will, and was subject to temptations, as we are; and the even greater difficulty of believing that the one who suffered on the Cross was co-equal with the Father. We are thus tempted, mistakenly, to think that as Jesus is mediator between ourselves and God, so he is intermediate as regards his being. He advises: 'If we ought to believe on the one hand, that the two natures remain unchanged, we ought to believe as firmly, on the other hand, that the person of the Mediator, as He is God and man, entered into all the humiliation, and that this person, as God and man, is now highly exalted'.[46]

As the Wesleyans contributed Clarke and Watson to the thought of the early decades of the nineteenth century, so they contributed William Burt Pope (1822–1903) to the last three decades. His position is clear: 'The Divine-human Person of our Lord is the mystery and the glory of the Christian faith.'[47] He insists that Christ was the Son incarnate, not a man united to God and, with echoes of the Chalcedonian Formula, he declares: 'Christ is "truly" God, "perfectly" man, "indivisibly" one Person, "unconfusedly" two natures.'[48] Among Nonconformists Pope is early in the field as having become acquainted with the kenoticism flowing in from Germany, but he repudiates it on the ground that it threatens God's immutability. It must also be said that whereas George Payne had stood at the threshold of modern biblical criticism, Pope's writings mark the end of a line of biblical exposition that could no longer be pursued with integrity.

IV. The Nonconformist Heyday

The period from 1890 to 1950 marks the heyday of Nonconformist writing on the person of Christ. The Baptist Samuel G. Green (1822–1905) published a paper titled 'Deity and humanity of Christ', in which he welcomes the fresh emphasis in biblical studies on the humanity of Christ, which balances up the earlier emphasis upon Christ's work. Green regards the humanity and deity of Christ as correlated truths, claims that they are properly held together in the Chalcedonian Formula, the Athanasian Creed and the *Westminster Confession*; and thinks that Christ's self-emptying is 'a phrase which perhaps more than any other in Scripture engages the best and deepest thought of our time',[49] though he is not persuaded by arbitrary divisions of Christ's attributes into immanent and relative ones, and he cautions that in Philippians 2 Paul was not concerned to propose a metaphysical theory. He repudiates both docetism and Nestorianism, and maintains that Jesus 'retained what was needful for man's salvation; of the rest he "emptied himself"'.[50]

The Congregationalist R. W. Dale (1829–95) was no less concerned to hold together Christ's humanity and divinity. The New Testament, he suggests, plainly reveals his humanity: he was hungry, susceptible to pain, and so forth; and likewise his divinity, which is presupposed by all the earliest Christian preaching and throughout the New Testament writings. In homiletic style he lets fly a series of questions the expected answer to which is clear:

> Who can this be through whom the sins of the race are forgiven, through whose death we ourselves have received the forgiveness of sins? We know that He is man; but surely He is more than man. Who is He? To Him the saved of all generations owe their eternal salvation. Who is He? Who? If you shrink from calling Him God, what other title adequate to the greatness of His work will you attribute to Him?[51]

It is interesting in passing to note that at precisely the time that many theologians, especially Anglican ones, were expounding an incarnationalism influenced by post-Hegelian immanentism, Dale remained rooted in the Bible; and notwithstanding his writings on the atonement, he observed: 'In theology the Incarnation lies deeper than the Atonement; and the great and august mystery of the Trinity lies deeper than the Incarnation.'[52]

The Unitarian scholar James Drummond (1835–1918), who had studied under Martineau, sailed closer to the orthodox wind than many of his co-religionists. 'A Christianity without Christ', he asserts, 'would be something fundamentally different from that by which [the great mass of believers] have lived'.[53] He criticizes classical Christological terms, disagrees that the Bible is a repository of infallible truths, and turns from the balder humanitarianism of some of his Unitarian forebears. He does not understand Jesus as simply the finest product of evolution, rather, he is the universal spirit who brings God close, and all Christians look to him, not so much as a model to be copied, but 'as a spirit of life which may diffuse itself, like a purifying atmosphere, through every variety of human vocation'.[54]

A number of writers took stock of the kenoticism that was propounded by Thomasius of Erlangen and others, among them the Presbyterian J. Oswald Dykes, who had studied under Thomasius. Dykes sums up the situation thus:

> Either Kenoticists suppose a suspension by the loving will of the Son of His divine activities (*all* His activities, save the will so to suspend them) which may be described as *total*, because it extends even to His universal activity as Lord of all worlds. Or they limit this surrender of His Divine ability to the sphere of His incarnate life as Man upon earth – leaving His cosmical and universal action as God otherwise unaffected.[55]

The former approach sanctions a human life only, and Dykes finds that the majority of English kenoticists take the latter approach, which yields a human consciousness, but not a unity of consciousness in one person; and hence the problem bequeathed by Chalcedon is not solved. Dykes will not take the way out offered by the Ritschlian emphasis upon practical religious certainty, preferring, in then increasingly fashionable mode, to speculate that psychologically, '[w]ithin Christ's complex and wonderful constitution, room might be found for a life-activity verily His own, yet of which He had on earth no human consciousness, or at most, it may be, an intermittent and imperfect knowledge'.[56] Dykes thinks that the psychology of human personality has nothing to say against this possibility, but it does not seem that, doctrinally, he has removed the dualistic danger that has haunted Christology through the ages.

Among other contemporary authors was the Welsh Presbyterian Thomas Charles Edwards (1837–1900), the son of Lewis Edwards, who briefly considers the Logos and *kenosis*, and does not hesitate to speak of the Son's subordination to the Father, thereby prompting disquiet among some of his Welsh readers. Indeed, he thinks that 'Origen's happy phrase, "eternal generation", implies subordination, without sacrificing equality'.[57]

In his *Studies in the Life of Christ* (1880) and *The Place of Christ in Modern Theology* (1893) the Congregationalist A. M. Fairbairn (1838–1912) blends the psychological interest of Dykes with the historical interest of Green, and makes the consciousness of Christ central to his theology. At the heart of this consciousness was 'His consciousness of God . . . and the relation He sustained to Him. God was His Father; He was God's Son'.[58] He understands the *kenosis* as being revelatory of the 'the supremacy of God's moral over His physical attributes'.[59] He pronounces (puzzlingly) that Christ is a unitary person who has two natures, otherwise he could not have accomplished his work. Christ was, 'in a sense, a double incarnation – of manhood and Godhood. In Him humanity was realized before God and revealed to man; in Him God was revealed to man by Godhood being realized before him'.[60]

In the opinion of many, *The Person and Place of Jesus Christ* (1909) is the greatest book by the Congregationalist P. T. Forsyth (1848–1921). He grants that we do not know how the eternal God could become man; he welcomes the way in which the Chalcedonian Formula closes the escape route to a number of heresies; but his great objection to it is that in the Formula Christ's two natures are united miraculously, not morally. In his view: 'The person was the resultant of the two natures, rather than the agent of their union.'[61] That is to say, in Christ '[w]e have within this single increate person the mutual involution of the two personal acts or movements supreme in spiritual being [religion and redemption], the one distinctive of man, the other distinctive of God'.[62] Forsyth endorses a modified kenoticism, but balances it with the view that in humbling himself the pre-existent Christ realized himself (*plerosis*). Throughout, Forsyth insists: 'The mighty thing in Christ is his grace and not His constitution.'[63] Not surprisingly, Forsyth stoutly opposed those liberals who pursued the intellectualist approach of expressing their Christian views through the medium of post-Hegelian immanentism. This, he was sure, landed them in either a mystical or an aesthetic mysticism. He was especially concerned to rebut the views of R. J. Campbell (1867–1956), at the time minister of London's (Congregational) City Temple. Campbell's reduced Christology appears in such an assertion as the following: 'What we succeed in doing some of the time Jesus did all the time; when all men are able to do it all the time the Atonement will have become complete, and love Divine shall be all in all.'[64] I cannot forbear to expostulate: (a) we cannot do it; and (b) the Atonement is already 'complete' and love Divine is already all in all – and that without any dependence upon, or help from, ourselves.

In welcoming the then current emphasis upon the historical Jesus, the Congregationalist A. E. Garvie (1861–1945) pulls no punches. He admits that past discussions of the person of Christ have too frequently set out from his divinity, and have then had the problem of associating his manhood with it. Indeed, '[t]he manhood has not been conceived in accordance with the historical evidence, but to secure consistency with an abstract idea of God which had no relevance to the facts'.[65] However, 'to assert the real humanity is not to affirm that Jesus was an ordinary man . . . We must allow the facts to modify our conception of real humanity.'[66] We must pay due heed to his moral development and to the development of his human consciousness, and we must maintain his sinlessness. Garvie pays careful attention to the Chalcedonian Formula, and finds its use of the term *ousia* ambiguous. It may mean an entity or a class. But

> Athanasius did not mean that Christ was an individual divine being belonging to the same class of divine beings as the Father. That would have been polytheism, and he was combating polytheism in resisting Arianism. Neither did he mean that Christ and God the Father were one individual subject, for that would have been a relapse into the modalism which had been condemned as a heresy . . . He meant . . . a relation of difference in unity.[67]

He finds an analogous ambiguity in the use of 'generation' in the Athanasian Creed. But the biggest fault of the Chalcedonian Formula and of the creeds was to repudiate the idea that Christ's divine nature is passible; for '[i]t is God who gives Himself and finds Himself in Christ, not an inferior deity, or a being partly divine; and the humanity, so far from being a limitation is the very condition of God's most fully giving and finding Himself'.[68] While trenchant in his criticism of earlier kenotic theories which parcelled out God's metaphysical and moral attributes, Garvie maintains that at the incarnation God's self-giving love entails his self-limitation, *kenosis*, which is at the same time love's *plerosis*.

Of the Congregational Christologies, that of D. Miall Edwards (1873–1941) is among the most liberal. To him Jesus reveals 'the sanctity of human life in all its interests and relations, the sacredness of that human nature which was found competent to be the abode of God'.[69] With religious experience as his starting-point, Edwards declares that thus far (fateful words) Jesus epitomizes the high point of religious experience. We learn this from the study of the Jesus of history, which study leads us to the conviction that the human, historical Jesus *'has in a unique sense "the religious value of God" for Christian experience'*.[70] He admits the echo of Ritschl's emphasis upon the value judgement, regarding the German's position as an interim one of use 'in the interval in which we are trying to get rid of the encumbrances of an obsolete metaphysic and have not yet found another to take its place'.[71] In a way that some found decidedly reductionist, Edwards does not find the idea of Christ's pre-existence essential because what we know of his consciousness is revealed only in his incarnate life. It is, however, essential that 'the values embodied in Christ be regarded as pre-existent in God and therefore as revealing the real and eternal nature of God, and not as first coming to be in the historical Jesus'.[72] As for the Chalcedonian Formula, Edwards agrees with Forsyth that its authors thought that two natures could be united by omnipotence or miracle; unlike Forsyth, however, he prefers to think in terms of the monothelite idea of one divine–human nature. That is, he begins from *'the spiritual affinity between God and man'*.[73] Unlike a number of his peers, then, he is not a kenotic theologian, for they accept the two nature doctrine that he rejects; and he eschews pantheism, for that would make Christ a phase or mode of God. To Edwards Christ's will is 'a distinct function not merged in the will of God though in the most perfect harmony with it'.[74]

Both Garvie and Edwards studied under Fairbairn at Mansfield College, Oxford. Two other Congregational theologians sat under P. T. Forsyth at Hackney College, London. The first is Sydney Cave (1883–1953). Like Miall Edwards, Cave is of the opinion that '[m]uch of our difficulty is due to the lack of a recognised philosophy, congruent with Christian values, and able to supply Christian theology with its necessary categories. And this difficulty is increased by the retention in theology of categories [such as "substance"] which have lost their meaning, and which belong to a philosophy pagan, and not Christian, in origin.'[75] He thinks that only a philosophy that makes personality its highest category will suffice. He examines the New Testament record regarding Jesus' life, and finds that it cannot be explained in terms of the noblest man who ever lived. Jesus is truly God and truly man, but to accept this is not to accept the two-natures doctrine. There is, for example, no suggestion in the New Testament that Jesus wills now as God, now as man. He argues that in the so-called Athanasian Creed the unity of the Godhead is emphasized to such a degree that the persons of the Trinity denote eternal aspects only of the Godhead; yet in the Creed's Christology Jesus is the Son of God incarnate. How can an aspect become incarnate, asks Cave? 'We must not', he advises, 'profess a unitary view of the Godhead and at the same time give an interpretation of Christ's person impossible on that unitary view'.[76] We must take a leaf from Ritschl's book and begin with the historic revelation of God in Christ, and not with a priori ideas regarding God's triune life. In any case, Christ did not come to tell us that God is triune; he came to reveal the wonder of God's holy love – the key conjunction of terms in the thought of Cave's teacher Forsyth. Thus, 'it is in the life and death of Jesus that we have the perfect revelation of the character of God'.[77]

H. F. Lovell Cocks (1894–1983) was equally inspired by his teacher Forsyth, from whom he learned that impersonal categories such as substance and being must not be allowed to obscure the religious and ethical datum of the communion of Jesus with God. From Garvie he learned some pointed criticisms of the Chalcedonian Formula. On his own account he argues that it will not suffice to regard Jesus as a religious genius or prophet or example. Though one of us, there is in him the unlikeness to us signified by the term 'only begotten': 'Though Christ is our brother, his sonship and ours are not of the same order. His is an absolute, ours a mediated sonship. He is for God only, we for God in him'.[78] In Jesus we see both what humanity at its highest is like, and also what human beings are not, namely free from sin. We cannot say that 'a sinless Jesus could not have been truly man, since all men have sinned. For, on any showing, sin, although part of the average man, is no part of the normal or typical man. It is definitely an intrusion into our humanity, a pathological element.'[79] Jesus is not a person who has two natures; 'he is not a man indwelt by the Spirit or human nature assumed by the Logos. He is the Son *as man*.'[80] As Son, he is both the revelation of God and the mediator of our sonship.

It remains only to add that the Congregationalist A. R. Vine (1900–73) published *An Approach to Christology* in 1948 – a somewhat abstruse defence of Chalcedonianism. It is replete with technical terms, which are supplemented by almost unpronounceable neologisms. With that the heyday of modern Nonconformist reflection on the person of Christ drew to a close.

V. Conclusion

There is little to report concerning the period 1950–2000. The Welsh Presbyterian Huw Parri Owen (1926–96) robustly defended Chalcedonianism: 'we must not expect that we can move outside the limits set by the Chalcedonian formula and the reflections of the Cappadocians';[81] the Congregational Church in England and Wales published a substantial *Declaration of Faith* in 1967 which sets out from the true manhood of Jesus and ends with his exaltation 'to be at all times God the Son eternally united with the Father in the one life of God';[82] the Baptists experienced, or endured, a flurry of Christological excitement following the address by Michael Taylor (b. 1936) to the Baptist Union Assembly under the title 'The Incarnate Presence: How Much of a Man Was Jesus Christ?' in which he said that while he encountered God in Christ he stopped short of saying categorically that Jesus is God;[83] and Colin Gunton (1941–2003) of the United Reformed Church, argued that from the New Testament onwards we may trace a continuous witness to Jesus as human and divine, and that in the incarnation is found both the basis of reconciliation and the value of human life.[84]

Among the reasons for the decline in the number of Nonconformist writings on the person of Christ between 1950 and 2000 are the following:

(a) the majority of the theologians active during the heyday of modern Christological writing had died, or ceased to publish, by about 1965; (b) meanwhile mainline Nonconformity had suffered significant numerical decline and had produced fewer systematic/historical theologians to replace them; (c) the attention of the remaining theologians was in some cases, owing to the needs of the ecumenical movement, directed towards ecclesiological topics; and (d) far from there being Christological heresies to be combated (the occasion of the Baptist skirmish was but mildly heretical, if heretical at all), there was widespread Christological complacency. Happily, reflection on the person of Christ has revived before, as it did following the relatively barren years from 1820 to 1890; and since the year 2000 a sufficient number of young Nonconformist theologians has arrived upon the scene – not all of them drawn from the ranks of the ministry – to make the hope for fresh treatments of the person of Christ by no means a forlorn one.[85]

Notes

1 P. T. Forsyth, *The Church and the Sacraments* (London: Independent Press, 1953 [1917]), p. 33.
2 William L. Lumpkin, *Baptist Confessions of Faith* (rev. ed., Valley Forge, PA: Judson Press, 1969), p. 84.
3 Ibid., p. 81.
4 Ibid., p. 100.
5 *The Westminster Confession* (numerous editions), II, VIII.
6 J. Owen, *Works*, ed. William H. Goold (1850–53) (London: The Banner of Truth Trust, 1965), I, p. 13.
7 Thomas Rees, *The Racovian Catechism, with Notes and Illustrations* (London: Longman et al., 1818), pp. 55–56.
8 J. Biddle, *A Confession of Faith* (London, 1648), p. 29.
9 Lumpkin, *Baptist Confessions*, p. 340.
10 Quoted by Francis Nicholson and Ernest Axon, *The Older Nonconformity in Kendal* (Kendal: Titus Wilson, 1915), p. 185.
11 J. Peirce, *The Evil and Cure of Divisions* (Exeter: Andrew Brice, 1719), p. 25.
12 S. Bourn, *An Address to Protestant Dissenters* (1736), p. 51.
13 G. Benson, *The Reasonableness of the Christian Religion as Delivered in the Scriptures*, 2 vols (London: J. Waugh, 1759), I, p. 158.
14 T. Emlyn, *An Humble Enquiry* (1702), p. 2.
15 S. Clarke, *The Scripture Doctrine of the Trinity* (London: James Knapton, 1712), p. 243.
16 See J. Peirce, *Plain Christianity Defended* (London: J. Noon, 1719), Pt. I, p. 29.
17 See William Whiston, *Memoirs of the Life and Writings of Mr. William Whiston* (London, privately printed, 1749), I, p. 220.
18 He turned Presbyterian in 1730. See *Oxford Dictionary of National Biography* (Oxford: Oxford University Press, 2004).
19 See *An Authentick Account of Several Things Done and Agreed upon by the Dissenting Ministers latterly assembled at Salters-Hall* (London: John Clark, 1719).
20 A. Taylor, *The Scripture Doctrine of the Trinity Vindicated* (London: J. Roberts, 1726), p. 115.

21 S. Chandler, *A Letter to the Reverend Mr. John Guyse* (London: John Gray, 1730), p. 28.
22 Ibid., p. 33.
23 T. Ridgley, *A Body of Divinity*, 2 vols (New York: Robert Carter, 1855 [1731]), I, p. 162.
24 J. Gill, *A Complete Body of Doctrinal and Practical Divinity*, 2 vols (Grand Rapids: Baker Book House, 1978 [1767]), I, pp. 206–7.
25 Ridgley, *A Body of Divinity*, I, pp. 162–63.
26 Walter Wilson, *The History and Antiquities of Dissenting Churches and Meeting-Houses in London, Westminster and Southwark*, 4 vols (London: W. Button, 1808), II, pp. 279–80.
27 Ibid., p. 280.
28 S. Bourn, *Discourses on Various Subjects*, 2 vols (London: R. Griffiths, 1760), I, pp. 142, 145.
29 William Morgan, *Memoirs of the Life of the Rev. Richard Price, D.D., F.R.S.* (London, 1815), p. 13.
30 J. Priestley, *The Theological and Miscellaneous Works of Joseph Priestley*, ed. J. T. Rutt (Bristol: Thoemmes Press, 1999 [1817–32]), V, p. 14; cf. XVIII, p. 443.
31 J. Wesley, *The Character of a Methodist* (7th edn, Bristol: Felix Farley, 1751), p. 3.
32 Andrew Gunton Fuller (ed.), *The Works of Andrew Fuller* (Edinburgh: The Banner of Truth Trust, 2007 [1841]), p. 944.
33 Ibid., p. 87.
34 Ibid., p. 82.
35 *Confession of Faith of the Calvinistic Methodists, or the Presbyterians of Wales* (Caernarfon: The Bookroom, for the General Assembly, 1823; E.T. 1827), pp. 62–63.
36 See Albert Peel, *These Hundred Years. A History of the Congregational Union of England and Wales 1831–1931* (London: Congregational Union of England and Wales, 1931), p. 68.
37 Ibid., p. 71. The most recent reprint of the *Declaration* is in David Bebbington et al. (eds), *Protestant Nonconformist Texts, Volume III: The Nineteenth Century* (Aldershot: Ashgate, 2006), pp. 39–44.
38 *The Savoy Declaration of Faith and Order*, ch. VIII, para. 2.
39 For this *Catechism* see D. Bebbington et al. (eds), *Protestant Nonconformist Texts, Volume III*, pp. 52–58. Clause 27 which lists the Ten Commandments is here omitted. The *Catechism* was drafted by the Presbyterian J. Oswald Dykes, and revised by the Wesleyan Hugh Price Hughes.
40 Clarke's *Commentary* (London: Ward, Lock, new edn in 6 vols, n.d., n.pag.).
41 Ibid.
42 G. Payne, *Lectures on Christian Theology*, ed. Evan Davies, 2 vols (London: John Snow, 1850), I, p. 249.
43 Ibid., pp. 249, 251.
44 Ibid., p. 268.
45 J. Martineau, *Essays, Reviews and Addresses* (London, 1891), III, p. 51.
46 L. Edwards, *The Doctrine of the Atonement* (London: Hodder and Stoughton, 1886), p. 108.
47 W. B. Pope, *The Person of Christ: Dogmatic, Scriptural, Historical* (2nd ed. London: Wesleyan Conference Office, 1875), p. 31.
48 Ibid., p. 27.
49 Samuel G. Green, 'Deity and humanity of Christ,' in *The Ancient Faith in Modern Light* (Edinburgh: T&T Clark, 1897), p. 173.
50 Ibid., p. 179.

51 R. W. Dale, *Christian Doctrine. A Series of Discourses* (London: Hodder and Stoughton, 1903 [1894]), p. 114.
52 Idem, *The Old Evangelicalism and the New* (London: Hodder and Stoughton, 1889), p. 49.
53 J. Drummond, *Via, Veritas, Vita* (London: Williams and Norgate, 1894), p. 291.
54 Idem, *Some Thoughts on Christology* (London: Philip Grees, 1902), p. 33.
55 J. O. Dykes, 'The Person of Our Lord,' *The Expository Times*, 17 (1905–6), p. 154.
56 Ibid., p. 156.
57 T. C. Edwards, *The God-Man* (London: Hodder and Stoughton, 1895), p. 9.
58 A. M. Fairbairn, *The Place of Christ in Modern Theology* (6th edn, London: Hodder and Stoughton, 1904), p. 48.
59 Ibid., p. 477.
60 Ibid., p. 479.
61 P. T. Forsyth, *The Person and Place of Jesus Christ* (London: Independent Press, 1961 [1909]), p. 223.
62 Ibid., p. 343.
63 Ibid., p. 10.
64 R. J. Campbell, *The New Theology* (London: Chapman and Hall, 1907), p. 174. Campbell later recanted his earlier views and returned to the Church of England whence he had come.
65 A. E. Garvie, *The Christian Doctrine of the Godhead* (London: Hodder and Stoughton, [1925]), p. 32.
66 Ibid.
67 Ibid., pp. 130–31.
68 Ibid., p. 469.
69 D. M. Edwards, 'The Christian Philosophy of Life in Its Relation to the Social Problem,' in Gwilym Davies, ed., *Social Problems in Wales* (Swansea, 1913), pp. 46–47.
70 D. M. Edwards, 'The Doctrine of the Person of Christ,' *The Hibbert Journal*, 23 (1924–25), p. 458; his italics.
71 Ibid., p. 460.
72 Ibid., p. 465.
73 Ibid., p. 466; his italics.
74 Ibid., p. 467.
75 S. Cave, *The Doctrine of the Person of Christ* (London: Duckworth, 1952 [1925]), p. 240.
76 Idem, *The Doctrines of the Christian Faith* (London: Independent Press, 1952 [1931]), p. 210.
77 Idem, *The Doctrine of the Person of Christ*, p. 243.
78 H. F. L. Cocks, 'Reinterpretation of the Fact of Christ,' p. 5; in Lovell Cocks Papers, Dr. Williams's Library, London.
79 Idem, 'The Manhood of Jesus,' p. 1; in Lovell Cocks Papers.
80 Idem, 'Reinterpretation of the Fact of Christ,' p. 10.
81 H. P. Owen, *The Christian Knowledge of God* (London: The Athlone Press, 1969), p. 44.
82 *A Declaration of Faith* (London: Congregational Church in England and Wales, 1967), p. 20.
83 See Ian M. Randall, *The English Baptists of the Twentieth Century* (Didcot: Baptist Historical Society, 2005), pp. 366–82.
84 See C. E. Gunton, *Yesterday and Today: A Study of Continuities in Christology* (London: Darton, Longman and Todd, 1983), p. 63. I may perhaps mention that my *Christ Our*

Saviour (Shippensburg, PA: Ragged Edge Press, 2000) is the middle member of my 'devotional systematics', *Doctrine and Devotion*.

85 In this highly selective account of a vast terrain I have stuck to my doctrinal task. It ought to be noted, however, that differences of interpretation of the person of Christ have had more denomination-shaping consequences for English and Welsh Nonconformity than any other doctrine. For a full-scale study of the doctrine in itself and in relation to those consequences see Alan P. F. Sell, *Christ and controversy: The Person of Christ in Nonconformist Thought and Ecclesial Practice* (Eugene, OR: Pickwick Publications, 2012).

9 Nonconformists and the Work of Christ: A Study in Particular Baptist Thought

Peter J. Morden

Charles Haddon Spurgeon, the nineteenth-century Baptist pastor of the Metropolitan Tabernacle in London, was the foremost popular Nonconformist minister of his age. On Sunday 15 February 1880 he preached a sermon based on Psa. 48.20–21, verses which include the words: 'He that is our God is the God of salvation.' The message was titled 'The Royal Prerogative' and the preacher was especially concerned to show that 'salvation is the most glorious of all God's designs'. The 'most delightful works . . . the Lord has performed', he insisted, 'have been works of salvation'.[1] Spurgeon returned to this subject the following Sunday, this time focusing on what he believed was the appropriate human response to God's saving work, that is, a response of faith. This second message was titled 'Your Personal Salvation' and concluded with a stirring appeal to those who had yet to exercise saving faith in Christ, an appeal which closed with the exhortation, 'O come to him and find salvation now'.[2] Those who had already been 'saved' he urged to reflect on all that God had done and would do for them, an exercise he was sure would lead to increased devotion and holiness of life.[3] Salvation was both God's 'royal prerogative' and something which a man or woman was required to make deeply 'personal'.

According to newspaper reports, Spurgeon preached with great 'force and vigour' on his chosen theme.[4] Not every Nonconformist has spoken about the doctrine of salvation – soteriology – with such passion, but it is certainly a subject to which Dissenters have given much attention. This chapter analyses Nonconformist approaches to soteriology, with a special focus on those who, like Spurgeon, were Calvinistic or Particular Baptists. The period under consideration will stretch from 1644, the date of the landmark Particular Baptist *London Confession*, to the end of the nineteenth century. Setting these parameters allows for a depth of analysis which would have been impossible if this chapter had included twentieth-century developments and sought to give comprehensive coverage of the other main Dissenting groups.[5] Nevertheless, Particular Baptists did not consider questions of soteriology in isolation, but worked out their approach in dialogue, not least with other Dissenters. Consequently, a study of Particular Baptist soteriology sheds considerable light on what was happening in other branches of Nonconformity, as well as illuminating more recent trends and debates.

The chapter analyses the two complementary dimensions of soteriology highlighted by Spurgeon's two sermons. The first half of the chapter considers belief about God's work in salvation; the second half analyses questions to do with human response. Common emphases will emerge, but there was much disagreement too, with thinking and praxis shifting considerably over time. One of the issues which taxed the thinking of Calvinistic Baptists was the nature of the relationship between the divine sovereignty and human responsibility in soteriology. In fact, the precise nature of the interplay between God's work in salvation and the human response to that work was a subject frequently debated in Particular Baptist life. Accordingly, I have given significant space to examining this interplay, although a range of other issues are followed up in this chapter as well.

I. The Sovereignty of God in Salvation

Particular Baptists from the seventeenth and eighteenth centuries would have agreed with Spurgeon: salvation was a sovereign work of God. For an individual to be saved he or she had to be one of the elect and had to be given the faith to believe. Put negatively, no one was saved unless God willed it. The Particular Baptist 1644 *London Confession* stated that salvation was 'onely for the elect' and that 'Faith is the gift of God wrought in the hearts of the elect by the Spirit of God'. Only through this supernatural gift of faith would anyone ever 'come to see, know, and beleeve the truth of the Scriptures'.[6] As Stephen Wright notes, the signatories of the Confession, who included John Spilsbury and William Kiffin, stopped short of stating unambiguously what some regarded as the logical corollary of election and effectual calling, namely that if salvation was foreordained by God then reprobation was similarly foreordained. They thus distanced themselves to a degree from what Wright calls the 'fiercer elements of predestinarian teaching'.[7] Nevertheless, the Confession bore the imprint of the 1618–19 Synod of Dort and predestination was clearly affirmed, along with the other five points of Dortian Calvinism such as the final perseverance of the saints.[8] Salvation was only for those people 'foreordained . . . to eternall life' before the 'foundation of the world' was laid; only those thus predestined would ever receive the gift of faith; once salvation had been received the Christian was eternally secure. The other class of people – those who were not of the elect – had no hope, and would be 'left in their sinne to their just condemnation'.[9]

The 1644 *London Confession*, appearing as it did at a formative time in Particular Baptist life, would prove significant in the subsequent shaping of Calvinistic Baptist belief.[10] The 1677 *Second London Confession* (with a revised edition appearing in 1688–89) was if anything even more influential,[11] and this contains similar statements of Calvinistic soteriology. The elect were saved as they were enabled by the Spirit to put their faith in Christ and they would persevere to the end. 'Others not elected', although they might exhibit 'some common operations of the Spirit', could not exercise saving faith, since they were 'not being effectually drawn by the Father'.[12] Although in substantial agreement with the 1644 *London Confession*, the 1677 document drew heavily from the 1646 *Westminster Confession* which had also shaped the Congregational *Savoy Declaration* of 1658.[13] At this point, Presbyterians, Independents and Particular Baptists were working with what was essentially a shared understanding of the sovereignty of God in salvation.[14]

This emphasis on the sovereignty of God in soteriology, with the accompanying stress on the inability of human beings to exercise saving faith apart from the regenerating grace of God, remained the standard Particular Baptist position in the eighteenth century. It was stated in personal confessions such as the one Andrew Fuller offered to the Calvinistic Baptist church at Kettering, the 'Little Meeting', at the time of his appointment as pastor there in 1783. Fuller stated that he believed 'the doctrine of eternal personal election and predestination' and also affirmed effectual calling and final perseverance.[15] As the authors of the 1644 *London Confession* had done, Fuller also hesitated to speak of double predestination. He declared: 'What has been usually, but, perhaps improperly, called the *decree of reprobation*, I consider as nothing more than *the divine determination to punish sin, in certain cases, in the person of the sinner.*'[16] Despite this caveat, Dortian orthodoxy was once again basically affirmed. This continuing commitment to Calvinistic decrees was not paralleled in Presbyterian churches, with the vast majority abandoning the older confessions.[17] In Congregationalism, a moderate Calvinism was represented in the eighteenth century by the influential theological educator Philip Doddridge.[18]

In the nineteenth century there was a movement away from the Calvinism of the seventeenth-century confessions in Congregational and Particular Baptist life too, although the process was more accelerated and thoroughgoing among the Independents. In 1813, English Particular Baptist churches had come together in a formal Union, the basis of which included commitment to 'eternal and personal election', 'particular redemption' and 'efficacious grace in regeneration'.[19] But in 1832 the constitution of the Union was thoroughly revised and all references to explicitly Calvinistic tenets were dropped, replaced instead by a much broader and rather vague reference to the 'sentiments usually denominated evangelical'.[20] In 1834, the year of his death, the veteran London Baptist pastor Joseph Ivimey lamented what he called the 'laxity' of the new crop of ministers in respect of the 'doctrines of grace', comparing them unfavourably with Fuller, whom he had known personally.[21] Ivimey had correctly identified a trend which was to gather pace in the ensuing years. By the 1850s Particular Baptists were increasingly cooperating with General, Arminian Baptists. There was growing talk of a more formal Union between the two groupings, something which finally happened in 1891.[22] The wider context for these developments was, as Ian Sellers states, 'the tide of nineteenth-century opinion [which] was running against religious particularism of any form, against any view of God as arbitrary and discriminating'.[23] Matthew Arnold, son of the famous headmaster of Rugby school, captured something of this mood when in 1870 he denigrated the Calvinism of the *Westminster Confession* as 'rigid', 'repelling' and lacking 'any trace' of 'delicacy of perception' or 'philosophical thinking'.[24] Particular Baptists were certainly influenced by these sorts of comments, with Arnold's strictures among those used against them by General Baptists.[25] The soteriology of Calvinistic Dissent, including many churches with Particular Baptist roots, was being remoulded by the spirit of the age.

Spurgeon was one nineteenth-century Baptist who, as we have seen, continued to proclaim vigorously the sovereignty of God in salvation. Indeed he had the 1688–89 version of the *Second London Confession* reprinted in 1855, adding his own recommendatory Preface.[26] He remained committed to the doctrines of election, predestination, effectual calling and final perseverance throughout a ministerial career which spanned the years 1851–92, attracting, unsurprisingly, some cutting personal criticism from Matthew Arnold.[27] Spurgeon was unrepentant in the face of this and other censures, delighting to stand for what he habitually referred to as the 'old theology'[28] in contrast to the 'new theology' advocated by men such as the Congregationalist J. Baldwin Brown.[29] He was not alone as a Baptist who continued to promulgate an essentially Calvinistic soteriology, although he was certainly the most prominent of those who did so, and many of the others who followed this line did so in part because of his influence. Many (although not all) of the students trained at his Pastors' College, founded in 1856, interpreted the Christian faith within a Calvinistic framework.[30] These men were shaped by Spurgeon himself and also by the lead tutor and principal of the College until 1881 George Rogers, who was himself a staunch Calvinist, described by Spurgeon as a man of 'Puritanic stamp'.[31] Rogers was an Independent, not a Baptist, and he stands as a reminder of the tradition of Calvinistic soteriology in Congregational life which took its cue from the *Savoy Declaration*.[32] By the late-nineteenth century, Rogers was unusual as a Congregationalist who remained wedded to the Calvinistic decrees.[33] Although still in the minority, those Baptists who were committed to similar tenets were more numerous. Nevertheless a shift in the general tenor of Particular Baptist soteriology, cemented by their 1891 Union with General Baptists, had taken place.

II. Salvation through the Cross of Christ

How did Calvinistic Baptists believe salvation was achieved? For them it was the work of Christ which was crucial in making salvation possible. The seventeenth-century open communion Baptist John Bunyan declared, in his short work titled *A Confession of My Faith*: 'I believe that Jesus Christ is he in whom the elect is alwayes considered, and that without him there is neither election, grace, nor salvation.'[34] Similar sentiments are present in each of the three seventeenth- and eighteenth-century Particular Baptist confessions discussed in the previous section of this chapter.[35] This christocentric emphasis is also beautifully captured by the eighteenth-century Baptist poet and hymn writer Anne Steele in her lines:

> Jesus, the springs of joys divine,
> Whence all my hopes and comforts flow;
> Jesus, no other name but Thine,
> Can save me from eternal woe.[36]

Salvation from 'eternal woe' was found in Christ and Christ alone. Of course, this was a stress Particular Baptists shared with other orthodox Dissenters, whether Calvinistic or Arminian.[37] But when other Nonconformists departed from this christocentric stance, Particular Baptists were often quick to respond. Andrew Fuller wrote his *The Calvinistic and Socinian Systems . . . Compared* as a response to the views of Joseph Priestley, the eighteenth-century Presbyterian minister who came to adopt and promulgate Unitarian views.[38] One of Fuller's complaints was that 'Dr Priestly does not appear to consider [Christ] as "the way of a sinner's salvation" in any sense whatsoever'.[39] This was simply unacceptable to Fuller. To state or even to imply that Christ was not 'the way of a sinner's salvation' was to strike at the very heart of the gospel. The road to Unitarianism was taken by a host of Presbyterians in the eighteenth century.[40] This was a path the vast minority of Particular Baptists staunchly refused to follow.[41] This of course was partly because they simply wanted to defend the deity of Christ and the doctrine of the Trinity as the revealed truth about God's nature. But concern over specifically soteriological issues was never far from the surface.

If salvation was found in Christ alone, that salvation was especially accomplished through the cross which for the vast majority of Particular Baptists was the locus of Christ's saving work. Once again, lines from Steele can be taken as an example of this pervasive emphasis. In a hymn titled 'Christ the Physician of Souls', Steele comments: 'Deep are the wounds which sin hath made', before posing the question: 'Where shall the sinner find a cure?' In answer she directed her readers to the atonement:

> See, in the Saviour's dying blood,
> Life, health, and bliss, abundant flow;
> 'Tis only this dear, sacred flood
> Can ease thy pain and heal thy woe.[42]

It was 'only' the 'dying blood' of Christ which could 'heal' the sinner. Christ was the great physician and he did his work through the cross.

John Bunyan's *The Pilgrim's Progress*, arguably the most influential book ever written by an English Dissenter, can be cited as a further example of this crucicentrism. One of the pivotal passages sees Bunyan's pilgrim, 'Christian', losing his heavy burden of sin at the cross. He comes to a place 'somewhat ascending' upon which stands a cross and, a little below it, a 'sepulchre'. The narrative continues:

> So I saw in my dream, that just as Christian came up with the cross, his burden loosed from off his shoulders, and fell from off his back, and began to tumble, and so continued to do till it came to the mouth of the sepulchre, where it fell in, and I saw it no more. Then was Christian glad and lightsome, and said with a merry heart, 'He hath given me rest by his sorrow, and life by his death'. Then he stood still a while, to look and wonder; for it was very surprising to him that the sight of the cross should thus ease him of his burden. He looked, therefore, and looked again, even till the springs that were in his head sent the waters down his cheeks.[43]

For Bunyan as later for Steele, the cross was the place where sin was decisively dealt with. The paradox was that life for the sinner came through Christ's death. Bunyan skilfully evokes deep feeling in his imaginative description of Christian's response to his burden coming loose and 'tumbling' out of sight. Christian was first 'glad', 'lightsome' and 'merry' and then, as he continued to contemplate the cross, wept tears of gratitude to his saviour. Such emotional responses to the work of Christ were not untypical of Particular Baptists, even though most of them would express themselves a little more prosaically than Bunyan or Steele. Particular Baptist spirituality could be heartfelt and emotional, especially when the atonement was in view.[44]

There were few who departed from this stress on the atonement, even in the nineteenth century, although a small minority of Baptist ministers did so. One such was J. G. Greenhough, minister from 1879 at Victoria Road in Leicester, a church with Particular Baptist roots. Greenhough, who was president of the Baptist Union for 1895, argued that what Paul intended to convey by the word 'cross' was not just the death of Christ but 'all that was included in the incarnation mystery'.[45] Such an approach was much more prevalent in Congregationalism. In Baldwin Brown's influential theology, said P. T. Forsyth, 'everything focused on the incarnation'.[46] But Greenhough was unusual in Baptist life in wanting to widen his focus so that in practice the cross became less prominent in his theology.[47] At the end of the nineteenth as in the seventeenth, crucicentrism prevailed.

III. Understanding the Atonement

The theory of the atonement propounded by both Bunyan and Steele was that of penal substitution. For Bunyan:

> If Christ . . . suffered for us, we were (even our sins, bodies and souls) reckoned in him when he so suffered. Wherefore, by his sufferings, the wrath of God for us is appeased, the curse is taken from us: for as Adam by his acts of rebellion made all that were in him guilty of wickedness; so Christ by his acts, and doings of goodness, and justice, made all who were reckoned in him good.[48]

Christ died in the place of sinners, whose sins were 'reckoned' in him as he suffered. In this way the wrath of God was 'appeased' and all those for whom Christ died could be reckoned 'good'. Anne Steele was even more explicit:

> Jesus the sacrifice became,
> To rescue guilty souls from hell,
> The spotless, bleeding, dying Lamb
> Beneath avenging justice fell.[49]

And,

> Was it for sin, for mortal guilt,
> The Saviour gave his vital blood?
> For sin the amazing anguish felt,
> The wrath of an offended God?[50]

Christ was righteous – the 'spotless' lamb of God – but he experienced the full force of God's wrath against sin on the cross. 'Avenging justice' fell on him, and through this substitutionary sacrifice 'guilty souls' were rescued from hell. The plain statements of penal substitution articulated by Steele were regularly sung by Particular Baptists both in public worship and in private family devotions. For example, two of her hymns on the cross were included in Rippon's famous *A Selection of Hymns* in the section 'The Sufferings of Christ'.[51] The first edition of Rippon's *Selection* was published in 1787 and it remained the hymn book of choice for many Particular Baptists well into the nineteenth century.[52] Her hymns appeared in many other books and her verses were available in several editions of their own.[53] As her lines were read privately and sung in worship up and down the land she helped shape the spirituality of many eighteenth- and nineteenth-century Particular Baptists – and other Dissenters. As far as soteriology was concerned, her verses consistently encouraged those who used them to reflect on the atonement and how on the cross Christ endured the wrath of God in the place of sinners.

Probably the first Particular Baptist of note to depart from an unambiguous commitment to penal substitution was Andrew Fuller.[54] During the course of a dispute with the London Calvinistic Baptist Abraham Booth, which took place at the beginning of the nineteenth century, Fuller argued that a person's sin was imputed to Christ and Christ's righteousness imputed to that person in a way that was 'figurative' rather than 'proper' or 'real'. Christ, he wrote, 'was accounted in the Divine Administration AS IF HE WERE, OR HAD BEEN, the sinner; that those who believe on him might be accounted AS IF THEY WERE, OR HAD BEEN, righteous'. Flowing from this view, Fuller was cautious about treating Christ's sufferings as punishment because Jesus was not, in any real sense, criminal. An innocent person could suffer but such a person could not, strictly speaking, be punished. Fuller's view was carefully nuanced. He could still speak of Christ's sufferings being 'penal', just as he could of 'our salvation' being a 'reward'. But, he reasoned, 'as [our salvation] is not a reward to us, so I question whether [his sufferings] can properly said to be a punishment to him'.[55]

Fuller may not have realized it but he was denying a strict understanding of penal substitution, since he did not believe that punishment could 'properly' be transferred from a guilty person to another, innocent one.[56] His opponent, Booth, vigorously resisted what he regarded as a dangerous innovation. He was adamant in rejecting Fuller's thinking, insisting that Christ had indeed been punished on the cross. Picking up on the words of Paul in Gal. 3.13, where it is stated that Christ became 'a curse for us', he commented: 'If, therefore Jesus was made a curse, he was punished – in a real and proper sense PUNISHED: for scarcely any words can convey the idea of punishment more forcibly than that of the apostle.'[57] Booth died in 1806 with the dispute still unsettled. Both men were evangelical Calvinists with an avowed commitment to the divine decrees, and both focused on the death of Christ as the fulcrum of God's saving work. They were unable, however, to agree on the 'mechanism' of atonement – how Christ's death actually 'worked' to save sinners. Booth believed that on the cross Christ was properly 'punished'; Fuller drew back from this because Christ was innocent of any crime and to talk of him being punished appeared to label God as unjust. Penal substitution was still the dominant way Particular Baptists spoke of the cross, but it was not the only way.

In his views on imputation, Fuller had been influenced by the 'moral government' theory of the atonement.[58] This had been originally propounded by the Dutch Jurist Hugo Grotius in the seventeenth century, although in advocating a 'moral government' approach Fuller was drawing especially from a number of New England theologians, disciples of Jonathan Edwards such as Joseph Bellamy and Samuel Hopkins.[59] God was seen as the benevolent moral governor of the universe. As Bellamy argued, Christ's death upheld and 'honoured' God's moral law, so that he could pardon the world consistently with his honour.[60] Hopkins developed this view arguing that no 'real' imputation of sin to Christ took place on the cross: real imputation was not honouring to God because to mete out punishment on an innocent party smacked of injustice. It was Hopkins' view which Fuller was to take up. The increasing popularity of the moral government theory of the atonement needs to be seen in the context of wider cultural trends with which it resonated, as David Bebbington shows. Contemporaries who used a similar intellectual framework and language to Fuller and the New England theologians included the Utilitarian philosopher Jeremy Bentham and the influential Italian thinker Cesare Beccaria.[61] Broader theological, philosophical and cultural streams were thus reshaping the approach to the cross advocated by one of the Particular Baptists' primary thinkers as he sought to remove stumbling blocks to belief and relate the gospel to the age in which he lived.

Fuller's moral government language was controversial in Particular Baptist life at the beginning of the eighteenth century, and not only with Booth. For example, in Wales the prominent Baptist leader Christmas Evans attacked the Kettering pastor's view in print in 1811,[62] with John Philip Davies, another Welsh Baptist, publishing in support of Fuller in 1822.[63] In England, the moral government theory continued to be influential.[64] It even found a place at Spurgeon's Pastors' College, with works which expounded the atonement within a governmental framework studied as part of the curriculum.[65] However, Spurgeon and his tutors remained absolutely committed to teaching an unambiguous form of penal substitution alongside this, seeing no contradiction between the two approaches. It was penal substitution which remained the dominant theory of the atonement propounded by them. When the Birmingham Independent R. W. Dale published his Congregational Union Lectures of 1875 under the title *The Atonement*, he too drew from the moral government theory.[66]

But now David Gracey, theology tutor at the Pastors' College (and, from 1881, principal in succession to Rogers) was alarmed. Dale appeared to be speaking of moral principles that were somehow 'beyond the will and mind of God',[67] an approach which he believed smacked of unhelpful metaphysical speculation with the potential to draw people away from a God-centred scriptural simplicity.[68] Gracey's theological lectures at the College included unambiguous affirmations of penal substitution alongside his firm critique of Dale.[69] But although the Pastors' College was unhappy with aspects of Dale's work, the Birmingham Independent's published lectures became influential in wider Baptist life in the latter quarter of the nineteenth century. For example, *The Atonement* was recommended reading for the students of Regent's Park Baptist College in the summer of 1877.[70] Ministerial students less conservative than Spurgeon's own were being shaped by new thinking about the cross, thinking that was increasingly at odds with the older Calvinism.

Further developments in the way the atonement was regarded were even less welcome to those who taught at the Pastors' College. Under the influence of the cultural mood known as Romanticism, some ministers turned from both penal substitution and moral government theories of the atonement. Once more, this shift was more pronounced in other branches of old Dissent, where it was typified in the theology of J. Baldwin Brown,[71] but it affected Baptist church life too. Whereas the eighteenth-century Enlightenment had emphasized reason, Romanticism exalted the will and emotion, and tended to dwell on concepts such as 'awe', 'wonder' and 'mystery'.[72] Influenced by this Romantic temper, some ministers and churches adopted an understanding of the cross which was far removed from penal substitution. Again, Greenhough can be cited as an example. Objective, 'legal' theories of the atonement were quietly dropped in favour of an approach which dwelt instead on the positive moral influence that reflection on the sacrificial love of Christ could have on people. God was seen as a rather 'kindly Heavenly Father', a God of love caring for his wayward family rather than a God of justice.[73] Not everyone who was affected by the Romantic mood adopted more liberal attitudes to the atonement. Spurgeon was a conservative who was imbued to a significant degree with Romantic sensibilities,[74] as was the prominent Baptist leader and Keswick speaker Frederick B. Meyer (who had been Greenhough's immediate predecessor at Victoria Road, Leicester).[75] But Romanticism did tend to shift the thinking of a number of Baptists in a more liberal direction as far as their interpretation of the cross was concerned. A range of different forces were reshaping Baptist commitments, not only the theology of the Congregationalists such as Dale and Baldwin Brown, but also the prevailing Romantic culture.[76] In addition, there was a desire (exhibited by both Dale and Greenhough) to communicate the Christian faith to nineteenth-century people in a way that was attractive and relevant, just as Fuller had aimed to state his soteriology in a way which would speak to his own times. The conservatives believed that something essential regarding biblical soteriology was being lost in the attempt to connect with the spirit of the age. The overarching issue, as noted by David Bebbington, was 'how far to go in accommodating the gospel to culture'.[77]

IV. The Extent of the Atonement

The extent of the atonement is another important theme to which Particular Baptists gave attention. Clearly, Particular Baptists (at least in the seventeenth and eighteenth centuries) believed in particular redemption: the atonement was, in some sense, limited. The seventeenth-century Congregationalist John Owen had forcefully argued, in his *The Death of Death in the Death of Christ* (1647), that Christ did not die, in any sense, for the non-elect. On the cross an identical payment (*solutio eiusdem*) was made by Christ for the sins of the elect, and for their sins only.[78] Owen provided the classic English statement of this position, but a number of Particular Baptists also propounded this view in print. The influential eighteenth-century Calvinistic Baptist John Gill conceived of the atonement as the literal and exact payment of a debt. Christ's sacrifice was a full and sufficient one – for the elect only.[79] But later in the eighteenth century this approach was challenged in Particular Baptist life.

Once more, Andrew Fuller was the theologian who questioned older ways of thinking. Following the publication of his seminal *The Gospel Worthy of All Acceptation* (1785), he became involved in a theological dispute with the New Connexion General Baptist leader Dan Taylor.[80] The New Connexion was founded by Taylor in 1770, following disillusionment with the unevangelical views of existing General Baptists. The New Connexion was both evangelical and Arminian (it was essentially this grouping that joined in Union with Baptist churches with Particular Baptist origins in 1891).[81] While rejecting universal salvation, Taylor insisted that in Christ's death propitiation was made 'for the sins of the whole world'.[82] The scriptures, he asserted, 'never give us any intimation . . . that Christ died for some and not for others'.[83]

In debate with Taylor, Fuller shifted his position on the extent of the atonement. Whereas previously he had held to the view outlined by Owen and Gill, in 1787 he argued that the particularity of redemption consisted 'not in the degree of Christ's suffering (as though he must have suffered more if more had been finally saved) . . . but in the sovereign purpose and design of the Father and the Son'. The sufferings of Christ, he continued, 'are of infinite value, sufficient to have saved all the world, and a thousand worlds, if it had pleased God . . . to have made them effectual to this end'.[84] Fuller was now locating the particularity of redemption in the application of the atonement, or more precisely 'in the design of the Father and the Son, respecting the persons to whom it shall be applied'.[85] This enabled him to continue to speak of a 'special design' in the death of Christ, because those to whom the atonement would be applied had been decided in the purposes of God 'before time'. This did not satisfy Taylor, but it was a significant modification of Fuller's previously held views, and his doctrine of the atonement could now properly be called 'general'. As he stated, 'if all the inhabitants of the globe could be persuaded to return to God in Christ's name, they would undoubtedly be accepted by him'.[86]

In adopting this new understanding of how particular redemption worked, Fuller was leaning on Jonathan Edwards, who had argued something very similar in his philosophical treatise *The Freedom of the Will*, first published in 1754. Christ's death, Edwards declared, was, in 'some sense' sufficient for the 'whole world', yet there was still 'something particular in the design of his death with respect to such as be saved thereby'.[87] Fuller had read and been profoundly influenced by *The Freedom of the Will*,[88] which was shot through with the spirit of the Enlightenment.[89] On the extent of the atonement as in other areas, Calvinistic soteriology was recast in ways which resonated with aspects of the prevailing intellectual and cultural mood. For those Baptists who wanted to continue to assert the particularity of redemption in the nineteenth century, Fuller's 'Edwardsean' approach became the standard one. Spurgeon continued to hold to particular redemption, as we have seen, but, like Fuller, he located this particularity firmly in the application of the atonement. As far as Christ's actual death was concerned, according to Spurgeon there was 'sufficient efficacy in the blood of Christ, if God had so willed it, to have saved not only all in this world, but all in ten thousand worlds'. The change from Fuller's one thousand worlds to ten thousand was a typical Spurgeonic flourish. For him, the thought of limiting the 'merit of the blood of Jesus' was 'near akin to blasphemy'.[90] Even allowing for a degree of hyperbole, Spurgeon's use of the phrase 'near akin to blasphemy' to describe the position he was opposing is striking. On one occasion he stated: 'Calvinism, pure and simple . . . is not perfect, for it lacks some of the balancing truths of a system [i.e. Arminianism] which arose as a remonstrance against its mistakes.' It was not, Spurgeon assured his readers, that he had thrown away the five points. But, he stated, he 'may have gained [an]other five'.[91] His theological framework always remained essentially Calvinistic, but this was not the Calvinism of John Gill or, indeed, of the seventeenth-century Westminster or Particular Baptist Confessions, whose authors would not have spoken of Arminianism in this eirenic way. Despite Spurgeon's reprint of the 1688–89 *Second London Confession*, even he represents a modification of some of the elements of the older Calvinism.[92]

By the end of the nineteenth century many ministers serving Particular Baptists churches were uninterested in such debates about Calvinistic soteriology, for adherence to what the older generations would have recognized as 'Calvinism' was fading. Writing in 1867, the New Connexion General Baptist George Coltman observed that the 'Calvinistic element in the Particular Baptist body is much weaker than it was fifty years ago' although it was still too strong for his liking.[93] By 1885 the New Connexion leader John Clifford was able to say that the 'Calvinism our fathers fought against is no longer able to walk uprightly, if indeed to walk at all'.[94] Clifford's comments, which relate to Calvinistic Dissent in general and Particular Baptist life especially, represent an overstatement, particularly given the continued influence of Spurgeon who, together with his students, planted a staggering fifty-three Baptist churches in London alone between 1865 and 1876.[95] But the trend away from doctrinal statements in Union life (in 1873 even the phrase 'the sentiments usually denominated evangelical' was dropped),[96] and the formal coming together of the Generals and Particulars in 1891 indicate that Coltman and Clifford were correct in their identification of a trend that was increasingly gathering speed as the century wore on. The 1891 Union took place, as Clifford stated, 'without respect to historical theological statements'.[97] The earlier hotly contested debates about subjects such as election, reprobation, effectual calling and the extent of the atonement, debates which took place within Particular Baptist life as well as with other Calvinistic Dissenters and with Arminians, seemed to many to belong to a past age. From the mid-seventeenth century to the end of the nineteenth Particular Baptists' soteriology may not have altered as drastically as that of the Presbyterians and Independents, but it had still undergone considerable change.

V. Receiving Salvation: Faith and Assurance

If these were some of the ways Particular Baptists viewed God's work in salvation, what did they think was the appropriate human response to God's action? Clearly, salvation needed to be appropriated by faith, although exceptions to this rule were made for unconscious infants who died having not had the opportunity or capacity to exercise saving faith. The 1677 *Second London Confession* declared: 'Elect Infants dying in infancy are regenerated and saved by Christ through the Spirit; who worketh when, and where, and how he pleaseth.'[98] Spurgeon took this a stage further. For him, all infants were unquestionably elect, so that all who died before being able to exercise faith sped 'their way to Paradise'.[99] Nevertheless, the normal way of receiving salvation was for an elect man or woman to be quickened by the Holy Spirit, who would lead them to exercise saving faith.[100]

It might be thought that the emphasis on the efficacy of saving faith, produced in the believer by 'no less power than that which raised up Christ from the dead',[101] coupled with the doctrines of election and final perseverance, would give great assurance of salvation to the Christian believer. This was not always the case, however. On the contrary, many Particular Baptists in the seventeenth and eighteenth centuries struggled with the question of assurance, a struggle which can be linked to Puritan spirituality. How could the one who had professed faith know that they had truly exercised a saving faith which had been given by God and not made a false profession, merely produced by the 'common operations of the Spirit' spoken of in the *Second London Confession*?[102] The standard Puritan answer to such a question involved regular, detailed self-examination.[103] And, as the seventeenth-century Puritan Thomas Brooks stated in *Heaven and Earth*, the Christian who wanted to attain assurance must engage in self-examination and 'must work, and sweat and weep . . . Assurance is such precious gold, that a man must win it before he can wear it.'[104] Attaining assurance through such means could be a long and painful business, with the outcome by no means certain.

John Bunyan was one who struggled to find assurance, as famously documented at book length in his *Grace Abounding to the Chief of Sinners*.[105] Andrew Fuller was another who found full assurance of salvation difficult to come by, as I have argued in detail elsewhere.[106] He eventually arrived at a more certain assurance as he embraced the theology and spirituality of the Evangelical Revival, with its Enlightenment influenced confidence that truth could be verified and known. Nevertheless, his struggles to throw off his fears concerning his eternal state were long and deep, continuing into the late 1780s.[107] At least one member of Fuller's congregation went through similar struggles. This was George Wallis, who was baptized and accepted into membership at Kettering in 1802.[108] Wallis kept a confessional diary in the Puritan tradition and the MS volume he began on 15 March 1805 survives. It is illustrative of a prolonged inner battle for assurance of salvation. For example, on 7 August 1808 he wrote:

> When I look at myself and see the barren state of my mind and my indisposedness *[sic]* to spiritual employment, I am ready to question whether such a state of mind can exist where there is any real Christianity, and from there am ready to conclude, I have *none*: yet I am not satisfied in this state and desire to have the impressions of divine things renewed on my soul; and *from the willingness of Jesus Christ to save sinners* I cannot give up my hope, that he will save even me: this is my antidote against despondency![109]

The seventeenth-century emphases on the search for 'impressions for divine things' and analysis of his 'barren state of mind' were tending to despair; the eighteenth-century evangelical stress that assurance was found by looking to

Christ and his promises, a stress which now characterized his pastor's preaching, offered hope. Wallis eventually walked the path his pastor had trodden, discovering a more confident assurance, although he could still slip back into old ways.[110] The older Puritan approach to assurance continued to influence Particular Baptist life.

Nevertheless, as the nineteenth century wore on, such agonizing about assurance became rarer. Few Calvinistic Baptists were more influenced by the Puritans than Spurgeon, indeed, he self-consciously sought to stand in the Puritan tradition.[111] But he did not follow the sixteenth- and seventeenth-century godly in their approach to assurance. The mature Spurgeon explicitly repudiated introspective self-examination,[112] saying that he did not believe those who felt themselves very poor would get rich by looking through all their 'empty cupboards'. '[I]f our graces are to be revived', he declared, 'we must begin with a renewed consciousness of pardon through the precious blood'. The way to get this was not for believers to look inside themselves for evidence they had a saving interest in Christ's death; rather they should go directly to the cross and simply trust in its power as they had done at their conversion.[113] Spurgeon had embraced what Wallis had earlier called the 'antidote against despondency' wholeheartedly: the work of Christ and his sure promises to save were the best grounds for hope. Moreover, for Spurgeon, assurance was the birthright of every believer, something it was vital to claim. While not essential to salvation, it was certainly essential to knowing the benefits of salvation in this life.[114] Particular Baptists in all of the three centuries considered in this study thought assurance of salvation was important, but, once again, the ways that they approached the issue altered over time.

VI. Living and Sharing Salvation

If salvation was received by faith, with assurance of salvation something to be prized, how should the saved life be lived? Particular Baptist theologians tended to emphasize the importance of conformity to Christ and they rejected antinomianism – the view that Christians were not subject to God's moral law. Fuller wrote a short MS on the subject which was posthumously published as *Antinomianism Contrasted with the Religion Taught and Exemplified in the Holy Scriptures* in which he engaged with the idiosyncratic preacher and 'coalheaver' William Huntingdon.[115] Spurgeon was similarly emphatic in rejecting antinomianism. One of the reasons for their clearly stated opposition to antinomianism is that it did impact Particular Baptist life at a popular level. If someone was saved because they were of the elect, and if final perseverance was assured, then (so the argument ran) whatever sins were committed, however heinous, salvation could not be lost.

Although antinomianism might appear the polar opposite of the Puritan striving after assurance, with its concomitant deep anxiety that one might, after all, be lost, the two approaches share a common root. If salvation is predestined then an individual cannot determine his or her own fate. For those with tender consciences this could lead to a lifetime of anxious searching for evidence of the impressions of God in their lives; those of a different temper could reason that, if all was predetermined, then their conduct was of no account. Spurgeon recorded that in the village of Waterbeach, Cambridgeshire, the place of his first pastorate, there had been a man who had once 'stood on the table of a public-house, and held a glass of gin in his hand, declaring all the while that he was one of the chosen people of God'. Spurgeon noted with approval that the other patrons wasted no time in throwing the man out. The young Spurgeon preached against antinomianism at Waterbeach chapel, saying that 'one of the first evidences that anyone is a child of God is that he . . . seeks to live a holy, Christlike life'.[116] 'Effectual calling', he maintained in one particular message, was a calling 'to holiness'. Continuing in this vein he exhorted all of his hearers who considered themselves 'Calvinistic Christians' to 'be holy'.[117] Salvation was from the penalty and the power of sin. Particular Baptist soteriology included a strong commitment to growth in holy living.

One of the ways salvation had to be lived out was by actively sharing the gospel with others, 'offering' Christ to them and calling them to repentance and faith, as Spurgeon had done in the two sermons cited in the introduction to this chapter. But although this was the dominant emphasis in Particular Baptist life, it was challenged by the theology known as High Calvinism (or, more pejoratively, hyper-Calvinism), which became prevalent in Particular Baptist life in the eighteenth century. Earlier, in the seventeenth century, Particular Baptists had not seen a contradiction between a strong adherence to Calvinistic tenets and invitational gospel preaching. John Bunyan combined a commitment to strict Calvinism with a vigorous evangelistic ministry,[118] during which he unashamedly called men and women to have faith in Christ. In his very first book *Some Gospel Truths Opened*, he addressed those who had not trusted Christ saying: 'In a word, you that have not yet laid hold on the Lord Jesus Christ, for eternal life, lay hold upon him; upon his righteousness, blood, resurrection, ascension, intercession, and wait for his second coming to "judge the world in righteousness".'[119] The title of one of his later works *Come and Welcome to Jesus Christ* aptly sums up his applied, invitational approach.[120] He always affirmed the sovereignty of God in salvation and was a lifelong proponent of a thoroughgoing Calvinism, declaring in *Come and Welcome*: 'Coming to Christ is by virtue of the gift, promise, and drawing of the Father.' But no sinner who wanted to trust in Christ need be afraid they were not one of the elect for, he reasoned, the very fact they wanted to come to Christ was *prima facie* evidence that God was drawing them. '[T]hou art a coming',

Bunyan said, 'therefore God hath given thee, promised thee, and is drawing thee to Jesus Christ'.[121] *Come and Welcome* was based on Jesus' words as recorded in Jn 6.37: 'Him that cometh to me I will in no wise cast out.' Bunyan was certain this verse gave him all the warrant he needed to reassure sinners who wanted to put their faith in Christ who were anxious they were not of the elect. He was also sure it gave him the mandate to apply himself unstintingly to evangelistic preaching.

In the eighteenth century, however, some Particular Baptists began to question the invitational approach typified by Bunyan. High Calvinism, most often associated with the aforementioned John Gill, combined with a number of other factors to cause a significant number of Particular Baptists to shrink from declaring, as Bunyan had done, 'you that have not yet laid hold on the Lord Jesus Christ, for eternal life, lay hold upon him'.[122] For the High Calvinist, it was wrong to 'offer' the gospel indiscriminately to all: only the elect could come; they would come anyway in God's good time; and invitational preaching might well induce false professions which would sully the purity of the church. The extent to which Gill was a High Calvinist has been questioned, but certainly he thought that the phrase 'to offer Christ' lacked any biblical foundation. Talk of 'gospel-commands, gospel-threatenings and gospel-duties' were to him a contradiction in terms, and smacked of 'loose and unguarded speech'.[123] In 1748 Gill wrote a Preface to the seventh edition of the hymns of Richard Davis, who from 1689 to 1714 had been the controversial minister of the Congregational church at Rothwell, Northamptonshire.[124] In it Gill commented on the fact that 'the phrase of offering Christ and grace is sometimes used in these hymns'. He continued:

> I can affirm, upon good and sufficient testimony, that Mr Davis, before his death, changed his mind in this matter, and disused the phrase, as being improper, and being too bold and free for a minister of Christ to make use of. And though I have not thought fit to alter any words or phrases in the revision of these hymns, yet in the use of them in public service, those who think proper may substitute another phrase in its room more eligible.[125]

Gill's own views are clear enough from this extract. Those who followed in this line of thinking were not to offer Christ or grace. To do so was to be too 'bold' and 'free'.

A significant number of early- to mid-eighteenth-century Particular Baptists resisted High Calvinism. As Roger Hayden has shown, there remained Calvinistic Baptist ministers, many of them trained at the Baptist Academy at Bristol, who adhered to a more evangelistically minded, expansive brand of Calvinism.[126] But there is still considerable evidence to suggest that High Calvinism was the dominant theology in many Particular Baptist churches in England. For example, John Fawcett Jr wrote of its prevalence in Particular Baptist churches in the 1760s in the north of England.[127] In Norfolk and Suffolk, High Calvinism was perhaps even more in the ascendant.[128] Even in Bath, just thirteen miles from Bristol and its Academy, High Calvinists were influential.[129] Fuller's own minister when he was a young man at Soham, Cambridgeshire, John Eve was a High Calvinist who had 'little or nothing to say to the unconverted'.[130] Andrew Fuller's tombstone biographer John Ryland Jr, stated that by the mid-eighteenth century the 'opinion had spread pretty much among the Baptist denomination [that] it was not the duty of the unregenerate to believe in Christ', and that consequently ministers were 'too much restrained from imitating our Lord and his apostles, in calling on sinners to repent and believe the gospel'.[131] Doubtless he was exaggerating, but High Calvinism was a significant theology in eighteenth-century English Particular Baptist life.

High Calvinism was challenged in Particular Baptist life by factors associated with the eighteenth-century Evangelical Revival. John Ryland Jr was Fuller's closest friend and colleague from the early 1780s onwards. He had himself been strongly inclined towards High Calvinism as a young man, but had been weaned away from it through his friendship and correspondence with the evangelical clergyman John Newton.[132] John Fawcett Sr, who in the late eighteenth century was a prominent Yorkshire Particular Baptist pastor, had in fact been a convert of Whitefield in 1755. Fawcett always kept a picture of Whitefield in his study and 'the very mention of his name inspired the warmest emotions of grateful remembrance'.[133] He refused to accept Gill's rejection of the 'open offer' of the gospel and composed the following lines,

> To be brief, my dear friends, you may say what you will
> I'll ne'er be confined to read nothing but Gill.[134]

Due to the influence of men like these and the continued work of the Bristol Academy, High Calvinism in Particular Baptist life was progressively on the wane during the last thirty years of the eighteenth century.

A number of writers directly challenged High Calvinism in print. Among these were Robert Hall Sr, who wrote *Help to Zion's Travellers* in 1779,[135] and the Welsh Congregationalist Edward Williams, who espoused a 'modern Calvinism' in the tradition of Doddridge which engaged effectively with aspects of High Calvinism and influenced some Baptists.[136] However, the most important figure breaking the power of High Calvinism for Calvinistic Baptists was Andrew Fuller, who was also the most significant of all the Dissenters writing on this issue. His *The Gospel Worthy of All Acceptation* impacted Particular Baptist life in ways that were both deep and broad. Fuller contended that it was the 'incumbent duty' of all who heard the gospel to trust in Christ. He advanced a number of arguments in favour of this, central among which was the fact that unconverted sinners were commanded to have faith in the scriptures. Indeed, in the New Testament, 'true saving faith [was] enjoined upon unregenerate sinners, as plain as words can express it'. He set out a catena of texts to support this contention, just one example being Jn 12.36: 'While ye have the light, believe in the light, that ye may be the children of light.' This he went on to expound:

> The persons to whom this was addressed were such, who though [Christ] had done so many miracles among them, yet believed not on him. Yet it seems they were given over to judicial blindness, and were finally lost. By the light they were commanded to believe in, he undoubtedly meant himself . . . and what kind of faith it was that they were called upon to exercise is very plain, for that on their believing they would not have abode in darkness, but would have been the children of light, which is a character never bestowed on any but true believers.[137]

In other words, those who were not believers (and in Fuller's view never became so) were commanded to have saving faith – by Christ himself. Surely it had been their 'duty' to respond to such a command, although in fact they had never done so.

In his conclusion, Fuller came to the two crucial, practical outworkings of his thesis. The first was that there was 'free and full encouragement for any poor sinner to . . . venture his soul on the Lord Jesus Christ'. No one need hold back from coming to Christ for the lack of a strong enough 'inner persuasion' that God was at work in their lives. The gospel itself and the exhortations to repentance and faith were all the warrant to believe that was needed. His second conclusion flowed naturally from the first. Christians, especially gospel ministers, should urge everyone, indiscriminately, to believe in Christ. The New Testament was full of such open 'offers' of the gospel. 'Calls, warnings, invitations, expostulations, threatenings and exhortations, even to the unregenerate', were perfectly consistent with Calvinistic belief.[138] Thus in *The Gospel Worthy* Fuller struck, quite deliberately, at two pillars of High Calvinist 'orthodoxy', insisting that it was the duty of ministers to proclaim the gospel to all, and the duty of all who heard to believe.

Once again, Jonathan Edwards was important in shaping Fuller's arguments, as I have sought to show at length elsewhere.[139] Alongside *The Freedom of the Will* Edwards' *Life of David Brainerd*, a work descriptive of evangelical action, was significant.[140] Overall, *The Gospel Worthy* was an evangelical tract, permeated throughout with the spirit of the eighteenth-century Evangelical Revival. Fuller's work was extraordinarily influential, helping to wean the majority of Particular Baptists away from High Calvinism. Ryland cites the example of an older minister Joshua Thomas, who initially opposed *The Gospel Worthy* but 'came over to Mr Fuller's views at last'.[141] He would have been one of many. In 1797 a group of deacons in a Baptist church in Hull wrote to the evangelical Baptist Pastor Joseph Kinghorn. The Hull church wanted Kinghorn to help them to find a minister, and specified the sort of man for whom they were looking. Among other things they were clear that he was to be a 'lively, zealous and affectionate preacher' and 'orthodox'. The letter has a marginal note explaining their understanding of 'orthodox'. It says 'of Mr Fuller's sentiments'.[142] The evangelical Calvinism represented by *The Gospel Worthy* was the catalyst for numerical growth in the existing churches at home, as well as church planting, and it underpinned the formation in 1792 and the subsequent early history of the Baptist Missionary Society.[143] In the nineteenth century what became known as 'Fullerism' (naturalized in Welsh as *Ffwleriaeth*)[144] predominated in Particular Baptist life, indeed, for those in the Baptist Union the question of the legitimacy of open offers was basically settled. The brand of soteriology which was characterized as Fullerism had far-reaching consequences.

Nevertheless Fuller's triumph was not quite complete. A minority of older High Calvinists would continue to reject 'duty faith', and their criticisms would be taken up by a new generation. The emergence of Strict and Particular Baptist groupings in the early nineteenth century should be seen in part as a reaction against Fuller's theology.[145] Key leaders of the Strict Baptist movement such as William Gadsby and J. C. Philpot regarded him as their *bête noire* and were scathing in their condemnation of him. For Gadsby, Fuller was 'the greatest enemy the church of God ever had, as his sentiments were so much cloaked in the sheep's clothing'.[146] This resistance is a reminder that, despite their shared heritage, those who identified as Calvinistic Baptists often found agreement in matters of soteriology hard to come by.

VII. Conclusion

Analysis of Particular Baptist soteriology from 1744 to 1899 has revealed a general movement away from the Calvinism of the 1644 *London Confession* to less strict forms of Calvinistic belief and, indeed, to no Calvinism at all. Spurgeon was a notable exception to this trend, even though his Calvinism was different in significant respects from that contained in the earlier confessions. This shift away from Dortian tenets did not happen as quickly or as thoroughly as it did with either the Presbyterians or indeed the Independents; nevertheless a clear trajectory can be traced.

As well as the differences in Particular Baptist soteriology which are apparent when one century is compared with another, there was heated debate between theologians within the movement at particular times over issues of both belief and practice. For example, Gill, Fuller and Booth, three of the most important eighteenth-century theologians, disagreed on a range of soteriological themes. The overarching issue which often created the fault lines between them was accommodation to contemporary culture. To what extent, and in what ways, was it appropriate to recast traditional doctrine to suit the spirit of the age? As Baptists encountered both the Enlightenment and Romanticism there were progressives who were willing to explore new paths and conservatives determined to stick to the old ways, as well as some who sought to find and traverse an alternative middle ground. Overall, Particular Baptist soteriology between 1744 to 1899 exhibits much movement and diversity.

There were, however, continuing commitments which were shared by the vast majority of Particular Baptists throughout our period. With just a few exceptions, they remained committed to Christ as the incarnate Son of God and as saviour. The journey undertaken by the English Presbyterians, from 'Elizabethan Puritanism to modern Unitarianism' was not one which was paralleled in Particular Baptist life.[147] Calvinistic Baptists remained committed (despite the odd exception) to maintaining the primacy of the atonement in their soteriological scheme. The loss of focus on the atonement, as represented, for example, by the theology of J. Baldwin Brown in nineteenth-century Congregationalism, did not happen in Particular Baptist life to any significant degree. One of the reasons for the continuing adherence to the deity of Christ and to the centrality of the atonement was the influence of the Evangelical Revival on Particular Baptist churches, with the eighteenth-century movement transfusing much life into the older Dissenting body. Most nineteenth-century Baptists with Particular Baptist roots remained 'evangelical' in their soteriology even when they abandoned strict Calvinism.

Calvinistic Baptists wrestled with the relationship between divine sovereignty and human responsibility, particularly in the eighteenth century. Despite the movement's dalliance with High Calvinism, the mainstream position for most of the period under discussion was that men and women could – indeed should – be exhorted to believe the gospel. A soteriology which stifled evangelistic effort was rejected. The decisive rejection of High Calvinism, represented by the publication of Fuller's *The Gospel Worthy*, coincided with a time of vigorous growth in Particular Baptist life, at home and abroad. Thus the story of English Particular Baptist soteriology is one not only of change and continuity but also one of great influence, in England and around the world.

Notes

1 C. H. Spurgeon, 'The Royal Prerogative', *New Park Street Pulpit/Metropolitan Tabernacle Pulpit (MTP)* (London: Passmore and Alabaster, 1856–1917), 26, Sermon Number (S. No.) 1523, Psa. 48.20, 21, delivered 15 February 1880, pp. 115–16.

2 C. H. Spurgeon, 'Your Personal Salvation', *MTP*, 26, S. No. 1524, 1 Pet. 1.9–12; Psa. 64.41, delivered 22 February 1890, p. 132.
3 Ibid., pp. 121–22.
4 See e.g. *Daily News* (16 February 1880), in 'Loose-Leaf Scrap Folder, October 1879 to April 1880', Spurgeon Archive, Spurgeon's College (2H), p. 34.
5 Even with this narrower focus, there are relevant themes which are not treated in this study due to constraints of space. E.g. the place of baptism in Particular Baptist soteriology is not considered. For this, see Anthony R. Cross, 'Baptismal Regeneration: Rehabilitating a Lost Dimension of New Testament Baptism', in Anthony R. Cross and Philip E. Thompson (eds), *Baptist Sacramentalism 2* (Milton Keynes: Paternoster, 2008), pp. 149–74, esp. pp. 155–57. Baptism occupied an important place in the soteriologies of some Particular Baptists, especially the minority who had a more 'sacramental' approach to the rite.
6 1644 *London Confession*, Clauses XXI and XXII, in William L. Lumpkin (ed.), *Baptist Confessions of Faith* (Valley Forge: Judson Press, 1969), pp. 162–63.
7 Stephen Wright, *The Early English Baptists, 1603–1649* (Woodbridge: Boydell, 2006), p. 134. For a useful survey of the 1618–19 Synod of Dort and its conclusions, see G. Michael Thomas, *The Extent of the Atonement: A Dilemma for Reformed Theology from Calvin to the Consensus* (Milton Keynes: Paternoster, 1997), pp. 128–59.
8 See especially 1644 *London Confession*, Clauses XXI–XXXII, in Lumpkin (ed.), *Baptist Confessions*, pp. 162–65 (Clause XXIII covers final perseverance). Cf. Barrie R. White, *English Baptists of the Seventeenth Century* (London: Baptist Historical Society, 1983), p. 64.
9 1644 *London Confession*, Clause III, in Lumpkin (ed.), *Baptist Confessions*, p. 157.
10 Ibid., pp. 146–47; 152.
11 See James M. Renihan, *Edification and Beauty: The Practical Ecclesiology of English Particular Baptists, 1675–1705* (Milton Keynes: Paternoster, 2005), passim.
12 1677 *Second London Confession*, Chapter X, 'Of Effectual Calling', in Lumpkin (ed.), *Baptist Confessions*, p. 265.
13 Ibid., p. 236.
14 A point made explicitly in the Preface to the 1677 *Second London Confession*. See ibid.
15 'Mr Fuller's statement of his religious principles', in John Ryland Jr, *The Work of Faith, the Labour of Love, and the Patience of Hope Illustrated in the Life and Death of the Rev. Andrew Fuller* (2nd edn, London: Button and Son, 1818), pp. 66 (Clause VIII), 67 (Clause XII) and 68 (Clause XIV).
16 Ibid., p. 66; italics original.
17 In Presbyterianism, Arminianism had been growing from the early years of the eighteenth century. See C. G. Bolam, Jeremy Goring, H. L. Short and Roger Thomas, *The English Presbyterians: From Elizabethan Puritanism to Modern Unitarianism* (London: George Allen and Unwin, 1968), pp. 135–37, 180–86.
18 See R. Tudur Jones, *Congregationalism in England: 1662–1962* (London: Independent Press, 1962), pp. 141–44, 148–51.
19 As cited by Ernest A. Payne, *The Baptist Union: A Short History* (London: Carey Kingsgate, 1958), p. 24.
20 Ibid., p. 61.
21 G. Pritchard, *Memoir of the Life and Writings of the Rev. Joseph Ivimey* (London: G. Wightman, 1835), p. 311.
22 For the gradual coming together of the 'Generals' and the 'Particulars', see John H. Y. Briggs, *English Baptists of the Nineteenth Century* (Didcot: Baptist Historical Society, 1994), pp. 96–157; for the events of 1891, see Payne, *Baptist Union*, pp. 146–47.
23 Ian Sellers, 'John Howard Hinton, Theologian', *Baptist Quarterly*, 33/3 (1989), p. 123.

24 Matthew Arnold, *St. Paul and Protestantism* (London: Smith and Elder, 1870), p. 19.
25 Briggs, *English Baptists of the Nineteenth Century*, p. 118.
26 C. H. Spurgeon, *Autobiography: Compiled from His Diary, Letters, and Records by His Wife and His Private Secretary*, 4 vols (London: Passmore and Alabaster, 1897–99), II, pp. 159–61.
27 Matthew Arnold, *Culture and Anarchy* (Cambridge: Cambridge University Press, 1935 [1869]), p. 31.
28 *Annual Paper Descriptive of the Lord's Work Connected with the Pastors' College During the Year 1870* (London: Passmore and Alabaster, 1871), p. 14.
29 For a detailed study of Baldwin Brown, see Mark Hopkins, *Nonconformity's Romantic Generation: Evangelical and Liberal Theologies in Victorian England* (Carlisle: Paternoster, 2004), pp. 17–45.
30 *Annual Paper Descriptive of the Lord's Work Connected with the Pastors' College During the Year 1870*, p. 5.
31 C. H. Spurgeon (ed.), *The Sword and the Trowel: A Record of Combat with Sin and Labour for the Lord* (London: Passmore and Alabaster, 1865–92), April 1870, p. 146.
32 Peter J. Morden, *'Communion with Christ and His People': The Spirituality of C. H. Spurgeon* (Oxford: Regent's Park College, 2010), p. 96.
33 For the drift away from Calvinism among the Independents in the nineteenth century, see Hopkins, *Nonconformity's Romantic Generation*, pp. 17–110.
34 John Bunyan, *A Confession of My Faith, and a Reason of My Practice* [1672] in *Miscellaneous Works of John Bunyan*, 13 vols, gen. ed. R. Sharrock (Oxford: Clarendon, 1976–94), IV, p. 146.
35 As shown in the clauses already discussed. See 1644 *London Confession*, Clause XXI; 1677 *Second London Confession*, Chapter 10, 'On Effectual Calling', both in Lumpkin (ed.), *Baptist Confessions*, pp. 162 and 264–65 respectively; 'Mr Fuller's statement of his religious principles', in Ryland Jr, *Andrew Fuller*, Clause VIII, p. 66.
36 Anne Steele, 'Christ the Way to Heaven', in J. R. Broome, *A Bruised Reed: The Life and Times of Anne Steele* (Harpenden: Gospel Standard Trust, 2007), Part 2, 'Hymns of Anne Steele', Hymn 23, p. 268.
37 For a Calvinistic example, see *The Savoy Declaration of Faith and Order Owned and Practised in the Congregational Churches . . .*, ed. A. G. Matthews (London: Independent Press, 1959 [1658]), Chapter VIII, pp. 86–88; for an Arminian example, see *The Standard [General Baptist] Confession, 1660*, Clauses IV and VI, in Lumpkin (ed.), *Baptist Confessions*, pp. 225–27.
38 For Priestley, see Isabel Rivers and David L. Wykes, *Joseph Priestley, Scientist, Philosopher, and Theologian* (Oxford: Oxford University Press, 2008).
39 Andrew Fuller, *The Calvinistic and Socinian Systems Examined and Compared . . .* [1802], in *The Complete Works of the Rev Andrew Fuller, with a Memoir of His Life by the Rev. Andrew Gunton Fuller*, ed. A. G. Fuller, rev. ed. J. Belcher, 3 vols (3rd edn, Harrisonburg, VA: Sprinkle Publications, 1988 [1845]), II, p. 118.
40 As charted by Bolam et al., *English Presbyterians: From Elizabethan Puritanism to Modern Unitarianism*, passim.
41 Robert Robinson, the late-eighteenth-century pastor of St Andrew's Street Church in Cambridge, was unusual among Particular Baptist ministers in that he became unorthodox on the Trinity later in life.
42 Steele, 'Christ the Physician of Souls', in Broome, *A Bruised Reed*, Part 2, 'Hymns of Anne Steele', Hymn 28, p. 271.
43 John Bunyan, *The Pilgrim's Progress* [1678], in *Works of John Bunyan*, ed. George Offor, 3 vols (London: Blackie and Son, 1856), III, p. 102.
44 Bunyan could evoke great emotion in those who heard him preach and lead services. See the words of Agnes Beaumont as cited by Raymond Brown, 'Bedfordshire Nonconformist Devotion', *Baptist Quarterly*, 35/7 (July 1994), p. 315. Cf. Richard

L. Greaves, *Glimpses of Glory: John Bunyan and English Dissent* (Stanford: Stanford University Press, 2002), pp. 309–12.
45 J. G. Greenhough, *The Cross in Modern Life* (London: Hodder and Stoughton, 1914 [1896]), p. 10.
46 P. T. Forsyth, *Baldwin Brown: A Tribute, a Reminiscence, and a Study* (London: James Clarke, 1884), p. 4.
47 David W. Bebbington, 'British Baptist Crucicentrism since the Late Eighteenth Century: Part 2', *Baptist Quarterly*, 44/1 (January 2012), p. 281.
48 John Bunyan, *A Defence of the Doctrine of Justification, by Faith* [1672], in *Miscellaneous Works of John Bunyan*, IV, p. 65.
49 Steele, 'Redemption by Christ Alone', in Broome, *A Bruised Reed*, Part 2, 'Hymns of Anne Steele', Hymn 71, p. 284.
50 Steele, 'Sin the Cause of Christ's Death', in Broome, *A Bruised Reed*, Part 2, 'Hymns of Anne Steele', Hymn 104, p. 294.
51 The hymns were No. 135, 'A View of Christ Crucified', and No. 137, 'A Dying Saviour'. See John Rippon, *A Selection of Hymns. . .* (London: W. Isbister, 1874 [1787]).
52 Ken R. Manley, *'Redeeming Love Proclaim': John Rippon and the Particular Baptists* (Carlisle: Paternoster, 2004), p. 112.
53 [Anne Steele] *Poems on Subjects Chiefly Devotional, by Theodosia* (Bristol: Pine, 1780 [1760]); Anne Steele, *Hymns, Psalms, and Poems: With a Memoir by John Sheppard* (London: C. Gordlier, 1882 [1863]).
54 Cf. Stephen R. Holmes, 'Ransomed, Healed, Restored, Forgiven: Evangelical Accounts of the Atonement', in D. Tidball, D. Hilborn and J. Thacker (eds), *The Atonement Debate* (Grand Rapids, MN: Zondervan, 2008), pp. 270–71. Holmes states that Fuller is the first evangelical that he is aware of to draw back from penal substitution.
55 Andrew Fuller, *Six Letters to Dr Ryland*, in *Fuller's Works*, II, pp. 703–4; emphases original. These letters were written in 1803 but not published until 1831, when they appeared in an early edition of Fuller's *Works*.
56 Cf. Stephen R. Holmes, *The Wondrous Cross: Atonement and Penal Substitution in the Bible and History* (Milton Keynes: Paternoster, 2007), p. 66.
57 Abraham Booth, *Divine Justice*, in *The Collected Works of Abraham Booth, with some Account of His Life and Writings*, 3 vols (London, 1813), III, p. 52; emphases original. For more on this dispute, see Peter J. Morden, *Offering Christ to the World: Andrew Fuller (1754–1815) and the Revival of Eighteenth Century Particular Baptist Life* (Carlisle: Paternoster, 2003), pp. 84–87.
58 Indeed, moral government language is included in Fuller's aforementioned personal confession of faith. See 'Mr Fuller's statement of his religious principles', Clause XIII, in Ryland Jr, *Andrew Fuller*, p. 68.
59 For this argument and the evidence in support of it, see Morden, *Offering Christ to the World*, pp. 89–92. Fuller corresponded directly with Hopkins.
60 Joseph Bellamy, *True Religion Delineated; Or, Experimental Religion . . .* (Boston: Henry P. Russell, 1804 [1750]), e.g. p. 310. Fuller wrote a Preface to the English edn of this work. See J. Bellamy, *True Religion Delineated; or, Experimental Religion . . . with a 'Recommendatory Preface' by A. Fuller* (3rd edn, London: T. Hamilton, 1809).
61 David W. Bebbington, 'British Baptist Crucicentrism since the late Eighteenth Century: Part 1', *Baptist Quarterly*, 44/4 (2011), pp. 230–31.
62 See Owen Thomas, *The Atonement Controversy in Welsh Theological Literature and Debate, 1701–1841* (Edinburgh: Banner of Truth, 2002), pp. 152–53, 188.
63 Ibid., pp. 221–22; R. Tudur Jones, *Congregationalism in Wales*, ed. Robert Pope (Cardiff: University of Wales Press, 2004), p. 135.

64 Speaking of Dissent as whole, Dale A. Johnson notes the prominence of the image of God as 'moral governor' in writing on the atonement in the nineteenth century. See his *The Changing Shape of English Nonconformity, 1825–1925* (Oxford: Oxford University Press, 1999), p. 131.
65 See the evidence cited by Bebbington, 'British Baptist Crucicentrism: . . . Part 2', p. 278.
66 R. W. Dale, *The Atonement* (London: Hodder and Stoughton, 1875). Dale was not uncritical of moral government principles, arguing in *The Atonement* that the moral theory on its own is inadequate to explain the cross. See A. W. W. Dale, *Life of R. W. Dale of Birmingham* (London: Hodder and Stoughton, 1902), p. 326.
67 David Gracey, *Sin and the Unfolding of Salvation, Being the Three Years' Course of Theological Lectures Delivered at the Pastors' College . . .* (London: Passmore and Alabaster, 1894), p. 81.
68 Ibid., p. 84.
69 See e.g. ibid., pp. 248–50.
70 See Hopkins, *Nonconformity's Romantic Generation*, p. 80.
71 For some of the changes in Congregationalism, see Johnson, *The Changing Shape of English Nonconformity*, pp. 134–40.
72 Sheridan Gilley, 'Introduction', in S. Gilley and Brian Stanley (eds), *World Christianities, c. 1815–c. 1914* (Cambridge: Cambridge University Press, 2006), p. 3; David W. Bebbington, *Holiness in Nineteenth-Century England* (Carlisle: Paternoster, 2000), p. 13.
73 Bebbington, 'British Baptist Crucicentrism: . . . Part 2', pp. 280–81.
74 See Morden, *'Communion with Christ and His People'*, e.g. pp. 113–14, 160–61, 272–74.
75 Ian M. Randall, *Spirituality and Social Change: The Contribution of F. B. Meyer (1847–1929)* (Carlisle: Paternoster, 2003), pp. 36–39.
76 Further forces, such as Darwin's evolutionary theories and the advent of liberal biblical criticism, also challenged the old certainties. See David W. Bebbington, *Baptists through the Centuries: A History of a Global People* (Waco, TX: Baylor University Press, 2010), p. 109.
77 Bebbington, 'British Baptist Crucicentrism: . . . Part 2', p. 288.
78 John Owen, *The Death of Death in the Death of Christ* [1647] in *The Works of John Owen*, 24 vols, ed. W. H. Goold (London: Banner of Truth, 1965–68 [1850–53]), pp. 173, 214; Thomas, *The Extent of the Atonement*, pp. 233–34.
79 John Gill, *The Cause of God and Truth* (London: Thomas Tegg, 1838 [1735–38]), pp. 180–81 Thomas J. Nettles, *By His Grace and for His Glory* (Grand Rapids: Baker, 1986), p. 79.
80 For details of this dispute, see Morden, *Offering Christ to the World*, pp. 63–76.
81 For biographical details of Taylor and the early history of the New Connexion see Adam Taylor, *Memoirs of the Rev. Dan Taylor* (London: Baynes and Son, 1820), passim; Frank W. Rinaldi, *The Tribe of Dan: The New Connexion of General Baptists 1770–1891: A Study in the Transition from Revival Movement to Established Denomination* (Milton Keynes: Paternoster, 2008), passim.
82 As stated on the title pages of Dan Taylor, *Observations on the Rev Andrew Fuller's Late Pamphlet Entitled The Gospel of Christ Worthy of All Acceptation* (St Ives, Cambridgeshire, 1786); and *Observations on the Rev. Andrew Fuller's Reply to Philanthropos* (St Ives, Cambridgeshire, 1788).
83 Taylor, *Observations on . . . Fuller's Reply to Philanthropos*, p. 29, cf. pp. 29–30, 'Christ died for all men, as the Scripture positively asserts'. Texts that Taylor cited include 2 Cor. 5.14–15 and 1 Tim. 2.6, 'Christ Jesus . . . gave himself as a ransom for all'.

84 Andrew Fuller, *Reply to the Observations of Philanthropos* [1787], in *Fuller's Works*, II, pp. 488–89.
85 From a 'Conversation with a friend at Edinburgh, on the subject of Particular Redemption, in 1805', recorded by John W. Morris, *Memoirs of the Life and Death of the Rev. Andrew Fuller* (2nd edn, London: Wightman and Cramp, 1826), p. 311.
86 Fuller, *Reply to Philanthropos*, in *Fuller's Works*, II, p. 506.
87 Jonathan Edwards, *The Freedom of the Will*, in *The Works of Jonathan Edwards*, I, ed. P. Ramsey (New Haven: Yale University Press, 1985 [1754]), p. 435.
88 See Morden, *Offering Christ to the World*, pp. 43–50.
89 David W. Bebbington, *Evangelicalism in Modern Britain: A History from the 1730s to the 1980s* (London: Unwin Hyman, 1989), p. 64.
90 Spurgeon, *Autobiography*, I, p. 174.
91 C. H. Spurgeon, 'The Present Position Of Calvinism In England', in Spurgeon (ed.), *Sword and Trowel*, February 1874, pp. 49–53.
92 For more on Spurgeon's particular approach to Calvinism, see Morden, *'Communion with Christ and His People'*, pp. 39–42.
93 George Coltman, 'The Present State of the Baptist Denomination', in the *General Baptist Magazine* (1868), p. 101, as cited by Rinaldi, *Tribe of Dan*, p. 185.
94 John Clifford, 'General Baptists in the Twentieth Century', in the *General Baptist Magazine* (1885), p. 5, as cited by Rinaldi, *Tribe of Dan*, p. 188.
95 Morden, *'Communion with Christ and His People'*, p. 201.
96 Payne, *The Baptist Union*, p. 109.
97 John Clifford, 'The Fusion of Baptists', in the *General Baptist Magazine* (1890), p. 368, as cited by Rinaldi, *Tribe of Dan*, p. 194.
98 1677 *Second London Confession*, Chapter X, in Lumpkin (ed.), *Baptist Confessions*, p. 265.
99 Spurgeon, *Autobiography*, I, p. 175.
100 1644 *London Confession*, Clause XXI, in Lumpkin (ed.), *Baptist Confessions*, p. 162.
101 1677 *Second London Confession*, Chapter X, in Lumpkin (ed.), *Baptist Confessions*, p. 265.
102 Ibid., p. 265.
103 John Coffey and Paul C. H. Lim, 'Introduction', in Coffey and Lim (eds), *The Cambridge Companion to Puritanism* (Cambridge: Cambridge University Press, 2008), p. 4. For an extended discussion of Puritan approaches to assurance, see J. Von Ruhr, *The Covenant of Grace in Puritan Thought* (Atlanta: Scholars, 1986), pp. 155–91.
104 Thomas Brooks, *Heaven on Earth* (London: Banner of Truth, 1961 [1654]), p. 139.
105 John Bunyan, *Grace Abounding to the Chief of Sinners* [1666], in *Bunyan's Works*, I, pp. 1–50.
106 Morden, *Offering Christ to the World*, pp. 158–65.
107 Ibid., pp. 165–71.
108 'Wallis Family Tree', Kettering Baptist Church Archive, Kettering. George Wallis was the son of Samuel Wallis and the great nephew of Beeby and Martha Wallis, prominent members at Kettering. For the importance of the Wallis family to the church at Kettering, see Ryland Jr, *Andrew Fuller*, pp. 372–73. George became a deacon of the church in 1813.
109 'Diary of George Wallis', Kettering Baptist Church Archive, Kettering, entry for 7 August 1808.
110 Ibid., see entries for 24 November 1816, 29 December 1816, 26 January 1817, 2 March 1817 (all on two facing pages). Three were positive about his state before God, one was more cautious. The fact that Wallis was writing less frequently in

his diary is a further sign he was moving away from the Puritan confessional approach.

111 Morden, *'Communion with Christ and His People'*, pp. 16–46.

112 Although he did practice this for a while in the early years of his Christian life. For a full discussion on Spurgeon and assurance, see Morden, *'Communion with Christ and His People'*, pp. 43–44, 71–76.

113 C. H. Spurgeon, 'Redemption through Blood, the Gracious Forgiveness of Sins', *MTP*, 37, S. No. 2207, Eph. 1.7, n.d., p. 311.

114 C. H. Spurgeon, 'The Blessings of Full Assurance', *MTP*, 34, S. No. 2023, 1 Jn 5.13, delivered 13 May 1888, pp. 273–76.

115 Andrew Fuller, *Antinomianism Contrasted with the Religion Taught and Exemplified in the Holy Scriptures*, 2nd edn [1st edn, 1816; 2nd edn, 1817], in *Fuller's Works*, II, pp. 737–62. For an analysis of the book, see Curt Daniel, 'Andrew Fuller and Antinomianism', in M. A. G. Haykin (ed.), *'At the Pure Fountain of Thy Word': Andrew Fuller as an Apologist* (Milton Keynes: Paternoster, 2004), pp. 74–82.

116 Spurgeon, *Autobiography*, I, pp. 258–59.

117 C. H. Spurgeon, 'Notebooks with Sermon Outlines, Vols 2–9', Spurgeon's College, Spurgeon Archive (U1), 'Nonconformity', S. No. 223, Rom. 12.2.

118 For details, see Robert W. F. Archer, 'The Evangelistic Ministry of John Bunyan' (unpublished MPhil dissertation, University of Wales [Spurgeon's College], 1959).

119 John Bunyan, *Some Gospel Truths Opened* [1656], in *Bunyan's Works*, II, p. 169.

120 John Bunyan, *Come and Welcome to Jesus Christ* [1678], in ibid., I, pp. 240–99.

121 Ibid., p. 284.

122 For some of these other factors, such as persecution and the geographical isolation of many churches, see Michael A. G. Haykin, 'A Habitation of God, through the Spirit: John Sutcliff (1752–1814) and the Revitalization of the Calvinistic Baptists in the Late Eighteenth Century', *Baptist Quarterly*, 34/7 (1992), pp. 304–19.

123 John Gill, *The Doctrines of God's Everlasting Love to His Elect . . . Stated and Defended. In a Letter to Dr Abraham Taylor* (London, 1752), p. 78.

124 For Davis, see Geoffrey F. Nuttall, 'Northamptonshire and the Modern Question: A Turning Point in Eighteenth-Century Dissent', *Journal of Theological Studies*, 16/1 (1965), pp. 104–8.

125 John Gill, 'Recommendatory Preface to the Hymns of Richard Davis' (1748), printed in G. T. Streather, *Memorials of the Independent Chapel at Rothwell* (Rothwell: Rothwell United Reformed Church, 1994), pp. 63–64.

126 Roger Hayden, *Continuity and Change: Evangelical Calvinism among Eighteenth-Century Baptist Ministers Trained at Bristol Academy, 1690–1791* (Didcot: Baptist Historical Society, 2006), passim.

127 J. Fawcett Jr, *An Account of . . . the late John Fawcett, DD* (London: Baldwin, Craddock and Joy, 1818), pp. 97–102.

128 As shown e.g. by the opposition to *The Gospel Worthy of All Acceptation* which was later to come from these counties. See e.g. A. Fuller to Thomas Steevens of Colchester, 18 May 1793, 'Andrew Fuller Letters', Regent's Park College, Oxford (4/5/1): 'I know the opposition made to "Andrew Fuller" in S[uffolk] and N[orfolk].'

129 Kerry J. Birch, 'The Contribution of the Baptists of Bath to the Religious and Social History of the City [1774–1837], with Special Reference to Somerset Street and Twerton Baptist Churches' (unpublished MLitt thesis, University of Bristol, 2008), passim.

130 The judgement is Fuller's own. Ryland Jr, *Andrew Fuller*, p. 11.

131 Ibid., p. 8.

132 Bruce Hindmarsh, *John Newton and the English Evangelical Tradition: Between the Conversions of Wesley and Wilberforce* (Oxford: Clarenden Press, 1996), pp. 142–49.
133 Fawcett Jr, *An Account of . . . the late John Fawcett*, p. 15.
134 Ibid., p. 108.
135 See R. Hall Sr, *The Complete Works of the Late Robert Hall*, ed. John W. Morris (London, 1828), pp. 47–199, for the second edition of Hall's work.
136 See Tudur Jones, *Congregationalism in Wales*, pp. 134–35.
137 Andrew Fuller, *The Gospel Worthy of All Acceptation* (Northampton: T. Dicey, 1785), p. 40. The text printed in *Fuller's Works*, II, pp. 328–416.
138 Fuller, *Gospel Worthy*, 1st edn, pp. 162–63, 166.
139 Most recently, Peter J. Morden, 'Baptist and Evangelical: Andrew Fuller and *The Gospel Worthy of All Acceptation*', in *Strict Baptist Historical Society Bulletin*, 38 (2011), pp. 10–14. This published lecture also contains a more complete analysis of the text of *The Gospel Worthy*.
140 See ibid., p. 10. For the text of Edwards' work, see Jonathan Edwards, *The Life of David Brainerd*, in *The Works of Jonathan Edwards*, VII, ed. Norman Pettit (London and New Haven: Yale University Press, 1985 [1749]).
141 Ryland Jr, *Andrew Fuller*, p. 131.
142 Cited by Arthur H. Kirkby, 'The Theology of Andrew Fuller in Its Relation to Calvinism' (unpublished PhD thesis, Edinburgh University, 1956), p. 11. The letter, dated 23 March 1797, is from three Deacons at George Street Baptist Church in Hull to Kinghorn, pastor of St Mary's Baptist Church, Norwich. The original is held in the archives at St Mary's. Cf. Michael R. Watts, *The Dissenters, Volume 1: From the Reformation to the French Revolution* (Oxford: Clarendon Press, 1978), p. 460, who states: 'Fullerism became the new orthodoxy of the [Particular Baptist] denomination.'
143 For growth in England, see Morden, 'Baptist and Evangelical: Andrew Fuller and *The Gospel Worthy*', pp. 15–18; for the BMS, see Peter J. Morden, 'Andrew Fuller and the BMS', *Baptist Quarterly*, 41/3 (2005), pp. 134–57.
144 Nuttall, 'Northants and *The Modern Question*', p. 101. Nuttall stated that at the time he was writing the word *Ffwleriaeth* was still in use and cites R. T. Jenkins, *Hanes Cymru yn y Deunawfed Ganrif* (Cardiff: University of Wales Press, 1945), p. 66.
145 Robert W. Oliver, 'The Emergence of a Strict and Particular Baptist Community among the English Calvinistic Baptists, 1770–1850' (Unpublished PhD thesis, CNAA [London Bible College], 1986), p. 119.
146 K. Dix, *Strict and Particular: English Strict and Particular Baptists in the Nineteenth Century* (Didcot: Baptist Historical Society, 2001), pp. 37 n.103; Michael A. G. Haykin, 'Particular Redemption in the Writings of Andrew Fuller', in David W. Bebbington (ed.), *The Gospel in the World: International Baptist Studies*, Studies in Baptist History and Thought (Carlisle: Paternoster, 2002), p. 108.
147 Bolam et al., *English Presbyterians: From Elizabethan Puritanism to Modern Unitarianism*.

10 Nonconformists and the Holy Spirit: A Dogmatic Overview

Robert Pope

In Christian history, pneumatology has often been eclipsed by other, apparently more pressing theological concerns. As a result, Gregory of Nazianzus, for example, could refer to the Spirit as 'the God about whom no one writes (*theos agraptos*)'.[1] While Christology has been dominated by discussion about the humanity and the divinity of Christ, the Spirit's divinity has, doubtless, been the cause of less debate than that of the Son, though 'Father' and 'Son' more 'readily function as personal symbols', a consideration which can cause concern over how best to answer the question, 'What (or who) is the Holy Spirit?'[2]

When the Spirit has been the focus of attention, controversy has often ensued, as with the second-century Montanists, for example, who, despite relative orthodoxy in their teaching, were condemned for stressing the immediate inspiration of the Holy Spirit and an ethic which suggested that personal sanctification, in a conservative ethical sense, was achievable. Pneumatological concern, then, has not revolved so much around the Spirit's divinity as around 'the identification of the Spirit and the location of his activity'.[3]

According to Colin E. Gunton (1941–2003), one of English Nonconformity's most prominent and prolific theologians of the twentieth century, there are three 'places' which offer 'highly varying accounts of the person and work of the Spirit'. The first he characterized as 'the mainstream dogmatic tradition', where the emphasis is on 'the work of the Spirit as applying to believer and Church the benefits of Christ'. The second is what he termed 'that amorphous group of phenomena known as the Charismatic movement', in which the Spirit is seen as 'the *cause* of particular religious phenomena', but where he considered that the Spirit's work is often viewed as separate from that of the Son. The third 'focus' sees the Spirit as identified 'with or in particular cultural and historical developments'. This so-called Hegelian approach emphasizes the essential immanence of the

Spirit, and Gunton rejected this as a misunderstanding. In his reappropriation of the 'mainstream dogmatic tradition', he attempted to maintain the *transcendence* of the Spirit: 'The Spirit may be active *within* the world, but he does not become identical with any part of the world. That is the function of the Son, who becomes flesh.'[4] For Gunton, both the 'charismatic' and 'Hegelian' approaches result in a weak pneumatology, where, in the former, the Spirit's person and work is indistinguishable from that of the Son and, in the latter, the Spirit is inseparable from historical events and cultural phenomena.

This chapter will focus on Nonconformist understandings of the 'mainstream dogmatic tradition'. There are inevitably points at which the charismatic and the Hegelian will receive passing reference, but only when they have impacted on the dogmatic tradition. A broadly historical approach will be adopted which will highlight how mainstream Nonconformists (Independents, Baptists and Presbyterians) in successive periods perceived the experience of the Spirit in the life of faith. The aim is to enable a clear, if general, overview of how Nonconformists have understood the work of the Holy Spirit.

I. The Spirit and the Puritans

Nonconformity and Dissent find their historical roots in the sixteenth-century movements which sought to reform the church. Although the result of social, political and religious developments, the Reformation, as Geoffrey Nuttall argued, could be seen as an outworking of the Holy Spirit and, as a result, the third person of the Trinity came to greater prominence in the life of faith. He wrote:

> The ecclesial system, with its centralization in an ultimate, single source of authority, was dissolved. The Bible was translated into the vernacular, for men to read for themselves, unchecked. The Renaissance of learning encouraged men to think for themselves, and the spirit of individualism became as potent in theological as in other mental disciplines. These and other influences combined to direct men's attention, for the first time in their lives and with some suddenness, to the nature of religion in the Bible, and more especially in the New Testament, as something individually experienced, a living, personal relationship, open to Everyman, between God and his soul. The doctrine bearing most nearly upon this experience and relationship on its Godward side was the doctrine of the Holy Spirit.[5]

According to Nuttall, the doctrine of the Holy Spirit 'received a more detailed consideration from the Puritans of seventeenth-century England than it has received at any other time in Christian history'.[6] A similar claim was made, slightly earlier, by Thomas Rees, at one time the principal of the Bala-Bangor Theological College, who wrote in 1915 that 'such men as John Owen, Thomas and John Goodwin, John Howe, and Richard Baxter bestowed upon the work of the Spirit the most elaborate exposition it has ever received'.[7] As will be seen, this treatment was not merely intellectual but *experimental*; the Spirit was only understood as he was perceived to be at work within the Christian's heart.

For most Puritans, it was the work of the Spirit which makes someone a Christian. In other words, it is the Spirit who effects both regeneration and sanctification. Protestants, in general, asserted that the Spirit was responsible for conversion and faith as 'initial acts of salvation', which contrasted with the prevailing Roman Catholic view of the 'efficacy of works and sacraments', where baptism itself had been seen to effect regeneration. In so doing, the Reformers allowed the closer and more direct 'association of the Spirit with the person and work of Christ'. In this way the Spirit both 'completes' and 'fulfils' 'the work of God in Christ, supplying the faith to accept the Gospel and the will to embrace the benefits of the Redeemer'.[8]

John Owen (1616–83), one of the most prolific and significant of Puritan authors and one who entered into an extended discussion of the Holy Spirit, maintained the theological importance of the Holy Spirit as a *hypostasis* of the divine Trinity while also asserting the Spirit's significance by delineating a specific task for 'him' within the redemptive scheme. For Owen (as for Augustine, and others, before him), it was the Holy Spirit who makes effective the gracious acts of God in salvation. Owen wrote: 'in every divine act, the authority of the Father, the love and wisdom of the Son, with the immediate efficacy and power of the Holy Ghost are to be considered'. Thus 'the Father designs salvation, the Son purchases it, and the Holy Spirit applies and accomplishes it, makes it effectual in us'.[9] Similarly Thomas Goodwin (1600–80), 'the Elder', one of the Independents in attendance at the Westminster Assembly, chaplain to Oliver Cromwell, president of Magdalen College, Oxford, and subsequently minister of the Congregational church in Fetter Lane, London, wrote in *Of the Work of the Holy Ghost and Our Salvation*, that 'election is appropriated to the Father, redemption to the Son, application to the Holy Ghost'.[10] For these Puritans it is the presence of the Spirit which makes redemption a lived and living reality. Without the Spirit, redemption might remain a historical event and even a theological datum, but it would remain unknown, and thus ineffective, in the human heart.

The Spirit makes redemption real to people because, in their utter depravity, they are unable to achieve salvation by their own efforts. Much of this discussion occurred within a wider debate about the justification only of God's elect. There were those, such as William Twisse (1578–1646) and Tobias Crisp (1600–43), who claimed that this implied that men and women were justified from eternity. The more mainstream view was that justification was the work of the Spirit in the present as expressed in the *Westminster Confession* (XI, 4): 'God did, from all eternity, decree to justify all the elect; and Christ did, in the fulnesse of time, die for their sins, and rise again for their justification; nevertheless they are not justified, until the Holy Spirit doth in due time actually apply Christ unto them.' The Westminster divines sought unambiguously to demonstrate that God alone was responsible for human salvation, that salvation was God's gracious gift made possible through Christ, but that salvation was made real only in each person's life in each successive age by the power of the Spirit rather than decreed from eternity. Later generations would debate what exactly this might mean (as we shall see later).

For the Puritans, sanctification followed regeneration. For Calvinists such as John Owen, sanctification, like salvation itself, could not be conceived in any sense as reliant on human effort. It was not the sum of moral endeavour. Instead it was the gracious act of God by the Spirit. In this way it is the Spirit who brings regeneration, or new birth, to people and sets them apart for godly living. Their sanctification does not make them morally perfect, but places God's seal upon them which will be perfected in eternity. The Spirit accomplishes this by his immediate presence within believers. According to John Owen:

> Sanctification . . . is the immediate work of God by his Spirit upon our whole nature, proceeding from the peace made for us by Jesus Christ, whereby being changed unto his likeness, we are kept entirely at peace with God, and are preserved unblameable, or in a state of gracious acceptance with him to the end.[11]

There are a number of points of significance here. Owen links the work of the Spirit to the work of Christ. Furthermore, sanctification is an 'immediate' work of God in the human heart, but holiness is eschatological. In other words, Owen did not believe that sanctification was accomplished suddenly, but that it could only be achieved by God working directly in the human heart by the Holy Spirit. As such, it is achieved fully only at the final resurrection. He described it thus:

> The work of holiness in its beginning is but like the seed cast into the earth; namely the *seed of God* whereby we are born again. And it is known how seed that is cast into the earth doth grow and increase: being variously cherished and nourished, it is in its nature to take root and to spring up, bringing forth fruit. So it is with the principle of grace and

holiness. It is small at first, but being received in good and honest hearts, made so by the Spirit of God, and there nourished and cherished, it takes root and brings forth fruit. And both these, even the first planting and the increase of it, are both equally from God by His Spirit.[12]

For the Calvinistic Puritans, this was the result of human impotence. William Dell (ca 1607–69), one-time chaplain to Cromwell's New Model Army and, until the Restoration, master of Gonville and Caius College, Cambridge, put it thus: 'By *Nature*, we are all without *strength*, weak, impotent Creatures, utterly *unable* to do any thing that is *truly* and *spiritually* righteous and good.' It is the power of love and unity which the Spirit brings which enables justification, and 'power is an inseparable adjunct of the *Spirit* as *weakness* is of *flesh*'.[13] For the Puritans the Spirit was not only the seal of true Christian belief but also the divine power in human beings turning them from sin to the living of the godly life. This confirmed that salvation was the work of God in Christ, made real through the Spirit. As a result, for some, the presence of the Spirit became the means by which a person's true conversion could be measured.

This was expressed, admittedly polemically, when the Puritans opposed the use of set and written services and prayers. Such an objection can be traced back to the sixteenth-century Separatists, such as the 'martyr' Henry Barrow (ca 1550–93) who had asked provocatively, 'may reading be said [to be] praying?' Around 1588, the Separatists were recorded as worshipping thus: 'They teach that all stinted prayers & red service is but babbling in the Lords sight & hath neyther promises of blessing or edification, for that they are but Cushyns for such idell Priests and Atheists as have not the Spirit of God.'[14] Joseph Hussey (1660–1726), a post-Ejectment non-conforming minister (initially Presbyterian but later Independent), wrote: 'Hath not flying to Notes upon every Sentence almost to be utter'd, under a Colour of refreshing Memory, griev'd the Spirit?' Indeed, he considered that the reading of a prayer or a sermon had so deadened church life 'that we may almost fear he [i.e. the Spirit] is gone'.[15]

Puritans differed over the extent to which written prayers were considered anathema. The Separatists seemed certain that they had no place in Christian life and worship; Presbyterians were not quite as extreme, though the Directory for Public Worship, compiled and approved at the Westminster Assembly, noted the need for extempore prayer. However, other written words were considered to be significant, whether meticulously prepared sermons or, more importantly, the words of scripture. These, too, comprised the Holy Spirit's specific sphere of influence. Indeed, Presbyterian and Independent Puritans insisted that the Spirit could not be divorced from the word of scripture, and the one was necessary in order to understand the other. According to the *Savoy Declaration* (1658), 'we acknowledge the inward illumination of the Spirit of God to be necessary for the saving understanding of such things as are revealed in the Word'.[16] While *sola Scriptura* became one of the watch-words of the Reformation, confirming that the scriptures were to be the final authority in the life of faith, in fact the Reformers had, on the one hand, a basic recognition of the authority of the orthodox Fathers of the church and, on the other, a profound sense of the need for the Spirit to illuminate the believer and to make Christ's benefits real in human life. Thus, for Zwingli, 'God teaches through his Spirit and through the letter that has been written by the inspiration of his Spirit and ordinance, and he says: "Search the Scriptures"'. Equally, for Calvin, the church was governed by the Spirit but he went on to insist that the Spirit had 'bound it to the word'; for it would be 'no less reasonable to boast of the Spirit without the word than it would be absurd to bring forward the word itself without the Spirit'.[17] Indeed, Calvin had argued that it was the 'inner testimony of the Spirit' which enabled people to hear and accept the Word of God when it was proclaimed to them.[18]

Most Puritans – whatever their ecclesiological preference – inherited and developed this sense that the Spirit and the scriptures worked together. Thus the Holy Spirit's activity both transformed the written words into God's word and also worked in the listeners enabling them to hear God's word in scripture. In this way, Nuttall explains: 'The work of the Holy Spirit in connexion with Scripture is thus twofold: the Spirit both inspired its writers and enlightens its hearers or readers.'[19] Richard Sibbes (1577–1635), whose Puritanism demanded neither separatism nor the rejection of set liturgies, put the case in this way:

> God, joining with the soul and spirit of a man whom he intends to convert, besides that inbred light that is in the soul, causeth him to see a divine majesty shining forth in the Scriptures, so that there must be an infused establishing by the Spirit to settle the heart in this first principle . . . that the Scriptures are the word of God. There must be a double light. So there must be a Spirit in me, as there is a Spirit in the Scripture, before I can see any thing.[20]

As a result, the Spirit was also responsible for human responses to the word of God. The Spirit's work in regeneration has already been discussed. But the Calvinistic Puritans confirmed that the Spirit prompted *all* human responses. The root of this assertion was the firm belief that God made provision for all human need and that God alone was responsible for the election of human beings to salvation. Thus the Spirit was at work in human hearts drawing them closer to God and enabling them to perform all religious acts. For John Owen, this meant that prayer itself was a work of the

Spirit which inspired in men and women the knowledge that they were recipients of God's grace. Thus the Spirit, rather than human ability or reading from a book, gave rise to true prayer:

> It is the work of the Holy Spirit to give unto believers such *a comprehension* of promised grace and mercy, as that they may constantly apply their minds unto that or those things in an especial manner which are suited unto their present daily wants and occasions, with the frame and dispositions of their souls and spirit. This is that which gives spiritual beauty and order unto the duty of prayer; namely, the suiting of wants and supplies, of a thankful disposition and praises, of love and admiration unto the excellencies of God in Christ, all by the wisdom of the Holy Ghost.[21]

It was this immanent presence of the transcendent Spirit which linked contemporary believers with the Apostles who were also indwelt by the same Spirit. The Spirit then spoke 'in', 'by' or 'through' the word of scripture which ensured that the message of contemporary proclamation was not some new invention but the same as that of the Apostles. Thus many were careful not to suggest that they relied more on the inner testimony of the Spirit than on the words of scripture. Indeed, the idea that the Spirit bore any revelation in addition to or surpassing that of scripture was generally considered to be false teaching. Calvin himself had declared that the Spirit does not have 'the task of inventing new and unheard-of revelations . . . but of sealing our minds with that very doctrine which is commended by the gospel'.[22] Richard Sibbes argued that the Spirit had to be tested by the scriptures: 'The breath of the Spirit in us is suitable to the Spirit's breathing in the Scriptures; the same Spirit doth not breathe contrary motions.'[23] Walter Cradock (ca 1606–59), the Welsh clergyman who helped to establish the first Independent church in Wales at Llanfaches, Monmouthshire, in 1639 and, as a preacher authorized by the Long Parliament, from 1641 played a prominent part among the parliamentary forces during the Civil Wars, claimed that by the Spirit 'God comes now with more light than wee had before', and 'the spirit is all in all in religion'. But he refused to accord more to the Spirit than could be found in scripture: 'I speak not this as if the Spirit were contrary to the Word, as some men to advance the Spirit, set the Word and Spirit by the ears; but the Spirit leads by the Word.'[24] John Owen was keen to instruct all 'that they diligently trye, examine and search into these things, by the safe and infallible Touchstone and Rule of the Word', in order to avoid the excesses that could emerge when preachers claimed to be inspired by the Spirit alone.[25] Richard Baxter (1615–91) asserted that the Holy Spirit did at one time effect new revelation from God. This he called 'extraordinary inspiration or impulse' which 'moved the prophets and apostles, to reveal new laws, or precepts, or events, or to do some actions without respect to any other command than the inspiration itself'. However he was emphatic in asserting: 'This Christians are not now to expect.' The Spirit's true work within the believer was clear: 'The other sort of the Spirit's working, is not to make new laws or duties, but to guide and quicken us in the doing of that which is our duty before by the laws already made. And these are the motions that all true Christians must now expect.'[26]

Despite these protestations, there were undoubtedly accusations of heterodoxy at the time which revolved around the immediacy of divine revelation, or the sense that the Holy Spirit could deliver a new message to believers apart from scripture. Independents were accused, by Robert Baillie (1602–62), professor of Divinity (from 1642) and principal (from 1661) of Glasgow University and one of the Scottish representatives at the Westminster Assembly, of including 'contemplations of God without Scripture';[27] John Robinson (1575–1625) is reported to have told members of his congregation as they prepared to leave for the New World: 'The Lord has more truth and light yet to break forth out of his holy word';[28] Oliver Cromwell wrote that God 'speaks without a written word sometimes, yet according to it'.[29] In fact, both Robinson and Cromwell stopped short of saying that there could be some new revelation delivered directly to the believer by the Holy Spirit. However, their belief that godly living meant a daily walk with God as a genuine and real experience, made possible by the Spirit, opened the way for the claim that extra-biblical revelation was possible.

As far as the historical context goes, there appears *prima facie* to have been much controversy over the issue, something which is reflected even in the *Westminster Confession* (V, 3), which reads: 'God, in His ordinary providence, maketh use of means, yet is free to work without, above and against them, at His pleasure.' Nevertheless, this clause sought not to safeguard a sense of special and immediate revelation, but instead its concern was the sovereign freedom of God. In other words, for most of the Puritans, special revelation had to remain a theoretical possibility simply because God was not to be restricted by any human construct, but the possibility was observed in the breach rather than in practice. Richard Baxter made the point in this way:

> It is possible that God may make new revelations to particular persons about their particular duties, events, or matters of fact, in subordination to the Scripture, either by inspiration, vision, or apparition, or voice; for he hath not told us that he will never do such a thing . . . Though such revelation and prophecy be possible, there is no certainty of it in general, nor any probability of it to any one individual person, much less a promise. And therefore to expect it, or pray for it, is but a presumptuous tempting of God.

For Baxter, Christians were to beware lest they fall prey to self-deception, because 'certain experience telleth us, that most in our age that have pretended to prophecy, or to inspirations, or revelations, have been melancholy, crack-brained persons, near to madness, who have proved deluded in the end'.[30]

The *Westminster Confession* (I, 1 – echoing the first verse of the letter to the Hebrews) noted that God has revealed himself 'at sundry times, and in divers manners' but that 'those former ways of God's revealing His will unto His people [are] now ceased' because the biblical canon is now closed. Puritan divines were largely agreed that the revelation contained in scripture was to be the final arbiter of truth for devotional, personal and civic life. In his study of the Puritans' attitude to 'special' or 'immediate' revelation by the Holy Spirit, Garnet Howard Milne has argued that there was a remarkably clear consensus among those who constituted mainstream Puritanism:

> Among the vast majority of the Westminster divines' sermons which deal with the subject of guidance, we discern an unwillingness to claim any sort of inspired extra-biblical revelation for guidance. Instead, we see a tendency to deny that there is still immediate revelation for both matters of religious truth and for daily living, whether the life of the individual or nation.[31]

Yet, as Thomas Rees explained, 'English Puritanism was a complex phenomenon' which upheld 'a rigid adherence to the letter of Scripture and the dogmas of Calvinism' while also issuing 'in almost every degree and form in the manifestation of the Spirit'.[32] Indeed, Geoffrey Nuttall argued that it was precisely the rediscovery of the idea of an experience of the Spirit (understood biblically as being filled with the Spirit), which characterized the Puritan movement, though he recognized too that it was the primacy given to experience which would ultimately lead to controversy over the role of the Spirit, both at the time and in subsequent generations.

The Quakers were intent on pursuing a sense of immediate revelation. As with other Puritans, they had recognized the same Spirit who was at work in the prophets and apostles to be at work in them. But whereas, generally, Independent and Presbyterian Puritans had declared that this activity of the Spirit had ceased, the Quakers believed that it had continued.[33] For George Fox (1624–91), the 'inner light' was not 'a naturall light & a made light' but rather 'divine & spirituall from Christ.' Indeed, 'the light is thoroughly supernatural. It is not conscience, or the light of nature, or the light of reason.'[34] Fox did not claim to have received anything that was contrary to the scriptures, but he did claim to have received them *independently* of the scriptures. 'These things I did not see by the help of man, nor by the letter, though they are written in the letter, but I saw them in the light of the Lord Jesus Christ, and by his immediate Spirit and power, as did the holy men of God, by whom the Holy Scriptures were written.'[35] Furthermore, for Fox, 'the Spirit of God . . . is the most fit, proper, and universal rule, which God hath given',[36] a claim which caused the Associated Ministers of Cumberland and Westmoorland (among others) to complain that the Quakers set up 'their Conceits and Experiences, as being of equal authority with the Scriptures'.[37]

In some ways the Puritan debates marked the territory for Nonconformist and Dissenting attitudes to the Holy Spirit certainly until the mid-nineteenth century. The Spirit's role in effecting regeneration both in justification and sanctification alongside the authority of the scriptures, read and understood under the inspiration and guidance of the Holy Spirit, were two prominent aspects. While the Society of Friends continued to uphold the guidance of the 'inner light', most Dissenters eschewed such teaching when it suggested that revelation was possible beyond the scriptures.

II. Confirming Orthodoxy

In the early debates between Puritans over the role of the Holy Spirit, there clearly emerged a battle for what could be considered to be orthodox Christian teaching. Early Independents and Baptists outlined their theological understanding in Church Covenants, a practice which continued to be widespread until the early nineteenth century. While those of the seventeenth century were fairly basic, as time went on covenantal statements became more detailed partly in order to declare the orthodoxy of a particular group of gathered Christians against one of the several heterodox teachings that had emerged by the end of the seventeenth and beginning of the eighteenth centuries. In some of these covenants and confessions, it is possible to see that, in their understanding of the work of the Holy Spirit, Nonconformists maintained a direct connection with their antecedents.

The Holy Spirit's place as a person of the Trinity was upheld by those keen to avoid the charge of Socinianism. This was more an affirmation of Trinitarian teaching than a direct rebuttal of Socinianism, but it was possibly all the more significant for that. In this way, the Alcester Baptists, in the early eighteenth century, echoed the Niceo-Constantinopolitan Creed when they confirmed that 'the Father is God, the Son of God, and the Holy Spirit is God; all equal in power, authority and glory & we believe this God is the only object of Divine worship and Adoration'.[38] The Walsall Independents, who incorporated their church as a result of doctrinal differences in the town's Presbyterian congregation, outlined a confession of faith in their covenant, dated 21 September 1763. For them, the Holy Spirit was the 'same in Substance, equal in power and glory' with the Father and the

Son. Furthermore, 'without regeneration by the Holy Spirit, we cannot enter into the Kingdom of Heaven'. Sanctification was also by the Holy Spirit, but whereas 'salvation is absolutely of grace', these Congregationalists firmly refuted the charge of antinomianism with the statement that 'we are firmly persuaded, that it is the indispensible Duty of every one that believeth to maintain good works'.[39] Slightly later, the Welsh Calvinistic Methodists, in their Confession of Faith (1823), proclaimed that 'the clear testimony of Holy Scripture' was 'that there are in the Godhead THREE persons . . . co-eternal and co-equal . . . nevertheless, there is only one God'. Furthermore, '[t]hough it is the Godhead of the three Persons that works all things, yet distinctive operations are ascribed to each Person: creation and election to the Father, redemption to the Son, sanctifying and sealing to the Holy Ghost'. As such, the Spirit is part of God's divine plan in order to ensure that the redemption wrought by Christ is applied to human beings:

> To save sinners, it is as necessary to apply as it was to provide the plan of salvation. To prepare and provide a plan of salvation without applying it would have been a vain thing. It must be applied, as well as provided, by an infinite Person . . . and God, foreseeing this from eternity, in decreeing, in his eternal love, the salvation of sinners, not only appointed his Son to provide a full salvation for them, but also, in the same eternal plan, appointed the Holy Ghost to apply it; that none of the objects of his love should perish for want of applying any more than for want of preparing and providing it.[40]

These various quotations demonstrate that the debates of the seventeenth century were continued into the eighteenth and nineteenth centuries, with what could be termed orthodox Nonconformists agreeing that the Spirit was a person of the Holy Trinity with the distinctive tasks of regenerating and sanctifying human beings and illuminating the scriptures. The Nonconformists sought both to affirm the reality of the Spirit's work in the present and to deny that this brought any additional revelation to that already given in the scriptures. Indeed, for Independents, Baptists and Presbyterians the scriptures not only possessed the final authority for the church and for Christian life but any hint that revelation could be found beyond them was still to be firmly rejected.

Further theological controversy, which included reference to the role of the Holy Spirit, emerged during the eighteenth century over Calvinist and Arminian views of salvation. The Evangelical Revival was 'a movement of the Spirit that affected churches and individuals without respect for denominational distinctions. Baptists, Anglicans, Quakers and Independents were to experience its vivifying influence.'[41] The Revival transformed Nonconformist proclamation and activity. Methodist itinerants travelled the length and breath of England and Wales offering the gospel to all with the implication that they were able to respond, an idea with which strict Calvinists could not agree. Nevertheless, Independents and Baptists were not unaffected and, under the especial influence respectively of Edward Williams of Rotherham and Andrew Fuller of Kettering, they modified their theology in order to incorporate such an open proclamation of the gospel.

For John Wesley, and the Methodists in general, justification is what God 'does for us' through the Son, and sanctification is what God 'works in us' by the Spirit. Thus the Holy Spirit is the agent of God's will on earth and grace in human hearts. For Wesley, it remained important to be able to distinguish between this experience of the Holy Spirit and 'popular enthusiasm, false assurance and special spiritual gifts and revelations'.[42] He continued: 'By the Testimony of the Spirit I mean an inward expression of the soul whereby the Spirit of God directly witnesses to my Spirit that I am a child of God; that Jesus Christ hath loved me and given Himself for me, that all my sins are blotted out, and I, even I, am reconciled to God.'[43] In this, Calvinists and Arminians would have been agreed. Indeed, there was, on both sides, a sense that salvation was the free gift of God, but, as Alan Sell has pointed out, they held different views about the meaning of the word 'free'. Did this refer to the 'free availability' of salvation to all, or did it refer to the idea that God could freely give or withhold salvation?[44] Furthermore, did God, through the Holy Spirit, inspire and produce conversion or did human beings contribute to it at all? There remained some staunchly Calvinistic ministers, such as Joseph Hussey, who were aghast at the idea that human beings, of their own nature, had the ability to respond to the preaching of the gospel. For Hussey,

> By offers of grace, tenders and proffers of salvation, it is evident, men do thereby imply that free grace and full salvation is propounded, tendered, and offered to all sinners within the sound . . . Is not this a piece of robbery against the Holy Spirit? . . . Does not the plea confine the operations of the Holy Spirit to common and eternal workings? Wherein does your plea give Jehovah the Spirit His due honour in the internal and mighty workings of His grace on sinner's hearts, that sinners may believe, repent, and be saved?[45]

Not all were as convinced as Hussey in their belief that the indiscriminate offer of the gospel to all – when God had predestined only the elect to salvation – did a disservice to the Holy Spirit. Nevertheless, there were those evangelical Calvinists who remained concerned that evangelical Arminianism was compromising God's sovereignty. Alan Sell has characterized it as the distinction between *offering* Christ to sinners and *preaching*

Christ to sinners, a difference between *the offer of grace* and *the gift of grace*. Clearly for a time the Calvinists, whether of an extreme or of a moderate and evangelical character, considered that God's sovereignty, active in salvation through the Son and the Holy Spirit, was at stake.[46]

Although the debate petered out over the course of the eighteenth century, there remained representations of a strict Calvinism throughout the nineteenth century, especially when it appeared that God's prerogative in salvation was being undermined. Robert Watts (1820–95), professor of Theology at the Presbyterian College, Belfast (1865–95), spoke on behalf of Calvinists when he said that they believe 'that the sinner cannot receive the things of the Spirit of God, or know them' and in order to do so 'he must be born again'. Regeneration is thus 'a fundamental change which precedes the existence and exercise of both faith and repentance', and this is, moreover, a change in which the sinner has no part to play at all for it 'is absolutely the result of the action of the Holy Ghost *immediately* upon the soul, whereby He creates it anew and implants a new moral *habitus* or principle of action'.[47]

In many ways the tide had turned by this time and Nonconformists in general were developing a system whereby God's initiative and human response were seen as equally significant even if this was couched in words where its human response was seen as a direct result of the inspiration of the Holy Spirit. In 1899, Principal Oswald Dykes of Westminster College, Cambridge, drafted an 'Evangelical Free Church Catechism' which was subsequently revised by the Methodist advocate of the Nonconformist Conscience, Hugh Price Hughes. The work of the Holy Spirit was said, significantly, to be 'the continuation of Christ's work of salvation', the 'secret power . . . working graciously in our hearts' enabling people to respond to the gospel with repentance and faith, and the means by which Christ dwells in his church.[48] The statement demonstrates a late-nineteenth-century evangelical consensus within Nonconformist circles whereby the human response to the gospel was enabled by the secret working of the Spirit in the human heart. Nevertheless, there remained a strong Arminian voice, most thoroughly advocated by W. B. Pope (1822–1903), who claimed that the Holy Spirit 'is powerless where the human energy is not put forth in co-operation with him'.[49] Nevertheless, this led to a degree of ambiguity: 'what we do in the power of God is no other than the work of God within us, Who fulfils His own promises through our instrumentality; and what the power of God accomplishes through our energies exerted in faith is counted by Him as our own act'.[50] It seems, then, that for Pope, the 'human energies' which co-operated with the Spirit were, at least at times, in fact inspired by that same Spirit. It is thus the Spirit at work within human beings who enables the response to the gospel, yet this is *counted* by God as if it were a human act.

III. Immanence, Experience and a Rediscovery of Orthodoxy

By the late nineteenth century, human and religious experience had begun to dominate theological discourse alongside the claim that Jesus had proclaimed a higher ethic and a message about God's love for his creation, encapsulated in his conception of the Kingdom of God and its coming, and the concomitant Fatherhood of God and brotherhood of man. This 'liberalizing' tendency could be seen as the result of Friedrich Schleiermacher's defence of religion to its 'cultural despisers' and his articulation of religion as the 'feeling of absolute dependence'. Further support for this tendency was found in the theology of Albrecht Ritschl and in the explanation of Christianity famously expounded by Adolf von Harnack. It received further support from Idealist philosophy especially as channelled through the work of F. H. Bradley (1846–1924), who insisted that the consciousness of the 'infinite whole' can be 'discovered immanently present within each one', and Edward Caird (1835–1908), who contended that 'what appear as disharmonies may be realised in a higher unity', all dependent on the fact that self-consciousness is in truth dependent on that greater consciousness we call God.[51] Immanent Spirit enabled people to sense their ultimate unity with all things, it informed and inspired consciousness and it lay behind all religious experience. Such thought was given expression by Nonconformist ministers such as R. J. Campbell, T. Rhondda Williams and Joseph Warschauer in England and David Adams in Wales, especially in what was called the 'New Theology' at the beginning of the twentieth century. Their 'New Theology' was considered, by some, to be somewhat extreme and it was vociferously opposed by Andrew Fairbairn and P. T. Forsyth to name but two. In the form in which Campbell advocated it, such 'theology' had virtually disappeared by the 1920s, though it is also true that elements of philosophical Idealism lingered in the thought of some Nonconformists throughout the twentieth century.

Alongside this, the emergence of psychology augmented the view of religious experience, even if its conclusions were not always altogether positive. Indeed, for H. Wheeler Robinson (1872–1945), principal of Regent's Park (Baptist) College (1920–42), the apologetic task was precisely 'to defend the reality of religious experience against the criticism that it is a psychological illusion'.[52] Thus religious consciousness came to be seen, for a time, as the vital aspect in the life of faith. The theological concomitant of this consciousness was the immanence of God not only in the believer but in the whole of creation. Both ideas inevitably leant heavily on an understanding of the Spirit, though not necessarily according to a traditionally Trinitarian formula.

The Wesleyan Methodist William T. Davison, principal of Richmond College, highlighted the role of experience in his *The Indwelling Spirit* (1911):

'[T]he Holy Spirit is God imparting Himself directly to the consciousness and experience of men.'[53] The Primitive Methodist A. Lewis Humphries (professor at his denomination's Hartley College in Manchester) looked to the 'underlying experience of the Spirit' which he identified as 'simply God moving upon man for the bestowal of truth and life'. This was enjoyed by 'the broad field of the human race'.[54] This sense of God's omnipresence which was known in creation as the experience of divine benevolence appeared to gain in significance over the course of the twentieth century. While H. Wheeler Robinson affirmed that the Spirit was part of the Godhead, 'the very life-breath of the conception of the Spirit is unity of operation with the Father and the Son. As God was present in the world through Christ, so is God through Christ present in the Holy Spirit', he further insisted that the Spirit is also present 'in the vast evolutionary process . . . immanent in method, transcendent in Nature'.[55] In the 1960s, the newly inaugurated Congregational Church in England and Wales asserted in its Declaration of Faith that the Holy Spirit 'is not confined to the Church; for even where the Spirit is not understood in relation to Jesus Christ, where his presence is undiscerned, where his very existence is denied, there too God works perpetually in the Holy Spirit to enlarge the possibilities of human life and to open the way for faith and sonship'.[56]

In some ways this sense that the Spirit is experienced by all people regardless of their particular confession stemmed from the biblical assertion that the Spirit 'blows where he wills' (Jn 3.8). However, its prominence, particularly during the early twentieth century, had as much to do with the importance of 'experience' as a theological category, the enduring influence of Idealist philosophy which had promoted the inherent unity of all things, and the growth of interest in fields such as psychology as it did to basic fidelity to scripture.

Thomas Rees (1869–1926) published his study of the Holy Spirit in 1915 and was duly awarded a PhD for it by the University of London. It was largely a historical account of the understanding of the Spirit through the ages with approximately half the book discussing biblical themes. His analytical framework for discussing this history was evolutionary theory. Thus as human beings became more sophisticated, both intellectually and morally, so their conception of the Spirit changed: 'At first the activities of the Spirit were alien, strange and abnormal, but in a more ethical medium, it became an inspiration, an inward monitor, an abiding principle, an immanent activity of God, until again, in a system of abstract ideas of God and man, the Spirit became a mediating hypostasis, outside both God and man.'[57] For Rees, the Spirit represented 'the personal activity of God' and 'its chief sphere of operation is human consciousness'.[58] Belief in the resurrection of Jesus Christ, and the experience of the Holy Spirit, were the 'two distinctive factors in the life of the Christian Church of the first generation'.[59] However, he interpreted 2 Cor. 3.17 – 'the Lord is the Spirit' – as meaning that the Spirit *is* Jesus Christ. The belief in the Spirit confirms that Jesus is alive in the churches and he is the principal truth and reality for the whole universe. In uniting the Spirit with Christ, Rees gave a definite meaning and character to the Spirit who should be understood according to the teaching, life, death, resurrection and principles of Jesus.[60] Nevertheless, his understanding of the Spirit as 'the principal truth and reality for the whole universe' belies his schooling in philosophical Idealism far more than a grounding in the Bible. It is hardly surprising, then, that Rees concluded his study with a call to restate eternal truths in the dress of contemporary thought-forms.[61]

Like Thomas Rees, H. Wheeler Robinson emphasized that 'the doctrine of the Holy Spirit is the doctrine of experience' which demanded a psychological treatment given that it is the 'consciousness of the inner content of the doctrine, the living experience of the presence of God' which is of real significance.[62] Christian experience is characterized by four aspects: the 'reality, the dignity, the eternal value of human personality'; the centrality of an ethical principle, namely 'agape'; the experience of God's grace which delivers humankind from adversity, moral evil and death; those who experience this 'have often described it as a new life initiated by a new birth'. It is the Holy Spirit who gives power for its creation and sustenance,[63] and who draws people into Christian society and fellowship of the church and in fellowship the experience of the Holy Spirit is manifest in moral, intellectual and aesthetic endeavour.[64] Although Wheeler Robinson and most other Nonconformists would have agreed that the Spirit was uniquely present in the church, the problem with the trajectory of such teaching was that it tended towards an emphasis on the generality of the Spirit as omnipresent rather than in the specificity of the Spirit, uniquely understood according to Christian teaching. During the twentieth century Nonconformist denominations in general gave increasing recognition to the Spirit's general presence throughout the universe and in all people and things, claims which prompted criticism not just from theological conservatives but from those who were most familiar with the dogmatic tradition.

Of all Nonconformist theologians of the early twentieth century, it was P. T. Forsyth (1848–1921) who retained a more exclusive role for the Spirit within the Christian fellowship. For Forsyth, 'the Holy Spirit is associated in the most close and exclusive way with the act of the Son, the action of the Word, and the existence of a Church of new souls . . . It has its source in the Cross, and its first action in the Resurrection and its Word.' Thus Forsyth could affirm that the Spirit is only understood within the context of the gospel. The Spirit's 'prime action' is 'miraculous', namely 'to regenerate, by organising men into Christ's new creation'. Morality and sanctification might follow, but they are secondary. The Spirit acts first in salvation. As such the Spirit is the sum total of the gift of the gospel to humankind which is known not generally in the world but specifically in the church: 'it is not one of Christ's gifts, as the Gospel is not, but the complete and effective gift of Christ Himself as the Saviour of the world brought home to the individual in the communion of God and the community of a Church'.[65] Forsyth identified the Spirit as God at work among humankind in a *saving* way, and thus pneumatology was best conceived in light of the detail of the gospel: 'We are raised from our death of sin not simply by the preaching of Christ to resurrection but by the same action of the same Spirit that raised Christ from the dead . . . The old gospel, preached with spirit, makes an impression; when preached with the Holy Spirit it makes regeneration.'[66]

Although influenced by the neo-Calvinism of Karl Barth, Hubert Cunliffe-Jones (1905–91, principal of the Yorkshire United Theological College in Bradford and later professor of theology in the University of Manchester) both confirmed the specifics of Christian teaching alongside a sense that the doctrine of the Spirit might not be domesticated. He contributed *The Holy Spirit* to the series of 'Forward Books' published by the Independent Press in the 1940s. He made the point that 'the Holy Spirit is God communicating himself to us and enabling us to respond to him'.[67] Again, for Cunliffe-Jones, there is a sense that the Holy Spirit is to be experienced and that the experience confirmed the utter dependence of the believer on God. The Holy Spirit is nothing less than the immanent presence of God, present through union with Christ made possible by faith, which transforms and empowers the Christian. Because the Spirit is God and not merely the gift of God, his presence within makes possible 'a real sharing in the divine life'.[68] As with the seventeenth-century Puritans, Cunliffe-Jones upheld that the Holy Spirit is not concerned only with reconciliation, 'whereby we enter into fellowship with God through the cross of Christ', but also in sanctification 'whereby we are cleansed from all unrighteousness and enabled to be holy even as God is holy'.[69] And this sanctification is not sudden. Instead the Christian life is marked by 'a constant struggle against sin'. Thus sanctification is 'growing in holiness through the love of God shed abroad in the heart by the Holy Spirit (cf. Rom. 5.5)'.[70] He quoted John Owen to clinch the point: 'The work of sanctification is progressive and admits of degrees.'[71]

Nevertheless, there is a paradox for Cunliffe-Jones where 'the gift of the Holy Spirit has meaning only as a witness to the risen and reigning Christ', but that

> the Holy Spirit means the indwelling power of God, and we are not entitled to limit this to something specifically Christian. In the first place, man is made in the image of God, and responds to God in the power of

> the Holy Spirit . . . so we must believe that every man, as man, is open to the Holy Spirit . . . this belief in the Holy Spirit is not peculiar to one religion but something that appears in all religions.[72]

It is possible to discern the impact of social and cultural factors on Cunliffe-Jones' understanding of the Spirit. While justified biblically and theologically by the need to avoid domesticating the Spirit, Cunliffe-Jones made his claims for the gospel in the context of a growing awareness of the non-Christian religions. By this time, too, a blanket dismissal of the non-Christian religions was both humanly and intellectually unacceptable. It is therefore understandable that Cunliffe-Jones gave the Spirit, whose work was at best mysterious, the role of working among those of non-Christian profession.

Colin E. Gunton was one of the few Nonconformists during the late twentieth century also to be an academic theologian. He sought to give a place and clear function to the Holy Spirit in a scheme that would avoid the extremes of tritheism and modalism and would seek to be consistently Trinitarian. Although Karl Barth was a lifelong theological companion, Gunton considered that Barth's doctrine of the Spirit merely confirmed Christ's benefits to the believer and indeed rendered the Spirit subordinate to the Son, leading to a less than fulsome – and thus rather suspect – Trinitarianism. Gunton found inspiration for his Trinitarianism in Patristic thought, especially that of Irenaeus, the third-century bishop of Lyons, 'one of Christianity's first great systematic theologians',[73] who offered 'a model of a theological integration of incarnation, saving death, resurrection and ascension, all embraced within a Trinitarian framework according to which the creating and redeeming work of God the Father is mediated by the Son and the Holy Spirit'.[74] As a result, the Spirit enables the life of the new creation, won in Christ, to be lived in anticipation in the present while also moving the creation towards its purpose according to the Creator's will. In this way the Spirit's presence was an eschatological reality in the believer's life, enabling a real foretaste of God's ultimate purposes and drawing the Creation towards its ultimate fulfilment.

Another prominent Nonconformist theologian of the twentieth (and early twenty-first) century Alan P. F. Sell has argued that the Spirit is only truly understood in Trinitarian terms. Thus, 'the Holy Spirit *is* God at work' and this is 'the fatherly God of holy love' who is 'known in the victorious Christ of the Bible', but is also 'generously active in the world; as life-givingly active in us; as drawing out and enabling our response of faith, love and service'. The Holy Spirit 'does not bring a new revelation, he bears witness to Christ (Jn 15.26). He is indeed, "the method of Christ's presence"' which unites the Christian to Christ and to other Christians in the church, 'ever renewing and refining our life in this world; and as holding us in fellowship with him eternally'.[75] This has two implications. The first is the assertion that 'the Spirit does nothing apart from or additional to what Christ does . . . Rather, the Spirit brings the risen Christ to us.'[76] The second is that the Spirit cannot be divorced from the Word where both work mutually to secure revelation: '[A]part from the objective Word we are at the mercy of our own subjective whims and fancies. Apart from the subjective work of the Spirit the Word is a dead letter.'[77] But while the Spirit is Christ's gift to the church, it is also true that the Spirit 'is at work even where it is unknown or unacknowledged'.[78] In this way, Alan Sell has continued to propagate the tradition outlined above where the Spirit is known through his *work*, bringing the benefits of Christ to the believer but also present throughout the Universe. Only the Spirit makes God known, but he does so through the revelation of scripture rather than in an immediate sense. Thus the charismatic and immediate inspiration of the Holy Spirit is acknowledged, but kept away from the excess which could lead to the claim of a further revelation.

IV. Conclusions

The foregoing discussion concentrated on the 'mainstream dogmatic tradition', outlining what Nonconformists identified as the Spirit's task, namely the application of Christ's benefits to the Christian and to the church and thus demonstrating the vital nature of pneumatology in historical Dissent. The Spirit was not thought, generally, to bring a new revelation, but the Spirit was absolutely necessary in order to reveal God's Word in the scriptures and to effect regeneration and sanctification of human beings. It must be said, however, that for various reasons the dogmatic, theological account of the Holy Spirt and his work did not receive extensive treatment by Nonconformists during the last half of the twentieth century.

A discussion of Pentecostalism and the Charismatic movement would undoubtedly have broadened the understanding of the Spirit outlined here. If both have offered a specific understanding of the Spirit's work, insisting on a dynamism and immediacy to those who live the life of faith, they might also, at times, have driven too great a wedge between the Spirit and the Son, something that the mainstream Nonconformist tradition would undoubtedly have sought to avoid. Nevertheless, it can be said with confidence that historical Dissent, the Charismatic movement and Pentecostals would all agree that the vitality of the Spirit is not merely a theological datum but an experience for each Christian believer. In other words, the Christian life, in terms of faith and belief, sanctification and morality, and in terms of regeneration itself, is dependent on the Sovereign act of God in Christ made known in human lives by the Spirit.

Notes

1 Veli-Matti Kärkkäinen, *Pneumatology: The Holy Spirit in Ecumenical, International and Contextual Perspective* (Grand Rapids, MI: Baker Academic, 2002), p. 16.
2 Joseph Haroutunian, 'Spirit, Holy Spirit, Spiritism', in Alan Richardson (ed.), *A Dictionary of Christian Theology* (London: SCM, 1969), pp. 318–19.
3 Colin E. Gunton, *Theology through the Theologians* (Edinburgh: T&T Clark, 1996), p. 105.
4 Ibid., pp. 105–8.
5 Geoffrey F. Nuttall, *The Holy Spirit in Puritan Thought and Experience* (Oxford: Blackwell, 1946), p. 4. Much use has been made in this chapter of Dr Nuttall's study, especially in the section on the Puritans.
6 Ibid., p. viii.
7 Thomas Rees, *The Holy Spirit in Thought and Experience* (New York: Charles Scribner & Sons, 1915), p. 191.
8 John McIntyre, *The Shape of Pneumatology: Studies in the Doctrine of the Holy Spirit* (Edinburgh: T&T Clark, 1997), pp. 24–25.
9 John Owen, *The Works of John Owen*, ed. William H. Goold (Edinburgh: T&T Clark, 1862), II, pp. 180–81; Rees, *The Holy Spirit*, p. 193.
10 Thomas Goodwin, *The Works of Thomas Goodwin*, 12 vols (Edinburgh, London, Dublin and Montreal: James Nichol, James Nisbet, W. Robertson and B. Dawson & Sons, 1863), VI, p. 47.
11 John Owen, *Pneumatologia*, abridged by George Burder (Philadelphia, PA: Wiolliam W. Woodward, 1810), p. 151.
12 John Owen, *The Works of John Owen*, II, p. 455.
13 R. Tudur Jones et al. (eds), *Protestant Nonconformst Texts, Volume 1: 1550–1700* (Aldershot: Ashgate, 2007), p. 338.
14 Quoted in Nuttall, *The Holy Spirit*, p. 66.
15 Joseph Hussey, *God's Operations of Grace*, pp. 453, 456, quoted in Geoffrey F. Nuttall, *Studies in English Dissent* (Weston Rhyn: Quinta Press, 2002), p. 176.
16 Alan P. F. Sell, *Enlightenment, Ecumenism, Evangel: Theological Themes and Thinkers, 1550–2000* (Milton Keynes: Paternoster, 2005), p. 42.
17 Quoted in Jaroslav Pelikan, *The Christian Tradition: A History of the Development of Doctrine: Volume 4: Reformation of Church and Dogma (1300–1700)* (Chicago, IL, and London: University of Chicago Press, 1984), p. 187.
18 John Calvin, *Institutes of the Christian Religion*, ed. John T. McNeill, trans. F. L. Battles (London: SCM, 1963), I vii 4, pp. 78–80.
19 Nuttall, *The Holy Spirit*, p. 22.
20 Quoted in ibid., p. 23.
21 Owen, *The Works of John Owen*, IV, p. 171.
22 Calvin, *Institutes of the Christian Religion*, I ix 1, pp. 93–94.
23 Richard Sibbes, *Works*, ed. A. B. Grosart (1862), V, p. 427; Nuttall, *The Holy Spirit*, p. 41.
24 Walter Cradock, *Gospel-Libertie* (1640), p. 41; idem, *Divine Drops Distilled* (150), pp. 315, 218. Quoted in Nuttall, *The Holy Spirit*, p. 24.
25 John Owen, *Pneumatologia*, quoted in Nuttall, *The Holy Spirit*, p. 43.
26 Richard Baxter, *Practical Works*, ed. W. Orme (London: J. Duncan, 1930), IV, p. 294.
27 Robert Baillie, *Dissuasive from the Errours of Our Time* (1645), p. 130; Quoted in Nuttall, *The Holy Spirit*, p. 24.
28 Nuttall, *The Holy Spirit*, p. 24 fn.3. Nuttall records that there was a degree of controversy over the provenance of the phrase.

29 Oliver Cromwell, *Letters and Speeches*, ed. T. Carlyle (1908), Speech IV; quoted in Nuttall, *The Holy Spirit*, p. 24.
30 Baxter, *Practical Works*, V, p. 556.
31 Garnet Howard Milne, *The Westminster Confession of Faith and the Cessation of Special Revelation: The Majority Puritan Viewpoint on Whether Extra-Biblical Prophecy Is Still Possible* (Milton Keynes: Patnernoster, 2007), p. 217.
32 Rees, *The Holy Spirit*, p. 191.
33 Nuttall, *The Holy Spirit*, pp. 21, 26.
34 George Fox, *Journal*, ed. N. Penney (1911), I, pp. 275, 260. Quoted in Nuttall, *The Holy Spirit*, p. 42.
35 Fox, *Journal*, ed. T. Ellwood (1901), I, p. 36. Quoted in Nuttall, *The Holy Spirit*, p. 36.
36 Fox, *Journal*, ed. T. Ellwood, II, p. 217. Quoted in Nuttall, *The Holy Spirit*, p. 27.
37 B. Nightingale, *The Ejected of 1662 in Cumberland and Westmorland* (London: Sherrat and Hughes, 1911), I, p. 101. Quoted in Nuttall, *The Holy Spirit*, p. 35.
38 Alan P. F. Sell, *Christ and Controversy: The Person of Christ in Nonconformist Thought and Ecclesial Experience, 1600–2000* (Eugene, OR: Pickwick, 2012), p. 35.
39 David W. Bebbington et al. (eds), *Protestant Nonconformist Texts, Volume 3: The Nineteenth Century* (Aldershot: Ashgate, 2006), p. 387.
40 Confession of Faith of the Calvinistic Methodists or the Presbyterians of Wales. Adopted at the Associations of Aberystwyth and Bala in the year 1823, sections 4, 20, 21. Found at www.creeds.net/cmwales/main.htm (viewed 14 December 2012).
41 R. Tudur Jones, *Congregationalism in England: 1662–1962* (London: Independent Press, 1962), p. 146.
42 Rees, *The Holy Spirit*, p. 199.
43 Ibid.
44 Alan P. F. Sell, *The Great Debate: Calvinism, Arminianism and Salvation* (Worthing: H. E. Walter, 1982), p. 70.
45 Hussey, *God's Operations of Grace but no Offers of Grace* (1707), quoted in ibid., p. 53.
46 Sell, *The Great Debate*, p. 54.
47 Alan P. F. Sell, *Dissenting Thought and the Life of the Churches: Studies in an English Tradition* (San Francisco, CA: Edwin Mellen Press, 1990) p. 567; see also R. Watts, *An Outline of the Calvinist System* (Edinburgh T&T Clark, 1865), p. 19.
48 Bebbington et al. (eds), *Protestant Nonconformist Texts, Volume 3*, pp. 52–58.
49 Sell, *Dissenting Thought and the Life of the Churches*, p. 568.
50 Ibid., p. 569.
51 See Alan P. F. Sell, *The Philosophy of Religion, 1875–1980* (London: Croom Helm, 1988), pp. 17–22.
52 H. Wheeler Robinson, *The Christian Experience of the Holy Spirit* (London: Fontana, 1962 [1928]), p. 225.
53 Quoted in Alan P. F. Sell, *Nonconformist Theology in the Twentieth Century* (Milton Keynes: Paternoster, 2006), p. 67.
54 Quoted in ibid., p. 66.
55 Wheeler Robinson, *The Christian Experience of the Holy Spirit*, pp. 121, 225; cf. Sell, *Nonconformist Theology in the Twentieth Century*, p. 70.
56 Sell, *Nonconformist Theology in the Twentieth Century*, p. 88.
57 Rees, *The Holy Spirit*, p. 3.
58 Ibid., pp. 17–18.
59 Ibid., p. 57.
60 Bangor University Archives: Bala-Bangor Collection: Principal Thomas Rees Papers, 'Now the Lord is the Spirit'; also Rees, *The Holy Spirit*, pp. 208–9, 212.

61 Ibid., p. 212.
62 Wheeler Robinson, *The Christian Experience of the Holy Spirit*, pp. 9, 11.
63 Ibid., pp. 28–39.
64 Ibid., p. 90.
65 P. T. Forsyth, *Faith, Freedom and the Future* (London: Hodder, 1912), pp. 12–13.
66 Sell, *Enlightenment, Ecumenism, Evangel*, p. 286.
67 H. Cunliffe-Jones, *The Holy Spirit*, The Forward Books (London: Independent Press, 1943).
68 Ibid., pp. 16–17.
69 Ibid., p. 37.
70 Vincent Taylor, quoted in ibid., p. 40.
71 Owen, *A Discourse Concerning the Holy Spirit*, quoted in Cunliffe-Jones, *The Holy Spirit*, p. 41.
72 Cunliffe-Jones, *The Holy Spirit*, p. 19.
73 Colin E. Gunton, *Yesterday and Today: A Study of Continuities in Christology* (2nd edn, London: SPCK, 1997), p. 173.
74 Ibid., p. 225.
75 Alan P. F. Sell, *Doctrine and Devotion, Volume 3: The Spirit Our Life* (Shippensburg, PA: Ragged Edge Press, 2000), pp. 8, 1.
76 Ibid., p. 76.
77 Ibid., p. 10.
78 Ibid., p. 1.

11 Nonconformist Hymnody

Ian Bradley

The singing and the writing of hymns have been among the most significant and widely recognized contributions of English and Welsh Nonconformity to the worship and witness of the wider Christian church in the British Isles and beyond.

Dissenters introduced hymn singing into public worship in the seventeenth century, an innovation that has been described as one of the greatest contributions ever made to Christian liturgy.[1] The two greatest English hymn writers of the eighteenth century, and arguably of all time, were the Congregational minister Isaac Watts, often described as the 'father of English hymnody', and Charles Wesley, the 'prince of English hymn writers' who, although he never renounced his Anglican orders, is remembered with his hymn-writing brother John as the founder of Methodism. Hymnody was at the heart of the identity and mission of nineteenth-century Nonconformity, as expressed in the remark by Robert William Dale, Congregational minister of Carrs Lane Chapel in Birmingham: 'Let me write the hymns of a church and I care not who writes the theology.'[2] The novels of George Eliot, Charlotte Bronte and Charles Dickens depict the distinctive atmosphere of Victorian Nonconformity through the medium of its hymns. Hymnody continued to constitute the main Nonconformist contribution to the worship of the wider church throughout the twentieth century through the work of such master practitioners as Fred Pratt Green, Fred Kaan and Brian Wren.

It is not difficult to establish the main reason behind the long-standing Nonconformist love affair with hymns. It is found in the statement by Bernard Lord Manning, the early-twentieth-century Congregationalist and historian, that 'hymns are for us Dissenters what the liturgy is for the Anglican'.[3] In the absence of a prayer book and set or prescribed liturgy, hymns have provided Nonconformists with both their personal devotional aids and their main expression of collective identity in worship. Hymn singing has taken on the role fulfilled in other traditions by participation in responsive prayers and become the principal vehicle for congregational and corporate expression of the great liturgical themes of adoration, confession, thanksgiving and intercession. As a result, hymns have also been hugely important in shaping Nonconformist theology and belief, bringing about a situation not so much of *lex orandi, lex credendi* as of *lex cantandi, lex credendi*. In the words of Josiah Conder, editor of the influential *Congregational Hymn Book* of 1836, 'instead of the rule of praying is the rule of believing, the rule of singing is the rule of believing'.[4]

In fact, the Nonconformist love affair with hymns had a somewhat uncertain and sticky beginning. Mid-seventeenth-century Dissenters were uncertain and deeply divided as to whether hymns of human composure should be sung in public worship. Baptists, almost certainly the first denomination to introduce hymn singing into public worship, were deeply divided over whether only the Psalms should be sung and there were further disagreements as to whether men and women should sing together, whether it was better to sing standing or sitting and over the correct method of singing. To a considerable extent these disagreements mirrored the different groupings within the Baptist movement. Most General Baptists disapproved of congregational hymn singing throughout the seventeenth century, fearing that the use of hymns would pave the way for fixed prayers and set liturgies, introduce a worldly element into worship and encourage hypocrisy by leading the uncommitted to join in Christian song and express sentiments that they did not believe or understand. In its deliberations on the subject of 'promiscuous singing', the General Baptist Assembly of 1686 resolved that 'it was not conceived anywise safe for the churches to admit such carnal formalities'.

Particular Baptists, who tended to be Calvinist rather than Arminian in their theology, were more favourably disposed towards congregational hymn singing in worship. It is from their ranks that some of the earliest English hymn writers came. Anna Trapnell, a Fifth Monarchy Baptist, published a collection of spiritual songs in 1654 and Thomas Tillan, a Seventh Day Baptist from the north of England, wrote and published three hymns in 1657. John Bunyan, himself a Particular Baptist at the time, often portrays his characters singing in *The Pilgrim's Progress*, although his own Bedford congregation did not sing hymns until after his death in 1688. The key figure in pioneering congregational hymn singing among English Baptists was Benjamin Keach (1640–1704), pastor of Horsley Down Church in London. From the early 1670s he wrote hymns for use after the breaking of bread, at baptisms, on thanksgiving days and on other special occasions. In 1692 he published a collection of hymns with the intriguing title *The Banquetting-House, or A Feast of Fat Things*. By then, his congregation were singing hymns in public worship every Sunday. This innovation did not go unchallenged. Isaac Marlow, an influential layman opposed to hymn singing, left Horsley Down Church in protest and launched a sustained attack on Keach, arguing that 'your singing of formal precomposed stinted matter is no better than counterfeiting that excellent gift of the Holy Spirit which was in the Primitive Gospel Church'.[5]

Keach's advocacy of congregational hymn singing prevailed among the Particular Baptists and by the end of the seventeenth century an increasing number of congregations were singing hymns of human composure with gusto. They included the verses of another important pioneer Baptist hymn writer Joseph Stennett (1663–1713), who published his first collection of hymns in 1697. Other denominations, notably Presbyterians and Independents, were also beginning to take up the practice and to produce their own hymn writers, notably George Wither (1588–1667), whose *Hymns and Songs of the Church* (1623) were written to counter the exclusive diet of psalmody in most Independent chapels, and Richard Baxter (1615–91), whose 'Ye holy Angels bright', published in his *Poor Man's Family Book* in 1674, was to become one of the best-loved dissenting hymns.

The outstanding early hymn writer from the Independent/Congregational tradition was, of course, Isaac Watts (1674–1748). Famously challenged by his father to 'write something better' after he had complained at the age of sixteen about the dull and profitless quality of what was sung in church, he did more than anyone else to end the stranglehold of metrical psalmody in Protestant worship, producing more than 700 hymns, many for use by his congregation at Mark Lane Chapel, London. Watts led a hymnological revolution not just by Christianizing the Psalms and turning them into robust statements of British patriotism in his *The Psalms of David, Imitated in the Language of the New Testament* (1719) but also by writing 'original songs of Christian experience' like the intensely personal 'When I Survey the Wondrous Cross' which became a classic of evangelical Nonconformist devotion. Enthusiastically taken up by all denominations, Watts' verses acquired almost canonical status within Congregational hymnals where they retained pride of place for over 150 years. The *Congregational Hymn Book* of 1836 was still styled on its title page as 'A Supplement to Dr Watts' Psalms and Hymns'. A second important early hymn writer from the Independent tradition was Philip Doddridge (1702–51) who, like Watts, wrote hymns, often in the form of fairly close metrical paraphrases of passages from scripture, to reinforce the message of his sermons. More than 370 of his hymns were published after his death.

Surpassing even Watts as the greatest English hymn writer of the eighteenth century, however, was Charles Wesley (1707–88). Whether he should feature in a survey of Nonconformist hymnody is a moot point. Like his hymn-writing brother John, he remained in Anglican orders throughout his life. This adherence to the Established Church led to his exclusion from the excellent volume of essays on Nonconformist hymnody *Dissenting Praise* (2011). Many of his hymns belong to a definably high Anglican eucharistic tradition and several came in for criticism from Dissenters for their perceived Catholic tendencies. Josiah Conder described Charles Wesley's more personal and devotional hymns as 'monastic, feminine and mawkish' and 'smacking of the devotion of the Roman mystic'. Yet despite these caveats, it is impossible not to acknowledge the importance of the Wesleys' work in the development of Nonconformist hymnody, especially within the denomination which, almost despite themselves, they are credited with founding. If it is true, as the preface to the 1933 *Methodist Hymn Book* famously stated, that Methodism was born in song, then it was the Wesleys' verses which provided its mother's milk.

Perhaps even more than their individual hymns, it was the hymn and tune books compiled by the Wesleys that played a key role in shaping Methodism's denominational identity and devotional life. John, much influenced by Moravian hymn-singing, produced his own hymnbook in 1737, the first of many that followed in quick succession. Hymns became an important instrument in the Wesleys' crusade to champion the principles of Arminianism against the narrower Calvinism of George Whitefield and his followers. In 1761 John Wesley compiled a book of over a hundred hymns and tunes 'designed chiefly for the use of the people called Methodists'. This was expanded in 1780 into a volume of 525 hymns. Entitled *A Collection of Hymns for the Use of the People Called Methodists*, and accompanied by a tune book *Sacred Harmony*, it was known popularly as 'the large hymn book' and stands as the first major denominational hymnbook published in Britain. More striking than its size was the arrangement of its contents which reflected the experience of a Christian who had been through the processes of awakening, repentance and conversion. Wesley himself described the book in the preface as 'a little body of experimental and practical divinity'. So, perhaps, was born the distinctively Nonconformist doctrine of *lex cantandi, lex credendi*. Within the narrower confines of Wesleyan Methodism, the 1780 collection remained the basis and template for all subsequent hymnals produced during the nineteenth century. The 1876 hymnal, which expanded the number of hymns to 1998, including 724 by the Wesley brothers, was still titled *A Collection of Hymns for the Use of the People Called Methodists, With a New Supplement*.

If the people called Methodists were in the van of promoting hymn singing in the later eighteenth century, other Dissenting denominations enthusiastically joined in. Among the earliest hymnbooks produced in England was one published in 1764 for use in the Countess of Huntingdon's chapels. An important and influential Baptist congregational hymnal was published in 1787 by John Rippon, a Baptist pastor in London. Spurred on by the Methodist revival, General Baptist churches gradually gave up their earlier antipathy to hymn singing and several hymnbooks were sanctioned by the General Baptist Assembly, notably *A Selection of Hymns* containing 746 items which was published in 1804 and later adopted as the *General Baptist Hymn Book* in 1830. *A Selection of Hymns for Public Worship* compiled in 1814 by the Calvinistically inclined William Gadsby, a Midlands stocking-weaver, found particular favour with the Strict Baptists, reinforcing a strong tendency within Nonconformist hymnody, and not least within Baptist ranks, for hymnals to be produced along clearly drawn theological lines. At the other end of the theological spectrum, one of the first explicitly Unitarian hymn books appeared in 1790. The work of Joseph Priestley, the core of its contents was made up of hymns by Isaac Watts suitably adapted 'for the sake of rendering the sentiment unexceptionable to Unitarian Christians'.

Among other Nonconformist hymn writers from this period, two deserve special mention. Anne Steele (1717–78) was almost certainly the leading Baptist hymn writer in terms of her influence and output. She wrote over 150 hymns, many of which first appeared in the *Collection of Hymns Adapted to Public Worship* published in 1769 by John Ash and Caleb Evans and popularly known as the Bristol book. James Montgomery (1771–1854) moved from his Moravian roots to Wesleyan Methodism and eventually became an Anglican. A radical journalist who supported the principles of the French Revolution, he wrote over 400 hymns, around a hundred of which were still in regular use fifty years after his death. He has been described as 'the greatest of English lay hymn writers'.[6]

Increasingly through the nineteenth century hymn singing came to define Nonconformity both in terms of the denominational distinctions within it and as it was seen from outside. Several of the Methodist groups which split away from the main Wesleyan body in the early nineteenth century earned nicknames on account of the heartiness of their singing. The Independent Methodists, who began in Lancashire in 1805–6, were known as the 'Singing Quakers'. Singing also featured prominently among the 'diversity of pious exercises' at the open-air meeting on Mow Cop, Staffordshire, in 1807, which gave birth to Primitive Methodism, some of whose early followers were dubbed 'Ranters' for singing in the streets of Belper, Derbyshire. Primitive Methodists, the most solidly working-class of all nineteenth-century British denominations, developed a distinctive hymnody which was genuinely popular and vulgar in the best sense of the word, interweaving the themes of work and worship, the secular and the sacred. The members of this particular branch of the Methodist family probably did as much as anyone in the nineteenth century to establish hymn singing as an everyday activity for all times and places. As the preface to one of its later hymnals proclaimed: 'Primitive Methodists do not require hymns for public worship only; they need them for the sick chamber, for the marriage feast, for funerals, for journeys by sea and land, for various social gatherings, for the home sanctuary, for personal and private use, for praising the Lord "secretly among the faithful" as well as in the "great congregation".'[7] Such was the enthusiasm with which working people took up this invitation that an anonymous anti-Methodist tract complained in 1805 that the typical labourer was returning from his daily toil and taking 'his wife and children from the wheel and other useful employments in the house' in order that they might sing hymns together.[8] Anglicans were often contemptuous of what they took to be the vulgarity of Primitive Methodist hymnody. John Julian, vicar of Wincobank, Sheffield, and author of the monumental *Dictionary of Hymnology* published in 1892, described the 1854 *Primitive Methodist Hymn Book* as 'the worst edited and most severely mutilated collection of hymns ever published'.[9]

More sympathetic Anglicans, especially those of an evangelical hue, pointed to the desertion of worshippers from the Established Church to Dissenting chapels because of their hearty hymn singing. As early as the 1760s, archbishop of Canterbury Thomas Secker had pointed to the dreariness of a diet made up exclusively of metrical Psalms and demanded that 'something must be done to put our psalmody on a better footing; the Sectarists gain a multitude of followers by their better singing'.[10] In 1787 William Vincent, rector of All Hallows in the City of London, noted the attraction people felt towards 'the psalmody of the Methodists' and suggested 'that for one who has been drawn away from the Established Church by preaching, ten have been induced by music'.[11] John Venn, rector of Clapham, and a leading member of the famous evangelical sect which included William Wilberforce, wrote to a friend in 1802: 'I am persuaded that the singing has been a great instrument in the Dissenters' hands of drawing away persons from the church, and why should not we take that instrument out of their hands?' Practising what he preached, Venn introduced congregational hymns and more singable versions of the Psalms into his services. When attendance at Clapham Parish Church subsequently improved he was quite sure that this was at least in part attributable 'to the improved state of our singing which has been the means of keeping many from the meetings who were allured to go by the excellence of the music'.[12]

Nineteenth-century novels confirm the extent to which hymn singing was seen as a characteristically Dissenting or Methodist activity. When Victorian novelists mention the practice (as they often do), the great majority of their references are to Nonconformists doing the singing and to verses by Wesley or Watts being sung. George Eliot's *Adam Bede*, published in 1859 but set at the beginning of the century, is a case in point. Although the novel begins with the eponymous hero, who is an Anglican, singing Bishop Ken's morning hymn, it is the singing of two Methodists, Dinah Morris and Adam's brother Seth, to which the author alludes much more frequently and, indeed, that provide her story with two of its most moving movements. The first is when Dinah has finished preaching on the village green and says: 'Let us sing a little, dear friends.' At this a stranger, who has looked on fascinated by her sermon, turns his horse aside and rides away 'and as he was still winding down the slope, the voices of the Methodists reached him, rising and falling in that strange blending of exaltation and sadness which belongs to the cadence of a hymn'. Later, Seth expresses his love for Dinah by turning to the words of a hymn by Isaac Watts, 'My God, the Spring of all My Joys'. Two further hymnological references in *Adam Bede* quote from hymns by Charles Wesley.[13]

Wesley is also chosen for what is surely the most extensive quotation from hymnody to be found in any Victorian novel. Charlotte Bronte's *Shirley*, published in 1849 but set around 1811–12, describes the scene in Briar Chapel, 'a large, new, raw, Wesleyan place of worship':

> As there was even now a prayer-meeting being held within its walls, the illumination of its windows cast a bright reflection on the road, while a hymn of a most extraordinary description, such as a very Quaker might feel himself moved by the spirit to dance to, roused cheerily all the echoes of the vicinage. The words were distinctly audible by snatches: here is a quotation or two from different strains; for the singers passed jauntily from hymn to hymn and from tune to tune, with an ease and buoyancy all their own.[14]

The 'quotation or two' that follows consists of two pages of verses from hymns in *The Collection of Hymns for the Use of the People Called Methodists*.

Charles Dickens' short story *George Silverman's Explanation* (1868) contains a vivid description of worship in a small exclusive Brethren chapel, further illustrating the extent to which Victorian writers turned to hymn singing when they wanted to conjure up the atmosphere of narrow Nonconformity:

> The service closed with a hymn, in which the brothers unanimously roared, and the sisters unanimously shrieked at me, that I by wiles

> of worldly gain was mocked, and they on waters of sweet love were rocked; that I with Mammon struggled in the dark, while they were floating in the second ark. I went out from all this with an aching heart and a weary spirit.[15]

By the end of the first decade of Queen Victoria's reign most Church of England congregations were singing hymns and hymnody later in the Victorian age was dominated by the publication and considerable impact of *Hymns Ancient and Modern* (1861). After a long period in which Nonconformists had been the main influence on English hymnody, Anglicans now took over. Compared to the output of Anglican hymn-writers, and indeed those from the Scottish Presbyterian and Roman Catholic churches, the contribution made by Nonconformist authors to Victorian hymnody seems small. The fact is that most Nonconformist congregations continued to rely largely on eighteenth-century hymns, especially those of Watts and Wesley, and saw little need to supplement them. The Dissenting denomination which perhaps provided most Victorian hymn-writers, certainly proportionately, was Unitarianism. Alongside two radical political figures, Sir John Bowring and Ebenezer Elliott, Unitarian hymn-writers included William Gaskell, Sarah Adams, whose 'Nearer, my God, to thee' ranked high in the Victorian Top Ten, and James Martineau (1805–1900) who re-wrote many of the great classics of nineteenth-century hymnody, including verses by John Henry Newman, to make them less Christocentric.

It was arguably new hymnbooks rather than new hymns which constituted Nonconformity's main contribution to nineteenth-century hymnody. The middle decade of the century saw both the General and the Particular Baptist Associations, the Primitive Methodist Conference and the Congregational Union all authorizing substantial hymn books which both clarified their denominational identity and brought greater uniformity and standardization into their worship. There were two outstanding hymnal compilers among Victorian Nonconformists who both did much to raise literary and cultural standards as well as greatly to increase the theological breadth of dissenting hymnody. James Martineau edited a series of Unitarian hymnals between 1830 and 1873 which drew on Catholic, mystical and other European traditions as well as on the rich seam of American Unitarian hymnody. In somewhat similar vein the Congregationalist William Garrett Horder (1841–1922) introduced many new treasures into English hymnody. John Greenleaf Whittier's 'Dear Lord and Father of Mankind' first appeared in his 1884 *Congregational Hymns*. Horder was also one of the first writers to take the whole study of hymns seriously, publishing his influential study *The Hymn Lover: An Account of the Rise and Growth of English Hymnody* in 1889.

English Nonconformity's golden age, or Indian summer, in the opening decade of the twentieth century, was marked by the publication of a series of substantial hymnals. They included Horder's *Worship-Song* (music edition, 1905) with 803 hymns, the 1904 *Methodist Hymn Book*, with 981, and, the biggest of all, the *Primitive Methodist Hymnal and Supplement* of 1912 which contained over 1,300 texts. All the major Nonconformist denominations continued to produce hymn books throughout the twentieth century, with new editions coming out at roughly thirty year intervals.

In terms of hymn writing, the Nonconformist contribution was almost certainly greater in the twentieth century than it had been in the nineteenth. The Methodist Fred Pratt Green (1903–2000) and Congregationalists Albert Bayly (1901–84) and Fred Kaan (1923–2010), who later joined the United Reformed Church (URC), stand among the century's leading hymn writers. Among contemporary English hymn-writers, several of the best known, most prolific and most represented in collections are Nonconformists: Brian Wren (born 1936), Alan Gaunt (born 1935) and Janet Wootton (born 1952) come from a Congregational background, with Wren and Gaunt later joining the URC, Andrew Pratt (born 1948) is a Methodist and Graham Kendrick (born 1950) is the son of a Baptist minister who has since worshipped in independent evangelical fellowships. Over the last decades of the twentieth century, Nonconformist writers have supplied a high proportion of the hymns expressing the social gospel and concerns relating to justice and peace.

However depleted their ranks were at the beginning of the twenty-first century, Nonconformists also continue to contribute considerably to the academic study of hymnody. The leading expert in the field, and editor of the *Canterbury Dictionary of Hymnology*, is the Methodist scholar Professor Richard Watson (born 1934), who follows in the footsteps of the Congregationalist Erik Routley (1917–82), the greatest authority on hymns in the twentieth century, while Nonconformist presence remained strong and significant among both the membership and the office bearers of the Hymn Society of Great Britain and Ireland. At the time of writing, the society's secretary Robert Canham is a minister in the URC and the editor of its bulletin, Andrew Pratt, a Methodist minister.

Welsh Nonconformist hymnody really needs a chapter in itself and the paragraph that follows hardly does it justice. The adage that Methodism was born in song is literally true in Wales where the first Methodist societies, or *seiadau*, resulted from Psalm singing classes held by John Games, precentor at Talgarth Church, at the conclusion of which Howell Harris exhorted those present to spiritual examination and encouragement. William Williams Pantycelyn (1717–91), who together with Harris was one of the key leaders of the eighteenth-century Welsh Methodist revival, is generally acknowledged as Wales' most famous hymn writer. His 'Arglwydd, arwain dwy'r anialwach', or 'Guide me, O Thou great Jehovah', sung to the tune 'Cwm Rhondda', which was composed by John Hughes, a Baptist deacon and preacher, for the anniversary of Capel Rhondda in Pontypridd in 1907, is the quintessential expression of Welsh Nonconformity, still bellowed out at rugby matches in Cardiff. The hymn singing festivals, or *cymanfaeodd canu*, which began in the mid-nineteenth century and continue to this day have been described as Wales' most distinctive contribution to the world of music. Hymns played a key role in the great Welsh religious revival of 1904–5, notably those of Howell Elvet Lewis (1860–1953), a Congregational minister who wrote over 200 hymns in Welsh. Although Welsh Nonconformity went into steep decline in the second half of the twentieth century, its hymns are kept alive by male voice choirs while there has also been a considerable revival of interest in the hymns of the Calvinistic Methodist writer Ann Griffiths (1776–1805).

This chapter has concentrated almost exclusively on hymn texts rather than tunes but it would be wrong to end without acknowledging the distinctive musical sound of Nonconformist hymnody. For a long time it was possible to tell at fifty paces whether someone was Anglican or Nonconformist by the tune to which they sang 'O for a thousand tongues to sing'. The hymnbooks of the established churches of both England and Scotland set Wesley's words to the measured and stately 'Richmond', whereas Nonconformist hymnals have tended to prefer the lively fuguing tune 'Lyngham', written for a Methodist village choir in Northamptonshire in 1803 by Thomas Jarman, a Baptist tailor, or the equally vigorous 'Lydia' which is mentioned in George Eliot's *Scenes of Clerical Life* as 'a meeting-house tune'. Nowadays, thank goodness, establishment snobbery is much diminished and 'Lyngham' is being sung in Anglican and Church of Scotland churches. Other characteristic Nonconformist tunes include 'Crediton', 'Warsaw' and 'Cranbrook' (long used for 'While shepherds watched' but later adopted for 'On Ilkley Moor Baht'at'), which were all the work of Thomas Clark, a cobbler and precentor at a Wesleyan Chapel in Canterbury; 'Sagina' by Thomas Campbell, first published in 1825; and 'Madrid' which was written by a Nottinghamshire stocking maker William Matthews.

Nicholas Temperley, who provides a stimulating chapter on the music of Dissent in *Dissenting Praise*, describes the tune 'Miles Lane', written for Edward Perronet's 'All hail, the power of Jesu's name' by William Shrubshole, who was dismissed from his post as organist at Bangor

Cathedral for frequenting conventicles, as 'the most brilliant specimen of a dissenting hymn-tune'.[16] I have to say that I regard the other tune regularly used for this hymn, James Ellor's vigorous 'Diadem' as much more characteristically Nonconformist with its repeated phrases and Handelian trill on the first appearance of the word 'crown'. Perhaps the last example of the great distinctive early-nineteenth-century Nonconformist hymn tunes, it was composed in 1837 by Ellor when he was an eighteen-year-old hatmaker for the choir of the Wesleyan Methodist Chapel at Droylsden near Manchester. If I was ever to put together a CD of Nonconformist hymn tunes (as I have of certain other categories), 'Diadem' would have pride of place along with 'Lyngham' and 'Sagina'.

Notes

In the preparation of this chapter, in addition to the sources cited in the notes, use has been made of the following articles from the forthcoming *Canterbury Dictionary of Hymnology*: 'Unitarian Hymnody' by Andrew Brown, 'Methodist Hymnody' by Andrew Pratt, 'Baptist Hymnody' by Michael Ball and 'Congregational Church Hymnody' by Andrew Goodall. The author is also grateful for the comments of Professor Dick Watson who read the chapter in draft form.

1 Michael R. Watts, *The Dissenters, Volume 1: From the Reformation to the French Revolution* (Oxford: Clarendon Press, 1978), p. 308.
2 L. E. Elliott-Binns, *Religion in the Victorian Era* (London: Lutterworth Press, 1946), p. 374.
3 B. L. Manning, *The Hymns of Wesley and Watts* (London: Epworth Press, 1942), p. 133.
4 J. Conder, *The Poet of the Sanctuary* (London: John Snow, 1851), pp. 95–96.
5 Quoted by E. Clarke, 'Hymns, Psalms, and Controversy in the Seventeenth Century', in I. Rivers and D. L. Wykes (eds), *Dissenting Praise: Religious Dissent and the Hymn in England and Wales* (Oxford: Oxford University Press, 2011), p. 24.
6 E. Routley, *A Panorama of Christian Hymnody* (Collegeville, MN: The Liturgical Press, 1979), p. 44.
7 G. Booth (ed.), *Primitive Methodist Hymnal* (London: Primitive Methodist Publishing House, 1889), p. iv.
8 Quoted in R. G. Woods, *Good Singing Still* (Ironbridge: West Gallery Music Association, 1995), p. 94.
9 J. Julian, *A Dictionary of Hymnology* (London: John Murray, 1892), p. 730.
10 N. Temperley, *The Music of the English Parish Church* (Cambridge: Cambridge University Press, 1983), I, p. 128.
11 W. Vincent, *Considerations on Parochial Music* (London, 1787), pp. 13–14.
12 M. Hennell, *John Venn and the Clapham Sect* (London: Lutterworth Press, 1958), p. 267.
13 G. Eliot, *Adam Bede* (Harmondsworth: Penguin Books, 1994), pp. 42, 46, 373 and 463.

14 C. Bronte, *Shirley* (Oxford: Oxford University Press, Clarendon Edition, 1979), p. 161.
15 C. Dickens, *Christmas Stories and Other Stories* (London: Chapman and Hall, 1891), p. 628.
16 N. Temperley, 'The Music of Dissent', in Rivers and Wykes (eds), *Dissenting Praise*, p. 209.

12 Nonconformist Preaching and Liturgy

Stephen R. Holmes

In different ways, preaching and liturgy have been central to Nonconformist identity. The iconic moment in the self-narration of Nonconformity centres, at least in classical presentation, on the ejection of clergy for maintaining a principled refusal to use (what was perceived to be) a flawed liturgy, the Book of Common Prayer; the presenting validation of Nonconformist principles has generally been fidelity to scripture, and the sermon was (with some exceptions, notably the Society of Friends) the principal way of disseminating or debating the teachings of scripture.

That said, it is not easy to propose a homiletic practice that is distinctively Nonconformist and common through history, and the crucial mark of Nonconformist liturgical practices might be seen to be variety. We might propose that it is not so much the practices of Nonconformity in these areas that is distinctive, so much as the importance attached to those practices: preaching is a central mode of Nonconformist discourse; similarly, it is often a mark of Nonconformity that liturgical uniformity is little-valued. This seems more successful as an analysis but, as will be seen, still fails to account for the sheer variety of practice visible in history.

We can usefully select three themes under which to explore these subjects: the centrality of the Bible; the expectation of the Spirit's inspiration; and the place of preaching.

I. The Bible the Only Rule of Practice

It is evident from reading Nonconformist texts that there is, or at least there was in the formative period, a profound commitment to a church practice based on scripture alone. Of course, all significant Christian traditions in Britain in the sixteenth century paid high respect to the teaching of scripture; the distinctive Nonconformist emphases might be listed as three: a sense that the reformation of the church required by scripture is much more far-reaching than others believed; a discounting of the authority of the early church in matters of liturgical practice; and a strong scripture principle which minimized the possibility of *adiaphora* in the area of Christian worship.

The characteristic early Separatist stance was a pressing sense of the need for urgent further reform of the practices of the English church. This included its ministry and governance, but also focused on liturgical practice. This is already visible in the 1572 *Admonition to the Parliament*, which asserts that 'we in England are so far off, from having a church rightly reformed, according to the prescript of God's word that as yet we have not come to the outward face of the same'.[1] This is spelt out first in a criticism of the multiple orders of ministry in the Church of England, and of the education and piety of those filling the offices; then in a complaint that in many and varied ways the order for celebrating the Lord's Supper is a departure from biblical practice: 'They had no introit, for Celestinus a pope brought it in, about the year 430. But we have borrowed a piece of one out of the mass book . . . They used no other words but such as Christ left: We borrow from the papists . . . They ministered the Sacrament plainly. We pompously, with singing, piping, surplice and cope waring.'[2] Similar complaints follow concerning baptism, and the liturgies laid down in the Prayer Book more generally.

When James VI of Scotland came to the English throne, a list of similar complaints was laid before him in the Millenary Petition (1603). The petitioners objected to many aspects of the authorized liturgy.[3] James was in no mood for reform, however, and the arguments continued. When William Bradshaw offered an account of the beliefs of *English Puritanisme* in 1605, he put this point, that liturgy ought to be conformed to scripture, first, in an impressively clear formulation: 'They hould and mainetaine that the word of God . . . is of absolute perfection, giuen by Christ the head of the Churche, to bee vnto the sam, the sole Canon and rule of all matters of Religion, and the worship and seruice of God whatsoeuer. And that whatsoeuer done in the same seruice and worship cannot bee iustified by the said word, is vnlawfull.'[4] He went on to state the negative corollary: 'They hould that all Ecclesiasticall actions invented & deuised by man, are vtterlie to bee excluded out of the exercises of religion.'[5]

Unsurprisingly, the same theme is prominent in the pleas for toleration after the imposition of the Clarendon Code following the restoration of the monarchy in 1660. John Milton argued for two principles that united all Protestant Churches: 'that the Rule of true Religion is the Word of God only; and that their Faith ought not to be an implicit faith [i.e., believing principles taught by a church without testing them against Scripture]'. He argued that from these two principles 'it directly follows that no true Protestant can persecute, or not tolerate his fellow Protestant'.[6] On this basis he saw an essential unity, not generally found by the groups themselves, it should be said, between Lutherans, Calvinists, Anabaptists, Arians, Socinians and Arminians.

Alongside the impressive uniformity of this call to reformation according to the word of God, Nonconformist history demonstrates almost endless diversity on the question of what a scriptural liturgical practice actually looks like. In Robert Browne's memoir we read of the gathering of a Separatist congregation in Norwich, which involved all present to test both the organization of the church, and its liturgical practice, against scripture. Where there was dispute (Browne records a question as to the propriety of raising queries in the assembly concerning the content of the teaching ministry), consensus was achieved on the basis of an appeal to scripture.[7] This is a fine story, and one repeated by many down the ages;[8] the sober historian has to judge that it is often also rather romantic. The reality of Nonconformist history suggests repeated failures to agree on what reformation is required by scripture, in the area of liturgy, and in many others.

Whereas the Anglican Prayer Book asserted the authority of 'ancient authors', and James I was prepared to accept matters on the basis of custom or 'comliness', Commonwealth Presbyterians would have asserted themselves equally bound to the text of scripture as the Independents, but (at least in matters of church order) found something different in the text. The notorious fissiparousness of Nonconformity stems, at least in self-presentation, from this problem of conflicting accounts of what is demanded by scripture. If there is an urgency to reform the church in accordance with the demands of scripture, and an inability to agree on what scripture demands, then repeated divisions will be the inevitable result. An impressive example of this may be seen in the well-known history of the Jacob-Lathrop-Jessey church in London, which saw many divisions, usually fairly amicable, over the proper practice of baptism, and the question of whether it was proper to have fellowship with parish churches.[9]

It is no surprise that, after toleration, the liturgical practices of Nonconformity became settled; there was less debate about the issue, and so less appeal to scripture.[10] It is difficult to find an example of a reflection on liturgical practice that does not at least acknowledge the idea that scripture is the crucial guide, however, even when other arguments seem to be more extensively in play. A classic example might be John Taylor's intervention in a mid-eighteenth-century debate about 'rational liturgy'. Taylor did not question the (characteristically eighteenth-century) call for 'rationality', but asserted that scripture teaches the duties of 'natural [i.e. rational] religion' 'most clearly,' and ends his comments with an appeal to 1 Corinthians 12.[11]

The nineteenth and twentieth centuries saw a general, if not quite universal, turn away from biblicist appeals in matters of liturgy to a broader willingness to explore the varied resources of the Christian liturgical tradition. This might be read, not so much as a rejection of biblicism, but as an acceptance that, as with models of church government, the biblical text was in fact less prescriptive than early generations had assumed. Exceptions included several renewal movements – the Brethren, for example – and the rise of the Charismatic movement (not, of course, confined to Nonconformity, but influential there also).

II. The Inspiration of the Spirit

Mention of the Brethren and the Charismatic movement points towards a second theme that is important in both liturgy and preaching in Nonconformist history: an expectation of immediate inspiration from the Holy Spirit in worship or preaching. Henry Barrow objected to the content of the Prayer Book as being unbiblical, but he also objected to the concept of a Prayer Book as acting to quench the Spirit.[12] Some early Baptists insisted that the preacher had no notes, or even an open Bible, so that he was cast entirely on the Spirit's work for his words.[13]

The Society of Friends were and are the purest example of this principle, in holding to a liturgical practice grounded entirely in openness to the immediate promptings of the Spirit. From the first, their detractors derided them for claiming the inspiration of the Spirit for everything they said;[14] Voltaire (who appears at this point to be reporting, not mocking) records that a Quaker acknowledged to him that some who spoke in the meeting were moved by folly, but that this was bearable, so that the Spirit may be heard.[15]

In broader Nonconformist circles, this commitment to seeking and expecting immediate inspiration became particularly focused in a commitment to extempore prayer that lasted from the beginnings of Nonconformity well into the eighteenth century. The Westminster Assembly, for example, criticized the Prayer Book, not just because the prayers were poor, but because having written prayers prevented ministers from exercising the 'gift of prayer' which, it was asserted, God gives to all who are ordained.[16] Even in 1745, Philip Doddridge could comment, almost in passing, that '[t]here is no particular *Form of Prayer* on this Occasion [viz, an ordination service], or on any other among us',[17] before going on to assume that the content of the prayer was the result of the leading of the Spirit. Doddridge's easy assumption no longer described a universal position, however. In 1760, John Taylor's defence of extempore prayer dismissed the notion that the practice should be a 'crude unpremeditated effusion, in an entire dependence upon some supposed sudden extraordinary motion or suggestion of the Spirit of God'.[18] Taylor's point, however, was not that the aid of the Spirit should not be expected, but that the Spirit would be at work in and through adequate preparation of the heart. He remained dismissive of written prayers.

The turn to liturgical forms in the nineteenth and twentieth centuries, already alluded to, and the arrival of Methodist denominations which (in some, but not all, cases) had borrowed a liturgy from the Church of England led to a less dismissive attitude towards written forms. This was not done to the detriment of the inherited practice of extempore prayer, however, which was always recognized as a necessary exercise of true piety (perhaps particularly among those strands of Nonconformity most influenced by evangelicalism), albeit one which required guidance and experience if it was to be done well,[19] and as a central part of the liturgical practice of Nonconformity. Even in publishing a book of set prayers in 1920, the Congregational Union described extempore prayer as a part of 'the inheritance of genius of the Free Churches', suggesting that '[t]he fervour of personal appeal informed with the impulses of the hour and pleading the hour's needs is frequently charged with sympathetic force such as no printed forms can supply'.[20]

Even Payne and Winwood's *Orders and Prayers*, arguably the high-point of the influence of liturgical renewal on British Baptist life, is extraordinarily wary of read prayers; the book commends the memorization of certain liturgical forms, particularly collects, but otherwise, 'in general the prayers are intended to help the minister in his [*sic*] own preparation for free prayer'.[21] The most recent Baptist manual *Gathering for Worship* (2005) is more ready for the minister to read the orders, but repeatedly, and at the central liturgical moments (the Eucharistic prayer; the prayer recalling God's mighty saving acts in preparation for a baptism; the prayer of ordination of a minister) the rubric invites the president to substitute extempore prayer for the set form.[22]

Here again the Charismatic movement has perhaps called Nonconformity back to its earlier traditions. It is striking that the twentieth-century examples I have quoted do not use the language of pneumatological inspiration in the way the earlier tradition did, rather speaking of 'free prayer'. Charismatic renewal invited churches to recover a sense of expectation of the Spirit's presence and action that had once been the common inheritance of Nonconformity (as previously had Pentecostalism; John Penry's account of Evan Roberts' ministry during the 1904–5 Welsh Revival offers a vivid illustration[23]).

III. Preaching

An expectation of the present work of the Holy Spirit distinguishes Nonconformist preaching as well. In the 1904–5 Welsh Revival, and before, the phenomenon of the *hwyl* was a striking example of this theme: a form of repetitive and almost musical extempore pulpit oratory which provoked a particular shared emotive reaction, perhaps not unlike certain traditions of African American preaching today. It would be possible to offer a merely psychological explanation of the *hwyl* (see David Davies' son's description of his father's preaching[24] for an example), and it seems likely that there is at least some truth in such an explanation, but preachers and listeners accounted for their experience by appealing to the work of the Spirit.

This is significant because of the central place of preaching in Nonconformist practice and identity. The sermon was the crucial way of discovering, defining, defending and distributing Nonconformist beliefs and practices, and, when the traditions became more settled, came to occupy the central place in the liturgical practices of almost every Nonconformist tradition (the Society of Friends are the only significant exception). A list of famous or influential Nonconformists is essentially a list of preachers.

It is not unreasonable to date the beginnings of organized Nonconformity to a debate over the place of preaching. Those who hoped for further or faster reformation in the national church at the beginning of the second half of the sixteenth century were active in promoting 'prophesyings', gatherings of clerics who came together, in public, to debate and discuss the interpretation of difficult or disputed texts of scripture. This became a widespread movement, generally supported by the bishops, through the 1560s, and was defended by Archbishop Edmund Grindal in a letter to the queen in 1576.[25] The queen was concerned that such gatherings might provoke dissension or disaffection, however, and rejecting Grindal's defence, banned such exercises.[26] This, for many, was the point at which the policy of pressing for further reformation of the national church was seen to have failed; a position which invited a move into Nonconformity.[27]

Grindal himself asserted the central importance of preaching on biblical grounds, and distinguished between the reading of the homilies, distinctly second-best, and the preaching of proper sermons, crafted to speak to the particular needs of the people. This argument was simply assumed by Browne, Barrow, and almost every later Nonconformist leader; sermons would become the central mode of communication of the new movement. The Millenary Petitioners, looking to James VI/I for the reform Elizabeth had been unwilling to grant, asked that all ministers should be competent and willing preachers;[28] Bradshaw's account of the nature of *English Puritanisme* identifies preaching of the gospel as 'the highest and supreame office' of a minister;[29] The *Westminster Directory* has preaching as 'one of the greatest and most excellent works belonging to the ministry of the gospel';[30] these examples could be multiplied almost endlessly.

There was, in the seventeenth century, a distinctive Puritan/Nonconformist tradition of preaching, classically illustrated in Perkins' famous *Arte of Prophesying*.[31] Perkins stresses plainness of speech and an eschewal of all literary pretension or form, in order that the message of the text may be presented simply and directly; when one compares this to Archbishop John Tillotson's justly famous sermons, the extent to which a simply different vision of the preaching task is at work is clear. Tillotson offered carefully crafted meditations on an idea, usually an ethical duty, suggested by the biblical text; Perkins rejects craft for clarity, and requires full and careful exposition of the text, followed by defence and application of the doctrine discovered therein. Perkins is concerned that the sermon should make the teaching of the scripture clear, and also make it obvious that the clear teaching is derived from the scripture; clearly, there is an echo of our first theme, biblicism, here: the preacher's only justification for his instruction is fidelity to the text.

In the eighteenth century, preaching became the primary vehicle of the evangelical revivals, at the same time remaining the basic mode of instruction of Old Dissent. At times there can be a simple clash here, as when Wesleyan Arminianism clashed with the Calvinistic commitments of (the majority of) Old Dissent: the Baptist John Collett Ryland, as a young man, records in his diary hearing Charles Wesley preach on Jn 5.1–14. 'Mr. Cha. Westley [*sic*] positively asserted falling from Grace, in the strongest Terms. I thank the Lord I thought at yt time on Mr. E. Coles *Discourse on Final Perseverence* . . . with an unusual Impression, and it seem's to Strengthen, Comfort and enlarge my heart.'[32]

The nineteenth century must be considered the great age of Nonconformist preaching. Ministers such as Joseph Parker, Alexander Maclaren, R. W. Dale, and supremely C. H. Spurgeon, could become major national figures through the power of their pulpit ministry. Of course, the same may be said of Anglicans such as Charles Simeon or John Henry Newman; the sermon had become a significant mode of national discourse – and one that could affect national life, at least from time to time.[33] The habit of referring to all else that happened in worship as 'the preliminaries' was often deplored,[34] but nonetheless speaks powerfully of the extent to which the sermon was elevated within worship to be almost the only significant religious exercise.

The nineteenth century also saw significant moves towards the opening of the preaching ministry to women. Catherine Booth, and the Salvation Army's practice of appointing couples to lead, is of course the most obvious example. Booth was inspired by the preaching of Phoebe Palmer, and defended Palmer's right to preach in *Female Ministry: A Woman's Right to Preach the Gospel* (1859/61); she borrowed arguments from Palmer's own *The Promise of the Father* (1859), which in turn borrowed arguments from the seventeenth-century Quaker Margaret Fell, who had defended a woman's right to speak in the assembly in her *Women's Speaking Justified* (1666). All three texts are deeply biblicist, arguing that a proper reading of the Bible, particularly the New Testament, establishes that the preaching ministry is indifferently open to women and men. Booth at one point quotes a pseudonymous anti-Roman controversialist who calls himself 'Presbuteros' who asserts that the denial of the pulpit to women is one more relic of papist superstition needing to be swept away:

> Habituated for ages, as men had been, to the diabolical teaching and delusions practiced upon them by the papal 'priesthood', it was difficult for them, when they did get possession of the Scriptures, to discern therein the plain fact, that among the primitive Christians preaching was not confined to men, but women also, gifted with power by the Holy Spirit, preached the gospel; and hence the slowness with which, even at the present time, this truth has been admitted by those giving heed to the word of God.[35]

The Salvationist position was pre-empted by other Nonconformist traditions, however, notably the Primitive Methodists, where the point was argued successfully by Hugh Bourne.[36] Bourne's arguments, focusing on Mary Magdalene and describing her as 'an apostle to the apostles, a preacher to the preachers, an evangelist to the evangelists' sound remarkably modern. Both the Baptist Union of Great Britain and the Congregational Union were to accept the ordination of women early in the twentieth century; Nonconformity was – not uniformly, but generally – remarkably progressive on the question of women's ministry.

The story of Nonconformist preaching in the twentieth century parallels the story of Nonconformist biblicism and Nonconformist accounts of pneumatological inspiration in worship: the liturgical movement led to a certain de-emphasizing of the distinctive, but preaching remains a central part of Nonconformist identity and practice; at the same time, it is a central part of evangelical identity and practice, and this complicates the picture somewhat: an evangelical Anglican church might have as much or more focus upon, and time given to, the sermon as a non-evangelical Nonconformist church; that said, taking two congregations in a similar theological tradition, it is likely that the Nonconformist congregation will have longer sermons that are perceived to be more central to its life and worship than the Anglican congregation.

IV. Conclusions

This chapter is necessarily brief, and has tried to cover a diverse tradition over several centuries; inevitably, much has been missed out. Other themes could be traced, and many anomalies or exceptions to the general points made could be offered. That said, a biblicist commitment to shaping worship according to the scriptures, and particularly the New Testament; a reliance upon and expectation of the immediate inspiration of the Spirit in worship, leading to a distrust, or at least downplaying, of set liturgical forms; and a focus on preaching as the central moment of the liturgy are each threads that seem to run through the tradition in all its variety, and mutually to reinforce each other. Nonconformity found in the Bible a source of authority to criticize the claims of the Established Church. In an account of the Spirit's work a justification of liturgical practices that were varied and local; and in the elevation of preaching both a way of exploring the claims of the Bible and experiencing the work of the Spirit, and a distinctive centre to congregational worship that distinguished the tradition from the establishment.

Further, the Bible was found to assert the work of the Spirit, and the centrality of preaching; a commitment to the work of the Spirit allowed people who were not necessarily scholars of the first rank to assert the correctness of their biblical interpretations, and to believe in the power of the preached word; a commitment to preaching placed the focus of the community on the biblical text, and provided occasion for the experienced work of the Spirit. The tradition was coherent and vibrant; it is no surprise that it has survived and prospered, even in the face of persecution and a changing culture.

Notes

1 R. Tudur Jones et al. (eds), *Protestant Nonconformist Texts, Volume 1: 1550–1700* (Aldershot: Ashgate, 2007), p. 37.
2 Ibid., pp. 39–40.
3 Ibid., p. 105.
4 Ibid., p. 109.
5 Ibid.
6 Ibid., p. 263.
7 Ibid., p. 61.
8 For a similar example, see ibid., p. 152.
9 There is a brief account of some of the divisions in ibid., pp. 370–71; a fuller account can be found in Murray Tolmie, *The Triumph of the Saints: The Separate Churches of London* (London: Cambridge University Press, 1977).
10 But see Alan P. F. Sell et al. (eds), *Protestant Nonconformist Texts, Volume 2: The Eighteenth Century* (Aldershot: Ashgate, 2006), pp. 16–18 for a Quaker document saturated in biblical citation.
11 Ibid., pp. 419–20.
12 Jones et al. (eds), *Protestant Nonconformist Texts, Volume 1*, pp. 76–78.
13 S. R. Holmes, *Baptist Theology* (London: T&T Clark, 2012), p. 110.
14 See, e.g., Jones et al. (eds), *Protestant Nonconformist Texts, Volume 1*, p. 204.
15 Sell et al. (eds), *Protestant Nonconformist Texts, Volume 2*, p. 62.
16 *Directory for the Public Worship of God*, Preface.
17 Sell et al. (eds), *Protestant Nonconformist Texts, Volume 2*, p. 165.

18 Ibid., p. 419.
19 See, for instance, Helen Herschell's advice of family prayer from ca 1840, in David Bebbington et al. (eds), *Protestant Nonconformist Texts, Volume 3: The Nineteenth Century* (Aldershot: Ashgate, 2006), pp. 180–81, in which she simply assumes the form of both solitary and family prayer will be extempore.
20 David M. Thompson et al. (eds), *Protestant Nonconformist Texts, Volume 4: The Twentieth Century* (Aldershot: Ashgate, 2007), pp. 144–45.
21 E. A. Payne and S. F. Winwood, *Orders and Prayers for Church Worship: A Manual for Ministers* (London: Carey Kingsgate, 1965), pp. xv–xvi.
22 C. J. Ellis and Myra Blyth, *Gathering for Worship: Patterns and Prayers for the Community of Disciples* (Norwich: Canterbury Press, 2005).
23 Thompson et al. (eds), *Protestant Nonconformist Texts, Volume 4*, pp. 25–26.
24 Bebbington et al. (eds), *Protestant Nonconformist Texts, Volume 3*, pp. 137–38.
25 See Jones et al. (eds), *Protestant Nonconformist Texts, Volume 1*, pp. 45–53.
26 Ibid., pp. 53–54.
27 Patrick Collinson, e.g., explores this at length in *The Elizabethan Puritan Movement* (London: Jonathan Cape, 1982), pp. 159–242.
28 See Jones et al. (eds), *Protestant Nonconformist Texts, Volume 1*, p. 105.
29 Ibid., p. 111.
30 *Directory*, 'Of the Preaching of the Word'.
31 William Perkins, *The Arte of Prophesying* (1606).
32 Recorded in H. Wheeler Robinson, *The Life and Faith of the Baptists* (London: Kingsgate, 1946), pp. 60–61.
33 The role of Nonconformist preachers in supporting the election of the Liberal Party (under Henry Campbell-Bannerman) in the 1906 election is the classic example.
34 See, e.g., Bebbington et al. (eds), *Protestant Nonconformist Texts, Volume 3*, pp. 135–36.
35 Booth, *Female Ministry*, the text can be found online at http://webapp1.dlib.indiana.edu/vwwp/view?docId=VAB7105, accessed on 12 November 2012.
36 Bebbington et al. (eds), *Protestant Nonconformist Texts, Volume 3*, pp. 247–48.

13 Nonconformist Architecture: A Representative Focus

Clyde Binfield

It took the buildings of Dissent three decades to turn into Dissenting architecture, initiating a natural if often awkward and frequently dismissed transition, to ensure a distinctive, visual, non-conformity. Within three generations religious Dissent was becoming institutionalized. This was a nationwide process and it required accommodation, tacit at a local level but statutory nationally. The latter was largely secured by the 'Toleration Act' of 1689. At that point, slowly and unevenly confirmed by subsequent legislation, Dissent became an inferior Establishment, second-rate and therefore second-best, deviating from normal national practice, witnessing to differing concepts of authority, consistently discriminated against but legally tolerated and within the pale of the Constitution. Its buildings reflected this. Where they became recognizable, architecture had a foothold; these buildings could now announce purpose and, increasingly, fitness for purpose. They indicated the means of the people for whom they were built, the skills of the artisans and craftsmen who built them and – again increasingly – their architects. Style came into the equation. The constraints of their status came into creative tension with their aspirations, their sense of mission and the economic opportunities which beckoned for a significant number of them.

The basic requirements were simple: room for people gathered in worship to hear the Word and observe the sacraments of Communion and baptism. The nature of the provision varied to suit the requirements of different sorts of Dissenter. Quakers needed separate rooms for men and women when meeting for church affairs as opposed to worship; they did not need provision for Communion or baptism, their ministry did not need a pulpit, although it made use of a raised platform or ministers' stand, and music played no part in their meetings. Baptists had to provide for believers' baptism by immersion. Paedobaptists moving towards Unitarianism placed decreasing emphasis on the sacraments. That was a later development, some generations down the line. Another, later, development was the provision for children which came with the Sunday School revolution. This broke in the 1780s and gathered exponential force for the next century and a quarter.

This is enough to suggest that there was nothing static about Dissenting architecture. It was vulnerable to constraints, including those of fashion, it was open to opportunity, it was flexible, and its buildings had no mystique. For Old Dissent – Baptists, Independents, Presbyterians, Quakers – the common form of building was the meeting house, which was exactly what those words suggested. This was the prevailing form from the late seventeenth to the mid-eighteenth century. Two surviving examples, both of them in Norwich, show the sophistication to which meeting houses could attain. The Independent Old Meeting (1693) is elegantly matter-of-fact; it expresses the corporate confidence of merchants who had seen good architecture in Amsterdam.[1] The Presbyterian, now Unitarian, Octagon Chapel (1754–56), expensively built following a competition to design by the leading local architect, Thomas Ivory (1709–79), famously impressed John Wesley who visited it a year after completion to find 'perhaps the most elegant [meeting house] in all Europe', its interior 'finished in the highest taste, and . . . as clean as any nobleman's saloon'.[2]

Wesley's was the response of an educated contemporary gentleman: sympathetic surprise at how cosmopolitan the provincial commercial classes could be. His response also marks a revolution. The Octagon Chapel was a meeting house, an effective gathering space for a comfortably settled congregation, but its architect was at the same time designing an Assembly Room for Norwich and Wesley saw how an octagon could accommodate an assorted assembly gathered for a more evangelistic purpose than the committed core of saints in a traditional meeting house. It was from the mid-eighteenth century that New Dissent, chiefly Methodist, dominated by the Wesleys, and in its own way as unwillingly Dissenting as Old Dissent had been, complicated the ecclesiastical building scene. Its buildings were more preaching boxes than meeting houses. Their arrangements for communion were significantly different and they frequently provided for travelling preachers, a different order of ministry from that called by Baptists or Independents or appointed by Presbyterians. They introduced a fresh building type, the chapel, a word which by the turn of the eighteenth century was to be found as much among English and Welsh Baptists and Congregationalists (as Independents were increasingly called) as among Methodists.

The chapel prevailed in the nineteenth century although from the 1840s it ceded place significantly to the church, a change of name that reflected denominational self-confidence, growing architectural sophistication and changing views of history as well as the human nature demonstrated whenever the Dissenting Joneses set out to keep up with the Anglican Joneses. In the twentieth century churches were in the Nonconformist ascendant while the meeting house was self-consciously rediscovered as all were subsumed by rising costs and declining membership.

I. Congregationalists as Representative Nonconformists: The Force of a Paper Read in Birmingham

If the nineteenth century saw Nonconformity's high noon, it might be argued that the Victorian age saw Congregationalists as England's and especially the political nation's representative Nonconformists. That suggests social and cultural standing and, since England was the driving force of an imperial nation, it also suggests far horizons. The rest of this chapter focuses on Congregational church building between the 1840s and the 1870s, arguing that there was a Congregational architecture which reflected a Congregational temper and that the organization of church building played a critical part in shaping and updating a truly national denomination. Similar arguments might be made for Baptists, Methodists and Unitarians but the relationship between Congregational building, architecture, and polity lends special force to such a focus. It allows for a representative narrative.

A particular date is pivotal to the argument: 24 August 1862, the bicentenary of 'Black Bartholomew's Day', 1662, when so many parsons were ejected from their livings that Protestant dissent from the reconstituted national church became a permanently structured part of the national polity. Most of the ejected were not Congregationalists but those who were formed the professional backbone of a fluid yet distinctive and persistent religious tradition. That it was more temper than denomination did not detract from its distinctiveness. Indeed, it allowed ample room for creative reflection to those who were beginning to examine the past that had formed them. Consequently that pivotal date, 24 August 1862, is less important than the use that was made of it: it was tailor-made to advance an already evolving strategy.

To explore both use and strategy the focus will be an organization, some theorists and a string-puller. The organization is a chapel-building society. The theorists are a succession of essayists who expressed the Congregational mind and its culture. The string-puller is an elderly man of antiquarian disposition, a retired barrister who had in fact never practised and who had lived for some years in Tunbridge Wells, enjoying the ill-health for which that resort catered. It was this man who seized the bicentennial moment and made it visibly fit for the purposes of Victorian England in general and its Congregationalism in particular.

In October 1861 a paper was read at the Birmingham Autumnals of the Congregational Union of England and Wales on the approaching bicentenary of the Great Ejectment. Its general drift was 'rapturously adopted'.[3] The paper had been prepared by our string-puller, Joshua Wilson, now in his mid-to-late sixties, but he was not present to deliver it, perhaps because public speaking had never been in his line but just as likely because of his health: Wilson was a martyr to chronic cystitis.[4] Robert Ashton, the man who read Wilson's paper for him, was not on the face of it a man to provoke rapturous applause, although he and Wilson were kindred spirits.[5] Ashton was in his earlier sixties and an *alumnus* of Hoxton, the theological college which had been largely founded and maintained by the Wilson family. He too had antiquarian inclinations. In 1851, as secretary of the short-lived Wycliffe Society, he had edited a three-volume edition of the works of John Robinson, pastor to the Pilgrim Fathers. For the past eleven years he had been out of pastoral charge and into denominational organization. In 1861 he was joint secretary of the Congregational Union, in reality a dogsbody post, picking up pieces mislaid by his better-known colleague George Smith of Poplar.[6] He also edited the *Congregational Year Book*, which one London preacher, the irrepressibly bombastic John Campbell of Moorfields Tabernacle, had recently praised for its 'peculiar achievement in English Ecclesiastical Literature':[7]

> It presents the most thorough analysis of the greatest, the most enlightened, and the most influential Dissenting community in the land, that can be imagined. It is a full and complete development of the ecclesiastical economy of the entire community, and everything appertaining to it . . . It is the most magnificent lecture on the power of the Voluntary Principle ever delivered.[8]

That rhetoric and those men, their interests, publications and connections, set the scene for what follows. Campbell's executive enthusiasm had saved Ashton's edition of Robinson's works from financial ruin. His orthodoxy was unimpeachable and if his style set the teeth of younger men on edge, he remained a famous warhorse. Perhaps Campbell, who had chaired the first annual meeting of the chapel-building society which is to be considered shortly, stoked up the rapture which greeted Ashton's reading of Wilson's paper.

The paper was an *omnium gatherum* of proposals, shrewd, practical, idealistic and antiquarian in turn, angled at Congregationalism's diverse constituencies, couched in a forcefully contemporary rhetoric and drawing on up-to-date observation, much of it provoked by the vogue for statistics which publication of the 1851 Religious Census had intensified in chapel circles. None of it was particularly original but the sum of it announced a curiously realistic strategy. Some of the proposals were piously anodyne: the reprinting of old Nonconformist histories, the formation of a Nonconformist history society, the erection of a memorial to the ejected in Bunhill Fields, Nonconformity's *Campo Santo* and of a Memorial Hall to house Congregationalism's representative communal activities. Specific weeks might be set apart for prayer on set subjects, popular tracts might be printed and lectures delivered in the Congregational colleges and more generally to propagate the foundational principles of Puritanism and Nonconformity. The rhetoric was uncompromising. The lectures, for example, were to 'let the people of England know on what an antichristian and sectarian foundation the Ecclesiastical Establishment in this country was reconstructed in 1661'.[9] A Congregational mind, spiritually forthright and popular, firmly grounded in national tradition, was to be released.

Central to these proposals was to be the construction of 100 memorial churches. Here strategy replaced rhetoric. None should be built in towns where fewer than 3,000 lived; none should seat fewer than 400 adults. All should accommodate the poor, 'especially that most interesting class – the working men and their families', and at least one 'plain, simple, commodious building' should be provided in each of the largest cities for their benefit.[10] Nonetheless, it remained 'an unquestionable fact that our strength as a denomination lies in the large cities and towns, as our special vocation is to the middle classes of the people, who form the chief portion of their inhabitants . . . Our watchword should now be "London and the large towns"'.[11] That secured, Congregationalists could then attend to evangelistic or agricultural out-stations in a programme of mission-planting which would avoid the debilitating multiplication of 'small chapels in villages . . . as the seats of small churches . . . generally . . . unable to support their own pastors'.[12]

To be fit for purpose a building needs an architect. To proclaim its purpose it needs a style. Architecture has entered the equation of denominational principle, temper and extension. It was promoted by Congregational architects, that is to say, men who were both Congregationalists and architects of Congregational buildings, and sustained by the English Congregational Chapel-Building Society.

II. The English Congregational Chapel-Building Society

The English Congregational Chapel-Building Society was formed in 1853. Although it never quite achieved what was hoped for it, it was a milestone in denominational organization and the development of chapel architecture. It was a crucible for networking, professionalism and mission.

It was not the first such Congregational society. Lancashire, England's 'empire county . . . whence issue so many of these mighty impulses which are changing the economical condition of the people, and the legislation of the country and of the world itself', had prepared the ground in 1852, preceded by London, the imperial capital, in 1848.[13] Lancashire aimed at fifty new chapels in five years but realistically settled for twenty. London, too, aimed at fifty but five years later only eighteen had been aided. The prospect was daunting. Even with fifty new chapels, London would still have under 200 Congregational chapels for a population 'which, ten years hence, will be three millions!!!'[14]

The London society was the reworking of an earlier Metropolitan Chapel-Building Society which had itself grown from the work of Joshua Wilson's father Thomas (1764–1843), a retired but far from retiring silk manufacturer who for nearly fifty years had been a one-man chapel-building society, if not a one-man Congregational Union.[15] That evolution explains the care with which the English Society's promoters set about their work and their anxiety 'to proceed with that caution which was likely to secure the confidence and co-operation of the entire denomination'.[16] The day of the representative committee, which had dawned in the 1790s, was now in its morning glory, accelerated and democratized by the railway age.

A national society needed national affirmation. This society was mooted at the Congregational Union's Northampton Autumnals in 1851. A committee was appointed to prepare a constitution at the Union's May Assembly in London, 1852, and at the following Bradford Autumnals the proposed constitution provided for a new committee to get things going. That committee promoted a conference in Derby in March 1853, at which the society was formed, its rules were adopted and an executive committee was elected. The process, committee on committee advancing, was then described for the benefit of the Union's Manchester Autumnals (October 1853) by the new society's secretary.[17] Northampton, London, Bradford, Derby, Manchester: the validation was nationwide.

The new society's aims were clear. It was to serve England outside London and Lancashire. It intended to erect fifty chapels in five years. It epitomized Victorian values; its leading principle was to aid local effort and promote good practice:

> This society, by holding out the inducement of a grant, steps in before the land is secured and the building is commenced, and endeavours to supersede the necessity of begging, by preventing unnecessary expenditure, and, if possible, the contraction of debt.[18]

The meeting of targets is a frustratingly inexact science, fraught with unintended consequences, but the society's achievement was respectable. In its first five years it aided seventy-four chapels, forty of them new causes. That could be translated into 41,271 sittings, provided at a cost of £106,967, of which £21,278 had been met by the society's grants and loans.[19] Encouraged by this, the society aimed at an annual income of £5,500, generated by society grants of £33,793 and loans of £47,321.[20]

The Bicentenary had accounted for much of this. It had encouraged the holding of conferences in July and September 1861, in Manchester and Darlington, and again in November 1861 and January 1862. The Manchester conference had introduced the idea of a hundred Memorial Chapels; the Darlington conference determined to raise £40,000 in four years, half of it for a Memorial Fund; and in 1862 itself, 132 applications had been received, fifty-eight had been accepted, it was decided to double the loan fund, and the society's secretary was justifiably up-beat: 'no year has witnessed such progress'.[21] Looking beyond his society's boundaries, he claimed that the 300 memorial chapels opened, commenced, or projected in 1862 would accommodate 150,000 hearers at a cost of £500,000. No wonder the *Year Book* found that 'the subject of Chapel-building is in an unprecedented degree enjoying the attention and stimulating the liberality of our denomination'.[22]

Such growth could not be maintained at a comparable rate. In the decade after 1863 the English society's income ranged from upwards of £8,000 to upwards of £9,000 with a peak of £11,000 in 1869; the London society's income in the same period ranged from £8,000 to £15,000 with its peak year in 1863–64.[23] Even so, it was reported at the society's jubilee that in fifty years 800 cases (338 of them for new causes) had been accepted, providing over 300,000 sittings, and upwards of £250,000 had been received and almost £230,000 disbursed. A manse fund had been instituted (and a hundred manses aided), and thirty-three grants had been made to causes in Ireland and the Colonies. Jubilee year itself had been the busiest since 1869, with nearly £6,000 disbursed.[24]

Taken as a whole, however, the society's significance outweighed its quantifiable achievement. It was certainly a catalyst in denominational credibility. It held firmly to its leading principle: 'Strictly speaking, this Institution occupies the position simply of an auxiliary to local operations.'[25] Fully aware of 'the dangers of undue and injurious centralisation, to which such a movement is peculiarly exposed', it went out of its way 'to guard against the suspicion of all undue central influence' and to demonstrate 'the compatibility of systematic action on a large scale with genuine Independency',[26] but its promoters were in no doubt as to the benefits of such action. In 1857, looking back on 'the old and vicious' Congregational system 'of deputing the Pastor upon errands of itinerant solicitation to gentlemen of well-known benevolence' too distant to investigate the facts, the committee spelt out the advantages of 'enlarged experience':

> We are willing to counsel you on all points . . . at the very *onset* of your undertaking, and having agreed with you as to the site, the plans, the cost, and the trust deed, we are willing to aid you with a pecuniary advance, on the condition that the local contribution be raised to a certain figure, and the system of general promiscuous begging be abandoned.[27]

At that year's Cheltenham Autumnals, Thomas Aveling, a prominent north London minister, turned his paper on 'Chapel Extension' into a carefully angled plea for the English society as a denominational responsibility.[28] The society had justified its existence for five years but '[t]hey must now say "No" to all further applicants, until the churches of the Denomination authorise them to say "Yes"':

> The Society is the willing servant of the Denomination, and is quite ready to engage in a course of prolonged obedience; but it cannot make bricks without straw, and cannot administer funds till they are entrusted to its care . . . Shall the Institution become permanent? Shall it continue for years, to be the condensed judgment and will of our denomination on the all-important point of chapel extension? Is this the pleasure of this Assembly?[29]

Of course it was, when put like that. The denominational note had been unerringly struck.

One reason for this had been the extent to which, from the first, the society had exploited Congregationalism's existing networks, its proliferation of like-minded provincials, 'faithful stewards of the world's riches', brought ever closer in business, leisure and public spirit by modern communication. Thus its committee comprised forty-two 'well-known and highly-respected individuals', all of course male, most of them laymen, drawn from thirty-one provincial centres; only eight lived in London.[30] They met quarterly, twice in different parts of the country and twice concurrently with the Union's May Assembly in London and Autumnal Assembly in the provinces. When meeting outside London – at least by the 1870s – the committee welcomed the pastor and deacons of the host church as *ex-officio* members, and invited those of all other Congregational churches in the town as observers. No business was transacted outside the committee and none was transacted that had not been announced in the papers prepared for each meeting. All was transparent and above board.[31] Since the society was a membership organization, it had an annual meeting and published an annual report. This listed subscribers, donations, committee members, cases considered and cases aided. The individuals named and celebrated record Congregationalism's movers and makers, as active in chapel extension as in politics, commerce, education, or overseas mission, in one sense the usual suspects but here testifying to the totality of their commitment and, as the Society's promoters so fervently hoped, to the 'great practical utility' of the Union in fostering those 'words of Christian aggression' which independent-minded Congregationalists could together undertake.[32]

III. 'Practical Hints': The English Chapel-Building Society and an Architectural Evolution

A professional evolution marched in step with the evolving denominationalism. In taking the stage in the chapel world, chapel architecture assumed a new significance in the architectural world. If the English society succeeded in its aims, the result could be transformative. At the least there would be 'increased economy and much practical improvement in our ecclesiastical architecture', but the ambition lay in those last two words: 'ecclesiastical architecture'.[33]

A chapel was 'a building adapted to public oral instruction, worship, and fellowship'.[34] The definition was as simple as the purposes were grand. Economy, improvement and architecture, especially ecclesiastical architecture, demanded expertise. In 1854 the *Civil Engineer's and Architect's Journal,* noting the society's recent formation, reported that 'various' architects (the society itself claimed to have approached over fifty), had been invited to submit model designs, some eighteen had responded, and five had been selected from firms in London, Bristol, Wolverhampton and Sunderland.[35] A snapshot from the society's report for 1857 catches the result as it impacted on Norwich: 'The local Committee, after advertising for plans, at length selected one in the Norman style, prepared by Joseph James, Esq., of London.' James was one of the five architects. His design for a new cause with an old name – Chapel in the Field – was for a 900-seater, costing (inclusive of site) £2,600.[36] In such a context the Union's 1860 *Year Book* could preface its ever-lengthening section of architectural descriptions with considerable confidence:

> Sites are no longer chosen because of their obscurity and seclusion; pews are no longer square, high-backed, and perpendicular; pulpits are no longer pitched at an angle to strain the eyes, and stiffen the necks of the worshippers; ventilation and drainage are no longer ignored. School, class, and lecture rooms are now a necessary appendage to the sanctuary; light, air, and comfort are essential to a quiet and healthful worship.[37]

Some matters still called for resolution. The *Year Book* noted the 'question of spires and columns, circular pews and pew doors, together with choir and pulpit', but time and experience would come to the aid of 'our chapel architects', as it would help resolve the question of nomenclature, now that 'meeting house' had all but vanished from our towns and 'chapel', which Methodism had brought into vogue, was found to have popish origins. That left 'church', a word as devoutly grand as it was properly popular, 'descriptive at once of the "house of the Lord" and the place where His people meet for worship'. One hears Robert Ashton's voice in this editorial comment: 'Time is a great innovator' in such matters. Only a historian could write such a thing.[38]

The society itself had an invaluable aid in its handbook-cum-manifesto *Practical Hints on Chapel-Building* (1855; 2nd edn 1862; 3rd edn 1874). *Practical Hints* was carefully persuasive. Here was a step-by-step guide for the most down-to-earth congregation. There were hints about form, site and size (allow seven feet of ground for each adult, recall that three adult sittings approximated to five children's sittings, note that galleries might increase space by a quarter to two-thirds).[39] There was advice about foundations, walls, roofs and roof trusses, windows, towers and spires, heating, lighting (and lightning conductors), ventilation, acoustics, floors, seats, passages, galleries, pulpit, table, font and insurance. A vital appendix reproduced the society's questionnaire for applicants and its recommended instructions to architects, as well as a model contract and trust deed.[40] There was even some bracing encouragement for congregations fearful of toppling too far: 'Stained glass, if the general effect be chaste and quiet, need not be refused as a *free gift*'; 'we can see no objection to the introduction of a neat font' (were there fears that baptismal regeneration might lurk there?), finding it 'unquestionably preferable to the occasional introduction of a white basin, or one adorned with the willow pattern'; the addition of a 'tower or spire gives that publicity to the building which may materially help to carry out some of its main designs, viz:– the attraction and accommodation of the public', not to mention the lobby, stair and ventilation space thus afforded.[41]

The annual reports stiffened the *Practical Hints*. The society had method, an office, office hours and a staff. From 1858 until 1875, when the Memorial Hall at last opened its doors in Farringdon Street, the office was two rooms in 1, Moorgate, entered from 118, London Wall. The hours were from 10 am to 4 pm (5 pm by 1863) on weekdays, and 10 am to 1 pm on Saturdays.[42] The staff consisted of James Charles Gallaway (1809–86), an architecturally trained minister who was the secretary from 1853 and author of *Practical Hints*. He could call on an elastic array of 'examining architects' – Bidlake, Habershon, Poulton, Pritchett, Trimen, as well as James, Oliver, all the usual suspects.[43] Their advice was largely superseded after 1860 by the appointment of an 'Accountant and Assistant' who would be in daily attendance.

He was in fact architecturally qualified, capable of examining plans, proffering practical advice and ensuring that the society stuck to its guns now that its brief covered Anglicized Wales, the Channel Islands and Ireland, as well as England.[44] That brief remained straightforward: to aid buildings for new causes, or better buildings for existing causes, in cities and towns, which might 'in certain circumstances' include villages; and to ensure that no grants were allocated until plans had been submitted for professional examination, and approved, and that no money was released until the building was covered, vested in trustees (and the deed enrolled) and at least 50 per cent paid for.[45]

At no point, however, was style far from the surface. The society and its well-wishers did their best to rise above the fray. 'It is obvious', noted the *Congregational Year Book* in 1860, 'that no uniform style . . . has been adopted . . . This is perhaps neither desirable nor practicable. The style of the building must be affected in some degree by the position selected, and the buildings in immediate contiguity'.[46] 'Your Committee', the society's annual report affirmed in 1859, 'altogether repudiate the idea of adhering exclusively to any particular order of architecture or of implicitly following any one prescribed course.'[47] The result, even so, was hardly in doubt. The annual report for 1858 categorized the styles of the seventy-four churches aided in the society's first five years: there were one each of Grecian Doric, Lombardic, Decorated Gothic and Early English; two Grecian; three Norman (and three unspecified); thirteen Italian, thirteen 'Modern'; and thirty-six 'Gothic'.[48] Whatever might be read into some of these rather slippery categories, that balance changed little, save in nuance, in the next twenty years.

IV. Medium and Message: Style and Mission

Practical Hints liked the fact that Gothic told its own tale: 'places of worship built in that style are never mistaken for Mechanics' Institutes, Post-offices, or Banks'.[49] It was, in its way, a manifesto for a missionary society:

> As the followers of Christ, we have a mission to *man*. In Chapel-building, we are presenting a permanently visible attitude to the *world* . . . in proportion as we thus evince a deference to public taste and convenience, we adapt the means of inducing the *public* to *attend*; and so turn Chapel-building into a most important instrument of making known the Gospel to all men.[50]

That missionary message was insistent. The 'main end of the whole thing is the salvation of man', said the 1876 report.[51] A year later the society urged that 'Church building in the hands of intelligent Congregationalists . . . is a method of teaching that acts upon the whole outlying community . . . These buildings are witnesses for Christ, for Protestantism, for willinghood, for liberty, for religious equality'. They were 'sermons in stones',[52] fit houses for worship and fellowship, fit for Gothic:

> Gothic is in itself as free from any vice as any style can be, because its essence, worth and charm lie not in mere detail, but in its truthfulness and inherent adaptability to the end proposed . . . We catch the true genesis of Gothic architecture when, having determined on our own ends, we study medieval and later models only to make them, in all respects, subservient to our own purposes.[53]

There is in such language – Pugin Protestantized, Ruskinized and updated – the assurance that was reflected by the mid-1870s in the work of James Cubitt, Joseph James, H. J. Paull and John Sulman.[54] That was the fruit of the time and experience which the *Congregational Year Book* had anticipated in 1860 but its boost had been the Bicentenary. The 1863 *Year Book* testified to this; it contained fifty-five pages of architectural descriptions, preceded by a three-page essay on 'Chapel Extension', reflecting on the 300 projected for 1862:

> What a demonstration of the vitality of those godly principles for which our forefathers suffered! What a triumph of freedom and Christian willinghood! What a voice for equality! And what fountains of good in every appropriate form! New chapels necessitate an earnest evangelical ministry, church organization, schools, Christian visiting, temporal relief, missionary enterprise. All the good works practised by good people have more or less their home and their support in these chapels; so that, in erecting them, we are originating, guiding, and stimulating every form of benevolence in which Christians take delight . . . Our fathers had no higher conception of Chapel-building than that of providing an asylum or new covering for an existing Christian community. They gathered to build. We build to gather. We are turning brick and mortar into an important auxiliary in our missionary service to the world at large.[55]

V. From Architecture to Ecclesiology: The Shaping of a Distinctive Mindset

Chapel architects wrote about their work and not only for advertisement. They rooted it confidently in history and annexed that boldly to their own tradition. As professional men verging on tradesmen they responded to need and opportunity but their response required justification; it acquired a moral and confessional dimension. The pattern was set by a London Wesleyan William Fuller Pocock (1779–1849). Pocock had graduated from superior joinery to architecture, making his money as a developer and consolidating his professional reputation with useful surveyorships. He was a safe pair of hands. Conviction and family connection embedded him into the building and Methodist worlds, with a Congregational admixture.[56] His own preferences were Classical but he was alert to the drift of fashion and turned his hand with equal dexterity to *cottages ornés* and Commissioners' Gothic. He demonstrated his workmanlike versatility in three well-timed pattern books for houses, the finishing of their interiors and churches, published between 1807 and 1819, each of them twice reprinted before 1837.[57] The book on churches and chapels has been fairly described as 'the only practical guide to the subject until the wave of Ecclesiologically-inspired publications in the 1840s . . . an invaluable summary of current thinking . . . on the eve of the biggest church building programme since the Middle Ages'.[58]

The Wesleyan Pocock's first major chapel was an austerely respectable Classical essay for Congregationalists just south of Sloane Square.[59] His son William Willmer Pocock (1813–99), who intensified the family's Methodism, was responsible for that most influential of Victorian Baptist chapels, the Metropolitan Tabernacle at Newington Butts (1861). The Tabernacle's style was a theatrical Grecian – in part, it was said, because Greek was the language of the New Testament – but W. W. Pocock's assistants included James Cubitt (1836–1912), a son of the Baptist manse and most scholarly and inventive of Dissenting Goths, whose *Church Design for Congregations* (1870) and *Popular Handbook of Nonconformist Church Building* (1892) provided – if confirmation were still needed – a lively rationale, at once intellectual and practical, for a truly Dissenting Gothic.[60]

Cubitt's sources for *Church Design* were comprehensive, indeed catholic, and up-to-date. They included G. E. Street's *Gothic Architecture in Spain* (1865), Viollet-le-Duc's *Dictionnaire Raisonné de l'Architecture Française* (1854–68) and Britton and Pugin's *Illustrations of Public Buildings of London* (1825–28).[61] The Pugin of Britton and Pugin was A. C. Pugin, the famous architect's draughtsman father, but the reference indicates the interconnectedness of the architectural and related worlds. Cubitt's books, moreover, continued and updated the work of older men such as J. C. Gallaway among Congregationalists and F. J. Jobson among Methodists. Jobson calls for comment at this point.

Frederick James Jobson (1812–81), like Gallaway, was a minister; unlike Gallaway, he had persevered with his architectural training and, once ordained, he became more prominent in his denomination.[62] It was his *Chapel and School Architecture* (1850) which brought Jobson to wide Wesleyan notice and it had been his training under the Roman Catholic E. J. Willson

(1787–1854) which had made a natural Goth of him. In the 1820s Willson had been associated with Britton, that 'highest authority among the writers on architectural antiquities', and with A. C. Pugin; in the 1830s he was associated with the younger Pugin.[63] In *Chapel and School Architecture* Jobson, who was the younger Pugin's contemporary, affirmed hardly less dogmatically that Gothic was Christian architecture 'as distinctly and emphatically, as the Egyptian, Greek, and Roman, are Pagan'. In 1850 that was almost a commonplace but Jobson pressed his point. Gothic architecture was 'ENGLISH CHURCH ARCHITECTURE'. It was the 'natural embodiment of Christian worship 'in our own land'. It was an expression of Truth. Here Jobson confronted his Wesleyan constituency: in 'these times of Tractarian heresy' it must be realized that truth in architecture was not 'necessarily connected with Error in Religion'; it ministered to evangelical need.[64]

Architectural truth is a precondition of architectural genius but it can no more guarantee that than it can flourish in a vacuum. What is noteworthy about the interconnected flurry of mid-nineteenth-century chapel building and architectural writing is how close it was to Anglican and Roman Catholic developments. Fashion can be intellectually as well as aesthetically infectious. It is sometimes indistinguishable from emulation. Emulation and fashion coincide with turns of mind. They colour, enlarge and transform them. Here too Congregationalists are representative. They indicate the networking impact of personalities rather than systems. All these trends collide in one man, John Blackburn (1792–1855).[65]

Blackburn was credible on several counts. He was a slightly older contemporary and friend of Robert Ashton, John Campbell and Joshua Wilson. As the son and brother of London liverymen (the family business was scale making), he was sufficiently respectable. As one of Thomas Wilson's men, an *alumnus* of Hoxton and minister at Claremont, Pentonville (1822–55), one of Wilson's most flourishing London chapels, he was ministerially prominent. As editor of the *Congregational Magazine* (1818–45), the *Congregational Calendar* (1840–48), and the *Congregational Year Book* (1846–47), and as secretary of the Congregational Union (1834–47), he was a key figure in a consolidating denomination. Few ecclesiastical or political trends escaped his judiciously conservative gaze. He had facts at his disposal and strategies in his mind with an abiding if not always sufficiently persuasive sense of history to cement them; in the 1840s he originated the ill-fated Wycliffe Society as a Nonconformist variant of the Parker and Camden Societies. He was also architecturally literate, composing a carefully seminal *Year Book* essay: 'Remarks on Ecclesiastical Architecture as Applied to Nonconformist Chapels'.[66]

John Blackburn's 'Remarks' struck all the right chords. An artfully shaped historical survey encompassed Herod's Temple ('reared rather for sacerdotal than congregational services and addressing the imagination rather than the judgment') and his people's synagogues (where worship was 'an exercise of the understanding rather than of the fancy', its duties 'not performed by the priests, but by the intelligence, zeal, and piety of the people').[67] The Congregational propriety of that comparison was steadily maintained as Blackburn measured one defective style against another (the Grecian 'identified with . . . all the abominable idolatries of a classical mythology', the Gothic 'adapted to . . . Popish superstition'), and as he considered the post-Constantinian evolution that encouraged Christians to recycle law courts and mercantile exchanges, basilicas adaptable to the needs of large assemblies.[68] The long view allowed Blackburn to be even-handed. He criticized the impact of Methodism on preaching-house style, especially in London (Wesley's City Road Chapel 'scarcely possesses an architectural character'; Whitefield's Tabernacle 'was a mass of architectural deformity'; Rowland Hill's Surrey Chapel was 'little better than an architectural eyesore'; Thomas Wilson's chapels, 'though well adapted to hold large audiences', were 'bare' and 'unsightly').[69] He alerted his readers to the perilous allure of symbolism: 'to take warning . . . against being led by the taste and terminology of architects into such mystic follies'. Here he had the Cambridge Camden Society in his sights, with its 'monkish efforts to vail again the truth of God in shadows, after we have been permitted, as "with open fire", to gaze upon it'.[70]

Such criticisms were as suggestive as they were predictable. They cleared the air. If symbolism were guarded against, if the architectural proprieties were heeded, if fitness for purpose (he did not use the phrase) were achieved, if 'the pulpit, not the altar, the teacher, not the symbol' were indeed conspicuous, and if costs were taken into proper account, then the English style 'popularly denominated the Gothic style', could be considered.[71] One example was tantalizingly appropriate. For the next seventy years, perhaps longer, Highbury Chapel, Bristol, was to rank among the most influential of English Congregational churches, notable for ministry and membership alike. The *Congregational Calendar*'s description was sparing with detail (its 'style . . . prevailed in England during the fifteenth century') and made no reference to William Butterfield, the young architect whose church this was.[72]

William Butterfield (1814–90) was new to practice but his hitherto impeccable evangelical credentials were cemented by his kinship to the Wills family, who were leading Bristol Congregationalists.[73] At exactly the same time he was encountering the Cambridge Camden Society and entering the world of the Ecclesiologists, interpreting and vigorously developing the Puginian ideal for High-Church Anglicanism. He came to regard his charming essay for his entrepreneurial kinsmen's co-religionists as an aberration. It was no such thing, even if he undertook no more such work for Dissenters.

VI. 'We have to build up for ourselves a Life'

John Blackburn's influence was blunted by the financial difficulties which clouded his last years and hastened his death, but the extent to which a cultural mindset was becoming engrained among Congregationalists is suggested by a cluster of essays published between 1869 and 1878. These were the work of an educated younger generation, out to demonstrate their confessional distinctiveness and their intellectual quality. In 1869 six of them collaborated in *Religious Republics*, a volume of essays by a republic of friends with no apparent editor and with no attribution beyond the table of contents.[74] Two were ministers, three were barristers and one was a medical man. All were in their late twenties or early thirties, all belonged to established Baptist or Congregational families, all had useful commercial, industrial and political connections. Their aim was to describe 'the religious system of Congregationalism, whether Baptist or Independent', its distinctive forms of character and opinion, and the basis of reason on which it rested.[75] They modestly thought it 'probable that the opinions they have expressed are commonly held by Congregationalists, or at least are prevalent in the younger generation of them'.[76]

Architecture was embraced in 'Congregationalism and Aesthetics' but each essay coloured the Congregational context for a distinctive approach. The essay on aesthetics was written by Thomas Harwood Pattison (1838–1904), then into his second pastorate as minister of Ryehill Baptist Church, Newcastle-upon-Tyne. Pattison was the model of an up-and-coming minister.[77] In his teens the family church had been Bloomsbury Baptist Church. His father, Samuel Rowles Pattison (1809–1901), was a successful London solicitor by secular profession, a Baptist by religious profession and a geologist by amateur preference; he was for years prominent in the legal and financial affairs of the Baptist Union until his connection with the Liberator Building Society brought his career and his reputation to a humiliating end.[78] The son inherited his father's intellectual curiosity; his aesthetic instinct had been developed by four years of architectural study before he turned to ministry.[79]

'Congregationalism and Aesthetics' was clearly driven by *Culture and Anarchy*, Matthew Arnold's latest goad to all thinking Nonconformists. It was a vigorous affirmation of Nonconformity's claim to sweetness and light (qualities which Matthew Arnold had made peculiarly his own) by a man who was advanced yet orthodox and commanded his pulpit. His rhetoric was enjoyably combative. Aesthetics was 'the science which concerns itself with the theory and philosophy of taste'.[80] This was no doubt bad news for Dissent, that 'species of eccentricity' (and the 'Englishman has a deep-seated horror of eccentricity'), for was not Dissent 'a direct violation of good taste?'[81] Pattison stirred harder. 'Our Nonconformity does affect materially our doctrine, our practice, our worship, our training, our modes of thinking, and indeed our whole life . . . Therefore it must be a power telling on taste'; and it was on the increase.[82] He was ready to counter-attack and annexed the New Testament:

> The Gospel and Acts of the Apostles are undoubtedly the records of what certain decided nonconformists thought and felt . . . said and did . . . Christ himself was a dissenter all His life . . . No one can read the Great Biography without being conscious of a fine harmony, or exquisite effortless unity, which plays freely through all Christ's words, thoughts, and actions. He came to bring sweetness and light to man. He was the preacher of the beautiful. By His miracles He restored physical health, by His parables He extolled moral beauty, by His life he exhibited saintly beauty, by His death He restored heavenly beauty.[83]

Harmony, unity, leading freely to true beauty and the enjoyment of fullness of life, was the prerogative of all who lived in the spirit of Christ. Pattison directed these key words to worship, education, architecture, amusement and recreation. In worship ('We aim at common worship') there 'is a marked simplicity' arising 'from the natural outworking of principle'; 'We reckon it to be right . . . to appeal through the ear to the reason, the intellect, and the heart.' Any resulting baldness might be 'in the most perfect taste. It is true to our belief; it refuses to introduce jarring elements. In this way we do homage to true aesthetic laws.' And as there must be 'clear and harmonious connexion between the various parts of the service' (no part running 'in its own peculiar groove'), so 'in Nonconformist meeting houses there ought to be implicit trust in the power of simplicity from floor to ceiling, from porch to pulpit'.[84]

Pattison's use of 'meeting house' is suggestive but he did not develop it and perhaps he meant no more by it than a simple village chapel. He dismissed Classical ('what teaching is there for us in classic plans or classic details?') and Gothic alike if it boiled down to fashion overcoming principle.[85] It hurt him that his co-religionists 'have been so enamoured of the national style, that they have sown the land over with miserable imitations of Gothic churches', but if principle were recalled:

> This abuse will cease. We want neither chancel nor transept, for we have no altars; we want no high-pitched roofs, for we have no incense to wreath up its curling smoke, and no surpliced choristers to pour forth chant and response . . . I believe that a refined and well-educated Congregationalist must reject Gothic, just because if it pleases his eye it will violate his convictions; or if . . . it satisfies his principles and demands, it must outrage his sense of beauty and harmony.[86]

What, then, was the way ahead? 'The Congregationalist is to think for himself, and to speak for himself . . . why should he not also design for himself?'[87] God's Palace Beautiful, moreover, had a democratic aspect: 'The beauty and ease of the theatre are matters of deeper interest to the audience than to the actors: it is just the same in our chapels'; and Pattison sought 'that quiet sense of pleasure which contributes much more than is generally supposed to worshipping with profit'. Thus a Congregational chapel, 'if intelligently planned, (becomes) an invaluable embodiment of the special tenets wherein we differ from the other Churches of Christendom'.[88]

Ryehill was in a rapidly growing labourers' suburb. In 1871 Pattison moved to the heart of the Manchester School, a town-centre church in Rochdale, and from 1875, having 'resolved to make a dash for freedom', he was in the United States, chiefly at Rochester Theological Seminary (NY) where an early pupil and later colleague was Walter Rauschenbusch, proponent of the Social Gospel.[89] For all the restlessness of his pastoral life, Pattison, friend of John Bright, correspondent of Spurgeon and R. W. Dale, tutor and colleague of Rauschenbusch, exemplified harmony. His emphasis on the spirit rather than the letter, on intelligent planning and honest materials, and on the godly democracy's pleasure principle, in fact precluded neither Gothic nor Classical styles.[90] What he advocated was not so much style-light as style-free; he pointed the way to a free style. He was in all essentials an Arts and Crafts man, a little ahead of his time.

One of T. H. Pattison's first outside engagements as a Baptist minister was to preach at the re-opening of Great Asby, a village cause in Westmorland which had been much helped by William Fawcett (1799–1874), a local minister of independent means.[91] Fawcett was a grandson of John Fawcett (1740–1817), the Yorkshire Baptist pioneer, and he was the father of William Mitchell Fawcett (b. 1839), one of the three barristers who contributed to *Religious Republics*.[92] W. M. Fawcett's essay 'The Congregational Polity' opened the collection.[93] It was written with an advocate's forceful clarity, readable, punchy, engaged and informative, with data drawn impartially from Baptist and Congregational churches.[94] With its picture of Christians bonded in free and essentially democratic spiritual association, it sets the scene for a visual, mental and political culture.

Fawcett's Congregational Church was 'an association of persons of spiritual character, united by voluntary consent for the accomplishment of spiritual objects'. Their leading consideration was 'not what is expedient, but what saith the Scripture?' Their conviction was that 'the New Testament contains all the principles of order and discipline requisite for constituting and governing Christian Societies' and where the Christian's 'statute book' was silent, he would be 'careful to base his procedure upon some general principle derived from inspired authority'. There was thus room for responsible expediency.[95]

Writing in the wake of a quietly revolutionary Reform Act, Fawcett was possessed of a spirit of judicious optimism: '[T]here must be some national benefit in the existence of a large number of communities, each member of which professes to conform his life to a high moral standard, and is bound under penalty of exclusion to abstain from open sin.'[96] And to any who urged that Congregationalism demanded too much of ordinary human nature he had this clinching response: 'It is no discredit to a Christian church that without Christianity it cannot succeed.'[97]

Spiritual democracy was the *leitmotiv* of the last and longest of the six essays. James Anstie's 'The Spirit of Nonconformity'.[98] Anstie (1836–1924) was the most solidly successful of the three barrister contributors. He lived comfortably in Kensington, took silk in 1882, became a Bencher of Lincoln's Inn and a Charity Commissioner.[99] In family tradition and in contemporary relevance he expressed the spirit of Nonconformity. His brother-in-law (and fellow barrister), H. S. P. Winterbotham, had been MP for Stroud since 1867 and was regarded as a rising Liberal star, a role model for young political Dissenters.[100] Anstie himself was a fifth-generation Baptist. His family had long been embedded in the commercial, legal, medical, educational and municipal life of Devizes.[101] By 1865, however, James Anstie had become, as he remained, a Congregationalist, transferring from New Baptist Church, Devizes, where he had been baptized in 1856, to John Stoughton's Kensington Chapel.[102]

Anstie took as epigraph a phrase from Eph. 4.3: 'The Unity of the Spirit is the bond of Peace'. His theme was the immediacy of faith, and its creation of 'a union and fellowship which is of its own nature free, unforced and spontaneous, determined and characterised by the fact of a spiritual presence and operation'.[103] Indeed, the 'whole history and structure of Christianity cry out against the alleged authority [of the Church] and summon men to believe in a spiritual creed and a free religion'.[104] Thus did spirit inform polity and thus might the spirit of the age come into its own and the local church, the essential Christian unit, be free to evolve as the harmonious expression of the individual and the communal.

Spiritual liberty, clear-eyed and responsible pragmatism and, most suggestive of all, the evolutionary principle, informed Philip Henry Pye-Smith's 'Congregationalism and Science'.[105] Its thesis was expressed in its epigraph ('Where the Spirit of the Lord is, there is Liberty'); and fellow feeling, the coincidences of personal friendship and traditional Dissent, quite as much as actual and potential distinction, explain his inclusion.

The inherited Dissent was flagged in all his names, Philip Henry after the Ejected divine and Pye-Smith, hyphenated after his grandfather's death.[106]

That grandfather, John Pye Smith (1774–1851), the 'Beloved Doctor', had been the essence of provincial social mobility, evangelical mental-artman style.[107] He had moved from the nervy political radicalism and edgy enlightenment of an as yet municipally unformed Sheffield (where Pye-Smiths long remained as municipal movers and moulders) to the tutorship of Homerton, a London Dissenting Academy evolving into a contemporary theological college. A discriminating fascination with geology marked the 'Beloved Doctor' rather as later it marked S. R. Pattison.

Pye-Smith was the instinctive Congregationalist,[108] convinced that the form of Christianity best able to cope with the contemporary science of natural selection 'is that which is the most free, the most varied, the most elastic'. He added an instructive rider:

> Uniformity is always artificial . . . Comprehension is yet more dangerous, for it makes religious differences seem unimportant, while differences in science are admitted to be all-important. It fosters the growth of esoteric doctrines of enlightenment, different from those publicly and officially expressed.[109]

His conclusion, Congregationally speaking, was almost foregone: '[I]t does appear that, now especially, the flexible and light-armed organization of this one branch of the great Christian army is better fitted than other more regularly and stiffly-drilled battalions to cope with the spirit of irreverence and unbelief.'[110]

Neither of the two remaining essayists, the brothers Edward Gilbert Herbert (1838–71) and Thomas Martin Herbert (1835–77), fulfilled his potential. The former died before achieving what his friends predicted, the latter died on the verge of fulfilment. Their essays, on 'The Congregationalist Character' and 'The External Relations of Congregationalism', respectively, complete and confirm the themes of *Religious Republics*; their inclusion completes the picture of a naturally evolving mentality; and they bring us back to the cultural, aesthetic and mental-artman background for the shaping of a specifically Nonconformist architecture.

They were the sons of Thomas Herbert (d. 1878), Nottingham lace manufacturer, mayor (1846), deacon and treasurer of his county Congregational Union.[111] They were London graduates and had been lay students at Spring Hill, Thomas Martin during its rebuilding by Joseph James and Edward Gilbert just after. Thomas continued as a ministerial student and completed his training at Lancashire Independent College.[112] Edward moved to London for University College, lodging in Doughty Street, followed by Lincoln's Inn, the Chancery Bar and chambers at 2 New Square. These he shared with Herbert Cozens-Hardy (a future Master of the Rolls), whom he had met at

Mrs Anstie's, in Queen Square, a short walk from Doughty Street, and whose 'dearest and most trusted friend' (and best man) he became.[113]

Their contemporaries were agreed as to Edward's flair and Thomas' steady application. The latter's health, complicated by a speech defect which was eventually cured, cut short his pastorates in otherwise eligible northern churches. One such was Nether Chapel, Sheffield, a vertiginously galleried Classical building by the elder Pritchett of York (1827). Herbert left after two years, 'warned that so large a building, planted . . . amidst a dense population, required a different style of preaching'.[114] That was in 1861. In 1869 he was happily settled at Cheadle, near Manchester, and in 1876 he would return to Lancashire Independent College as professor of philosophy and history. Locals 'thought we had found the very man for the church's needs' but he died suddenly, late in 1877.[115]

Thomas Herbert's essay celebrated a variant of Pye-Smith's 'flexible light-armed' Congregationalism in which, since 'spiritual convictions are the determining considerations' for membership, no rigid conditions could be imposed 'because such convictions are but partially revealed to human observation'.[116] The fundamental, formative, condition was 'personal allegiance to the Divine Christ':

> Christ . . . is . . . the Divine Head of a kingdom or society, the animating principle of which is personal allegiance to Himself, expressed in worship and in service if the subjects of this invisible empire, some are pilgrims on earth, and some have arrived in heaven, and their muster-roll is a sealed book in the keeping of Christ.[117]

The local church, as the visible expression of that invisible society, 'in admitting an applicant, proceeds upon evidence that the more momentous step has already been taken'. This allowed for responsible flexibility: 'there is substantial agreement . . . as to the great outline of Christian doctrine, greater diversity exists in details, and greater freedom in expression than existed formerly'.[118] It also allowed for a family spirit and if, as in families, 'internal dissensions and unbecoming exclusiveness are to be found in Christian societies', the following remained true:

> A church of moderate size, whose members meet often to survey their Christian heritage, and revive their Christian allegiance, attains to a unity of feeling like that which animates a family; the social instinct, which is inseparable from the idea of a church, obtains scope for development.[119]

Many such churches were 'brotherhoods in which a broad equality of need and of privilege sets social distinction aside'; their 'democratic constitution' demonstrated this and their fundamental condition of membership demonstrated that Congregational churches were 'not exclusive in any sense inconsistent with universal brotherhood'.[120] T. M. Herbert's message was one of tolerance made possible by the awareness of due limits. His rhetoric – family, brotherhood, equality, 'the social instinct', 'scope for development' – looks ahead. It lends force to the regret – given his 'almost unrivalled knowledge of the feud between science and theology' – that he had died before he could exercise his 'rare faculty for abating their unnatural strife'.[121]

Edward Herbert built on the familial revolution. His was the most alluring of the essays.[122] He began with the observation that 'character is never a definitely settled thing; it is always moving'.[123] He set the characteristics of contemporary Congregationalism against the broader religious scene: '[T]he Congregationalist has many both of the virtues and of the faults of other sects, but these qualities are cast in a distinctive mould of his own.'[124] To explain the nature of that mould he drew on family recollections.[125] There was the impact of public prayer.[126] There was the sermon ('in harmony with this simplicity of form and strenuous vigour of spirit . . . The preaching of the Word was one of the leading elements in his Sabbath privileges') and there was the weekday outworking: the Congregationalist 'had a high appreciation of the virtue of industry, and a constraining sense of the value of time, as a talent for the full employment of which, to its last fractions, he was responsible . . . Thus his life in the world, while he strove to keep it distinct from the life of the soul, ministered to his soul's health'.[127] This spirit infused more recent changes. In obedience to a new and 'almost universal' feeling for art, Congregational worship had 'conformed to highest aesthetic standards'; Herbert gently warned against what he nonetheless welcomed: 'No doubt, they sometimes attach an undue measure of importance to their music and their architecture'.[128] Even so, the older fellowship and simplicity remained fundamental to the reality of what was experienced. Herbert focused on the fellowship at communion:

> The sacredness of the service depends on the confidence in each other's faith and spiritual love which the communicants may confess. This confidence is the basis of that sympathy, that communion of saints, which to the Congregationalist is essential to the due celebration of the Lord's Supper. To him the elements have no mysterious agency. The words of Christ, 'Do this in remembrance of me', cannot be obeyed by a solitary act. He regards them as enjoining on a church an act of communion, that is, of united remembrance of Christ, and thus he recognises in the institution not only an efficient aid to the religious life, but also one of the strongest bonds of Christian fellowship.[129]

He described the ritual: no altar, but bread and wine on a table covered with a white cloth; a hymn; St Paul's words 'describing the Last Supper'; perhaps a short address, its tone 'more subdued than at other times'; a short prayer; then the minister 'repeats the words of the apostle, which tell how our Lord broke bread, and puts a plate into the hands of the deacons, who so carry the broken bread round to the people, as they sit in the pews'; and the same is done with the cups of wine.[130]

That was the spirit which meeting house, chapel or church should be designed to promote.

Notes

1 C. Stell, *An Inventory of Nonconformist Chapels and Meeting-Houses in Eastern England* (Swindon: English Heritage, 2002), pp. 256–59.

2 Ibid., pp. 260–62.

3 J. Wilson, 'The Second Centenary of the Ejectment of the Nonconformist Ministers from the Established Church' [hereafter 'Second Centenary'], *Congregational Year Book* [hereafter *CYB*] (1862), p. 72.

4 For Joshua Wilson (1795–1874) see A. Argent, 'Joshua Wilson', in D. M. Lewis (ed.), *The Blackwell Dictionary of Evangelical Biography 1730–1841* (Oxford: Blackwell, 1995), II, p. 1209; R. Halley, 'Recollections of the Old Dissent. No. V', *The Congregationalist* (1875), pp. 93–101; S. S. England, 'The Late Joshua Wilson, Esq.', *Evangelical Magazine* (1874), pp. 661–63. For further information I am indebted to Mr J. Creasey, Miss Alice Ford-Smith and Mr D. Powell.

5 For Robert Ashton (1798–1878) see *CYB* (1879), p. 297.

6 For George Smith (1803–70) see *CYB* (1871), pp. 346–49; R. Balgarnie, *Brief Memoir of the Rev. George Smith, D.D.* (London, 1870).

7 For John Campbell (1794–1867) see J. H. Y. Briggs, 'John Campbell', in Lewis (ed.), *The Blackwell Dictionary of Evangelical Biography*, I, p. 190.

8 Quoted in A. Peel, *These Hundred Years. A History of the Congregational Union of England and Wales, 1831–1931* (London: Congregational Union of England and Wales, 1931), p. 197.

9 'Second Centenary', p. 66.

10 Ibid., pp. 64–65.

11 Ibid., pp. 63–64. Here he was recalling what Thomas Binney had urged in his Congregational Union address of 1848.

12 Ibid., p. 63.

13 Lancashire's successive chapel-building campaigns (1852–59, ca 1862, and 1868 onwards) are described in B. Nightingale, *The Story of the Lancashire Congregational Union 1806–1906 Centenary Memorial Volume* (Manchester: John Heywood Ltd, n.d [1906]), pp. 78–80, 94–98.

14 *CYB* (1854), p. 283.

15 For Thomas Wilson see *Oxford Dictionary of National Biography* (Oxford: Oxford University Press, 2004) [hereafter *ODNB*]; J. Wilson, *Memoir of Thomas Wilson* (London, 1846).

16 *CYB* (1854), p. 75.

17 Ibid., pp. 75–79.

18 English Congregational Chapel-Building Society (1854), *Report of the Committee to the Members of the Society* [hereafter E.C.B.S, *Report*], p. 7.

19 ECBS, *Report* (1858), p. 7.
20 ECBS, *Report* (1859), p. 9; (1863), p. 10.
21 ECBS, *Report* (1862), pp. 2, 12–14.
22 *CYB* (1863), pp. 289–90.
23 *CYB* (1864–74) passim, esp. (1871) p. 345; (1865) p. 314.
24 ECBS, *Report* (1904), p. 9.
25 ECBS, *Report* (1857), p. 5.
26 *CYB* (1854) p.76; ECBS, *Report* (1855), p. 10; (1865), p. 8.
27 ECBS, *Report* (1857), pp. 5, 6.
28 For Thomas William Baxter Aveling (1815–84) see *CYB* (1885), pp. 176–79.
29 *CYB* (1858), p. 73.
30 *CYB* (1854), p. 76.
31 Ibid.; ECBS, *Report* (1877), p. 12.
32 *CYB* (1854), p. 79.
33 Ibid.
34 *Practical Hints on Chapel-Building* [hereafter *Practical Hints*] (London: English Congregational Chapel-Building Society, 1855), p. 8; 3rd edn issued as *Practical Hints on the Erection of Places of Public Worship* (London: John Snow & Co., 1874).
35 *The Civil Engineer's and Architect's Journal*, XVII (1854), p. 117. I am indebted to the Revd Michael Hopkins for this reference.
36 ECBS, *Report* (1857), p. 23
37 *CYB* (1860), p. 231.
38 Ibid.
39 *Practical Hints*, p. 10.
40 Ibid., pp. 49–63.
41 Ibid., pp. 26–27, 34, 28.
42 ECBS, *Report* (1859), p. 14; (1863), p. 10.
43 For George Bidlake (ca 1829–92), Edward Habershon (d. 1901), W. G. Habershon (ca 1818–91), W. F. Poulton (ca 1820–1900), James Pigott Pritchett, father (1789–1868) and son (1830–1911), Joseph James (1828–75) and Thomas Oliver (1824–1902), see A. Felstead et al., *Directory of British Architects 1834–1900* (London: Mansell Publishing, 1993), pp. 80, 390, 733, 741, 495, 675. Andrew Trimen was a London architect whose best surviving Congregational (now United Reformed) chapel is in Allen Street, Kensington (1854–55). For Gallaway, see *CYB* (1887), pp. 197–201.
44 ECBS, *Report* (1860), p. 16; (1863), p. 10; (1859), p. 12.
45 *CYB* (1860), p. 264.
46 Ibid., p. 231.
47 ECBS, *Report* (1859), p. 14.
48 ECBS, *Report* (1858), p. 7.
49 *Practical Hints*, p. 16.
50 Ibid., p. 9.
51 ECBS, *Report* (1876), p. 14.
52 ECBS, *Report* (1877), p. 10.
53 ECBS, *Report* (1876), p. 14.
54 For James Cubitt (1836–1912), Henry John Paull (d. 1888) and Sir John Sulman (1849–1934) see Felstead et al., *Directory of British Architects*, pp. 225, 696, 889.
55 *CYB* (1863), p. 290.
56 C. Binfield, 'Architects in Connexion: Four Methodist Generations', in J. Garnett and C. Matthew (eds), *Revival and Religion since 1700* (London: The Hambledon Press, 1993), pp. 153–65.

57 W. F. Pocock, *Architectural Designs for Rustic Cottages .... Villas etc.* (London: J. Taylor, 1807); idem, *Modern Finishings for Rooms* (London: J. Taylor, 1811); idem, *Designs for Churches and Chapels of Various Dimensions and Styles* (London: J. Taylor, 1819).
58 C. Webster, in W. F. Pocock, *Designs for Churches and Chapels* (3rd edn, Reading: Spire Books, 2010 [1835]), p. 4.
59 Ibid, pp. 18–20, plates 9–12. Ranelagh Chapel opened in 1818; it passed from Congregational to Presbyterian use in 1845; its congregation moved to Halkin Street as Belgrave Presbyterian Church in 1866 and Ranelagh Chapel was demolished ca 1870; what is now the Royal Court Theatre occupies part of its site.
60 Binfield, 'Architects in Connexion', pp. 166–72. For Cubitt, see C. Binfield, *The Contexting of a Chapel Architect: James Cubitt 1836–1912* (London: The Chapels Society, 2001).
61 J. Cubitt, *Church Design for Congregations: Its Developments and Possibilities* (London: Smith, Elder and Co., 1870), p. 1.
62 For Jobson, Connexional book steward from 1864 and president of Conference 1869, see J. A. Vickers (ed.), *A Dictionary of Methodism in Britain and Ireland* (Peterborough: Epworth Press, 2000), p. 182.
63 F. J. Jobson, *Chapel and School Architecture, as Appropriate to the Buildings of Nonconformists, particularly to Those of the Wesleyan Methodists* (London: Hamilton, Adams, Co., 1850), pp. vii, 16; for Willson, see Felstead et al., *Directory of British Architects*, p. 1003. Willson and Britton (1771–1857) are best followed in Rosemary Hill's *God's Architect: Pugin and the Building of Romantic Britain* (Harmondsworth: Penguin, 2008); his collaboration can be charted in A. C. Pugin and J. Britton, *Specimens of the Architectural Antiquities of Normandy* (1828); A. C. Pugin and E. J. Willson, *Specimens of Gothic Architecture Selected from Various Antient Edifices in England*, 2 vols (1821–23); A. C. Pugin, E. J. Willson, A. W. Pugin, *Examples of Gothic Architecture*, 3 vols (1831–36).
64 Jobson, *Chapel and School Architecture*, pp. 15, 24, 40.
65 For John Blackburn see *CYB* (1856), pp. 208–10; A. Peel, *The Congregational Two Hundred 1530–1948* (London: The Independent Press Limited, 1948), pp. 138–39. The broad context of his interests is indicated by his correspondence held in Dr Williams's Library (NC. L52).
66 *CYB* (1847), pp. 150–63.
67 Ibid., p. 150.
68 Ibid., pp. 153, 151.
69 Ibid., p. 156–57.
70 Ibid., p. 152. He had particularly in mind two frequently reissued publications, John Mason Neale's *A Few Words to Church Builders*, and *A Few Words to Church Wardens on Churches . . .*, both of 1841.
71 *CYB* (1847), pp. 158–61.
72 *The Congregational Calendar and Family Almanac* (1844), p. 121. Stone laid on 3 October 1842; opened 6 July 1843. [C. Stell], *An Inventory of Nonconformist Chapels and Meeting-Houses in Central England* (London: HMSO, 1986), p. 64. In 1863 E. W. Godwin added a tower.
73 For Butterfield see *ODNB*; Curl, *A Dictionary of Architecture*, pp. 134–35.
74 *Religious Republics: Six Essays on Congregationalism* (London: Longman, Green, & Co., 1869).
75 'Preface', Ibid.
76 Ibid.
77 For information about T. H. Pattison and his family, I am indebted to Mrs Faith Bowers and Mrs Susan Mills.

78 *Baptist Magazine* (1902), pp. 31–32; also (1890), pp. 98–100; see also D. McKie, *Jabez: The Rise and Fall of a Victorian Rogue* (London: Atlantic Books, 2004), esp. pp. 21, 191, 203–4.
79 *The Examiner*, 82/11 (1904), p. 328. The architect's office is not specified; it is likeliest to have been that of John Gibson (1817–92), architect of Bloomsbury Chapel, or C. G. Searle (1816–81), who transferred his membership to Bloomsbury in the year of Pattison's baptism there.
80 T. H. Pattison, 'Congregationalism and Aesthetics', in *Religious Republics*, p. 134.
81 Ibid.
82 Ibid., p. 137.
83 Ibid., pp. 145–46.
84 Ibid., pp. 147, 148, 150.
85 Ibid., p. 160.
86 Ibid., pp. 159–60.
87 Ibid., p. 160.
88 Ibid., pp. 162–63.
89 *The Examiner*, 82/11 (1904), p. 328.
90 That was just as well. West Street, Pattison's church in Rochdale, was a Classical building (1833) enlarged and improved in his time there. His senior deacon G. T. Kemp (1810–77) was a leading Rochdale manufacturer who had been a founder member and deacon at Bloomsbury Chapel and was a brother-in-law of Bloomsbury's founder S. M. Peto (1809–89).
91 In 1862. A. P. F. Sell, *Church Planting. A Study of Westmorland Nonconformity* (Worthing: H. E. Walter, 1986), p. 98. The Fawcetts had property at Crosby Garrett and useful mercantile and industrial connections with Hebden Bridge and Hull.
92 In 1861, while Pattison was still a student at Regent's Park College, Fawcett was a law student lodging in St John's Wood. For John Fawcett see *ODNB*.
93 W. M. Fawcett, 'The Congregational Polity', in *Religious Republics*, pp. 1–59.
94 Fawcett's own allegiance has yet to be determined. He was the author of *A Compendium of the Law of Landlord and Tenant* (London, 1871; 3rd edn 1905); by 1891 he was living comfortably in Hampstead Hill Gardens.
95 Fawcett, 'The Congregational Polity', pp. 1–5.
96 Ibid., p. 58.
97 Ibid., p. 59.
98 J. Anstie, 'The Spirit of Nonconformity', *Religious Republics*, pp. 202–78.
99 For Anstie, see *Who Was Who 1916–1928* (London: A. & C. Black, 1929), p. 26. I am indebted to Mrs K. Spackman for further information.
100 For H. S. P. Winterbotham (1837–73), Under-Secretary of State at the Home Office, 1871–73, see *ODNB*. The Winterbothams replicated the Ansties as a broad-based Dissenting family; originally Baptist, they became increasingly Congregational, Henry among them. He died in Rome, and was buried in the Protestant cemetery, his funeral attended and his tombstone designed by a close friend, the architect Alfred Waterhouse (*Stroud Journal*, undated cutting, ca 20 December 1873).
101 See L. Haycock, *John Anstie of Devizes 1743–1830. An Eighteenth-Century Wiltshire Clothier* (Stroud: Wiltshire Archeological and Natural History Society/Alan Sutton, 1991); B. and J. Hurley, *The New Baptist Church, Devizes: Brief History and Membership Book 1805–1942* (Devizes, 1991).
102 I am indebted to Mr J. Hurley for this information.
103 Anstie, 'The Spirit of Nonconformity', p. 206.
104 Ibid., p. 244.

105 P. H. Pye-Smith, 'Congregationalism and Science', in *Religious Republics*, pp. 169–201.
106 For Philip Henry (1631–96) see *ODNB*; young Pye-Smith, however, was 'Harry' to his family.
107 For John Pye Smith, see *ODNB*.
108 Perfectly caught in his comment: 'Let [the humble seeker after truth] "read the Bible like any other book", and he will soon find that there is no other book like it.' Pye-Smith, 'Congregationalism and Science', p. 199.
109 Ibid.
110 Ibid., pp. 200–1. Over and against this surprisingly military language is the meliorism possible before 1914, not least to the missionary-minded (Pye-Smith was a medical consultant for the London Missionary Society), and understandable in one who had studied in Paris, Berlin and Vienna, and been honoured by Dublin and Philadelphia: he believed in the international spirit of science and its 'influence in neutralizing national prejudice, and promoting comity of thought and feeling'.
111 Surman Lay Index, DWL.
112 *CYB* (1847), p. 161. In 1848 T. M. Herbert had briefly been at Mill Hill School, which Blackburn noted had rejected 'a beautiful plan and elevation in the English style' for a more costly Grecian which, despite its noble portico, was 'very destitute of appropriate decoration'. A nephew of Sir William Tite, Mill Hill's architect was a school contemporary of Herbert's: Hampden-Cook, *The Register of Mill Hill School*, p. 89.
113 Census Return 1861; Cozens-Hardy MSS, pp. 39, 44. Mrs Anstie was James' widowed mother. For Herbert Hardy Cozens-Hardy (1838–1920), Congregationalist and Master of the Rolls, see *ODNB*.
114 *CYB* (1879), p. 320. Yet Pritchett prided himself on his acoustics; he was architect (and senior deacon) of Lendal (1816) and Salem (1839) chapels, York, whose minister, James Parsons (1799–1877) was equally famed for his weak voice and his preaching. Perhaps it was the content of Herbert's preaching which unsettled a relatively conservative congregation: his obituary picks its phrases – 'simplicity and clearness . . . choice beauty of phrase . . . exact sequence and coherence of thought, and . . . ingenious and often strikingly original conceptions of his subject'. Nether was the chapel of the Sheffield Pye-Smiths.
115 F. J. Powicke, *A History of the Cheshire County Union of Congregational Churches* (Manchester: Thomas Griffiths & Co., 1907), p. 180. T. M. Herbert's son, Thomas Arnold Herbert (1863–1940), followed in E. G. Herbert's footsteps and fulfilled his promise: Lincoln's Inn, Chancery Bar, K.C., and Liberal MP Wycombe 1906–10: *Who Was Who 1929–1940*, p. 628.
116 T. M. Herbert, 'The External Relations of Congregationalism', *Religious Republics*, p. 60.
117 Ibid., pp. 63–64.
118 Ibid., pp. 64, 66.
119 Ibid., pp. 75, 74.
120 Ibid., pp. 75, 76.
121 Powicke, *A History of the Cheshire County Union*, p. 180.
122 E. G. Herbert, 'The Congregationalist Character', *Religious Republics*, pp. 91–132.
123 Ibid., p. 91.
124 Ibid., pp. 95–96.
125 Especially of his maternal grandfather: J. Gilbert, *Autobiography and Other Memorials of Mrs. Gilbert (Formerly Ann Taylor)* (4th edn, London: Kegan Paul & Co, 1879).

126 Herbert, 'The Congregationalist Character', p. 98.
127 Ibid., pp. 99–100.
128 Ibid., p. 106.
129 Ibid., pp. 108–9.
130 '[N]o rule is violated when the ordinance is administered by a layman'. Ibid., p. 109.

14 Nonconformists, the Home and Family Life

Karen E. Smith

Drawing from their Puritan roots, Nonconformists in England and Wales traditionally viewed the home as a place for the development of character and morals, as well as the shaping of life in community. While chapel services, which emphasized scripture reading, sermons and prayers, were seen to be important to spiritual growth, home and family life were considered essential for nurturing genuine devotion and the promotion of godliness. Hence, while Nonconformists differed in their approach to church polity and doctrine, in the seventeenth and early eighteenth centuries there was widespread agreement that home and family life were at the heart of genuine piety and true holiness of life. Indeed, it was in the home that life was ordered and maintained.

As part of a burgeoning middle-class society in Britain, in the nineteenth century Nonconformists in England shared in the idealized concept of the Victorian home and family and sought to use this ideal as a means for shaping the values of children.[1] While Welsh Nonconformists did not culturally share in the same kind of middle-class development, they, too, were shaped by the idea that the home is where piety is taught and nurtured.[2] With the growth of the Sunday School movement, however, the focus of religious education shifted from the home to the chapel. By the early twentieth century, as different patterns of family life began to emerge, Nonconformists looked more and more to organized groups meeting in chapels to provide the moral grounding and spiritual guidance that had originally been the province of the home.

As the century wore on and chapels ceased to be the centre of the social and community life, Sunday School attendance and religious youth clubs and organizations were often over-shadowed and replaced by team sports and leisure activities in the wider community. In the twenty-first century the voice of Nonconformists with regard to home and family life has rarely been heard and the influence of the chapel on family life as a whole has diminished if not almost disappeared. This chapter will seek to offer a broad overview of some of these changing views toward home and family among Nonconformists in Britain from their Puritan beginnings to the present day.

I. Puritans and the Scriptural Order of the Home

The Puritan ideal for family life was shaped by their belief that all of life had been ordered and planned by God; men, women, children, servants, masters – indeed, all who were part of society – had their proper place and a role which had been plainly described in scripture. As Puritans interpreted scripture, the class or rank of every individual was decreed by God and conformity to patterns of behaviour deemed appropriate to a particular station in life was a sign of spiritual maturity and growth in godliness. Indeed, from a Puritan perspective, it was the duty of all true believers to accept their particular sphere. Hence, servants were to be obedient to their masters. Women were to keep silent in the church and remain subservient to their husbands. Children were to obey their parents who were to remember that 'sparing the rod' could spoil the child.

The Puritans' emphasis on 'godly order' was to be reflected in every area of life and, naturally, shaped their approach to family life and devotion.[3] Indeed, from a Puritan perspective family worship was to provide a constant reminder of the divinely decreed hierarchy of relationship among human beings and with God, too. Indeed, the biblical order of the family was taught and maintained by regular family worship.

Puritan writer William Perkins (1558–1602) wrote a manual for marriage and family relationships, *Christian Oeconomie, or, A short survey of the right manner of erecting and ordering a familie according to the Scriptures*, which was published posthumously in 1609. Here he argued that the 'onely rule of ordering the family is written within the word of God'.[4] After explaining his view on the appropriateness of marriages which avoid any hint of incest or scandal, he then described the particular duties and responsibilities in family life. In addition to the practical aspects of relationship, Perkins insisted that family worship was essential in every home and that every household should gather for scripture reading and prayer several times a day: in the morning in order to 'call on the name of the Lord before they begin the works of their calling',[5] in the evening and also before and after meals. Solemnly, Perkins insisted that these occasions of family worship 'are, as it were, little churches, yea, even a kind of paradise on earth'.[6]

The understanding of a divine order of relationship was at the heart of Puritan life and a theme taken up by many different writers. In 1622, William Gouge (1575–1653) wrote a popular guide to home, marriage and family titled *Of Domesticall Duties*, in which he explained that the man is head of the house and 'a king in his own household' and that women and children were to be subservient to men. Although the book underwent a number of editions, Gouge was aware that his views were not enthusiastically received by everyone. By the time the third edition was printed in 1634, he addressed his critics by arguing that he was no 'hater of women', but suggested that 'many that can patiently enough heare their duties declared in generall termes, cannot endure to heare those generals exemplified in their particular branches'.[7] 'This', he claimed, 'commeth too neere to the quicke, and pierceth too deepe'.[8] Yet, while he continued to insist that there was a particular biblical order and pattern in relationships which should be maintained, he conceded that mutuality in relationship when possible was important, too. He then suggested that the husband should seek to treat his wife as a 'joynt Governour of the family with himself' and should in fact 'referre the ordering of many things to her discretion'.[9]

In reading Gouge's work, it appears that while he argued for a biblical pattern that the man is head of the household, he conceded that women have their sphere of service as well. In *Of Domesticall Duties*, he addressed different kinds of situations which he believed might arise between parents and children, husbands and wives, servants and masters. In order to maintain the proper order in relationship, Gouge, like Perkins and other Puritan writers, stressed that family prayers were a duty which should never be neglected. Family devotions provided the opportunity to teach children and servants and to underscore the importance of obedience, discipline and order in all aspects of life. In short, it appears that for Puritans, family prayers became a means by which social relationships were taught and maintained. Writing of the household, for example, Richard Baxter (1615–91) set out very clearly the duties of servants and masters. 'Holy families', he claimed, 'must be preservers of the interest of Religion in the world'.[10]

As Nonconformity emerged and developed out of Puritanism, there was a continuing belief that genuine Christians could be distinguished from others by the way they conducted worship in their homes. By the end of the seventeenth century, however, it seems that some Nonconformists may not have been regularly observing family devotions. In 1694 Samuel Slater (d. 1704), Presbyterian minister at Crosby Square in London, wrote a tract in which he lamented the fact that family worship had waned among Nonconformists.

> Alas! there is a wonderful abatement and decay in the Practical part of Religion, and an apparent vast difference between the generality of Professors at this day, and those who lived in former times. The Sun hath gone ten degrees backward, we have quarrelled and fought, disputed and wrangled the life and power of Godliness almost out of the Nation . . . There is so little done for God in the Houses of many who call themselves Christians, that one would take them not for Christians, but Atheists, and conclude them without God in the world, yea, and that altogether; for there is no Praying in their Families, no Reading of

> the Scriptures, no Singing of the Psalms, no Repeating of Sermons, no Catechizing of young ones, who would not take these for Heathens, if they did not call themselves something else?[11]

Although some Nonconformists may have agreed with Slater's assessment about the overall decline in family worship, the idea of gathering as a household for worship certainly had not disappeared. Indeed, there were those who still emphasized that the family was divinely ordained and important for the overall good of the church and society. Samuel Stennett (1727–95), Baptist minister and hymn writer, wrote *Discourses on Domestic Duties* in which he reasserted the belief that that family was divinely inspired and ordered: A family then is a little society, consisting of man and wife, their children, their servants and such other relations or friends as may either dwell or occasionally sojourn with them.'[12] Refuting claims that family worship was no longer important, Stennett argued that children who were catechized were not being denied their freedom to inquire into religious matters, as some had claimed.[13] Moreover, in response to Calvinists who wanted to argue that Christian faith was 'God's work', he claimed that it was still important to gather children and servants together and explained the various aspects of family devotion.[14] Insisting that scripture, hymns and prayer were important to family worship, he wrote:

> The morning and the evening seem each a fit season for this social exercise. That time, however, should be chosen which may best conduce to the right discharge of the duty: not a late hour of the morning, for that will clash with the hurries of business; nor a late hour at night, for that will indispose persons to serious attention. The service, for obvious reasons, should not be protracted to an undue length: the whole may perhaps be comprehended within about a quarter of an hour. Every one [*sic*] in the house should consider it as his duty to attend. The scriptures should be read in regular order, that so their connection may be understood, and the whole in a course of time gone through. A particular attention should be paid to the circumstances of the family in the prayers addressed to God. And as variety and brevity should be aimed at, to prevent tediousness, so formality should be carefully guarded against.[15]

Stennett insisted that 'the orderly management of the business of the day' was helped by having at least two fixed times a day for family worship.

> Shall we have fixed times for our meals, our going to rest, and our various civil businesses; and no fixed season for worshipping God? On urgent occasions it may be necessary to depart from the established rule. But if there be no certain known time, it is much if the service is not every now

> and then omitted . . . On the contrary, regularity will in many respects have a very good effect . . . The indecent hurrying manner, in which this duty is too often performed, where no regard is had to a fixed time, will be prevented. And indeed an attention to this one point, will have no small influence on the orderly management of all the other businesses of the day.[16]

Stennett goes on to give advice about the type of reading and the way to approach prayer suggesting:

> The Bible should be read in regular order, especially the historical books of it. The portion allotted to be read should not be large, that the memory may not be overburdened. Perhaps the devotional parts of scripture may best suit the morning, and the historical the evening. Whoever reads should speak audibly, distinctly, and slowly. In some houses, where there are children, it has been the practice for the master to call upon each of them to repeat a verse of the chapter that has been read, and in a few words to explain it to them. And in others, a section of a chapter has been read, and the comment of some practical expositor upon it. This part of the service may be comprised within the compass of about ten-minutes. But we mean not to dictate on these matters. If edification is the grand object, and there is prudence to direct, no doubt such mode of instruction will be adopted, as best suits the circumstances of the family.[17]

As a hymn writer, Stennett appreciated the contribution of song to worship. He claimed that 'by singing a few stanzas of a psalm or hymn, if it can be conveniently practised, will greatly enliven the service'.[18] Finally Stennett discussed prayer offered at family worship. He claimed that this should be conducted by 'the master of the family, or upon some other person properly qualified who happens to be present'.[19] Significantly, he urged them not to rush, but to remember that the way they led worship would have an impact on the members of the family.

> When you go down on your knees, remember that you are in the presence of Almighty God, that you are the representative as it were of your whole family, and that the proper or improper discharge of this duty will be likely to have an important effect on their temper and conduct. Be, therefore, serious, and self collected. Do not hurry over the service in a thoughtless, negligent, customary manner. If you do, you will not only offend God, but unhappily contribute to the habituating those around you to a careless trifling mode of treatment of divine things.[20]

While it is difficult to assess the actual practice of prayer in the homes of Nonconformists in the eighteenth century, certainly there was concern expressed by some writers that family prayers were being neglected. Stennett suggested that people had abandoned family prayers because they were indifferent to religion or they claimed to be too busy with work or they simply felt too timid or weak to lead prayer in front of others. Whatever the reason given, however, Stennett claimed it was a duty which must be performed.

For those who practised family devotion, the difficulty in knowing what to read or how to pray was addressed by a variety of writers. Many Nonconformist ministers would have insisted that effective preaching is dependent on the work of God as Holy Spirit, and therefore the best sermons are delivered extempore and without dependence on manuscripts or notes. However, some volumes of sermons were printed and were sometimes used in family devotions. William Jay (1769–1853) a well-known Congregational minister who served as minister in Bath for sixty years wrote *Short Discourses to be Read in Families*.[21] Likewise, Philip Doddridge's work *The Family Expositor* had been written 'chiefly to promote family religion and to render the reading of the New Testament more pleasant and improving'.[22]

Hymn collections were printed, such as *Hymns Adapted to Public Worship or Family Devotion* by Benjamin Beddome (1717–95)[23] and the well-known *Divine Hymns for the Use of Children* by Isaac Watts. Watts also produced a popular catechism for children, *Young Child's Catechism and Prayers to Teach Children to Pray.*

The role of family prayers in the education of children particularly in the latter part of the eighteenth century was noted by Paul Sangster in his book *Pity My Simplicity: The Evangelical Revival and the Religious Education of Children, 1738–1800*. Stating that the home, schools and church became the three spheres of influence in education, Sangster suggests that increasingly in the second half of the century in England at least, 'parlour religion' became the recognized medium of education.[24] While the idea of parlour religion may not have been realized in the same in rural Wales, among Nonconformists in general family worship was a means of educating the household in matters of faith and morals. Good Nonconformist parents were expected to assert a strong religious influence upon the children. Women in particular were expected to take a lead in this domestic religious sphere.

Those who were responsible for household worship realized that it was not just children, but adults, too, who needed catechetical instruction and instruction in prayer. Samuel Palmer (1741–1813) who is best remembered for his *Protestant Dissenters' Catechism* and *Nonconformist's Memorial* drew together a collection of prayers in 1783 to be used in family worship.[25] Born in Bedford and having studied for the ministry at Daventry Academy under Caleb Ashworth, Palmer's collection included prayers from earlier Nonconformist writers, including Richard Baxter, Matthew Henry, Philip Doddridge, Henry Grove and Isaac Watts.

Although he was aware that many Dissenters would claim that prayer, like preaching, should be extempore and led by God as Holy Spirit, Palmer claimed that he had compiled the volume because he believed that 'family prayer is an indispensable duty and an important means of religion'.[26] However, he was also concerned that some had claimed they did not have family prayers because they do not have the 'ability or the courage to pray in the presence of others'.[27] While this work was written primarily to help those who felt they were unable to pray even to lead family prayers, Palmer claimed that 'others who can and do pray extempore, would better promote the edification of their families, if they were, occasionally at least, to adopt some good printed compositions'.[28]

Predictably, the collection of prayers includes prayers for many of the common experiences of human existence, that is, journeys, times of sickness and grief, etc. There are also prayers for the beginning and close of the year, as well as for before and after participation at the Lord's Supper. Palmer obviously intended the work to be of use to all Nonconformists and carefully edited one prayer for use 'after the baptism (or dedication) of a child' so that it could be used by those who had differing theological views of baptism. There was also a prayer for 'a young person journeying from home with an eye to business', which perhaps indicates an awareness of changing cultural circumstances and growing urbanization.

The alignment between nineteenth-century English Nonconformity, and the structures of social class and culture is evident in some of the prayers. For instance, a good example of the way the respective spheres of service and order were maintained may be seen in the prayer 'for a servant just come into the family':

> We pray for the servant who is brought to reside in this house. May [he] [she] be faithful to us, and to thee; may [he][she] diligently conform to the orders of this family, seriously attend the worship of it, and carefully improve every religious advantage to be enjoyed, so as to have everlasting reason to bless God that [he][she] was brought under our roof.[29]

Prayers like this leave no doubt that religion was enmeshed in culture and at times was used as an agent of socialization. Yet, this does not negate the fact that throughout the eighteenth and nineteenth centuries many Nonconformists genuinely believed that they had a divinely appointed responsibility toward all of those who were in their household. Indeed, they claimed that the souls of members of the household had been entrusted into the care of the head of the family. In 1792, an address 'On Evangelical Obedience' was given to an association meeting of Baptist churches who had gathered in Lyme in Dorset which outlined the duties towards children and servants:

> Let your servants also, if you have any, be your care: let them see how the religion of Jesus actuates you . . . whether you are husbands or wives,

> parents or children, masters or servants let it be your great care in every relation, to do credit to your profession of Christianity, and prove to all around you that you are in reality what you are in profession.[30]

The concern that family devotions were being neglected by Nonconformists continued to be expressed into the nineteenth century. In 1838, *The Evangelical Magazine* printed an article under the title 'Is the Practice of Family Prayer Incumbent upon the Christian?' The answer, of course, was a resounding 'yes'. In fact, it was claimed that family devotions were as important as public worship.[31] Again the way this 'duty' of prayer was suggested as a tool to socialize and modify the behaviour of children was made plain. It was suggested that as a child hears

> his father fondly commit his child into the hands of his God beseeching him to bless and preserve and help him through life, he is induced by a principle of gratitude, and reciprocal affection, to love, honour and obey his father; and in return for his earnest concern for his welfare, the child strives to please and meet the favour of his parent.[32]

It is tempting to doubt the veracity and credibility of religious belief that seems to have been so crassly used to control and manipulate the lives of others. Davidoff and Hall, however, have suggested that the desire by people in the middle ranks to control behaviour was the result of uncertainty.[33] Not just the uncertainty of shifting economic interests, but also the insecurity of the susceptibility to sudden illness and accident.[34] The emphasis on home and family which was grounded in a theology of providential ordered care was perhaps one way of trying to gain control over what must have seemed to be an insecure existence.

Whether the idealized picture of family worship was to gain control or to feel greater security, it is difficult to judge. What is clear is that the picture of family worship became romanticized in poetry and fiction, and into the nineteenth century was promoted as the standard to which all true Christians should aspire. For example, in a book published in Boston in 1844, titled *The Family Altar: Or the Duty, Benefits, and Mode of Conducting Family Worship*, the compiler (having already claimed to have depended heavily on British writers such as Doddridge and Watts), cites some verses from the Scottish poet Robert Burns and claims: 'In hundreds of families you might witness all that is pure and sublime in the scene contemplated by the Scottish bard.'[35] The verses depict a family gathering for worship after supper:

> The cheerfu' supper done, wi' serious face,
> They, round the ingle, form a circle wide;
> The sire turns o'er, with patriarchal grace,

The big ha'bible, *ance* his father's pride:
His bonnet rev'rently is laid aside,
His *lyart haffets* wearing thin and bare;
Those strains that once did sweet in Zion glide,
He wales a portion with judicious care;
And 'Let us worship God!' he says with solemn air.

They chant their artless notes in simple guise,
They tune their hearts, by far the noblest aim;
Perhaps Dundee's wild-warbling measures rise;
Or plaintive Martyrs, worthy of the name;
Or noble Elgin beets the heaven-ward flame;
The sweetest far of Scotia's holy lays:
Compar'd with these, Italian trills are tame;
The tickl'd ears no heart-felt raptures raise;
Nae unison *hae* they with our Creator's praise.

The priest-like father reads the sacred page,
How Abram was the friend of God on high;
Or Moses bade eternal warfare wage
With Amalek's ungracious progeny;
Or how the royal bard did groaning lie
Beneath the stroke of Heaven's avenging ire;
Or Job's pathetic plaint, and wailing cry;
Or rapt Isaiah's wild, seraphic fire;
Or other holy seers that tune the sacred lyre.[36]

II. The Picture of an 'Ideal Home'

While the practice of family devotions may have waxed and waned throughout the seventeenth and eighteenth centuries, by the nineteenth century it appears that the concept of an idealized family life became significant in British culture and society. Victorian home life was depicted as a place of comfort and warmth. A place where everyone was to have their separate sphere of service. The home was viewed as a central feature of a well-ordered society. In 1846, *The Evangelical Magazine* printed an article titled 'Maternal Responsibility' in which women were reminded of their duty within the home.

> Mothers of England! let us arouse from our lethargy and criminal indifference . . . Ours is a Protestant country, a land of Bibles where true Christianity is widely diffused amongst all classes, so there are

> fewer hindrances and counteractives to blight our hopes and check our efforts . . . There is we are compelled to fear, a low state of piety in our families, and that too at a time when the enemy is unusually busy in alluring the young from the church to the world and when more ordinary grace is required to hold fast the faith once delivered to the saints . . . Childhood is our golden opportunity. Now they are, as it were, shut up to domestic influence, and in a great measure to the operation of maternal love. May we have grace wisely to employ the sacred interval.[37]

The emphasis on domestic virtues was readily embraced and promoted by Dissenters and members of the Established Church alike. The separate sphere of women as the guardians of domesticity was highlighted in a work by Sarah Stickney Ellis. A Congregationalist, her volume *The Duties of Wives of England: Their Relative Duties, Domestic Influence and Social Obligations* gained acceptance in Britain and America. Claiming that women should remember that a 'good marriage was important', Ellis goes on to describe the 'duty of wives to be the helpmeet of their husbands' and the responsibilities women had in relationships within the household.[38]

Ellis' emphasis on home duty echoed the picture of a good woman which was also promoted in Nonconformist publications such as the *Evangelical Magazine* and the *Baptist Magazine* through the medium of death-bed testimonies. These denominational publications in the nineteenth century were replete with the testimonies of women who were presented as pious, good, subservient 'mothers of Israel' who cared for their families and stayed within the sphere of service to which they had been divinely placed.[39] Significantly, too, the testimonies allow the voice of women to be heard, albeit in a way that did not challenge, but confirmed the acceptable view of 'Christian womanhood' and family life. Deathbed testimonies reinforced the culturally accepted view that women belonged in the home, supporting their husbands and caring for children.[40]

Similar views of domestic virtues and the sanctity of home life were also presented in Victorian novels and magazines. Magazines such as *The Sunday Home, Family Magazine for Sabbath Reading* not only included Bible readings, but also poems, stories, and sermons which depicted good Christian character.[41] Some of the magazines which were specifically for women were considered by evangelicals to be a distraction from the serious matters of the soul which they believed should be the primary concern of good Christian women. Others no doubt were afraid that women's magazines would affect subscriptions to denominational publications.[42] However, for Nonconformists, devotional reading was central to their faith and a magazine specifically for women continued to have a certain appeal. The publications were conservative in nature and may have encouraged the development of a middle class which was recognized by its 'church going, family worship, the observance of the Sabbath and an interest in religious literature'.[43] Yet, although these periodicals and novels often seemed to reinforce middle-class values which kept women in the domestic sphere, they also gave women a voice to speak beyond their own household. Indeed, the cheap press was used to great effect by women. The Baptist writer Marianne Farningham, author, editor and lecturer, is one example of a woman who developed a sphere of service outside the home.[44] However, while she never married and, indeed, according to Linda Wilson, felt that 'single women should take control of their lives', Farningham also used the idealized view of home and family in many of her stories.[45] A reflection on an experience of worship after the death of a loved one is the focus of this poem:

Four Sundays since. We read the grand old psalm,
'Lord, thou hast been our dwelling-place.' He spake
In faith's strong words of the eternal calm
Of those who in the Lord's glad beauty wake.

We sang, 'Nearer to Thee,' and unseen hands
Knitted our hearts to God's great heart of love;
We bent our knees in prayer, and angel bands
Brought us the echoes of the choir above.

Two Sundays since. The hands were growing cold
That clung to mine beside the parting wave:
The spirit looking his eyes grew bold,
His strength had failed him, faith had made him brave.

'I know in whom I have believed.' Heaven's light
Became too strong for his poor mortal eyes:
I closed them; and there came to me the night,
To him, the morning in the upper skies.

Only two Sundays since. The weeks seem years.
I read the grand old psalm alone to-day;
I bathe the holy words in human tears,
Since he who read with me has passed away.

How far away, and yet how very near!
The door that hangs between is only air;
I put my hand within the Father's here,
He dwells in his immediate presence there.

I weep, and he rejoices. But a word
Spoken in softest tones shall reach me soon,
And I shall be as he is, with the Lord –
Mine the bright morning, his the blissful noon.[46]

While some managed to extol the virtues of family in poems, and stories, even while working themselves in other spheres, there are examples of Nonconformist women who crossed the boundaries of domesticity in other ways. Many Nonconformist women began to involve themselves in philanthropic activities and used their organizational skills to good effect within and outside chapel life. Fundraising itself was not a new task for women; they had long been supporting various causes. In his work *Women and Philanthropy in Nineteenth Century England*, F. K. Prochaska has noted that women's involvement in charitable fundraising and their claims to a wider role in nineteenth-century society were, they believed, supported by the examples of women who had served in scripture (Phoebe, Rebekah, Dorcas and Priscilla).[47] Yet, even though they were still seen to be under the authority of men, women began to assume more independence as they used their fundraising skills.

In an article titled 'Victorian Women with Causes: Writing, Religion and Action', Suzanne Rickard noted that in the mid-nineteenth century 'a new type of woman was beginning to clearly emerge from the shadows of men, of literary caricature and of household obscurity'.[48] This woman, according to Rickard, had 'a social conscience and a public cause to champion'.[49] While this kind of stand for social reform has often been associated with the more outspoken and often radical voices calling for women's rights and suffrage, Rickard notes that many of these women were highly motivated by religious faith and zeal as well as by 'women-centred concerns'.[50] Much of their concern and action may have been shaped by their religious views, but it seems also to have flowed out of a deep passion about injustice, as well as a desire for service.

Among Nonconformist women, the efforts outside the home were mainly concentrated on evangelical and missionary activity. Since many missionary societies refused to send single women to the mission field (or indeed refused to recognize married women as missionaries in their own right), Nonconformist women formed auxiliaries which appointed and supported women in missionary service. Groups such as the Ladies Association for the Support of Zenana Work and Bible Women in India (the name was changed to The Baptist Zenana Mission [BZM] in 1897), proved highly efficient and successful as they sent women to serve as teachers, nurses, and doctors.[51] It is ironic, of course, that the call for women to be allowed to serve in foreign climes came out of a concern that there were women who were bound in their own experience of domesticity and had not been able to hear the gospel proclaimed.

Although there are examples of Nonconformist women, who actively gave time and energy to such things as denominational work, evangelistic causes, or social reform, they still insisted that attention should be given to the home. Temperance reform leader Clara Lucas Balfour who travelled and lectured widely to promote the cause of total abstinence was adamant that a Christian home and family were essential to the defeat of 'demon drink'.[52] Independent-minded and an able speaker, Balfour was not seeking the rights of women or desiring freedom from domesticity. However, Kristin Doern has suggested that in her own way Balfour did much to encourage a new understanding of the role of women among Nonconformists as she 'manipulated Victorian "domestic ideology", which situated women exclusively in the private sphere' and in so doing promoted a view of the 'ideal Victorian woman'.[53]

In addition to missionary work within the local church and in the denomination, some Nonconformist women balanced home life with social action in their communities. Their social concern included work in orphanages, establishing homes for unwed mothers and shelters for the poor, and support for the temperance movement. This kind of involvement may be seen clearly in the work of Sarah Anne Edwards who was married to William Edwards, the principal of the Baptist College in Cardiff.[54] A member of Tredegarville Baptist Church, Cardiff, she gave her support to women's groups locally, in Wales and as part of the Baptist Union of Great Britain, too.[55]

While acknowledging her work locally and in the denomination, it should also be noted that her influence as a Baptist leader extended beyond denominational bounds and into civic life. In 1926 she was named as a magistrate of the city of Cardiff.[56] She also served as an official visitor appointed by the Home Office, to the women at Cardiff prison. She devoted a great deal of time to the British Women's Temperance Association and was president of the Cardiff and District Union of the British Women's Temperance Association for many years. Her temperance work brought her into contact with other women's groups which were agitating for equal voting rights for women. She attended meetings of the Cardiff Women Citizen's Association when they were demanding equal franchise for women and was a member of the last deputation to go to the government prior to the granting of the franchise for women. She also served as leader of a deputation to the prime minister, Lord Asquith, to ask for legislation condemning drinking clubs.

Politically involved, she was vice-president for several years of the Cardiff Women's Liberal Association in Cardiff and in addition to being a member of the board of management for the Royal Infirmary, she served as a member of the visiting committee to the Institution for the Mentally Defective, a member of the local National Insurance Committee (the first woman to be appointed), government representative on the unemployment tribunal's board for Cardiff and the Rhondda valley and a referee under the old age pensions act. She was also an honorary member of the Gorsedd of Bards of the National Eisteddfod of Wales.[57]

Edwards is a good example of the kind of new Nonconformist woman who was emerging in the late nineteenth and early twentieth centuries. These women were active outside the home in chapel and in the community, but at the same time they would have continued to hold traditional views of the importance of home and family life. Indeed, most would have echoed the sentiments of John Angell James (1785–1859), Independent minister of Carrs Lane Chapel, Birmingham, who wrote *The Family Monitor or A Help to Domestic Happiness* in which he speaks of mutuality in relationship between a husband and wife, but then makes it clear that the man is always king of the home. Claiming that in every society there must be some ultimate authority, James wrote:

> In the domestic constitution this superiority rests in the husband: he is the head, the lawgiver, the ruler. In all matters touching the little world in the house, he is to direct, not indeed without taking counsel with his wife, but in all discordancy of view, he, unless he choose to waive his right, is to decide; and to his decision the wife should yield, and yield with grace and cheerfulness. No man ought to resign his authority as head of the family, no woman ought to wish him to do it: he may give up his predilections, and yield to her wishes, but he must not abdicate the throne, nor resign his sceptre.[58]

Although this traditional hierarchical view of hearth and home as the place of guidance and Christian nurture continued to be expressed, in the second half of the nineteenth century it seems that more and more responsibility for Christian education was passing to the chapels. In 1863, *The Baptist Magazine* printed an article, 'On the Nurture of Converts', in which it was argued that the church and the family were similar and that the church could learn 'many instructive hints from the nurture and discipline of the family'.[59] The author continued by offering a number of characteristics of the home which the church could provide, including personal contact and conversation, a system of discipline, instruction and the habit of action exercise and work. Finally, the point is made that the elder members of the church may make 'religion beautiful and attractive in the eyes of younger members'.[60]

It appears that a shift of responsibility was taking place. No longer was home the place where morals and conduct were to be shaped, but now, it seems the church was assuming more responsibility for this role. Addressing Baptists at the Wiltshire and East Somerset Association meeting in 1875, William Burton argued that it was the duty of the church to provide spiritual nurture for young inquirers and converts. He noted that many did not have the loving care of parents and family but are 'surrounded by deadening influences'.[61] He argued that the church should form young members' classes. He wrote:

> Our young people might then become acquainted with the reasons that lie at the foundation of our Protestantism and Nonconformity, and with the principles we hold as Congregationalists and Baptists. Everything in such a class, it is scarcely necessary to say, should be made subservient to the upholding of Christian character, the deepening of spiritual experiences, the intensifying of love and zeal in the cause of the Redeemer.[62]

III. Twentieth and Twenty-First Centuries: The Changing Face of Home and Family in Nonconformity

As the twentieth century dawned, many, if not most, Nonconformists would have readily embraced the view that the church must assume the role of nurturing converts. To be sure there were still those who aspired to have family devotions and gathered the household daily to read a work such as C. H. Spurgeon's devotional guide *Morning by Morning, Daily Readings for the Family or the Closet*. Yet, there were signs that life was changing and the responsibility for the education and nurture of the church was being assumed by organized groups meeting within the chapels. The Sunday School movement had continued to grow since its beginnings in the 1780s and became an important place for education as well as spiritual nurture. Other meetings such as the Band of Hope which began as a temperance group for young people also drew young people together for Christian meetings outside the home. In Wales, chapel choir practice became a focal point for many young people and adults who gathered on one evening during the week to sing and socialize.

As well as reflecting a growing dependence on denominational organization and structures, the shift away from domestic worship may in part have been due to the changing political and social landscape.[63] In the twentieth century British Nonconformists were confronted with drastic change in social, economic and political spheres. Two world wars which called men to the battle field and women to work outside the home meant that the nineteenth-century picture of an 'ideal home' was no longer applicable. After each war, many men never returned and those who did had experienced unimaginable suffering, which called into question the views of God they had been taught in chapel.[64] Some returned home unable to discover or create domestic happiness; after years of separation from families many children did not recognize or know their fathers. Widows were now head of the house and many single women had little prospect of marriage. The conflict of battle had changed the contours of home and family life irrevocably.

By the end of the twentieth century, family life had taken on different configurations in culture. Women often work alongside men. Marriage is no longer viewed as normative. Child-rearing patterns include the use of paid nurseries and after school programmes. Moreover, parents in the twenty-first century who are shaped by consumerism often emphasize the freedom of choice for children, especially when it comes to religious views. Sporting events, leisure activities and Sunday openings have all been blamed for a decline in attendance at Sunday worship. Reflecting on religious life in Wales, Howell and Baber claim: 'The wireless, cinema, development of bus services and the secularising influence of schools were all eroding the old cultural isolation and dogmatic beliefs and the hold of the chapel suffered accordingly.'[65] However, it may also be true that Nonconformity as it is understood in its historical and theological context no longer seems to have a place in a world that now defines itself as 'post modern' and even 'post-Christian'.

Still, religion and culture have remained aligned. While it would be too simple to say that the collapse of the family life in the twentieth century has had an effect on Nonconformity or that the collapse of Nonconformity has had an effect on family life, the two are closely linked. This is particularly true in Wales, for example, where Nonconformity was at the heart of Welsh life for so many years.[66] In a study of social change and family formation, a survey conducted in 2002 was compared with an earlier survey taken in 1960. One aspect of the study examined the influence of religion on family and identity. In the 1960 survey, 98 per cent responded affirmatively to a question asking them to identify the religious denomination to which they belonged. However, in 2002 when individuals were asked if they felt any belonging or identification to any religious organization or group only one-third said 'yes'.[67]

Such a fall in numbers may be the result of a collapse of Nonconformist churches in Wales in the twentieth century. However, decline may also be traced to the strong links between chapel culture, and class structure, as well as family identity. Commenting on Nonconformity in Wales, Howell and Baber boldly claimed: 'Increasingly from the last decades of the nineteenth century people were appointed deacons because they were of the emerging class and others passed over because of poverty and this doubtless contributed to the chapel's decline.'[68]

Family identity and the links with chapel culture in Wales, in particular, has played its part in the support of Nonconformity. Significantly, one twenty-two-year-old (who was Welsh speaking and the son of a minister) was interviewed for the aforementioned survey, and claimed that while his parents would have liked he and his four siblings to have a more 'religious nature', they stopped attending chapel in their teens. However, he commented that one brother had now married and returned to the chapel because he had children of his own, and the family went there together.[69]

Naturally the future of Nonconformity, or indeed Christian faith, may not depend on family identity with a particular religious outlook. Realizing the declining number of adherents, some Nonconformists churches have responded by reaching out to local communities through discipleship programmes and youth groups. Others have altered the style of worship services to include more emphasis on friendship and fellowship, rather than preaching and prayer. In many instances, hymns have been replaced by worship songs and organs have been replaced by worship bands.

On a wider scale, for some time denominations have noted with alarm the decline in membership and financial support. In November 2005, the Baptist Union of Great Britain noted a decline in numbers, especially in the numbers of children and younger people within the denomination, and called for a special time of prayer.[70] The General Assembly of the United Reformed Church (URC), which meets every two years, plans a youth assembly at the same time. This allows young people to take part in a special programme which covers some of the same issues of the main assembly gathering. In this way the URC hopes to educate children and enable them to experience something of how the URC is governed.[71]

None of this, of course, has anything to do with family prayers or nurturing devotion within the home. Denominational concerns often reflect institutional matters which focus on finance and membership and rarely touch on issues of spirituality such as prayer, Bible reading or the disciplines of the Christian life. The concerns over family prayer and devotion among Nonconformists have long ago faded from view. Yet, while the notion of an 'idealized home' and domestic virtues supported by a hierarchical worldview were never to be an appropriate response of Christian faith in a changing and uncertain world, the importance of nurturing Christian faith in the context of relationship is an important legacy of Protestant Nonconformity.

Notes

1 Leonore Davidoff and Catherine Hall, *Family Fortunes: Men and Women of the English Middle Class, 1780–1850* (rev. edn, London: Routledge, 2002), p. 77.

2 Smelser has noted that the understanding of a middle class cannot be applied to Wales in the same way. Rural Wales into the nineteenth century had largely a two-class system with 'overlapping cleavages of wealth, political power, administration of justice, religion, cultural aspirations, regional identification, style of life and language'. See Neil J. Smelser, *Social Paralysis and Social Change: British Working-Class Education in the Nineteenth Century* (Oxford: University of California Press, Russell Sage Foundation, 1991), p. 149. See also, D. W. Howell and C. Baber, 'Wales', in F. M. L. Thompson (ed.), *The Cambridge Social History of Britain, 1750–1950, Volume I: Regions and Communities* (Cambridge: Cambridge University Press, 1990), pp. 286–90.

3 Gordon S. Wakefield, *Puritan Devotion: Its Place in the Development of English Piety* (London: Epworth Press, 1957), p. 55.

4 William Perkins, *Christian Oeconomie, or, a short survey of the right manner of erecting and ordering a familie according to the Scriptures first written in Latine by the author M. W. Perkins; and now set forth in the vulgar tongue for more common use and benefit by Tho. Pickering* . . . (London: Imprinted by Felix Kyngston, 1609), p. 1.

5 Ibid., p. 6.

6 Ibid., p. 8.
7 William Gouge, *Of Domesticall Duties: Eight Treatises* (3rd edn, London: Printed by George Miller for Edward Brewster, 1634), p. v.
8 Ibid., p. iv.
9 Ibid., p. v.
10 Richard Baxter, *The poor man's family book in plain familiar conference between a teacher and a learner: with a form of exhortation to the sick, two catechisms, a profession of Christianity, forms of prayer for various uses, and some Psalms and hymns for the Lords day: with a request to landlords and rich men to give to their tenants and poor neighbours either this or some fitter book* (London: Printed for Benjamin Cox, 1691), p. 282.
11 Samuel Slater, 'The Epistle Dedicatory', in *An Earnest Call to Family-Religion or, A Discourse Concerning Family Worship Being the Substance of Eighteen Sermons* (London: Thomas Parkhurst, 1694), pp. 2–3.
12 Samuel Stennett, *Discourses on Domestic Duties* (Edinburgh: J. Ritchie, 1800), p. 327.
13 Ibid., p. 62.
14 Ibid.
15 Ibid., p. 65.
16 Ibid., p. 94.
17 Ibid., p. 97.
18 Ibid., p. 94.
19 Ibid., p. 98
20 Ibid.
21 William Jay, *Short Discourses to Be Read in Families* (Hartford: Oliver D Cooke, 1812).
22 Philip Doddridge, *The Family Expositor or a Paraphrase and Version of the New Testament: With Critical Notes and a Practical Improvement of Each Section* (London: J. Waugh, 1845), I.
23 B. Beddome, *Hymns Adapted to Public Worship or Family Devotion* (London: Burton and Briggs, 1818).This collection was left in manuscript form by Beddome for his family to use in family worship, but was reprinted for wider use with a recommendatory preface by Baptist minister, Robert Hall (1764–1831) in 1818.
24 Paul Sangster, *Pity My Simplicity: The Evangelical Revival and the Religious Education of Children, 1738–1800* (London: Epworth Press, 1963), p. 71.
25 Samuel Palmer, *A Collection of Family Prayers* (6th ed. London: Sherwood, Neely and Jones, 1815 [1783]).
26 Ibid., preface.
27 Ibid.
28 Ibid.
29 Ibid., pp. 191–92.
30 William Clarke, 'On Evangelical Obedience', The Western Letter, 1792, in John Rippon, *The Baptist Annual Register for 1790, 1791, 1792 and part of 1793* (London: Dilly, Button and Thomas, 1793), pp. 443–44.
31 'Is the Practice of Family Prayer Incumbent upon the Christian?', in *The Evangelical Magazine*, n.s. XVI (London: Thomas Ward and Co, 1838), p. 477.
32 Ibid.
33 Davidoff and Hall, *Family Fortunes*, p. 22.
34 Ibid.
35 (No Author), *The Family Altar: Or the Duty, Benefits, and Mode of Conducting Family Worship* (Boston: Gould, Kendell and Lincoln, 1844), p. 41.
36 Robert Burns, 'The Cotter's Saturday Night' (1785). A 'Cotter' was a poor peasant who was given the use of a Cottage by the property owner in exchange for labour as opposed to paying rent. The poem relates how the Cotter and his family take time to relax on a Saturday evening after a week of work. In the poem the family

eat their meal and then gather for family worship as the father reads from the Bible.

37 'Maternal Responsibility', in *The Evangelical Magazine*, NS XXIV (London: Ward and Co., 1846), pp. 68–69.

38 Sarah Stickney Ellis, *The Wives of England: Their Relative Duties, Domestic Influence and Social Obligations* (New York: J. & H. G. Langley, 1843), pp. 5–8.

39 This literary genre is an important source for the study of Nonconformists. Although they follow a similar stylistic pattern (perhaps similar to the Purtian conversion narratives of the seventeenth century) these testimonies also serve as 'obituary notices' for women.

40 See Karen E. Smith, 'Forgotten Sisters: The Contributions of Some Notable but Un-noted British Baptist Women', in Philip E. Thompson and Anthony R. Cross (eds), *Recycling the Past or Researching History?* Studies in Baptist History and Thought, Vol. 11 (Milton Keynes: Paternoster, 2005).

41 *The Sunday Home: Family Magazine for Sabbath Reading* (London: The Religious Tract Society, 1874).

42 This concern appears to have been behind an appeal made to Baptist women in the nineteenth century to continue supporting the *Baptist Magazine*. See Karen E. Smith, 'What about the Widows? An Appeal to Nineteenth Century Baptist Women', in John H. Y. Briggs and Anthony R. Cross (eds), *Baptists and the World: Renewing the Vision*, Papers from the Baptist Historical Society Conference, Prague, Czech Republic, July 2008 (Oxford: Centre for Baptist History and Heritage, 2011), Chapter 6.

43 Davidoff and Hall, *Family Fortunes*, pp. 78ff as cited in Margaret Beetham, *A Magazine of Her Own? Domesticity and Desire in the Woman's Magazine, 1800–1914* (London: Routledge, 1996), p. 49.

44 Linda Wilson, *Marianne Farningham: A Plain Woman Worker* (Milton Keynes: Paternoster, 2008).

45 Linda Wilson, '"Afraid to be Singular": Marianne Farningham and the Role of Women, 1857–1909', in Sue Morgan (ed.), *Women Religion and Feminism in Britain, 1750–1900* (Basingstoke, Hampshire: Palgrave Macmillan, 2002), p. 108.

46 Marianne Farningham, 'Sundays at Home', in *Poems* (London: James Clarke, 1866), pp. 74–75.

47 F. K. Prochaska, *Women and Philanthropy in Nineteenth Century England* (Oxford: Clarendon Press, 1980), pp. 16–17.

48 Suzanne Rickard, 'Victorian Women with Causes: Writing, Religion and Action,' in Sue Morgan (ed.), *Women Religion and Feminism in Britain 1750–1900*, p. 141.

49 Ibid.

50 Ibid.

51 Karen E. Smith, 'Women in Cultural Captivity: British Women and the Zenana Mission', in *Baptist History and Heritage*, XLI/1 (Winter 2006), pp. 30–41.

52 See Kristin G. Doern, 'Equal Questions: The "Woman Question" and the "Drink Question" in the Writings of Clara Lucas, 1808–78', in Sue Morgan (ed.), *Women, Religion and Feminism in Britain, 1750–1900*, pp. 159–76.

53 Kristin G. Doern, 'Balfour, Clara Lucas (1808–78)', *Oxford Dictionary of National Biography*, Oxford University Press, 2004, www.oxforddnb.com/view/article/1183, accessed 12 October 2011.

54 Edwards served the College, which was located in Pontypool, and later moved to Cardiff, from 1880 to 1925. His work as an educator and Baptist leader are well documented. Establishing himself as an able administrator and scholar he wrote a number of works in Welsh and English, but is probably best known for his translation of the New Testament into Welsh and his translation of many hymns. He served as president of both the Baptist Union of Wales and the Baptist Union of

Great Britain and founded the Welsh and English Baptist Sunday School Unions in Wales. T. W. Chance (ed.), *The Life of Principal William Edwards* (Cardiff: Priory Press, 1934). Sarah Ann Evans (1865–1947) was born in 1865 in Pontlottyn in the Rhymney Valley where she attended Zoar Baptist Church. She trained as a vocalist at the Royal Academy of Music. In 1891 she married William Edwards, just after he had taken over as principal of the College in Pontypool. This was his second marriage, as his first wife had died in 1880 after giving birth to their third child. Sarah and William had four children. Irene Myrddin Davies (ed.), *Memory: An Inspiration* (Cardiff: Priory Press, 1957), p. 30.

55 Irene Myrddin Davies (ed.), *Memory: An Inspiration*, p. 30.

56 *The Cardiff Year Book* (1926), p. 24.

57 Irene Myrddin Davies (ed.), *Memory: An Inspiration*, p. 13.

58 John Angell James, *The Family Monitor or A Help to Domestic Happiness* (from the third London edition corrected and enlarged, Boston: Crocker and Brewster, 1830), p. 39.

59 Rev. C. Short, 'On the Nurture of Young Converts', in *The Baptist Magazine*, Vol. LV (London: Pewtress Brothers, 1863), p. 615.

60 Ibid., p. 618.

61 'The Duty of the Church towards Young Inquirers and Converts', A Paper read at the Wilts and East Somerset Association of Baptist Churches, 17 June, by the Revd William Burton, 9 July 1975, p. 352.

62 Ibid.

63 See W. R. Lambert, 'Some Working-Class Attitudes toward Organized Religion in Nineteenth-Century Wales', in Gerald Parsons (ed.), *Religion in Victorian Britain, Vol. IV: Interpretations* (Manchester: Manchester University Press, 1988), pp. 96–114.

64 This is noted by D. Densil Morgan in *The Span of the Cross, Christian Religion and Society in Wales 1914–2000* (Cardiff: University of Wales Press, 1999), p. 76.

65 Howell and Baber, 'Wales', p. 330.

66 For an overview of some of the changes in Welsh culture and the effects on Nonconformist chapels, see ibid., p. 310.

67 Nickie Charles, Charlotte Aull Davis and Christopher Charles Harris, *Families in Transition: Social Change Family Formation and Kin Relationships* (Bristol: University of Bristol, 2008), p. 107.

68 Howell and Baber, 'Wales', p. 330.

69 Charles Davis et al., *Families in Transition*, p. 108.

70 www.christianpost.com/news/british-baptists-call-for-day-of-prayer-for-children-to-revive-new-generation-8478/, accessed 2 August 2012.

71 United Reformed Church General Assembly, 2012, http://generalassembly.urc.org.uk/?page_id=478, accessed 2 August 2012.

15 Nonconformists and Education

Stephen Orchard

Biblical scholarship was fundamental to the Reformation. It was critical that the Reformers had an authentic text of scripture and an agreed canon. It is in this sense that the Reformation flows from the Renaissance and the new humanism of that era. In order to challenge the traditional teachings of the Church, it was necessary to establish the earliest possible texts for the Bible and to begin understanding them in new ways. For some people scholarship was enough. Others were more radical and linked the reinterpretation of scripture with change at every level of church and society. Translating the scriptures into the vernacular could transform the nature of the Church itself by equipping all Christians to reach their own conclusions on matters of faith. For this to happen, learning had to move out of the university. The skill of literacy needed to accompany the technological change of printing books. A new spectrum of learning opened out. At one end were the scholars, establishing and translating the manuscripts, and at the other end was the plough-boy with his printed Bible. The plough-boy end of the spectrum was hyperbole. At the beginning of the Reformation printed books were too expensive and popular education too sparse for all but the exceptional plough-boy to have his own access to the Word of God. However, the aspiration was real. The historic Church had always had a role in fostering scholarship and popular education. The Reformers were committed to it with new energy. The Puritan part of the Elizabethan Church of England, who saw themselves as the heirs of the Reformers, did everything they could to promote preaching and lecturing with a view to educating the people at large. Their zeal was resisted and checked by more conservative forces who were in favour of scholarship and learning but not when it was used to promote Puritan ideas.

I. Learning during the Commonwealth

In the seventeenth century the Puritan party gained ascendancy during the English Civil War and attempted to legislate for a Church of England in the Presbyterian mould. Not all Puritans had arrived at Presbyterian conclusions; a sizeable minority were Independents in their view of the Church and a part of that group were Baptists. Though they were agreed in opposing prelacy on the one hand and the Quakers on the other, there was not enough common ground to settle the Church of England before the Restoration and the consequent re-establishment of the bishops and the Book of Common Prayer. In the window of time between monarchs, which was the Commonwealth, Puritan learning flourished. The Puritan scholar who cultivated the widest reach within the academic community was Samuel Hartlib (ca 1600–62).[1] Although his origins were in the Polish Protestant community of the Baltic port of Elbing, Hartlib spent most of his adult life in England, his merchant father having taken an Englishwoman for his third wife. Her name is unknown but she was well-connected; one of her sisters was married to Sir Richard Smith, a privy councillor to James I. Hartlib was in Cambridge in 1625–26, and possibly earlier, under the patronage of John Preston, master of Emmanuel College, a Puritan stronghold. Hartlib returned to Elbing from Cambridge but war and the end of the English merchant privileges in Elbing drove him back to England in 1628. He married in London in 1629 and set up a private academy in Chichester. It was there that he first met John Pell (1610–85), the mathematician, and the local minister William Speed, through whom it is possible he came to know the agriculturalist Adolphus Speed (fl. 1647–59) who was active in promoting new ways of farming during the Commonwealth.[2]

Hartlib's academy did not prosper and William Speed advised him to return to London, possibly to try setting up a school there. In fact, Hartlib's London life took another turn. From his house in Duke's Place in the City of London he established an international correspondence with Protestant scholars all over Europe. One of his chief sources of information at first was John Durie, who had ministered to Calvinists in Elbing from 1625 to 1630. Eventually, from all over Europe, Hartlib learnt of rare books, new inventions, technological change and the beginnings of modern science. He supplied a newsletter in his own hand to circulate this information widely among his correspondents. People visiting London came to stay at his house and added to his knowledge and his networks. He also began to be interested in pedagogy in its own right – how did people best learn anything? In this he believed he was building on the work of Francis Bacon. His own efforts were admired eventually by John Milton, who was stimulated to write on education and on the free exchange of ideas. Hartlib's interests overlapped with his prominent contemporary Jan Amos Komensky, the Czech educationalist better known as Comenius. This drew him into promoting the pansophical ideas of Comenius, who believed the world would discover harmony through the universal spread of knowledge and the Protestant Reformation.

By the time of the Civil War, Samuel Hartlib had a reputation for his erudition and during the Commonwealth period he flourished. He was paid to think and to circulate ideas, because there were advantages to be gained economically and politically. Having advised Parliament about weapons to pursue the war he was now a promoter of new technology to boost the economy. With his wide circle of European Protestant contacts he could provide intelligence that would support foreign policy. Although the 'Office for the Address of Communications' which Hartlib proposed was never formally instituted he was voted a salary by parliament in order to promote the wide exchange of ideas. He met senior officials in the government and was present at audiences with Cromwell himself. In addition, in 1642, he, Durie and Comenius had formed a pact to promote religious peace, education and scholarly reform. Their ambition was to see Bacon's dream of a new Solomon's House, a model college of learning, established in London, possibly at Chelsea College. This was of a piece with Puritan thinking about the possibility of new universities and the reform of Oxford and Cambridge.

The scholarly friendships of this period of Hartlib's life are often characterized by the title 'the invisible college'. Hartlib was anticipating the World Wide Web by some 450 years. There was no academic foundation, but there was a virtual community of Protestant scholars across Europe circulating ideas. Hartlib saw it as an altruistic concern. Durie and he equated the idea of such communication with the Greek *koinonia*, more regularly rendered in English as the communion or fellowship of the Holy Spirit. Releasing the full human potential which God has given to humanity required this opening up of knowledge. He sought and disseminated information on a diversity of subjects, from chemistry, medicine and engineering to horticulture, agriculture and charitable enterprise. He was involved in over half the patents for new inventions issued at this time. Both his Puritanism and his involvement with the government told against him after 1660. It had always been irksome for him to get the previous administration actually to pay the salary they had awarded him; now he got nothing and died in relative poverty. The 'invisible college' is reckoned to be the precursor of the Royal Society, formed after the restoration of the monarchy and including many of Hartlib's contacts. Although the new regime attempted to expunge the Commonwealth and all its works the pursuit of new knowledge, especially what we would now call scientific knowledge, continued. The Puritans were out of favour but their dreams of changing the world by extending learning and setting up a pan-European Protestant alliance continued.

II. The 1662 Ejectment

The immediate difficulty for Puritan scholars after the restoration of the monarchy was the church settlement. Schoolmasters were once more to be licensed by bishops. University matriculation at Oxford and graduation at Cambridge required conformity to the Church of England. Some Puritans conformed and continued their academic careers in the hope of better days to come. Others, especially those ordained by presbyters during the Commonwealth period, who were now required to submit to Episcopal ordination, refused to conform and were ejected from their livings and barred from teaching posts and the universities. The ejected Taunton minister Joseph Alleine (1634–68), kept school with his wife in Ilchester and promoted catechizing and religious instruction in families, in spite of suffering imprisonment for his views.[3] This was at the level of elementary education. By contrast Samuel Ogden (1628–97), ejected from Mackworth, near Derby, kept school in Derby until he was prosecuted and then withdrew to Wirksworth, under the protection of the local squire, Sir John Gell. Ogden then presided over a school in Wirksworth and ministered to Dissenters there before and after the 'Toleration' of 1689. Ogden followed a grammar school syllabus, which is described in detail by his assistant and son-in-law, Zachary Merrill.[4] This account mentions pupils from Nonconformist families around the county, so we deduce there were boarding arrangements at the school in Derby. It begins:

> Mr Ogdens Method of School Mastering, as it was practised by him near 40 years with good success, and observed by me sometime his Usher and written as a fit pattern for my self or others to imitate.
>
> First I will observe the way that he usually took in grounding a young Schollar and what authors he caused them to read, what helps of translations he allowed of, what exercises. &c.
>
> Secondly, I will note his carriage on part of discipline, what his customs were in ye ordering his Schooles:

The mention of 'near 40 years' tells us that Ogden ran his school, whether in Derby or Wirksworth, from 1662 onwards until his death and, possibly, for a few years before the Ejectment. The boys studied Latin by rote from an early age, reciting the conjugations of verbs and learning the parts of grammar. Ogden was not above using a silly rhyme to reinforce the learning and used proverbs for the first exercises in translating from English to Latin. The senior pupils were given translation exercises and subjects for original composition. Merrill's account of how the school was conducted gives a picture of such establishments.

> Touching his carriage towards his schollars, I shall observe it first as it relates to his Schollars in School and then to his boarders in his own house. As to his ordering his school his custom was to come to school all summer at 7 a clock in morning unless hindered by chance or otherwise and then we his ushers did constantly observe that hour and to retain them till Eleven, but usually it would be ½ an hour past before.

There follows a description of the content of the lesson, which was entirely devoted to Latin and then remarks about discipline.

> For his discipline it was not found very seldom whipping any unless for some gross miscarriage as truanting or laughing . . . When he did beat any he was usually severe, tho it were but Elder, which made them very fearfull, but if he whipt any it was with so much mildness that a boy of 4 years of age might well abide it. Sometimes he would walk to and fro and then by no means suffer any to stare him in the face or laugh.

Ogden was careful not to fall foul of the laws on public worship in his conduct of the school: 'Before we gave over at noon or night one of his boys vicissime read a psalm or chapter in English out of Proverbs and after every boy repeated his verse in Latin. Nor had public prayers in school but as soon as he came in in a morning his custom was to sit down and take off his hat and looking upward to pray for a blessing.' This was, however, a Puritan school and religion had a prominent place in it: 'On Saturdays he made all his boys to stand forth together and say their catechism, then would mind them of duty to parents and to God, charge them to read Chapters on Sabbath come to church. He never taught any other mode all to learn it immediately after catechism they would all home with a Chapter.'

The Nonconformist involvement in what we would now term primary and secondary education is exemplified by Alleine and Ogden and many like them around the country. Other ejected ministers found posts as tutors in private households sympathetic to the Nonconformist cause. Although the schools were subject to complaint and persecution they were able to continue by one means or another and domestic arrangements for education fell foul of none of the new laws. The difficulty came, as has been already noted, if a university education was sought.

Zachary Merrill relates an anecdote told to him by a Mr Pawling long after the event.

> The present Dr Birch[5] and his brother were educated at Oxford for many years before they were matriculated; their father a worthy parson would not permit them to be entered, only they lodged in the town & were tutored by Dr Ashton, author of the proposal for widows. Some were angry at the Dr for teaching them, but Dr Wallis[6] said He might teach who he would. Mr Pawling.[7]

The motive for compromising religious belief in order to go to Oxford or Cambridge was a strong one. These were the places where scholars gathered to debate and where libraries were to be found. The alternative was to go to a Scottish university or to gather an alternative group of students in a private house around a learned tutor and his library. This last course led to the emergence of what we now term the Dissenting Academies.

III. Dissenting Academies

Here the picture is more complex than traditional studies have suggested and a major research programme was begun in 2008 to gather information and subject it to renewed analysis. 'Academies' is an imprecise term and covers what we might now term secondary education as well as higher education. Dissenters were involved in both. A further problem is that academies took on the personal idiosyncrasies of their tutors, including doctrinal variations. These religious differences were important in their time but have come to dominate the study of the academies at the expense of considering their broader impact. Because academies were originally personal to the tutor they came and went. Students might also move between them. A few of the early ones can be claimed as the lineal predecessors of subsequent institutions in the Unitarian, Baptist and Congregational traditions. Academies might be defined as those institutions from which people went into ministry, so long as it is not assumed that all those who completed the course did so. Anything termed an academy where the curriculum was largely a grounding in the Classics, such as might be found in a contemporary grammar school, and where some students went on to more demanding academies, is clearly a school rather than a college. Ejected ministers taught in both.

The records of academies in the years between 1662 and 1689 are sketchy. This is partly because of the informal nature of such institutions and partly because of the need to keep a low profile to avoid harassment by the authorities. An example is Samuel Craddock's academy at Wickhambrook, near Newmarket in Suffolk. We know the names of some of the students from biographical references, from which we infer it was an academy proper, but the detail of how it was conducted eludes us.[8] The object was clearly to offer the academic advantages of a university by mimicking the teaching with the aid of scholars who would otherwise have been candidates for university posts. In the years immediately after 1662 there was a pool of such scholars, some ejected from their existing posts and all university educated. The passing of the years diminished this resource and other means had to be found.

The passing of the 'Toleration Act' in 1689 enabled academies to emerge from the shadows, although academies and schools kept by Dissenters again became imperilled by the Schism Act towards the end of the reign of Queen Anne. Her death marked the end of attempts to pass laws against religious dissent, although the English universities and many public offices remained closed to non-Anglicans. The history of academies becomes clearer, although they remain personal to their founders rather than continuing institutions. A very full account of the academy at Findern and Derby (ca 1712–54) has been compiled by Dr David Wykes.[9] It is known to have been in existence already in 1712 when the tutor Thomas Hill was prosecuted for keeping a school in Derby. By the time of Hill's death in 1720 it was at Findern, some five miles to the south-west, and was taken over by Ebenezer Latham and Samuel Brentnall, a former student. Brentnall subsequently ministered from his own house, Oslaston Hall, west of Derby, and after a malicious prosecution, at Duffield, north of the town, in the household of the Cope family. Latham ran the academy for many years, combining it with a ministry in Derby towards the end of his life. He was reckoned a good biblical scholar; he also studied natural philosophy (science), mathematics and astronomy. The Presbyterian Fund Board made a grant to him for the purchase of apparatus for conducting experiments. Latin remained fundamental to the curriculum. Ministerial candidates during the Commonwealth period had been expected to defend a thesis in Latin and this tradition continued, along with an expectation that they should have some competence in Greek and Hebrew as well. Most of them served Presbyterian meetings but some conformed and took Anglican livings and at least one, John Bennet, became a prominent Methodist preacher. The lay students included Thomas Bentley, partner of Josiah Wedgwood. David Wykes' assessment is that Findern was the most important academy in the English Midlands in the first half of the eighteenth century, to be succeeded in eminence by the later academy of Philip Doddridge at Northampton. In his last years in Derby, Latham had fewer students and on his death in 1754 the academy closed. The impact of such an academy is difficult to assess, since its students scattered into different places and occupations. However, it is entirely reasonable to trace Latham's interests into the next generation, as represented by Joseph

Priestley, who knew some of the former students, and the Lunar Society. The same pattern of an academy associated with a local pastorate is to be found beyond Findern and Northampton. The Bristol Baptist Academy was run in association with the Broadmead church and, unlike Findern, accepted only candidates for ministry. The curriculum was dominated by theological and classical studies.

a. Funding the Academies

The tutor who kept an academy had two main sources of funding. The first was from the fees paid by students. These were the lay students, sons of gentry sympathetic to Dissent. The second was from ministerial students whose fees were met by sponsors. The sponsor might be a private individual. However, from the first Dissenters gathered common funds to sponsor ministerial students and poor ministers. The holders of such funds became influential by exercising judgement about which academies should be supported. The Presbyterian Fund supported tutors moving towards Arianism and Rational Dissent. Those who wished to retain the old Calvinist orthodoxies joined in such bodies as the King's Head Society, named after the inn where it first met. The Coward Trust, established by the will of William Coward (1647/48–1738), a London merchant and Dissenter, favoured academies of varying schools of thought until settling for trinitarian orthodoxy in the early nineteenth century.[10] The Bristol merchant Edward Terrill (1634–85), a wealthy scrivener involved in the sugar trade between Bristol and the West Indies and a member of Broadmead Baptist Church, Bristol, provided the basic endowment for the academy there by a deed of gift made in his will of 1679, supplemented by other endowments from wealthy Baptists.

b. The Academies and the Evangelical Revival

As the century went on the Evangelical Revival and the rise of Methodism created a new strand of academy. William Bull at Newport Pagnell, with the encouragement of his friend John Newton, opened an academy in 1783 whose object was to train effective preachers. The original curriculum was devised with advice from Newton, whose Plan of Academical Preparation for the Ministry describes an ideal evangelical and non-denominational education, designed to attract evangelical subscribers. It emphasized biblical studies and excluded the systematic study of doctrine, rhetoric and science. The students preached in the surrounding countryside. The London banker John Thornton, friend of Newton, underwrote the costs. It was assumed that the benefits would be enjoyed by the Church of England as well as by Dissenters. In practice it had become a college for Congregationalists by the time it closed in 1850. A yet more radical approach was taken by the Countess of Huntingdon in 1768, when she founded her college at Trevecka, near Talgarth in the south Wales countryside. She avoided the model of the Dissenting Academy and called her modest establishment a college. Itinerant preaching was part of the duty of her students, not just locally, but across England and into Ireland. She challenged students to go to Savannah and even Sumatra. She was a reluctant Dissenter from the Church of England, rather taking the view that it had left her more than she had left it. However, her college, which moved to Cheshunt in Hertfordshire and eventually to Cambridge, became a Dissenting institution.[11] The Evangelical Revival generally strengthened those academies devoted to preparing ministers to serve the growing number of Baptist and Congregational churches. Those without the backing of a rich patron or trust relied on subscriptions for their income. After the death of the Countess of Huntingdon a trust took over the funding of her college.

The Bristol Education Society was formed in 1770 to gather subscriptions and donations to supplement the endowment of the Baptist academy. Annual reports of such bodies were produced, directed towards the subscribers, and providing an apologia for ministerial education to the evangelical constituency, which rated personal conviction the *sine qua non* for ministry, rather than scholarship. The academies tried to avoid doctrinal controversy in order to protect their reputation. By the late nineteenth century their alumni were preachers and literary figures and they had ceased to produce leading scientists. The founding of new universities, beginning in London, offered Dissenters new opportunities in the arts and sciences. The old academies became colleges which were effectively seminaries for ministerial formation. Where they pursued theological studies to graduate status they looked to the new universities for partnership or validation, or required their students to take a Scottish degree.

IV. Elementary Education

A boy who had studied under Samuel Ogden was fully prepared for entry to an eighteenth-century academy. The opportunities for such study were limited by economic and social circumstances. The general provision of elementary education in England and Wales during the eighteenth century was haphazard. Parish schools were widely promoted in Presbyterian Scotland but were dependent on local circumstances elsewhere. Parents with money could secure an education for their children, but did not necessarily do so. People who made their mark on legal documents of the period came from among the more prosperous tradesmen as well as the poor. There were charity schools and dame schools for the very young but literacy, like manners, was usually accessed through the home. Although by no means typical of Dissenters in his later life, we do know something of the education of William Blake, whose father was a hosier in Broad Street, London. All his biographers are agreed that Blake was steeped in the Bible in his upbringing by Nonconformist parents. He always gave thanks in later life that he never attended school, where pupils were routinely beaten, and he picked up his education as he went along, encouraged by his parents. His older brother was brought up to run the family business, and did so successfully. William's love of art was cultivated by his parents, and offered him a way of making a living other than the hosiery trade. He subsequently became an engraver.[12] The example of Blake prompts the thought that Dissenters were especially likely to be autodidacts. An ever more rarefied example is Michael Faraday, brought up in a Sandemanian family, who never attended school, yet became a distinguished scientist. Blake and Faraday are not examples of what all Dissenters became, but what we know of their upbringing provides insight into the lives of their many unsung contemporaries.

Dissenters might also take the lead in establishing charity schools. One example is the Orphan Working School. On 10 May 1758, a group of 'city men and men of business', under the leadership of the Revd Edward Pickard, a Presbyterian minister, met at the George Tavern, Ironmonger Lane, in the City of London, to establish a Charitable Foundation for orphans. The object was to provide them with a basic education as a preparation to take up apprenticeships. A house was leased in rural Hoxton and the first pupils, aged from six to nine, admitted in 1760. From 1761 a partner school for girls was added. The venture prospered and moved to purpose-built premises on the City Road in London in 1774. Eventually in 1847 it moved to splendid premises at Maitland Park, Haverstock Hill, and enjoyed royal patronage. William Wilberforce was a supporter, indicating this was a cooperative venture between Dissenters and evangelical Anglicans. Admissions were not restricted to London children. This is evident in the case of James Gawthorn (1775–1857), whose family was associated with Doddridge's church in Northampton and who was admitted soon after the death of his father in 1779.[13]

At the other end of the scale a small chapel might provide a room for its minister to offer schooling to local children. There might be a small charge for this. In 1791 the Independents in Keld, Upper Swaledale in Yorkshire, called the preacher Edward Stillman to be their minister. Once a chapel and an adjoining room had been built he opened a school for local children. The schoolroom was rebuilt in 1842, the minister continuing to be the school master until the various educational changes brought in qualified teachers and assistants. Like many rural schools it became absorbed by national provision, although the local congregation still retained trusteeship. The school was finally closed in 1972, when the number of children in the village no longer justified a separate school. Although they may not have had so long a history the story exemplifies the many local initiatives among Congregational and Baptist congregations.[14]

By the late eighteenth century the limitations of domestic education and individual initiative were becoming obvious. The Industrial Revolution demanded new patterns of knowledge and skill in the working population and the gathering of people in towns and cities created concentrations of children on a scale not seen before. The same phenomenon is found in the developing world today. The rural poor move to cities in search of an enhanced income. They live in crowded conditions in the urban margins and their children are left to roam the streets or be taken up as cheap labour. Only a small proportion of these children are orphans; most have parents too busy to care for them during the day. Just as NGOs and individuals respond to their needs in the modern world so there were charitable instincts at work in the late eighteenth and early nineteenth centuries. These were not distinctively Nonconformist, although their disestablished status left more room for innovation and flexibility in responding to need.

V. The Evangelical Revival and Popular Learning

The Sunday School movement was popularized by Robert Raikes, an Anglican and proprietor of a Gloucester newspaper, but was largely interdenominational in its origins. It was a charitable work among the poor; the argument was that the idle children who were free from work on Sunday should be given the opportunity to learn rather than roam the streets. The people offering this learning were from the pious middle classes and so the literacy was based on the Bible; there was a break in the school day to attend public worship, but this was not primarily a religious exercise. Many of the original Sunday Schools employed paid teachers. The middle-class sponsors acted as inspectors and visitors. Religion sometimes got in the way of the good educational intentions as arguments developed along sabbatarian lines. Was it right to teach practical skills such as writing and arithmetic on the Lord's Day? These arguments were especially powerful among Nonconformists, who had inherited a sabbatarian tradition. However, Dissenters were enthusiastic collaborators in local non-denominational societies which promoted Sunday Schools and from one of these, founded at the Surrey Chapel in Southwark, the National Sunday School Union traced its origins. The prime mover of the Surrey Chapel Sunday School Union was William Brodie Gurney, a Baptist, active in various forms of social improvement.[15]

The limitations of Sunday Schools in meeting the need for popular education were evident, even at the time. The educational needs of those families who could not meet the cost themselves could only be addressed by charitable means. Although Adam Smith had argued that it was in the economic interest of the state to subsidize the education of the poor there was no general acceptance of such a proposal at the turn of the eighteenth and nineteenth centuries. The idea that education was the province of voluntary societies of charitable persons persisted for decades. Particularly among Dissenters there was a fear that state control would follow state funding and that such control would favour the Established Church. The limits of charitable funds were obvious. A single teacher could only teach so many children at one time. Finding teachers for the large numbers of unschooled children was prohibitively expensive. The problem was addressed by devising new forms of education. Andrew Bell in Madras and Joseph Lancaster in London both devised systems which utilized senior pupils as monitors to supplement the work of a single teacher and increase the classroom population. In his prime Lancaster boasted that the only limitation on the number of pupils to be taught was the size of the schoolroom.

Two societies were formed around these educational theories. The National Society was exclusively Anglican and favoured Bell's Madras system. The British and Foreign School Society brought Dissenters and Low Church Anglicans together around Lancaster's methods. On 22 January 1808 Lancaster met with William Corston and Joseph Fox to consider how his pioneering school at Borough Road in Southwark might be continued, for it was burdened with debt. Corston was a Moravian while Fox was a Baptist, a surgeon-dentist at Guy's hospital and an enthusiast for vaccination, which became a subsidiary concern of the Society. Later in the year two rich Quakers joined the committee. One was the manufacturing chemist William Allen, a friend of Fox. The other was Joseph Foster, a banker. Corston was a City figure, the owner of a large hat-making business, and was the person who introduced Lancaster to the royal family, to whom he was a supplier. Fox had capital of his own, which he brought into the Society, along with his enthusiasm for vaccination.[16] However, it was with the advent of two wealthy Quakers in July of 1808 that the new Society began to have hopes of survival and growth. William Allen took over from Corston as Treasurer, taking care of the debts.

Lancaster himself was a Quaker, although it is not obvious that this was always the case. He is known to have had aspirations, as a teenager, to be a missionary, and it has recently been discovered that he applied for admission to Cheshunt College for ministerial training in 1794 but was turned down.[17]

He finally made his mark as a schoolmaster, innovative and controversial, at a school he founded among the poor children of Southwark, on the Borough Road. He had an uneasy relationship with the Society formed to promote his ideas but the essentials remained the same. British Schools, as they were generally known, were non-denominational and used monitors to maximize their capacity. A Lancastrian schoolroom had a raked floor and lines of benches, the weakest pupils being at the front, where they learnt the alphabet. Only when progress in writing and spelling had been made in the first few rows did pupils move on to arithmetic. Silence reigned in the schoolroom. A monitor would correct the work of the pupils on his row (the first schools set up were for boys), but not speak to them. At the side of the school room hung charts which were substitutes for textbooks. A row of pupils would be led out by their monitor to gather around a chart in a semi-circle. Each pupil was challenged in turn to perform a simple task, such as spelling, beginning with the first boy. Failure led to demotion within the semi-circle. Pupils could earn tokens for good work and good behaviour, which were traded in against simple toys which hung from the ceiling. Bad behaviour resulted in demerit marks and public humiliation. The ultimate punishment was to be hoisted to the ceiling in a wicker basket and left there in great discomfort. The aim of the school was to give basic skills in literacy and numeracy, along with a good diet, cleanliness and social conformity. This was not the education which a Dissenting minister or merchant would wish for his own children. It was a kind of industrialized schooling for an industrial age.

The non-denominational principle in education was popular with Dissenters, especially with those referred to as the 'New Dissenters', who formed Independent churches in the wake of the Evangelical Revival, rather than being members of congregations which had existed since 1662. They wished to exist outside the Established Church in order to have freedom of action, even if their doctrinal convictions sat easily with the Thirty-Nine Articles. Non-denominational organizations enabled them to cooperate with Low Church Anglicans, such as Wilberforce. They wore the contempt of High Churchmen as a badge of pride. Among the institutions they set up by way of alternative provision to that of the Church of England were schools. Some of these were attached to congregations, as we have seen in the example of Keld. Such schools tended to look to the British and Foreign School Society for teacher training and classroom resources. The middle-class Dissenters looked for more than this; they wanted an alternative to proprietary schools run by Anglicans and the ancient endowed grammar-schools, which were also in Anglican hands. This was part of a general campaign to show that the voluntary association of Christians was preferable to a religious establishment which was perpetuated by historic endowments and church taxes.

VI. Independent Schools

In 1807 the Protestant Dissenters Grammar School was formed, more familiarly known by its name of Mill Hill School, from its site north of London. It aimed to provide a non-denominational boarding school where Dissenters might feel at home and offered reduced rates for the sons of Baptist and Congregational ministers as well as a few free scholarships. By the middle of the nineteenth century it was describing itself as a public school for Free Churchmen. In 1811 a specifically Congregational school was also formed in London, with the aim of providing a boarding education for the sons of Congregational ministers, many of whom had stipends well below the level at which they might afford school fees. This school secured its own premises in Lewisham in 1815 and opened a new site at Caterham in 1890. By then it had broadened its intake, while remaining under Congregational influence. The present independent school at Caterham is the result of a merger between this and the Eothen School for Girls. From 1809 onwards attempts were made to run a Yorkshire Protestant Dissenters Grammar School at Silcoates, near Wakefield. This was an attempt to replicate for northern England what had been done in the south. After two false starts the school was refounded in 1831 with an aim of providing education for the sons of ministers, a charitable object which increased the subscription base essential for the school to thrive. This wish to serve the children of ministers and missionaries, who now constituted a substantial body of people, lay behind schools founded in Walthamstow, in 1838 for girls and in 1842 for boys. Baptists and Congregationalists joined in these ventures. The boys' school subsequently moved to Eltham.

More deliberate attempts to mimic the emerging public school system, with an eye to Eton, Harrow and Rugby, were the West of England Dissenters Proprietary School founded at Taunton in 1847 and the Midland Counties Proprietary School at Tettenhall in 1863. Both these schools were promoted by strong local churches. In the case of Tettenhall, the deacons of Queen Street Congregational Church in Wolverhampton took the lead. They wanted to have a school suitable for evangelical Nonconformists, especially Baptists and Congregationalists. Both these schools widened their objectives and their constituencies in the twentieth century. Taunton was provided with a fine chapel, whereas the founders had expected pupils to be taken to local places of worship. In the case of all the schools mentioned the liberal nature of their founding trusts or companies enabled them to transform as institutions to meet the needs of particular times. Historically they always suffered from a lack of general support among the local churches across England. Their immediate locality and the rich merchants within the denominations were their principal contributors. Over time the Baptist and Congregational denominations became cooler towards private education. One might suspect that even in the nineteenth century a local church at a distance from one of these schools might have given preference to its own local voluntary school projects. In the late twentieth century a smaller proportion of a declining cohort of ministers with children looked to independent boarding education as a first choice.[18]

The role of Dissenters in girls' education extended beyond Walthamstow. Gender prejudices restricted the opportunities for girls to go to school and the subjects they were offered there. This did not go uncontested by women such as Mary Woolstonecraft, whose radical circle included people like Coleridge and Hazlitt, who had backgrounds in Unitarianism. The bulk of Dissenters took longer to embrace the rights of women to a broader education. It needed the advocacy of ministers to commend it. Lectures given in the 1830s by Benjamin Parsons, Congregational minister of Ebley in Gloucestershire, were published as *The Mental and Moral Dignity of Women* in 1842 and *Education: The Birthright of Every Human Being* in 1845. Parsons argued that mathematics and science were essential parts of any woman's education and that singing and languages should not be seen as mere accomplishments but as part of a total education in Truth. He believed that the woman's crucial role in the family and society more than justified a full and rounded education, quite apart from his argument in principle.[19] It was in this spirit that Milton Mount School at Gravesend, for the education of the daughters of ministers, was opened in 1873. The deacons of Richmond Hill Congregational Church, Bournemouth, took offence when the local girls' grammar school fell entirely into Anglican hands and founded an alternative Wentworth School for Girls in 1899. This was a deliberate attempt to secure 'a Mill Hill for girls' and when local circumstances altered in 1918, so that the town's provision became acceptable once more, the school enlarged its boarding capacity to ensure its continuance. Unlike Taunton, the girls attended Richmond Hill church services of worship through most of the twentieth century.

VII. The Politics of Education

Independent boarding education was a small, though important, part of the Dissenting scene. Popular education, often on Lancaster's scheme, was the main preoccupation of the Dissenting denominations. It became increasingly politicized as the nineteenth century progressed, being one factor in the rivalry between Church and Dissent, sometimes played out in bitter local feuds. The national players were the British and Foreign School Society, non-denominational but in competition with the National Society of the Church of England; the new denominational bodies formed to further the interests of Dissenters, especially the Baptist Union and the Congregational Union; and the Dissenting Deputies, the historic body which represented Dissenters' interests to the government.

The British and Foreign School Society was characterized by a belief in voluntarism and a commitment to non-denominational education. Joseph Lancaster believed that his schools should accept all children, but he was not wedded to the non-denominational principle. As his ideas spread around Europe he often found himself working with Roman Catholics. He was never able to work under the direction of others or to be answerable for his expenditure and this led to a breach with the Society in 1812. The Rules adopted then still tried to represent Lancaster's openness: 'No catechism or peculiar religious tenets shall be taught in the schools, but every child shall be enjoined to attend regularly the place of worship to which its parents belong.'[20] In practice, the chosen extracts from scripture, which made up the reading scheme, conveyed an evangelical Protestant ethos. The Rules also represent the delicate political balance in the committee between men like James Fox, with avowedly missionary intentions, and Francis Place, motivated by the utilitarian thinking he shared with John Stuart Mill and Jeremy Bentham. Place failed to get the committee to modify the content of the reading scheme or to run the schools and training institutions on more economic principles and he eventually withdrew.

The Society continued to try and define an inclusive and non-denominational approach to education, not always realizing that this constituted an ideology in its own right. The first generation of the Society nailed their colours to the mast in 1838 with a declaration that national education should be inclusive, 'based on the Scriptures, but positively excluding from all schools aided by Parliament the formularies of any particular church'.[21] This principle became historically associated with the Free Churches but was supported by some evangelical parts of the Church of England. The Hon. and Revd Baptist Noel, admittedly on his way out of the Church of England to become a Baptist in denomination as well as name, believed that it was possible to teach religion without denominational bias.[22] Lord John Russell, a long-time supporter of both the Society and the rights of Dissenters, expressed the view that the scriptures must be taught in school in order to provide a guide to conduct. He opposed the view that, in order to cut the Gordian knot of denominationalism, all state-supported schools should be secular. He foresaw that many children would not receive any religious instruction and feared that they would be left with no moral compass.[23] The radicals continued to oppose this approach. Richard Cobden based his opposition to non-denominational religious education on the injustice this did to Roman Catholics and Jews. They would contribute to the provision of education without deriving benefit from it. He was prepared to allow the

Bible into schools on the basis of local option, without note or comment, when Roman Catholics were present, but no other books favouring the doctrines of any Christian sect.[24]

In 1843, the question of non-denominational education became acute in a dispute over the education clauses of Sir William Graham's Factory Bill. Among the regulations proposed to protect children who worked in factories were clauses requiring them to have a minimal education. This would require them to produce a certificate to show they attended school. Where schools did not exist there was provision for local taxation to fund one. The schedules of schools virtually excluded those provided by Dissenters and a great many private ones. The new provision of schools lay in the hands of the Church of England and allowed for Roman Catholic schools too. Dissenters were already agitating about civil disabilities. These clauses ignited fierce opposition. The ghosts of Latimer and Ridley, burnt for their religion, and John Hampden, unjustly taxed, were invoked at large public meetings. Even the resolutions of the Congregational Union of England and Wales were belligerent.

> RESOLUTIONS OF THE CONGREGATIONAL UNION ON THE FACTORIES' EDUCATION BILL.
>
> At a Meeting of the Committee of the Congregational Union of England and Wales, held on Tuesday, the 4th of April, B. Hanbury, Esq. in the chair, the following resolutions were unanimously adopted, upon consideration of a Bill now before Parliament, entitled, 'A Bill for Regulating the Employment of Children and Young Persons in Factories, and for the Better Education of Children in Factory Districts.'
>
> That the Members of this Committee have brought to the consideration of this Bill all the sentiments and solicitudes of most sincere friends of its professed object, – the religious education of the young, – yet they cannot but regard the provisions of this measure with deep alarm, and strong disapprobation.
>
> First. As Protestant Dissenters – Because in respect to the education of the people, the Bill places all Dissenters under heavy disadvantages. It will be impossible that a Dissenter should be a Teacher, and all but impossible that a Dissenter should ever be a Trustee of any school established by the act; while should Dissenters find themselves unjustly compelled by this exclusive scheme to establish separate schools at their own cost, after paying the tax levied for the government schools, even then education in such schools will not form a legal qualification for factory employment, unless they shall be reported by inspectors, not likely to regard them with favour, to be 'efficiently conducted'.

> Second. As Friends of British Freedom – They object to the enormous increase of irresponsible church power conferred under this Act, at a time when such power is most dangerous.
>
> Third. As Evangelical Christians – They deprecate, especially in these days of Anti-Protestant doctrine and feeling, in the Church of England, the extended and compulsory use, in schools sustained by general taxation, of that most erroneous formulary, the Church Catechism, in which the doctrine of sacramental religion and salvation is so plainly taught.
>
> Fourth. As sincere Friends of Education – They strongly protest against the education of the people being placed so exclusively under the control of the clergy, a body of men long the avowed opponents of general education, and never, till this time, its advocates and supporters.
>
> Fifth. As Friends of the Poor, especially of the Dissenting Poor – They object to the education of their children being made a matter of the stringent compulsion enforced by this law, – as in many cases there will be no choice of schools for their children in the power of parents, – in all cases there will be heavy penalties on parents for non-attendance of their children, – a school certificate will be made a legal qualification for factory employment, – and, in the government schools, the children of Dissenters will be compelled to learn the Church Catechism, which they cannot recite with truth, or to be registered and separated as Dissenters in the view and scorn of all the school, and of the hostile clerical trustee.
>
> Sixth. As those attached to the great principle of the British Constitution, – 'that the people shall not be taxed without their own consent.' – They decidedly object against a system worked throughout by force of law, – allowing no popular voice in the laying of the School Rate, – no suffrage of the rate-payers in the choice of the Trustees, – no control over the expenditure and application of the funds.[25]

The expressions of grievance were strong enough to lead to the clauses being dropped from the Bill, thus gaining a point of Dissenting principle at the expense of securing more education for children. Dissenters were sensitive to this criticism and determined to increase voluntary provision of schools. Strenuous attempts were made by the Congregational Union to encourage local churches to raise funds for school provision. This created tension between the denominations and the British and Foreign School Society, which also needed to raise funds for its national work as well as its local schools. The Society trained teachers and provided curriculum material and guidance, all of which were beneficial, if not essential, to the running of local voluntary schools. The Baptist Union made no attempt to urge local congregations to start schools but called upon them to back the British and Foreign School Society.[26] The thirty-five Baptist day-schools of 1843 were augmented by only thirty-eight more in 1844.[27]

From 1732 the interests of Dissenters in London, Baptist, Independent, Presbyterian and Unitarian, were promoted by a Board of Deputies. Because London was the seat of parliament this body spoke for Dissenting interests in general. The usefulness of the Dissenting Deputies in 1843 was to provide a meeting place for the denominations, where notes could be compared and strategies planned. In the years leading up to 1843 they had not been dogmatically voluntarist in their approach and had taken part in the negotiations which led to government grants being extended to the National Society and the British and Foreign School Society for the opening of schools in areas with no provision. The Deputies were driven to outright opposition of Graham's Bill by the naked assertion of the need for Church of England control over the extended system of national education.[28] A United Conference was organized by the Deputies, which brought in Methodist and Quaker representatives. The committee of this Conference met daily for ten weeks, corresponding with local churches and individuals and gathering thousands of names in petitions. Graham first tried to revise the clauses and make a stand there, but finally saw that the opposition was so strong it would be better to withdraw completely. The opposition of Wesleyan Methodism alongside old Dissent was probably decisive. The other factor was the Puseyite controversy, which weakened the resolve of evangelical Anglicans to ride out the storm.

The increases in voluntary schools after 1843 did not match the growing need for popular education. It was, however, the starting point for subsequent educational debates. There was broad agreement on the need to extend elementary education. By 1870, the need for state support out of taxation was generally recognized. The points of difficulty for Nonconformists were always the nature of religious education in school and the denominational management. The prominent Congregationalist R. W. Dale was chairman of the Congregational Union of England and Wales in 1870. With Joseph Chamberlain, his Unitarian ally in Birmingham, Dale opposed the dual system proposed in the 1870 Act in an effort to meet the objections of Nonconformists. He and his followers believed it was better to keep religion out of state schools than allow the state to prescribe in matters of religion. This caused a rift in the opposition and is one of the reasons a Liberal government, elected with Nonconformist support, failed to deliver a more sympathetic act. The Church of England knew exactly what it wanted. The majority of Nonconformists, who did not take Dale's view, were fatally compromised by their past acceptance of government money for their schools on condition they gave religious instruction based on the Bible in the 'Authorized Version'. This was tantamount to accepting state prescription in matters of religion.

The dual system, which Nonconformists had to accept, gave power to school boards to set up new schools without specifying that they should be non-denominational. The compromise was a clause introduced by William Cowper-Temple, giving parents the right to withdraw their children from religious education lessons on the grounds of conscience and banning the use of catechisms or religious formularies distinctive of any particular denomination. This principle has been preserved in legislation until the present day, except for an easing of the law in respect to distinctive religious opinions in order to allow comparison and discussion. Dale and his Birmingham friends tried to run the city's schools with a total exclusion of religious teaching, which the Act allowed, but this was not popular and they eventually moved to a Bible-based religious curriculum. School Board elections, especially in the early years, were keenly contested and where an approved list of Anglican candidates was offered local Nonconformists made every effort to see they were defeated. The reality of school provision in areas of great need tended to take priority over religious scruples. When it was proposed in 1902 to replace the school boards with local authority control Nonconformists were loud in defence of the system they had approached so warily thirty years before.

What grieved them most was the generous provision for running church schools with a public subsidy. This would benefit Anglicans the most, but also gave benefits to Roman Catholics. Opposition was not only vocal but also took the form of passive resistance to paying the local rate which would go towards schools. 'Rome on the rates' was the slogan of the protesters. Goods were distrained and some people gaoled for refusing to pay: 190 people went to prison in 1907 alone. These numbers were made up of sixty Primitive Methodists, forty-eight Baptists, forty Congregationalists, fifteen Wesleyans and twenty-five from smaller denominations.[29] This was the first major use of passive resistance in the twentieth century; the tactic was developed further by Mahatma Gandhi, who was familiar with it from his conversations with Nonconformists while in England and as a result of his experiences in South Africa in 1893–94. This campaign coincided with the emergence of a greater 'Free Church' consciousness; Methodists joined with the old Dissenters to create Free Church institutions in contradistinction to the Establishment. Two long-term consequences of the 1902 Act for Nonconformists in general were the creation of places for Free Church nominees on local education committees and the abandonment of school management by the British and Foreign School Society, which concentrated on its role as a provider of teacher training.

The 1944 and 1988 Education Acts secured rights for 'other denominations' to play a role in religious education, along with the Church of England (but not the Church in Wales), teachers' and local authority representatives. This grouped Nonconformists with Roman Catholics and, eventually, other major world faiths. By 2012 the Free Church places on committees had been abolished and the role of local education authorities in religious education diminished. The institutional involvement of the original Dissenting denominations in national provision of schooling was virtually at an end.

VIII. Adult and Continuing Education

Something of a similar change was apparent in adult education. Just as all denominations had joined in school provision so they offered various forms of evening classes during the nineteenth and early twentieth centuries. Some of this was through sponsorship of organizations such as Mechanics Institutes and YMCAs; some of it was through societies offering programmes of speakers and classes on church premises. After the 1870 Education Act, the role of Sunday Schools was affected by the expansion of elementary education to all children. This changed the Sunday School curriculum towards Christian formation rather than the acquisition of skills, and also created an expectation among young people that they should leave Sunday School when they left school, at the beginning of their teens. Adult education was one answer to this, along with the development of sport as a means of keeping young people within the ambit of churches.[30] The need for more educational sophistication in the Sunday School approach was recognized among the Free Churches, who supported the opening of Westhill College in 1912 at Selly Oak, in Birmingham, to improve the training of Sunday School teachers.[31] It had been intended to style it the National Training Institute for Sunday School Workers but after failing to secure Anglican cooperation in the venture the Free Church sponsors decided to drop the term 'National'. Westhill College eventually developed a teacher training course for schools and a Community Work course before being taken over by the University of Birmingham in 2002. Until the end it sponsored a course in church education which attracted students from a worldwide constituency. It was perhaps this broad agenda which influenced one Westhill principal, Basil Yeaxlee (1930–35), to develop the influential concept of 'life-long' education and another, H. A. (Bert) Hamilton (1945–54), to be a powerful advocate of 'Family Church' as an all-age approach to worship and learning.

Individual Nonconformists played important roles in the development of interdenominational and ecumenical organizations for the promotion of education. The Institute of Christian Education at Home and Abroad promoted best educational practice for schools sponsored by missionary societies around the world. The Student Christian Movement in Schools offered study material for school groups and summer camps for pupils. These two organizations combined to create the Christian Education Movement, which in 2000 combined with the National Christian Education Council, formerly the National Sunday School Union, to form the charity Christian Education. People such as John Sutcliffe, Simon Oxley and Donald Hilton all played key roles in this process. In the wider world of academic education Professors Roy Niblet and John Hull were enormously influential.

IX. Conclusion

The distinctiveness of the Nonconformist contribution to education diminished over the course of the twentieth century. As they were drawn into the establishment by the provision of schools and colleges and adopted conventional approaches the new educational dissenters came from all denominations and none. Changes in university education meant that the Church of England moved to a seminarian approach for the education of its clergy. With the growth of ecumenical cooperation the surviving Nonconformist theological colleges established federal relationships and even union with the old enemy. All Christians were becoming dissenting minorities in a society dominated by secular values. These secular values influenced the expectations of education. Not even religious people were ready to see the sharing of knowledge as an extension of *koinonia*. Education was seen as essential for World Development but not reckoned to be a certain route to universal peace. Learning was much more closely related to employment prospects than to the need to uncover truth. Those who dissented from such views were not identified by religious denomination. Milton is not remembered for his educational ideas; Comenius and Hartlib are known only to a few specialist historians. The opponents of faith schools are led by humanists, opposed and supported by Christians across the denominations. The 1662 Ejectment left its mark on the educational history of England and Wales, as did the Evangelical Revival, but insofar as there are competing sects in contemporary education they are not characterized by their loyalty to Church or Dissent as once they were.

Notes

1 Details of Samuel Hartlib's life may be found in an extended entry by M. Greengrass in *Oxford Dictionary of National Biography* (hereafter *ODNB*; Oxford: Oxford University Press, 2004) and G. H. Turnbull, *Samuel Hartlib: A Sketch of His Life and His Relations to J. A. Comenius* (London: Oxford University Press, 1920).

2 *ODNB*.
3 *The Life and Death of that Excellent Minister of Christ Mr Joseph Alleine* [by Theodosia Alleine, his widow] (London, 1672).
4 Information about Ogden's school and a collection of anecdotes and observations by Zachary Merrill, Bodleian Library, Rawlinson, D. 1120.344.
5 Peter Birch (ca 1652–1710), a High Churchman, in spite of his Presbyterian upbringing.
6 John Wallis (1616–1703), professor of geometry at Oxford.
7 Robert Pawling, Whig politician in Oxford and then controller of the Stamp Office, Lincoln's Inn, friend of Locke and a Nonconformist.
8 Details of this and other academies are to be found on the website of the Centre for Dissenting Studies, run jointly by Queen Mary's College and Dr Williams's Trust: http//dissacad.english.qmul.ac.uk.
9 This account is to be found on the website mentioned in note 8.
10 See article on William Coward by J. H. Thompson in *ODNB*.
11 Stephen Orchard, 'Selina, Countess of Huntingdon', *The Journal of the United Reformed Church History Society*, 8/2 (2008), pp. 77–90.
12 Peter Ackroyd, *William Blake* (London: Sinclair-Stevenson, 1995), pp. 22–23.
13 Stephen Orchard, 'James Gawthorn and Derbyshire Congregationalism', *The Journal of the United Reformed Church History Society*, 9/1 (2012), pp. 3–21.
14 K. W. Wadsworth, 'Keld Congregational School', *The Journal United Reformed Church History Society*, 1 (1973), pp. 118–21.
15 Philip B. Cliff, *Rise and Development of the Sunday School Movement in England: 1780–1980* (Birmingham: National Christian Education Council, 1986), p. 74.
16 *ODNB*. Fox had worked with Jenner on inoculation. When Fox died Brougham told the House of Commons that he had been the saviour of the Lancastrian system.
17 E. Welch, *Cheshunt College: The Early Years: A Selection of Records* (Rickmansworth: Hertfordshire Record Society, 1990), p. 78.
18 For a survey of the history of Congregational schools, their influence and financing, see A. Argent, 'Nursed by the Church', *The Journal United Reformed Church History Society*, 6 (1998), pp. 72–97.
19 See Clyde Binfield, *Belmont's Portias: Victorian Nonconformists and Middle-Class Education for Girls* (London: Dr Williams's Trust, 1981), p. 3.
20 H. B. Binns, *A Century of Education* (London, J. M. Dent & Co., 1908), p. 73. Rules as adopted in 1814.
21 Ibid., p. 128.
22 Ibid., p. 149.
23 Ibid., p. 150.
24 Ibid., p. 156.
25 *Congregational Year Book* (1844).
26 John H. Y. Briggs, *English Baptists of the Nineteenth Century* (Didcot: Baptist Historical Society, 1994), p. 350.
27 Ibid., p. 352.
28 B. L. Manning, *The Protestant Dissenting Deputies*, ed. O. Greenwood (Cambridge: Cambridge University Press, 1952), p. 342.
29 D. W. Bebbington, *The Nonconformist Conscience: Chapel and Politics, 1870–1914* (London: G. Allen & Unwin, 1981), p. 147, drawing on contemporary reports in *The Christian World*.
30 See especially, Hugh Macleod, 'Sport and the English Sunday School', in Stephen Orchard and John H. Y. Briggs (eds), *The Sunday School Movement: Studies in the*

Growth and Decline of the Sunday Schools (Milton Keynes: Paternoster, 2007), pp. 109–23.

31 Jack Priestley, 'The Lumber Merchant and the Chocolate King: The contributions of George Hamilton Archibald and George Cadbury to the Sunday School Movement in England and Wales', in Orchard and Briggs (eds), *The Sunday School Movement*, pp. 124–41.

16 Nonconformity and Culture

Timothy Whelan

Matthew Arnold (1822–88), the Victorian literary and social critic, experienced Nonconformist culture first-hand, spending some twenty years as a school inspector, primarily among Methodist and other Nonconformist schools. Though he recognized the literary artistry of John Milton (1608–74), John Bunyan (1628–88), Daniel Defoe (ca 1660–1731) and Isaac Watts (1674–1748), Arnold nevertheless believed that Nonconformists, in general, were moral, social and intellectual 'Philistines', devoid of 'sweetness and light', culturally deficient and replete with religious bigotry, political uncharitableness and mental poverty. To Arnold, Nonconformist culture was marked by 'jealousy of the Establishment, disputes, tea meetings, openings of chapels, [and] sermons'[1] – not completely inaccurate, but considering the achievements of Nonconformist culture between 1650 and 1850, extremely shortsighted. As William H. Dawson argued at the beginning of the twentieth century, Arnold looked at Nonconformists with 'a certain spirit of curiosity and wonderment, as though a Dissenter were a social oddity of which he, for his part, did not quite know what to make'.[2] Even Dawson was not entirely free of his own prejudices, observing that Nonconformity, in its detachment from the Established Church, had lost touch with

> the nation's larger life. By shutting itself within the walls of a self-contained sectarianism its entire conception of things was dwarfed, its sense of proportion was distorted; its own concerns became for it all-important . . . Hence proceeded the stunted life, the limited outlook, the partial view of things, which to Arnold as a cultured man of the world, who strove 'to see life truly and to see it whole', were so sore an offence, so profound a regret.[3]

Henry Crabb Robinson (1775–1867), the prolific nineteenth-century Unitarian diarist, was, like Arnold, a 'cultured man of the world'. He was reading Arnold when he made his last entry to his diary on 31 January 1867, his death occurring during the same year that Arnold's essays began to appear in the *Cornhill*

Magazine, essays that later formed the basis of *Culture and Anarchy* (1869). Robinson's life as a Nonconformist, however, bears little resemblance to Dawson's description of a 'dwarfed', 'distorted', or 'stunted life'. To Robinson, the creative arts constantly intersected with his social activities; he never felt that his Nonconformity excluded him from enjoying art and literature, engaging in philosophical speculation, or critiquing nearly every writer of note in the first half of the nineteenth century. Robinson was an avid reader (from classical texts to contemporary English and European literature), member of several literary and social clubs from the 1790s onward, successful journalist and lawyer, friend and correspondent of numerous Romantic writers, regular attendant at the theatre and art exhibitions, translator and critic of works of German philosophy, contributor to literary and religious periodicals, frequent traveller throughout Great Britain and Europe, advocate for rigorous collegiate education for Nonconformists (he was involved with the founding of London University in 1828 and University Hall in 1849), ardent abolitionist and supporter of effective political reform and governmental accountability, and relentless defender of the right of freedom of conscience for all Englishmen – hardly a 'partial' view of life or a failure to 'see life truly and to see it whole'.

The picture of Nonconformity created by Arnold and Dawson (though belied by the example of Robinson) underwent considerable correction in the first half of the twentieth century as a result of the work of such scholars as William Haller, Perry Miller and Geoffrey Nuttall.[4] This resurgence, however, which continued into the second half of the twentieth century, focused mainly on Nonconformist ministers and their theology (primarily seventeenth-century divines), Nonconformist denominations (Presbyterian, Independent and Baptist) and case studies of local congregations. In some instances, the isolated nature of Nonconformity and what many perceived to be its anti-cultural, anti-intellectual characteristics (Arnold's chief criticisms) were reinforced.[5] Not until the late 1970s and 1980s, however, did scholars such as J. R. Watson, Clyde Binfield, Donald Davie, Isabel Rivers, Doreen Rosman, John Morgan and N. H. Keeble begin to examine the distinct *literary* culture of Nonconformity (though often in connection with the rise of evangelicalism, which crossed all denominational lines in the late eighteenth and early nineteenth centuries), a culture that operated largely under the rubric of its own aesthetic and yet, when necessary, moved easily within the larger political, religious and social culture of England, Scotland, Wales and America.[6] Recent studies by James Bradley, Jon Mee, Paul Corby Finney, David Bebbington and Timothy Larsen, Dan White and Felicity James have further broadened our understanding of the distinctive culture of Nonconformity.[7] In fact, Arnold's despised purveyors of 'Hebraism', though clearly at odds at times with certain aspects of British culture, may have been more 'Hellenistic' than he thought.[8]

I. Nonconformity and the Theatre

Nonconformity was probably at its most 'Hebraistic' when opposing the theatre. Shakespeare's Malvolio from *Twelfth Night* has served for nearly four centuries as a popular literary representation of the irritable, priggish, killjoy Puritan, the forerunner of the Nonconformist 'social oddity' of which Dawson claimed Arnold 'did not quite know what to make'. If Malvolio had a counterpart in the real world, it might have been William Prynne (1600–69), whose *Histriomastix* (1632) depicted actors, actresses and playwrights as licentious rogues, vagabonds and scandalous women seducing their audience (which often included King Charles I and his wife Henrietta Maria) and debasing English culture through an activity Prynne believed unlawful, immoral and unscriptural. During the time of Milton and the political ascendancy of Cromwell and the Puritans, the theatres were closed for nearly two decades. For the next two centuries, Nonconformists continued to debate theatre attendance and the moral inadequacies of stage performances (though the *reading* of Shakespeare's plays, since they were mostly poetry, rarely met with disapproval).

In the second half of the eighteenth century, however, scattered voices from within the Nonconformist community began to speak more favourably of theatre attendance. Benjamin Flower (1755–1829), radical editor of the *Cambridge Intelligencer* (1793–1803), was raised a Calvinist in Edward Hitchin's Independent congregation at White Row, Spitalfields; he became an Arian in the 1780s, though he worshipped primarily in Particular Baptist churches for most of 1793–1818. He described his youthful attraction to novel-reading and the theatre in a letter to his fiancée Eliza Gould (1770–1810) (formerly a Particular Baptist from Bampton, Devon) on 30 August 1799, noting that there were 'few scenes or characters' in either that could not be found 'in real life'. 'It is this reflection', he adds, 'which has made me shew as much weakness (must I use the word) as almost any one, at the Theatre, when witnessing those affecting scenes, and impassioned representations, in which a [Sarah] *Siddons* and a [Fanny] *Kemble* have so frequently engaged and rivetted me'.[9] Just a few months before Flower's letter, Mary Steele (1753–1813) of Broughton, Hampshire, granddaughter of a Baptist minister, niece of the popular Baptist hymn writer Anne Steele (1717–78) and, like her, a gifted poet, also extolled the pleasures of the theatre and the powerful acting of Siddons. She wrote to her younger half-sister Martha (in London) on 14 May 1799:

> Of all the varied Amusements the Town affords none appear to me so rational & interesting as the Theatre that I suppose you will often visit if the Friends you are with do not disapprove it – but shall I own that to me the Pomp the Grace especially at a first view diminishes the higher

> pleasure which the Drama inspires & I should feel Mrs Siddons powers still more I think in a Scene less magnificent, but this I fancy soon goes off, external decoration may strike the Eye but comes not near the heart.[10]

Despite these examples – not to mention the life-long attraction to the theatre by Crabb Robinson[11] and the strict Sandemanian (Scotch Baptist) Michael Faraday (1791–1867),[12] or the unusual career of the dramatist turned Baptist preacher James Sheridan Knowles (1784–1862)[13] – a contentious, puritanical attitude towards the theatre continued to accompany Nonconformity well into the nineteenth century.[14] This became a matter of public debate during a controversy that erupted in 1803–4 between Richard Ryland (1747–1832), a corn-factor at 5 Great Tower Hill and member of the Independent congregation meeting in the Weigh-House, and John Clayton (1754–1843), the church's minister and estranged brother-in-law to Benjamin Flower. Clayton refused to grant to Ryland and his wife letters of transfer to W. B. Collyer's congregation in Peckham because of their attendance at the theatre (they were also guilty of card playing and dancing). A bitter pamphlet war ensued between Clayton and the Rylands, with several Nonconformist ministers and laymen contributing pamphlets as well.[15] The controversy was still simmering in 1808, provoking the following comment on theatre attendance from Sydney Smith, editor of the influential *Edinburgh Quarterly*:

> Methodists [a term Smith is using, most likely, to refer to all evangelicals, both Anglican and Nonconformists] hate pleasure and amusements; no theatre, no cards no dancing, no punchinello, no dancing dogs, no blind fiddlers; all the amusements of the rich and poor must disappear wherever these gloomy people get a footing . . . it is not only wicked to hear the licentious plays of Congreve, but wicked to hear Henry the Vth or the School for Scandal.[16]

The Ryland/Clayton controversy was emblematic of a tendency within Nonconformity that would persist well into the twentieth century (particularly so among Baptists and Methodists) in which certain social activities, such as theatre attendance, card playing and dancing, were viewed as detrimental to one's evangelical witness and a 'stumbling block' to unbelievers, a tendency that, to minds like Smith and Arnold, however, was emblematic of the inadequacy of Nonconformity's cultural character.[17]

II. Nonconformity and the Enquiring Self

Arnold's low opinion of Nonconformists, those he termed the 'every-day middle-class Philistine', was also bolstered by his dislike of their dogmatism, which he believed was the result of 'feeding and stimulating . . . [the] ordinary self' instead of 'annulling' it.[18] To Arnold, a Nonconformist was 'pleased at hearing no opinion but his own, by having all disputed points taken for granted in its own favour, by being urged to no return upon itself, no development'.[19] Arnold's comments miss the point, however, for to most Nonconformists, the 'self' that ultimately mattered was *precisely* Arnold's despised 'ordinary' self. That was the self the Nonconformist began each day with, struggled with throughout the day and retired to bed with every night. It was a self to be analysed, exposed, interrogated, humiliated and repressed (if necessary) in order to be a reflection of the 'mind of Christ' and worthy repository of 'the temple of the Holy Ghost' (1 Cor. 2.16, 6.19). It was not, as Arnold saw it, a provincial self (in a religious sense) to be annulled or 'lost in the greatness of a public body',[20] such as the Established Church. Nor was it the arrogant, ascetic self as depicted nearly a century later by Helen Corke, who argued that '[e]ighteenth- and nineteenth-century Nonconformity walled itself round with a crude individual arrogance uglier than the walls of its ugly chapels'.[21]

Without question there were some 'ugly chapels', and Nonconformists did indeed divide over doctrine: sometimes orthodox Calvinists rooted out the vestiges of Arminianism, Arianism and Socinianism in their congregations (and sometimes vice versa); at other times, Baptists and Congregationalists chose sides in the debate over the 'Modern Question' between 'moderate' evangelical Calvinism (the legacy of a group of prominent seventeenth-century Puritan divines as well as the writings of Jonathan Edwards [1703–58] of New England and Andrew Fuller [1754–1815] of Kettering), and High Calvinism (best expressed by the writings of two London Baptist ministers, John Gill, 1697–1771 and John Brine, 1703–65). 'Liberal' attitudes and a non-dogmatic approach to religion, however, were not uncommon among Nonconformists, despite claims to the contrary by those loyal to the Established Church. As Thomas Madge, one of Crabb Robinson's favorite Unitarian preachers, often said: 'Let it never be forgotten that *Christianity is not thought, but action; not a system, but a life*',[22] though Robinson also believed that Nonconformists should always exhibit 'a degree of rationality compatible with sound doctrine'.[23] The Unitarians cherished the label 'rational Christian'; orthodox Calvinists, though generally uncomfortable with that label, never considered themselves 'irrational', despite their reluctance to grant as much prominence to 'reason' as the Unitarians believed it should receive. To the orthodox (and evangelicals in general), human knowledge and worldly endeavours were perfectly acceptable provided they did not exceed their proper bounds in relation to faith and Christian character. At times some seventeenth-century Ranters exhibited behaviour many Nonconformists considered irrational, but Nonconformity as a whole was never *anti*-rational; reason had its proper place, but when elevated too highly (as the Deists and the 'rational' Dissenters were accused of doing), it tended to thwart an 'experimental' faith. Joseph Priestley, the noted Unitarian minister, scientist, political writer and biblical commentator, argued that reason was not only necessary to a proper understanding of the scriptures but that certain doctrines held by the orthodox (the virgin birth and substitutionary death of Christ, predestination and the absence of free will) were objectionable primarily because they violated human reason, the ultimate test of all religious doctrine and opinions. Priestley was the foremost scientist among Nonconformists, yet, despite his discoveries in the fields of electricity and gases, his advocacy of reason and science, much like his theology, did not always meet with the approval of the orthodox. In the late 1770s, Mrs Noah Symonds, a liberal-minded schoolmistress and wife of the Particular Baptist minister at Bampton, after having invited a gentleman to lecture to her students upon some '*Philosophical Instruments*', discovered that one member of the church believed her and the minister to be having '*Dealings with the Devil* under his Roof'. 'Those Dealings proved to be no more', the Revd Symonds later wrote in the Church Book, 'than our innocent *Explaination* [*sic*] of a few of the *Laws of Nature*',[24] a tension that would surface again with the rise of Darwinism in the mid-nineteenth century.

Crabb Robinson, though a Rational Dissenter himself, frequently examined his faith, valuing opinions other than his own and rarely taking disputed points for granted until he had vigorously sought an answer for himself, a *self* that was always in a state of 'development', despite Arnold's assertion to the contrary. 'I was very ill educated', Robinson confessed to his friend Wilhelm Benecke on 26 January 1834,

> or rather I had no regular instruction, but heard what are called orthodox notions preached in my childhood, when I like other children believed all that I heard uncontradicted – But before I was 20 years old, I met with anti-religious books, and had nothing to oppose to sceptical arguments – I sprang at once from one extreme to another. And from believing every thing I believed nothing. My German studies afterwards made me sensible of the shallowness of the whole class of writers whom I before respected And one good effect they wrought on me. They made me conscious of my own ignorance and inclined me to a favorable study of religious doctrines.[25]

Mary Steele shared Robinson's inquiring spirit, though with a different result. As her spiritual autobiography (composed ca 1780) reveals, she moved from something in the proximity of High Calvinism during her school days in London in the late 1760s to a more moderate, evangelical Calvinism espoused by two Baptist ministers Robert Hall Sr of Arnsby and Steele's friend Caleb Evans of Bristol. In the mid-1770s she adopted a Baxterian compromise between Arminianism and Calvinism, and by 1780 had arrived at an Arminian position on free will more in line with the New Connexion General Baptists, the Wesleyan Methodists and the Arian/Unitarians.[26] Steele finally joined the Baptist church in Broughton when she was forty-two, though she continued to maintain theological opinions at odds with the moderate Calvinism of her friend and pastor William Steadman. As Steadman's biographer notes, Steele's rejection of predestination and adherence to free will did not disallow her membership. 'It does not appear that the church at Broughton required actual subscription to a particular creed', Thomas Steadman writes, 'otherwise it is most likely that a Christian of the cultivated intellect and refined susceptibilities which distinguished Miss Steele, would have been virtually excluded from their communion; in which case it is not easy to determine which party would have been the greater loser'.[27] Arnold seems to have had little knowledge of this kind of Nonconformist introspection and tolerance. Robinson and Steele were by no means anomalies within early-nineteenth-century Nonconformity. Both individuals possessed 'cultivated intellect[s] and refined susceptibilities' and relished open enquiry, exhibiting a willingness to hear opposing viewpoints as a means not only of examining and strengthening their intellectual adherence to their faith but also of measuring and maintaining their civility toward those with differing opinions.

III. Nonconformist Poetry and a New Literary Aesthetic

Arnold's pontifications on the shortcomings of Nonconformist culture also reveal an inadequate understanding of the nature of the Nonconformist literary aesthetic. In fact, the bulk of Nonconformist literature composed between 1650 and 1850, especially its poetry, is marked by an aesthetic vastly dissimilar to that employed by most seventeenth- and eighteenth-century poets. As a rule, Nonconformist artists believed, as Mason Lowance has argued, 'that art should be purposefully didactic, and that literature especially should contain only enough art to guide one to the truth'.[28] Eschewing the typical Renaissance poet's reliance on the 'flowers of Rhetoricke' and 'wittie Sophistrie',[29] Nonconformist poets, beginning in the second half of the seventeenth century, frequently imitated the poetry of the Psalms and Song of Solomon, the forceful expression of the prophets, the homely metaphors and illustrations of Christ and the familiar discourse of the Pauline epistles.[30] They also sought by means of 'holy endeavours', as the Puritan Thomas Brooks contended, 'to edify others, to instruct others, to enlighten and inform others in the knowledge of spiritual and heavenly things'.[31] They did not believe this necessarily produced dull literature (i.e. *Paradise Lost* or *Pilgrim's Progress*), but rather, as N. H. Keeble makes clear, they 'recognized that the edificatory and the enjoyable were not inimical; the one might serve the other'.[32]

The same applied to their hymns, spiritual autobiographies and, later, to their moral fiction as it developed in the early nineteenth century. Isaac Watts made no attempt to imitate the powerful cadences of Milton's *Paradise Lost* (1667) or the exquisite diction of Alexander Pope's 'Essay on Criticism' (1711). Watts knew his hymns would not satisfy all his critics, yet he was adamant that he 'would neither indulge any bold metaphors, nor admit of hard words, nor tempt the ignorant worshipper to sing without his understanding'.[33] His hymns and psalms were not only devotional aids to the individual 'saint' but also collective aids to the doctrines espoused within the 'gathered church', the congregation of believers that, along with the Bible, served as the central focus in the private lives and 'gathered' communities of Nonconformists. At war with the carnal world, the believer in the privacy of his or her closet gained spiritual strength and assurance of faith through scripture, prayer and hymns, three powerful 'means of grace' made visible through the fellowship of believers in the local church. Seventeen-year-old John Ryland Jr (1753–1825), a future leader among the Particular Baptists, also hoped his poetry would serve a 'useful' purpose and not merely entertain his readers. He admitted his poems did not possess the 'sweetness' of the sonnets of the Scottish poet Ralph Erskine or the 'sublimity' of the epics of Milton, nor would he have ever assumed they would achieve the popularity of the poems of Watts, Pope or Edward Young (poets highly revered by Nonconformists), but he did believe he could be 'an instrument' to comfort believers 'who may live in a cottage, or be cast upon a dunghill'.[34] 'Sweetness' and 'sublimity' may have been worthy aims for a young Nonconformist poet's attitude toward his art object (a painting or engraving would have generated a similar desire), but Donald Davie's trinity of 'simplicity, sobriety, and measure'[35] may be a more apt description of the 'Calvinist aesthetic' employed by Watts and lesser poets like Ryland. This was an aesthetic that mirrored attitudes towards church architecture as well, in which the poet's attempt to suffuse a simple yet succinct verbal picture of human spirituality within the confines of a poem reflected the architect's desire for simplicity in the typical Nonconformist chapel, Watts' 'garden wall'd around'.[36] Though Nonconformist writers utilized many literary genres and aesthetic techniques between 1650 and 1850, the majority of their writings demonstrate one overriding aesthetic purpose: a sincere presentation of divine truth through means of a plain style, grounded in the language of scripture, for the edification of their readers.[37]

Nonconformist hymns and prayers, as well as the private meditations inserted in their diaries and journals, reflect the 'language of Canaan', the imagery and diction found in the King James Bible. This 'language', as

J. R. Watson has pointed out concerning Watts, employed a 'plain and unfigurative' versification marked by 'a restrained and dignified simplicity of language, rhythm, and metre'.[38] The *emotions* gendered by spiritual warfare, however, were anything but 'restrained' to the Nonconformist spiritual autobiographer, hymn writer and poet. It was that emotion, far more than their 'simplicity of language' (not unlike the simplicity of the Nonconformist chapel), that Arnold and his early-twentieth-century commentator William Dawson considered undignified and dull. An 'exalted idea of worship' was undermined, Dawson believed, when piety was attached to poetic language. Dawson denigrated the 'solemn tones' employed by Nonconformists in worship, both communal and private, arguing that the 'adoration of the Deity [was] degraded to a species of morbid introspection, the worshipper busying himself with the analysis of his own feelings and describing these in the language of rhapsodical and often illiterate hymnology for the common edification',[39] certainly a skewed assessment by an unsympathetic spectator.

Donald Davie confessed that as a twentieth-century Baptist youth possessing a strong desire to write *poetry* (the literary 'graven images' many considered only slightly removed from the pictorial icons Cromwell so hated), he initially felt his desire was 'self-contradictory' and in league with the 'enemy'[40] until he discovered that the history of Nonconformity (at least through the first half of the nineteenth century) revealed a continuous stream of poets, not just hymn writers. In fact, what would have seemed even more 'self-contradictory' to students of British poetry ca 1950 is that the poetic heirs of Milton within Nonconformity were primarily *women*. Hester Chapone advised her women readers in *Letters on the Improvement of the Mind* (1777):

> Nothing you can read will so much contribute to the improvement of this faculty as poetry; which, if applied to its true ends, adds a thousand charms to those sentiments of religion, virtue, generosity, and delicate tenderness, by which the human soul is exalted and refined.[41]

John Ash (1724–79), educator, lexicographer and Baptist minister at Pershore, echoed Chapone's opinions that same year in his *Sentiments on Education* (1777).[42] Such views of poetry among Nonconformists, however, had been in place by that time for more than a century. In 1650 Anne Bradstreet's brother-in-law published in London her collection of poems, *The Tenth Muse lately Sprung up in America*, prefaced by commendatory verses from several London Puritan ministers. Her posthumous collection, *Several Poems Compiled with Great Variety and Wit and Learning*, appeared in 1678. Bradstreet (1612–72), a member of one of Massachusetts' leading Puritan families, exhibited not only the literary aesthetic that would come to distinguish so much of Nonconformist poetry but also the poetic genres and themes Nonconformist poets, both men and women, would employ into the nineteenth century: blank verse, common metre and heroic couplets in lyric poems on love, friendship, retirement and solitude, nature, affliction and death, as well as occasional poems (both private and public, including poems on politics), verse narratives and, of course, religious and philosophical poems.[43] Though numerous Nonconformist men published poetry (other than hymns) during the eighteenth and early nineteenth centuries, none came close to challenging the greatness of a Milton or Marvell, nor were any as prominent as the women poets.[44]

IV. Nonconformists and the Elevation of Spiritual Autobiography and Moral Fiction

The language of emotional piety was even more prevalent in the 'spiritual relation', a common requirement for membership in Nonconformist congregations, especially those that were Calvinist in doctrine. These highly particularized accounts of an individual's coming to faith in Christ were often expanded (and sometimes published) as 'spiritual autobiographies', the most famous example being Bunyan's *Grace Abounding to the Chief of Sinners* (1666). Diaries and journals, some kept weekly and others daily, were commonly used by Nonconformists to maintain a more detailed record of their spiritual progress, such as the journals of the Quaker George Fox (1794), the Presbyterian Richard Baxter (1696), the American Congregationalist David Brainerd (1746), the American Quaker John Woolman (1774) and the Methodist leader John Wesley (1827).[45] Spiritual autobiography was the most pervasive form of writing among Nonconformists for more than two centuries; it was also the least gendered. Its primary aim was to delineate the believer's progress from an initial state of doubt and unbelief through the regenerative work of divine grace to an eventual state of spiritual enlightenment, religious affection and assurance of faith. In these informal writings Nonconformist men and women raised their spiritual 'Ebenezers' (as Robert Robinson put it in 'Come, Thou Fount of Every Blessing'), verbal pillars that forever reminded them of their hard-fought spiritual victories. The 'pilgrimage' of the saint through the enticements of a temporal Vanity Fair towards the eternal pleasures of heaven was difficult for all Christians, whether male or female. The journey of Bunyan's Christian in *Pilgrim's Progress* (1678) (both 'Christian' and 'Pilgrim' bespeaking the androgynous nature of the spiritual quest) required an unyielding reliance upon a persevering faith that sustained each pilgrim in his or her 'progress' to the Celestial City.

Doctrinal discourses, religious meditations, spiritual autobiographies, diaries and journals were all accepted forms of edificatory prose writing for Nonconformists between 1650 and 1850. Imaginative fiction, however, despite Defoe's success in the early 1700s, was generally considered outside the bounds of proper literary activity (though the novels of Samuel Richardson, especially *Sir Charles Grandison*, appear to have been exceptions). Not until the appearance of *Caleb Williams* (1794) by William Godwin (1756–1836), a former Independent minister turned sceptic, and *Emma Courtney* (1796) by Mary Hays (1760–1843), an acquaintance of Godwin and Crabb Robinson who grew up in a Baptist Church in Southwark before becoming a Unitarian, did novel-writing regain a place (though still marginal) within Nonconformist culture.[46] The novel that more closely exemplifies the Nonconformist literary aesthetic is *The Coquette* (1797) by Hannah Foster (1758–1840), an American writer and wife of a Congregational minister. Not even a clear didactic purpose – to warn young women of the danger of being seduced by allowing their imagination ('fancy') to rule their reason – could mask the more titillating parts of the novel of seduction, a staple of the circulating libraries during the late eighteenth and early nineteenth centuries. Not only did these novels glorify sensual desires and uncontrolled passions, they also distorted reality (an early indicator of the later desire among Nonconformists for more 'realistic' didactic fiction) and promoted an unhealthy vanity among young female readers. In 1810, the Unitarian writer Anna Lætitia Barbauld suggested in *An Essay on the Origin and Progress of Novel-Writing* that it might be better to read romance novels primarily for 'entertainment' and not for moral or social instruction, warning that they exalted 'virtue and delicacy' in their heroes and heroines to a level impossible for any young person to attain.[47]

In 1792 Maria Grace Andrews (1772–1858), seven years prior to her marriage to John Saffery (1763–1825), Baptist minister at Salisbury, published her only novel, *The Noble Enthusiast*, having composed it as a teenager when she was still an Anglican and avid reader of sentimental romance novels. Her novel (marred by excessive diction, over-drawn characters and a convoluted plot) sanctioned all the fears of the critics of the novel, including Barbauld. Within three years of her novel's publication, Andrews had removed from London to Salisbury and become immersed (in more ways than one) into evangelical Christianity and Nonconformity through her membership in the Brown Street Baptist church in Salisbury. During that time her attitude toward her own novel became one of regret and embarrassment, opinions possibly shaped by her friend Mary Egerton Scott (ca 1765–1840), second wife of the popular evangelical biblical commentator Thomas Scott (1747–1821). Mary Scott's first published work, *The Path to Happiness* (1796), argued that those who are 'fascinated in early life by the perusal of novels and romances have deluded themselves with the hope of enjoyments never to be realized, qualifications neither to be attained or even desired, and characters which are no where to be found'.[48] Though not a Nonconformist, Scott's views towards fiction were in line with Barbauld, Hannah More and the vast majority of Nonconformists who also identified as evangelicals, believing that the imagination was designed to serve a moral, social and spiritual purpose, not merely an aesthetic one. Even though she would never write another work of fiction, Maria Grace Andrews Saffery refused to allow her Nonconformity to be an excuse for a retreat from literary culture, becoming the leading Baptist woman poet in England during the first half of the nineteenth century.

As a reaction to the popular sentimental romance novel, Nonconformist and evangelical prose writers, both men and women, turned to a new genre – the short moral tale – and a new class of readers emerging from among the poorer working classes, a readership largely created through the work of Sunday Schools, charity schools, adult learning societies, the Religious Tract Society (1799) and the British and Foreign Bible Society (1804). Hannah More's Cheap Repository Tracts (1795–97) enjoyed a phenomenal success and established the model the non-denominational Religious Tract Society would quickly follow. These works glorified middle-class domesticity with plots that were often a blend of romantic and realistic elements (partially the legacy of Barbauld's criticism of the romance novel). From Sally Idle of Poverty Lane to Ragged Dick of the Bowery of New York, from Mrs Wilkins of Fleet Street in London to Jenny Hickling of Wimeswold in Leicestershire,[49] these characters and individuals joined the moral virtues of industry, frugality and prudence with the biblical imperatives of faith, salvation, and good works, all with the design of effecting a social and spiritual transformation of the self.[50] Though far removed in style, form and content from the 'high' literary culture Arnold preferred, many of these works had immense circulations, having 'passed the wall of China' by the end of the nineteenth century and 'entered the palace of the Celestial emperor'. They had also

> gone to the sons of Africa to teach them, in their bondage, the liberty of the Gospel. They have preached Christ crucified to the Jew and also to the Greek; while in the home land they have continued to offer the truths and consolations of religion to soldiers, to sailors, to prisoners, to the inmates of hospitals, and, in short, to rich and poor in every circumstance of life.[51]

Like the thousands of Nonconformist missionaries labouring in India, China, Jamaica and various parts of the world, these short prose works became ambassadors (in a literary sense) of British culture and evangelical Christianity, a remarkable achievement for any body of literature.

After 1800 Nonconformists continued to produce full-length novels, usually historical romances or novels of domestic life, though increasingly coloured, at times, with a tint of realism. Women writers dominated, including two Unitarians, Elizabeth Cleghorn Gaskell (1810–65), wife of William Gaskell (1805–84), Unitarian minister at Cross Street Chapel, Manchester, and Harriet Martineau (1802–76), originally from Norwich and sister of James Martineau (1805–1900), one of the leading Unitarian preachers, writers and educators in the last half of the nineteenth century.[52] Both women formed a link among Unitarian women writers that began with Barbauld and Hays in the last quarter of the eighteenth century, writers who consistently granted imaginative fiction an important role in promoting and defining the moral imperatives of Nonconformist culture. The prejudice against fiction within Nonconformity weakened considerably after 1850, as evidenced by the popularity of George Macdonald (1824–1905), a Congregational minister from Scotland, and William Hale White (1831–1913) (who was raised a Congregationalist and wrote under the pseudonym 'Mark Rutherford'), especially the latter's *Mark Rutherford's Deliverance* (1885) and *The Revolution in Tanner's Lane* (1887). These four novelists – Gaskell, Martineau, Macdonald and White – helped restore Nonconformist fiction to a level of sophistication and popularity not enjoyed since Defoe's novels more than a century earlier. Macdonald, however, replaced the episodic and picaresque forms used so effectively by Defoe and the realism of the mid-nineteenth century novelists with elements of fantasy more akin to the work of Lewis Carroll and two Christian writers of the twentieth century whose work was clearly influenced by Macdonald: C. S. Lewis (1898–1963) and J. R. R. Tolkien (1892–1973).

V. Nonconformists and Print Culture

The role of Nonconformist booksellers, printers and publishers, both in London and the provinces, in promoting Nonconformist culture has received little scholarly attention. One prominent example is Joseph Cottle (1770–1853) of Bristol, early publisher of the Romantic poets William Wordsworth, Samuel Taylor Coleridge and Robert Southey, and best known for his involvement in the publication of *The Lyrical Ballads* (1798). Cottle's lifelong devotion to his Calvinistic faith (shaped and nurtured among several Baptist and Independent congregations in Bristol) and his forty-year association with the Bristol Education Society, however, dictated his career as a bookseller/publisher far more than his attraction to romantic poetry. Though often ridiculed by literary historians as incompetent and ultimately a failure, Cottle was by no means a minor figure as a bookseller in Bristol in the 1790s.[53] By the end of the eighteenth century, Nonconformists like Cottle were operating bookshops throughout the provinces, from Salisbury, Taunton and Bristol in the West Country to Cambridge and Norwich in the East and Liverpool, Newcastle and Edinburgh in the north. Though the actual number of Nonconformist booksellers/printers is difficult to ascertain (given the scarcity of existing Nonconformist church records and a general lack of biographical details), at least sixty Nonconformist men and women operated shops in London between 1650 and 1850, with several occupying prominent addresses in Paternoster Row, adjacent to St Paul's Cathedral. In fact, most of the leading women booksellers/publishers in London during the eighteenth century were Nonconformists, beginning with the Quaker Tace Sowle (1666–1749) and ending with Mary Lewis (1705?–91) and Martha Gurney (1733–1816). Lewis, an Independent, took over her husband's shop in 1 Paternoster Row in 1754, having served as the primary printer for two prominent evangelists, George Whitefield and John Cennick. Gurney, a member of the Baptist congregation in Maze Pond, Southwark, and sister to Joseph Gurney (1744–1815), stenographer for the Old Bailey and parliament, operated a bookshop at 128 Holborn Hill from 1782 to ca 1810.[54] Other successful individual booksellers and publishers in London at the end of the eighteenth century included the Independent Thomas Conder (1746?–1841), the Baptist Thomas Vernor (d. 1793), the Methodist Joseph Butterworth (1770–1826) and his nephew Henry (1786–1860), all of whom would give way in the nineteenth century to much larger publishers, such as the Quaker firm of Darton and Harvey and three prominent Congregational publishers: the Unwin Brothers, Jackson and Walford, and Hodder and Stoughton.

Aside from Benjamin Flower's work as editor of the *Cambridge Intelligencer* (1793–1803) and the *Political and Monthly Review* (1807–11), other Nonconformists who left their mark in journalism include the MP Edward Baines (1774–1838), publisher and editor of the *Leeds Mercury* (1801–ca 1830); William Ward (1769–1823), who, before he left England for the Baptist Mission at Serampore to work with William Carey, edited the Derby *Mercury*, Staffordshire *Advertiser* and Hull *Advertiser* between 1789 and 1796; Josiah Fletcher (fl. 1830–50), deacon in the Baptist church at St Mary's, Norwich, who, along with his fellow church-member Simon Wilkin, published the *East Anglian, Norfolk and Suffolk and Cambridgeshire Herald* and the *Norfolk News*; John Edward Taylor (1791–1844), son of the Unitarian poet Mary Scott (a close friend of Mary Steele) and founder of the Manchester *Guardian*, one of the most influential newspapers in British history; and Robertson Nicoll of Aberdeen, minister in the Scottish Free Church and editor of *The Expositor* (1884–1923). In Wales, the Presbyterian Josiah Rees (1744–1804) founded one of the earliest Welsh magazines, *Trysorfa Gwybodaeth, neu, Eurgrawn Cymraeg* in 1770, though it ran for only a few months. More important was the work of Joseph 'Gomer' Harris (1773–1825), Baptist minister, writer and journalist from Llangloffan, who collaborated with Titus Lewis (1773–1811) in 1806 in publishing the periodical *Y Drysorfa Efengylaidd*. In 1814 he established the first newspaper in the Welsh language, *Seren Gomer* (it continued in print until 1983), and later the Baptist magazine *Greal y Bedyddwyr*.

Early periodicals that were popular among (though not exclusive to) Nonconformists were the influential (and largely secular) *Monthly Review*, founded by the Nonconformist bookseller Ralph Griffiths, whose editors were almost exclusively Nonconformists from 1749 until 1825; the High Calvinist *Royal Spiritual Magazine*, founded by John Allen in 1752, who served as a Particular Baptist minister for a time in the 1760s in London prior to becoming a writer of pro-American political pamphlets in the early 1770s; the *Gospel Magazine* (1766–1805; 1838–present), of which the first editor and publisher was Joseph Gurney, who was a bookseller/printer before he became a stenographer; the *Protestant Magazine* (1781–82), which emerged in the aftermath of the Lord George Gordon Riots in 1780; the short-lived *Protestant Dissenters' Magazine* (1794–99); and the *Evangelical Magazine* (1793–1904), initially a joint Baptist–Congregationalist venture. Various periodicals served the interests of each denomination, such as the *Arminian Magazine* (1778–97), which became the *Methodist Magazine* (1798–1821) and then the *Wesleyan Methodist Magazine* (1822–1913); the *General Baptist Repository* (1802–53), which was followed by the *General Baptist Magazine* (1854–91); *Baptist Magazine* (1809–1904); *Monthly Repository* (1806–38) (Unitarian); *Congregational Magazine* (1818–45); and the *New Methodist Magazine and Evangelical Repository* (1812–32), to name a few.[55] The *Nonconformist* (1841–1900), an influential weekly paper founded by the Congregational minister Edward Miall (1809–81), advanced an aggressive platform for the disestablishment of the Anglican Church, primarily from the perspective of the Liberal Party, under whose banner Miall served as MP for Rochdale (1852–57) and Bradford (1860–74). A periodical of equal importance, though related less to politics and more to art and literature, was the *Eclectic Review* (1805–68), founded by Daniel Parken (1785–1812), a Baptist layman. He was succeeded by Josiah Conder (1789–1855), son of the Congregational bookseller Thomas Conder; the younger Conder retained his editorship until 1837, when he was replaced by the retired Baptist minister Thomas Price (1802–68), who continued until 1850. The *Eclectic* was among the first periodicals to review the Romantic writers, such as Wordsworth, Coleridge and Byron, as well as the Victorian novelist Charles Dickens and numerous American writers, such as Washington Irving and Ralph Waldo Emerson. Among its contributors were the Moravian poet James Montgomery (1771–1854), abolitionist George Thompson (1804–78), social reformer Andrew Reed (1787–1862), philanthropist Thomas Chalmers (1780–1847), Methodist theologian Adam Clarke (1762–1832) and three Baptists – Robert Hall (1764–1831), J. E. Ryland (1797–1866) (editor, 1855–68) and Olinthus Gregory (1774–1841). The *Eclectic Review* published more than 180 essays of the Baptist minister John Foster (1770–1843), who, after the publication of his *Essays in a Series of Letters* (1805) and *An Essay on the Evils of Popular Ignorance* (1821), became one of the leading Nonconformist journalists of his day.

VI. Nonconformity and the Visual Arts

Besides its contributions to literary culture through poetry, prose, fiction and periodicals (little of which seems to have impressed Arnold), Nonconformity produced a host of visual artists (primarily portrait and landscape painters) who were regular exhibitors at the Royal Academy and the British Institution during the second half of the eighteenth and first half of the nineteenth centuries. These artists, however, had to overcome a general antipathy to 'graven images' (fostered by Calvin himself) that seriously hampered sixteenth- and seventeenth-century Nonconformist attitudes towards the visual arts, an antipathy that far exceeded Nonconformity's rejection of Catholic and Greek Orthodox iconography. During the eighteenth century, however, the relationship between Nonconformists and the visual arts grew more congenial. John Harvey's comments concerning Welsh Nonconformists at that time are apropos to the larger Dissenting culture in general, in which 'invisible religious concepts such as doctrine, biblical narrative, and spiritual experience, [were] given tangible expression in visual, literary and conceptual imagery'.[56] Nonconformist artists include Edward Kennion (1744–1809) of Liverpool and his son, Charles John Kennion (1789–1853), both Independents; Samuel Medley Jr (1769–1857) of Liverpool, son of the Particular Baptist minister and hymn writer Samuel Medley (1738–99); the 'Smiths of Chichester' – George Smith (1713/14–76), William (1707–64), and John (1717–64) – sons of the General Baptist minister William Smith (d. 1719) of Chichester; J. de Fleury (fl. 1773–1823), brother of the Baptist poet Maria de Fleury and engraver for the *Protestant Magazine* in 1781–82; the water-colourist Joshua Cristall (1768?–1847), brother of the Unitarian poet Anne Batten Cristall; Thomas Fisher (1772–1836), prominent Congregational historian, best known for his drawings of interior church monuments; Maria Ann Spilsbury Taylor (1777–1820), daughter of a Methodist print-maker and portrait painter and wife of a Calvinist philanthropist and Nonconformist, who exhibited some eighty paintings at the Royal Academy and the British Institution between 1792 and 1813; and the landscape painter John Linnell (1792–1882), friend and benefactor of the radical Romantic poet and engraver William Blake (1757–1827).

A professed mystic and prophet, Blake once wrote: 'A Poet, a Painter, a Musician, an Architect: the Man or Woman who is not one of these is not a Christian'.[57] Blake, who remained apart from any organized religion most of his life, contended that 'Christianity is Art & not Money',[58] demonstrating an idealism in his personal and artistic life that both fascinated and confounded his friends and critics, especially Crabb Robinson.[59] Blake was an engraver as much as he was a painter or poet, and he was not alone among Nonconformists in this area of artistic expertise. Other engravers worth noting include William Burgess (1754/55–1813), Baptist minister at Fleet, Lincolnshire; Isaac Taylor Sr (1730–1807), an Independent layman in London, and his son Isaac Taylor (1759–1829), father of the poets Ann and Jane Taylor; and Robert Bowyer (1758–1834), a Baptist layman from Portsmouth, who eventually became miniaturist to George III and whose famous collection of prints of biblical settings and characters became known as the Bowyer Bible.[60] Thomas Sheraton (1751–1806), Baptist minister at Darlington (1800–6), had previously lived in London, where he earned considerable fame as a furniture designer, sharing honours with Thomas Chippendale and George Hepplewhite as the three giants of the craft during the eighteenth century. Another form of artistry that deserves attention is pottery, a trade in which several Nonconformists engaged with remarkable success, primarily in Staffordshire and Worcestershire. Among these are the Independent layman Martin Barr of Worcester and his partners, Thomas Flight, a prominent Baptist layman from Southwark, and his sons, John and Joseph Flight; the Unitarian Josiah Wedgwood of Burslem, Staffordshire; the Baptist W. H. Grose of Stoke-on-Trent; and the Methodist Ridgways (William and E. J.) of North Staffordshire.[61]

In his Preface to *Milton* (ca 1810) Blake had made an impassioned plea for a new kind of visual art and artist (though hardly the kind most Nonconformists of his day fully understood):

> Painters! on you I call. Sculptors! Architects! Suffer not the fashionable fools to depress your powers by the prices they pretend to give for contemptible works, or the expensive advertizing boasts that they make of such works; believe Christ and his Apostles that there is a class of man whose whole delight is in destroying. We do not want either Greek or Roman Models if we are but just and true to our own Imaginations, those worlds in which we shall live for ever in JESUS OUR LORD.[62]

Forty years later, Thomas Binney (1798–1874), successor to John Clayton as Congregational minister at the King's Weigh House, London, may have thought that Blake's prophecy was coming true. Binney told an audience of YMCA supporters that evangelical Christianity (and he clearly meant the kind propagated in his home church) was now dedicated to promoting intellectual improvement and cultural engagement among its adherents. Such Christians, he concluded, echoing Blake, find beauty in 'poetry or eloquence, in writing or discourse, in painting, music, statuary, and song' and thus become 'of necessity a thinker and reader'.[63] Binney's 'thinker', however, was clearly not the powerful, imaginative artist Blake had in mind. Blake's idea of Nonconformity demanded a radical break between the individual and what he perceived to be a corrupt culture of church and state ca. 1800, between private conscience and public 'Greek or Roman Models' that, like the priest in his poem 'The Garden of Love', bind 'with briars, [our] joys & desires'.[64] On the other hand, as David Bebbington and Timothy Larsen point out, Binney believed that 'the enjoyment of wealth . . . was entirely legitimate' for Nonconformists, encouraging his listeners to 'acquire a taste for the elegant and the beautiful'.[65]

After the success of the Crystal Palace Exhibition of 1851 and its celebration of British culture, a culture that now circled the globe, Binney was convinced that Nonconformity had reached a degree of cultural prowess many of its eighteenth-century adherents would never have thought possible or even desirable. As living embodiments of Binney's ideal of a Nonconformist *nouveau riche*, Samuel Morley (1809–86) of London (a member of Binney's congregation) and John Rylands (1801–88) of Manchester, two Congregational millionaire manufacturers and philanthropists, left a distinct mark on Victorian and twentieth-century British culture. After Rylands' death, his third wife, Enriqueta Augustina Tennant Rylands (1843–1908), built an opulent library in Manchester in his honour. When the John Rylands Library opened on 6 October 1899, the building was described in the *Baptist Magazine* as 'an addition of rare value to the architectural wealth of Manchester', the speaker that day boasting that the architect 'had adorned Manchester and enriched England with one of the most distinguished and the most perfect architectural achievements of this century'.[66] Binney's vision of an integrated, validated, accommodationist Nonconformist culture in 1852 had become a reality by the end of the century, embodied in the impeccable gothic beauty and grandeur of the Rylands Library, a cultural vision that proved itself far more powerful and relevant to Nonconformists than Blake's radical romantic ideals would ever be.[67]

VII. Conclusion

Arnold's suggestion, quoted previously, that the chief legacy of Nonconformist culture was its 'disputes, tea meetings, openings of chapels, [and] sermons' was answered by one Baptist minister, who declared in 1869 (the year of Arnold's *Culture and Anarchy*) that his denomination had 'left the old Puritan error. We no longer despise the beautiful and artistic, but claim them as divine things, and enlist them in the divine service. We no longer consider retirement from the world a sign of holiness, but believe that all man's life and work can be dedicated to heaven'.[68] However, to say that Nonconformists prior to 1869 despised 'the beautiful and artistic' belies more than two centuries of creative achievements in poetry, fiction, painting, engraving, pottery and numerous other artistic and cultural endeavours.[69] Nor was there ever a ubiquitous belief among Nonconformists (as a wealth of recently uncovered 'informal' writings, primarily letters and diaries, makes clear) that 'retirement from the world' was held to be a badge of holiness. Evidence shows that Nonconformists, especially writers and artists, moved easily between their denominational subcultures and the larger culture in which they lived, whether in England, Ireland, Scotland or Wales, embracing their faith and doctrine at the same time they sought after the 'beautiful and artistic', unleashing imaginations attuned to their private, spiritual and domestic lives just as much as it was societal concerns, whether cultural, ecclesiastical or political. As this brief examination has demonstrated, the cultural and aesthetic life of Nonconformists between 1650 and 1850 is far richer and intellectually stimulating than the one Arnold critiqued so harshly, and, despite considerable scholarly interest in recent decades, one that has yet to be fully drawn.

Notes

1 Matthew Arnold, *Culture and Anarchy: An Essay in Political and Social Criticism* (London: Smith, Elder and Co., 1869), p. 29.

2 William H. Dawson, *Matthew Arnold and His Relation to the Thought of Our Time* (New York: Putnam's, 1904), p. 305.

3 Ibid., pp. 312–13. The nineteenth-century historian W. E. H. Lecky (*A History of England in the Eighteenth Century* (1878–90), III, pp. 150–52) also criticized Evangelicals and Dissenters for a general lack of intellectual curiosity.

4 William Haller, *The Rise of Puritanism* (Philadelphia, PA: University of Pennsylvania Press, 1938); Perry Miller, *The New England Mind: The Seventeenth Century* (Cambridge, MA: Harvard University Press, 1939); Geoffrey F. Nuttall, *The Holy Spirit in Puritan Faith and Experience* (Oxford: Blackwell, 1946).

5 See R. W. Dale, *A History of English Congregationalism* (London: Hodder and Stoughton, 1907); Ford K. Brown, *Fathers of the Victorians: The Age of Wilberforce* (Cambridge: Cambridge University Press, 1961). For a more sympathetic treatment of evangelicalism and its relationship to English culture and society, see W. R. Ward, *Religion and Society in England 1790–1850* (London: B. T. Batsford, 1972).

6 J. R. Watson, *The English Hymn: A Critical and Historical Study* (Oxford: Clarendon, 1977); Clyde Binfield, *So Down to Prayers: Studies in English Nonconformity, 1780–1920* (London: J. M. Dent and Co., 1977); Donald Davie, *A Gathered Church: The Literature of the English Dissenting Interest, 1700–1930* (Oxford: Oxford University Press, 1978); Isabel Rivers, *Classical and Christian Ideas in English Renaissance Poetry* (London: Allen and Unwin, 1979); Doreen Rosman, *Evangelicals and Culture* (London: Croom Helm, 1984); John Morgan, *Godly Learning: Puritan Attitudes towards Reason, Learning and Education, 1560–1649* (Cambridge: Cambridge University Press, 1986); N. H. Keeble, *The Literary Culture of Nonconformity in Later Seventeenth Century England* (Athens, GA: University of Georgia Press, 1987). Despite Davie's evident appreciation of the literature and culture of Dissent (he was raised a Baptist) and his rejection of Arnold's bigotry, he nevertheless confesses that the 'Puritanism' of Bunyan and Knox, though 'grand', was also 'bigoted, ferocious and uncharitable', and later notes that Nonconformity in the nineteenth century (in contrast to that in the eighteenth century) became 'as philistine as the Church had always said it was' (Davie, *A Gathered Church*, pp. 10, 56–57), sentiments echoed by such historians as J. H. Plumb, *England in the Eighteenth-Century* (Harmondsworth: Penquin Books, 1950), pp. 91–97 and E. P. Thompson, *The Making of the English Working Class* (London: V. Galloncz, 1963), pp. 26–54.

7 James Bradley, *Religion, Revolution and English Radicalism: Non-Conformity in Eighteenth-Century Politics and Society* (Cambridge and New York: Cambridge University Press, 1990); Jon Mee, *Dangerous Enthusiasm: William Blake and the Culture of Radicalism in the 1790s* (Oxford: Clarendon Press, 1994); idem, *Romanticism, Enthusiasm and Regulation: Poetics and the Policing of Culture in the Romantic Period* (Oxford: Oxford University Press, 2003); Paul Corby Finney, *Seeing Beyond the Word: Visual Arts and the Calvinist Tradition* (Grand Rapids, MN: Eerdmans, 1999); David W. Bebbington and Timothy Larsen (eds), *Modern Christianity and Cultural Aspirations* (London and New York: Sheffield Academic Press, 2003); Dan White, *Early Romanticism and Religious Dissent* (Cambridge: Cambridge University Press, 2006); Felicity James, *Religious Dissent and the Aikin-Barbauld Circle, 1749–1860* (Cambridge: Cambridge University Press, 2012). Recent scholarship has expanded the definition of culture itself far beyond Arnold's advocacy of a 'high' culture. Besides the seminal study by Raymond Williams, *Culture and Society, 1780–1850* (London: Chatto and Windus, 1958), see Davie, *A Gathered Church*; Clyde Binfield, 'Hebrews Hellenized? English Evangelical Nonconformity and Culture, 1840–1940', in S. Gilley and W. J. Sheils (eds), *A History of Religion in Britain: Practice and Belief from Pre-Roman Times to the Present* (Oxford: Blackwell, 1994), pp. 322–45; John Harvey, *The Art of Piety: The Visual Culture of Welsh Nonconformity* (Cardiff: University of Wales Press, 1995); Alan Kreider and Jane Shaw (eds), *Culture and the Nonconformist Tradition* (Cardiff: University of Wales Press, 1999).

8 Other studies of Nonconformity worth noting include David M. Thompson, *Nonconformity in the Nineteenth Century* (London: Routledge and Kegan Paul, 1972); John H. Y. Briggs and Ian Sellers (eds), *Victorian Nonconformity* (London: Edward Arnold, 1973); Ian Sellers, *Nineteenth-Century Nonconformity* (London: Edward Arnold, 1977); Patricia Caldwell, *The Puritan Conversion Narrative: The Beginnings of American Expression* (Cambridge: Cambridge University Press, 1985); Dale A. Johnson, *The Changing Shape of English Nonconformity, 1825–1925* (Oxford: Oxford University Press, 1999); John H. Y. Briggs (ed.), *Pulpit and People: Studies in Eighteenth Century Baptist Life and Thought* (Milton Keynes: Paternoster, 2009). The Centre for Dissenting Studies, in affiliation with Dr Williams's Library, London, and Queen Mary, University of London, has also made significant contributions to recovering the writings and history of Nonconformity. Among the publications appearing under its auspices are Isabel Rivers and David Wykes (eds), *Joseph Priestley: Scientist, Philosopher and Theologian* (Oxford: Oxford University Press, 2008); idem (eds), *Dissenting Praise: Religious Dissent and the Hymn* (Oxford: Oxford University Press, 2011); Elizabeth J. Clapp and Julie Roy Jeffrey (eds), *Women, Dissent and Anti-Slavery in Britain and America, 1790–1865* (Oxford: Oxford University Press, 2011), as well as the forthcoming *History of the Dissenting Academies in the British Isles, 1660–1860* (ed. Isabel Rivers and David Wykes, along with Richard Whatmore) and *Reliquiae Baxterianae* (gen. ed. N. H. Keeble).

9 Timothy Whelan (ed.), *Politics, Religion and Romance: The Letters of Benjamin Flower and Eliza Gould Flower, 1794–1808* (Aberystwyth: The National Library of Wales, 2008), p. 75.

10 Timothy Whelan (ed.), *Nonconformist Women Writers, 1720–1840*, 8 vols (London: Pickering and Chatto, 2011), III, p. 350.

11 Eluned Brown (ed.), *The London Theatre 1811–1866: Selections from the Diary of Henry Crabb Robinson* (London: Society for Theatre Research, 1966).

12 Davie, *A Gathered Church*, pp. 68–69.

13 Knowles, a relation of the playwright/politician Richard B. Sheridan and friend of the Romantic figure William Hazlitt and the actor William Macready, wrote several

successful plays in the 1820s and 1830s prior to becoming a Baptist preacher and writer in 1844, though he maintained his literary interests until his death. I am indebted to John Briggs for calling my attention to Knowles.

14 Besides Knowles, other playwrights connected with Nonconformity include Joanna Baillie (1762–1851), an occasional worshipper at the Rosslyn Hill Unitarian Chapel in her later years, and Thomas Noon Talfourd (1795–1854), writer, judge, politician and son-in-law of the Unitarian John Towill Rutt (1760–1841), the biographer of Joseph Priestley.

15 Among the contributors to the pamphlet war were George Burder (1752–1832), Independent minister at Fetter Lane, London; Rowland Hill (1744–1833), minister for forty years at the Surrey Chapel, London; and two laymen, D. W. Harvey, Esq., and John Styles, a Quaker. For a complete discussion of the controversy, see Whelan (ed.), *Politics, Religion and Romance*, pp. 352–56.

16 *Edinburgh Quarterly* (1808), p. 357.

17 In the 1880s Spurgeon reinforced this image in many minds, frequently inveighing against the theatre from his pulpit at the Metropolitan Tabernacle, even rejecting an invitation to speak at a conference sponsored by Joseph Parker, Congregational minister at London's City Temple, because of Parker's theatre-going. See John H. Y. Briggs, *The English Baptists of the Nineteenth Century* (Didcot: The Baptist Historical Society, 1994), pp. 179–80.

18 Matthew Arnold, *Passages from the Prose Writings of Matthew Arnold* (New York: Macmillan and Co., 1880), p. 195.

19 Ibid.

20 Ibid.

21 Helen Corke, *D. H. Lawrence: The Croydon Years* (Austin, TX: University of Texas Press, 1965), p. 127.

22 Thomas Sadler (ed.), *Diary, Reminiscences and Correspondence of Henry Crabb Robinson*, 2 vols (London and New York: Macmillan, 1872), II, p. 282.

23 Ibid., I, p. 8.

24 See Bampton Church Records, f. 203, Angus Library, Regent's Park College, Oxford.

25 Crabb Robinson to Wilhelm Benecke, 26 January 1834, Crabb Robinson Correspondence, Dr. Williams's Library, quoted by permission of the director and trustees of the Library.

26 Whelan (ed.), *Nonconformist Women Writers*, III, pp. 179–95.

27 Thomas Steadman (ed.), *Memoir of the Rev. William Steadman DD* (London: Thomas Ward, 1838), pp. 127–28.

28 Mason Lowance, 'Religion in Puritan poetry: The Doctrine of Accommodation', in Peter White (ed.), *Puritan Poets and Poetics* (University Park, PA: Pennsylvania State University Press, 1985), p. 40.

29 John Downame, *The Christian Warfare* (London: Felix Kingston, 1608), p. 342.

30 Milton's poetry, though at times didactic, reflected a more ornate Renaissance poetic style; his political prose, however, would remain popular among Nonconformists well into the nineteenth century. The biography of Milton by the London Baptist minister Joseph Ivimey (1773–1834) sought to correct all previous accounts of Milton which had depicted him 'principally in his character as a poet, but have obscured his features as a patriot, a protestant, and non-conformist'. Ivimey, *John Milton: His Life and Times* (London: E. Wilson, 1833), p. iii.

31 Thomas Brooks, *Heaven on Earth: A Treatise on Christian Assurance* (Edinburgh: Banner of Truth Trust, 1961 [1654]), pp. 191–92.

32 Keeble, *The Literary Culture of Nonconformity in Later Seventeenth-Century England*, p. 155.

33 Isaac Watts, *The Works of Isaac Watts*, 9 vols (London: Longman, Hurst, Rees [and others], 1813), IX, p. 35.

34 John Ryland Jr, *Serious Essays on the Truths of the Glorious Gospel, and the Various Branches of Vital Experience* (London: J. W. Pasham, 1771), p. xxii.

35 Davie, *A Gathered Church*, p. 25.

36 Isaac Watts, *Hymns and Spiritual Songs* (21st edn, London: R. Ware [and 8 others], 1753), Book 1, Hymn 74.

37 Nonconformity produced great hymn writers during the eighteenth and nineteenth centuries, but not many musicians. Aside from the sons of Charles Wesley, Charles (1757–1834) and Samuel (1766–1837), the most important Methodist composer was James Leach (1761?–98), who had 48 hymn tunes included in James Evans's *David's Companion, or, The Methodist Standard* (1810). Others worth noting include John Freeth (1731–1808), a Birmingham innkeeper and Unitarian who placed some 400 songs in various collections between 1766 and 1805, many of which were collected in *The Political Songster* (1790); and Eliza Flower (1803–46), daughter of Benjamin Flower, who composed 63 hymn tunes for *Hymns and Anthems* (1845), a collection designed for W. J. Fox's Unitarian congregation at South Place Chapel, Hackney.

38 J. R. Watson, 'The Hymns of Isaac Watts and the Tradition of Dissent', in Rivers and Wykes (eds), *Dissenting Praise*, p. 58.

39 Dawson, *Matthew Arnold and His Relation to the Thought of Our Time*, p. 316.

40 Davie, *A Gathered Church*, pp. 3, 2.

41 Hester Chapone, *Letters on the Improvement of the Mind* (London: J. Walter . . . and E. and C. Dilly, 1777), pp. 177–78.

42 John Ash, *Sentiments on Education*, 2 vols (London: Edward and Charles Dilly, 1777), II, pp. 6–12.

43 Bradstreet's literary descendants among Nonconformist women include, from among the Independents, Elizabeth Singer Rowe (1674–1737), Mary Chandler (1687–1745), Ann (1782–1866) and Jane Taylor (1783–1824), Susanna Harrison (1752–84), and Maria Jane Jewsbury [Fletcher] (1800–33); Baptists Anne Dutton (1691/92–1765), Anne Steele (1717–78), Maria de Fleury (fl. 1773–94), Hannah Neale (1758?–98) and Alice Flowerdew (1769–1830); Unitarians Mary Scott (1751–93), Anna Lætitia Aikin Barbauld (1743–1825), Helen Maria Williams (1761?–1827), Anne Batten Cristall (bap. 1769–1848) and Sarah Flower Adams (1805–48); and the Methodist Hannah Wallis (fl. 1787).

44 Some names worth noting include Samuel Bowden (fl. 1733–61), an Independent; two Particular Baptists, John Sheppard (1785–1879) of Frome and Henry Smithers (fl. 1790–1805) of Southwark, London; Unitarians Francis Webb (1735–1815), George Dyer (1755–1841) and Samuel Rogers (1763–1855); and three Welsh bardic poets from Glamorgan, the Congregationalist Lewis Hopkin (1707/8–71) and his two pupils, Edward Evan (1716–98) and Edward Williams (1747–1826), who later changed his name to Iolo Morganwg and became a Unitarian, assisting in the founding of the South Wales Unitarian Society in 1802.

45 Crabb Robinson's massive diary, which he maintained daily from January 1811 to February 1867, diverges from most Nonconformist diaries in that it primarily chronicles Robinson's intellectual progress and social life, not his spiritual concerns, though the latter's quest for a satisfying 'rational' faith is nevertheless a recurring theme.

46 Helen Maria Williams's *Julia* (1790) precedes Hays' *Emma Courtney*, as does Mary Wollstonecraft's *Maria: or, The Wrongs of Woman* (not published, however, until 1798). Though Williams and Wollstonecraft moved in London Unitarian circles in the 1780s and early 1790s, their association with Nonconformity is marginal in

comparison to Hays, and neither can be viewed as representatives of Nonconformist culture in general.

47 William McCarthy and Elizabeth Kraft (eds), *Anna Letitia Barbauld: Selected Poetry and Prose* (Peterborough, Ontario: Broadview Press 2002), pp. 407, 411.

48 Mary Scott, *The Path to Happiness, Explored and Illustrated* (2nd edn, London: Jacques and Thomas [and others], 1797), p. 6.

49 For these characters and historical personages, see Elizabeth Coltman, *Plain Tales, Chiefly Intended for the Use of Charity Schools* (London: Vernor and Hood, 1799); Horatio Alger, *Ragged Dick: or, Street Life in New York* (Boston: Joseph H. Allen, 1867); Mary Scott, *The Happiness of Having God for a Friend in Time of Trial, or the History of Mrs. Wilkins* (London: Jacques and Thomas, 1796); Elizabeth Coltman, *The History of Jenny Hickling: A Living Character* (London: Tilling and Hughes, 1817). Elizabeth Coltman (1761–1838), a close friend of Mary Steele, was raised a Presbyterian in Leicester but became a Baptist after the arrival of Robert Hall in 1807; Horatio Alger (1832–99) was a New England Unitarian minister and writer best known for his series of books for young boys.

50 For instance, Alger's Ragged Dick is transformed from a street arab to a counting clerk, from a pagan to a Christian, signing his name 'Richard Hunter, Esq.' at the end of the novel, a graphic instance of the power of the verbal iconography of middle-class success.

51 John McClintock and James Strong (eds), *Cyclopaedia of Biblical, Theological and Ecclesiastical Literature*, 12 vols (New York: Harper and Brothers, 1894), X, pp. 513–14.

52 Other women novelists include Mary Hughes (fl. 1810–20), a Unitarian from Bristol; Catherine Hutton (1768–1842), a Unitarian from Birmingham (though her letters suggest she flirted with Quakerism in the early 1820s); Mary Margaret Blair Busk (1779–1863) of London; Esther Copley [Hewlett] (1786–1851), a Baptist from Oxford; Anne Knight [*née* Waspe] (1792–1860), a Quaker from Suffolk; and Hannah Lawrance (1795–1875), a Congregationalist from London.

53 More than one hundred imprints bearing Cottle's name were issued between 1791 and 1802, sixty-three of which were sermons and other forms of religious writings by Baptists and Unitarians.

54 Briggs (ed.), *Pulpit and People*, pp. 165–201; Clapp and Jeffrey (eds), *Women, Dissent and Anti-Slavery in Britain and America, 1790–1865*, pp. 44–65.

55 For a detailed analysis of the *Monthly Repository*, see F. E. Mineka, *The Dissidence of Dissent* (Chapel Hill, NC: University of North Carolina, 1944).

56 Harvey, *The Art of Piety*, p. 1.

57 David V. Erdman (ed.), *The Complete Poetry and Prose of William Blake* (Berkeley, CA: University of California Press, 2008), p. 273.

58 Ibid., p. 274.

59 Edith Morley (ed.), *Blake, Coleridge, Wordsworth, Lamb etc.: Being Selections from the Remains of Henry Crabb Robinson* (Manchester: Manchester University Press, 1922), p. 8.

60 In its final form the Bowyer Bible consisted of forty-five volumes and nearly seven thousand engravings; it now resides in the Bolton Museum, Lancashire.

61 For a complete account of Nonconformist pottery makers, see John H. Y. Briggs, 'Nonconformity and the Pottery Industry', in Bebbington and Larsen (eds), *Modern Christianity and Cultural Aspirations*, pp. 47–77.

62 Erdman (ed.), *The Complete Poetry and Prose of William Blake*, p. 95. For more on Linnell, Blake and a group of artists associated with the Baptist congregation in Keppel Street, London, between 1810 and 1825, see Ernest Payne, 'John Linnell, the World of Artists and the Baptists', *Baptist Quarterly*, 40 (2003), pp. 22–35.

63 Thomas Binney, *Is It Possible to make the Best of Both Worlds? A Book for Young Men* (London: James Nisbet and Co., 1853), pp. 38, 75.
64 Erdman (ed.), *The Complete Poetry and Prose of William Blake*, p. 26.
65 Bebbington and Larsen (eds), *Modern Christianity and Cultural Aspirations*, pp. 1, 2.
66 James Stuart, 'The John Rylands Library', *Baptist Magazine*, 91 (1899), pp. 511, 513. The first manuscript collection purchased by Mrs Rylands for her new library was the autograph letter collection of Thomas Raffles (1788–1863), Congregational minister at Great George Street in Liverpool, 1812–63. His biographer declared that Raffles was known not only for his fame as a preacher but also for his 'reputation as a man of cultivated taste', demonstrated by his impressive letter collection. See James Baldwin Brown, *Thomas Raffles DD, LLD: A Sketch* (London: Jackson, Walford and Hodder, 1863), p. 39.
67 Two other examples of the radical change in Nonconformist church architecture was Samuel M. Peto's impressive Bloomsbury Baptist Church (1848), and Spurgeon's massive colonnaded Metropolitan Tabernacle (1861).
68 Binfield, *So Down to Prayers*, p. 19.
69 Arnold appears to have been unaware (or, at best, unappreciative) of the work of the Baptist minister, antiquarian and British Museum librarian Andrew Gifford (1700–84); the Presbyterian encyclopaedist Abraham Rees (1743–1825); Baptist mathematician and educator Olinthus Gregory (1774–1841); the Quaker architect Thomas Rickman (1776–1841); the Unitarian botanist William Roscoe (1753–1831); literary translators Thomas Chevalier (1767–1824) and James Martin (1821–77) (both Baptists) and the Quaker Jeremiah Holmes Wiffen (1792–1836); the Welsh cartographer Emanuel Bowen (1693/94–1767) (mapmaker to the king), his son Thomas Bowen (1732/33–90), and two of his apprentices, Thomas Kitchin (1719–84) and Thomas Jefferys (ca 1719–71), all of whom were connected with the Baptist chapel in the Barbican, London; and the Gurney family of London – Thomas (1705–70), Joseph (1744–1815), William Brodie (1777–1855) and Joseph (1804–79) – Baptist stenographers at the Old Bailey and parliament for more than one hundred years.

17 Nonconformists and Home Mission

David Ceri Jones

In 1742, Philip Doddridge, the Independent minister at Northampton, and without doubt the most prominent English Dissenting minister of his day, published *The Evil and Danger of Neglecting the Souls of Men.*[1] The text of a sermon preached to fellow dissenting ministers in Kettering, Doddridge passionately made the case for the formation of voluntary societies 'towards assisting in the Propagation of Christianity Abroad, and spreading it on some of the darker Parts of our own Land'.[2] Some, he wrote, 'who once were our Hearers, and it may be our dear Friends too, have perished through our Neglect . . . Multitudes to this day surround us, who stand exposed to the same Danger, and on the very brink of the same Ruin.'[3] Preaching as population levels in Britain were beginning to grow rapidly and the drift from the countryside to the towns and cities was accelerating, Doddridge's generation responded imaginatively to these new circumstances, developing innovative ways to respond to the highly challenging evangelistic task with which they were faced. But he was not the first, and would certainly not be the last, to grapple with the need to secure the conversion of his contemporaries. Indeed, since the emergence of Protestantism in England following Henry VIII's break with Rome in the 1530s, successive generations of Protestants had struggled with issues associated with encouraging the inhabitants of the British Isles towards something approaching an educated and enthusiastic embrace of the gospel.[4] The Reformation was always more of a process than an event.

Adopting a broadly chronological approach, this chapter examines specifically Dissenting attempts to bridge the gap between the 'godly' and the 'multitude'. Beginning with the first generations of Protestants, focusing particularly on the Puritans, it examines their efforts to make the idea of a Protestant nation a reality, an endeavour which was only finally killed-off following the 'Great Ejectment' in 1662 and the effective acceptance of religious plurality with the creation of Nonconformity. It then looks at the use of more voluntary evangelistic techniques, particularly the religious revival, which seemed for a time during the eighteenth century to offer the best opportunity to secure the conversion of the nation. It charts the way that these revivals, rather than bringing about national reformation, effectively replenished the ranks of Nonconformity from one generation to the next throughout the nineteenth century. From a position of numerical strength these Nonconformists were able to broaden out their concept of mission and address many of the social ills of Victorian Britain with varying degrees of success. These different approaches to home mission ran like a fault line through much of twentieth-century Nonconformity, at precisely the time when the evangelistic task became almost impossible in light of rampant secularization and endemic decline.

I. The Perennial Problem of the 'Dark Corners of the Land'

The success or failure of the Reformation was the subject of an increasing amount of historical literature during the last quarter of the twentieth century. While certainly Protestant by 1603, if not well before, the extent to which England and Wales were nations of committed Protestants has been hotly contested.[5] It was one thing to attempt to suppress the vestiges of the old Catholic faith, and to secure Protestant conformity at an official level, it was quite another to secure the informed allegiance of the masses to the new faith. For many this conversion to Protestantism was best pursued through the existing parochial system, through the securing of godly preachers at the local level, determined to preach regularly, catechize their parishioners and take responsible pastoral care for their flocks. Yet this inevitably slow and gradual policy was too conservative for many, and by the mid-sixteenth century there were other voices calling for new and innovative evangelistic strategies to speed up the conversion process.[6]

When John Penry, the Separatist martyr, complained in 1586 about 'the spirituall miserie wherein wee nowe liue in the country of WALES, for want of the preaching of the Gospel',[7] his comment betrayed the enormity of the task that lay before his fellow Protestants. His comments could equally well have been made about the north of England or the West Country, of course, since beyond its urban heartlands in the south-east of England, more committed Protestantism had barely secured a toehold. Penry's preference for a state-funded body of preachers to address this problem fell largely on deaf ears, at least during the last years of Eliazabeth I's reign.[8] Yet the appointment of six itinerant ministers in 1551 to tour Wales, Lancashire, Yorkshire, the Scottish borders, Devon and Hampshire, including among their number a young John Knox, was an early admission that effective itinerant evangelism might be the key to the long term securing of allegiance to the Protestant faith.[9] They were not alone. Patrick Collinson has written about the occasionally itinerating preachers who were often followed around the countryside by erstwhile supporters, sometimes referred to as the 'gadding' people.[10] Christopher Haigh's work on itinerant Puritan preaching in Lancashire has shown the nature and extent of the obstacles that the godly faced as they confronted the evangelistic challenge before them.[11]

That the penetration of the gospel into some of the remoter parts of England and Wales had reached little further by the middle of the seventeenth century bothered the consciences of the Puritans sufficiently to ensure that parliament placed the evangelistic task near the top of its agenda during the early months of the Commonwealth. John Owen, in a sermon before the House of Commons in 1647, argued that it was the duty of the state to ensure that all had the opportunity to hear gospel preaching.[12] When the Puritan regime did turn its attention to the provision of a godly ministry, necessity forced it to fall back on an army of itinerant ministers. Taking the advice of Hugh Peter, the Cornish Puritan who had urged the ploughing of tithe revenues into the provision of godly preachers, the Rump Parliament devoted much of its efforts to the provision of preachers in poorly evangelized areas of the country. The Act for the Better Propagation of the Gospel in Wales (1650) set up a commission to examine preachers, deprive poorly performing ones of their livings, and replace them with better qualified alternatives. Of course, it was far easier to turn out inadequate ministers than it was to find sufficient numbers of evangelical preachers to replace them. Consequently, parliament was forced to fall back upon the use of itinerants, who could at least be relied upon to carry the gospel into otherwise virgin territory.

The terms of the Propagation Act were not solely confined to Wales; there were also Commissioners for Propagation concerned with the north of England, particularly Cumberland, Westmorland, Northumberland and Durham, and their attentions also turned to the equally problematic southwest.[13] Despite all of the obstacles which they faced, the Welsh itinerants often laboured heroically. Vavasor Powell preached tirelessly up and down the Welsh border, often 'in two or three places a day, and seldom two days in a week throughout the year out of the Pulpit . . . he would sometimes ride a hundred miles in a week, and preach in every place where he might have admission both day and night.'[14] Yet their often pioneering activities were cut short by the political instability surrounding the fall of the Rump Parliament; just when the most propitious circumstances for the evangelization of the country seemed to be within reach, the opportunity evaporated.

There were, of course, plenty of other itinerants who did not rely upon state sponsorship. The Baptists gained a not entirely undeserved reputation for 'sheep-stealing'; John Myles' itinerancies throughout south Wales in the late 1640s picked up followers from all over the region which were later organized into a network of Baptist congregations.[15] George Fox sustained a ministry that saw him make a series of extended itineraries around England, Wales, Scotland, Ireland, the Netherlands, Germany and America.[16] Beginning in 1647, these preaching tours created a network of Quaker meeting houses; working with John ap John in Wales during the later 1650s, Fox capitalized on the disillusionment that many felt with the Puritans' abortive evangelistic strategy.[17] Puritan evangelism a little further afield was often an even greater challenge. The Irish remained a perennial problem. The preachers that rode on the coat tails of the Cromwellian invasion of Ireland in 1649 were hampered by internal conflicts and theological disagreements. While there is evidence that some preached in Gaelic, the battle to save the souls of the Irish was never going to be won.[18] Yet by contrast, Calvinist Presbyterian ministers in the Scottish *Gaidhealtachd* had remarkable success in adapting to a largely oral culture and presenting Protestantism in culturally more accessible terms.[19]

If the work of the Puritan itinerants proved ephemeral, and difficult to sustain in the medium to longer term, there were plenty of examples of the kind of inroads that could be made by dedicated patient pastoral ministry. At Taunton, Joseph Alleine assiduously pastored the people of his own parish through regular preaching and house-to-house visitation, and also frequently itinerated beyond its boundaries. His example pointed to the benefits that might accrue were a similar strategy to be adopted more extensively.[20] But it was the ministry of Richard Baxter at Kidderminster that proved most inspiring, where a parish-based approach was adopted which, while certainly prioritizing regular preaching, in fact put far more emphasis on systematic house-to-house visitation and the reform of behaviour through close ministerial supervision. Baxter's vision, and equally important his success, was written up for all to see and emulate in his *The Reformed Pastor* (1656).

Having lost their parishes in the Great Ejectment in 1662, many newly Nonconformist ministers were forced to alter their approach to mission.[21] The dream of a national reformation was suddenly further away than ever, and many were now forced to reach out to the unevangelized from within the confines of their gathered congregations. The evangelistic techniques which they used still included itinerancy, but placed considerably more emphasis on the printed word. Stephen Hughes travelled clandestinely throughout Carmarthenshire during the height of the restrictions of the Clarendon Code, offering pastoral support to suppressed Nonconformist congregations, and was one of the leading supporters of the Welsh Trust, a London-based charity committed to establishing charity schools and translating some of the classics of English devotional literature into Welsh.[22] Following the granting of toleration in 1689, when Nonconformist ministers had greater freedom of operation, Richard Davis, an Independent minster at Rothwell in Northampton, was criticized for going 'up and down to such places

Babbling'.[23] His commitment to itinerant preaching bore fruit in the establishment of a significant number of new congregations in Northamptonshire and neighbouring Cambridgeshire.[24]

Despite being the preserve of Anglicans, many Nonconformists inevitably benefitted from the activities of the Society for Promoting Christian Knowledge, which after 1699 ploughed its resources into opening schools and publishing godly literature. In Wales, as Geraint H. Jenkins has shown, the years between 1660 and 1730 saw a marked increase in the number of books printed, the vast majority of which were either evangelistic or devotional in tone.[25] They included Welsh translations of Alleine's *An Alarm to Unconverted Sinners* (1672)[26] and Baxter's, *Call to the Unconverted* (1658),[27] both of which were proven tools in the armoury of English Nonconformists intent on maintaining an awakening ministry. More widely these decades saw a flood of godly literature; distributed relatively cheaply by chapmen, books which held out the necessity of repentance and conversion found their way into the homes of more people than ever before.[28]

For Eamon Duffy, the approach to mission that had been perfected by Richard Baxter represented something of a 'pastoral revolution'; his shift from a narrow focus on preaching, to one that was much more holistic flagged up an alternative route to the kind of national reformation of which the Puritans had long dreamed.[29] His was a model taken up with enthusiasm by Nonconformist ministers after 1662, and perhaps more effectively still by the Methodists, during the Evangelical Revival of the mid-eighteenth century.

II. The Methodist Evangelistic Strategy

If the Restoration and the ejection of almost two thousand of the most evangelistically minded minsters in 1662 put paid to the chances of a parish-by-parish transformation of the nation, the early eighteenth century saw the rise in popularity of another evangelistic technique that seemed to offer greater opportunities for many more conversions.[30] While the communal religious revival was by no means an eighteenth-century – still less a Methodist – innovation,[31] it had not previously been used to quite such stunning effect. Intimations of its potential were felt in Penmain, Monmouthshire, in the early 1720s when 'the Lord returned, and visited this church . . . divers joined in communion with them; amongst others, some young men, who became gifted men and preachers of the gospel, helped much to increase the church . . . It was a glorious time with the church at Penmain again . . . above a hundred persons joined the congregation.'[32] But it was the revival that took place at Northampton, Massachusetts, in 1734 under the ministry of Jonathan Edwards that really showed the full potential of community revivals. Writing in the preface to the English edition of Edwards' account of that revival, *A*

Faithful Narrative of the Surprising Work of God (1735), the English Dissenting ministers John Guyse and Isaac Watts urged that Edwards' account be read carefully in the expectation that 'a plentiful effusion of the blessed Spirit, also, descend on the British Isles, and all their American plantations, to renew the face of religion there!'[33]

When Howell Harris compared the revival underway in Wales as very much like that which had taken place just a few years previously in New England,[34] he was referring primarily to the transformation which his exhorting ministry had brought about in some areas. Having initially begun by 'exhorting' to those who lived in the immediate vicinity of his home in Trevecka, Breconshire, Harris soon began to organize those who responded to his message into small *seiadau* (societies). Within a few years he had established a network of these societies in south-east Wales,[35] and once he had linked up with his contemporary Daniel Rowland, an Anglican clergyman from Llangeitho in south-west Wales, the Welsh revival movement began to take shape. Its success was based on the use of a number of evangelistic techniques. Passionate evangelical preaching of individual conversion, tireless itinerancy and the organization of converts into societies which could be adequately supervised, ensured that the Welsh revival did not fizzle out once its initial energy had waned. By 1750, the Welsh Methodists had established a network of 450 societies, containing perhaps as many as 10,000 members who submitted themselves to exacting Methodist discipline. While this was perhaps not quite the great awakening of Methodist myth, it was nonetheless significant, especially within the context of the difficulties which previous generations of Welsh Protestants had faced in winning their contemporaries over to anything more than a nominal Protestantism.[36]

As in Wales, the Evangelical Revival in England was also at first predominantly Anglican. Both George Whitefield and John Wesley (who quickly came to represent different strands of the English revival, one Calvinist the other Arminian) used the same evangelistic techniques as Harris had used to such good effect in Wales. George Whitefield, 'the Grand Itinerant' had begun preaching to very large crowds in Bristol and London as early as 1736; working initially among the existing religious societies, Whitefield's message of the immediate attainability of the new birth, communicated through the novel means of open-air preaching, provoked an enthusiastic response. Using many of the latest communication techniques, easier travel, cheap print and advertising, Whitefield became ubiquitous in the late 1730s.[37] He kick-started revivals in various parts of England, Scotland and down the whole length of the eastern seaboard of the American colonies. He also established societies, although his constant itinerating and decision to divide his time between Britain and America after 1738 meant that he rarely stayed in one place long enough to build a sustainable Methodist movement. Whitefield's itinerancy broke much new ground, but the majority of those who owed their conversion to his ministry, or who had at one time or another belonged to one of the Calvinist societies that he or one of his followers had set up, eventually found their way into the arms of Nonconformity, whether in the form of the Countess of Huntingdon's Connexion or older Dissenting communities such as the Independents. Where Whitefield sowed, others often watered and reaped the most plentiful harvest.

This was in marked contrast to John Wesley. Lacking the charismatic oratory of Whitefield, Wesley more than made up for this with his flair for organization. For Wesley, the weakness of Whitefield's approach was his inability to make adequate provision for his converts. Wesley wrote: 'But those who were more or less affected by Mr Whitefield's preaching had no discipline at all . . . They were formed into no societies: They had no Christian connexion with each other, nor were ever taught to watch over each other's souls.'[38] Wesley rectified this shortcoming by creating a Connexional structure. No less committed to itinerancy than Whitefield, as he travelled around the country, Wesley took the important additional step of leaving those who had responded to his preaching under the care of one of his many travelling preachers. Where this itinerancy was particularly successful and the number of converts dictated larger societies, they were sub-divided into classes and bands. Slowly, Wesley evolved a system of monthly meetings and an annual conference to maintain his iron grip on a movement that by the end of the eighteenth century had grown to such an extent that it effectively acted as an alternative to the Church of England in which for much of the time it still professed to belong. The step of joining the ranks of Nonconformity was not easily taken; ultimately it was pressure from his itinerants at home and in America, as well as Wesley's old age and impending demise, that forced him into the ordination of his own ministers in 1784.[39] Wesley's itinerancy and its accompanying revivalism was therefore a highly regulated affair, and his preference for order became enshrined within the structures which he created. W. R. Ward has suggested that by the end of the eighteenth century this may in fact have blunted the effectiveness of the Methodist evangelistic strategy, leaving the way open for more unregulated revivalism of the kind which originated in the 'Camp Meetings' on the American frontier and which found their way into sections of British Methodism after the Mow Cop revivals of the early nineteenth century.[40]

The Evangelical Revival initially provoked a hostile response from many within the Dissenting community who saw its tendency towards enthusiasm and chaos as something to be avoided. John Evans thought that some of the 'disorderly scenes' which he witnessed at services led by some of the Countess of Huntingdon's preachers 'cannot be of any service to the deluded individuals, nor can they prove beneficial to society'.[41] For others the whole idea of Methodist evangelism with its indiscriminate preaching of the gospel to all was suspect. The Baptist John Gill's High Calvinism led him to 'utterly deny . . . that there are universal offers of grace and salvation to all men'.[42] It was left to Andrew Fuller to mount the most persuasive challenge to Gill's position, arguing that for a 'minister to withhold the invitations of the gospel till he perceives the sinner, sufficiently as he thinks, convinced of sin, and then to bring them forward as something to which he is entitled . . . to think of himself one of God's elect and warranted to believe in Christ, is doing worse than nothing.'[43] There had also been signs of a moderating of High Calvinism elsewhere as well. Father and son Hugh and Caleb Evans, largely through their influence on successive generations of Baptist ministerial students at the Bristol Baptist Academy, married Calvinism to an interest in itinerancy and mission, both at home and abroad.[44] Those prepared to moderate, even soften, their Calvinism were to benefit most from the Evangelical Revival.

In the second half of the eighteenth century, many of the Dissenting denominations received what John Walsh has called 'an enormous blood transfusion from the veins of the Evangelical Revival'.[45] Perhaps the most persuasive factor of all for many Nonconformist ministers was the overwhelming evidence of the good results that revivals produced. Edmund Jones, the Independent minister at Pontypool in Monmouthshire, was profoundly challenged by Howell Harris' ministry, and, as well as being one of his earliest Dissenting supporters, expressed a desire that the 'Lord will yet raise my head, and will yet own me to cast a light about me'.[46] At Bourton-on-the-Water in Gloucestershire, the fifty-five-year ministry of the Baptist Benjamin Beddome witnessed a series of remarkable local religious revivals 'blest for restoring decayed religion, the increasing of our church . . . and the raising up gifts for the help of other Churches'.[47] In Wales, the largest Dissenting denomination, the Independents, was transformed via a more moderate Calvinism, a new urgency in its ministers' preaching and less passive congregations largely by means of emotive hymn-singing and less structured, more participatory, services.[48]

Critical in giving form to this new energy was undoubtedly Philip Doddridge. Holding a 'kind of council' with seventeen fellow ministers at Denton in Norfolk in 1741, where they discussed 'the methods to be taken for the Revival of Religion',[49] Doddridge recommended the formation of societies for the spreading of Christianity 'in some of the darker parts of our own Land'.[50] Copying many of the techniques perfected by the Methodists, direct, enthusiastic and pastoral preaching, ministerial visitation, societies and bands, catechizing, regular communion and associations of like-minded ministers at a local or regional level, Doddridge had already experimented with such a society at Northampton. Freely admitting that 'the effects of it in one congregation can be but very small', he had seen enough of its potential in the hands of the Methodists to know that if 'it were generally to be followed, who can tell what a Harvest such a little grain might at length produce?'[51] It was societies such as those with which Doddridge and others had experimented that mushroomed in the closing years of the eighteenth century, and which alongside mass itinerancy seemed to present the best chance of bringing about the kind of national conversion for which Puritans and Dissenters had worked since the Reformation.

III. Enthusiasm and Inventiveness

The growth and spread of Nonconformity over the course of the century following the Evangelical Revival was fuelled by these two things; further religious revivals, inspired and sustained by the extension of Methodist-style itinerancy, and the proliferation of a vast array of home mission societies, each designed to respond to different kinds of evangelistic need. They became the two arms of the evangelical assault on irreligion and godlessness throughout the nation; the scale of the task was only matched by the sheer inventiveness of the response. It was undoubtedly among the Wesleyan Methodists that the full potential of religious revivals was first realized. Faced with a rapidly increasing population, and the industrialization and urbanization of large swathes of the country, the Methodists were able to take full advantage of the slowness of the Church of England to adapt to these new communities through the extension of itinerant preachers. At John Wesley's death in 1791, his Methodists had numbered over 56,600, but in little more than forty years that number had swollen to over 230,000, amounting to about 1.5 per cent of the population.[52] Areas such as Yorkshire, the East Midlands, Durham and Cornwall were serviced by itinerant Methodist preachers who operated on a circuit-like system, preaching emotive but often highly relevant sermons to the newly coalescing working classes. At Mow Cop in Staffordshire in May 1807 a new type of revival took place. Led by a layman, Hugh Bourne, 'camp meeting' revivals of this kind were at once elemental and chaotic, and were characterized by charismatic preaching and unrestrained congregational participation as individuals experienced the agony and ecstasy of conversion in a short space of time. However, to many these revivals simply looked uncontrolled and improper; they attracted some and repelled others,[53] and in the process contributed still further to the fracturing of a Wesleyan Methodism that under the leadership of Jabez Bunting was making a determined bid for respectability.

Yet neither itinerancy nor revival were limited solely to the Methodists; in the north-west of England, for example, William Roby, an Independent minister in Manchester, founded the Lancashire Independent Association in

1806 specifically to promote the sort of itinerant evangelistic work deemed essential to the encouragement of frequent revivals.[54] In Wales revivals became commonplace, especially following the outbreak of an awakening at Llangeitho in 1762. Over the course of the following eighty years, there were at least fifteen national religious revivals in Wales; that which occurred in 1859 was merely the best known, widespread revivals also swept the country in 1796–97, 1807–9 and 1817. In between, there were countless more local occurrences.[55] From Bala, Thomas Charles, armed with his system of Sunday Schools, reaped the harvest from these successive waves of revivals.[56] In the generation that followed, and led by gifted preachers such as the Calvinistic Methodist John Elias, the Baptist Christmas Evans and the Independent William Williams of Wern, community revivals became the chief means by which successive generations made the transition from a nominal to a more committed Christian profession. Wales seemed particularly susceptible to regular religious revivals.

While those that championed religious revivals most fervently had always struggled with the tension between the role of divine initiative and human agency in their propagation, as the nineteenth century progressed and as the benefits of revivals seemed so obvious, the balance shifted decisively towards the latter.[57] From around the 1820s, 'New Measures' revivalism, championed by the American Presbyterian Charles G. Finney, who thought that revival could be produced by the 'right use of the appropriate means',[58] increasingly became the norm. His *Lectures on Revivals of Religion* (1835) were first published in Britain in 1837, and translated into Welsh almost immediately.[59] Encouraging a more mechanistic and utilitarian view of revivals, the publication of Finney's book breathed new life into the revivalist enterprise. Awakenings took place in various parts of England and Scotland as a result, but it was in Wales that the most dramatic events occurred in a revival that was quickly dubbed 'Finney's revival'.[60] Although Finney never visited Wales, the application of some of his techniques, including direct, even theatrical preaching, women's participation, spontaneous prayer, with individuals often being specifically named, protracted meetings late into the night or over a number of days, and the high pressure technique of the 'anxious seat' were all in evidence.[61] Responses were unsurprisingly often highly emotional. From this point onward, more obvious planning went into revivals, and they almost always contained some or all of these elements.

Revivals proved remarkably well-suited to the evangelistic task that confronted the churches in early decades of the nineteenth century. In Wales evangelical Nonconformity grew rapidly; by 1815 the Independents could boast an impressive 257 congregations,[62] while the Baptists increased their membership six-fold between 1760 and 1800.[63] By the time of the 1851 Religious Census, over three quarters of the Welsh population could be comfortably accommodated within Welsh places of worship, and the overwhelming majority preferred to attend a Nonconformist chapel rather than an Anglican parish church.[64] In England, the number of Dissenting congregations rose from fewer than 1,700 in the 1770s to in excess of 17,000 by 1851.[65] Yet that growth often came at a high price; if these years saw spectacular rates of increase, they also saw the splintering of Nonconformity into a myriad of sects. The pressures of the missionary task at home far from encouraging unity often set the Nonconformist bodies against one another as they competed for souls in an increasingly crowded marketplace.

When revival broke out in New York in 1857, following an economic crash in the city, the businessmen who lay behind the prayer meetings that were its engine ensured that it avoided many of the excesses of more rural awakenings.[66] Meticulously organized, the awakening like many before it crossed the Atlantic reaching Scotland, Ulster and Wales by 1859.[67] In Wales it has been estimated that as many as 110,000 professed conversion,[68] but the awakening was the culmination of successive waves of revivals. What proved to be most remarkable about the 1859 revival was not so much its global reach, but that it proved to be the last major international awakening of its kind. In its aftermath, the nature and pattern of religious revivals evolved further. Continued urban growth throughout Britain led revivalists to concentrate their efforts in urban areas. Like the 1857 awakening in New York, businessmen began to take an increasingly prominent role in organizing revivals in the major British cities. Focusing on large-scale preaching rallies, usually staged in vast halls, they were led by professional revivalists who were specifically invited for their proven success in harvesting souls. There was little scope for overt displays of enthusiasm in these revivals, those seeking spiritual help were not directed to an 'anxious seat', but invited to a separate after-meeting at which they were counselled in private by specially trained evangelists. Mirroring the industrial enterprises in which many in urban Britain worked by this time, this was a highly organized and carefully regulated style of revival.

The most gifted exponent of this type of revival was the Chicago-based evangelist Dwight Lyman Moody. His crusade-like revivals were held with the funding and support of commercial and business leaders, and always made extensive use of mass advertising. Accompanied by his assistant, the gospel singer Ira D. Sankey, Moody's crusades were a combination of the evangelical and the cloyingly sentimental. Although not all agreed with either his theology or his methods, his winsomeness, personal sanctity and obvious success did help break down denominational barriers, as evangelicals began to come together in pursuit of a common evangelistic goal. During two major tours of British cities in 1873–75 and 1883–84, at which he preached in such vast auditoria as the Manchester Free Trade Hall and the Agricultural Hall in Islington, it was estimated that in excess of 2.5 million people heard him.[69] However, despite his desire to reach out to the unchurched, Moody's efforts were in fact most successful in drawing in those already on the fringes of the churches to more committed membership. There were few home-grown preachers or evangelists who could match his appeal. The Baptist C. H. Spurgeon regularly attracted 8,000–10,000 to Surrey Gardens Music Hall in the late 1850s, and similar numbers to his Metropolitan Tabernacle for decades after, but he consciously eschewed many aspects of contemporary revivalism.[70] The crusade-style of revival was very much an American import; it was to be perfected during the twentieth century.

If revival was one approach to the nineteenth-century evangelistic challenge, the formation of voluntary home mission agencies mushroomed alongside them. Of course, for the majority of Nonconformist churches in the nineteenth century it was the Sunday School that became the chief means of inculcating a lifelong commitment to the Christian faith. Although their chief instigators had been the Anglicans Robert Raikes in England and Thomas Charles in Wales, Sunday Schools quickly became integral to Nonconformist church life. By 1803 the Nonconformists had established the national Sunday School Union which co-ordinated efforts more centrally, leading to the proliferation of schools across the country. By 1833, 45 per cent of English children were attending Sunday Schools, although not all of these were of the Nonconformist variety.[71]

Yet Sunday Schools could be less successful in drawing in the unchurched, especially in the growing industrial and urban centres. To address this problem the Nonconformists established a plethora of home mission societies, channelling the energies of those converted in revivals into a life of activism through evangelism and social and moral reform. Critical in conditioning evangelical attitudes to social reform, especially in the cities, was the Church of Scotland minister Thomas Chalmers. In his parish on the eastern edge of Glasgow's city centre between 1815 and 1823, Chalmers developed an innovative approach to urban mission. Dividing his parish into a number of smaller areas, each consisting of less than a hundred families, he then set an elder or deacon over each; elders were to look after the spiritual needs of the parishioners, the deacons their material needs. He hoped that each of these localities would become self-sustaining communities, mirroring the patterns of mutual support that Chalmers had witnessed in some of the more rural Scottish parishes he had served before his arrival in Glasgow. His ideas were published in his *The Christian and Civic Economy of Large Towns* (1819–26), and although his scheme achieved only patchy success, Chalmers' ideas had a powerful impact on evangelical and Nonconformist attitudes to the growing problem of the urban poor.[72]

For many evangelicals it was the system of systematic pastoral visitation that was the most attractive element of Chalmers programme. In 1826 David Nasmith adapted Chalmers' plan and founded the Glasgow City Mission; specifically nondenominational, laymen were employed as scripture readers and visitors especially among the poor, and the scheme was soon taken up by many in other cities in both Britain and America. The London City Mission was established in 1835, but it was only the largest and most varied in its activities.[73] The Manchester City Mission employed thirty-five lay workers between 1842–43 engaging in such activities as the distribution of tracts, systematic house-to-house visitation, the reclamation of drunkards and the restoration of prostitutes to their friends and families. The report of this mission for these months confidently proclaimed that there were almost five thousand 'inquirers' dependent on its workers for 'religious instruction'.[74] The Unitarian Domestic Mission Station at Spicer Street in London similarly held classes, maintained a library, sponsored lectures, but also supported a savings bank and a benevolent fund for sick members.[75]

To facilitate the work of both the Sunday Schools and the city missions, a complementary array of tract and Bible societies were established. The Society for Promoting Religious Knowledge among the Poor had been established by Nonconformists as early as 1750; dedicated to printing and distributing tracts, Bibles and other godly literature, it was a precursor to the larger and more ambitious societies of the early nineteenth century.[76] By 1849 the Religious Tract Society, which had been formed in 1799, had distributed over five-hundred million tracts, broadsheets and handbills to the poor throughout the country.[77] The British and Foreign Bible Society (1804) similarly produced inexpensive Bibles for distribution among the poor, including in languages other than English for circulation in Wales and parts of Scotland where Gaelic was still the predominant language.[78] Societies such as these made the work of the other Nonconformist voluntary mission agencies possible.

Over time a whole range of more specialized mission societies evolved in response to specific needs. Maintaining the interests of the young, especially when there were other activities, good and not so good, to occupy their leisure time in the major cities was a perennial concern. George Williams, a Congregationalist and lowly apprentice draper, founded the Young Men's Christian Association in London in 1844, specifically to provide social, recreational and educational activities for young men who ran the risk of turning their backs on their earlier religious commitments following their arrival in the city.[79] Similarly, Hugh Stowell Brown, a Baptist minister in Liverpool, began Sunday afternoon lectures to the working men of the city,[80] although attempts to offer free food were often more successful inducements to attract those who might otherwise have been reluctant to attend divine service. William Carter's evangelistic Tea Meetings, directed at the barrow-sellers of fruit and vegetables around his Brethren assembly in south London, were not untypical.[81] But it was in the realm of philanthropy that the nineteenth-century evangelicals were at their most innovative. David Bebbington has argued that the nineteenth century saw evangelicalism reach a dominant position in British society,[82] both on account of the significant harvests which evangelical revivals reaped, and also the sense that evangelicals were behind nearly every philanthropic agency that was established. However, disentangling Nonconformist activity from wider evangelical activity in this area is difficult, since at least after the establishment of the Evangelical Alliance in 1846 very real attempts at pan-evangelical unity were attempted as Anglicans and Nonconformists worked alongside each other to combat many of society's moral ills.

Nonetheless, Nonconformists were involved in major philanthropic ventures, especially concerning the care of orphaned children. George Müller opened his first orphanage in Bristol in 1836 and soon had thousands of children under his care.[83] Charles Spurgeon opened his Stockwell Orphanage in 1867,[84] and a year later Thomas Barnardo opened his East End Juvenile Mission which ran both schools and a home for abandoned boys.[85] In 1848 the Congregationalist Andrew Reed established a home for children with learning difficulties at Highgate in north London, pioneering innovative therapeutic techniques that were to change the way in which disabilities of this nature were regarded.[86] Others were concerned with the poor housing conditions in which many lived; the Congregationalist Titus Salt, a Yorkshire woollen manufacturer, built a new community called Saltaire outside Bradford, providing improved housing and many modern amenities for his employees.[87] Another Congregationalist, William Hesketh Lever, provided similar facilities at his soap manufactory at Port Sunlight on the Wirral.[88] Other Nonconformists were prominent in campaigns to secure better medical provision, improve the quality of popular schooling, safeguard the sanctity of the Lord's Day, ameliorate the conditions of prisoners and stamp out vice in all its forms.[89]

Yet if there was one issue guaranteed to rouse Nonconformists to action in greater numbers it was alcohol. Despite the foundation of a national United Kingdom Alliance in 1853, in most instances temperance advocates preferred to use voluntary means, especially the persuasion of the young to sign a pledge of total abstinence.[90] Indeed, such was the close affiliation of Nonconformity and temperance that for many the decision to remain teetotal became as much a rite of passage as baptism or one's first Communion. Attempts to tighten up the licensing laws, however, proved frustratingly difficult, except in Wales where the Liberal Party, which drew much of its strength from a dominant Nonconformity, managed to secure the passing of the Welsh Sunday Closing Act in 1881.[91] Some Welsh counties were to remain dry on a Sunday until the closing years of the twentieth century.

During the last quarter of the nineteenth century attitudes towards mission among Nonconformists clearly underwent a change. While many still thought of mission almost exclusively in terms of individual salvation, others took a more holistic approach that stressed social reform as much as personal redemption.[92] When Andrew Mearns, secretary of the London Congregational Union, published *The Bitter Cry of Outcast London* in 1883, many were horrified at the poverty and degradation which he described in such unremitting detail.[93] Among the first to respond was William Booth. Having started life among the New Connexion Methodists, Booth was a typical exponent of Wesleyan revivalism, albeit with the novel idea of taking the gospel to the poor rather than expecting them to come to the churches. However, the reality of work among the poorest in society soon forced him to change tack, and in 1890 he published *In Darkest England and the Way Out* in which he, like Mearns before him, laid bare in often shocking detail the extent to which those at the very bottom of society lived lives of chronic poverty and despair.[94] Seeing social and spiritual needs as inextricably linked, Booth was compelled to shift the focus of his Salvation Army to stress practical relief as much as spiritual redemption to those to whom it ministered. It was an innovation that was to have a profound effect on what many felt should be the evangelistic priorities of the churches on the cusp of the twentieth century.

IV. Mission in the Face of Secularization

Any discussion of Nonconformist home mission in the twentieth century is inevitably overshadowed by the catastrophic decline in influence and membership experienced by every single Christian denomination. Yet as the century began, optimism was the order of the day. When revival broke out in south-west Wales in 1904, under the charismatic leadership of a trainee for the Calvinistic Methodist ministry, Evan Roberts, the twin engines of growth that had served the Nonconformist churches so well, revival and home mission societies, seemed primed and ready to continue their delivery of generation upon generation of souls to fill the pews of their increasingly cavernous new chapels. The members of Tabernacle Chapel in Morriston, near Swansea, took immense pride in their new building. Opened in 1872 and built at phenomenal cost, this cathedral of Welsh Nonconformity could accommodate 3,000 worshippers at a time. While it was the largest of its kind in Wales, chapels with a seating capacity in excess of 1,500 shot up in practically every town in Wales in the closing decades of the nineteenth century.[95] They were testimony to the optimism and confidence of their Nonconformist congregations; the irony was that many of them were never filled. Despite the harvest of souls garnered by the 1904–5 revival, by 1906 the high water mark of Nonconformist church membership had already passed.[96]

The revival of 1904–5 was the last national religious awakening that Wales experienced. While the revival was always about more than the activities of Evan Roberts, the publicity that surrounded him meant that the predominant impression of the revival for many was the histrionic behaviour of Roberts himself. There were certainly many thousands of converts,[97] but with a message that often concentrated more on holiness and total consecration than evangelical conversion, Roberts' revival appealed more to those already within the churches, heightening the spiritual experience of many. For others, though, Roberts' manipulative style and some of his more outlandish claims, led to charges that the revival was little more than fool's gold.[98] Although it attracted considerable international attention,[99] the revival did not spread to other parts of Britain in any significant way. Despite considerable interest, English Nonconformity, with the exception of those congregations which contained a significant Welsh contingent, remained largely untouched.

This is not to say that the era of mass evangelism was at an end. Between February and June 1905, the American evangelists Reuben A. Torrey and Charles M. Alexander held 202 meetings in London's Royal Albert Hall, attracting over 1.1 million attendees and securing an estimated 17,000 conversions. Similar meetings were held in Edinburgh, Liverpool and Birmingham.[100] Indeed, filling the Royal Albert Hall remained a badge of achievement for evangelists throughout the early part of the twentieth century. George Jeffreys, the founder of the Elim Pentecostal denomination, held regular Easter evangelistic and healing campaigns there in the late 1920s, attracting major American preachers including the controversial Californian revivalist Aimee Semple Macpherson in 1926 and 1928.[101] Yet events such as these tended to create an overly positive impression. As early as 1912 the Wesleyans, for example, were beginning to despair at statistics which revealed, in real terms, their sixth annual decline in membership,[102] while in Wales, one of Nonconformity's strongest bastions, by the 1930s the four main Nonconformist denominations were haemorrhaging members.[103] By the eve of the Second World War, that decline had become endemic.

Yet for many Nonconformists traditional styles of evangelism had lost their attraction. The early decades of the twentieth century were the heyday of the social gospel. Many within the Free Churches, some influenced by liberal theological trends, but most simply overwhelmed by the poverty that they witnessed among the working classes, felt that the church's traditional emphasis on personal salvation meant that they had little to say to their present circumstances. It was a problem thrown into still sharper relief by the harrowing experience of trench warfare in northern France during the 1914–18 war. Mirroring the work of the New York Baptist Walter Rauschenbusch, who had emphasized the establishment of the kingdom of God in social and economic, rather than solely spiritual terms,[104] many Nonconformist leaders were inspired to recast their mission in terms of the creation of a full-blown social Christianity. Among the social gospel's most ardent champions was R. J. Campbell, minister of the City Temple in London, whose 'New Theology' was an eclectic mix of philosophical idealism and collectivist social theory. Along with the Baptist John Clifford, who published *Socialism and the Teaching of Christ* in 1898,[105] Campbell argued that socialism was nothing other than the practical application of Christianity.[106] With the Labour's Party's electoral breakthrough in 1906 many influential Nonconformist leaders anticipated that the kind of reordering of society which they had thought and spoken about for decades was closer than ever.

In practical terms, those influenced to a greater or lesser extent by social teaching of this kind, re-orientated the mission of their churches in a number of ways. For some the idea of the 'institutional church' seemed to offer the best solution. The church, it was held, should look after its members from the cradle to the grave; church was to be more like a home than a place of worship. The first thing required was the flattening or refitting of chapels whose primary purpose had been worship and preaching. In came purpose built auditoriums with a warren of smaller rooms attached in which the plethora of activities now on offer could be accommodated. Lecture halls, reading rooms, facilities for amateur dramatic societies, gymnasia and games rooms were typical additions.[107] For the Wesleyan Methodists it was the building of Central Halls that was thought the best response. While some of these were cavernous and ostentatious buildings, the Methodist Central Hall in London, strategically positioned opposite Westminster Abbey and adjacent to the Houses of Parliament, for example, was always more of a statement of Wesleyan self-confidence than anything else,[108] others were more attuned to the needs of the communities in which they were erected. Hugh Price Hughes had been one of the most successful innovators in this area. Originally opened in 1887, his Wesleyan West London Mission combined, seemingly successfully, a plethora of social programmes as well as Sunday evening evangelistic services.[109] J. Arthur Rank funded the building of a vast auditorium in Tooting in 1910,[110] and there were similar initiatives in most other major English cities.

In south Wales where the social conditions of the working classes were exacerbated by the regular depressions in the mining industry, the Central Halls really came into their own. Under the leadership of R. J. Barker, for example, the Central Hall at Tonypandy in the Rhondda proved especially effective during the extreme hardship of the General Strike in 1926. Barker's idea was that mutual care could alleviate the worst of the social conditions; as well as the usual distribution of food and clothing, families in neighbouring communities were encouraged to adopt unemployed families in the Tonypandy area. The opening of a Community House in Trealaw in 1928 provided a milk bar, lecture rooms, training in basic craft skills and a gymnasium.[111] Among the Calvinistic Methodists, Wales' largest Nonconformist body, the Society for the Establishment of new and missionary causes', better known as the Forward Movement, although established by John Pugh in 1891 as a stripped back evangelistic agency to some of the more deprived areas of south Wales,[112] had through its large purpose built halls begun to fulfil a similar function to the Wesleyan Central Halls. That Martyn Lloyd-Jones saw fit to disband the church football team, cancel the programme of musical evenings and chop-up the wooden stage used by the amateur dramatic society for firewood, when he began his ministry at a Forward Movement hall in Aberavon,[113] is indicative of the extent to which social activities of this sort had become indispensable in Nonconformist attempts to connect with the working classes.

For some evangelicals preoccupation with social matters was therefore a diversion from the true calling of the church, winning souls. At a local level this task continued unabated; roving evangelists, tent missions, open air preaching, tract distribution, Gospel Mission carts and later cars were all common sights. Yet where many Nonconformists had adopted a more incarnational approach to mission, seeking to be part of society and work towards its transformation, many evangelicals, especially those of a more fundamentalist bent, took a more confrontational approach. Often cowed by the extent to which some of the main Nonconformist denominations had been won over to liberal theological positions, some evangelicals withdrew into their own sub-cultures. For them evangelism was more akin to a raid on enemy territory, and their presentation of the gospel was often couched in negative, even denunciatory, terms. R. B. Jones, the Baptist minister at Porth in the Rhondda was as well known for his condemnation of the cinema, jazz music, the League of Nations and the newly founded Welsh nationalist party Plaid Cenedlaethol Cymru (later Plaid Cymru), as he was for a more positive presentation of the gospel.[114] However, there were other evangelical voices in the 1930s freer of such denunciatory language; Martyn Lloyd-Jones was able to attract large congregations throughout south Wales to hear preaching that while certainly evangelistic could also be intellectually and theologically challenging.[115]

Unlike the experience of the First World War, the Second World War did not bequeath quite the same legacy of disillusionment with the churches. Indeed, the 1950s were to usher in something of a hiatus in the long process of declining church attendance.[116] There were a number of more successful evangelistic initiatives that seemed to offer a way forward. The hope of revival was still seen by many as the ultimate panacea; the formation of the Baptist

Revival Fellowship in 1938[117] and the London ministry of Martyn Lloyd-Jones, which was marked by an increasing emphasis on revival following a series of sermons he preached in 1959 to mark the centenary of the 1859 revival, kept the possibility of revival at the forefront of the minds of many conservative evangelicals.[118] Yet neither the East Anglian Revival in 1921 nor the Hebridean Revival between 1949 and 1952, became anything more than localized quickenings of the evangelistic pace. Despite the publicity, the likelihood of revival seemed further away than ever.[119]

There were still many who maintained the emphasis on seeing the evangelistic task in primarily social terms. None was more influential in post-war Britain than the Methodist Donald Soper. As minister of the Kingsway Hall, a Central Hall that housed the West London Methodist Mission, Soper married his socialist politics to his liberal theology. As well as being a prominent open-air preacher, a fixture at Speaker's Corner in Hyde Park, Soper's Mission did much to serve the poor and marginalized in his west London locality. Yet his was always a controversial voice, most often heard over his favourite issues of teetotalism, in criticism of blood sports and in favour of pacifism and the Campaign for Nuclear Disarmament.[120] These concerns were a far cry from traditional evangelistic priorities. Traditional approaches to evangelism were given an enormous shot in the arm in post-war Britain by the American evangelist Billy Graham. Callum Brown has called the 1950s the 'crusade decade'.[121] When Graham arrived in London in early 1954 the churches had been alive with talk of the reconversion of England for some time, but as worthy as some of these efforts proved to be,[122] it was Graham who captured the public and church-going imaginations. His Greater London Crusade packed the Harringay Arena for twelve weeks, and culminated in 120,000 filling Wembley Stadium on the final evening. His simple style, and simplistic message, combined with a dash of American razzmatazz, went down especially well in a Britain still suffering from post-war austerity. While there was plenty of opposition from among the old Nonconformist denominations, for every dissenting voice raised there were others prepared to leap to Graham's defence. Conservative estimates suggested that well in excess of a million people attended a crusade meeting during these months;[123] further crusades followed in 1966 and Graham's ambitious Mission England campaign filled English football stadiums in 1984, but neither of these had quite the impact of the 1954 extravaganza. However, there was a sense in which these crusades were worlds away from the lives of the average church member; while they initially brought in significant harvests of converts they could leave others feeling beleaguered, unable to offer the kind of experience to new converts that Harringay had promised. Their contribution to the evangelistic task confronting the churches in the 1950s and beyond was inevitably mixed.

Yet if the 1950s bred a certain evangelistic optimism the decade that followed threw the churches into confusion, and then accelerated decline. The 1960s were deeply disorientating for many Nonconformist Christians in Britain. The gathering tide of permissiveness, the first inkling of which was the *Lady Chatterley's Lover* case in 1960, saw the loosening of long assumed behavioural standards. By the late 1960s a whole raft of legal changes saw the decriminalization of homosexuality, the passing of more liberal abortion laws, the provision of legislation to make divorce easier and the wider availability of contraception. For many Nonconformists these were welcome changes, but for the majority they were sharply divergent from the values that the churches had held dear for centuries. They may well have precipitated the final death of Christian Britain.[124] Certainly many churches saw some of the evangelistic agencies on which they had relied so heavily become increasingly ineffective. The spread of car ownership and the ubiquity of television meant that for many there were simply other things to do on a Sunday. Sunday School attendance consequently plummeted, removing one of the chief means by which the Nonconformist churches in particular had traditionally recruited new members.[125]

Yet it is easy to paint an overly pessimistic picture of the fortunes of the Nonconformist churches in the 1960s and 1970s. Some channelled their energies into opposing aspects of the new permissive society. Mary Whitehouse's National Viewer's and Listener's Association and Malcolm Muggeridge's 'Festival of Light' in 1971, although not led by Nonconformists, received much of the grass roots support on which they relied from disaffected Baptist, Brethren and infant Pentecostal denominations. They became a rallying point for many who were outraged at the amount of sex and violence which they saw on their televisions and in the media.[126] The expansion of higher education during the 1960s led to a growth in the number of Christian Unions, run by students for students as non-denominational bodies whose *rasion d'être* was the strategic evangelization of generations of students who would go on to be leaders in many facets of British life. In Wales many migrated into the independent evangelical churches represented by the separatist Evangelical Movement of Wales once their student days were over, bringing their considerable evangelistic experience and expertise with them.[127]

Yet little of this did much to arrest the decline in the mainline Nonconformist denominations. However, in the mid-1960s the advent of the Charismatic movement, although primarily concerned with a reintegration of the gifts of the Holy Spirit into the lives of the churches, revolutionized the culture of many evangelical churches. Charismatic renewal encouraged a more relaxed, less stuffy attitude towards church; freer forms of worship, a stress on the community life of the local church and a new flexibility towards the task of evangelism were all among the benefits reaped, even by churches which disagreed with charismatic pneumatology. The old evangelistic techniques that Nonconformists had relied upon for generations, preaching rallies, open-air evangelism and literature or tract distribution all suddenly looked old-fashioned and ill-suited to the late twentieth century. By the early 1970s most Nonconformist denominations had groups within them which had been influenced to some extent by charismatic renewal.[128] While not all necessarily agreed with approaches to mission such as John Wimber's 'power evangelism', in which signs and wonders were encouraged as an authentication of the gospel message,[129] many benefitted from such 'seeker sensitive' approaches as that which emanated from the Willow Creek Community Church in Chicago. Encouraging churches to craft their worship services in a way that would prove attractive and accessible to the unchurched made some Nonconformist churches more adaptable and better able to build bridges into their local communities.[130] With the advent of the Alpha Course in the 1990s, a form of relational low-pressure evangelism which allowed those often alienated from the traditional churches an opportunity to explore the Christian faith in a relaxed and non-confrontational way, many churches found an evangelistic technique that reaped significant results. By 2008, over 7,150 Alpha Courses had been run in churches throughout Britain, including in many of the older Free Churches.[131] The irony of this new initiative, of course, was that it harked back to the catechetical techniques that had been used with such success by Nonconformists of earlier centuries.

However, for many charismatics the old Nonconformist denominations had simply outgrown their usefulness. Beginning in house churches, small fellowships of those committed to exploring the gifts and ministry of the Holy Spirit proliferated during the 1970s and beyond. Knit together by conferences, and occasionally the presence of a charismatic leader, some of these groups coalesced into formal denomination-like networks. They were supplemented by the rapid growth of Black-majority churches. While immigration from the Caribbean had been a reality since the 1950s, the 1980s witnessed the proliferation of African-led church planting, especially in London.[132] These New Churches became, in the words of David Bebbington, the 'new Nonconformity'.[133] Where the Free Churches had defined themselves against the Established Church, these New Churches defined themselves over against the traditional denominations. As the twentieth century drew to a close it was among these groups that signs of evangelistic success were to be detected.

When examining the evangelistic effectiveness of the Nonconformist churches, especially during the second half of the twentieth century, it can be very difficult to move beyond the dominant narrative of decline. While secularization clearly overshadows the story, recent research has shown that there have been areas of the United Kingdom where that decline has been checked and in some cases even reversed. Among the New Churches and the Black-majority Churches in contemporary Britain, in particular, there has been significant growth since the early 1980s.[134] Much of this growth has occurred in London and along the various major trade routes of contemporary Britain, areas where there has been a degree of economic flexibility and a significant multicultural population. And in many of these churches there has also been a breaking down of the old division between traditional evangelism and social action; many of the New Churches blend both approaches to the evangelistic task with some measure of success. In Wales, for example, while the older Nonconformist denominations have, in the main, struggled to escape from the cycle of decline, there have been other churches, especially on the economically more diverse M4 corridor, which have been prepared to engage with their communities in targeted social action, adapt some of their inherited structures and carefully enculturate their presentation of the gospel. Some have experienced a measure of growth. Many have found their sense of mission revitalized during the early years of the twenty-first century.[135]

V. Conclusion

This overview of Nonconformist efforts at home mission from the sixteenth century to the present day has shown that there has been enormous diversity in the approaches that have been adopted over time. While the hope and expectation of revival has tended to overlay all of their efforts, where there has been a willingness to adapt and experiment with new evangelistic means and techniques, those efforts have often been met with success. Conversely, where there has been a tendency to retreat from the public sphere, to disengage with wider society, to circle the wagons and wait for better days, Nonconformist churches have tended to ossify, become culturally irrelevant and become locked in a downward spiral of decline and declension. While the revival for which many still long appears at best only a distant possibility, there are signs among some contemporary Nonconformists that the evangelistic challenge is being taken up with renewed vigour and that the inventiveness that has traditionally characterized the Nonconformist approach to mission still survives.

Notes

1 Philip Doddridge, *The Evil and Danger of Neglecting the Souls of Men . . .* (London: M. Fenner, 1742).
2 Alan P. F. Sell et al. (eds), *Protestant Nonconformist Texts, Volume 2: The Eighteenth Century* (Aldershot: Ashgate, 2006), p. 202.
3 Ibid., pp. 202–3.
4 See Nicholas Tyacke (ed.), *England's Long Reformation, 1500–1800* (London: Routledge, 1998); Peter Wallace, *The Long European Reformation* (Houndmills: Palgrave, 2004).

5 Patrick Collinson, 'Elizabethan and Jacobean Puritanism as Forms of Popular Religious Culture', Christopher Durston and Jacqueline Eales (eds), *The Culture of English Puritanism, 1560–1700* (Basingstoke: Palgrave, 1996), p. 46.
6 Eamon Duffy, 'The Long Reformation: Catholicism, Protestantism and the Multitude', in Tyacke (ed.), *England's Long Reformation, 1500–1800*, p. 34.
7 R. Tudur Jones et al. (eds), *Protestant Nonconformist Texts, Volume 1: 1550 to 1700* (Aldershot: Ashgate, 2007), pp. 91–92.
8 See J. Gwynfor Jones, 'John Penry: Government, Order and the "Perishing Souls" of Wales', *Transactions of the Honourable Society of Cymmrodorion* (1993), pp. 47–81.
9 Christopher Hill, *Change and Continuity in Seventeenth Century England* (London: Yale University Press, 1974), p. 5.
10 Patrick Collinson, *The Religion of Protestants: the Church in English Society, 1559–1625* (Oxford: Oxford University Press, 1984), p. 249.
11 Christopher Haigh, 'Puritan Evangelism in the Reign of Elizabeth I', *English Historical Review*, XCII/362 (1977), pp. 30–58.
12 Michael R. Watts, *The Dissenters, Volume 1: From the Reformation to the French Revolution* (Oxford: Clarendon Press, 1978), p. 139.
13 Hill, *Change and Continuity in Seventeenth Century England*, p. 38.
14 Edward Bagshaw, *The Life and Death of Mr Vavasor Powell* (London, 1671), p. 107.
15 T. M. Bassett, *The Welsh Baptists* (Swansea: Ilston House, 1977), pp. 13–33.
16 Watts, *The Dissenters, Volume 1*, pp. 195–97.
17 Geraint H. Jenkins, *Protestant Dissenters in Wales, 1639–1689* (Cardiff: University of Wales Press, 1992), pp. 35–36.
18 See Crawford Gribben, *God's Irishmen: Theological Debates in Cromwellian Ireland* (Oxford: Oxford University Press, 2007).
19 Jane Dawson, 'Calvinism and the Gaidhealtachd in Scotland', in Andrew Petegree, Alastair Duke and Gillian Lewis (eds), *Calvinism in Europe, 1541–1620* (Cambridge: Cambridge University Press, 1994), pp. 231–53.
20 Duffy, 'The Long Reformation: Protestantism, Catholicism and the Multitude', pp. 46–47.
21 For the extent of this ejection in different parts of England and Wales, see Alan P. F. Sell (ed.), *The Great Ejectment of 1662: Its Antecedents, Aftermath, and Ecumenical Significance* (Eugene, OR: Wipf and Stock, 2012).
22 Eryn M. White, 'Popular Schooling and the Welsh Language, 1650–1800', in Geraint H. Jenkins (ed.), *The Welsh Language before the Industrial Revolution* (Cardiff: University of Wales Press, 1997), pp. 319–21.
23 Sell et al. (eds), *Protestant Nonconformist Texts, Volume 2*, p. 191.
24 Geoffrey F. Nuttall, 'Northamptonshire and *The Modern Question*: A Turning Point in Eighteenth Century Dissent', *Journal of Theological Studies*, XVI/1 (1965), p. 104.
25 Geraint H. Jenkins, *Literature, Religion and Society in Wales, 1660–1730* (Cardiff: University of Wales, 1978).
26 Joseph Alleine, *Hyfforddwr Cyfarwydd i'r Nefoedd* (London: Thomas Whitledge and R. Everingham, 1693).
27 Richard Jones, *Galwad i'r Annychweledig* (London, 1659).
28 See Eamon Duffy, 'The godly and the multitude in Stuart England', *The Seventeenth Century*, I/1 (1986), pp. 44–49.
29 Duffy, 'The Long Reformation: Protestantism, Catholicism and the multitude', pp. 48–49.
30 Bruce Hindmarsh, 'The Reception of Jonathan Edwards among Early Evangelicals in England', in David W. Kling and Douglas A. Sweeney (eds), *Jonathan Edwards at Home and Abroad: Historical Memoires, Cultural Movements, Global Horizons* (Chapel Hill, SC: University of South Carolina Press, 2003), pp. 203–4.

31 Communal revivals had been commonplace in Scotland in the seventeenth century. See Leigh E. Schmidt, *Holy Fairs: Scotland and the Making of American Revivalism* (Grand Rapids, MI: Eerdmans, 2001). For their late-seventeenth and early-eighteenth-century versions, see W. R. Ward, *The Protestant Evangelical Awakening* (Cambridge: Cambridge University Press, 2002).
32 Sell et al (eds), *Protestant Nonconformist Texts, Volume 2*, p. 192.
33 Jonathan Edwards, *A Faithful Narrative of the Surprising Work of God* (London: John Oswald, 1737), pp. xv–xvi.
34 David Ceri Jones, '"Sure the Time Here now Is Like New England": What Happened When the Welsh Calvinistic Methodists Read Jonathan Edwards?', Kenneth E. Minkema, Adriaan Neele and Kelly van Andel (eds), *Jonathan Edwards and Scotland* (Edinburgh: Dunedin Academic Press, 2011), p. 49.
35 Geraint Tudur, *Howell Harris: From Conversion to Separation, 1735–50* (Cardiff: University of Wales Press, 2000), chapter 4.
36 See David Ceri Jones, '"A Glorious Morn"? Methodism and the Rise of Evangelicalism in Wales, 1735–1762', in Mark Smith (ed.), *British Evangelical Identities: Past and Present* (Milton Keynes: Paternoster, 2008), I, pp. 110–11.
37 David Ceri Jones, Boyd Stanley Schlenther and Eryn Mant White, *The Elect Methodists: Calvinistic Methodism in England and Wales, 1735–1811* (Cardiff: University of Wales Press, 2012), pp. 6–10.
38 Sell et al (eds), *Protestant Nonconformist Texts, Volume 2*, p. 227.
39 Frank Baker, *John Wesley and the Church of England* (London: Epworth Press, 1970), chapters 13 to 16.
40 W. R. Ward, 'Was there a Methodist evangelistic strategy in the eighteenth century?', in Tyacke (ed.), *England's Long Reformation, 1500–1800*, pp. 299–302.
41 Sell et al. (eds), *Protestant Nonconformist Texts, Volume 2*, p. 241.
42 'John Gill on the Gospel to be Preached, and John Wesley's Rejoinder', in Sell et al. (eds), *Protestant Nonconformist Texts, Volume 2*, p. 204.
43 'Baptist Evangelism', in Sell et al. (eds), *Protestant Nonconformist Texts, Volume 2*, p. 207.
44 Roger Hayden, *Continuity and Change: Evangelical Calvinism among Eighteenth-Century Baptist Ministers Trained at Bristol Academy, 1690–1791* (Milton under Wychwood: Baptist Historical Society, 2006).
45 John Walsh, 'Methodism at the end of the Eighteenth Century', in Rupert Davies and Gordon Rupp (eds), *A History of the Methodist Church in Great Britain* (London: Epworth Press, 1965), I, p. 293.
46 Sell et al. (eds), *Protestant Nonconformist Texts, Volume 2*, p. 238.
47 Ibid., p. 195.
48 R. Tudur Jones, *Congregationalism in Wales*, ed. Robert Pope (Cardiff: University of Wales Press, 2004), chapter 8.
49 Sell et al. (eds), *Protestant Nonconformist Texts, Volume 2*, p. 199.
50 Ibid., p. 202.
51 Ibid.
52 Alan D. Gilbert, *Religion and Industrial Society in England: Church, Chapel and Social Change, 1740–1914* (London: Longman, 1976), p. 31.
53 See John Kent, *Holding the Fort: Studies in Victorian Revivalism* (London: Epworth Press, 1978), chapter 2.
54 David Bebbington et al. (eds), *Protestant Nonconformist Texts, Volume 3: the Nineteenth Century* (Aldershot: Ashgate, 2006), pp. 25–60. See also Deryck W. Lovegrove, *Established Church, Sectarian People: Itinerancy and the Transformation of English Dissent, 1780–1830* (Cambridge: Cambridge University Press, 1988).

55 These have been helpfully catalogued in Geraint Jones, *Favoured with Frequent Revivals: Revivals in Wales, 1762–1865* (Cardiff: Heath Christian Trust, 2001), pp. 9–43.
56 Jones, Schlenther and White, *The Elect Methodists*, pp. 197–98.
57 David W. Bebbington, *Victorian Religious Revivals: Culture and Piety in Local and Global Contexts* (Oxford: Oxford University Press, 2012), pp. 9–13.
58 'Charles Finney on Revivals, 1839', Bebbington et al. (eds), *Protestant Nonconformist Texts, Volume 3*, p. 262.
59 Charles G. Finney, *Darlithiau ar Adfywiadau Crefyddol* (Swansea, 1839).
60 Richard Carwardine, 'The Welsh Evangelical Community and "Finney's Revival"', *Journal of Ecclesiastical History*, 29 (1978), pp. 463–80.
61 Richard Carwardine, *Trans-Atlantic Revivalism: Popular Evangelicalism in Britain and America, 1790–1865* (Westport, CT: Greenwood Press, 1978), p. 8. See also Dyfed Wyn Roberts, 'The Effect of Charles Finney's Revivalism on the 1858–60 Awakening in Wales', in idem (ed.), *Revival, Renewal and the Holy Spirit* (Milton Keynes: Paternoster, 2009), pp. 36–44.
62 Jones, *Congregationalism in Wales*, p. 149.
63 Bassett, *The Welsh Baptists*, p. 93.
64 Ieuan Gwynedd Jones, *Explorations and Explanations: Essays in the Social History of Victorian Wales* (Llandysul: Gomer Press, 1981), p. 21.
65 Gilbert, *Religion and Society in Industrial England*, pp. 36–37.
66 See Kathryn T. Long, *The Revival of 1857–58: Interpreting an American Religious Awakening* (New York: Oxford University Press, 1998).
67 Janice Holmes, *Religious Revivals in Britain and Ireland, 1859–1905* (Dublin: Irish Academic Press, 2000), chapters 1–2; Kenneth S. Jeffrey, *When the Lord Walked the Land: The 1858–62 Revival in the North-East of Scotland* (Carlisle: Paternoster Press, 2002).
68 Eifion Evans, *Revival Comes to Wales: The Story of the 1859 Revival in Wales* (3rd edn, Bridgend: Evangelical Press of Wales, 1979), p. 97.
69 See D. W. Bebbington, 'Moody as a Transatlantic Evangelical', in Timothy George (ed.), *Mr Moody and the Evangelical Tradition* (London: T&T Clark, 2004), pp. 79–80.
70 Mark Hopkins, *Nonconformity's Romantic Generation: Evangelical and Liberal Theologies in Victorian England* (Milton Keynes: Paternoster, 2004), p. 128.
71 Thomas Walter Laqueur, *Religion and Respectability: Sunday Schools and Working Class Culture, 1780–1850* (New Haven, CT: Yale University Press, 1976), p. 44.
72 For an evaluation, see John Roxborogh, *Thomas Chalmers: Enthusiast for Mission* (Carlisle: Paternoster, 1999).
73 Donald M. Lewis, *Lighten Their Darkness: The Evangelical Mission to Working-Class London, 1828–1860* (Westport, CT: Greenwood Press, 1986).
74 Bebbington et al. (eds), *Protestant Nonconformist Texts, Volume 3*, p. 263.
75 Ibid., p. 264.
76 Isabel Rivers, 'The First Evangelical Tract Society', *The Historical Journal*, 50/1 (2007), pp. 1–22.
77 Quoted in Mark Hutchinson and John Wolffe, *A Short History of Global Evangelicalism* (Cambridge: Cambridge University Press, 2012), p. 72.
78 Leslie Howsam, *Cheap Bibles: Nineteenth Century Publishing and the British and Foreign Bible Society* (Cambridge: Cambridge University Press, 1991), pp. 3–4, 80–82, 95.
79 See Clyde Binfield, *George Williams and the YMCA: A Study in Victorian Social Attitudes* (London: Heinemann, 1973).
80 Bebbington et al. (eds), *Protestant Nonconformist Texts, Volume 3*, pp. 264–65.
81 Ibid., pp. 265–67.

82 David W. Bebbington, *The Dominance of Evangelicalism: The Age of Spurgeon* (Leicester: Inter-Varsity Press, 2005).
83 For the background, see Roger Steer, *Delighted in God: The Life of George Müller* (London: Hodder and Stoughton, 1975).
84 Patricia Stallings Kruppa, *Charles Haddon Spurgeon: A Preacher's Progress* (New York: Garland, 1982), pp. 170–71.
85 See Gillian Wagner, *Barnardo* (London: Weidenfeld and Nicholson, 1979).
86 Ian J. Shaw, *Churches, Revolutions & Empires, 1789–1914* (Fearn: Christian Focus, 2012), p. 227.
87 Ian Campbell Bradley, 'Titus Salt: Enlightened Entrepreneur', in Gordon Marsden (ed.), *Victorian Values: Personalities and Perspectives in Nineteenth-Century Society* (London: Longman, 1990), pp. 89–100.
88 David J. Jeremy, 'The Enlightened Paternalist in Action: William Hesketh Lever at Port Sunlight before 1914', in David J. Jeremy and Geoffrey Tweedale (eds), *Business History*, IV (London: SAGE Publications, 2005), pp. 300–22.
89 For an overview of some of these efforts, see Ian Bradley, *The Call to Seriousness: The Evangelical Impact on the Victorians* (Oxford: Lion, 1976).
90 Brian Harrison, *Drink and the Victorians: The Temperance Question in England, 1815–1872* (London: Faber & Faber, 1971).
91 Kenneth O. Morgan, *Rebirth of a Nation: Wales, 1880–1980* (Oxford: Oxford University Press, 1981), pp. 36–37.
92 Some of the far-reaching implications of this often subtle and gradual change have been explored in Dominic Erdozain, *The Problem of Pleasure: Sport, Recreation and the Crisis of Victorian Religion* (Woodbridge: Boydell, 2010).
93 Ian M. Randall, 'The Social Gospel: A Case Study', in John Wolffe (ed.), *Evangelical Faith and Public Zeal: Evangelicals and Society in Britain, 1780–1980* (London: SPCK, 1995), p. 157.
94 Harry Gariepy, *Christianity in Action: The International History of the Salvation Army* (Grand Rapids, MI: Eerdmans, 2009), chapter 9.
95 Anthony Jones, *Welsh Chapels* (Stroud: Allan Sutton, 1996), p. 73.
96 Robert Currie, Alan Gilbert and Lee Horsley (eds), *Churches and Churchgoers: Patterns of Church Growth in the British Isles since 1700* (Oxford: Clarendon Press, 1977), p. 34.
97 Noel Gibbard, *Fire on the Altar: A History and Evaluation of the 1904–05 Welsh Revival* (Bridgend: Bryntirion Press, 2005), pp. 132–36.
98 R. Tudur Jones, *Faith and the Crisis of a Nation: Wales, 1890–1914*, ed. Robert Pope (Cardiff: University of Wales Press, 2004), p. 337.
99 Noel Gibbard, *On the Wings of a Dove: The International Effects of the 1904–05 Revival* (Bridgend: Bryntirion Press, 2002).
100 Callum G. Brown, *Religion and Society in Twentieth-Century Britain* (Harlow: Pearson Educational, 2006), pp. 60–61.
101 Andrew Walker and Neil Hudson, 'George Jeffreys, Revivalist and Reformer: A Revaluation', in Andrew Walker and Kristin Aune (eds), *On Revival: A Critical Examination* (Carlisle: Paternoster, 2003), pp. 139–46; Edith L. Blumhoffer, *Aimee Semple McPherson: Everybody's Sister* (Grand Rapids, MI: Eerdmans, 1993), pp. 212–13.
102 Quoted in David Bebbington, 'Evangelism and Spirituality in Twentieth-Century Protestant Nonconformity', in Alan P. F. Sell and Anthony R. Cross (eds), *Protestant Nonconformity in the Twentieth Century* (Milton Keynes: Paternoster, 2003), p. 186.
103 D. Densil Morgan, *The Span of the Cross: Christian Religion and Society in Wales, 1914–2000* (Cardiff: University of Wales Press, 1999), p. 162.

104 See Christopher H. Evans, *The Kingdom Is Always But Coming: A Life of Walter Rauschenbusch* (Grand Rapids, MI: Eerdmans, 2004).
105 Bebbington, *The Dominance of Evangelicalism*, p. 234.
106 See Robert Pope, *Seeking God's Kingdom: The Nonconformist Social Gospel in Wales, 1906–1939* (Cardiff: University of Wales Press, 1999), pp. 11–16.
107 See Clyde Binfield, *So Down to Prayers: Studies in English Nonconformity, 1780–1920* (London: Dent, 1977), pp. 162–85.
108 John A. Vickers (ed.), *A Dictionary of Methodism in Britain and Ireland* (Peterborough: Epworth Press, 2000), p. 389.
109 See Christopher Oldstone-Moore, *Hugh Price Hughes: Founder of a New Methodism, Conscience of a New Nonconformity* (Cardiff: University of Wales Press, 1999).
110 Keith Robbins, *England, Ireland, Scotland, Wales: The Christian Church, 1900–2000* (Oxford: Oxford University Press, 2008), p. 56.
111 See Robert Pope, *Building Jerusalem: Nonconformity, Labour and the Social Question in Wales, 1906–1939* (Cardiff: University of Wales Press, 1998), pp. 202–3.
112 Jones, *Faith and the Crisis of a Nation*, pp. 81–82.
113 Iain H. Murray, *D. Martyn Lloyd-Jones: The First Forty Years, 1899–1939* (Edinburgh: Banner of Truth, 1982), pp. 134–35.
114 Brynmor Pierce Jones, *The King's Champions: Revival and Reaction, 1905–1935* (Cwmbran: Christian Literature Press, 1986), pp. 150–51.
115 David Ceri Jones, 'Lloyd-Jones and Wales', in Andrew Atherstone and David Ceri Jones (eds), *Engaging with Martyn Lloyd-Jones: The Life and Legacy of 'the Doctor'* (Nottingham: Apollos, 2011), pp. 62–72.
116 S. J. D. Green, *The Passing of Protestant England: Secularization and Social Change, c.1920–1960* (Cambridge: Cambridge University Press, 2010), chapter 7.
117 Ian M. Randall, 'Baptist Revival and Renewal in the 1960s', in Kate Cooper and Jeremy Gregory (eds), *Revival and Resurgence in Christian History* (Woodbridge: Boydell Press, 2008), pp. 341–53.
118 Ian Randall, 'Lloyd-Jones and Revival', in Atherstone and Jones (eds), *Engaging with Martyn Lloyd-Jones*, pp. 91–113.
119 See S. C. Griffin, *A Forgotten Revival: East Anglia and NE Scotland – 1921* (Bromley: Day One Publications, 1992); Colin and Mary Peckham, *Sounds from Heaven: The Revival on the Isle of Lewis, 1949–1952* (Fearn: Christian Focus, 2009).
120 See Mark Peel, *The Last Wesleyan: A Life of Donald Soper* (Lancaster: Scotforth Books, 2008).
121 Brown, *Religion and Society in Twentieth-Century Britain*, p. 188.
122 Kenneth Hylson-Smith, *Evangelicals in the Church of England, 1734–1984* (Edinburgh: T&T Clark, 1988), pp. 287–88, 314.
123 Ian Randall, 'Conservative Constructionist: The Early Influence of Billy Graham in Britain', *Evangelical Quarterly*, 67/4 (1995), pp. 309–33.
124 Callum G. Brown, *The Death of Christian Britain: Understanding Secularization, 1800–2000* (London: Routledge, 2001).
125 Bebbington, 'Evangelism and Spirituality in Twentieth-Century Protestant Nonconformity', p. 204.
126 See Amy C. Whipple, 'Speaking for Whom? The 1971 Festival of Light and the Search for the Silent Majority', *Contemporary British History*, 24/3 (2010), pp. 319–39.
127 Geraint D. Fielder, *'Excuse Me, Mr Davies – Hallelujah!': Evangelical Student Witness in Wales, 1923–1983* (Bridgend: Evangelical Press of Wales, 1983), pp. 198–203, 207–8.
128 Peter Hocken, *Streams of Renewal: The Origins and Early Development of the Charismatic Movement in Great Britain* (Exeter: Paternoster, 1986), chapter 21.

129 Andrew Lord, *Spirit-Shaped Mission: A Holistic Charismatic Missiology* (Milton Keynes: Paternoster, 2005), pp. 16–21.

130 See, for example, Ian M. Randall, 'Baptist Growth in England', in David Goodhew (ed.), *Church Growth in Britain: 1980 to the Present* (Aldershot: Ashgate, 2012), pp. 66–67.

131 James Heard, *Inside Alpha: Explorations in Evangelism* (Milton Keynes: Paternoster, 2009), p. 21.

132 Hugh Osgood, 'The Rise of Black Churches', Goodhew (ed.), *Church Growth in Britain*, pp. 107–25.

133 Bebbington, 'Evangelism and Spirituality in Twentieth-Century Protestant Nonconformity', p. 215.

134 For an exploration of some of the reasons for this, see David Goodhew, 'Church Growth in Britain: 1980 to the Present Day', in idem (ed.), *Church Growth in Britain*, pp. 3–14.

135 Paul Chambers, *Religion, Secularization and Social Change in Wales: Congregational Studies in a Post-Christian Society* (Cardiff: University of Wales Press, 2005). See also Paul Chambers, 'Out of Taste, Out of Time: The Future of Nonconformist Religion in Wales in the Twenty First Century', *Contemporary Wales*, 21 (2008), pp. 86–100.

18 Nonconformists and Overseas Mission

Ian M. Randall

In *The Evil and Danger of Neglecting the Souls of Men*, the published version of his address delivered to Independent ministers in Kettering in 1741, Philip Doddridge made the suggestion that something might be done 'towards assisting in the Propagation of Christianity Abroad' as well as at home. As a practical step, Doddridge proposed that 'we endeavour to engage as many pious people of our respective congregations as we can, to enter themselves into a society, in which the members may engage themselves to some peculiar cares, assemblies, and contributions, with regard to this great end'.[1] It was to be several decades before English Nonconformists took up Doddridge's suggestion. There had, however, been some initiatives by Protestants before this: the Society for Promoting Christian Knowledge (1699) had a concern for overseas mission and David Brainerd worked among Native Americans through the Scottish Society for the Propagation of Christian Knowledge, formed in 1710.[2] In 1732 the Moravians, in their community in Herrnhut, Germany, committed themselves to what proved to be a remarkable Protestant missionary work. Doddridge, like many others in England in the eighteenth century who sought to promote overseas mission, had contact with Moravians.[3] This chapter examines shaping influences on Nonconformist mission such as the Moravians; early Nonconformist missionary advances and setbacks; the relationship between mission and society; and the dimensions of Nonconformist overseas mission in the nineteenth century. The main focus will be on Congregationalists and Baptists.[4] Finally the Faith Missions and the changes in Nonconformist overseas mission in the twentieth century will be explored.

I. Early Influences

Nonconformists were inevitably influenced by imperialism. Kathleen Wilson, in *The Island Race* (2003), suggests that the London Missionary Society (LMS) – which became one of the major Nonconformist missionary bodies – demonstrated powerful imperatives 'to convert, subdue and possess the world through the cultural power and superiority of English Protestantism'.[5]

This interpretation, however, contrasts sharply with the way early LMS leaders themselves spoke of what had shaped their thinking. David Bogue, an Independent (increasingly the word Congregational was used) minister in Gosport, Hampshire, and a founder of the LMS in 1795, spoke admiringly a year earlier about the example and spiritual influence of the Moravian missionaries, who in their 'number and substance' had 'excelled . . . the whole Christian world'. Another early supporter of the LMS, Rowland Hill, of Surrey Chapel in London, hoped that the LMS would learn from the 'amazing' example of the Moravians.[6] Since the Moravians were primarily a central European refugee community, it is difficult to see their influence as one that promoted a sense of English Protestant cultural power. Indeed the LMS, as Jeffrey Cox notes, was marked by its willingness to take recruits of a lower social standing than those recruited for mission associated with the Church of England.[7] By the end of 1760, more than two hundred Moravians were in far-flung parts of the world under the auspices of the Moravian Brethren's Society for the Furtherance of the Gospel among the Heathen. Moravian publications and personal connections with Moravians in the Caribbean had an impact on a Welshman Thomas Coke in the 1780s, and this helped to spur Coke on to initiate Wesleyan Methodist missionary work in the region in 1786.[8]

The Moravians also had a crucial influence on a young Baptist minister and former cobbler William Carey, and on the thinking that led to the formation in October 1792 of the Particular Baptist Society for Propagating the Gospel among the Heathen, later known as the Baptist Missionary Society (BMS).[9] Carey was baptized in 1783 by John Ryland, a Baptist minister in Northampton who had developed a friendship with Francis Okely, a Moravian minister in the same town. Ryland and Okely exchanged missionary reading material.[10] William Carey's vision for mission was set out in a book published in 1792 (although written four years earlier), *An Enquiry into the Obligation of Christians, to Use Means for the Conversion of the Heathens*. Carey argued that Roman Catholic missionaries had surmounted great obstacles in their early missionary endeavours, and he then moved on to talk about the more recent example of the Moravians. 'Have not the missionaries of the *Unitas Fratrum*, or Moravian Brethren', he asked, 'encountered the scorching heat of Abyssinia, and the frozen climes of Greenland and Labrador . . .?' Carey looked at various efforts in world mission and concluded, in words that Bogue would echo: 'But none of the moderns have equalled the Moravian Brethren in this good work.'[11] Moravians were not only being held up as an example but new questions were being asked about how that example could be followed.

How did William Carey obtain details about the Moravians and how did he go about using his information? It is quite possible that Carey drew some of his information from Ryland, and also from another Baptist minister in the Northamptonshire Baptist Association, John Sutcliff. At the October 1792 meeting at which the BMS was formed it seems likely that Carey referred to the Moravian missionary magazine *Periodical Accounts*. Joseph Hutton writes that, at the meeting, 'Carey flung down on the parlour table some numbers of a missionary magazine entitled *Periodical Accounts*', and as he argued for Baptist missionary enterprise he exclaimed: 'See what these Moravians have done!'[12] S. Pearce Carey, who was Carey's biographer and his grandson, claimed that Carey was a reader of *Periodical Accounts* 'from the first', and that in speaking to, as well as writing for, his fellow-Baptists, some of whom were sceptical or cautious about world mission, he challenged them to take note of 'what Moravians are daring, and some of them British like ourselves, and many only artisan and poor'.[13] Carey was interested in how Moravians lived together in communities and proposed that in Baptist mission a similar policy be adopted.[14] Andrew Fuller, the first secretary of the BMS, commented: 'The experience of the Moravians seems to sanction it'.[15] One of Carey's colleagues in India, William Ward, had a strong attachment to the 'spirit of the Moravians' and wrote in his diary: 'Thank you, ye Moravians, you have done me good. If I am ever a missionary worth a straw, I shall owe it to you under our Saviour.'[16] The Moravian vision rather than an imperialistic one helped to shape Baptist mission overseas.

Another influence on Nonconformist mission was the Evangelical Revival. Andrew Porter writes in *Religion versus Empire?* that 'the context and direct experience of domestic revivals, both in Britain and in the American colonies, brought out not only the possibility but also the ease with which Christians themselves could become evangelists'.[17] This was extrapolated to overseas mission. The seeds of this global dimension were present in John Wesley's thinking. 'I look upon all the world', he famously stated, 'as my parish'.[18] There are well-known links between Wesley's spiritual development and the witness of the Moravians. Indeed Colin Podmore argues that the story of the English Evangelical Revival begins not in Aldersgate Street, with Wesley's experience of the 'warmed heart', but in Central Europe.[19] However, Wesley himself did not introduce the Moravian vision for world missionary endeavours into his Methodist societies. Despite this, individual Methodists in the 1760s and 1770s, such as Nathaniel Gilbert in Antigua and Thomas Coke with his call in 1778 for missionaries to go to West Africa, became convinced that conversionist theology was to be translated into overseas mission. But Coke's plans were rejected by Wesley and a 'deflated Coke' (as Cox puts it) had to – and did – find other ways to proceed.[20] The activism which was apparent among the Methodists widened into an 'evangelistic impulse' that came to 'dominate orthodox Dissent'.[21] A young Baptist minister in Birmingham Samuel Pearce, one of the ministers who encouraged William Carey, was one of those whom Thomas Coke affected. Pearce had his missionary zeal 'fanned into a flame' by a sermon preached in Birmingham by Coke.[22]

While Wesleyan Arminianism was one eighteenth-century stream of revival that affected world mission, another was represented by the American Calvinistic theologian Jonathan Edwards. His *An Humble Attempt to Promote Explicit Agreement and Visible Union of God's People in Extraordinary Prayer*, with its postmillennial hope for 'the Advancement of Christ's Kingdom on Earth', was crucial in the story of evangelical missionary developments. A 'Prayer Call' in 1784 by the Northamptonshire Baptist Association flowed from this. At a meeting in June 1784 Andrew Fuller preached a message that was deeply indebted to the *Humble Attempt*, and another minister present, John Sutcliff, moved that churches should meet on the first Monday of each month to pray for revival at home and 'the spread of the Gospel to the most distant parts of the habitable globe'. This prayer movement spread well beyond Northamptonshire.[23] Following the June meeting of the Association, Fuller spent some months preparing a profoundly significant book (which was published in 1785) *The Gospel Worthy of all Acceptation*. This sought to refute the High Calvinism which inhibited evangelistic endeavour, and its stress on human responsibility was crucial. As Peter Morden argues: '*The Gospel Worthy* was *the* key text in creating the ecclesiastical climate (among the Particular Baptists) where a venture such as the BMS could be accepted and supported, and would prosper.'[24] Far from Nonconformist mission being simply an extension of the colonial enterprise, the evidence is that the shaping forces were spiritual and theological.

II. Advances and Setbacks

William Carey lacked the social standing and the access to resources that characterized some other evangelical figures of his period, but what he did have was the ability to make things happen and to ensure missionary advance. His efforts led to the organization of what was the first voluntary missionary society established in Britain and he went as a missionary himself to India.[25] Carey also influenced others. In July 1794 a letter from Carey, the first since he sailed, was passed to David Bogue and the result was an appeal 'To the Evangelical Dissenters who practise Infant Baptism' to follow the example of the Baptists in setting up a missionary society.[26] The LMS drew primarily upon Congregationalists, but also on members of the Countess of Huntingdon's Connexion, and had support from a few evangelical Anglican leaders such as Thomas Haweis (most evangelical Anglicans were sceptical), and some Scottish Presbyterians from both the Church of Scotland and dissenting denominations.[27] In 1795, Bogue preached a memorable sermon at the formation of the LMS. This inaugural event, for Bogue, marked 'the funeral of *bigotry*'.[28] By contrast the BMS took the view that 'in the present divided state of Christendom it seems that each denomination by exerting itself seperately [*sic*] is most likely to accomplish the great ends of a mission'.[29] However, the LMS was not to fulfil the 'ecumenical' hopes and it became the missionary society of the Congregationalists.

The way in which LMS advance was anticipated and hopes were expressed is reflected in a letter of 5 May 1795 from John Eyre, another founding leader of the LMS and editor of the *Evangelical Magazine*, to Andrew Fuller. In this letter, which reported on an Editors' Meeting of the *Evangelical Magazine*, Eyre noted: 'The Missionary Society in whose success we are so much interested, will certainly obtain, through the medium of the magazine: numerous friends, who will generously come forward both for its formation & support: – and what advantages may be desired from such an Institution cannot be calculated.' For Eyre, what was happening in England, as a new and optimistic vision of world mission developed, had a transatlantic dimension. It was, specifically, linked with united prayer taking place in Britain and America. Eyre continued:

> The late Intelligence from America may incline some to wish for similar prayer meetings upon the plan recommended by President [Jonathan] Edwards . . . At the quarterly Meetings a recital might be made of what is doing in the Churches at home and abroad, which would not only enliven Devotion, but afford matter for prayer in public & private, & be a guide to many by instructing them how they should best direct their efforts to promote the glory of the Redeemer.[30]

These efforts soon produced the first major overseas initiative by the LMS leaders.

The LMS raised money to purchase a 'missionary ship' and issued a call for missionaries. Bogue was interested in India, but there were objections from the East India Company. It was therefore decided to send the first LMS missionaries to the South Seas – which was not an area under British colonial rule. Porter comments that it was Anglicans who tended to follow in the footsteps of territorial empire.[31] The LMS purchased the 300-ton ship the *Duff* for £4,800 and appealed for ordained ministers and lay people. Cox notes that there was criticism of the low social standing of those who responded: twenty-five were artisans including bricklayers, tailors, weavers, carpenters and a blacksmith. One was a surgeon, four were ordained ministers and there were several missionary wives. Critics who spoke of the missionaries seeking material wealth or being social climbers were not able to document their rather bizarre charges.[32] On 10 August 1796 the *Duff* sailed from Blackwall Dock in London flying a newly designed flag: three white doves with olive branches.[33] After 208 days the *Duff* reached Tahiti. Seventeen of the missionaries, including the married couples, were left in Tahiti where they were welcomed by Pomare, the ruler whom Captain Cook had praised. Pomare and his wife Idia gave protection to the missionaries. But over the succeeding years there was a series of setbacks and the first phase of the enterprise in Tahiti ended, as Horne put it, in 'blank defeat and absolute failure'.[34] If anything the situation was more disastrous on the island of Tonga. The *Duff* left nine men there, of whom three were killed – the first martyrs of the LMS – and one abandoned Christianity to indulge in what was described as 'a life of immorality'.[35] The remaining five became destitute. It was painfully evident that resources were being wasted.[36]

The Baptist mission in India experienced a similar mixture of advances and setbacks. In another example of the inadequacy of the theory that mission was an arm of imperialism, the Baptists generally had a closer association with people of all levels of Indian society than did government officials.[37] From 1794, Carey set about educating a few local youths and by 1799 he had forty students among whom he hoped to stimulate enquiry about a range of subjects. Oriental scholars and East India Company officials in Britain and India considered whether English, Persian, Sanskrit or Arabic was the language that should be cultivated in connection with British rule in Bengal, but for Carey the answer was the vernacular – Bengali.[38] Baptists encouraged the education of the people in their native language. Serampore College, which was established in order to train Indians to be missionaries in India, was another aspect of the educational vision. The curriculum included science and Oriental languages, as well as theology. In 1805 a 'Form of Agreement' was adopted by the missionaries in Serampore which stated that Indians who were ordained to the ministry of the word and sacraments should be allowed freedom to work

> as much as possible without the interference of the missionary of the district who will constantly superintend their affairs, give them advice in cases of order and discipline, and correct any errors into which they fall; and, who joying and beholding their order, and the steadfastness of their faith in Christ, may direct his efforts continually to the planting of new churches in other places, and to the spread of the gospel in his district, to the utmost of his power.[39]

This is hardly imperialistic imposition. It was reported that local Christians 'have chiefly been the immediate means by which our church has been increased'.[40] But despite the areas of advance, there were disappointments, such as the relative paucity of converts, and numerous obstacles, not least the hostility of government officials. However, BMS activity expanded into new fields in Asia and the work of the BMS was augmented by that of the General Baptist Missionary Society, formed in 1816.[41]

Meanwhile, the LMS was seeking to recover from the public relations disaster of the *Duff*. On its second voyage, in 1798, the ship was captured by a French frigate. However, in the same year the recruitment to the LMS of Johannes Theodorus Van der Kemp marked a turning point for the Society. Van der Kemp, a Dutchman, had been attracted to the LMS through Moravian contacts in Holland. He was over fifty when he began his missionary service and unlike the artisans who had joined the *Duff* he was an ex-dragoon officer. In addition he had been a rationalist and an author prior to his conversion. All these factors were significant in enabling him to function in a hostile environment.[42] The field opened up by Van der Kemp on behalf of the LMS was Cape Colony, South Africa, where he and a small group arrived in 1799, intent on reaching the Xhosa. In 1802 they established a settlement, Bethelsdorp (near present-day Port Elizabeth), and gave refuge to dispossessed Khoi. As he saw the way white settlers pushed indigenous people off their own land, Van der Kemp became a severe critic of white settler society. His work was regarded with favour by one Anglican missionary visitor, the famous Henry Martyn, who was associated with Charles Simeon in Cambridge, but with disfavour by the Moravians, who wanted a better-ordered mission station.[43] However, Van der Kemp was one of those, like the Moravians, who showed that missionaries could make a difference. This was well received by local people. In 1803 a leading British Baptist John Rippon recognized the Moravians as those whose ministry was designed 'to humanise and christianise the world'.[44] This vision spread.

The LMS moved into several new fields, such as British Guinea and Madagascar. In Madagascar William Ellis and other LMS missionaries saw typical setbacks and advances. As a mark of advance, Ellis wrote in 1871 expressing his worry that 'our Society should not be able to meet the large demand [for education] which has so suddenly arisen out of the great numbers who have asked for instruction since the general burning of idols'.[45] New BMS areas included the West Indies, Cameroons and the Congo, Ceylon and China. The possibilities for advance meant that overseas mission became, increasingly, an integral part of Nonconformist identity. In 1800, David Bogue opened the first missionary training academy in Gosport to complement his academy for training Nonconformist ministers. When he died in 1825 he had trained over one hundred missionary candidates. Later the academy closed and LMS missionary recruits trained alongside ministerial students.[46] For Baptists, home and foreign mission distinctions were not as marked. Until 1815–16, the BMS sponsored itinerant evangelistic preaching in parts of England.[47] However, overseas mission had a quality of 'otherness' which was attractive. Nonconformist Sunday Schools increasingly raised money for overseas mission, and more generally in the late 1830s and early 1840s, Stanley notes, that there were very substantial – 'in some cases spectacular' – increases in giving.[48] This was at a time of national economic depression and hardship. Joseph Angus, later principal of Regent's Park College, assumed administrative responsibility of the BMS in 1841 and raised a large amount of money. The Society was able to establish itself in offices in Moorgate, London.[49]

Angus was one among many Nonconformists who saw opportunities for missional advance increasing. In 1863, at the request of the Baptist Union, he spoke about Baptist resources and responsibilities, outlining BMS advances in India, Burma, the Caribbean and Africa. He spoke about the continent of Europe and the emergence of 1,000 Baptist churches and preaching stations largely as a result of (and in the lifetime of) Johann Oncken. Angus had a vision of 2,000 British Baptist churches, walking 'in love and in the power of the Holy Ghost', with the Bible as their rule and agreeing in 'evangelical doctrines' and Baptist principles, being 'the surest means' of 'evangelizing the world'.[50] In 1871, Angus gave a major address to the BMS on 'Apostolic Missions'. Over the course of 100 years, Angus said, the Bible had been translated into more than 150 languages, spoken by more than half the globe. He described the endeavours of 3,000 Protestant foreign missionaries and, highly significantly, of 30,000 native preachers. Angus suggested that 'as mighty a work has been done in these last hundred years as in any hundred since the beginning of the Gospel'.[51] He argued that Christians of his time were more able to preach the gospel to the whole world than Christians of the first century – and this could be done in the next ten to twenty years.[52] He then embarked on remarkable – and at points bizarre – suggestions about resources required, suggesting that from Europe and America 50,000 Christian workers would be needed. Financial support was also estimated: £15 million a year for ten years. He concluded, 'It can be done'.[53] A. T. Pierson, the American missionary statesman, asked Angus to reprint this address, and Pierson suggested it was from Angus' address that the motto 'The World for Christ in Our Generation' – often expressed in Student Volunteer Movement (SVM) circles as 'The Evangelization of the World in This Generation' – was drawn.[54] In 1904, John R. Mott, a central figure in the SVM and the Ecumenical Movement, suggested that 'some of the greatest discourses ever preached were missionary sermons', and instanced Angus on 'Apostolic Missions'.[55] John Briggs argues that no history of Baptists in the nineteenth century can be properly focused unless it underlines Baptist commitment to world mission.[56] Across Nonconformity the picture was, to a large extent, similar.

III. Nonconformist Mission and Society

As Porter argues, in the early phase of the Protestant missionary movement from Britain, most missionaries thought they were probably better off without the state and its aid, while the imperial government was deeply suspicious of popular religious enthusiasm and the threat it posed to social and political order, for example, in India.[57] These religio-political tensions were particularly noticeable in the case of the Nonconformists. As an example of radical Nonconformist attitudes, David Bogue preached a provocative sermon in 1792:

> But what effects of Christian zeal can we boast? It would be easy to mention distant countries discovered by the skill of our mariners and the munificence of our rulers – countries where we have planted colonies to cultivate the soil – countries where we carry on with the natives an extensive commerce – countries which our armies have overrun, and which we have seized as our own – countries which our troops are now wetting with the tears and with the blood of the innocent inhabitants – countries from which we have for a long course of years been dragging the wretched natives to worse than Egyptian bondage. But where is the country which we have exerted our zeal to rescue from pagan darkness or Mahometan delusion, and to bring to the knowledge and consolations of the gospel?[58]

Bogue was subpoenaed as a witness during a treason trial two years later, and it was suggested that he was personally involved in naval mutinies. Although he denied these charges, and they were never proved, it is clear that he opposed the established order.[59] The nineteenth century saw Nonconformists engaging in a range of political activities, with their sense of responsibility – their 'conscience' – driving them to action.[60] A sense of solidarity with those who were oppressed – reflecting the profound Nonconformist awareness of being themselves discriminated against – was transmitted through overseas mission.

Carey was not overtly political like Bogue, but he believed in social change. Carey and the other Baptist missionaries in India took up the cause of widows who were burned on their husband's funeral pyres – the practice of *sati*. The East India Company did not want to interfere, but the missionaries' campaign brought the issue to the attention of British public opinion, and in 1829 *sati* was declared illegal in Bengal.[61] This kind of involvement did not impress all religious observers. For Sydney Smith, an Anglican clergyman and editor of the *Edinburgh Review*, Nonconformist missionaries in India were not fit to represent Christianity. 'If a tinker is a devout man', Smith complained, 'he infallibly sets off for the East'. He suggested that those involved in the 'Anabaptist missions', by which he meant Baptists, were 'benefiting us much more by their absence, than the Hindooes by their advice'.[62] Such comments showed a lack of interest in the conditions of people in other countries. Yet Nonconformist missionaries in India could at times fail to distinguish between the injustices they saw and the religious traditions they encountered. Early encounters with Hinduism tended to create conflict rather than build bridges. Henry Martyn, a sympathetic fellow-evangelical, said about the preaching of Carey's associate

Joshua Marshman: 'I feel pain that he should so frequently speak with contempt of the Brahmins, many of whom were listening with great respect and attention.'[63] Oddie argues that a growing *feeling* in India of being Hindu in a 'socio-religious communal sense' was intensified by missionary activities.[64] The BMS 'Form of Agreement' (1805) recognized the importance of love, not 'acrimony', in mission, and another of the BMS missionaries William Ward acknowledged the achievements of Hindu civilization.[65]

The Nonconformist approach did not focus on non-Christian religions as the primary source of social evil. William Ward's biographer spoke of Ward showing that India was like other places in being full of cruelty.[66] In Cape Colony it was white settlers who were accused by LMS missionaries of acts of cruel mistreatment of blacks. Van der Kemp and other LMS missionaries also sought evangelical conversions. Before long, as Elphick notes, 'a number of blacks had undergone such an experience, while most whites had not. Thus the identification of European ancestry with Christianity, and of both with privileged status, threatened to unravel – and with it the fabric of the hierarchical social order.'[67] When John Philip was appointed LMS director of operations in Southern Africa in 1817, he turned his attention to the plight of the Khoi. Philip also became minister of the Presbyterian congregation in Cape Town in 1820, an English-speaking congregation, but his missionary duties took precedence.[68] For him this mission involved social change. He became convinced that the Cape authorities would not support submissions made by the missionaries on behalf of the Khoi and he applied to the government. In the preface to a crucial book he wrote in 1828, *Researches in South Africa*, Philip hoped 'that the friends of humanity and of religion in England, will see it to be their duty to petition the British throne and the British parliament, that the natives of South Africa may have those rights secured to them'.[69] Philip was determined to work for the native converts' freedom from colonial oppression. His denunciation of the colonial authorities caused a storm.[70] Support came from T. F. Buxton, the Anglican antislavery campaigner, an indication of the way in which there was a shared abolitionist drive which united evangelical Anglicans and Nonconformists. Legislation was passed to secure the equality under the law of the Khoi.[71]

LMS directors insisted in 1828 that missionaries respect the government, indication that as well as radicalism there was caution.[72] Church–state issues were debated within the LMS in the 1830s.[73] In southern Africa, Robert Moffat is often cited as a major LMS figure who opposed missionaries taking on political functions.[74] Moffat had a strict Scottish Calvinistic upbringing and despite having had almost no formal schooling he was accepted by the LMS and commissioned for overseas mission at Surrey Chapel, London, in 1816. He and his wife Mary served for over fifty years with great distinction. The allegation – much repeated – that Robert Moffat did not uphold the rights of oppressed native people has been comprehensively refuted by Steve de

Gruchy, who shows that throughout his life 'Moffat remained passionately concerned about issues of justice and peace for the black inhabitants of southern Africa'.[75] The Moffats' famous son-in-law David Livingstone had been a member of an Independent Chapel in Hamilton, Scotland, and his approach to faith was influenced not by Scottish Presbyterianism but by the kind of revivalism represented by Charley Finney.[76] The fact that Livingstone 'denounced the whole British colonial set-up in the Cape Colony' is often passed over.[77] Perhaps his most famous book is *Missionary Travels and Researches in South Africa* (1857) but he had earlier prepared a significant, long piece about the situation in South Africa in 1842 for the *British Quarterly and the Morning Herald*. The *Quarterly*, however, did not publish it. Ross, noting that many biographers have not drawn attention to its existence, argues that Livingstone showed unambiguously that he shared with Philip a belief in 'the equality of all human beings in terms of human rights': Livingstone was fully aware that his own Scottish ancestors had been seen as 'degraded' and 'savage'.[78] In 1873 the LMS warned: 'Do not ANGLICISE YOUR CONVERTS.'[79] Leading LMS missionaries in Africa established a tradition of criticism of imperialism that remained important right up to the mid-twentieth century.[80]

There were other examples of the way in which Nonconformist missionaries were more critical than Anglicans of 'the empire's official classes'.[81] One case, which helped to alter British public opinion, was that of the 'Demerara Martyr', the LMS missionary John Smith. Originally, from Northamptonshire, Smith moved to London with his mother and became a trainee baker. In his twenties he married Jane Godden and he was ordained at Tonbridge Chapel, Kent, in 1816. A year later the couple went to Demerara, British Guiana, with the LMS. John Smith preached in a chapel near Georgetown and attracted large congregations, including slaves and former slaves to whom he offered help, which enraged plantation owners. In 1823 a massive slave rebellion took place, which was brutally suppressed. Smith and one of his senior deacons Quamina, who was a slave, urged those in revolt to avoid violence, and this advice was heeded, but Quamina was shot by the authorities (one of two hundred killings by the troops on the plantation) and Smith was arrested and imprisoned.[82] Smith had refused to take up arms and he was accused at his trial – which was a court martial – of inciting the slaves to rebel. He was sentenced to be hanged, although there was also a recommendation of mercy. It was clear that the intention was that Nonconformist missionary enterprise should be crushed.[83] After seven weeks in dreadful prison conditions, Smith died. Jane Smith was prevented from being present when her husband was buried. Instead of showing any remorse the colonial authorities redoubled their efforts to force LMS missionaries out and replace them with Anglican clergymen.[84] The LMS published a book in 1824 *The Case of John Smith*, and the publicity generated helped to fuel debates in the House of Commons which ultimately led to the abolition of slavery in British colonies, against strong opposition from the planters and their supporters in Britain. William Wilberforce mentioned Smith in his last abolitionist appeal to the House.[85] The editor of a memoir of John Smith saw him as an example of the kind of missionary who would 'always be obnoxious to the . . . *higher classes* of their fellow Colonists, because of their efforts to protect the emancipated people from gross injustice'.[86]

In the same year as the Demerara uprising took place, William Knibb, a Baptist, decided to become a missionary with the BMS in Jamaica. He had become an apprentice in Kettering in 1816 but his thinking about his life changed in 1822: in that year he was baptized and his brother Thomas became a missionary in Kingston, Jamaica, pursuing a calling which began to inspire William. Thomas died after only a year in Jamaica and the BMS accepted William's offer to replace him. As William and his wife, Mary, settled into Jamaica he was shocked by the treatment of the slaves and ashamed that he belonged to a race that was indulging in such atrocities. Catherine Hall notes that these missionaries – Knibb's colleagues included fellow BMS missionaries Thomas Burchell and J. M. Phillippo – were the first white men in Jamaica who were not primarily interested in making a fortune. Their concern was Christian mission, and in this they were successful. In 1827 there were eight Baptist chapels with 5,000 members while in 1835 there were 13,795 members.[87] Many others were attending chapels without becoming members. In the meantime the planters were becoming irritated by the Dissenting preachers and a new Slave Law was passed in Jamaica 1826 to restrict what the preachers could do.[88]

Undaunted by the difficulties, Knibb took up the cause of the slaves, and in 1830 he supported a deacon in his congregation, Sam Swiney, a slave, who had been sentenced to a whipping and hard labour for preaching and teaching. What he had done was lead a prayer meeting. Knibb clashed with the magistrates and with George Bridges, the nearby Anglican Rector, who defended the slave owners. For Bridges the Dissenting missionaries were dangerous enemies of the established order.[89] As E. A. Payne put it, Knibb became politically disruptive through his crucial evidence to Britain's political leaders about how British landowners were treating slaves.[90] There was an intensified Colonial backlash against the missionaries following a slave revolt led by a Baptist deacon Sam Sharpe in 1831, and in the following year, back in Britain, Knibb addressed a large meeting at the Exeter Hall in London. The BMS leadership had been very wary about being drawn into political campaigning, and Knibb stated that his cause was not political but religious and moral. He continued:

> [T]here is nothing more delightful than to stand forward as the advocate of the innocent and persecuted; and when I consider that on the present

> occasion I appear before an assembly of my countrymen on behalf of the persecuted African, I find in the fact a reward for all the sufferings, in character and person, which I have endured in the cause as a missionary for the last eight years . . . All I ask is, that my African brother may stand in the family of man; that my African sister shall, while she clasps her tender infant to her breast, be allowed to call it her own.[91]

The theological point made by Knibb was that God 'views all nations as one flesh', while his practical plea was that slavery should be abolished, and his wish was that this should be done before the death of William Wilberforce. Knibb's address was greeted with deafening applause. Knibb mobilized public opinion across the country and also gave evidence to Parliamentary committees. The reluctance by the BMS to enter politics was overcome. Freedom came, and very large numbers of freed men and women joined Baptist chapels in Jamaica.[92] Mission was inextricably linked with social change.

IV. Dimensions of Nonconformist Mission

Although Nonconformist attitudes to social issues marked them off from many Anglicans in the nineteenth century, in other respects missionaries with the LMS and the BMS adopted similar policies to those in other missionary societies. A notable feature was the encouragement to local Christians to take up the work of evangelism alongside foreign missionaries. Carey was committed to this vision, and it was regularly replicated. In Africa, for example, many new converts were involved in speaking about the Christian message in villages, market places and along trade routes. David Killingray comments that these evangelists, 'few of whom had functional literacy', founded churches 'often . . . in ways and with results which outside observers saw as worryingly chaotic and irregular'.[93] The growth of Christianity outside the West arguably subverted Western Christianity rather than being an extension of Christendom. Indeed Andrew Walls wrote in 1996 in *The Missionary Movement in Christian History* of 'the fortunate subversion of the church' through the world Protestant missionary movement and especially voluntary missionary societies.[94] Both Robert Moffat and David Livingstone aimed to train local African Christians, and Moffat was frustrated when one protégé of his, John Serian Mokitera, was apparently spoiled by the fulsome attentions of some LMS supporters in Britain. The LMS directors had hoped Mokitera would be a useful teacher, but Moffat wrote in 1843 to LMS Foreign Secretary Arthur Tidman to express his disappointment at the results of the misguided (as he saw it) LMS approach.[95] As an indication of his belief in Africa, Moffat concluded his letter: 'Our kindest regards to Murray & your dear son. If God spares him send him out to S. Africa. I am persuaded he would improve in health there.'[96]

It is certainly not that foreign missionaries were regarded as unimportant: Moffat was seeking more, not less. However, the ideal was communication between Africans. This way of thinking led to the sending out to Africa not only of white missionaries but also of Jamaicans and African Americans. In 1878 Thomas Johnson and Calvin Richardson, two African Americans who had come to England and trained at C. H. Spurgeon's Pastors' College in London, went to West Africa with the BMS. C. H. Spurgeon – like other Nonconformist leaders – had in mind the possibility of considerable numbers of African Americans going to Africa as missionaries.[97] Thomas Johnson became well known through his telling of his remarkable story in *Twenty-Eight Years a Slave*. The BMS already had a Black missionary in West Africa, Joseph Jackson Fuller, a Jamaican, who had been serving in the Cameroons since the 1850s.[98] However, the fact that Spurgeon, the most prominent Baptist of the nineteenth century, gave his full support to Johnson and Richardson was of great significance.[99] After their arrival in West Africa, Mr and Mrs Johnson and Mr and Mrs Richardson spent time in Freetown, Sierra Leone, and in Monrovia, Liberia, and then settled in the Cameroons, but soon after this illness struck the Johnsons. In *The Sword and the Trowel* (the magazine of Spurgeon's church, the Metropolitan Tabernacle) for January 1880, Spurgeon included a letter from Johnson about his wife's suffering. The fever which she contracted led to her death. Johnson expressed his thankfulness for the support of the Tabernacle and concluded, 'Yours truly, for Africa'.[100] Johnson returned to the United States and had a long ministry. C. H. Richardson continued to work in Bakundu, Cameroons, reporting in 1886 that he had distributed (among traders who could speak English) Spurgeon's sermons, sent by Mrs Spurgeon, and that he was also translating them.[101]

Another significant development in this period was the way in which missionary societies began to utilize the gifts of women. In the BMS, Carey wanted women involved in reaching out to other women, and this was often done by the wives of missionaries, but in 1866 Marianne Lewis, who was promoting female education in Bengal, urged British Baptist women to form a society in connection with the BMS. The particular concern was women in 'zenanas', the parts of high-caste Hindu family dwellings that were restricted to women and males in the immediate family. Lewis spoke of the 'imprisoned inmates' of the zenanas.[102] The response was rapid. The BMS Committee had already given approval in principle to developing zenana work and in May 1867 twenty-four women and E. B. Underhill, the secretary of the BMS, met and formed the Ladies Association for the Support of Zenana Work and Bible Women in India – later the Baptist Zenana Mission. Most of those initially supported by the Association were Indian Bible women, but 1871 saw the first missionary recruited from Britain, Miss Fryer of Bristol, and by 1880 the Association employed twenty-seven European or Euroasian women and forty-four Indian women. Amelia Angus, wife of Joseph Angus, was from 1869 to 1893 the foreign secretary of the Association.[103] Later the work was extended to include missionary service in China. Women who were accepted had first to attend rigorous interviews and were then directed to a training school. A number were in medical work or were teachers. All had to study the local language or languages.[104]

Within the LMS, Robert Morrison, who (having been influenced by David Bogue) went to Canton in 1807 with the LMS as the first Protestant missionary to China, suggested to the directors of the Society as early as 1824 that they consider recruiting unmarried women for overseas mission.[105] At that point the Society was doubtful about taking this step. It was only in the 1860s that thinking began to change, in part due to the religious revival of the late 1850s and early 1860s which opened up new possibilities for women in ministry – it was in 1860 that Catherine Booth, for example, the founder with her husband of the Salvation Army, began to preach – and also stimulated new thinking about world mission.[106] From 1864 to 1875 nine female teachers were appointed by the LMS, and LMS female missionary work officially started in 1875. By the early 1890s there were more than sixty women serving. As with the BMS, there was a concern to reach Indian zenana women. The LMS required its female missionaries to have the education and culture to minister to the higher classes of women in India. Many of the LMS female missionaries were teachers, governesses or nurses and in the 1880s and 1890s there was a particular stress on medical zenana mission. However, fees for medical training for women (in Schools for Medicine for Women in London, Edinburgh and Glasgow) were high, and few LMS candidates had the resources required. From 1900, China was a major field for the LMS and in the period 1900–14 sixty women went to China, thirty-eight to India, and smaller numbers to Madagascar and the South Seas. In 1914 there were 310 LMS missionaries. Of these eighty-six were single women and in addition there were 186 wives of missionaries.[107] Thus by this stage the majority of those in active service with the LMS were women.

Involvement in medical work became an increasingly important dimension of mission. Robert Morrison and John Livingstone, who was a surgeon to the East India Company, were pioneers in this area in China through their founding of a public dispensary for Chinese at Macau in 1820. While Morrison was not a medical missionary, he had studied medicine briefly at St Bartholomew's Hospital, London. Progress was slow, but the LMS role was significant. In 1844, Dr William Lockhart of the LMS founded the 'Chinese Hospital', operated by the LMS in Shanghai. Lockhart was one of the first Western missionaries in China after the Opium War, when numbers of missionaries were small. There was an explosion of foreign missionary personnel in China in the 1870s and 1880s, from 100 to 2,800.[108] The medical aspect of what was offered, in China and elsewhere, was part of a vision that Lockhart and others had for human betterment. Brian Stanley, in *The Bible and the Flag*, argued for two parallel British missionary traditions, one understanding mission as embracing a broader humanitarianism, and the other that was more inclined to limit the Christian message to one of individual salvation.[109] While always emphasizing conversion, Nonconformist missionaries tended to embrace the broader view. Thus John Williams considered that as an LMS missionary in the South Seas he was spreading not only Christianity but also 'civilization and the acquisition of useful arts'.[110] Charles Darwin, during the voyage of the *Beagle*, having been dubious about missionary activity, came to the view that missionaries contributed to 'civilization' and was prepared to defend the missionaries of the South Seas.[111]

But for BMS and LMS missionaries 'civilizing' was never an aim in and of itself. Even medical work and education were always seen as being undertaken in connection with the gospel. Thus Carey wrote to his brother Thomas about what was done at Serampore: 'The work of the Mission divides itself into three parts, viz. the Translation and publishing of the Word of God, The preaching of the Gospel, gathering and superintending of Churches and the formation and superintendence of Schools.'[112] Carey particularly gave time to translation of the Bible. In 1831 he wrote to the publisher Samuel Bagster against a background of savage criticism of Carey's Marathi Bible from an anonymous contributor to the *Asiatic Journal*. This work had taken Carey eighteen years to complete. William Greenfield, editor of Bagster's Syriac New Testament, defended the translation. Bagster then published it. Carey thanked Bagster and added: 'I therefore just mention that beside the translation of the Scriptures I have published a Bengalee, a Telinga, a Punjabi, a Karnata; and a Sangskrit Grammar. A Dictionary of the Bengalee Language. A hist[ory] of the Sangskrit roots. Three v[olume]s of a translation of the Ramayana and some smaller pieces which I cannot now recollect.'[113] Andrew Walls argues that it was probably the linguistic work of these missionaries which led to the recognition of their contribution to scholarship. Robert Morrison, who as well as working for the LMS also (reluctantly) became Chinese secretary and translator for the East India Company, was awarded a Glasgow University DD in 1817.[114] His main objective and his major work was in fact the translation of the Bible.[115] Timothy Richard, a Baptist, is an example of a missionary in China who sought, later in the nineteenth century, to address questions about 'comparisons between religions, the significance and impact of scientific knowledge, and the political benefits of reform', as he communicated the Christian gospel.[116] The motivation of these missionaries was, above all, to spread the Christian message.

V. The Changing Face of Nonconformist Mission

The rise and growth of what became known as the Faith Missions in the second half of the nineteenth century was to have a profound effect on Nonconformist overseas mission. The work of J. Hudson Taylor, the founder in 1865 of the China Inland Mission (CIM), has commonly been regarded as defining 'Faith Missions'.[117] The CIM was committed to interdenominationalism – recruiting Anglicans and Nonconformists – and to missionaries wearing Chinese dress and identifying with the local people. Taylor was from a Methodist family, but he was one of those – together with Grattan and Fanny Guinness and their East London Institute – influenced by the Brethren movement, with its propagation of the concept of 'living by faith', without any guaranteed stipend.[118] In the mid-1850s he worked for a time in China with William Chalmers Burns, of the English Presbyterian Mission. Thus there were strong Nonconformist impulses in the development of the Faith Missions, but also new dimensions. In 1866, Hudson Taylor's first group went to China. They were known as the Lammermuir Party, because they sailed on the tea clipper *Lammermuir*, and of the sixteen missionaries who sailed with Taylor and his family, nine were unmarried women, mostly in their twenties. The impact of Taylor's vision was such that the sympathies of C. H. Spurgeon began to incline towards the Faith Missions.[119]

Spurgeon is an example of the way new currents of thought were to affect the approach of many Nonconformists to overseas mission. Preaching the BMS sermon in April 1858, Spurgeon had opposed the view – put forward earlier in the century by Edward Irving – that missionaries should be sent out without guaranteed support. Spurgeon argued then that churches should assure missionaries whom they sent out that 'the least we can do is to provide for your needs'.[120] However, in December 1858 Spurgeon expressed his sympathy with the philosophy of George Müller, in Bristol, who never approached people to ask for money for his orphanage work but relied on prayer.[121] This was at odds with the BMS system of seeking subscribers. In 1863 Spurgeon, citing Müller, argued that mission activities should be 'in the highest degree works of faith' and also suggested that the BMS had become an 'interposing medium' between churches and missionaries.[122] Spurgeon invited Taylor to speak at a mid-week meeting at the Tabernacle, and a friendship began. It is not that faith missions and the BMS were in opposition to one another. BMS Secretary E. B. Underhill assisted Taylor, introducing him to the Royal Geographical Society,[123] and the two missions worked side by side in areas of China, with one former student of Spurgeon's Pastors' College, J. J. Turner, together with his wife, transferring from the CIM to the BMS in 1883.[124] But from the late nineteenth century and through the following century the admiration of Spurgeon for the entrepreneurial energy of the Faith Missions was evident among many who would earlier have been firmly committed to specifically Nonconformist enterprises.

Faith Missions gave an enormous boost to world mission. From the 1880s the CIM recruited many new missionaries at the annual Keswick Convention, designed to promote the life of holiness.[125] By the mid-1890s the CIM had about 650 missionaries. The Brethren also became notable for their involvement in overseas mission, co-ordinated and publicized through a home office and a magazine, *Echoes of Service*. In the 1930s, up to four thousand people were attending the Brethren's annual London Missionary Meetings. This level of interest was not maintained, and the proportion of Brethren members going overseas declined later in the twentieth century, but even at the end of the century that proportion was higher than in any other Protestant denomination.[126] Another of the newer Nonconformist bodies to engage in overseas mission was the Salvation Army. In India its missionaries – women and men – were recruited 'to an unprecedented degree' directly from the working classes. As with the CIM in China, Salvationists who came to India adopted local dress.[127] The early twentieth century saw the powerful Welsh Revival of 1904–5, which had a significant international impact.[128] The Revival played a crucial part in the birth of Pentecostalism, which has been by far the fastest growing section of the evangelical movement worldwide over the past hundred years.[129] Before the First World War, British Pentecostal leadership lay largely with Alexander Boddy, vicar of All Saints, Monkwearmouth, Sunderland, and Cecil Polhill, one of the famous 'Cambridge Seven' CIM missionaries to China in 1885. Polhill later formed the Pentecostal Missionary Union, which was to become the missionary arm of one of the leading Pentecostal denominations, the Assemblies of God.[130] Among early British Pentecostal missionaries, William Burton, with his multifaceted work in the Congo, was the most remarkable.[131]

The CIM – which was to become the Overseas Missionary Fellowship – was followed by many other Faith Missions, some of which emerged in the early twentieth century, such as the Worldwide Evangelization Crusade, started by another member of the 'Cambridge Seven', C. T. Studd.[132] A further development took place after the Second World War, with the growth of short-term mission. Richard Tiplady, in *World of Difference*, speaks about three important waves in Protestant mission. The first, in the eighteenth century, is associated especially with William Carey and the BMS. The mid-nineteenth century saw the rise of the second wave, the Faith Missions. Tiplady sees the third wave as coming in the 1950s and 1960s, with mission organizations such as Youth with a Mission (YWAM), Operation Mobilisation (OM), Frontiers and World Horizons, all of which have combined training, mission and discipleship within their programmes. He draws attention to generations of Christian students being trained through these movements.[133] In Britain, many hundreds of young people became involved in summer programmes with OM from the 1960s onwards, and OM also developed a 'year programme'. By the later 1960s, over four hundred young people were involved in OM's year teams. The year programme became, for many who participated, a pathway into longer-term missionary work with OM. India became the largest OM field of operation.[134] Although OM drew from all denominations, Brethren influence was crucial. Notes published for a Brethren conference in Britain spoke about the denominational make-up of OM and described the Brethren representation as 'by far the largest'.[135]

Whereas there was a strong Nonconformist identity in the nineteenth century, Cox notes the importance of 'the disappearance of a distinctive Nonconformist social identity' and suggests that this phenomenon awaits its historian.[136] In terms of world mission, in China the Communist Revolution forced all missionaries – LMS, BMS and CIM among them – to leave the country by the early 1950s, and this had a profound impact. The end of the British Empire also contributed to a decline in missionary activity. John Stuart suggests that just prior to the Second World War the number of Protestant missionaries from the United Kingdom was 9,300 and that this had fallen to 4,475 by 1962.[137] Despite these changes, the Free Church (the term Nonconformist dropped out of use) tradition continued to play its part in overseas mission. In 1966 the LMS and the Commonwealth Missionary Society combined to form the Congregational Council for World Mission. In 1977, following the formation in 1972 of the United Reformed Church, the Council for World Mission was inaugurated. The early 1960s saw Baptists involved in seeking to address the treatment of Angolans by the Portuguese regime of Dr Salazar. Rebellion against the regime broke out in that year and in response to a massacre of Portuguese settlers there were terrible reprisals by the authorities. At the 1961 Baptist Assembly, Clifford Parsons, BMS Africa secretary, gave a moving speech which led to a resolution being passed that registered 'grave disquiet at the reports of large-scale terrorism by the armed European community' and appealed to the Portuguese authorities for restraint.[138] Baptist leaders saw Lord Home, foreign secretary, and met various MPs and government under-secretaries.[139] The Methodist George Thomas, MP, later speaker of the House, presented a petition to the Commons and it was announced in parliament that Britain would no longer send arms to Portuguese territories overseas.[140]

In 1982 a periodic analysis of Protestant overseas missionaries from Britain, which included short-term missionaries, showed that 40 per cent were Anglican, with the remainder largely being from various 'Nonconformist' denominations – Baptist (26 per cent), Brethren (10 per cent), Presbyterian (9 per cent), Pentecostal (6 per cent), Methodist (5 per cent) and other (4 per cent). The total number of British overseas Protestant missionaries was estimated at about eight thousand. By 1998 Baptists had declined significantly to 16 per cent (Anglicans were still the largest group, at 34 per cent) and the most dramatic change was in the 'others', which was now 25 per cent, reflecting the growth of independent/charismatic evangelical churches and ethnically based evangelical denominations.[141] By the beginning of the twenty-first century the ebullient expressions of Nonconformity represented by the LMS and the BMS (by now BMS World Mission) in the nineteenth century had long gone. The key events in world Christianity were increasingly taking place in Africa, Asia and Latin America.[142] The growth of the church in the non-Western world was having a highly significant impact in Britain through large and growing Black-majority and ethnically diverse churches – the phenomenon of 'reverse mission'. Thus the largest Baptist churches in London were Black-majority congregations, with Kingsley Appiagyei, pastor of a congregation of 2,000 people in Trinity Baptist Church, West Norwood, saying in 2001 that he saw himself as a missionary seeking to strengthen the church in the United Kingdom.[143] However, there was evidence of a new Nonconformity in Britain having a continuing commitment to mission elsewhere, with almost two-thirds of the British overseas Protestant missionary force, long-term and short-term, coming from the Free Church constituency.

VI. Conclusion

This chapter has sought to examine some of the influences that shaped Nonconformist overseas mission over the course of two centuries. The question of how Nonconformists expressed their convictions in overseas contexts has been explored. I have argued that Nonconformist mission was not a by-product of an imperialist vision. Indeed Nonconformists were often at odds with the colonial authorities. Porter comments that at different times and in various places, relationships between missionaries and authorities 'varied considerably from the mutually supportive to the deeply hostile'. Although Porter identifies changes over time, he suggests that the 'shifting, complex picture' points to it being impossible to give a straight answer to the traditional question 'was missionary enterprise a tool of imperialism?'[144] Also, any attempt at an answer needs to take into account the quite different approaches that at times characterized Anglican clergy on the one hand and Nonconformist leaders on the other. What is not always clearly identified in historical analysis of the history of Protestant mission is that because the Nonconformist tradition has rejected the idea of an Established Church at home it has also often been at odds with the 'Establishment' abroad. It is, however, the case that with the rise of interdenominational missions and with the end of Empire the picture has altered. There is much less that can be identified as distinctively 'Nonconformist'. At the same time, there is a widespread desire for a 'Post-Christendom' paradigm of mission.[145] The Free Church vision of pioneers such as William Carey has largely prevailed. It could be argued that Carey also foresaw interdenominational co-operation, since in 1806 he proposed that a meeting of all Protestant missionary organizations be held every ten years.[146] Carey did not see the emergence of 'reverse mission' to the West. But this development is fully consistent with a Nonconformist missional vision.

Notes

1 Philip Doddridge, *The Evil and Danger of Neglecting the Souls of Men* (London: M. Fenner, 1742), pp. vii–ix.
2 After Brainerd's death in 1747 his work was made famous through Jonathan Edwards' *An Account of the Life of the Late Reverend Mr. David Brainerd* (1749).
3 E. A. Payne, 'Doddridge and the Missionary Enterprise', in G. F. Nuttall (ed.), *Philip Doddridge* (London: Independent Press, 1951), pp. 87–93.
4 Methodist overseas mission is dealt with in Charles Yrigoyen Jr (ed.), *T & T Clark Companion to Methodism* (London: T&T Clark, 2010). See also essays in William J. Abraham and James E. Kirby (eds), *The Oxford Handbook of Methodist Studies* (Oxford: Oxford University Press, 2009).
5 Kathleen Wilson, *The Island Race: Englishness, Empire and Gender in the Eighteenth Century* (London and New York: Routledge, 2003), p. 81; cf. Brian Stanley, 'Nineteenth-Century Liberation Theology: Nonconformist Missionaries and Imperialism', *Baptist Quarterly*, 32/1 (1987), pp. 5–18, for a balanced perspective.
6 For these LMS details see J. C. S. Mason, *The Moravian Church and the Missionary Awakening in England, 1760–1800* (Woodbridge: The Boydell Press, 2001), pp. 145–66, 170.
7 Jeffrey Cox, *The British Missionary Enterprise since 1700* (London: Routledge, 2008), p. 83.
8 See John Vickers, *Thomas Coke: Apostle of Methodism* (London: Epworth, 1969); idem, *Thomas Coke and World Methodism* (Bognor Regis: World Methodist Historical Society, 1976).
9 For the Baptist Missionary Society, see B. Stanley, *The History of the Baptist Missionary Society, 1792–1992* (Edinburgh: T&T Clark, 1992).
10 See Mason, *The Moravian Church*, pp. 84–89.
11 The full text of Carey's *Enquiry* is in T. George, *Faithful Witness: The Life and Mission of William Carey* (Leicester: IVP, 1991).
12 J. E. Hutton, *A History of Moravian Missions* (London: Moravian Publication Office [1923]), p. 3; cf. D. A. Schattschneider, 'William Carey, Modern Missions and the Moravian Influence', *International Bulletin of Missionary Research*, 22/1 (1998), pp. 8–12.
13 S. P. Carey, *William Carey* (London: Hodder and Stoughton, 1923), p. 90.
14 T. G. Carter, *The Journal and Selected Letters of William Carey* (Macon, GA: Smyth and Helwys, 2000), p. 136.
15 Mason, *The Moravian Church*, p. 174.
16 Ibid., p. 169.
17 Andrew Porter, *Religion versus Empire?: British Protestant Missionaries and Overseas Expansion, 1700–1914* (Manchester: Manchester University Press, 2004), p. 33.
18 J. Telford (ed.), *The Letters of the Rev. John Wesley, A.M.* (London: Epworth Press, 1931, reprinted 1960), I, p. 286.
19 C. Podmore, *The Moravian Church in England, 1728–1760* (Oxford: Clarendon Press, 1998), p. 5; cf. W. R. Ward, *The Protestant Evangelical Awakening* (Cambridge: Cambridge University Press, 1992), chapters 2 and 4.

20 Cox, *The British Missionary Enterprise*, p. 64.
21 D. W. Bebbington, *Evangelicalism in Modern Britain: A History from the 1730s to the 1980s* (London: Routledge, 1995), p. 41.
22 Stanley, *History of the Baptist Missionary Society*, p. 11.
23 E. A. Payne, *The Prayer Call of 1784* (London: Baptist Laymen's Missionary Movement, 1941).
24 Peter J. Morden, *Offering Christ to the World: Andrew Fuller (1754–1815) and the Revival of Eighteenth Century Particular Baptist Life* (Carlisle: Paternoster, 2003), p. 139.
25 Cox, *The British Missionary Enterprise*, pp. 70–71.
26 Richard Lovett, *The History of the London Missionary Society, 1795–1895*, (London: Henry Frowde, 1899), I, p. 5.
27 Cox, *The British Missionary Enterprise*, p. 74.
28 J. Bennett, *Memoirs of the Life of the Revd David Bogue, DD* (London: Westley and Davis, 1827); cf. R. H. Martin, *Evangelicals United: Ecumenical Stirrings in Pre-Victorian Britain, 1795–1830* (Metuchen, NJ, and London: The Scarecrow Press, 1983), p. 43.
29 BMS Committee Minutes, 2 October 1792, pp. 1–2, Angus Library, Regent's Park College, Oxford.
30 John Eyre to Andrew Fuller, 5 May 1795. P. R. Conlan's private archive.
31 Porter, *Religion versus Empire?* p. 71.
32 Cox, *The British Missionary Enterprise*, p. 84.
33 C. S. Horne, *The Story of the L.M.S., 1795–1895* (London: London Missionary Society, 1895), p. 23.
34 Ibid., p. 35.
35 Ibid., p. 27.
36 Porter, *Religion versus Empire?* pp. 55–56.
37 E. D. Potts, *British Baptist Missionaries in India, 1793–1837* (Cambridge: Cambridge University Press, 1967), p. 114.
38 Cox, *The British Missionary Enterprise*, p. 81.
39 *Periodical Accounts Relative to the Baptist Missionary Society*, III (1804–9), p. 206, cited in Brian Stanley, 'Planting Self-Governing Churches: British Baptist Ecclesiology in the Missionary Context', *Baptist Quarterly*, 34 (1991–2), p. 381.
40 *Periodical Accounts*, III, cited by Eleanor Jackson, 'From Krishna Pal to Lal Behari Dey: Indian Builders of the Church in Bengal, 1800–1894', in Dana L. Robert (ed.), *Converting Colonialism: Visions and Realities in Mission History, 1706–1914* (Grand Rapids, MI: Eerdmans, 2008), pp. 177–78.
41 Stanley, *History of the Baptist Missionary Society*, pp. 54–57.
42 Andrew F. Walls, 'The Eighteenth-Century Missionary Awakening in Its European Context', in B. Stanley (ed.), *Christian Missions and the Enlightenment* (Grand Rapids, MI: Eerdmans, 2001), p. 39.
43 Porter, *Religion versus Empire?* pp. 76–79.
44 J. Rippon, *A Discourse Delivered at the Drum Head* (London: Barnard and Sultzerpp, 1803), pp. 37–38, cited by K. R. Manley, *'Redeeming Love Proclaim': John Rippon and the Baptists* (Carlisle: Paternoster Press, 2004), pp. 252–53.
45 William Ellis to John Peckover, 15 July 1871, P. R. Conlan archive. See also A. Porter Ellis, 'The Career of William Ellis: British Missions, the Pacific and the American Connection', in A. Frost and J. Samson (eds), *Pacific Empires* (Melbourne: Melbourne University Press, 1999), pp. 193–214.
46 Cox, *The British Missionary Enterprise*, pp. 102–3.
47 Stanley, *History of the Baptist Missionary Society*, pp. 18–19.
48 Brian Stanley, 'Home Support for British Overseas Mission in Early Victorian England, c.1838–1873' (unpublished PhD thesis, University of Cambridge, 1979), pp. 25–27.

49 Stanley, *History of the Baptist Missionary Society*, pp. 212–13.
50 Joseph Angus, *The Baptist Denomination in England, Wales, Scotland and Ireland* (London: J. Heaton and Son, 1863), p. 11. On Oncken, see I. M. Randall, *Communities of Conviction: Baptist Beginnings in Europe* (Prague: IBTS, 2009), especially chapters 5 and 6.
51 Joseph Angus, *Apostolic Missions: The Gospel for Every Creature. A Sermon First Preached before the Baptist Missionary Society, April 26th, 1871* (new edn, London: James Nesbit, 1892 [1871]), p. 8.
52 Ibid., p. 20.
53 Ibid., pp. 23–27.
54 Ibid., p. 4.
55 J. R. Mott, *The Pastor and Modern Missions: A Plea for Leadership in World Evangelization* (New York: Student Volunteer Movement, 1904), pp. 67–68. I am grateful to Darrell Jackson, then director, Nova Research Centre, and lecturer in European Studies, Redcliffe College, for this reference.
56 J. H. Y. Briggs, *The English Baptists of the Nineteenth Century* (Didcot: Baptist Historical Society, 1994), p. 293.
57 Andrew Porter, 'Church History, History of Christianity, Religious History: Some Reflections on British Missionary Enterprise since the Late Eighteenth Century', *Church History*, 71/3 (2002), p. 563.
58 John Morison, *The Founders and Fathers of the London Missionary Society* (London: Fisher, 1844), p. 187. From a sermon preached by David Bogue in 1792, not 1705, as in Susan Thorne, *Congregational Mission and the Making of an Imperial Culture in Nineteenth-Century England* (Stanford, CA: Stanford University Press, 1999), p. 183.
59 Thorne, *Congregational Mission*, pp. 44–45.
60 D. W. Bebbington, 'The Baptist Conscience in the Nineteenth Century', *Baptist Quarterly*, 34/1 (1991), pp. 13–24.
61 Potts, *British Baptist Missionaries in India*, pp. 144–57.
62 Sydney Smith, 'Indian Missions', *Edinburgh Review*, 12 (April 1808), p. 180.
63 Potts, *British Baptist Missionaries in India*, p. 218.
64 G. A. Oddie, 'Constructing "Hinduism": The Impact of the Protestant Missionary Movement on Hindu Self-Understanding', in R. E. Frykenberg (ed.), *Christians and Missionaries in India* (Grand Rapids, MI: Eerdmans, 2003), p. 166.
65 This was in William Ward's massive study, *A View of the History, Literature and Religion of the Hindoos* (Calcutta, 1806).
66 Samuel Stennett, *Memoirs of the Life of the Rev. William Ward* (London: Haddon, 1825), p. 255.
67 Richard Elphick, 'Evangelical Missions and Racial "Equalization" in South Africa, 1890–1914', in Robert (ed.), *Converting Colonialism*, p. 114.
68 Helen Ludlow, '"Working at the Heart": The London Missionary Society in Cape Town, 1819–1844', in John de Gruchy (ed.), *The London Missionary Society in Southern Africa, 1799–1999* (Athens, OH: Ohio University Press, 2000), pp. 101–2.
69 J. Philip, *Researches in South Africa* (London: J. Duncan, 1828), I, p. xxix.
70 Andrew Porter, 'An Overview, 1700–1914', in Norman Etherington (ed.), *Missions and Empire* (Oxford: Oxford University Press, 2005), pp. 50, 67.
71 Porter, *Religion versus Empire?* pp. 80–83.
72 Laurence Kitzan, 'The London Missionary Society and the Problem of Authority in India, 1798–1833', *Church History*, 40 (1971), pp. 468–69.
73 See Michael A. Rutz, 'The Problems of Church and State: Dissenting Politics and the London Missionary Society in 1830s Britain', *Journal of Church and State*, 48/2 (2006), pp. 379–98.

74 Jean and John Comaroff, *Of Revelation and Revolution: Christianity, Colonialism and Consciousness in South Africa* (Chicago, IL: University of Chicago Press, 1991), p. 252.
75 Steve de Gruchy, 'The Alleged Political Conservatism of Robert Moffat', in J. de Gruchy (ed.), *The London Missionary Society*, pp. 17–36 [p. 34].
76 Andrew C. Ross, *David Livingstone: Mission and Empire* (London: Hambledon and London, 2002), pp. 6, 17.
77 Andrew Ross, 'David Livingstone: The Man Behind the Mask', in J. de Gruchy (ed.), *The London Missionary Society*, p. 45.
78 Ross, *David Livingstone: Mission and Empire*, pp. 70–74.
79 *General Regulations for the Guidance of the English Missionaries of the Society* (London: LMS, 1873), Part II, cited in Porter, *Religion versus Empire?* p. 328.
80 Porter, 'Church History, History of Christianity, Religious History', p. 565.
81 Thorne, *Congregational Mission*, p. 41.
82 For the rebellion, see Emilia Viotta da Costa, *Crowns of Glory, Tears of Blood: The Demerara Slave Rebellion of 1823* (Oxford: Oxford University Press, 1994).
83 Lovett, *The History of the London Missionary Society*, II, p. 349.
84 Horne, *The Story of the L.M.S.*, pp. 165–66.
85 The entry in Wilberforce's diary reads: 'Poor Smith the missionary died in prison at Demerara! The day of reckoning will come'. See Robert and Samuel Wilberforce *The Life of William Wilberforce*, (Philadelphia: Henry Perkins, 1841), II, p. 262.
86 *The Case of John Smith* (Newcastle: J. Clark, for the London Missionary, 1824); E. A. Wallbridge, *Demerara Martyr* (London: C. Cilpin, 1848), p. 418.
87 Catherine Hall, *Civilising Subjects: Colony and Metropole in the English Imagination, 1830–1867* (Chicago, IL: University of Chicago Press, 2002), pp. 88–89.
88 Ibid., pp. 98–100.
89 Stanley, *History of the Baptist Missionary Society*, pp. 74–75. Hall, *Civilising Subjects*, pp. 101–2.
90 E. A. Payne, *Freedom in Jamaica: Some Chapters in the Story of the BMS* (London: Carey Press, 1933).
91 J. H. Hinton, *Memoir of William Knibb* (London: Houlston and Stoneman, 1847), pp. 154–55.
92 Ibid., pp. 155–56; Hall, *Civilising Subjects*, pp. 113–15.
93 David Killingray, 'Empire and Christian Missions: Opposition, Opportunities, Obstacles', *CHF Bulletin* (Summer 2010), p. 31; cf. Richard Elphick and Rodney Davenport (eds), *Christianity in South Africa: A Political, Social and Cultural History* (Berkeley, CA: University of California Press, 1997); David Maxwell, *Christians and Chiefs in Zimbabwe. A Social History of the Hwesa People c.1870s-1990s* (Edinburgh: Edinburgh University Press, 1999).
94 A. F. Walls, *The Missionary Movement in Christian History* (Edinburgh: T&T Clark, 1996), chapter 18.
95 Robert Moffat to Arthur Tidman, from the ship *Fortitude*, 3 July 1843. P. R. Conlan archive.
96 Mungo Murray, of Lintrose, Cupar Angus, Forfarshire, took part, along with William Cotton Oswell, in David Livingstone's discovery of Lake Ngami in 1849.
97 *The Sword and the Trowel* (April 1874), p. 192. For background on the 'Black Atlantic' endeavour see D. Killingray, 'Black Baptists in Britain 1640–1950', *Baptist Quarterly*, 40 (2003), pp. 69–89.
98 Stanley, *History of the Baptist Missionary Society*, p. 109.
99 T. L. Johnson, *Twenty-Eight Years a Slave, or The Story of My Life in Three Continents* (Bournemouth: W. Mate & Sons, 1909), pp. 78–90.
100 *The Sword and the Trowel* (January 1880), pp. 42–43.

101 Ibid. (February 1886), p. 92.
102 E. A. Payne, *Marianne Lewis and Elizabeth Sale: Pioneers of Missionary Work among Women* (London: Carey Press, 1937), pp. 4–7; cf. Karen Smith, 'Women in Cultural Captivity: British Women and the Zenana Mission', *Baptist Quarterly*, 42/1 (2007), p. 105.
103 Stanley, *History of the Baptist Missionary Society*, p. 231.
104 Smith, 'Women in Cultural Captivity', pp. 107–10.
105 Rosemary Seton, '"Open Doors for Female Labourers": Women Candidates of the London Missionary Society, 1875–1914', in R. A. Bickers and R. Seton (eds), *Missionary Encounters: Sources and Issues* (Richmond, Surrey: Curzon Press, 1996), pp. 50–51.
106 I. M. Randall, *Rhythms of Revival: The Spiritual Awakening of 1857–1863* (Milton Keynes: Paternoster, 2010), pp. 61–68, 119–24.
107 Seton, '"Open Doors for Female Labourers": Women Candidates of the London Missionary Society', pp. 64, 67.
108 Porter, *Religion versus Empire?* p. 207; Norman Goodall, *A History of the London Missionary Society, 1895–1945* (London: Oxford University Press, 1954), p. 508.
109 See B. Stanley, *The Bible and the Flag* (Leicester: IVP, 1990), p. 172.
110 Porter, *Religion versus Empire?* pp. 145–46. Williams was murdered in 1839.
111 M. W. Graham, '"The Enchanter's Wand": Charles Darwin, Foreign Missions, and the Voyage of H.M.S. *Beagle*', *Journal of Religious History*, 31/2 (2007), pp. 131–50.
112 William Carey to Thomas Carey, 2 January 1817, a letter addressed to his merchant nephew Jesse Hobson, c/o Mrs Hardy, Jerusalem Coffee House, London, 'for Mr T. Carey'. P. R. Conlan archive.
113 Carey began the letter on 6 June 1831. He added a list of philological Serampore publications on 2 August. Carey's spellings have been maintained. 'Karnata' (Karnada) is the old word for Kanarese.
114 Walls, *The Missionary Movement*, p. 192. Walls cites William Ellis' *Polynesian Researches* (1829), John Williams' *Narratives and Missionary Enterprises in the South Seas* (1837) and Robert Moffat's *Missionary Labours and Scenes in Southern Africa* (1837) as examples within the LMS of the 'Missionary as Scholar'.
115 A letter of introduction from George Burder, director of the LMS, to John Mason, New York, 26 January 1907, stated that Morrison had been studying the Chinese language and was going to China 'with an ultimate view to the Translation of the Holy Scriptures'. P. R. Conlan archive.
116 Lauren F. Pfister, 'Rethinking Mission in China: James Hudson Taylor and Timothy Richard', in A. Porter (ed.), *The Imperial Horizons of British Protestant Missions, 1880–1914* (Grand Rapids, MI: Eerdmans, 2003), pp. 208–9.
117 See K. Fiedler, *The Story of Faith Missions* (Oxford: Regnum Books, 1994), p. 32.
118 H. H. Rowdon, 'The Concept of "Living by Faith"', in A. Billington, A. N. S. Lane and M. Turner (eds), *Mission and Meaning: Essays Presented to Peter Cotterell* (Carlisle: Paternoster, 1995), pp. 339–56.
119 Brian Stanley, 'C. H. Spurgeon and the Baptist Missionary Society', *Baptist Quarterly*, 29/7 (1982), pp. 323, 326. I. M. Randall, '"The World Is Our Parish": Spurgeon's College and World Mission', in I. M. Randall and A. R. Cross (eds), *Baptists and Mission: Papers from the Fourth International Conference on Baptist Studies* (Milton Keynes: Paternoster, 2007), pp. 64–77.
120 C. H. Spurgeon, 'The Desolations of the Lord, the Consolation of His Saints', *New Park Street Pulpit*, Vol. 4, sermon on Psalm 46, vv. 8 and 9, preached 28 April 1858 (London: Passmore and Alabaster, 1892), pp. 206–7.
121 C. Ray, *The Life of Charles Haddon Spurgeon* (London: Passmore and Alabaster, 1903), p. 257; Stanley, 'C. H. Spurgeon and the Baptist Missionary Society', p. 320.

122 Stanley, 'C. H. Spurgeon and the Baptist Missionary Society', pp. 320–21.
123 A. J. Broomhall, *Hudson Taylor and China's Open Century*, (London: Hodder and Stoughton, 1982), III, p. 390.
124 H. R. Williamson, *British Baptists in China, 1845–1952* (London: Carey Kingsgate Press, 1957), pp. 49, 52.
125 For Keswick and mission see Andrew Porter, 'Cambridge, Keswick and Late Nineteenth Century Attitudes to Africa', *The Journal of Imperial and Commonwealth History*, 5 (1976), pp. 5–34.
126 Tim Grass, *Gathering to His Name: The Story of the Open Brethren in Britain and Ireland* (Milton Keynes: Paternoster, 2006), pp. 343, 489.
127 Cox, *The British Missionary Enterprise*, pp. 207–8.
128 For wider effects see N. Gibbard, *On the Wings of the Dove: The International Effects of the 1904–05 Revival* (Bridgend: Bryntirion Press, 2002).
129 E. L. Blumhofer, 'Transatlantic Currents in North American Pentecostalism', in M. A. Noll, D. W. Bebbington and G. A. Rawlyk (eds), *Evangelicalism: Comparative Studies of Popular Protestantism in North America, the British Isles, and Beyond* (Oxford: Oxford University Press, 1994), pp. 354–57.
130 P. Hocken, 'Cecil H. Polhill – Pentecostal Layman', *Pneuma*, 10/2 (1988), pp. 131, 135.
131 For aspects of Burton's work, see David Maxwell, 'Photography and the Religious Encounter: Ambiguity and Aesthetics in Missionary Representation of the Luba of South East Beligian Congo', *Comparative Studies in Society and History*, 53/1 (2011), pp. 38–74.
132 See I. M. Randall, *'Entire Devotion to God': Wesleyan Holiness and British Overseas Mission in the Early Twentieth Century* (Ilkeston: Wesley Fellowship, 1998), incorporating a paper for the North Atlantic Missiology Project.
133 Richard Tiplady, *World of Difference* (Carlisle: Paternoster, 2003), p. 110.
134 For OM see I. M. Randall, *Spiritual Revolution: The Story of OM* (Milton Keynes: Authentic, 2008).
135 Grass, *Gathering to His Name*, p. 494.
136 Cox, *The British Missionary Enterprise*, p. 258.
137 John Stuart, *British Missionaries and the End of Empire: East, Central and Southern Africa, 1939–64* (Grand Rapids, MI: Eerdmans, 2011), p. 189.
138 Stanley, *History of the Baptist Missionary Society*, p. 454.
139 *Baptist Times* (15 June 1961), p. 1; (29 June 1961), p. 1; (13 July 1961), p. 3; (20 July 1961), p. 4; (2 November 1961), p. 1.
140 L. Addicott, *Cry Angola!* (London: SCM, 1962), p. 104.
141 P. Brierley and H. Wright (eds), *UK Christian Handbook*, 3/5 (London: HarperCollins, 2000/2001), no. 2; cf. Cox, *The British Missionary Enterprise*, pp. 258–59.
142 A. F. Walls, *The Cross-Cultural Process in Christian History* (Edinburgh: T&T Clark, 2002), p. 69.
143 *Spurgeon's College Record* (April 2001), p. 3.
144 Porter, 'Church History, History of Christianity, Religious History', p. 563.
145 W. R. Shenk, 'New Wineskins for New Wine: Towards a Post-Christendom Ecclesiology', *International Bulletin of Missionary Research*, 24/2 (2005), pp. 73–79.
146 Potts, *British Baptist Missionaries in India*, p. 53. Carey proposed that the first be in Cape Town in 1810, which was why the Lausanne 2010 was held in Cape Town.

19 Nonconformist Business Leaders, ca 1880–1940: The Uses and Abuses of Wealth

David J. Jeremy

Collectively, Nonconformists in religion made remarkable contributions to the industrial world of the late nineteenth and early twentieth centuries. Their involvement in business, begun in the seventeenth and eighteenth centuries and traceable to the present, had its heyday during the years between 1880 and 1940, before being largely swallowed by unbelief, war, the managerial revolution and materialism. However, traces of their activities remain in names that have long conveyed commercial goodwill: Austin Reed clothing, Beechams pills, Boots the chemist, Bryant & May matches, Cadbury's chocolate, Carr's biscuits, Clark's shoes, Chubb locks, Coats sewing thread, Colman's mustard, (Thomas) Cook travel agencies, Crossley carpets, Courtauld fabrics, Doulton china, Harland & Wolff ships, Laing construction, Mackintosh toffees, Pilkington glass, Rank flour, Rowntree pastilles, Sunlight soap, Tate & Lyle sugar, T&N brake systems, Unilever (originating as Lever Bros), Wills cigarettes, to name the best known.[1] This chapter examines some of the achievements and ethics of Nonconformist entrepreneurs behind these and other products and services.[2] First, how much wealth did Nonconformists in business have at their disposal?

I. How Wealthy Were Nonconformists in the Period 1880–1940?

Hitherto this question has produced only anecdotal answers. However, two national funds organized by the Wesleyans, largest of the Nonconformist (or 'Free Church') denominations, provide a much larger quantitative view of the antecedent decades, out of which later wealth sometimes sprang. The Centenary and Thanksgiving Funds, subject to the Wesleyans' characteristic practices of accountable and transparent stewardship of church monies, published donors' names and their gifts in detail.[3] The salient point affirmed in the analysis of these funds (see Table 19.1), assuming that generosity was an indication of wealth, is that rich Wesleyans comprised a tiny proportion – less than 1 per cent – of total church membership.[4] In many traceable cases their wealth derived from intergenerational capital accumulation flowing from Britain's prime-mover role in international industrialization.[5]

Other features of Wesleyan wealth and generosity come into sharp focus in Table 19.1. Noticeably, the pool of donors (an approximate figure[6]), increasing by nearly 50 per cent between 1839 and 1878, expanded much faster than Wesleyan membership, which managed only a 10 per cent rise. At the same time it was the wealthier donors (giving £100 or more) who were also growing in numbers more rapidly (36 per cent increase) than the wider membership. Simultaneously their total share of the fund grew much bigger, by 59 per cent. The rising prosperity of the Wesleyan middle classes has long been noted. Their willingness to subscribe to national denominational enterprise, and their extraordinary generosity in an age when an agricultural labourer might earn about £50 a year, is conclusively demonstrated by these data: at 2010 prices £1,000 would equate to £100,000. Wesleyans were reckoned to be the wealthiest among other branches of Methodism and their collective generosity grew with their collective wealth. Old Dissent (Presbyterians, Unitarians, Baptists and Quakers) had enjoyed many more decades to accumulate wealth.[7] Unlike the Wesleyans they did not advertise it.[8]

For the Nonconformist business élite after 1880 there is evidence from the *Dictionary of Business Biography* (*DBB*). This is summarized in Tables 19.2 and 19.3. Of the 188 cases in Table 19.1, where estates at death are analysed, three were bankrupts (Balfour, Hooley and Peto). The Methodists were pulled down by the exceedingly small estate of William Henry Holland (who in later life became a Roman Catholic). By far the wealthiest were the Congregationalists, both in their average and median sizes of estate. Their showing was massively pulled up by the Wills family, Bristol tobacco manufacturers. As can be seen from Table 19.3, the Wills family produced two millionaires (and several more were not included in the *DBB*).

The difficulty with the data derived from the *DDB* is that they relate to the enclosed world of business, rather than to the population as a whole. An attempt to overcome this is displayed in Table 19.3 where the estates at death of Nonconformists in the *DBB* are compared to the largest estates left just before the First World War and then again in the years 1923–25, as analysed by Josiah Wedgwood.[9] Assuming that all the premises are sound, Table 19.4 demonstrates that just before the First World War the Baptists, Congregationalists, Methodists and Unitarians had up to half a dozen individuals who were so wealthy that they were among the richest 0.1 per cent in England and in the richest 10 per cent of estates left at that time. Again

Table 19.1 Wesleyan Methodist funds compared

	Approx. number of donors	Total sum collected (£s)	Number of WM members at fund opening	Average per member gift (£s)	Number of £100+ donors	Number of £1,000+ donors	Largest donation (£s)	Aggregate share from £100 donors (%)	Number of £100+ donors as % of WM members
Centenary, Fund									
1839–44	31,800	207,961	436,109	0.48	255	13	1,500	24.8	0.058
Thanksgiving Fund									
1878–83	47,500	297,518	477,832	0.62	348	35	10,000	39.5	0.073
Increase,									
1839–78 (%)	49	43	10	31	36	169	567	59	25

Note: Each fund included gifts from foreign mission stations but only the Centenary Fund included gifts from Ireland. To achieve comparability, Irish numbers and gifts have been omitted.

Sources: Author's analysis of the two fund reports: *General Report of the Wesleyan Centenary Fund* (Leeds: Anthony Pickard, 1844); *Report of the Wesleyan-Methodist Thanksgiving Fund, 1878–1883* (London: Wesleyan-Methodist Book-Room, 1884); Wesleyan Methodist Church, *Minutes of Conference* 1844, p. 61; 1883, p. 163.

Table 19.2 How wealthy were business leaders with adult Nonconformist involvements? The relative sizes of business leaders' estates at death, 1870–1990 (£s)

	Baptists	Congregationalists	Methodists	Presbyterians	Quakers	Unitarians	
Number in *DBB* with adult loyalties to denomination	16	48	47	25	30	18	185
Average size of estate	267,769	647,835	435,511	386,175	234,254	322,302	
Median size	146,263	229,723	165,883	133,855	96,280	175,365	
Number of millionaires	2	6	5	3	2	1	19
Largest estate	1,291,462 (Philip Henman)	10,000,000 (George Alfred Wills)	5,993,323 (J. Arthur Rank)	2,432,810 (Donald Currie)	1,332,525 (Joseph S. Fry)	1,130,907 (James Kitson)	
Smallest estate (excluding bankrupts)	2,731 (Thomas Cook)	3,155 (William Woodall)	25 (Wm Henry Holland)	1,496 (Fred Geo Creed)	10,000 (Ernest Bader)	2,000 (Swinton Boult)	
Bankrupts	Samuel M. Peto Ernest T. Hooley	Jabez S. Balfour					

Notes: Inflationary effects are ignored.
Bankrupts excluded from calculations in Tables 19.2 and 19.4.

Source: *DBB*.

Table 19.3 Nonconformist millionaires, 1883–1983, by fortunes left at death

	Denomination	Upbringing	Adult faith	Name	b-date	d-date	Industrial activity	Estate at death (£m)
1	Baptist	u	A	Coats, Thomas	1809	1883	Thread mfr	1.309
2	Congregationalist	u	A	Lever, William Hesketh	1851	1925	Soap mfr	1.625
3	Congregationalist	u	A	Pilkington, William Henry	1905	1983	Glass mfr	1.88
4	Congregationalist	u	A	Rylands, John	1801	1888	Cotton mfr	2.575
5	Congregationalist	u	A	Wills, George Alfred	1854	1928	Tobacco mfr	10
6	Congregationalist	u	A	Wills, William Henry	1830	1911	Tobacco mfr	2.548
7	Meth, Primitive	u	A	Hartley, William Pickles	1846	1922	Jam mfr	1.1
8	Meth, United MFC	u	A	Furness, Christopher	1852	1913	Ship owner	1.844
9	Meth, Wesleyan	u	A	Rank, Joseph Arthur	1888	1972	Flour miller & film maker	5.993
10	Meth, Wesleyan	u	A	Runciman, Walter	1847	1937	Ship owner	2.896
11	Meth, Wesleyan	u	A	Smith, Prince	1840	1922	Worsted mchy mfr	1.175
12	Presbyterian	u	A	Clark, George Smith	1861	1935	Shipbuilder	1.544
13	Presbyterian	u	A	Currie, Donald	1825	1909	Ship owner	2.433
14	Presbyterian: UFC	u	A	Coats, Archibald	1840	1912	Thread mfr	1.365
15	Quaker	u	A	Cadbury, George	1839	1922	Cocoa mfr	1.071
16	Quaker	u	A	Fry, Joseph Storrs	1826	1913	Cocoa mfr	1.333
17	Seventh Day Adventist	u	A	Wellcome, Henry Solomon	1853	1936	Pharmaceutical mfr	3.014
18	Unitarian		A	Kitson, James	1835	1911	Machine maker	1.126
19	Unitarian	u		Loyd, Samuel Jones	1796	1883	Banker	2.119
20	Unitarian	u	A	Tate, Henry	1819	1899	Sugar refiner	1.264
	Other wealthy, *inter vivos*							
	Meth, Wesleyan		A	Rank, Joseph	1854	1943	Flour miller	Disp. 3.5

Table 19.4 How wealthy were business leaders with adult Nonconformist involvements? Comparisons with England's richest people (at death) in the early twentieth century

The richest 10% of estates left in England, 1911–14	**England**							
	0.10% (1 in 1,000)	**0.20% (1 in 500)**	**Baptists 16 in *DBB***	**Cong'ists 47 in *DBB***	**Methodists 48 in *DBB***	**Presby'ns 25 in *DBB***	**Quakers 29 in *DBB***	**Unit'ns 18 in *DBB***
			3 of 16	1 of 47	3 of 48	3 of 25	0 of 29	2 of 18
Minimum value of estate (£s)								
Age at death								
55–64	69,000	41,000	120,907	n/a	55,209	14,287	n/a	n/a
65–74	100,000	57,800	35,340	n/a	169,559	n/a	n/a	n/a
75–84	141,000	82,000	n/a	2,548,210	168,218	59,608	n/a	43,763
Average value of estate (£s)								
Age at death	0.10%	Next 0.20%						
55–64	251,000	56,000	120,907	n/a	949,757	14,287	n/a	n/a
65–74	273,000	84,100	35,340	n/a	169,559	n/a	n/a	n/a
75–84	386,000	113,000	n/a	2,548,210	168,218	59,608	n/a	433,388

The richest 10% of estates left in England, 1923–25	England							
	0.20% (1 in 500)	0.50% (1 in 200)	Baptists 16 in *DBB*	Cong'ists 47 in *DBB*	Methodists 48 in *DBB*	Presby'ns 25 in *DBB*	Quakers 29 in *DBB*	Unit'ns 18 in *DBB*
Minimum value of estate (£s)								
Age at death								
55–64	54,700	26,600	n/a	n/a	n/a	n/a	n/a	n/a
65–74	69,000	33,900	n/a	1,625,409	n/a	n/a	n/a	n/a
75–84	85,000	41,700	n/a	n/a	685,462	175,841	193,119	n/a
Average value of estate (£s)								
Age at death								
55–64	205,000	45,200	n/a	n/a	n/a	n/a	n/a	n/a
65–74	229,000	56,800	n/a	1,625,409	n/a	n/a	n/a	n/a
75–84	272,000	68,000	n/a	n/a	714,201	175,841	193,119	n/a

Sources: Josiah Wedgwood, *The Economics of Inheritance* (Harmondsworth: Penguin, 1939 [1929]), pp. 193–95); *DBB*.

in the early 1920s up to half a dozen individuals in business and from the Congregational, Methodist, Presbyterian and Quaker denominations were among the wealthiest 0.2 per cent of the population and again in the richest 10 per cent of estates. Nonconformists in business could be very rich.

II. Wealthy Nonconformists in Their Business Settings

Before the First World War and sometimes after, Nonconformist national-level lay leaders were frequently recruited from the world of business, not least because they had useful skills, flexible time and disposable income. Of seventy-six Wesleyan laymen most active on their national committees in 1907, nearly two-thirds were in business. Among Primitive Methodists, over 90 per cent of their forty-nine vice-presidents (the denomination's highest lay position) 1872–1932 were in business, or had business experience, though only one (Sir William Hartley) was a millionaire.[10]

Whatever advantages Nonconformists may have had in business, in aspiring to industrial eminence they could hardly avoid three attributes: hard work, the ability to spot a market opportunity and possession of some kind of competitive advantage. Long hours and long working lives were legendary in nineteenth-century Britain. A classic example was William Carnelly, chairman of John Rylands & Sons, one of Lancashire's largest cotton manufacturing firms, and a Wesleyan who wrote two books about the Bible. In fifty years he never took a full week's holiday from work and retired just before his ninety-fourth birthday in 1916, dying soon afterwards.[11]

Wesley's criticism of commercial men who 'ran in the same dull track as their forefathers' was often heeded in later generations of Nonconformists searching for new market opportunities.[12] David Davies of Llandinam was a good example. A devout Calvinistic Methodist all his life and originally a sawyer, he demonstrated his skills when he had the opportunity to build a bridge over the River Severn near his home. From this modest base he gained railway contracts in mid-Wales and then in the 1860s he was prime mover in developing the upper Rhondda coalfield, securing additional capital through his Ocean Coal Company Ltd (1884). That in turn led to bitter rivalry with the Bute Estate who controlled the obsolete Cardiff docks and the Taff Vale Railway. Davies bypassed and overtook both by promoting the Barry docks as an alternative coal port and the Barry Railway (1884) to bring the coal down the Rhondda valleys. They proved to be 'a brilliant success'.[13]

Competitive advantage took many forms. Becoming an early (if not prime) mover in a more expansive industry could bring personal or corporate competitive advantage. Henry Adams, a Sheffield coalminer, in his twenties chose to become a local insurance agent and two decades later was the highly remunerated director of the very successful Refuge Assurance Company, only outdone in the field of industrial insurance (life insurance based on weekly or monthly collection of premiums) by the Prudential: corporate competitive advantage based on the spreading insurance habit of the Victorian working classes.[14] The introduction of labour-saving technology, despite its difficulties for employee relations, offered a widely pursued competitive advantage. Joseph Rank, Wesleyan Methodist, exploited steam driven roller flour milling in the 1880s. Among the Quakers, Fowlers of Leeds and Ransomes of Ipswich (agricultural implement makers) were introducing new machinery in the 1850s; Cadbury (chocolate) in the 1860s; and Clarks of Street (footwear), similarly in the 1870s.[15] Rather differently, Charles Mudie, Congregationalist, pioneered circulating libraries in London. Others left their rivals behind by rejecting adulteration, demonstrating their superior product quality. The Quaker chocolate manufacturers, Cadbury, Fry and Rowntree, or the Congregational dairyman Edmund Charles Tisdall with his distribution of high-quality milk to his Kensington customers, exemplified this approach.[16] Improved working conditions gave an advantage when it came to labour recruitment. Organizational restructuring, most easily imposed when a family firm converted into a limited liability company (usually to secure injections of new capital), offered yet another competitive advantage. Of course, all these, and other, advantages were not confined to Nonconformists. Sometimes, however, they excelled in exploiting particular ones.

Were Nonconformists any different from other employers? Did they treat their employees better? Were wages, hours, working conditions, pensions superior in Nonconformist firms? Were they swift to recognize trade unions? Were they concerned about worker health and safety? Did they admit employees to company direction (board membership) as well as management? Were they any more innovative?

It is impossible to make definite generalizations. Apart from the usual problem of inadequate evidence, no historian has made a comprehensive and systematic study of Nonconformists as employers. There is much anecdotal evidence and a few case histories. Michael Watts noted that while some Nonconformist employers could be severe and hypocritical, others reputedly were considerate paternalists, given to acts of charity. In general, he argues, Dissent promoted social harmony in the industrial districts and respectability among the working classes.[17] Presumably this was not achieved by exploitive, canting Nonconformist employers, who were as numerous in the cotton industry (largest of the country's manufacturing industries) before 1850 as their Church of England counterparts.[18]

Tony Corley's valuable survey of Quaker businessmen suggests that they were benevolent employers but, for some, their workers put in hours just as long as elsewhere, with Rowntrees leading the way in shortening hours.[19] Cadbury's, one of the very few truly major British companies lacking a thorough scholarly company history, has been the subject of desultory debate. Smith, Rowlinson and Child, coming from a sociological perspective, have noted that Cadbury's, like other English chocolate manufacturers, imitated continental and American practice in product development, personnel and scientific management, except that Cadbury's rejected a ruthless version of Taylorism (scientific management).[20] Comparisons between the Cadburys at Bournville and William Lever at Port Sunlight show the former in a better light.[21]

Two things can be said about Nonconformists as employers. First, they had no excuse for ignorance about ideals. Besides the Bible, there were Quaker instructions, John Wesley's rules and in the 1850s a profile of a model Nonconformist businessman, the Bristol dry goods merchant and Wesleyan Samuel Budgett (1794–1851).[22] William Arthur's pious biography firmly declared: 'You cannot press men to a point that stings their feelings and endangers their health, without sin.'[23] Samuel Budgett's slogans for his assistants were 'tact, push, principle' and 'order, punctuality, just dealing'. Within six years of its appearance in 1852, *The Successful Merchant* was in its twentieth edition and 50,000 copies had been printed.[24] Wesleyans and Methodists would have been among the first Nonconformists to read the biography not least because its author was one of the secretaries of the Wesleyan Methodist Missionary Society and later president of the Wesleyan Conference.[25]

If Budgett's was a model, Sir Samuel Morton Peto's career was a warning. Once the greatest railway contractor in the world (according to Brunel), an enlightened employer of 30,000 workers across Europe and North America as well as Britain, and the leading Nonconformist layman of mid-Victorian England, Peto was felled by financial incaution and the collapse of his bankers Overend, Gurney and Company in 1866. After Peto's bankruptcy proceedings were concluded in 1868, the deacons of his church, Bloomsbury Baptist Chapel (the £18,000 cost of which he had mostly funded), investigated his commercial morality. They concluded that he had held too much power, assumed excessive liability and sometimes gave the appearance of wrongdoing.[26]

Second, with respect to working and welfare conditions, Nonconformist employers reached the highest standards in the development of model industrial villages in the period 1760–1940. Of 135 such model villages and housing schemes built by industrialists, 21 per cent were constructed by Nonconformist employers.[27] The pinnacle of their achievement was seen in three of them. Saltaire, built between 1853 and 1872 by the Bradford worsted manufacturer and Congregationalist Sir Titus Salt, was hailed as a 'magnificent establishment . . . the factory is made the centre around which a complete colony lives and thrives . . . a town in the midst of the country'. Over time the hyperbole gave way to criticism as social standards and expectations changed.[28]

The most ambitious of them all architecturally, Port Sunlight, was begun in 1888, by the Merseyside soap manufacturer and Congregationalist William Hesketh Lever. Organizationally, even higher standards arrived after the brothers George and Richard Cadbury, chocolate manufacturers and Quakers, moved their works from the centre of Birmingham to Bournville in 1879 and in 1893–94 started to build a factory village around the works. In contrast to other model estates, Bournville houses were open to all to rent. To avoid private capital gains, they were eventually owned and controlled by an independent non-profit-making trust. The architectural, organizational and philosophical examples set at Port Sunlight and at Bournville, shaped the garden city movement and influenced modern town planning.[29] The major difference between Port Sunlight and Bournville lay in the personalities and philosophies of their founders. Lever, uncertain of his own faith, was a compulsive power seeker and at Port Sunlight he did all he could to control the minds and behaviour of his 3,000 workpeople, first through religious institutions and later through freemasonry. In contrast, George Cadbury was an evangelical Quaker whose outlook was tempered and shaped by the Quaker respect for the dignity and individuality of all people. If he felt the temptation to play the ubiquitous feudal magnate, his upbringing and his principles enabled him to resist it. Having a keenly attuned sense of stewardship, however, he was not indifferent to the spiritual needs of his employees. Like fellow Quaker, Joseph Storrs Fry in Bristol, he followed Samuel Budgett in holding a morning service for his workpeople, limited to three times a week by 1911 when there were up to five thousand employees.[30] (Other Nonconformist employers, such as the Wesleyan coal factor John Cory of Cardiff, and the Baptist shoe manufacturer and retailer Sir George White, of Norwich, prayed with their fellow managers.[31])

On one labour relations front nearly all Nonconformist employers were agreed. Workers' representatives were to be denied a seat in the boardroom. Company direction belonged to company owners. Even the Quaker employers resisted any boardroom interference by workers and most of all opposed worker knowledge and decision-making about corporate financial matters. In this they were no different from any other employers in the British economy. Exceedingly rarely, a highly talented worker would be co-opted as a director. In this British business lagged behind German best practice and, by the 1920s, the policies of the Labour and Liberal parties. Not until the 1950s did the picture change much.[32] Profit-sharing was as far as Nonconformists or anyone else would go in giving labour a share of capital. The merits of profit-sharing have been disputed by historians.[33]

III. Nonconformists in Business and Their Private Use of Wealth

Conscious of the warnings against the deceitfulness and dangers of riches issued by their denominations' founding fathers and their successors, Nonconformists in business struggled with temptations in the private use and disposal of wealth. Wesley was quite definite about what Methodists should not do with their wealth: avoid wasting your resources in indulging carnal desires, he advised, by which he meant not merely avoiding gluttony, drunkenness, even 'elegant epicurism', but also 'curiously adorning your houses' with books, pictures, 'elegant rather than useful gardens' and also expenditures on one's person 'to gain the admiration or praise of men'. Nor should Christians throw money away on their children. 'If you have good reason to believe they would waste what is now in your possession, in gratifying, and thereby increasing, the desire of the flesh, the desire of the eye, or the pride of life; at the peril of theirs and your own soul, do not set these traps in their way. Do not offer your sons or your daughters unto Belial, any more than unto Moloch.' Only if the child 'knew the value of money' should the parent entrust it with 'a considerable fortune'.[34] A casual survey might conclude that George Cadbury (Quaker) carefully observed these advices while William Lever (Congregationalist) happily succumbed to them.

In his mid-forties in 1897 Lever, after fourteen years of manufacturing and marketing his enormously popular Sunlight soap, possessed assets worth more than £1 million and an income of £92,000, of which up to 30 per cent was disposable. By 1912 his assets were worth almost £3 million and his income £242,000.[35] His hobbies were re-shaping houses, laying out gardens and collecting *objets d'art*. Paintings, furniture, porcelain, Wedgwood china, embroidery, Masonic jewels, and after his soap empire extended to Africa and the Pacific, ethnographic and archaeological collections. Like a magpie he could seldom resist the finest available. At first his Pre-Raphaelite, and other, paintings hung on the walls of the 800-seat works dining room in the Gladstone Hall at Port Sunlight. Eventually, in 1922 all the collections were displayed in the Lady Lever Art Gallery built there in memory of his wife. This ionic-columned temple to the fine arts cost over £25,000, at a time when a comfortable three-bedroom house was under £500.[36]

In contrast, George Cadbury, on the whole, agreed with Wesley. He told his biographer: 'My pictures are not remarkable. If I had spent a fortune in pictures I should not have had it to spend in other ways which seemed to me more important. Why should I hang fortunes on my walls while there is so much misery in the world?'[37] Nor did he pour large sums into his children's pockets. When he set up the Bournville Trust in 1900 with a gift of £172,000, to establish the Bournville estate for his employees and local people, he said:

> I am not rich as an American millionaire would count riches. My gift is the bulk of my property outside my business. I have seriously considered how far a man is justified in giving away the heritage of his children, and have come to the conclusion that my children will be all the better for being deprived of this money. Great wealth is not to be desired, and in my experience of life it is more a curse than a blessing to the families of those who possess it. I have ten children. Six of them are of an age to understand how my actions affect them, and they all entirely approve.[38]

Why did Nonconformist millionaires such as Lever, Sir Henry Tate and Sir Donald Currie become accumulators of this world's treasures? First, human nature is naturally acquisitive. Even an ascetic Nonconformist such as John Rylands, the self-effacing millionaire Manchester cotton merchant, indulged a collecting habit, creating at his home, Longford Hall, Salford, a library dedicated to literature, history, religion and general reference, with over 1,780 titles in five out of nineteen bookcases.[39] As landed tycoon, Lever exceeded them all. After the First World War he purchased the islands of Lewis, Harris and St Kilda in the Outer Hebrides. With a total of 570,000 acres and containing nearly 35,000 people they made him the biggest private landowner in the United Kingdom at that time.[40]

Second, there was a long tradition of Nonconformist patronage of the arts. By indulging their tastes, Lever, Tate and others were both enabling creativity and, by making art (particularly English art) available to a wider public, diffusing one of life's elevating influences.

Another justification Nonconformist millionaires might have advanced in defence of their indulgences, at least in collecting fine paintings, was a commercial one. In response to the challenges of mass production, entrepreneurs sometimes appropriated paintings by well-known artists for advertising purposes. William Lever, unrivalled marketing man and self publicist who spent about £2 million on advertising Sunlight soap between 1886 and 1906, soon seized such opportunities. In 1889 he purchased *The New Frock* by William P. Frith and used it to advertise Sunlight soap. While Millais had been half annoyed and half amused by Barrett's use of *Bubbles*, Frith was furious with Lever. A change in copyright law in 1911 favoured the creator, rather than the possessor, of a work of art and thereafter Lever was more cautious in using the works of top flight artists and Royal Academicians. However, this did not stop him from utilizing a range of outstanding illustrators and commercial artists to design advertisements for Lever Bros.[41]

Fourth, the social and economic trappings of these millionaires – country estates, London houses, art collections, titles – might also have been part of the long process of the assimilation of Dissent into English society. It was only in 1908 that the first Methodist entered the Lords, when Henry Fowler was elevated to the peerage as First Viscount Wolverhampton.

Last, a colossus like Lever might have retorted that he invested as much money, at one period in time at least, in his model company village Port Sunlight for the benefit of his employees, as he spent on his private art collections. After the Lady Lever Art Gallery was open to the general public, he could argue that his art collections brought more benefit and pleasure than his model village, the advantages of which were confined to his employees.

Yet, in his day-to-day lifestyle Lever was far from hedonistic. He arose each morning at 4.30 am, awoken by a night watchman. After exercising with Indian clubs for twenty minutes and plunging into a cold bath, he began the day's work. At 7.30 am he breakfasted. He then had ten minutes with the newspapers, half-an-hour for personal correspondence and by 9.00 am was in his office. He allowed himself fifteen minutes for lunch at his desk, followed by forty minutes' sleep. From 2.15 until 5.30 pm he again worked. At 7.00 pm he had dinner, at which no business talk was allowed. At 10.00 pm he went to bed. While living at Thornton Manor, his fine home three miles from Port Sunlight, between 1888 and 1919, he slept in a bed on a platform half-open to the skies. Sometimes he and his uncomplaining wife awoke under cover of snow. Whether he submitted to this discipline for his health or as a form of self-control is unknown. He rarely drank and after 1896 never smoked. Perhaps he slept under the stars to harden himself 'against the flabbiness latent in great wealth'.[42] His son recalled that he abhorred betting and gambling. To fill his mind with the values to which he aspired, he read a brief portion of the Bible every day. 'He loved it as literature, but, above all, he valued it as a book of practical advice.' However, the gospel of the Golden Rule ('Do as you would be done by'), not the Sermon on the Mount, was his creed. Unsurprisingly, he regarded the book of Proverbs as most applicable to the world of business.[43]

Nonconformists in business were also very generous towards the churches to which they belonged. John Wesley reminded his fellow believers that they were to 'give all you can' because God had placed the individual in the world 'not as a proprietor, but a steward'.[44] Some were inspired by the concept and practice of systematic beneficence developed among evangelicals. Essentially it entailed a regular scrutiny of the individual's personal finances and application of the principle that the more received, the greater the proportion given away. It originated with a lecture, later published, by the Wesleyan Methodist minister William Arthur (Budgett's biographer) in 1855.[45] An outstanding practitioner was William Hartley the jam maker and Primitive Methodist lay leader who, by the time he died in 1922, was giving away a third of his income and still managed to leave over £1 million.[46] To an inquiry from Bishop Gore, George Cadbury confidentially reported: 'I have for many years given practically the whole of my income for charitable purposes, except what is spent upon my family.'[47]

While systematic beneficence removed a conscience-scratching problem of how much to give away, it did not offer any guidance about the directions of charitable donations, nor did it solve the troublesome difficulty of how much to give to individual beneficiaries. Hartley eventually had to employ a trusted full-time assistant to deal with the disposal of his philanthropic funds. Furthermore, these private acts of charity had little impact on the wider problems of society. At the beginning of the twentieth century, Nonconformists struggled with this issue. Perks promoted schemes to enable the poor to emigrate to the colonies. George Cadbury advocated doubled death duties, graduated income tax and a land tax.[48] Joseph Rowntree's son Benjamin Seebohm Rowntree pioneered exposés of the scale of poverty in society.[49] Within the Society of Friends, Seebohm Rowntree's sociological study influenced the formation of the Friends Social Union (1903), committed to grappling with 'the sort of social disintegration which reflected a deeper spiritual malaise in modern society'.[50]

Nor was the charity of Nonconformists in business confined to their churches. Educational, medical and civic causes, in considerable numbers, were among the recipients of their largesse. A few examples have to suffice: Josiah Mason, pen manufacturer and Wesleyan, gave £200,000 to establish Birmingham University; the Wills family, cigarette manufacturers and Congregationalists, provided more than £500,000 for the fully independent Bristol University; Jesse Boot, manufacturing and retail chemist and Wesleyan, donated well over £500,000 and thirty acres to University College Nottingham. Of course these Nonconformists and others benefited because universities potentially supplied their companies with trained graduates.[51]

Differently, the widow of John Rylands, Enriqueta Rylands, ensured that her husband's memory was preserved in the foundation of a great library, the John Rylands Library on Deansgate, Manchester, dedicated to theology and the humanities.[52] Altogether it cost her about £1 million, despite which she still left an estate of £3.6 million in 1908.[53]

While the benefits that rich businessmen brought to their churches are undoubted, their presence also introduced treacherous shoals. There was the hazard of regarding secular wealth, status and power as sufficient qualification for leadership in the chapel or the denomination. In south Wales, promotion to colliery manager in some chapels almost automatically elevated them to the deacons' 'big seat'.[54]

Then there was the blurring of the line between secular and religious roles and relationships. On the one hand, church could imprudently envelop trade. For instance, a minister could become too powerful in the commercial counsels of one of his members in business. Examples of this were reported in south Wales.[55] Equally, a businessman's involvement in the affairs of his chapel or denomination could damage his business. For example, Joseph Storrs Fry immersed himself in Quaker and evangelical enterprise to the detriment of his family chocolate manufacturing business, apart from its welfare and employee aspects. Out of tune with commercial realities, he adamantly refused to move to a new site to escape the inefficiencies of the scattered premises in the centre of Bristol.[56]

On the other hand, it was possible for the chapel to be no more than the extension of a business enterprise. A classic example of this was William Lever and Christ Church, the church he built and controlled in his company village Port Sunlight. Faced with socialist rumblings among his employees, Lever appointed a Wesleyan minister of Christian Socialist convictions to Christ Church and simultaneously made him welfare officer for his company, Lever Bros. It was a clever move. The minister concerned, Samuel Gamble Walker, proved to be Lever's tame poodle but in the end the tactic failed because most of Lever's employees worshipped elsewhere.[57]

Even where company and church were kept apart, the presence of the rich man could distort or usurp the democratic structures of the chapel. And for the congregation, it could produce an enfeebling dependence, accompanied by deference, obligation and diminished reliance on spiritual resources – to say nothing of dissatisfactions within a congregation when the rich individual inserted his family members into leading posts in the chapel. The prudent declined to do no more than pump-prime chapel or denominational money-hungry projects. This seems to have been John Mackintosh's policy at Queens Road, Halifax. It was also the policy of the wealthy Wesleyan businessmen who, in 1900, at the annual conference, publicly and impulsively pledged large sums towards the Twentieth Century Fund's target of one million guineas.[58]

IV. Nonconformists in Business and the Abuses of Wealth

The most convincing test of any religious faith appears in its ethical standards and the moral behaviour of its adherents. What is clear is that the flaws of a very small number of Nonconformist business leaders shaded from the dubious to the immoral, the illegal and the criminal. Religious convictions have not always preserved entrepreneurs and executives from ethical dilemmas and irresponsible choices. Kirk's work on casuistry emphasizes that the assessment of ethical behaviour has to be set in the context of a community or social institution of values; this makes possible a verdict case-by-case.[59] Here that community of values must include the standards established by the various Nonconformist bodies. Space prevents more than the presentation of three cases (out of a possible nine affecting major businesses, 1880–1940), one each from the Quaker, Free Church of Scotland and Methodist traditions.

In their teaching and pursuit of integrity in business, the Quakers (Society of Friends) were ahead of other Nonconformists. Their seventeenth-century founder George Fox enjoined his Meetings to appoint two or three members to admonish any Friends who 'profess the Truth [but] follow pleasures, drunkenness, gaming, or are not faithful in their callings and dealings, nor honest, but run into debt, and so bring a scandal upon the Truth'.[60] Those who persisted in such behaviour would be disowned (excluded). When Friends ran into financial difficulty, commercially experienced members of the Meeting would inspect the pertinent financial records, give advice and render assistance. A bankrupt would be investigated by fellow Friends and, if judged morally guilty, would be disowned.[61] The overarching principle motivating the Quakers was expressed in 'Advices and Queries' issued in the eighteenth century by the Yearly Meeting of Ministering Friends (the Quakers' governing body): 'Finally, dear Friends, let your whole conduct and conversation be worthy of disciples of Christ.'[62]

This Quaker commitment to good neighbourliness failed to restrain Joseph Rowntree's adoption of underhand methods in trying to catch up with industry leaders. In 1872 he placed an advert in the London newspapers for workmen in the cocoa and chocolate making industry, set himself up at a temporary London address and proceeded to interrogate applicants. In this way he recruited several key foremen and learned about rivals' methods and recipes. Nor did he stop at London. He travelled to Bristol and Birmingham, and effectively stole recipes from Fry and Cadbury, fellow Quakers.[63] The ruses he deployed were practised fifty years earlier by some of the early industrialists.[64] Joseph Rowntree, however, stooped below his high Quaker ideals, to say nothing of the Seventh and Tenth Commandments, allowing custom and self-interest to dictate his commercial behaviour.

Why did he do this? Only three years before, he had left his grocery shop and joined a younger brother in a chocolate and cocoa manufacturing business employing about a dozen men. His brother, Henry Isaac Rowntree, was better at engineering than the commercial side of the business and the firm was in some difficulty – by 1873 it incurred a loss of £500. In addition Joseph Rowntree, in his mid-thirties, had remarried in 1867 after being widowed several years before, and had three children to look after. So there were strong economic and family pressures on him to achieve a quick turnaround in his firm's fortunes.[65] The alternative to stealing his fellow Quakers' business and technical secrets would have been to negotiate openly with Cadbury and Fry and to pay them for their closely guarded information and artisan skills. Perhaps he ranked his employees as closer neighbours than his commercial rivals, despite the latter being coreligionists and the former possibly not. Although Joseph Rowntree's labour piracy and industrial espionage tactics paid off because his firm survived and grew to two-thirds the size of its two Quaker rivals by 1907, he kept this episode in his early career quite secret; it was nothing to be proud of according to his espoused Quaker principles.[66]

A second case involved the Free Church of Scotland. Here principles of business ethics would have derived from Revd Thomas Chalmers, leader of the 1843 Disruption and first Moderator of the Free Church which it created.[67] In his discourses on *Commercial and Ordinary Affairs of Life,* Chalmers defined the golden rule taught by Jesus – 'whatsoever ye would that men should do to you, do ye even so to them; for this is the law and the prophets' (Mt. 7.12) – as 'the great Christian law of reciprocity between man and man'.[68] In the light of this the behaviour of John Campbell White seems extraordinary.

White was the third-generation inheritor of the partnership of J. & J. White, chemical manufacturers at Rutherglen near Glasgow, and he appeared to be the very model of an evangelical layman. At his death in 1908 he was president or vice-president of a score of religious societies or hospital trusts. He had been leader of a 500-strong Bible class in Dumbarton; promoter of the United Evangelistic Association (1873) doing mission and charitable work among Glasgow's poor; a generous supporter of the Christian Institute, the Bible Training Institute and the YMCA in Glasgow; and always a staunch member of the Free Church of Scotland to whose Livingstonia Mission in central Africa he had given, over the years, £50,000. He was deputy- and then lord lieutenant of Dunbartonshire and was raised to the peerage in 1893 as Baron Overtoun.

Simultaneously he seemed entirely oblivious to working conditions in the family firm which was Britain's largest chrome producer. At his Shawfield works his employees, mostly young Irishman, endured miserable wages, long hours and hazardous exposure to chemicals which caused 'chrome holes' in the skin and nasal passages. Accumulated decades of chemical sludge polluted the environment of the River Clyde. Awareness of conditions burst upon the public in 1899 when his workers at last went on strike, their case vigorously and viciously publicized by Keir Hardie, then editor of the *Labour Leader*. Hardie knew the community of values to which Overtoun subscribed because he had had an evangelical conversion experience in his early twenties and became an active lay preacher; though drifting from organized religion when he moved into socialism, he still called himself a Christian.[69] Most embarrassingly for Overtoun, the strike coincided with a 'grand religious revival campaign' being organized by fellow evangelicals. Eventually Overtoun published a weak defence of the situation, arguing that his wages were the going rate for unskilled workers. The men went back to work, Hardie moved to other concerns, and the scandal received scant notice in Overtoun's obituaries.

It seems, as Sydney Checkland has suggested, that Overtoun was partly deceived by two nephews, to whom he entrusted the works management, and partly by self-deception, imagining that appalling working conditions had changed for the better since his father's time – which implies that he made few visits to see what was going on at Shawfield. Of course working conditions were just as bad in many other works in Scotland and elsewhere. The difference was that Overtoun before 1899 was regarded as a paragon of evangelical virtue and energy north of the Border. The revelations of 1899 seen in the light of the ethical code outlined for merchants by Chalmers, to say nothing of the plain teaching of the New Testament, suggested that Overtoun was guilty of hypocrisy, one of the worst sins in the evangelical canon, as well as cruelty to his employees.[70]

In the first decades of the twentieth century a different community of values emerged. Nonconformist concepts of business ethics were being modified in response to radical changes in society, not least the proliferation of limited companies and the rise of socialism and the trade unions. All denominations between the 1890s and the 1920s reasserted the sovereignty of religion and morality over economics and the market.[71] In this context the behaviour of the Turners, members of the United Methodist Church (UMC) and asbestos manufacturers at Rochdale, Lancashire, has to be assessed.

The Turners were dominant in the newly emergent asbestos industry (where asbestos was mixed with cotton fibres to form fireproof materials).[72] In 1920 when their forty-year-old firm of Turner Brothers Asbestos Ltd (TBA) merged with Newalls Insulation, of Washington, County Durham, to form Turner and Newall (T&N), the new business had several thousand employees at home and abroad. It proved extremely profitable and each of the three Turner brothers became very wealthy. Each lived in his own acred residence and left fortunes: John, £260,079 in 1906; (Sir) Samuel II, £609,770 in 1924; Robert, £661,516 in 1931. All were generous in their civic as well as their Nonconformist philanthropies. Like their father they were strong Liberals as well as Methodists. All three were elected to Rochdale town council, served as mayors and became aldermen.

Robert Turner (1847–1931), youngest of the three brothers, was partner in the family asbestos firm and then director of T&N when that was formed. After the death of his brother Sir Samuel in 1924, he became chairman of TBA and vice-chairman of T&N until 1927. He remained on the T&N board another year. As a senior director when the asbestos hazard was first identified, Robert Turner's values are of particular significance.

At Baillie Street, Rochdale (a 2,000-seat 'cathedral' of United Methodism), he was a trustee but his chapel allegiance was to the UMC chapel at Spotland, the location of the family asbestos works. Here he was Sunday School teacher, trustee and member of the 'sale of work' committees in the 1880s. In 1896 he was treasurer of the new chapel fund and president of the bazaar committee which raised £1,963 towards the £5,325 cost of a new chapel and schoolroom for Spotland village.[73]

Robert's chapel networks reached far beyond Rochdale. He became an important figure in the national life of the United Methodist Free Churches (UMFC). At the century's turn he was treasurer of the UMFC Twentieth Century Fund (which raised 100,000 guineas). In 1907, the last year of the existence of the UMFC (before it merged with the Methodist New Connexion and the Bible Christians to form the UMC), he was a member of the denomination's Chapel and Superannuation Funds Committee, treasurer of its Twentieth Century Extension Fund and a trustee of the denomination's Free Methodist College in Manchester. That year the governors of the College reported Robert Turner's 'munificent generosity' in donating a sum of £1,340 that allowed them to discharge the whole of the debt on the College.[74]

His generosity and talents continued to be utilized in the UMC. In 1911 one of his public profiles noted that he took 'a very considerable interest in the missionary work of the United Methodist Church, and has traveled a good deal on its behalf, having visited several of the foreign missionary centres, and having also represented the denomination at an Ecumenical Conference in the United States' (in Washington, DC, 1891).[75] He was a 'Guardian Representative', or organizational trustee of the denomination (the UMC's highest position for a layman), and strongly supported the union of the Methodist branches, 1909–31; Twentieth Century Fund treasurer, 1907–21; Thanksgiving Fund treasurer, 1907–13; Home Mission Extension treasurer, 1915–22. For sixteen years (until 1928) he was chairman of the Finance Board of the UMC. In 1932, when his memory was eulogized and when the UMC merged with the Wesleyan Methodists and the Primitive Methodists, Robert Turner was remembered for his 'business sagacity and conservative guidance' which allowed the UMC, financially speaking, 'to look the Wesleyans in the face'. His national recognition came not only from his shrewd financial judgement but also from his own generosity to the UMC. In 1920 he gave £30,000 to the Chapel Fund on condition that the UMC circuits responded more generously to the claims of the Fund. In his will he left £12,500 to the UMC for a variety of its funds.[76] It was scarcely possible for a layman in the UMC to attain a higher standing than that of Robert Turner, JP.

Robert Turner was also the major property owner in Spotland. Significantly, in 1911 when the recent completions of Port Sunlight and

Bournville were fresh in the public mind, the newspaper simply reported that 'Mr [Robert] Turner has built and is the owner of much of the house property in the Spotland district, and has proved himself a most considerate landlord'.[77] Noticeably the estate was not described as an example of model housing.

The UMC history reported: 'When the cotton debacle [depression of 1921] came to Lancashire, he gave vast sums of money to lessen the effect of the catastrophe on his own work people.'[78] A very different picture emerges from the company papers of T&N and its subsidiary TBA. While Robert Turner, his brother Sir Samuel II and his son Samuel III were in charge, the toxic nature of asbestos, long suspected, was confirmed. In 1922 a Rochdale physician Dr Walter Scott Joss diagnosed Mrs Nellie Kershaw, a rover in the spinning room of TBA and wife of a slater's labourer, as suffering from 'asbestos poisoning'. The finding was confirmed in the inquest on Mrs Kershaw in 1924 by a Wigan pathologist Dr William Edmund Cooke, who published his account of the disease in the *British Medical Journal* in 1924 and 1927. He gave it the name 'pulmonary asbestosis'. Meantime another general practitioner Dr Ian Grieve, some of whose patients worked for another T&N subsidiary, J. W. Roberts Ltd of Armley, Leeds, had been studying lung diseases for his Edinburgh University MD thesis on 'Asbestosis' and concluded that asbestos particles were the unique cause of his patients' complaint. T&N rejected these findings. In 1928 the government commissioned the factory inspectorate to investigate. The Merewether and Price report of 1930 led to government regulations in 1931 which brought asbestosis within the Workmen's Compensation Act. What were the responses of the Turners?

After Mrs Kershaw applied to the Newbold Approved Society (one of the societies administering the government's health insurance scheme under the National Insurance Act of 1911) for National Health benefits in 1922, the TBA managers informed the Newbold Approved Society, 'We repudiate the term "Asbestos Poisoning". Asbestos is not poisonous and no definition or knowledge of such a disease exists. Such a description is not to be found among the list of industrial diseases in the schedule published with the Workmen's Compensation Act.'[79] Consequently Mrs Kershaw was denied any National Health benefits on the grounds that 'asbestos poisoning' was not covered by the scheme.

The TBA directors took the matter a stage further. They contested the notion of 'asbestos poisoning', informing their insurers, the Lancashire and London Insurance Company, 'because we feel that it will be exceedingly dangerous to admit any liability whatever in such a case'.[80] They were clearly concerned that admission of liability would open the floodgates to future claims against them.

What about Mrs Kershaw? Her situation is caught in the letter she wrote to TBA in September 1922, shortly after giving up work for the final time:

> Sept 25th 1922
> 45 Clementina Street
> Rochdale
>
> Dear Sir
>
> I am writing waiting to know what you are going to do about my case. I have been at home nine weeks now and not received a penny; as I think it is time there was something from you, as the national Health refuses to pay me anything. I am needing nourishments and the money I should get would buy them. I have lost nine weeks with wages now, through no fault of my own.
>
> Hoping you will answer me as soon as possible.
>
> Yours
> Mrs N. Kershaw.[81]

She died, painfully and spitting blood, eighteen months later.[82] During the last seven months of her life she secured seven shillings a week under the National Health Insurance scheme, but never a penny from her employers, TBA or its parent T&N.

Her widower Frank Kershaw was still struggling to get assistance in July 1924, three months after the inquest on his wife.[83] In the company archives, at the end of depositions made in the Kershaw inquest, is a memo 'made at Mr Rupert's [Robert's youngest son and a T&N director] request for future reference'. It noted that Frank Kershaw had appealed to the company early in July 1924. Mr Ellison [William M. Ellison, employment manager at TBA] of the company explained 'that he [Kershaw] was not entitled to any payment whatever as it was not a case coming under the Workmen's Compensation Act, but that it was a National Health Insurance case and he would not be entitled to any payment after the death of his wife'. Kershaw had pleaded that 'he was in need of money due to the builders strike. He said his wife's funeral expenses had not yet been met and there was money owing for the furniture.' Ellison promised to 'put the case before the Directors. Mr Ellison also told Kershaw that he was not entitled to anything from the Relief Section [of TBA] as he did not work here, and his wife had not been a member of the Benevolent Society'. The T&N directors soon decided that none of their profits would be diverted into *ex gratia* payments to relatives of asbestos victims: 'Mr Bussy [Frank Bussy, departmental manager at TBA and lifelong member of Syke Methodist Church[84]] advised that no payment should be made, and Mr Rupert decided likewise, as it would create a precedent, and admit responsibility which has hitherto been repudiated, and furthermore if a payment be made there would no doubt be further applications by Kershaw later.'[85]

That the Turner family were guilty of applying double standards in their religious and business activities seems clear. Why did they do this? The most obvious explanation is that they simply separated chapel and mill on grounds of expediency: in this way they could operate most effectively in each of the very different spheres of their lives. There was some theological defence from a spurious version of Luther's two kingdoms doctrine. Emerging in the 1860s, it split Christian moral law from worldly moral law.[86] Such a transmission of theological ethics, through pulpit sermons or church conferences, into the worlds of Robert Turner, his brothers and his sons has yet to be demonstrated. In fact, while this German thinking led to the fatal rise of Nazism, diametrically opposed positions advanced in Britain in the 1920s and 1930s.

As noted, a more insightful understanding comes from Kirk's suggestion that consciences are informed by communities and institutions. As Methodists, manufacturers, directors of a limited company and civic leaders, the Turners belonged to communities with diverging communal values. A brief consideration of some of these moral traditions suggests which may have exerted the stronger pulls.

The seismic effects of the First World War, particularly on membership figures, drove the churches to a new self-examination which *inter alia* from some of the denominations produced statements and positions clearly defining a Christian industrial morality. In 1918, the UMC Conference adopted the report of its Spiritual State Commission, ordered its printing and commended it to members. Published as *Facing the Facts*, the Commission report deplored the Church's neglect of 'huge tracts of life . . . like commerce and public questions in which ordinary people are most interested'. It spoke of the need to 'Christianise labour, commerce, and professional life', and the Christian's 'continual conflict with worldly standards'. [87] Yet it tended to pull its punches, when compared to the report of the (Church of England) Archbishops' Fifth Committee of Inquiry *Christianity and Industrial Problems*, also published in 1918: '[W]e think it our duty to point out that Christianity claims to offer mankind a body of moral teaching which not only is binding upon individuals in their personal and domestic conduct but also supplies a criterion by which to judge their economic activity, their industrial organization and their social institutions.'[88]

More significantly for the Turner family, in 1925 the UMC Conference expressed 'its sense of the value of the reports and findings of the great Conference on Christian Politics, Economics and Citizenship'[89] held in Birmingham the previous year – when 1,500 delegates from all the churches, inspired by Bishop (later Archbishop) William Temple, met to discuss a dozen reports prepared by commissions informed by study groups across the country. COPEC's ninth report *Industry and Property* was heavily influenced by *Christianity and Industrial Problems* and, like it, asserted that wealth, property, and capital must be subordinated to Christian ethics and morality. Among the objectives set by COPEC was one that with laser sharpness brought to bear on the Nellie Kershaw case (and hundreds of others in the decades to follow) the traditional biblical and Methodist moral teaching: 'The first charge on industry should be a remuneration sufficient to maintain the worker and his family in health and dignity.'[90] As a leading national layman in the United Methodist Church, Robert Turner almost certainly saw a copy of *Industry and Property*. For him and his sons, it would have been disturbing reading. However, it was new teaching and the Turners evidently ignored it.

For them the textile and asbestos industries exhibited a rather different community of values. As a second-generation textile manufacturer Robert Turner would have grown up accustomed to unhealthy working conditions. In his early days in his father's cotton mill he would have inhaled as much cotton dust in the carding, spinning and weaving rooms as any of his employees. As for dust removal, there were extractor fans in the better spinning mills and weaving sheds but even these were not entirely effective. Consequently, over 600,000 cotton industry employees in Lancashire commonly tolerated a dusty working environment.[91] The Turners' cotton mill manufactured a mixture of cotton and asbestos fibres and before the early 1920s they evidently regarded asbestos dust as no more dangerous than cotton dust; lung complaints from both were inevitable

The merger of Turner's with Newall's in 1920 introduced yet another community of values to the Methodist directors from Rochdale. Now they were legally obliged to share control of the business. No longer could Robert Turner or his sons regard themselves as free to act as Christian stewards of their family businesses: these now belonged to the new holding company T&N, initially a private limited company. In 1924 T&N became a public limited company and immediately this led to the increasing dispersion of shares and ownership. The directors became accountable to new and fluctuating groups of investors whose common interest was T&N's profitability. Head of the Newall side of the boardroom was Frederick Stirling Newall, son of a science-educated family (his father was an FRS, his mother a Quaker) and himself a prominent member of the science-orientated industrial community centred on Newcastle-upon-Tyne.[92] F. S. Newall religious affiliation was Established Church.[93] Serving as T&N chairman (1924–29), he doubtless reinforced a strict attention to the corporate pursuit of profits.

Confronted by this clash of values, primarily between a new, sharpened Christian ethic and, on the other hand, market morality framed by English company law, the Turners chose the market ethic and profit maximization. They could publicly rationalize this on grounds of job creation for Rochdale and elsewhere, promise technological improvements for their plants' health and safety conditions and deny the toxic effects of asbestos exposure. For decades these and other devices satisfied many private and public consciences alike.

Robert Turner shared with his two sons, fellow directors, the critical, culture-shaping decisions about Nellie Kershaw. Of those sons, Samuel Turner III became chairman of T&N in 1929 and retired in 1946. In early manhood he had led the Sunday School at Baillie Street chapel. Like his father he contributed to the national-level work of the UMC, serving as treasurer of its Chapel Fund (1924–32) and donating £7,000 for the support of UMC ministers and their dependants.[94] However, after the death of his father in 1931, Methodist union in 1932 and an astonishing growth in asbestos markets and the mushrooming of T&N and its subsidiaries in the 1930s, Samuel Turner III bowed out of national level activities in the Methodist Church.[95] Under his and his successors' chairmanship, the company's tactics in denying the lethal effects of exposure to asbestos continued through most of the rest of the twentieth century.[96]

V. Conclusion

This chapter has tried to establish the extent of wealth among Nonconformist members of the British business élite, demonstrating that by the 1900s several were among the richest in the land. It has then attempted to discover how that wealth was used in business and in the private lives of individual Nonconformist business people, revealing a range of attitudes, from the self-denying stewardship of George Cadbury to the much more complex and mixed applications of wealth by William Lever. Last, it has examined three cases (among half a dozen more, 1880–1940, including the criminal Jabez Spencer Balfour[97]) illustrating ethical failures among Nonconformist business people. Perhaps the most important finding of these investigations is that Nonconformist teaching about business ethics before the 1930s was inadequately understood and espoused by the Nonconformist business community. It should be noted that the essay is confined to the most successful and the most wealthy Nonconformist capitalists. It says nothing about outstanding Nonconformist business executives of the period, such as Harold Bellman or Josiah Stamp; and it is silent about the thousands of Nonconformists who in their working lives ran small businesses and in their faith lives exercised leadership of their chapels, circuits, associations, regional assemblies and national conferences.

Notes

I am indebted to the staff and resources of the John Rylands Library, Manchester, especially for their Methodist and Nonconformist collections; Manchester Metropolitan University Library, for interlibrary loan services; Manchester Central Library, for access to electronic library resources. Professor Geoffrey Tweedale has kindly facilitated my access to the Turner and Newall archive formerly at the Manchester Metropolitan University Business School.

1 See David J. Jeremy, 'Religious Links of Individuals Listed in the *Dictionary of Business Biography*', in idem (ed.), *Business and Religion in Britain* (Aldershot: Gower, 1988), pp. 188–205.

2 David J. Jeremy, 'Introduction: Debates about Interactions between Religion, Business and Wealth in Modern Britain', in idem (ed.), *Religion, Business and Wealth in Modern Britain* (London: Routledge, 1998), pp. 1–31.

3 *General Report of the Wesleyan Centenary Fund* (Leeds: Anthony Pickard, 1844); *Report of the Wesleyan-Methodist Thanksgiving Fund, 1878–1883* (London: Wesleyan-Methodist Book-Room, 1884).

4 This fits Watts' finding that the majority of Nonconformists in the first four decades of the nineteenth century, though increasing in numbers, were going down the social scale. Michael R. Watts, *The Dissenters, Volume II: The Expansion of Evangelical Nonconformity* (Oxford: Clarendon Press, 1995), pp. 325–27.

5 Israel Worsley, *Observations on the State and Changes in the Presbyterian Societies of England during the Last Half Century; also, on the Manufactures of Great Britain Which Have Been for the Most Part Established and Supported by the Protestant Dissenters* (London, 1816); Geoffrey E Milburn, 'Piety, Profit and Paternalism: Methodists in Business in the North-East of England, ca 1760–1920', *Proceedings of the Wesley Historical Society*, 44 (1983), pp. 45–92; Clyde Binfield, 'Victorian Values and Industrious Connexions', *Proceedings of the Wesley Historical Society*, 55 (2006), pp. 141–68; Watts, *The Dissenters, Volume II*, pp. 327–46.

6 Based on a guesstimate of a hundred names per page.

7 Michael R. Watts, *The Dissenters, Volume I: From the Reformation to the French Revolution* (Oxford: Clarendon Press, 1978), pp. 346–66.

8 A notable demonstration of Wesleyan business-derived wealth was the seemingly reckless, faith-inspired manner in which half a dozen businessmen stood up at the Wesleyan Conference of 1900 and pledged thousands of guineas at a time to complete the one million guinea Twentieth Century Fund. David J. Jeremy, 'Late-Victorian and Edwardian Methodist Businessmen and Wealth', in Jeremy (ed.), *Religion, Business and Wealth*, pp. 71–73.

9 Josiah Wedgwood, *The Economics of Inheritance* (rev. edn, Harmondsworth: Penguin Books, 1939 [1929]), pp. 186–98.

10 David J. Jeremy, *Capitalists and Christians: Business Leaders and Churches in Britain, 1900–1960* (Oxford: Clarendon Press, 1990), pp. 298, 304; idem, 'Laity in Denominational Leadership: Vice-Presidents of the Primitive Methodist Church, 1872–1932', *Proceedings of the Wesley Historical Society*, 57 (2010), p. 256.

11 *Manchester Guardian* (27 July 1916).

12 John Wesley advised his followers to 'gain all you can' in 'worldly business' using 'all possible diligence in your calling' and seek improvements 'by using in your business all the understanding which God has given you. It is amazing how few do this; how men run on in the same dull track with their forefathers'. John Wesley, *Forty-Four Sermons* (London: Methodist Conference Office, n.d.), pp. 617–21. These sermons have been the final authority on doctrine for all the branches of Methodism and, after 1932, of the Methodist Church.

13 D. S. M. Barrie, 'David Davies', in David J. Jeremy and Christine Shaw (eds), *Dictionary of Business Biography*, 6 vols (London: Butterworths, 1984–86) [hereafter *DBB*]; Kenneth O. Morgan, 'David Davies', *Oxford Dictionary of National Biography* (Oxford: Oxford University Press, 2004) [hereafter *ODNB*]; Jack Simmons, *The Railways of Britain: An Historical Introduction* (London: Routledge & Kegan Paul, 1961), p. 29; Ivor (Bulmer) Thomas, *Top Sawyer: A Biography of David Davies of Llandinam* (reprint, Carmarthen: Golden Grove, 1988 [1938]).
14 *Sheffield Daily Telegraph* (12 December 1906); Barry Supple, *The Royal Exchange Assurance: A History of British Insurance, 1720–1970* (Cambridge: Cambridge University Press, 1970), pp. 218–24.
15 T. A. B. Corley, 'How Quakers Coped with Business Success: Quaker Industrialists, 1860–1914', in Jeremy (ed.), *Business and Religion in Britain*, pp. 171, 177; see entries on these and many more in Edward H. Milliken, *Biographical Dictionary of British Quakers in Commerce and Industry, 1775–1920* (York: Sessions Book Trust, 2007).
16 Peter J. Atkins, 'Edmund Charles Tisdall', *DBB*.
17 Watts, *The Dissenters, Volume II*, pp. 630–34. 649–56.
18 Anthony C. Howe, *The Cotton Masters, 1830–1860* (Oxford: Clarendon Press, 1984), p. 62.
19 Corley, 'How Quakers Coped with Business Success'. See also Milburn, 'Piety, Profits and Paternalism'.
20 Chris Smith, Michael Rowlinson and John Child, *Reshaping Work: The Cadbury Experience* (Cambridge: Cambridge University Press, 1990).
21 Jeremy, *Capitalists and Christians*, pp. 143–45; idem, 'The Enlightened Paternalist in Action: William Hesketh Lever at Port Sunlight before 1914', *Business History*, 33 (1991), pp. 58–81.
22 Peter Wardley, 'Samuel Budgett', *ODNB*.
23 William Arthur, *The Successful Merchant: Sketches of the Life of Samuel Budgett* (London: Hamilton, Adams, & Co, 1858), p. 219.
24 See title page of the 1858 edition.
25 David N. Hempton, 'William Arthur', *ODNB*.
26 Philip L. Cottrell, 'Samuel Morton Peto', *DBB*; Michael H. Port, 'Samuel Morton Peto', *ODNB*; Faith Bowers, *A Bold Experiment: The Story of Bloomsbury Chapel and Bloomsbury Central Baptist Church, 1848–1999* (London: Bloomsbury Central Baptist Church, 1999).
27 Compiled from Budgett Meakin, *Model Factories and Villages: Ideal Conditions of Labour and Housing* (London: Fisher Unwin, 1905); Gillian Darley, *Villages of Vision* (London: Architectural Press, 1975; revised 2007) and Walter L. Creese, *The Search for Environment. The Garden City: Before and After* (New Haven, CT: Yale University Press, 1966), with a number of the present author's additions.
28 Jack Reynolds, *The Great Paternalist: Titus Salt and the Growth of Nineteenth Century Bradford* (London: Maurice Temple Smith, 1983), pp. 281–86.
29 Enid Gauldie, *Cruel Habitations: A History of Working Class Housing, 1780–1918* (London: George Allen and Unwin, 1974), pp. 192–94 sees Bournville and Port Sunlight as 'middle-class affairs' with little impact on working class housing. Nevertheless they predated and informed the garden city concept published by Ebenezer Howard in his book *Tomorrow* (1898): Mervyn Miller, 'Ebenezer Howard', *ODNB*.
30 For Lever's attempts to control, see Jeremy, 'Enlightened Paternalist'; and for Cadbury see A. G. Gardiner, *The Life of George Cadbury* (London: Cassell & Co., 1925), pp. 27–29, 137, 279–302.
31 Williams, 'John Cory', *ODNB*; Keith Brooker, 'George White', *DBB*.
32 Jeremy, *Capitalists and Christians*, pp. 162–73, 230–31.

33 Derek Matthews, 'The British Experience of Profit-Sharing', *Economic History Review*, 42 (1989).
34 Wesley, *Forty-Four Sermons*, pp. 621–24.
35 Andrew M. Knox, *Coming Clean: A Postscript after Retirement from Unilever* (London: Heinemann, 1976), pp. 72–75. Lever's female employees' maximum earnings in 1909 were £60 a year while those of his male workers reached £75 a year. W. L. George, *Labour and Housing at Port Sunlight* (London: Alston Rivers, 1909), pp. 43, 47.
36 See essays in Edward Morris (ed.), *Art and Business in Edwardian England: The Making of the Lady Lever Art Gallery* (Liverpool: National Museums and Galleries on Merseyside, 1992); John Burnett, *A Social History of Housing, 1815–1970* (Newton Abbot: David & Charles, 1978), p. 246.
37 Gardiner, *George Cadbury*, p. 103.
38 Ibid.
39 Douglas A. Farnie, *John Rylands of Manchester* (Manchester: John Rylands University Library, 1993), pp. 21–36.
40 Nigel Nicolson, *Lord of the Isles: Lord Leverhulme in the Hebrides* (London: Weidenfeld & Nicolson, 1960), pp. 25, 122.
41 Morris (ed.), *Art and Business.*
42 Nicholson, *Lord of the Isles*, pp. 7–9.
43 Second Lord Leverhulme, *Viscount Leverhulme* (London: George Allen & Unwin, 1927), pp. 275–76.
44 Wesley, *Forty-Four Sermons*, p. 624.
45 Jane Garnett, '"Gold and the Gospel": Systematic Beneficence in Mid-Nineteenth Century England', in W. J. Sheils and Diana Wood (eds), *The Church and Wealth* (Oxford: Blackwell, 1987), p. 355. An 1863 reprint of Arthur's lecture can be found in the Methodist Archives at the John Rylands Library, Manchester.
46 Over two-thirds of his known charitable gifts supported causes serving the whole community, not solely his fellow Nonconformists. Arthur S. Peake, *The Life of Sir William Hartley* (London: Hodder & Stoughton, 1926), passim.
47 Gardiner, *George Cadbury*, p. 105.
48 Ibid., pp. 103, 108.
49 With his famous investigation, *Poverty. A Study of Town Life* (London: Macmillan & Co., 1901). See entries in the *DBB* by Shirley Keeble and in the *ODNB* by Brian Harrison.
50 Thomas C. Kennedy, *British Quakerism, 1860–1920: The Transformation of a Religious Community* (Oxford: Oxford University Press, 2001), pp. 190, 280.
51 Michael Sanderson, *The Universities and British Industry, 1850–1970* (London: Routledge & Kegan Paul, 1972); Stanley Chapman, *Jesse Boot of Boots the Chemists* (London: Hodder & Stoughton, 1974) pp. 185–88.
52 Douglas A. Farnie, *Enriqueta Augustina Rylands (1843–1908), Founder of the John Rylands Library* (Manchester: John Rylands University Library of Manchester, 1989).
53 Farnie, *John Rylands*, p. 63; idem, 'Money-Making and Charitable Endeavour: John and Enriqueta Rylands of Manchester', *The Journal of the United Reformed Church History Society*, 6 (2000), pp. 429–39.
54 E. T. Davies, *Religion in the Industrial Revolution in South Wales* (Cardiff: University of Wales Press, 1965), pp. 149–50.
55 Ibid., pp. 64–65.
56 Gillian Wagner, 'Joseph Storrs Fry', *DBB.*
57 Jeremy, 'Enlightened Paternalist'.

58 Jeremy, 'Chapel in a Business Career'; idem, 'Late-Victorian and Edwardian Methodist Businessmen and Wealth', pp. 71–85.
59 Kenneth E. Kirk, *Conscience and Its Problems: An Introduction to Casuistry*, Introduction by David H. Smith (Cambridge: James Clark & Co., 1999), pp. 58–105. His concern was the Church of England.
60 Religious Society of Friends in Great Britain, *Church Government, Being the Third Part of Christian Discipline in the Religious Society of Friends* (London: Central Offices of the Religious Society of Friends, 1931), pp. xviii–xix.
61 James Walvin, *The Quakers: Money and Morals* (London: John Murray, 1997), pp. 73–79.
62 Religious Society of Friends, *Church Government*, p. 39. Bankruptcy also disqualified from church membership Baptists, Congregationalists and those in the several branches of Methodism from the eighteenth century to the formation of the Methodist Church in 1932 when the disqualification was included in its Constitution.
63 Walvin, *The Quakers*, pp. 162–65. Walvin appears to be the first to discover this dubious episode. It is not mentioned by Fitzgerald in his company history.
64 John R. Harris, *Industrial Espionage and Technology Transfer: Britain and France in the Eighteenth Century* (Aldershot: Ashgate 1998), passim; David J. Jeremy, *Transatlantic Industrial Revolution: The Diffusion of Textile Technologies between Britain and America, 1790–1830s* (Cambridge MA: MIT Press, 1981), pp. 78, 95, 114, 130–36, 257.
65 Anne Vernon, *A Quaker Business Man: The Life of Joseph Rowntree, 1836–1925* (London: George Allen & Unwin Ltd, 1958), passim.
66 Robert Fitzgerald, *Rowntree and the Marketing Revolution, 1862–1969* (Cambridge: Cambridge University Press, 1995), pp. 220–21; Peter Wardley, 'The Emergence of Big Business: The Largest Corporate Employers of Labour in the United Kingdom, Germany and the United States *c.*1907', *Business History*, 41 (1999).
67 Stewart J. Brown, 'Thomas Chalmers', *ODNB*.
68 Thomas Chalmers, *The Application of Christianity to the Commercial and Ordinary Affairs of Life: in a Series of Discourses* (Glasgow: Chalmers & Collins, 1820), Discourse V.
69 Kenneth O. Morgan, 'James Keir Hardie', *ODNB*.
70 Sydney Checkland, 'John Campbell White', in Anthony Slaven and Sydney Checkland (eds), *Dictionary of Scottish Business Biography, 1860–1960* [hereafter DSBB], 1860–1960, 2 vols (Aberdeen: Aberdeen University Press); Lionel Alexander Ritchie, 'John Campbell White', *ODNB*.
71 Jeremy, *Capitalists and Christians*, pp. 53–72.
72 For which see Geoffrey Tweedale, *Magic Mineral to Killer Dust: Turner & Newall and the Asbestos Hazard* (Oxford: Oxford University Press, 2000).
73 Spotland Methodist Centenary Committee, *The Story of a Hundred Years. United Methodist Church, Spotland, 1826–1926* (Rochdale: *Observer* General Printing Department, 1926), pp. 26–38, 49, 75, 78, 88.
74 United Methodist Free Churches, *Minutes of Annual Assembly* (1907), pp. 122, 198, 204.
75 *Rochdale Times* (17 June 1911).
76 UMC, *Minutes of Conference* (1923), pp. 1, 293; (1925), p. 362; (1926), p. 329; (1932), pp. 9, 86. Henry Smith, John E. Swallow and William Treffry, *The Story of the United Methodist Church* (London: Henry Hook, 1932), pp. 24, 58–59, 80, 89, 113, 163, 170, 221, 223. His will shows that he left £12,000 to the UMC to be invested in 4 per cent stock.
77 *Rochdale Times* (17 June 1911).

78 Henry Smith et al., *Story of the United Methodist Church*, p. 89.
79 T&N Papers, TBA to Newbold Approved Society, 15 September 1922, Nellie Kershaw case file, 68/1704.
80 T&N Papers, TBA to the Lancashire & London Insurance Co Ltd, 21 September 1922, Nellie Kershaw case file, 68/1706.
81 T&N Papers, Nellie Kershaw case file, 68/1662–1663, 1710–1711.
82 T&N Papers, Frank Kershaw's deposition, Nellie Kershaw case file, 68/1751. See also Tweedale, *Magic Mineral*, pp. 15–16.
83 T&N Papers, Memo, 25 July 1924, Nellie Kershaw case file, 68/1766.
84 *Rochdale Observer* (2 October 1957).
85 T&N Papers, Memo, 25 July 1924, Nellie Kershaw case file, 68/1766.
86 William J. Wright, *Martin Luther's Understanding of God's Two Kingdoms: A Response to the Challenge of Skepticism* (Grand Rapids, MI: Eerdmans, 2010), pp. 17–36.
87 UMC, *Minutes of Conference* (1918), pp. 4–9; UMC, *Facing the Facts: A Challenge to United Methodism, Being the Report of the Commission on the Spiritual State of the Churches together with Notes on the Recommendations and a Summary of the Replies to the Questionary* [*sic*] (London: UMC Conference, 1918), pp. 14, 17. Although 25,000 were printed (UMC, *Minutes of Conference* (1919), p. 31), this is now a rare pamphlet. My thanks to E. Alan Rose for the loan of his copy.
88 *Report of the Archbishops' Fifth Committee of Inquiry, Christianity and Industrial Problems* (1918), 9. John Oliver, *The Church and Social Order: Social Thought in the Church of England, 1918–1939* (London: Mowbray, 1968); Edward R. Norman, *Church and Society in England, 1779 to 1970: A Historical Study* (Oxford: Clarendon Press, 1976).
89 UMC, *Minutes of Conference* (1925), pp. 10–11.
90 Conference on Christian Politics, Economics and Citizenship, *Industry and Property* (London: Longmans, Green & Co., 1924), p. 194.
91 Allen Clarke, *The Effects of the Factory System* (London: Grant Richards, 1899), pp. 45, 75.
92 F. S. Newell was one of the eight directors of the Newcastle-upon-Tyne Electricity Supply Company, which claimed to be the largest electric power company in the world before 1914. *The Times* (10 October 1913), p. 14.
93 His memorial service was held at St Nicholas's Cathedral, Newcastle-upon-Tyne. *Newcastle Journal* (27 June 1930). My thanks to James Crosthwaite of the City Library for this.
94 UMC, *Minutes of Conference* (1924), p. 10; (1925), p. 362; (1927), p. 13; (1929), p. 273; (1932), p. 304.
95 Henry Smith et al., *Story of the United Methodist Church*, pp. 80, 220. He does not, for example, appear in *Who's Who in Methodism* (1933).
96 As Geoffrey Tweedale has fully demonstrated in *Magic Mineral*.
97 Entries on Jabez Spencer Balfour by Edmund J. Cleary in *DBB* and by Duncan Bythell in *ODNB*.

20 The Nonconformist Conscience

Robert Pope

It was in November 1890, during the public scandal which surrounded the divorce of Captain William and Mrs Katharine O'Shea, that the phrase 'the Nonconformist Conscience' first came to prominence. Although Mrs O'Shea had begun an affair with Charles Stewart Parnell, leader of the Irish Parliamentary Party, some ten years previously, it made the headlines when a divorce suit was filed by Captain O'Shea on Christmas Eve 1889. The case was heard in November the following year and neither Parnell nor Mrs O'Shea contested the charge, primarily because they wished to be married. The lack of defence suggested an admission of guilt, and the divorce was granted on 17 November 1890. While the adultery of Mrs O'Shea with Parnell might have appeared sordid and thus offensive to Victorian sensibilities, few initially believed that the scandal would offer anything but a minor and fleeting distraction from the ongoing affairs of state. At that point the media took over, ably assisted by some of the prominent Nonconformist leaders of the day.

The day after the *decree nisi* was granted, *The Times* condemned Parnell for his adultery and suggested that an apparently immoral private life was unacceptable in a public figure: 'Even the least prudish draw the line for public men above the level of a scandalous exposure like this.'[1] On the same day, the Baptist minister John Clifford, who had a long pedigree of social involvement motivated by a highly attuned moral sense, wrote to *The Star* warning that unless the Irish parliamentary party insisted on Parnell's 'immediate retirement', all sympathy would be lost for the greater issue, namely the granting of home rule to Ireland. 'He must go', he wrote, basing his demand on the principle that 'men legally convicted of immorality will not be permitted to lead in the legislature of the Kingdom'. As a result, Parnell's withdrawal from public life, whether voluntary or forced, was 'the only right course'.[2] 'Parnell must go' became something of a rallying cry. It was repeated by Clifford in a letter jointly composed with Joseph Parker, the popular, if rather earthy, pastor of London's (Congregational) City Temple, in the *Pall Mall Gazette* of 19 November, while the following day Hugh Price Hughes, who had already established himself as a mover and shaker both within Wesleyan Methodism and in the communities in which he ministered, commented: 'Of course, Mr Parnell must go. We apologise to our readers for discussing so obvious a point.'[3] In a letter published in the *Times* on 28 November, Hugh Price Hughes demanded once again that Parnell retire altogether from public life. Given the extent of the moral turpitude, 'nothing less will satisfy the Nonconformist conscience', he wrote.[4] And the chief motivation behind his protest was that 'we stand immovably on this eternal rock; what is morally wrong can never be politically right'.[5] For Hughes, 'the sacred cause of social purity would never be secured until all notoriously immoral men were expelled from the House of Commons'.[6]

Though not formally ousted from his position, Parnell certainly lost much support as a result of this public moralizing with the Irish party divided between a minority Parnellite section and the majority anti-Parnellites. Circumstance finally resolved the affair. Parnell married Mrs O'Shea on 25 June 1891 and died from a heart attack on 6 October the same year. Nevertheless, it was the campaign by Nonconformists, whose consciences had been aggrieved by the adultery of a public figure, that ensured that, though previously immensely popular, Parnell lost the hold he once had on a great number of his supporters as well as the political significance and influence he had formerly possessed.[7]

It is worth pausing over the bare facts of the Parnell case. This was the catalyst which caused the phrase 'Nonconformist Conscience' to enter the public domain and it also casts some light on the phenomenon which gave rise to the term. For those Nonconformists involved in the debate, there could be no separation of politics and morality: 'what is morally wrong can never be politically right' became a slogan for Nonconformist comment on national and even international events. But in order to be moral, politics required politicians of unimpeachable character. Thus there could be no separation of public and private life. Even if private immorality did not spill over into public life, a country's leaders were expected to set an example and, as a result, no politician could exercise his role fully unless he was also a model of upright and righteous living. It would have been naïve of the Nonconformists to believe that all politicians led completely blameless lives, and this was certainly not the position they held. Instead the Nonconformist Conscience, as it came to prominence during the Parnell affair, was concerned precisely with moralizing politics and ensuring that redress was made when moral ideals were violated. Once moral principle had been breached, there was no way forward but to expunge the offence (or the offender) completely. Thus Parnell could not apologize, show remorse or repent (none of which he showed any desire to do), he simply had to go. The Parnell case showed that, for Nonconformists, politics itself was to be Christianized, where politicians were governed by the highest moral principles, lived blameless lives and thus could be trusted to help inaugurate God's kingdom on earth through righteous, and even Christian, legislation. Having become respectable over the course of the nineteenth century and possessing what they thought was a degree of influence over the Liberal Party, the Nonconformists believed that their role was to assist in that task.

As a result, the association of the Nonconformist Conscience with the Parnell case raises important questions about the nature of Nonconformist public witness. Did it reveal that the so-called Nonconformist Conscience had emerged by the late nineteenth century due to the particularities of late-Victorian society and the place the Nonconformists were able to play within it, or was it something that characterized the witness of Nonconformity and Dissent even from the dawn of the movement in the sixteenth and seventeenth centuries? Both the Nonconformists at the time and subsequent commentators have failed to agree entirely over the answers to these questions.

I. A Nonconformist Conscience?

According to John Kent, it is possible to argue that there was no such thing as a 'Nonconformist Conscience', for 'the nonconformists simply shared the conscience of other people'.[8] In other words, the Nonconformists were merely pursuing a moral agenda which either corresponded with Christian teaching and therefore with the expectations of other ecclesiastical groups or that their activity reflected a rigid adherence to certain Victorian mores. Either way it would appear that the Nonconformists *qua* Nonconformists brought nothing in particular to public debate while the historical context played a significant role in the emergence of the Nonconformist Conscience. Yet, while there were Nonconformists who believed themselves to enjoy 'special circumstances' through their relationship with the Liberal Party during the last quarter of the nineteenth century, there were also those who highlighted that the Nonconformist Conscience had been forged over a longer period and in a very different socio-political context.

J. Guinness Rogers, for thirty-five years the minister of Clapham Congregational Church and considered by both Gladstone and Lord Rosebery to be a trusted spokesman for Nonconformist views on the issues of the day, suggested that it was a 'slang' term and, like John Kent after him, he asserted that the Nonconformists had no 'keener sense of what is due to right than other Christians'.[9] However, Guinness Rogers was well aware of the contribution Nonconformity was making to public life and this led him almost to affirm the uniqueness of the Nonconformist Conscience as a phenomenon even if he was dissatisfied with the name. He claimed that the Parnell case had demonstrated that the Nonconformists had 'obeyed their moral instincts and these instincts have proved right' even if some 'action may have been unwise or hasty, or Pharisaic'. He insisted that Nonconformity was 'something more than a mere objection to a particular Church. It is an assertion of the right of the individual conscience, a protest against invidious class privilege and distinction, an emphatic testimony on behalf of liberty and progress.'[10] The distinction was significant. Here was the assertion that Nonconformity stood for *something*, and thus it had a positive contribution to make to public life. Thus even if Guinness Rogers refuted the term 'Nonconformist Conscience', he recognized that it reflected something deeply rooted within Nonconformity.

Guinness Rogers was not alone in his belief that Nonconformists had a particular witness to public life. There were others who referred to the fact that Nonconformists had suffered for their deeply held beliefs over several centuries, and this enabled them to identify wrongdoing – whether immorality or injustice – in the seat of government. Others held similar views and considered Nonconformity to be the expression of the willingness to make a stand for a moral, righteous, even holy ideal. R. F. Horton, minister at Hampstead but darling of the working classes as well as the professionals who graced his congregation, wrote: 'Dissenters *as such* are more religious than they who conform just because their convictions are strong enough to compel thought and to nerve them for suffering in a cause which is despised.'[11] W. B. Selbie, also a progressive thinker and the second principal of Mansfield College, the Congregationalists' seminary in Oxford, said it was a voice 'which the forces of privilege and reaction have every reason to fear'.[12] In other words, Nonconformity possessed a public role to fulfil, its presence in society would be a constant reminder to the State that it should fulfil its proper role under the providence of God and that 'freedom of conscience', 'liberty and progress' and the highest 'moral instincts' should be established as fundamental principles for the conduct of public life. For Rogers, Horton and Selbie, Nonconformity was a matter of conviction, of commitment to an ideal which deserved not merely religious but also political and social attention. It may well be significant that such men were influenced by the prevailing theological liberalism which motivated the younger generation within evangelical Christianity to consider the social implications of the gospel alongside the matter of personal salvation and ensured that they upheld the notion that Christianity represented the highest moral ideal. It could also be significant that all three were Congregationalists and thus to some degree rooted in historical Dissent.

This sense of inheriting a historical witness was captured by Charles Silvester Horne, one of the younger stars of the Congregational pulpit, when he wrote his *Popular History of the Free Churches* (1903). In the book, he made reference to 'an unconquerable spirit dedicated to the service of an indestructible ideal' which had been its primary motivation for two centuries. This 'ideal' was the freedom of conscience which, by the nineteenth century, was expressed in terms of the voluntary principle, whose influence ought to extend beyond a person's religious life into the whole of society. Writing in the middle of the campaign against the 1902 Education Act, Horne continued: 'While men and women of the Free Churches are bracing themselves to renew the fight for unsectarian education and religious equality it may be well that they refresh their memories of those illustrious forbears who helped to make England great.'[13] The significance of this statement cannot be over-emphasized. While it says more about Horne's perception of the importance of nineteenth-century Nonconformity than his grasp of history, it also demonstrates his conviction that, because they were motivated by ideals, principles and values, the Nonconformists of the past 'helped to make England great' despite their exclusion from social and political structures. Their language owed much to the nineteenth century, and their Nonconformity was, on the surface, very different from the Dissent of the seventeenth. And yet these Nonconformists believed that they stood in direct relationship with their dissenting forebears and that their own political and social stance was motivated by the same principles which had led to the Puritan rejection of the post-Restoration church settlement, not as a matter of ecclesiastical nit-picking, but as the assertion of a God-given privilege.

In that sense, nineteenth-century Nonconformists, particularly those who represented 'Old Dissent', believed that their consciences had been forged, under the guidance of scripture and the Holy Spirit, in the seventeenth century. At that time, the battle had been fought simply for the recognition of the sacred nature of conscience in the matter of religious faith rather than any attempt to exercise moral influence over politics or society. Baptists appear to have been the first to argue for the liberty of conscience in matters of religion, as they refuted the right of the state to coerce religious belief through the offices of the magistrate. John Smyth, the Separatist church leader who came under Anabaptist influence while in exile in Amsterdam, formulated a confession which highlighted that conscience was to be free from such interference. 'The magistrate', he averred, 'is not by virtue of his office to meddle with religion, or matters of conscience'. Furthermore, the officers of the state were not 'to force or compel men to this or that form of religion, or doctrine: but to leave Christian religion free to every man's conscience . . . for Christ only is the king and Lawgiver of the Church and conscience'.[14] Innocent as such a principle might at first appear, in the seventeenth century it was novel, even revolutionary. For it suggested that there was a divine law which could be known in the conscience and could by-pass the state's political structures. In an England whose establishment had accepted and promoted the kind of erastianism explained forcefully by Samuel Parker, bishop of Oxford, with the words: 'Where a Religion is Establish'd by the Laws . . . whoever openly refuses obedience plainly Rebels against the Government, Rebellion being properly nothing else but an open denial of obedience to the Civil Power',[15] the potentially seditious nature of the liberty of conscience was all too clear. It is exemplified in Thomas Helwys, credited with establishing the first Baptist church on British soil at Spitalfields, London, in 1612, who could daringly warn 'the earthly power' that it had no right 'to punish . . . in the least measure' anyone, whether they 'be hereticks, Turcks, Jewes, or what soever'.[16] But, as a consequence, Helwys would suffer imprisonment in Newgate, where he died by 1616.

Over the following half-century or so, throughout the Civil Wars, the Commonwealth and Restoration periods, this witness to the freedom of the religious conscience became increasingly significant. The Independents gradually moved towards this position as the dominance of Presbyterians at the Westminster Assembly ensured that they began to recognize that they, too, could suffer exclusion. Thus, whereas the Westminster Conference upheld the role of the civil authority in punishing heretics and eradicating 'false religion', the *Savoy Declaration*, penned by prominent Independents a decade or so later, at least recognized the 'right to be vouchsafed a tolerance and mutual indulgence unto saints of all perswasions' so long as their doctrine was orthodox and they upheld holy living. Thus *Savoy* did not embrace full toleration, but in the work of John Owen, the doyen of Independent divines, can be discerned the dawning realization that, theologically, this was the only logical conclusion based on a proper division of responsibilities between the church and the state. For Owen: 'The sole question is, whether God has authorized and doth warrant any man . . . to compel others to worship and serve him contrary to his way and manner that they are in their conscience persuaded that he doth accept and approve . . .'[17] Thus Owen came to speak out against persecution of those considered to be heretics as 'pernicious, fatal and dreadful to the profession and professors of the gospel'.[18] Perhaps most daringly, he declared in a sermon before parliament, on 19 April 1649: 'The time shall come when the *earth* shall disclose her slain, and not the simplest *heretic* . . . shall have his blood unrevenged: neither shall any atonement be made for this blood, or expiation be allowed.'[19]

These seventeenth-century debates were concerned with defining a proper boundary between the state and its responsibilities and the church, rather than establish the principle that the church should police the state. And yet they ensured that subsequent generations of Nonconformists held dearly to the principle that the state's responsibilities did not extend to forcing uniformity in religious belief and practice. The law of God existed above the state, which meant that the state and its officers could be held to account by that higher law. While Charles I was tried for treason, the very fact that the king could be tried was a direct result of this sense that even he was subject to God's laws. Over subsequent years, during which Dissenters suffered persecution ameliorated only by periods of 'regal indulgence' and restricted toleration after 1689, they also forged a more determined approach to public life, where they sought the repeal of the Test and Corporation Acts and the amelioration of other disabilities through the offices of the Committee of the Three Denominations and the Dissenting Deputies and where they also recognized that the state's role was to treat all citizens equally regardless of religious persuasion.

Thus a conscience which had been claimed as sacred as far as matters of faith were concerned was inevitably politicized by drawing attention to social and political injustice based on religious difference and working towards its mitigation. Consequently, at least in part, the 'Nonconformist Conscience' of the late nineteenth century, as a public witness to the highest principles, can be traced back to events of the seventeenth.

II. The Conscience of 'Old Dissent' Renewed

By 1880, all the particular Nonconformist grievances against oppressive and repressive legislation had been resolved. The repeal of the Test and Corporation Acts in 1828 paved the way for Nonconformists formally to contribute in the political arena. Alongside this, parliamentary reform was gradually including more of the population in the political system. Although the 1832 Reform Act still restricted the franchise to around 8 per cent of the population,[20] it began a movement which led finally to the establishment of universal suffrage after the First World War. The last inequality to be considered by parliament concerned the ability of Nonconformist ministers to conduct services in the parish graveyard according to their own rites, and this was granted through the Burials Act of 1880.[21]

Over the century and a half since the 'Toleration Act', Nonconformists had not merely campaigned for better conditions; they were concerned with the very foundations and fabric of society itself. By the mid-nineteenth century Nonconformists had come to believe that the oppressions they formerly suffered[22] were symptoms; the root cause was that the Church of England enjoyed social and economic privileges because of its association with the state, privileges denied to other denominations and to those who professed non-Christian religion. Various campaigns were instituted as an outworking of a fundamental principle; they were the result of a conviction that legislation should ensure that all citizens enjoy similar legal rights rather than give certain privileges to some and not to others because the state, and thus true citizenship, happened to be associated with an established church. As a result, the Nonconformists initiated the campaign for disestablishment, in effect giving religion over to the voluntary principle and creating a free market in matters spiritual. More theologically, it recognized the principle that neither ecclesiastical hierarchy, priest, monarch or government should come between the soul and its God.

The principle that the Anglican Church should not be established in parts of the United Kingdom where Anglican communicants formed a minority of religious observers appeared to have been conceded when the Irish Church Act was passed in 1869. Reasons other than this principle led to Gladstone's zealous support for the measure, and he was equally enthusiastic in opposing the Bill to Disestablish the Anglican Church in Wales which came before parliament in 1870 and gained the support of only forty-five MPs. Disestablishment in Wales continued to be debated, largely on the democratic principle that the vast majority of Welsh Christians were Nonconformists, until finally becoming law in 1914 (its implementation being delayed until 1920 because of the First World War).

At least some English Nonconformists were initially keen to pursue the cause and the first Bill for disestablishment came before parliament on 9 May 1871, introduced by the Congregational minister, journalist and MP Edward Miall. Miall was a fervent campaigner for disestablishment and founded the British Anti-State Church Association in 1844 in order to pursue the cause. In 1853 the Association changed its name to the Society for the Liberation of Religion from State Patronage and Control, though it was more commonly known as the Liberation Society. Its aim was to ensure the selection of parliamentary candidates who supported the cause of disestablishment. Following the success of Irish disestablishment it appeared that there was some momentum in favour of the notion of disestablishment in England, but the bill, in 1871, was defeated by 374 votes to 89.[23]

There were some voices which made a stand against the establishment on religious principles alone. The Baptist Union had made the point as early as 1839 that an established church was 'a palpable departure from the laws of Christ' and 'the most formidable obstacle in the land to the diffusion of true piety'.[24] A further voice raised in support of this standpoint was that of John Clifford. For him, disestablishment was not a cause to be pursued because of social injustice but because it was a fundamental misunderstanding of Christianity itself. 'We must aim not so much to right ourselves', he said, 'as to right Christianity'.[25] Here can be seen the Nonconformist Conscience at its best. Clifford did not seek redress for specific Nonconformist grievances; he did not seek the promotion of Nonconformity to the status he believed it deserved. Rather he saw the claims of the gospel as having the first call on the Christian's allegiance which included calling for the removal of obstacles placed in its path by the state.

However, the argument for disestablishment revolved around a variety of factors, and rarely did it depend fully on the theological principle that state and church should be separate. Instead, Nonconformists drew attention to the fact that, since the Oxford Movement appeared to be drawing the Church of England towards Catholic ritualism, its continued support by parliament and legislation, not to mention the economic privileges which came as a result, was simply wrong. Here spokesmen such as Miall discovered the factor on which they could build a crusade, inspired by a sense of righteous indignation: this was conversion to Rome through the back door, aided and abetted by the establishment. Such a situation could not be permitted to continue, while it made a mockery of the fact that the law existed to assist all citizens rather than to uphold the privilege of one group over and above another.[26] While the argument was governed by moral principle, it was not necessarily driven by theological or religious concern. Indeed, there was a tendency to recognize that in order to make progress, the argument had to have wider resonance and adapt to what could be seen as secular principles primarily revolving around whether or not a majority of religious believers practised their faith according to the rites and liturgy of the Established Church. The Liberation Society tended to move in this direction, resulting in the withdrawal of support from such prominent ministers as R. W. Dale, Joseph Parker and C. H. Spurgeon.[27]

It was the matter of undue religious privilege which came to the fore in debates about state provision of education, especially of religious instruction which, Nonconformists believed, was the task of the churches and not of the government. They raised their voices in protest at each new Education Act that continued to offer public money to support Church Schools. The Forster Education Act of 1870, for example, did not bring the financial support of Church Schools to an end, it established school boards to which Nonconformists could be elected. This, alongside a 'conscience clause' in the Act, which enabled Nonconformists to withdraw their children from lessons in which the catechism was taught, left Nonconformists reasonably, if not fully, content. However, the Balfour Education Act of 1902 abolished the school boards, which had been popular with the Nonconformists and had placated them over the greater issue of state sponsorship of sectarian schooling, and handed over their duties to local borough or county councils. They in turn established Local Education Authorities to maintain the schools in their areas and the Nonconformists once again began to find themselves excluded in favour of those who represented the Established Church. Alongside this, the Act continued to offer provision to supply financial support to (primarily Anglican but, even more controversially, also to Catholic) Church Schools and ultimately sought to impose a state-centred system of primary, secondary and technical schools.

The forces of Nonconformity rallied to the cause with 'passive resistance', and rate refusal began in spring 1903. By 1906 over 170 men had been imprisoned for non-payment. But despite the sense of injustice, the moral and religious principle which was at stake, the rallying of the Free Churches behind the cause, the commitment to suffer in the pursuit of a righteous ideal and the symbolic martyrdom suffered by those whose goods were confiscated or those who were imprisoned, the campaign was almost totally unsuccessful. The truth was that when it came to the crunch, the Nonconformists in fact possessed very little political influence. As David Bebbington notes, the leaders of the Liberal Party knew that the Nonconformists had nowhere else to turn and thus they were among 'their most loyal supporters'. Once in power, the Liberals could simply ignore many of their claims because they no longer needed their direct support: 'That is why it was possible for the greatest Nonconformist campaign of the period, the uprising against the 1902 Education Act, with all its rhetoric, central organisation and local enthusiasm, to achieve virtually nothing.'[28]

Despite the lack of achievement, the campaigns for disestablishment and non-sectarian education were based on principles which were firmly rooted in Dissent. The state should not interfere in matters of conscience nor should it coerce people into a particular religious confession. As such, these expressions of the 'Nonconformist Conscience' reflected the same principles that could be discerned at the Great Ejectment in 1662 and, in a sense, could be seen as forming the bed-rock of religious Dissent and Nonconformity. As such, the 'Nonconformist Conscience' was a peculiarly *Nonconformist* phenomenon; it was possessed of something essential which was not part of the witness of other Christian denominations. However, the peculiar context of the nineteenth century also gave rise to other expressions of the 'Nonconformist Conscience' which, at the very least, demonstrated that these principles had been widened to incorporate other socio-political standpoints and, more expansively, that this principle had been transformed by the clear emphasis placed on morality and purity during the Victorian age.

III. Social Developments

Nonconformist presence in the public sphere certainly became more potent as a result of the Evangelical Revival, and this had an effect on their 'conscience'. According to Lovell Cocks: 'The monolith of Victorian ethics had been reared by the Evangelical revival; for the despised preacher and practitioners of personal holiness had succeeded in transforming private convictions into public conventions.'[29] This is where the particular context in which Nonconformists found themselves in the nineteenth century did have an effect. Indeed, as Timothy Larsen has shown: 'A reforming ethos was nurtured by a rising belief in their own importance and power: they saw themselves as a force in the land that had the potential to provoke change.'[30] They felt that they held the upper hand for, when considered collectively, it could be argued that there were more members of Nonconformist chapels than regular Anglican worshippers.[31] They could thus appeal to the democratic principle which was gaining ground in political circles that they ought to be listened to because they represented the majority voice. Perhaps more realistically, they gained a degree of influence because of the presence of industrialists and entrepreneurs in their midst. Men such as John Rylands, W. H. Lever, Sir Henry Tate, Titus Salt, Samuel Courtauld, John Crossley, Samuel Morley, W. D. and H. O. Wills and many others contributed to the nation's economic well-being as well as to a number of philanthropic causes. Justice, as well as naked economics, demanded that they have political and social influence, and many of them sat for a time in parliament.

Within such a context, and with so many of its prominent members taking an active interest in political, social and economic matters, the greater politicization of Nonconformity was unavoidable and it was natural that any political engagement would revolve around matters of religious principle. Given their evangelical zeal, it was inevitable that their political pronouncements would be characterized by a crusading temper. John Kent has argued that what was 'particularly nonconformist' in the 'Late Victorian Conscience' was Evangelical Pietism (particularly a sense of social purity), Cobdenite Radicalism (which sought to prevent intervention in international affairs and resulted in an isolationist tendency) and Social Imperialism (which paradoxically saw the expansion of the Empire as beneficial for the whole world). This resulted in a 'clash of ideas' for the first two would suggest a degree of retreat, whether from 'everything that was non-Christian' or 'the non-English', while the third 'wanted to expand, to dominate other countries'.[32] Nevertheless, it remains true that this combination of moralism, numerical strength, crusading zeal and the absolute conviction of the difference between right and wrong, all of which were expressed alongside general support for the Empire and for *laissez faire* economics, was characteristic of Nonconformist public witness by the late nineteenth century.

As such, the Nonconformist Conscience can be seen to have responded to the context in which it found itself. In Old Dissent it had been moulded by convictions about religious freedom as a God-given right. In a revivified Nonconformity, rapidly transforming itself into Free Churchmanship, it was primarily seen as a campaign to ensure ethical political policies pursued by morally upright public figures. But underlying both was the same basic dictum that, on the basis of divinely revealed principles, society should be moulded ever more closely to the kingdom of God.

During the nineteenth century, born from their own experience of suffering, the sense of righting wrongs became more pronounced and Nonconformist comment on public policy tended to adopt a moralizing tone. Indeed, the Nonconformists' conscience came to prominence in the debate on public matters when great principles or the highest morality seemed to be at stake. The Anti-Slavery campaign of the 1830s was just such an instance because it was grounded in the argument that slavery was 'criminal before God'. As such, Christians simply could not tolerate it.[33] This was essentially a political campaign fought under the conviction that current policy was contrary to God's will. Neither public opinion nor the likelihood of success were paramount. It could simply be asserted that slavery was *wrong*. The difference in the late Victorian era was that Nonconformists possessed both the numerical strength and the kind of charismatic leadership to suggest that they might exert a greater influence on public policy than at any time since the Commonwealth.[34] And they did so by taking the role of the nation's moral guardian.

Given the interest in personal holiness held by many in their ranks, the Wesleyans seemed to hold this ideal of moralizing public affairs most dear. Unlike the Dissenters, the Wesleyans had previously eschewed political activity and Conference itself led the way in viewing political issues as a 'distraction from the work of the gospel'.[35] Gradually their opinion changed. In 1891, the Wesleyan Methodist Conference resolved that 'the responsible representatives of the nation ought to be men of unstained character'. The following year, Conference asked for legislation to exclude from 'our Houses of Legislature' any man 'judicially convicted of flagrant immorality'.[36] Hugh Price Hughes publicly championed the stance. In June 1888, he argued in provocative terms that gamblers should be expelled from the House of Commons: 'Nothing would do more to impress the public conscience than to make gambling a moral disqualification for a seat in Parliament. Rational Christians can already see that debauchees, drunkards, and gamblers are utterly unfit to make the laws of England. We must agitate for the rigid exclusion of such enemies of mankind.'[37]

Hughes was relentless in pursuing this ideal. His motive was theological, but his theology was fundamentally moralistic. Thus, he declared in 1894, all 'impure' men had to be expelled from parliament. Immoral men, he believed, could not embody righteousness in law. As a result, he insisted, it was 'men of pure character, high intelligence [and] true humanity [who should] make and administer our laws'.[38] For him, laws themselves could help to promote social purity by upholding an ideal of what could be considered to be the moral life.[39] Indeed, 'the real character of every nation', he declared, 'is determined by the character of its laws'.[40]

This belief in being right, exercised from a base which appeared to be growing in numerical strength and in civic confidence, developed into the conviction that Nonconformists needed to enter into a dynamic partnership with politics. For example, George White told the Baptist Union in 1903: 'If we make politics a part of our religion, as I claim we should, then in the conduct of our national policy, moral principles must be supreme.'[41] As Silvester Horne put it: 'We believe politics may be as truly sacred a task as theology; and that how best to safeguard youth against cruelty, manhood against temptation, and a human life against poverty and disease is as Christian a study as to expound the doctrine of election, the ecclesiastical use of incense, or the legitimacy of the chasuble.'[42] According to W. B. Selbie, his biographer, it was Horne's 'conviction that it was necessary to bring religion into politics and reconstruct both municipal and national affairs on a Christian basis'.[43] Such a conviction led Horne into pursuing a political career and he entered parliament as member for Ipswich in 1910 while retaining his pastorate at Whitefield's Tabernacle in London and while also engaged in frenetic public activity. Motivated by religious conviction, he attempted to bring the light of the gospel to bear on all his activity. But the effort took its toll and he died, aged only forty-nine, having resolved to give up his pastorate as well as his parliamentary seat in order to work for international peace. Here, too, he had found a cause which called for conviction, commitment and zeal. In all this, he appeared to embody the Nonconformist Conscience; it was convinced, committed, tireless (even relentless), moralistic and political, but it seemed almost to blow itself out and its real achievements were few and far between while, in effect, those committed to the ideal, such as Horne and Hughes, were burnt out in its pursuit.

Nevertheless, over the course of the nineteenth century, the Nonconformists came to believe that political activity itself, when properly informed and policed, could help in the task of establishing God's kingdom on earth.[44] While it could be argued that 'freedom of conscience' could be seen lying behind much of their activity, in fact their motivation was often the defence of morality which enabled them to nurture a sense of outrage. Nowhere is this seen more clearly than in the campaign to repeal the Acts for the Spread of Contagious Diseases.

Successive legislation in 1864, 1866 and 1867 sought to enforce a system of regulation of prostitution in places around army camps and naval ports whereby women could be registered as prostitutes, subjected to regular medical examination and detained if found to be suffering from sexually transmitted diseases. The campaign to repeal the acts was led by Josephine Butler who described the medical examination as 'surgical rape'. Hugh Price Hughes was present at one of her meetings, was moved to tears by her account and was won over to the cause.

Some reference was made to the 'scandalous injustice' of the Acts. Hugh Price Hughes identified the exploitation of 'thousands and tens of thousands of weak and deluded women' who 'should no longer be sacrificed to the lusts of brutal men' and condemned the 'scandalous injustice' which 'metes out forgiveness to the more culpable man and infamy to the partner of his sin'.[45] Nevertheless, the vast majority of Nonconformist support for the repeal of the Acts came as a result of the conviction that the state, in legislating in this way, appeared to be condoning fornication.[46] Unlike disestablishment and education, this was more clearly a matter of public morality, specifically the appearance that the state had legalized prostitution (rather than the immoral and unjust treatment of the women).

The campaign to repeal the Acts was conducted along the lines of a moral, if not religious, crusade and the language used by Nonconformists in pursuit of their goal predated but also resonated with that used during the Parnell case. William Morley Punshon, president of the Wesleyan Methodist Conference in 1874, claimed that the campaign raised the issue of 'whether expediency or right is to govern a Christian people',[47] while the Wesleyan solicitor Henry Fowler insisted in 1876 that the Acts infringed the principle that 'whatever is morally wrong can never be politically right',[48] a slogan which was reiterated over the next thirty years or so in association with the Nonconformist Conscience. The Wesleyan Society for Securing the Repeal of the Contagious Diseases Acts was formed in 1874, thus becoming 'the first organisation in Methodist history to prompt overt political action by Wesleyan ministers against existing legislation'.[49] Nevertheless, it took until 1883 for the Acts to be suspended and 1886 for them to be fully repealed.

Similar motivation, as well as tactics, can also be discerned in the campaign to improve the living conditions of the urban poor unleashed by the publication in 1883 of *The Bitter Cry of Outcast London.* Though published anonymously, the report had been written by Andrew Mearns, secretary of the London Congregational Union. A close look at the furore which erupted after its publication demonstrates that it was not the ideal of good housing per se which was upheld, for it was not the living conditions themselves which had provoked Nonconformist ire. Instead, the Nonconformists had been incensed by the report's revelation of housing problems as the cause of incest. 'Mearns could point to a street of 35 houses where 32 were brothels. In another district, 43 brothels housed 428 prostitutes, some of them no more than 12 years old. Most horrifying of all, he explained that among families occupying single rooms incest was common.'[50]

Nonconformists were motivated to act by the spectre of immorality. Hugh Price Hughes declared in 1889: '[T]he state must . . . secure for the poorest . . . the right to live as something better than the uncleanest of brute beasts.'[51] According to Christopher Oldstone Moore: 'What stirred Hughes "to the depths of his being" when he read Mearns's pamphlet was the perception that poverty and overcrowding were direct causes of immorality and a barrier to salvation.'[52] It is noteworthy that here, too, it was the recognition of a *moral evil* which enabled the crusading mindset of contemporary Nonconformist leaders to support the issue. Both preventing the spread of contagious diseases and poor housing were seen as symptoms of an underlying malaise where society seemed oblivious to the way in which social conditions promoted immorality and while Nonconformist efforts were rallied against the specific issues at hand, their crusading zeal was seen more clearly in their efforts to organize themselves in favour of social purity. The National Vigilance Association was launched in 1885 and promoted the establishment of local associations dedicated to the protection of women and girls by seeking the proper enforcement of the Criminal Law Amendment Act (1885). The leading force in the movement was Percy Bunting, a lawyer and member of Hughes' West London Mission, and the work revolved around seeking to raise the age of consent to sixteen and forcing the of closure of brothels. As such the Nonconformist Conscience became a force which sought to hold government to its professed convictions and to ensure that adherence to the highest ideals, as encapsulated in its legislation, were achieved in practice.[53]

International affairs also came under scrutiny from time-to-time, especially the 'eastern question' which revolved around the expansionist aspirations of the Ottoman Empire. The brutal suppression of the Bulgarian rising in 1876, the massacre as Sassoon in 1894 and a number of events in between all served to fuel Nonconformist protests. Nonetheless, the Nonconformists' outspoken criticism, characterized by a sense of shame at the British government's attempt to uphold Turkish authority as well as a popular aversion to Islam (a revulsion which was exacerbated following reports of sexual assaults perpetrated by Turkish soldiers) changed over the years. Whereas they initially favoured non-intervention, from the mid-1890s Nonconformist leaders began to uphold the idea that Britain's moral duty was to fight for what was right. The *Christian World* in September 1895 declared that Britain must be prepared to go to war to defend the Armenians,[54] while Alexander Maclaren, for forty-five years minister of Union Baptist Chapel in Manchester, appeared to support war at a rally in Manchester when he suggested that this was the only course of action which would ensure that the right thing was done.[55] Initially, John Clifford (who would later make a stand for peace) maintained that 'this wholesale butchery and robbery, this ravishing of maidens that was going on against the Armenians was worse than war'.[56] Hugh Price Hughes, who maintained a more consistent approach to the issue, demanded British intervention which, in practice, meant going to war against what he called Turkish 'devilry'.[57] Thus, '[i]nstead of believing that it was best to approximate a policy of non-intervention they were beginning to endorse the use of force in righteous causes'.[58]

These examples of the Nonconformist Conscience as it came to light in the nineteenth century were the result of a Nonconformity 'come of age'. They reflected a social and political confidence born from a sense of numerical strength and moral superiority: their support was voluntary rather than legally enforced. When driven by a sense of morality rather than purely by principle, these campaigns were, on the whole, more successful than those for disestablishment and education, probably because they appealed to the wider public's imagination. Nevertheless, not all were satisfied, and the Nonconformist Conscience was subjected to widespread criticism at the time.

IV. Critique

The Nonconformist Conscience came to prominence at the very time that the socialist and labour movements began to grow in strength and influence. Yet the Nonconformist Conscience itself had very little interest in industrial questions.[59] This is most clearly highlighted by the events of 1911, the year of the National Railwaymen's Strike. Nonconformists were silent over the justice or otherwise of the Railwaymen's cause, with the Free Church Council called on its members to pray for peace between the two sides as well as to offer assistance to women and children who might have suffered most from the affects of the strike. Nevertheless, during the same year the Baptist F. B. Meyer successfully campaigned against the World Heavyweight Boxing Championship which was to be held at Earls Court because racial tensions, he claimed, would be exacerbated given that Jack Johnson, the defending champion and likely winner, was black while 'Bombardier Billy' Wells, the challenger, was white.[60] Clearly, there was a moral principle at stake in the Railwaymen's dispute, and there might well have been one at stake in the proposed boxing match, but appeals to a higher morality were rarely made when the major questions of the day revolved around a fair wage and decent working and living conditions.

It is hardly surprising, then, that the Nonconformist Conscience had its critics. J. A. Newbold, a Wesleyan teacher from Manchester, accused the Free Church Councils of being 'overbearing, partisan and hypocritical' in a publication entitled *The Nonconformist Conscience a Persecuting Force.*[61] A rather scurrilous booklet was published in 1903 castigating the Nonconformist Conscience, written under the pseudonym 'by one who has had it'. The book contained the accusation that the Nonconformist Conscience was characterized by hypocrisy and attempts at personal gain and public recognition. The truth is that the Nonconformists had opened themselves to such criticism by giving the impression that the primary concerns of the working class were subordinate to the call to adopt a higher morality. All too often, or so it seemed, their protests appeared to coalesce with the policies of the Liberal Party.[62] Thus an anonymous pamphlet, published in 1909, criticized the Nonconformist Conscience for precisely this reason: '[M]odern Nonconformity, in making corporate political action bulk so large in its programmes, is forsaking its first ideals, substituting a smaller thing for a greater.'[63]

Given the crusading nature of the late-Victorian Nonconformist Conscience, perhaps it is understandable that the Nonconformists were often portrayed as those who sought, by means of legislation, to impose their religious and moral views – especially temperance and sabbatarianism – on others.[64] In reality, this is far from the *whole* truth. Nonconformists were not merely, if at all, seeking their own elevation. Many of them truly believed in the cause of religious equality and, by the late nineteenth century, they were willing to concede this even to those with whom they profoundly disagreed.[65] In this way, at its best, the Nonconformist Conscience combined its moralizing with the principles it had inherited from Puritan Dissent, something articulated during the height of the education controversy by John Clifford, when he said:

> I am resolutely opposed to any man, a Mahometan or a Methodist, a Ritualist or a Romanist, a Quaker or a Baptist, being made to suffer in the slightest degree for his religious opinion. In my fixed conviction those opinions are entirely outside the functions of the State. Parliament has nothing whatever to do with them. I am strongly opposed to the establishment by Parliament of what is called 'undenominational teaching', as I am to Romanism; i.e., I protest with all my might against teaching at the expense of ratepayers a set of dogmatic theological opinions on which Christians generally are supposed to be agreed, as I protest against the teaching of any distinctively Roman or Anglican doctrine. I wish theological dogma to be taught, but taught by the Churches, and entirely at the expense of

> the Churches; and not by the officers of Parliament; and at the expense of the ratepayers. I have fought for Roman Catholics in municipal and Parliamentary contests. I shall again. What I oppose is anybody's effort to *compel* me to pay for the propagation of Romanist or any other Christian doctrines, or to use the Parliament of the people for that purpose.[66]

For Clifford, from the very beginning of his long ministry, 'the business of a Christian church is to find out the real needs of the people in the neighbourhood in which it is placed and, as far as it can, supply all that will make for brightness and joy, for strength and service, for manhood and brotherhood'.[67] In other words, the Christian life 'is more than working for one's personal good. Rather is it working with God for the regeneration of the world'.[68] This, at its best, was the aim and intention of the Nonconformist Conscience.[69]

V. Conclusion

For a short period during the late nineteenth and early twentieth centuries, Nonconformists were able to exercise a degree of influence over political policy largely through the offices of their political allies, the Liberal Party. This influence was characterized by agitation and the moulding of public opinion based on moralism pursued with a crusading zeal. There was a paradox pertaining to it in that while the numbers of Nonconformist members of parliament increased after 1870, the Nonconformist leaders found their greatest support in W. E. Gladstone, the High Churchman who seemed at ease with their moralizing and recognized their usefulness when it came to ensuring that his policies gained the support required to see them enshrined in law. There was a paradox too in the fact that this political influence, characterized at the time as the Nonconformist Conscience because of its concentration on moralism, tended to focus on the negative reaction against the prevailing issues of the day rather than on a positive contribution to the shaping of social life and the body politic. At the same time that chapel folk began to embrace the title 'Free Church' in an effort to propagate a more positive image, they were also fully engaged in political activity, but the image conveyed was that of moral police castigating those whose standards did not match their own and demanding that their grievances be addressed. And there was, finally, an irony in the fact that, when it really mattered, their influence counted for very little and their claims and demands were ignored, even by their Liberal allies, when it was clear that their opposition would not hinder the progress of a particular policy through parliament. Ultimately, the Nonconformist Conscience led to accusations – perhaps fairly levelled against it – that Nonconformists had become over-politicized, that this had led to a secularization of the chapels and contributed to numerical decline both in membership and attendance, certainly from 1907.

Having said this, it is also true that the period of the Nonconformist Conscience was in itself one when the Nonconformists learnt how best to approach the social and political problems of the day. There was something about it which had been inherited from their dissenting forebears, even if this was clothed in the mores and rhetoric of late-Victorian society. At that point, they had the numerical strength and confidence to enter into a crusade to see the highest moral values established in public life. But this approach was unable to deal with the complexities of public concerns as they emerged towards the end of the nineteenth century. In the early twentieth century, the growth of the ecumenical movement, as well as a general weariness with the issue, caused the campaign for disestablishment to be quietly set aside and Nonconformists in general recognized the need for the specialist study of the social problem characterized by considered and expert comment rather than an ethical verdict and moral campaigning. Nonconformists played their part in this through the Welsh School of Social Service, established in 1911, through denominational social committees and through both the Conference on Christian Politics, Economics and Citizenship held in Birmingham in 1924 and the Life and Work movement inaugurated at Stockholm in 1925. To their credit, the Nonconformists adapted when they realized that social problems required specialist study and even compromise in order to achieve improvement. As a result, they entered the new century with a commitment and a zeal that demonstrated that the Nonconformist Conscience, though in one sense at an end, had left a legacy that would remain with them certainly until, and to some extent beyond, the Second World War.

Notes

In this chapter, I have drawn extensively on D. W. Bebbington, *The Nonconformist Conscience: Chapel and Politics, 1870–1914* (London: G. Allen & Unwin, 1981) and James Munson, *The Nonconformists: In Search of a Lost Culture* (London: SPCK, 1991), pp. 204–43.

1 *The Times* (17 November 1890); Munson, *The Nonconformists*, p. 205.
2 *The Star* (18 November 1890); Munson, *The Nonconformists*, p. 205.
3 *The Methodist Times* (20 November 1890); Munson, *The Nonconformists*, pp. 206–7.
4 *The Times* (28 November 1890); Munson, *The Nonconformists*, pp. 206–7;
5 See *The Methodist Times* (27 November 1890), p. 1211; cf. H. F. Lovell Cocks, *The Nonconformist Conscience* (London: Independent Press, 1943), p. 7; Christopher Oldstone-Moore, *Hugh Price Hughes: Founder of a New Methodism, Conscience of a New Nonconformity* (Cardiff: University of Wales Press, 1999), p. 214; Munson, *The Nonconformists*, p. 213.
6 Oldstone-Moore, *Hugh Price Hughes*, p. 213.

7 See J. F. Glaser, 'Parnell's Fall and the Nonconformist Conscience', *Irish Historical Studies* 12 (1960).
8 John Kent, 'Hugh Price Hughes and the Nonconformist Conscience', in G. V. Bennett and J. D. Walsh (eds), *Essays in Modern English Church History* (Oxford and New York: Oxford University Press, 1966), p. 181.
9 J. G. Rogers, 'Nonconformists in Political Life', in *Contemporary Review*, LXI (1892), pp. 502–3; see also Munson, *The Nonconformists*, p. 207.
10 Rogers, 'Nonconformists in Political Life', pp. 506, 498; Munson, *The Nonconformists*, p. 220.
11 R. F. Horton, *The Dissolution of Dissent* (London, 1902), p. 16; Munson, *The Nonconformists*, p. 208.
12 Munson, *The Nonconformists*, p. 243.
13 C. Silvester Horne, *A Popular History of the Free Churches* (London: James Clarke & Co., 1903), p. vii.
14 W. L. Lumpkin, *Baptist Confessions of Faith* (rev. ed. Valley Forge, PA: Judson Press, 1969), p. 140.
15 Samuel Parker, *A Discourse of Ecclesiastical Politie* (London: John Martyn, 1670 [1659), p. lvi. I am grateful to Professor Alan Sell for this reference.
16 Thomas Helwys, *The Mistery of Iniquity* (1612), p. 69.
17 John Owen, *The Works of John Owen*, ed. Thomas Russell (London: Richard Baynes, 1826), XIII, p. 530.
18 Ibid., VIII, p. 163.
19 Ibid., XV, pp. 360–61.
20 Bob Whitefield, *The Extension of the Franchise, 1832–1932* (Oxford: Henemann Educational Publishers, 2001), p. 72.
21 See Bebbington, *The Nonconformist Conscience*, p. 30.
22 These were listed by the Dissenting Deputies, in 1833, as the enforced use of the marriage service of the Established Church; the lack of legal registration of births and deaths outside the Established Church; compulsory Church Rates; the possibility of poor rates being charged to Dissenting places of worship; the inability of Dissenters to bury their own in churchyards without their own ministers officiating; religious tests in the universities. See Bernard Lord Manning, *The Protestant Dissenting Deputies* (Cambridge: Cambridge University Press, 1952), p. 274; Albert Peel, *These Hundred Years* (London: Congregational Union, 1931), p. 104; Timothy Larsen, *Friends of Religious Equality: Nonconformist Politics in Mid-Victorian England* (Milton Keynes: Paternoster, 1999), p. 43.
23 Bebbington, *The Nonconformist Conscience*, p. 18.
24 Quoted in ibid., p. 26.
25 Charles T. Bateman, *John Clifford: Free Church Leader and Preacher* (London: National Council of the Evangelical Free Churches, 1904), pp. 199–200.
26 Arthur Miall, *Life of Edward Miall, formerly Member of Parliament for Rochdale and Bradford, etc.* (London: Macmillan and Co., 1884), p. 281; Bebbington, *The Nonconformist Conscience*, p. 26.
27 Bebbington, *The Nonconformist Conscience*, p. 28.
28 Ibid., p. 154.
29 Lovell Cocks, *The Nonconformist Conscience*, p. 9.
30 Timothy Larsen, *Contested Christianity: The Political and Social Contexts of Victorian Theology* (Waco TX: Baylor University Press, 2004), p. 146.
31 As Bebbington notes, chapel membership required a fair degree of commitment. See Bebbington, *The Nonconformist Conscience*, p. 2.

32 John Kent, 'Hugh Price Hughes and the Nonconformist Conscience', pp. 184–85.
33 Bebbington, *The Nonconformist Conscience*, p. 14.
34 So claimed Guinness Rogers in 1884: 'Nonconformity has not been so powerful a force in the nation since the days of Long Parliament', quoted in Bebbington, *The Nonconformist Conscience*, p. 1.
35 The point is made by Bebbington, in ibid., p. 8.
36 Wesleyan Methodist Minutes of Conference (1891), p. 333; (1892), p. 306; Munson, *The Nonconformists*, p. 217.
37 Hugh Price Hughes, *Social Christianity: Sermons* (London: Hodder and Stoughton, 1889), p. 266; cf. John Kent, 'Hugh Price Hughes and the Nonconformist Conscience', pp. 186–87.
38 Munson, *The Nonconformists*, p. 218. See also Wesleyan Methodist Minutes of Conference (1898), p. 429.
39 Hugh Price Hughes, *Social Christianity: Sermons*, pp. 139–45; Bebbington, *The Nonconformist Conscience*, p. 13.
40 Hugh Price Hughes, *Social Christianity*, p. 139; Oldstone-Moore, *Hugh Price Hughes*, p. 175.
41 'The Nonconformist Conscience in Its Relationship to Our National Life', *Baptist Hand Book* (1904), p. 113; quoted in Bebbington, *The Nonconformist Conscience*, p. 3.
42 C. Silvester Horne, *Pulpit, Platform and Parliament* (London: Hodder and Stoughton, 1913), pp. 193–96; Bebbington, *The Nonconformist Conscience*, p. 12.
43 W. B. Selbie (ed.), *The Life of Charles Silvester Horne* (London: Hodder and Stoughton, 1920), p. 175.
44 D. W. Bebbington, 'The Evangelical Conscience', in *The Welsh Journal of Religious History*, 3 (2007), p. 38.
45 *Methodist Protest* (16 November 1877), p. 99; Bebbington, *The Nonconformist Conscience*, p. 41; Oldstone-More, *Hugh Price Hughes*, p. 35.
46 See Bebbington, *The Nonconformist Conscience*, p. 39.
47 *Methodist Protest* (15 May 1874), p. 48.
48 Ibid. (15 February 1876), p. 96; Bebbington, *The Nonconformist Conscience*, p. 40.
49 Bebbington, *The Nonconformist Conscience*, p. 39.
50 Ibid., p. 42; *The Bitter Cry of Outcast London*, ed. A. S. Wohl (Leicester: Frank Cass and Co., 1970), p. 61.
51 Bebbington, *The Nonconformist Conscience*, p. 43.
52 Oldstone-Moore, *Hugh Price Hughes*, p. 111.
53 Bebbington, *The Nonconformist Conscience*, p. 44.
54 *Christian World*, (19 September 1895), p. 708.
55 Ibid. (23 May 1895), p. 397; Bebbington, *The Nonconformist Conscience*, p. 117.
56 *Christian World* (19 December 1895), p. 961; Bebbington, *The Nonconformist Conscience*, p. 117.
57 *Christian World* (8 October 1896), p. 760; Bebbington, *The Nonconformist Conscience*, p. 118.
58 Bebbington, *The Nonconformist Conscience*, p. 118.
59 Ibid., p. 55.
60 Bebbington, *The Nonconformist Conscience*, p. 82.
61 J. A. Newbold, *The Nonconformist Conscience: A Persecuting Force* (Manchester: John Heywood, 1908), pp. 191, 193; Bebbington, *The Nonconformist Conscience*, p. 79.
62 *The Times* (29 December 1890), p. 4; Bebbington, *The Nonconformist Conscience*, p. 100.
63 'A Nonconformist Minister', *Nonconformity and Politics* (London: Sir Isaac Pitman and Sons, 1909); Stephen Koss, *Nonconformity in Modern British Politics* (London:

Batsford, 1975), p. 102; see also David M. Thompson (ed.), *Nonconformity in the Nineteenth Century* (London: Routledge and Kegan Paul, 1972), pp. 269–70.
64 Larsen, *Friends of Religious Equality*, p. 171.
65 Larsen, *Contested Christianity*, p. 152.
66 Bateman, *John Clifford*, pp. 283–84.
67 Ibid., p. 115.
68 Ibid., p. 180.
69 Larsen, *Friends of Religious Equality*, p. 269.

21 Nonconformity and the Labour Movement

Peter Catterall

In 1921 the Wesleyan and future Labour MP C. G. Ammon told a Brotherhood meeting: 'A working man founded the Church.'[1] The speeches of many of the founders of the modern British labour movement in the nineteenth and early twentieth centuries indeed regularly assured their audiences of the concern of the Carpenter of Nazareth for the lot of working men, or even that Jesus was the first socialist. The Wesleyan journal *The Watchman* protested in the 1850s that this was to 'degrade our Lord into a Socialist model man'.[2] For Keir Hardie, however, this is exactly what the churches should have been doing: Christ's teaching in his interpretation was focused upon salvation in this world through a re-ordering of human society. This was because late-nineteenth-century *laissez-faire* destroyed human dignity. Arguing that Christ did not preach competition, the Quaker Alfred Salter complained that the churches nevertheless unquestioningly accepted the existing economic order and its un-Christian consequences. In language borrowed from the pulpit he and his fellow Nonconformists in the labour movement lambasted the churches for failing to practise what they preached.[3]

On the other hand, however, the subsequent rise of the Labour Party led Nonconformist historians and commentators to suggest the Free Churches played a prominent role in the origins of the new movement. In a series of books published on labour and Methodism between 1937 and 1959, R. F. Wearmouth wrote extensively about the personnel his church contributed to the development of the trade unions.[4] 'The Labour Movement in this country', claimed Harry Jeffs, 'was cradled in our little Free Church chapels – Methodist, Baptist and Congregationalist'.[5] Such views reflected ideas both of the relative prominence of the working classes in Nonconformity and that the chapels provided opportunity for them to develop their speaking talents in the pulpit and their organizational skills in the diaconate. The chapel inculcated service, self-discipline and study: this working-class autodidactism made men like the Primitive

Methodist George Edwards the obvious people to turn to for Norfolk farm labourers seeking to protect their livelihoods by forming a union in the 1870s.[6] Accordingly, long-time Labour Party secretary, the Wesleyan Arthur Henderson, reflecting in 1929 on his own origins in the trade union movement fifty years before, recalled:

> [T]he majority of the leaders locally and nationally were actively engaged in religious work as lay-preachers, church deacons, Sunday School superintendents and teachers, Bible-class teachers, Band of Hope workers, etc. . . . I found in all parts of the country that many of the most active religious workers were often also the most influential leaders of the local trade union branches.[7]

Such a contribution became something of a historiographical commonplace down to the 1960s, at least as applied to the leaders of the founding generation of the Labour Party such as Henderson. Nor, it was suggested, was this confined to lay involvement in the development of the trade unions. Individual Nonconformist activity in most of the socialist movements which began to emerge around the 1880s may have been less noticeable. Nevertheless, some leading lights of the Fabian Society – such as Beatrice Webb – were of Unitarian background, while its long-term secretary E. R. Pease was a Quaker. Walton Newbold, even claimed that the Independent Labour Party (ILP), founded in Bradford in 1893, was shaped by Nonconformity.[8]

In this he was suggesting that the relationship between Nonconformity and such organizations was more than one merely of personnel. Nonconformity was felt, not least by German observers, to have given the British labour movement distinctive characteristics.[9] Elsewhere in Europe socialist organizations developed marked anti-clerical tendencies in response to Erastian churches or Catholic hierarchies felt to be pillars of established order. In Britain Nonconformity was relatively strong, while its traditional witness for religious liberty was itself mildly anti-clerical. This helped to produce an atmosphere in which the emergence of the British labour movement was less shaped than on the continent by conflict with organized religion. Indeed, in the midst of a war for the liberty of Europe, W. G. Symons could in 1941 conclude his remarks on the Nonconformist roots of British labour with: 'It is not fanciful to connect the failure of political democracy on the Continent with the absence there of a strongly religious tradition of the Free Church type.'[10]

Since the 1960s, however, the idea that the labour movement was nurtured by the Free Church tradition has come under critical scrutiny. The exemplary lives cited by Wearmouth have been shown by David Hempton to exaggerate the numerical contribution Methodism made to the nascent trade union movement in the early nineteenth century.[11] Paul Stigant revisited the Halévy thesis that Wesleyanism provided forms of social control to contain radical political movements during and following the French Revolution.[12] And Stephen Yeo, Stanley Pierson and Leonard Smith all argued that any mantle labour inherited from Nonconformity in the closing decades of the nineteenth century was lightly worn.[13] A close relationship for them was generally brief, and only at the level of personnel essentially moving from Nonconformity towards a new religion of socialism.

Meanwhile, K. S. Inglis' work prompted examination of the hitherto relatively neglected issue of how the Free Churches as organizations responded to the rise of the labour movement in 1880–1900.[14] Stephen Mayor's study of the Nonconformist press in that period suggested that increasing coverage of the issues which concerned the labour movement did not lead to close alignment with their cause.[15] Peter d'A. Jones instead argued that the small proportion of Nonconformist ministers who were so converted set up inward-looking denominational socialist societies.[16] In the face of the conflicts between capital and labour at the end of the century these were in turn subsumed into Social Service Unions. In place of the pulpit policy entrepreneurs of the nineteenth century these organizations bureaucratized Nonconformist political witness into broad statements on social questions designed in large measure to maintain consensus within denominations increasingly characterized – certainly by the inter-war years – by divided partisanship among the people in the pews. This divided partisanship was by then also equally marked in the pulpits. It had, J. D. Jones argued in 1938, sapped the assertive self-confidence of the late-nineteenth-century Nonconformist Conscience. Accordingly, R. Tudur Jones lamented in 1962, Congregationalism could speak with unanimity on Premium Bonds, but not on nuclear weapons.[17]

The Nonconformist Conscience had been closely aligned with the Liberal Party at the very moment that Labour began to emerge politically. However, even though many of the leading ministers associated with it were sympathetic to Labour's aspirations and the needs of the working classes, like C. Silvester Horne, they tended to regard it as a junior partner of the Liberal Party he represented in parliament (1910–14). From the point of view of those in the new party, Nonconformity's relationship with Liberalism in general however created a sense of rivalry that was partly political and partly theological.

It is no coincidence that the literature on Nonconformity and the labour movement concentrates on the period 1880–1914 when these rivalries were at a height. Responses to labour are still generally treated as peripheral in works on the earlier period of mid-nineteenth century Nonconformity and politics.[18] Engagement with the needs of the labouring poor hitherto had largely been local, such as the Unitarian the Revd Robert Robinson's involvement in Lancashire weavers' combinations in the 1740s.[19] The fact that the leading Baptist Minister Robert Hall felt required to defend supporting such combinations in 1819 suggests, however, that they remained frowned upon.[20] Trade unionism was treated with distrust as an alternative source of authority, discipline and socialization, the Calvinistic Methodists of Wales going so far as to ban members from joining such organizations in 1831.[21]

National developments were however changing such attitudes by the time R. W. Dale became chairman of the Congregational Union in 1869. Improving communications and denominational development meant that the Free Churches increasingly presented a corporate and, by the close of the century, national voice. The franchise reform of 1867 ensured that this voice now spoke for greatly enhanced numbers of Nonconformist voters often noisily aligned with the Liberal Party. It also, for the first time, enfranchised many working-class voters. This led, in turn, to growing interest in working-class representation either through or in opposition to the Liberals. The rise of labour was also marked in 1867 by the Royal Commission on Trade Unions, before which union officials challenged the notion of a reciprocity of interests between masters and men so redolent of mid-Victorian (and contemporary Nonconformist) political economy.[22] The following year the Trades Union Congress was founded. This and the contemporary emergence of socialist organizations on the continent prompted Dale to warn his audience that the questions working people were now discussing 'with the keenest interest affect the whole structure and order of society'.[23]

Following the Royal Commission, in 1871 the trade unions acquired a much improved, if still insufficiently clear, legal status. With state legitimation went greater Nonconformist condoning of lay involvement in trade unionism.[24] Meanwhile, Nonconformist employers responded to the rise of labour in ways ranging from the profit-sharing introduced by the Congregationalist Theodore Cooke Taylor of Bradford to the model towns and workplace conciliation machinery promoted by, for instance, the chocolate-manufacturing Quakers, the Cadburys and Rowntrees.

Conciliation rather than class conflict was also a characteristic emphasis of their Nonconformist counterparts in the trade unions.[25] However, industrial conflict was to become more common from the late 1880s, prompted partly by growing international competition. In such circumstances the self-help and conciliation – which fitted well with the ethos of the chapel and its alignment with Gladstonian Liberalism – of an older generation of trade unionists came to be challenged by those, such as the Congregationalist Fred Jowett, who felt that the industrial system did not need to be managed but transformed. The lock-outs in Bradford in 1892 in response to American textile tariffs, for instance, were an important backdrop to the founding in that town of the Independent Labour Party (ILP) by Hardie the following year.[26]

Such circumstances helped to undermine traditional Nonconformist opposition to interference by an Erastian state in the sphere of personal responsibilities. For instance, concerns about housing (and immorality) highlighted by the 1883 Congregationalist pamphlet *The Bitter Cry of Outcast London*, led the *Congregationalist* to proclaim: '[T]here is a certain socialism which Christianity sanctions . . . the State may lawfully be called upon to deal with a mass of evil which is . . . beyond the capacity of private benevolence.'[27] Similar concerns led the eminent Wesleyan Hugh Price Hughes to call in 1884 upon the churches 'to do their long-neglected duty in caring for the social welfare of the people', not least because in so doing they might 'bring back the alienated masses to the social brotherhood of Christ'.[28] Attempts to reach out to those alienated masses included in 1875 the founding of Pleasant Sunday Afternoon (later known as Brotherhood) meetings in a Congregational church in West Bromwich, and in the 1880s, the inner city Central Halls and settlements established in order to reconnect with the urban poor. To do so, however, the *Nonconformist and Independent* warned, the churches 'will certainly have to enlarge their conception of Christianity'.[29] The challenge was to address matters of more than individual salvation. John Clifford, for instance, set up a committee on social questions at Westbourne Park Baptist Church in 1885, the year after he became one of the first members of the Fabian Society.[30]

A fellow Baptist and early Fabian was J. C. Carlile, who ran the short-lived Christian Socialist journal *Duty* before going on to join Clifford in 1887 in setting up the Christian Socialist League (CSL).[31] The CSL lasted into the 1890s, thereafter gradually being replaced by various denominational social service departments. Carlile, meanwhile, as a docklands minister, was among a number of Nonconformists prominently involved in supporting the 1889 London Dock Strike, culminating in his becoming one of the joint trustees of the new dockers' union. Many of his colleagues were, however, scandalized by his presence on a strike committee, reflecting concern that ministers who become so involved might drift off into purely secular activities.[32]

This certainly happened – as demonstrated by Pope's analysis of the subsequent careers of several Welsh Nonconformist ministers who committed to Socialism[33] – though not in Carlile's case. It might be supposed that this reflected the attenuated nature of his Socialism: notwithstanding the CSL's support for nationalization of natural monopolies, Carlile and Clifford were primarily motivated to demonstrate a Christian concern for social issues.

There were however, more thoroughgoing socialists, such as the Wesleyan Samuel Keeble, one of the few English socialists to read Marx in the original German, whose 1896 tract *Industrial Day-Dreams* began with an attack on the immorality of competitive capitalism.

The handful of Nonconformist ministers who were self-ascribed socialists at this time could be found in all denominations. They included Carlile's fellow CSL member Bruce Wallace, the Congregationalist founder of the anarchist Brotherhood Church in north London. This was an early example of a congregation moving leftwards, in some cases establishing agrarian communes. Leonard Smith gives examples of several others, but shows that this movement was often resisted by Liberal-supporting chapel stalwarts. For instance, H. Bodell Smith was effectively driven from the pulpit at Beech Road Unitarians, Crewe, in 1895, a year after he founded the local ILP branch.[34] Similar political divisions were palpable in the Bradford chapels during the labour disputes of the early 1890s. The Revd R. Roberts, a Congregational minister who played a leading role in the early ILP, was the most prominent to be ejected from his pastorate.[35] Most of his colleagues, however, were conspicuous in their support instead for the Liberal millowner and Congregationalist Alfred Illingworth in his successful election fight with the dockers' leader (and Congregational lay preacher) Ben Tillett in the 1892 general election.[36] Such hostility towards Labour candidates long continued.[37] As the erstwhile Ulster Quaker S. G. Hobson later recalled: 'I soon realised that the ILP had appeared at a moment in time when Yorkshire Nonconformity was in a process of disruption [and] . . . accordingly set out to capture the soul of Nonconformity.'[38] These social tensions within the chapels helped to create a sense of conflict between Nonconformity and labour which, as Pope's work on Wales shows, was by no means confined to Yorkshire.

Tillett had warned the Unitarians' triennial conference in 1891 that, unless Nonconformity provides 'churches where the people could get what they needed . . . the workers would provide churches for themselves'. In his audience was John Trevor, who the following year responded by founding the Labour Church movement. Jowett, severing his connections with Congregationalism, became the first president of the Bradford Labour Church.[39] These Labour churches, however, have been subjected to disproportionate historiographical scrutiny. Few thrived for long and the movement was moribund by the First World War.[40]

In part this may be because the ILP to some extent replaced religion, and indeed the Labour Church. This was not least because it was able to tap into existing immanentist theological trends to which Trevor was also responding.[41] An exclusive stress upon personal salvation was diminishing in all the denominations. T. Rhondda Williams later reflected on his early ministry: 'I did not hesitate to promise heavenly mansions to the good, without even seeing any duty in regard to the hovels in which they lived on earth.'[42] For him such attitudes were undermined by the higher criticism of the Bible of the late nineteenth century; its focus upon the historical Jesus leading to a growing stress on God's activity in the world. His position as minister of the City Temple gave R. J. Campbell a particular platform to launch the most celebrated example of this trend when he published *The New Theology* in 1907. Its association of sin with the selfishness seen as producing the un-Christian slums and sweatshops of capitalism also provided an obvious link to the growing, if still small, socialist movement.

For Leonard Smith this theological modernism was resisted in chapels dominated – not least financially – by middle-class Liberals, leading to a growing gap between Nonconformity and the labour movement.[43] A possible exception was the Brotherhood: 'Here at any rate has come into being a movement that is bridging the gulf that for so many years has existed between the churches and the working classes', claimed its former president William Ward.[44] Yet, Smith maintains that the link which Ward saw the Brotherhood as providing was often weak. Certainly, many chapels remained cool towards the Brotherhood down to the First World War.[45] It was, however, strongly supported in others, serving as an arena wherein people like Ammon could express the intimate relationship between their politics and their faith. The ILP's newspaper subsequently commented that in the Edwardian period the Brotherhood was substantially a religious counterpart of the labour movement.[46] Brotherhood branches helped to distribute Labour propaganda in the run-up to the 1918 election. It was a different Brotherhood movement, however, which emerged from the First World War. Two-thirds of its membership enlisted, a figure not unadjacent to the 65 per cent drop in subscriptions reported in 1919.[47] Over the next twenty years the Brotherhood was much smaller, more ecumenical and much less political than it had been before 1914.

Strains of theological modernism, in contrast, continued to advance. In 1918 its chairman, E. Griffith-Jones, told the Congregational Union that, in contrast to the simple evangelicalism of his youth that 'redemption is a social as well as an individual fact'.[48] His predecessor in 1917, B. J. Snell, responded to the common challenge presented by total war by calling for fellowship, observing: 'The first Labour government can be trusted to see to the laws that impede fellowship.'[49] The Liberal Party split from 1916 onwards perhaps helped to make Labour identification among ministers both more common and more acceptable than had often been the case before 1914. Theological modernism also became more acceptable, exemplified when in 1929 Rhondda Williams, who had previously been denied a platform at the Congregational Union, now became its chairman.

The significance of theological modernism, however, should not be misrepresented. Rhondda Williams may have argued that people 'cannot be saved from their sin until they are saved from their systems', but he still recognized the need to do both.[50] Nor should liberal modernism be overstated, coming under challenge as it did from Barthianism in the inter-war years.[51] Furthermore, it was not the only route for Nonconformist ministers to socialism. A sacramental sense of a common life could also lead in the same direction. This was perhaps particularly significant among Wesleyans: several leading figures in the Methodist Sacramental Fellowship such as Donald Soper became ardent socialists, while R. J. Barker at Tonypandy Central Hall in 1928 established a Community House both to express this sacramental vision and to provide an alternative to the then widespread communist activity in the valleys.[52] There were, however, other examples, such as W. E. Orchard's ministry at the King's Weigh House before his eventual conversion to Catholicism.[53]

Earlier Orchard had been among the few Nonconformists to attempt a detailed refutation of Marx and Lenin in response to the Bolshevik revolution and the 1920 founding of the Communist Party of Great Britain (CPGB).[54] The Marxist challenge was expressed thus by a former Wesleyan turned communist: 'Dope and hope are poor substitutes for vigorous action.'[55] A desire for such vigour, in the form of class conflict, led Walton Newbold to leave the Quakers to become Britain's first elected Communist MP in 1922. He was an exception, though there was little Nonconformist enthusiasm for British intervention in the 1918–21 Russian civil war, some radical chapels even contributing to famine relief funds.[56] The atheism of Soviet Russia ensured that the CPGB never acquired the religiosity of tone that had made the ILP a rival before 1914. This atheism drew considerable Nonconformist hostility in the 1920s, particularly among Baptists.

In the 1930s, however, there was a spate of books and articles on the relationship between religion and Communism, including the Left Book Club volume on *Christianity and the Social Revolution* edited by the Unitarian minister John Lewis, in 1937. Some even became Communists, such as Unitarian P. N. Harker, attracted in part by the activism of the CPGB in the face of mass unemployment and the perceived international need to combat the rise of fascism.[57] Similar influences seem to have led to the Free Church support for Communist candidates in the 1935 election lamented by Barker.[58] Active Free Church involvement in the CPGB, however, remained very limited, held in check by its antipathy to religion and emphasis on class conflict.

There was, in contrast, by the 1930s a considerable Free Church presence in the Labour Party. The Quaker C. H. Wilson even organized a short-lived Nonconformist parliamentary group of fellow Labour MPs in 1931.[59] This consciously aped the similar group of Liberal MPs convened by Robert Perks in the Edwardian years. Free Church Labour MPs portrayed their party as having succeeded to the historic witness of Liberalism (and Nonconformity) in other ways as well. As the Congregationalist Somerville Hastings put it in 1934: 'We who are Free Churchmen must never forget the debt we owe to our forefathers for the measure of political and religious liberty that is ours . . . But civil and religious liberty can never be complete without economic liberty as well.'[60]

The mechanisms adopted to achieve that economic liberty, however, did not always appeal to Free Church leaders. Liberal businessmen, such as the Congregationalist Angus Watson, could agree (in debate with Ammon) that industry should be primarily for service not profit.[61] This did not mean that there was general Nonconformist agreement on the benefits of nationalization. There was great Nonconformist and Brotherhood interest in the ultimately fruitless Mond–Turner talks about better industrial relations following the 1926 General Strike.[62] That event, however, for Carlile indicated the rise of a different kind of Labour man motivated by class conflict.[63] By now the editor of the *Baptist Times*, in the 1930s, in common with many Nonconformist leaders, he supported the National government.

A lack of enthusiasm for nationalization was still apparent after 1945.[64] Nationalization was often seen as redolent of a doctrinaire (and potentially illiberal) view of economic order to which Nonconformity had by no means been wholly converted. The Nonconformist Conscience had been, at its best, a revolt against injustice, oppression and vested interests. Traditionally Nonconformity reflected a search for a moral order established by people striving for betterment, rather than a belief that a moral order can be established by particular economic measures. The planned social perfection Keeble sketched out in his vision of a socialist society in 1936 only worked because '[e]veryone controls himself'.[65] To those Marxists who argued that all that was needed for a good society was good conditions, Salter had therefore replied in 1931: 'We may equalise wealth and abolish all kinds of wrongs and injustices so that there will be plenty for each and for all, and yet these changes in themselves will provide no guarantee at all that people will be happier than they are now, unless spiritual progress attends progress in material things.'[66]

The appeal of nationalization to the labour movement originated in the idea that it would provide greater job security and a better distribution of social goods than the seeming chaos of late-nineteenth-century competitive capitalism. The Nonconformist Labour MPs George Thomas led in singing 'Cwm Rhondda' as they trooped through the division lobbies to vote for the nationalization and welfare state measures of the post-war Attlee government certainly believed that these were righteous measures that would enlarge the economic liberty of which Hastings had written. Yet, as Thomas subsequently noted, there was a risk that 'Social security is treated as an end in itself, rather than as a means to enable men to give greater service to their fellows'.[67] It became an entitlement, rather than a Christian duty.

Many of the welfare services now nationalized by central government had been started by the churches. Indeed, a number of the architects of the Welfare State in the 1945–51 Attlee government, both Anglican and Nonconformist, had started their public lives in such work. Since around 1900, when Clifford transferred the adult education work founded by his church to his local authority, the idea that the state had greater resources to deliver these services had gathered ground. In the process, state welfare was imbued with the idea that it delivered the common brotherhood encapsulated by much contemporary theological modernism. In other words, the welfare formerly provided by the churches was increasingly seen as the Christian duty of the state. In the post-war years accordingly, remaining church-based welfare became increasingly professionalized, regulated, secularized and financially dependent upon government funding.[68] This undermined the social Christianity which, as Pope has shown, was a key element in the Free Church response to the rise of the labour movement.[69] Social Christianity helped to pave the way for the Welfare State, but after 1948 it became in attenuated form more associated with that state than any of the churches. The result was to weaken the social significance of the Free Churches and blunt their message.

Meanwhile, once established, the Labour Party became its own training ground: it no longer needed the chapels to train its speakers and organizers. Accordingly, the distinctive Nonconformist presence in the Parliamentary Labour Party still so discernible throughout the inter-war years, had virtually disappeared by the end of the twentieth century.

Claims about the relationship between Nonconformity and Labour nevertheless arguably reached their peak in the 1950s in the various speeches the party's Methodist general secretary, Morgan Phillips, gave (usually abroad) about Labour owing more to Methodism than Marx. Since, however, Labour clearly owed little to Marxism, this was not necessarily as much of a claim as first met the eye. Meanwhile, at the start of the following decade, Christopher Driver suggested that any debt to Nonconformity was likely to be a positive disadvantage to Labour.[70] Methodist trade union dinosaurs with puritanical attitudes, he argued, prevented the party responding effectively to the liberalizing social and personal morals of the 1960s. Tony Crosland, in contrast, having thrown off his Brethren upbringing, was urging Labour to embrace these developments. Post-war affluence led to a growing search for cultural liberalization and moral relativism that did not sit easily with the historic message of Nonconformity.

Certainly, Wertheimer linked the cultural conservatism he discerned as particular to the British labour movement in the 1920s to Nonconformity. He also linked its righteousness of tone to the same source. Unlike the Marxists of his native Germany, Labour found a ready form of political communication in the religious idealism of Nonconformity already made familiar to electors through its exposition on late Victorian Liberal platforms. This illustrates that the relationship between Nonconformity and the labour movement was complex, operating on levels from the electoral to the rhetorical.[71]

It also operated within a wider context. For instance, Nonconformity was already numerically in decline before it was confronted by the rise of labour in the late nineteenth century. The latter, notwithstanding some commentators, seems to have had little influence on this process. Furthermore, while Leonard Smith rightly draws attention to the role of theological modernism in creating an atmosphere conducive to the rise of labour, he overstates the extent to which it became merely a stepping stone for leaving the Free Churches altogether. Many shared Rhondda Williams' view that there remained a need to transform both people and systems. As Ammon warned in 1948: 'Advances in education and standards of living . . . tend to obscure the dangers arising from spiritual decline . . . It is right that such things be sought and gained; but by themselves they are not enough.'[72] Without committed and converted individuals how could better systems be maintained?

Notes

1 *Southampton Times* (12 December 1921).
2 Quoted in M. L. Edwards, *Methodism and England: A Study of Methodism in Its Social and Religious Aspects during the Period 1850–1932* (London: Epworth, 1943), p. 166.
3 A. Salter, 'The Modern Messianic Movement', in C. G. Ammon (ed.), *Christ and Labour* (London: Jarrold and Sons, 1912), p. 27.
4 See P. Catterall, 'The Distinctiveness of British Socialism? Religion and the Rise of Labour *c*.1900–39', in M. Worley (ed.), *The Foundations of the British Labour Party: Identities, Cultures and Perpsectives, 1900–39* (Farnham: Ashgate, 2009), pp. 131–52 [p. 132].
5 *Brotherhood Outlook* (September 1928).
6 N. Edwards, *Ploughboy's Progress: The Life of Sir George Edwards* (Norwich: Centre of East Anglian Studies, University of East Anglia, 1998), chapters 2–4.
7 A. Henderson, 'British Labor and Religion', in J. Davis (ed.), *Labor Speaks for Itself on Religion* (New York: Macmillan, 1929), pp. 140–50 [pp. 144–46].
8 J. Walton Newbold, 'The ILP: A Marxist Study', *Socialist Review*, 17 (1920), pp. 77–86 [p. 82].
9 Catterall, 'The Distinctiveness of British Socialism?', p. 138.

10 Quoted in E. A. Payne, *The Free Church Tradition in the Life of England* (London: SCM, 1944), p. 151.
11 D. Hempton, *Methodism and Politics in British Society, 1750–1850* (London: Hutchinson, 1984).
12 P. Stignant, 'Wesleyan Methodism and Working-Class Radicalism in the North, 1792–1821', *Northern History*, 6/1 (1971), pp. 98–116; E. Halévy, *Histoire du people Anglais au 19e siècle* (Paris: Hachette, 1913).
13 S. Yeo, *Religion and Voluntary Organisations in Crisis* (London: Croom Helm, 1976); S. Pierson, 'John Trevor and the Labour Church Movement, 1891–1900', *Church History*, 28/2 (1960), pp. 463–78; L. Smith, *Religion and the Rise of Labour: Nonconformity and the Independent Labour Movement in Lancashire and the West Riding, 1880–1914* (Keele: Ryburn, 1993).
14 K. S. Inglis, *Churches and the Working Class in Victorian England* (London: Routledge and Kegan Paul, 1963).
15 S. H. Mayor, *The Churches and the Labour Movement* (London: Independent Press, 1967)
16 P. d'A. Jones, *The Christian Socialist Revival in England, 1877–1914* (Princeton, NJ: Princeton University Press, 1968).
17 R. Tudur Jones, *Congregationalism in England 1662–1962* (London: Independent Press, 1962), p. 425.
18 See, e.g., T. Larsen, *Friends of Religious Equality: Nonconformist Politics in Mid-Victorian England* (Woodbridge: Boydell Press, 1999); R. Floyd, *Church, Chapel and Party: Religious Dissent and Political Modernisation in Nineteenth-Century England* (Basingstoke: Palgrave, 2008).
19 R. V. Holt, *The Unitarian Contribution to Social Progress in England* (London: Lindsey Press, 1939), p. 204.
20 Payne, *The Free Church Tradition in the Life of England*, p. 99.
21 Robert Pope, *Building Jerusalem: Nonconformity, Labour and the Social Question in Wales, 1906–1939* (Cardiff: University of Wales Press, 1998), p. 4.
22 See D. Kynaston, *King Labour: The British Working Class, 1850–1914* (London: Allen and Unwin, 1976); H. F. Lovell Cocks, *The Nonconformist Conscience* (London: Independent Press, 1943), pp. 30f.
23 Quoted in J. C. G. Binfield, 'Dale and Politics', in idem (ed.), *The Cross and the City: Essays in Commemoration of Robert William Dale, 1829–1895* (Cambridge: United Reformed Church History Society, 1999), pp. 91–119 [p. 105].
24 On 1 January 1892, the *Nonconformist and Independent* noted 'our churches . . . have extended a welcome to labour questions and to labour leaders which twenty years ago would have seemed incredible'.
25 E.g. *The Christian Witness and Congregationalist Magazine*, n.s. 3 (March 1867), pp. 127–28 observed: 'It is the object of Christianity to teach all classes to behave properly to each other – to teach employers to be just, and workmen to be conscientious.'
26 K. Laybourn, 'Trade Unions and the Independent Labour Party: The Manningham Experience', in T. Jowitt and R. Taylor (eds), *Bradford 1890–1914: The Cradle of the Independent Labour Party* (Bradford: University of Leeds Centre for Adult Education, occasional paper 2, 1980).
27 Quoted in J. Wolfenden, 'English Nonconformity and the Social Conscience, 1880–1906' (unpublished PhD thesis, Yale University, 1954), p. 33.
28 Quoted in C. Oldstone-Moore, *Hugh Price Hughes: Founder of a New Methodism, Conscience of a New Nonconformity* (Cardiff: University of Wales Press, 1999), p. 114.
29 *Nonconformist and Independent* (3 January 1884).

30 J. Marchant, *Dr John Clifford CH: Life, Labours and Reminiscences* (London: Cassell, 1924), p. 63; Wolfenden, 'English Nonconformity and the Social Conscience, 1880–1906', p. 67.
31 J. C. Carlile, *My Life's Little Day* (London: Blackie, 1935), pp. 49–51.
32 Ibid., pp. 88–93.
33 Pope, *Building Jerusalem*, pp. 39f.
34 Smith, *Religion and the Rise of Labour*, chapter 6.
35 Laybourn and Reynolds, *Religion and the Rise of Labour, 1890–1914*, pp. 34, 80.
36 B. Diggle, 'Illingworthism: Alfred Illingworth and Independent Labour Politics' (unpublished MA thesis, University of Huddersfield, 1984), pp. 30–31.
37 See, e.g., B. Turner, *About Myself: 1863–1930* (London: Cayme Press, 1930), p. 175.
38 S. G. Hobson, *Pilgrim to the Left: Memoirs of a Modern Revolutionist* (London: Arnold, 1938), pp. 38–39.
39 S. Pierson, *British Socialists: The Journey from Fantasy to Politics* (London: Harvard University Press, 1960), pp. 465–67.
40 J. Turner, 'Labour's Lost Soul? Recovering the Labour Church', in M. Worley (ed.), *The Foundations of the British Labour Party: Identities, Cultures and Perspectives, 1900–1939* (Farnham: Ashgate, 2009), pp. 153–70 [p. 168].
41 M. Bevir, 'Labour Churches and Ethical Socialism', *History Today*, 47/4 (1997), pp. 50–54.
42 T. Rhondda Williams, *How I Found My Faith: A Religious Pilgrimage* (London: Cassell, 1938), pp. 23, 44–46.
43 Smith, *Religion and the Rise of Labour*, pp. 170–71.
44 W. Ward, in W. Forbes Gray (ed.), *Non-Church Going: Its Reasons and Remedies* (Edinburgh: Oliphant, Anderson and Ferrier, 1911), pp. 174–83 [p. 181].
45 Smith, *Religion and the Rise of Labour*, pp. 68–69; *Brotherhood Year Book* (1913–14), p. 26.
46 *Labour Leader* (18 September 1919).
47 *Methodist Times* (13 June 1935); *Baptist Times* (16 May 1919).
48 *Congregational Year Book* (1919), pp. 26, 36.
49 *Congregational Year Book* (1918), p. 36.
50 *Socialist Christian* (August 1929).
51 Pope, *Building Jerusalem*, chapter 6.
52 R. J. Barker, *Christ in the Valley of Unemployment* (London: Hodder and Stoughton, 1936), pp. 30–31, 81–110.
53 E. Kaye and R. Mackenzie, *W. E. Orchard: A Study in Christian Exploration* (Oxford: Education Services, 1990).
54 *The Crusader* (2 February 1923).
55 *Methodist Times* (21 December 1922).
56 P. Ackers, *Labour and Capital in the Wigan Churches of Christ, c.1845–1945* (Loughborough: Loughborough University Business School, research series paper 4, 1994), p. 14.
57 *Bolton Evening News* (2 November 1932).
58 Barker, *Christ in the Valley of Unemployment*, p. 60.
59 Catterall, 'The Distinctiveness of British Socialism?', p. 141.
60 *Free Churchman* (December 1934).
61 *Free Church Year Book* (1923), p. 53.
62 *Brotherhood Outlook* (November 1927; May 1928).
63 Carlile, *My Life's Little Day*, p. 242.
64 G. I. T. Machin, *Churches and Social Issues in Twentieth-Century Britain* (Oxford: Clarendon, 1998), p. 142.
65 *Methodist Times* (3 December 1936).

66 *Christian World* (15 January 1931).
67 George Thomas, *The Christian Heritage in Politics* (London: Epworth, 1959), p. 50.
68 P. Catterall, 'Slums and Salvation', in P. Ballard and L. Husselbee (eds), *Free Churches in Society: The Nonconformist Contribution to Social Welfare, 1800–2010* (London: Continuum, 2012), pp. 111–32.
69 Pope, *Building Jerusalem*, chapter 2.
70 C. Driver, *A Future for the Free Churches?* (London: SCM, 1962), p. 37.
71 Catterall, 'The Distinctiveness of British Socialism?', pp. 136–38.
72 Hull History Centre: Ammon Papers, U. DMN/9/1, 'Whither?', draft article ca 1948.

22 Nonconformists and Ecumenical Relationships

Noel A. Davies

Nonconformist churches and denominations in Britain and Ireland, as in Europe and worldwide, have been at the heart of initiating and developing ecumenical relationships from the last decades of the nineteenth century onwards. They have given priority, at different times within this period, to developing new partnerships and unions within the various traditions as well as collaborations between Nonconformist denominations and, later in the twentieth century, deeper ecumenical relationships with Anglican, Roman Catholic and Orthodox churches. They have consistently been key participants in ecumenical councils, nationally and locally, as well as partners in church union negotiations. This chapter will explore a range of examples of these ecumenical relationships but it cannot hope to be in any way comprehensive. It will focus on England and Wales in the twentieth century but will also explore some key developments in the first decade of the twenty-first century. Here and there, also, we will touch on events that predated this period.

The ecumenical enterprise embraces all aspects of the life and witness of its participating churches. However, since other chapters in this volume cover aspects such as church and state, social responsibility, mission and education, this chapter will focus predominantly on ecumenical relationships and union. It will end by reflecting on ways in which these ecumenical relationships, in their various aspects, may shape the future of the Nonconformist traditions in the coming decades.

Although this chapter will not attempt a comprehensive and detailed examination of all the Nonconformist churches and denominations, from time to time some reference will be made to most of those churches that have come to be regarded as Nonconformist both historically and in their present realities. Negatively, these churches may be understood as those that are not Anglican, Roman Catholic or Eastern or Oriental Orthodox churches but, more positively, much of the chapter will explore ways in which Nonconformist churches have related to these other traditions.

Two other factors need to be recognized, namely geography and language. Some of the ecumenical relationships that this chapter will explore have involved the churches and denominations in Britain and Ireland as a whole, whereas others have been limited to one or other of the nations or to England and Wales. In Britain and Ireland as a whole, of course, most, if not all, ecumenical relationships have been conducted through the medium of English although some of the churches concerned in Scotland and, to some degree, in Ireland have used Scottish or Irish Gaelic in their worship and witness. However, ecumenical relationships in Wales have always been bilingual in nature. This is not just a matter of ecumenical communication but rather a matter of how cultural issues, such as language and the identities that have been shaped by language, among other factors, contribute to both the richness and complexities of ecumenical engagement. Language, in ecumenical as well as in other aspects of human relationships, is never merely a tool of communication. It shapes culture, character and identity and thus becomes an ingredient in the ecumenical enterprise.

I. Collaborative Ecumenical Organizations

It was in 1846 that the Evangelical Alliance (for England and Wales)[1] was formed in order to foster common bonds between those who shared a doctrinal understanding. Unity and Catholicity were its defining principles. It was conceived as a global organization but its history and development were predominantly British, with 84 per cent of the delegates at the inaugural conference held in London in August 1846 being from Britain. In November of the same year the British organization of this 'World's Evangelical Alliance' was established in Manchester. By 1859 it had 6,000 members. By the 1890s annual Free Church Congresses began to be held and in 1892 the National Council of the Free Churches (for England and Wales) was formed that drew together local Free Church Councils rather than national denominational representatives. Its successor, the National Council of the Evangelical Free Churches, formed in 1896, did, however, include denominational representatives. The Welsh Nonconformists Council, formed a few years earlier, was replaced in Wales by the new body. But in 1907 a National Council of Wales was formed 'under (the) wing' of the newly established body. By 1908, it had 167 local branches throughout Wales.[2] R. Tudur Jones' judgement on this creative period in Nonconformist relationships in Wales is that 'there was a strong conviction that it could do no more than foster co-operation within a federal framework and that there was little point in raising the issue of seeking union between the denominations'.[3]

However, twenty years after its formation, the National Council of the Evangelical Free Churches (covering England and Wales) was challenged by its chairman J. H. Shakespeare, then general secretary of the Baptist Union of Great Britain and Ireland, to 'consider the possibilities and implications of Free Church union'.[4] Shakespeare himself concluded two years later that '(such) a vision hung for a brief moment over the conference and then vanished. The moment was not ripe for corporate union.'[5] So the churches agreed to move towards a federal relationship with one another, defined by Shakespeare as a 'fuller, richer and various life of the Churches which compose it . . . [that] aims at the practical reconciliation of autonomy with co-operation, liberty with order and unity with diversity'.[6] The Federal Council of the Evangelical Free Churches was formed in 1917. Thompson comments that Shakespeare was 'more far-sighted and prepared to be more realistic than many other Nonconformists of his own day and since; but his words . . . found no echoes at the time, and provoked hostility among his Baptist colleagues'.[7] These two bodies, the National Council and the Federal Council, continued in existence until they were merged in 1940 to form the Free Church Federal Council, which adopted as its doctrinal statement the detailed Declaratory Statement of Common Faith and Practice agreed by the Federal Council in 1917.[8]

During this same period, steps were being taken to strengthen ecumenical relationships within Wales between the Nonconformist churches and the newly founded (Anglican) Church in Wales. This movement was largely driven by the disestablishment of the Church of England in Wales in 1920 to form the Church in Wales, a non-established, independent Anglican province. It was also influenced by the call of the Lambeth Conference of Anglican Bishops also in 1920 for deeper Christian union based on what came to be known as the Lambeth Quadrilateral (namely Holy Scriptures, the historic creeds, the sacraments of Baptism and Holy Communion and the historic Episcopate) – a call that also inspired further efforts towards unity between Anglican and Nonconformist churches, such as the Anglican–Methodist conversations in the 1950s and 1960s. Many Nonconformist leaders in Wales had encouraged the movement towards disestablishment because they believed that it would give the Anglican community in Wales greater freedom – without what many regarded as the encumbrance of establishment relationships – to develop different kinds of relationships with the other church communities in Wales and to undertake Christian witness that would be more in tune with the religious and cultural context in Wales.

As a consequence of this greater freedom, 1929 saw the formation, following considerable negotiation during the intervening years, of the Joint Committee for the Promotion of Mutual Understanding and

Co-operation between the Christian Communions in Wales. The Joint Committee included among its members the newly formed Church in Wales as well as Welsh-language and English-language Nonconformist churches and denominations. The responses to the Joint Committee were mixed. Some regarded it as no more than a 'talking shop' for church leaders. But others recognized that it provided a focus and a space to enable church leaders to grow in their friendship with and understanding of each other and hence a foundation for their churches' growth into greater unity and mutual understanding.

On a world level and following the 1910 Edinburgh International Conference for Missionary Societies and organizations, which is generally recognized as providing the main impetus for the creation of the modern ecumenical movement during the early decades of the twentieth century, a number of key international events led to the formation of the World Council of Churches as the main instrument of the global ecumenical enterprise. Thus, the first international Life and Work conference in Stockholm in 1925, the first international Faith and Order conference in Lausanne in 1927 and the international missionary meeting in Jerusalem in 1928 contributed in fundamental ways to a desire to forge an instrument that would reflect the vision of Edinburgh 1910 and be a focus for an ecumenical approach to the agenda being developed through these ecumenical forums. The Nonconformist denominations of England and Wales, especially those that included churches in England and Wales within their membership (such as the Methodist Church of Great Britain) as well as the Church of England and the other Anglican provinces participated in these international developments and this, in turn, had an impact on their ecumenical engagement at home.

In 1938, it was agreed that the World Council of Churches (WCC) should be formed to give expression to the growing global mutual understanding and collaboration that had developed through the international conferences that were fruits of Edinburgh 1910. However, the Second World War (1939–45) meant that the first Assembly could not be held until 1948. At that first Assembly in Amsterdam the Baptist Union of Great Britain and Ireland, the Baptist Union of Scotland, Churches of Christ in England and Wales, the Congregational Union of England and Wales, the Methodist Church, the Presbyterian Church of England, the Presbyterian Church of Ireland, the Presbyterian Church of Wales and the United Free Church of Scotland were represented, as well as the Anglican Churches in the four nations of Britain and Ireland, and the national Church of Scotland (Presbyterian).[9] Soon after the inaugural Assembly, the Union of Welsh Independents (a Welsh-language Congregational denomination) joined. In addition, the British Province of the Moravian Church is a WCC member church, as is the United Reformed Church (see later).

This international process towards the formation of the WCC was, at least in part, an inspiration also for setting up the British Council of Churches (BCC) in 1942. The inaugural service was held at St Paul's Cathedral. In his sermon as president of the Council, Dr Geoffrey Fisher, later to become archbishop of Canterbury, said:

> Today we inaugurate the British Council of Churches, the counterpart in our country of the World Council, combining in a single organisation the chief agencies of the interdenominational co-operation which has marked the last five years . . . Our differences remain . . . but we take our stand on the common faith of Christendom, faith in God, Creator, Redeemer, Sanctifier.[10]

All the churches listed above as being members of the WCC were also members of the BCC together with the Society of Friends and the Unitarian Church which were able to become members through a clause that enabled 'any body which has hitherto been represented on the Commission (of the Churches for International Friendship and Social Responsibility)' to continue in membership of the Council.

Alongside their developing commitment within the BCC, the churches were also engaged in ecumenical organizations within Ireland and Scotland as well as in Wales. These inevitably impinged on the wider relationships and conversations across these nations – not least because the 'troubles' in Ireland during much of this period had effects beyond Ireland itself and affected, indeed in many ways strengthened, ecumenical relationships within Ireland itself and between Irish churches and other churches in these islands, particularly through the Irish Council of Churches and, later, the Ballymascanlon Inter-Church Meetings. Similarly the Scottish Churches' Council and the Multilateral Conversations in Scotland had wider implications for the broader ecumenical family.

In Wales, the Council of Churches for Wales was established as a successor to the Joint Committee (see earlier) at the inaugural meeting in Swansea in 1956.[11] The founding members were the Church in Wales, the Union of Welsh Independents, the Methodist Church, the Baptist Union of Wales, the Congregational Union of England and Wales, the Baptist Union of Great Britain and Ireland and the Salvation Army. The Society of Friends became an observer and the Roman Catholic Church became consultant observers in 1968, largely following the encouragement of the Second Vatican Council. This initiative was stimulated both by a concern that a British ecumenical organization could not adequately understand the Welsh inter-church context at national and local levels (not least its bilingual nature) and by a recognition that adequate engagement with the cultural, socio-economic and political issues that challenged the churches of Wales at this time required an ecumenical body that was rooted in the soil and context of Wales. On both of these issues, that is, the Welsh inter-church context and engagement with what the text of the Covenant for Union in Wales (see later) referred to as 'the land and people of Wales', the Nonconformist churches were at the forefront of this attempt to ensure that the churches had at their disposal an ecumenical structure that could foster within Wales the vision of unity represented by the WCC.

In a chapter such as this, it is not possible to provide a full account of the ways in which the Nonconformist churches became engaged in the very many diverse activities of the BCC and its partner ecumenical bodies in Ireland, Scotland and Wales. However, some aspects of these areas of collaboration deserve to be mentioned. First, a predominant concern for all the churches within these bodies was local ecumenism. Often growing out of commitments to organizations such as Christian Aid and working in collaboration with local Free Church councils and increasingly after the Second Vatican Council with the Roman Catholic Church, local councils of churches came into being throughout England, Scotland and Wales most especially. Local Free Church councils continued to be important as expressions of the Free Church (or Nonconformist) identity, even when they had become less effective in enabling the collaboration of the Free Churches in their local communities, but during recent years this expression of Free Church 'solidarity' has been considerably weakened.

One significant result of this pattern of growing local collaboration was a considerable growth in more committed local collaborations and partnerships, mainly through Local Ecumenical Projects (LEPs) subsequently renamed Local Ecumenical Partnerships. These involved partnerships not only between the Church of England and the Methodist Church but also Baptist, United Reformed, Congregational, Presbyterian and, in some cases, Catholic churches. The main impetus for this development was the historic Faith and Order conference held, under the auspices of the BCC, in Nottingham in 1964 which called for the setting up of 'areas of ecumenical experiment'.[12]

A Church of England report (2011) helpfully points to the importance of LEPs within the ecumenical scene, a scene in which most of the Nonconformist churches were involved in very committed ways:

> The LEP concept emerged as a pioneering venture pointing the way to a reconciliation of the churches and an integration of their resources and ministry, – finding particular expression as new Christian communities

> in new towns and housing developments. They were exceptions seeking exception from denominational patterns, and acknowledgement and support from the denominations sponsoring them.[13]

But it also true to say, not least in the light of the experience of recent years, that LEPs have truly tested and challenged the structures of all the churches, confronting the churches with the need to find ways within inherited patterns and orders, to allow the ecumenical vision to be translated into truly local partnerships shaped by and for mission.

Secondly, many of these local councils of churches gave priority to issues of community relationships within their neighbourhoods. Within the BCC, the Community and Race Relations Unit sought to encourage churches both locally and nationally to find ways of fostering closer relationships within increasingly multiracial communities, not least in partnership with Black-majority churches. Nonconformist churches were often at the forefront of these efforts both locally and nationally and many churches and denominations developed a range of programmes to foster greater understanding. The 'People Next Door' campaign in 1966 was intended to encourage local churches to build bridges with their local communities so that there would be greater mutual understanding and greater opportunities for Christian service and witness. There is a question about its long-term effectiveness but, at the time, it did engage local Nonconformist as well as other churches in new ways of community involvement and service.

Thirdly, patterns of governance within these nations became a key ecumenical concern.[14] As early as 1939, there was debate in Wales about nationalism, self-government and National Socialism in Europe. In those early days, supporters of national self-government were frequently accused of fascist tendencies and of sympathy with Hitler, even by fellow Nonconformists. But thirty years later, when the political debate about self-government became a politically contentious issue, attitudes had changed. During the Council of Churches for Wales Church and Society Conference in 1970 (following up the very significant WCC Church and Society Conference in Geneva in 1966), some denominational representatives (including especially those from the Welsh-language Nonconformist churches) declared that 'some form of self-government is necessary to ensure the greatest benefit to the people of Wales'. Others were more cautious or, in some cases, fundamentally antagonistic towards such a political policy. In 1969 many of the Nonconformist churches presented evidence to the Crowther Commission and urged that '(o)nly the authority of the people of Wales over their own lives'[15] (i.e. through some form of self-government) would enable them to foster the Christian values that had been foundational in Wales over the centuries.

In 1977, the BCC set up a working group to bring a report on devolution to its Assembly in March 1977. Its members were the archbishop of Wales G. O. Williams, Bill Johnson (who would later become moderator of the Church of Scotland) and Derek Pattinson (secretary general of the General Synod of the Church of England). None of these was a Nonconformist in the strict sense of that word. However, they were unanimous in their view that 'devolution for both (Scotland and Wales) is necessary now and . . . legislative devolution for Wales (is) as necessary as for Scotland'.[16] Receiving this report the BCC Assembly expressed its support for devolved powers for Scotland and Wales while also seeking to preserve the unity of the United Kingdom. Whereas this was a historic commitment by a British ecumenical body, there remains a question as to the degree of commitment to devolution there would be at that time within the individual member churches and denominations, including some of the Nonconformist denominations, especially in England.

The referenda in Scotland and Wales did not lead to devolution. But by the 1990s there was a growing consensus across the church traditions, certainly in Wales and Scotland, and increasingly in England that a degree of devolved government within these two nations would be desirable. There would be many within Nonconformist denominations in Scotland and Wales that would argue for political independence but the majority would probably have argued for political devolution within a continuing United Kingdom political reality. When a Scottish parliament and a Welsh Assembly were established in 1998, there was a general welcome within the churches of the two nations and recognition in England that these moves might raise fundamental questions about governance within England itself.

Fourthly, these national ecumenical bodies were at the forefront of campaigns and programmes that focused on two issues that were a priority for the worldwide ecumenical movement, namely nuclear disarmament and opposition to apartheid in South Africa. Many of the Nonconformist churches, as well as key leaders in the Catholic and Anglican communities, gave considerable priority to both of these key issues on the international agenda.

Efforts to secure nuclear disarmament should be seen within the context of a long-standing commitment to peace and reconciliation among Nonconformist as well as other church traditions. There were ambiguities within many of these traditions. Keith Robbins suggests: 'Nonconformity did not as a whole stand out for the belief that war was always wrong.'[17] This may well have been true in England but, generally, though not exclusively, the Welsh-language Nonconformist churches had a stronger pacifist tradition more in tune with, for example, the Religious Society of Friends (the Quakers).

Throughout the post–Second World War decades all the Nonconformist churches were fully engaged in the efforts of national, British and worldwide ecumenical organizations (such as the BCC and the WCC) to build a strong consensus in support of nuclear disarmament. Indeed, here as in other fields, it can be argued that the attempt to speak with one voice against what was conceived to be an evil force (even if some people regarded nuclear deterrence as an important guarantee of peace – or at least a powerful disincentive to go to war – among the nations) was a more important contribution to Christian unity than the explicit engagement with ecclesial questions of unity and union sometimes proved to be.

The same could be said of the churches' common efforts in opposition to apartheid in South Africa. The role of leaders such as Pauline Webb (formerly vice-president of the [British] Methodist Conference and vice-moderator of the WCC Central Committee) in the anti-apartheid struggle was highly significant. Reponses to events such as the banning of the Christian Institute of South Africa, the efforts to ban official visits by sports teams from South Africa in accordance with the Gleneagles agreement (accepted by the British government in 1977), support for South African leaders such as Desmond Tutu and the debates around the Programme to Combat Racism (set up by the WCC in 1969) engaged the Nonconformist churches (sometimes in antagonistic ways) in what was a crucial international concern and fostered among them a sense of worldwide ecumenical partnership in common cause.

II. The Inter-Church Process and New Ecumenical Instruments

In 1984, following the visit by Pope John Paul II in 1982 and the growing partnership with the Roman Catholic Church, the failure of the English Covenant, based on the ten propositions (see endnote 51 in this chapter) to secure support from all the churches, the continuing commitment to the Covenant for Union in Wales, the Multilateral Conversations in Scotland and the growing significance of the Inter-Church Meeting between the Irish Council of Churches and the Roman Catholic Church in Ireland, an inter-church process was inaugurated focused on 'the nature and purpose of the church in the light of its mission in and for the world'. Most of the Nonconformist churches of the United Kingdom and Ireland were participants in this process alongside Anglican, Orthodox and Black-majority and Pentecostal churches, most of which had been members of the BCC and the other national councils. However, the notable factor in this process was the full participation of the Roman Catholic Church in England and Wales and the Roman Catholic Church in Scotland. The Roman Catholic Church in Ireland had observer status within the process.

Catholic involvement was the transforming factor. It placed new questions and challenges before the churches about the nature of the unity they sought to express in their developing ecumenical relationship and the ecumenical witness of the churches in relation to personal, social and public morality. But it also caused some difficulty for some churches and denominations for whom closer partnership with the Catholic Church and a deeper commitment to Christian unity within the proposed new ecumenical instruments raised serious historical and theological questions. However, it was encouraging that the majority of the Nonconformist churches were able to agree to become members of the new ecumenical instruments, following conferences for England, Scotland and Wales and for Great Britain and Ireland as a whole in 1987. It was agreed to set up new ecumenical instruments: Churches Together in England (CTE), Action by Churches Together in Scotland (ACTS) and Cytûn: Churches Together in Wales as well as Churches Together in Britain and Ireland (CTBI). These new bodies came into being in inaugural services held at the beginning of September 1990. The Roman Catholic Church in England and Wales and in Scotland became full member churches of these bodies while the Roman Catholic Church in Ireland has observer status within CTBI. At the heart of these new ecumenical instruments was (and is) a commitment to partnership. They were not to be organizations that acted in ways that all the churches could not necessarily follow. Rather they were to be the point at which the member churches decided and acted together in those areas upon which they had a common mind and in which they shared a common purpose and commitment. The Roman Catholic Church in Ireland also collaborates closely with member churches of the Irish Council of Churches through the Irish Inter-Church Meeting whose remit is 'to survey the whole field of ecumenism, to initiate a general review of relations between the Christian Churches in Ireland and to explore the possibilities of further dialogue on both practical and doctrinal issues'.[18]

III. The Search for Visible Unity: The Denominations

Thompson comments that 'the twentieth century saw the decisive moves [in relation to church unity], even though less was achieved in the end than many had hoped'.[19] This may well be true in relation to the achievement of visible unity as such – although the period under consideration was not without its achievements, as we shall see. Nevertheless, the search for unity, whatever its achievements did have a significant influence on all the participating churches, not least the Nonconformist churches.

a. Unity within Methodism

In 1907, three communities of Methodist churches came together to form the United Methodist Church. The United Methodist Free Church had been formed in 1857 when the Wesleyan Association and the Wesleyan Reformers came together. The Bible Christian Church had been formed in 1815, in Cornwall, but had gradually spread to various parts of England, as well as Canada, the United States, Australia and New Zealand. The Methodist New Connexion (also known as the Kilhamite Methodists, after the founder Alexander Kilham) had been formed in 1797 by secession from the Wesleyan Methodists. This process of unity meant that there were three streams of Methodism in Great Britain from 1907 onwards, the United Methodist Church, the Primitive Methodist Church (originating in 1807) and the Wesleyan Methodist Church (which was the main Methodist Connexion in Great Britain and was in legal continuity with the Methodist societies founded by John Wesley). In 1918, negotiations towards further union began between these churches[20] and led to the formation of the Methodist Church of Great Britain in 1932. Thompson notes that a number of issues such as 'the ratio of ministers and lay in the Conference . . . the Wesleyan demand for continuing ministerial or "pastoral" session . . . and even lay Presidency at Holy Communion . . . were solved quickly'.[21] However, he identifies two doctrinal issues that took longer to resolve, namely the role of scripture and of Wesley's sermons and *Notes on the New Testament*.

The first scheme of union was presented in 1920, but three further versions of the scheme were presented in 1922, 1924 and 1926, the latter of which 'became the basis of the doctrinal clauses of the Deed of Union'. These clauses are illuminative not just in terms of Methodism but also as an approach to the foundational tradition which is often seen as being fundamental to an agreement on union:

> The Doctrines of the Evangelical Faith, which Methodism has held from the beginning and still holds, are based upon Divine revelation recorded in Holy Scriptures . . . These Evangelical Doctrines to which the Preachers of the Methodist Church both Ministers and Laymen are pledged are contained in Wesley's Notes on the New Testament and the first four volumes of his sermons . . . (which) are not intended to impose a system of formal speculative theology . . . but to set up standards of preaching and belief which should secure loyalty to the fundamental truths of the Gospel of Redemption and ensure the continued witness of the Church to the realities of the Christian experience of salvation.[22]

Two other related aspects of the Methodist doctrinal standards as stated in the 1932 Deed of Union are also worthy of note: 'The Methodist Church claims and cherishes its place in the Holy Catholic Church . . . (and) rejoices in the inheritance of the Apostolic Faith and loyally accepts the fundamental principles of the historic creeds and the Protestant Reformation',[23] words that, at the time of writing, are quoted on the current website of the Methodist Church in Great Britain.[24] Here is a significant reminder that, both in terms of their own self-identity and their relationships and growing unity with other Christian families, all the Nonconformist traditions treasure their distinctive and formative history and doctrinal positions but do so in full awareness also of their being within the Apostolic faith confessed by the One, Holy Catholic Church of the historic creeds.

b. United Churches in India

Two unions of churches – both of which involved Nonconformist churches that came into being as a result of the missionary enterprise – had a major influence on the search for union worldwide during the second half of the twentieth century. The Church of South India (CSI) was established in 1947, the year of Indian Independence, at a service of inauguration in St George's Cathedral, Chennai (then known as Madras) in Tamil Nadu. It brought together Anglican, Presbyterian, Congregational, Reformed and Methodist traditions to form a united church that is now the largest church in India after the Roman Catholic Church. The Church of North India (CNI) was established in 1970. As with the CSI this followed a fifty-year process of formation. It brings into unity the Anglican Province, Congregational and Presbyterian Churches (that had already formed a United Church), Baptist churches (having their origins in the British missionary movement), Methodist churches having their origins in the British and Australian Conferences of the Methodist Church and the Disciples of Christ (Churches of Christ) denominations.[25]

For many within the worldwide Anglican Communion, especially those in the Anglo-Catholic tradition, the formation of these two united churches and, most especially, their understanding of the church and its ministry, had already posed a particularly challenging problem. How could churches that had not had the three-fold ministry of bishop, priest and deacon within an apostolic succession now be regarded, without any further act of re-ordination, as having a ministry that could be recognized as being of equal validity as Anglican ministers in the new church? This issue was not, of course, a challenge within India itself. But for the wider church it raised particularly difficult questions with regard to church order.

c. Dialogues towards Union

(i) Dialogues with the Church of England

The issues raised by the process of formation of the CSI were the primary motivation for the suggestion made by archbishop of Canterbury Geoffrey Fisher, in a sermon in Cambridge in 1946 (i.e. the year prior to the inauguration of the CSI) that the non-episcopal churches should 'take episcopacy into their systems' in order to ease the path towards union negotiations involving the Church of England and other Anglican provinces. He believed that such a step would avoid the painful questions that had to be faced during the formation of the CSI. As Thompson comments: 'It is not surprising that Baptists, Congregationalists and Presbyterians, who might perhaps have been prepared to adopt episcopacy in a united church, could see no point in making their existing churches episcopal without further steps towards union.'[26]

However, the Methodist Church of Great Britain did take the invitation seriously. As a result, initial conversations began in 1956 with the aim of bringing a scheme of union before the Methodist Church and the Church of England on the basis of 'one Church renewed for mission and service'.[27] An initial report was published in 1963 and a revised report in 1967. A Service of Reconciliation was proposed which involved acts of commitment, acts of reconciliation of members and acts of integration of ministries.

> A mutual laying on of hands between the bishops of the Church of England and representatives of the Methodist Church, in mutual recognition of the incompleteness of their ministries and the gifts that each brought to the union, was originally envisaged . . . (and) was intended to result in the integration of ministries.

Here was an indication of the willingness of the Methodist Church to take episcopacy into its system within a mutual commitment by the two churches to seek union. However, the initial report of 1967 and the final revised report of 1972, while being approved by the Methodist Conference, were rejected by the Church of England General Synod, the latter by only seven votes in the House of Clergy.[28] Thus, despite Methodist generosity and commitment in this matter (as well as continuing debate about some of the key questions raised for Methodists by the report), ultimately there was disappointment and discouragement at the inflexibility of the Church of England. As Thompson comments, at the heart of the matter was the mutual laying of hands by bishops and senior representatives, which 'attracted the hostility both of those who felt that it implied ordination and of those who felt that it was not made sufficiently clear that it was (ordination)'.[29]

Thirty years after the General Synod's rejection of the proposal for Anglican–Methodist unity in 1972, the Church of England and the Methodist Church agreed, at their Synod and Conference respectively in 2002, a covenant that was subsequently signed in November 2003.[30] The preamble to the covenant recognizes the common ground of faith upon which the two churches stand and acknowledges the failures and errors of the past. The covenant itself commits the churches to seek to 'remove the obstacles to organic unity . . . on the way to the full visible unity of Christ's Church' and looks forward to the day 'when the fuller visible unity of our churches makes possible a united, interchangeable ministry'.

(ii) The Formation of the United Reformed Church

The year of the failure of the Anglican–Methodist scheme was also the year when many years of negotiation and developing friendship and partnership bore fruit in the inauguration of what was then the United Reformed Church in England and Wales (URC). The inaugural service that was held in Westminster Abbey in October 1972 celebrated the bringing into union most of the congregations belonging to the Congregational Church in England and Wales with the Presbyterian Church of England. This was the result of conversations between these churches that had resumed in 1963. The Re-formed Association of Churches of Christ joined with the URC in 1981 and the majority of the congregations of the Congregationalists in Scotland joined in 2000.

The ecumenical journey was at the heart of this newly formed united and uniting church, as a note on ecumenical relations, posted on its website, indicates:

> It has often been said of the URC that it is a church which came into existence in order to die. We are almost unique in that but it reflected the belief, back in 1972, that we were on the way to a wider union of churches which would itself be a step on the route to the long dreamed of goal of the organic unity of the whole of Christ's church . . . The journey has taken other routes and the landscape has changed so that today we speak of 'churches together'. This means that the URC is still here as a distinct denomination but none the less committed to the ecumenical journey and to the belief that God still wills the unity of his Church but that the timescale and the shape of that unity is yet to be perceived.[31]

During the forty years since its formation, the URC has been deeply committed to forging local partnerships in LEPs with a high proportion of its local congregations involved in a variety of forms of committed partnerships. It is a member of the ecumenical instruments in England, Scotland and Wales. It continues its engagement with the Free Church councils as well as the European and worldwide ecumenical bodies.

On 7 February 2012 a joint service for the URC and the Church of England was held at Westminster Abbey to mark the Great Ejectment of 1662 and to enable the churches to make a new commitment to deeper partnership on their ecumenical journey. It was a service that included 'Reconciliation, Healing of Memories and Mutual Commitment [as well as] testimonies about martyrs of the past and stories of shared work in the present, leading to an act of commitment for the future'.[32] It marked the URC's growing engagement with a church whose formation, following the Reformation in England, was the stimulus and cause for the actions and words of the Dissenters which were formative in its foundations and can still provide energy and encouragement for its contemporary ecumenical journey.

d. Towards Visible Union in Wales

So far we have examined union negotiations and agreements involving the Methodist Church of Great Britain, the URC and the Church of England. These have largely focused on England and that is inevitable. But it is worth noting that these conversations have had repercussions also in the other nations of these islands. Any such conversations with the Church of England inevitably raise questions about these churches' relationships with the Anglican Provinces in Ireland, Scotland and Wales, not least since both the Methodist Church of Great Britain and the URC have churches in Scotland and Wales as well as in England and the Methodist Church of Great Britain works in close collaboration with the Methodist Church in Ireland in the whole island of Ireland. These interconnections can be both enriching and challenging for the churches' ecumenical journey. But there have also been wider conversations in the four nations of Great Britain and Ireland aimed at visible union, conversations that have had variable success.

It was in Wales in 1965 that the earliest of such conversations began following the 1964 Nottingham Faith and Order conference.[33] We have already touched on the motion agreed by that conference urging churches to move towards areas of ecumenical experiment (or local ecumenical projects or partnerships as they have later been called). But another significant motion was the main impetus for a consideration of the possibility of a covenant for union. The motion called on the member churches of the BCC, which included nearly all the Nonconformist churches as well as the National (Presbyterian) Church of Scotland and the Anglican Provinces in England, Ireland, Scotland and Wales

> in appropriate groupings such as nations, to covenant together to work and pray for the inauguration of union by a date agreed among them. We dare to hope that this date should be no later than Easter Day 1980.[34]

Norman Goodall, one of the Nonconformist pioneers of the ecumenical movement in the United Kingdom and worldwide, called this resolution 'splendidly irrational but authentic'.[35]

As a response to this call, the Council of Churches for Wales set up a Joint Covenanting Committee and invited all its member churches to consider the possibility of forging and entering into such a covenant. The majority of the Nonconformist churches (the Baptist denominations did not accept the invitation at that time) as well as the Anglican Church in Wales accepted the invitation and in 1966 its report *The Call to Covenant* was published. The churches were invited to respond to this report and in due course a new Joint Covenanting Committee was formed chaired by the then bishop of Bangor (later to become archbishop of Wales), G. O. Williams. In 1968 it published its report, *The Call to Covenant*, and invited the participating churches to respond. Two further reports were published in 1971 which set out the terms of the Covenant and included essays on key issues raised by the Covenant proposals.

By 1974 four churches had accepted the terms of the Covenant and agreed to proceed to covenant with one another, namely the Church in Wales, the Methodist Church of Great Britain, the Presbyterian Church of Wales and the URC in England and Wales. A number of significant Nonconformist denominations in Wales did not accept the covenant. The Union of Welsh Independents had been part of the conversations but the majority of its churches were not in favour of proceeding with the covenant. The Baptist Union of Wales and the Congregational Federation had not been part of the original committee. The majority of the churches in Wales that were affiliated to the Baptist Union of Great Britain and Ireland rejected the proposals but a small group of twelve churches in the South Wales Area voted in favour of the covenant and entered individually into covenant with the other churches.

In due course, the Commission of the Covenant Churches was established to further the Covenant and to bring before the churches proposals for ways forward towards visible unity in Wales. A number of reports, such as *The Principles of Visible Unity in Wales* (1979) and *Ministry in a Uniting Church* (1986), were published by the Commission. These set out some of the key theological, ecclesiological and liturgical issues raised for the churches by the covenant. Debates on some of these issues have continued during ensuing years. Can Episcopal, Presbyterian and Congregational understandings of the church and the consequent patterns of authority and decision-making be reconciled with one another in a united church? Is it possible to find ways of reconciling the ordained ministries of the churches within a united church in such a way as to bring into unity the Nonconformist understanding of ministry and the Anglican tradition of a three-fold ministry in apostolic succession? Can all the churches recognize that women as well as men are not only called to ministry but can be recognized and accepted by all the churches for all orders of their ordained ministry? Can all members in good standing of all the churches be accepted by all the churches as true members in full sacramental communion within the united church?

The reality, more than three decades after the original covenant, was that agreement on these and other questions has not been reached and no specific steps towards visible union as such in Wales have been taken by the Covenanted Churches. This has been as much the result of the Nonconformist churches' desire to be faithful to what they see as the scriptural understanding of these issues as it has been the consequence of the Church in Wales' commitment to be faithful to its inherited Catholic and Reformed traditions. However, a Trefecca Declaration of 2005 re-committed the covenanted churches to the covenant by reaffirming their commitment to the goal of visible unity by 'a fuller sharing of . . . ministries . . . undertaking new work jointly . . . pooling resources (for) witness . . . (and) listening to what the nation is saying to the Church'.[36]

In preparation for the Covenant Sunday celebrations in June 2011, the final year of the period to which the Trefecca Declaration relates, the following paragraph highlighted key aspects of the Commission's work and the churches' working out of the Covenant for Union:

> (The) agenda is broad and exciting and includes work in areas such as seeking common ground among the churches on matters of Church Governance and Pastoral Oversight, identifying areas where a Local Ecumenical Partnership might be established and holding local conversations to facilitate this, identifying specific communities, such as new housing developments, which could act as experimental models for ecumenical ministerial deployment, revising the Commission of Covenanted Churches' Baptism and Eucharistic rites, and working locally with other denominations who are members of Cytûn.

Laudable as these commitments may be – and there is no doubt that they remain fundamental to the churches' covenant – it has to be said that these are a very long way from the original vision of the pioneers of the covenant for *visible unity* in Wales almost half a century ago. It remains to be seen, in what the URC has called 'a changed (ecumenical) landscape' (see earlier), in Wales as much as elsewhere, whether the original goals of the covenant are still achievable or whether the goal of visible unity will have to be transformed into what many, at least, will see as a more inadequate vision of ecumenical partnership within a churches together model.

Two other attempts at forging a united church in Wales deserve a mention here. The *Tuag at Uno* (Towards Unity) report was presented to the Welsh-language Nonconformist churches in Wales in the late 1960s but despite considerable debate did not receive adequate support among the churches. Around the year of the millennium, *Y Ffordd Ymlaen* (The Way Forward) was presented to the Nonconformist churches in Wales. But these proposals too were rejected partly because of the failure to agree on how Presbyterian and Congregational understandings of the church could be reconciled but partly because some of the churches did not want to endanger through a 'narrower' union their commitment to the broader vision of the covenant for union in Wales.[37]

e. Summary

To sum up, the Nonconformist churches' involvement with the search for visible union, especially during the decades since the Nottingham Faith and Order Conference in 1964, has, in some ways, been frustrating. This has been largely because both Nonconformist and Anglican traditions have struggled with finding common ground that would enable them to be faithful to their traditions (not least in relation to ordained ministry) as well as to discover sufficient common ground in fundamental areas of faith and, more especially, of order to enable them to recognize each other's ministry and thus develop deeper partnerships and fuller visible unity. Yet the challenge of visible unity (fulfilled in the United Kingdom only by the formation of the URC in 1972) has nevertheless enabled both Nonconformists and Anglicans to reach agreement on essential theological issues and develop collaborative ways of working locally, regionally and nationally so that deeper partnerships in mission and service have been possible. What appears from one perspective to have been a failure of nerve (and sometimes of imagination) has been mutually enriching for all the churches involved. They would not be the churches they are today had they not faced the opportunities and challenges that their search for unity presented for them. And the door is not yet closed. In England and Ireland, in Scotland and Wales the commitment to visible unity is still present as some of the Nonconformist denominations continue to engage with their partners in this painful but enriching search. While this commitment continues we cannot know how the Holy Spirit will use the churches to fulfil what they believe to be the will and purpose of God.[38]

III. Conclusions

This study has shown that the Nonconformist churches in these nations have been deeply committed to the ecumenical journey during the period under consideration and have constantly sought ways to foster collaboration, partnership and deeper unity, locally, nationally and internationally through conciliar and collaborative instruments and, more recently, through the churches together relationships. Many of these churches, but clearly not all, have also seen the search for visible unity not only with other Nonconformist churches but also with churches of the Anglican Communion and, at a different level of understanding, with the Roman Catholic Church, as a fundamental commitment for their church.

However, within this search for visible unity, reaching agreement on issues of common faith has been more easily achieved than finding agreement on the more challenging issues of order such as church polity and ordained ministry. There is also a question about whether the new churches together models for ecumenical partnership and collaboration have served to strengthen or to weaken the churches' ecumenical resolve and commitment for the future.

At the beginning of the twenty-first century, the numerical decline of many of these churches and denominations, the shift (not least among young people) from the traditional Nonconformist churches to the more recently formed Evangelical, Charismatic and Pentecostal churches as well as the shift in the centre of gravity of global Christianity and the increasingly multicultural and multifaith nature of our communities, all began to shape a new landscape but have also challenged the churches with critical questions of survival in their present form.

There is, therefore, a need to choose between inward looking entrenchment and risk-taking ecumenical engagement, between holding on to our own threatened self-identity and tradition and risking 'our' tradition as we explore ways in which our diverse traditions may be brought into a richer whole. Many of these churches were born in Dissent. In one sense, we are all, of whatever tradition, 'dissenters' now. Now more than ever we need one another to articulate Christian dissent to the cultural and intellectual norms of our contemporary societies. In order to be effective, such dissent requires a deeper ecumenical engagement.

The signs are that the Nonconformist churches, as well as the other churches, no longer have the energy or the commitment for the search for visible unity in the ways, and using the models, that previous generations have forged. This failure of nerve may yet prove to be to the impoverishment of our church life and worship as well as (more significantly) of our shared witness and service in and for these nations.

Perhaps, then, we need a new vision of unity. Mary Tanner suggests:

> It is more constructive not to opt for any controlling model of visible unity and instead to go on exploring a portrait of what life in unity may be like. A convincing portrait should challenge churches to renew their own lives now in the light of that portrait, as well as challenge churches in different places, in different partnerships, to move together towards that portrait for the sake of a more effective mission and more authentic

> worship of the God whose gift is unity . . . (in a way that takes) more account of the multifaith, multicultural world in which the Church is called to live out its vocation.[39]

So Nonconformist churches (and, indeed, all the churches) may need not so much ecumenical architects that can construct structures that can incorporate our denominational diversities but ecumenical artists that can draw on our richly diverse Christian kaleidoscope of faith and worship, ministry and witness, to portray with greater and more creative imagination than we have so far managed what 'the one holy, catholic and apostolic church' may look like in our challenging and enriching contemporary context.

Notes

1 See I. Randall and D. Hilborn, *One Body in Christ* (Carlisle: Paternoster Press, 2001) and a web-based summary of this official history at www.eauk.org/about/loader.cfm?csModule=security/getfile&pageid=9566, accessed 6 January 2010.
2 R. Tudur Jones, in his Foreword to N. A. Davies, *A History of Ecumenism in Wales* (Cardiff: University of Wales Press, 2008), p. xiii.
3 Ibid.
4 J. H. Shakespeare, *The Churches at the Cross-Roads* (London: Williams & Norgate, 1918), taken from an extract in D. M. Thompson et al. (eds), *Protestant Nonconformist Texts, Volume IV: The Twentieth Century* (Aldershot: Ashgate, 2007), p. 345.
5 Ibid.
6 Ibid., p. 346.
7 Ibid., p. 337.
8 For the full text of the Statement, see ibid., pp. 361–64.
9 See W. A. Visser 'T Hooft (ed.), *The First Assembly of the World Council of Churches: The Official Report* (London: SCM, 1949), pp. 236ff for a full list of founding churches and their representatives.
10 C. Davey, The History of the BCC, at www.ctbi.org.uk/pdf_view.php?id=100, accessed 10 January 2012.
11 For a comprehensive history of the Council of Churches for Wales, see Davies, *A History of Ecumenism in Wales, 1956–1990*.
12 *Unity Begins at Home: A Report of the British Faith and Order Conference* (London: British Council of Churches, 1964), p. 79.
13 D. Hawtin and R. Paul, *The Origin and Development of Local Ecumenical Partnerships (LEPs): Telling the Story* (London: The Council for Christian Unity, 2011), p. 17 at www.churchofengland.org/media/1344960/telling%20the%20story%2018%20 11%202011.pdf, accessed 24 February 2012.
14 For a review of 'The churches and self-government in Wales' and the wider debate within the BCC, see Davies, *History of Ecumenism in Wales, 1956–1990*, p. 83.
15 Quoted in Paul H. Ballard and D. Huw Jones (eds), *This Land and People* (Cardiff: Collegiate Centre of Theology, 1979), p. 51.
16 British Council of Churches, *Devolution and the British Churches* (London: BCC, 1977), p. 38, quoted in Davies, *History of Ecumenism in Wales, 1956–1990*, p. 90.

17 Alan P. F. Sell and A. R. Cross (eds), *Protestant Nonconformity in the Twentieth Century* (Carlisle: Paternoster Press, 2003), pp. 221–22; quoted in Thompson et al. (eds), *Nonconformist Texts, Volume IV*, p. 267.
18 See www.irishchurches.org/about/iicm, accessed 3 February 2012.
19 Thompson et al. (eds), *Nonconformist Texts, Volume IV*, p. 337.
20 For an account of these negotiations see R. E. Davies, *A History of the Methodist Church in Great Britain* (London: Epworth Press, 1983), III; K. Kent, *The Age of Disunity* (London: Epworth Press, 1966); J. Munsey Turner, *Conflict and Reconciliation: Studies in Methodism and Ecumenism in England 1740–1982* (London: Epworth, 1985). These are all cited in Thompson et al. (eds), *Nonconformist Texts*, p. 344.
21 Thompson et al. (eds), *Nonconformist Texts*, p. 338.
22 Ibid., p. 355.
23 Ibid., p. 354.
24 www.methodist.org.uk/index.cfm?fuseaction=opentogod.content&cmid=1360, accessed 14 February 2012.
25 For more information on the significance of the United Churches in the Indian subcontinent see, e.g., K. C. Abraham and T. K. Thomas, in Briggs et al. (eds), *A History of the Ecumenical Movement, Volume 3: 1968–2000* (Geneva: WCC Publications, 2004), p. 503.
26 Thompson et al. (eds), *Nonconformist Texts, Volume IV*, p. 340.
27 D. Hawtin and R. Paul, *The Origin and Development of Local Ecumenical Partnerships (LEPs): Telling the Story*, p. 3.
28 Voting in the General Synod requires either a simple majority or a two-thirds majority (depending on the topic under consideration) in each of the Houses of Bishops, Clergy and Laity for any proposal to be carried by the Synod.
29 Thompson et al. (eds), *Nonconformist Texts, Volume IV*, p. 340.
30 For the full text of the covenant see www.anglican-methodist.org.uk/text.htm, accessed 24 February 2012.
31 See www.urc.org.uk/mission/ecumenical-relations.html, accessed 24 February 2012.
32 See www.urc.org.uk/news/500-rowan-williams-to-preach-at-reconciliation-service.html, accessed 24 Feburary 2012.
33 For a fuller account of the beginnings of these conversations see Davies, *History of Ecumenism in Wales, 1956–1990*, pp. 21ff and for a historical evaluation of the Nottingham Faith and Order Conference, see A. Hastings, *A History of English Christianity, 1920–1985* (London: Collins, 1987), pp. 87f.
34 *Unity Begins at Home*, p. 43.
35 Ibid., p. 45.
36 For further information about the Commission of Covenanted Churches and the text of the Welsh Covenant, see www.cytun.org.uk/covenantedchurches.html, accessed 28 February 2012, from which the text of the Trefecca Declaration has been taken.
37 For an account of developments towards unity in Ireland and an evaluation of the current situation, see *Methodist Anglican Dialogue* (October 2007) author not named, at www.irishchurches.org/files/MethodistAnglicanDialogue.pdf, accessed 29 February 2012; and *The Covenant Council: History* (2012) at www.covenantcouncil.org/history.htm, accessed 29 February 2012.
38 Space does not permit a detailed review of the Ten Propositions towards a Covenant in England (1980) nor of the Multilateral Conversations in Scotland and its successor The Scottish Church Initiative for Union (SCIFU). For a brief evaluation of the former and some of the key documents, see Thompson et al. (eds), *Nonconformist Texts, Volume IV*, pp. 343, 386–97. For the latter, see *Multilateral Church Conversation*

in Scotland (Interim Report), (Edinburgh: St Andrew Press, 1972) and the Methodist website at www.methodist.org.uk/index.cfm?fuseaction=opentogod.content&cmid=359.

39 M. Tanner, 'The Goal of Visible Unity – Yet Again', in J. Morris and N. Sagovsky (eds), *The Unity We Have the Unity We Seek: Ecumenical Prospects for the Third Millennium* (London: T&T Clark, 2003), pp. 187–88.

23 Sources for Protestant Nonconformity in England and Wales since 1662: A Structured Bibliography

Clive D. Field

This chapter provides an introduction to the sources for Protestant Nonconformity in England and Wales. It takes the form of a structured bibliography, with some interlinking notes. Given space constraints, a number of exclusions have been implemented. The focus is on the period since 1662, rather than on the movement's antecedents in the late sixteenth and early seventeenth centuries. Primary and tertiary (reference tools and the like) literature is emphasized, with little treatment of secondary works, including the standard histories of Nonconformity and its constituent denominations. No attempt has been made to cover the overseas mission field. Huguenots and other foreign Protestants are omitted. URLs, where cited (generally only when they lead to a free web resource), were current on 23 January 2012.

I. Generalia

This section sets out some of the basic reference tools available to support research into Nonconformist history. These are fairly uneven in their denominational coverage (Methodism perhaps being best served), and many are obviously quite dated, requiring to be used with circumspection. Only the Methodists and Presbyterian Church of Wales are the subjects of regular historical bibliographies. Nonconformist periodicals and newspapers are a crucial resource, but indexing and even basic listing of them remain inadequate. Titles which have been digitized are most accessible (theoretically, since subscriptions or pay-per-view models are usually in operation), such as those made available as part of Proquest's *British Periodicals* collection. There are also some denomination-specific initiatives, including *Wesleyan and Primitive*

Methodist Periodicals from Microform Academic Publishers. Secondary articles in modern periodicals are best identified through *Bibliography of British and Irish History*, *ATLA Religion Database*, *Index Theologicus* or *Religious and Theological Abstracts*, although only the third of these is free. Of particular interest are the journals of the various denominational historical societies, which are generally better indexed, and which contain transcriptions of unpublished sources, as well as secondary research, notes and queries and book reviews. Most of the encyclopaedias come from the Scarecrow Press historical dictionaries series, which has an international focus. Of the various selections of primary documents, the four-volume *Protestant Nonconformist Texts*, under the overall editorship of Alan Sell, provide a good entry-point to the printed primary evidence (few archives and manuscripts are tapped in this work), with relevant secondary commentary.

a. Bibliographies: General and Old Dissent

Caulfield, Anna Breiner, *Quakers in Fiction: An Annotated Bibliography* (Northampton, MA: Pittenbruach Press, 1993).

[Crippen, Thomas George], 'Bibliography of Congregational Church History', *Transactions of the Congregational Historical Society*, 2 (1905–6), pp. 119–35, 337–38.

Crippen, Thomas George, 'Early Nonconformist Bibliography', *Transactions of the Congregational Historical Society*, 1 (1901–4), pp. 44–57, 99–112, 171–84, 252–65, 410–20; 2 (1905–6), pp. 61–71, 219–29, 432–44.

Dexter, Henry Martyn, *The Congregationalism of the Last Three Hundred Years, as Seen in Its Literature* (London: Hodder and Stoughton, [1880]).

English Dissenters [to 1660], www.exlibris.org/nonconform/engdis/index.html.

Evans, Humphrey Turner, *A Bibliography of Welsh Hymnology to 1960* ([Caernarfon]: Welsh Library Association, 1977).

Foxton, Rosemary, *Hear the Word of the Lord: A Critical and Bibliographical Study of Quaker Women's Writing, 1650–1700* (Melbourne: Bibliographical Society of Australia and New Zealand, 1994).

Gill, Athol, *A Bibliography of Baptist Writings on Baptism, 1900–1968* (Rüschlikon-Zürich: Baptist Theological Seminary, 1969).

Hall, David J., 'The Earlier Bibliographers of Quakerism', in Robin Myers and Michael Harris (eds), *Pioneers in Bibliography* (Winchester: St Paul's Bibliographies, 1988), pp. 58–72.

Hill, Andrew McKean, *Bibliography of Unitarian History*, www.unitarianhistory.org.uk/hsbib.html.

McIntyre, Willard Ezra, *Baptist Authors: A Manual of Bibliography, 1500–1914* (Montreal: Industrial and Educational Press, [1914]), 3 parts [A-Day].

Nuttall, Geoffrey Fillingham (ed.), *The Beginnings of Nonconformity, 1660–65: A Checklist* (London: Dr Williams's Library, 1960).

Smith, Joseph, *Bibliotheca Anti-Quakeriana* (London: Joseph Smith, 1873).

—, *Bibliotheca Quakeristica* (London: Joseph Smith, 1883).

—, *A Descriptive Catalogue of Friends' Books*, 2 vols (London: Joseph Smith, 1867); supplement (1893).

Starr, Edward Caryl, *A Baptist Bibliography, Being a Register of Printed Material by and about Baptists, including Works Written against the Baptists* (Philadelphia, PA: Judson Press, 1947–76), 25 vols and www.baptistheritage.com/resources/starr.htm.

Thomas, John A., 'Nonconformist Architecture in Britain: A Bibliography', *University of Birmingham Institute for the Study of Worship and Religious Architecture Research Bulletin*, 11 (1976), pp. 74–80.

Thorne, Roger Frank Sidney, *Chapels!! Their Architecture and Distribution: A Preliminary Bibliography* (Ottery St Mary: The Author, 1994).

Whitley, William Thomas, *A Baptist Bibliography*, 2 vols (London: Kingsgate Press, 1916–22).

b. Bibliographies: Methodism

Beckerlegge, Oliver Aveyard, *A Bibliography of the Bible Christians* (Westcliff-on-Sea: Gage Postal Books, 1988).

—, *A Bibliography of the United Methodist Church* (Westcliff-on-Sea: Gage Postal Books, 1988).

—, *A Bibliography of the United Methodist Free Churches* (Westcliff-on-Sea: Gage Postal Books, 1988).

—, *A Bibliography of the Wesleyan Methodist Association and other Branches* (Westcliff-on-Sea: Gage Postal Books, 1988).

Beckerlegge, Oliver Aveyard and Rose, Edward Alan, *A Bibliography of the Methodist New Connexion* (Westcliff-on-Sea: Gage Postal Books, 1988).

Decanver, H. C. [*pseud.* for Curtis H. Cavender], *Catalogue of Works in Refutation of Methodism, from Its Origin in 1729 to the Present Time* (Philadelphia, PA: John Penington, 1846; 2nd edn, New York: [no publisher], 1868).

Field, Clive Douglas, 'Anti-Methodist Publications of the Eighteenth Century: A Revised Bibliography', *Bulletin of the John Rylands University Library of Manchester*, 73/2 (1991), pp. 159–280.

—, 'Bibliography', in Rupert Eric Davies, Alfred Raymond George and Ernest Gordon Rupp (eds), *A History of the Methodist Church in Great Britain, Volume IV* (London: Epworth Press, 1988), pp. 651–830.

—, 'Bibliography of Methodist Historical Literature' [1974 to date], *Proceedings of the Wesley Historical Society*, 40 (1975–76), pp. 145–49 and annually to date.

—, *The People Called Methodists: A Documentary History of the Methodist Church in Great Britain and Ireland on Microfiche – Instalments 1–11* (Leiden: IDC Publishers, 1998).

—, 'Preparing for the Wesley 250th: British Methodist Studies, 1980–88', *Epworth Review*, 15/2 (1988), pp. 95–109.

Gage, Laurie E., *English Methodism: A Bibliographical View* (Westcliff-on-Sea: Gage Postal Books, 1985).

Green, Richard, *Anti-Methodist Publications Issued during the Eighteenth Century: A Chronologically Arranged and Annotated Bibliography* (London: C. H. Kelly, 1902).

Hatcher, Stephen George, *A Primitive Methodist Bibliography* ([Leigh-on-Sea]: Laurie Gage Books, 1980).

Osborn, George, *Outlines of Wesleyan Bibliography* (London: Wesleyan Conference Office, 1869).

Rack, Henry Denman, 'Recent Books on Methodism', *Epworth Review*, 7/1 (1980), pp. 82–88.

Rowe, Kenneth Elmer (ed.), *Methodist Union Catalog, Pre-1976 Imprints*, 7 vols (A-Le) (Metuchen, NJ: Scarecrow Press, 1975–94).

Thornborow, Philip, 'Online Sources for Methodist Historians', *Heritage: Journal of the East Midlands Branch of the Wesley Historical Society*, 10/2 (2009), pp. 26–30 and *Methodist Recorder*, 7936 (28 January 2010), p. 13.

Thorne, Roger Frank Sidney, *The Bible Christians, 1815–1907: A Catalogue of the Collection of Roger F. S. Thorne* (2nd imp., Ottery St Mary: The Author, 1989).

Turner, John Munsey, 'Wesley and Early Methodism Studies, 1993–2003', *Epworth Review*, 30/4 (2003), pp. 65–72.

Warrick, Susan Eltscher, 'Bibliography', in Charles Yrigoyen (ed.), *T & T Clark Companion to Methodism* (London: T&T Clark, 2010), pp. 515–32.

c. Bibliographies: Other Denominations

Allen, James B., Walker, Ronald Warren and Whittaker, David J., *Studies in Mormon History, 1830–1997: An Indexed Bibliography* (Urbana, IL: University of Illinois Press, 2000).

Brady, David, 'The Brethren: A Bibliography of Secondary Sources', *Brethren Archivists and Historians Network Review*, 2/2 (2003), pp. 104–9.

Brady, David and Johnson, Graham, *The Brethren: A Bibliography of Secondary Studies*, www.library.manchester.ac.uk/searchresources/guidetospecialcollections/brethren/printed/bibliography/.

Copinger, Harold Bernard, *Catholic Apostolic Church: A Bibliography* ([no place: no publisher, ?1955]).

Crawley, Peter and Whittaker, David J., *Mormon Imprints in Great Britain and the Empire, 1836–1857: An Exhibition, Friends of the Brigham Young University Library Newsletter*, 30 (Provo, UT: The Friends, 1987).

Dennis, Ronald D., *Welsh Mormon Writings from 1844 to 1862: A Historical Bibliography* (Provo, UT: Religious Studies Center, Brigham Young University, 1988).

Ehlert, Arnold D., *Brethren Writers: A Checklist* (Grand Rapids, MI: Baker Book House, [1969]).

Flake, Chad J. (ed.), *A Mormon Bibliography, 1830–1930* (Salt Lake City, UT: University of Utah Press, 1978; with supplement, 1989; and indexes, 1992).

Madden, John Lionel, 'Cyhoeddiadau diweddar/Recent Publications, 2003–04' [on the history of the Presbyterian Church of Wales], *Cylchgrawn Hanes*, 28 (2004), pp. 92–96 and annually to date.

Moyles, Robert Gordon, *A Bibliography of Salvation Army Literature in English (1865–1987)* (Lewiston, NY: Edwin Mellen Press, 1988).

Whittaker, David J., 'Mormonism in Victorian Britain: A Bibliographic Essay', in Richard L. Jensen and Malcolm Ray Thorp (eds), *Mormons in Early Victorian Britain* (Salt Lake City, UT: University of Utah Press, 1989), pp. 258–71.

d. Guides to Periodicals

Altholz, Josef Lewis, *The Religious Press in Britain, 1760–1900* (New York: Greenwood Press, 1989), pp. 57–96.

ATLA Religion Database, http://admin.atla.com/products/catalog/Pages/rdb-db.aspx.

Bibliography of British and Irish History, www.brepolis.net/.
Billington, Louis, 'The Religious Periodical and Newspaper Press, 1770–1870', in Michael Harris and Alan J. Lee (eds), *The Press in English Society from the Seventeenth to Nineteenth Centuries* (Rutherford, NJ: Fairleigh Dickinson University Press, 1986), pp. 113–32, 231–39.
British Periodicals, www.proquest.com/en-US/catalogs/databases/detail/british_periodicals.shtml.
Index Theologicus, www.ixtheo.de/.
Religious and Theological Abstracts, http://rtabstracts.org/.
Rogal, Samuel J., 'A Survey of Methodist Periodicals Published in England, 1778–1900', *Victorian Periodicals Review*, 14 (1981), pp. 66–69.
Rose, Edward Alan, *A Checklist of British Methodist Periodicals* (Bognor Regis: W.M.H.S. Publications, 1981).
Taylor, Rosemary, 'English Baptist Periodicals, 1790–1865', *Baptist Quarterly*, 27 (1977–78), pp. 50–82.
Wesleyan and Primitive Methodist Periodicals, www.britishonlinearchives.co.uk/.

e. Denominational Historical Society and Equivalent Journals

Annual Journal of the New Church Historical Society, 2000 to date.
Baptist Quarterly, 1922 to date [preceded by *Transactions of the Baptist Historical Society*], full text available online at www.biblicalstudies.org.uk/articles_bq_01.php.
Bathafarn: Cylchgrawn Hanes yr Eglwys Fethodistaidd yng Nghymru [Historical Society of the Methodist Church in Wales], 1946–2003, full text available online at http://welshjournals.llgc.org.uk/browse/listissues/llgc-id:1050541.
Y Cofiadur: sef Cylchgrawn Cymdeithas Hanes Annibynwyr Cymru [Welsh Independents' Historical Society], 1923 to date, full text available online at http://welshjournals.llgc.org.uk/browse/listissues/llgc-id:1085539.
Congregational History Circle (Society) Magazine, 1979 to date.
Cylchgrawn Cymdeithas Hanes y Methodistiaid Calfinaidd [Historical Society of the Presbyterian Church of Wales], 1916–76 [continued by *Cylchgrawn Hanes: Cymdeithas Hanes y Methodistiaid Calfinaidd*].
Cylchgrawn Hanes: Cymdeithas Hanes y Methodistiaid Calfinaidd [Historical Society of the Presbyterian Church of Wales], 1977 to date [preceded by *Cylchgrawn Cymdeithas Hanes y Methodistiaid Calfinaidd*].
Journal of the Friends' Historical Society, 1903 to date.
Journal of the Presbyterian Historical Society of England, 1914–72.
Journal of the United Reformed Church History Society, 1973 to date.
Proceedings of the Charles Wesley Society, 1994 to date.
Proceedings of the Wesley Historical Society, 1897 to date, full text available online at www.biblicalstudies.org.uk/articles_whs_01.php.
Quaker Studies, 1996 to date.
Strict Baptist Historical Society Bulletin, 1961 to date.
Trafodion Cymdeithas Hanes Bedyddwyr Cymru [Welsh Baptist Historical Society], 1906–89 [continued by *Trafodion Cymdeithas Hanes y Bedyddwyr*].
Trafodion Cymdeithas Hanes y Bedyddwyr [Welsh Baptist Historical Society], 1990 to date [preceded by *Trafodion Cymdeithas Hanes Bedyddwyr Cymru*].
Transactions of the Baptist Historical Society, 1908–21 [continued by *Baptist Quarterly*], full text available online at www.biblicalstudies.org.uk/articles_tbhs_01.php.

Transactions of the Congregational Historical Society, 1901–72.
Transactions of the Unitarian Historical Society, 1916 to date.
Wesley and Methodist Studies, 2009 to date.

f. Encyclopaedias

Abbott, Margery Post, Chijioke, Mary Ellen, Dandelion, Ben Pink and Oliver, John William, *Historical Dictionary of the Friends (Quakers)* (Lanham, MD: Scarecrow Press, 2003).

Abraham, William James and Kirby, James Edmund (eds), *The Oxford Handbook of Methodist Studies* (Oxford: Oxford University Press, 2009).

Benedetto, Robert and McKim, Donald Keith, *Historical Dictionary of the Reformed Churches* (2nd edn, Lanham, MD: Scarecrow Press, 2010).

Bitton, Davis and Alexander, Thomas G., *Historical Dictionary of Mormonism* (3rd edn, Lanham, MD: Scarecrow Press, 2008).

Brackney, William Henry, *Historical Dictionary of the Baptists* (Lanham, MD: Scarecrow Press, 1999).

BrethrenPedia: An Encyclopedia of 'Plymouth' Brethren History, www.brethrenpedia.com/Main_Page.

Briggs, John Henry York (ed.), *A Dictionary of European Baptist Life and Thought* (Milton Keynes: Paternoster, 2009).

Cathcart, William (ed.), *The Baptist Encyclopedia*, 2 vols (Philadelphia, PA: L. H. Everts, 1881).

Chryssides, George D., *The A to Z of Jehovah's Witnesses* (Lanham, MD: Scarecrow Press, 2009).

Edwards, Eric, *Yr Eglwys Fethodistaidd* (Llandysul: Gwasg Gomer, 1980; supplement, 1987).

Gibson, William, Forsaith, Peter Stuart and Wellings, Martin (eds), *The Ashgate Research Companion to World Methodism* (Farnham: Ashgate, 2013).

Harmon, Nolan Bailey (ed.), *The Encyclopedia of World Methodism*, 2 vols (Nashville, TN: United Methodist Publishing House, 1974).

Land, Gary, *Historical Dictionary of Seventh-Day Adventists* (Lanham, MD: Scarecrow Press, 2005).

Merritt, John G. (ed.), *Historical Dictionary of the Salvation Army* (Lanham, MD: Scarecrow Press, 2006).

Vickers, John Ashley (ed.), *A Dictionary of Methodism in Britain and Ireland* (Peterborough: Epworth Press, 2000).

—, *Dictionary of Methodism in Britain and Ireland*, [expanded edition], http://wesleyhistoricalsociety.org.uk/dmbi/.

Yrigoyen, Charles (ed.), *T & T Clark Companion to Methodism* (London: T&T Clark, 2010).

Yrigoyen, Charles and Warrick, Susan Eltscher (eds), *The A to Z of Methodism* (Lanham, MD: Scarecrow Press, 2009).

g. Collections of Primary Documents

Bebbington, David William, with Dix, Kenneth and Ruston, Alan Robert (eds), *Protestant Nonconformist Texts, Volume 3: The Nineteenth Century* (Aldershot: Ashgate, 2006).

Briggs, John Henry York and Sellers, Ian (eds), *Victorian Nonconformity* (London: Edward Arnold, 1973).
Cameron, Richard Morgan (ed.), *The Rise of Methodism: A Source Book* (New York: Philosophical Library, 1954).
Carile, Sergio (ed.), *I metodisti nell' Inghilterra della rivoluzione industriale (sec. XVIII–XIX)* (Torino: Claudiana Editrice, 1989).
Hamm, Thomas D. (ed.), *Quaker Writings: An Anthology, 1650–1920* (London: Penguin Books, 2010).
Jones, Robert Tudur, with Long, Arthur and Moore, Rosemary (eds), *Protestant Nonconformist Texts, Volume 1: 1550–1700* (Aldershot: Ashgate, 2007).
Sell, Alan Philip Frederick, with Hall, David J. and Sellers, Ian (eds), *Protestant Nonconformist Texts, Volume 2: The Eighteenth Century* (Aldershot: Ashgate, 2006).
Thompson, David Michael (ed.), *Nonconformity in the Nineteenth Century* (London: Routledge & Kegan Paul, 1972).
Thompson, David Michael, with Briggs, John Henry York and Turner, John Munsey (eds), *Protestant Nonconformist Texts, Volume 4: The Twentieth Century* (Aldershot: Ashgate, 2007).
Vickers, John Ashley, 'Documents and Source Material', in Rupert Eric Davies, Alfred Raymond George and Ernest Gordon Rupp (eds), *A History of the Methodist Church in Great Britain, Volume IV* (London: Epworth Press, 1988), pp. 1–649.
Whelan, Timothy (ed.), *Nonconfirmist Women Writers*, 1720–1840, 8 vols (London: Pickering & Chatto, 2011).

II. Libraries and Archives

Although there is some concentration of the sources of Protestant Nonconformity (notably in Dr Williams's Library, the John Rylands University Library, Manchester, and the National Library of Wales), much of the material is widely dispersed, in this country and overseas. For books and pamphlets online library catalogues are usually a good starting-point, especially the two principal union catalogues: *COPAC* (which covers selected UK libraries) and *WorldCat* (which is international in scope). Serials are additionally recorded in *Suncat*. For pre-1801 publications, the *English Short Title Catalogue* is an essential guide, with researchers whose institutions subscribe to *EEBO* and *ECCO* having access to the full-text versions of many of the works. Digital copies of numerous other out-of-copyright primary and secondary books and pamphlets are also freely available on the internet and may be traced via search engines. They have either been digitized as part of mass programmes run by Google, Microsoft and other major players or are the outcome of niche initiatives, such as those run by various Baptist websites. It should be remembered, however, that many legacy collections in libraries often lie uncatalogued or are recorded only in card and other non-electronic catalogues. The ABTAPL directory provides some indication of the collecting strengths of British theological libraries. The *National*

Register of Archives performs a similar service for religious archives, now often enhanced by links to full-text handlists, while there are several specialist online archive portals, including *Mundus*, which covers missionary collections, and *Archives Wales*. A recent general overview of archives of Free Church interest has been provided by Clive D. Field.[1]

Dr Williams's Library in London opened in 1729 and is the premier library for the study of Old Dissent. It is essentially a private institution, run by a trust. Its foundation collections comprised the personal libraries of the Presbyterian ministers Daniel Williams (after whom the Library is named) and William Bates (bought by Williams in 1699). However, much other material has been added over the years, by donation, purchase and transfer, including the libraries of many Dissenting academies. Denominationally, the Library's greatest strengths lie in Presbyterianism/Unitarianism (augmented by the Unitarian archives from Essex Hall, incrementally deposited from 1987) and Congregationalism. The latter holdings were immeasurably strengthened by the acquisition of New College Library in 1977 and the co-location with Dr Williams's Library of the Congregational Library (formed in 1831) in 1982, although it remains the property of the Congregational Memorial Hall Trust (1978) Ltd. This should not be confused with the small Congregational History Society Library stored at Bunyan Meeting, Bedford. A current initiative of the Friends of the Congregational Library is to encourage retired or retiring United Reformed or Congregational ministers to donate their personal papers. There are also records of several national interdenominational Nonconformist organizations at Dr Williams's Library; others will be found at the Guildhall Library in London and the London Metropolitan Archives.

The John Rylands University Library, Manchester, is steeped in Nonconformist tradition. It came into being in 1972 as a result of the merger between the library of Manchester University (founded in 1851) and the John Rylands Library (opened in 1900). The former developed from Owens College which was established under the endowment of John Owens, a Manchester merchant and Congregationalist, who was passionately committed to the ideals of religious equality. The College library owed its origins to the gift, in 1851 and 1860, of 1,200 volumes from James Heywood, a Dissenting MP who waged a successful campaign in Parliament in the mid-1850s to secure the removal of religious tests at Oxford and Cambridge Universities. The John Rylands Library was erected in memory of another Congregationalist John Rylands, by his third wife Enriqueta Augustina Rylands. In planning the library she was guided by a quartet of north-western Nonconformists, and to dedicate it she chose, not royalty but, Andrew Fairbairn, principal of Mansfield College, Oxford. Both libraries steadily acquired Nonconformist holdings from their earliest days, but it was only during the librarianship of Frederick Ratcliffe (1968–80) that large-scale accessions in this field were made, by donation, permanent loan and purchase. These included the national archives of the Methodist Church (formally inaugurated in 1961 and transferred to Manchester in 1977) and of the Christian Brethren (created *ex nihilo* in 1979, but incorporating earlier collections formed by the editorial office of Echoes of Service in Bath, the Bristol Library for Biblical Research and by George Cecil Douglas Howley). The historic libraries and archives of the local Baptist, Independent, Unitarian and Methodist theological colleges also came during the Ratcliffe years.

The National Library of Wales was established by Royal Charter in 1907 and opened in 1909, moving to its present site in Aberystwyth in 1916. It has a special remit to collect material about Wales and has strong holdings in Welsh Nonconformity. These include the central archive of the Presbyterian Church of Wales, which was gathered together in 1919 and has been on deposit at the National Library since 1934. This comprises corporate documents, local chapel records and personal papers of prominent Welsh Calvinistic Methodists. The National Library also houses the archives of the Congregational Federation in Wales, the United Reformed Church's Synod of Wales and Welsh (especially Welsh-speaking) Wesleyanism (notably the Cymru District). It has many Baptist, Congregational and Wesleyan chapel records, among them those of Welsh churches in England, although official policy is now to direct new accessions of this sort to local repositories, of which the Archives and Welsh Library of Bangor University has an especially important holding. The National Library's printed collections have been enriched by the incorporation of elements of the libraries of Welsh Nonconformist theological colleges, such as those of the Baptists in Bangor, the Independents in Swansea, the Calvinistic Methodists in Aberystwyth and Trefeca and the archival material from the Presbyterian College, Carmarthen.

Other denominations also have their own central libraries and archives. For the Baptists this role is discharged by the Angus Library at Regent's Park College, Oxford. This originated in the personal library of Joseph Angus (principal of the College, 1849–93) but has since been considerably enlarged, especially in the 1980s through the accession of the Baptist Union Library and archives, the Baptist Historical Society Library and the Baptist Missionary Society archive. Two branches of the Baptist family have their own dedicated facilities, the Strict Baptist Historical Society Library in Dunstable and the Gospel Standard Baptist Library in Hove, while Dr Williams's Library is an important resource for the General Baptists. The Religious Society of Friends, or Quakers, has a national library and archive at Friends House in London, embracing records of Britain Yearly Meeting and its committees from the 1670s, other Quaker organizations not part of Yearly Meeting, and the papers of many individual Friends from the days of George Fox and William Penn onwards. This was established as early as 1673, although the first librarian was not appointed until 1901. The British Province of the Moravian Church and the New Church (or Swedenborgians) in Britain likewise maintain their respective libraries and archives in London, but the Countess of Huntingdon's Connexion is with the Cheshunt Foundation at Westminster College, Cambridge.

There are similar central libraries and archives for denominations which emerged during the nineteenth and twentieth centuries. That for the Independent Methodists is at Wigan. Those for the Presbyterian Church of England and Churches of Christ (the latter formerly at the University of Birmingham) are now in the care of the United Reformed Church History Society at Westminster College, Cambridge (that denomination having been formed when the Presbyterian Church of England united with most congregations of the Congregational Church in England and Wales in 1972 with further union with the Re-formed Association of Churches of Christ in 1981 and the Congregational Church of Scotland in 2000). The Christadelphian Office Library in Birmingham is the national repository for the Christadelphians. Although there is apparently no official archive for the Catholic Apostolic Church or Irvingites, partly connected with the veil of secrecy under which the church operated, several private collections have found their way to the university libraries of Birmingham, Oxford and St Andrews. The British Library also has the Boase Collection, and there is Irvingite archival material at the West Yorkshire Archives Service, Bradford, and the Borthwick Institute for Archives, University of York.

The Salvation Army International Heritage Centre is in London. This has been formally constituted only since 1979, and, despite substantial losses as a result of the wartime bombing of its offices in May 1941 and very haphazard record-keeping, this is still a rich resource, comprising the archives of both the international headquarters and the UK territory, with records of its corps, rescue homes, social service centres and overseas work, and personal papers of the Army's leaders. Since 1989 the Donald Gee Centre for Pentecostal and Charismatic Research, at Mattersey Hall (the Assemblies of God Bible College), has been retrospectively gathering the historical records of the principal Pentecostal and charismatic movements in Britain; its strongest holdings are said to be for the pre-1920 and post-1960 periods. However, the West Glamorgan Area Record Office in Swansea has held since 1991 much material on the Apostolic Church, whose national headquarters were, until recently, situated in the vicinity. The Church of the Nazarene in Britain Archive Centre is located at its college in Manchester, and the Seventh Day Adventists have a similar facility in the Ellen G. White Research Centre Europe at Newbold College, Bracknell.

In the case of some denominations, in addition to the principal national centre, there are subsidiary libraries and archives in Great Britain. Examples include: (for the Baptists) Bangor, Bristol and Spurgeon's Colleges; (for the Unitarians) Harris Manchester College, Oxford; Woodbrooke Quaker Study Centre, Birmingham; (for the Methodists) Oxford Brookes University, the Royal Institution of Cornwall and Wesley College, Bristol (the last-named now closed and the collection awaiting relocation); (for the Swedenborgians) the British Library, the Mitchell Library, Glasgow, and New Church College, Manchester; and (for the Plymouth Brethren) Middlesbrough Reference Library. Also, in the case of overseas mission archives, those for the Congregational, Presbyterian Church of England and Methodist traditions are at the School of Oriental and African Studies, London. The National Archives hold a considerable amount of Nonconformist-related records, notably non-parochial registers to 1837, chapel trust deeds, registrations of meeting houses and the 1851 ecclesiastical census returns. The British Library has the archive of the Muggletonians and the largest single collection on the Southcottians, as well as numerous personal papers about Nonconformist ministers and laity. The Thomason Tracts there are a major source for studying the nascent Dissenters of the 1640s and 1650s, while the runs of Nonconformist newspapers are extensive. Lambeth Palace Library is especially rich in manuscripts touching on Anglican–Nonconformist relations from the eighteenth to twentieth centuries.

Overseas libraries and archives should not be ignored. Indeed, in the case of denominations imported from America, the main historical resources may well be abroad, as with the Church of Jesus Christ of Latter-Day Saints (at Salt Lake City) and the Christian Scientists (at Boston, MA). Other United States libraries and archives with important holdings on British Nonconformity include: Haverford and Swarthmore Colleges (for the Quakers); Harvard Divinity School and Meadville/Lombard Theological School (for the Unitarians); and Drew, Duke, Emory and Southern Methodist Universities (for Methodism). The University of Toronto Libraries have the late-seventeenth-century Dissenting library of James Forbes and the Wesleyana collection of Richard Green. The international Unity Archive in Herrnhut, Germany, is an important source for the British Moravians.

a. Overviews

Archives Wales, www.archivesnetworkwales.info/.

Association of British Theological and Philosophical Libraries Theological and Religious Studies Collection Directory, www.abtapl.org.uk/database/contents.html.

Batts, John Stuart, *British Manuscript Diaries of the Nineteenth Century: An Annotated Listing* (London: Centaur, 1976).

Bodley, Alison, 'Museums of Dissent', in Crispin Paine (ed.), *Godly Things: Museums, Objects and Religion* (London: Leicester University Press, 2000), pp. 120–31.

Briggs, John Henry York, 'Image and Appearance: Some Sources for the History of Nineteenth Century Nonconformity', *Baptist Quarterly*, 23 (1969–70), pp. 15–31, 59–72.

COPAC National, Academic and Specialist Library Catalogue, www.copac.ac.uk.

Directory of Methodist Libraries [in the United Kingdom] (rev. edn, Oxford: Applied Theology Press, 1999).

Early English Books Online [*EEBO*], http://eebo.chadwyck.com/home.

Eighteenth Century Collections Online [*ECCO*], http://gdc.gale.com/products/eighteenth-century-collections-online/.

English Short Title Catalogue [*ESTC*], http://estc.bl.uk.

Field, Clive Douglas, 'Preserving Zion: The Anatomy of Protestant Nonconformist Archives in Great Britain and Ireland', *Archives*, 33 (2008), pp. 14–51.

—, *Protestant Nonconformist Archives in Great Britain and Ireland* (2007), http://rylibweb.man.ac.uk/rag2/news/newsletter/2007autumn/pncarchives-field07.pdf.

Hall, David J., 'Quaker Meeting Libraries', *Library & Information History*, 27 (2011), pp. 255–62.

Hodson, John Howard, 'The Manuscript Sources of Presbyterian History', *Transactions of the Unitarian Historical Society*, 12 (1959–62), pp. 97–110.

Kay, William Kilbourne, *Pentecostalism: Archives and Histories* (2010), http://rylibweb.man.ac.uk/rag2/activities/conference/2007/documents/Pentecostalismarchives.ppt#256,1,Pentecostalism.

Kelley, Lillian Winifred, *Some Sources of English Presbyterian History* (London: Presbyterian Historical Society of England, 1950).

—, 'Some Sources of Presbyterian History', *Journal of the Presbyterian Historical Society of England*, 9 (1948–51), pp. 131–46.

Lloyd, Gareth, 'Methodist Printed and Archival Research Collections: A Survey of Material in UK/USA Repositories', in Charles Yrigoyen (ed.), *T & T Clark Companion to Methodism* (London: T&T Clark, 2010), pp. 369–86.

Mills, Susan J., *Probing the Past: A Toolbox for Baptist Historical Research* (Didcot: Baptist Historical Society, 2009).

Mullett, Michael, *Sources for the History of English Nonconformity, 1660–1830* ([London]: British Records Association, 1991).

Mundus: Gateway to Missionary Collections in the UK, www.mundus.ac.uk.

National Register of Archives, www.nationalarchives.gov.uk/nra/default.asp.

Powell, William Raymond, 'Bibliographical Aids to Research, XII: The Sources for the History of Protestant Nonconformist Churches in England', *Bulletin of the Institute of Historical Research*, 25 (1952), pp. 213–27.

Richards, Thomas, 'Some Disregarded Sources of Baptist History', *Baptist Quarterly*, 17 (1957–58), pp. 362–79.

Royal Commission on Historical Manuscripts, *Papers of British Churchmen, 1780–1940* (London: Her Majesty's Stationery Office, 1987).

Suncat: Serials Union Catalogue for the UK, www.suncat.ac.uk/.

Tibbutt, Harry Gordon, 'Sources for Congregational Church History', *Transactions of the Congregational Historical Society*, 19 (1960–64), pp. 33–38.

Welch, Charles Edwin, 'The Early Methodists and Their Records', *Journal of the Society of Archivists*, 4 (1970–73), pp. 200–11.

Whittaker, David J. (ed.), *Mormon Americana: A Guide to Sources and Collections in the United States* (Provo, UT: BYU Studies, 1995).
Wilson, John, 'Sources for the History of the Christian Brethren', *Local Historian*, 14 (1980–81), pp. 478–80.
WorldCat, www.worldcat.org/.

b. Dr Williams's Library and Congregational Library

Author Catalogue of Additions, Dr Williams's Library [1900–32], 2 vols (Cambridge: printed by W. Heffer and Sons, 1923–33).
Baker, William, *The George Eliot-George Henry Lewes Library: An Annotated Catalogue of Their Books at Dr Williams's Library, London* (New York: Garland, 1977).
Catalogue of Accessions, Dr Williams's Library, London [1900–80], 4 vols (London: Dr Williams's Trust, 1955–83).
A Catalogue of the Congregational Library, 2 vols (London: Congregational Union of England and Wales, 1895–1910), (with supplements, 3 vols [1981–82]).
Catalogue of the Library in Red Cross Street, Cripplegate, Founded Pursuant to the Will of the Reverend Daniel Williams, D.D., 3 vols (London: Richard and John E. Taylor, 1841–70; 2 supplements, 1878–85).
Congregational Memorial Hall and Library: Their Rise and Progress (London: A. Southey, 1873).
Creasey, John, *The Congregational Library* (London: Congregational Memorial Hall Trust (1978) Limited, 1992).
—, *Dr Williams's Library: The Last Fifty Years*, Friends of Dr Williams's Library Lecture, 53 (London: Dr Williams's Trust, 2000).
Fletcher, Irene M. and Taylor, John Horace, 'Blomfield Street Mission House and Congregational Library', *Transactions of the Congregational Historical Society*, 19 (1960–64), pp. 256–62.
Godfrey, Peter Bertram and Ditchfield, Grayson McClure, 'The Unitarian Archives at Essex Hall', *Archives*, 26 (2001), pp. 58–70.
Herford, Robert Travers and Jones, Stephen Kay, *A Short Account of the Charity and Library Established under the Will of the Late Rev. Daniel Williams* (London: Dr. Williams's Trust, 1917).
Jones, Stephen Kay, *Dr Williams and His Library*, Friends of Dr Williams's Library Lecture, 1 (Cambridge: printed by W. Heffer & Sons, 1948).
Nuttall, Geoffrey Fillingham, *New College, London and Its Library* (London: Dr Williams's Trust, 1977).
Payne, Ernest Alexander, *A Venerable Dissenting Institution: Dr Williams's Library, 1729–1979*, Friends of Dr Williams's Library Lecture, 33 (London: Dr Williams's Trust, 1979).
Peel, Albert, 'The Congregational Library', *Transactions of the Congregational Historical Society*, 12 (1933–36), pp. 340–45.
Surman, Charles Edward, 'The Congregational Library, London', *Bulletin of the American Congregational Association*, 1/2 (1950), pp. 5–15.
Thomas, Roger, *Notes on the Bibliography of Early Nonconformity in Dr Williams's Library* (London: Dr Williams's Trust, 1957).
Twinn, Kenneth, *Dr Williams's Library: Guide to the Manuscripts* (London: Dr Williams's Trust, 1969).

—, 'Sources for Church History, 2: Dr Williams's Library', *Local Historian*, 9 (1970–71), pp. 115–20.

Woodward, Gwendolen and Thomas, Roger, *Early Nonconformity, 1566–1800: A Catalogue of Books in Dr Williams's Library, London*, 12 vols (Boston, MA: G. K. Hall, 1968).

c. John Rylands University Library

Brady, David, 'The Christian Brethren Archive in the John Rylands University Library of Manchester', in Lorenza Giorgi and Massimo Rubboli (eds), *Piero Guicciardini, 1808–1886* (Firenze: Leo S. Olschki, 1988), pp. 175–91.

Calkin, Homer L., *Catalog of Methodist Archival and Manuscript Collections (Part 6), Great Britain and Ireland: Section 1, Methodist Archives and Research Centre, The John Rylands University Library* ([Arlington, VA]: World Methodist Historical Society, 1985).

Field, Clive Douglas, 'Sources for the Study of Protestant Nonconformity in the John Rylands University Library of Manchester', *Bulletin of the John Rylands University Library of Manchester*, 71/2 (1989), pp. 103–39.

—, 'Unitarian College Collection and other Unitarian Materials in the John Rylands University Library of Manchester', in Leonard Smith (ed.), *Unitarian to the Core: Unitarian College, Manchester, 1854–2004* (Manchester: The College, 2004), pp. 177–84.

Johnson, Graham, *The Christian Brethren Archive* (2007), http://rylibweb.man.ac.uk/rag2/activities/conference/2007/documents/RAGtalk_000.pdf.

Leary, William, 'The Methodist Archives', *Archives*, 16 (1983–84), pp. 16–27.

Lloyd, Gareth, 'The Methodist Archives and Research Centre at the John Rylands University Library of Manchester', in Charles Yrigoyen (ed.), *The Global Impact of the Wesleyan Traditions and Their Related Movements* (Lanham, MD: Scarecrow Press, 2002), pp. 285–92.

—, *Sources for Women's Studies in the Methodist Archives* (Manchester: John Rylands University Library of Manchester, 1996).

Manchester – John Rylands University Library of Manchester: Methodist Archives and Research Centre, *Methodist Archives and Research Centre, The John Rylands University Library, The University of Manchester: Archive Accessions, 1977–2011* (Manchester: The Library, 2011), www.library.manchester.ac.uk/searchresources/guidetospecialcollections/methodist/methodistarchivescollectioncatalogue/_files/Public-Report-of-All-Accessions.pdf.

McLachlan, Herbert, *The Story of a Nonconformist Library* [Unitarian College], (Manchester: University Press, 1923).

—, *The Unitarian College Library* (Manchester: printed for private circulation, 1939).

Midgley Reference Library: Catalogue of Books Relating to the Society of Friends (Manchester: printed by Wm. Irwin, 1866).

Nockles, Peter Benedict, 'The Work of the Methodist Archives & Research Centre, John Rylands University Library of Manchester', in *Religious Archives Group: Proceedings of a Conference Held at Wesley College, Bristol, 14th September 1992* ([London: The Group, 1993]), pp. 1–8 and *Catholic Archives*, 14 (1994), pp. 44–52.

[Riley, David Woodward], 'The Methodist Archives and Research Centre', *Bulletin of the John Rylands University Library of Manchester*, 60 (1977–78), pp. 269–74.

[Sharp, John Alfred], *A Catalogue of Manuscripts and Relics, Engravings and Photographs, Medals, Books and Pamphlets, Pottery, Medallions, etc. belonging to the Wesleyan Methodist Conference* (London: Methodist Publishing House, 1921).

Whelan, Timothy, 'A Chronological Calendar of Baptist Autographs at the John Rylands University Library of Manchester, 1741–1907', *Baptist Quarterly*, 42 (2007–8), pp. 577–612.

—, 'Baptist Autographs in the John Rylards Library, Manchester, 1741–1907', *Bulletin of the John Rylands University Library of Manchester*, 89/2 (2013), pp. 203–25.

d. National Library of Wales

Catalogue of the Contents of Four Exhibitions of Ecclesiastical Archives, Relics, etc. The Presbyterian Church of Wales, the Baptists, the Congregationalists, the Church in Wales (Aberystwyth: National Library of Wales, [1948]).

[Huws, Daniel], *Guide to the Department of Manuscripts and Records, the National Library of Wales* (Aberystwyth: The Library, 1994).

Madden, John Lionel, 'Trysorfa hanes: ffynonellau Methodistaidd yn Llyfrgell Genedlaethol Cymru' [Methodist sources], *Bathafarn*, 31 (2000), pp. 50–54.

Roberts, Brynley Francis, 'Welsh Nonconformist Archives', *Journal of Welsh Ecclesiastical History*, 3 (1986), pp. 61–72.

Schlenther, Boyd Stanley and White, Eryn Mant, *Calendar of the Trevecka Letters* (Aberystwyth: National Library of Wales, 2003).

Tibbott, Gildas and Davies, K. Monica, 'The Archives of the Calvinistic Methodist or Presbyterian Church of Wales', *National Library of Wales Journal*, 5 (1947–48), pp. 13–49.

Tomos, Merfyn Wyn, 'Methodist by Name, Methodical by Nature: The Calvinistic Methodist Archive at the National Library of Wales', *Capel Newsletter*, 38 (2001), pp. 16–19.

e. Other Libraries and Archives

Andrews, John Samuel, 'Some Early Quaker Material in the University of Lancaster Library', *Gutenberg Jahrbuch* (1976), pp. 333–39.

Banks, Joyce, 'Religious and Theological Societies: 1. The Wesley Historical Society', *Bulletin of the Association of British Theological and Philosophical Libraries*, 2/7 (1990), pp. 9–13.

Barber, Melanie, 'Records of Quaker Interest in Lambeth Palace Library', *Journal of the Friends' Historical Society*, 53 (1972–75), pp. 165–69.

—, 'Tales of the Unexpected: Glimpses of Friends in the Archives of Lambeth Palace Library', *Journal of the Friends' Historical Society*, 61 (2006–9), pp. 87–123.

Blewitt, Paul and Reynolds, Simon, 'The Moravian Church Archives and Library', *Journal of the Society of Archivists*, 22 (2001), pp. 193–203.

Crozier, David J., *Methodism: A Bibliography of the Present Collection of Material Held at St Deiniol's Library, Hawarden* (Hawarden: The Library, [1996]).

Fortescue, George Knottesford (ed.), *Catalogue of the Pamphlets, Books, Newspapers and Manuscripts Relating to the Civil War, the Commonwealth and the Restoration Collected by George Thomason, 1640–1661*, 2 vols (London: British Museum, 1908).
Henderson, Janet, 'The Special Collections and Manuscripts Held at Wesley College, Bristol', *Wesley Historical Society Bristol Branch Bulletin*, 91 ([2005]), pp. [A]1–8.
Heyworth, Peter Lorriman, 'Unfamiliar Libraries: The Forbes Library', *Book Collector*, 19 (1970), pp. 317–27.
Hicks, Muriel A., 'Friends' Reference Library, 1901–1959', *Journal of the Friends' Historical Society*, 49 (1959–61), pp. 123–36.
—, 'Manuscript Resources of the Friends Libraries: The Library, Friends House, London', in Anna Cox Brinton (ed.), *Then and Now: Quaker Essays, Historical and Contemporary, by Friends of Henry Joel Cadbury* (Philadelphia, PA: University of Pennsylvania Press, 1960), pp. 203–8.
Kemp, Beverley, 'The Library of the Religious Society of Friends', *Bulletin of the Association of British Theological and Philosophical Libraries*, 16/1 (2009), pp. 4–8.
Lamont, William Montgomerie, 'The Muggletonian Archive', in Christopher Hill, Barry Reay and William Montgomerie Lamont, *The World of the Muggletonians* (London: Temple Smith, 1983), pp. 1–5.
Lively, Robert L., 'Bodleian Sources for the Study of Two Nineteenth-Century Millenarian Movements in Britain' [Catholic Apostolic Church and the Mormons], *Bodleian Library Record*, 13 (1988–91), pp. 491–500.
Morgan, Paul, 'Manchester College and Its Books', in Barbara Smith (ed.), *Truth, Liberty, Religion: Essays Celebrating Two Hundred Years of Manchester College* (Oxford: The College, 1986), pp. 111–26.
Mortimer, Russell Stanley, 'The Archives of the Society of Friends (Quakers) from c.1673', *Amateur Historian*, 3 (1956–57), pp. 55–61.
Orchard, Stephen Charles and Welch, Charles Edwin, 'Archives at Cheshunt College, Cambridge', *Transactions of the Congregational Historical Society*, 20 (1965–70), pp. 202–4.
Porter, Dennis, *A Catalogue of Manuscripts in Harris Manchester College, Oxford* (Oxford: The College, 1998).
Sheils, William Joseph, 'Sources for the History of Dissent and Catholicism at the Borthwick Institute', *Borthwick Institute Bulletin*, 3/1 (1983), pp. 11–28.
Shorney, David, *Protestant Nonconformity and Roman Catholicism: A Guide to Sources in the Public Record Office* (London: PRO Publications, 1996).
Spittal, Charles Jeffrey, 'The New Room Library', *Wesley Historical Society Bristol Branch Bulletin*, 91 ([2005]), pp. [B]1–6.
Welch, Charles Edwin, *Calendar and Index of Cheshunt College Archives*, List & Index Society Special Series, 14 (London: Swift, 1981).

III. People Sources

Finding information about individual Nonconformists can be challenging. Only a tiny minority (typically in national leadership roles) will have been sufficiently important to have left behind personal papers (which are best traced in the *National Register of Archives*), and/or to have written autobiographies, diaries or journals or to have been the subject of book-length biographies (all genres which can be identified from bibliographies or library catalogues). However, a much larger number, especially in the case of ministers, may have featured in biographical directories and/or been the subject of a published obituary. For the main Nonconformist denominations at least, there is a reasonably good spread of collective biographies and indexes, as listed below, the Methodists again being best served (but the Unitarians not far behind). Additionally, the principal library or archive for each denomination typically has unpublished biographical tools. For example, the Angus Library holds Samuel Couling's manuscript biographical dictionary of Baptist ministers in Great Britain and Ireland who died between 1800 and 1875 and William Thomas Whitley's card index of Baptist ministers, while the Baptist Historical Society keeps a consolidated list of obituaries which have appeared in Baptist publications. Friends' House Library maintains a typescript dictionary of Quaker biography and has an index to obituaries in *The Friend*, 1894–1980. The Methodist Archives at Manchester have a variety of unpublished biographical indexes to Methodist magazines and newspapers in the century or so before Methodist reunion in 1932, largely prepared by William Leary when he was the Methodist Church Connexional archivist.

For the Nonconformist rank and file, the net will need to be cast more widely than these collective biographies. Although only the Quakers have their own family history society, the Society of Genealogists has commissioned practical guides for those wishing to trace ancestors with connections to the mainstream denominations. Frequent articles about Nonconformist records also appear in the monthly genealogical magazines such as *Family History Monthly*, *Family Tree Magazine*, *Who do You Think You are? Your Family History* and *Your Family Tree*. Much genealogical research can now be undertaken online, either through general searches of the web or through family history portals which provide access to digitized nominal data from secular and religious sources. The best known of these websites is familysearch.org, home of the International Genealogical Index, which has been developed by the Church of Jesus Christ of Latter-day Saints and which is international in reach. More United Kingdom–specific are sites such as ancestry.co.uk, familyhistory.uk.com, findmypast.co.uk and genesreunited.co.uk. These offer some basic searching for free, with micro-payments for access to original documents.

Such websites make extensive use of non-parochial registers, especially those which were surrendered to the state by Nonconformist chapels on the inauguration of civil registration in England and Wales in 1837. These particular registers are now in the National Archives and are indexed at bmdregisters.co.uk/. Many of these pre-1837 registers, which mainly record births or baptisms, have also been transcribed by local family history societies and published in paper, microfiche or CD-ROM format. Later registers, including marriages and monumental inscriptions, have also been published by these societies, albeit rarely beyond the First World War. Availability of these transcripts for purchase can be checked via online stores such as genfair.co.uk or parishchest.com. The originals of registers will be held either at local record offices or remain with the chapels. Several local record offices have printed lists of their holdings of Nonconformist registers, while Dafydd Ifans has edited an excellent guide to the Welsh ones.[2] Registers also feature prominently in the Society of Geanlogists' series, with, for instance, David Clifford giving the location of registers for all Congregational churches formed before 1850.[3] The best-known aggregate academic use of the non-parochial registers is the occupational analysis undertaken by Michael Watts.[4]

a. Genealogical Guides

Breed, Geoffrey Ralph, *My Ancestors Were Baptists* (4th edn, London: Society of Genealogists, 2002).

Clifford, David J. H., *My Ancestors Were Congregationalists in England and Wales* (2nd rev. edn, London: Society of Genealogists, 1997).

Evans, Muriel Bowen, 'Nonconformity', in John and Sheila Rowlands (eds), *Welsh Family History: A Guide to Research* (2nd edn [Birmingham]: Federation of Family History Societies, 1998), pp. 39–58.

Gandy, Michael, *Basic Facts about English Nonconformity for Family Historians* (Birmingham: Federation of Family History Societies, 1998).

—, *Tracing Nonconformist Ancestors* (Richmond: Public Record Office, 2001).

Leary, William, *My Ancestors Were Methodists* (rev. edn, London: Society of Genealogists, 1999).

Lloyd, Gareth, *Use of the Methodist Archives and Research Centre by Family Historians* (Manchester: John Rylands University Library of Manchester, 1995).

McLaughlin, Eve, *Nonconformist Ancestors* (Haddenham: Varneys Press, 1995).

Milligan, Edward Hyslop and Thomas, Malcolm J., *My Ancestors Were Quakers* (2nd edn, London: Society of Genealogists, 1999).

My Methodist History: Recording and Sharing the Family History of the Methodist Church, www.mymethodisthistory.org.uk.

My Primitive Methodist Ancestors: Connecting People and Places Through Sharing Photos, Stories, and Research, www.myprimitivemethodists.org.uk.

My Wesleyan Methodist Ancestors: Recording and Sharing Methodist Family Memories and Memorabilia from 1790s–1930s, www.mywesleyanmethodists.org.uk.

Oates, Paul James, *My Ancestors Were Inghamites* (London: Society of Genealogists Enterprises, 2003).

Quaker Connections: Magazine of the Quaker Family History Society, 1994 to date.

Ratcliffe, Richard, *Basic Facts about Methodist Records for Family Historians* (Bury: Federation of Family History Societies, 2005).

Ruston, Alan Robert, *My Ancestors Were English Presbyterians or Unitarians* (2nd edn, London: Society of Genealogists, 2001).
Steel, Donald John, *Sources for Nonconformist Genealogy and Family History* (London: Society of Genealogists, 1973).
Waller, Ian H., *My Ancestor was a Mormon* (London: Society of Genealogists Enterprises, [2011]).
Wiggins, Ray, *My Ancestors Were in the Salvation Army* (2nd edn, London: Society of Genealogists, 1999).

b. Collective Biographies: General

Baylen, Joseph Oscar and Gossman, Norbert Joseph (eds), *Biographical Dictionary of Modern British Radicals*, 3 vols (Hassocks: Harvester Press, 1979–88).
Bellamy, Joyce Margaret and Saville, John (eds), *Dictionary of Labour Biography*, 12 vols (London: Macmillan, 1972–2005).
Boase, Frederic, *Modern English Biography*, 6 vols (Truro: Netherton & Worth, 1892–1921).
The 'Christian World' Year Book . . . A Complete Alphabetical List of Ministers of all the Nonconforming Churches of Great Britain and Ireland (London: James Clarke, 1883–86).
Cox, Janice V. (ed.), *The People of God: Shrewsbury Dissenters, 1660–1699*, Shropshire Record Series, 9–10, 2 vols (Keele: Centre for Local History, Keele University, 2006–7).
Creasey, John, *Index to the John Evans List of Dissenting Congregations and Ministers, 1715–1729 in Dr Williams's Library* (London: Dr Williams's Trust, 1964).
Dissenting Academies Online: Database and Encyclopedia [tutors and students], http://dissacad.english.qmul.ac.uk/new_dissacad/phpfiles/.
Free Church Directory (1965/6–70/1).
Free Church Year Book (1911–16).
Greaves, Richard Lee and Zaller, Robert (eds), *Biographical Dictionary of British Radicals in the Seventeenth Century*, 3 vols (Brighton: Harvester Press, 1982–84).
Harrison, Brian, *Dictionary of British Temperance Biography* (Coventry: Society for the Study of Labour History, 1973).
Howes, Charles, *Free Church Musicians* (London: Novello, [1909]).
Jeremy, David John (ed.), *Dictionary of Business Biography*, 5 vols and supplement (London: Butterworths, 1984–86).
Jones, Robert Tudur and Owens, Benjamin George, 'Anghydffurfwyr Cymru, 1660–1662', *Y Cofiadur*, 32 (1962), pp. 3–93.
Larsen, Timothy (ed.), *Biographical Dictionary of Evangelicals* (Leicester: Inter-Varsity Press, 2003).
Lewis, Donald M. (ed.), *The Blackwell Dictionary of Evangelical Biography, 1730–1860*, 2 vols (Oxford: Blackwell, 1995).
Light, Alfred W., *Bunhill Fields*, 2 vols (London: C. J. Farncombe & Sons, 1913–33).
Matthews, Arnold Gwynne, *Calamy Revised: Being a Revision of Edmund Calamy's Account of the Ministers and Others Ejected and Silenced, 1660–2* (Oxford: Oxford University Press, 1934).
—, *Walker Revised: Being a Revision of John Walker's Sufferings of the Clergy during the Grand Rebellion, 1642–60* (Oxford: Clarendon Press, 1948).

Middleton, Erasmus, *Biographia Evangelica, or an Historical Account of the Lives and Deaths of the Most Eminent and Evangelical Authors or Preachers, both British and Foreign, in the Several Denominations of Protestants, from the Beginning of the Reformation to the Present Time*, 4 vols (London: printed by J. W. Pasham for the author, 1779–86).

Morgan, John Vyrnwy (ed.), *Welsh Religious Leaders in the Victorian Era* (London: James Nisbet, 1905).

Nappo, Tommaso, *British Biographical Index*, 8 vols (3rd edn, Munich: K. G. Saur, 2008), and *British Biographical Archive* on microfiche (Munich: K. G. Saur, 1984–2003).

Oxford Dictionary of National Biography (Oxford: Oxford University Press, 2004), www.oxforddnb.com/.

Pine, Leslie Gilbert (ed.), *Who's Who in the Free Churches (and Other Denominations)* (London: Shaw Publishing Co., 1951).

Ruston, Alan Robert, *Obituaries and Marriages of Dissenting Ministers in the Gentleman's Magazine in the 18th Century* (Watford: The Author, 1996).

—, *Obituaries of Dissenting Ministers in the Gentleman's Magazine, 1801–1837* (London: Dr Williams's Trust and Library, 2008).

Stenton, Michael, *Who's Who of British Members of Parliament*, 4 vols (Hassocks: Harvester Press, 1978–81).

Welsh Biography: A Bibliography of Welsh Biographical Sources, www.llgc.org.uk/index.php?id=biography0.

Welsh Biography Online, http://yba.llgc.org.uk/en/index.html.

Who was Who, 1897 to date.

Winskill, Peter Turner, *Temperance Standard Bearers of the Nineteenth Century*, 2 vols (Manchester: printed by Darrah Bros., 1897–98).

c. Collective Biographies: Baptist

The Baptist Who's Who ([London]: Shaw Publishing, [1933]).

Bebbington, David William, 'Baptist M.P.s in the Seventeenth and Eighteenth Centuries', *Baptist Quarterly*, 28 (1979–80), pp. 245–62.

—, 'Baptist M.P.s in the Nineteenth Century', *Baptist Quarterly*, 29 (1981–82), pp. 3–24.

—, 'Baptist Members of Parliament in the Twentieth Century', *Baptist Quarterly*, 31 (1985–86), pp. 252–87.

—, 'Baptist Members of Parliament: A Supplementary Note', *Baptist Quarterly*, 42 (2007–8), pp. 148–61.

Breed, Geoffrey Ralph, 'Indexes to the Careers of Baptist Ministers', *Baptist Quarterly*, 44 (2011–12), pp. 420–32.

Gordelier, Charles, *Our Contemporaries: An Appendix to Mr Cornelius Slim's Brief Memorials of Gospel Ministers during the Present Century* ([London]: printed for the author, 1872).

Haykin, Michael Anthony George (ed.), *The British Particular Baptists, 1638–1910*, 3 vols (Springfield, MO: Particular Baptist Press, 1998–2003).

Landels, William, *Baptist Worthies: A Series of Sketches of Distinguished Men Who Have Held and Advocated the Principles of the Baptist Denomination*, 2 vols (London: Baptist Tract and Book Society, 1883–84).

Nettles, Tom J., *The Baptists: Key People Involved in Forming a Baptist Identity, Volume One: Beginnings in Britain* (Fearn: Mentor, 2005).

Payne, Ernest Alexander, *The First Generation: Early Leaders of the Baptist Missionary Society in England and India* (London: Carey Press, [1936]).

—, *The Great Succession: Leaders of the Baptist Missionary Society during the Nineteenth Century* (2nd edn, London: Carey Press, 1946).

Shakespeare, John Howard, *Baptist and Congregational Pioneers* (London: National Council of Evangelical Free Churches, 1906).

Slim, Cornelius, *My Contemporaries of the Nineteenth Century: Brief Memorials of more than Four Hundred Ministers of the Gospel of Various Denominations* [particularly Baptist and Congregational] ([London]: Elliot Stock, 1870).

Swaine, Stephen Albert, *Faithful Men, or Memorials of Bristol Baptist College and Some of Its Most Distinguished Alumni* (London: Alexander and Shepheard, 1884).

Thomson, Ronald William, *Heroes of the Baptist Church* (London: Kingsgate Press, 1937).

Whelan, Timothy (ed.), *Baptist Autographs in the John Rylands University Library of Manchester, 1741–1845* (Macon, GA: Mercer University Press, 2009), pp. 345–472.

d. Collective Biographies: Congregationalist

Bebbington, David William, *Congregational Members of Parliament in the Nineteenth Century*, United Reformed Church History Society Occasional Publication, 1 (Cambridge: The Society, 2007).

Binfield, John Clyde Goodfellow and Taylor, John Horace (eds), *Who They Were in the Reformed Churches of England and Wales, 1901–2000* (Donington: Shaun Tyas, 2007).

Peel, Albert, *The Congregational Two Hundred, 1530–1948* (London: Independent Press, 1948).

Shakespeare, John Howard, *Baptist and Congregational Pioneers* (London: National Council of Evangelical Free Churches, 1906).

Slim, Cornelius, *My Contemporaries of the Nineteenth Century: Brief Memorials of more than Four Hundred Ministers of the Gospel of Various Denominations* [particularly Baptist and Congregational] ([London]: Elliot Stock, 1870).

The Surman Index Online, www.english.qmul.ac.uk/drwilliams/surman/intro.html.

Who's Who in Congregationalism ([London]: Shaw Publishing, [1933]).

e. Collective Biographies: Unitarian

Bebbington, David William, *Unitarian Members of Parliament in the Nineteenth Century: A Catalogue*, *Transactions of the Unitarian Historical Society*, supplement to 24/3 (2009).

Dictionary of Unitarian and Universalist Biography, www25.uua.org/uuhs/duub/.

Memorable Unitarians, Being a Series of Brief Biographical Sketches (London: British and Foreign Unitarian Association, 1906).

Ruston, Alan Robert, *Index to the Obituaries of Unitarian Ministers, 1800–1899*, www.unitarianhistory.org.uk/ministerobit1800.html.

—, *Monthly Repository Obituaries, 1806 1832: Index and Synopsis* ([Watford: The Author], 1985).
—, *Obituaries of Unitarian Ministers, 1800–1849: Index and Synopsis, Transactions of the Unitarian Historical Society*, supplement to 24/1 (2007).
—, *Obituaries of Unitarian Ministers, 1850–1899: Index and Synopsis, Transactions of the Unitarian Historical Society*, supplement to 23/4 (2006).
—, *Obituaries of Unitarian Ministers, 1900–1999: Index and Synopsis, Transactions of the Unitarian Historical Society*, supplement to 22/2 (2000).
—, *Obituaries of Unitarian Ministers, 1900–1999: Corrections and Additions, Transactions of the Unitarian Historical Society*, supplement to 23/3 (2005).
—, *Obituaries of Unitarian Ministers, 1900–2004: Index and Synopsis*, www.unitarian-history.org.uk/ministerobit.html.
—, *Unitarian Obituaries from Various Denominational Journals, 1794–1850: Index and Synopsis* (Watford: The Author, 1990).
Spears, Robert, *Record of Unitarian Worthies* (London: E. T. Whitfield, [1876]).
Turner, William, *Lives of Eminent Unitarians, with a Notice of Dissenting Academies*, 2 vols (London: Unitarian Association, 1840–43).
Unitarian Obituaries, Harris Manchester College Library, www.unitarianobituaries.org.uk/index.php.

f. Collective Biographies: Quaker

The Annual Monitor (1813–1919/20).
Besse, Joseph, *A Collection of the Sufferings of the People called Quakers*, 2 vols (London: printed by Luke Hinde, 1753).
Evans, William and Evans, Thomas (eds), *Piety Promoted: In a Collection of Dying Sayings of Many of the People Called Quakers*, 4 vols (new edn, Philadelphia, PA: Friends' Book Store, 1854).
Green, Joseph Joshua, *Quaker Records, Being an Index to 'The Annual Monitor', 1813–1892* (London: Edward Hicks, 1894).
Harrison, Richard S., *A Biographical Dictionary of Irish Quakers* [including British-born and Irish active in Britain] (2nd edn, Dublin: Four Courts Press, 2008).
Milligan, Edward Hyslop, *Biographical Dictionary of British Quakers in Commerce and Industry, 1775–1920* (York: Sessions Book Trust, 2007).
Robinson, William (ed.), *Friends of a Half Century: Fifty Memorials with Portraits of Members of the Society of Friends, 1840–1890* (London: Edward Hicks, 1891).

g. Collective Biographies: Methodist

Atmore, Charles, *A Chronological List of the Itinerant Preachers in the Connexion of the Late Rev. John Wesley* (Manchester: printed at the Office of W. Shelmerdine & Co., 1801).
—, *The Methodist Memorial* (Bristol: printed by Richard Edwards, 1801).
Barrass, Edward, *A Gallery of Deceased Ministers* (London: T. Holliday, 1853).
Beckerlegge, Oliver Aveyard, *United Methodist Ministers and Their Circuits* (London: Epworth Press, 1968).
Brownson, William James, Gair, John, Mitchell, Thomas and Prosser, David Samuel, *Heroic Men: The Death Roll of the Primitive Methodist Ministry* (London: Joseph Toulson, [1889]).

A Chronological and Alphabetical List of All the Itinerant Methodist Preachers in the Connexion of the Late Rev. John Wesley (Exeter: printed by E. Woolmer for A. B. Seckerson, [1814]).

Edwards, Eric, *O gylchdaith i gylchdaith: cronicl o daith un gweinidog yng ngweinidogaeth yr Eglwys Fethodistaidd, 1932–1975* ([Caernarfon: Methodist Church, 2001]).

[Everett, James], *Wesleyan Takings; or, Centenary Sketches of Ministerial Character, as Exhibited in the Wesleyan Connexion during the First Hundred Years of Its Existence*, 2 vols (London: Hamilton, Adams & Co., 1840–51).

F., J., *Recollections of Methodist Worthies* (London: Beveridge & Co., [1881]).

Garlick, Kenneth Benjamin, *Garlick's Methodist Registry, 1983* (London: Edsall, 1983).

—, *Mr Wesley's Preachers* (London: Pinhorns for the World Methodist Historical Society (British Section), 1977).

Gorrie, Peter Douglass, *The Lives of Eminent Methodist Ministers* (Auburn, AL: Derby and Miller, 1852).

Graham, Ena Dorothy, *Chosen by God: A List of the Female Travelling Preachers of Early Primitive Methodism* (2nd edn, Evesham: Wesley Historical Society, 2010).

Greeves, Edith, *From the Cradle to the Pulpit, Being Sketches of the Youthful Days of Some Wesleyan Methodist Ministers* (London: C. H. Kelly, 1892).

Gunstone, William Dance, *Companion to the Minutes of Conference; Being an Alphabetical Arrangement of the Ministers of the Methodist New Connexion* (Dewsbury: Darley Terry, 1896).

Hall, Joseph, *Memorials of Wesleyan Methodist Ministers; or, the Yearly Death Roll from 1777 to 1840* (London: Haughton & Co., 1876).

Herod, George, *Biographical Sketches of Some of Those Preachers Whose Labours Contributed to the Origination and Early Extension of the Primitive Methodist Connexion* (London: T. King, [1855]).

Hill, William, *An Alphabetical Arrangement of all the Wesleyan Methodist Preachers and Missionaries* (Bradford: printed and sold by T. Inkersley, 1819 [with 24 further editions to 1926]).

Holroyd, James, *A Chronological and Alphabetical List of all the Itinerant Preachers that Have Been and now Are in the Wesleyan Methodist Connexion* (Haslingden: J. Walton, 1819).

Hurd, F. H., *Earnest Men: Sketches of Eminent Primitive Methodists* (London: F. H. Hurd, 1872).

Index of Methodist Ministers, www.library.manchester.ac.uk/searchresources/guidetospecialcollections/methodist/using/indexofministers/.

[Jackson, Francis Marris], *An Index to the Memoirs, Obituary Notices and Recent Deaths, together with the References to the Local Histories of Methodism, as Contained in the 'Arminian Magazine', 1778–1797, the 'Methodist Magazine', 1798–1821, and the 'Wesleyan Methodist Magazine', 1822–1839, Proceedings of the Wesley Historical Society*, supplement to 7 (1910).

Jackson, Thomas (ed.), *The Lives of Early Methodist Preachers, Chiefly Written by Themselves*, 6 vols (3rd edn, London: Wesleyan Conference Office, 1865–66).

Jeremy, David John, 'Laity in Denominational Leadership: Methodist Vice-Presidents, 1932–2000', *Proceedings of the Wesley Historical Society*, 58 (2011–12), pp. 12–33.

—, 'Laity in Denominational Leadership: Vice-Presidents of the Primitive Methodist Church, 1872–1932', *Proceedings of the Wesley Historical Society*, 57 (2009–10), pp. 246–72.

Jones, John, *Y Bywgraffydd Wesleyaidd* (Machynlleth: J. Williams, 1866).

Keeling, Annie E., *Eminent Methodist Women* (London: Charles H. Kelly, 1889).

[Lawson, William D.], *Wesleyan Local Preachers* (Newcastle-upon-Tyne: William D. Lawson, 1874).

Leary, William, *The Early Methodist People of Lincolnshire* (Loughborough: printed by Teamprint, 2000).

—, *For all the Saints: Lincolnshire Methodists of the Twentieth Century* (Loughborough: printed by Teamprint, 2000).

—, *Lincolnshire Born Methodist Ministers* (Loughborough: printed by Teamprint, 2001).

—, *The Methodist Church: Ministers Who Have Died, 1968–1989* (Peterborough: printed by Methodist Publishing House, [1990]).

—, *Ministers & Circuits in the Primitive Methodist Church: A Directory* (Loughborough: Teamprint in association with the World Methodist Historical Society, 1990; supplement, 1993).

—, *Some Lincolnshire Methodists* (Loughborough: Teamprint, 1998).

Lenton, John Herriott, 'Sources for the History of British and Irish Methodism and Genealogy: Some Printed Donation Lists', *Proceedings of the Wesley Historical Society*, 55 (2005–6), pp. 43–52, 121–2.

—, *Wesley's Preachers, 1740–1791*, www.gcah.org/site/c.ghKJI0PHIoE/b.3945307/.

Lloyd, Gareth, *Index of Obituaries of Members of the Wesleyan Methodist Association, 1838–1857, and of the United Methodist Free Church from 1857–1907* (Manchester: John Rylands University Library, 1993).

—, *The Methodist Archives Biographical Index*, www.library.manchester.ac.uk/searchresources/guidetospecialcollections/methodist/using/biographicalindex/.

Madden, John Lionel, *Yr Eurgrawn (Wesleyaidd), 1809–1983: mynegai i ysgrifau am weinidogion* [index to writings about ministers in the Welsh Wesleyan magazine] (Aberystwyth: Yr Eglwys Fethodistaidd, Cymdeithas Hanes Talaith Cymru, 2006).

The Methodist Local Preachers' Who's Who, 1934 (London: Shaw Publishing Co., 1934).

The Methodist Who's Who, 1910[-15] (London: Robert Culley, 1910–15).

Michell, William John, *Brief Biographical Sketches of Bible Christian Ministers and Laymen*, 2 vols (Jersey: Beresford Press, 1906).

Milburn, Geoffrey Eden, 'Piety, Profit and Paternalism: Methodists in Business in the North-East of England, c.1760–1920', *Proceedings of the Wesley Historical Society*, 44 (1983–84), pp. 45–92.

Ministerial Portrait Gallery of the United Methodist Free Churches (Manchester: John Heywood, [1860]).

Ministers and Probationers of the Methodist Church (London: Methodist Publishing House, 1933 [with 6 further editions to 1968]).

Moister, William, *Missionary Worthies; Being Brief Memorial Sketches of Ministers Sent Forth by the Wesleyan Missionary Society Who Have Died in the Work from the Beginning* (London: T. Woolmer, 1885).

Mosley, Albert Watson, 'The Methodist Missionary Data Base Project', *Wesley Historical Society West Midlands Bulletin*, 9/7 (2011), pp. 129–36.

Myles, William, *A List of all the Methodist Preachers Who Have Laboured in Connexion with the Late Rev. John Wesley and with the Methodist Conference* (Bristol: printed for the author by R. Edwards, [1801]).

Pawson, John, *A Chronological Catalogue of all the Travelling Preachers Now in the Methodist Connexion* (Liverpool: printed by J. M'Creery, 1795).

Pearce, Joseph, *Burning and Shining Lights: A Souvenir of Primitive Methodist Radiant Personalities* (Halesowen: H. Parkes, 1935).

—, *Dinna Forget: A Souvenir of Primitive Methodist Soul-Winning Personalities* (Leominster: Orphans' Printing Press, 1932).

Portraits of the Wesleyan Methodist Ministers; with Biographical Memoirs (London: Simpkin and Marshall, 1837).

Rogal, Samuel J., *A Biographical Dictionary of 18th Century Methodism*, 10 vols (Lewiston, NY: Edwin Mellen Press, 1997–99).

Smith, Henry, *Sketches of Eminent Methodist New Connexion Ministers* (London: J. C. Watts, [1893]).

Smith, Samuel, *Anecdotes, Facts and Biographical Sketches Connected with the Great Revival of the Work of God in Raising up and Progressing the Primitive Methodist Connexion* (Douglas, Isle of Man: Matthew Glover, 1872).

Stevenson, George John, *Methodist Worthies: Characteristic Sketches of Methodist Preachers of the Several Denominations*, 6 vols (London: Thomas C. Jack, 1884–86).

Taft, Zechariah, *Biographical Sketches of the Lives and Public Ministry of Various Holy Women*, 2 vols (London: published for the author, 1825–28).

Wesley and His Successors (London: Charles H. Kelly, 1891).

West, Robert Athow, *Sketches of Wesleyan Preachers* (London: Simpkin, Marshall & Co., 1849).

Whiteley, David (ed.), *Illustrious Local Preachers* (Bradford: Thornton & Pearson, 1891).

Who's Who in Methodism, 1933 (London: Methodist Times and Leader, 1933).

Wilkes, Arthur and Lovatt, Joseph, *Mow Cop and the Camp Meeting Movement: Sketches of Primitive Methodism* (Leominster: Orphans' Printing Press, [1942]).

Withrow, William Henry, *Makers of Methodism* (London: C. H. Kelly, 1903).

h. Collective Biographies: Other Denominations

Anderson, James, *They Finished Their Course: A Record of Some Brethren Who Were Called Home in the 1970s* (Kilmarnock: J. Ritchie, 1980).

—, *They Finished Their Course in the Eighties: A Record of Some Brethren Who Were Called Home in the 1980s* (Kilmarnock: J. Ritchie, 1990).

Bayley, Jonathan, *New Church Worthies* (London: James Speirs, 1884).

Evans, Joseph, *Biographical Dictionary of Ministers and Preachers of the Welsh Calvinistic Methodist Body or Presbyterians of Wales* (Caernarvon: D. O'Brien Owen, 1907).

Jones, John Morgan and Morgan, William, *The Calvinistic Methodist Fathers of Wales* [translation of *Y Tadau Methodistaidd*, Abertawe: Lewis Evans, 1895–97], 2 vols (Edinburgh: Banner of Truth Trust, 2008).

Pickering, Henry, *Chief Men among the Brethren* (2nd edn, London: Pickering & Inglis, [1932]).

Plant, Robert, *They Finished Their Course in the 90s* [Brethren] (Kilmarnock: J. Ritchie, 2000).

i. Bibliographies of Individuals: General

Benedetto, Robert, *P. T. Forsyth Bibliography and Index* (Westport, CT: Greenwood Press, 1993).

Crook, Ronald Eric, *A Bibliography of Joseph Priestley, 1733–1804* (London: Library Association, 1966).

Fletcher, Harris Francis, *Contributions to a Milton Bibliography, 1800–1930* (Urbana, IL: University of Illinois Press, 1931).

Greaves, Richard Lee, *An Annotated Bibliography of John Bunyan Studies* (Pittsburgh, PA: Clifford E. Barbour Library, Pittsburgh Theological Seminary, [1972]).

Hanford, James Holly and McQueen, William Ashley, *Milton* (2nd edn, Arlington Heights, IL: AHM, 1979).

Harrison, Frank Mott, *A Bibliography of the Works of John Bunyan*, supplement to the Bibliographical Society's *Transactions*, 6 (Oxford: Oxford University Press, 1932).

Huckabay, Calvin, *John Milton: A Bibliographical Supplement, 1929–1957* (Pittsburgh, PA: Duquesne University Press, 1960).

—, *John Milton: An Annotated Bibliography, 1968–1988* (Pittsburgh, PA: Duquesne University Press, 1996).

Klemp, Paul Jerald, *The Essential Milton: An Annotated Bibliography of Major Modern Studies* (Boston, MA: G. K. Hall, 1989).

Patrides, Constantine A., *An Annotated Critical Bibliography of John Milton* (Brighton: Harvester Press, 1987).

Roberts, Richard Owen, *Whitefield in Print: A Bibliographic Record of Works by, for and against George Whitefield* (Wheaton, IL: Richard Owen Roberts, Publishers, 1988).

Shawcross, John Thomas, *John Milton: A Bibliography*, www.itergateway.org/resources/id=3.

—, *Milton: A Bibliography for the Years 1624–1700* (Binghamton, NY: Medieval & Renaissance Texts & Studies, 1984).

Thomas, David Oswald, Stephens, John and Jones, Peter Alun Lewis, *A Bibliography of the Works of Richard Price* (Aldershot: Scolar Press, 1993).

Thompson, Elbert Nevius Sebring, *John Milton: Topical Bibliography* (New Haven, CT: Yale University Press, 1916).

j. Bibliographies of Individuals: Wesleys

Baker, Frank, *A Union Catalogue of the Publications of John and Charles Wesley* (Durham, NC: Divinity School, Duke University, 1966; 2nd edn, Stone Mountain, GA: George Zimmermann, 1991).

Bullen, Donald Alfred, 'Bibliography', in Kenneth George Charles Newport and Ted Allen Campbell (eds), *Charles Wesley: Life, Literature and Legacy* (Peterborough: Epworth, 2007), pp. 533–64.

Collins, Kenneth Joseph, *A Wesley Bibliography* (Wilmore, KY: First Fruits Press, [2012]), http://place.asburyseminary.edu/firstfruitspapers/4/.

Field, Clive Douglas, 'Charles Wesley Bibliography, 1985–2009', *Bulletin of the John Rylands University Library of Manchester*, 88/2 (2006), pp. 179–214.

Green, Richard, 'A List (Chiefly) of Published Biographies and Biographical Notices of John Wesley, Arranged in Alphabetical Order', *Proceedings of the Wesley Historical Society*, 3 (1901–2), pp. 217–36.

—, *The Works of John and Charles Wesley: A Bibliography* (2nd edn, London: Methodist Publishing House, 1906).

Jarboe, Betty M., *John and Charles Wesley: A Bibliography* (Metuchen, NJ: American Theological Library Association and Scarecrow Press, 1987).

Judson, Sandra, 'Biographical and Descriptive Works on the Rev. John Wesley' (unpublished University of London Diploma in Librarianship, 1963).

McIntosh, Lawrence Dennis, 'The Place of John Wesley in the Christian Tradition: A Selected Bibliography', in Kenneth Elmer Rowe (ed.), *The Place of Wesley in the Christian Tradition* (Metuchen, NJ: Scarecrow Press, 1976), pp. 134–59.

Melton, John Gordon, 'An Annotated Bibliography of Publications about the Life and Work of John Wesley, 1791–1966', *Methodist History*, 7/4 (1969), pp. 29–46.

Rogal. Samuel J., *A Bibliographical Survey of the Published Works of the Eighteenth-Century Wesleys (Samuel the Elder, Samuel the Younger, Mehetabel, John and Charles)* (Lewiston, NY: Edwin Mellen Press, 2008).

Sommer, E. F., 'John Wesley: eine bibliographische Skizze', *Mitteilungen der Studiengemeinschaft für Geschichte des Methodismus*, 4 (1966–67), pp. 4–47.

Trouten, Edsel Russell, 'A Select Bibliography of Primary and Secondary Literary Data on the Founder of Methodism, John Wesley' (unpublished M.A. thesis, Cincinnati Bible Seminary, 1988).

k. Non-Parochial Registers

Ambler, Rodney William, 'Sources for Church History, 5: Non-Parochial Registers and the Local Historian', *Local Historian*, 10 (1972–73), pp. 59–64.

General Register Office: Registers of Births, Marriages and Deaths Surrendered to the Non-Parochial Registers Commissions, RG 4 and RG 8, List & Index Society, 265–66, 2 vols (Richmond: The Society, 1996).

General Register Office: Society of Friends' Registers, Notes and Certificates of Births, Marriages and Deaths (RG 6), List & Index Society, 267 (Richmond: The Society, 1996).

Ifans, Dafydd (ed.), *Nonconformist Registers of Wales* (Aberystwyth: National Library of Wales and Welsh County Archivists' Group, 1994).

Townsend, Sheila and Townsend, Stephen, *Nonconformist Registers for Cornwall held at the Public Record Office*, 6 vols (St Austell: Shelkay, 2000).

Watts, Michael Robert, *The Dissenters, Volume 2: The Expansion of Evangelical Nonconformity* (Oxford: Clarendon Press, 1995), pp. 303–27, 718–88.

Welch, Charles Edwin, 'Nonconformist Registers', *Journal of the Society of Archivists*, 2 (1960–64), pp. 411–17.

IV. Chapel Sources

The chapel or congregation was the lowest and most fundamental unit of Nonconformist organization, even in denominations which had a national framework of governance. Although there is no comprehensive record of Nonconformist chapels over time, there are numerous lists. Sources from outside Nonconformity are especially important here. For instance, after the 'Toleration Act' (1689) it was a requirement to register meeting houses with the authorities in England and Wales, licenses being issued by county and borough quarter sessions or episcopal and archidiaconal registries. With the Protestant Dissenters Act (1852) responsibility was transferred to the registrar general, with whose successors it still resides, although registration became permissive in 1855 except in connection with the solemnization of marriages. Most of these records are unpublished, being held by the National Archives or the Office for National Statistics in Southport, but some county editions have been published.

Church of England clergy visitation returns also shed much light on local Nonconformity, particularly for the eighteenth and early nineteenth centuries, and a good many of these have also been printed in recent years. The returns from the 1851 religious census are likewise steadily being published, with the whole of Wales now covered and about half of England (Bedfordshire, Berkshire, Buckinghamshire, Derbyshire, Devon, Hampshire, Hertfordshire, Kent, Lincolnshire, Norfolk, Northamptonshire, Nottinghamshire, Oxfordshire, Rutland, Shropshire, Suffolk, Surrey, Sussex, Worcestershire and Yorkshire). Nonconformist lists of congregations are available from the eighteenth century, the Evans and Thompson surveys being best known. There were also several denominational efforts, the Baptists, for example, compiling periodic lists of their meetings, commencing with John Rippon's *Baptist Annual Register* in the 1790s and continuing in the *Baptist Magazine* at intervals between 1811 and 1835. Thereafter, denominational handbooks increasingly recorded the locations of chapels, with the conspicuous exception of the Methodists (who, in their minutes of conference, mostly only listed the circuits into which chapels were grouped). There are also a number of bibliographies of chapel histories and gazetteers of chapels.

a. Bibliographies of Chapel Histories and Sources

Barton, David Anthony, 'Methodism in Derbyshire: A Provisional Bibliography of Printed Works Relating to Methodism in Derbyshire', *Heritage: Journal of the East Midlands Branch of the Wesley Historical Society*, 2/2 (1985), pp. i–viii.

Calkin, Homer L., *Catalog of Methodist Archival and Manuscript Collections (Part 6), Great Britain and Ireland*, 8 vols ([Arlington, VA]: World Methodist Historical Society, 1985–91).

English, James Seymour, *A Bibliography of Lincolnshire Methodism* (Gainsborough: The Author, 1994).

Farrar, Michael, 'Records of Nonconformity in Cambridgeshire', in Norma Virgoe and Tom Williamson (eds), *Religious Dissent in East Anglia: Historical Perspectives* (Norwich: Centre of East Anglian Studies, University of East Anglia, 1993), pp. 149–52.

Field, Clive Douglas, 'The Protestant Churches', in Carl Chinn (ed.), *Birmingham: Bibliography of a City* (Birmingham: University of Birmingham Press, 2003), pp. 78–110.

Hill, Andrew McKean, *English Presbyterian/General Baptist/Unitarian Congregations in Great Britain: Location List of Records*, www.unitarianhistory.org.uk/hsrecords.html.

Independent Chapels of Wales, www.llgc.org.uk/index.php?id=independentchapelsofwales.

Jones, Gwenith, *The Descent of Dissent: A Guide to the Nonconformist Records at the Leicestershire Record Office* (Leicester: Leicestershire Museums, Arts and Records Service, 1989).

Leary, William, *Local Methodist Records: A Brief Explanation of Local Methodist Archival Material Deposited in County Record Offices* (Bognor Regis: W.M.H.S. Publications, 1981).

Lloyd, Gareth, *Researching the History of a Chapel at the Methodist Archives and Research Centre* (Manchester: John Rylands University Library of Manchester, 1995).

Nonconformist Congregations in Great Britain: A List of Histories and other Material in Dr Williams's Library (London: Dr Williams's Trust, 1973).

Nonconformist Records: A Brief Introduction (Kingston upon Thames: Surrey Record Office, 1988).

Owen, Bob, 'Llyfryddiaeth Crynwyr Meirionydd' [bibliography of Merionethshire Quakerism], *Journal of the Welsh Bibliographical Society*, 7 (1950–53), pp. 1–17.

Owen, David Huw, 'Capeli sir Ddinbych' [chapels of Denbighshire], *Transactions of the Denbighshire Historical Society*, 56 (2008), pp. 133–60.

—, 'Chapels of Glamorgan: A Bibliographical Survey, 1981–2006', *Morgannwg*, 50 (2006), pp. 166–84.

Parsons, Kenneth, 'Printed Sources for the History of Dissent in Cambridgeshire', in Elisabeth Somerville Leedham-Green (ed.), *Religious Dissent in East Anglia* (Cambridge: Cambridge Antiquarian Society, 1991), pp. 125–33.

Rawlins, Bert J., *The Parish Churches and Nonconformist Chapels of Wales: Their Records and Where to Find Them – Volume 1: Cardigan, Carmarthen and Pembrokeshire* (Salt Lake City, UT: Celtic Heritage Research, 1987).

Richardson, Sidney Yearsley, 'Methodism in Leicester, City and County: A Provisional Bibliography', *Heritage: Journal of the East Midlands Branch of the Wesley Historical Society*, 1/10 (1984), pp. i–viii.

Roberts, Helen E., *Researching Yorkshire Quaker History: A Guide to Sources* (Hull: Brynmor Jones Library, University of Hull, 2003).

Robson, R. S., 'Our Congregational Bibliography', *Journal of the Presbyterian Historical Society of England*, 6 (1936–39), pp. 220–28, 340–41 and 7 (1940–43), p. 39.

Rose, Edward Alan, *A Register of Methodist Circuit Plans, 1777–1860* [with supplements to 1907], 6 vols ([Manchester]: Society of Cirplanologists, 1961–80).
Ruston, Alan Robert, *Nonconformity in Hertfordshire: A Guide to Sources for Family and Local Historians* (Barnet: Hertfordshire Family History Society, 2005).
—, *Bibliography of Unitarian Congregations which have Existed since 1800*, www.unitarianhistory.org.uk/hsbib4.html.
Spittal, Charles Jeffrey, *Wesley Historical Society: Index to the Proceedings of the Local Branches, Volume 2: 1995–2005* ([Bristol: New Room, 2009]).
Spittal, Charles Jeffrey and Nichols, George, *Wesley Historical Society: Index to the Proceedings of the Local Branches, 1959–1994* (Manchester: John Rylands University Library of Manchester, 1995).
Stampe, George, 'List of Local Histories, Compiled Chiefly by Mr George Stampe from His Collection', *Proceedings of the Wesley Historical Society*, 1 (1897–98), pp. 3–14.
—, 'A Supplemental List of Local Methodist Histories in George Stampe's Collection', *Proceedings of the Wesley Historical Society*, 6 (1907–8), pp. 70–74.
Surman, Charles Edward, *A Bibliography of Congregational Church History* ([Birmingham]: Congregational Historical Society, 1947).
Swarbrick, Judith, *The Sacred Annals Speak: Methodist History in Lancashire County Library Local Studies Collections – A Bibliography* (Preston: Lancashire County Council Library, Museums and Arts Committee, 1996).
Swift, Wesley Frank, *How to Write a Local History of Methodism* (5th rev., with additions by Thomas Shaw and Edward Alan Rose, Nantwich: Wesley Historical Society, 1994).
Sydenham, George, 'Source Material for the History of Suffolk Congregationalism', *Suffolk Review*, 4/2 (1973), pp. 41–52.
Thorne, Roger Frank Sidney, *Methodism in Devon: A Handlist of Chapels and Their Records* (Exeter: Devon Record Office, 1983; 2nd edn, 1989).
—, *Methodism in the South-West: An Historical Bibliography* ([Topsham: The Author, 1983]).
—, '"Our Providential Way": A Bibliography of the History of Dissent in Devon', *Devonshire Association Report and Transactions*, 127 (1995), pp. 201–46.
Walters, Huw, 'Eglwysi Annibynnol Cymru: llyfrau a llyfrynnau' [bibliography of Welsh Independent chapels], *Y Cofiadur*, 51 (1986), pp. 26–29; 52 (1987), pp. 27–35; 58 (1993), pp. 42–43.
Ward, Graham, *Sources for Researching Nonconformists in Northamptonshire* ([Northampton]: Northamptonshire Family History Society, 2004).

b. Gazetteers of Chapels

Butler, David M., *The Quaker Meeting Houses of Britain*, 2 vols (London: Friends' Historical Society, 1999).
—, *Quaker Meeting Houses of the Lake Counties* (London: Friends' Historical Society, 1978).
Chambers, Ralph Frederick, *The Strict Baptist Chapels of England*, 5 vols ([London: Strict Baptist Historical Society, 1952–68]).
The Churches of Britain and Ireland [photographs], www.churches-uk-ireland.org/.
Collett, Pauline, *Rutland in Dissent: 350 Years of Protestant Meeting-Houses and Chapels* (Stamford: Spiegl Press, 2011).

Cox, Janice V., *Shropshire's Nonconformist Chapels*, www.users.waitrose.com/~coxfamily/.

Ede, Janet, Virgoe, Norma and Williamson, Tom, *Halls of Zion: Chapels and Meeting-Houses in Norfolk* (Norwich: Centre of East Anglian Studies, University of East Anglia, 1994).

Edwards, Eric, *Yr Eglwys Fethodistaidd* (Llandysul: Gwasg Gomer, 1980; supplement, 1987).

Edwards, Huw, *Capeli Llanelli: Our Rich Heritage* (Carmarthen: Carmarthenshire County Council Libraries and Heritage Section, 2009).

Evans, George Eyre, *Vestiges of Protestant Dissent* (Liverpool: F. & E. Gibbons, 1897).

Hague, Graham, *The Unitarian Heritage: An Architectural Survey of Chapels and Churches in the Unitarian Tradition in the British Isles* (Sheffield: Unitarian Heritage, 1986).

Hall, John, *Britain Quaker Meeting Houses*, www.flickr.com/photos/qmh/.

—, *Friends Meeting Houses*, 11 vols (2011–12), www.magcloud.com/user/dangerfield.

Jones, Alan Vernon, *Chapels of the Cynon Valley* (Aberdare: Cynon Valley History Society, 2004).

Jones, Anthony, *Welsh Chapels* (rev. and expanded edn, Stroud: Alan Sutton Publishing in association with National Museums & Galleries of Wales, 1996).

Jones, Geraint I. L., *Capeli Môn* [Anglesey chapels] (Llanrwst: Gwasg Carreg Gwalch, 2007).

Jones, J. Eric, *Gardens of Faith: Unitarian Heritage Sites in Wales* ([no place]: Unitarian Welsh Department, 2006).

—, *The Good Ground: Unitarian Places of Worship in Wales* ([Aberdare]: Unitarian Welsh Department, 2010).

Jones, Penri, *Capeli Cymru* (Talybont: Y Lolfa, 1980).

Kaye, Rosalind, *Chapels in Essex* ([Colchester]: Chellow Dean Press, 1999).

Lake, Jeremy, Cox, Jo and Berry, Eric, *Diversity and Vitality: The Methodist and Nonconformist Chapels of Cornwall* (Truro: Cornwall County Council Archaeological Unit, [2001]).

Methodist Church Buildings: Statistical Returns [1940, 1960, 1970, 1980, 1990, 2000], 6 vols (Manchester: Department for Chapel Affairs, [1947–2001]).

National Monuments Record, www.englishheritagearchives.org.uk/.

Neave, David and Neave, Susan, *East Riding Chapels and Meeting Houses* (Beverley: East Yorkshire Local History Society, 1990).

Oakley, Ray, *To the Glory of God: A History of the Development of the Salvation Army in the British Isles as Expressed, Illustrated and Symbolised through Its Buildings and some Paintings* (Leamington: The Author, 2011).

Owen, David Huw, *Capeli Cymru* (Talybont: Y Lolfa, 2005).

—, *The Chapels of Wales* (Bridgend: Seren, 2012).

Paul, Sydney Frank, *Further History of the Gospel Standard Baptists*, 6 vols ([Brighton: The Author], 1951–69).

Percival, David, 'Inventory of Nonconformist Chapels and Sunday Schools in Cardiganshire', in Geraint Huw Jenkins and Ieuan Gwynedd Jones (eds), *Cardiganshire County History, Volume 3: Cardiganshire in Modern Times* (Cardiff: University of Wales Press, 1998), pp. 508–39.

Returns of Accommodation Provided in Wesleyan Methodist Chapels and other Preaching Places [1873, 1881, 1891, 1901, 1911, 1931], 6 vols (London: Wesleyan Conference Office, 1875–1932).

Rushton, Tim, *Capeli – Chapels* (Talybont: Y Lolfa in association with the Royal Commission on the Ancient and Historical Monuments of Wales, 2012).

Sinclair, J. B. and Fenn, R. W. D., *Marching to Zion: Radnorshire Chapels* (Kington: Cadoc Books, 1990).

Smith, Ian, *Tin Tabernacles: Corrugated Iron Mission Halls, Churches & Chapels of Britain* ([Pembroke]: Camrose Organisation, 2004).

Stell, Christopher Fyson, *An Inventory of Nonconformist Chapels and Meeting-Houses* [in England], 4 vols (London: HMSO, 1986–2002).

Temple, Philip, *Islington Chapels: An Architectural Guide to Nonconformist and Roman Catholic Places of Worship in the London Borough of Islington* (London: Royal Commission on the Historical Monuments of England, 1992).

United Methodist Church, *A List of Our Churches Classified in Alphabetical Order in Circuits and Districts* (London: Henry Hooks, [1926]).

Webb, Nigel, *Rutland Nonconformist Chapels and Meetings* (substantially rev., 2011), www.rutlandhistory.org/pdf/rutlandchapels.pdf.

Williams, Ned, *Black Country Chapels* [photographs], 3 vols (Thrupp: Sutton Publishing, 2004–8).

c. Registrations of Meeting Houses

Chandler, John Howard (ed.), *Wiltshire Dissenters' Meeting House Certificates and Registrations, 1689–1852*, Wiltshire Record Society, 40 (Devizes: The Society, 1985).

Dissenters' Places of Worship: List of Returns Made to the Registrar General of the Number of Certified Places of Religious Worship of Protestant Dissenters, House of Commons Papers, Session (1852–53), p. 78.

Donaldson, Barbara (ed.), *The Registrations of Dissenting Chapels and Meeting Houses in Staffordshire, 1689–1852*, Collections for a History of Staffordshire, Fourth Series, 3 ([Stafford]: Staffordshire Record Society, 1960).

Emanuel, Hywel David, 'Dissent in the Counties of Glamorgan and Monmouth', *National Library of Wales Journal*, 8 (1953–54), pp. 399–418; 9 (1955–56), pp. 22–41, 216–34.

'Register of Places of Worship, 1689 to 1852', The National Archives, RG 31, 11 vols.

Spurrier, Lisa (ed.), *Berkshire Nonconformist Meeting House Registrations, 1689–1852*, Berkshire Record Society, 9–10, 2 vols (Reading: The Society, 2005).

Welch, Charles Edwin (ed.), *Bedfordshire Chapels and Meeting Houses Official Registration, 1672–1901*, Publications of the Bedfordshire Historical Record Society, 75 (Bedford: The Society, 1996).

—, 'The Registration of Meeting Houses', *Journal of the Society of Archivists*, 3 (1965–69), pp. 116–20.

Willis, Arthur James (ed.), 'Dissenters' Meeting House Certificates in the Diocese of Winchester, 1702–1844', in Arthur James Willis (ed.), *A Hampshire Miscellany* (Lyminge: The Editor, 1963–67), pp. 109–200.

d. Published Editions of Church of England Visitation Returns

Details of published editions of the returns, and of *specula* derived from them, will be found in:

Field, Clive Douglas, 'Appendix 4: Church of England Clergy Visitation Returns of the Eighteenth and Nineteenth Centuries', in Clive Douglas Field, *Religious Statistics in Great Britain: An Historical Introduction* (Manchester: Institute for Social Change, University of Manchester, 2010), pp. 66–69, www.brin.ac.uk/wp-content/uploads/2011/12/development-of-religious-statistics.pdf.

e. Other Non-Recurrent Listings to ca 1850

Ambler, Rodney William, 'A Lost Source? The 1829 Returns of Non-Anglican Places of Worship', *Local Historian*, 17 (1986–87), pp. 483–89.

Bate, Frank, *The Declaration of Indulgence, 1672* (London: Archibald Constable for the University Press of Liverpool, 1908).

Creasey, John, *Index to the John Evans List of Dissenting Congregations and Ministers, 1715–1729 in Dr Williams's Library* (London: Dr Williams's Trust, 1964).

[Crippen, Thomas George (ed.)], 'A View of English Nonconformity in 1773', *Transactions of the Congregational Historical Society*, 5 (1911–12), pp. 205–22, 261–77, 372–85.

'Evangelical Baptist Churches in England', *Baptist Magazine*, 27 (1835, supplement).

Evans, John, 'List of Dissenting Congregations and Ministers in England and Wales, 1715–29', Dr Williams's Library MS. 38.4.

Gordon, Alexander (ed.), *Freedom after Ejection: A Review (1690–1692) of Presbyterian and Congregational Nonconformity in England and Wales* (Manchester: University Press, 1917).

Return of the Number of Parish Churches and Chapels and Chapels of Ease of the Church of England, and of the Number of Places of Worship not of the Church of England; so far as Regards the County of Lancaster, House of Commons Sessional Papers (1830), 19.

Thompson, Josiah, 'List of Dissenting Congregations in England and Wales, 1772–3', Dr Williams's Library MS. 38.6.

Turner, George Lyon (ed.), *Original Records of Early Nonconformity under Persecution and Indulgence*, 3 vols (London: T. Fisher Unwin, 1911–14).

Whiteman, Anne (ed.), *The Compton Census of 1676: A Critical Edition* (London: Oxford University Press, 1986).

[Whitley, William Thomas], 'The Baptist Interest under George I', *Transactions of the Baptist Historical Society*, 2 (1910–11), pp. 95–109.

Wykes, David L., 'The 1669 Return of Nonconformist Conventicles', in Kathryn M. Thompson (ed.), *Short Guides to Records, Second Series, Guides 25–48* (London: Historical Association, 1997), pp. 50–54.

f. Published Editions of Local Returns to the 1851 Religious Census

Details of published editions of the returns, and of secondary analysis of them, will be found in:

Field, Clive Douglas, 'Appendix 2: Recent Publications on the 1851 Religious Census of England and Wales', in Clive Douglas Field, *Religious Statistics in Great Britain: An Historical Introduction* (Manchester: Institute for Social Change, University of Manchester, 2010), pp. 60–63, www.brin.ac.uk/wp-content/uploads/2011/12/development-of-religious-statistics.pdf.

—, 'The 1851 Religious Census: A Select Bibliography of Materials Relating to England and Wales', *Proceedings of the Wesley Historical Society*, 41 (1977–78), pp. 175–82.

—, 'The 1851 Religious Census of Great Britain: A Bibliographical Guide for Local and Regional Historians', *Local Historian*, 27 (1997), pp. 194–217.

—, *The 1851 Religious Census of Great Britain: A Bibliographical Guide for Local and Regional Historians* (Salisbury: British Association for Local History, 1999).

V. Other Sources

I have described Nonconformity's involvement in statistics-gathering and social surveys elsewhere,[5] so only a brief account is necessary here. Although elements within the Free Church tradition have been suspicious of statistics, sometimes citing King David's sin in numbering the people of Israel as biblical foundation for their opposition, the Nonconformist movement as a whole has not been averse to deploying quantitative data in its cause, when it has suited its purposes. During the eighteenth and early nineteenth centuries the Old Dissent in particular saw value in demonstrating its numerical importance as a means of influencing government to relax the legislative restrictions which still remained after the 'Toleration Act' (1689). However, much of this early quantification was around ministers and places of worship. While Methodism commenced the regular collection of membership figures, in 1766, soon followed by the New Connexion of General Baptists, from 1770, it was not until the second half of the nineteenth century that Baptists, Congregationalists, Quakers, Welsh Calvinistic Methodists and other, smaller bodies followed suit at national level. Statistics were invariably published in the relevant denominational annual handbook, but some collation of the figures of membership, Sunday School work, ordained and lay ministry and so forth was undertaken for many years after 1900 by the National Council of the Evangelical Free Churches and the Free Church Federal Council. *Churches and Churchgoers* is the best modern guide to statistical series until 1970. Attendance data have been less systematically gathered, but publication in 1854 of the results of the 1851 Religious Census in England and Wales did lead to Nonconformist-inspired attempts to enumerate sittings and worshippers at the local level in the late Victorian and Edwardian eras. National censuses are only available periodically after 1979, thanks to the efforts of the Bible Society and Christian Research. Various ad hoc surveys of specific denominations were also conducted during these same decades. It should be noted that, apart from statistics of the solemnization of marriages from 1837, the state has undertaken little regular quantification of Nonconformity, with the 1851 Religious Census and the Royal Commission on the Church of England in Wales (the survey took place in 1905) being the main non-recurrent exceptions.

Audio-visual materials constitute a seriously underexploited resource for studying Nonconformity, partly because they are often inadequately catalogued, lack curatorial oversight and are unusually widely dispersed. The British Library and the British Film Institute are the national archives for sound and moving image, respectively, but it should be noted that there is still no legal deposit of publications in these media. The National Screen and Sound Archive of Wales (part of the National Library of Wales) is a significant Welsh collection, as is the Museum of Welsh Life for the nation's oral history. For the rest, much other sound and moving image material is held locally, although the Wesley Historical Society and the Baptist Historical Society have national oral history programmes for their own traditions. Some Nonconformist archives have large photographic collections, especially the Quakers and the Salvation Army, and photographs also feature strongly in overseas missionary archives. However, many images pertaining to Nonconformity will be found in more general photographic collections, including commercial picture libraries such as the Mary Evans Picture Library and the Francis Frith Collection. The British Museum's Department of Prints and Drawings is a good starting-point for caricature, while paintings and pottery are particularly important for Methodism.

Since the mid-1990s the world wide web has become the dominant medium for the dissemination of current information, and the Free Churches have not been immune from this trend, with official and unofficial websites proliferating. Much of the information on these sites has not been published in parallel in conventional printed form, and a great deal of it is ephemeral. Therefore, students of contemporary Nonconformity will increasingly need to use the web as a source of primary evidence. Unfortunately, websites are often transient, and much valuable content has already been lost, partly because it has been deemed out-of-date and hence has been over-written, and partly because digital preservation technology is in its infancy. Nevertheless, some early sites may still be retrievable from the *Internet Archive*, while, since 2004, the *UK Web Archive* has been endeavouring to capture UK websites on a selective basis, where permissions have been forthcoming. The latter has two so-called special collections on the Free Churches and the Quakers, the second being especially impressive, since the Society of Friends has co-operated at national and local levels to ensure that its web presence is archived. The web is also a mechanism for publishing secondary and tertiary sources, many of which have already been individually noted, above. Additionally, major research programmes into Nonconformity will typically have their own websites, two examples being *Dissenting Academies Online*, a joint initiative of Dr Williams's Centre for Dissenting Studies and the Sussex Centre for Intellectual History, and the Manchester Wesley Research Centre.

a. Statistics: General

Barley, Lynda M., Field, Clive Douglas, Kosmin, Barry Alexander and Nielsen, Jørgen S., *Religion*, Reviews of United Kingdom Statistical Sources, 20 (Oxford: Pergamon Press, 1987), www.brin.ac.uk/commentary/documents/eBook-RUKSS-Religion.pdf.

Brierley, Peter William, *A Century of British Christianity: Historical Statistics, 1900–1985* (London: MARC Europe, 1989).

—, *Religion in Britain, 1900 to 2000* (London: Christian Research, 1998).

— (ed.), *UK Church Statistics, 2005–2015* (Tonbridge: ADBC Publishers, 2011).

British Religion in Numbers, www.brin.ac.uk.

Currie, Robert and Gilbert, Alan David, 'Religion', in Albert Henry Halsey (ed.), *Trends in British Society since 1900* (London: Macmillan, 1972), pp. 407–50.

Currie, Robert, Gilbert, Alan David and Horsley, Lee, *Churches and Churchgoers: Patterns of Church Growth in the British Isles since 1700* (Oxford: Clarendon Press, 1977).

Field, Clive Douglas, 'Counting Religion in England and Wales: The Long Eighteenth Century, *c.*1680-*c.*1840', *Journal of Ecclesiastical History*, 63 (2012), pp. 693–720.

—, *Religious Statistics in Great Britain: An Historical Introduction* (Manchester: Institute for Social Change, University of Manchester, 2010), www.brin.ac.uk/wp-content/uploads/2011/12/development-of-religious-statistics.pdf.

Royal Commission on the Church of England in Wales and other Religious Bodies in Wales and Monmouthshire, 6 vols, House of Commons Sessional Papers (1910), 14–19.

UK Christian Handbook (1982–2009).

UK Christian Handbook: Religious Trends (1997–2008).

Williams, Lawrence John, *Digest of Welsh Historical Statistics*, 2 vols (Cardiff: Welsh Office, 1985), II, pp. 249–354.

—, *Digest of Welsh Historical Statistics, 1974–1996* ([Cardiff]: Government Statistical Service, 1998), pp. 299–307.

b. Statistics: Church Attendance

Brierley, Peter William, *'Christian' England: What the 1989 English Church Census Reveals* (London: MARC Europe, 1991).

— (ed.), *Prospects for the Eighties: From a Census of the Churches in 1979 Undertaken by the Nationwide Initiative in Evangelism*, 2 vols (London: Bible Society, 1980–83).

—, *Prospects for the Nineties: Trends and Tables from the 1989 English Church Census* (London: MARC Europe, 1991).

—, *Pulling Out of the Nosedive: A Contemporary Picture of Churchgoing – What the 2005 English Church Census Reveals* (London: Christian Research, 2006).
—, *The Tide Is Running Out: What the English Church Attendance Survey Reveals* (London: Christian Research, 2000).
Brierley, Peter William and Evans, Byron, *Prospects for Wales: Report of the 1982 Census of the Churches* (London: Bible Society, 1983).
Census of Great Britain, 1851: Religious Worship, England and Wales – Report and Tables, House of Commons Sessional Papers (1852–53), 89.
Gallacher, John, *Challenge to Change: Results of the 1995 Welsh Churches Survey* ([Swindon]: British and Foreign Bible Society, [1997]).
Mearns, Andrew, *The Statistics of Attendance at Public Worship, as Published in England, Wales and Scotland by the Local Press between October 1881 and February 1882* (London: Hodder and Stoughton, 1882).
Mudie-Smith, Richard (ed.), *The Religious Life of London* (London: Hodder and Stoughton, 1904).
The Newspaper Religious Census and Its Lessons: A Summary of the Statistics of Attendance at Public Worship, Published between October 1881 and April 1882 (London: Society for the Liberation of Religion from State Patronage and Control, 1882).
The Religious Census of London: Reprinted from 'The British Weekly' (London: Hodder and Stoughton, 1888).

c. Paintings and Pottery

Forsaith, Peter Stuart, 'Methodism and Its Images', in Charles Yrigoyen (ed.), *T & T Clark Companion to Methodism* (London: T&T Clark, 2010), pp. 350–68.
—, 'Oxford Brookes University', in *Oil Paintings in Public Ownership in Berkshire, Buckinghamshire & Oxfordshire* (London: Public Catalogue Foundation, 2009), pp. 288–305.
—, 'Material and Cultural Aspects of Methodism: Architecture, Artefacts, and Art', in William Gibson, Peter Stuart Forsaith and Martin Wellings (eds), *The Ashgate Research Companion to World Methodism* (Farnham: Ashgate, 2013), pp. 387–406.
Harvey, John, *The Art of Piety: The Visual Culture of Welsh Nonconformity* (Cardiff: University of Wales Press, 1995).
—, *Image of the Invisible: The Visualization of Religion in the Welsh Nonconformist Tradition* (Cardiff: University of Wales Press, 1999).
Lee, Roger, *Wesleyana and Methodist Pottery: A Short Guide* ([London: The Author], 1988).
Miller, John, *Religion in the Popular Prints, 1600–1832* (Cambridge: Chadwyck-Healey, 1986).
Rogal, Samuel J., *The Historical, Biographical and Artistic Background of Extant Portrait Paintings and Engravings of John Wesley (1742–1951)* (Lewiston, NY: Edwin Mellen Press, 2003).
Ryan, Donald Holt, *The Doughty Collection of Wesleyana* [at Epworth Old Rectory] (Wolverhampton: The Author, 2008).
—, *The Horace Hird Collection of Wesleyana* [at Mount Zion Methodist Church and Heritage Centre, Halifax] (Wolverhampton: The Author, 2004).

—, *The Sidney Lawson Collection of Wesleyana* [at the John Rylands University Library of Manchester] (Wolverhampton: The Author, 2003).
—, *John Wesley's Chapel, The New Room, Bristol: Collection of Wesleyana and Artefacts* (Wolverhampton: The Author, 2012).
Wollen, Roger A., *Catalogue of the Methodist Church Collection of Modern Christian Art, with an Account of the Collection's History* (Oxford: Trustees of the Collection, Wesley Centre, Oxford Brookes University, 2003).
Your Paintings: Uncovering the Nation's Art Collection, www.bbc.co.uk/arts/yourpaintings/.

d. Websites

Baptist Historical Society, www.baptisthistory.org.uk.
Capel: The Chapels Heritage Society [Wales], www.capeli.org.uk/.
Centre for Baptist History and Heritage, www.rpc.ox.ac.uk/index.php?pageid=16&tln=ResourceCentres
Chapels Society, www.chapelssociety.org.uk/.
Dissenting Academies Online, www.english.qmul.ac.uk/drwilliams/portal.html.
Dr Williams's Centre for Dissenting Studies, www.english.qmul.ac.uk/drwilliams/index.html.
Dr Williams's Library, www.dwlib.co.uk/dwlib/.
Friends Historical Society, www.f-h-s.org.uk/.
Internet Archive, www.archive.org/.
Manchester Wesley Research Centre, www.mwrc.ac.uk/.
UK Web Archive, www.webarchive.org.uk/ukwa/.
Unitarian Historical Society, www.unitarianhistory.org.uk/.
Wesley Historical Society, www.wesleyhistoricalsociety.org.uk/.

Notes

The author is grateful to Dr Lionel Madden, Dr Robert Pope and Professor Isabel Rivers for their comments on an initial draft of this chapter.

1 Clive Douglas Field, 'Preserving Zion: The Anatomy of Protestant Nonconformist Archives in Great Britain and Ireland', *Archives*, 33 (2008), pp. 14–51.
2 Dafydd Ifans (ed.), *Nonconformist Registers of Wales* (Aberystwyth: National Library of Wales and Welsh County Archivists' Group, 1994).
3 David J. H. Clifford, *My Ancestors were Congregationalists in England and Wales* (2nd rev. ed., London: Society of Genealogists, 1997).
4 Michael Robert Watts, *The Dissenters, Volume 2: The Expansion of Evangelical Nonconformity* (Oxford: Clarendon Press, 1995), pp. 303–27, 718–88.
5 Clive Douglas Field, *Religious Statistics in Great Britain: An Historical Introduction* (Manchester: Institute for Social Change, University of Manchester, 2010), pp. 16–23.

Part II

ABC of Nonconformity

Act of Uniformity

Various Acts of Uniformity sought to ensure common practice and order throughout the English church, thus rendering illegal any religious practice that was not found in the Book of Common Prayer (BCP). The first such act was passed in 1548 and it upheld the BCP as containing the only legal form of worship. A first offence was to be punished by loss of earnings and six months imprisonment; a second offence would result in a year's imprisonment; a third offence would lead to life imprisonment. The BCP was revised in 1552 rendering necessary a further act, though this was revoked during the reign of Mary I who tried to convert England back to Roman Catholicism. On the accession of Elizabeth I in 1559, a revised BCP was published and the new act went further than the previous two by trying to enforce attendance at worship in the parish church at least once a week. Those who did not attend were liable to be fined 12d.

The Act which had the most significant impact was that of 1662. While various attempts were made, following the restoration of the monarchy in 1660, to arrive at a church settlement which would include the more moderate Presbyterian Puritans within an Episcopalian structure, the Cavalier-dominated parliament still debated a Bill for Uniformity from early 1661 with the expectation that ministers would conform to the requirements of a revised BCP. The revisions were completed in early 1662 and the Bill passed into law on 19 May as 'An Act for the Uniformity of Publique Prayers and Administracion of Sacramentes & other Rites and Ceremonies and for establishing the Form of making, ordaining and consecrating Bishops, Priests and Deacons in the Church of England'. Although all of its clauses were amended over the following two centuries or so, the Act has never been formally repealed.

Under the terms of the Act, ministers, school teachers and university lecturers had to conform to the services and the requirements of the BCP, to declare that it was unlawful to take up arms against the king and to renounce the Solemn League and Covenant (1643) as unlawful. Those who had been episcopally ordained had to demonstrate proof that this had been the case; those who could not had to submit to ordination by a bishop. All had to be episcopally licensed. Assent had to be given publicly, either on or before 24 August, the Feast of St Bartholomew.

The 1662 Act sought the eradication of religious dissent by imposing uniformity of Faith and Order. Its motivation was political; it was implemented in order to quell religious enthusiasm of the sort which had led to, and condoned, the execution of the king in 1649. It has been calculated that between 1660 and 1662 a total of 1,760 ministers and 149 University and School teachers were ejected from their livings. The basis for their Nonconformity in 1662 was theological, whether it was because of objection to episcopal order, the refusal to allow the state to interfere in matters of faith, or the belief that an oath, once made, could not be broken. Not all ejected ministers held to all three principles and some of them later conformed, though it seems that this was probably as low as 10 per cent of them. Those who continued to preach after their ejection faced three months imprisonment. Not all ejected clergy were removed on 24 August, but the date entered into the Nonconformists' consciousness as 'Black Bartholomew's Day', recalling the slaughter of thousands of Huguenots on St Bartholomew's Day 1572.

There had been ejectments of ministers during the reigns of Queen Mary and King James, as well as during the Commonwealth. However, in 1662 many Nonconforming ministers were able to command popular support. As a result the Act failed in its purpose, namely the eradication of religious dissent. Instead it gave birth to a movement in England and Wales which would have major social and spiritual significance for three centuries and more.

RP

Arminianism

Arminianism is the word normally used to describe those who reject the confining of salvation to a predetermined number of the elect whose salvation had been ordained before the foundation of the world. Instead, Arminians focus on the exercise of human free will, promoted by the Spirit, in responding to the call of Christ. This way of systematizing theology has played a large part in Nonconformist thought, not only through those of Puritan origin in the Presbyterian, Congregational and General Baptist traditions who were unable to accept five-point Calvinism but also through those who followed the theology of the Wesleys in the Evangelical Revival and the birth of Methodism.

Jacobus Arminius (Jacob Harmenz, 1559–1609) was a Dutch Reformed pastor who had studied at Leyden, Marburg and in Geneva under Theodore Beza, who commended him back to the Dutch Church. He served as a pastor in Amsterdam from 1588 before becoming a professor at Leyden in 1603. Older historians were of the view that Arminius was initially an orthodox Calvinist and only later developed his revisionist views, but modern scholarship has argued that Reformed theology was only slowly developing an orthodoxy and that in the second half of the sixteenth century there was a considerable amount of permitted theological flexibility. Some scholars, such as Barrie White, speak of Arminianism as a form of revisionist Calvinism. Indeed Arminius' conflict with the authorities was one of the *causes célèbres* which served to reduce the range of acceptable beliefs, for Reformed theology as defined by the Synod of Dort (1618–19) clearly excluded his views of free will as heterodox.

Arminius' concern was essentially Christological, his problem being that if a person's destiny was already determined before the foundation of the world, the work of Christ was confined to effecting a salvation already determined. In other words, Christ's work was confined to a subordinate aspect of human redemption. Accordingly Arminius placed emphasis on God's foreknowledge rather than his prior determination of the fate of individuals. His part here was to determine the categories of persons to be saved or damned, that is to receive into favour those who believed and to exclude those who did not. Another way of expressing this is to say that Arminius reversed the orders of election and grace; for Reformed orthodoxy the operation of grace was dependent on election, but for Arminius election was subsequent to grace seen in God's determination to save all who repent and believe. Salvation then becomes dependent on the human response to the gospel which is an act of free choice though prompted by the Spirit and not something coerced by irresistible grace. This response God in his wisdom wholly foresaw, and thus his ability to count all such among the names of the elect. At the same time there is clear rejection here of any idea of a limited atonement.

After his death, Arminius' sympathizers drew up the Remonstrance to the States General asking for a revision of the Belgic Confession. The so-called five points of Arminianism were: (1) predestination is conditional on a person's response, being grounded in God's foreknowledge; (2) Christ died for all, but no one enjoys the forgiveness of sins except the believer; (3) human beings do not have saving grace of themselves, for in a state of sin they cannot do anything good, so they must be born again of the Spirit; (4) God's grace is the beginning, continuing and the accomplishing of all good, so all that a regenerate man succeeds in doing must be ascribed to the grace of God in Christ; such grace is not irresistible because scripture speaks of those who resisted the Holy Ghost; (5) in Christ and through his life-giving Spirit, the believer is equipped with all things necessary to resist temptation if only he or she will seek his assistance. These propositions were condemned at the Synod of Dort in 1618–19, when a Calvinist orthodoxy was established.

Scholars have distinguished between a seventeenth-century Arminianism 'of the head' and an eighteenth-century Arminianism 'of the heart' as incarnated in the Wesleyan revival. In the nineteenth century the fact of revivalism seemed to challenge all restricted views of the exercise of God's grace. In the writings of Jonathan Edwards it led to widespread amendment of Bezan Calvinism, and in the thinking of Charles Finney, during the nineteenth century, it found ample justification in an updated version of evangelical Arminianism.

JHYB

Baptist Missionary Society

The Baptist Missionary Society (BMS), or to give it its full title 'the Particular Baptist Society for the Propagation of the Gospel among the Heathen', was founded in 1792 during the dark years of conflict with Revolutionary and Napoleonic France, the first of the societies devoted to foreign missions to be established as a result of the Evangelical Revival. William Carey, its principal mover, would have preferred to establish a society with broad evangelical support, but deemed that impractical at that time. Behind the founding of the society lay the exposition, following the works of Jonathan Edwards of a newly shaped evangelical Calvinism articulated for British Baptists by Andrew Fuller who became the first secretary of the society. Operating from his Kettering pastorate, it was not until after Fuller's death in 1815 that the society opened a London office in 1819. Carey and Dr John Thomas, the society's first missionaries, were sent to Bengal in 1793 establishing themselves in Danish territory at Serampore. The first missionaries, very active in translation work, were bi-vocational, investing much of their private remuneration in the plant at Serampore, which they believed gave them distinct interests in its use and brought them into conflict with the committee in London. This, combined with differences over the breadth of curriculum and of student entry at the Serampore College, became the source of a rift between the Serampore missionaries and the London committee, which meant that at the end of his life Carey was not employed by the BMS but by a separate Serampore Mission Committee.

In 1812, the BMS began work in Sri Lanka, and two years later in Jamaica, where former slaves from the United States had already planted a number of Baptist churches not responsible to any mission organization. The Jamaica missionaries inevitably became involved with the issue of slavery with William Knibb becoming a notable campaigner for emancipation, secured by legislation in 1833 but not implemented until after the end of the Apprentice System in 1836. Baptist work among former slaves prospered and became the source of mission activity in Africa when Jamaicans under BMS auspices helped to found the Cameroon mission in 1841. On the reassignment of the

Cameroons to German sovereignty, this was, for the most part, transferred to the Basel Mission, prompting the BMS to relocate its activities to the Congo River in 1879, aided by munificence of Robert Arthington of Leeds who entertained a grand design for the evangelization of Central Africa.

The BMS had already begun work among the people of the ancient culture of China in 1859. Here the Welsh missionary Timothy Richard (1845–1919) developed new strategies for missionary work, challenging many evangelical orthodoxies. The approach that he commended was one of holistic mission, seeking to meet the needs of 'the whole man, body and soul', saving him 'from hell in this world as well as in the next' rather than pietistically focusing on salvation for the soul only. A focus on general education challenging the whole nation on issues of religion and ethics was to replace the concentration on Sabbath instruction of a religious minority. With a nod to Romans 13, believing that the strategy should be unashamedly élitist, missionaries should seek the support of 'God's appointed rulers', and those influential in education, exploiting the indigenous press rather than the foreign pulpit.

The fruits of the labours of BMS missionary personnel, at their highest in 1921–22, were seen in the establishment of substantial Baptist churches in north-east India, Jamaica the Democratic Republic of Congo and Angola, while also working to establish the church in China. The older missiology of a sending church assigning its personnel to receiving mission fields gave way to a pattern of partnership with a number of autonomous churches. Since the 1980s missionary organizations have contained more short-term personnel and fewer career missionaries, working in smaller teams in a wider spread of countries. While engaging in educational, agricultural and medical missions, and engaging in relief activities, the BMS remains committed to evangelism as a priority.

JHYB

Baptist Union of Great Britain and Ireland

At the end of the eighteenth century, Baptist life in England was becoming more organized. Baptists were proud of their leadership in the modern missionary movement with the establishment of the Baptist Missionary Society in 1792; new regional associations with a missionary purpose, and new colleges had come into being to provide a properly trained ministry, and the denomination now had its own periodicals. In 1813 a first (Particular) Baptist Union serving the whole nation was founded, but within twenty years it was remodelled to allow evangelical General Baptists churches to become members, a process which came to full fruition in 1891 when the two streams of Baptist life fully united. However the Union was slow to win the affections of British Baptists. Apparently the 182 Baptist ministers who attended the meeting of the Anti-Corn Law League in Manchester in 1841 was a larger number than had at that time attended a Baptist Union meeting.

At the time of the launch of the 1833 Union, there were at most 70,000 Baptists in England. This had risen to just short of 411,000 with some 570,000 Sunday School scholars enrolled, by the high point of 1906, but by 1991 this had fallen back to ca 160,000 members (or rather less than a quarter of a million, if strict and independent Baptists as well as those in Wales, Scotland and Ireland are added to those in churches in membership with the Union) with some 136,000 associated young people.

Superficially the two most significant figures in Baptist life in the nineteenth century Charles Haddon Spurgeon and John Clifford might be seen to represent the old Particular and General Baptist traditions; both of them in their differing ways helped the denomination to engage with the emerging urban industrial culture. Spurgeon, ever anxious to defend the faith of the Puritans, did so with homely interpretation of scripture, bringing the great doctrines of the faith within the reach of the large congregations that filled his Metropolitan Tabernacle every Sunday. This great church also supported a battery of agencies and organizations which sought to meet the social and spiritual needs of the people of south London. However his concern at the developments in liberal theology, representing a 'departure from Scriptural truth' led to the Down Grade Contoversy of 1887–88, and Spurgeon's resignation from the Union. While John Clifford was deemed to hold advanced views in many areas of theology, wrote socialist tracts for the Fabian Society and led the 'Passive Resistance Movement' against the British government's determination to give rate aid to denominational schools, he, like Spurgeon was passionately committed to the promotion of personal evangelism. By contrast with Spurgeon he was elected in turn to the presidencies of the Baptist Union and the Baptist World Alliance.

Such disparate endeavours were forged into a working denomination by J. H. Shakespeare who served as general secretary of the Union from 1898 to 1924. Symbolic of his work was the opening of Baptist Church House on Southampton Row in Holborn in 1903 giving the Union a fitting home for the first time, an intelligence centre for the denomination, housing its various departments and agencies and providing facilities for its members to take counsel together. J. H. Rushbrooke did not exaggerate when in his obituary he described Shakespeare as 'the real founder of the Baptist Union' giving its mission and ministry both shape and power.

In more recent years Baptists have emerged as a bridge denomination between the mainstream denominations with their ecumenical concerns and the world of evangelical religion. Ecumenically they have taken a leading role in the several councils of the Free Churches in England, and were founding members of both the British Council of Churches (as later of Churches Together in England, and Churches Together in Britain and Ireland) and the World Council of Churches. At the same time many Baptists have given service to the Evangelical Alliance of which body many Baptist churches are members. None of this ecumenical involvement has been adversely affected by the Union moving its headquarters out of central London, which was a fear upheld by the 9 per cent of council members who voted against the Union moving its offices to Didcot in 1989, a move which enabled the fulfilment of long-held desires for BUGB and BMS to share offices in the same building.

Denominational agencies and departments are now more developed than in 1900, offering resources to the local church in various areas of ministry and mission. A system of regional ministry seeks to interpret the principles of *episcope* within a free-church context with particular emphases on the pastoral care of ministers and equipping the churches for mission each in its own locality. Worship patterns have changed with the denomination open to charismatic influences and enriched by them. A further change is the way in which the so-called mission fields of Asia, Africa and Latin America have come to Britain with the largest congregations in the nation representing their diaspora communities. By contrast an increasing Celtic consciousness, seen politically in the development of separate patterns of government in Scotland, Wales and Ireland, has led to much greater emphasis on those nations' separate Unions with fewer churches in those nations in membership resulting in the Baptist Union of Great Britain, which never had any considerable influence in Ireland, dropping 'and Ireland' from its title in 1988.

JHYB

Baptist Union of Wales

The Baptist tradition in Wales began in the 1640s with the evangelistic work of Hugh Evans (d.1656), a native of Radnorshire, who returned to his home county having been converted to the Baptist position under the influence of Jeremiah Ives, the London General (or Arminian) Baptist leader. Despite local lore asserting the existence of a Particular (or Calvinistic) Baptist congregation at Olchon in the Welsh-speaking border country between Herefordshire and Breconshire as early as 1633, the earliest evidence for the planting of the Particular Baptist faith in Wales is of the work of John Myles in the parish of Ilston, Glamorganshire, in 1649. Myles (1621–83) had been sent by the London Particular Baptists to gather churches of a distinct ecclesiastical order, closed communion and closed membership, in south Wales, and by 1652 an association of interlinked congregations between Abergavenny in Monmouthshire and Carmarthen in west Wales had been planted.

Following the Restoration Myles emigrated to New England and the Welsh Association, its churches having merged with Hugh Evans' Radnorshire General Baptists (who now assented to closed communion Calvinism), perpetuated their witness in the face of great hardship and persecution. With the granting of liberty of conscience to Dissenters in 1689, Baptists emerged from the shadows and by the mid-eighteenth century had established themselves as a sturdy if minority religious body in Wales, evangelistically active and doctrinally sound. With the impact of the Evangelical Revival in the 1780s, however, growth increased substantially. The movement spread into north Wales, and in 1790 the single Welsh Association was divided into the North Wales Association, the South-East Association and that of the South-West.

It was during the early nineteenth century that the Baptist movement expanded exponentially. Popular preaching, as exemplified by Christmas Evans (1766–1838), was astoundingly effective, and by mid-century Nonconformity, its Baptist contribution well to the fore, seemed to be claiming the whole of Wales. By then the three associations had become nine, following roughly the pattern of municipal counties, though the Carmarthen and Cardigan Association in west Wales, the Denbigh, Flintshire and Merioneth Association in north Wales and the Radnorshire and Montgomery Association in mid-Wales overran county boundaries. It was soon felt that the Welsh Baptist body needed a central focus for its expanding witness.

The Baptist Union of Wales and Monmouthshire was established in 1866. (Only in 1959 did it adopt the title Baptist Union of Wales.) A union of churches and associations, it would meet annually in different locations to discuss matters of mutual concern, to serve as a focal point for joint witness, to forge connections with other orthodox Nonconformist denominations and to nurture links with the wider Baptist community in the United Kingdom and abroad. Following the appointment of William Morris (1843–1922), minister of Noddfa chapel in Treorchy, Rhondda, as secretary in 1879, the Union became a power in Welsh Nonconformist life. A platform for the Nonconformist Conscience and for the increasingly radical social involvement of the churches, it also established a pension scheme for ministers (1872), a temperance association (1879), a Sunday School union (1887), an insurance company and building fund (1888), a historical society (1901) and a publishing house, 'the Ilston Press' (1912).

By 1901, 950 churches were in fellowship with the Baptist Union of Wales representing 143,000 members. Despite sharp twentieth-century decline, the

Union still functions as the representative body of mainstream Baptists in Wales.

DDM

Baptists

It has long been debated whether Baptists find their roots in continental Anabaptism or in English Separatism. It appears that there were connections with both. What is quite clear is that its foundation represents a new beginning because their assertion that only the baptism of believers was in accord with New Testament principles seemed to unchurch the rest of Christendom. The first Baptists were John Smyth, sometime Cambridge don, and Thomas Helwys who was trained in law, who, fleeing persecution sought freedom of worship in Holland. In 1609 Smyth, convinced that all existing churches were in error in their practice of baptism, first baptized himself and then Helwys and his other followers. Smyth soon came to the judgement that he should have sought baptism from the Waterlander Mennonites but Helwys took a contrary view convinced that a new beginning was necessary and that it was wrong to seek institutional succession, believing that true succession was to be found in the spiritual experience of each generation of believers. Accordingly Helwys broke with Smyth and led a minority group back to England where he founded the first Baptist church on British soil in London (Spitalfields) in 1612.

This group has often been called General Baptists because of their belief in a general atonement potentially available to all, though denominational associations as such did not emerge until the 1640s. The other group often called Particular Baptists emerged slightly later and were orthodox Calvinist in their doctrine. Indeed the emergence of exclusively Baptist churches was a slow process and so, for purely pragmatic reasons, a number of congregations were happy to embrace both Paedobaptists and believer Baptists. Later the 'open membership' position received a theoretical justification for their constitution from the writings of John Bunyan, who, as a matter of principle, objected to different patterns of baptism being made a source of divisions in the church. All groups initially baptized by affusion but by the 1640s it was not only the subject of baptism that came to define the Baptist position as the several groups adopted immersion as the biblical mode with its clear rehearsing of a death/resurrection imagery in keeping with Paul's teaching on the symbolism of baptism.

Baptists were caught up in the religious debates of the Civil War period but few of them were prepared to serve even within a Puritan reformed state church. By 1660 it has been estimated there were about three hundred Baptists churches spread across the different traditions, facing the persecution of the Restoration years. While the 'Glorious Revolution' of 1689 brought about a modest measure of toleration, the fledgling Baptist movement which had lost some members to more sectarian groups, and more particularly to the Quakers, in the late seventeenth and early eighteenth century suffered internal difficulties which gravely affected Baptist witness in the world. While the Generals suffered Christological disputes parallel to those faced by the Presbyterians, the Particulars found their outreach impeded by a brittle hyper-Calvinism though not all were persuaded of this interpretation of reformed doctrine.

Baptists were not therefore in a position immediately to benefit from the new life born of the Great Awakening, though in due course it was to bring new life to both parts of the Baptist family. Some midland labourers formed evangelical groups under the influence of preachers associated with the Countess of Huntingdon together with a group of Yorkshire miners led by a Methodist preacher Revd Dan Taylor. They sought baptism from and tried to co-operate with the Old General Baptists but eventually discovered that their evangelical Arminianism was very different from the theological latitude of the Old Connexion, and in 1770 a New Connexion of General Baptists was formed with its strength in the East Midlands and South Yorkshire. Some Old Connexion churches transferred to this new organization leaving the majority to become Unitarians

New life came to the Particulars through the work of three ministers from Northamptonshire where a new outreach-orientated association was set up in 1764. John Sutcliff who called ministers and churches to more urgent prayer; William Carey who invited them to consider the wider horizons of mission and Andrew Fuller who, much influenced by Jonathan Edwards, offered the churches a new evangelical Calvinism which served to underpin theologically mission both at home and abroad, for commitment to overseas missions seems to have revived the health of the churches at home – 400 particular churches in 1789 had become more than 1,000 by 1835. Membership peaked in 1906 when Union-related churches had just under 411,000 members (with just under 570,000 children in Sunday School), which had declined to just under 135,000 in 2011, though church attendance was 25 per cent higher than this.

In 1813 Baptists established their first national union but within twenty years it was re-founded to allow General Baptists to join, a process which was completed when the two strands of Baptist life were fully integrated. Together with other free churchmen they campaigned for full civil rights starting with the abolition of the Test and Corporation Acts in 1828. Later in the century they also shared in the implementation of the 'Nonconformist Conscience' with its concern not only for issues of private morality but also broader structural issues of slavery in the colonies, poverty, employment, housing and education.

Superficially the two most prominent Baptists in the nineteenth century, Charles Haddon Spurgeon and John Clifford, might seem to represent the unresolved tension between Particular and General Baptists. But Spurgeon while defending traditional doctrine was far from being simply nostalgic, and was anxious to take the measure of developments in the modern world in his attempts to woo new worshippers to his Metropolitan Tabernacle, which was not only a great centre of evangelism but also an Institutional Church in so far as it supported a battery of organizations meeting the social and spiritual needs of the people of south London. John Clifford in West London held advanced views on many theological topics, wrote tracts for the Fabians and led the 'Passive Resistance' movement in opposition to governmental grants to denominational schools. But for all their differences both were dedicated to the cause of personal evangelism.

Domestically, Baptist congregations have been open to sharing with other denominations in establishing Local Ecumenical Partnerships while, in many situations, their worship has been influenced by the charismatic movement.

JHYB

Baxter, Richard (1615–91)

Richard Baxter was a Puritan minister and writer whose career spanned the turbulent years of the mid-seventeenth century. He was a noted moderate who strove all his life for the comprehension and peace of the church. Ordained deacon in 1638, and probably priested soon after, he held a number of short-term appointments before being installed as preacher and lecturer at Kidderminster in 1641. The demands of the Civil War intervened and Baxter served as an Army chaplain, intent on countering the radical sectarianism which flourished there with his own brand of moderate Presbyterianism.

A period of illness during his service in the Army led to a retreat in 1647 to the home of landed supporters where he began his most famous devotional book *The Saints Everlasting Rest* (1650). Later in 1647 he returned to Kidderminster where he exercised a pastorate that was to become a model of Reformed ministry, based on catechetical instruction and systematic pastoral care. His *The Reformed Pastor* (1656) lent the experiment a permanence and became one of the most influential texts of pastoral theology.

Baxter's commitment to the quest for the unity of Christ's church was remarkable. In 1652 he founded the Worcestershire Association, a monthly ministers' meeting which brought together those of Presbyterian and Independent persuasions, as well as some Episcopalians, for mutual education and encouragement. He did all that he could during the religiously anarchic years of the Commonwealth to create a comprehensive church settlement. At the Restoration he was offered the bishopric of Hereford, but refused it because he felt acceptance would stop his search for the unity of the church. When positions hardened, and it became clear that comprehension was not a pragmatic option, Baxter persevered. Forced to leave Kidderminster, he continued his ministry as best he could within the harrying of the law, yet always scrupulously avoiding the disturbance of parish worship. When he had no other option (after 1672), he reluctantly applied for a licence as a 'nonconformist', yet throughout the 1670s and 1680s he continued to publish works promoting the unity of the church. He continually refused to accept any label beyond that of 'mere Christian' or 'mere Catholick'.

He married Margaret Charlton in 1662. They faced the difficult and dangerous years of the Restoration together, sharing the distraint of goods and imprisonment which were consequent on his preaching. She died in 1681. In 1685 Baxter was imprisoned by Judge George Jeffreys on the grounds that his *Paraphrase of the New Testament* was seditious. He was released after eighteen months during which he spent his time studying the New Testament book of Revelation.

Baxter was the most prolific man of letters of the seventeenth century; scholar, devotional writer, pastoral theologian and, indeed, autobiographer, because his sprawling, unwieldy *Reliquiae Baxterianae*, although never published in full and known mainly through Matthew Sylvester's edition (1696), is a significant early example of the genre.

N. H. Keeble, *Richard Baxter: Puritan Man of Letters* (Oxford: Oxford University Press, 1982).

DGC

Binney, Thomas (1798–1874)

Thomas Binney was born in Newcastle-upon-Tyne to a Presbyterian family but became a Congregationalist in his teens, while working as an apprentice bookseller. He was trained for Congregational ministry at Wymondley College, Hertfordshire, and began his ministry at Bedford in 1823, moving to Newport, Isle of Wight, in 1824 and to the King's Weigh House, London, in 1829. This church was rebuilt on Fish Street Hill in 1832, and Binney made a strong attack on church establishment at the opening. In later life he followed a more conciliatory approach to the Church of England. Among the members of King's Weigh House Chapel were Samuel Morley, patron of many Congregational causes, and Sir George Williams, the founder of the YMCA. Binney was a popular preacher, less formally dressed than his predecessors and with a conversational style. He wrote and published many hymns, of which only 'Eternal light' is in the modern repertoire. His distinctive contribution was in liturgical studies. He aspired to improve the hymn singing in his congregation and introduced anthems and chants. His hymn collection is the first notable one following the formation of the Congregational Union (1832). In his day he was one of the most influential figures in Congregationalism and his distinction was recognized by the award of various honorary degrees.

SCO

Black-Majority Churches

At the time of writing, people of African and Caribbean origin constitute approximately 2 per cent of the population of the United Kingdom, they account for some 7 per cent of worshippers nationwide and in the region of two-thirds of Sunday churchgoers in London. Christian Research Association figures show that in the first decade of the twenty-first century the membership of Black-majority churches has grown by 18 per cent while other churches have declined on average by 5 per cent. Britain's Black-majority churches are associated with immigrants from the Caribbean and what has come to be known as the 'Windrush era' which began shortly after the end of the Second World War. In response to advertisements aimed at filling gaps in post-war labour markets, the *Empire Windrush* arrived at London's Tilbury docks on 22 June 1948 with 490 West Indians on board who were buoyed by hopes of a new way of life. The first of many such migrations, few could have foreseen that this would come to mark a new departure in colonial and race relations, and that it would alter both the social fabric and the religious topography of mainland Britain.

The first wave of Afro-Caribbean immigrants, who were already deeply attuned to a dynamic church culture, encountered severe challenges in this as in other spheres of their adopted society. With separatism all but foisted upon them, independent ventures, initially small-scale and lacking in resources, were undertaken almost immediately. Overwhelmingly inclined towards a Pentecostal ethos and style of worship these Black-led, or Black-majority, churches, as they have more recently been designated, exert a holistic appeal reflecting the strength of Christianity in their respective countries of origin and a vibrant ministry that has proven to be attractive to people of all ages. In addition to those of Caribbean origin and extraction, believers of direct African heritage, as well as Asians from both Africa and Asia have added their presence to these churches. Casting an appraising eye, Dr Joe Alfred, a spokesperson and observer, has noted that 'theologically Black churches in Britain have stuck uncritically to a mainly Pentecostal code that owes its existence to the modern non-conformist revivals that emerged in the U.S. around the end of the 19th and the beginning of the 20th century'. These were 'transplanted churches' that came 'doctrinally pre-packaged and often "theology averse"'. Black Theology began to be articulated in Britain but the originators of such developments are rarely from within Black-majority Churches per se but rather Black Christians in mainstream churches. Yet none of this can detract from the inescapable fact that in terms of growth and adherence, this movement continues in its startling reversal of the stubbornly consistent trajectory of decline exhibited by the historic indigenous denominations. Boasting in excess of three thousand mainly urban-based congregations, and with a number of these qualifying for 'mega-church' status, the Black-majority churches are widely considered to be the most prosperous, stable and influential institutions within the African and Caribbean communities. Overall the Black-majority churches continue to exhibit vibrancy and autonomy, self-belief and potential for wider social impact rarely seen in British church life since the heyday of Victorian Nonconformity.

Joe Alfred's address to the University of Birmingham is available from the Churches Together in England website: www.cte.org.uk/Articles/82343/Churches_Together_in/Features_Reviews/Features/Black_Churches.aspx.

TBW

Brethren

The origins and formation of this strand of religious Nonconformity is synonymous with John Nelson Darby (1800–82). A member of the Anglo-Irish aristocracy whose ancestors acquired Leap Castle in County Offaly as a reward for loyalty to Cromwell in the 1640s, he was educated at Trinity College Dublin, from whence he graduated with recognition as a Classical scholar in 1819. After a time at the Bar, he took orders and was appointed to a parish in Wicklow. He attended conferences hosted by Lady Theodosia Powerscourt, a keen student of the scriptures who had been inspired by Henry Drummond's Albury Circle. It was in this context that Darby encountered Anthony N. Groves, J. V. Parnell and George Müller among others. Meeting to pursue devout scholarship in the febrile atmosphere that followed the French Revolution, clergy and laymen debated a range of issues prominent among which were biblical eschatology and the true nature of the church. Having come to doubt both the Anglican system and church structures generally, Darby relinquished his parish in 1827.

Almost simultaneously Benjamin Wills Newton (1807–99), previously a Quaker and for a time a fellow of Exeter College, Oxford, underwent a similar process which likewise rendered him disillusioned with Anglicanism. Leaving Oxford, he purchased a Nonconformist place of worship, Providence Chapel on Rayleigh Street in Plymouth. Darby was invited to Plymouth and meetings were conducted in a manner which was notable for its biblical simplicity and primitivism. In similar vein to an assembly established by Groves in Dublin, the 'Brethren in Plymouth' sought to emphasize the priesthood of all believers (clergy were not recognized or required) and to welcome Christians from all backgrounds in a deliberately non-sectarian fashion. Early Brethren worship took place with 'no priest, no ritual, no festivals, no ornament of any kind, nothing but the Lord's Supper and the exposition of Holy Scripture drawing these austere spirits into any sort of cohesion' (Edmund Gosse).

Yet it is the case that after a time of evangelism and teaching on the Continent, Darby felt compelled to return to Plymouth to 'battle for the soul of Brethrenism'. Contentious issues had arisen in connection with views on the nature of Christ, the finer points of end-time teaching (while Newton expected believers to undergo a time of tribulation, Darby had come to espouse a pre-tribulation rapture), and the implications of the priesthood of all believers. That Newton's publication *Thoughts on the Apocalypse* (1842) received an unflattering critique, some 490 pages long, from the pen of Darby, serves to demonstrate the deterioration in relations between these two erstwhile protagonists of the Brethren cause. Lacking support Newton left the movement in 1847 and established an independent gathering in London. Darby had sought a universal condemnation of his perceived heretical views but this was not forthcoming and when George Müller welcomed members of Newton's congregation to the Bethesda, a Brethren assembly in Bristol, it was summarily disenfranchised by Darby. This development, a pronounced departure from earlier ideals of evangelical simplicity, served to establish a faction which came to be known as the Exclusive ('Darbyite') Brethren.

While the incipient phase of the movement was characterized by gentry and clergy, certainly in terms of its leadership profile, the second generation experienced a rise of evangelists and itinerant teachers. The years 1850–1914 saw new converts acquired as opposed to an earlier appeal to those disaffected with existing denominations. During the Evangelical Awakening of 1859 the Brethren were among those religious bodies that underwent numerical growth and scores of mission halls were opened. This expansionary phase continued until 1914 and beyond with Open Brethren in particular being evangelistically active, biblically informed and boasting an entrepreneurial lay leadership who were frequently dynamic and attuned to the issues of the day. Post–Second World War Britain raised particular challenges for Brethrenism such as the success of the Billy Graham Crusades of 1950 which caused much soul-searching as Brethren found themselves confronted by the fact that church bodies they had denounced as apostate appeared to be experiencing divine favour. Among the factors that militated against the movement were, in addition to a general malaise and decline in religious worship, the rise of Reformed theology, the widening appeal of the Charismatic movement and unfavourable media coverage of the extremes of the Exclusive wing. Demographic haemorrhage came to reverse earlier gains yet it remains the case that many ministries, not least among the House Church and Third Wave Charismatic movements, attribute long-standing positive influence to formative years in Brethren circles. In addition, figures such as the biblical scholar F. F. Bruce (1910–90) have contributed significantly to the cause of evangelical scholarship. The Brethren movement overall emphasized and accentuated certain key features of the British Nonconformist character and outlook, at times pursuing them to extremes, and in a manner which was not always pragmatically sustainable. Their story could with justification be described as another 'chapter in the history of idealism'.

Edmund Gosse, *Father and Son: A Study of Two Temperaments* (London: Penguin Books, 1989); Tim Grass, *Gathering to His Name: The Story of the Brethren in Britain and Ireland* (Milton Keynes: Paternoster, 2006).

TBW

Brotherhood Movement

The modern Brotherhood Movement in Britain had its origins in the Pleasant Sunday Afternoon (PSA) classes which developed in the West Midlands after 1875. The founder John Blackham, a Congregationalist in West Bromwich, was concerned that young men had ceased to attend church. To 'reclaim the lapsed masses' he began an informal Sunday afternoon Bible Class that was 'brief, bright, and brotherly'. The idea spread and within ten years 35,000 men regularly met in PSA classes in Nonconformist churches in the Birmingham area. The popular term 'brotherhood' was adopted by the class in Leamington Spa, a title also preferred by the Revd F. B. Meyer for his class at Christ Church, Lambeth. By the early twentieth century there were over 250,000 members meeting in 1,200 societies across the country, organized in regional federations. In 1906 a national Brotherhood Federation was formed. By 1910, the Brotherhood had grown to over 350,000 members, with a parallel Sisterhood. The Movement was strong in Nonconformist churches in the midlands, London, and in many small rural towns, although not in Wales where chapel attendance was strong. There was a publishing house, local journals and overseas branches in the British Dominions and North America.

In origin, PSA classes were primarily evangelical, offering the gospel to the working and artisan classes along with ideas of self-help, temperance, opposition to gambling and a strong emphasis on fraternity irrespective of race or colour. However, the autonomy of classes inevitably led to different theological and social emphases. Many espoused social gospel ideas of action to change economic and political institutions, along with strong anti-imperial and pacifist strands. Certain classes closely identified with the politics of the Independent Labour Party and the Labour Party; Keir Hardie and Arthur Henderson were active members. The Baptist leader Dr John Clifford, with his Christian socialist movement, was also active in promoting the Brotherhood idea.

The outbreak of the First World War in 1914 challenged the idea of international brotherhood. For many PSA/Brotherhood members patriotism and participation in the conflict overrode ideas of pacifism, and membership fell. At the end of the War attempts were made to rally the Brotherhood as a body to promote internationalism and also to secure industrial peace. The World Brotherhood Confederation, meeting in London in September 1919, endorsed the League of Nations. The Brotherhood revived and many prominent Nonconformists were associated with its continuing work in adult education, labour–employer relations and measures to reduce unemployment. Optimism was high when a recruitment drive was begun in the 1930s, but as the tide of pacifism steadily receded later in the decade the Brotherhood lost members.

By the 1980s a small number of Nonconformist churches and chapels continued to have independent weekly 'brotherhood' and 'sisterhood' classes. A national Brotherhood Movement survived but with no more than 2,000 adherents. A once large and influential Nonconformist movement had almost disappeared.

David Killingray, 'The Pleasant Sunday Afternoon Movement: Revival in the West Midlands, 1875–1900?' in Kate Cooper and Jeremy Gregory (eds), *Studies in Church History. Vol. 44. Revival and Resurgence in Christian History* (Woodbridge: The Boydell Press, 2008), pp. 262–74; A. E. H. Gregory, *Romance and Revolution: The Story of the Brotherhood Movement 1875–1975* (Sevenoaks, n.d. [1975]).

DK

Bunhill Fields

The name 'Bunhill' derives from 'Bone Hill', suggesting that the site was used as a cemetery at least from Saxon times. Located in the London Borough of Islington, burials took place in the area in the mid-sixteenth century, while in 1665 the City of London used it as a burial site for those who had died from the plague. From the mid-seventeenth century, under the ownership of a Mr Tindal, Bunhill Fields, or 'Tindal's Burial Ground', became a popular place for the interment of Nonconformists because it fell outside the jurisdiction of the Established Church. The graves of many notable Dissenters can be found there, including John Bunyan, Isaac Watts, Daniel Defoe, George Fox, John Gill, John Owen and Daniel Williams, as can those of other famous figures whose Nonconformity was not mainstream, such as William Blake. Bunhill Fields closed as a burial ground in 1854, by which time some 120,000 burials had taken place. After closure as a cemetery, the land was opened as a common park in 1869. There was also a Quaker Burial Ground alongside Bunhill Fields, used from 1661 until 1855.

RP

Bunyan, John (1628–88)

John Bunyan was born in 1628, at Elstow near Bedford. His father was a tinker (brazier), a trade also pursued by John. He served as a private in the Parliamentary Army during 1644–47 and was married at the age of nineteen (his wife's name is unknown). The period 1650–57 was, according to his *Grace Abounding to the Chief of Sinners* (1666), one of intense spiritual struggle as he sought assurance of salvation. His wife died in 1658 and he married his second wife, Elizabeth, a year later.

Bunyan had joined John Gifford's Separatist congregation in Bedford in 1653 and despite having little by way of formal education he soon began to preach. Following the Restoration in 1660 he was tried and imprisoned for leading worship at an illegal conventicle. The sentence was initially for three months although the imprisonment was to last for nearly twelve years. Bunyan was finally released in 1672 under the Declaration of Indulgence, although he was locked up again, briefly, in 1676–77. While in prison he composed a number of works, including *The Pilgrim's Progress*.

In 1672 he became pastor of his Bedford congregation and gave himself to ministry both in his home town and as an itinerant. In his preaching he tended to spiritualize the biblical text and his published messages reveal a strong mystical strain allied to some rather fanciful typologizing, particularly evident in his figurative interpretations of Old Testament passages. But he was popular, becoming well-known in London, where the 'mechanic preacher' could draw large crowds for a weekday sermon. John Owen is reported to have said that he would willingly exchange his learning for the tinker's ability to 'touch men's hearts'. Theologically, Bunyan emphasized justification by faith and Puritan covenant theology. As to ecclesiology, he held to gathered church principles. He was almost certainly baptized as a believer around the time he joined Gifford's congregation, but he was committed to open communion, defending this position in print against the Particular Baptist William Kiffin. He died of a fever on 31 August 1688 while on a visit to London, and was buried in Bunhill Fields.

Bunyan has been portrayed in various ways, for example, as a class conscious social radical (by Christopher Hill) and as psychologically disordered (with such accounts tending to draw especially from the agonized, introspective soul searching of *Grace Abounding*). There is some truth in these portraits, but many recent studies have focused instead on his literary achievements. His output was prodigious, with over sixty works published during his lifetime or soon after. They include controversial writings, books of popular theology, devotion and poetry. He is best known for his allegories *The Holy War* (1682) and, especially, *The Pilgrim's Progress* (1678). This extraordinary work of the imagination was popular in Bunyan's lifetime, and, with a second part added in 1684, it became established as one of the classics of English literature. It influenced authors as diverse as Samuel Taylor Coleridge, Christina Rossetti and George Bernard Shaw, and contributed, particularly during the Victorian era, to people's self-understanding of what it meant to be English. Due to its use by nineteenth-century Protestant missionaries, the book attained a transnational circulation, thus exercising a formative influence on the spirituality of countless individuals and Christian communities around the world. Bunyan was one of the most significant figures in all of English Nonconformity, one who continues to cast a long shadow.

Richard L. Greaves, *Glimpses of Glory: John Bunyan and English Dissent* (Stanford, CA: California: Stanford University Press, 2002); Christopher Hill, *A Tinker and a Poor Man: John Bunyan and His Church, 1628–1688* (New York and London: W.W. Norton, 1990); Isabel Hofmeyr, *The Portable Bunyan: A Transnational History of* The Pilgrim's Progress (Princeton, NJ: Princeton University Press, 2004).

PJM

Caird, George Bradford (1917–84)

Caird was, without doubt, one of Nonconformity's most distinguished biblical scholars. He was born in London on 19 July 1917 and educated at

Peterhouse, Cambridge, where he graduated BA in Classics in 1939, and Mansfield College, Oxford, where he graduated MA in 1943 and DPhil in 1944. From 1943 to 1946 he was pastor of Highgate (Congregational) Chapel, London, before embarking on an academic career which initially took him to Canada where he was professor of Old Testament at St Stephen's College, Edmonton, and later also professor of New Testament at McGill University and principal of the United Theological College of Montreal. In 1959 he returned to Mansfield, initially as senior tutor and then as principal from 1970 to 1977. During this time he established himself as a popular lecturer on the New Testament and he was given the title of Honorary Reader in Biblical Studies in the University. In 1975–76 he was moderator of the General Assembly of the United Reformed Church and in 1977 he was appointed Dean Ireland's Professor of the Exegesis of Holy Scripture in Oxford University and fellow of Queen's College. He was elected a fellow of the British Academy and awarded its Burkitt Medal for Biblical Studies. He served on the panel which translated the Apocrypha for the New English Bible as well as on the panel working on the Revised English Bible. It was his conviction that biblical translation was concerned not with finding the correct word but with accurately conveying the meaning of a text.

Caird was a scholar and a pastor, a theologian and a preacher. His interests were wide-ranging and eclectic and this was reflected in his publications. He wrote on the historical Jesus, the Apostle Paul and New Testament ecclesiology, eschatology, biblical lexicography and exegesis (he published commentaries on 1 and 2 Samuel, the gospel of Luke and the book of Revelation). Alongside his scholarship, he took an interest in the application of faith, demonstrating his convinced pacifism in 'War and the Christian' (1979), taking a stand against the South African churches which had colluded in the apartheid regime (outlined in *South Africa: Reflections on a Visit*, 1976), upholding the role of women against what he considered to be poor exposition of the apostle's teaching in 'Paul and Women's Liberty' (the Manson Memorial Lecture, 1972), and a dedication to ecumenism (he was an official observer at Second Vatican Council, as described in *Our Dialogue with Rome: The Second Vatican Council and After*, 1967). He argued that the New Testament documents are basically trustworthy witnesses not only to the thought of the early church but to Jesus' teaching itself and he consistently and effectively opposed the demythologizing of Rudolf Bultmann and what he considered to be the scepticism of German biblical scholarship regarding the historical Jesus.

Caird died from a heart attack in his study at home in Wantage on 21 April 1984, at Easter. His major work *New Testament Theology* was left to be completed by a former student L. D. Hurst, while other projects, such as a commentary on Hebrews, were left unstarted.

John Taylor and Clyde Binfield (eds), *Who They Were in the Reformed Churches of England and Wales, 1901–2000* (Donnington: Shaun Tyas/United Reformed Church History Society, 2007), pp. 24–25.

RP

Calamy, Edmund (1671–1732)

Edmund Calamy was the son of a father with the same name as, indeed, had his grandfather before him. The two older Edmund Calamys were among the ejected ministers of 1662. The Edmund with whom we are here concerned is chiefly known as the historian of ejected ministers, although he also played an important role as a representative of Presbyterians to government and an apologist for Nonconformity. Barred from the English universities by his religion he studied at the University of Utrecht. In 1791 he stayed for a year with the Presbyterian minister in Oxford Joshua Oldfield, and this led him to seek ministry among Nonconformists. He was ordained in London in 1694 by a group of ministers which included Dr Daniel Williams whose assistant he then became. In 1703 he became minister of Tothill Street Meeting in Westminster. After Williams' death, Calamy took his place as a leader of London ministers and as one of the trustees of his will secured the extra funding needed to establish Dr Williams's Library in appropriate premises. Calamy had met the aged Richard Baxter and, given the poor editorial work which lay behind the *Reliquiae Baxterianae*, prepared *An Abridgement of Mr Baxter's Narrative* in 1702. A substantial chapter of this was concerned with the history of ejected ministers. Calamy carried out further researches and expanded the chapter as a separate work, culminating in a four-volume edition of 1727. The work is accurately summarized for modern readers in A. G. Matthews' *Calamy Revised*, but the full biographical sketches are only to be found in the original. To complete the confusion he left a son also called Edmund Calamy.

SCO

Calvinism

Calvinism is a product of the Reformation. While retaining a number of common theological points, Calvinists have also held significant differences, synchronically and diachronically, over the interpretation of particular doctrines. Furthermore, there has been much debate as to the extent of Calvinism's dependence on the work of John Calvin (1509–64). While Calvin deplored such use of his name, the scholarly consensus at the beginning of the twenty-first century would suggest that there is a foundational connection between the two. 'Calvinism' tends to denote a doctrinal stance rather than ecclesiastical and political order, though the latter two were certainly aspects of the Genevan Reformer's sphere of interest and influence.

Fundamental to Calvin's theology was the place of scripture as the final authority for the Christian life and for the church. From the Bible, Calvin gleaned a sense of God's sovereignty; he is the creator, the source of all truth and the redeemer of the elect. This revelation, according to Calvin, was not the result of rational argument but a work of the Holy Spirit. While double predestination (which included the election to eternal punishment of the reprobate) was taught by Calvin as a proper inference from scripture and from God's sovereignty, it did not hold a central place in his theological system as it did for some of his successors. Calvin also promoted discipleship focused on the weekly celebration of the Lord's Supper (something he never achieved in Geneva), though it was his successors who would elevate godly discipline to the status of a third mark of the church alongside the pure preaching and hearing of the word and the administration of the sacraments according to their dominical institution.

Initially, 'Calvinist' referred to those who shared Calvin's view of Christ's presence at the Lord's Supper. However, Calvinism became synonymous with a particular view of salvation, clearly defined as a result of conflict with the followers of Jacobus Arminius (1560–1609) who appeared to suggest that there was human co-operation with God in the work of salvation. Arminius could be seen as one who modified, rather than opposed, Calvinism, but the controversy which accompanied his teaching gave rise to the convening of the Synod of Dort by the States General of the Netherlands. The Synod met from 13 December 1618 until 9 May 1619 and debated the five points of Arminianism as formulated in the Remonstrance of 1610. Arminianism was condemned and, while the Synod did not articulate its own five points in response, subsequent commentators have identified the 'five points of Calvinism' as expressed by the Synod as: (1) the total depravity of humankind, or that human beings are so corrupted by sin that they cannot, by their own power, know anything of God or achieve their own salvation; (2) unconditional election, or that God elects people to salvation regardless of their personal righteousness; (3) limited atonement, or that Christ's atoning death was effective only in securing salvation for those whom God has elected; (4) irresistible grace, or that God's call cannot in any way be rejected by those whom he elects; and (5) the perseverance of the saints, which meant that the elect could not fall from grace. As a result, Calvinism is often associated with soteriology and specifically with debates about predestination, though in fact it deals with all aspects of Christian doctrine.

While there were Puritans whose theological system was substantially different, Calvinism was the prevailing theology among the vast majority of them during the sixteenth and seventeenth centuries, though some, such as Richard Baxter (1615–91), held to a slightly modified version, sometimes called Amyraldism after its founder Moses Amyraut (1596–1664), who rejected limited atonement. Most Calvinists upheld the federal theology that emphasized the unity of the biblical material and 'covenant' as the interpretative key for theological discourse. Debates with Arminians continued throughout much of the eighteenth century, exacerbated by the apparent open offer of salvation proclaimed by the itinerant preachers of the Evangelical Revival. At this time 'High [or sometimes "hyper"] Calvinism' emerged, represented by such figures as Joseph Hussey (1660–1726) and John Gill (1697–1771), whose fidelity to God's sovereignty led them to assert that regeneration was the work of the Holy Spirit and in no way the result of any human action. Independents and Baptists generally considered the success of the Revival to undermine their doctrinal position and were led to 'modify' or 'moderate' their Calvinism by Edward Williams (1750–1813, for the former) and Andrew Fuller (1754–1815, for the latter). Developing ideas which could be traced back to the Dutch jurist and theologian Hugo Grotius (1583–1645), these men advocated the governmental view of atonement which argued for God's forgiveness of human beings without punishing them directly. The cross was a demonstration of God's displeasure at sin, though it in no sense corresponded exactly to the punishment deserved by sinful humankind or the elect. Alongside this, the salvation wrought by the cross was not applied to individuals. Instead men and women received the benefit of Christ's saving work by faith through membership of the church (or body of Christ). The intention behind such thought was to retain the primacy of God's sovereign justice, to continue to restrict salvation to true members of the church and to uphold the necessity of freely preaching Christ to all.

By the late nineteenth century, liberalizing tendencies associated with biblical criticism could be discerned within Congregationalism and among Baptists with the result that Calvinism was eclipsed denominationally, despite its advocacy by prominent ministers such as C. H. Spurgeon (1834–92, who nevertheless seemed to formulate his own interpretation of it). Calvinism re-emerged in a modified form following the First World War, especially as mediated through the dialectic theology of Karl Barth (1886–1968) and others. It was also championed by a number of evangelical ministers, D. Martyn Lloyd-Jones (1899–1981), the influential minister of Westminster Chapel, London, being a particularly prominent Nonconformist example. In the hands of both groups Calvinism was adapted, in the former as a result of insights gained from liberal methodologies and in the latter as a result of the primacy of personal conversion in evangelical circles.

Thus, in the early twenty-first century, it is difficult, if not impossible, to identify a 'pure' Calvinism. Instead it remains diverse, its adherents often having fashioned their theology according to movements in thought which have emerged since the days of the Genevan Reformer.

RP

Campbell, Reginald John (1867–1956)

R. J. Campbell came to prominence in the early twentieth century partly as the pastor of the City Temple in London (at the time one of Congregationalism's most significant pulpits), and primarily for his advocacy of the 'New Theology' and the controversy which surrounded it. His father had rejected the *Westminster Confession* and thus the Presbyterianism in which he had been raised and, by the time Campbell was born at Bermondsey, London, on 29 August 1867, he was working as a minister of the United Methodist Connexion. Brought up by his maternal grandparents in Ulster due to ill health, R. J. Campbell was raised a Presbyterian but he was later confirmed an Anglican while employed as a junior master in a school in Cheshire. In 1852 he went up to Christ Church, Oxford, where he read history, though he intended to be ordained and to continue a career in school teaching. While he came under the influence of Charles Gore, work with the YMCA brought him into contact with Oxford Nonconformists and although his knowledge of and connections with Congregationalism were almost non-existent, he was ordained at Union Church, Brighton, in July 1895. His reputation as a preacher quickly grew and he was called to the City Temple as successor to the celebrated Joseph Parker in 1902.

Campbell was possessed of personal charm and charisma and his popularity quickly grew. As chair of the London Congregational Board of Ministers in 1906, his philosophical and almost mystical ideas about religion began to receive a wider airing, leading to an interview with the *Daily Mail* and to considerable controversy. He published *The New Theology* in 1907 in order to give a systematic account of his beliefs. He openly confessed that he rejected the doctrines of the Fall and the Atonement and, in their place, he offered a spiritualized account of philosophical Idealism. Reality, he believed, is constituted by consciousness, which shares in a common unity. Thus there could be no absolute dichotomies between human beings and God, between sin and righteousness, or between good and evil. Campbell's theology did not merely emphasize God's immanence but instead adopted a pantheism which he preferred to call monism, for all things were expressions of the same fundamental reality. Jesus' uniqueness was to be seen in the way in which he revealed the moral ideal of love. The kingdom of God was an inner spiritual reality which drew people to work for humankind as a whole rather than for themselves. This led to Campbell's adoption of Socialism and to him joining the Independent Labour Party. He was frequently employed in speaking on behalf of its parliamentary candidates, including Keir Hardie. Indeed, Campbell claimed that the New Theology was the spiritual articulation of Socialism, famously asserting: 'Wherever you see a man trying to do something for the common good, you see the uprising of the Spirit of Christ; what he is doing is a part of the Atonement' (*The New Theology*, p. 210). He articulated his views more fully in *Christianity and the Social Order* (1907).

Over the next few years, Campbell suffered from ill health and also began to modify his theological opinions. He withdrew *The New Theology* early in 1915, resigned from his pastorate in September that year and, five days after leading his final act of worship in the City Temple, he was received back into the Church of England by Charles Gore. He subsequently served in that Church's ministry at Birmingham Cathedral, Christchurch, Westminster, Brighton and Chichester, where he was canon and chancellor of the Cathedral and a theological tutor. He died on 1 March 1956.

RP

Cartwright, Thomas (1534/35–1603)

Thomas Cartwright was a fellow of Trinity College, Cambridge (from 1562), who became the leading English proponent of Presbyterianism during the reign of Elizabeth I. Born in Royston and educated at St John's College, Cambridge, his first post was as domestic chaplain to the bishop of Armagh. He returned to Cambridge by 1567, and as Lady Margaret's Reader in Divinity in 1570 he lectured to a packed Great St Mary's Church on the early chapters of Acts, proclaiming them to present a normative church order to which the English church should align itself.

Such radicalism ensured both his popularity among younger scholars and his marginalization by the senior echelons of the university. His ideas lay behind John Field and Thomas Wilcox's *Admonition to the Parliament* (1572). His part in the ensuing controversy about the shape of the English church (he published two books on the subject in reply to Archbishop John

Whitgift) led to his exile from 1574 to 1584 which encompassed the universities of Heidelberg and Basel, as well as ministry in the Reformed Merchant Adventurer's church in Antwerp and Middelberg. William Travers was the first minister, but when he returned to England in 1580, Cartwright succeeded him. Elizabeth's spy-master, Sir Francis Walsingham, tried to neutralize the dangerous Cartwright in 1582 by turning his attention to anti-Catholic polemic in the wake of the publication of the Rheims version of Scripture. It did not work.

In 1584 he was unwise enough to return to England where he was promptly arrested and imprisoned. Influential friends managed to negotiate his freedom and, after a brief return to the Netherlands, he was installed as the master of the earl of Leicester's hospital in Leicester. It was a post that he held for the rest of his life.

However, he was soon further engaged in controversy when his name was linked with the scurrilous anti-episcopal Marprelate Tracts (1588/9), although it is highly unlikely that he had anything to do with them. Nevertheless, the investigation of the Presbyterian underworld that followed laid bare Cartwright's continuing commitment to the Presbyterian way, and he was duly arrested, although nothing was proved and the case eventually ran into the sands.

After release from prison in 1592, he served for a period as the chaplain to the governor of Guernsey before returning to Warwick in old age where he died in 1603.

A. F. S. Pearson, *Thomas Cartwright and Elizabethan Puritanism: 1535–1603* (Cambridge: Cambridge University Press, 1925).

DGC

Cennick, John (1718–55)

John Cennick ran almost the full gamut of eighteenth-century Methodist options. Having experienced an evangelical conversion in 1737, following a nominal Anglican upbringing, Cennick soon made the acquaintance of George Whitefield who appointed him a teacher at the school he had established at Kingswood near Bristol. However, the arrival of John Wesley in Bristol in 1739, following Whitefield's departure for the American colonies, saw the Bristol Calvinist societies riven by doctrinal dispute. Wesley, determined to exclude all Calvinists from the Bristol society, dismissed Cennick from the school, and reorganized the society under his own leadership. Cennick took on the leadership of a new Calvinist society in the city and, in 1740, a new school under the control of Whitefield. Whitefield's frequent absences from England meant that, following the division between Wesleyan and Calvinistic Methodism, Cennick was pressed into the leadership of the Calvinist wing of the English revival. Despite the assistance of Howell Harris, Cennick was ill-suited to this role, preferring the life of an itinerant evangelist.

In 1744, Cennick left the Calvinistic Methodist movement altogether, taking over four hunded members of Whitefield's London Tabernacle Society with him to the Moravians. He first took charge of Moravian congregations in his native Berkshire, but in 1746 sailed for Ireland. He initially itinerated around Dublin, before moving north to Ulster where he founded a series of Moravian societies, including the large settlement at Gracehill, near Ballymena. A prolific hymn writer, Cennick published a number of collections including his *Sacred Hymns for the Use of Religious Societies* in 1743. Never enjoying robust health, Cennick died at the age of thirty-six in 1755.

DCJ

Chamberlain, Elsie Dorothea (1910–91)

Elsie Chamberlain, Congregational minister and radio broadcaster, was born on 3 March 1910 in Islington, London, the third child of James Arthur Chamberlain, Post Office clerk, and his wife, Annie Maria Hayward. Her father attended the Anglican parish church while her mother went to Islington Chapel (Congregational). She was educated at Dame Alice Owen School (1916–20) and Channing School for Girls, a fee-paying Unitarian school in Highgate (1920–27). She then became a dress designer. Intending to become a Congregational minister, Chamberlain studied theology 1936–39 at King's College, London, where she met her future husband, John St Clair Garrington (1912–78), who was soon ordained into the Church of England. Before their marriage, they struggled against the Anglican hierarchy, which found her becoming a minister unacceptable. In 1939 Chamberlain became assistant to Revd Muriel Paulden, in Berkley Street, Liverpool. In 1941, she moved to become minister of Christ Church, Friern Barnet.

Chamberlain's friendship with Margaret, Viscountess Stansgate, beginning when both were theological students at King's, led to her becoming in 1946 the first woman chaplain in the RAF. In reaction Geoffrey Fisher, archbishop of Canterbury, demanded of Viscount Stansgate, secretary of state for Air, that Church of England adherents should not attend communion services when she presided. Due to ill-health Chamberlain left the RAF in 1947. Bishop Wand of London stressed that Garrington would not be commended to a parish while Chamberlain was a serving Congregational minister, given that an Anglican clergyman's wife was then expected to support his ministry. Eventually Garrington obtained a living in Hampton, Middlesex, through Viscount Stansgate's intervention, and they married in July 1947. In November 1947, Elsie became part-time minister of Vineyard Congregational Church, Richmond-upon-Thames, managing also to be an active vicar's wife. At this time they adopted Janette who later wrote her mother's biography.

In 1950, Chamberlain joined the BBC. She produced 'Lift up your Hearts', a morning radio talk programme, and was the first ordained woman to lead the Daily Service. She hoped to attract listeners on the fringes of the churches but in 1967 resigned from the BBC, which was moving away from advocacy towards analysis.

Chamberlain was elected chairman of the Congregational Union of England and Wales 1956–57, the only woman to hold that position. In 1968 she became associate minister of the City Temple, London, under the Revd Kenneth Slack. He favoured, but Chamberlain came to oppose, the union of the Congregational Church with the English Presbyterians which created the United Reformed Church in 1972. Chamberlain joined the Congregational Federation comprising about 300 churches, and from 1971 ministered to Hutton Free Church, Essex.

John Garrington died in 1978 and, refusing to rest, she rescued Kentish Town Congregational church from closure. In 1980 she became minister of two churches, North Street, Taunton and Chulmleigh, Devon, and in 1983 settled in Nottingham at the Congregational Centre church. She died on 10 April 1991 in Nottingham.

AA

Chapel

Contrasting images provide a good starting point. Consider first the ambience of a seventeenth-century meeting house, and note the language, this is not a church, for such high language is for people, not for bricks and mortar. The building is domestic in scale, perhaps with thatched roof. It will be twice as wide as it is deep, with the pulpit set against the long wall opposite the entrance. In front of the pulpit will be the big pew encircling the communion table, where the deacons may well have had their seats. John Betjeman says it will have the quality of a well-scoured farmhouse kitchen, for this is a building built for business – it is where the saints, well-versed in scripture meet around the open Bible and the Table for their nurture and growth in grace. All is good quality, the best that men and women of modest means can provide.

Good examples of such buildings include the Baptist Meeting House at West End, Stevington, in Bedfordshire, the Old Meeting House (Congregational) at Walpole in Suffolk, or Maes-yr-Onnen (now United Reformed Church) in Powys.

Next to this consider a 'Tabernacle' or a 'Salem' Chapel of the late eighteenth or early nineteenth centuries. The language has changed, and although this may be a Nonconformist Tabernacle it will be found to be far from temporary or portable, especially if equipped with classical portico to spell out a proper defiance of Catholic Gothic. The interior is changed as well. The scale and the orientation have both been altered. The pulpit, or perhaps now more correctly a rostrum, to house the preacher's supporters as well as himself, is set against the short wall opposite the entrance. Behind it are ranged, in commanding fashion, an array of impressive organ pipes, as if these trumpets, great and small, were of major theological significance. The model is now not so much the domesticity of farm house, but the performance of a theatre, with the preacher lifted above the congregation as a symbol of the authority of the proclaimed Word of God. Everything is done to accommodate as many hearers as possible, in serried ranks of pitch pine pews, with galleries taking the seating up the rear and side walls. There is much less sense of sharing here: the preacher has the message and the people, many of whom may be here for the first time, are present to receive it, not to engage in theological debate. This is a building for mission, a building to accommodate the unbeliever as much as the committed disciple. What may appear to be a communion rail is there for a different purpose, for this is the penitents' bench, where those seeking to make a decision to follow Christ may make public display of that intention. The invitation, now called an 'appeal', will surely both be made and pressed, so that we can legitimately speak of it as a part of the liturgy, especially at the Sunday evening service, when the preacher will be anticipating, among those in attendance, the presence of sinners needing conversion. He is preaching for a verdict. Indeed the whole service will be constructed to lead up to a climax which will be found as those present respond to the gospel. While this change could be illustrated by examples from all denominations, examples might include the Wesleyan (Epworth Street) and New Connexion (Bethesda) Methodist chapels in Stoke-on-Trent, or the New Room, Bristol. Those two pictures spell out the dialectic of church and mission, an essential part of the calling of evangelical dissent.

In the nineteenth century most Nonconformists expanded their buildings, adding to the sanctuary a Sunday School either next to the church or on a neighbouring site. These substantial additions involving the deployment of much capital also spelt out a broadening of community activities, in the first instance for children, but then for adolescents and the adult members of the church community. This enabled the development of 'chapel' in a cultural sense, that is, not just a focus for worship and Christian service but an almost complete educational and recreational programme for the congregation and its associates. Chapel was now not just for Sundays but was a seven-day a week network of activity.

At the same time as Nonconformists became more prosperous there was a further change in chapel architecture, with an increasing tendency from the second half of the nineteenth century to aspire to all the outward signs of 'church' with an imitation of Anglican styles of architecture, and so the emergence of Gothic chapels, with patronal dedication or perhaps such designations as 'Holy Trinity' or 'Emmanuel'. The pulpit was now displaced from its Puritan and evangelical centrality to one side and the dynamics of the worship space altered with the introduction of stained glass, chancels and transepts. Not all designs went this far, but this was the trend in chapel architecture. Nonconformist Gothic is well represented by two Yorkshire Unitarian Churches, the very early Mill Hill, Leeds, and the Todmorden chapel of the factory reformer John Fielden. All of the Free Churches produced similar examples during this time.

After the Second World War costly Gothic edifices became an increasing burden on shrinking congregations. New churches tended to be of more utilitarian design with less elaborate decoration. Very often space now had to fulfil dual purpose functions for worship and other activities. Indeed as Nonconformist congregations became more engaged with the community with increasing pressures on space, Sunday-only sanctuaries were increasingly seen as a poor stewardship of resources. In addition new styles of worship also impinged on the space needed for worship. Accordingly in many situations there was an attack on traditional elements in chapel furnishing such as organs, pulpits and pews, with the introduction of more free space for music groups and overhead projection of hymns, worship songs and other visual images. This meant fewer signs in the building of the basic commitments of the covenant people of God, which became increasingly dependent upon congregational action, rather than what earlier had been spelt out by the presence of specially devoted space and foci in the building itself.

JHYB

Charismatic Movement

A broad-ranging movement which occurred within the Christian Church during the middle to late twentieth century, the Charismatic movement emphasizes biblical *charismata* – speaking in tongues (*glossolalia*) and prophecy being most prominent – and a pronounced sense of divine immediacy. While the movement looks back to the book of Acts and the pages of the New Testament for its template for spiritual practice and behaviour, a more immediate precursor is to be found in the Pentecostal phenomenon that spread from inauspicious beginnings in an unprepossessing mission in Azusa Street, Los Angeles ca1906.

While Pentecostal denominations began to solidify in the decades that followed, an outward and more embracing orientation came to be fostered by certain isolated, if ultimately influential figures, such as South African-born Pentecostal minister David du Plessis (1905–87), who is now considered to be a founding father of the Charismatic Movement. Departing from received perspectives and restrictions, du Plessis became convinced of the merits of ecumenical engagement. He attended and involved himself in the World Council of Churches and later the Second Vatican Council. The title of his autobiography *The Spirit Bade Me Go* (1963) encapsulated his conviction in a divine mandate to take the Pentecostal message to other churches and denominations, yet the efforts of the man who became known affectionately as 'Mr Pentecost' were not always welcomed (his own denomination the American Assemblies of God removed his preaching credentials which were only restored in 1980). The denominations established in the aftermath of Pentecostal revival, frequently termed 'Classical Pentecostalism', proved suspicious of this attempt to embrace historic churches generally and, in particular, displayed an abiding Protestant antipathy towards Roman Catholicism. Interestingly during the 1960s and 1970s it was frequently Catholics who were among the keenest to embrace charismatic experience, typically under priestly guidance, and the movement came to enjoy the blessing of Pope Paul VI and his successors. Protestantism, as a whole, was more resistant and critiques, indeed outright denunciations, have since been issued from conservative evangelical and Reformed branches of the Protestant churches.

Those involved in Charismatic Renewal, unlike classic Pentecostals, purposefully remained within their historic denominations and, by and large, resisted the urge to secede and form new religious bodies. Ironically groups such as the Elim Pentecostal Churches of Britain and Ireland – by then well into the cycle of routinization – found themselves challenged and discomfited by the fresh wave of charismatic activity emanating from what were to their minds some very unlikely sources during the 1960s and 1970s. By the 1980s there had emerged what Peter Wagner of Fuller Theological Seminary termed the 'Third Wave'. This encompassed a range of charismatic expressions, drawn largely from evangelical sectors in Britain and America, which crystallized around leaders such as John Wimber from California and Terry Virgo from Brighton, England. This neo-Charismatic stream differentiated itself by its espousal of a new ecclesiological paradigm in that it came to embrace a separatist ethos. Leaders embarked on the establishment of networks of churches and forms of association while remaining ostensibly resistant to the trappings of denominationalism. 'House Churches' became 'New Churches' (including Vineyard, New Frontiers, Pioneer, Ichthus) and, fuelled by biblical restorationism and primitivist ideals, they have been and continue to be characterized by vibrant spirituality and charismatic expression while remaining outside both historic denominational structures and the classical Pentecostal tradition.

It has been noted that there exists something of a 'charismatic concensus' across the church spectrum with worship and liturgical styles displaying characteristics derived from Charismatic Renewal. While in no sense claiming overtly charismatic credentials many church bodies and congregations have adopted patterns of spirituality and expression undeniably influenced by the movement. Pentecostals too, in spite of initial reluctance and resistance have, over time, found their congregations, structures and wider outlook to have been rejuvenated by both the second and third waves of a century of charismatic activity.

TBW

Charles, Thomas (1755–1814)

Thomas Charles was born on 14 October 1755 in the parish of Llanfihangel Abercowin, Carmarthenshire, south Wales, the son of a fairly prosperous farmer. He was educated at the Carmarthen Dissenting academy and Jesus College, Oxford, graduating in 1779. Ordained a year earlier as an Anglican clergyman, he held various curacies in Somerset before returning to Wales in 1783 where he married Sally Jones, a shopkeeper's daughter from Bala, Merionethshire. Although he had been appointed curate at Llanymawddwy, some ten miles from his Bala home, his evangelical preaching caused consternation among his flock and drew the bishop's censure. By the summer of 1784 he had joined the Methodist society in Bala and although his Anglican orders were never revoked, he would thereafter fulfil his ministry among the Welsh Calvinistic Methodists. As well as rising to prominence as the leader of that movement, his chief contribution during the last decades of the eighteenth century was to provide a network of circulating schools in north Wales where illiteracy was remedied and the scriptures taught. Along with exercising considerable administrative oversight, he supplied his scholars with copious reading matter in order to ground them in the faith. A series of catechisms became massively influential while his scriptural dictionary *Y Geiriadur Ysgrythurol* (1805–11) became the mainstay of popular Welsh biblical scholarship throughout the nineteenth century. His zeal to provide cheap Welsh Bibles was one of the contributing factors in the establishment of the British and Foreign Bible Society in 1804.

By the second decade of the nineteenth century, the anomalous ecclesiastical position of the Welsh Calvinistic Methodists became unbearable. Neither wholly Anglican nor formally Dissenters, in 1811 Charles ordained twenty-one Methodist preachers in order to administer the sacraments of baptism and the Lord's Supper within the Methodist societies, thus severing the link with the establishment and creating a new Nonconformist denomination, the Welsh Calvinistic Methodist Connexion. This was a momentous step for a man who retained his Anglican sensibilities to the end, but it was one that he never regretted. He died on 5 October 1814 and was buried in Llanycil churchyard, Bala.

DDM

Chauncey, Isaac (1632–1712)

Isaac Chauncey was an Independent minister, the son of Charles, the vicar of Ware, who sought refuge from Laudian persecution in New England. He eventually became president of Harvard, and Isaac was educated in theology and medicine there.

He came to England in 1654, serving in the Cromwellian church as rector of Woodbury, from which he was ejected in 1660. Chauncey became a convinced and determined Independent. Like many ministers during the years of persecution, he practised medicine, and ministered as and when he could. In 1687 he was called to minister to the Mark Lane meeting in London and became one of the leaders of London Independency in the generation after the Ejectment. As such he played a role in the establishment of the Common Fund for the relief of poverty among Independent and Presbyterian ministers, and was one of those who helped design the so-called Happy Union of 1690–91.

Later scholars have suggested that the Heads of Agreement between ministers which created the Union papered over the cracks between the two ecclesiologies. Those cracks were painfully exposed by the Richard Davis affair. Davis' evangelistic ministry at Rothwell in Northamptonshire was predicated on a Calvinism which verged on antinomianism, and it aroused the suspicions among the Presbyterians of the United Ministers who called him for interview. The Presbyterian Daniel Williams accused him of antinomianism, and the old theological battles began again, as the Independents swung into polemic action by charging the Presbyterians with Arminianism. Chief among them was Chauncey, especially in *Neonomianism Unmask'd* (1692–93) and *A Rejoynder to Mr D. Williams* (1693). He left the union, the Common Fund was divided and Chauncey became one of the architects of the Congregational Fund.

From that point onwards, Chauncey's Independent views intensified, and he wrote widely on the subject in the 1680s and 1690s – *Ecclesia enucleata* (1684), *The interest of Churches* (1690), *Ecclesiasticum* (1690) and *The Divine Institution of Congregational Churches* (1697) are among his principal studies.

He served as a tutor at the Hoxton Academy, but his pulpit ministry at Mark Lane became so obsessed with his ecclesiological pet subjects that the congregation dwindled to such an extent that there were only just over forty members present to call Isaac Watts to succeed him in 1701. He was married three times and had two sons (who predeceased him) and one daughter who survived into adulthood. He died in London in 1712.

Oxford Dictionary of National Biography (Oxford: Oxford University Press, 2004).
DGC

Church Covenant

The principal covenants in scripture are God's covenant with humanity after the Flood, giving the rainbow as a sign that the earth will never again be destroyed; God's covenant with Israel, giving the nation a land of its own; and God's covenant of redemption for all people through Jesus Christ. There are also covenants between individuals and God and, by extension, covenants between people in which God is called as witness. From the latter example arises the legal convention, which extends to the present day, that a covenant is a promise enforceable by law. In the Middle Ages such covenants might be made by members of a trade guild, to obey its rules and keep its secrets.

The Puritans turned to the covenant as a device for separating the godly and ungodly. For those who took the view that living in a Christian country did not automatically make someone a Christian and a worthy recipient of the Lord's Supper the requirement to make a covenant with God, to walk in the ways of righteousness, was a solemn test of sincerity. Early Congregational and Baptist churches invited members to swear a simple covenant with God and with each other to be obedient to scripture and keep fellowship together. This was a reinforcement of their theological view that they were part of the elect but also an expression of solidarity against their opponents. Presbyterians in Scotland took things further and devised a National Covenant which was first signed in Greyfriars Kirk, Edinburgh, by nobles, ministers and citizens over several days in February 1638 and then offered to the whole nation. This covenant had political implications, contesting the king's prerogative in church affairs. It was one of the immediate causes of the so-called Bishops' Wars in Scotland, which led eventually to the Civil Wars which convulsed England, Scotland and Ireland for years afterwards. The Scots made their support of the English Parliament conditional on agreement to the Solemn League and Covenant (1643) binding Presbyterians in both nations together in opposition to the High Church aspirations of Archbishop Laud and the king. The Act of Uniformity of 1662 required, among other things, renunciation of any oaths taken in support of this covenant.

The early covenants of local churches in the seventeenth century expanded to include doctrinal matters. This was an important reassurance to other congregations with whom they shared fellowship, since there were no common confessions of faith beyond the requirement of all Protestant Dissenters who claimed the privileges under Toleration after 1689 to be in general agreement with the Thirty-nine Articles. The idea of covenant was taken up by Methodists in the late eighteenth century and used as an annual means of reaffirming personal commitment. The expansion of Independent and Congregational churches in the early nineteenth century was not always based on the use of a founding covenant in the historic sense. An alternative was a set of rules to which members were expected to adhere. The Congregational Union of England and Wales produced a Confession of Faith in 1836 to express the general beliefs of the denomination.

There are examples of covenants being made by new congregations into the twentieth century, though in language and doctrine they are far removed from those of the seventeenth. To some extent the covenant of local membership was superseded by the forms of words made nationally available for the reception of church members. The simple handshake which follows the ceremony, 'the right hand of fellowship', is a sign of a covenant relationship in many human interactions. The idea of covenanting found favour with the leaders of the Congregational Union of England and Wales in the 1960s, who made it the basis for turning the Union into the Congregational Church in England and Wales. John Huxtable introduced the idea to the talks for Church Union in the 1970s, but the Church of England failed to reach the required majority in favour of a scheme based on a covenant. It subsequently rejected proposals on covenanting to resolve the problems of the Anglican Communion in 2012. It would appear that covenanting sits easily with the idea of the gathered church but becomes contentious when it is extended on a wider scale.

SCO

Churches of Christ

In 1981, the Re-formed Association of Churches of Christ and the United Reformed Church united to form a new denomination, still known as the United Reformed Church, but committed to recognizing baptism of either infants or believers, non-stipendiary ministry alongside stipendiary, and having some local congregations in Scotland. This gave prominence to a group of local churches in Britain whose origins lay in the early nineteenth century, which had come to be known as the Churches of Christ although this was not a title the founders claimed for themselves.

The philosophical movement we now know as the Enlightenment and changing nature of society as the industrial age gained pace lent itself to the emergence of radical ideas in politics and theology. Critics of the Establishment saw the idea of Primitive Christianity, based on the New Testament, as an alternative religious path. Such people were to be found throughout Britain. One group in Scotland, Baptists, who opened their first church in Edinburgh in 1765, were committed to this idea, especially the unpaid ministry and believers' baptism they traced in scripture. Although not following their Baptist convictions, Scottish Independents were similarly enthused, notably the Haldane brothers and Greville Ewing. They were particularly struck by the models of evangelism in the New Testament. A Presbyterian group with similar ideas concerning Establishment was the Anti-Burgher Secession Presbyterian Church. Their minister in Ahorey, near Armagh in Ireland, Thomas Campbell (1763–1854), was distressed by the factionalism in his own denomination. He subsequently emigrated to the United States, where he met people who were also impatient of the divisions which historic denominations seemed to represent and anxious for a new start based on first principles. His son Alexander Campbell (1788–1866), who had met the Haldanes and Ewing, then joined him and expressed the new thinking in his *Declaration and Address* (1809). At this stage there was no formal movement, rather the circulation of ideas for reform, to which some responded with enthusiasm. Similar thinking would lead to schism among the Wesleyans and to the formation of other new religious groups. Some of the energy was simply absorbed by existing denominations. What differentiated Campbell's writings was their promotion in Britain through the networks of Scotch Baptists after an American enthusiast Peyton C. Wyeth joined their congregation in Windmill Street, Finsbury Square, London, in 1833. William Jones, an elder there, first circulated news of Campbell's writings around the denomination. After his enthusiasm cooled, James Walker (b. 1793) of Nottingham became the principal advocate, publishing the *Christian Messenger* from 1837, again with a circulation mostly among Scotch Baptists.

The early followers set great store by evangelism and what we would now call apologetics. Campbell and his more prominent followers engaged in public debate with sceptics. In this they had the advantage of sharing the scepticism about the existing churches and offering a more egalitarian perspective on church life, based on the New Testament rather than tradition. The congregations which formed around Campbell's writings employed no ministers and appointed their own elders to lead worship and preside at communion. They practised believers' baptism and excluded paedo-Baptists from the Lord's Table. They avoided denominationalism to the point of refusing to constitute trusts for their own buildings, on the argument that this would commit them to credal statements. They held a first Cooperation meeting in 1842, to promote their ideas, especially through evangelism, and resisted the idea that it should consist of appointed delegates from each congregation. The congregations in the United States came together as the Disciples of Christ. The relation between the British and American groups was not always easy. The British were grateful for American help with evangelism, but suspected them of denominational ambitions, and distrusted their communion discipline, which extended to allowing other Christians to communicate on an occasional 'guest' basis. Campbell believed that Christian unity could only come about by returning to a New Testament ordering of the church and this unity remained an objective of Association churches even when they were at their most factional.

Fifty congregations were represented at the first Cooperation meeting. This number had risen to eighty-five by the next meeting in 1848. From the beginning the North and Midlands were the most favourable territory for churches, but this was never a large denomination, even when it was prepared to acknowledge that it was a denomination at all. At its peak, in 1930, there were 16,596 members. From 1881 to 1917 there were rival factions, happily reunited at that point. Among the disputed ideas were communion discipline, theological education, temperance and overseas mission. The more conservative forces resisted the denominationalism which followed from combining on public questions or missions, arguing that cooperation in evangelism was the sole task of any association. With the passing of time a new generation succeeded in creating a structured body, with staff and paid evangelists, but the autonomy of congregations remained. After the establishment in 1920 of Overdale, a theological college in Birmingham, which from 1931 associated with the Selly Oak Colleges, its principals were able to exercise influence and to represent the Churches of Christ ecumenically. The most distinguished of these William Robinson was an influential member of the World Council of Churches. He was also instrumental in recalling his colleagues to an original aim of Campbell – to bring about church unity by returning to the New Testament for guiding principles.

The Churches of Christ, led by their then-general secretary Philip Morgan, expressed an interest in unity during the original negotiations of the 1960s which led to the union of English Presbyterians and the majority of English and (English-speaking) Welsh Congregationalists in 1972. A scheme was prepared for widening that union, which failed to win acceptance by a sufficient majority among the Churches of Christ. Accordingly the Association dissolved itself in 1978 so that the individual churches could go their different ways. The majority opted to join the Re-formed Association which concluded the union with the United Reformed Church. A few independent congregations of the Churches of Christ remain in Britain. The Disciples of Christ and other bodies with their origins in Campbell's movement remain significant in the United States.

SCO

Clarendon Code

Edward Hyde (1609–74), first earl of Clarendon, was Chancellor of the Exchequer for Charles I during the Civil Wars and guardian of the Prince of Wales who, on his accession as Charles II in 1660, made him both chancellor of the University of Oxford and lord chancellor. A man of moderate views, he has in the past been directly associated with the drafting of the four statutes passed between 1661 and 1665 which are collectively known as the 'Clarendon Code'. Scholarly opinion now suggests that he had little to do with formulating the detail of these Acts and that he favoured a comprehensive church settlement. However, as chief minister, and as one who was left to enforce the Acts, they have borne his name ever since.

The four statutes were intended to maintain the faith and order of the Church of England as the sole legal form and practice of faith and to render Nonconformity illegal. The first, the Corporation Act of 1661, required municipal officials to celebrate the Lord's Supper in the parish church and to reject the Solemn League and Covenant of 1643 in effect excluding Nonconformists from public office. The second, the Act of Uniformity of 1662, made acquiescence to the services of the Book of Common Prayer compulsory as well as assent to the church order contained within it. The Act further insisted that ministers declare it unlawful to take up arms against the king and to renounce as illegal the Solemn League and Covenant (1643). The third, 'An Act to prevent and suppresse seditious Conventicles' (the Conventicle Act) of 1664 made it illegal for groups of more than five people, who did not belong to the same household, to meet for worship. The sole purpose of the Act was to render illegal any Nonconformist meeting, the title of the Act demonstrating that holding a religious conventicle was deemed by its very nature to be seditious. The final part of the Code was 'An Act for Restraining Non-Conformists from inhabiting Corporations' which prevented Nonconforming ministers from coming within five miles either of incorporated towns or of their former livings, giving rise to its popular title 'The Five Mile Act'. The Act sought to prevent Nonconformist ministers from preaching and teaching in schools unless they were prepared to swear an oath never to resist the king or to attempt to alter the government of the Church and the state. They were also to agree to the services, rites and other requirements of the Book of Common Prayer.

The Acts that make up the penal code rendered impossible any settlement between the rival ecclesiastical parties whether radical or moderate. More than that, they enshrined in law an intolerance which became not simply a part of religious but also social life, which caused Nonconformists to suffer direct persecution and to keep them excluded from public life for over two centuries.

Hyde fell out of favour with Charles II and, in 1667, he was forced into exile in France where he died in 1674. While in exile he completed his *History of the Rebellion and Civil Wars in England.*

RP

Clifford, John (1836–1923)

Happy to be associated with the Evangelical Alliance, Clifford also believed that there was a social dimension to Christian commitment and that integrity of mind involved new accommodations of both scientific understanding and critical method. While in many respects the antithesis of Charles Haddon Spurgeon, there was no personal antipathy between them. The most articulate of the New Connexion General Baptists (Arminian in theology, born out of the experience of the Methodist Revival), Clifford, who was born at Sawley, Derbyshire, on 16 October 1836, had little formal education before going to work, aged eleven, for sixteen hours a day in a lace mill. Converted in November 1850 he was baptized seven months later as a mark of his personal commitment to the service of Christ. His subsequent call to the ministry was followed by study at the Midland Baptist College.

During the early years of his only pastorate at Praed Street, Paddington (subsequently Westbourne Park), London, the largely self-educated Clifford successfully completed his studies in arts, science and law through London University. Westbourne Park became the archetypal 'Institutional Church' sponsoring a diversity of programmes – philanthropic, educational, recreational, cultural and spiritual – all of which attracted a large, intelligent and influential membership. So extensive was its educational work that it was known as a 'people's university'. Clifford was instrumental in securing the full integration of the New Connexion and the Particular Baptists within the life of the Baptist Union, which he twice served as president.

Clifford's *The Inspiration and Authority of the Bible* (1892) guardedly sought to show an evangelical openness to reverent criticism. He first used the language of 'social gospel' as a campaigning slogan in addressing the Baptist Union in 1888; sacred was not to be separated from secular, rather God's sovereignty extended over the whole realm of human activity, for every social problem had a spiritual dimension. But the church was not to be taken over by mere socialist utopian talk; political change could do so much for humankind but could never do all it needed.

Politically, Clifford worked through the Liberal Party which he saw as the best instrument for implementing the Nonconformist Conscience, whether in terms of a moral foreign policy abroad, or issues of social purity or confessional education at home. Critical of theologians who thought they could exhaust the meaning of the atonement in wordy definitions, worked out in their 'verbal controversies and creed-fights', he nevertheless rejoiced in 'the free and full pardon it offers and the hope it creates'.

As the first president of the Baptist World Alliance (1905–11) he was a familiar figure in Europe. In 1907, for example, he led a delegation to Hungary in an attempt to reconcile the two Baptist groups then in conflict there. Active at the European Congresses in Berlin in 1908 and Stockholm in 1913, he also travelled in the cause of European Peace. In 1920, he chaired the important London Conference on Baptist reconstruction and mission in Europe. Committed throughout his life to the evangelistic imperative – 'Our first business is to make men see Christ' – it was in fact during a debate on this in which he intended to speak, that he died at Baptist Church House on 20 November 1923.

J. H. Y. Briggs, 'John Clifford', in T. Larsen (ed.), *Biographical Dictionary of Evangelicals* (Leicester: IVP, 2003); Sir James Marchant, *Dr John Clifford, C.H., Life, Letters and Reminiscences* (London: Cassell, 1924).

JYHB

Coltman (née Todd), Constance Mary (1889–1969)

Born in London on 23 May 1889, Constance Todd read History at Summerville College, Oxford, from 1908 to 1911. She pursued her sense of calling to

Christian ministry with the Presbyterian Church of England, in which she had been raised. That particular door being closed, she persuaded W. B. Selbie, principal of Mansfield College, Oxford, that her call was genuine. She entered the college in 1913 and read for the London BD while training as a Congregational minister. Her course ended in 1916 and there was no immediate call. Her pacifism led her to join W. E. Orchard's King's Weigh House and, on 17 September 1917 she and her fiancée Claud Coltman (1889–1971, who had been a fellow student at Mansfield) were ordained as joint ministers of the King's Weigh mission on Darby Street in the East End. They were married the following day. While she inspired and supported women's ministry, she was not disposed to agitating for it. Nevertheless, she believed that women had a unique contribution to make to ministry and to the interpretation of Christian faith. She ministered jointly with her husband at Kilburn, Oxford, Wolverton and Haverhill before they returned to the King's Weigh House in 1946. She retired from ministry in 1949, her husband continuing until 1957. They retired to Bexhill where she died on 26 March 1969.

Elaine Kaye, Janet Lees and Kirsty Thorpe, *Daughters of Dissent* (London: United Reformed Church, 2004).

RP

Congregational Federation

The Congregational Federation (CF) is an association of Congregational churches, formed for purposes of mutual help. In accordance with Congregational principles, it neither has the power nor the desire to legislate for the internal affairs of any church, although a church may appeal to the CF for help and advice. The CF began life in 1972 as an alternative for Congregational churches which decided not to join the United Reformed Church. It aimed to continue the theological breadth of the former Congregational Union of England Wales (CUEW), hoping to include both liberals and evangelicals. However the separate existence of the Evangelical Fellowship of Congregational Churches, and the fact that some Congregational churches chose to remain unaffiliated to any wider body, served in part to limit this ambition. The CF arose from the earlier Congregational Association, a group of individuals who were concerned at trends within the CUEW, in the 1960s and 1970s, towards union and away from Congregationalism.

The CF's churches are grouped together in twelve geographical regions. Two regions coincide with national boundaries – Scotland and Wales – and there is also a category for overseas churches – with one member in Brittany at the time of writing. The CF's council is served by three main committees, dealing with mission and society, Christian ministries, and finance and support services. Subsidiary boards have specific responsibilities. The CF's twelve area associations cover England, Wales and Scotland. These area associations of churches elect representatives to CF committees, and co-operate over common concerns. The CF holds an annual assembly, usually in May. Nevertheless, local churches remain autonomous and possess the authority to make their own decisions concerning their life and witness.

Although churches may call whom they wish to their ministry, the CF is able to advise confidentially on the suitability of candidates, male and female, prior to the issuing of a 'call'. The CF recognizes ordination, carried out by the local church to which a minister is first called, as authentic for future ministries, and it maintains a list, published in its year book, of accredited ministers who have concluded satisfactory levels of training. The CF accepts its responsibility to offer training, principally through its integrated course. This training, which has thus far received University validation, enables some to move towards ordination, others to qualify as lay preachers and church members to know more about the faith.

CF churches are broadly orthodox in doctrine, upholding the Trinity. In general, Congregationalists baptize both the children of believers and those adults who seek Christian baptism but have not previously been baptized. CF churches normally have an 'open table' at the Lord's Supper, at which 'all who love the Lord in sincerity and truth' are welcome.

The CF works with Christians of other denominations in the Council for World Mission, Churches Together in Britain and Ireland, Action of Churches Together in Scotland, CYTUN (Churches Together in Wales), Churches Together in England and other external bodies.

AA

Congregational Union of England and Wales

During the eighteenth century the number of Independent churches in England and Wales grew markedly, influenced by the Evangelical Revival. Pastors and churches saw benefits in combining for fellowship and mission and, consequently, county unions developed. Independent churches envisaged similar benefits deriving from a national union and in 1831 the Congregational Union of England and Wales was founded. This was always a voluntary organization, to which churches might choose to affiliate or not. It had advisory powers only, but gradually came to exercise a centralizing force, which significantly increased during the twentieth century, from its offices in Memorial Hall, London, which opened in 1875. Memorial Hall, built to commemorate the ejections of Nonconformists in 1660–62, was an imposing stone building, which stood on the site of the former Fleet Prison, where Nonconformists were at one time incarcerated. It included a hall which held 1,500 people and also housed the Congregational Library. The CUEW consisted of very different county unions. Some, like Lancashire, London and Yorkshire, were large and wealthy, employing their own full-time secretaries. Others like Dorset were small and rural. Bedfordshire and Huntingdonshire were joint associations with the Baptist churches of those counties.

From 1831, organized Congregationalism faced a tension between the centripetal and the centrifugal. The dilemma for Congregationalists, posed by the existence of the CUEW, was always to respond to demands for effective organization, witness, training, mission, publications, etc., without forsaking the distinctive independency which must be the *raison d'être* of Congregationalism. Yet the colleges which trained ministers for the churches were independent in foundation, with no direct responsibility to the CUEW. The Congregational churches chose to channel their missionary efforts principally through the independent London Missionary Society but also through the smaller Colonial (later Commonwealth) Missionary Society. The two merged in 1966 to become the Congregational Council for World Mission.

Throughout the twentieth century the CUEW functioned largely on the basis of a constitution adopted in 1904 (occasionally amended) which left executive control and initiative with a council of 300 members to which a number of committees (nineteen in 1947) reported. The CUEW met in assembly in the spring and autumn of each year. After the Second World War, the autumn assembly, which had moved between the large provincial towns, was discontinued and only the spring meeting in London resumed. The churches elected an honorary chairman to serve CUEW for a year.

The amassing of large central funds, particularly associated with John Daniel Jones, the CUEW honorary secretary 1919–42, to finance desired central initiatives, and the popular support thereby engendered, further enhanced the power and prestige of the CUEW. The appointment of nine provincial moderators in November 1919 was a move to consolidate the churches into something approaching a unified denomination and to regularize the standards required to enter the Congregational ministry.

Also during the twentieth century, the CUEW's bureaucracy grew and its general secretaries enjoyed unprecedented influence. Notable among these were Sidney Berry (secretary 1923–48 and 1955–56), who offset the marked expansion of the CUEW's activities under his management with his repeated stress that the Congregational churches should see themselves as a family, and John Huxtable (secretary 1964–72), who campaigned ceaselessly for ecumenism and persuaded most Congregational churches to leave behind much of their independency when they united with the Presbyterian Church of England in 1972 to form the United Reformed Church (URC). Huxtable sought for the URC a wider union with other churches in England but, in this, was largely frustrated.

The CUEW remained in existence until the majority of its constituent churches formed themselves into the Congregational Church in England and Wales in 1966. At this point a number of churches, mostly conservative evangelicals unhappy at the drift towards denominational union, elected not to join the CCEW and formed an Evangelical Fellowship of Congregational Churches. In 1972 over two-thirds of the churches within the CCEW voted in favour of union with the Presbyterian Church of England and the URC came into being. Most of those churches which preferred to continue in the Congregational tradition formed the Congregational Federation, while a few churches remained unaffiliated to any of the new groupings.

AA

Congregationalism

Congregationalism is that ecclesiastical system in which each church is autonomous and decisions are made in regular meetings of the church members, who together seek the mind of Christ for their affairs, guided, as they believe, by the Holy Spirit. Its apologists claim it is rooted in the Apostolic churches. Congregational church government is based on the equality of all believers. No formal ecclesiastical hierarchy exists, since Christ is in principle the immediate head of each church. A Congregational church is considered to be the microcosm of the macrocosm, namely the representation of the entire Church. Like other Protestants, Congregationalists recognize only two sacraments (often known as ordinances), namely baptism and the Lord's Supper.

Congregationalists have insisted, following scripture, that churches should be independent of the state. No higher earthly authority than the church meeting exists within Congregationalism. Congregational churches, through their church meetings, call ministers to their pastorates, although ministers are not considered essential for the church's existence. Normally the minister leads worship, preaches and performs pastoral duties. Ordination rests with the local church, though the wider church is normally represented at such services. Some administrative duties, assistance in distributing the Lord's Supper and pastoral duties are undertaken by deacons who are lay people elected by the church meeting.

Congregationalism arose from the Reformation and represents a natural extension of the doctrine of the priesthood of all believers. Those impatient with the pace of reform in the Elizabethan Church of England felt impelled to separate and gather their own churches. Among these was Robert Browne who in 1581 gathered in Norwich a church of like-minded believers, bound to God and each other by mutual covenant. Members of such gathered churches were called Brownists (by outsiders), Separatists and, later, Independents. The Separatists were forced underground and some fled to the Netherlands, from whence the Mayflower pilgrims migrated in 1620 to New England. The first Independent church in Wales was founded in 1639 at Llanfaches, Monmouthshire. The Independents set out their faith and order in the *Savoy Declaration* of 1658. The 1662 Act of Uniformity drove Independents to become Nonconformists (with Presbyterians, Baptists and Quakers). Denied the right to attend the universities, they set up academies.

During the eighteenth and nineteenth centuries, pastors and churches, influenced by evangelicalism, associated in county unions, for fellowship and mission. They were among the founders of the (London) Missionary Society in 1795 and, in 1831, formed the Congregational Union of England and Wales. The younger Congregational churches of Scotland, influenced by the Evangelical Revival, founded the Congregational Union of Scotland in 1812. The (Welsh-speaking) Union of Welsh Independents was founded in 1872. These national unions exercised advisory roles rather than legislative authority but expressed the common mind of their churches.

The Congregational Church in England and Wales (incorporated in 1966) merged with the Presbyterian Church of England in 1972 to create the United Reformed Church (URC), although approximately five hundred churches opted to stay independent and Congregational, while the Union of Welsh Independents continued its separate life. In 2000 just over half of the churches in the Congregational Union of Scotland united with the URC. Congregationalists have joined interdenominational unions in other countries.

AA

Council for World Mission

The Council (CWM) comprises a partnership of thirty-one Protestant church bodies worldwide related to the missionary work of the London Missionary Society (LMS), founded in 1795, as the Missionary Society; Commonwealth Missionary Society (founded by the Congregational Union of England and Wales – CUEW – as Colonial Missionary Society, 1836); Foreign Missions of

Presbyterian Church of England (1847) and work supported by the British conference of Churches of Christ in Malawi.

Impelled by the philosophy of successive international missionary conferences that 'the Church is mission', CUEW moved to transform the London Missionary Society into a churchly body. The intention was to forge a closer relationship with CUEW's 1966 successor, the Congregational Church in England and Wales (CCEW), while keeping links with Congregational Unions in Scotland and Wales. First as the Congregational Council for World Mission (CCWM) and, following CCEW's union with Presbyterian Church of England in 1972, as CWM (Congregational and Reformed), its recognition of former mission field churches as equal partners began a process which led to parity between them and the former sending churches in the 1977 structure of CWM.

CWM retained a London headquarters until 2012, when the global office moved to Singapore with regional offices in Africa, Caribbean, East Asia, Europe, Pacific and South Asia.

The LMS's first mission field, Tahiti and neighbouring Polynesian islands, passed to the Paris Missionary Society following French colonization. Missionaries went to many other Pacific island groups, from which emerged present day member Churches of CWM in Samoa, Kiribati, Tuvalu, Nauru, the Solomon Islands and Papua-New Guinea. Major nineteenth-century LMS mission fields were China, India, South and Central Africa, Madagascar and the Caribbean, including Guyana. English Presbyterian missions were principally active in Formosa (Taiwan), Amoy (Xiamen), Rajshahi (now in Bangladesh) and the Malay Straits. Welsh Presbyterian missionary interest through north-east India, especially Mizoram, impelled the receiving church to evangelize in Burma (Myanmar) and elsewhere. Likewise missionaries went from one Pacific island group to others, creating cross-currents of mission long before the modern theme 'from everywhere to everywhere' was promoted.

For the British public, however, it was the romantic stories of missionary pioneers, their courage, adventures, endurance and (in some cases) deaths on duty which created heroes. John Williams (b. 1796, killed at Erromanga, Vanuatu, 1839) gave his name to a line of seven missionary ships which sustained the South Pacific mission until the 1970s. Robert Morrison (1782–1834, solitary in Canton from 1807, translated the Bible into Mandarin Chinese). Robert Moffat (1795–1883) served in southern Africa from 1839, David Livingstone (1813–73) married Moffat's daughter Mary but soon moved on from missionary duty to exploration, celebrity and conflict with the slavers. James Chalmers (1841–1901) with W. G. Lawes pioneered the mission in Papua-New Guinea from 1877, via Torres Straits islands.

LMS missionaries transcribed oral languages, wrote grammars and dictionaries in order to achieve their main goal, publication of the scriptures in local languages. In some countries they set up the first printing presses, distributed tracts, portions and whole Bibles and established schools. Medical services were offered at an elementary level by most mission stations and introduced Western medicine at a professional standard where clinics or hospitals could be established. LMS and shared mission schools and colleges made significant contributions to education, particularly in opening opportunities for women.

Relationships with power were varied: in some fields LMS missionaries formed alliances with existing power structures, while in others (e.g. Vanderkemp among the South African Xhosa and John Smith in Demerara) they championed the interests of indigenous and oppressed peoples against settlers, slave-masters and colonizers.

The process by which twentieth-century LMS and Congregational church leaders transformed a self-financing and substantially lay-led London society into an international partnership of church professionals falls broadly into two stages. In the first, world missionary conferences in Edinburgh (1910), Jerusalem (1928), Tambaram (1938), Willingen (1952), Mexico City (1963) and Bangkok (1974) and world church conferences especially those at Amsterdam (1948) and New Delhi (1961) provided the theory: mission, the voluntary interest of a minority, had to be recognized as the essence of what it is to be a church. In practice what emerged became more remote from erstwhile mission supporters; fund-raising for overseas mission was folded into church budgets and there was less report-back from missionaries or overseas churches. In the second stage, these trends continue: Churches of former mission-field areas take equal places around the meeting table; proceeds from sale of a mission hospital site in Hong Kong provide finance; each member church develops its own mission plans which the collective support.

Richard Lovett, *The History of the London Missionary Society 1795–1895*, 2 vols (London: Oxford University Press, 1899); Norman Goodall, *A History of the London Missionary Society, 1895–1945* (London: Oxford University Press, 1954); Bernard Thorogood (ed.), *Gales of Change: Responding to a Shifting Missionary Context: The Story of the London Missionary Society, 1945–1977* (Geneva: World Council of Churches, 1994).

GEHR

Cradock, Walter (1610?–59)

The Welsh Puritan leader Walter Cradock was born in Llangwm, Monmouthshire, into a substantial yeoman family and was educated at

Jesus College, Oxford. He first emerges in 1634 as curate of St Mary's parish in Cardiff where he was censured for Puritan irregularities and described by his bishop as 'a bold, ignorant young fellow'. The revoking of his licence did not prevent him from ministering, and within a matter of months he had made a reputation as a powerful preacher at Wrexham, Denbighshire, the one stronghold of Puritanism in north Wales. During the next few years he moved between the Welsh borders and London, spending time at Shrewsbury, Llanfair Waterdine in Shropshire where a Puritan congregation had been established, and at Llanfaches in his home county, helping establish Wales' first Independent church in 1639.

During the Cromwellian regime Cradock rose to a position of prominence in London, and used his influence to support evangelistic initiatives in his native Wales. His sermon before the House of Commons published as *The Saints Fullness of Joy* (1646) conveys the sense of his winsome spirituality while his description of spiritual awakening in south-east Wales – 'the most glorious work that ever I saw in Britain, unless it were in London; the Gospel is run over the mountains between Brecknockshire and Monmouthshire, as the fire in the thatch', *Glad Tidings from Heaven* (1648) – is memorable. Partly as a result of his influence parliament passed the Act for the Better Propagation of the Gospel in Wales (1650) under whose terms he became one of the 'approvers' appointed to oversee its implementation.

As one of Cromwell's principal Welsh supporters, he challenged Vavasor Powell's Fifth Monarchist rejection of the Lord Protector's authority, and displayed his loyalty to the regime in his *Humble Representation and Address* (1655). By that time he had been instituted Puritan incumbent of his home parish of Llangwm, where he died, aged forty-nine, in December 1659.

DDM

Cromwell, Oliver (1599–1658)

Oliver Cromwell was born in Huntingdon in 1599. In 1620 he married Elizabeth Bourchier in St Giles Cripplegate, London, and they had nine children. During the 1630s Cromwell was a yeoman farmer living in St Ives in Cambridgeshire. In 1640 he became MP for Cambridge, and by 1653 he was Lord Protector, in effect head of state. Such a rise speaks both of the uniqueness of the times and of personal greatness.

As the breakdown of relationships between Charles I and parliament turned to armed conflict in 1642, Cromwell rose to power as an instinctive soldier and military strategist, gaining a series of remarkable victories from Marston Moor in 1642 to Naseby, Langport and Bristol in 1645. Later, during the Interregnum, his ill-fated Irish campaign (1649/50) and Scottish campaign (1651) which culminated in a victory against all odds at Dunbar confirmed his military pre-eminence. That success determined his political prominence.

Little is known of Cromwell's early life, but he experienced a religious conversion ca 1628/29, and might have been further radicalized by the preaching of Job Tookey at St Ives. What is certain is that he ascribed the triumph of parliament through the Civil Wars to the providence of God. His political career was to be predicated on the need to respond to that divine favour by reforming the country into a godly society, which (as he put it in 1650) would relieve the oppressed, hear the groans of poor prisoners, reform the abuses of the professions and produce greater economic equality. It was a manifesto that floundered on the rocks of political pragmatism – the English Republic did not have a blueprint.

Cromwell was one of those who signed the king's death warrant in 1649, but he only did so after extensive negotiations had rendered his favoured solutions of first, a divided sovereignty between king and parliament, and second, abdication, impossible. It was only after the failure of Rump and Barebones parliaments to govern competently that Cromwell accepted the Lord Protectorate in 1653. Although he accepted many of the trappings of monarchy after 1657, there was no rhetoric to match them, his favoured images being those of the good constable or the faithful watchman.

Cromwell's religious vision was of a national church with a publicly accredited ministry, with the proviso that those who in conscience could not accept it would be allowed to worship and organize themselves in freedom. In the latter years of the Protectorate he became increasingly irritated with sectarians who refused to live contentedly in their parishes. He was as generous to Catholics as it was possible for him to be, and it was at his sole behest that Jews were re-admitted to England in 1655. His personal religious views remain an enigma. He seems to have attended his parish church but also to have been active in conventicles. His personal chaplains were Independents, but of the variety who were happy to accept office in the national church of the 1650s.

John Morrill, *Oliver Cromwell* (Oxford, Oxford University Press, 2007).
DGC

Dale, Robert William (1829–95)

A Congregational minister, R. W. Dale was born in December 1829 in Newington, London. His parents, Elizabeth and Robert Dale, a hat-trimmer, were members of Tabernacle, Moorfields, where John Campbell ministered.

In 1844 Dale became an assistant teacher in Andover, and a member of East Street Congregational Church. He studied for the ministry at Spring Hill College, Birmingham, 1847–53, taking first class honours in his London BA, and an MA with the gold medal in philosophy.

Dale first preached at Carrs Lane Church, Birmingham, in 1849, and from September 1852 he took services there monthly. Admiration replaced earlier criticism of the minister John Angell James, with Dale becoming his biographer. In July 1853, Dale was chosen assistant preacher and in July 1854 co-pastor with James. When James died, in 1859, Dale became sole pastor, remaining there until his death. In time Dale founded new churches at Edgbaston, Moseley, Yardley and Acocks Green. He was a formidable preacher and speaker, given his intellect and ethical teaching. He provoked gossip by smoking a pipe and declining to don the dissenting pastor's traditional black coat and white tie. He refused to accept the title 'Reverend', conceding that of 'Doctor' after Glasgow University conferred on him an honorary doctorate in 1883. These attitudes revealed his objections to treating ministers as priests.

He maintained that political participation was binding on Christians. Dale's was a newer Liberalism. By the late 1860s, the campaign to improve Birmingham's education and social conditions had begun. Although Joseph Chamberlain applied the ideals, Dale ensured Nonconformist support. Hardly any facet of municipal life was untouched by Dale. He became famous as a result of the education controversy. In the 1860s he championed compulsory state education, free for all unable to pay. He criticized the Education Bill of 1870 because, by allowing denominational teaching in schools, it violated the principle of religious equality. His opposition, with Baptist and Congregational backing, contributed to Gladstone's election defeat in 1874. He also favoured the disestablishment of the Church of England, but found the Liberation Society too combative. With James Guinness Rogers, he conducted an independent disestablishment campaign in 1875–76.

In April 1886, Gladstone's Irish Home Rule Bill caused such arguments among Congregationalists that Dale withdrew from participation in the Congregational Union of which he had been chairman in 1869. He was chairman of the first International Congregational Council, in London in 1891. Alongside these activities, he was instrumental in removing Spring Hill College to Oxford, where it opened in 1889 as Mansfield College. He chaired its council until 1894.

Dale's *Christian Doctrine* (1894) affirmed orthodox teaching on the Trinity, incarnation, and resurrection. He defended the Congregational understanding of the church, arguing that evangelical individualism had denuded this understanding, in *The Evangelical Revival* (1880). He criticized Calvinist teaching on total depravity and double predestination. In *The Atonement* (1875) he substituted, for traditional evangelicalism, the view that Christ's death was a voluntary sacrifice which vindicated God's righteousness. Overall he rendered evangelical theology more ethical and more in accord with divine love.

In 1855 Dale married Elizabeth Dowling. Their son Sir Alfred William Winterslow Dale (1855–1921), vice-chancellor of Liverpool University 1903–19, edited his father's *History of English Congregationalism* (1907) and wrote the *Life of R. W. Dale* (1899). Dale died on 13 March 1895 in Birmingham.

Dale was among the most important Nonconformists in England. He taught Nonconformists to realize their social and political powers. In all Dale published sixty-four titles and edited *The Congregationalist* (1871–78).

AA

Defoe, Daniel (ca 1660–1731)

The son of a Presbyterian London tallow-chandler, Defoe became one of the most important journalists and writers of the early eighteenth century (he authored more than three hundred works) and is generally recognized as the father of the modern British novel. For many years he attended the ministry of the Presbyterian Samuel Annesley (1620?–96) in Bishopsgate Street and later in Spitalfields. Annesley was ejected in 1662 from his ministry at St Giles, Cripplegate, for his refusal to conform to the Established Church. His daughter, Susanna (1669–1742), was the mother of John and Charles Wesley. Defoe attended two academies conducted by Independent ministers: first as a young boy at James Fisher's school in Dorking, and later at Charles Morton's academy in Newington Green, where Defoe studied for the ministry, though he did not enter the profession. Morton's Dissenting Academy was considered the finest of his day, and he taught in English, leaving a lasting mark on Defoe and his future career as a writer. Though raised in a Puritan home, Defoe developed an appreciation for music, art and literature, believing, as did John Calvin, that these forms of artistic expression, when created in the fear of God and devoted to the service of humankind, were eminently useful. Defoe's early life as a Dissenter was marked by an eclectic spirit: he was raised a Presbyterian, trained by Independents, befriended the Quakers (most notably William Penn) and revered the works of John Bunyan, who has long been claimed by both Independents and Baptists. Defoe's conduct books and fiction owe an obvious debt to Bunyan's *Pilgrim's Progress* (1678), which provided Defoe with a valid defence as a Nonconformist for the creation of allegorical and moral fiction.

Though his energies were focused on business, politics and religious controversy for most of his adult life (he did not publish his first novel until he was nearly sixty years of age), Defoe's successes in business (he operated a brick and pantile factory in Tilbury for many years, as well as investing heavily in the export-import business) were overshadowed by his lapses in judgement and bad luck, experiencing numerous bankruptcies and incarcerations for debt as well as harassment from the authorities due to his outspoken allegiance to Whig politics and religious Nonconformity. Though devoted to William III, he later worked (virtually as a spy among Dissenters, much of it in Scotland) for the Tory leader Robert Harley during the reign of Queen Anne. Defoe's writings, whether political, religious or fictional, were consistently shaped by his adherence to a Whig culture and ideology that stressed individualism, equality, wealth, happiness and religious and political freedom, yet acknowledged at the same time the role of government in creating a society that would nourish and preserve these rights for all its citizens, whether Anglican or Nonconformist, what Leon Guilhamet terms Defoe's 'secularization of Puritan attitudes' (*Defoe and the Whig Novel: A Reading of the Major Fiction* (Newark, DE: University of Delaware Press, 2010), p. 15). These ideals were first embodied in his popular poem, *The True-Born Englishman* (1698) (which went through some fifty editions by 1750), and given fuller treatment in his philosophical verse essay *Jure Divino* (1706).

Defoe's controversial career as a pamphleteer and journalist, however, began with his inflammatory exposé *An Inquiry into Occasional Conformity* (1698), a practice he felt weakened the testimony of Nonconformists, though many Churchmen and Dissenters disagreed with his position. This was merely the first of many pamphlets that would find Defoe defending what he believed was a central feature of Nonconformity only to be attacked by foes and friends alike. This was most true of his controversial pamphlet *The Shortest Way with the Dissenters* (1702), written in the persona of a rabid High Churchman (patterned somewhat after the anti-nonconformist Anglican preacher Henry Sacheverell) who advocated the subjection and even abolition of Dissenters. After his authorship of the pamphlet became known, Defoe was charged with sedition and spent three days in the pillory in 1703. The following year Defoe commenced publication of *The Review*, which ran from February 1704 to June 1713, one of the most important contributions by a Nonconformist to the early history of British journalism.

Defoe was also widely known among Dissenters for his conduct books, most notably his two volumes of *The Family Instructor* (1715, 1718, which went through twenty editions by the end of the century), followed by *Religious Courtship* (1722), *The Complete English Tradesman* (1726) and *Conjugal Lewdness* (1727), all employing various narrative devices (primarily dialogues with carefully constructed character types) that Defoe would perfect in his novels.

Robinson Crusoe appeared in 1719, the first of a series of novels exploiting travel and picaresque narrative forms that would propel Defoe into the first rank of British novelists (the novel would eventually become one of the most widely translated works in English history and has never been out of print). Crusoe and his island offered Defoe a laboratory in which he could work out many of his political and religious ideals, emphasizing in Crusoe's instruction of Friday the supremacy of scripture, revelation and the sovereignty of God, with occasional asides to such contemporary controversies among Nonconformists as that which occurred at Salters' Hall in 1719 concerning Arianism. Defoe's other novels include *Moll Flanders* (1722), *Col. Jack* (1722), *Journal of the Plague Year* (1722) and *Roxana* (1724).

Throughout his long career as a writer and controversialist, Defoe espoused a belief in moderation as a rule of life, yet in certain areas he was never one to compromise. He was worldly, yet devoutly religious; loyal to Dissent, yet tolerant of other Christians, knowing that, in the end, being a Christian and exhibiting an allegiance to Protestant Christianity was society's greatest bulwark against infidelity, scepticism and vice. The Calvinism of his youth was gradually modified by his emphasis upon individual accountability and human ability and reason, yet still he maintained a conviction of God's providential rule in this world and the ever-present role of Satan in subverting man's fallen nature and his obligation to adhere to the law of God. Though evil was real, God was sovereign and good would ultimately prevail. In this regard, his Calvinism remained firm.

Paula R. Backscheider, *Daniel Defoe: His Life* (Baltimore, MD and London: The Johns Hopkins University Press, 1989).

TW

Dissenting Academies

The events of 1662 excluded Nonconformists from a university education in England. The need to provide higher education was met on a domestic scale. Ejected ministers who could claim the right credentials took in pupils to mimic the studies that a tutor might direct at Oxford or Cambridge. Such academies might have a short life and were not originally educational institutions as such. Nonconformists prized a university education for ministers and the new generation was educated in this fashion, although academies also educated lay people and conformists. Funding was always a problem, being reliant on fees paid to tutors. A number of funds were established to offer bursaries to suitable students who could not afford the fees. The curriculum was built around the classic and philosophical subjects. Records of early academies are by their very nature sparse. They emerged as more public institutions after the 'Toleration Act' of 1689, but were threatened once more by penal legislation which failed to pass into law because of the death of Queen Anne. Eighteenth-century academies remained modest and personal enterprises, although the seeds of later institutions were sown in some of them. Throughout this period some Nonconformists took advantage of the Scottish universities to pursue study to degree level. Some academies moved towards what would now be termed Unitarianism.

The scene changed after the Evangelical Revival. When six Methodist students were expelled from Oxford in 1768 the Countess of Huntingdon opened a theological college at Trevecka in south Wales. This was followed by another at Newport Pagnell, sponsored by John Newton and his evangelical friends and under the care of William Bull, the town's Independent minister. These institutions rejected the traditional university course and, although they still taught classics and biblical languages, put a far greater emphasis on popular preaching. Students were only admitted to train for ministry and they were usually unable to pay fees from their own resources. The Bristol Baptist Academy, run in association with the Broadmead church, similarly only admitted ministerial students. Congregationalists made use of the new breed of academies and began to copy the model. The result was the emergence of theological colleges in the nineteenth century. These were larger institutions than the former academies and their buildings were more obviously designed for the purpose. The opening of a university accessible to Dissenters in London and the growth of other new civic universities providing a range of courses removed the need for the old academies to offer a general education and the ones which survived became essentially seminaries. Through the twentieth century the demand for theological college places diminished and many were closed or amalgamated.

SCO

Dodd, Charles Harold (1884–1973)

Born in Wrexham on 7 April 1884 and raised a Congregationalist, Dodd studied Classics at Magdalen College, Oxford (1902–5), the numismatics of the Roman Empire in Berlin (1907), then theology at Mansfield College, Oxford (1908–11). He was minister at Brook Street, Warwick, during 1912–15 and again in 1918–19. In 1915 he was appointed tutor at Mansfield, later becoming professor of New Testament Greek and Exegesis. He remained at Mansfield until 1930 when he became the Rylands Professor of Biblical Criticism and Exegesis in the University of Manchester. In 1935 he became the first Nonconformist to hold a theological chair in either of England's ancient universities when he was appointed Norris-Hulse Professor of Divinity in the University of Cambridge, a post he held until his retirement in 1949. He was a prolific author and although the suppositions behind some of his work have been subsequently challenged, his ideas had a profound impact on New Testament during his lifetime and have continued to be the subject of debate since his death on 21 September 1973.

His first two books *The Meaning of Paul for Today* (1920) and *Parables of the Kingdom* (1935) demonstrate his aversion to apocalyptic and his thinking about 'realized eschatology', namely that the realities of the kingdom of God did not belong to the future but to the present. He subsequently modified his thinking to suggest that the kingdom was in process of realization. For Dodd the New Testament is grounded in historical event and this provides it with an essential unity. This event was the apostolic preaching or *kerygma* which meant that the New Testament writings were trustworthy witness accounts of the early church, the details of which could be discovered by means of the historical-critical method. He believed that historical study could reveal much about Jesus, though his *The Interpretation of the Fourth Gospel* (1953), while still read, has been criticized by some for giving insufficient space to the gospel's Jewish background.

Dodd was proud of his roots as a Welshman and a Congregationalist, but he was also international and ecumenical in outlook. He made a significant contribution to the translation of the *New English Bible*. There can be little doubt that he was the foremost British biblical scholar of the twentieth century.

F. W. Dillistone, *C. H. Dodd: Interpreter of the New Testament* (London: Hodder & Stoughton, 1977).

RP

Doddridge, Philip (1702–51)

Born in London, Doddridge was destined for a career as a Dissenting minister, his grandfather having been one of those ejected from the Church of England in 1662. In 1719 he entered the Dissenting Academy at Kibworth, Leicestershire, and after briefly succeeding one of his tutors left to become pastor of the Independent congregation at Northampton in 1723. Alongside this he became tutor at the newly established Dissenting Academy at Market Harborough, later known as the Daventry Academy. He combined these two roles for the whole of his life. He quickly gained a reputation as a gifted preacher, and his devotional approach was much imitated. It was this that made him an early encourager of the evangelical revivalists, particularly those of Calvinistic theological opinions. Although not averse to criticizing their tendency to enthusiasm, Doddridge saw in the early Calvinistic Methodists the same commitment to a warm and mission-orientated evangelicalism that he himself prized. Like them he preferred a moderate Calvinism that encouraged rather than inhibited evangelistic endeavour. He was genuinely innovatory in his recommendation that Nonconformists establish voluntary societies to spread the gospel both at home and abroad. Doddridge was also a prolific author, and his most famous book *The Rise and Progress of Religion in the Soul* (1745) has been translated into numerous languages and remained in print almost continuously. He taught in excess of two hundred students, many of whom went on to become prominent figures in the world of Dissent. He majored in philosophy and theology, but Doddridge was really a polymath, keeping abreast of the latest scientific discoveries of his day. A prolific letter writer, his correspondence, encapsulating as it does his position at the heart of the English Dissenting world, remains perhaps his greatest legacy.

M. Deacon, *Philip Doddridge of Northampton, 1702–1751* (Northampton: Northamptonshire Libraries, 1980).

DCJ

Edwards, Jonathan (1703–58)

Born in East Windsor, Connecticut, Edwards entered Yale at the age of just thirteen. Heavily influenced by the philosophy of John Locke, Edwards served as a tutor at Yale before being appointed as the assistant minister to his grandfather Solomon Stoddard at Northampton, Massachusetts, in 1727. One of the most influential congregations in New England, Edwards' profile was raised still further in 1734 when the town was convulsed by an intense revival. Edwards' account of the awakening, *A Narrative of the Surprising Work of God*, was published the following year, and it quickly became the classic explanation and defence of revival. When the Great Awakening broke out in 1740 largely under the inspiration of George Whitefield, Edwards, despite reservations about aspects of contemporary revivalism, become one of the chief defenders of the revivals. In subsequent publications: *The Distinguishing Marks of the Works of the Spirit of God* (1741) and *The Religious Affections* (1746), Edwards offered a nuanced account of genuine religious experience. Other major publications followed, including his magnum opus *The Freedom of the Will* (1754). Yet Edwards ran foul of his own congregation on account of his determination to revoke the Halfway Covenant that had been introduced by his grandfather in 1750. He left to become the pastor of a church at Stockbridge, Massachusetts, in effect a frontier post where his parishioners were chiefly native Americans. In 1757 he was appointed president of the College of New Jersey, but shortly after taking up the post in 1758 he died as a result of a smallpox vaccination.

Edwards was enormously influential on the young evangelical movement, especially in Britain. His *Narrative of the Surprising Work of God* was published in London in 1737, with the fulsome recommendation of two of the most influential Dissenting ministers of the day, Isaac Watts and John Guyse. It was read by the Welsh Methodists almost immediately, and bowdlerized by John Wesley in his *Christian Library*, albeit shorn of its Calvinist references. During the nineteenth century, Edwards' main theological works appeared in British editions and some were also translated into Welsh. Among the Independents, in particular, there was extended engagement with his writings and with the New England theology developed by some of Edwards' successors. However, it was his theology of religious experience and revival that remained most influential. In the twentieth century, Edwards' theology became malleable in the hands of a wide variety of groups, from post-war Reformed evangelicals to those on the charismatic and Pentecostal wing of the evangelical movement. To various groups Edwards appeared to legitimize a wide range of religious experiences.

George Marsden, *Jonathan Edwards: A Life* (New Haven, CT: Yale University Press, 2003).

DCJ

Edwards, Lewis (1809–87)

The Welsh Calvinistic Methodist theologian and educator Lewis Edwards was born on 27 October 1809 in Llanbadarn Fawr, Cardiganshire, to humble parents. He was educated locally before becoming a schoolmaster and Methodist preacher. A burning desire for higher education took him, much to the consternation of Connexion leaders, first to the newly established London University in 1831, and between 1833 and 1836 to Edinburgh where he graduated *magna cum laude* within three rather than the normal four years. Returning to Wales he married Jane, grand-daughter of Thomas Charles, and along with David Charles, his brother-in-law, established in Bala a preparatory school for the training of ministers.

Edwards' years in Edinburgh, where he had been taught by Scotland's premier theologian Thomas Chalmers, had instilled in him Presbyterian values and an insight into the ecclesiology of the best Reformed churches of Europe. As his connexion was no longer Episcopalian, nor had it inherited the tradition of the Older Dissent, its ecclesiastical character was ambiguous. It was through Edwards' influence, not least in his debate with the Independent Samuel Roberts, that the Welsh Calvinistic Methodists embraced a Reformed ecclesiology to become, in the fullness of time, the Presbyterian Church of Wales.

Through his work at Bala Edwards convinced his fellow Methodists of the importance of a learned ministry. Between its foundation in 1837 and Edwards' death fifty years later, hundreds of young men had been imbued with the ideal of piety, sound learning and catholic breadth. These values were disseminated in the churches and beyond through the quarterly magazine *Y Traethodydd* ('The Essayist') founded in 1845 on the pattern of *The Edinburgh Review*, through which he as editor shared information on the latest trends in theology, philosophy, science and literature. His work blended the Calvinism of his upbringing with a catholicity born of a profound knowledge of the Western Christian past.

Along with his educational work and Connexional leadership, Edwards contributed to theology in Wales through his groundbreaking series of essays 'The Consistency of the Faith' (1845–58) which eschewed polarizing dualities between predestination and free will, and his volume on the atonement (1860). His eldest son Thomas Charles Edwards (1837–1900) was the founding principal of Aberystwyth University before succeeding his father as principal of the Bala college.

Lewis Edwards died on 19 July 1887 and is buried beside the grave of Thomas Charles at Llanycil churchyard, Bala.

DDM

Evangelical Alliance

Founded in 1846, the Evangelical Alliance today claims to be the largest single body representing evangelicals in the United Kingdom with a purported million strong constituency. Emerging out the rapid expansion of evangelicalism in the early nineteenth century across all denominations, Anglican and Dissenting, the Evangelical Alliance was a genuine attempt to give expression to the unity that many felt despite their varied denominational allegiances. Its immediate catalyst was the controversy surrounding the government's continued support for the Maynooth College in Ireland, which focused evangelical minds on the necessity of united opposition to apparent Catholic advance. Yet unifying such a disparate group as the evangelicals proved difficult at this stage.

At the opening meeting of the Alliance in London in August 1846, attended by evangelicals from North America, Continental Europe and all parts of the United Kingdom, the diversity of the evangelical constituency was laid bare. When it came to agreeing on a basis of faith it was difficult to come to a consensus on a number of controverted issues, and the American delegation baulked at plans to include critical views of slavery in the document. The American branch of the Alliance soon faltered, and was not revived after the Civil War. For its part, the British branch of the Alliance was primarily concerned with facilitating co-operation among evangelicals in the face of the pressing evangelistic problems of the urban and industrial parts of the country. It sponsored regular conferences, many of which were focused on the pressing social and ethical issues of the day.

Some have assumed that the Alliance was a precursor to the twentieth-century ecumenical movement. While represented at the forming of the World Council of Churches in Amsterdam in 1948, it maintained a position of benevolent neutrality to the movement for much of the time. Towards the end of the twentieth century, the Alliance saw something of a resurgence and reinvention. Beginning under the leadership of Gilbert Kirby from 1956, the Alliance's range of interests have gradually diversified. If there were divisions among evangelicals over attitudes to ecumenism in the 1960s, the Charismatic movement injected new life and a new confidence into the evangelical community and the Alliance became one of the chief beneficiaries. Among the Alliance's most innovative contributions was the establishment of the Evangelical Alliance Relief Fund (TEAR Fund), a testimony to the importance which many evangelicals had come to place on social issues. The 1980s saw the emergence of a more youthful leadership under Clive Calver, and a measure of organizational devolution occurred as separate bodies for the Evangelical Alliance in England, Wales, Scotland and Northern Ireland were established. While representing a growing and highly diverse evangelical constituency, at the time of writing the Alliance sees representing the evangelical voice to government at a whole range of levels as being at the very heart of its mission.

Ian Randall and David Hilborn, *One Body in Christ: The History and Significance of the Evangelical Alliance* (Carlisle: Paternoster, 2001).

DCJ

Evangelicalism

Although the term evangelical has a long lineage (William Tyndale was possibly the first English Protestant to identify himself as such in print in

1531), evangelicalism had its origins in the religious revivals that occurred throughout the British Isles, parts of Europe and the American colonies in the middle decades of the eighteenth century. According to the widely accepted definition of David Bebbington, evangelicals have tended to be marked by four emphases. They have stressed the central place of the Bible, the crucial importance of the cross of Christ, the need for individual conversion and the necessity of a life of Christian activism and service. However, evangelicalism has never been an entirely homogeneous movement. At its heart has been a common understanding of how an individual experiences the grace of God in Christ. Beyond this evangelicals have remained a diverse group, often giving expression to these characteristics in different ways, and within a wide range of ecclesiastical communities.

The experience of revival has continually shaped the evangelical movement. Born in trans-Atlantic revivals, the English evangelist George Whitefield arguably emerged as the first widely recognized leader of the evangelical movement. His international itinerant ministry brought a series of individual religious awakenings together into a loosely unified movement. But the evangelical impulse quickly permeated other religious traditions. In the American colonies Jonathan Edwards, a Congregationalist, gave shape to an evangelical tradition that soon spilled over into most American religious groupings. In England, Methodism under the leadership of John Wesley became the engine of evangelical growth, although Wesley's eclectic theology limited his appeal beyond the confines of the Methodist movement which he controlled. A split between Wesley and Whitefield over the relative merits of Arminian and Calvinist theology became a fault line that was to run right through the evangelical movement well beyond the eighteenth century. Nonetheless, the evangelical enthusiasm of Methodism rejuvenated many of the older dissenting groups in England and Wales in the second half of the eighteenth century. Facing a rapidly growing population, with many migrating to new industrial and urban areas, evangelical forms of religious belonging proved remarkably adaptable, and successive waves of religious revival drew many into the life of the churches.

In the nineteenth century the majority of denominations in England and Wales were either thoroughly evangelical in ethos, or contained a large proportion of evangelical members. The nineteenth century was undoubtedly the evangelical century. Fuelled by regular revivals, the Second Great Awakening lasted from the 1790s until perhaps the 1840s, a major international revival occurred in 1859 and an important awakening took place in Wales in 1904–5 that had far reaching consequences on the pattern of evangelicalism in the twentieth century, giving an important impetus for the growth of Pentecostalism. During the nineteenth century evangelicals turned their attention to the spread of the gospel overseas; following William

Carey's establishment of the Baptist Missionary Society in 1792, other denominations responded to the task and inaugurated their own societies. Protestant missionaries benefitted from and were often in the vanguard of English colonial expansion in the nineteenth century. Evangelicals were equally concerned with spreading the gospel at home, and for much of the nineteenth century they were marked by a commitment to social involvement that saw significant achievements. William Wilberforce's parliamentary campaign against the slave trade which resulted in the outlawing of the trade in the British Empire in 1807 showed evangelicals what could be achieved through concerted action. Others attempted to improve the educational, medical and living conditions of those in urban and industrial Britain, while all the Nonconformist denominations sponsored a proliferation of home mission societies that published and distributed evangelical literature, and sponsored evangelists and street workers determined to take the gospel out of the churches and into the streets of urban Britain. The nineteenth century was also the age of the great preacher; individuals such as the Baptist Charles Haddon Spurgeon who preached to thousands every week from the pulpit of his Metropolitan Tabernacle in London and hundreds of thousands through his weekly printed sermons, or the Chicago evangelist D. L. Moody, exemplified the entrepreneurial energy of Victorian evangelicals and the success with which their efforts were often met.

Yet by the end of the nineteenth century evangelical forms of religious life were facing enormous challenges. First, revivals, one of the chief agencies of growth at their disposal, were becoming less frequent and more routinized. Numerical increase was no longer guaranteed. But a combination of evolutionary science, following the publication of Charles Darwin's *Origin of Species* in 1859, and the spread of Higher Critical attitudes to the Bible, called into question some of the theological certainties upon which evangelicals had traditionally rested. While many evangelicals attempted an accommodation with the latest learning, scientific and biblical, others in the early twentieth century retreated into an anti-intellectual fundamentalism. Bewildered by modernity, some evangelicals retreated from the life of their denominations, especially where they had been won over to liberal theological ideas, and from wider public engagement.

During the twentieth century evangelicalism became enormously diversified. Pentecostalism, which emerged in the opening decade of the century, became a major force especially in the two-thirds world. Within the evangelical movement more broadly, some evangelicals sought to move beyond the fundamentalist impasse. Neo-evangelicalism which emerged in the immediate post-war years in the United States was determined to develop a more positive and engaged outlook. It was an agenda exemplified by the ministry of Billy Graham. In England, some evangelicals within the

Church of England began to engage more creatively with the life of their denomination, although there were others under the leadership of D. Martyn Lloyd-Jones who were determined to abandon the Free Churches altogether for the life of evangelical separatism. From the 1960s much of evangelicalism was revolutionized by the Charismatic movement; while its stress on the gifts of the Holy Spirit was not to everybody's taste, the Charismatic movement contributed much to the development of a more emotive spirituality, even among evangelicals who rejected its pneumatology. While evangelicals have experienced decline and the shrinking of congregations in the same way as the broader Nonconformist constituency, some congregations have been more able both to resist secularization and experience growth. Among the New Churches – the new Nonconformity – there has been expansion, and the presence of substantial ethnic minority communities in some major cities has done much to reverse decline.

At the beginning of the twenty-first century the evangelical movement is both diverse and multi-faceted. Many evangelicals deem it necessary to add an adjective to the term evangelical to define themselves more precisely. There are therefore conservative, liberal, confessional, reformed, neo-, open, post and red letter evangelicals to name just a few. However, the most dramatic development in recent times has been the globalization of the evangelical movement; where once Britain and America contained the largest concentration of evangelical Christians, the centre of gravity of the movement has shifted to south-east Asia and sub-Saharan Africa. Evangelicalism today is a global movement.

Mark Hutchinson and John Wolffe, *A Short History of Global Evangelicalism* (Cambridge: Cambridge University Press, 2012).

DCJ

Fairbairn, Andrew Martin (1838–1912)

For a variety of reasons, Fairbairn exercised a profound effect on theological education in England and Wales. Born near Edinburgh on 4 November 1838, he was educated at the Evangelical Union College in Glasgow, and at the universities of Edinburgh and Berlin. He was ordained minister at Bathgate Evangelical Union Church, Edinburgh, in 1860, moving to St Paul's Congregational Church, Aberdeen, in 1872. While based in that city, he delivered Sunday evening lectures and one who attended was a young P. T. Forsyth. In 1877 he was appointed principal of the Airedale College in Bradford. While there, he transformed ministerial training by arranging that students would go to Edinburgh University to study for an Arts degree before returning to Bradford for their theological studies. This arrangement remained in place during the twentieth century when the Yorkshire United College in Bradford taught a BD scheme to its students who, on completion of the course, were awarded Edinburgh degrees. Fairbairn's standing in the denomination was demonstrated by his election to the chair of the Congregational Union of England and Wales in 1883.

With the removal of the religious tests from England's ancient universities, it was decided to move the Spring Hill College from Birmingham to Oxford. Fairbairn was the first principal of the new Mansfield College from 1886 and oversaw the construction and opening of its new building in 1889. Fairbairn believed that theological training and research had to occur in dialogue with other disciplines rather than uphold a particular theological stance or tradition, which meant that theology should not be sidelined in the seminary, but a subject that retained a central place in the modern university. For him, theology was a living discipline, engaging with currents in modern thought, rather than a collection of ancient truths to be handed from generation to generation. He was a consultant when the universities of Wales and Manchester established theological faculties while he also delivered the Gifford Lectures in Aberdeen in 1892–94 as well as lecturing in the United States and India. He served on the Royal Commission on Secondary Education (1894–95) and on the Royal Commission on the Endowments of the Welsh Church (1906). His most important books were *Studies in the Philosophy of Religion and History* (1876), *The Place of Christ in Modern Thought* (1893) and *The Philosophy of the Christian Religion* (1902). He died on 9 February 1912.

W. B. Selbie, *The Life of Andrew Martin Fairbairn* (London: Hodder & Stoughton, 1914).

RP

Farmer, Herbert Henry (1892–1981)

Born in Highbury, London, on 27 November 1892, Farmer won a scholarship to Peterhouse, Cambridge, where he graduated with first class honours in Moral Sciences in 1914. A conscientious objector, he worked on a farm at Histon before entering Westminster College, Cambridge (1916–19), to train for ministry in the Presbyterian Church of England. He was ordained and served the church at Stafford (1919–22) and then St Augustine's, New Barnet (1922–31), before he was appointed professor of Christian Doctrine, at Hartford Seminary Foundation, Connecticut, USA (1931–35). In 1935, he was appointed Barbour Professor of Systematic Theology at Westminster College in succession to his friend and former teacher John Oman. He remained in post until his retirement in 1960 while also being Stanton Lecturer in the Philosophy of Religion in Cambridge University in 1937, Norris-Hulse Professor of Divinity from 1949 (in succession to C. H. Dodd), and fellow of Peterhouse (1950–60).

For Farmer, all religious experience (Christian and non-Christian) was the experience of the one true Reality, though he always maintained that Christ is the definitive revelation of that Reality, which makes Christianity the one, true, 'living' religion. He posited an 'epistemic distance' between the Creator God and the human creation which was compounded by human sin. Thus, while all people can experience God, they will not all interpret that experience correctly; further, not all interpretations of this general revelation can provide 'saving knowledge'. For Farmer, where religious claims contradicted the Christian claim, they can said to be wrong. Conversely, if they concur, they can be known to be true.

Farmer's theological system was marked by a sense of a general encounter with God but found its motivation in the specific forgiveness of God and reconciliation between God and human beings as expressed in the Christian gospel. This experience was marked by awe and mystery as it was constituted by holy love.

Farmer was Gifford Lecturer at the University of Glasgow in 1950–51, an institution which had awarded him an honorary DD in 1936. He died at Birkenhead on 13 January 1981.

RP

Forsyth, Peter Taylor (1848–1921)

Of all Nonconformist theologians, P. T. Forsyth ranks among the most significant. His theology reflected the critical methods of the prevailing theological liberalism, but went beyond the stress on immanent Spirit and moral value to assert the necessity of the atonement as the heart of the Christian good news and the motivation for the moral life. In his theology he rejected the evolutionary optimism of the prevailing liberalism and rediscovered God's holy love which was not merely revealed but active on the cross.

Born in Aberdeen on 12 May 1848, Forsyth studied in the University there and attended lectures in the city's St Paul's Congregational Church, delivered by its minister A. M. Fairbairn. He studied at Göttingen under Albrecht Ritschl and then attended New College, London, before ordination in 1876 at Shipley in Yorkshire. In 1879 he moved to St Thomas' Square, Hackney. At this point he was known for his advanced modernist views which rendered him suspect within his denomination and particularly in the Yorkshire and London Congregational Unions. However, while at Hackney he underwent a transformation, famously confessing later that he 'was turned from a Christian to a believer, from a lover of love to an object of grace'. As a result, Forsyth emphasized that only grace could reconcile sinful humanity to a holy God and that God's grace, in Jesus Christ, had actively secured redemption and reconciliation. From then on, Jesus Christ and his cross were central to the gospel which he proclaimed. At successive pastorates in Cheetham Hill, Manchester (1885–88), Clarendon Park, Leicester (1888–94) and Emmanuel, Cambridge (1894–1901), his reputation as the epitome of the learned minister, both theologian and preacher, grew within and beyond the denomination. He became principal of Hackney College in 1901 and remained there until his death on 11 November 1921.

Alongside the 'cruciality of the cross' which Forsyth consistently emphasized (see *The Person and Place of Christ* and *The Cruciality of the Cross*, both published in 1909), he also pioneered a rediscovery of Reformed Churchmanship, particularly in *The Church and the Sacraments* (1917). For Forsyth, the church was the society of the redeemed who were bound up with the gospel. As a result the church is founded on its doctrine and thus on the cross. It therefore had to defend its teaching.

Forsyth was rediscovered by his fellow Congregationalists later in the twentieth century and a number of his books were reprinted. His style was considered by some to be obscure, but for many it stimulated an appropriation of the atonement through which God poured forth grace on humankind. As such his work has an enduring value which continued to inspire and stimulate thought long after his death.

Alan P. F. Sell (ed.), *P. T. Forsyth: Theologian for a New Millennium* (London: United Reformed Church, 2000).

RP

Fox, George (1624–91)

George Fox was the founder of the Religious Society of Friends (Quakers). He was the son of Christopher Fox, a prosperous weaver, and Mary, and was born in Drayton-in-the-Clay (Fenny Drayton), Leicestershire, in June 1624. The earliest years of his life are not recorded as sixteen pages of his earliest memoirs have not survived, but it is suggested that he did have a formal education and was clearly able to read and write. The unsettling nature of the first Civil War (1642–46) and his own religious doubts made him introspective and he shunned the company of his contemporaries, preferring instead to dispute religious issues with scholars and clergymen. In ca 1647 he underwent a profound spiritual experience and accepted that the inward guide was the guiding authority. Although fully conversant with the Bible, he felt drawn to proselytize the primacy of the Spirit and repudiated the doctrine of the Trinity. Furthermore, like other radical sectaries, he rejected oath-taking and the collecting of tithes. His initial missionary work in the Midlands was largely unsuccessful, but he was able to draw a small number of adherents together, notably in the north of England. Among his earliest adherents were James Nayler (1616–60), Richard Hubberthorne (1628–62) and Margaret Fell (1614–1702) of Swarthmoor Hall in Cumbria whom he married in 1669. She helped to organize the missionary activities of Fox's followers (the 'Valiant Sixty') in the 1650s, particularly as throughout these years Fox was regularly arrested after advocating novel social, economic and religious beliefs, and challenging the civil and ecclesiastical authorities. Fox was a prolific writer and he wrote frequently to Friends, offering advice or admonishing those who were wavering in their commitment or were accused of 'ranterism'. After the charge of blasphemy was levelled against Nayler in Bristol in 1656, Fox increasingly sought to secure the future of the Quaker gatherings by creating a series of monthly meetings and later quarterly meetings which would help to maintain order and discipline. In 1659 he unsuccessfully attempted to counter allegations that Friends were religious and social deviants by writing the *Great Mistery of the Great Whore Unfolded*. Similarly, in the early Restoration years, he sought to allay fears that the Friends were violent sectaries. He was nevertheless imprisoned for five months, but shortly after the Thomas Venner Fifth Monarchist uprising (January 1661) he and Hubberthorne wrote *Harmless and Innocent People of God, Called Quakers* in which they eschewed carnal warfare. The ambiguity of the peace testimony was not, however, universally accepted by all Friends and many were still classified as dangerous radicals by the authorities.

Fox also had to deal with unrest among members who opposed Foxian centralization. In the early 1660s John Perrot resisted the attempts of George Fox and other leading Friends to restrict their activities and pronouncements. The schism continued even after Perrot's death in 1665, while additional divisions (Wilkinson-Story controversy) occurred in the 1670s when some members opposed the establishment of business meetings, and more specifically the decision to allow women's meetings. Fox and other leading Friends also had to negotiate the penal code which led to the frequent disruption of meetings, distraint of property and imprisonment. He was imprisoned three times: Lancaster, Scarborough (1664–66) and at Worcester (1673–75) where he began to dictate his *Journal*. Indefatigable in his missionary activity, Fox sought to proselytize new areas and, along with other Quaker missionaries, embarked on preaching tours to continental Europe in the 1660s and 1670s, and between 1671 and 1673 he visited the Caribbean and North America. While on Barbados he questioned the nature of slavery, stressed the amelioration of their conditions and ultimately sought emancipation, but accepted that this would be a long-term goal. He also produced a further declaration of Quaker faith which reaffirmed Quaker dogma as within Christian orthodoxy.

From the mid-1670s, Fox worked on his *Journal* which, although being a personal account, remains a focal point for many interested in early Quaker history. During the latter years of his life Fox saw the fortunes of Friends change markedly. The close relationship between William Penn (1644–1718) and James II provided members with a modicum of toleration, but the revolution of 1688–89 led to a loss of influence. Consequently, relations with Penn soured as Fox believed that he had become too close to the royal court. The 'Toleration Act' of 1689 nevertheless provided Friends with the right to hold religious meetings and to license their meeting houses. Fox remained concerned, however, that such a measure might diminish Friends' steadfastness and result in a decline in membership. It is true that until the early years of the eighteenth century there was recruitment, but as the century wore on numbers declined in many areas. Fox continued to attend meetings in this period, but on 11 January 1661 while attending Gracechurch Street meeting he was taken ill and died two days later at the home of Henry Gouldney. He was later buried in Bunhill Fields.

Fox's legacy is mixed. He was determined to enforce a more coherent organizational structure, but his temperamental nature and the significant changes in the management of the Society as well as the imposition of a code of discipline aroused internal divisions. Nevertheless he was a charismatic and inspirational leader who helped provide members with the means to see them through the difficult penal years.

RCA

Free Church Federal Council

The term 'Free Church' first came into general use after the disruption of the Church of Scotland in 1843. Those who wished to see a complete separation of Church and state broke away from the established Church of Scotland to form the Free Church of Scotland, which enjoyed warm links with English Dissenters, sharing moderate Calvinism as well as anti-establishment sentiments. By this time English Methodism, especially in the Wesleyan Connexion, did not share the Calvinist heritage. Historically Methodists had been forced to register their chapels under the legislation which provided for Nonconformists. This gave them some common interests, but only the more radical Methodist groups, such as the Wesleyan Reform Union, shared aspirations with Nonconformists. The common interests were dominated by politics and the need to seek parity of esteem with the Church of England.

By the end of the nineteenth century, Methodists were more likely to share with Baptists, Congregationalists and Presbyterians a commitment to the Liberal Party and to causes such as teetotalism. Local Free Church Councils were formed. At a congress in Manchester in 1892 a National Free Church Council was formed to which local councils could affiliate. A doctrinal difference arose, since historic Nonconformity included Unitarians who, although small in numbers, were influential in local activities. In 1919 the Baptist J. H. Shakespeare organized a Federal Council of the Evangelical Free Churches, designed to exclude Unitarians and to which representatives were appointed by denominations. It was not until 1940 that the two bodies were brought together in the Free Church Federal Council. By this time most of Methodism had been brought together in the Methodist Church and it was hoped the new Council might promote further Free Church union. It performed an administrative role in the provision of Free Church chaplains to the armed forces, hospitals and the prison service. The annual presidency rotated between the member denominations and the president took part in national events alongside the archbishop of Canterbury and archbishop of Westminster. The Council's offices in Tavistock Square were the gift of the Baptist Robert Wilson Black. The representation of Free Church interests to government was increasingly shared with the British Council of Churches. The last prominent campaigning issue in which it was involved in its own right was opposition to the Sunday Trading Bill of 1984.

The rise of the British Council of Churches from 1942 served to diminish the role of the Free Church Federal Council and denominations were reluctant to fund a plurality of inter-church bodies. Through the 1980s and 1990s the staffing was reduced and many local Free Church Councils merged with Councils of Churches. Attendance at the Annual Assembly declined steeply. When Churches Together in England (CTE) was established in 1990 it was decided to bring the remaining Free Church activities into the new body under a Free Church secretary, the whole organization being housed in the former Free Church Federal Council offices in Tavistock Square. The Council still exists as a legal entity, to administer the historic assets. The Free Churches Group within CTE offers membership to denominations which do not wish to join CTE, of which the president of the Free Church Federal Council is a vice-president.

SCO

Fry, Elizabeth (1780–1845)

Elizabeth Fry was a Quaker prison reformer and philanthropist. She was born in Norwich to John Gurney and Catherine Bell (both established Quaker families). Although her parents were 'cultural' Quakers, Elizabeth experienced a conversion in 1798, and from that moment her faith became determinative. Two years later she married Joseph Fry, a member of a wealthy Bristol Quaker family. They had eleven children, all but one of whom survived into adulthood. Only one remained a Friend, which may reflect the perpetual tension which Elizabeth felt between her Quaker vocation and domestic life. By 1811 she was recorded as a Quaker minister, and sought to move Quakerism in a more evangelical direction.

At the behest of a fellow Friend, she first visited the women's prison at Newgate 1813, and was appalled by what she found. Convicted and unconvicted women, many with their children, were crowded into large, unsanitary cells. Although family responsibilities kept her away in the following years, she returned in 1816 to try to create a school for the children, and for illiterate prisoners. She also made provision for the supply of decent clothing, and fought for the appointment of a matron. Her method was simple, she saw prisoners as fellow human beings who needed kindness, not cruelty and neglect. Sydney Smith visited Newgate with her in 1821 and was deeply impressed, writing: 'She is very unpopular with the clergy; examples of living, active virtue disturb our repose, and give birth to distressing comparisons: we long to burn her alive.'

In 1817 she founded the Ladies Association for the Reformation of Female Prisoners in Newgate, which in 1821 became the British Ladies Society for Promoting the Reformation of Female Prisoners. As she travelled as a Quaker minister, she took the opportunity to visit women's prisons, and to do as much fact-finding as possible. In 1827 she published *Observations on the Visiting, Superintendence, and Government, of Female Prisoners*. Her brother-in-law Thomas Fowell Buxton became MP for Weymouth in 1818. He too was an enthusiast for penal reform and it was at his behest that she became the first woman to give evidence to a House of Commons Committee – on conditions in women's prisons.

Joseph's bank went bankrupt in 1826, and he was disowned by the Quakers. The family had to downsize. Later in her life, supported by her brothers, she journeyed across Europe meeting with fellow reformers and inspecting prisons. She died in Ramsgate in 1845. Although many of her attitudes (distinguishing the 'worthy' from the 'unworthy' poor, and seeking sobriety and industriousness) now seem dated, she was a remarkable pioneer whose ministry changed many lives.

A. Van Dreth and F. De Haan, *The Rise of Caring Power: Elizabeth Fry and Josephine Butler in Britain and the Netherlands* (Amsterdam: Amsterdam University Press, 1999).

DGC

Fuller, Andrew (1754–1815)

Andrew Fuller was born on 6 February 1754, in Wicken, Cambridgeshire. His early religious experiences were in the Particular Baptist church in nearby Soham, where his mother was a member. This church was High Calvinistic in theology. According to Fuller, its pastor, John Eve, had 'little or nothing to say to the unconverted'. Nevertheless, Fuller did experience conversion in 1769 and, despite having very little by way of formal education, he became pastor in succession to Eve in 1775.

As minister at Soham, Fuller came into increasing contact with Particular Baptists who were not High Calvinists, especially John Ryland Jr and John Sutcliff. He embraced an evangelical Calvinism that was imbued with the spirit of the eighteenth-century Evangelical Revival and which was especially influenced by the writings of Jonathan Edwards and other New England theologians such as Joseph Bellamy and Samuel Hopkins. Fuller was called to be minister of the Particular Baptist church at Kettering in 1783, and published *The Gospel Worthy of All Acceptation* in 1785 (with an important second edition appearing in 1801). This was the most developed statement of evangelical Calvinism the Particular Baptists produced. *The Gospel Worthy* was an important milestone in Nonconformist soteriology. Fuller wrote a number of other theological, apologetic and practical works, for example, *The Gospel Its Own Witness* (1799), which engaged with the thought of Thomas Paine and repudiated deism. Fuller's writings were warmly commended by a wide range of Anglican evangelicals, with William Wilberforce, Thomas Scott and John Newton among his admirers.

Fuller was involved in the 1784 'Call to Prayer' which encouraged Particular Baptists and others to establish monthly prayer meetings for the worldwide spread of the gospel. In 1792 he became the founding secretary of the 'Particular Baptist Society for Propagating the Gospel among the Heathen' (BMS), the first fruits of a renewed Protestant cross-cultural missionary endeavour which was to have huge global significance. Fuller remained pastor at Kettering until his death, but also gave himself unstintingly to the work of the BMS. He spent up to three months of each year travelling in order to raise support for the new society, whose first missionary was his young friend, William Carey. In this capacity he visited Scotland five times between 1799 and 1813, with much of his ministry taking place among the Independent congregations associated with Robert and James Haldane. Thus, while remaining a committed Particular Baptist (indeed, he was a lifelong defender of closed communion principles), his work for the BMS saw him practising a form of evangelical ecumenism. He died on 8 May 1815, possibly of cancer (he had a snuff habit), and is buried in the graveyard of his church in Kettering.

Peter J. Morden, 'Andrew Fuller and the Gospel Worthy of All Acceptation', in J. H. Y. Briggs (ed.), *Pulpit and People: Studies in Eighteenth-Century Baptist Life and Thought* (Milton Keynes: Paternoster, 2009), pp. 128–51; idem, *Offering Christ to the World: Andrew Fuller (1754–1815) and the Revival of Eighteenth Century Particular Baptist Life* (Carlisle: Paternoster, 2003).

PJM

Garvie, Alfred Ernest (1861–1945)

Garvie's grandparents on both sides had emigrated from Scotland to Poland in the 1820s and worked in the linen and flour trades. He was born in Zyrardow in Poland, a town under Russian rule, on 29 August 1861. He was plagued by illness and a serious eye inflammation left him with poor sight for the rest of his life. He was fluent in German and Russian as well as English. He attended George Watson's College in Edinburgh (1874–78) and was then apprenticed to a draper for four years. He attended worship at the United Presbyterian Church and was involved in street mission. He studied Classics at Glasgow University and graduated MA in 1889 being awarded the Logan medal as most distinguished arts graduate. His dissatisfaction with the *Westminster Confession* led him to the Congregationalists and he attended Mansfield College, Oxford (1889–92), and graduated from Oxford University with first class honours in theology. Pastorates followed at Macduff (1893–95) and Montrose (1895–1903) and he was chairman of the Congregational Union of Scotland in 1902–3. In 1903 he became professor of Christian theism, comparative religion and ethics at the Hackney and New Colleges in London. He became principal of New College in 1907 and principal of the merged New and Hackney Colleges from 1924 until his retirement in 1933.

Garvie was a prolific author. He styled himself a 'liberal evangelical', by which he meant that Christian theology needed to fuse a commitment to the exposition of the scriptures with the recognition that experience was fundamental to the religious life, especially the experience of the early church. He gained some of this insight from the Ritschlian theology, having lectured on the subject at Mansfield College in 1899, subsequently publishing the lectures, though he denied being a Ritschlian. He was chair of the Congregational Union of England and Wales in 1920. Alongside this, he was committed to social reform being vice-chair of the Conference on Christian Politics, Economics and Citizenship (COPEC) held in Birmingham in 1924, a post which also demonstrated a life-long dedication to ecumenism. He was co-president of the Conference on Life and Work held at Stockholm in 1925 and deputy chair of the first World Conference on Faith and Order held at Lausanne in 1927. He was moderator of the Free Church Council in 1928. His major publications are probably his three volumes *The Christian Ideal for Human Society* (1920), *The Christian Doctrine of the Godhead* (1925) and *The Christian Belief in God* (1932). Widely respected in his day for his scholarship as well as his commitment to social improvement and ecumenism, his work is bound to the philosophical and ecclesiastical concerns of the time, which has meant that his publications have had little impact upon subsequent generations. He died in London on 7 March 1945.

Alfred E. Garvie, *Memories and Meanings of My Life* (London: Allen & Unwin, 1938).

RP

Gill, John (1697–1771)

John Gill was born in 23 November 1697 in Kettering, Northamptonshire. Converted at the age of twelve, as a young man Gill taught himself Latin, Greek and Hebrew, laying the foundations for a lifetime of scholarly work. In 1720 he was called to be the minister of the Particular Baptist church meeting at Horslydown, Southwark. This pastorate was not without its challenges, but Gill would serve this historic congregation (the church had been established by Benjamin Keach) for the rest of his life, becoming probably the best known Baptist minister of his generation.

For much of his time in London, Gill was the leading figure on the London Baptist Board, a group of pastors whose advice on a wide range of matters was sought by Calvinistic Baptist churches from all over the country. But he was best known as a voluminous writer. He was the first Baptist both to write a detailed exposition of the whole Bible (published in nine volumes between 1748 and 1766) and also to produce a systematic theology (his three-volume

Body of Divinity which appeared in 1769–70). Earlier his reputation had been established by *The Cause of God and Truth* (originally published in four volumes between 1735 and 1738), which was a trenchant defence of Calvinistic tenets. These and other works exercised a huge influence at a time when many pastors had not been formally educated in the Academy.

Gill has often been associated with the growth of High Calvinism in Particular Baptist life. In summary, Gill consistently rejected open offers of the gospel, and his writings exhibit a number of other features associated with High Calvinism, although the charge that he was an antinomian, one that has often been levelled against him, is not borne out by his published work. His scholarship, particularly his ability as a Hebraist, was widely recognized and he was awarded an honorary DD by the University of Aberdeen in 1748. In later years he suffered failing health and his congregation dwindled, but he was loved by those who remained, and when he tendered his resignation a year before his eventual death the congregation refused to accept it. He died on 14 October 1771 and was buried in Bunhill Fields.

Gill has not fared well at the hands of most Baptist writers. His works were memorably described by Robert Hall Jr early in the nineteenth century as a 'continent of mud', and later theologians and historians have tended to share Hall Jr's negative view. Conversely, those in the Strict Baptist movement which emerged at the beginning of the nineteenth century have usually been positive. A fair assessment of Gill needs to resist reading him against the background of these later debates. Such an assessment might conclude that, while the High Calvinism with which he was associated encouraged a narrow, insular ecclesiology, his works did help to hold Particular Baptists to a basic Trinitarian orthodoxy at a time when many Nonconformists were embracing Socinianism and Unitarianism. Certainly Gill was a significant figure, and any study of eighteenth-century and indeed nineteenth-century Baptist life needs to reckon with his influence.

John Gill, *The Cause of God and Truth* (London: Aaron Ward, 1735–38); John Rippon, *A Brief Memoir of the Life and Writings of John Gill D.D.* (London: John Bennett, 1838); Michael A. G. Haykin (ed.), *The Life and Thought of John Gill (1697–1771): A Tercentennial Celebration* (Leiden: Brill, 1997).

PJM

Goodwin, Thomas (1600–80)

Thomas Goodwin was born in Great Yarmouth, the son of a prosperous merchant and educated at Christ's College, Cambridge. In 1619 he became a Fellow of St Catharine's College, where he remained until he resigned in 1638 to marry Elizabeth Prescott, the daughter of a well-connected London alderman. He was a theologian and clergyman who also served town churches St Andrew the Great and Holy Trinity as curate, lecturer and vicar between 1628 and 1632. Like many Cambridge theologians in Stuart England, he had Puritan sympathies. His posthumous *Works* reveal him to have been interested in pastoral theology, the Trinity and the peace of the church as well as other themes.

Soon after his marriage he took up a post as teacher in the English congregation at Arnhem in the Netherlands. This might have been prompted simply by the need to earn a living, or to the imposition of Laudian values on the English church, or both. He seems to have put Independency into practice at Arnhem, emphasizing both covenantal theology and the need for ecclesiastical discipline.

He returned to London in 1641 and was to play a significant role in the future shaping of the English Church. He was a member of the Westminster Assembly and was part of the sub-committee that drew up The Directory for Public Worship. He was clearly identified in the Assembly as an Independent, dissenting from its decisions on church government.

When Cromwell came to power, Goodwin was appointed president of Magdalen College, Oxford (1650), and along with John Owen and Philip Nye helped fashion the Cromwellian church settlement. During the Cromwellian period he was at the centre of power. Unlike Owen, he continued his support of Cromwell after 1657, and was one of the Privy Councillors who attested that the Protector had named his son Richard as his successor. In 1658 he played a central role in the Savoy Conference which produced the *Savoy Declaration* which was to be so influential on later Congregationalism.

It would be anachronistic to judge Goodwin a Congregationalist. He was a Puritan reformer in late Stuart England who sought to reform the church with an Independent polity. After the Restoration he was not persecuted under the Clarendon Code but he found ways to continue preaching and lecturing, and was much in the company of John Owen. His health declined in the 1670s, and he died in 1680. He was one of the few ejected ministers who was of independent means and wealth.

Oxford Dictionary of National Biography (Oxford: Oxford University Press, 2004).
DGC

Happy Union (1690–91)

During the period of persecution following the Act of Uniformity of 1662, it proved impossible to sustain the Presbyterian system of synods and councils, leading to a degree of rapprochement between the various dissenting groups. This was, in part, motivated by practical concerns, including the relief of poverty among ministers and the education of future church leaders. In order to make provision for both, a 'Common Fund' was established in 1690 and administered by a committee made up of Independent and Presbyterian ministers. This was the catalyst to seek further union, with John Howe leading the quest. On 6 March 1691 virtually all Presbyterian and Congregational ministers in London signed the *Heads of Agreement* and on 6 April the 'Happy Union' was inaugurated at the Stepney Meeting House. The scheme sought to unite Presbyterians and Independents around the idea of a gathered church of saints who adhered to the basic doctrines of Christian faith. The gathered church was given authority to elect its own officers and to call its own pastors, providing they were competent in Christian learning and morals and their ministry was approved by the calling congregation and confirmed by neighbouring churches.

Controversy emerged from the beginning with Presbyterians accusing Independents of antinomianism and Independents suggesting that Presbyterians were leaning towards Socinianism, accusations which grew in strength after Richard Davis, Independent minister at Rothwell, Northamptonshire, was called to a meeting of Presbyterian ministers who accused him of having embraced an antinomian position. In effect this squabbling put an end to the 'Happy Union', with Isaac Chauncey for the Independents and Daniel Williams for the Presbyterians articulating their objections. R. Tudur Jones notes that a 'rift' was created 'between Presbyterians and Congregationalists that was never closed' (p. 118).

R. Tudur Jones, *Congregtionalism in England: 1662–1962* (London: Independent Press, 1962).

RP

Harris, Howell (1714–70)

A native of Breconshire, Harris worked as a schoolmaster before experiencing an evangelical conversion in 1735. Almost immediately he began 'exhorting' to his immediate neighbours, and by early 1736 had established his first religious society. This activity quickly mushroomed so that within a couple of years Harris was supervising a small network of societies in south-east Wales. In 1737 he and Daniel Rowland, who had been attracting large congregations to Llangeitho in south-west Wales, fused their activities creating the Welsh Methodist movement. A convinced

Anglican, Harris' attempts to secure ordination in the Church of England were repeatedly thwarted on account of his refusal to abandon his irregular exhorting activity. His status as a layman was to cause significant problems in his relations with the other ordained leaders of the Welsh revival.

Harris' great skill was in the organization of the Welsh Methodist revival; the system of societies, various levels of officers to oversee them and a system of monthly, quarterly and annual meetings to manage them served the movement well. In early 1739, he made the acquaintance of the English revivalist George Whitefield. It was a friendship which saw Harris work closely with Whitefield, and effectively become second-in-command of the English Calvinistic Methodist movement following the split with the Wesleys over Calvinism in 1741. In 1743 Harris and Whitefield established the English and Welsh Calvinistic Methodist movement, a series of revivals under a single organizational structure. For much of the 1740s, particularly with Whitefield absent in the American colonies, Harris divided his time between the leadership of the English Calvinistic and the Welsh revivals. However, by the later 1740s Harris had become an increasingly contentious figure. A combination of overwork, fragile mental health, his growing acceptance of aspects of Moravian theology and an unhealthy friendship with a female prophetess, Mrs Sidney Griffith, prompted both Whitefield and the Welsh Methodist leadership to separate from him.

No longer welcome at Whitefield's London Tabernacle, and excluded from the Welsh revival which now fell under the leadership of Daniel Rowland, Harris gradually withdrew to Trevecka where he devoted his attention to the creation of the Trevecka 'Family'. Modelled on Moravian communities, the 'Family' was a self-sustaining quasi-monastic community, under Harris' authoritarian rule. Its membership ebbed and flowed, but among its most notable achievements was the impetus its agricultural activities gave to the newly established Breconshire Agricultural Society. Harris only gradually emerged from his self-imposed exile, joining the Breconshire Militia in 1759 in the middle of the Seven Years War (1756–63). The outbreak of a fresh revival at Llangeitho in 1762 brought about reconciliation between Harris and his old friends in the Methodist movement. He took up many of his old responsibilities, began to visit the London Methodists again, and was behind the Countess of Huntingdon's decision, in 1768, to open a college at Trevecka at which to train preachers for her chapels. However, in reality he had lost much of his old verve.

By the time of his death, the movement which Harris had done so much to shape was firmly in the hands of his friend and old rival Daniel Rowland. Ironically, it was just entering upon a phase of significant growth that would see it become the largest Nonconformist denomination in Wales, following its eventual secession from the Church of England in 1811. Its growth was built on the structures put in place by Harris.

Geraint Tudur, *Howell Harris: From Conversion to Separation, 1735–1750* (Cardiff: University of Wales Press, 2000); David Ceri Jones, Boyd Stanley Schlenther and Eryn Mant White, *The Elect Methodists: Calvinistic Methodism in England and Wales, 1735–1811* (Cardiff: University of Wales Press, 2012).

DCJ

Hastings, Selina, Countess of Huntingdon (1707–91)

Born at Astwell House, Nottinghamshire, little is known of the Countess of Huntingdon's early life beyond the fact that she stayed with her father, Earl Ferrars, following her parents' separation in 1712. She married Theophilus, ninth earl of Huntingdon, in 1728 and they lived on his estate at Donington Park, Leicestershire. The details of her conversion are unclear, but in 1741 she initiated a relationship with the Wesley brothers, but by 1744 had parted company with them and aligned herself with George Whitefield and his Calvinistic Methodists. Following the death of her husband in 1746, the countess took an increasingly prominent role in the leadership of Calvinistic Methodism. In 1749 she appointed Whitefield her personal chaplain, part of an audacious bid to secure the conversion of many from the upper reaches of society to the evangelical cause. The relative failure of this policy forced her to change tack and during the 1760s she began opening chapels in some of the major spa towns in England. Appointing prominent evangelical clergymen as her chaplains, she opened chapels in Brighton (1761), Bath (1765) and Tunbridge Wells (1769). Others followed in subsequent years.

Following the death of Whitefield in 1770, she inherited responsibility for his orphanage in Georgia. The project proved an unmitigated disaster, and by 1774 had been razed to the ground by fire. Although a member of the Church of England, the countess' irregular activities soon got her into trouble with the ecclesiastical hierarchy. When she converted an amusement house at Clerkenwell, London, into a chapel the bishop of London ordered its closure. In 1780 following further attempts by the bishop to close down the newly named Spa Fields Chapel, the Countess seceded from the Church of England altogether. Her chapels were registered as Dissenting meeting houses and in 1783 the Countess of Huntingdon's Connexion was born. The college which she established at Trevecka in 1768 and which relocated to Cheshunt, Hertfordshire, in 1792, provided the ministers for the new denomination.

By the time of her death, her Connexion consisted of sixty chapels. During her lifetime the countess' entrepreneurial energies resulted in the birth of many projects, both at home and abroad, but the financial burden that so many commitments placed upon her meant that few of them had a long life. Her Connexion, which at the time of writing consists of twenty-three chapels, remains her most lasting legacy.

Boyd Stanley Schlenther, *Queen of the Methodists: The Countess of Huntingdon and the Eighteenth-Century Crisis of Faith and Society* (Lancaster: Scotforth Books, 1997); Alan Harding, *The Countess of Huntingdon's Connexion: A Sect in Action in Eighteenth-Century England* (Oxford: Oxford University Press, 2003).

DCJ

Helwys, Thomas (ca 1575–1615/16)

Thomas Helwys, a wealthy lawyer, together with the Lincolnshire clergyman John Smyth (ca 1570–1612), founder of the modern Baptist movement, were among a small group of English Separatists who left England for Amsterdam in 1608 to escape persecution, exercising leadership there in an English-speaking congregation. In 1609 this group formed a Baptist church, when Smyth baptized himself and then the other members, including Helwys. Later, thirty-one members of this group, including Smyth, had doubts about Smyth's re-baptism, and applied to join the Mennonites. Helwys, and a minority of Smyth's congregation, upholding the correctness of the baptism they had received from Smyth, opposed this move, and decided to return to England where in 1612 they established the first Baptist church in Spitalfields, just outside the city of London. Stephen Wright suggests that two traditions developed among the early General Baptists, one followed the Dutch Mennonites and was both clerical and pacifist in character, while the other owed more to 'English erastianism' and gave prominence to local, lay leadership; Smyth represented the first of these, Helwys the second. They also differed over the idea of securing a true 'succession' of churches and of ministry. Helwys opposed such a search, which he saw as grounded in the Old Testament rather than the New, where the emphasis was on a succession of faith and spiritual life rather than on an institution. Smyth, however, having changed his views, subsequently held to the importance of succession, which underlay his desire to join the Waterlanders. Helwys argued that since John the Baptist was unbaptized and yet preached a baptism of repentance and baptized others who 'believed and confessed their sins' it remained legitimate for those similarly moved by the Holy Spirit to do likewise.

Knowledge of the beliefs of the Spitalfields congregation can be traced back to a 'Synopsis of the Faith of the true English Church', which indicates clear distance from Mennonite beliefs, in favour of Arminian teaching. This was the beginning of the stream in Baptist life, later called General (so called because of belief in a general redemption). In 1612 Helwys published *A Short Declaration of the Mistery of Iniquity*, an historic document on religious toleration addressed to James I, the first argument in favour of the toleration not simply of Christian diversity but of all faiths. Helwys argued that while God had given the king 'all worldly power' there was also a heavenly kingdom and 'with this kingdom our lord the king hath nothing to do (by his kingly power) but as a subject himself: and that Christ is king alone.' The 'earthly sword' exacted justice, but had no authority over consciences. In some of the most famous words of the Short Declaration, Helwys bravely announced that 'men's religion to God is betwixt God and themselves; the king shall not answer for it, neither may the king be judge between God and man. Let them be heretics, Turks, Jews or whatsoever, it appertains not to the earthly power to punish them in the least measure.' Helwys was not destined to see the fruit of his call for liberty. He was imprisoned in Newgate prison and died in 1615 or 1616.

JHYB

Heywood, Oliver (ca 1630–1702)

Oliver Heywood was the most important bridge between Puritanism and post-Restoration Nonconformity in the north of England. The child of pious Puritan parents, he was born in Bolton. He was educated at Trinity College, Cambridge, returning home after graduating in 1650, becoming a preacher at Coley, one of the chapels in the parish of Halifax. Halifax was a noted centre of Puritan activity, and Heywood was ordained by the Bury classis in 1652. He introduced monthly communion and presbyterian discipline at Coley. It was inevitable that he would fall foul of the authorities after the Restoration, and he duly took his place among the ejected.

He continued to preach and minister on both sides of Pennines, becoming an itinerant after the passing of the Five Mile Act. Following the Declaration of Indulgence in 1672 he applied for a licence as a presbyterian preacher and a hundred members of his former congregation at Northowram covenanted with him. The licence was revoked three years later, and Heywood became an itinerant once more, his ministry developing almost as an informal, Nonconformist form of Episcopacy, keeping in touch with a number of congregations, supporting and nurturing them.

Once the political climate improved in 1687 he concentrated on Northowram once more, building a meeting house. He was also instrumental in spreading the 'Happy Union' (1690–91) of Presbyterians and Congregationalists to the north. During the 1690s as the strains in the relationship became obvious over the Richard Davis affair, Heywood worried about the orthodoxy of some of his fellow Nonconformists. He continued ministering and preaching throughout the Pennine region until his death. Younger ministers treated him as a kind of 'father-in-God'. He was noted for his pastoral gifts and the depth of his prayer life. He published a number of works of practical divinity and sermon series, and was deeply conscious of passing on a dissenting heritage which reached back (in his view) to the Marian martyrs.

He died in 1702 and was buried in Halifax parish church, so respected that his funeral was attended by large number of clergy from both the Church of England and Nonconformity. His two sons, John and Eliezar, entered the ministry and served in the north of England.

Oxford Dictionary of National Biography (Oxford: Oxford University Press, 2004).
DGC

Hill, Rowland (1744–1833)

Rowland Hill was an anomaly. He was an evangelical preacher. Educated at Shrewsbury, Eton, and St John's College, Cambridge, where he formed a small group of the religiously like-minded which had some similarities to Wesley's much better-known Holy Club. He was deeply influenced by George Whitefield and after his graduation undertook itinerant ministry (much to his family's consternation).

Although he wished to be ordained, it was unclear which denomination might ordain him. After six Anglican bishops refused, the bishop of Bath and Wells ordained him deacon in 1773 and he became a curate at Kingston in Somerset. However, his continuing commitment to itinerancy meant that no bishop would ordain him priest. He therefore remained in deacon's orders for the rest of his life. Theologically he was a Calvinist. His ministry developed as a blend of Anglicanism and Nonconformity, which might explain his enthusiasm for evangelical unity.

After his marriage to Mary Tudworth in 1773, he moved to Wootton-under-Edge in Gloucestershire where he built a chapel, almshouses and a woollen mill to provide employment for the poor. He used the Book of Common Prayer in the liturgy, but kept his pulpit open to evangelical preachers of any persuasion. This was replicated in his other chapels – Surrey Chapel at

Blackfriars in London, Cheltenham and Leamington. He spent the summer months in Gloucester and Surrey Chapel was his base for the rest of the year.

His ministry was a telling blend of evangelical preaching and passionate social concern. Surrey Chapel spawned thirteen Sunday Schools, providing education for more than three thousand children. He also created a Dorcas Society to provide relief for married women in poverty and a school of industry to provide employment for young girls. After meeting Edward Jenner he created a clinic in Surrey Chapel where thousands of children were vaccinated.

Hill was deeply involved in many evangelical causes and societies, among them the Religious Tract Society, the British and Foreign Bible Society and the London Missionary Society. He was a remarkably popular preacher who, like Whitefield, could attract massive crowds as he itinerated.

He wrote a number of books, including *Village Dialogues* and the hymn-book *Collection of Psalms and Hymns* (1783). Witty, passionate, aristocratic and singular, he continued preaching almost daily well into his eighties. He died in 1833 and was buried under the pulpit of Surrey Chapel.

Oxford Dictionary of National Biography (Oxford: Oxford University Press, 2004).
DGC

Horne, Charles Silvester (1865–1914)

Born at Cuckfield, Sussex, on 15 April 1865, his father was Charles Horne, the local Congregational minister, and his mother was Harriet Silvester. Six weeks after his birth, the family moved to Newport, Shropshire, where Charles senior became editor of the local newspaper. Horne attended Glasgow University, where he graduated MA in 1886, and then became one of the first six students to enter Mansfield College in Oxford. His fame grew rapidly and he was called to the Allen Street Church in Kensington before he had completed his course. So impressed were they by Horne's clear pastoral gifts that the church was willing to wait eighteen months for their new minister. Horne was much in demand both as a preacher and a platform speaker, being contrasted favourably even with Lloyd George. He was also driven by compassion for the plight of the poor, especially the working classes who seemed to be estranged from the churches. As a result, he was an advocate of the 'Institutional Church' while at Kensington and, in 1903, he accepted a call to the debt-ridden, run-down Whitefield's Tabernacle on Tottenham Court Road. He transformed that church by incorporating a library, classrooms and canteen and by offering cooking and sewing lessons.

Over one thousand men regularly attended his Sunday afternoon lectures. He was chairman of the Congregational Union of England and Wales in 1910–11 and was elected to parliament as junior member for Ipswich in 1910. His was a public and thus inevitably political witness and he epitomized the Nonconformist Conscience. Personal morality was a priority, but such morality had to extend to the social structures which kept people in poverty and prevented them from doing anything about it. The combination of a radical message and a gift for public speaking made him much in demand and he selflessly and tirelessly dedicated himself to the cause. Never in the most robust of health, he departed in spring 1914 for North America where a lecture series on the history of preaching was well-received at Yale University and a short holiday was taken near Niagara Falls. A speaking engagement in Toronto was booked, but Horne collapsed and died on 2 May, on deck of ship as it crossed Lake Ontario. His passing was widely mourned, and Nonconformists felt that with his death they had lost their greatest champion.

W. B. Selbie (ed.), *The Life of Charles Silvester Horne, MA, MP* (London: Hodder & Stoughton, 1920).

RP

Horton, Robert Forman (1855–1934)

Born in London on 18 September 1855, Horton was educated at Shrewsbury School and New College, Oxford, where he was president of the Oxford Union in 1877, graduated with a first in Classics and was elected to a fellowship of his college in 1879, lecturing for a time in history. He turned his back on Oxford in 1880 when he accepted a call to the Lyndhurst Road Congregational Church in Hampstead, where he helped to erect a grand chapel to replace the tin hut in which, as a student, he had first ministered. Possessed of a clear and brilliant mind, Horton had been attracted to the higher criticism of the nineteenth century and published two works about it, *Inspiration and the Bible* (1888) and *Revelation and the Bible* (1892), though he later opposed his friend R. J. Campbell over his New Theology. Theological and political liberalism led him towards the social gospel movement and he turned the church on Lyndhurst Road into an 'Institutional Church' which attracted the likes of H. H. Asquith to hear his preaching, and large audiences of working men to hear his lectures. He considered the Boer War to be a tragedy and joined a group of Congregational ministers who called for a degree of self-government for the African colonies. He believed the First World War to be a 'conflict of principle' and supported it, though he protested against the treatment of conscientious objectors, failing in an attempt to have the matter debated in the Congregational Union's meetings. Horton was primarily concerned with the living of the Christian life which led him to take a stand on social issues such as the consumption of alcohol, gambling and the length of the working day. He inaugurated an Adult School Movement in Hampstead and alongside the diaconate he introduced an eldership into his church in order to secure pastoral care of the congregation. He was chair of the Congregational Union of England and Wales in 1903–4 and president of the Free Church Council in 1904–5. He died on 30 March 1934.

Albert Peel and J. A. R. Marriott, *Robert Forman Horton* (London: Allen & Unwin, 1937).

RP

Howard, John (1726–90)

John Howard was an Independent layman who pioneered the reform of prisons. His father had made his fortune in the upholstery and carpet business, and was determined that his son should succeed in business, so he apprenticed him to a wholesale grocer. Howard hated it, and when his father died in 1742 leaving a substantial fortune to be divided between him and his sister, he set out on a grand tour of France and Italy.

He was dogged by ill health, and returned home to his lodgings in Stoke Newington where he married his landlady Sarah Loidore. She died in 1755. He then set out for Lisbon, but his ship was captured by French privateers and he was imprisoned for six days, which may have spurred his interest in prisons. He returned to his family estate in Cardington in Bedfordshire and set about improving it for his tenants, becoming a model landlord. In 1758 he married Henrietta Leeds. They had one child, Jack, before she too died in 1765.

In an attempt to escape grief Howard travelled again. In 1783 he was elected high sheriff of Bedfordshire, a position from which he was disqualified as a Dissenter by the Test Act. However, the provisions of the Act (as often) were ignored. Among his duties was that of keeper of the County Gaol. Howard performed the role diligently. His discovery that prisoners who were acquitted were thrown back into gaol until they could afford to pay the fees of their gaolers appalled him, and it may have been this discovery and the subsequent unravelling of many other abuses which determined his single minded quest for prison reform.

Over the next seventeen years he travelled the length and breadth of Britain and Europe collecting information and making observations about the state of the penal system. He collected statistics about space, food, air and water, and in 1777 published at his own cost *The State of Prisons in England and Wales, with Preliminary Observations, and an Account of some Foreign Prisons*. It was a record of some 350 visits to 230 different institutions. Over a century later his method appeared to some to be a pioneering work of social science. He had provided the systematic evidence which is necessary for pressure and policy change. In 1774 he gave evidence to the House of Commons about the fees prisoners had to pay for gaolers, and was called to the bar to receive the thanks of the House.

He died in Kherson in southern Russia in 1790 while inspecting Russian army hospitals because he had embarked on a tour to discover how plague victims were treated across Europe. The Howard League for Penal Forum perpetuates his memory.

Tessa West, *The Curious Mr Howard: Legendary Prison Reformer* (Hook: Waterside Press 2011).

DGC

Hughes, Hugh Price (1847–1902)

Born in Carmarthen on 9 February 1847, Hughes entered Richmond College in 1865 in order to train for ministry in the Wesleyan Connexion. He ministered in Dover, Brighton, Tottenham, Dulwich, Oxford, Brixton Hill and finally at the West London Mission from 1887. Although initially socially conservative, he was gradually radicalized, especially after hearing Josephine Butler speak on the abolition of the Contagious Diseases Acts. It was at the West London Mission that he came into his own, establishing a number of organizations and activities designed at offering social as well as religious services such as a labour bureau, a poor man's lawyer, a soup kitchen among others. Alongside this he was committed to social purity, playing a prominent part in the downfall of Charles Stewart Parnell following his adultery with Mrs Katharine O'Shea. As a result, he came to embody the Nonconformist Conscience, popularizing the aphorism that 'what is morally wrong cannot be politically right'. Hughes sought improvement for the lot of the poor while also preaching the need for individual conversion, connecting the cause of social reform with evangelical Christianity. He held to the belief that a believer could be sanctified following the baptism of the Holy Spirit, and he worked tirelessly for numerous causes, seeking improved recreational facilities, sanitation, housing and medical services for the working class as well as prison reform, child welfare and women's emancipation. He served his denomination as founding editor of the *Methodist Times* (1885) and he was elected president of the Welseyan Conference in 1898. He was also a firm advocate of free church unity. Plagued by ill health, he died on 17 November 1902.

Christopher Oldstone-Moore, *Hugh Price Hughes: Founder of a New Methodism, Conscience of a New Nonconformity* (Cardiff: University of Wales Press, 1999).
RP

Huxtable, William John Fairchild (1912–90)

John Huxtable was the son of a Congregational minister. His father died while on a posting at Leghorn when John was aged only twelve and he was subsequently educated in Barnstaple and at Western College, Bristol. After graduation he took the ministerial course at Mansfield College, Oxford, where he was heavily influenced by the views of Nathaniel Micklem. He became a member of the Church Order Group in Congregationalism and was identified with those who emphasized the denominational debt to the Reformed tradition. After a ministry at Newton Abbot from 1937 he was called to Palmers Green, London, in 1942 and began to exert his influence in the denomination. He was appointed a delegate to the first meeting of the World Council of Churches in 1948 and to the Translation Committee of the New English Bible. In 1954 he became principal of New College, London, where he enjoyed a cordial friendship with Geoffrey Nuttall although the two had differing views on the nature of Congregationalism. He was invited to become general secretary of the Congregational Union of England and Wales in 1964 and led to completion the shift to its becoming the Congregational Church and then its union with the Presbyterian Church of England in 1972 although, to his regret, not all Congregationalists were persuaded to join the new United Reformed Church. He was the first moderator of the General Assembly of the new Church. From 1974–78 he led the Churches Unity Commission, which then became the Churches Council for Covenanting. On his retirement in 1978 he feared that this initiative might fail, as indeed it did. Although forceful in his views John Huxtable was a cheerful companion and patient with his critics. His scholarship was considerable, although he did not produce many books, being first and foremost a church leader.

SCO

'Intolerable Sects'

Following the 'Elizabethan Settlement', there emerged those who considered that the Reformation of the English church had not gone far enough. Puritans of Presbyterian persuasion and Separatists who sought the establishment of gathered congregations of believers appeared while there were others whose interpretation of Reformation principles sought a more extensive role for the freedom of the religious conscience. They came to public notice during the first half of the seventeenth century while political uncertainties associated with the Civil Wars and the establishment of the Commonwealth offered an unprecedented opportunity to express liberty of the religious conscience. This liberty was interpreted in terms of thought and behaviour, though the general consensus still tended to balk at full freedom of expression and there remained those whose beliefs and practices were considered to be 'intolerable'. The most prominent among the sects were the Religious Society of Friends (or Quakers) and the Socinians who later developed into the Unitarians. However, there were also a number of other groups, some of which were fairly short-lived. Although they are treated here as if they were distinct groups, in fact there was considerable confusion at the time and, as with many other terms during the sixteenth and seventeenth centuries, the different appellations seem, on occasion, to have been interchangeable.

The origins of the Familists, or 'Family of love', can be traced to Anabaptist and naturalistic beliefs which were promoted on the European continent by the mystical German Hendrik Niclaes (ca 1501–ca 80). The doctrine of the Trinity was eschewed, as was infant baptism, but tolerance of religious belief was promoted while the taking of oaths and the carrying of arms were repudiated. Outwardly conformist, Familists tended not to seek to convert others to their views but remained instead as members of the established churches of Europe. Familists were known to be active in Guildford around 1560 as well as in Cambridge, Balsham, Surrey, Ely and Wisbech and the chief spokesperson in England was Christopher Vitells (fl. 1543–79), born in Holland but settled in Southwark by the mid-sixteenth century and who translated Niclaes' work into English. He recanted his views when threatened with execution. Elizabeth I issued a proclamation condemning the group in 1580, though the teaching prevailed in some quarters, with James Pardage, curate at Reading during the Civil Wars, known to have been receptive of Familist teaching, while the group known as the Grindletonian Familists (or Grindletonians) emerged in Yorkshire around 1660. Though accused of moral excess, there is no evidence to suggest that the accusation was based on the group's practices. They were seen to be antinomian and placed significance on the leading of the 'inner light'. Groups remained extant until the eighteenth century, though the Familists are more significant as one antecedent of the Society of Friends.

The Seekers are thought to have derived from the Familists, though their origins are shrouded in mystery. They emerged certainly from around 1600, though the name 'Seeker' is not known much before the 1640s. Their teaching derived from the Legate brothers, Walter, Thomas and Benjamin, and as a result they are sometimes known as the Legatine Arians. The movement was Puritan but not Calvinist, eschewing predestination but embracing millenarian and anti-Trinitarian thinking. They believed that Anti-Christ had taken control of the church and therefore rejected all contemporary ecclesiastical systems as well as clerical leadership, expecting instead that God would send new apostles who would establish a renewed and purified church. Walter was apparently drowned in an accident; Thomas and Benjamin were accused of Arian views, the former dying in Newgate gaol and the latter being burned to death at Smithfield. A follower of the Legates was Edward Wightman, who was the last person to be burned at the stake in England as a result of religious belief (he was brought first to the stake in Lichfield in March 1612 but recanted and was taken down, only to be burned to death in the following month). The Seekers, too, seem to have been antecedents of the Society of Friends.

The Levellers and the Diggers were closely related. Basing his teaching on an exposition of Acts 2.44–45, where believers held all things in common and sold their personal belongings in order that they be distributed according to need, Gerard Winstanley (1606–76) developed an early form of Christian communitarianism. In *The New Law of Righteousness* (1649) he suggested that all men were descended from a common ancestor, Adam, and advocated the abolition of both property and aristocracy. A further tract *The Law of Freedom and Platform* (1652) advocated the abolition of property and of wages. His movement, which numbered somewhere between one and two hundred, appropriated land in Surrey, Buckinghamshire and Northamptonshire, cultivating it and distributing the crops to its members free of charge. This earned for the group the epithet 'Diggers'. Winstanley fell foul of landlords who employed thugs to destroy the crops and the movement petered out. Winstanley characterized his movement as 'True Levellers' against the teaching of those such as John Lilburne (1614–57) who sought not so much the abolition of property as the establishment of basic freedoms which were, he believed, based on God-given rights. Lilburne argued for common manhood suffrage, equality before the law and religious tolerance. As a result his opponents branded him a Leveller, but he referred to himself as a 'Leveller so-called' and preferred the title 'Agitator'. Lilburne was a constant thorn in the side of both the royalist and parliamentarian factions and was brought before the courts on several occasions. While sentenced to be flogged, pilloried and imprisoned under the monarchy, his several appearances in court under the Commonwealth resulted in his acquittal. Like Winstanley, it seems that Lilburne later became a Quaker. There was some kind of organization to the Leveller movement, with offices located in several London taverns and those who belonged to the movement wore green ribbons on their clothing. Yet there also remained a wider constituency on the periphery of the movement which demonstrates the complexity of the situation; a host of religious views came to light as radicals sought to explore what true liberty might mean. Diggers and Levellers might well have been related to each other, but they were not necessarily joined in any single organization. By 1650, the Levellers were no longer considered a threat.

The most radical of the sects was probably the Ranters who were in vogue between 1641 and 1654. Very little is known about them apart from the fact that they upheld pleasure as a goal in life and they were associated with a lack of moral values. They seem to have upheld the teaching about the all-sufficient indwelling Spirit and were held to be antinomian. It is possible that they were simply the victims of propaganda, though the Blasphemy Act of August 1650 seems to have been passed with the Ranters in view. Many of its adherents subsequently became Quakers.

The Muggletonians were apparent from around 1651 with John Reeve (1608–58) and his cousin Lodowicke Muggleton (1609–98) promoting the imminent millennium and the idea that formal religious ceremonies were unnecessary. The movement held to some heretical teachings such as that Jesus is God (not a person of the Trinity), that God was between five and six feet tall, and that heaven was about six miles above the earth. It is known that they were active in London but there is evidence also of Muggletonian groups in Bristol, Cork, Faversham and East Anglia. The movement survived into the twentieth century, though the final known member was Philip Noakes who died on 26 February 1979.

The most influential of the groups, at least for a time, were the Fifth Monarchists who were active from around 1649 to 1661. Based on an exposition of Daniel 2, they argued that world history was separated into a succession of empires – Assyria, Persia, Greece and Rome – and that the fourth monarchy had come to an end with the execution of Charles I on 30 January 1649. They believed that the fifth monarchy, that of Jesus Christ, was about to be inaugurated and, through an analysis of the book of Revelation, they calculated that this would occur in 1656 or 1660 or 1666. They sought to replace the Long Parliament with the rule of the saints and to turn England into a godly nation. Several prominent Puritans were counted in their number including Thomas Harrison, Christopher Feake, John Carew, Robert Blakebone, John Rogers, Vavasor Powell, Morgan Llwyd and John Bunyan. They lost impetus after the Instrument of Government

(1653) declared Cromwell to be Lord Protector. At the Restoration, several of the fifth monarchists, including Carew and Harrison, were executed as regicides while others, such as Powell and Bunyan, were to spend years in prison. The final stand of the Fifth Monarchists was the uprising led by Thomas Venner from 6 to 10 January 1661. Venner marched from his meeting house in Coleman Street, London, accompanied by fifty of his followers. The rebellion was easily crushed and Venner was executed on 19 January outside his meeting house.

The general sense of religious liberty during the 1640s and 1650s enabled the emergence of groups intent on pushing the limits of both theological and, apparently, moral propriety, though the latter might owe more to the accusation of opponents than to an accurate reflection of their practice. They seem to have shared similar views in rejection of the contemporary church as irredeemably corrupt, in adopting millenarian teaching and exalting both confidence in and reliance on the 'inner light'. The fact that many of these sects were short-lived, or lacked popular support, is not only the result of the legal clamp down which followed the Restoration in 1660 but also because mainstream groups successfully challenged the legitimacy of their religious and moral teaching. Those that prevailed did so because they were able to defend themselves reasonably, theologically and morally and to command more than a modicum of support, or else because they did not seek the approval of the majority and opted instead to establish a clandestine existence.

Christopher Hill, *The World Turned Upside Down: Radical Ideas during the English Revolution* (new edn, Harmondsworth: Penguin, 1991).

RP

Jacob, Henry (1562/63–1624)

Henry Jacob was an Oxford trained theologian, a former precentor at Corpus Christi College, who was one of the organizers of the Millenary Petition which the Puritan 'party' presented to James I on his accession in 1603.

His early career is difficult to trace before 1616. He certainly had contact with Separatist ideas because in 1596 he had visited Francis Johnson in prison and tried to convince him of the error of his ways in seeking to separate from the Church of England. He published *A Defence of the Churches and Ministry of England* (1599). By 1604, however, he had modified his views and was arguing for the reform of the Church in a Separatist direction – 'Only a particular ordinary constant congregation . . . is appointed and reckoned a visible church' (*Reasons Taken out of God's Word . . .*, 1604). However, unlike other Separatists, Jacob believed that it was possible for gathered congregations to maintain communion with the Church of England. Historians, not quite knowing how to label Jacob, have called this 'semi-Separatism'. He was imprisoned for eight months for his pains.

It seems that he then went to the Netherlands, his *The Divine Beginning and Institution of Christes True Visible Church* reveals that he was in Leyden in 1610. It was probably while he was in the Netherlands that he engaged in conversation with other Separatists such as John Robinson whom he seems to have influenced in a more moderate direction.

In 1616 he re-emerged from obscurity in the Netherlands to establish a covenanted gathered congregation in Southwark. This is the first known Independent congregation to be founded in England. Although all male members of the congregation were deemed capable of 'prophesying', Jacob still maintained that this was not 'Separatism' because they were happy to communicate in their parish church 'on occasions'. In this crucial respect he had modified the rigid separatism of thinkers such as Francis Johnson and Henry Ainsworth.

Like most proponents of compromise, Jacob found himself reviled by both sides. Separatists accused him of 'idolatry' for daring to attend parish churches and he received short shrift from the authorities in the Church.

He emigrated to Virginia in 1622, and died there in 1624. He left a widow, Sarah, and three children (one adopted). He seems to have expected that they would follow him to Virginia. Sarah seemingly shared his views because she too fell foul of the authorities for belonging to a separatist congregation in 1632–37.

S. Brachlow 'The Elizabethan roots of Henry Jacob's churchmanship', *Journal of Ecclesiastical History*, 36 (1985), pp. 228–54.

DGC

James, John Angell (1785–1859)

Born on 6 June 1785 at Blandford Forum in Dorset, James was initially apprenticed to a linen-draper at Poole before sensing a call to preach and entering David Bogue's Gosport Academy in 1802. This had a lasting effect for Bogue had helped to establish both the London Missionary Society and the British and Foreign Bible Society, two causes for which James worked tirelessly.

During the summer vacation of 1804, James was invited to occupy the pulpit at Carrs Lane Church in Birmingham. So impressed were the church with his abilities as a preacher that they called him to be their minister. He settled in Birmingham the following year, having completed his course at Gosport, and was ordained in May 1806. Over the course of his ministry, attendance at the church grew from a couple of hundred to nearly two thousand, and a larger building was opened in August 1820. Carrs Lane was his one and only charge, but from there he exercised a fairly significant influence over wider Congregationalism.

James' was not a theological approach; he was no Calvinist and his preaching tended to be imaginative, demonstrative but equally attractive because of its directness and because his style, if earnest, was also, in its broadest sense, entertaining. He was possessed of a commanding pulpit presence with an attractive voice, and his sermons, though well-prepared, were delivered from memory and were designed to appeal as much to the emotions as to the intellect. As such he was one who led a transformation in Nonconformist preaching.

James believed in the need for unity among Protestant evangelicals. He had little time for Roman Catholicism and opposed ritualism in the Church of England, though he had little interest in the Anti-State Church Society established by Edward Miall. He was instrumental in the establishment of the Congregational Union of England and Wales in 1831 and, through his oratorical gifts, was able to persuade a number of his fellow ministers of the wisdom of establishing such an organization. He also helped to establish the Evangelical Alliance which he saw as a means to unite true Protestant Christians in the face of Anglican ritualism and Roman Catholic militancy. He published a number of books, the most important of which was *The Anxious Enquirer after Salvation Directed and Encouraged* (1834) which, by 1839, had sold over 200,000 copies and been translated into Gaelic, Welsh, German, French, Swedish and Malagasy. He was convinced of the need for proper ministerial training which saw him support the establishment of the Spring Hill College in 1838 and to chair its Board of Education from its inception until his death. He supported the movement against slavery and was instrumental in securing the services of R. W. Dale, at that time a student at Spring Hill, as his successor in Carrs Lane. He died on 1 October 1859.

RP

Laud, William (1573–1645)

William Laud was archbishop of Canterbury, 1633–41. Educated at St John's College, Oxford (of which he later became president), he was dean of Gloucester (1616–21), bishop of St Davids (1621–26), Bath and Wells (1626–28) and London (1628–33; which he combined with being chancellor of Oxford University from 1629). He was translated to Canterbury in 1633. His archiepiscopate therefore coincided with Charles I's years of personal rule (1629–41).

Laud was convinced of the symbiotic relationship between church and state, arguing that the well-being of the commonwealth depended on the church. His life's work was dedicated to enhancing the honour, dignity and power of the church. From his earliest days in Oxford he developed a theology which understood the episcopate as of the essence of the church, an order ontically distinct from the presbyterate. He also sought church unity through uniformity of practice rather than doctrine. Practice, in his view, should be determined by reverence and decency, by a sense of holiness. Ceremony was therefore important – altars should be at the east, railed, and bowed to, appropriate vestments should be worn, the liturgy properly followed, the sacrament received kneeling.

Those core beliefs brought him into direct conflict with the Puritan party in the church. He in turn regarded them as a dangerous threat to church and state. The conflict played itself out through the 1630s. Puritan radicals chose exile in the Netherlands or New England rather than conform. Ill-judged acts such as the persecution of Prynne, Bastwick and Burton in 1637 and the attempt, during the same year, to enforce the Prayer Book on Scotland heightened the crisis between crown and parliament, and hastened Laud's fall from power. He was impeached for high treason in 1641 – an absurd charge – imprisoned in the Tower, and after a trial which did no credit to his accusers, was executed in 1645.

Puritan polemic turned Laud into the source of all the woes of the 1630s and 1640s, and scholarly opinion about him remains divided. He was a humble rather lonely man whose diaries show him continually caught on tides of fear. To handle such vulnerability and seek to reform the church as consistently as he did, despite the cost, speaks of bravery. Puritans in the 1630s, however, believed him sorely mistaken, and there is little doubt that his harrying of them simply strengthened their resolve and exacerbated the deep divisions within the English church.

H. R. Trevor-Roper, *Archbishop Laud, 1573–1645* (London: MacMillan 1965).
DGC

Lloyd-Jones, D. Martyn (1899–1981)

Trained as a surgeon, Lloyd-Jones turned his back on a potentially glittering medical career in 1927 to become the minister of a struggling Welsh Calvinistic Methodist Forward Movement mission at Aberavon in south

Wales. He stripped back many of the activities of the church and through the force of his own preaching, and a certain celebrity status born of his high profile following his resignation from the medical profession, witnessed remarkable growth in the congregation during the early 1930s. In 1938, feeling that there were few opportunities for wider influence in his native Wales, he became assistant minister to the famous G. Campbell Morgan at Westminster Chapel, London, becoming sole pastor in 1943. For the next thirty years until his retirement in 1968, Lloyd-Jones turned the chapel into a magnet for those wanting a diet of Reformed theology and detailed biblical exposition. Lloyd-Jones preached two mammoth series on Paul's letters to the Romans and the Ephesians, published following his retirement in eight and fourteen volumes respectively.

A resolute Calvinist, Lloyd-Jones was the moving figure behind a number of agencies, including the Banner of Truth Trust and the Puritan (later Westminster) Conference, established to stimulate interest in the Reformed faith. Alongside John Stott and James I. Packer, Lloyd-Jones did much in the immediate inter-war years to revitalize British evangelicalism, especially through agencies such as the Inter-Varsity Fellowship. However, from the mid-1960s Lloyd-Jones became a more controversial figure. Alarmed at the ambitions of the Ecumenical Movement, in an address to the National Association of Evangelicals in 1966, Lloyd-Jones called evangelicals in doctrinally mixed denominations to secede and come together in a new loose association of independent evangelical churches. His call was ignored by many, including the vast majority of evangelicals in the Church of England, but some ministers and congregations did secede from the various Free Church denominations, aligning themselves with separatist groups such as the Fellowship of Independent Evangelical Churches, the British Evangelical Council and the Evangelical Movement of Wales. Thereafter, Lloyd-Jones' influence on the broader evangelical scene was much more limited.

Following his retirement in 1968, Lloyd-Jones devoted much of the final decade of his life to the editing of his sermons for publication and supporting those congregations which had responded positively to his secessionist call. He died on St David's Day 1981. While his continuing influence on the British evangelical scene remains relatively insignificant, within those networks in which he was involved during his lifetime he continues to be widely venerated.

John Brencher, *Martyn Lloyd-Jones (1899–1981) and Twentieth-Century Evangelicalism* (Carlisle: Paternoster, 2002); Andrew Atherstone and David Ceri Jones (eds), *Engaging with Martyn Lloyd-Jones: The Life and Legacy of 'the Doctor'* (Nottingham: Apollos, 2011).

DCJ

Manning, Bernard Lord (1892–1941)

Congregationalist, church historian and lay preacher Bernard Lord Manning was born at Caistor, Lincolnshire, on 31 December 1892, the only son of George Manning and his wife, Mary Ann, the daughter of William Short Lord, a businessman and farmer. George Manning had been a Wesleyan and, when young, Bernard often attended the Methodist chapel in Caistor with his grandfather. In 1898, Manning's father became a Congregational minister, which led to Bernard living first at Ravenstonedale, in Westmorland, which he loved, and later at Caistor.

Bernard was educated at Caistor Grammar School and Jesus College, Cambridge, having won an open scholarship there in 1912. He obtained a double first in the history tripos in 1914, won the Lightfoot scholarship in 1915, a Thirlwall prize in 1917, and was a bye-fellow of Magdalene College and editor of the *Cambridge Review* (1916–18). Chronic illness during his childhood left him physically frail, with only one serviceable lung. His brief national service at the Ministry of Munitions in 1918 was ended abruptly by a bout of tuberculosis. Manning recovered sufficiently well to be elected in 1919 a fellow of Jesus College. He was bursar (1920–33), senior tutor from 1933 until his death and a university lecturer in medieval history from 1930. In addition he was director of studies in church history at Cheshunt College, Cambridge, from 1920 and honorary bursar there from 1932. He was a governor (later chairman of governors) of Cheshunt College from 1934 and sat on the editorial board of *The Congregational Quarterly*. He never married and died, at Evelyn Nursing Home, Cambridge, on 8 December 1941. He was buried in the graveyard of High Chapel, the Congregational church at Ravenstonedale, as were his parents and later his sister.

Manning had a practical and level-headed side to his nature, while he was also profoundly spiritual. As bursar of Jesus College he was shrewd in his business dealings and a good administrator. As tutor he revealed a talent for upholding discipline, while managing to befriend his students and to retain friendships. His scholarship and wit are evident in his writings. He published, among others: *The People's Faith in the Time of Wyclif* (1919, his Thirlwall prize essay); *The Making of Modern English Religion* (1929); *Why not Abandon the Church?* (1939); *Essays in Orthodox Dissent* (1939); *The Hymns of Wesley and Watts* (1942); and two chapters ('Edward III and Richard II' and 'Wyclif') in vol. 7 of the *Cambridge Medieval History*. *The Protestant Dissenting Deputies* (edited by Ormerod Greenwood, 1952) and two volumes of sermons were published posthumously.

He was a loyal Congregationalist (a member of Emmanuel Church, Cambridge), with friends in all denominations, and had a broad ecumenical understanding, partly deriving from his studies, especially of the late medieval church. He vigorously defended what he termed 'orthodox dissent', allying himself in the 1930s with John S. Whale and Nathaniel Micklem against the lack of rigour in liberal and modernist theology which, they believed, was then evident in Congregational ministers.

AA

Martineau, James (1805–1900)

James Martineau was born in Norwich, the seventh child of a Huguenot merchant and his wife. The whole family worshipped in the nearby Octagon Chapel and it was on this fellowship that its social and cultural life was centred. The Octagon Chapel was a stimulating place; over the years several famous people had worshipped there, including Sir James Edward Smith, the botanist; John Taylor, the hymn writer, and William Smith, member of parliament and grandfather of Florence Nightingale.

At the age of sixteen, James was sent to Lant Carpenter's school in Bristol. Carpenter was an inspirational schoolmaster; alongside his lessons in science, history, geography, mathematics, classics and biblical criticism, he read the daily papers to his pupils around the dinner table, and kept them in touch with parliamentary debates.

On leaving school Martineau became an apprentice to an engineer in Derby but soon moved to Yorkshire to train for the Ministry at Manchester College, York. On completing his five years of study he was engaged as a school teacher in Bristol for a year before taking up his first ministerial appointment, in 1828, as assistant minister of Eustace Street Presbyterian Meeting House, Dublin. However his ministry in Dublin lasted only four years due to his refusal to accept any part of the *Regium Donum*, an annual grant bestowed by parliament on Presbyterian ministers.

In 1832 he was appointed minister of Paradise Street Chapel, Liverpool. Here he formed a close association with J. H. Thom and Charles Wicksteed of Liverpool, and J. J. Tayler of Manchester. These four ministers met regularly at Tayler's home to edit the *Prospective Review*. Alongside his ministerial duties he ran classes for young ladies, where he taught Anna Swanwick, Catherine and Suzanne Winkworth; all of whom remained indebted to him. Having studied in Berlin, he built a new church in Hope Street, Liverpool, and having taken on a part time lectureship at Manchester New College, Martineau was appointed full-time professor of Moral Philosophy at the College, by then established in London, and of which institution he was shortly to become principal. From there he launched his great assaults on the agnosticism of Herbert Spencer, the materialism of John Tyndall and the ethics of Henry Sidgwick. These together with his books, hymns, sermons and addresses were to be vital contributions to nineteenth-century English Christianity and caused A. M. Fairbairn to say: 'It is largely owing to him that our age was not swept off its feet by the rising tide of materialistic and pseudo-scientific speculation.' William Gladstone ranked him as first among British thinkers.

Martineau worked hard on the ecumenical front to build bridges between churches, and strongly argued against his own Church taking the doctrinal name Unitarian. He made an important contribution to Nonconformist liturgy, through his hymns prayers and orders of service. These, alongside his sermons, are perhaps his lasting contribution to the Christian Church. He retired from Manchester New College at the age of eighty and over the next fourteen years wrote some of his most famous works.

His major books are: *The Rationale of Religious Inquiry* (1836); *Endeavours after the Christian Life* (1843) (which influenced F. D. Maurice and Bishop Colenso); *Hours of Thought on Sacred Things* (1876); *Hymns for the Christian Church and Home* (1840); *Hymns of Praise and Prayer* (1873); *Home Prayers* (1891); *Types of Ethical Theory* (1885); *A Study of Religion* (1888); *The Seat of Authority in Religion* (1890); *National Duties and Other Sermons and Addresses* (1903). His collected articles are published in the four volumes of *Essays, Reviews and Addresses* (1893).

J. Estlin Carpenter, *James Martineau, Theologian and Teacher: A Study of His Life and Thought* (London: Philip Green, 1905).

RW

Matthews, Arnold Gwynne (1881–1962)

A. G. Matthews, Congregational minister and historian, was born in East Barnet on 7 August 1881 and died in Oxted, Surrey, on 6 December 1962. He was the second son of John Matthews, a Congregational minister, and his wife, Mary. He was educated at Mill Hill School, New College, Oxford, and Mansfield College, Oxford. He was a shy, eccentric man who served two pastorates, Tettenhall Wood, Wolverhampton (1907–22) and Oxted, Surrey (1922–27). While at Tettenhall he researched the history of the county's Nonconformist churches which resulted in his first book *The Congregational Churches of Staffordshire* (1924). This book covers a wider field than its title suggests and set him on the path to further study.

He left Tettenhall after his brother, in an insane fit, had killed their cook in the manse. His brother was detained in Broadmoor Hospital and Matthews moved, against the wishes of the Tettenhall church, in order to make visits easier. The episode resulted also in the ending of his engagement to be married and he remained a bachelor. Matthews was happy at Oxted and lived there for the rest of his life. Yet he retired early from his ministry in 1927 to devote himself to historical study. Later he was for a time church secretary there. In older age, he would also regularly attend evensong in the parish church.

His comprehensive works of scholarship *Calamy Revised* (1934) and *Walker Revised* (1948) reveal a meticulous application to research and remain essential reading for any seventeenth-century specialist. The former details all Nonconformist ministers who were ejected (1660–62) and the latter treats similarly all those Anglican clergymen ousted during the Civil War and Interregnum. Both books contain thorough mini-biographies of every minister identified and the titles again reveal Matthews' innate modesty and his generous breadth of mind. Both works were reissued in 1988.

Matthews was editorial secretary of the committee which produced the hymn book *Congregational Praise* (1951) and regularly contributed to the *Transactions of the Congregational Historical Society*, of which society he was president (1951–57). In addition, he compiled an annotated list of the works of Richard Baxter, and edited and provided a scholarly introduction to *The Savoy Declaration of Faith and Order 1658* (1959). He published a collection of essays, *Mr Pepys and Nonconformity* (1954), and wrote on Puritan worship and other subjects. Nevertheless, his two main works are his finest legacy for he was an amateur scholar of the highest calibre.

AA

Methodism

Methodism had its birth in the evangelical revivals that took place in the British Isles in the middle decades of the eighteenth century. Traditionally, Methodism has been closely associated with the name of John Wesley largely because he founded the Methodist church, following his ordination of ministers for America in 1784. However, Methodism was initially a disparate movement, decidedly Anglican in tone and ethos. As originally conceived Methodism in all its guises was a renewal movement within the Church of England. The term Methodist was first used to refer to those who gathered in the Holy Club in Oxford, but a Methodist movement began to coalesce around the Fetter Lane Society in London following the awakening that accompanied the London ministry of George Whitefield in 1737, and the conversion of the Wesley brothers in 1738. This initial feeling of common purpose did not last long, and by 1741 the English revival had splintered into Calvinistic, Wesleyan and Moravian factions.

Under the leadership of George Whitefield, Calvinistic Methodism enjoyed only fitful growth. Whitefield linked his English Calvinists with the Welsh Methodist revival, establishing the joint English and Welsh Calvinistic Methodist Association in January 1743. However, Whitefield's commitment to his transatlantic itinerant ministry meant that the English Calvinists lacked consistent and inspirational leadership, despite the best efforts of John Cennick and Howell Harris to stand in for him. When Whitefield relinquished his leadership altogether in 1749, the English Calvinistic Methodist movement unravelled. Some of his converts came under the oversight of the Countess of Huntingdon, others stayed nominally under Whitefield's oversights, while still others, maybe the majority, found their way into independent Dissent. By contrast, Welsh Calvinistic Methodism under the leadership of Howell Harris and Daniel Rowland went from strength to strength, with a meticulously worked out organizational structure and an army of willing lay workers. By the later part of the eighteenth century, fuelled by waves of revivalism, a fresh generation of leaders headed by Thomas Charles led the Welsh Methodists out of the Established Church in 1811. While Calvinistic Methodism struggled to become a viable option in England, by the mid-nineteenth century it had become the largest Nonconformist denomination in Wales.

By contrast John Wesley's brand of Methodism quickly established itself as the mainstream version in England. Through a system of Class meetings under the oversight of lay preachers and, from 1744, the Methodist Conference, Wesleyan Methodism proved flexible enough to respond to the rapidly growing population of industrial Britain in the second half of the eighteenth century. After Wesley's death in 1791, waves of revival fuelled further growth, but as Wesleyan Methodism took on the accoutrements of a denomination, especially under the authoritarian leadership of Jabez Bunting (1779–1858), there followed a series of secessions. The Methodist New Connexion (1797), the Primitive Methodists (1811), the Bible Christians (1815) and the United Methodist Free Churches (1857) were each in their own way reactions against a perceived loss of fervour within mainstream Methodism, and an attempt to recapture the primitive spirit of Methodism as originally conceived. In the later nineteenth century there were further spin-offs; inspired by Wesley's teaching on entire sanctification, groups such as the Church of the Nazarene sought to give expression to his teaching on holiness. Indeed, it could be argued that the various Pentecostal churches which proliferated in the early twentieth century owed much to the holiness movements of the later nineteenth century. If the nineteenth century saw a series of Methodist secessions, the early twentieth century saw attempts to repair many of these divisions. The Methodist New Connexion, the Bible Christians and the United Methodist Free Churches united in 1907 to form the United Methodist Church, and then that new denomination merged with the Wesleyan Methodist Church and the Primitive Methodists in 1932 to form the Methodist Church in Great Britain. The ecumenical impulse in the second half of the twentieth century set in motion attempts to bring about the reintegration of Methodism into the Church of England. First mooted in 1963, the most serious union plans were put before both churches in 1968; while the Methodist Conference accepted them, they were comprehensively rejected by the General Synod of the Church of England.

DCJ

Methodist Missionary Society

The Methodist Missionary Society was formed in 1932 to administer the overseas missions of the three uniting churches which until then had autonomous mission agencies. From its origins Methodism was a mission-minded faith, first in Britain, and then more formally overseas from the 1780s. Wesleyan Methodist Missionary Society work began in 1813 in the Caribbean, gradually extending to India, Africa and Europe; Primitive Methodist missions were organized from the 1840s, focused largely on Africa, while United Methodists worked in China, Africa and the Caribbean. The MMS constitution of 1942 stated that 'every member of the Methodist Church is a member of the Methodist Missionary Society', reiterating the founding purpose of Methodism of active evangelism at home and overseas. Following an Overseas Consultation in the 1960s, and influenced by the ideas of Edgar W. Thompson, the Society changed its focus from 'overseas missions' to emphasize 'World Church Partnerships' between autonomous Churches. As such, in 1973 the MMS became one of the seven divisions of the Methodist Church.

All the earlier Methodists missions had regular journals. After Methodist Union, the four journals were merged into *The Kingdom Overseas*, the new MMS magazine. This became *NOW* in 1970 and after 1992 *Connect*. The budget for the Methodist World Mission Fund in 2010–11 totalled over £6 million for a variety of partnership, aid and development programmes. British mission personnel serving overseas ('mission partners' as they were called from 1996) declined in number during the latter part of the twentieth century, but an increasing number of ministers from overseas came to work in Britain.

Edgar W. Thompson, *The Methodist Missionary Society: Its Origin and Name* (London: Methodist Missionary Society, 1955).

DK

Meyer, Frederick Brotherton (1847–1929)

F. B. Meyer was educated at Brighton College and partly through the influence of William Brock, minister of Bloomsbury Chapel, he felt drawn towards Baptist ministry and trained for this at Regent's Park College. After pastorates in Liverpool and York, where he encountered the evangelist Dwight L. Moody, he moved, in 1874, to Victoria Road Church in Leicester, where his commitment to reaching the unchurched, especially industrial workers, was not shared by his deacons. He resigned in 1878 to become the first pastor of the newly founded Melbourne Hall, which was built to Meyer's specifications as a centre for evangelistic, educational and social activity, drawing congregations of up to 1,500. In 1888, Meyer moved to Regent's Park Chapel, London, which grew rapidly under his care. The remainder of his life was spent in London, at Regent's Park (1888–92 and 1909–15), and at Christ Church, Westminster Bridge Road, Lambeth (1892–1907 and 1915–20), a church affiliated to the London Congregational Union.

Meyer represents the saintly mystic who is also the ever-on-the-move ecclesiastical manager and organizer, summarized by one wit in the phrase 'St Francis with a Bradshaw', for his travelling in six continents in an age innocent of jet engines was truly remarkable. He was both a contemplative, schooled in the spirituality of the ages, and an activist, demanding urgent social change; the pastor of the gathered people of God, who is ever the evangelist, restlessly seeking the lost wherever they are to be found. He was also a prolific writer.

So many movements bear the touch of his personality: Christian Endeavour, the Sunday School movement – locally, nationally and internationally – the Free Church Movement which at different times he served as editor, secretary and president, and the YMCA, on the one hand, and Keswick, the Advent Testimony and Preparation Movement and non-denominational missions like the Regions Beyond Missionary Union on the other. This freedom of movement had its root in his theology, which was devotional rather than doctrinal, a theology experiential rather than academic, developed within a consciousness powerfully affected by nineteenth-century romanticism, which for ever emphasized the overwhelming power of the love of God. Thus for Meyer the cross was 'not simply a dogma or a doctrine but an experience'. In particular this made for practical modification of a received Calvinism and any notion that election constructed 'a high wall enclosing a favoured few', though retrospectively he was always convinced of the divine initiative.

Before the First World War, Meyer, in a generally optimistic frame of mind, was concerned for the unity of the whole church exercising a ministry of reconciliation not only among different varieties of evangelicals but also among the Free Churches, and between Nonconformists and those of the Established Church. A passion to address the social degradation in which many of the unchurched existed sat happily alongside Meyer's deeply rooted concern for evangelism and his own search for a deeper holiness. But after the war a more pessimistic expectation of human affairs generally, tempered only by his confidence in the work of the Spirit made his ministry more pietist and less concerned with institutional change. After the war he was more concerned with adventist emphases in spirituality, as urgent expectation of Christ's return came to dominate his thinking.

JHYB

Miall, Edward (1809–81)

For much of the nineteenth century, Edward Miall was the most prominent representative of radical Nonconformity. His life and work reflected the fact that English Nonconformity had reached a state of social prominence and public confidence by the 1830s and 1840s.

Born in Portsmouth, Miall was ordained to Congregational ministry at Ware, Hertfordshire, in 1831, moving to Bond Street, Leicester, in 1834, but resigning his pastorate in 1839 in order to devote his life to agitation for Nonconformist rights. In 1841, he founded *The Nonconformist* which became the mouthpiece for all radical Nonconformist thought and, particularly, for Miall's own agenda. He edited the paper until 1878 and through it he championed the campaigns for religious equality and, most significantly, for the disestablishment of the Church of England. To that end, Miall was instrumental in the formation of the British Anti-State Church Association in 1844 which became the Society for the Liberation of Religion from State Patronage and Control in 1853, known more popularly as the Liberation Society.

For Miall, the collusion of Church and State in the Anglican establishment had resulted in creating an identifiable group of second class citizens whose consciences did not allow them to conform to the church established by law. This, he believed, ran contrary to the gospel and to those rights which were God-given and inherent in each person to follow conscience in matters of faith. As a result, he opposed the Established Church and the denial of privileges to those who refused to conform. But, most significantly, he realized that this was a political battle which meant that Nonconformist beliefs and rights had to be fought for from inside parliament. Though initially unsuccessful when standing for parliament as member for Halifax, he represented Rochdale (1852–57) and Bradford (1868–74). During this time he opposed the Education Act of 1870 because it would result in the promotion of the Established Church.

Miall retired from public life in 1874. He had received a public testimonial, significantly in 1862 (the year of the bi-centenary of the Great Ejectment), and he died in 1881. He was a pioneer and leader of a militant Nonconformity which came to prominence during the nineteenth century but had receded by the outbreak of the First World War in 1914.

RP

Milton, John (1608–74)

John Milton was the son of a London musician and was educated by tutors at home and then at St Paul's School before entering Christ's College, Cambridge, in 1625. Cambridge was particularly under Puritan influences at this time. Milton was at odds with his tutor, the Puritan William Chappell, and was rusticated for some months before returning to complete his degree. There is evidence of his writing poetry from his school days onwards. He continued to study after graduating. His first significant publication was the poem *Lycidas* in 1637, to mark the death by drowning of his friend Edward King. In the poem his attack on prelates is the first sign of any discontent with the Church of England. He travelled extensively in Italy in 1638 and 1639, returning when he judged the outbreak of the Civil War as too serious a time to be abroad. He ran a school in London and wrote pamphlets on the issues of the day. His contact with Samuel Hartlib and his circle of European Reformed thinkers led to his writing on education as a liberating discipline. He married in 1642 but was soon at odds with his wife and her family and wrote a pioneering pamphlet on divorce. He was increasingly critical of Episcopacy and was moving towards Republicanism in his political philosophy. He wrote in defence of the execution of Charles I in 1649 and soon afterwards was given a government post as secretary for Foreign Tongues, which mostly involved translating diplomatic correspondence into Latin. He would seem to have shared Cromwell's views on monarchy, that it was unnecessary, and his Independent church polity. Like Cromwell he was opposed to the more radical and popular politics of the Levellers, Diggers, Fifth Monarchists and others whom they termed 'sectaries'. From the time of his government appointment his sight began to fail and by 1652 he was completely blind. His wife died and he remarried, only to be widowed again within two years. By the end of the Interregnum he was writing against Erastian views and offering a variety of solutions for the constitutional crisis, all falling short of a restoration of the monarchy. He was arrested in 1660 and held in the Tower of London, but secured a pardon at the expense of a large fine. It was at this period that his papers were confiscated and his books burned. Some of his manuscripts, including the first drafts of his intended theological work, were not rediscovered until the nineteenth century. He may be seen as Arian in his theology. In spite of his identification with the broadly Calvinist Puritans he was Arminian in his view of salvation. This theological profile anticipates the path many Nonconformists subsequently took, influenced by the rationalism they learnt from the classics. He married a third time in 1663 and his widow outlived him by many years. His greatest contribution to English literature is *Paradise Lost* (1667). Like many great works it has spawned a range of interpretations. It embodies Milton's religious thinking rather more eloquently than his lost theological tome might have done, to judge from the drafts. His continuing fame rests on this epic, followed by *Paradise Regained and Sampson Agonistes* (1671). Milton was claimed as a founding father of the denomination by Victorian Congregationalists and stained glass representations of him and of Cromwell are to be found in some of the larger churches of that period, along with Bunyan and Wycliffe.

SCO

Moravians

The Moravians trace their origins to Jan Hus in Bohemia and Moravia at the beginning of the fifteenth century. Although executed for heresy in 1415, groups that looked to Hus had organized themselves as the Bohemian Brethren or Unity of the Brethren at Kunvlad in Bohemia by 1457. In effect, they constituted the first Protestant church. Deeply committed to education, they established schools throughout the Czech lands in the sixteenth century. However, they were persecuted and dispersed throughout Europe following the Battle of White Mountain in 1621, a consequence of the imposition of a Catholic monarch on the Bohemian throne during the Thirty Years War.

In 1722 one of these dispersed groups of Bohemian Brethren arrived at the estate of Nikolaus Ludwig von Zinzendorf at Berthelsdorf where they sought refuge. They established a new community at Herrnhut nearby, and in 1727 the town experienced a dramatic religious revival. The renewal transformed the community with the result that similar communities were established further afield. The Herrnhut experience effectively represented the rebirth of the Moravians as a viable denomination.

The Moravians were committed to overseas expansion and can legitimately be regarded as the first Protestant missionary movement, sending evangelists to North America, the Caribbean, Africa and even the Arctic.

Moravian missionaries first arrived in England in 1728. Initially, they were at the heart of the Evangelical Revival, and it was at a Moravian dominated meeting at Fetter Lane that the Wesley brothers were converted. However, by 1741 the English revival had fragmented into Calvinistic, Wesleyan and Moravian factions. The Moravians experienced a measure of growth in the 1740s, substantial settlements were established at Fulneck in Yorkshire in 1746, and Ockbrook in Derbyshire in 1750, and their activities were extended to Ireland under the ministry of John Cennick from 1746 leading to the establishment of the Gracehill settlement in Ulster in 1765.

While the Moravians were certainly part of the evangelical movement they tended to be reluctant to define themselves in theological terms. A liturgical church that held to the threefold order of ministry, it was communal spiritual life that lay at the heart of their vision, and it was this philosophy that lay behind their founding of settlements. Elements of Moravian spirituality, especially the Love Feast and the Watchnight service, found their way into the practice of other denominations, especially Methodism. For many today the most recognizable Moravian innovation can be seen in the prominence of the Christingle service during Advent and Christmas.

Being an Episcopal church the Moravians had obvious affinities with the Church of England; in 1749 an act of parliament was passed which granted official recognition to another Episcopal church in Britain and her colonial possessions, a move that ensured that the Moravians were no longer regarded as Dissenters. The Moravians have remained a small grouping of churches; committed to the ecumenical agenda in the twentieth century, they have often worked closely with Methodist and Anglican Christians on a local level, although no organizational unity has been achieved. Today, the British and Irish province of the Moravian church boasts thirty congregations, although the majority of these are small in size. Internationally, the story is very different. There remains a thriving settlement at Herrnhut, and the American province, based at Bethlehem in Pennsylvania, boasts a college and theological seminary. The largest concentration of Moravians in the world today is in the east African country of Tanzania.

DCJ

Nayler, James (1616–60)

Born in Ardsley, Yorkshire, in 1616, Nayler (or Naylor) joined the parliamentarians during the Civil Wars, serving from 1642 to 1650. He began to seek spiritual direction and believed he had received it following a meeting with George Fox in 1652. Charismatic and energetic, he was one of the 'Valiant Sixty' Quaker preachers, though he attracted a personal following which left him under suspicion. He fell out with Fox and their relationship became even more strained following Nayler's procession into Bristol in October 1656, riding a donkey and accompanied by his friends who threw their garments along the road and sang 'Holy, holy, holy'. Whatever the intention might have been, and Nayler denied any claims to messianic status, the incident appeared to suggest that he believed himself to be the returned Christ. The times were turbulent and Quakers were commonly held to be guilty of spiritual excess and thus belonging to the 'intolerable sects'. This was sufficient to see him convicted of blasphemy and to be condemned by Fox. His sentence was to be pilloried and whipped through the streets of London, to be branded with the letter 'B' on his forehead, to have his tongue pierced with a hot iron and then to be whipped through the streets of Bristol before enduring two years' hard labour in prison. He left prison in 1659 a broken man, though he engaged in strident criticism of the Commonwealth. He was formally reconciled with Fox, but in October 1660, he was robbed and left for dead while returning to his family home in Yorkshire. He died on 21 October 1660.

RP

Newbigin, Lesslie (1909–98)

Lesslie Newbigin is a figure of towering importance in twentieth-century church history. He was born in Newcastle-upon-Tyne on 8 December 1909, the son of Edward, a shipping merchant, and his wife Anne. Educated at Cambridge and trained for ministry at Westminster College, Cambridge, he was ordained to missionary service in India by the Church of Scotland.

His importance is threefold. As a missionary he discovered both what it meant to be a Christian in a predominantly Hindu culture, and the depth of spirituality in the villagers among whom he ministered. A sharp and incisive theologian (his first book *Christian Freedom in the Modern World* had been finished on the boat to India), as well as a remarkable pastor, it was inevitable that he would be one of the first bishops of the newly united Church of South India in 1947. He was bishop of Madurai.

Second, that experience prepared him for a phase of work as an ecumenical theologian and statesman. His theological defence of the South India scheme, and the more popular *South India Diary* (1948) led to engagement with the World Council of Churches in its formative years. He was appointed general secretary of the International Missionary Council in 1958, and his hand lay behind the integration of the International Missionary Council and the WCC. However, he was never entirely happy as a bureaucrat and was glad to return to India as bishop of Madras in 1965.

However, his lasting contribution was as a theologian. He wrote widely and deeply on mission, but *The Household of God* (1953) was the first major ecclesiological work to recognize Pentecostalism as a distinctive and significant Christian tradition. In 'retirement' after 1974 he returned to England which he called the hardest mission field he had ever encountered. He chose to minister in the United Reformed Church despite offers of assistant bishoprics from several dioceses. It was during these years that he sought to engage theologically with post-Enlightenment Western culture, and that led to a series of studies – *The Other Side of 1984* (1983), *Foolishness to the Greeks* (1986), *The Gospel in a Pluralist Society* (1989), and *Truth to Tell: The Gospel as Public Truth* (1991), the last of which lent a new vitality to the role of theology in the public square. He also produced *The Light Has Come: An Exposition of the Fourth Gospel* (1985) which in spiritual depth and intellectual penetration deserves to stand alongside William Temple's *Readings in St John's Gospel* (1945).

He married Helen Henderson in 1936, and died in south London on 30 January 1998. He was awarded the CBE, and received six honorary doctorates.

Geoffrey Wainwright, *Lesslie Newbigin: A Theological Life* (Oxford: Oxford University Press, 2000).

DGC

'New Genevans'

The 'New Genevans' was a collective title applied to a number of influential Congregationalists who led a revival in worship and ecclesiology from the 1930s. Though not tightly coordinated, those involved were linked through various common activities, especially contributing to the journal *The Presbyter* (1943–48), and belonging to the Church Order Group, founded in 1946. Their aim was the re-statement of Reformed Orthodoxy, salvaging gospel faithfulness from what they considered to be the excesses of both liberal and conservative thought, and to assert the primacy of the visible church as the historical medium for God's purposes in the world. This latter aim produced a 'high' churchmanship which sought the renewal of liturgical forms, due respect for the office of ministry and commitment to work for the visible unity of the church.

The 'New Genevans' were inspired by a number of sources. The neo-Calvinistic reaction against theological liberalism, led on the European continent by figures such as Karl Barth, certainly played a part, but a genuine rediscovery of the Reformation and of their English Puritan heritage was probably more significant. There had also been antecedents, if not precursors; P. T. Forsyth's theology was rediscovered by some, while his pupils, by this time themselves in positions of denominational influence, seemed to welcome the resonances between the new movement and their mentor's thought. Their unofficial manifesto was published in 1939 in the form of a letter 'To the Ministers of Christ's Holy Gospel in the Churches of the Congregational Order'.

This 'Call to Reformation' was drafted by the historian Bernard Lord Manning (1892–1941) and revised by Nathaniel Micklem (1888–1976), principal of Mansfield College, Oxford (1932–53), and John Seldon Whale (1896–1997), at the time president of Cheshunt College, Cambridge (1933–44). Micklem's desire to see renewal in theology, ecclesiology and liturgy was driven by a sense that to be truly Protestant meant to be truly Catholic, and he became increasingly interested in scholasticism, especially that of Thomas Aquinas. Whale was largely responsible for the rediscovery of Calvin's theology within Congregationalism. Other signatories included Sydney Cave (principal of New College, London, and a former student of Forsyth who, as a former missionary, had retained a degree of respect for the older liberalism as essential for the apologetic task), H. F. Lovell Cocks (principal of the Scottish College, soon to become principal of Western College, Bristol, who was influenced by the Barthian theology but more profoundly indebted to his former teacher Forsyth), E. J. Price (principal of the Yorkshire United College, Bradford), J. D. Jones (Congregationalism's elder statesman) and John Short (one of Congregationalism's leading ministers who had ministered at Lyndhurst Road, Hampstead, and was at that time Jones' successor at Richmond Hill, Bournemouth). For a time, Whale was a virtual household name among British Nonconformists. He spent the 1950s as guest or visiting professor in a host of North American universities, but in reality he seemed to lose his way after he resigned his presidency of Cheshunt to take up the headmastership of Mill Hill School, north London (1944–51). Micklem, however, influenced many of his students who continued his work, particularly Daniel T. Jenkins (1914–2002), whose Reformed credentials were forged while a student in Scotland), John Huxtable (1912–90) and Erik Routley (1917–82).

The support commanded by the so-called New Genevans was not inconsiderable and they were able to instigate a rediscovery of Reformed theology and a renewal of worship within Congregationalism. As a result, they played an important part in preparing the way for the inauguration of the United Reformed Church in 1972. While debates surrounding the nature of the Reformed tradition continued after that time, there were no identifiable and prominent successors to any of these men, while their direct influence appeared to have faded, certainly by the last quarter of the twentieth century.

RP

New Theology

As new philosophical or other intellectual insights are brought into dialogue with the church's belief systems, so 'new theologies' come to prominence. In the 1850s, the theological liberalism which emphasized God's fatherhood over Calvinistic predestination and eternal punishment was known by some in Congregationalism as the 'new theology'. However, the name is most commonly associated with the attempt by several Nonconformist thinkers, at the end of the nineteenth century and beginning of the twentieth, to accommodate philosophical Idealism and contemporary scholarship in their system and to give greater prominence to social rather than individual and personal salvation.

The influence of two philosophers F. H. Bradley (1846–1924) and Edward Caird (1835–1908) can be discerned as playing a prominent role in the Nonconformist theology of the period. Bradley had emphasized that the infinite was immanently present in human consciousness and thus demonstrated the basic unity of all things. For Caird, any disharmony was a pale reflection of a greater harmony, which emphasized the fundamental unity of the whole of the universe in all its aspects. The New Theology gave prominence to this thinking. It championed divine immanence and insisted that the God who is thus immanently present in the universe is also present in each person. Thus all humans are united in one 'brotherhood' as well as united with the divine. There could thus be no absolute dichotomies. Evil was necessary to demonstrate the excellence of the good. Sin is merely the result of pursuing self-interest over the interest of humankind.

There were several prominent expositors of the New Theology. By nature of his charismatic personality, R. J. Campbell was undoubtedly the best known. When Campbell's book was published in 1907, T. Rhondda Williams claimed that he had been teaching the new theology for years. Perhaps more able than both men were the Unitarian Joseph Warschauer and the Congregationalists W. E. Orchard and Kerr Crummon Anderson. Campbell established the New Theology League in 1907 to promote his work while 'The Progressive League' was established later that year when the controversy broke. This later became the Liberal Christian League.

The New Theology faced much opposition both from theological traditionalists and from the greatest Nonconformist minds of the generation, especially A. M. Fairbairn and P. T. Forsyth. While some of its insights continued to be propounded throughout the twentieth century, the 'New Theology', in this form, had all but disappeared by the 1920s.

RP

Nuttall, Geoffrey Fillingham (1911–2007)

Congregational minister and church historian Geoffrey Nuttall was born in Colwyn Bay, Denbighshire, on 8 November 1911, the second of three children of Harold Nuttall, general medical practitioner, and his first wife Muriel Fillingham, *née* Hodgson. He learned Welsh as an adult but considered himself English. Descended from generations of Congregational ministers, his early resolve was to be a minister. From Baswich House School, Stafford, he won a scholarship to the Quaker Bootham School, York, which confirmed his lifelong pacifism. Advised by W. B. Selbie, principal of Mansfield College, Oxford, he entered Balliol College in 1929 to read *literae humaniores*. He explained his third class degree (1933) by his having assisted Percy Allen with his *Opus epistolarum* of Erasmus in whom Nuttall was always interested, as he was in Dante, for the study of whom he learned Italian.

Nuttall trained for the ministry (1933–36) at Mansfield College but had little sympathy for the new principal Nathaniel Micklem. He studied in Marburg (1936–37), attending Bultmann's lectures and meeting Theodor Sippell, the scholar of Puritanism, but also witnessing Nazism. In 1938 he graduated BD, and became minister of Warminster Congregational church, Wiltshire. In 1943 he was research fellow at Woodbrooke, the Quaker college in Birmingham, where he wrote *The Holy Spirit in Puritan Faith and Experience* (1946). In early 1945 he became only the second Nonconformist to gain an Oxford DD. In September 1944, he married Mary Powley, *née* Preston, secretary of Woodbrooke, a widow.

Nuttall was lecturer in church history (1945–77) at New College, London, which trained Congregational ministers. As college librarian also, when it closed in 1977, he ensured that its collections, stretching from the days of the Dissenting Academies, transferred to Dr Williams's Library, where he was a trustee for almost fifty years until 1997.

The outstanding historian of religious dissent, Nuttall wrote on Richard Baxter, George Fox, John Bunyan, Isaac Watts, Philip Doddridge, George Whitefield, John Wesley and Selina, Countess of Huntingdon. His calendars of the Quaker Swarthmore letters, the correspondence of Baxter (with Neil Keeble), and of Doddridge, his introduction to Fox's *Journal*, and his analysis of the manuscript of *Reliquiae Baxterianae* are exceptional. Besides *Holy Spirit*, he wrote *Visible Saints, 1640–1660* (1957; 2nd edn 2001), *The Welsh Saints, 1640–1660* (1958; 2nd edn 1971), *Richard Baxter* (1965), *The Puritan Spirit* (1967) and over six hundred items. His interests included monasticism, Swiss and Dutch church history, and Welsh poetry.

Nuttall was an honorary DD of the University of Wales (1969) and a rare English vice-president of the Honourable Society of Cymmrodorion

(1978). He was president of the Friends' Historical Society (1953), of the Congregational History Society (1965–72), the Ecclesiastical History Society (1972), and the United Reformed Church History Society (1972–77). He was elected a fellow of the British Academy in 1991. On retirement he received a *Festschrift* and was a visiting professor of King's College, London.

In 1979 Nuttall moved from Hampstead Garden Suburb to Bournville. Having suffered a stroke in 2000 he entered a nursing home near Bromsgrove where he died on 24 July 2007.

The breadth of his sympathetic understanding of Christian faith in general, and religious dissent in particular, should ensure his work will long be consulted.

AA

Nye, Philip (ca 1595–1672)

Born in Sussex and baptized on 19 January 1595, Nye was educated at Brasenose College and Magdalen Hall, Oxford, where he came under Puritan influence. He graduated BA in 1619 and MA in 1622, and was curate of All Hallows Staining from 1627 and lecturer at St Michael Cornhill from 1630. Although he seems to have attempted to secure the conformity of John Cotton in 1632, by 1633 he was counted among the dissenters, with John Robinson mentioned as the one responsible for his conversion to Independency. He had close connections with New England, and was the financial beneficiary of several investments made there. It was rumoured that he would go to the colonies, but he stayed in England, apart from a period when he was exiled in Arnhem in the Netherlands (1633–40) where he was joint pastor of a gathered church.

Nye seems to have held a variety of views in tension. He certainly adopted the Independent way, and advocated the establishment of gathered congregations of believers which were to be autonomous and exempt from 'Presbyterall authority', but he maintained that authority lay with the minister and elders and not with the church meeting. He appeared to support toleration, especially in his criticism of the New England persecution of Anabaptists, yet he consistently advocated the role of the magistrate in the enforcement of orthodoxy and argued for the king's authority over the church in his *The Lawfulness of the Oath of Supremacy* (1662). He was sent to Edinburgh in 1643 successfully negotiating the wording of the Solemn League and Covenant in order to satisfy Independent sensibilities by the inclusion of the clause 'according to the Word of God' and the removal of references to Presbyterian polity. It was Nye who presented the agreement to Parliament on 25 September that year. He led the Independent delegation at the Westminster Assembly (which included Thomas Goodwin, William Bridge, Jeremiah Burroughes and Sidrach Simpson), while he sat on the committee which drew up the confession adopted by the Savoy Conference of 1658. He was a member of the Committee for the Approbation of Publique Preachers (the Triers), but he opposed turning the protectorate into a hereditary monarchy. He approved of the Declaration of Breda, but was considered among the regicides at the Restoration, his life being spared on condition that he refrain from public ministry. He seems to have advocated 'occasional conformity' at least from 1683, but Richard Baxter blamed him (together with John Owen) for the divisions in the English Church.

According to Edmund Calamy, Nye was 'a man of uncommon depth'. He demonstrated political skill and profound intellect, but it seems he was neither widely trusted nor liked during his lifetime. He is certainly remembered as a powerful advocate of the Congregational Way, but his activities suggest a willingness to compromise both over church order and in response to social developments.

RP

Oman, John Wood (1860–1939)

John Oman was born in Orkney on 23 July 1860, the son of a mariner turned farmer, who also piloted the local ferry to the mainland. He was fortunate enough to share the services of a neighbour's tutor in his early years and proved to be a superb scholar, entering Edinburgh University in 1877 and securing a First in Philosophy along with several prizes. As a trained academic he was disturbed by the conservative reaction to new biblical criticism and his thoughts turned to ministry. Accepted for training by the United Presbyterian College in Edinburgh he also visited German universities. This bore fruit when early in his ministry he was the first to translate Schleiermacher for a British readership. After a short assistantship at St James' Church, Paisley, he was called by a majority of one vote to be minister of Clayport Street Church, Alnwick, in 1889. Always a better writer than speaker he nevertheless earned the respect of his congregation for his systematic teaching in sermons and Bible class. His scholarly publications during these years at Alnwick earned him a reputation as a philosophical theologian of distinction and he was elected to the chair of systematic theology and apologetics at Westminster College, Cambridge, in 1907. This was the newly-built institution of the Presbyterian Church of England, a conscious bid for influence in the ancient university, although not a formal part of it. Oman's talent was soon employed by the

Faculty of Divinity, on whose board he served for many years. He was made a member of Queens' College in 1909 and an honorary fellow of Jesus College in 1935.

Oman was not an orator and his writing is not in a popular style. It was the depth of the themes he identified as important which commended him to his academic peers. Two of his most celebrated titles, *Faith and Freedom* and *Grace and Personality*, give the flavour of the fundamental theological issues he addressed. By the 1930s he had recognized that the scientific challenge to Christianity was as great as the philosophical one and he produced *The Natural and the Supernatural*. He had a deep conviction that new knowledge and fresh insights were always compatible with orthodox faith so long as that faith was not trapped in conservative shibboleths. His pupil, John Hick, was to take this further in the late twentieth century. Contemporaries, such as Rudolph Otto, held Oman in high regard. Oman set great store by personal integrity and living reverently in order to enjoy the gifts and graces God gives to humankind. His ability to express his beliefs in his own personality and conduct impressed all who met him. He was active in the affairs of his adopted denomination, especially after he became Principal of the college in 1922. He was elected Moderator of its General Assembly in 1931. The universities of both Edinburgh and Oxford conferred honorary degrees on him. His wife, Mary, came from Northumberland and they had four daughters. John Oman died in Cambridge on 7 May 1939.

SCO

Orchard, William Edwin (1877–1955)

W. E. Orchard was one of the most winsome Christian apologists of the twentieth century. Born on 20 November 1877, his faith journey began in the heartlands of English Presbyterianism, at Willesden Presbyterian Church where the ministry of Charles Anderson Scott (later of Westminster College, Cambridge) was determinative, albeit coupled with an evangelical conversion at the hands of an un-named lay evangelist at College Park Church. Training for ministry at Westminster College was to follow, and in 1904 Orchard was ordained to St Paul's Enfield. His ten year ministry there was marked by a brief flirtation with the New Theology, a deepening socialism and pacifism, and an increasing sacramental devotion.

In 1914 he was called to the distinctive Congregational King's Weigh House in Mayfair where John Hunter had ministered with rare liturgical taste and decorum between 1901 and 1904. By 1914 the membership had declined to just over forty, so Orchard accepted a challenge. His ministry there (1914–32) was singular. His pacifism was uncompromising, but so too was his commitment to the reconciliation of evangelicalism and catholicism within the life of a local Congregational church. It was a remarkable experiment, combining apologetic, evangelistic preaching of the highest order with a catholic liturgy – the juxtaposition was most stark in the evening service where the preaching of an evangelistic sermon for about forty minutes was followed by Benediction when the host was taken from the tabernacle, reverenced with incense and shown to the people who were then blessed with it. Reservation, incense, vestments, the ancient Latin hymns of the church, all ensured that this was no ordinary Congregational Church.

Orchard's quest to reconcile the evangelical and the catholic led to one of the most quixotic episodes in the history of twentieth century Nonconformity. Orchard sought to respond to the 1920 Lambeth Appeal to All Christian People by offering the Weigh House as a 'bridge church'. It was brave, principled and hopeful, yet such an individual approach was doomed to failure, and in 1931 it finally failed.

Orchard faced a dilemma, but he felt he could do no other than resign and take steps to be received into the Roman Catholic Church. He was accepted in 1932 and, in 1933, published his autobiography *From Faith to Faith*. He settled faithfully, yet not comfortably, into the Catholic Church. He was much in demand as a preacher, mission and retreat leader in Britain and America throughout the 1930s and into the Second World War. Cardinal Hinsley felt it politic to curtail his pacifist enthusiasms, and in 1943 he was appointed as chaplain to a small religious community at Brownshill near Stroud, where he died on 20 June 1955.

Elaine Kaye and Ross Mackenzie, *W. E. Orchard: A Study in Christian Exploration* (Oxford: The Education Service 1990).

DGC

Owen, John (1616–83)

Born into a Puritan family in Stadhampton, Oxfordshire, and educated at Queen's College, Oxford (BA, 1632; MA 1635), Owen was one of the most prolific authors and significant thinkers of his age and undoubtedly the intellectual force within Congregationalism. Forced to leave Oxford in 1637 due to his Puritanism, he became a private chaplain and tutor. On the outbreak of the Civil War, he sided with parliament and he carefully, and at times courageously, defended a republican position throughout his life.

He first came to prominence in 1642 on the publication of *The Display of Arminianism* in which he demonstrated a solid and committed defence of Calvinism. This gained him the favour of parliament and he was installed as pastor at Fordham in Essex, later moving to Coggeshall. Thereafter he was a regular preacher before parliament, most notoriously on the day following the execution of Charles I when he famously managed to preach without making any direct reference to the event. His preaching brought him the friendship of Oliver Cromwell and he accompanied Cromwell on tours of Ireland and Scotland in 1649–50. Cromwell made him Dean of Christ Church, Oxford, in 1651 and vice-chancellor of the University in 1652, the degree of DD being conferred on him in the following year. He was a firm disciplinarian and, while at Oxford, he opposed ecclesiastical garb to the extent that he was known to dress fashionably, even pretentiously. At this point Owen was at the height of his powers and constantly involved in the affairs of State. In the Spring of 1657 he openly opposed the attempt to make Cromwell king, complaining that in practice the protectorate had usurped the powers of the Long Parliament. He gradually fell out of favour, despite being a prominent participant at the Savoy Conference which published its declaration of the Congregational Way in 1658 (based on the *Westminster Confession*, but promoting Congregational polity and removing the powers of the magistrate to interfere in the life of the church or in matters of conscience). He was removed from the vice-chancellorship of Oxford University in October 1658. He certainly participated in the discussions of the Wallingford House group, though he denied any responsibility in the downfall of Richard Cromwell. As the Presbyterian party gained the upper hand, so he was deprived of the Deanery of Christ Church in March 1660. He retired to Stadham and spent the rest of his life engaged in writing, despite invitations to become minister at Boston, New England in 1663, and to become president of Harvard College in 1670.

Though initially attracted to Presbyterian polity, by 1644 he had clearly been convinced of the scriptural warrant for the Congregational way and defended it in his *Country Essay for the Practice of Church Government*. He advocated Calvinism primarily because of the conviction that human beings played no part in their salvation; God alone could bestow salvation and that by grace alone. Perhaps his most famous publication, *The Death of Death in the Death of Christ* (1651), made his position clear. This brought him into a bitter dispute with, among others, Richard Baxter who accused such a stance of antinomianism. He was a staunch defender of the liberty of conscience and opposed any form of religious persecution. Thus he campaigned for toleration, a stance which led to him being considered suspect by the majority Presbyterian party. He was accused of being a co-conspirator in the Rye House plot (1683), but there was no evidence to support this. He married

Mary Rooke (d.1675) in 1644. Together they had eleven children, only one of whom (a daughter) survived into adulthood only to pre-decease her parents when she succumbed to consumption. He died on 24 August 1683 and was buried in Bunhill Fields.

RP

Parker, Joseph (1830–1902)

In an age of pulpit princes, Parker was among the most popular and impressive of preachers. Born at Hexham, Northumberland, on 9 April 1830, he became assistant to Dr John Campbell, minister of Whitefield's Tabernacle, in 1852. At that time he attended lectures in philosophy at University College London, which amounted to the sum of his formal education. He was ordained at Banbury in 1853, moving to Cavendish Chapel, Manchester, in 1858. In 1869 he moved to the Poultry Lane Chapel in London but undertook a project to erect the far more impressive, Cathedral-like City Temple off Holborn Viaduct. The City Temple was opened in May 1874 at a cost of £80,000 and quickly became a centre for Congregationalism in London. Parker remained minister there until his death on 28 November 1902.

Parker was a striking figure and possessed a voice of impressive range and volume. His style was direct and colloquial, speaking to the heart of his congregations. His fame spread and he drew large crowds to his services. He published sermons and some expository work and he was awarded an honorary DD from the University of Chicago. In 1884 and again in 1901 he was chairman of the Congregational Union of England and Wales, using his latter address to advocate a scheme to create a 'United Congregational Church' where an assembly made up of representatives from the County Unions would administer combined funds, colleges, buildings and literature. The scheme failed to win support, though in some ways it predicted the formation of the Congregational Church in England and Wales in 1966 (though the later scheme was not so centralized as the one suggested by Parker).

Parker married Ann Nesbitt in 1851. She died in 1863 and Parker paid for a memorial window to be installed in the Congregational church in Hexham. In 1864 he married Emma Jane Common. Parker was devastated by her death in 1899 and, it is said, he never truly recovered.

RP

Payne, Ernest Alexander (1902–80)

Ernest A. Payne, who came from an East London professional family of committed Baptists, was to become one of the best known European Baptists of the twentieth century. For his higher education he undertook studies in London (King's and Regent's Park), Oxford (Mansfield) and Marburg (Germany). Although he did not possess an earned doctorate he was probably the most distinguished church historian among British Baptists, writing on the radical wing of the Reformation, the modern missionary movement, the Free Church tradition, the history and ecclesiology of the denomination and on a number of ecumenical themes. He had one pastorate at Bugbrooke, Northamptonshire (1928–32) and thereafter served with the Baptist Missionary Society (1932–40) before becoming a tutor at Regent's Park College (1940–51), at that time in process of establishing itself within the University of Oxford. His historical studies made him a valued member of the Baptist Historical Society which he saw as a valuable instrument in cultivating denominational identity. Sometime editor of the *Baptist Quarterly*, he contributed more than seventy articles to the journal during his lifetime. In particular he argued in favour of the denomination's Anabaptist roots and against those who contrary to this maintained its origins were exclusively in English Separatism.

Payne played an increasingly significant role in the governing bodies of both the Union and the Missionary Society, and internationally in the Baptist World Alliance (BWA), making a notable visit to Russia in 1954 which showed him to be remarkably perceptive of the situation in the Russian churches. It was he who avoided acrid conflict over membership of the World Council of Churches at the BWA Congress in Copenhagen in 1947, by pointing out that the Alliance could not legislate for member unions, while the proposed World Council of Churches only provided for membership by churches, not world confessional families. Attempts to persuade him to take senior appointments in the Bible Society, the BMS, the BWA were all rejected (as later one from the British Council of Churches), but in 1951 he was persuaded to succeed M. E. Aubrey as general secretary of the Baptist Union. This he did with some fear and trepidation because he confessed he did not have close association with the Spurgeonic part of the denomination, but was encouraged by the promise of Dr Percy Evans, principal of Spurgeon's College and the Chairman of the Search Committee, to help him with that. Within days of Payne taking up office Evans was dead; temperament as much as theology made for difficulties in securing the sympathy of the most conservative members of the denomination, though under his leadership the denomination remained united.

In Europe he was the principal architect of the constitution of the European Baptist Federation (EBF) and the interpreter of that constitution in the 1950s when the EBF sought to establish itself as a body with integrity and self-government and not simply as a 'European Committee' of the BWA. Beyond the denomination Payne gave leadership to the English Free Church Federal Council, the infant British Council of Churches, whose executive he chaired from 1962 to 1971. No other Baptist was so widely respected in the counsels of the World Council of Churches where he was Vice-Moderator of the Central Committee (1954–68) and a much respected and effective member of the Presidium (1968–75). He was Chairman of the Preparatory Committee for the Evanston Assembly of the WCC, and, because of death, the presiding officer at the Uppsala Assembly in 1968. He was involved in securing the success of the BWA Congress in London in 1955, and was the architect of the Baptist Union of Great Britain's Tercentenary Celebrations. His service to British Baptists was completed when he was called to be President of the Union in 1977–78.

His general secretaryship of the British Baptist Union was not only administratively well-founded, but was notable for his endeavours to deepen the theological thinking of the denomination to enrich its worship. His service, nationally and internationally, received civil recognition when he was appointed a Companion of Honour, an exceptionally rare distinction in British life, by Queen Elizabeth II. Although externally he might appear a rather shy, remote, academic figure he was keenly interested in people and possessed a quite unique ability in encouraging young men and women in their Baptist heritage, inspiring them in the service of the denomination. His service of and commitment to the whole of British Christendom led the dean of Westminster to issue an invitation for his memorial service to be held in Westminster Abbey, London, which was crowded for the event.

JHYB

Pentecostalism

The roots of Pentecostalism in Britain are associated with an Anglican vicar based in the north-east of England. The Revd Alexander A. Boddy had been appointed to All Saints' parish, Monkwearmouth, Sunderland, in 1884 by Bishop J. B. Lightfoot. Having travelled extensively and written of these journeys, been elected a Fellow of the Royal Geographical Society, campaigned on behalf of Durham miners, become active in the promotion of temperance, Boddy along with a later bishop of Durham, H. C. G. Moule, became interested in the Keswick Convention and other manifestations of Holiness teaching. While different understandings arose, the central notion of an experience subsequent to conversion and promoting spiritual power became signally influential. The Welsh Revival of 1904–5 served as a further catalyst – Boddy himself visited Evan Roberts and returned to Sunderland with the injunction from the Calvinistic Methodist mystagogue that ardent believers must fight heaven down. 'Waiting meetings', a phenomenon that would become characteristic of early Pentecostalism, were established. The aim was to seek and secure a divine encounter, an experience of heavenly power. Cecil Polhill, one of the celebrated Cambridge Seven who travelled to China in a missionary capacity during the 1880s, described the purpose of such meetings as similar to the spiritual ministrations of the Salvationist penitent form or the Keswick after-meeting. Yet there was an additional and distinctive feature: he had visited Azusa Street in Los Angeles where speaking in tongues had occurred in a revivalist context from 1906. *Glossolalia* was to become the defining characteristic of Pentecostalism in Britain, as elsewhere, in spite of severe criticism from fellow evangelicals and Holiness advocates.

On Boddy's invitation, T. B. Barratt, a British-born Methodist minister based in Norway, conducted a mission in Sunderland during the autumn of 1907. This was to be the prelude to an annual conference held each Whitsuntide until the First World War. This event, and a magazine, *Confidence*, provided the nucleus of an as yet disparate movement. Boddy himself vaunted the fact that these gatherings saw 'a unity which nothing but the Holy Spirit could give. We were Anglicans, Methodists, Friends, Salvationists, Congregationalists, Mission members etc., but "denomination" was forgotten. All one in Christ Jesus, was true'. Much like the Charismatic Movement some half a century later, he promulgated the ethos that this 'blessing' was to benefit existing churches and denominations and separatism (frequently termed 'come-out-ism') was strongly discouraged. These ideals did not, however, render the movement immune from tensions, divergent views, extremist tendencies, sharp criticism from without – all of which hastened the drive to establish norms, parameters and orthodoxies. The drift toward greater cohesion and ultimately denominationalism proved irresistible.

The first recognizable Pentecostal body to be established in Britain was the Apostolic Church – itself the offshoot of an earlier controversial faction – founded in Pen-y-groes, Carmarthenshire, in 1916. Approximately a decade later, and following developments in North American (transatlantic exchange remained as potent among Pentecostals as it had been for earlier sectors of evangelicalism) the Assemblies of God was founded. Many congregations and hitherto independent missions opted to associate with this grouping. Welsh evangelist George Jeffreys returned from several years campaigning in Ireland in the 1920s and his Elim Evangelistic Band brought their particular brand of Pentecostal revivalism to a variety of locations across the British mainland. By the end of the decade crusades reminiscent of Moody and Sankey, but with the added element of divine healing, made a notable impact on urban centres. Significant influx of converts necessitated leadership training (a Bible School was established in Clapham) and the denominational structures of the Elim Pentecostal churches were refined during the 1930s.

In post-war Britain the Pentecostal churches along with other denominations felt the effects of widespread decline in religious observance. In keeping with patterns observed among revivalist and enthusiastic movements, they also began to encounter the onset of routinization. In addition the emergence of the Charismatic movement in the second half of the century caused suspicion, questioning and discomfort among Pentecostals. Historic denominations frequently rejected as spiritually bankrupt appeared to have encroached into the realm of the Holy Spirit, a development which majority Pentecostal opinion was far from ready to applaud much less embrace. The House Church and Third Wave phenomenon with its vibrancy and contemporary styles of worship precipitated further unease and upheaval. Some, frustrated by the perceived recalcitrance and traditionalism of a Pentecostalism well advanced into its maintenance/stability phase, left Pentecostal ranks to join these newer streams. The rise to prominence of Britain's Black-majority Churches, a largely African and Caribbean-led phenomenon displaying strong Pentecostal leanings – sometimes toward extremes – has also presented both stimulus and challenge to indigenous denominations. Increasing engagement with para-church networks such as the Evangelical Alliance and Churches Together in Britain and Ireland has rendered earlier anti-clerical, isolationist and exclusivist tendencies less prevalent in the Pentecostal outlook. Classical denominations such as Elim have, in the face of significant challenges within and without, succeeded in reflecting, re-adjusting and revitalizing their structures and methods while remaining true to core Pentecostal preoccupations. After almost a century, these churches are now on a stable footing, confident in their identity, clear in their mission, committed to activism and eager to see the glories of the past re-enacted and re-transmitted to meet the needs of a new generation.

William K. Kay, *Pentecostals in Britain* (Carlisle: Paternoster, 2000); Timothy B. Walsh, *'To Meet and Satisfy a Very Hungry People': The Origins and Fortunes of English Pentecostalism, 1907–1925* (Milton Keynes: Paternoster, 2012).

TBW

Pilgrim Fathers

The Separatist congregations in the Netherlands, under the authority of ministers such as John Robinson, found themselves persecuted following the coup effected by Prince Maurice of Orange in 1618 and the subsequent spectre of war with Spain. From that point the Dutch Reformed churches came to prominence and the continued existence of the Separatist congregations appeared to be under threat. The English exiles, numbering around four hundred families in 1618, secured a charter to found a colony at the mouth of the Hudson River and, in 1620, a number emigrated. The *Speedwell* left Holland on 1 August 1620 for Southampton and the intention was that it would travel to New England in the company of the *Mayflower*. The *Speedwell* was found to be unseaworthy and, in the end, 101 passengers and thirty crew boarded the *Mayflower* at Plymouth on 6 September 1620 and left for the Americas. Poor weather threw the ship off course and instead of reaching Virginia, the ship landed at Plymouth, Cape Cod, on 11 November that year. Robinson is reputed to have bidden farewell to the pilgrims with the words 'The Lord has more truth and light yet to break forth out of his holy word', though historians have questioned the provenance of this phrase. He intended to travel to New England later with the rest of his congregation, but died in Holland in 1625. The term 'pilgrim fathers' appears to have been coined in the eighteenth century.

RP

Powell, Vavasor (1617–70)

The Welsh Puritan leader Vavasor Powell was born in Cnwc-las, Radnorshire, in 1617 and following education, possibly at Jesus College, Oxford (according to Wood's *Athenae Oxoniensis*, though there is no verification in college records), became a schoolmaster at Clun in his native county. While there he came under Puritan influence through reading Sibbes' *Bruised Reed* and the preaching of Walter Cradock. He soon began itinerating, and was arrested several times between 1638 and 1642 for contravening ecclesiastical authority.

The turbulence of the Civil War found him in London and in 1644 Powell was appointed vicar of Dartford, Kent, though there is no record of how, or if, he had been ordained. During the conflict he served with Cromwell's forces though he lost little opportunity to itinerate whenever he could. Like his colleague Walter Cradock, he preached before parliament in 1650 and became an 'approver' under the Act for the Better Propagation of the Gospel in Wales. As well as ejecting from their livings those clergy who were deficient according to the Puritan norm, Powell, the so-called 'Metropolitan of the Itinerants', supported zealously the sending out of travelling preachers to serve in vacant parishes.

Possessed of a radical personality, he acquired millenarian convictions and strenuously opposed Cromwell's appropriation of the title and role of Lord Protector. His *Word for God* (1655) expressed this view, and brought him into open conflict not only with Cromwell but with his erstwhile collaborator and friend. The fall of the protectorate by 1659 brought him no comfort, and he was arrested in April 1660, a month before the Restoration officially began. Between then and his death he spent seven years and four different spells in various prisons, though he would invariably engage in vigorous evangelism during his short periods of release. He returned to Wales in 1668 only to be arrested again, and died aged fifty-three in the Fleet Prison, London, on 27 October 1670, and was buried in Bunhill Fields.

DDM

Presbyterian Church of England

The Presbyterian Church of England (PCOE) was formed in 1876 from a union of the Presbyterian Church in England (PCIE) and the English Synod of the United Presbyterian Church. It existed until 1972 when all but two congregations (Guernsey and Jersey) united with the Congregational Church in England and Wales to form the United Reformed Church.

It was composed of two distinct presbyterian strands. The English church was in theory presbyterian in order during the Interregnum (1649–60) after the prescription of the Westminster Assembly (1646), but in practice little was done to create the necessary conciliar structures. As a consequence all but a very few Presbyterian congregations created after the Great Ejectment of 1662 lapsed into Unitarianism during the next century. In the far northern counties of Northumberland and Cumberland and in the city of Newcastle-upon-Tyne, indigenous English classes were founded in the eighteenth century, although the churches were ministered to mainly by Scots. In 1836 those two strands of Presbyterianism joined a number of thriving ex-patriate Scottish congregations in the north-west of England (brought south by the growth of 'cottonopolis') and London to form the Presbyterian Church in England. It considered itself a little piece of Scotland in England and sought union with the Mother Church. Legally that was impossible because of the territorial relationship between the two Established Churches of England and Scotland, but it was not until 1844, in the wake of the Scottish Disruption of 1843, that the PCIE realized that its vocation was to be an English Church.

The United Presbyterian Church was a union of the two main Scottish dissenting traditions, the Secession and Relief of 1731 and 1751 respectively, in 1847. Their dissent was grounded in objection to the power of patrons to intrude ministers on congregations. United Presbyterian strength was centred in the Lowlands. It tended to liberalism and it brought into English Presbyterianism wealth and scholarship in almost equal measure. It is no accident that Agnes Smith-Lewis and Margaret Dunlop-Gibson, the two pioneering women English Presbyterian biblical scholars, and Samuel Stitt the Liverpool ship-owner and church benefactor, came from that tradition. So too did English Presbyterianism's greatest theologian, John Oman.

The PCOE was to make its own contribution to English church life – it nurtured the great missionary theologian Lesslie Newbigin the philosophers of religion H. H. Farmer and John Hick, and the ecumenical statesman Kenneth Slack who served as general secretary of the British Council of Churches from 1955–65.

At the time of union in 1972 the church had 246 congregations in England and just over 71,000 members.

David Cornick, *Under God's Good Hand* (London: The United Reformed Church, 1998).

DGC

Presbyterian Church of Wales

The Presbyterian Church of Wales is the product of the Evangelical Revival. Around Easter time 1735 an Anglican layman, Howell Harris (1714–73) of Trevecka, Breconshire, and a clergyman, Daniel Rowland (1713–90), curate of the parish of Llangeitho, Cardiganshire, experienced evangelical conversions and began preaching in a way that encouraged conversion. Both Harris' itinerant evangelism and Rowland's parish based ministry had a startling effect, and before long the spirit of revivalism was being felt throughout their respective vicinities. In order to provide spiritual nurture for their converts, fellowship or 'society' meetings were organized, and by 1737 a network had been established in many parts of south Wales. Each 'society' had its exhorter or 'steward', usually an unordained layman, though wider leadership was provided by the evangelical or 'Methodist' clergy who had united themselves with the movement. Oversight of the societies was provided mostly by Harris, though the leaders came together in an 'association' which consisted of both awakened clergy and sympathetic Dissenting ministers.

By the 1740s the network of societies and the association had taken on a quasi-Presbyterian form. Soon, however, the Dissenting ministers withdrew, and for the next sixty years the Welsh Methodist movement, which unlike Wesley's parallel English movement was Calvinistic in creed, functioned nominally as a renewal movement within the Established Church but in reality as an increasingly influential independent sect. Following the death of Rowland in 1790 and his clerical colleague, William Williams of Pantycelyn, in 1791, it became increasingly difficult to preserve the movement's Anglican identity. The clamour from the people to be allowed to receive the sacraments from the hands of their own preachers, by then few of whom were episcopally ordained, resulted in the next generation of leaders, Thomas Charles of Bala (1755–1814) and Thomas Jones of Denbigh (1756–1820), taking the momentous step of breaking with the mother church. This occurred in 1811 when Charles, himself an ordained Anglican clergyman, set apart twenty-one preachers to administer baptism and the Lord's Supper within the societies.

The new body, the Welsh Calvinistic Methodist Connexion, perpetuated the quasi-Presbyterian form inherited from Howell Harris, laid out its doctrinal views in its 1823 Confession of Faith and was incorporated by Constitutional Deed in Chancery three years later. Nevertheless it was still unsure of its true ecclesiolgy. No longer Episcopalian and never having inherited the gathered church principles of historic Dissent, it was through the vision of Lewis Edwards (1809–87), Wales' premier nineteenth century theologian, that it discovered its mature ecclesial identity. Edwards had studied in Edinburgh under Thomas Chalmers in the 1830s, and returned intent on bringing his Connexion into an alliance with churches of the Presbyterian order. As a result of his 1839–41 controversy with the Independent Samuel Roberts, Edwards forged a consensus among his co-religionists in favour of a strengthened Presbyterianism, and thereafter the body moved closer to the Reformed churches of Scotland. The Presbyterian ideals of a learned and salaried ministry and settled pastorate were accepted, with a General Assembly being established in 1864.

By the 1880s the Welsh Calvinistic Methodist body, now called the Presbyterian Church of Wales, was the largest of the nation's Nonconformist denominations and the most influential. The changed theological presuppositions of the age registered forcibly by the early twentieth century, and the Reconstruction Commission of the 1920s and the Amendment Act passed by parliament in 1933 altered the status if not the letter of the Confession of Faith. Later in the century the Church became ecumenically involved and more socially active, though retaining its ecclesiological nature as a Presbyterian body.

DDM

Presbyterianism

Presbyterianism is a form of church government which was formulated during the sixteenth and seventeenth centuries consisting of government by 'presbyters'. It is particularly associated with the ecclesiology of John Calvin (1509–64) the Genevan reformer. Calvin's exegesis of 1 Tim. 5.17 led to a distinction between 'ruling' and 'teaching' presbyters (or elders – *presbuteros* in Greek means 'older' or 'elder'). Calvin took this to mean that the government of the church was to be shared between lay people who were 'ruling' elders and ministers who were 'teaching' elders. Later Presbyterian theologians have disputed this, but it does mean that one characteristic of Presbyterianism is the office of the lay, ordained elder (which seems to its critics a contradiction in terms).

Presbyterianism expresses this government through a hierarchy of interlocking courts. Locally ministers and elders join together in what was classically known as the 'consistory', but which is now known by other names such as 'Session' or 'Elders' meeting'. One or more regional courts (presbyteries and synods) provide regional oversight, and they in turn are subject to a national General Assembly which is the ultimate source (under Christ) of all law and authority. Each of these courts would consider itself to be meeting under the headship of Christ and to be actively seeking his will for the church. In that sense Presbyterianism is a theocratic form of church government.

Presbyterian churches take many different forms. In Scotland the (Established) National Church is Presbyterian in government, and in the Netherlands the Reformed Church was the major partner in the creation of the new Protestant Church of the Netherlands. Elsewhere Presbyterian churches are minority churches.

Doctrinally Presbyterian churches are Trinitarian and orthodox, and historically they place a high premium on confessions. The *Westminster Confession* (1646), which became the principal subordinate standard of the Church of Scotland, has been particularly influential in the English-speaking world. All Presbyterian churches would consider that scripture is the ultimate authority under which they order their lives and worship. However, although its original theorists (such as Calvin and Thomas Cartwright) considered Presbyterianism to be the only pattern of church life seen in the New Testament, most would now accept that it reveals a variety of patterns of church organization.

The worship of Presbyterian churches is simple and dignified. In most churches the determinative service is the Ministry of the Word which emphasizes the reading of scripture, its interpretation, and a congregational response. Eucharistic celebration is either monthly or quarterly, despite Calvin's plea that it be the weekly, determinative act of worship.

Most churches of a Presbyterian order are members of the World Communion of Reformed Churches (WCRC).

G. D. Henderson, *Presbyterianism* (Edinburgh: The University Press 1952).
DGC

Price, Richard (1723–91)

Price was born in south Wales, the son of a dissenting minister, on 23 February 1723. His early education included attendance at the academies at Talgarth, Breconshire, and Moorfields, London. By the time he left the latter, in 1744, he had already begun to forge his rationalist and libertarian views as well as to reject Trinitarian teaching. He became personal chaplain to the family of George Streatfield at Stoke Newington and an assistant to Samuel Chandler at Poor Jewry Lane meeting house. From 1758, he was minister of the Presbyterian chapel, Newington Green, where he remained until 1783. Alongside this, he ministered at Poor Jewry Lane (1758–78) and at the Gravel-Pit Meeting, Hackney (1778–91).

Price was well-connected. Through William Petty, second earl of Shelbourne, he met Benjamin Franklin and knew Pitt the younger. His *Observations on the Nature of Civil Liberty* (1776), which defended the American side in the war of independence, brought him to the attention of Congress who invited him to advise them on financial matters, though he declined the invitation. He was politically vocal. A founder member of the Society for Constitutional Reform (1780), he advocated reform of parliament, universal manhood suffrage and the reform of electoral boundaries. When the French Revolution broke out he hailed it as the means of establishing religious and civil liberty. Politics was one interest among many. He also pursued enquiries into probability theory, actuarial science and demography.

As a moral philosopher, he sought to establish the objectivity of moral judgement as a function of reason. He also upheld the libertarian view that all were free and able to pursue what they considered to be their duty. As a theologian, he was convinced of God's benevolence and omnipotence, which led him to advocate the idea that everything which occurred did so because it contributed to the fulfilment of the divine will. He was an Arian and rejected the idea that the Son was consubstantial with the Father, but he maintained that the Son existed prior to the incarnation. Although he advocated the fulfilment of duty, salvation came not as a result of human effort but as the response to the grace poured out at the crucifixion.

Price died on 19 April 1791 and was buried in Bunhill Fields. Some of the ideas which he advocated have been established as essential to civil society, including the sense that the state and its social institutions are servants of the people and that all should participate in the government of society. However, his advocacy of the French Revolution, and the trenchant criticism of this by Edmund Burke, as well as his inaccurate claim that the population of England and Wales was falling, both contributed to a tendency to dismiss much of his work. Furthermore, Unitarians have tended to favour the work of Joseph Priestley (1733–1804) and his understanding of Christ's humanity as opposed to Price's more complex Arianism. Nevertheless, Price was rediscovered during the twentieth century and celebrated for the breadth of his scholarship, his political insight and courage, and his pursuit of a reasonable faith while faithfully ministering to his congregation. His ideas may not have prevailed, and his influence might have quickly waned, but he was, in many senses, the epitome of Rational Dissent.

Oxford Dictionary of National Biography (Oxford: Oxford University Press, 2004).

RP

Priestley, Joseph (1733–1804)

A theologian and scientist, Joseph Priestley was in fact a polymath of remarkable energy who not only discovered oxygen and other gases but also pioneered radical religious thought in the eighteenth century. He evolved into a radical political thinker who addressed the relationship between church and state, the role of government and education in a new way. Born in humble circumstances, he was brought up as a Calvinist in the Independent tradition and was mainly taught by Dissenting ministers. He entered Daventry Academy in 1752, and when he left three years later the seeds of his later heretical theology had been laid.

His first ministry at Needham Market was not a success due to his developing Arian opinions and a decided stammer. In 1758 he moved to Nantwich for three years where he kept a school. He joined the staff of the newly created Warrington Academy (1757) widening his knowledge, and making contact with both scientific and religious dissenters in London. In 1767 with a wife and family and a growing reputation as a grammarian and scientist, he moved to the ministry of Mill Hill Chapel, Leeds, a Presbyterian foundation.

At Leeds Priestley came to adopt Socinianism as a result of his own reading. He then published a series of brilliantly controversial works setting out his new position. Priestley launched *The Theological Repository* (1769–71, but later reconstituted) and he met Theophilus Lindsey in 1771 who became his long-term friend and was the founder of the first Unitarian congregation in London in 1774. In 1773 Priestley took an appointment with the liberal earl of Shelbourne as his librarian. During the next seven years he developed his theological and scientific ideas. In 1780 he became minister of the New Meeting, Birmingham, again Presbyterian. During this period his reputation as a radical figure developed, for which he became known. His *History of the Corruptions of Christianity* (1782) argued that the beliefs of primitive Christianity were Unitarian and that all departures from that faith were 'corruptions'. His anti-Trinitarian views on the position of Christ caused the greatest upset, not only in England but in Europe as well.

Priestley entered into a controversy with Samuel Horsley, archdeacon of St Albans and later bishop of St Davids, which lasted eight years and became a battle of wills as well as insults. Priestley's *History of Early Opinions concerning Jesus Christ* (1786) was a significant work of scholarship which Horsley ignored. The controversy became enmeshed in attitudes towards the French Revolution, and Burke's *Reflections etc.* (1790) were in response to a sermon by Richard Price, Priestley's friend and dissenting collaborator. Feelings ran high against the liberal Dissenters which boiled over in July 1791 when not only the New Meeting, Birmingham, was burned down but also Priestley's house; he and his family narrowly escaped. Priestley had to leave Birmingham and went to Hackney near London to minister to the Gravel Pit Meeting. In February 1794 he left for America where most of his family had already gone; if he had stayed the government is likely to have taken action against him. He preached materialism and a necessarian philosophy to Unitarian congregations in America until his death. His writing continued unabated and his non-scientific publications have been estimated to exceed 150.

With Lindsey, and to a lesser extent Price, he created the Unitarian movement in England, mainly among the Presbyterian congregations, which became a recognized grouping during the following century. It was Priestley, the strong controversialist, whose theological and social views strengthened Dissenters in the face of the hostile government. He saw the Church of England as an overgrown fungus upon the body of true Christianity. While called an infidel and an atheist by many, he drew his religious beliefs from the Bible though he rejected sections which he regarded as accretions. He held that Christianity is less a system of opinions than a rule of life and that the welfare of all humanity depends upon its acceptance of Christianity.

AR

Protestant Dissenting Deputies

The passing of the 'Toleration Act' in 1689 eased the situation of Nonconformists but did not give them parity with those who accepted the pre-eminence of the Church of England. In particular, the Test and Corporation Acts remained in force, requiring at least a nominal allegiance to the national church by those who held public office. This did not apply to members of parliament but did affect local government. Nonconformists, or Dissenters as they tended to style themselves after 1689, were prominent in the City of London and it was there that attempts to change the legislation were most concentrated. A series of meetings was held in London in 1732 to consider how best to lobby the government for the abolition of the Test and Corporation Acts and from these emerged the formal constitution of a body known as the Protestant Dissenting Deputies. Baptist, Congregational and Presbyterian congregations within a ten mile radius of the City of London were invited to send two lay members to represent them at a general meeting, which elected a committee of twenty-one to carry out their business. The committee encompassed members of parliament and City figures who might exert political influence on the government of the day. In practice they relied on Whig governments to give a sympathetic hearing to their grievances. Sympathy was in ample supply in order to attract the votes of Dissenters in elections but change was always postponed until a better time. Although there was some criticism from provincial Dissenters about the constitution of the Deputies the nature of communications in the eighteenth century dictated that the London body had to act for all. Over time Dissenters from all parts of England and Wales wrote to the Protestant Dissenting Deputies to take up grievances on their behalf, when individuals or congregations felt they had been harshly treated by the authorities.

The Deputies controlled their own membership. Presbyterian congregations which moved into Unitarianism were excluded. In the nineteenth century the boundary for membership was extended to congregations within a twelve mile radius. The repeal of the Test and Corporation Acts, almost one hundred years after the Deputies came into being, did not end their work. They had already assumed general lobbying activities on behalf of Dissenters and took up major causes, such as education, as the nineteenth century progressed. The Deputies continued into the twentieth century, their importance and influence declining as other bodies, with a wider denominational spread, came into existence. Their administration was taken over by the Free Church Council, which itself became a sub-set of Churches Together in England. At the beginning of the twenty-first century an annual meeting and lecture was still called in the name of the Protestant Dissenting Deputies but it ceased to have any political purpose.

SCO

Puritans

'Puritan' is a word that began life as a term of abuse for those who engaged in over-zealous criticism of the Church of England in the sixteenth and seventeenth centuries. More accurately it represented those who thought that the Established Church, with an outlook both catholic and reformed, represented an imperfect or incomplete reformation, and were anxious for the process to be pursued to its completion. The Puritans pursued their goal in terms of deepening personal piety so that the church visible more nearly corresponded to the church invisible, which also entailed the reform of the government of the church, though they were divided as to whether this should have a Presbyterian or a Congregational order. Concerned both for purity of life and purity in the church, defined according to biblical principles rather than by church traditions or state legislation, they sought the ending of all corruption and the establishment of a better educated and more disciplined clergy, and most obviously a more thorough reform of the church's worship, with the elimination of all those elements which they deemed too 'Roman'. Because the church was established, the Puritans necessarily were cast in the role of political agitators, and indeed in the 1650s, after the execution of Charles I (30 January 1649), the Puritans wielded political power and patronage in England. But the very notion of an Established Church was unsatisfactory to many Puritans, who took the argument one step further in becoming Separatists: such were, for example Robert Browne, Francis Johnson and John Robinson as well as the early Baptist leaders. Thus Nonconformity finds it roots in Puritanism, but not all Puritans were Nonconformists, indeed some scholars would limit the term to those who, remaining within the Established Church rather than separating from it, sought more forthright reform. Puritan theologians, aided by the publication of the Authorized (King James) Version of the Bible in 1611, expounded, developed and applied an English version of Calvinist doctrine, which became their unifying *lingua franca*, especially as it was enshrined in such documents as the *Westminster Confession* (1646), and the *Savoy Declaration* (1658) under the leadership of men such as William Perkins (1558–1602), William Ames (1573–1633), John Owen (1616–83), Thomas Goodwin (1600–80) and Richard Baxter (1615–91). This Puritan theology finds poetic expression in the works of John Milton (1608–74), who did as much as any theologian to disseminate a Puritan world view, while Puritan imagination is best seen in the allegorical writings of John Bunyan (1628–88), author of *The Pilgrim's Progress*.

JHYB

Regicides

Following the restoration of the monarchy in 1660, the 'Indemnity and Oblivion Act' identified the fifty-nine commissioners who acted as judges at the trial of Charles I and who signed the death warrant as 'regicides' along with officials who participated in the trial and execution and Hugh Peter, a prominent Republican, minister and vocal supporter of the king's execution (who nonetheless had not participated in the king's trial). Twenty-one had died before the restoration and three were ordered to be posthumously executed (including Oliver Cromwell). Nine fled to Europe or North America and six of them escaped the reprisals of the restored monarch and Cavalier parliament, three being captured, returned to England and executed. Five were still in England at the time of the restoration but managed to escape and to elude capture. Ten were sentenced to death with two dying before the sentence was carried out; the other eight were hanged drawn and quartered including Major General Thomas Harrison, a Fifth Monarchist, who reportedly met his fate with great courage. Fourteen spent the rest of their lives in prison, some having initially been sentenced to death. One, Richard Ingoldsby, who had been an officer in the New Model Army, was pardoned after claiming that he was forced to sign the death warrant by Cromwell (who was his cousin). Of the nineteen commissioners who did not sign the death warrant, four died before the Restoration and five would suffer life imprisonment. Thomas Fairfax, though Commander in Chief of the Parliamentary Forces during the Civil Wars and head of the commissioners at the king's trial, was given a royal pardon partly because he refused to take any part in the proceedings once he realized that the intention was to execute Charles and partly because he was at the head of the parliamentary force sent to welcome back the restored Charles II. Henry Vane the younger, a leading parliamentarian during the Civil Wars and a close associate of Cromwell, was condemned to death probably because he argued that sovereignty lay with parliament and the people rather than with the monarch. Though sentenced to be hanged, drawn and quartered, he was allowed a nobleman's death and was beheaded on Tower Hill on 14 June 1662. John Lambert, a general in the parliamentary forces and a commissioner who was absent from London during the king's trial, was imprisoned for life. Lambert had opposed the Restoration, but at his trial threw himself on the mercy of the court, an act which doubtless spared his life. Neither man signed Charles I's death warrant. A further two officers were executed (Colonels Daniel Axtell and Francis Hacker, again neither signed the death warrant) while five named officers escaped to Switzerland, one was pardoned, one not tried and two were assassinated. While *prima facie* these actions were made against those who played a part in the trial and execution of Charles I, it is clear that there were other forces at work and both Charles II, and his Cavalier-dominated parliament, took the opportunity to silence those it considered to represent a continued threat to the monarchy and the political *status quo*.

RP

Religious Society of Friends (Quakers)

The Religious Society of Friends (Quakers) is regarded as a Christian religious organization that has its origins in the mid-seventeenth century. At the time of writing, there are approximately 340,000 Quakers worldwide with a membership that reveals the various theological traditions of Quakerism (Evangelical, Liberal and traditional/Conservative). Before accepting the name of the Religious Society of Friends, the early members of the Society were known as the 'Children of the Light' or simply as 'Friends'. In 1650 in Derby the term 'Quaker' was coined as a term of abuse by Justice Bennett. This reflected the way early Friends behaved during worship. The diversity of belief among Quakers is apparent in the organizational structure of the various Yearly Meetings. These meetings reflect the different range of religious expressions while the composition of the membership of the Society includes agnostics, Christians, atheists as well as those who hold universalist beliefs. Quakers are, however, best known for their pacifism and social witness which came out of their expressions of social equality, most notably in their opposition to slavery and the promotion of prison reform.

The origins of the Society can be dated from ca 1652 in the north-west of England and closely linked with the activities of George Fox (1624–91) who is accredited with founding the movement. Initial converts to Quakerism, who came from a variety of backgrounds, turned away from Anglicanism and from the dissenting congregations largely because they failed to meet their spiritual needs. Many Friends in the 1650s and in the post-Restoration period, including Fox, Margaret Fell, James Nayler and other preachers (the 'Valiant Sixty') as well as Quaker theologians, especially Robert Barclay and William Penn, helped disseminate the Quaker message and develop a coherent organizational basis. There are four main theological ideas which are held in common by most Friends: (1) the direct and inward experience of God;

(2) the priesthood of all believers and spiritual equality; (3) a consensual approach to church business rather than a voting system; and (4) a testimony for peace. Friends thereby seek peaceful resolutions to conflict and offer (where possible and practical) assistance to find solutions to prevailing social concerns.

As a result of the missionary efforts of early Friends, meetings were held throughout the British Isles, Europe, the Caribbean and in the Americas. In their earliest days meetings were held wherever Friends could gather, for example, in their homes (conventicles), in barns and even in their own burial grounds. Purpose-built meeting houses were nevertheless quickly erected or existing properties used for holding meetings for worship, despite the risk of prosecution during the imposition of the penal code between the 1660s and 1680s, and a number of these meetings have continued to exist to the present day. During the earliest years, meetings were held in silence where members awaited the presence of the Spirit, but in reality the 'ministry' of members, including the unusual sight of women preachers, often meant that lengthy preaching sessions were more common than silence. Members were also actively encouraged to disseminate their beliefs to the wider public in 'threshing' meetings. These and other activities, such as walking naked as a sign or disrupting a clergyman during divine service, often provoked a hostile reaction, arrest and lengthy periods of imprisonment for many Friends. Gradually, however, the Society adopted an organizational framework (ca 1660s onwards). This comprised structured meetings, a body of ministers and elders, regular epistles providing members with information and guidance and a code of behaviour to which Friends were expected to adhere. Consequently, the Society naturally ceased to be an amorphous movement, developing into a sect and post-Toleration (1689) it was legally accepted as part of the religious make-up of Britain and elsewhere. There was still prosecution for the non-payment of tithes and occasional local or regional prejudice, but Friends became increasingly respected for their business acumen and fair-dealing. Schism has led to the development of different strains of Quakerism worldwide, but the Society is still a highly respected and influential religious organization. Although Friends are recognized and respected, they are not always fully understood as part of the Christian community.

RCA

Robinson, Henry Wheeler (1872–1945)

A Baptist minister and biblical theologian, Robinson was the son of a Northampton butcher, who abandoned wife and son before his birth.

Baptized on profession of faith in March 1888 at College Street Baptist Church, Robinson began to think about possible ordination. After a year at Regent's Park College, London, he entered Edinburgh University, where, influenced by J. S. Blackie, Alexander Whyte and Henry Drummond, he graduated in 1895. Proceeding to Mansfield College, Oxford, he received encouragement from its principal A. M. Fairbairn. Having concentrated on Old Testament studies, he was placed in the second class of the School of Oriental Studies (1898), but was awarded no fewer than five prizes and scholarships.

While in pastoral ministry in Pitlochry (1900–3), and in Coventry (1903–6), he studied Hebrew psychology, preparing himself for future literary work. From 1906 to 1920 he served as tutor at Rawdon Baptist College (1906–20), where his gifts as a teacher soon became apparent, while his first three books – a commentary on *Deuteronomy and Joshua* (1907), *The Christian Doctrine of Man* (1911) and *The Religious Ideas of the Old Testament* (1913) – established his reputation. A serious illness in 1913 directed his thinking towards the doctrine of the Holy Spirit and the problem of suffering.

Robinson's appointment in 1920 as principal of Regent's Park College, still located in London, set the scene for the greatest achievement of his life, the moving of the college, notwithstanding hesitation among many of his Baptist colleagues, to Oxford. A site was secured in 1927, but the stone-laying of the new buildings was not possible until 1938, while a formal opening had to be abandoned owing to the outbreak of war. By then Robinson had become a valued member of the London Society for the Study of Religion and a leading figure in the Society for Old Testament Study. With Dr W. R. Matthews he planned and edited the Library of Constructive Theology, an important series of volumes taking religious experience as its starting point. Robinson himself contributed *The Christian Experience of the Holy Spirit* (1928) and *Redemption and Revelation* (1942). In his thinking an emphasis on human experience is always balanced by insistence on the work of the Holy Spirit. He also published many smaller books and essays on the Old Testament, including a notable work on the Hebrew conception of corporate personality and the idea of the suffering of God.

One of Oxford's best-known theological lecturers, he was appointed Reader in Biblical Criticism in 1934, and in 1937–39 was the first free churchman to be chairman of the theology faculty. On his retirement from his college principalship in 1942, he was elected speaker's lecturer in Biblical Studies and planned to give himself to the writing of a major work on Old Testament theology. The posthumously published lectures *Inspiration and Revelation in the Old Testament* (1946) were intended as prolegomena, but his health failed shortly after his retirement and he died in Oxford three years later.

For many years president of the Baptist Historical Society, his *Baptist Principles before the Rise of Baptist Churches* (1911) and *The Life and Faith of the Baptists* (1927) had a wide circulation. Recipient of honorary DDs from Edinburgh (1926) and Manchester (1943), the wide range of his intellectual interests and influence and the volume of work he accomplished were possible only by rigid self-discipline strengthened by unusual spiritual understanding and power. His personal faith was most clearly and simply set forth in *The Veil of God* (1936) and *Suffering, Human and Divine* (1940).

JHYB

Robinson, John (1575–1625)

Born in Nottinghamshire, Robinson was educated at Corpus Christi College, Cambridge, where he graduated BA (1596) and MA (1599) and spent some time teaching. Although apparently destined for holy orders, Robinson came under the influence of Puritanism, possibly while at home but certainly while at Cambridge. He came to believe that the parish system was unbiblical and that a church could only be made up of Christian believers. Due to increased persecution designed to enforce conformity in religion, Robinson resigned his teaching post in Cambridge in 1604. He was pastor in Norwich for a short time, but there too he found he could not, in all conscience, submit to the new book of canons, as was required in law, and he returned home to Nottinghamshire. He appears to have been a member of John Smyth's Separatist church in Gainsborough before becoming assistant pastor at the Separatist church in Scrooby in 1606. By 1608 the members of the church had emigrated to Amsterdam, where Smyth and his church had also relocated the previous year. Smyth adopted Baptist principles and modified his theology to the extent that Robinson and he parted company, Robinson's church relocating to Leyden.

While Robinson believed that the Church of England was falsely constituted, he did not think that it was utterly devoid of Christian people. As a result, he advocated maintaining communion with other genuine Christians, wherever they may be found, for God's grace was certainly at work wherever the godly minister. Thus he encouraged his own church members to attend the parish church to hear godly preaching even while he opposed the formal order of the Church of England. This came to be known as 'semi-Separatism' or 'occasional conformity'.

The church at Leyden suffered poverty and hardship and found themselves increasingly alienated from the local language and culture. War was brewing between Holland and Spain and the church believed that it would be destroyed unless it relocated. In 1619, it was resolved to emigrate to the Americas. Around thirty-five members set sail, along with sixty-six others (whose motives were not to seek religious liberty) in the *Mayflower* in September 1620. Robinson had decided to remain with the majority of his church in Leyden, the plan being to join the initial party at a later date. However, Robinson died before he could make the journey.

RP

Ryland Jr, John (1753–1825)

John Ryland Jr was born on 29 January 1753 in Warwick, the son of John Collett Ryland, a prominent Baptist minister. A precocious child, by the age of ten, Ryland Jr was able to read and translate Latin, Hebrew and Greek. He experienced conversion in 1766. An early book of his poems, which his father published, reveals a tendency to High Calvinism. But Ryland Jr was helped to a more evangelical position through a friendship with John Newton, curate at Olney while the Rylands were based at nearby Northampton. This friendship, carried on mainly through correspondence, was to last for over thirty years.

Ryland was appointed his father's co-pastor at Northampton in 1781, becoming sole minister in 1785. He was a prominent figure in the revitalization of Particular Baptist life which took place towards the end of the eighteenth century. Along with his contemporaries Andrew Fuller, John Sutcliff and William Carey he advocated a theology that was both evangelical and Calvinistic, helped establish the 1784 Call to Prayer, and promoted vigorous evangelistic efforts at home and abroad. He was one of the founders of the Baptist Missionary Society (BMS) and became its joint secretary in 1815. Although from 1818 John Dyer was the full time 'co-secretary' and did the bulk of the work, Ryland remained an enthusiastic advocate of the BMS, taking particular interest in its activities in the Caribbean. Both in theology and practice he was indebted to the writings of Jonathan Edwards (he named one of his sons Jonathan Edwards Ryland), and he was also influenced by other New England theologians such as Joseph Bellamy and Samuel Hopkins.

In 1793 he accepted a call to be president of Bristol Academy and pastor of Broadmead Baptist church in the city. The Academy was strategic for Particular Baptist life. Ryland was able to continue and develop its work, ensuring that it turned out pastors and missionaries who shared the brand of Edwardsean evangelical Calvinism that was characteristic of the coterie of Particular Baptist ministers who had founded the BMS.

He wrote over thirty books. These included *The Difficulties of the Christian Ministry and the Means of Surmounting Them* (1802), *The Practical Influence of Evangelical Religion* (1802) and an important 'tombstone' biography of his friend Andrew Fuller (1st edn 1816; 2nd edn 1818). Ryland himself was never the subject of a major biography (partly because he outlived those of his friends who might have undertaken this task). He has also been neglected in recent scholarly study, but he was a significant figure, one who was at the heart of many important developments. He died in Bristol, on 25 May 1825.

Jonathan E. Ryland (ed.), *Pastoral Memorials: Selected from the Manuscripts of the Late John Ryland DD, with a Memoir of the Author*, 2 vols (London: Holdsworth, 1826–28).

PJM

Rylands (*née* Tennant), Enriqueta Augustina (1843–1908)

Born on 31 May 1843 in Havana, Cuba, Enriqueta's father was Stephen Cattley Tennant (1800–48), a merchant, while her mother was Juana Camila Dalcour (1818–55). The family retired to Liverpool but within a year Tennant was dead. Dalcour removed to Paris and remarried. Enriqueta was raised a Roman Catholic and educated in New York, London and Paris. She later became a Congregationalist and was personally known to, and supportive of, a number of prominent ministers such as A. M. Fairbairn and C. Silvester Horne. From around the year 1860, she became companion to Martha Carden, wife of the Lancashire businessman John Rylands, and, eight months after Martha's death, she married him and they subsequently adopted two children. When he died in 1888, she inherited the vast majority of his estate. Like her husband, she was strong-willed but committed to various philanthropic and missionary causes, including Horne's Whitefield's Tabernacle, various hospitals, ragged schools and other foundations and charities. She built the John Rylands Library, Manchester, in honour of her husband, engaging Basil Champneys, architect of Mansfield College, Oxford, for the task. It was inaugurated on 6 October 1899, some twenty-four years after the day of her marriage, when an address was delivered by Fairbairn. At the same time, she was admitted to the Freedom of the City of Manchester, the first woman to be so honoured. She died on 4 February 1908 and her ashes were buried with her husband.

RP

Rylands, John (1801–88)

The third son of Joseph Rylands, John was born on 7 February 1801 and entered into partnership with his elder siblings, Joseph and Richard, in the family firm before he was eighteen years of age. The firm of Rylands and Sons was established in 1819 and engaged in various activities in Lancashire, all concerned with the manufacture of cotton goods. In 1823 he opened a warehouse in Manchester and the firm expanded by purchasing a dye works and a bleach works as well as the opening of extensive and valuable coal seams under property purchased in Wigan. The business continued to expand until Joseph Jr and Richard retired around 1839, with John in sole control from 1847. A warehouse was opened in London in 1849. The firm became the largest textile manufacturer in Britain with seventeen mills and factories and a capital of £2 million.

Although reserved by nature, Rylands was typical of nineteenth-century Nonconformist businessmen in that he supported charitable causes including orphanages, homes for the aged and retirement homes for ministers, as well as providing for a town hall, public baths and a library in Stretford, where he lived at Longford Hall. He also supported the poor of Rome and he was awarded the Order of the Crown of Italy from its king. He engaged scholars in the translation of the Bible and made that and other publications available free of charge. He was a Congregationalist, but not a sectarian. Possessed of Baptist sympathies (he was baptized as an adult following the death of his mother), he provided finance for a number of Union Chapels in the north-west of England.

He married three times, first, in 1825, to Dinah Raby who bore six children, none of whom survived their father; second, in 1848, to Martha Carden; and third to Enriqueta Augustine Tennant who survived him and was responsible for the erection of the John Rylands Library in Manchester as a tribute to her husband. John Rylands died on 11 December 1888. At that time he was the richest of all of Britain's cotton manufacturers with a personal estate valued at £2,574,922.

RP

Salt, Titus (1803–76)

Sir Titus Salt was a Congregational layman and industrialist who perfected a technique for making fabric from blending alpaca with other materials. As a consequence he dominated the market and accumulated a fortune.

Bradford was the centre of the worsted industry, and his father, who was a wool-stapler, had moved there in 1822. Titus began his working life in the family firm, but after ten years he started his own company. The family were Congregationalists, and deeply involved in the emergence of civic Bradford. He served as mayor of Bradford (1848–49) and as one of its MPs (1859–61).

Bradford was gaining a reputation for the squalor and misery which accompanied industrialization, and it is against this background that Salt's employment practice needs to be seen. By 1850 he had five separate mills, and had the reputation of being an excellent employer. In that year he decided to move his entire operation to a new plant and model village by the river Aire three miles outside Bradford in Saltaire. The mill was opened in 1853 and the model village followed. It eventually consisted of just over eight hundred houses. All of them had drainage and lavatories, and they were built to ensure that each was open to the sun. The village also had public baths, a school, an Institute, almshouses, both a Congregational Church and Methodist chapel and a landscaped park.

For Salt this seems to have been both an outworking of the gospel, and sound business sense. He cared deeply about his workforce, and the effect that industrialization was having on the environment. His new mill had been engineered to reduce noise and its chimneys were fitted with state of the art technology to reduce air pollution. His village provided an ideal environment for his workers, and contemporaries noted how much more healthy they were than workers in the surrounding cities. His foresight in creating this 'industrial colony' was warmly commended by the pioneering economist Alfred Marshall who proposed a similar process of reform for London. Others, like Ruskin, dismissed the initiative as a way of producing a captive labour force.

Salt's achievements were lauded, and he was knighted in 1869. He was married to Caroline Whitlam and they had eleven children. He died in 1876 and at his funeral 100,000 people lined the streets of Bradford. He was buried in the Congregational Church at Saltaire, which is now part of a World Heritage site.

J. Reynolds, *The Great Paternalist: Titus Salt and the Growth of Nineteenth Century Bradford* (London: Temple Smith, 1983).

DGC

Salvation Army

The Salvation Army was formed in 1878 out of what was William Booth's East London Christian Mission established in 1865. In a sense the Salvation

Army was one of the last groups to break away from Methodism, Booth having been a New Connexion Methodist preacher and evangelist for the best part of ten years. The new society was formed 'to bring under the Gospel those who were not in the habit of attending any place of worship'. Booth had deep insight into what would make his new movement popular: the military image with its associated chain of command and use of uniforms, the sanctification of band music for evangelistic purposes – Booth was reputedly the author of the quip 'Why should the Devil have all the best tunes?' – its offering of leadership positions to women, the much respected 'Salvation Army Lassies', its particular blend of social work and evangelism, and the broadcasting of its concern for the 'submerged tenth' of the inner cities in Booth's influential *In Darkest England and the Way Out* (1890). The Army exposed such abuses as the white-slave trade, founded hostels for the homeless, ran numerous soup kitchens, worked to create employment for the unemployed and ran a missing persons bureau among other social tasks. The work of the Army rapidly spread around the world being introduced to France in 1881 and Sweden in 1882. The Salvation Army sees itself as an 'integral part and element of the Great Church, a living fruit-bearing branch of the True Vine'. Other churches have often seen the Army as a specialized agency undertaking work on behalf of all the churches, but at the same time it has developed its own denominational identity, responding to the need to relate ecumenically. In 1948 when the World Council of Churches was formed the then–presiding general argued that it seemed to him that 'for the Army to take its full place in this great world gathering of the spiritual forces of Christendom is a logical development of the Army's policy of co-operation'. Later this was to prove problematic, for the Army had joined the World Council through its international headquarters, when the basic unit of council membership was a member church normally in one nation. When difficulties emerged over the Council calling 'the churches to the goal of visible unity in one faith and in one Eucharistic fellowship', and when it established its programme to Combat Racism with its Special Fund to aid the welfare work of aggressive bodies such as the African National Congress, the Army, in 1981, deemed the moment right to withdraw from the Council as a member church, but to associate with it as a World Confessional Family.

JHYB

Savoy Conference and Declaration (1658)

On 15 June 1658, Henry Scobell, secretary of the Council of State under Oliver Cromwell, sent out invitations to Independent ministers in London for a preliminary meeting to consider whether a national meeting might be held to consider a statement of faith and church order which would carry the confidence of Independents (or Congregationalists), generally. On 21 June they agreed to summon a national meeting of ministers and lay people, to be held at the Savoy Palace, beginning on 29 September. It is reckoned that this meeting carried the tacit approval of Cromwell, though it was summoned in the name of the London ministers. Cromwell died on 3 September but the meeting went ahead. Independents were dissatisfied with the *Westminster Confession of Faith* of 1646 and although they set out to create a new confession their eventual agreed text bears many similarities with that of the *Westminster Confession*, suitably modified to represent their theological position. Overall there is a stronger emphasis on grace and a less rigorous treatment of law and sin, and the magistrate is denied any authority to enforce religious belief or practice. A document giving guidance on the nature of Congregational churches was also prepared. The whole work was completed by 12 October. Although it was of the same Calvinist family as the Presbyterian text it was denounced by people such as Richard Baxter as a barrier to future Presbyterian and Congregational union. Had Cromwell lived it might have become the basis for a church settlement in England, but in the event the Restoration of the Monarchy in 1660 and the rebuilding of Episcopacy, with the imposition of the Prayer Book, left the work stranded so far as practical politics were concerned. The Savoy Declaration was taken up by Congregationalists in New England and used in the development of church polity there. It was given new importance in England when Congregationalism enjoyed a great expansion in the nineteenth century.

SCO

Separatism

Although Separatism is acknowledged to be the antecedent of Congregationalism, little is known about the early Separatists because, by their very nature, the Separatist congregations had to meet in secret for fear of reprisal from the state and its church. Early Separatists were united in their opposition to Rome and its influences on the English church established by law and in their belief that their own ecclesiology was formed by an understanding of the New Testament. There were separatist congregations meeting at Bocking in Essex and Faversham in Kent during the mid-sixteenth century. When their members were arrested in 1551, they confessed that they had not celebrated Communion in the parish church for two years. It seems that these churches rejected the doctrine of predestination and emphasized free will and human responsibility, earning them the epithet 'Arminian'. During the reign of Mary I, a 'privy church' met in London and its minister, John Rough, and deacon, Cutbert Symson, were burned at the stake during the Marian persecutions. A Puritan congregation was meeting at the Plumbers' Hall by 1567, though it is uncertain that it met on strictly Separatist lines; its pastor, William Bonam, and twenty-four of its members, were discharged from prison in 1568 only after vowing not to observe Communion 'Contrarie to the state of religion nowe by publique authoritie established, or Contrarie to the Lawes of this Realme of *England*'. Richard Fitz seems to have attracted some members from the Plumbers' Hall who entered into a solemn church covenant with each other, while a church was meeting at the home of James Tynne, a goldsmith, in the parish of St Martin's in the Fields by March 1568 when it was raided by the authorities.

Though patchy, this evidence suggests that Separatist tendencies were emerging in the English church in the sixteenth century, even if it lacked the organization which would normally pertain to a specific movement. Separatism gained theological justification in the work of Robert Browne (1550–1633), educated at Corpus Christi College, whose publications included the polemical tract *A Treatise for Reformation without Tarrying for Anie* (1582). For Browne, the members of the church did not need to wait for the officers of the state in order to secure reformation. He initially opposed the parish system, arguing that the church was composed of believers and that no Christian required an Episcopal licence in order to preach the gospel. Robert Harrison (1540?–85?) gathered a church at Norwich around the year 1580 with the members binding themselves to each other in a formal church covenant. Both Browne and Harrison, and their respective churches, found themselves in exile in Holland in the early 1580s, but by 1584 Browne was in Scotland and rapidly refuting his former position. In 1585 he conformed to the Established Church. Browne's works were widely circulated and in 1583 a Royal Declaration denounced as 'seditious, schismatical and erroneous' a list of books by him and by Harrison. In June of that year, John Copping and Elias Thacker were both hanged at Bury St Edmunds for promoting Brownist views, while William Denys followed at Thetford for the same reason. To advocate an alternative ecclesial order to that of the Established Church was clearly considered to be a seditious act and the 1581 Act 'for retaining the Queen's subjects in their due obedience' though aimed at Catholics, prescribed exile or death for all who refused to attend church or sought to persuade others to do so.

While early Separatism was centred around London, Cambridge appears to have continued to have been its intellectual locus. Henry Barrow (ca 1550–93) was an alumnus of Clare Hall while his friend John Greenwood (?–1593) had been at Corpus Christi. Greenwood was imprisoned after

1586 for worshipping in a conventicle while Barrow was arrested in 1588 while visiting Greenwood in the Clink. By 1590 it is estimated that there were fifty-two Separatists housed in various London prisons. Barrow and Greenwood were finally brought to trial and executed together on 6 April 1593. John Penry (ca 1563–93), also educated at Cambridge (and Oxford) followed them to the gallows on 29 May 1593. All three appear to have been victims of the desire by the bishops to make an example of those who refused to conform to the requirements of the Book of Common Prayer by linking religious nonconformity with political sedition.

Separatism came into its own in the early years of the seventeenth century. In 1606, John Smyth (ca 1570–1612), a fellow of Christ's College, Cambridge, gathered a church in Gainsborough, John Robinson (1575–1625), a Corpus Christi man, was involved in the gathering of a church at Scrooby and Richard Bernard (1568–1641), formerly of Christ's College, gathered a church at Worksop. By 1608 Smyth and Robinson emigrated to Amsterdam with their congregations. While there, Smyth began to propound Baptist ideas and Robinson eventually settled his congregation at Leyden. Robinson came to support 'occasional conformity' where the parish ministers were demonstrably godly and this became the pattern for the separatist cause. These principles were taken to North America in 1620 with the departure of the Pilgrim Fathers and this was the ecclesiology adopted by Thomas Helwys (ca 1575–ca 1616) who established the first Baptist church in Spitalfields, London, in 1612 and by Henry Jacob (1563–1624) who gathered the first church along Independent lines at Southwark in 1616. The separatists went into exile in Holland and New England in the 1630s, but came to prominence during the Civil Wars and the Commonwealth due to the support given to Independency by Oliver Cromwell. By that time the cause was being propounded by Thomas Goodwin, Philip Nye, Hugh Peter, Thomas Hooker, John Owen and others who gradually developed these ideas into a clearer form of church polity which would become Congregationalism.

Champlin Burrage, *Early English Dissenters* (Cambridge: Cambridge University Press, 1912); M. M. Knappen, *Tudor Puritanism: A Chapter in the History of Idealism* (Chicago, IL: University of Chicago Press, 1966).

RP

Shakespeare, John Howard (1857–1928)

A son of the manse, Shakespeare was born on 16 April 1857 in Yorkshire. Trained for the Baptist ministry at Regent's Park College, he also gained an

MA in philosophy at University College (1883). On completing his studies, at a remarkably early age he was called to the notable pastorate of St Mary's Baptist Church, Norwich, and soon gained a national reputation. On becoming secretary of the Baptist Union in 1898, exercising firm leadership, he immediately set about making the Union a strong, centralized organization directing the affairs of the denomination, bringing previously disparate agencies under its control. The birth of a new century provided the occasion to raise a large national fund, primarily for the purpose of building new churches, as well as an impressive London headquarters for the denomination, opened in 1903. A modern denomination, he believed, needed a system both to facilitate the movement of ministers between local churches, and to support those who were in financial need. A significant part of his scheme, as it was eventually implemented in 1916, involved the division of Britain into areas, each overseen by a superintendent minister who was answerable to the Union. Some saw this controversial step as a dangerous aping of the Episcopacy of the Established Church. Shakespeare played a major part in the formation of the Baptist World Alliance, organizing its inaugural congress in London in 1905 and serving as its European secretary.

A keen advocate of Free Church unity, he sought to increase the influence of the Free Churches in national life, and supported by fellow Baptist David Lloyd George he persuaded the War Office to allow new recruits to register as free churchmen, and to commission Free Church chaplains, creating the United Army and Navy Board to nominate Baptist and Congregational ministers to serve as chaplains.

In 1916 Shakespeare, as president of the National Free Church Council, proposed the formation of a United Free Church of England. At an early stage in that process, in 1919, the denominations agreed to come together into a federation, and the Federal Council of the Evangelical Free Churches was formed, with Shakespeare as its first moderator. His major ecumenical exploration *The Churches at the Cross Roads* (1918) advocated the possibility of the reunion of the Free Churches with the Established Church, but in this he was far ahead of his constituency.

Passionate and energetic, he frequently worked for fifteen hours a day. Often suffering from periodic bouts of nervous and physical exhaustion, during the Third Baptist World Alliance in Stockholm he was invited by Archbishop Söderblom to preach in Uppsala Cathedral. Most unfortunately the Bible fell from the pulpit which he interpreted as a sign that his life's work was over. He retired from the secretaryship of the Baptist Union on grounds of ill health in 1924 and died following a stroke on 12 March 1928 in London.

JHYB

Social Gospel

While the language of the 'Social Gospel' dates to the end of the nineteenth century, it was preceded by the older exploration of what Christian Socialism might entail, an exercise mainly undertaken by Anglicans. R. Tudur Jones identifies Benjamin Parsons, the Chartist-sympathizing minister of the Independent Church in Ebley in Gloucestershire, as one of the earliest pioneers of 'The Social Gospel', with his claim that 'the *true Gospel* includes temporal and spiritual salvation. The King of kings is the Father of all, and he expects that we shall show our spiritual pre-eminence by attending to the physical, social, intellectual and religious emancipation of all his creatures, but especially of his poor children' (*Congregationalism in England* (London: Independent Press, 1962), p. 210). Another programme which fed into a concern for a 'Social Gospel' was the emphasis on a 'Civic Gospel' or 'Municipal Socialism' in the government of the city of Birmingham, expounded and implemented by the less than orthodox George Dawson, but popularized by the orthodox and respected Congregationalist R. W. Dale. Such concerns were also promoted by theological developments which began to emphasize the Fatherhood of God and the Brotherhood of Man, more than election and substitutionary atonement. They were further endorsed by the revelation by Christian writers of the appalling conditions prevailing in the nation's slums, in an increasingly class-structured society, coupled as it was with the rise of organized labour. Thus, while the dictum that the Labour Party owed more to Methodism than Marx has enjoyed widespread consideration, Tudur Jones illustrated the links between Congregationalism and various workers' movements whether agricultural labourers or dockers or boot-makers, also telling the story of F. W. Crossley's attempt to show his solidarity with his Manchester workers by going himself to live in the slums.

Hugh Price Hughes, leading Methodist advocate of the new emphasis, argued against too individualistic a focus in the practice of evangelism, to the detriment of the promotion of 'the social welfare of the people'. Among Congregationalists, teaching on the Social Gospel became associated with modernist theology as espoused by R. J. Campbell, minister of the City Temple, London. In 1907 Campbell wrote both his provocative *The New Theology* and *Christianity and the Social Order*. For Campbell, the older theology's emphasis on the universal fall of man and the consequent need for blood-atonement was 'not only misleading but unethical'. With similar views, Campbell's friend and supporter, and most radical of Congregational social gospellers, Thomas Rhondda Williams, who occupied the chair of the Congregational Union in 1928–29, had earlier penned his volume on *The Social Gospel* in 1902. Thus there were a number of issues at stake – traditional soteriology, the accusation that Nonconformity had been concerned with the individual to the exclusion of the corporate and the nature of the church's mission in the contemporary world.

While Campbell's 'new theology' was widely condemned by senior Congregationalists, including A. M. Fairbairn and P. T. Forsyth, the wider agenda of 'The Social Gospel', even amid fears of secularizing the pulpit and the church, received much support from successive chairmen of the Congregational Union. Critics have been harsh: James Munson has suggested that the concern with reforming society resulted in confusion in the church's message where the 'secular world' was incorporated into the Christian message. His overall judgement was that while Nonconformity did produce its extreme social gospellers, for whom the new evangelism required a new theology which displaced orthodox views of the atonement, a larger number saw their concern for social change as an out-working of an orthodox evangelicalism which did not supplant the historic obligation to invite individuals to undergo conversion.

Whatever names were used, the influence was widespread. For example, one normally known for his commitment to evangelism and deepening spirituality, the Baptist pastor F. B. Meyer defended political action working 'for the betterment of the people', co-operating with the Congregationalist J. B. Paton in forming the Christian Union for Social Service in 1895 which established a farm colony for the unemployed. Two years earlier, another Baptist minister John Clifford had formed 'The Ministers' Union' to bring together ministers who felt that 'the Gospel has a Social message for today'. In 1894, with Clifford as its first president, this union became the Christian Socialist League and later the Christian Social Brotherhood. In 1889, the layman T. W. Bushill, director of a box-making company in Coventry, and deacon of the Queen's Road Baptist Church, an advocate of profit-sharing and industrial partnership, who was to give evidence to a Royal Commission on Labour in 1892, addressed the Baptist Union Assembly on 'The relationship between employer and employed in the light of the Social Gospel'. That John Clifford also urged the Baptist Union to pursue the 'social gospel' at the same assembly demonstrates early use of the term.

The fullest exposition of the Social Gospel is to be found in the work of a group of North American theologians, the most notable of whom was the Baptist Walter Rauschenbusch. Before becoming a professor of Church History, he had exercised a remarkable ministry in the slums of New York in the 'Hell's Kitchen' area, which persuaded him that the church had to find in the scriptures a message which spoke to the exploitation and destitution that the processes of industrialization had produced. In the Bible he found much relevant material in the denunciation by the prophets of the corruption of their day and in Jesus' own warnings about letting service of Mammon, which could be interpreted as living by the profit motive, motivate the way one lived one's life in the world, and in his teachings about the coming of the kingdom. Rauschenbusch wrote a number of significant books such as *Christianity and the Social Crisis* (1907), *Prayers of the Social Awakening* (1910), *Christianizing the Social Order* (1912) and *A Theology for the Social Gospel* (1917). Rauschenbusch's work was known among the Nonconformists of England and Wales, though it served more as a confirmation of their own thought rather than a catalyst for it.

A progressive concern to implement the Social Gospel seemed to fit well with evolutionary theory. In so doing it was clearly post-millennial in emphasis and therefore provoked attacks from dispensationalists and conventional pre-millennialist writers. Emerging neo-orthodox thinkers were also critical of a movement which tended to seek specialist knowledge of the social problem and philanthropic engagement in solving it rather than the exposition of the scriptures and the proclamation of salvation. While many of its insights continued to be propounded throughout the twentieth century, the Social Gospel, in effect, appeared to ebb by the outbreak of the Second World War.

JHYB

Solemn League and Covenant (1643)

During the first English Civil War (1642–46), parliamentary forces were faced with the possibility of Irish Catholics sending an army to fight on the Royalist side. They entered into a contract with Scottish Covenanters who agreed to send an army south providing that parliament support the reformation of religion in England and Ireland 'according to the word of God and the example of the best reformed churches'. In practice this meant opposition to Roman Catholicism and Episcopacy and the adoption of a Presbyterian system. The final document, the Solemn League and Covenant, made no explicit mention of Presbyterianism thus enabling the support of Independents, who formed a significant group in the parliamentary forces. It was approved by the Long Parliament and, with some minor amendments, by the Westminster Assembly. Subsequently, during the second Civil War (1648–49), the Scottish Covenanters entered into an 'engagement' with Charles I against the English Independents, but they were defeated at the Battle of Preston in 1648. The Covenanters persuaded Charles II, while he was in exile, to agree to the terms of the Solemn League and Covenant during the Treaty of Breda (1650). However, at the Restoration, the Sedition Act (1661) declared the Solemn League and Covenant to be unlawful while the Corporation Act (1661) and the Act of Uniformity (1662) required that public officials and ministers of religion respectively swear an oath repudiating it as unlawful. The text was ordered to be publically burned by the hangman.

RP

Soper, Donald Oliver (Baron Soper, 1903–98)

Born in London on 31 January 1931, Soper was raised in Methodism. His father was an accomplished public (open air) speaker while his mother took him to suffragette meetings from an early age. He was educated at St Catharine's College and trained for ministry at Wesley House, both in Cambridge. He began ministry in 1926 at Oakley Place Wesleyan Church off the Old Kent Road, though his liberalism brought him into conflict with the local Wesleyan authorities. From 1927 he engaged in public speaking, first at Tower Hill and, from 1942, from Speaker's Corner in Hyde Park where he gained a favourable reputation for his ability to respond to hecklers in a witty but informed manner. In 1929, he was awarded a PhD from the University of London for a thesis on Gallicanism and was also ordained at Plymouth, becoming minister at Islington Central Hall, Highbury. He was theologically and emotionally predisposed for ministry in such a context. In 1936 he moved to the West London Mission at Kingsway Hall and remained there for forty-two years. Since his undergraduate days he had been convinced that total war was an ever-present danger. He adopted the pacifist position, but was at times overly confident that it would prevail in a Europe rapidly succumbing to the Nazi menace. Nevertheless, he continued throughout his life to support the Campaign for Nuclear Disarmament and the Fellowship of Reconciliation. A convinced Socialist, he became a vocal supporter of the Labour Party, outspokenly condemning the policies of Margaret Thatcher as incompatible with Christian teaching and he regularly defended his position in radio and television broadcasts. Despite his radicalism, he did not reject contact with the establishment, preaching at Sandringham in 1971 and, after accepting a life peerage in 1965, he spoke on 230 occasions in the House of Lords.

Always a controversial figure, Soper's relationship to his denomination was, at best, strained. Despite being elected president of Conference in 1953, he was considered suspect for his theological liberalism, his sacramentalism and his willingness to accept episcopal reordination in order to move beyond the stalemate in church-unity discussions. Despite suffering debilitating arthritis, and finally being forced to use a wheelchair, he continued to exercise local ministry and to be a public figure into his nineties. He died on 22 December 1998.

RP

Spurgeon, Charles Haddon (1834–92)

Charles Haddon Spurgeon was born in Kelvedon, Essex, on 19 June 1834. Both his father and paternal grandfather were Independent ministers, but it was not until January 1850 that he experienced evangelical conversion. He came to Baptist convictions and was baptized as a believer on 3 May 1850. For the next three years he preached at Waterbeach Baptist Chapel near Cambridge and in numerous villages around Cambridge, causing a sensation and earning the epithet 'the boy preacher of the Fens'. In 1853 he was called to the pastorate of the historic New Park Street Chapel, Southwark. Spurgeon revived a failing cause, becoming so successful that he was described in the press as the nineteenth-century George Whitefield. In 1861 his congregation moved into the specially built Metropolitan Tabernacle in Newington Butts. Spurgeon would continue to fill the 5,500 seat auditorium for the rest of his ministry.

In 1856 he founded a College for training pastors and evangelists which had the avowed aims of encouraging 'spiritual fervour' and equipping students for practical ministry. His orphanage in Stockwell was opened in 1869 and helped give expression to a strong social conscience. These and other ventures were funded by an extensive network of supporters, which included both the members of his Tabernacle congregation and a much wider group who read his printed sermons. His church planting work, carried on with the help of successive generations of students, redrew the religious map of Britain, particularly in London. In 1887 he resigned from the Baptist Union as a protest against what he saw as the 'downgrading' of certain doctrines – among them the infallibility of scripture and penal substitutionary atonement – by some Baptist ministers. The strenuous efforts of the Union's leadership to get him to reconsider are indicative of his standing not only in Baptist life but in the wider Christian world. He died on 31 January 1892 in Mentone, France.

In theology, Spurgeon was an evangelical Calvinist who married a commitment to God's sovereignty in salvation with applied, evangelistic preaching which was couched in the language of the people. Covenant theology was important to him, and he was indebted to the Puritan works that were the staple of his personal library. But he was also shaped by factors and personalities that were neither Puritan nor Calvinistic. For example, nineteenth-century evangelicals such as J. Hudson Taylor and George Müller, who were committed to raising funds for Christian ventures through 'faith and prayer' significantly impacted Spurgeon. He was appreciative of aspects of High Church spirituality (while he dissociated himself vigorously from its accompanying ecclesiology), and he was also moulded by aspects of culture, with a popular Romanticism helping to shape, for example, his pre-millennial eschatology. In addition, he exhibited many of the characteristics of the 'Victorian self-made man' and he was an admirer of Samuel Smiles, author of the quintessential Victorian guide to self-improvement *Self Help* (1859). Spurgeon's ministry therefore exhibits a complex range of influences.

The effect suffering had on him was also important. From 1867 he began to experience severe pain from rheumatic gout, as well as struggling with kidney and liver problems which became increasingly acute. Allied to these physical difficulties was a tendency to depression. He developed a theology of suffering which emphasized the ways that 'sanctified affliction' could draw a person closer to Christ, the crucified God. Overall, felt 'communion with Christ' was extremely important to Spurgeon. It was one of the key-notes of his ministry and the pursuit of such communion was at the heart of his spirituality.

Charles H. Spurgeon, *Autobiography: Compiled from His Diary, Letters, and Records by His Wife and His Private Secretary*, 4 vols (London: Passmore and Alabaster, 1897–99); Peter J. Morden, *'Communion with Christ and His People': The Spirituality of C. H. Spurgeon (1834–92)* (Oxford: Regent's Park College, 2010).

PJM

Stead, William Thomas (1849–1912)

Born in Embleton, Northumberland, on 5 July 1849, the son of a Congregational minister, Stead was educated at Silcoates School, Wakefield, and after an apprenticeship in a merchant's finance office, he began a career in journalism becoming editor of the *Northern Echo* in April 1871 aged only twenty-one. His approach was innovative leading to increased sales. His was a radical agenda which included overt support for the Liberal Party as well as initiating campaigns for compulsory education at primary and secondary levels, universal suffrage (for women as well as men), the repeal of the Contagious Diseases Acts, a regulated working day, collectivism in industry, social purity in politics and Home Rule for Ireland. In July 1880 he became assistant editor of the *Pall Mall Gazette*, becoming editorial director in August 1883 in succession to John Morely. He was in the vanguard of the 'new journalism', advocating bold, cross-column headlines, illustrations, provocative leading articles and introducing interviews with prominent individuals. One of the more sensational stories he covered concerned the campaign against child prostitution during which he 'purchased' the thirteen-year-old Eliza Armstrong from her father in order to demonstrate the ease with which children could be procured. This led to his conviction for abduction and a three month spell in prison. In January 1890, he founded the *Review of Reviews* in which he advocated morality in public life, ultimately helping to prevent the adulterer Charles Dilke from resuming his political career. His attempts to establish a daily paper in 1904 failed and led him to the brink of bankruptcy, a situation avoided only through the intervention of well-heeled friends.

Alongside his pioneering journalistic tactics, Stead had a life-long interest in psychic phenomena, regularly attending sceances and practising automatic writing. He was committed to the peace movement and sought to establish processes of international arbitration in order to avoid the devastation of war which would result from the build up of arms. He had long predicted that he might die either by lynching or by drowning and in fact met his demise on board the Titanic, though there is evidence that he selflessly assisted others to safety. He revitalized, if not transformed, journalism by means of the personal interview and by the use of sensationalism in order to mould public opinion, believing that the media should influence the forming of political policy. While some of his judgements were, even at the time, considered to be misplaced, he was clearly motivated by his faith to pursue righteous causes and to seek the creation of a better world.

RP

Steele, Anne (1717–78)

Anne Steele was born in April/May 1717 into a prominent dissenting family in Broughton, Hampshire. Her father, William, was a successful timber merchant who also served the Baptist chapel at Broughton as a part-time minister. The family was relatively wealthy, with William able to pastor the congregation without remuneration while at the same time contributing significantly to its finances. Anne Steele experienced conversion and was baptized as a believer on 9 July 1732, joining her father's church.

Anne received some limited formal education at a boarding school in Trowbridge. She had a lifelong love of learning and her own writings reveal a wide breadth of reading; the writers she engaged with include Milton, Hervey and Pope. Her life was marked by suffering, although some popular biographies and web-based articles exaggerate this. The story of the death by drowning in 1737 of her supposed fiancé James Elcome has often been told, despite the absence of firm evidence that they were actually engaged. Although she did know him, his death is unlikely to have affected her to the extent that is often claimed. Nevertheless, her life was not easy, as she experienced prolonged bouts of physical illness and the death of well-loved family members. The context of suffering certainly shapes her published work. She died on 11 November 1778 and is buried in Broughton.

Her fame largely rests on her *Poems on Subjects Chiefly Devotional* (1760), which appeared under the pseudonym 'Theodosia', with a second, posthumous, edition in 1780. Many of these poems were sung as hymns which became popular on both sides of the Atlantic, with an important edition of her work published in Boston, Massachusetts, in 1808. Her writing lacked the confidence of Isaac Watts or Charles Wesley, being more introspective, although it certainly exhibits an emotional, evangelical piety. What sets her work apart is her ability to fuse this ardent piety with some beautifully expressed reflections on suffering, faith and hope, which are both intensely personal and appropriate for congregational singing. Her most famous hymn was 'Father of Mercies in Thy Word', but 'Dear Refuge of My Weary Soul', which was also well-known in both the eighteenth and the nineteenth centuries, is perhaps more typical:

> Dear refuge of my weary soul,
> On thee when sorrows rise:
> On thee when waves of trouble roll,
> My fainting hope relies.
>
> While hope revives, though prest with fears,
> And I can say, my God,
> Beneath thy feet I spread my cares,
> And pour my woes abroad.
>
> To thee, I tell its rising grief,
> For thou alone can heal;
> Thy word can bring a sweet relief
> For every pain I feel.

The lines take seriously both the reality of suffering and the confidence in God to bring relief. Her writings helped shape the spirituality of generations of Nonconformists more profoundly than many better-known theologians, and she is a significant figure in both Dissenting and women's history.

Anne Steele, *Poems on Subjects Chiefly Devotional, by Theodosia* (Bristol: Pine, 1780 [1760]); Cynthia Y. Aalders, *To Express the Ineffable: The Hymns and*

Spirituality of Anne Steele (Milton Keynes: Paternoster, 2008); J. R. Broome, *A Bruised Reed: The Life and Times of Anne Steele* (Trowbridge: Gospel Standard Trust, 2007).

PJM

Temperance

Drunkenness is abhorred in the Judaeo-Christian tradition but abstinence from beverage alcohol is restricted to groups taking particular vows of asceticism, as distinct from the Muslim tradition which bars alcohol altogether. Consequently Christian Europe and its colonists took the line that alcohol was to be enjoyed in moderation. In the late eighteenth century, the large-scale production and consumption of gin became a cause for concern. From 1750 onward the British parliament passed legislation to license alcohol consumption and tax spirits. There was some reduction in consumption but problems of drunkenness and alcoholism persisted. This was not an age in which society in general looked to government legislation to solve such problems but one where great store was set by voluntary activities. The first societies dedicated to the promotion of temperance are traced to the United States in the early years of the nineteenth century. By 1830 the beginnings of such societies, usually on a local basis, can be seen in England and Wales, Ireland and Scotland. These societies invited people to join on the basis that they would renounce 'ardent spirits' and restrict their consumption to beer and table wine. Even then there were clauses to allow for spirits to be drunk if health required it, since it was widely believed that they had medicinal properties. In Scotland the publisher William Collins supported the Scottish Temperance Society from 1830 and published *The Temperance Record*. In England such societies were most successful in the manufacturing towns of the north-west. They played into the economic and political aspirations of the rising mechanical class. By cutting alcohol consumption not only was money saved to support individual prosperity but wealth was denied to brewers and distillers.

The weakness of temperance societies was evident when habitual or addictive drinkers joined. Although not taking the fast path to drunkenness through spirits it was still possible to move well beyond temperance by consuming beer and wine. This moved temperance reformers in various places to conclude that total abstinence from alcohol was the best course. The best-remembered of these is Joseph Livesey, a printer of Preston, an autodidact and Free Trader. He, with six colleagues, signed a pledge on 1 September 1832 at a meeting in the Cockpit at Preston, to abstain from all intoxicating liquor, except as medicine. Livesey went on to become a campaigner for total abstinence. In 1834 he won the support of the Cadbury family in Birmingham. The temperance movement of these years was largely a working-class movement aimed at self-improvement. As a result, it became particularly strong in chapels and among Quakers, although it was resisted initially by the Wesleyan leadership. The Reform parliament of 1832 had three members who were total abstainers – John Silk Buckingham, Joseph Brotherton and George Wilson, all representing northern urban constituencies. Edward Baines of Leeds, a powerful Congregationalist, became an abstainer in 1837. From this time, 'temperance' usually was taken to mean total abstinence. John Bright became a supporter. It is well known that Thomas Cook started his travel business with a temperance excursion from Leicester. In Ireland the Capuchin Father Matthew recruited thousands of abstainers among the Catholic population. Temperance reform became part of a radical agenda, alongside the drive for popular suffrage, trade unions, Free Trade and education.

Friendly Societies were historically associated with public houses where they met. Temperance reformers established new ones, such as the Order of the Sons of Temperance, started in New York in 1842 but soon spreading in Britain. The Order of Rechabites (1835) was a British friendly society. The Independent Order of Good Templars (1876) was a campaigning organization but exhibited many of the characteristics of Free Masonry, with secret handshakes, passwords and a hierarchy of officers. Temperance hotels and cafés, a Temperance Building Society and insurance through the Temperance and General Providence Institution were all provided. Children were recruited to the movement, most notably in the Band of Hope, which had a branch at most chapels. By the end of the century the changing status of women was reflected in the British Women's Total Abstinence Union, part of a worldwide federation. Very few Nonconformist ministers admitted to being drinkers at that time and the clause in early pledges providing an exception for Communion wine had been made redundant by the almost universal use of non-alcoholic grape juices when they conducted the sacrament. The Church of England had a smaller proportion of abstainers, but there was a vigorous Church of England Temperance Society enjoying the support of evangelicals. The movement used its parliamentary influence to tighten the licensing laws, establish Sunday closing and regularly press for total prohibition. The United Kingdom Alliance was formed to join abstainers and moderate drinkers in pushing for more stringent restrictions on the drinks trade, with a long-term aim of suppression. Lloyd George's first parliamentary speech was against recompensing licensees for the forced closure of public houses.

The apogee of temperance influence was during the First World War (1914–18) when concern about the effect of drink on productivity brought about the strictest licensing the country was to experience. From this point, a long slow decline in the temperance movement followed, with much of the moral energy it had once enjoyed transferring to other causes, such as disarmament and world development. The churches distanced themselves from temperance, which seemed old-fashioned and a cultural barrier to recruitment. Politicians assumed that societal problems with alcohol were contained. It was only in the first decade of the twenty-first century that some of the consequences of increased consumption across the board became evident once again.

SCO

Theological Colleges

The Dissenting Academies had offered Higher Education on an essentially domestic scale. Those who attended them went on to a variety of professions and some were conformists. The creation of new universities in England from 1828 onwards provided broader opportunities for Nonconformists who could not conscientiously make the necessary declarations to graduate at Oxford or Cambridge. At the same time the evangelical academies of the late eighteenth century had developed to cater solely for ministerial candidates, funded by sponsors or endowments. The nineteenth century saw the development of theological colleges which were effectively seminaries for ministerial training. Smaller academies became uneconomic and closed or amalgamated. The colleges and the trusts which supported them became more overtly denominational.

Such development might be illustrated by the history of the academy founded at Ottery St Mary in 1752 with four students under John Lavington. This was an initiative of the Congregational Fund Board in London to create a consciously Trinitarian academy in the West Country to compete with what they regarded as the Arian one at Taunton. In the manner of academies as tutors changed the Ottery St Mary Academy moved to Bridport and then Taunton. In 1828, when support from the Congregational Fund Board failed for lack of funds the academy was rescued by subscription from local churches and moved to Exeter and became known as the Western Academy. In 1845, as support waned in Exeter the academy moved to Plymouth, where it was first termed Western College, though still with a handful of students at any one time. A succession of principals developed new courses, which offered students the opportunity to matriculate in the University of London, and numbers increased as Congregationalism flourished, so that a recognizably collegiate building in the Gothic style was opened in 1861. In 1901 it was decided to move the college to Bristol where, not only would local support be stronger, but the possibility of joint work between the Baptist College and the university beckoned. Western College flourished there until the decline of religious institutions after the Second World War and in 1968 amalgamated with the Northern Congregational College in Manchester, itself a union of various colleges from Lancashire and Yorkshire and Paton College, Nottingham. The trajectory from Ottery St Mary to Manchester could be replicated many times in the histories of other theological colleges.

The move from the tutor housing a few pupils to a college, with public rooms and a chapel, was dictated partly by economies of scale, partly by changing expectations in ministerial preparation and made possible by the enlarged constituency of Nonconformists. Denominational ambition extended to having a presence in Oxford and Cambridge once their degrees and academic posts were open to all. In Cambridge the Methodists opened Wesley House (1921), the Presbyterian Church of England's Westminster College moved from London (1897) and Cheshunt College, by then almost exclusively Congregational, moved there from Hertfordshire (1905). In Oxford the Baptists opened Regent's Park College, moved from London (1927), while the Congregationalists opened Mansfield College (1886), replacing the Spring Hill College in Birmingham and intended not only to prepare ministers but to offer a rallying ground for Nonconformists in the rest of the university. Overall the theological colleges represented a shift from the view that a minister had a good classical education with a bias towards philosophical theology and apologetics to what would now be termed 'vocational education'. In the nineteenth century this was particularly evident in cultivating skills in preaching. In the twentieth century there was a shift to pastoral skills and missiology.

SCO

Toleration

The emergence of Protestantism as the established religion of England was accompanied by the attempt to coerce conformity and uniformity of worship, supported with the full force of the law. The argument for toleration emerged only gradually within the Puritan movement, initially gaining support among Baptists but later being commonly adopted by those who found themselves outside the establishment as a result of the 1662 Act of Uniformity.

In the early seventeenth century, John Smyth and Thomas Helwys were pioneers of the view that religious faith should be disentangled from the organs of the state with both men denying the magistrate the right to coerce people in matters of religion or conscience. During the 1640s, the Independents were at the forefront of the debate. Initially they sought to ensure that their own convictions would be respected spurred by the realization that they were themselves excluded to some extent by the Presbyterian majority at the Westminster Assembly. But as they explored the biblical and theological reasons for religious toleration, so they gradually adopted a more general approach. Oliver Cromwell opposed attempts to enforce religious conformity and, during the Commonwealth, hopes were high that there could be a comprehensive settlement recognizing the validity of different forms of church order and, more importantly, that religious practices were matters of conscience and not something to be dictated by law. Independents generally adopted such a stance; Presbyterians generally were unwilling to extend toleration to those they perceived to be unorthodox including Quakers, Socinians and Roman Catholics, and they tended to seek intervention by the magistrate in order to quell heresy.

The Restoration in 1660 caused much concern, with Independents in particular believing that the Stuarts would not recognize the liberty of conscience. Charles II's Declaration of Breda, read to parliament on 1 May 1660, appeared to offer some comfort due to the apparent promise to defend 'liberty to tender consciences, and that no man shall be disqualified or called in question for differences of opinion in matters of religion'. The scholarly consensus is that Charles' words were sincere, partly because he sought greater freedom for Roman Catholics, but he was thwarted by an intransigent parliament dominated by 'High Church' Cavaliers who were intent on revenge for their suffering during and since the Civil Wars. Initial attempts at a comprehensive settlement failed. The Presbyterian party, rapidly losing the influence it had once possessed, hoped for limited Episcopacy modified by a Presbyterian order. However, the Fifth-Monarchist insurrection of January 1661, led by Thomas Venner, did not help the political situation and all religious conventicles, except those held in parochial churches and chapels, were forbidden on 10 January 1661. The Act of Uniformity (1662) and the so-called Clarendon Code of which it was a part, saw an end to any real hope of a comprehensive settlement. Nonconformity among clergy was outlawed and, between 1661 and 1688, those who sought to practice it suffered almost continuous persecution.

Nonconformist ministers gained popular respect for their courage during the plague of 1665 and the Great Fire of London in 1666, while the king continued to look for opportunities to liberate the Catholics. In February 1668, Charles II announced his hope that 'a better union and composure' in matters of religion could be sought. Parliament remained resolutely opposed and voted instead for a more rigorous application of the Act of Uniformity. In 1670 an act to Prevent and Suppress Seditious

Conventicles (the Second Conventicle Act) was passed. Alongside upholding the liturgy of the Church of England, the Act allowed a single Justice of the Peace to convict offenders without trial. Confession, testimony of two sworn witnesses, or 'notorious evidence and circumstance of the fact' were sufficient to convict. Those found guilty were fined 5s for the first offence and 10s for any subsequent offence. If they could not afford to pay, and had no goods to be confiscated, then the fine passed to wealthier members of the congregation. Preachers and owners of meeting houses were fined £20 for the first offence and £40 for any subsequent offence. Most tellingly, informants were offered one-third of the fines collected from each incident while magistrates who failed to comply were to be fined £100. The Act was declared to be permanent.

On 15 March 1672, Charles, recognizing that the religious question had not been settled by repression, issued a Declaration of Indulgence which suspended the penal acts against Nonconformists (and Catholic Recusants). The Declaration required that buildings and preachers belonging to Protestant Dissent be approved by relevant authorities while Catholics would be free to worship in their own homes. The Declaration was met with a mixed response. While it relaxed the persecution of Nonconformists, it did not repeal the penal code against them. Furthermore, it only granted them the liberty to exercise what they considered in any case to be their God-given right. It was also a demonstration of regal power and prerogative. A year later parliament decreed that only it could suspend penal laws and the declaration was withdrawn on 7 March 1673. Persecution re-emerged, aided by an unfortunate sequence of events including the rumours of a Jesuit plot to kill the king, ably propounded by the villainous Titus Oates, rumours of a rebellion perpetrated by Dissenters in 1682 and the Rye House plot of 1683 to assassinate the king while he returned from the races in Newmarket.

From his accession to the throne in February 1685, James II sought the repeal of the penal code for Catholics but he faced stiff opposition in parliament and in the Church of England, with many Nonconformists entering into alliance with Anglicans in order to prevent further concession to Catholics. James tried to unite the Protestant Dissenters with the Catholics and in a Declaration of Indulgence, published on 4 April 1687, the penal code was again suspended as were the consequences of the Test Acts of 1673 and 1678. As a result, some Nonconformists appeared in the corporations, with Sir John Shorter, member of the Independent church which met at Plumbers' Hall, becoming Lord Mayor of London. A second Declaration of Indulgence was made on 27 April 1688 but it was openly resisted by the clergy and the bishops. By this time, James' reign had become unsustainable. William of Orange set sail for England declaring 'to endeavour a good Agreement between the Church of England, and all Protestant Dissenters'. He landed in Torbay on 5 November and on 11 December James went into exile.

From at least the Restoration, Independents had sought toleration rather than inclusion in the Established Church while Presbyterians had hoped for a more comprehensive church settlement (which, in turn, would exclude intolerable sects). A Comprehension Bill was read in the House of Lords on 11 February 1689. However, before it could be made law, the earl of Nottingham introduced 'An Act for exempting their Majesties' Protestant Subjects, Dissenting from the Church of England, from the Penalties of Certain laws', commonly referred to as the 'Toleration Act', on 28 February. It received Royal Assent on 24 May.

The 'Toleration Act' enabled orthodox Dissenters and Quakers to pursue their own form of worship and ecclesiastical order, though it did not extend to Roman Catholics or to Unitarians. However, its effects were severely limited. Trinitarian Dissenters had to accept the doctrine of the Church of England as contained in the Thirty-Nine Articles (with the exception of the 34th *Of the Traditions of the Church*, the 35th *Of Homilies*, the 36th *Of Consecration of Bishops and Ministers* and the opening of the 20th on *The Authority of the Church*; Baptists were also exempted from the clauses of the 27th which referred to infant baptism), and the Oaths of Allegiance and Supremacy had to be sworn and assent given to the Declaration against Transubstantiation and other Roman doctrines. This had to occur before, and be registered by, a JP at the Quarter Sessions. Dissenting meeting places had to be certified by the local bishop, archdeacon or a JP.

The Act did not repeal the penal code; it merely suspended its effects. Dissenters generally welcomed the Act, but it reinforced their position as second class citizens because they remained exempt from the corporations and offices of public trust. From 1689, some (especially the Presbyterians) tried to get round this by occasional conformity. However, the dominance of the Tory party after 1702 resulted in further attempts to eradicate Nonconformity first with the passing of 'An Act for preserving the Protestant Religion', usually known as 'The Occasional Conformity Act', in December 1711. The Act defined the Protestant religion solely in terms congruent with the contents of the Book of Common Prayer and prescribed a fine not exceeding £40 for attending a conventicle after fulfilling the demands of the Corporation Act. The Schism Act followed, which sought to prevent anyone keeping school without a bishop's licence, and the bishops would only issue a licence to applicants who had received Communion in the Church of England during the previous twelve months. This was clearly an attack on the Dissenting Academies and its effect would have been substantial had Queen Anne not died on the very day it was to become law (1 August 1714). The Hanoverian monarchs proved to be unwilling to enforce these Acts and they went into abeyance before finally being repealed in 1718 (the Schism Act) and 1719 (the Occasional Conformity Act). Nevertheless, Nonconformists continued to suffer persecution by Tory mobs who opposed the succession of the Hanovers while a rightful Stuart heir remained alive. The Nonconformists allied themselves to the Whigs, now in the ascendant, who paid compensation for damaged property.

While a degree of toleration was granted in 1689, full equality before the law was only achieved over the course of the next 200 years. It was not until 1828 that the Test and Corporation Acts were repealed, thus allowing Nonconformists to take a role in public life, while the Catholic Relief Act (1829) had a similar effect on the Catholic population. However, other dissenting disabilities remained in force only to be gradually reformed over the course of the nineteenth century. The compulsory payment of Church Rates was not repealed until 1868, religious tests at Oxford and Cambridge were dissolved in 1871 but not extended to degrees and professorships in divinity, and only in 1880 were Nonconformists granted the legal right to bury their dead in a parish graveyard according to their own rites.

John Coffey, *Persecution and Toleration in Protestant England, 1558–1689* (London: Longman, 2000).

RP

Union of Welsh Independents

Although the Congregational cause in Wales dates back to 1639 when the first Welsh Independent church was established in Llanfaches, Monmouthshire, it was not until the nineteenth century that a strong inter-congregational structure was put in place. The network of churches which was formed during the Commonwealth, which survived the persecution of the Restoration and perpetuated the Congregational way during the long eighteenth century, exercised fraternal relations with one another though the ideal of each church's individual autonomy was jealously preserved. Following the Evangelical Revival Welsh Independency, along with the Baptist denomination and the Calvinistic Methodists, became a highly popular religious movement, and by the turn of the nineteenth century expediency dictated that a more practical means of inter-church cooperation was required. It was then that the Quarterly Meeting, local assemblies including laymen as well as ministers, became a focus for local denominational presence. The Quarterly Meeting was a voluntary gathering with no authority over the local church though a means of organizing Sunday Schools, social witness and evangelistic outreach.

By this time the Welsh Independents had become a thriving movement, its twenty-six churches in 1715 had risen to a hundred in 1775 and 684 by 1851. From having forty-six ordained ministers in 1800, there were as many as 319 in 1851 with an estimated membership of some 50,000. There were two opposing forces at work within the movement, one in favour of a more centralized polity, the so called systematized Independency, the other which rejected vehemently anything which threatened the sovereignty of the individual church fellowship. By 1872, when Wales itself was undergoing rapid social, industrial and cultural transformation, sufficient Independents – individual ministers and laymen, not churches – had overcome their separatist scruples to support the creation of a new denominational structure: the Union of Welsh Independents.

Its leading light was Dr John Thomas (1821–92), minister of the Tabernacle church, Great Crosshall Street, Liverpool, and the Welsh Congregationalists' most skilful ecclesiastical politician. Formerly a Calvinistic Methodist, he was held in rank suspicion by a powerful band of more traditionalist Independents, led by Michael D. Jones (1822–98), principal of the Independent Bala College. Notwithstanding the tensions between the opposing parties, by the end of the Victorian era the Union had secured its position as the body through which Welsh Congregationalism expressed its corporate identity.

The denomination's statistical high point was 1905, the year of the Welsh religious revival, when membership reached 175,000. The liberalism championed by Thomas Rees (1869–1926), John Morgan Jones (1873–1946) and others which had become the doctrinal norm during the early decades of the twentieth century was challenged by a younger generation of ministers much influenced by J. D. Vernon Lewis (1879–1970), professor of doctrine at the Brecon College, and more especially by J. E. Daniel (1902–62) who held the corresponding chair at the Bala-Bangor College in north Wales. Whereas the Union has been sufficiently wide to accommodate a variety of doctrinal views, its churchmanship has remained that of 'systematized Independency' at best. Even during the twenty-first century, Welsh Congregationalists remain wary of Presbyterianism in any form.

DDM

Unitarianism

The word Unitarian was first applied to those who were called 'deniers of the Trinity' in Britain in the 1670s. Disputes about the Trinitarian formula arose as soon it became a creed in the early centuries of the Church. However it was the upheaval created by the Reformation which made Unitarian thinking into a movement in Italy, Poland and Transylvania (modern Romania and Hungary). It went under the name of Socinianism, after one of its early leaders, Faustus Socinus (1539–1604), a sixteenth-century Italian. Those who maintained a non-Trinitarian stand suffered persecution and even death, like Michael Servetus, a Spanish doctor, burned at the stake at Geneva in 1553. Socinianism, after Socinus' death, was suppressed as part of the Counter Reformation but the influential *Racovian Catechism* (1605) was translated into English and printed secretly, mainly in Holland, and distributed. This work was officially burned in Britain on more than one occasion before 1660.

The Socinian approach to looking at God spread in the Church of England in the seventeenth century, mainly out of Oxford. John Biddle (1615–62), a Gloucester schoolmaster often called the father of English Unitarianism, wrote and spoke extensively on his views and died in prison. Samuel Clarke (1675–1729), rector of St James' Piccadilly, came under severe censure when his book *The Scripture Doctrine of the Trinity* appeared in 1712 in which he argued that supreme honour should be given only to God, the Father.

For the rest of the eighteenth century Unitarianism spread, not only in the Church of England but most significantly among the Dissenters, mainly the English Presbyterians who had hitherto been orthodox in theology. Many of their churches, among the oldest in Dissent, adopted Unitarian views in the second half of the century, to be followed by the old General Baptists, their Assembly having been formed in 1653. Not that it was called Unitarianism, as this belief was specifically proscribed by the 'Toleration Act' of 1689; Unitarianism did not become legal until 1813. The term applied to erstwhile Unitarians was Rational Dissenters, though evangelicals still incorrectly used the term Socinian as an insult. Its polity has always been congregational.

Joseph Priestley (1733–1804), the scientist and discoverer of oxygen, was the organizer of modern Unitarianism although not before Theophilus Lindsey (1723–1808), vicar of Catterick, Yorkshire, left the Church of England to found the first avowed Unitarian congregation in Essex Street, near the Strand in London, in 1774. The site remains to this day the headquarters of Unitarianism in Britain. It is from this time that modern Unitarianism can be said to date. A national association of churches was formed in 1825 (British and Foreign Unitarian Association), though it was not until 1928 that a more formal denominational organization was created (General Assembly of Unitarian and Free Christian Churches).

Unitarianism has always been a reform movement both in religion and in politics. Opposition to the state church and support for the principles of the French Revolution did not make its adherents popular in Britain. These affirmations led to renewed persecution in the 1790s which disappeared with the arrival of the nineteenth century, the age of confidence and influence for Unitarianism with its strong belief in individual liberty.

In Britain, James Martineau (1805–1900) revolutionized the traditional Unitarian reliance on citation of biblical texts, leading it towards a wider faith-based German biblical criticism, and the application of reason and the enlightened conscience. Unitarians of all shades of opinion were much influenced by their American co-religionist William Ellery Channing (1780–1842). The existence of Unitarian opinion was still attacked by other Nonconformists and the Church. Long-running legal disputes centred on the illegality of Unitarian belief before 1813 nearly deprived Unitarians of most of their older chapels. However the government came to their aid and passed the Dissenters' Chapels Act of 1844 which secured the right of Unitarians to ownership of their buildings and charities.

Unitarianism was possibly the only church organization within the nineteenth-century Christian fold not blown off course by the Darwinian revolution; indeed the movement embraced the new thought, as it has, in the main, subsequent scientific advances as well as aspects of rationalist thought. It has consistently placed emphasis on the intellect and reason rather than emotion.

AR

United Reformed Church

The United Reformed Church was formed in 1972 from a union of the Presbyterian Church of England and 74 per cent of the congregations of the Congregational Church in England and Wales (which accounted for 82 per cent of its membership). The united church was from its inception committed to the quest for visible unity. Two further unions have marked its history – in 1981 with the Re-formed Association of the Churches of Christ and in 2000 with the Congregational Union of Scotland. As institutional unity waned in popularity during the later decades of the twentieth century, the church expressed its ecumenical commitment through energetic commitment to local unions – in 2011 the United Reformed Church was a partner in 55 per cent of Local Ecumenical Partnerships in England (nearly a third of its total congregations) and similar partnerships are also evident in Wales and Scotland.

The church unites three different Reformed traditions – Presbyterianism, Congregationalism and the 'restorationism' of what became the Disciples movement in America. It plays an active part in the World Communion of Reformed Churches and other appropriate world confessional bodies. Its Reformed understanding can be seen in its conciliar government (thirteen Synods and a biennial General Assembly), the ordering of its worship which emphasizes the preaching of the Word and the administration of the sacraments, the parity of its ministers and the ministry of elders.

The traditions within the United Reformed Church are diverse. Classical Presbyterianism looks back to Calvin's Geneva and Zwingli's Zurich for its theological compass, whereas Congregationalism was far more eclectic, blending Calvinism with the free leading of the Spirit, and open to the ideas of the radical left-wing of the Reformation such as Conrad Grebel and the Swiss Brethren. The restorationism of Thomas Campbell (1763–1854) and his son Alexander Campbell (1788–1866) was an attempt to 'restore' the primitive church of the New Testament among their contemporaries – in itself an echo of the work of the sixteenth-century Reformers. Balancing those traditions has resulted in the United Reformed Church in the development of a polity which seeks to hold seemingly irreconcilable differences in creative tension, for example, both believer's and paedo-baptism (although not re-baptism) are practised and honoured in the belief that such creative tolerance will be necessary in any future united church.

In 2012 the United Reformed Church had 1,529 congregations in England, Scotland and Wales and a membership of 63,380.

David Cornick, *Under God's Good Hand* (London: The United Reformed Church, 1998).

DGC

Watts, Isaac (1674–1748)

Isaac Watts was an Independent minister, hymn writer and scholar. He is remembered as the pre-eminent hymn writer of the early eighteenth century, forging a bridge between the forms of the metrical psalm and the religious poem to create the hymn. Hymns were written to be sung and understood, so metrical structure and simple, elegant language were essential. It was, in effect, a new art form. Watts published four main collections: *Horae Lyricae* (1706/9), *Hymns and Spiritual Songs* (1707/9), *Divine Songs in Easy Language for the use of Children* (1715) and *Psalms of David Imitated in the New Testament* (1719). 'Give to our God immortal praise', 'Jesus shall reign where'er the sun', 'This is the day the Lord has made', 'Our God our help in ages past', and the incomparable 'When I survey the wondrous cross' are just part of his heritage. His intent was to modernize the psalms, so Jesus replaced Jehovah and Israel became Great Britain, and the experience of Christians and reflection on the faith became legitimate subject matter.

Watts was secure in his dissent. His father had been imprisoned for his Nonconformity, but as Isaac reached maturity the political tone of the country had changed from persecution to toleration. When faced with the choice of education in the Anglican university system or the Dissenting Academy Watts did not hesitate, and chose Thomas Rowe's Academy in the Dissenting heartland of Stoke Newington. After leaving he spent time as a personal tutor to the son of Sir John Hartopp until in 1699 he accepted the post of assistant to the unpopular Isaac Chauncey at Mark Lane Chapel, London. This was a significant congregation. John Owen had ministered there, and its members included significant descendants of the Cromwellian regime. Watts succeeded Chauncey in 1702.

He was never in good health, and suffered a breakdown during 1712–16. In 1712 Sir Thomas Abney and his family took Watts into their household. He acted as tutor to their children, but mostly devoted himself to writing, and to the affairs of Independency; for example, he attended meetings of the Congregational Fund Board with punctilious regularity.

His interests were polymathic. He wrote significant works about educational method, a textbook on logic which was widely used, catechisms for children, devotional treatises and works of theology and philosophy. He believed that reason and faith were complementary ways of exploring the wonder of God and the gospel of Jesus Christ. 'Nature with open volume stands / To spread her Maker's power abroad', yet not even 'the whole realm of Nature' could be a sufficient offering for the 'love so amazing, so divine' seen on the cross.

Harry Escott, *Isaac Watts, Hymnographer: A Study of the Beginning, Development, and Philosophy of the English Hymn* (London: Independent Press, 1962).

DGC

Waugh, Benjamin (1839–1908)

Eldest son of James, a saddler, and his wife Mary, Benjamin was born on 20 February 1839 in Settle, North Yorkshire. He attended Airedale College in Bradford before ministering in Newbury (1865–66), then in Greenwich (1865–85) and New Southgate (1885–87). While working in the slums, he was appalled at the results of the Poor Law and the workhouse systems, especially the effects they had on children. He advocated a separate system of justice to deal with juvenile crime in *The Gaol Cradle, Who Rocks It* (1873) and served on the London School Board (1870–76). Mirroring an initiative which had been established in Liverpool, he founded the London Society for the Prevention of Cruelty to Children in 1884, and in turn this became the National Society for the Prevention of Cruelty to Children on 14 May 1889. Waugh was its first director; Queen Victoria its first patron. He played a significant role in promoting the Anti-Cruelty Act (1889) which enshrined in law a child's right to be fed and clothed and enabled the removal of children from abusive parents. He died at Wescliff-on-Sea on 11 March 1908.

RP

Weatherhead, Leslie Dixon (1893–1976)

Born in Harlesdon, London, on 14 October 1893, and trained for the Methodist ministry at Richmond College, Weatherhead became one of the most popular, but controversial, exponents of theological liberalism in the twentieth century. He ministered at Farnham, Surrey, in 1915–16 before serving in various posts in India (1916–22), Oxford Road, Manchester (1922–25), and Brunswick, Leeds (1925–36). He was then called to the Congregational City Temple and remained there until his retirement in 1960. Remarkably, he was elected president of the Methodist Conference in 1955–56 despite not then ministering in a Methodist circuit, a tribute to the fact that he was both a celebrated preacher and public figure due to his radio broadcasts and the popularity of his published work.

His approach was eclectic and he drew on non-Christian faiths, psychology and psychotherapy as well as spiritualism as offering means of ministering in the twentieth century. He established the City Temple Psychology Clinic where doctors, ministers and psychotherapists worked side-by-side in order to offer holistic healing to members of the congregation and to the wider public. He was awarded a PhD from the University of London for his book *Psychology, Religion and Healing* (1951). He frequently attended séances during one of which he claimed to have been visited by John Wesley. He was a consummate communicator, but his sermons were not theological. He eschewed traditional ideas about the atonement, the bodily resurrection of Christ and the Virgin Birth, claiming that creeds and confessions were no more than 'museum specimens'. As time went on, he became a firm advocate of the doctrine of reincarnation and tended to treat his preaching ministry as an exercise in psychotherapy. He was a prolific author, but there is a dispute as to whether he has had a lasting influence. Some claim that his books are largely ignored, while others suggest that his approach had a significant impact on the ministry of the traditional, liberal Free Churches.

After the City Temple was destroyed by enemy bombs during the Second World War, Weatherhead kept its congregation together in various locations for seventeen years, being the primary fund-raiser to rebuild the chapel. In October 1958 the church was re-opened in the presence of Queen Elizabeth the Queen Mother, in part the result of a large donation from J. D. Rockefeller, secured personally by Weatherhead while he was on a preaching tour of the United States. In January 1959, he was appointed CBE, while he received honorary doctorates from Scottish and American universities.

He retired to Bexhill-on-Sea, where he died on 5 January 1976.

Kingsley Weatherhead, *Leslie Weatherhead: A Personal Portrait* (London: Hodder & Stoughton, 1975).

RP

Wesley, Charles (1707–88)

Despite being overshadowed by his older brother John, Charles Wesley was very much his own man. Following education at Westminster School, he entered Christ Church, Oxford, and was a founder member of the Holy Club in 1727. Ordained an Anglican clergyman in 1735, following an abortive attempt at the life of a missionary in Georgia in 1736, Charles experienced an evangelical conversion shortly after his brother's famous Aldersgate experience in May 1738. Charles took a full role in the early revival, but largely remained in the shadow of this brother. His main contribution to the Methodist movement in its early years was his prolific hymn writing. In 1743 he published *Hymns and Sacred Poems*, and over the course of his life published the words of over six thousand of them in various collections. They were important in encapsulating the core doctrines and emphases of Methodism in an easily accessible and memorable idiom. Many of his compositions have been widely used well beyond Methodism.

Charles' marriage to Sarah Gwynne in 1749 marked an important transitional point in his career. After marriage he settled in Bristol, and domestic responsibilities meant that he became increasingly reluctant to engage in itinerant ministry. After 1756 he confined himself to Bristol and London. This put a measure of strain on his relationship with his brother, but it was his opposition to John's increasing conviction that the Methodists needed to ordain their own ministers and thereby split from the Church of England that damaged their relationship irrevocably. Charles remained deeply loyal to the Church professing towards the end of his life: 'I have lived and I die, a member of the Church of England.'

Kenneth C. G. Newport and Ted A. Campbell (eds), *Charles Wesley: Life, Literature and Legacy* (London: Epworth, 2007); Gareth Lloyd, *Charles Wesley and the Struggle for Methodist Identity* (Oxford: Oxford University Press, 2007).

DCJ

Wesley, John (1703–91)

The son of the rector of Epworth in Lincolnshire, the strongest influence on Wesley's formative years was undoubtedly his mother Susanna. Her commitment to his education resulted in a scholarship at Charterhouse and then a place at Christ Church, Oxford, in 1720. The first evidence of serious religious concern occurred in 1725 when, after reading William Law, Wesley resolved to strive after Christian perfection. He was ordained deacon in the same year, but after a period as his father's curate he returned to Oxford as a tutor in 1729. There he threw in his lot with the Holy Club, an attempt at capturing the spirit of primitive Christianity. In 1735, Wesley sailed for the newly founded colony of Georgia where he hoped to establish a Christian society along primitive lines in virgin territory. Perhaps the most significant result from his missionary endeavours was his encounters with the Moravians; he returned from Georgia doubting whether he had ever been a Christian at all. Relief eventually came in an evangelical conversion at Aldersgate Street, London, in May 1738. The Evangelical Revival had already been underway for some time, and Wesley encouraged by the example of George Whitefield, soon took the step of preaching in the open air for the first time.

The revival that was initially focused on the Moravian-dominated Fetter Lane society did not remain unified for long. Wesley first divided from the Moravians and then still more dramatically from George Whitefield and his Calvinists in 1741. He had already established his own headquarters at the Foundry in London and quickly fanned out from there, soon also securing footholds in Wales, Cornwall and the north-east of England. Ireland and Scotland were both added to his sphere of operations shortly afterwards. In all of these localities he either established societies or took control of ones established by others. They were divided into bands and class meetings, groups of them were later organized into circuits, and the whole came under the control of the Methodist Conference in 1744. It was a structure which Wesley devoted much of the rest of his life to making work smoothly.

Inevitably such a tightly regulated Methodist movement sat awkwardly within the larger structure of the Church of England. Wesley fought a constant rear guard action against those who wished to separate from the Established Church; his brother Charles withdrew from his itinerant responsibilities and urged that all Methodist preachers submit to the authority of their local Anglican incumbents. Controversy was endemic to the life of Methodism. A major secession took place in the early 1760s surrounding the claim of some to Christian perfection, and the whole movement was convulsed by further disagreement over Calvinism between 1770 and 1775.

In the last decade of Wesley's life the accelerating pace of population and urban growth in Britain fed the rapid growth of Methodism. Preoccupied with issues relating to his posthumous legacy, Wesley eventually ordained Thomas Coke as superintendent of Methodism in America as well as two preachers to assist him in 1784. The ordination of three further preachers in 1788 who stayed in England effectively signalled the end of the Methodists' membership of the Church of England.

Theologically, Wesley was an eclectic mix. He drew from a wide range of traditions, Anglican, Pietist, Puritan, the Catholic mystics and some Patristic writers. While he professed to focus on the central doctrines of original sin, justification by faith and holiness, his interpretation of them was often idiosyncratic. His lifelong fascination with the possibility of Christian Perfection was indicative of this. He had an uncanny knack of backing the right positions on many of the key issues of the day. An early supporter of the American revolutionaries, he was also a deeply committed and vocal opponent of slavery.

Wesley was enormously prolific as an author. He kept a journal from 1725 and wrote thousands of letters. In addition, his *Christian Library* included abridged copies of classic Christian literature; although drawn from an eclectic range of authors and Christian traditions, Wesley's abridgements could sometimes have little resemblance to the originals. As well as sermons, he also published a volume of medical remedies *Primitive Physic* (1761) and from 1778 edited the *Arminian Magazine*.

Following his death in 1791, the structures that Wesley had put in place functioned well without his guidance, and Methodism continued to grow into the nineteenth century. His greatest legacy, of course, remained the Methodist movement and then the denomination that had been created in his image.

Henry D. Rack, *Reasonable Enthusiast: John Wesley and the Rise of Methodism* (London: Epworth Press, 1989); Kenneth J. Collins, *The Theology of John Wesley: Holy Love and the Shape of Grace* (Nashville, TN: Abingdon, 2007).

DCJ

Westminster Assembly and Confession

The Westminster Assembly was, in effect, a think-tank established by parliament in 1643 to provide resources to re-shape the Church of England after the beginning of the Civil War. It was composed of 151 members, made up of 121 divines and thirty lay assessors. The divines represented a range of opinion from moderate Episcopalian to Independent although the main bulk were Presbyterian. Bishops Ralph Brownrigg of Exeter and James Ussher of

Armagh were among the Episocopalians, the Presbyterians included Edward Reynolds, Edmund Calamy and Anthony Tuckney, and the Independents Thomas Goodwin and Philip Nye. The lay Assessors included such significant politicians as John Pye and Bulstrode Whitlock, and the Scottish commissioners included Robert Baillie and Samuel Rutherford. In practice, the Episcopalians rarely attended, and the small group of Independents (who had Cromwell's ear) continually campaigned against the adoption of Presbyterianism.

The Assembly met at Westminster Abbey some 1,163 times between 1643 and 1649, and continued meeting until 1653. It led the attack on Episcopacy, church courts, the Prayer Book and the liturgical year, yet, oddly, in political terms was fairly ineffective. Its true influence lay in the production of documents which were to be determinative of Presbyterianism – the Directory for Public Worship which was a guide to ministers on how to replace the liturgy of the Prayer Book with a liturgy based on extempore prayer, the *Westminster Confession* and the Shorter and Longer *Catechisms*.

The *Westminster Confession*, drafted largely by Anthony Tuckney, the vicar of Boston, was based on the Articles of Religion which Ussher had drafted for the Irish church in 1615. It was the quintessence of orthodox Reformed and Puritan thought. It became the principal subordinate standard of the Church of Scotland and has been immensely influential within the English-speaking Reformed world. Puritan influence can be seen in its espousal of covenant theology. It also exhibits the contemporary European Reformed orthodoxy of Dort (several members of the Assembly had been at Dort in 1619) – total depravity, unconditional election, limited atonement, irresistible grace and the perseverance of the saints. It also bears witness to the supreme authority of scripture, the real presence of Christ in the sacraments and the catholicity of the church.

During the eighteenth and nineteenth centuries many Reformed churches began to modify their attitude to the *Westminster Confession*, in relation first to its teachings about the relationship between the church and the civil magistrate, but then in relation to its teaching about limited atonement.

Chad Van Dixhoorn, *The Minutes and Papers of the Westminster Assembly 1643–1653* (Oxford: Oxford University Press, 2012).

DGC

Whitefield, George (1714–70)

Raised at the Bell Inn in Gloucester, Whitefield entered Pembroke College, Oxford, as a servitor in 1732. He soon became a member of the Holy Club, but its strict regimen of devotional duties brought him to the edge of a nervous breakdown. He experienced an evangelical conversion in 1735, and was ordained at Gloucester cathedral in 1736, before the usual age. The 'boy parson' became an instant sensation attracting large crowds to hear him preach, especially in London, and by 1737 he had published his first sermon *The Nature and Necessity of Our New Birth in Christ Jesus*. Whitefield's theatrical style of preaching, and his gift for self-promotion fed his celebrity status – he published regular updates of his journal, and a group of secretaries flooded the press with positive proof about his activities. After almost a year in the new American colony of Georgia in 1738, Whitefield took the momentous step of preaching in the open air for the first time at Kingswood in Bristol. By this point he had made the acquaintance of the Welsh revivalist Howell Harris and John Wesley had joined the infant revival movement, having at last experienced his own evangelical conversion.

Along an axis from London to Bristol and south Wales, Whitefield preached incessantly during 1739, up to nine times a week, but his commitment to the American colonies meant that the leadership of the revival fell increasingly on John Wesley. A virulent opponent of Calvinism, Wesley purged the Bristol societies of Calvinists during Whitefield's absence through much of 1740. He then audaciously began a pamphlet war against Calvinism and by extension Whitefield himself. The controversy split the English revival in two. When Whitefield returned in 1741, he found many of his former followers no longer ready to listen to him. Wesley, now at the head of the revival, opened his own headquarters and began to put in place a structure that facilitated the growth and spread of a distinctly Wesleyan brand of Methodism. Whitefield from his headquarters at the Tabernacle in Moorfields tried to rebuild his work with the assistance of John Cennick and Howell Harris; despite his best efforts to put a system of pastoral care and control in place which saw the amalgamation of English and Welsh Calvinistic Methodism under one administrative structure, the more fissiparous English Calvinistic Methodists proved resistant to such regulation.

Whitefield was probably temperamentally unsuited to the day-to-day running of the Methodist movement which he had created. He preferred the life of a roving evangelist. In 1741 he made his first trip to Scotland, and the following year helped fan the flames of revival at Kilsyth and Cambuslang outside Glasgow. Having preached along the whole length of the eastern seaboard of America during 1740, the draw of the colonies remained strong, and Whitefield spent a further four years there from 1744. His orphanage at Bethesda in Georgia was his first commitment, and his ministry became increasingly bound up with raising funds for its support. Questions about its financial management dogged Whitefield throughout his life, and his use of slave labour on its adjoining plantation ensured that he became one of the strongest evangelical advocates of the institution of slavery.

In 1749 the Countess of Huntingdon appointed Whitefield one of her chaplains, but her attempts to win over members of the aristocracy to the evangelical cause bore little tangible fruit. For the remainder of his life, Whitefield continued to split his time roughly equally between England and the American colonies, thus leaving English Calvinistic Methodism with no effective leadership. Many found their way into the welcoming arms of Dissent, or gravitated toward the Countess of Huntingdon for guidance. In his final years Whitefield became more of an evangelical figurehead, respected for his charismatic preaching, but unable to head-up a Calvinistic version of Methodism capable of challenging the Wesleyan movement.

Whitefield's posthumous reputation has been mixed. He was certainly a divisive figure during his lifetime, and has remained so ever since. He has a claim to being the father of the evangelical movement; his preaching of the new birth and commitment to itinerant evangelism were to become hallmarks of evangelicalism. For some he remains the model Calvinistic evangelist. For others Whitefield is seen as the original revivalist who through his combination of theatrical preaching and self-publicity managed to create and then extend a revival movement across two continents. For a time in the eighteenth century he was certainly the most famous and sensational preacher in the whole British Atlantic community.

Harry S. Stout, *The Divine Dramatist: George Whitefield and the Rise of Modern Evangelicalism* (Grand Rapids, MN: Eerdmans, 1991); Frank Lambert, *'Pedlar in Divinity': George Whitefield and the Trans-Atlantic Revivals* (Princeton, NJ: Princeton University Press, 1994).

DCJ

Williams, Daniel (ca 1643–1716)

Williams is chiefly remembered today for the library which bears his name. Dr Williams's Library in Gordon Square is the successor institution to that opened in Red Cross Street in 1729 by the trustees of his will. Over the years it has become the chief repository of Nonconformist books and archives. Williams was born in Wrexham. He became a Nonconformist preacher in his late teens and from 1664 took up ministry in Ireland, where he acquired experience of the country which was an asset in his subsequent career. His ministry was among both Presbyterians and Independents. He married a rich widow, Elizabeth Juxon. The couple moved to London in 1687, during the political crisis, with an intention of returning, which was never fulfilled.

In London he became a friend of leading Nonconformists, such as John Howe and Richard Baxter. After Baxter's death Williams succeeded him as Pinners' Hall Lecturer in 1691. Although the leaders of Presbyterians and Independents pursued a policy of co-operation and union at this time a doctrinal dispute centred on antinomianism drove them apart. Williams was one of the protagonists in a pamphlet war which led to the Presbyterians withdrawing from Pinners' Hall to set up their own lectureship at Salters' Hall in 1694. Williams was by now one of the Nonconformist leaders consulted by the king and leading politicians. His wife died in 1698 and, in 1701, he married Jane Barkstead, another rich widow. Williams led the deputation of Nonconformists to greet Queen Anne on her accession. This deputation of Baptists, Independents and Presbyterians was the historical origin of the Dissenting Deputies, who continued to make joint representations to the crown until the present day. Although Williams was an active lobbyist, Nonconformists found their liberties curtailed during the reign of Queen Anne and Williams only just lived into the reign of George I when matters began to improve once more. He was awarded honorary doctorates at Edinburgh and Glasgow in 1709. Williams husbanded his fortune with care and left a long and complicated will which made provision for his relatives (he had no children), and made a range of charitable provisions, of which the library was one. The trustees of his will had to secure further support to bring the library into being in the way he wished. Williams' own books now represent a fraction of the total holding, to which various collections have been added over the centuries, most recently the Congregational Library and that of New College, London. Unitarianism is well-represented and Dr Williams's Library is partner with Queen Mary, University of London, in the Centre for Dissenting Studies.

SCO

Williams, Edward (1750–1813)

Though brought up in the Vale of Clwyd by staunchly Anglican parents, Williams was impressed by the preaching of the Methodist revivalist Daniel Rowland of Llangeitho. Convinced from an early age of the importance of the intellect, he entered the Church of England with a view to studying at Oxford University, only to abandon this plan when he encountered a group of Anglican ordinands in a debauched state. He finally settled on Congregationalism and, in 1771, he entered the academy at Abergavenny with a view to becoming a Congregational minister. In 1775 he was ordained at Ross on Wye and then, in 1777, he proceeded to Oswestry where he began to teach students under the patronage of Lady Glenorchy. Following an approach to become principal of the Abergavenny Academy, he encouraged its relocation to Oswestry in 1782 and combined teaching and pastoral work in the town until he moved to Carrs Lane Church in Birmingham in 1791. In 1795 he became principal of Rotherham Academy and pastor to the church at Masborough. He remained there until his death in 1813.

Williams combined the intellectual seriousness and rigour of the Puritans with the evangelistic zeal of the Methodists. He was involved in the establishment of the London Missionary Society in 1795 and, through evangelistic work, helped to establish the Sunday School movement in north Wales. He was a prolific author and his defence of infant baptism, *Antipaedobaptism Examined* (1789) earned him the DD of Edinburgh University. His primary theological contribution was to help modify the prevailing Calvinism of Old Dissent with its emphasis on election, limited atonement and God's active reprobation of the impenitent. He argued that salvation as achieved in Jesus Christ was universal in scope and thus had to be proclaimed to all people. At the same time, salvation remained a gift of God's grace and mercy and not subject to human response. Thus human beings are the passive recipients of divine benefits and made holy only by God's merciful grace. But as human beings are also free moral agents, who, without God's predestination, opt to sin, they are wholly responsible for their reprobation.

Williams' theological system attempted to maintain the sovereignty of God and demonstrate the significance of a proclamation of the good news to all. He is often attributed with having done for Congregationalists what Andrew Fuller had done for the Baptists. He edited works by John Owen, Philip Doddridge, Isaac Watts and Jonathan Edwards while his two major works, where he expounded his moderate Calvinism, were *An Essay in the Equity of Divine Government and the Sovereignty of Divine Grace* (1809) and *A Defence of Modern Calvinism* (1811).

W. T. Owen, *Edward Williams, DD, 1750–1813: His Life, Thought and Influence* (Cardiff: University of Wales Press, 1963).

RP

Wilson, Joshua (1795–1874)

Son of the industrialist millionaire Thomas Wilson and inheritor of his father's fortune, Joshua was born in London on 27 October 1795. He studied law at the Inner Temple and qualified as a barrister, though he never practised. A relatively accomplished historian of early Dissent, he continued his father's philanthropic work through support of New College, London, and the founding of the Congregational Library in Bloomfield Street, to which he donated 4,000. By 1866, the library had outgrown its premises and the building had to be vacated due to the expansion of the Metropolitan Railway. The books were placed in store. He was a key figure in the bi-centenial commemoration of the Great Ejectment in 1862, advocating and helping to finance the scheme to see fifty new Congregational churches opened by 24 August 1862 with a further fifty foundation stones being laid on that date. By this time, several prominent Congregationalists were claiming the emerging middle class as their special field of mission, Wilson included, and he expressed the hope that the 100 commemorative churches would be established in towns with more than 3,000 inhabitants. His crowning achievement was to propose the erection of the Congregational Memorial Hall and Library and the building was opened on Farringdon Street in 1875. The site had previously been occupied by the Fleet Prison, where many early Dissenters had been incarcerated for their nonconformity. Wilson did not live to see the move. He died at Tunbridge Wells on 24 August 1874.

RP

Wilson, Thomas (1764–1843)

One of the most significant of Nonconformist philanthropists of the Victorian era, Thomas Wilson was born on 11 November 1764 in London. He made his fortune in the manufacture of silk ribbon. He retired in 1798 at the age of thirty-four and held many significant posts such as treasurer of the Hoxton Academy and its successor Highbury College (from 1794 to 1843), institutions which eventually became New College, London. Involved in re-opening abandoned chapels, as well as building new ones, he was committed to the Congregational Way and served it both through being a founding member of the Metropolitan Chapel Fund Association in 1837 and by engaging in lay preaching from 1804. He was a founding member of the Council of University College, London, in 1825 and a director of the London Missionary Society.

Wilson was at the forefront of establishing the radical democratic nature of nineteenth-century Nonconformity. He supported parliamentary reform and was present at Peterloo in 1819 when a crowd of between 60,000 and 80,000 gathered to demand reform. Following a cavalry charge, fifteen people were killed and 400 to 700 were injured. He described this as 'a wanton, cruel attack of despotism'. He was an enthusiastic supporter of the 1831 Reform Bill and advocated standing to sing hymns. He died on 17 June 1843.

RP

AA Alan Argent is a Congregational minister, a former President of the Congregational Federation and the editor of the *Congregational History Society Magazine*.

AR Alan Ruston is President of the Unitarian History Society and former editor of its *Transactions*.

DCJ David Ceri Jones is Lecturer in History and Welsh History, Aberystwyth University.

DK David Killingray is Emeritus Professor of History, Goldsmiths University, London.

DDM D. Densil Morgan is Professor of Theology, University of Wales, Trinity St David, Lampeter.

DGC David Cornick is a United Reformed Church minister, General Secretary, Churches Together in England and Fellow and Director of Studies in Theology and Religious Studies, Robinson College, Cambridge.

GEHR Geoffrey Roper is a retired minister of the United Reformed Church and a former General Secretary of the Free Churches' Council and of Churches Together in England.

JHYB John H. Y. Briggs is Professor Emeritus in the University of Birmingham and Director Emeritus of the Baptist History and Heritage Centre, Regent's Park College, Oxford.

PJM Peter J. Morden is Tutor in Church History and Spirituality and a College Chaplain, Spurgeon's College, London.

RCA Richard C. Allen is Reader in History, University of Wales, Newport.

RP Robert Pope is Reader in Theology, University of Wales, Trinity St David, Lampeter.

RW Ralph Waller is Principal of Harris Manchester College, Oxford, and Pro-Vice Chancellor of Oxford University.

SCO Stephen Orchard is a former Principal of Westminster College, Cambridge.

TBW Timothy B. Walsh is Associate Lecturer in History and Spirituality at Regents Theological College, West Malvern.

TW Timothy Whelan is Professor of English, Georgia Southern University, Statesboro, GA, USA.

Contributors to the Volume

Clyde Binfield, OBE, is Professor Emeritus in History at the University of Sheffield. He is a past president of the Chapels Society, a Trustee of the Historic Chapels Trust and of Dr Williams's Trust and Library. His academic interests have been in the social, cultural and political contexts of English Nonconformity in the nineteenth and twentieth centuries, as reflected in *So Down to Prayers: Studies in English Nonconformity 1780–1920* (London: J. M. Dent, 1977) and *The Contexting of a Chapel Architect: James Cubitt, 1836–1912* (London: The Chapels Society, 2001).

Ian Bradley is Reader in Church History and Practical Theology in the University of St Andrews. His publications include *Abide with Me: The World of Victorian Hymns* (London: SCM, 1997), *The Daily Telegraph Book of Hymns* (London: Continuum, 2005). His most recent book is *Grace, Order, Openness and Diversity: Reclaiming Liberal Theology* (London: Continuum, 2011). He is currently working on a study of the sacred and church music of Arthur Sullivan.

John H. Y. Briggs, President of the Baptist Historical Society and Visiting Professor at the International Baptist Theological Seminary in Prague, is Professor Emeritus in the University of Birmingham and Director Emeritus of the Baptist History and Heritage Centre, Regent's Park College, Oxford. He is the author and editor of a number of books including *The English Baptists of the Nineteenth Century* (Didcot: Baptist Union of Great Britain, 1994), and the editor of other books, including (with Stephen Orchard), *The Sunday School Movement: Studies in the Growth and Decline of the Sunday Schools* (Milton Keynes: Paternoster, 2007).

Peter Catterall is Reader in History at the University of Westminster, London. He is a founder editor of *National Identities*, has recently edited for publication *The Macmillan Diaries: Prime Minister and After, 1957–1966* (London: Macmillan, 2011) and is currently completing a monograph on Nonconformity and the Labour Party in the inter-war years.

John Coffey is Professor of Early Modern History at the University of Leicester. He has published on various aspects of early modern Protestant culture: toleration debates, the English Revolution, Puritanism, Evangelicalism and abolitionism. He is the author of *Persecution and Toleration in Protestant England, 1558–1689* (London: Longman, 2000) and *John Goodwin and the Puritan Revolution* (London: Boydell and Brewer, 2006), and has co-edited *The Cambridge Companion to Puritanism* (Cambridge: Cambridge University Press, 2008) and *Seeing Things Their Way: Intellectual History and the Return of Religion* (Notre Dame, IN: University of Notre Dame Press, 2009).

Noel A. Davies, OBE, is a Welsh Congregational minister in Swansea. He has been General Secretary of the Council of Churches for Wales and the Commission of the Covenanted Churches (1977–90) and Cytûn: Churches Together in Wales (1990–98). He has taught at Cardiff University, the Open University and Trinity College, Carmarthen, and written *A History of Ecumenism in Wales* (Cardiff: University of Wales Press, 2008) and *SCM Core Text and Reader on Christianity in the Twentieth Century* (with Martin Conway, London: SCM, 2008). In March 2013 he delivered the Pantyfedwen Lecture on 'Contemporary Christian Ethics: An Ecumenical Perspective'.

Clive D. Field, OBE, is Honorary Research Fellow in the School of History and Cultures, University of Birmingham and in the Institute for Social Change, University of Manchester. He is a former director of Scholarship and Collections at The British Library. He has researched and published widely in the field of British religious history from the eighteenth century to the present and is a particular authority on religious statistics and the history of Methodism. His trilogy of articles, 'Zion's People: Who Were the English Nonconformists?' appeared in *The Local Historian* in 2010.

Stephen R. Holmes is Senior Lecturer in Systematic Theology at the University of St Andrews. His research interests include the classical theological tradition, evangelical theology and constructive approaches, as reflected in publications such as *God of Grace and God of Glory: An Account of the Theology of Jonathan Edwards* (Edinburgh and Grand Rapids, MI: T&T Clark and Eerdmans, 2000), *Listening to the Past: The Place of Tradition in Theology* (Carlisle and Grand Rapids, MI: Paternoster Press and Baker Academic, 2002), *The Wondrous Cross: Atonement and Penal Substitution in the Bible and History* (Carlisle: Paternoster, 2007), *The Holy Trinity* (Milton Keynes: Paternoster, 2012).

David J. Jeremy is Emeritus Professor of Business History at Manchester Metropolitan University. He is the author of *Capitalists and Christians: Business Leaders and the Churches in Britain, 1900–1960* (Oxford: Oxford University

Press, 1990) and 'Ethics, Religion and Business in Twentieth Century Britain', in Richard Coopey and Peter Lyth (eds), *Business in Britain in the Twentieth Century* (Oxford: Oxford University Press, 2009), pp. 356–84.

David Ceri Jones is Lecturer in History and Welsh History at Aberystwyth University. He is the author of *'A Glorious Work in the World': Welsh Methodism and the International Evangelical Revival, 1735–1750* (Cardiff: University of Wales Press, 2004) and co-author of *The Elect Methodists: Calvinistic Methodism in England and Wales, 1735–1811* (Cardiff: University of Wales Press, 2012). In addition, he has written extensively on contemporary church history including *Engaging with Martyn Lloyd-Jones:The Life and Legacy of 'the Doctor'* (edited with Andrew Atherstone, Leicester: Apollos, 2011). He also serves as an Associate Curate in the Church in Wales.

John Gwynfor Jones is Emeritus Professor of Welsh History at Cardiff University. He has published extensively in Welsh and English on early Welsh religious, administrative, social and cultural themes. Among his recent publications are *Aspects of Religious Life in Wales, c.1536–1660: Leadership, Opinion and the Local Community* (Cardiff: University of Wales Press, 2004) and *Crefydd a Chymdeithas: Astudiaethau ar Hanes y Ffydd Brotestannaidd yng Nghymru, c.1559–1750* (Cardiff: University of Wales Press, 2007).

Peter J. Morden is Tutor in Church History and Spirituality, and Chaplain, Spurgeon's College, London. His research interests encompass evangelical history and spirituality and the way in which they relate to ministry today. His publications include *Offering Christ to the World: Andrew Fuller (1854–1815) and the Revival of Eighteenth-Century Particular Baptist Life* (Carlisle: Paternoster, 2003), and *'Communion with Christ and His People': The Spirituality of C.H. Spurgeon (1834–92)* (Oxford: Regent's Park College, 2010).

D. Densil Morgan is Professor of Theology and Provost of the Lampeter Campus, University of Wales, Trinity St David. He is the author of numerous books in English and in Welsh, the most recent of which include *Wales and the Word: Historical Perspectives on Welsh Identity and Religion* (Cardiff: University of Wales Press, 2008), *Lewis Edwards* (Cardiff: University of Wales Press, 2009), *Barth Reception in Britain* (London: T&T Clark, 2010) and *Edward Matthews, Ewenni* (Caernarfon: Gwasg Pantycelyn, 2012). He is a member of the Center of Theological Inquiry, Princeton, NJ, USA, and a Baptist minister.

Stephen Orchard is a former Principal of Westminster College, Cambridge (2001–7), and President of the Cambridge Theological Federation. Before that, he served as General Secretary and Director of the Christian Education Movement. His research interests have included Christian education and Nonconformity in Derbyshire, as reflected in two recent publications *The Sunday School Movement: Studies in the Growth and Decline of the Sunday Schools* (Milton Keynes: Paternoster, 2007) which he edited with John H. Y. Briggs, and *Nonconformity in Derbyshire: A Study in Dissent, 1600–1800* (Milton Keynes: Paternoster, 2009).

Robert Pope is Reader in Theology at the University of Wales, Trinity St David, based at Lampeter, Wales. His publications include *Building Jerusalem: Nonconformity, Labour and the Social Question in Wales, 1906–1939* (Cardiff: University of Wales Press, 1998), *Seeking God's Kingdom: The Nonconformist Social Gospel in Wales, 1906–1939* (Cardiff: University of Wales Press, 1999), *Salvation in Celluloid: Theology, Imagination and Film* (London: T&T Clark, 2007) and *Lloffion ym Maes Crefydd: Diwinyddiaeth y Byd Cyfoes* (Cardiff: University of Wales Press, 2007). He is a member of the Center of Theological Inquiry, Princeton, NJ, USA, and a minister of the United Reformed Church.

Ian M. Randall is a Baptist minister who has had local church pastorates in the south of England. He also taught church history and spirituality for a number of years at Spurgeon's College, London, and at the International Baptist Theological Seminary (IBTS), Prague. He is a Senior Research Fellow of Spurgeon's and IBTS. He is the author of several books and many articles on aspects of Nonconformist and evangelical history. Among his recent books are *Communities of Conviction: Baptist Beginnings in Europe* (Schwarzenfeld: Neufeld Verlag, 2009) and *Rhythms of Revival: The Spiritual Awakening of 1857–1863* (Milton Keynes: Paternoster, 2010)

Keith Robbins was formerly Professor of History at the universities of Bangor and Glasgow and vice-chancellor of the University of Wales. He has written over twenty books, edited eight books and published 120 scholarly articles on political and international topics. His writing on church history includes *History, Religion and Identity in Modern Britain* (London: Continuum, 1993) and *England, Ireland, Scotland, Wales: The Christian Church 1900–2000* (Oxford: Oxford University Press, 2008). He is a former president of the Ecclesiastical History Society. His most recent book is *Transforming the World: Global Political History since World War II* (London: Palgrave Macmillan, 2013).

Alan P. F. Sell is an Honorary Research Fellow of the University of Wales, Trinity St David. A philosopher-theologian and ecumenist, employed in research, writing and lecturing in the United Kingdom and abroad, he has held academic posts in England, Canada and Wales, and ecclesiastical posts in England and Geneva. He is the author or editor of over thirty books, of which the most recent are *Convinced, Concise and Christian: The Thought of Huw Parri Owen* (Eugene, OR: Pickwick, 2012) and *Christ and Controversy: The Person of Christ in Nonconformist Thought and Ecclesial Experience* (Eugene, OR: Pickwick, 2012) while he also edited *The Great Ejectment of 1662* (Eugene, OR: Pickwick, 2012).

Karen E. Smith has been teaching at the South Wales Baptist College and Cardiff University since 1991. Her research interests include Baptist History and spirituality. She has written primarily in the area of eighteenth- and nineteenth-century Baptist life with a special interest in spirituality and women in Christian community.

David M. Thompson is Emeritus Professor of Modern Church History at the University of Cambridge and a non-stipendiary minister of the United Reformed Church. His academic specialism encompasses religious history since the Evangelical Revival, with a particular interest in the history of Protestant Nonconformity and his most recent books have included *Baptism, Church and Society in Modern Britain: From the Evangelical Revival to 'Baptism, Eucharist and Ministry'* (Carlisle: Paternoster, 2005), *Cambridge Theology in the Nineteenth Century* (Aldershot: Ashgate, 2008) and *Protestant Nonconformist Texts, Volume 4: The Twentieth Century* (Aldershot: Ashgate, 2007) which he edited with John H. Y. Briggs and John Munsey Turner.

Timothy Whelan is Professor of English, at Georgia Southern University, Statesboro, GA, USA. Among his publications are *Nonconformist Women Writers, 1720–1840*, 8 vols (London: Pickering & Chatto, 2011), for which he was General Editor; *Baptist Autographs in the John Rylands University Library of Manchester, 1741–1845* (Macon, GA: Mercer University Press, 2009); and *Politics, Religion, and Romance: The Letters of Benjamin Flower and Eliza Gould Flower, 1794–1808* (Aberystwyth: National Library of Wales, 2008).

John Tudno Williams is a former Principal of the United Theological College (Presbyterian Church of Wales), Aberystwyth, and Moderator of the Free Church Council. He has published on various aspects of biblical interpretation, encompassing both the Old and New Testaments. He has also published studies of various biblical scholars, including the Welshmen C. H. Dodd and W. D. Davies.

Index